交通运输与现代物流管理

朱道立 著

科学出版社
北京

内 容 简 介

交通运输与现代物流是关系到国家经济建设和人民生活的重要的两个产业。随着全球经济和信息技术的发展，交通运输、现代物流与供应链管理中的重大问题研究的重要性和复杂性越来越凸显出来。自20世纪90年代以来，这两个产业和相应的学科得到了很大的发展。本书介绍了作者和合作者在交通运输和现代物流领域多年的研究成果，着重介绍两个领域中具有重大理论研究意义和重大应用价值的前沿研究内容。全书包括交通均衡和变分不等式、动态交通流配载和网络均衡、具有多类出行者多目标的交通均衡和有效收费问题、用于交通网络系统设计的二层优化与控制研究、全球运输和港口竞争分析、多产品需求和供应链竞争协调策略、物流金融等七章内容。

本书可作为高等学校交通运输、物流管理、管理科学、运筹学、经济学等专业的教师与研究生研究和教学的参考用书，也可为从事交通运输和现代物流管理实践的工程技术人员及政府管理人员了解相关领域的国内外前沿研究提供参考。

图书在版编目(CIP)数据

交通运输与现代物流管理/朱道立著. —北京：科学出版社，2009
ISBN 978-7-03-024793-3

Ⅰ. 交…　Ⅱ. 朱…　Ⅲ. ①交通运输管理②物流-物资管理　Ⅳ. F502
F252

中国版本图书馆CIP数据核字(2009)第096866号

责任编辑：马　跃 / 责任校对：陈玉凤
责任印制：张克忠 / 封面设计：耕者设计工作室

科学出版社 出版
北京东黄城根北街16号
邮政编码：100717
http://www.sciencep.com

中国科学院印刷厂 印刷
科学出版社发行　各地新华书店经销
*
2009年5月第 一 版　开本：787×1092 1/16
2009年5月第一次印刷　印张：36 1/2
印数：1—2 000　字数：930 000

定价：85.00元
(如有印装质量问题，我社负责调换〈环伟〉)

作 者 简 介

朱道立，1968 年毕业于复旦大学，1970 年进入中国航空电子研究所工作，任助理工程师、工程师，从事航空电子计算机、导航系统的系统设计与仿真工作。1979 年，作为我国第一批留学生到法国国立巴黎高等矿业学院留学，师从著名的自动化专家 G. Cohen 教授，研究大系统优化，并于 1983 年获工学博士学位。1985～1989 年，为上海交通大学管理学院副教授、决策科学系副主任，从事管理决策的科研和教学工作 1989 年赴加拿大，在 McGill 大学、Montreal 大学做访问教授。1993～1997 年，进入 Montreal 大学交通运输研究所工作，任研究员，从事交通运输和决策科学研究工作。1998 年受复旦大学邀请回国工作，任复旦大学管理学院教授、管理科学系主任，从事管理科学与工程、物流和供应链管理等教学研究工作。现任复旦大学上海物流研究院院长，中国物流学会副会长和中国系统工程学会常务理事。

鉴于其在工程科技和管理的成就和贡献，2006 年被授予中国“管理学杰出贡献奖”一等奖和“中国有突出贡献物流专家”奖，为我国管理学和物流管理领域首届全国大奖；2008 年被授予“中国物流改革开放 30 年杰出贡献奖”。

前　　言

2009 年 3 月，国务院发布《物流业调整和振兴规划》，指出物流业是融合运输、仓储、货代和信息等的复合型服务产业，是国民经济的重要组成部分，对于促进我国产业结构调整、转变经济发展方式和增强国民经济竞争力有着重要的战略意义。2009 年 4 月，国务院又公布了关于上海建设金融航运中心的意见，要求，到 2020 年在上海基本建成航运资源高度集聚、航运服务功能健全、航运市场环境优良、现代物流服务高效，具有全球航运资源配置能力的国际航运中心。国家关于物流与航运中心建设的两大发展战略，充分体现了交通运输和现代物流对国家经济建设和人民生活的重大战略意义和作用。

本书共分两部分，分别介绍了笔者和合作者在交通运输和现代物流领域多年的研究成果，特别是介绍了这两个领域中具有重大理论研究意义和重大应用价值的前沿研究成果。

本书第一部分(第一章至第四章)主要介绍笔者和合作者们在交通分配和交通系统设计方面的前沿研究成果。

世界上有很多区域和城市面临着交通拥挤、事故频发、环境污染、资源过度消耗等交通问题的严峻挑战。解决交通问题成为保证社会经济可持续发展、提高居民生活质量、提升国家竞争力的关键。相关的重要研究内容有交通规划、交通和土地协调规划、交通需求管理、交通分配问题、交通基础设施和网络设计、交通收费、智能交通系统、公共交通结构分析和政策、交通可持续发展等。

交通分配是将出发地-目的地(origin-destination)的交通需求按出行者择路行为分配到交通网络中，得到网络上的流量，即出行状态。交通分配问题的主要研究内容包括出行者路径选择行为、交通网络均衡模型、有效的求解方法。1952 年 Wardrop 提出了描述出行者路径选择行为的用户均衡原理和系统最优原理。Beckman 等人(1956)建立了交通分配的网络均衡优化模型。而 Dafemos(1969)提出了更完善的优化模型。20 世纪 70 年代，交通科学工作者致力于发展有效的优化算法和交通实践应用。自 80 年代起，特别是在 90 年代，学者们致力于建立完备的变分不等式理论，包括映射理论、解的性质、求解方法和分析等。其中，交通科学工作者更关心解决交通分配问题的有应用价值的计算方法。本书的第一章即介绍了笔者和合作者在交通分配问题和变分不等式方面的前沿研究成果。

自 90 年代起，交通学术界和工业界极其重视动态交通分配问题，原因是它比传统的静态交通分配问题模型更能客观地反映现实，在动态交通分配问题中，着眼于估计和预测交通网络在短时间内的动态变化，包括需求和流量。动态模型在智能交通中有巨大的应用潜力。交通问题动态性能的复杂性和人的动态交通行为问题建模的困难性，使得我们要在数学严格建模、问题求解和实际应用之间作一个折中。本书的第二章介绍了笔者和合作者在动态交通分配问题分析理论上的前沿研究成果。它们是动态交通分配理论和实践的基础。

由于交通出行者出行行为和社会经济特征(如收入、年龄、偏好、习惯)是不同的,他们乘坐的交通工具(如汽车、卡车、火车、飞机等)也是不同的。所以把单用户的交通均衡扩展到多用户的交通均衡是非常自然和必要的。由于不同用户有不同的经济特征,其时间、费用、舒适偏好决定了他们对交通方式与路径选择的不同行为。各类用户具有的特征一般是满足某些分布的。他们按照自己的行为来选择出行路线与工具,选择标准也经常是多种目标的,如费用、时间和舒适程度等。研究多类出行者多目标的交通均衡问题是 90 年代中期,特别是新世纪以来交通界最重要的研究方向之一。在最优收费问题中,人们试图找到一个合理收费(补贴)策略以使多目标多用户交通系统的均衡状态达到预期的状态,例如系统最优状态,或者让系统达到某个系统目标,如污染排放小于某个值等。本书的第三章介绍了笔者和合作者在多类出行者、多目标交通均衡和有效收费(补贴)方面的前沿研究成果。由于这一研究方向具有重大的理论意义和应用价值,笔者仍在继续进行深入的理论和应用研究工作。

交通拥挤、安全和环境关系到每个人的生活、生命和健康,以及经济的发展。随着社会经济的发展,设计和管理一个可靠和有效的交通网络系统、为用户提供高效快捷的服务是交通科技工作者非常紧迫的任务。交通系统设计的问题是要在有限可利用资源的前提下,设计各类网络方案,使之最大限度为顾客服务。交通系统设计的典型问题有网络通行能力设计、道路拥挤收费、信号灯控制优化。很多交通系统设计以及交通收益管理问题都可用一类带有网络均衡约束的优化问题来描述。在数学上可表示为二层优化与控制问题,它是一个较为困难的科学问题。由于解决这些交通问题现实需求的直接推动,二层优化和控制理论、算法和应用的研究在近十年中有很大的发展。本书的第四章介绍了笔者和合作者关于二层优化在交通网络系统设计和收益管理方面的应用研究,以及二层优化的前沿理论研究成果,包括最优化条件和计算方法等。

本书的第二部分(第五章至第七章)主要介绍笔者及合作者在物流和供应链管理方面的创新研究成果。

物流是国民经济重要组成部分。现代物流是以提高效率和成本效益、满足顾客需要为目的,从商品的生产地到消费地,对包括原材料、在制品、最终成品和相关信息的流动与存储进行设计、实施和控制的过程。当前,现代物流的研究和实践的主要发展趋势是全球化、集成化、网络化和信息化;现代物流管理强调全球物流,物流资源优化配置,物流和制造、贸易流通及金融的融合;强调地区的合作和竞争;强调资源节约、环境和安全的可持续发展。

随着经济全球化和融入世界经济步伐的加快,中国已成为世界上航运最繁忙的区域。航运业在经历了船舶大型化和集装箱化革命之后已进入现代物流时代。航运企业间的竞争将从简单的航运价格提升到完整价值链意义上的集成物流服务价值上。港口不再是运输的终点,而是国际运输和物流链中的一环。港口货源的形成分析、港口之间的合作和竞争已成为现代港口管理的重要内容。本书第五章介绍了笔者和合作者利用现代管理科学和经济学的方法研究全球运输网络和港口竞争分析的前沿研究成果，对我国建设现代航运中心及加速发展航运物流的实践以及航运物流科学研究有重要的参考价值。

信息和供应链管理已成为现代物流的核心技术。供应链是供应商、制造商、批发商及零售商通过运输、库存、信息及金融设施互连而成的一个有机整体，它的目标是为最终客户提供产品和服务的有效价值，为供应链各个成员创造收益。近年来，供应链管理研究和实践发展的新趋势包括多产品需求和供应链竞争环境下的供应链协调，供应链网络，金融物流和供应链，供应链风险管理，绿色和逆向供应链，推动制造和服务融合、贸易和物流融合的供应链技术，基于可视化可跟踪信息通信技术的供应链管理，基于电子商务的供应链网络等。本书第六章介绍了笔者和合作者在国家自然科学基金委员会的重点项目“供应链协调理论，供应链协调应用技术和运营策略”支持下取得的部分研究成果，包括多产品需求理论及其竞争环境下的供应链协调策略、应用交通科学和超网络理论研究、信息不对称供应链契约、供应链竞争和协调策略、供应链网络结构等。

随着国内外先进企业物流、信息流和资金流集成管理实践的发展，物流金融管理的概念被提出并得到广泛研究。物流金融管理是面向物流运作的全过程，应用各种集成式的服务与产品，通过信息共享、协调和组织合作等方法集成物流、资金流、信息流，从而达到降低资金流运作成本并为供应链创造价值的管理系统。融通仓是一种有重大应用价值的物流金融管理方法和技术。它是笔者和学生在 2002 年提出的并在实践中得到广泛应用，具有了重要经济价值。本书第七章介绍了笔者和合作者在金融物流方面的部分研究成果，包括融通仓的理论、运作模式、定价决策和价值分析等。

本书的研究得到国家自然科学基金项目“物流管理的随机决策”（编号：79870106）、“二层网络决策理论和企业竞争策略设计方法”（编号：70171010），重点项目“供应链协调理论、应用技术和运作策略研究”（编号：70432001）和加拿大科学基金 NSERC，FQRNT 的支持。

本书包括了笔者和国外合作者蒙特利尔大学 P. Marcotte 教授，维克多利亚大学 J. Ye 教授的合作成果，以及我和同事、学生共同的研究成果，特别是徐庆教授、徐兵、陈祥峰副教授、鲁奇辉、吉阿兵、胡一泓、徐最、朱文贵博士等，在此，谨表深切谢意。另外也感谢科学出版社马跃编辑的精心工作。由于水平有限，缺点、错误在所难免，殷切希望读者不吝指正。

朱道立

2009 年 5 月

目　　录

第一章　交通均衡和变分不等式

运输需求和网络模型以及交通分配模型是交通运输科学和工程中的主要研究内容。交通流分配模型是用来描述交通网络中的出行者组成的交通出行状态的，交通网络可包括城市街道交通系统、铁路或航空交通系统。假设网络的性能特征已知，出行需求可以用起讫点(origin-destination)需求矩阵来描述，或者由需求函数来确定。在系统最优交通流分配模型中，出行者的路径选择所导致的路径流会使得网络实现公众利益最大化。而在交通用户均衡问题中描述这样一种状态：路网上的出行者选择路径，使得没有一个单独用户可以单方面改善出行的成本。这就是著名的 Wardrop 均衡(Wardrop，1952)，它是纳什均衡的一个特例，在 Wardrop 用户均衡中只有最小成本的路径被使用，所有的路径的交通流总和等于出行需求。这个问题通常称为网络均衡模型(NEM)。它在其他许多领域中也得到了应用，包括电力网络、水网络和空间价格均衡问题。一个有趣而又重要的关系是，从边际成本的概念来看系统最优解是均衡的，而用户均衡解在平均成本意义下是均衡的。值得注意的另一个事实是，在对于边上的成本函数的合适假设下，NEM 下的总的弧流量可以是唯一的，但是按 OD 对或按路径的总交通流量却不是唯一的。

在交通规划中使用的基本 NEM 模型中，如果成本和需求函数是可分离的，那么它可以用优化模型来表示。如进一步假设成本函数是凸的，需求函数是严格单调的，这时，用户最优化问题可以用凸规划来表述。Beckman 等人(1956)建立了基本的网络均衡模型。如果成本函数是不可分离的，或者其 Jacobian 矩阵是不对称的，这时，交通均衡问题是不能用最优化问题来描述的。Smith(1979)和 Dafermos(1980)分别发现不对称网络均衡问题可以用变分不等式来描述。20 世纪 70 年代交通科学工作者做了很大努力，发展解决网络均衡问题的最优化求解算法。而在 80 年代，特别是 90 年代，学者们致力于发展求解网络均衡问题的变分不等式理论和算法，并取得了一系列的研究成果。本章主要介绍作者在计算交通均衡变分不等式理论和算法方面的研究成果，包括映射单调性、求解变分不等式迭代算法、下降法和割平面法、解的性质，以及对于求解交通均衡尤为重要的有效分解算法。交通网络均衡问题的原始观察信息都是关于弧的，如流和费用等，而在计算过程中，需要把弧形式的变分不等式转换为路径形式的变分不等式。这时会改变映射的单调性，从而不能证明其算法收敛性。Zhu 和 Marcotte(1997)提出了关于 co-coericivity 变分不等式迭代算法，解决了这个困惑了交通运输领域多年的计算问题。

CO-COERCIVITY AND ITS ROLE IN THE CONVERGENCE OF ITERATIVE SCHEMES FOR SOLVING VARIATIONAL INEQUALITIES*

D. L. ZHU** AND P. MARCOTTE***

Abstract. This paper stresses the role of co-coercivity and related notions in the convergence of iterative schemes for solving monotone but not necessarily strongly or even strictly monotone variational inequalities. The analysis will be conducted within the conceptual framework of the "auxiliary problem principle."

Key words. mathematical programming, variational inequalities, monotonicity, auxiliary problem, co-coercivity

AMS subject classifications. 47H05, 49J40, 49M27, 90C25

1. Introduction

Let C denote a nonempty, closed, convex subset of R^n, F a continuous mapping from C into R^n, and f a continuous convex function from C into R. We say that a point x^* is a solution of the variational inequality VIP if it satisfies

$$\text{VIP:} \qquad \langle F(x^*), x - x^* \rangle + f(x) - f(x^*) \geq 0 \quad \forall x \in C, \tag{1}$$

where $\langle .,. \rangle$ denotes the standard dot product in R^n. Throughout the paper, we assume that the mapping F is monotone over C and that the function f is convex over C.

Various iterative schemes have been proposed for solving variational inequalities. The interested reader may consult the survey of Harker and Pang [6] for a good introduction to the subject. For several iterative methods, the convergence proof requires the mapping F to be strongly monotone over C. Recently, Tseng [12] and Marcotte and Wu [8] studied the convergence of iterative processes when the mapping F is affine and

*Received by the editors June 1, 1994; accepted for publication (in revised form) February 20, 1995.

**Centre de recherche sur les transports, Université de Montréal, Montréal, Québec, Canada H3C3J7 (daoli@crt.umontreal.ca).

***Département d'informatique et de recherche opérationnelle, Université de Montréal, C. P. 6128, Succursale A, Montréal, Québec, Canada H3C 3J7 (marcotte@iro.umontreal.ca)

co-coercive. It is the main purpose of this paper to investigate iterative schemes for solving nonlinear variational inequalities under the co-coercivity assumption.

The paper will proceed as follows. Properties of co-coercive mappings are introduced in § 2; in § 3 we address the global convergence of a very general iterative scheme; in § 4 we study a variant of the iterative scheme introduced in § 3 and consider various realizations of this method. In particular, we will stress the relationships with asymmetric projection methods and consider its application to the traffic equilibrium problem. Next we introduce the notion of partial co-coercivity that will prove useful in the analysis of algorithms for solving systems of variational inequalities. Finally we will propose a primal-dual realization of our general algorithmic framework.

2. Co-coercive mappings and their properties

In this paper we will denote by $\| x \|_B$ the norm induced by the positive definite matrix B, i. e. ,

$$\| x \|_B = \langle Bx , x \rangle^{1/2}.$$

Also, $\| x \|_2$ will denote the standard norm in R^n. For any vector norm $\| \cdot \|$, the corresponding matrix norm is

$$\| A \| = \max_{\| x \| = 1} \| Ax \| .$$

DEFINITION 2. 1. *The mapping F is co-coercive on C if there exists a positive-constant a such that*

$$\langle F(y) - F(x), y - x \rangle \geq \alpha \| F(y) - F(x) \|^2 \qquad (2)$$

for all x, y in C.

It is clear that co-coercive mappings are monotone but not necessarily strongly monotone (consider a constant mapping). Conversely, strongly monotone and Lipschitz continuous mappings are co-coercive, and it follows that co-coercivity is an intermediate concept that lies between simple and strong monotonicity.

The sum of co-coercive mappings is trivially co-coercive. As shown below, cocoercivity is also preserved under affine transformations, which inciude scalings and translations as particular cases.

PROPOSITION 2. 2. *Let A be an $m \times n$ matrix. If the mapping F from R^m into R^m is co-coercive with modulus α, then the mapping $y \to A^t F(Ay) + d$ is co-coercive with modulus $\alpha / \| A \|^2$.*

Proof. Assume that A is nonzero (otherwise the result holds trivially). We have

$$\begin{aligned}\langle [A^t F(Ay) + d] - [A^t F(Ax) + d], y - x \rangle &= \langle (F(Ay) - F(Ax), Ay - Ax \rangle \\ &\geq \alpha \| F(Ay) - F(Ax) \|^2 \\ &\geq \frac{\alpha}{\| A \|^2} \| A^t F(Ay) - A^t F(Ax) \|^2\end{aligned}$$

$$= \frac{\alpha}{\| A \|^2} \| [A^t F(Ay) + d] - [A^t F(Ax) + d] \|^2$$

and $A^t F(Ay) + d$ is co-coercive, as claimed. □

Co-coercive mappings are monotone and Lipschitz continuous over their domain of definition. Although the converse does not hold in general, it does hold in R^1, where a function is co-coercive on an interval if and only if it is monotone(increasing) and Lipschitz continuous on that interval. The next properties of co-coercive mappings will be required in subsequent sections of this paper.

PROPOSITION 2. 3. *Let F be a mapping from a closed convex subset C of R^n into R^n. If the mapping F-αI is Lipschitz continuous with Lipschitz constant $\beta(\beta \leq \alpha)$ over C, then F is co-coercive on C. Conversely, if F is co-coercive with modulus $\beta(\beta \geq \frac{1}{2\alpha})$ on C, then F-αI is Lipschitz continuous on C, with Lipschitz constant α.*

Proof. Denote $G = F - \alpha I$. For any x, y in C we can write

$$\begin{aligned} \| F(y) - F(x) \|^2 &= \| G(y) - G(x) + \alpha y - \alpha x \|^2 \\ &= \| G(y) - G(x) \|^2 + 2\alpha\langle G(y) - G(x), y - x\rangle + \alpha^2 \| y - x \|^2 \\ &\leq (\beta^2 + \alpha^2) \| y - x \|^2 + 2\alpha\langle G(y) - G(x), y - x\rangle \\ &\leq 2\alpha\langle [G(y) + \alpha y] - [G(x) + \alpha x], y - x\rangle, \end{aligned}$$

and this implies

$$\langle F(y) - F(x), y - x\rangle \geq \frac{1}{2\alpha} \| F(y) - F(x) \|^2,$$

i. e. , that F is co-coercive on C with modulus $\frac{1}{2\alpha}$.

As for the second claim, observe that

$$\begin{aligned} \| (F - \alpha I)(y) - (F - \alpha I)(x) \|^2 &= \| F(y) - F(x) \|^2 \\ &\quad - 2\alpha\langle F(y) - F(x), y - x\rangle + \alpha^2 \| y - x \|^2 \\ &\leq \alpha^2 \| y - x \|^2, \end{aligned}$$

i. e. , F-αI is Lipschitz continuous on C. □

PROPOSITION 2. 4. *Let the mapping $F: C \to R^n$ be invertible. Then F is co-coercive on C if and only if F^{-1} is Lipschitz continuous and strongly monotone on the range F (C) of F.*

Proof. The proof of the proposition is straightforward from the definitions. □

As shown by Marcotte and Wu [8], a sufficient condition for a mapping F to be co-coercive on a closed convex set C is that the Jacobian $F'(x)$ and the *square* of the Jacobian $F'(x)^2$ be both positive semidefinite on C.

In the affine case, the concept of co-coercivity can be related to that of psdplus matrices. By definition, a matrix M is psd-plus if it is positive semidefinite, and $Mx = 0$ whenever, $\langle Mx, x\rangle = 0$. Recently, Luo and Tseng [7] characterized the class of psd-plus matrices as follows: a matrix M is psd-plus if and only if it can be decomposed into the product

$$M = E^t A E,$$

where A is a positive definite matrix. From this result, the following result can be shown.

PROPOSITION 2.5. *A matrix M is psd-plus if and only if the mapping $x \to Mx$ is co-coercive.*

Proof. The result holds trivially if $M=0$. Assume that M is nonzero. If Mx is co-coercive, then we have

$$\langle Mx, x\rangle \geq \alpha \| Mx \|^2,$$

which implies that M is psd-plus.

Conversely, let M be a psd-plus matrix. Decompose M as $M=E^tAE$, where A is a positive definite matrix. Let α be the smallest eigenvalue associated with the symmetric part of A. The number α is positive and we can write

$$\langle Mx, x\rangle = \langle E^tAEx, x\rangle = \langle A(Ex), Ex\rangle \geq \alpha \| Ex \|^2. \tag{3}$$

Also, since M is nonzero, $\| E^tA \|$ is nonzero and we have

$$\| Mx \|^2 = \| E^tAEx \|^2 \leq \| E^tA \|^2 \| Ex \|^2. \tag{4}$$

Coupling (3) and (4) gives

$$\langle Mx, x\rangle \geq \frac{\alpha}{\| E^tA \|^2} \| Mx \|^2,$$

and the mapping Mx is co-coercive on R^n. □

3. A general iterative scheme.

The co-coercivity condition can be used to analyze the convergence behavior of iterative schemes based upon the auxiliary problem framework developed by Cohen [4]. The following lemma will be required in our analysis.

LEMMA 3.1. *Let h be a continuously differentiable function defined on a convex subset C of R^n.*

(i) *If h is strongly convex with modulus b over C, then*

$$h(x_2) - h(x_1) \geq \langle h'(x_1), x_2 - x_1\rangle + \frac{1}{2}b \| x_2 - x_1 \|^2 \quad \forall x_1, x_2 \in C.$$

(ii) *If the the gradient h' is Lipschitz continuous over C, with Lipschitz constant B, then*

$$h(x_2) - h(x_1) \leq \langle h'(x_1), x_2 - x_1\rangle + \frac{1}{2}B \| x_2 - x_1 \|^2 \qquad \forall x_1, x_2 \in C.$$

Proof. (i) See [1].

(ii) For any x_1, $x_2 \in C$, define the function

$$\phi(t) = h((1-t)x_1 + tx_2) - h(x_1) - t\langle h'(x_1), x_2 - x_1\rangle \quad \forall t \in [0, 1].$$

We have

$$\phi'(t) = \langle h'((1-t)x_1 + tx_2) - h'(x_2), x_2 - x_1\rangle$$

and

$$\phi(1) = h(x_2) - h(x_1) - \langle h'(x_1), x_2 - x_1 \rangle$$
$$= \phi(0) + \int_0^1 \phi'(t)dt \text{ by the fundamental theorem of calculus}$$
$$\leq 0 + \int_0^1 |\phi'(t)| dt \text{ since } \phi(0) = 0$$
$$\leq \int_0^1 B \| t(x_2 - x_1) \| \cdot \| x_2 - x_1 \| dt$$
$$= \frac{B}{2} \| x_2 - x_1 \|^2. \qquad \square$$

We now introduce the basic algorithmic framework. From now on, we assume that the solution set of VIP is nonempty. Let ϵ be a positive parameter and consider, for a given iterate x^k, the auxiliary VIP that consists of finding a point x^{k+1} that satisfies the variational inequality

$$\langle \epsilon F(x^k) + \Gamma(x^{k+1}) - \Gamma(x^k), x - x^{k+1} \rangle + \epsilon (f(x) - f(x^{k+1})) \geq 0 \quad \forall x \in C, \quad (5)$$

where F is a mapping approximating the mapping F.

If we select F to be a gradient mapping, e. g. , $F(x) = h'(x)$, we have the following convergence result.

THEOREM 3. 2. *Let F be co-coercive over C (with modulus γ) and $F = h'$. Let h be strongly convex over C (with modulus b) and its derivative h' be Lipschitz continuous over C (with Lipschitz constant B). Then there exists a unique solution x^{k+1} to (5).*

If in addition we take $0 < \epsilon < 2b\gamma$, then the sequence $\{x^k\}$ is bounded and converges to a solution of the VIP.

Proof. Since the function h is strongly convex over C, the solution x^{k+1} of (5) is unique. Let x^* denote *any* fixed solution of the original variational inequality VIP and consider, for x in C, the function

$$\Lambda^*(x) = h(x^*) - h(x) - \langle h'(x), x^* - x \rangle$$
$$\geq (b/2) \| x - x^* \|^2,$$

where the last inequality follows from the strong monotonicity of h'. We have

$$\Lambda^*(x^k) - \Lambda^*(x^{k+1}) = h(x^{k+1}) - h(x^k) - \langle h'(x^k), x^{k+1} - x^k \rangle$$
$$+ \langle h'(x^{k+1}) - h'(x^k), x^* - x^{k+1} \rangle \quad (6)$$
$$\geq \frac{b}{2} \| x^k - x^{k+1} \|^2 + \epsilon \langle F(x^k), x^{k+1} - x^* \rangle + \epsilon [f(x^{k+1}) - f(x^*)], \quad (7)$$

where the second term of the inequality is obtained by setting $x = x^*$ in equation (5). If we set $x = x^{k+1}$ in (1) and combine (1) and (7), we obtain

$$\Lambda^*(x^k) - \Lambda^*(x^{k+1}) \geq \frac{b}{2} \| x^k - x^{k+1} \|^2 + \epsilon \langle F(x^k) - F(x^*), x^{k+1} - x^* \rangle$$
$$= \frac{b}{2} \| x^k - x^{k+1} \|^2 + T.$$

Now

$$T=\epsilon\langle F(x^k)-F(x^*),x^{k+1}-x^*\rangle$$
$$=\epsilon\langle F(x^k)-F(x^*),x^k-x^*\rangle+\epsilon\langle F(x^k)-F(x^*),x^{k+1}-x^k\rangle.$$

Since F is co-coercive, we obtain

$$T\geq\epsilon[\gamma\|F(x^k)-F(x^*)\|^2+\langle F(x^k)-F(x^*),x^{k+1}-x^k\rangle]$$
$$\geq-\frac{\epsilon}{4\gamma}\|x^{k+1}-x^k\|^2.$$

Therefore

$$\Lambda^*(x^k)-\Lambda^*(x^{k+1})\geq\frac{1}{2}\left(b-\frac{\epsilon}{2\gamma}\right)\|x^{k+1}-x^k\|^2.$$

If $x^{k+1}=x^k$, it is easily shown that x^k is a solution of the variational inequality. Otherwise, the assumption $\epsilon<2b\gamma$ implies that the sequence $\Lambda^*(x^k)-\Lambda^*(x^{k+1})$ is nonnegative, and we must have

$$\lim_{k\to\infty}\|x^{k+1}-x^k\|=0.$$

Furthermore, since $\|x^k-x^*\|^2\leq(2/b)\Lambda^*(x^k)$ and the sequence $\{\Lambda^*(x^k)\}$ is decreasing, we can affirm that the sequence $\{x^k\}$ is bounded. Let $\bar{x}$ be any cluster point of the sequence $\{x^k\}$. Taking the limit in (5), we conclude that $\bar{x}$ is a solution of thevariational inequality.

If we replace x^* by $\bar{x}$, the analysis remains valid for $\bar{x}$ and its associated metric function $\bar{\Lambda}$. The sequence $(\bar{\Lambda}(x^k))$ still strictly decreases and, from Lemma 3.1, we have

$$\bar{\Lambda}(x^k)\leq\frac{1}{2}B\|\bar{x}-x^k\|^2.$$

This shows that the sequence $\bar{\Lambda}(x^k)$ converges to zero. This result, together with the inequality

$$\bar{\Lambda}(x^k)\geq\frac{b}{2}\|x^k-\bar{x}\|^2,$$

allows us to conclude that the entire sequence $\{x^k\}$ converges to $\bar{x}$. □

Remark 3.3. The previous convergence result constitutes an extension of Cohen's result to the co-coercive case. Cohen [4] gave an example, involving a monotone mapping F, where the iterative method did not converge. In his example, however, the mapping F failed to be co-coercive.

Remark 3.4. A related algorithm has been studied in Mataoui [10] in the case $f=0$, where the author proved only the existence of a convergent subsequence.

From a practical point of view, the solution of the auxiliary variational inequality cannot be obtained in closed form, and a trade-off must be achieved between the amount of work spent on solving the auxiliary problem and the accuracy of the corresponding solution. More precisely one can, at step k, find an approximate solution of the auxiliary problem, i. e. , a point x^{k+1} of C satisfying

$$\langle \epsilon F(x^k) + h'(x^{k+1}) - h'(x^k), x - x^{k+1} \rangle + \epsilon (f(x) - f(x^{k+1})) \geq -\rho k \quad \forall x \in C', \tag{8}$$

where ρ_k is a positive number. If C is bounded we let $C' = C$. Otherwise, we define $C' = C \cap \{x \mid \|x\| \leq R\}$, where R is a suitably large constant. Although such a number always exists (recall that the sequence $\{\|x^k - x^*\|\}$ is bounded), it could be difficult to estimate in practice. One possibility is to update R whenever the sequence of iterates converges to a nonequilibrium point at the boundary of the set C'.

THEOREM 3. 5. *If the conditions of Theorem* 3. 2 *are fulfilled and the sequence* $\{\rho_k\}$ *satisfies*

$$\rho_k \geq 0, \quad \sum_{k=1}^{\infty} \rho_k < \infty,$$

then the sequence $\{x^k\}$ *converges to a solution of VIP.*

Proof. Following the steps of the proof of Theorem 3. 2 we have

$$\Lambda^*(x^{k+1}) - \Lambda^*(x^k) \leq -\frac{1}{2}\left(b - \frac{\epsilon}{2\gamma}\right) \|x^{k+1} - x^k\|^2 + \rho_k.$$

Since $2b\gamma - \epsilon > 0$ and $\sum_{k=1}^{\infty} \rho_k < \infty$ we have, for any N and any solution x^* to VIP,

$$\frac{b}{2} \|x^{N+1} - x^*\|^2 - \Lambda^*(x^1) \leq \sum_{k=1}^{N} (\Lambda^*(x^{k+1}) - \Lambda^*(x^k)) \leq \sum_{k=1}^{\infty} \rho_k.$$

This implies that the sequence $\{x^k\}$ is bounded and that the limit of $\|x^{k+1} - x^k\|$ is zero. It is then easy to show, exactly as in the proof of Theorem 3. 2, that the entire sequence converges to a solution of the variational inequality. □

4. A modified auxiliary mapping and its use in the decomposition of variational inequalities.

In this section we present a more general iterative scheme that converges under less stringent monotonicity assumptions on the mapping F.

4. 1 A general method.

For a given $x^k \in C$, let us consider the variational inequality that consists of determining $x^{k+1} \in C$ such that

$$\langle \epsilon F(x^k) + \Gamma_\epsilon(x^{k+1}) - \Gamma_\epsilon(x^k), x - x^{k+1} \rangle + \epsilon (f(x) - f(x^{k+1})) \geq 0 \quad \forall x \in C, \tag{9}$$

where Γ_1 and Γ_2 are nonlinear mappings and $\Gamma_\epsilon = \epsilon \Gamma_1 + \Gamma_2$. We will focus our attention on the choice

$$\Gamma_1(x) = Mx + L(x),$$
$$\Gamma_2(x) = h'(x),$$

where M is a symmetric matrix, L a monotone mapping, and h is a convex function with Lipschitz continuous gradient. If $\Gamma_1 = 0$ we recover the preceding method. Let us denote by $\lambda_{\min}(\Delta)$ the smallest eigenvalue of a matrix Δ.

THEOREM 4.1. *Let h' be strongly monotone with modulus b over C and $F-L$ be co-coercive with modulus γ over C. Select ϵ such that*

$$0<\epsilon\leq\frac{2b\gamma}{1-2\gamma\lambda_{\min}(M)} \qquad if\ \frac{1}{2\gamma}-\lambda_{\min}(M)>0, \tag{10}$$

$$0<\epsilon<\infty \qquad if\ \frac{1}{2\gamma}-\lambda_{\min}(M)\leq 0. \tag{11}$$

Then there exists a unique solution x^{k+1} to (9). Also, the sequence $\{x^k\}$ is bounded and converges to a solution of VIP.

Proof. Let x^* be any fixed solution of VIP. Let $G=I+(\epsilon/b)M$ and consider the function

$$\begin{aligned}\Lambda^*(x)&=h(x^*)-h(x)-\langle h'(x),x^*-x\rangle+\frac{\epsilon}{2}\langle M(x-x^*),x-x^*\rangle\\&\geq\frac{b}{2}\|x-x^*\|^2+\frac{\epsilon}{2}\langle M(x-x^*),x-x^*\rangle\\&=\frac{b}{2}\|x-x^*\|_G^2.\end{aligned}$$

From the assumptions, the matrix G is positive definite and symmetric. We have

$$\begin{aligned}\Lambda^*(x^k)-\Lambda^*(x^{k+1})&=h(x^{k+1})-h(x^k)-\langle h'(x^k),x^{k+1}-x^k\rangle\\&\quad+\langle h'(x^{k+1})-h'(x^k),x^*-x^{k+1}\rangle+\frac{\epsilon}{2}\langle M(x^k-x^*),x^k-x^*\rangle\\&\quad-\frac{\epsilon}{2}\langle M(x^{k+1})-x^*),x^{k+1}-x^*\rangle\\&\geq\frac{b}{2}\|x^k-x^{k+1}\|^2+\frac{\epsilon}{2}[\langle M(x^k-x^*),x^k-x^*\rangle\\&\quad-\langle M(x^{k+1}-x^*),x^{k+1}-x^*\rangle]\\&\quad+\epsilon[\langle F(x^k)+M(x^{k+1}-x^k)+L(x^{k+1})-L(x^k),x^{k+1}-x^*\rangle]\\&\quad+\epsilon[f(x^{k+1})-f(x^*)],\end{aligned}$$

where the inequality results from setting $x=x^*$ in (9). On the other hand, if we set $x=x^{k+1}$ in (1) and combine the resulting inequality with the preceding, we obtain

$$\begin{aligned}\Lambda^*(x^k)-\Lambda^*(x^{k+1})&\geq\frac{b}{2}\|x^k-x^{k+1}\|^2\\&\quad+\epsilon[\langle F(x^k)-F(x^*)+L(x^{k+1})-L(x^k),x^{k+1}-x^*\rangle]\\&\quad+\epsilon[\langle M(x^{k+1}-x^k),x^{k+1}-x^*\rangle\\&\quad+\frac{1}{2}(\langle M(x^k-x^*),x^k-x^*\rangle-\langle M(x^{k+1}-x^*),x^{k+1}-x^*\rangle)]\\&=A_1+A_2+A_3\end{aligned}$$

with

$$A_1=\frac{b}{2}\|x^k-x^{k+1}\|^2,$$

$$A_2=\epsilon[\langle(F-L)(x^k)-(F-L)(x^*),x^{k+1}-x^*\rangle+\langle L(x^{k+1})-L(x^*),x^{k+1}-x^*\rangle]$$

$$\geq \epsilon [\langle (F-L)(x^k)-(F-L)(x^*), x^k - x^* \rangle$$
$$+ \langle (F-L)(x^k)-(F-L)(x^*), x^{k+1} - x^k \rangle]$$
$$\geq \epsilon [\gamma \| (F-L)(x^k)-(F-L)(x^*) \|^2$$
$$+ \langle (F-L)(x^k)-(F-L)(x^*), x^{k+1} - x^k \rangle]$$
$$\geq -\frac{\epsilon}{4\gamma} \| x^{k+1} - x^k \|^2,$$

and

$$A_3 = \frac{\epsilon}{2} \langle M(x^k - x^{k+1}), x^k - x^{k+1} \rangle.$$

Next

$$A_1 + A_3 = \frac{b}{2} \| x^k - x^{k+1} \|^2 + \frac{\epsilon}{2} \langle M(x^k - x^{k+1}), x^k - x^{k-1} \rangle$$
$$= \frac{b}{2} \| x^k - x^{k+1} \|_G^2$$
$$\geq \frac{b}{2} \lambda_{\min}(G) \| x^k - x^{k+1} \|^2$$

and

$$\Lambda^*(x^k) - \Lambda^*(x^{k+1}) \geqslant \frac{1}{2} \left[b\lambda_{\min}(G) - \frac{\epsilon}{2\gamma} \right] \| x^k - x^{k+1} \|^2.$$

As in the preceding proofs, the sequence $\{\Lambda^*(x^k)\}$ is nonnegative, strictly decreasing (unless $x^{k+1} = x^k$), and must therefore converge. The inequality $\Lambda^*(x^k) \geq \frac{b}{2} \| x^k - x^* \|_G^2$ holds for all solutions x^* to VIP and implies that (i) the sequence $\{x^k\}$ is bounded and (ii) the sequence $\| x^{k+1} - x^k \|$ converges to zero. The proof of convergence of the entire sequence to a unique solution uses the same arguments as the proof of Theorem 3. 2.

□

4. 2 Decomposition.

The preceding result is important. Indeed, it allows the decomposition of monotone, but not necessarily co-coercive, variational inequalities. In particular, assume that F can be expressed as the sum of a co-coercive mapping F_1 and a monotone mapping F_2. If we set $\Gamma_1 = F_2$ in the modified auxiliary problem method, x^{k+1} is then characterized as the solution to the auxiliary variational inequality

$$\langle \epsilon (F_1(x^k) + F_2(x^{k+1})) + \Gamma_2(x^{k+1}) - \Gamma_2(x^k), x - x^{k+1} \rangle + \epsilon (f(x) - f(x^{k+1})) \geq 0$$

for all x in C. If F_2 happens to be symmetric or separable, the previous auxiliary problem is easier to solve than the original variational inequality.

Since any monotone mapping can be expressed as the sum of the zero mapping (which is trivially co-coercive) and itself, we recover as a special instance the general proximal variational inequality

$$\langle \epsilon F(x^{k+1}) + \Gamma_2(x^{k+1}) - \Gamma_2(x^k), x - x^{k+1} \rangle + \epsilon (f(x) - f(x^{k+1})) \geq 0 \quad \forall x \in C.$$

If, more specifically, $f(x)=0$ and we take $\Gamma_2(x)=x$, then we recover Martinet's regularization method [9] as a special case of our general method.

4.3 Relation to the asymmetric projection algorithm.

Let $f=0$; let D be an $n\times n$ positive definite matrix; and consider the algorithm where, at iteration k, the original variational inequality is approximated by the affine, but not necessarily symmetric, variational inequality

$$\langle F(x^k)+D(x^{k+1}-x^k), x-x^{k+1}\rangle \geq 0 \quad \forall x\in C. \tag{12}$$

Tseng [12] showed that the convergence of this algorithmic scheme followed from general convergence conditions given by Gabay for a forward backward splitting algorithm [5]. This "asymmetric projection" method is indeed a special instance of our general algorithm if one takes $M=0$, $L(x)=[(D-D^t)/2]x$, and $h'(x)=[(D+D^t)/2]x$. Dividing by ϵ, the auxiliary variational inequality can be written as

$$\langle F(x^k)+\left(\frac{D-D^t}{2}+\frac{D+D^t}{2\epsilon}\right)(x^{k+1}-x^k), x-x^{k+1}\rangle \geq 0 \quad \forall x\in C \tag{13}$$

and Tseng's asymmetric projection method is obtained for $\epsilon=1$.

Now denote by $\overline{D}$ the symmetric part of the matrix D. From Proposition 2.2, the mapping $F-L$ is co-coercive(with modulus γ) if and only if the mapping $\widetilde{F}-\widetilde{L}$ is co-coercive (with modulus $\widetilde{\gamma}$), where $\widetilde{L}=\widetilde{D}^{-\frac{1}{2}}LD^{-\frac{1}{2}}$, $\widetilde{F}=\widetilde{D}^{-\frac{1}{2}}FD^{-\frac{1}{2}}$, and $\widetilde{\gamma}=\gamma/\|\widetilde{D}^{-\frac{1}{2}}\|^2$. Our convergence condition can now be expressed as $0<\epsilon\leq 2\widetilde{\gamma}$. This reduces to Tseng's condition $2\widetilde{\gamma}\geq 1$ when $\epsilon=1$.

4.4 Application to the traffic equilibrium problem.

Let A be a matrix representing the arc-path incidence relationships over a multicommodity network. In this case, the feasible set C assumes the very simple form

$$\sum_p x_{pc}=d_c,$$
$$x_{pc}\geq 0, \tag{14}$$

where p is a path index, c a commodity index, and d_c the demand for commodity c.

Let F be a monotone cost mapping from R^m into R^m. Bertsekas and Gafni [3] proposed the projection iteration

$$x^{k+1}=\mathrm{Proj}_D[x^k-\epsilon D^{-1}A^tF(Ax^k)] \tag{15}$$

for solving network equilibrium problems modeled as the variational inequality

$$\langle A^tF(Ax^*), x-x^*\rangle \geq 0 \quad \forall x\in C, \tag{16}$$

where $\epsilon>0$; D is a positive definite, symmetric matrix; and Proj_D denotes the projection operator over the set C with respect to the norm induced by the matrix D. Under the assumptions that C be a polyhedral set, F be strongly monotone and Lipschitz continuous on C, and ϵ be sufficiently small, they proved the convergence of the previous projection algorithm. Their method clearly fits into our general framework, and convergence follows directly from the co-coercivity of the mapping $A^T F(Ax)$, which in general is not strongly monotone. In our analysis, the set C is only required to be a general convex set, not necessarily a polyhedron.

5. Partially co-coercive mappings and systems of variational inequalities.

In this section we consider the system of variational inequalities

$$\langle F_1(x^*, y^*), x - x^* \rangle \geq 0 \quad \forall x \in C_x, \tag{17}$$

$$\langle F_2(x^*, y^*), y - y^* \rangle \geq 0 \quad \forall y \in C_y, \tag{18}$$

where C_x (respectively, C_y) is a nonempty, closed convex subset of R^n (respectively, R^m) and F_1, F_2 are continuous mappings from $C_x \times C_y$ into R^n and R^m, respectively. Furthermore, assume that $F_1(x, y)$ is strongly monotone on C_x with respect to the variable x, and denote by α_y its modulus.

DEFINITION 5.1. *The mapping* $F(x,y) = (F_1(x,y), F_2(x,y))$ *is partially co-coercive if for any* $x_1, x_2 \in C_x$ *and any* $y_1, y_2 \in C_y$, *there exists a constant* γ *such that*

$$\langle F_1(x_1, y_1) - F_1(x_2, y_2), x_1 - x_2 \rangle + \langle F_2(x_1, y_1) - F_2(x_2, y_2), y_1 - y_2 \rangle$$
$$\geq \gamma \| F_2(x_1, y_1) - F_2(x_2, y_2) \|^2. \tag{19}$$

Consider the algorithm based on the iteration

$$\langle F_1(x^{k+1}, y^k), x - x^{k+1} \rangle \geq 0 \quad \forall x \in C_x, \tag{20}$$

$$\langle \epsilon F_2(x^{k+1}, y^k) + h'(y^{k+1}) - h'(y^k), y - y^{k+1} \rangle \geq 0 \quad \forall y \in C_y, \tag{21}$$

where the gradient h' is strongly monotone (with modulus b) over C_y and Lipschitz continuous over C_y with constant L.

THEOREM 5.2. *Let* F_1 *be strongly monotone on* C_x *with respect to the variable* x *with modulus* α_y, $F = (F_1, F_2)$ *be partially co-coercive with modulus* γ, *and either* (i) a_y *is independent of* y *or* (ii) $F_1(x, y)$ *is Lipschitz continuous in* y *and its Lipschitz constant is independent of* x. *Then the sequence* $\{(x^k, y^k)\}$ *generated by the algorithm converges to a solution of the system* (17), (18) *whenever* $0 < \epsilon < 2b\gamma$.

Proof. Let (x^*, y^*) be any fixed solution of the variational system (17), (18) and consider the function

$$\Lambda^*(y) = h(y^*) - h(y) - \langle h'(y), y^* - y \rangle. \tag{22}$$

We have

$$\Lambda^*(y^k) - \Lambda^*(y^{k+1}) = h(y^{k+1}) - h(y^k) - \langle h'(y^k), y^{k+1} - y^k \rangle$$
$$+ \langle h'(y^{k+1}) - h'(y^k), y^* - y^{k+1} \rangle$$
$$\geq \frac{b}{2} \| y^k - y^{k+1} \|^2 + \epsilon \langle F_2(x^{k+1}, y^k), y^{k+1} - y^* \rangle.$$

If we let $y = y^{k+1}$ in (18) and combine the corresponding inequality with the preceeding, the result is

$$\Lambda^*(y^k) - \Lambda^*(y^{k+1}) \geq \frac{b}{2} \| y^k - y^{k+1} \|^2 + \epsilon \langle F_2(x^{k+1}, y^k) - F_2(x^*, y^*), y^{k+1} - y^* \rangle$$

$$=\frac{b}{2}\|y^k-y^{k+1}\|^2+T.$$

Now

$$T=\epsilon\langle F_2(x^{k+1},y^k)-F_2(x^*,y^*),y^{k+1}-y^*\rangle$$
$$=\epsilon\langle F_2(x^{k+1},y^k)-F_2(x^*,y^*),y^k-y^*\rangle$$
$$+\epsilon\langle F_2(x^{k+1},y^k)-F_2(x^*,y^*),y^{k+1}-y^k\rangle.$$

Setting $x=x^{k+1}$ in (17) and $x=x^*$ in (20) and using the partial co-coercivity of F, we get

$$T\geq\epsilon[\gamma\|F_2(x^{k+1},y^k)-F_2(x^*,y^*)\|^2+\langle F_2(x^{k+1},y^k)-F_2(x^*,y^*),y^{k+1}-y^k\rangle]$$
$$\geq-\frac{\epsilon}{4\gamma}\|y^{k+1}-y^k\|^2$$

and

$$\Lambda^*(y^k)-\Lambda^*(y^{k+1})\geq\frac{1}{2}\left(b-\frac{\epsilon}{2\gamma}\right)\|y^{k+1}-y^k\|^2.$$

Since $\epsilon<2b\gamma$, $\Lambda^*(y^k)-\Lambda^*(y^{k+1})$ is positive and the sequence $\{\Lambda^*(y^k)\}$, which is strictly decreasing unless $y^k=y^{k+1}$, must converge to some number. Now, the fact that $\Lambda^*(y^k)\geq\frac{b}{2}\|y^k-y^*\|^2$ and $\{y^k\}$ is bounded imply that $\|y^{k+1}-y^k\|$ converges to zero. Thus there exists a subsequence $\{y^{k'}\}$ that converges to some limit point $\bar{y}$ of C_y.

Now let $x(y)$ satisfy the variational inequality

$$\langle F_1(x(y),y),x-x(y)\rangle\geq0\quad\forall x\in C_x\tag{23}$$

and let $\bar{x}=x(\bar{y})$. From our assumptions, the mapping $x(y)$ is continuous in y (see Harker and Pang[6], for instance). Since $y^{k'}\to\bar{y}$, it follows that $x^{k'+1}\to\bar{x}$ and $(\bar{x},\bar{y})$ satisfies(17)with$(x^*,y^*)=(\bar{x},\bar{y})$. On the other hand, since $\|y^k-y^{k+1}\|$ converges to zero, $(\bar{x},\bar{y})$satisfies(18). This implies that $(\bar{x},\bar{y})$ is a solution of the system(17),(18).

The previous convergence analysis holds for any solution (x^*,y^*) of the system of variational inequalities. Taking$(x^*,y^*)=(\bar{x},\bar{y})$, we can prove that the entire sequence $\{(x^k,y^k)\}$converges to $(\bar{x},\bar{y})$. Using the Lipschitz constant L of h', we can indeed write

$$\frac{b}{2}\|\bar{y}-y^k\|^2\leq\Lambda^*(y^k)\leq\frac{1}{2}L\|\bar{y}-y^k\|^2.$$

This, together with the convergence. of the sequence $y^{k'}$ to $\bar{y}$, implies that the entire sequence $\{y^k\}$ converges to $\bar{y}$. Then it follows from the continuity of $x(y)$ that the entire sequence $\{x^{k+1}\}$ converges to $\bar{x}$. □

Although the previous method can be applied to any asymmetric variational inequality satisfying the partial co-coercivity condition, it is more specifically suited to problems that are "partially" asymmetric, i. e., where the mapping F_1 is a gradient mapping, in which case (20) reduces to an optimization problem.

6. A primal-dual framework.

In this section we consider the variational inequality

$$\langle F(x^*), x-x^* \rangle \geq 0 \quad \forall x \in E = C \cap \{x \in R^n \mid B(x) \leq 0\}, \tag{24}$$

where C is a nonempty closed convex subset of R^n, F is strongly monotone (with modulus a) on E, and $B(x)=(f_1(x), f_2(x), \cdots, f_m(x))$ is a constraint mapping explicitly defined by the convex, Lipschitz continuous, and continuously differentiable functions f_i, $i=1,\cdots,m$. Assume that there exists $x_0 \in C$ such that $f_i(x_0)<0, i=1,\cdots,m$ (Slater's constraint qualification). Then the variational inequality (24) is equivalent to the Kuhn-Tucker-like system

$$\langle F(x^*) + (\nabla B(x^*))^t y^*, x-x^* \rangle \geq 0 \quad \forall x \in C, \tag{25}$$

$$\langle -B(x^*), y-y^* \rangle \geq 0 \quad \forall y \geq 0. \tag{26}$$

Let $F_1(X, y)=F(x)+(\nabla B(x))^t y$, $F_2(x, y)=-B(x)$, and $\Gamma=(F_1, F_2)$. We have, for y_1, y_2 nonnegative and x_1, x_2 in C,

$$\begin{aligned} S &\overset{\text{def}}{=} \langle F_1(x_1,y_1) - F_1(x_2,y_2), x_1-x_2 \rangle + \langle F_2(x_1,y_1) - F_2(x_2,y_2), y_1-y_2 \rangle \\ &= \langle F(x_1) - F(x_2), x_1-x_2 \rangle + \langle (\nabla B(x_1))^t y_1 - (\nabla B(x_2))^t y_2, x_1-x_2 \rangle \\ &\quad - \langle B(x_1) - B(x_2), y_1-y_2 \rangle. \end{aligned}$$

Since y_1 and y_2 are nonnegative and the functions f_i are convex, the functions $x \to \langle B(x), y_1 \rangle$ and $x \to \langle B(x), y_2 \rangle$ are convex. Therefore we can write

$$\langle (\nabla B(x_1))^t y_1 - (\nabla B(x_2))^t y_2, x_1-x_2 \rangle \geq -\langle B(x_1) - B(x_2), y_1-y_2 \rangle \tag{27}$$

and

$$S \geq \langle F(x_1) - F(x_2), x_1-x_2 \rangle \geq a \| x_1-x_2 \|^2.$$

Denoting by L_B the Lipschitz constant of B, we obtain

$$S \geq (a/L_B^2) \| B(x_1) - B(x_2) \|^2 = (a/L_B^2) \| F_2(x_1,y_1) - F_2(x_2,y_2) \|^2,$$

which implies that the mapping Γ is partially co-coercive.

We can apply the iterate (20), (21) of the previous section to the system (25), (26) to obtain the primal-dual algorithm

$$\langle F(x^{k+1}) + (\nabla B(x^{k+1}))^t y^k, x-x^{k+1} \rangle \geq 0 \quad \forall x \in C_x, \tag{28}$$

$$\langle -\epsilon B(x^{k+1}) + h'(y^{k+1}) - h'(y^k), y-y^{k+1} \rangle \geq 0 \quad \forall y \geq 0. \tag{29}$$

In particular, if we take $h(y)=\| y \|^2/2$, the solution of the auxiliary variational inequality is given by the closed-form expression

$$y^{k+1} = \max\{0, y^k + \epsilon B(x^{k+1})\}, \tag{30}$$

and our algorithm reduces to a Uzawa-type method (see Bensoussan, Lions, and Temam [2]).

If F and ∇B are separable our primal-dual algorithm lends itself naturally to decomposition. Otherwise, decomposition can still be achieved by applying the auxiliary problem technique to the pair of variational inequalities. (25), (26).

REFERENCES

[1] A. AUSLENDER, *Optimisation: Méthodes Numériques*, Masson, Paris, 1973.

[2] A. BENSOUSSAN, J. L. LIONS, AND R. TEMAM, *Sur les méthodes de décomposition et de coordination et applications*, Sur les Méthodes Numériques en Sciences Physiques et Économiques, J. L. Lions and G. I. Marchouk, eds., Dunod, Paris, 1974.

[3] P. BERTSEKAS AND M. GAFNI, *Projection methods for variational inequalities with application to the traffic assignment problem*, Math. Programming Stud., 17 (1982), pp. 139-159.

[4] G. COHEN, *Auxiliary problem principle extended to variational inequalities*, J. Optim. Theory Appl., 59 (1988), pp. 325-333.

[5] D. GABAY, *Applications of the method of multipliers to variational inequalities.*, in Augmented Lagrangian Methods: Applications to the Numerical Solution of Boundary-Value Problems, M. Fortin and R. Glowinski, eds., North-Holland, Amsterdam, 1983.

[6] P. T. HARKER AND J. S. PANG, *Finite-dimensional variational inequalities and nonlinear complementarity problems: A survey of theory, algorithms and applications*, Math. Programming, 48 (1990), pp. 161-220.

[7] Z. Luo AND P. TSENG, *A decomposition property for a class of square matrices*, Appl. Math. Lett., 4 (1991), pp. 67-69.

[8] P. MARCOTTE AND J. H. Wu, *On the convergence of projection methods: Application to the decomposition of affine, variational inequalities*, J. Optim. Theory Appl., 85 (1995), pp. 347-362.

[9] B. MARTINET, *Régularisation d'indquations variationnelles par approximations successives*, Revue française d'informatique et de recherche opérationnelle, R-3 (1970), pp. 154-159.

[10] M. A. MATAOUI, *Contributions à la Décomposition et à l'Agrégation des Problémes Variationnels*, Thése de Doctorat, École des Mines de Paris, Paris, 1990.

[11] J. M. ORTEGA AND W. O. RHEINBOLDT, *Iterative Solution of Nonlinear Equations in Several Variables*, Academic Press, New York, 1970.

[12] P. TSENG, *Further applications of a splitting algorithm to decomposition in variational inequalities and convex programming*, Math. Programming, 48 (1990), pp. 249-264.

Published in *SIAM J. Optimization*, 1996, 6(3)

WEAK SHARP SOLUTIONS OF VARIATIONAL INEQUALITIES*

PATRICE MARCOTTE** AND DAOLI ZHU***

Abstract. In this work we give sufficient conditions for the finite convergence of descent algorithms for solving variational inequalities involving generalized monotone mappings.

Key words. sharp solution, variational inequality, descent algorithm, generalized monotonicity

AMS subject classifications. 90C33, 49M99

PII. S1052623496309867

1. Introduction.

Recently, Burke and Ferris [5] introduced sufficient conditions for the finite identification, by iterative algorithms, of local minima associated with mathematical programs. To this aim, they introduced the notion of a weak sharp minimum, which extends the notion of a sharp or strongly unique minimum to mathematical programs admitting nonisolated local minima. In our work, we extend their results and those of Al-Khayyal and Kyparisis [1] to generalized monotone variational inequalities and provide a characterization of their solution sets. Our work is also closely related to that of Patriksson [14], who analyzed the finite convergence of approximation algorithms for solving monotone variational inequalities under a sharpness assumption.

The paper is organized as follows. Section 2 introduces the main definitions. In section 3, we reformulate the variational inequality problem (VIP) as a convex program and show that its objective is continuously differentiable at any solution of the VIP, un-

*Received by the editors September 27, 1996; accepted for publication (in revised form) September 2, 1997; published electronically December 2, 1998. This research was supported by NSERC (Canada) and FCAR (Québec).

http://www.siam.org/journals/siopt/9-1/30986.html

**DIRO, Université de Montréal, C.P. 6128, succursale Centre-Ville, Montréal, Québec, H3C 3J7 Canada (marcotte@iro.umontreal.ca).

***CRT, Université de Montréal, C.P. 6128, succursale Centre-Ville, Montréal, Québec, H3C 3J7 Canada (daoli@crt.umontreal.ca).

der a regularity assumption. In section 4 we introduce the notion of weak sharpness for the VIP and derive a necessary and sufficient condition for a solution set to be weakly sharp. Finally, section 5 addresses the finite convergence of iterative algorithms for solving variational inequalities whose solution set is weakly sharp.

2. Notation and definitions.

Let X denote a nonempty, closed, and convex subset of R^n and let F be a mapping from X into R^n. We consider the VIP that consists of finding a vector $x^* \in X$ that satisfies the variational inequality:

$$\langle F(x^*), x - x^* \rangle \geq 0 \quad \forall x \in X, \tag{2.1}$$

where $\langle x, y \rangle$ denotes the Euclidean inner product of two vectors in R^n. Throughout the paper, we will denote by X^* the set of solutions of the variational inequality (2.1). If X is a subset of R^n, its *polar set* X° is defined as

$$X^\circ := \{y \in R^n : \langle y, x \rangle \leq 0 \quad \forall x \in X\}.$$

We denote by $\operatorname{int}(C)$ the interior of a set C. The *projection* of a point $x \in R^n$ onto the set X is defined as

$$\operatorname{proj}_X(x) := \arg\min_{y \in X} \| x - y \|.$$

If X is a convex set, its *normal cone* at x is

$$N_X(x) := \begin{cases} \{y \in R^n : \langle y, z - x \rangle \leq 0 \quad \forall z \in X\} & \text{if } x \in X, \\ \phi & \text{otherwise}, \end{cases} \tag{2.2}$$

and its *tangent cone* at x is $T_X(x) := [N_X(x)]^\circ$. Using this notation, a vector x^* is a solution of the VIP if and only if

$$-F(x^*) \in N_X(x^*) \tag{2.3}$$

or, equivalently,

$$\operatorname{proj}_{T_X(x^*)}(-F(x^*)) = 0. \tag{2.4}$$

A mapping F from a convex set X into R^n is *monotone* on X if, $\forall x$, y in X,

$$\langle F(y) - F(x), y - x \rangle \geq 0. \tag{2.5}$$

It is *strongly monotone* on X if there exists a positive number α such that, $\forall x$, y in X,

$$\langle F(y) - F(x), y - x \rangle \geq \alpha \| y - x \|^2. \tag{2.6}$$

It is *pseudomonotone* on X if, $\forall x$, y in X,

$$\langle F(x), y - x \rangle \geq 0 \Rightarrow \langle F(y), y - x \rangle \geq 0. \tag{2.7}$$

It is *strongly pseudomonotone* on X if there exists a positive number β such that, $\forall x$, y in X,

$$\langle F(x), y - x \rangle \geq 0 \Rightarrow \langle F(y), y - x \rangle \geq \alpha \| y - x \|^2. \tag{2.8}$$

It is *monotone*$^+$ on C if F is monotone and for every pair of points x, y in X,

$$\langle F(y) - F(x), y - x \rangle = 0 \Rightarrow F(y) = F(x). \tag{2.9}$$

It is *pseudomonotone*$^+$ on X if F is pseudomonotone and, $\forall x$, y in X,

$$\langle F(x), y - x \rangle \geq 0 \text{ and } \langle F(y), y - x \rangle = 0 \Rightarrow F(y) = F(x). \tag{2.10}$$

It is *quasimonotone* on X if, $\forall x$, y in X,

$$\langle F(x), y-x\rangle > 0 \Rightarrow \langle F(y), y-x\rangle \geq 0. \qquad (2.11)$$

Several results concerning mappings satisfying the above monotonicity or generalized monotonicity conditions can be found in Schaible [15] and Zhu and Marcotte [11, 17]. Finally, a mapping F from the set X into R^n is *Lispchitz continuous* on X, with Lipschitz constant L, if, $\forall x$, y in X,

$$\| F(x) - F(y) \| \leq L \| x - y \| . \qquad (2.12)$$

3. The dual gap function for the pseudomonotone VIP.

If the mapping F is pseudomonotone, then the solution set of the VIP can be characterized as the intersection of half-spaces, i. e. , x^* is a solution of the VIP if and only if it satisfies

$$\langle F(x), x - x^* \rangle \geq 0 \quad \forall x \in X. \qquad (3.1)$$

It follows that the solution set of the VIP is closed and convex. The proof of this result is identical to that given in Auslender [2] for monotone variational inequalities. Note that we cannot substitute quasimonotonicity for pseudomonotonicity in (3.1), as shown by the VIP involving the quasimonotone function $F(x)=x^2$ and the set $X=R$. We define the *dual gap function* $G(x)$ associated with the VIP as

$$\begin{aligned} G(x) &= \max_{z\in X}\langle F(z), x - z\rangle \\ &= \langle F(\tilde{y}), x - \tilde{y}\rangle, \end{aligned} \qquad (3.2)$$

where $\tilde{y}$ is any point in the set $\Lambda(x) := \arg\max_{z\in X}\langle F(z), x-z\rangle$.

Since the function G is the pointwise supremum of affine functions, it is closed and convex on X. Moreover, G is nonnegative and achieves its minimum value (zero) only at points of X that satisfy the original variational inequality. Thus, any solution of the VIP is a global minimum for the convex optimization program

$$\min_{x\in X} G(x). \qquad (3.3)$$

If F is pseudomonotone$^+$, the dual gap function G enjoys the nice properties given in the theorem below.

Theorem 3.1. *Let F be continuous and pseudomonotone$^+$ on X. Then*

(i) *F is constant over X^*;*

(ii) *for any x^* in X^*, F is constant and equal to $F(x^*)$ over $\Lambda(x^*)$;*

(iii) *$\Lambda(x^*)=X^*$ for any x^* in X^*;*

(iv) *if X is compact, then G is continuously differentiable over X^*, and $\nabla G(x^*) = F(x^*)\ \forall x^*$ in X^*.*

Proof. (i) Let x^* and x^{**} be any two solutions of the VIP. It follows from (2.1) and (3.1) that

$$\langle F(x^{**}), x^{**} - x^* \rangle \geq 0,$$

$$\langle F(x^{**}), x^{**} - x\rangle \leq 0,$$

from which we deduce

$$\langle F(x^{**}), x^{**} - x^{*}\rangle = 0.$$

Now, the inequality

$$\langle F(x^{*}), x^{**} - x^{*}\rangle \geq 0,$$

together with the pseudomonotonicity^{+} of F, yields $F(x^{*})=F(x^{**})$.

(ii) For every $x^{*}\in X^{*}$ and y^{*} in $\Lambda(x^{*})$,

$$G(x^{*}) = \langle F(y^{*}), x^{*} - y^{*}\rangle = 0 \tag{3.4}$$

holds. Now, $\langle F(x^{*}), y^{*}-x^{*}\rangle \geq 0$ (x^{*} is a solution of the VIP) and $\langle F(y^{*}), y^{*}-x^{*}\rangle =0$ imply, by the pseudomonotonicity^{+} of F, that $F(x^{*})= F(y^{*})$.

(iii) Let $\tilde{x}\in\Lambda(x^{*})$. From (ii) we have that $F(x^{*})=F(\tilde{x})$ and $\langle F(\tilde{x}), x^{*}-x\rangle=0$. This implies that, for any y in X,

$$\langle F(\tilde{x}), \tilde{x}-y\rangle = \langle F(\tilde{x}), \tilde{x}-x^{*}\rangle + \langle F(\tilde{x}), x^{*}-y\rangle \tag{3.5}$$

$$= \langle F(x^{*}), x^{*}-y\rangle \tag{3.6}$$

$$\leq 0 \tag{3.7}$$

and $\tilde{x}$ is in X^{*}. Conversely, for any x^{*} in X^{*},

$$\tilde{x} \in X^{*} \Rightarrow \langle F(\tilde{x}), x^{*}-\tilde{x}\rangle = 0 \tag{3.8}$$

$$\Rightarrow \tilde{x} \in \Lambda(x^{*}). \tag{3.9}$$

(iv) From a result of Danskin[4] the derivative of G at x^{*} in the direction d is given by the expression

$$G'(x^{*}; d) = \max\{\langle F(y), d\rangle : y\in\Lambda(x^{*})\}$$
$$= \langle F(x^{*}), d\rangle,$$

since, by (ii), F is constant and equal to $F(x^{*})$ over $\Lambda(x^{*})$. Thus, G is continuously differentiable at every point $x^{*}\in X^{*}$, with gradient . $\nabla G(x^{*})= F(x^{*})$. □

4. Sharp solutions of variational inequalities.

Recently, in the context of convex smooth optimization, Burke and Ferris [5] have extended the notion of a strongly unique solution to optimization problems whose solution set is not necessarily a singleton. To this aim, they introduced the notion of a weak sharp solution for a convex minimization problem. We recall that the solution set X^{*} is *weakly sharp* for the program $\min_{x\in X} f(x)$ if there exists a positive number α (*modulus* of sharpness) such that

$$f(x) \geq f(x^{*}) + \alpha\,\mathrm{dist}(x, X^{*}) \quad \forall x^{*}\in X^{*}, \tag{4.1}$$

where $\mathrm{dist}(x, X^{*}) := \min_{x^{*}\in X^{*}} \| x-x^{*} \|$. These authors proved that if f is a closed, proper, and convex function and if the sets X and X^{*} are nonempty, closed, and convex, then the solution set of the convex optimization program (4.1) is weakly sharp if and only if the geometric condition

$$-\nabla f(x^{*}) \in \mathrm{int}\left(\bigcap_{x\in X^{*}} [T_X(x) \cap N_{X^{*}}(x)]^{\circ}\right) \quad \forall x^{*}\in X^{*} \tag{4.2}$$

holds. Since the VIP lacks a "natural" objective function, it is natural to define weak sharpness of the solution set of a variational inequality with reference to (4.2). Precisely, following Patriksson [14], we say that the solution set of the VIP is *weakly sharp* if we have, for any x^* in X^*,

$$-F(x^*)\in \text{int}\,(\bigcap_{x\in X^*}[T_X(x)\cap N_{X^*}(x)]^\circ). \tag{4.3}$$

Alternatively, one could have defined weak sharpness with respect to an "artificial" convex programming reformulation of the VIP. If F is pseudomonotone, an obvious choice for such a reformulation is the one based on the dual gap function defined earlier (see (3.2) and (3.3)). This would have led to the definition

$$G(x)\geq \alpha\text{dist}(x,X^*) \tag{4.4}$$

$\forall x$ in X. If this condition is fulfilled, the function G provides an error bound for the distance from a feasible point to the set of solutions to the VIP. The constant α is again called the *modulus* of sharpness for the solution set X^*. Note that the very evaluation of G at a point x requires the solution of a possibly nonconvex mathematical program.

From this point on, we will adopt the geometric condition (4.3) as the definition of weak sharpness and show that both definitions are actually equivalent whenever F is pseudomonotone$^+$.

THEOREM 4.1. *Let F be continuous and pseudomonotone$^+$ over the compact set X. Let the solution set X^* of the VIP be nonempty. Then X^* is weakly sharp if and only if there exists a positive number α such that*

$$G(x)\geq \alpha\text{dist}(x,X^*)$$

$\forall x$ in X.

Proof. Let B denote the unit ball in R^n. We first prove that the inclusion

$$\alpha B\subset F(x^*)+[T_X(x^*)\cap N_{X^*}(x^*)]^\circ \tag{4.5}$$

holds at $x^*\in X^*$ if and only if we have

$$\langle F(x^*),z\rangle\geq\alpha\|z\|\qquad\forall z\in T_X(x^*)\cap N_{X^*}(x^*). \tag{4.6}$$

Indeed, if (4.5) holds, then for every $y\in B$, we have

$$\alpha y-F(x^*)\in[T_X(x^*)\cap N_{X^*}(x^*)]^\circ. \tag{4.7}$$

Thus, for every $z\in[T_X(x^*)\cap N_{X^*}(x^*)]$, we have $\langle\alpha y-F(x^*),z\rangle\leq 0$. Taking $y=z/\|z\|$ in the above inequality, we obtain (4.6).

Now assume that (4.6) holds. Then there exists a positive number α such that, for $x^*\in X^*$, $y\in B$, and $z\in T_X(x^*)\cap N_{X^*}(x^*)$,

$$\begin{aligned}\langle -F(x^*)+\alpha y,z\rangle &= \langle -F(x^*),z\rangle+\alpha\langle y,z\rangle\\ &\leq\langle -F(x^*),z\rangle+\alpha\|y\|\,\|z\|\\ &\leq\langle -F(x^*),z\rangle+\alpha\|z\|\\ &\leq 0 \text{ by (4.6).}\end{aligned}$$

This implies that (4.5) holds as well.

If $-F(x^*) \in \text{int}\,(\bigcap_{x\in X^*}[T_X(x)\cap N_{X^*}(x)]^\circ)$ $\forall x^*$ in X^*, then there must exist a positive number α such that (4.5) is satisfied for every $x^* \in X^*$. From the above derivation, we have that $\langle F(x^*),z\rangle \geq \alpha \|z\|$ for every z in $T_X(x^*)\cap N_{X^*}(x^*)$. Now set, for x in X, $\bar{x}=\text{proj}_{X^*}(x)$. Clearly, $x-\bar{x}\in T_X(\bar{x})\cap N_{X^*}(\bar{x})$ and there follows

$$\langle F(\bar{x}),x-\bar{x}\rangle \geq \alpha \|x-\bar{x}\| = \alpha \text{dist}(x,X^*).$$

Since G is a convex function, differentiable at $\bar{x}\in X^*$, we have

$$\begin{aligned} G(x) &= G(x)-G(\bar{x}) \\ &\geq \langle \nabla G(\bar{x}),x-\bar{x}\rangle \\ &= \langle F(\bar{x}),x-\bar{x}\rangle \\ &\geq \alpha\ \text{dist}(x,X^*). \end{aligned}$$

Conversely, let X^* satisfy (4.4) for some positive number α and let x^* be a point in X^*. If $T_X(x^*)\cap N_{X^*}(x^*)=\{0\}$, then $[T_X(x^*)\cap N_{X^*}(x^*)]^\circ = R^n$ and $\alpha B\subset F(x^*)+[T_X(x^*)\cap N_{X^*}(x^*)]^\circ$, trivially. Otherwise, let d be a nonzero vector in $T_X(x^*)\cap N_{X^*}(x^*)$. For any $y^*\in X^*$, we have

$$\langle d,y^*-x^*\rangle \geq 0 \quad \text{since } d\in T_X(x^*),$$
$$\langle d,y^*-x^*\rangle \leq 0 \quad \text{since } d\in N_{X^*}(x^*).$$

Those inequalities imply that $\langle d,y^*-x^*\rangle = 0$, and X^* is a subset of a hyperplane H_d orthogonal to d. Let $\{d^k\}$ be a sequence converging to d such that $x^*+t_kd^k\in X$ for some sequence of positive numbers $\{t_k\}$. We can write

$$\begin{aligned} \text{dist}(x^*+t_kd^k,X^*) &\geq \text{dist}(x^*+t_kd^k,H_d) \\ &= \frac{t_k\langle d,d^k\rangle}{\|d\|} \end{aligned}$$

Since X^* satisfies (4.4) with modulus α, we obtain

$$G(x^*+t_kd^k) \geq \alpha\text{dist}(x^*+t_kd^k,X^*) \geq \alpha\, t_k\frac{t_k\langle d,d^k\rangle}{\|d\|}$$

and

$$(G(x^*+t_kd^k)-G(x^*))/t_k \geq \alpha\frac{\langle d,d^k\rangle}{\|d\|}.$$

Taking the limit as $t_k\rightarrow 0$ and $d^k\rightarrow d$ leads to

$$\langle \nabla G(x^*),d \geq \alpha\|d\|$$

$\forall d$ in $T_X(x^*)\cap N_{X^*}(x^*)$. Therefore, for any w in B,

$$\begin{aligned} \langle \alpha w-F(x^*),d\rangle &= \langle \alpha w,d\rangle - \langle \nabla G(x^*),d \\ &\leq \alpha\|d\| - \alpha\|d\| \\ &= 0, \end{aligned}$$

and it follows that $\alpha B\subset F(x^*)+[T_X(x^*)\cap N_{X^*}(x^*)]^\circ$. Since F is constant over X^*, we conclude that (4.3) holds. □

We now show, by means of an example, that pseudomonotonicity of F is too weak a condition for the above result to hold. Indeed, consider the variational inequality defined by the two-dimensional mapping $F(x)=(-x_2, 2x_1)$ and the set $X=\{0\leq x_1\leq 1, 0\leq x_2\leq 1\}$. One can check that the mapping F is pseudomonotone but not pseudomonotone$^+$ on X. Indeed, F is not constant over its solution set $X^*=\{x\in X: x_2=0\}$, in contradiction with the first statement of Theorem 3.1. We have

$$\begin{aligned} G(x) &= \max_{y\in X}\langle(-y_2, 2y_1), (x_1-y_1, x_2-y_2)\rangle \\ &= \max_{y\in X} -x_1y_2 - y_1y_2 + 2x_2y_1 \\ &= 2x_2 \\ &= 2\mathrm{dist}(x, X^*), \end{aligned}$$

and X^* satisfies (4.4) with modulus $\alpha=2$. However, for any x^* in X^*, we have $[T_X(x^*)\cap N_{X^*}(x^*)]^\circ=\{x_2^*\leq 0\}$. Consequently $-F(x^*)$ does not lie inside

$$\bigcap_{x^*\in X^*}[T_X(x^*)\cap N_{X^*}(x^*)]^\circ$$

for any x^* in the solution set X^*, and the solution set X^* is not weakly sharp.

Our second characterization of weak sharpness involves the notion of *minimum principle suffciency* introduced by Ferris and Mangasarian [6]. Consider the refor-mulation of the VIP as the (possibly nonconvex and/or nonsmooth) optimization problem $\min_{x\in X} g(x)$, where the *primal gap function* g is defined as

$$g(x):=\max_{y\in X}\langle F(x), x-y\rangle, \tag{4.8}$$

and let

$$\begin{aligned} \Gamma(x) &:= \arg\max_{y\in X}\langle F(x), x-y\rangle \\ &= \arg\min_{y\in X}\langle F(x), y\rangle. \end{aligned}$$

We say that the VIP possesses the *minimum principle suffciency* (MPS) property if $\Gamma(x^*)$ coincides with the solution set X^*, for every x^* in X^*.

THEOREM 4.2. *Assume that F is continuous on X and that the set*

$$K:=\mathrm{int}\left(\bigcap_{x\in X^*}[T_X(x)\cap N_{X^*}(x)]^\circ\right)$$

is nonempty. Then, for each z in K, one has that $\mathrm{argmax}\{\langle z, y\rangle: y\in X\}\subset X^*$. Moreover, if F is pseudomonotone and $-F(x^*)\in K$ for every $x^*\in X^*$, then the VIP possesses the MPS property.

Proof. Let $x\in X$, $x\notin X^*$, and $\bar{x}=\mathrm{proj}_{X^*}(x)$. We have that $x-\bar{x}\in T_X(\bar{x})\cap N_{X^*}(\bar{x})$, and, for any given z in K, there exists a positive number δ such that $\langle z+w, x-\bar{x}\rangle<0$ $\forall w$ in δB. Thus,

$$\langle z, x\rangle < \langle z, \bar{x}\rangle - \delta\|x-\bar{x}\|;$$

i.e., $x\notin \mathrm{argmax}\{\langle z, y\rangle: y\in X\}$, which brings about the conclusion by contradiction.

Next, let $-F(x^*)\in K$ for $x^*\in X^*$. In the first part of the proof, it has been established that

$$\mathrm{argmax}\{\langle -F(x^*), y\rangle: y\in X\}\subset X^*.$$

Let $\hat{x}$ be in X^*. We have, as before, $\langle F(x^*), \hat{x}-x^*\rangle=0$. Now, for any y in X,

$$\langle F(x^*),\hat{x}-y\rangle=\langle F(x^*),\hat{x}-x^*\rangle+\langle F(x^*),x^*-y\rangle$$
$$\leq 0.$$

Therefore, $\hat{x}\in\Gamma(x^*)$ and $X^*\subset\Gamma(x^*)$. By gathering the two preceding inclusions, we conclude that arg max $\{\langle -F(x^*),y\rangle: y\in X\}=X^*$, as claimed. □

Theorem 4.3. *Let F be pseudomonotone*$^+$ *and continuous on the compact poly-hedral set X. Then the VIP possesses the MPS property if and only if it is weakly sharp, i.e.,* $X^*=\Gamma(x^*)=\Lambda(x^*)$.

Proof. The " if " part of the statement is a consequence of Theorem 4.2. To prove the converse, first observe that the solution set $\Gamma(x^*)=X^*$ of the linear program

$$\min_{x\in X}\langle F(x^*),x\rangle$$

is weakly sharp (see appendix in Mangasarian and Meyer [10], for instance) with positive modulus α, and that α only depends on the constant vector $F(x^*)$ and X. We develop

$$\begin{aligned}G(x)&=\max_{y\in X}\langle F(y),x-y\rangle\\&\geq\langle F(x^*),x-x^*\rangle\qquad\forall x^*\in X^*\\&=\langle F(x^*),x-\hat{x}\rangle\qquad\forall\hat{x}\in\Gamma(x^*)\\&\geq\alpha\,\|x-\mathrm{proj}_{\Gamma}(x^*)(x)\|\\&=\alpha\,\|x-\mathrm{proj}_{X^*}(x)\|\\&\geq\alpha\,\mathrm{dist}(x,X^*),\end{aligned}$$

and from Theorem 4.1, X^* is weakly sharp. □

5. Finite convergence of algorithms for solving the VIP.

In this section we will derive finite convergence results for classes of algorithms under the condition that the solution set of the VIP be weakly sharp. The first such result generalizes a result of Al-Khayyal and Kyparisis [1] to the case where the solution set is not necessarily a singleton.

THEOREM 5.1. *Let F be continuous and pseudomonotone*$^+$ *over the set X, and let the solution set* X^* *of the VIP be weakly sharp. Also let* $\{x^k\}$ *be a sequence in* R^n. *If either*

(i) *the sequence* $\{\mathrm{dist}(x^k,X^*)\}$ *converges to zero and the mapping F is uniformly continuous on an open set containing the sequence* $\{x^k\}$ *and the set* X^*, *or*

(ii) *the sequence* $\{x^k\}$ *converges to some* $x^*\in X^*$, *then there exists a positive integer* k_0 *such that, for any index* $k\geq k_0$, *any solution of the linear program*

$$\min_{x\in X}\langle F(x^k),x\rangle\qquad(5.1)$$

is a solution of the VIP.

Proof. First assume that (i) holds. From Theorem 3.1, $-F(x^*)$ is constant over X^* and there must exist a uniform positive constant α such that

$$-F(x^*)+\alpha B\in\bigcap_{x\in X^*}[T_X(x)\cap N_{X^*}(x)]^\circ \tag{5.2}$$

for every x^* in X^*. Since F is uniformly continuous and $\operatorname{dist}(x^k,X^*)\to 0$, there exists an integer k_0 such that

$$\| F(x^k)-F(x^*)\| <\alpha\, \forall\, k\geq k_0,$$

i. e., $-F(x^k)\in \operatorname{int}(\bigcap_{x\in X^*}[T_X(x)\cap N_{X^*}(x)]^\circ)$. Therefore, by Theorem 4.2,

$$\arg\min_{x\in X}\langle F(x^k),x\rangle\subset X^*.$$

Under condition (ii) the result (5.2) is still valid for every $x^*\in X^*$, and we obtain the result as a consequence of the convergence of the sequence $\{\| F(x^k)-F(x^*)\|\}_k$ to zero. □

If Ω is a nonempty, closed, and convex subset of X, Burke and Ferris [5] have proved the inclusion

$$\Omega+\bigcap_{x\in\Omega}[T_X(x^*)\cap N_\Omega(x)]^\circ\subset\bigcup_{x\in\Omega}[x+N_X(x)]. \tag{5.3}$$

We will now use this result to provide a geometric characterization of sequences that achieve the finite identification of a solution to the VIP.

THEOREM 5.2. *Let F be pseudomonotone$^+$ and continuous over the compact set X. Let the solution set X^* of the VIP be weakly sharp. Let $\{x^k\}$ be a subsequence with elements in X such that the real sequence $\{\operatorname{dist}(x^k,X^*)\}$ converges to zero. If F is uniformly continuous on an open set containing $\{x^k\}$ and X^*, then there exists a positive integer k_0 such that, for any index $k\geq k_0$, x^k is a solution of the VIP if and only if*

$$\lim_{k\to\infty}\operatorname{proj}_{T_X(x^k)}(-F(x^k))=0. \tag{5.4}$$

Proof. If $x^k\in X^*$, then $-F(x^k)\in N_X(x^k)$ and (5.4) holds trivially.

Otherwise, assume that (5.4) is satisfied. The Moreau decomposition of $-F(x^k)$ along $T_X(x)$ and its polar cone $N_X(x)$ yields

$$-F(x^k)=\operatorname{proj}_{T_X(x)}(-F(x^k))+\operatorname{proj}_{N_X(x)}(-F(x^k)).$$

By Theorem 3.1, we have that F is constant over X^*. Thus, for any $x^*\in X^*$, the assumptions imply

$$\| F(x^*)+\operatorname{proj}_{N_X(x)}(-F(x^k))\|\to 0,$$

and so

$$\operatorname{dist}(x^k+\operatorname{proj}_{N_X(x^k)}(-F(x^k)),X^*-F(x^*))\to 0.$$

But, from the weak sharpness property, one has

$$X^*-F(x^*)\subset\operatorname{int}(X^*+\bigcap_{x\in X^*}[T_X(x)\cap N_{X^*}(x)]^\circ)$$

Now, for x^k close to x^* in X^*, we have, using (5.3),

$$x^k+\operatorname{proj}_{N_X(x^k)}(-F(x^k))\in\operatorname{int}(X^*+\bigcap_{x\in X^*}[T_X(x)\cap N_{X^*}(x)]^\circ)$$
$$\subset\bigcup_{x\in X^*}[x+N_X(x)].$$

Therefore, $\forall\, k$ suffciently large,

$$x^k=\operatorname{proj}_X(x^k+\operatorname{proj}_{N_X(x^k)}(-F(x^k)))$$

$$\in \mathrm{proj}_X\Big(\bigcup_{x\in X^*}[x+N_X(x)]\Big)$$
$$\subset \bigcup_{x\in X^*}\{x\}$$
$$= X^*.$$

This completes the proof. □

Several authors have proposed general iterative frameworks for solving variational inequalities. For instance, Cohen [3], or Zhu and Marcotte [18] investigated a scheme in which x^{k+1} is a solution of the variational inequality

$$\langle \sigma F(x^k)+H(x^{k+1})-H(x^k), x-x^{k+1}\rangle \geq 0 \quad \forall x\in X, \tag{5.5}$$

where σ is a positive constant and H is an auxiliary mapping, usually taken to be strongly monotone. Under suitable assumptions on F (strong monotonicity or co-coercivity[1]) and σ, the sequence $\{x^k\}$ is known to converge to a solution of the original variational inequality. From now on, we restrict our attention to those cases where the algorithm returns a convergent sequence $\{x^k\}$ whose limiting point is a solution of the VIP, and provide a sufficient condition for itsfinite termination.

LEMMA 5.1. *Let F and H be uniformly continuous on X and* $\{x^k\}\to x^*$. *Then the sequence* $\{\mathrm{proj}_{T_X(x^{k+1})}(-F(x^{k+1}))\}$ *converges to zero.*

Proof. Since the sequence $\{x^k\}$ is convergent, $\|x^{k+1}-x^k\|\to 0$. From (5.5), we have

$$-[\sigma F(x^k)+H(x^{k+1})-H(x^k)]\in N_X(x^{k+1}).$$

The Moreau decomposition technique yields

$$\|\mathrm{proj}_{-T_X(x^{k+1})}(F(x^{k+1}))\| = \min_{v\in N_X(x^{k+1})}\|-(x^{k+1})-v\|$$

$$= \min_{z\in -F(x^{k+1})-N_X(x^{k+1})}\|z\| \leq \left\|[F(x^{k+1})-F(x^k)]+\frac{1}{\sigma}[H(x^{k+1})-H(x^k)]\right\|.$$

From the uniform continuity of F and H, the right-hand side of the above inequality converges to zero, and we obtain that $\{\mathrm{proj}_{TX(x^{k+1})}(-F(x^{k+1}))\}$ converges to zero, as claimed. □

Combining Theorem 5.2 and Lemma 5.1, we obtain the following result.

Theorem 5.3. *Under the assumptions of Theorem* 5.2 *and Lemma* 5.1, *the general iterative algorithm for solving the VIP based on the auxiliary problem* (5.5) *generates a sequence* $\{x^k\}$ *such that, for all k sufficiently large,* x^k *is a solution of the VIP.* *

Recently, Zhu and Marcotte[18]have proposed a descent framework for the VIP, based on the auxiliary variational inequality (5.5), that includes as particular cases Fukushima's projective method [7] and Taji, Fukushima, and Ibaraki's Newton meth-

*1 The mapping F is co-coercive on the set X if there exists a positive number β such that $\langle F(x)-F(y), x-y\rangle \geq \beta \|F(x)-F(y)\|^2$ for all x, y in X; i.e., its inverse mapping is strongly monotone.

od [16] (see also Fukushima [8] or Larsson and Patriksson [9] for a survey of de-scent methods for the VIP). Given a mapping $H(w,x)$ defined on $X \times X$, continuous and strongly monotone with respect to the variable x and such that $H(x,x)$ coincides with the values $F(x)$ of the original mapping, a direction d^k is speci al, at iteration k, as $d^k = w^k - x^k$, where w^k is the unique solution of the auxiliary variational inequality

$$\langle H(w^k,x^k) - H(x^k,x^k), x - x^k \rangle \geq 0 \quad \forall x \in X. \tag{5.6}$$

The iterate x^{k+1} is then obtained by minimizing some merit function (related to the auxiliary mapping H) along the direction d^k. Under a suitable assumption, we have that d^k is a descent direction for the merit function at the point x^k, and it can be shown that d^k converges to zero, while both w^k and x^k converge to a solution of the VIP. If F and H are both uniformly continuous, respectively, on X and $X \times X$, we then obtain that pro $\mathrm{j}_{T_{X(w^k)}}(-F(w^k))$ converges to zero. If, furthermore, the assumptions of Theorem 5.2 are satisfied, the sequence $\{x^k\}$ converges to x^* after a finite number of iterations.

REFERENCES

[1]F. A. AL-KHAYYAL AND J. KYPARISIS, *Finite convergence of algorithms for nonlinear program-ming and variational inequalities*, J. Optim. Theory Appl., 70 (1991), pp. 319-332.

[2] A. AUSLENDER, *Optimisation, Méthodes numériques*, Masson, Paris, 1976.

[3]G. COHEN, *Auxiliary problem principle extended to variational inequalities*, J. Optim. Theory Appl., 59 (1988), pp. 325-333.

[4]J. M. DANSKIN, *The theory of min-max with applications*, SIAM J. Appl. Math., 14 (1966), pp. 641-664.

[5]J. V. BURKE AND M. C. Ferris, *Weak sharp minima in mathematical programming*, SIAM J. Control Optim., 31 (1993), pp. 1340-1359.

[6]M. C. FERRIS AND O. L. *Mangasarian, Minimum principle sufficiency*, Math. Programming, 57 (1992), pp. 1-14.

[7] M. FUKUSHIMA, *Equivalent diffierentiable optimization problems and descent methods for asym-metric variational inequality problems*, Math. Programming, 53 (1992), pp. 99-110.

[8] M. FUKUSHIMA, *Merit functions for variational inequality and complementarity problems*, Non-linear Optimization and Applications, G. Di Pillo and F. Giannessi, eds., Plenum Press, 1996, pp. 155-179.

[9]T. LARSSON AND M. PATRIKSSON, *A class of gap functions for variational inequalities*, Math. Programming, 64 (1994), pp. 53-80.

[10] O. L. MANGASARIAN AND R. R. MEYER, *Nonlinear perturbation of linear programming*, SIAM J. Control Optim., 17 (1979), pp. 745-752.

[11]P. MARCOTTE AND D. L. ZHU, *Monotone$^+$ mappings and variational inequalities*, in Fifth International Symposium on Generalized Convexity, Luminy, France, June 1996.

[12]J. J. MOREAU, *Décomposition orthogonale dans un espace hilbertien selon deux cônes mutuellement polaires*, Comptes Rendus Hebdomadaires des Séances de l'Académie des Sciences (Paris), S'erie A, 255 (1962), pp. 233-240.

[13]S. NGUYEN AND C. DUPUIS, *An e. cient method for computing traffic equilibria in networks with asymmetric transportation costs*, Transportation Sci., 18 (1984), pp. 185-202.

[14]M. PATRIKSSON, *A unified framework of descent algorithms for nonlinear programs and varia-tional inequalities*, Ph. D. thesis, Department of Mathematics, Link¨oping Institute of Tech-nology, Link¨oping, Sweden, 1993.

[15]S. SCHAIBLE, *Generalized monotonicity*, in Proceedings of the 10th International Summer School on Nonsmooth Optimization, Analysis and Applications, Erice, Italy, 1991, F. Gi-annessi, ed., Gordon and Breach, Amsterdam, The Netherlands, 1992.

[16]K. TAJI, M. FUKUSHIMA, AND T. IBARAKI, *A globally convergent Newton method for solving strongly monotone variational inequalities*, Math. Programming, 58 (1993), pp. 369-383.

[17]D. L. ZHU AND P. MARCOTTE, *New classes of generalized monotononicity*, J. Optim. Theory. Appl., 87 (1995), pp. 457-471.

[18]D. L. ZHU AND P. MARCOTTE, *An extended descent framework for variational inequalities*, J. Optim. Theory. Appl., 80 (1994), pp. 349-360.

[19]D. L. ZHU AND P. MARCOTTE, *Co-coercivity and its role in the convergence of iterative schemes for solving variational inequalities*, SIAM J. Optim., 6 (1996), pp. 714-726.

Published in *SIAM J. Optimization*, 1998, 9(1)

An Extended Descent Framework for Variational Inequalities *

D. L. ZHU** AND P. MARCOTTE***
Communicated by F. Giannessi

Abstract. In this paper, we develop a very general descent framework for solving asymmetric, monotone variational inequalities, We introduce two classes of differentiable merit functions and the associated global convergence frameworks which include, as special instances, the projection, Newton, quasi-Newton, linear Jacobi, and nonlinear methods. The generic algorithm is very flexible and consequently well suited for exploiting any particular structure of the problem.

Key Words. Mathematical programming, variational inequalities, descent methods.

1. Introduction

The aim of this paper is to present an extended framework of globally convergent methods for solving monotone variational inequality problems (VIP). For a good survey of solution methods for solving VIP, the reader is referred to Harker and Pang [1]. Several unifying algorithmic frameworks have already been proposed in the literature. In particular, Dafermos[2] has presented a class of approximation methods whose iterates contract to the unique solution of a strongly monotone VIP. However, it has recently been shown by Zanni[3] that the estimate of the contraction constant was often close to unity. Independently, Cohen[4] has presented related iterative methods based upon the auxiliary problem principle. More recently, authors have proposed descent al-gorithms for VIP that proceed by minimizing surrogate objectives (gap functions). A linesearch strategy allows these algorithms to converge globally from any starting point Marcotte [5], Marcotte and Dussault [6][7], Fukushima [8]. In particular, it has been shown

*This research was supported by the National Science and Engineering Research Council of Canada, Grant A5789, and by the Department of National Defence of Canada, Grant FUHBP.

**Invited Researcher, Center for Research on Transportation, Université de Montréal, Montréal, Québec, Canada.

***Professor, Département d'Informatique et de Recherche Opérationnelle, Université de Montréal, Montréal, Québec, Canada.

by Marcotte and Dussault [7] that Newton's direction is gap-decreasing, thus providing a global convergence framework for Newton's method applied to VIP. In this paper, we study a very general gap function that provides an equivalent differentiable optimization formulation for VIP. It includes, as special cases, the projective gap function of Fukushima [8] as well as extensions thereof proposed by Wu, Florian, and Marcotte [9] and Taji et al. [10].

The paper will be organized as follows. Basic notations are introduced in Section 2. Section 3 addresses a general descent formulation for VIP. Section 4 defines the auxiliary problem which will be used in the definition of the general framework (Section 5) and its two realizations (Sections 6 and 7). A conclusion (Section 8) will close the paper.

2. Notations and Basic Definitions

Let V be a closed, nonempty, convex subset of R^n, and let F be a mapping from V into R^n. We say that F is monotone on V if

$$\langle (F(v) - F(u), v-u\rangle \geq 0, \quad \forall v, u \in V; \tag{1}$$

it is strictly monotone on V if the above inequality is strict for $v \neq u$; it is strongly monotone on V with modulus μ if there exists a positive constant μ such that

$$\langle F(v) - F(u), v-u\rangle \geq \mu \| v-u \|^2, \quad \forall v, u \in V, \tag{2}$$

where $\| \cdot \|$ denotes the Euclidean norm in R^n; and it is strongly pseudo- monotone on V with modulus $\beta, \beta > 0$, if for every u, $v \in V$ we have that

$$\langle F(u), u-v\rangle \geq 0 \text{ implies } \langle F(v), v-u\rangle \geq \beta \| v-u \|^2. \tag{3}$$

We say that F is coercive with respect to v if there exists a vector $v^0 \in V$ such that

$$\lim_{v\in V, \|v\| \to \infty} \langle F(v), v-v^0\rangle / \| v-v^0 \| = \infty. \tag{4}$$

Every strongly monotone mapping is strongly pseudomonotone and coer- cive. Furthermore, if f is coercive and monotone, the solution set to VIP is convex and compact.

If F is differentiable on V, then F is monotone [respectively, strongly monotone] on V if and only if the Jacobian matrix $\nabla F(v)$ is positive semidefinite [respectively, positive definite] on V. The mapping F is Lipschitz continuous on V, with Lipschitz constant $L < \infty$, if

$$\| F(u) - F(v) \| \leq L \| u-v \|, \quad \forall u, v \in V. \tag{5}$$

Finally, a function $f: V \to R$ is said to be strongly convex on V with modulus $a(a>0)$ if, for all u, $v \in V$ and $\alpha \in [0, 1]$, we have

$$f(\alpha u + (1-\alpha)v) \leq \alpha f(u) + (1-\alpha) f(v) - a[\alpha(1-\alpha)/2] \| u-v \|^2. \tag{6}$$

If furthermore f is continuously differentiable on V, then f is strongly convex on V if and only if its gradient is strongly monotone on V.

Now we consider the variational inequality problem: Find $v^* \in V$ such that

$$(\text{VIP}) \langle F(v^*), v-v^*\rangle \geq 0, \quad \forall v \in V.$$

Definition 2.1. A gap function for VIP is a nonnegative function g defined on V such *that* $g(v)=0 \Leftrightarrow v$ is a solution to VIP, i. e. , the solution set of VIP coincides with the global solutions of the mathematical pro gramming problem $\min_{v\in V} g(v)$.

Gap functions have been introduced to monitor the convergence of sequences to a solution of a variational inequality. The standard nondiffer entiable gap function, defined as

$$g(v) = \max_{u\in V}\langle F(v), v-u\rangle,$$

has been shown by Marcotte and Dussault (Ref. 6) to be closely related to the duality gap associated with VIP.

3. Extended Differentiable Gap Function Formulation

Let $\Omega(u, v): V\times V \to R$ be nonnegative, continuously differentiable on $V\times V$, strongly convex on V with respect to u for all $v\in V$ and satisfy

$$\Omega(v, v) = 0 \text{ and } \nabla_u\Omega(v, v) = 0, \quad \text{for all } v\in V.$$

Define

$$h(u, v) = \langle F(v), v-u\rangle - \Omega(u,v), \tag{7}$$

$$g(v) = \max_{u\in V} h(u, v) = h(H(v), v), \tag{8}$$

where the maximizer $H(v)$ is unambiguously defined, since h is the sum of a linear and a strongly convex term.

Theorem 3. 1. g is a gap function.

Proof. Since $h(v, v) = 0$, it is clear that $g(v)\geq 0$ for every $v\in V$. Now, assume that v solves VIP. Then,

$$h(u, v) = \langle F(v), v-u\rangle - \Omega(u, v)\leq 0,$$

which implies that

$$g(v) = 0 .$$

Conversely, assume that $g(v) = 0$. This implies that

$$h(u, v)\leq 0, \qquad \text{for all } u\in V,$$

and that v is a solution to the optimization problem $\max_{u\in V} h(u, v)$. Thus, v satisfies the variational inequality

$$\langle \nabla_u h(v, v), u-v\rangle \leq 0, \quad \forall u\in V,$$

i. e. ,

$$\langle F(v), u-v\rangle + \langle \nabla_u\Omega(v, v), u-v\rangle \geq 0, \qquad \forall u\in V.$$

Hence,

$$\langle F(v), u-v\rangle \geq 0, \qquad \forall u\in V,$$

since

$$\langle \nabla_u\Omega(u, v), u-v\rangle = 0.$$

Consequently, v solves VIP. □

Theorem 3. 2. If the mapping F is continuous on V, then the function g defined by

(8) is also continuous. Furthermore, if F is continuously differentiable, then g is also continuously differentiable and its gradient is given by

$$\nabla g(v) = F(v) - (\nabla F(v))^T(H(v) - v) - \nabla_v \Omega(H(v), v), \qquad (9)$$

where $H(v)$ is the unique solution of the maximization problem appearing on the right-hand side of (8).

Proof. The first part of the statement follows from the continuity of the max operator. If F is continuously differentiable, it follows, from the uniqueness of the maximizer $H(v)$ of (8), that g is differentiable with gradient

$$\begin{aligned}\nabla g(v) &= \nabla_v h(H(v), v)\\ &= F(v) - \langle \nabla F(v), H(v) - v\rangle - \nabla_v \Omega(H(v), v).\end{aligned}$$

□

Theorem 3.3. Let v^* be a solution to VIP. If F is strongly pseudo- monotone with modulus μ on V and if the gradient of Ω with respect to u is Lipschitz continuous with constant L_Ω on V, then there exists a positive constant α such that

$$g(v) \geq \alpha \| v - v^* \|^2, \qquad \forall v \in V. \qquad (10)$$

Proof. Since F is strongly pseudomonotone with modulus μ on V and

$$\langle F(v^*), v - v^* \rangle \geq 0, \qquad \forall v \in V,$$

we have

$$\langle F(v), v - v^* \rangle \geq \mu \| v - v^* \|^2, \qquad \forall v \in V. \qquad (11)$$

Set

$$v_t = v + t(v^* - v), \qquad \text{for } t \in [0, 1].$$

Since Ω is convex in u and its gradient with respect to u is Lipschitz continuous, we get

$$\begin{aligned}\Omega(v_t, v) - \Omega(v, v) &\leq \langle \nabla_u \Omega(u_t, v), v_t - v\rangle\\ &= \langle \nabla_u \Omega(u_t, v) - \nabla_u \Omega(u, v), v_t - v\rangle\\ &\leq L_\Omega \| v_t - v \|^2.\end{aligned}$$

Then, we have

$$\begin{aligned}g(v) &\geq \langle F(v), v - v_t\rangle - \Omega(v_t, v)\\ &= \langle F(v), v - v_t\rangle - (\Omega(v_t, v) - \Omega(v, v))\\ &\geq t\langle F(v), v - v^* \rangle - L_\Omega \| v_t - v \|^2\\ &\geq t\langle F(v), v - v^* \rangle - L_\Omega t^2 \| v - v^* \|\\ &\geq (t\mu - t^2 L_\Omega) \| v - v^* \|^2\\ &= [\mu^2/4L_\Omega - L_\Omega (t - \mu/2L_\Omega)^2] \| v - v^* \|^2.\end{aligned}$$

In particular, if we let

$$t = \min\{1, \mu/2L_\Omega\},$$

we obtain

$$g(v) \geq \alpha \| v - v^* \|^2,$$

where

$$\alpha = \begin{cases} \mu - L_\Omega, & \text{if} \mu \geq 2L_\Omega, \\ \mu^2/4L_\Omega, & \text{if} \mu \leq 2L_\Omega, \end{cases}$$

which proves the result. □

4. Auxiliary Variational Inequality

Let $\Gamma(u, v): V \times V \to R^n$ be a mapping (the auxiliary mapping), contin uous and strongly monotone with respect to u, and continuous with respect to v. Let us consider the auxiliary variational inequality problem: Find $w \in V$ such that

$$(\text{AVIP}(v)) \quad \langle \Gamma(w, v) - \Gamma(v, v) + F(v), u - w \rangle \geq 0, \qquad \forall u \in V. \tag{12}$$

In view of the strong monotonicity of $\Gamma(u, v)$ with respect to $u \in V$, this auxiliary variational inequality has a unique solution, which we denote $W(v)$.

Proposition 4.1. The mapping $W: V \to V$ is continuous on V. Further more, v is solution of VIP if and only if it is a fixed point of W, i.e., $v = W(v)$.

Proof. The first half of the proposition follows from Ref. [1], Theorem 5.4. To prove the second half, we first suppose that $v = W(v)$. This yields

$$\langle F(v), u - v \rangle \geq 0, \qquad \forall u \in V,$$

and v solves VIP. Conversely, suppose that v solves VIP. Then,

$$\langle F(v), W(v) - v \rangle \geq 0,$$

and it follows from (12) that

$$\langle \Gamma(W(v), v) - \Gamma(v, v) + F(v), v - W(v) \rangle \geq 0.$$

Adding the two preceding inequalities, one obtains

$$\langle \Gamma(w(v), v) - \Gamma(v, v), v - W(v) \rangle \geq 0,$$

and we conclude, from the strong monotonicity of Γ with respect to u, that the equality $v = W(v)$ must hold. □

5. Extended Framework for Solving VIP

Proposition 4.1 suggests a fixed-point algorithm for solving VIP. For given $v^k \in V$, consider the auxiliary variational inequality problem: Find $v^{k+1} \in V$ such that

$$(\text{AVIP}(v^k)) \; \langle \Gamma(v^{K+1}, v^k) - \Gamma(v^k, v^k) + F(v^k), u - v^{k+1} \rangle \geq 0, \quad \forall u \in V, \tag{13}$$

i.e., $v^{k+1} = W(v^k)$. In our approach, we will instead use

$$d^k = W(v^k) - v^k \tag{14}$$

as a descent direction.

The strong monotonicity of Γ with respect to u ensures that the auxiliary problem always has a unique solution $W(v^k)$. For specific choices of F, AVIP(v^k) will be easier to solve than the original VIP. In this paper, we will present a very general decent framework for solving monotone variational inequalities, which incorporates a line search strategy of Armijo type. If $v^k = W(v^k)$, we obtain the solution to VIP. Otherwise, the vector $d^k = W(v^k) - v^k$ is a descent direction for g at v^k under conditions to be considered later. Let us first state the generic algorithm.

Generic Algorithm A1.

(i) Select a feasible vector v^0, a tolerance factor ϵ, and parameters γ, β, σ in the open interval (0, 1). Set k to zero.

(ii) At step k of the algorithm, determine the search direction d^k by solving the auxiliary variational inequality problem AVIP (v^k); see formulas (13) and (14). If $g(v^k+d^k)<\gamma g(v^k)$, set $v^{k+1}=v^k+d^k$. Otherwise, select the smallest integer m such that

$$g(v^k)-g(v^k+\beta^m d^k)\geq -\sigma\beta^m\langle\nabla g(v^k), d^k\rangle,\ \text{set } \alpha_k=\beta^m$$

and $v^{k+1}=v^k+\alpha_k d_k$.

This step follows the Armijo linesearch rule.

(iii) Stop if $\| v^{k+1}-v^k \| <\epsilon$. Otherwise, increase k by one and return to Step (ii).

The gap function g monitors the convergence of the iterates to a solution of VIP. Through suitable choices of the auxiliary function Ω, alternative gap functions can be derived. Each combination of Ω and Γ will generate a different descent algorithm. The function Ω should be chosen such that the gap function g and its gradient ∇g are easily computed at every point of V. In the following sections, we introduce two types of gap functions and the associated convergence frameworks.

6. First Class of Gap Functions

Let

$$\Omega(u, v)=(1/2)(u-v)^T G(u-v),$$

where G is any $n\times n$ symmetric positive-definite matrix. Define

$$h_1(u, v)=\langle F(v), v-u\rangle-(1/2)(u-v)^T G(u-v) \tag{15}$$

and the associated gap function

$$g_1(v)=\max_{u\in V} h_1(u, v), \tag{16}$$

which coincides with the gap function considered by Fukushima[8].

Let $H(v)$ be the unique solution of the maximization problem $\max_u h_1(u, v)$, which is equivalent to the problem

$$\min_{u\in V}\| u-(v-G^{-1}F(v)) \|_G^2 \tag{17}$$

We have that

$$H(v)=\mathrm{Proj}_{V,G}(v-G^{-1}F(v)),$$

the projection of the point $v-G^{-1}F(v)$ on the set V with respect to the matrix norm $\|\cdot\|_G$. By construction of $H(v)$, we have

$$\langle F(v)+G(H(v)-v), v-H(v)\rangle\geq 0.$$

Thus,

$$\langle F(v), v-H(v)\rangle\geq \| H(v)-v \|_G^2, \tag{18}$$

and we obtain

$$\nabla g_1(v) = F(v) - (\nabla F(v) - G)^T (H(v) - v). \tag{19}$$

This leads to the following procedure.

Genetic Algorithm A2. This algorithm differs from Generic Algorithm Al in that the gap function g_1 is used as the objective in place of the gap function g. Clearly, this algorithmic scheme is subsumed by that of Generic Algorithm Al.

Convergence conditions for the preceding algorithm will use the following assumption.

Assumption 6.1. Let the mapping $\Gamma(u, v)$ be continuous differentiable in u and satisfy

$$\| \nabla_u \Gamma(u, v) - \nabla F(v) \| \leq \delta, \quad \forall u, v \in V, \tag{20}$$

for some positive constant δ.

Proposition 6.1. Let F be continuously differentiable and strongly monotone with modulus μ on V. Let $\Gamma(u, v)$ be continuously differentiable and strongly monotone with respect to u(with modulus λ) and continuous with respect to v on V. Let G be an $n \times n$ symmetric positive-definite matrix with minimum eigenvalue $\lambda_{\min}(G)$. Moreover, assume that one of the following conditions is satisfied:

(a) Assumption 6.1 is met, with $\delta < \lambda$ and $\delta < \lambda_{\min}, (G) \leq \| G \| < 2\lambda - \delta$.

(b) Assumption 6.1 is met, with $\delta < \mu$ and $\delta \leq \lambda_{\min}(G) \leq \| G \| < 2\mu - \delta$.

(c) $\Gamma(u, v) = \nabla F(v)(u - v)$(modified Newton method) and $\| G \| < 4\mu$.

(d) $\Gamma(u, v) = G(u - v)$ (projection method).

Then, the vector $d^k = W(v^k) - v^k$ satisfies the inequality

$$\langle \nabla g_1(v^k), d^k \rangle \leq -\xi \| d^k \|^2, \tag{21}$$

for some $\eta > 0$, i. e. , d^k is a feasible descent direction for g_1 at v^k, whenever v^k is not a solution to VIP.

Proof.

(a) For simplicity of presentation, we temporarily omit the super script k. Since $d = W(v) - v$, it follows from (19) that

$$\begin{aligned}
\langle \nabla g_1(v), d \rangle &= \langle F(v), W(v) - v \rangle - \langle \nabla F(v)^T (W(v) - v), H(v) - v \rangle \\
&\quad + \langle W(v) - v, G(H(v) - v) \rangle \\
&= -\langle \Gamma(W(v), v) - \Gamma(v, v) + F(v), H(v) - W(v) \rangle \\
&\quad + \langle F(v), H(v) - v \rangle + \| H(v) - v \|_G^2 \\
&\quad + \langle \Gamma(W(v), v) - \Gamma(v, v) - \nabla F(v)^T (W(v) - v), H(v) - W(v) \rangle \\
&\quad - \langle d, \nabla F(v)^T d \rangle - (1/2) \| W(v) - H(v) \|_G^2 \\
&\quad - (1/2) \| H(v) - v \|_G^2 + (1/2) \langle d, Gd \rangle.
\end{aligned} \tag{22}$$

Since $W(v)$ is a solution to AVIP(v), the first two lines in (22) are nonpositive; see (18). Let us rewrite the third term T as

$$\begin{aligned}
T &= \langle \Gamma(W(v), v) - \Gamma(v, v) - \nabla F(v)^T (W(v) - v), H(v) - W(v) \rangle \\
&= \langle \Gamma(W(v), v) - \Gamma(v, v) - \nabla F(v)^T (W(v) - v), v - W(v) \rangle
\end{aligned}$$

$$+\langle \Gamma(W(v), v)-\Gamma(v, v)-\nabla F(v)^T(W(v)-v), H(v)-v\rangle$$
$$=T_1+T_2.$$

We have

$$T_1\leq -\lambda \| d \|^2+\langle d, \nabla F(v)d\rangle$$

and

$$T_2=\left\langle\int_0^1[\nabla_u\Gamma(v+t(W(v)-v),v)-\nabla F(v)]^T(W(v)-v)dt, H(v)-v\right\rangle$$
$$\leq \left\|\int_0^1[\nabla_u\Gamma(v+t(W)(v)-v),v)-\nabla F(v)]^T(W(v)-v)dt\right\|\cdot \| H(v)-v\|$$
$$\leq \int_0^1 \| [\nabla_u\Gamma(v+t(W)(v)-v),v)-\nabla F(v)]^T(W(v)-v)\| dt\cdot \| H(v)-v\|$$
$$\leq (1/2)\delta[\| W(v)-v\|^2+\| H(v)-v\|^2]$$
$$\leq (1/2)\delta\| W(v)-v\|^2+(1/2)\delta(\lambda_{\min}(G))^{-1}\| H(v)-v\|_G^2.$$

Regrouping the terms we obtain

$$\langle \nabla g_1(v), d\rangle <-[\lambda-(1/2)(\delta+\| G\|)]\| d\|^2$$
$$-(1/2)(1-\delta(\lambda_{\min}(G))^{-1})\| H(v)-v\|_G^2.$$

Let

$$\eta=\lambda-(1/2)(\delta+\| G\|).$$

According to our assumptions, we have that η is positive and $1-\delta(\lambda_{\min}(G))^{-1}$ is nonnegative. Thus,

$$\langle \nabla g_1(v), d\rangle <-\eta\| d\|^2.$$

(b) In this case, we estimate T directly from (22),

$$T=\langle \Gamma(W(v), v)-\Gamma(v, v)-\nabla F(v)^T(W(v)-v), H(v)-W(v)\rangle$$
$$=\left\langle\int_0^1[\nabla_u\Gamma(v+t(W(v)-v), v)-\nabla F(v)]^T(W(v)-v)dt, H(v)-W(v)\right\rangle$$
$$\leq \left\|\int_0^1[\nabla_u\Gamma(v+t(W(v)-v), v)-\nabla F(v)]^T(W(v)-v)dt\right\|\cdot \| H(v)-W(v)\|$$
$$\leq \int_0^1 \| [\nabla_u\Gamma(v+t(W(v)-v), v)-\nabla F(v)]^T(W(v)-v)\| dt\cdot \| H(v)-W(v)\|$$
$$\leq (1/2)\delta[\| W(v)-v\|^2+\| H(v)-W(v)\|^2]$$
$$\leq (1/2)\delta\| W(v)-v\|^2+(1/2)\delta(\lambda_{\min}(G))^{-1}\| H(v)-W(v)\|_G^2.$$

Thus, we have

$$\langle \nabla g_1(v), d\rangle <-[\mu-(1/2)(\delta+\| G\|)]\| d\|^2$$
$$-(1/2)(1-\delta(\lambda_{\min}(G))^{-1})\| H(v)-W(v)\|_G^2.$$

Let

$$\eta=\mu-(1/2)(\delta+\| G\|).$$

Our assumptions imply that η is positive and

$$1-\delta(\lambda_{\min}(G))^{-1}\geq 0.$$

Therefore,

$$\langle \nabla g_1(v), d\rangle < -\eta \| d \|^2.$$

(c) In this case, we have $T=0$ and

$$\begin{aligned}\langle \nabla g_1(v),\ d\rangle &= -\langle d,\ \nabla F(v)d\rangle - (1/2)\ \| w(v) - H(v) \|_G^2 \\ &\quad - (1/2)\ \| H(v) - v \|_G^2 + (1/2)(d,\ Gd\rangle \\ &\leq -\langle d, \nabla F(v)^T d\rangle + (1/4)\langle d, Gd\rangle \\ &\leq -(\mu - \| G \| /4)\ \| d \|^2.\end{aligned}$$

Let

$$\eta = \mu - \| G \| /4,$$

which is positive. Then,

$$\langle \nabla g_1(v),\ d\rangle < -\eta \| d \|^2.$$

(d) In this case, $W(v)=H(v)$ and $T=0$. From (22), we have

$$\begin{aligned}\langle \nabla g_1(v),\ d\rangle &= -\langle d,\ \nabla F(v)d\rangle - (1/2)\ \| H(v) - v \|_G^2 + (1/2)\langle d, Gd\rangle \\ &= -\langle d, \nabla F(v)d\rangle \\ &\leq -\mu \| d \|^2,\end{aligned}$$

and with $\eta=\mu$, we have

$$\langle \nabla g_1(v),\ d\rangle < -\eta \| d \|^2.$$ □

Theorem 6.1. (Global Convergence). Let F, $\Gamma(u, v)$, and G be given as in Proposition 6.1. Then, for any starting point $v^0 \in V$, the sequence $\{v^k\}$ converges to the unique solution of VIP.

Proof. Since v^k and v^k+d^k both belong to V and since $0<\alpha_k<1$, it follows from the convexity of V that the sequence $\{v^k\}$ is feasible. From Proposition 6.1 and the linesearch rule, the sequence $\{g_1(v^k)\}$ is strictly decreasing. From Theorem 3.3, the sequence $\{v^k\}$ is bounded, and hence has at least one accumulation point. Let the sequence $\{v^k\}$, $k\in K$, be any convergent subsequence of $\{v^k\}$, and let $\bar{v}\in V$ be its limit point.

If

$$g_1(v^k + d^k) \leq \gamma g_1(v^k), \qquad k \in K, \qquad \gamma < 1,$$

holds infinitely, there exists a subsequence $\{v^k\}$, $k\in K'\subset K$, such that

$$\operatorname{lira}_{k\to\infty} g_1(v^k) = 0, \qquad k \in K'.$$

Since g_1 is continuous, $g_1(\bar{v}) = 0$. Moreover, from Theorem 3.1, $\bar{v}$ is a solution of VIP.

Next, we consider the case were

$$g_1(v^k + d^k) \leq \gamma g_1(v^k)$$

holds for only finitely many values of the index k, i. e., there exists $\bar{k}_1$ such that

$$g_1(v_k + d^k) > \gamma g_1(v^k), \qquad k \geq \bar{k}_1.$$

Since $d^k=W(v^k)-v^k$ and W is continuous, the sequence $\{d^k\}$ must converge to some $\bar{d}=W(\bar{v})-\bar{v}$. To prove that $\bar{v}$ is a solution of VIP, it will be sufficient to show that $\bar{d}=$

0. Assume the contrary. Then, there exists $\epsilon>0$ and $\bar{k}_2$ such that $\|d^k\|\geq\epsilon$ for all values of k larger than $\bar{k}_2$. It then follows from (21) that

$$\langle\nabla g_1(v^k),\ d^k\rangle<-\eta\epsilon^2,\qquad \forall k\in K,\ k\geq\bar{k}_2, \tag{23}$$

from which we obtain

$$\langle\nabla g_1(\bar{v},\bar{d}\rangle<-\eta\epsilon^2<0. \tag{24}$$

On the other hand, it follows from the linesearch rule that

$$g_1(v^k)-g_1(v^{k+1})\geq-\sigma\alpha_k\langle\nabla g_1(v^k),d^k\rangle>0 \tag{25}$$

and

$$g_1(v^k)-g_1(v^k+(\alpha_k/\beta)d^k)<-\sigma(\alpha_k/\beta)\langle\nabla g_1(v^k),d^k\rangle, \tag{26}$$

for all $k\in K$, $k\geq\bar{k}_1$. Inequality (25) implies that the nonnegative sequence $\{g_1(v^k)\}$ is monotonically decreasing and therefore converges. Then, we have

$$\lim_{k\in K}\alpha_k\langle\nabla g_1(v^k),d^k\rangle=0.$$

Hence from (23), we get

$$\lim_{k\in K}\alpha_k=0.$$

Dividing both sides of (26) by α_k/β and taking the limit, we obtain

$$-\langle\nabla g_1(\bar{v}),\bar{d}\rangle\leq-\sigma\langle\nabla g_1(\bar{v}),\bar{d}\rangle,$$

and since $\sigma<1$,

$$\langle\nabla g_1(\bar{v}),\bar{d}\rangle\geq0,$$

which contradicts (24). Consequently, we must have $\bar{d}=0$, i. e., $\bar{v}$ is a solution of VIP. Moreover, the strong monotonicity of F ensures that VIP has a unique solution, and we can conclude that the entire sequence $\{v^k\}$ converges to the unique solution of VIP. □

Remark 6.1. In each of the following situations, Assumption 6.1 is satisfied with $\Gamma(u,\ v)=A(v)(u-v)$:

(i) $A(v)=\nabla F(v)$;

(ii) $A(v)\approx\nabla F(v)$ and $\|A(v)-\nabla F(v)\|\leq\delta$, $\delta>0$;

(iii) $A(v)=(1/2)[\nabla F(v)+\nabla F(v)^T]$ and $\|1/2[\nabla F(v)-\nabla F(v)^T]\|\leq\delta$, $\delta>0$;

(iv) $A(v)=D(v)$, the diagonal of $\nabla F(v)$, and $\|\nabla F(v)-D(v)\|\leq\delta,\delta>0$;

(v) $A(v)=\begin{cases}L(v)+D(v)/\omega \text{ and } \|D(v)(1/\omega-1)+U(v)\|\leq\delta,\\ U(v)+D(v)/\omega \text{ and } \|D(v)(1/\omega-1)+L(v)\|\leq\delta,\end{cases}$

where $L(v)$ [respectively, $U(v)$] denotes the lower triangular [respectively, upper triangular] part of $\nabla F(v)$, and $\omega\in(0,2)$. Here, (i) refers to Newton's method, (ii) refers to the quasi-Newton method, (iii) refers to the symmetric Newton method, (iv) refers to the linear Jacobi method, and (v) refers to the SOR, linearized Gauss-Seidel method ($\omega=1$).

If one sets

$$\Gamma(u,\ v)=\nabla F(v)(u-v),$$

the auxiliary variational inequality of Algorithm Al becomes

$$\langle \nabla F(v^k)(w - v^k) + F(v^k), u - w \rangle \geq 0, \qquad \forall u \in V,$$

which corresponds to the modified Newton method of Taji et al. (Ref. 10), for which we give the weaker convergence condition

$$\| G \| < 4\mu.$$

Such a condition, which is not required in the gap-decreasing algorithm of Marcotte[5], is essential here. Indeed, if G were arbitrary, the algorithm would not necessarily yield a descent direction for the gap function, as may be observed on the following counter example.

Example 6.1. Let

$$F(v) = \begin{bmatrix} 1 & -2 \\ 3 & 5 \end{bmatrix} v + \begin{bmatrix} 40 \\ -24 \end{bmatrix}, \qquad C = \{v \mid v_1 \geq 0, v_2 \geq 0\}$$

We note that F is strongly monotone with modulus

$$\mu = 3 - (1/2)\sqrt{17}.$$

This problem has the solution $v^* = (0, 4.8)^T$. Take

$$G = I/\alpha, \qquad \alpha > 0.$$

At $v^0 = (10, 0)^T$, we have

$$H_\alpha(v^0) = \begin{cases} (0, 0)^T, & \text{if } \alpha \geq 0.2. \\ (10 - 50\alpha, 0)^T, & \text{otherwise.} \end{cases}$$

From (19), if $\alpha < 0.2$, we have

$$\nabla g_1(v^0) = (50\alpha, 6 + 150\alpha)^T,$$

$$\langle v^* - v^0, \nabla g_1(v^0) \rangle = 220\alpha + 28.8 > 0.$$

If $\alpha > 0.2$, we have

$$\nabla g_1(v^0) = (60 - (10/\alpha), 36)^T,$$

$$\langle v^* - v^0, \nabla g_1(v^0) \rangle = -427.2 + 100/\alpha.$$

Only for $\alpha > 0.234$ is $\langle v^* - v^0, \nabla g_1(x^0) \rangle$ negative, yielding a descent direction of g_1 at v^0. Our lower bound on α is 0.266, while Taji et al.'s is 0.533.

Remark 6.2. Under some regularity assumption, it can be proven that there exists an index $\bar{k}$ such that

$$\alpha_k = 1, \qquad \text{for all } k \geq \bar{k},$$

thus ensuring a quadratic rate of convergence; see Ref. [7].

Corollary 6.1. Let F be as in Theorem 6.1, and let $\nabla F(v)$ have positive diagonal elements. Let

$$\nabla F(v) = D(v) + C(v),$$

$D(v)$ and $C(v)$ are the diagonal and off-diagonal parts of $\nabla F(v)$, respectively. If

$$\| C(v) \| \leq \delta \text{ and } \delta < \lambda_{\min}(D(v)),$$

choose a matrix G such that

$$\delta \leq \lambda_{\min}(G) \leq \| G \| < 2\lambda_{\min}(D(v)) - \delta.$$

Then, for any starting point $v^0 \in V$, the sequence $\{v^k\}$ generated by the modified linear Jacobi method is well defined and converges to the unique solution of VIP.

Proof. Set

$$\Gamma(u, v) = D(v)(u - v),$$

which is strongly monotone with respect to u with modulus $\lambda_{\min}(D(v))$. Since

$$C(v) = \nabla F(v) - D(v) = \nabla F(v) - \nabla_u \Gamma(u, v)$$

and

$$\| C(v) \| \leq \delta, \qquad \text{with } \delta < \lambda_{\min}(D(v)),$$

the conclusion of Theorem 6.1 holds. □

Corollary 6.2. Let F be as in Theorem 6.1. Let $A(v)$ and $S(v)$ denote the symmetric and skew-symmetric parts of the positive-definite matrix $\nabla F(v)$, respectively. If $\| S(v) \| \leq \delta$ and $\delta < \mu$, choose the matrix G such that

$$\delta \leq \lambda_{\min}(G) \leq \| G \| < 2\mu + \delta.$$

Then, for any starting point $v^0 \in V$, the sequence $\{v^k\}$ generated by the modified symmetric Newton method is well defined and converges to the unique solution of VIP.

Proof. As in the proof of Corollary 6.1,

$$\Gamma(u, v) = A(v)(u - v)$$

is strongly monotone uniformly in u, with modulus $\lambda = \mu$. Since

$$S(v) = \nabla F(v) - A(v) = \nabla F(v) - \nabla_u \Gamma(u, v)$$

and

$$\| S(v) \| \leq \delta, \quad \delta < \mu,$$

the conclusion of Theorem 6.1 holds. □

We note that the conditions of Corollaries 6.1 and 6.2 are sufficient conditions for local convergence of the linear Jacobi and symmetric Newton methods (Harker and Pang, [1]). Thus, there exists an integer $\bar{k}$ such that we can switch to the true iterative method from the $\bar{k}$ th iteration on. In real applications, one would resort to trial and error to determine $\bar{k}$.

7. Second Class of Gap Functions

In this section, Ω assumes the general form introduced in Section 3, and the auxiliary mapping is chosen as

$$\Gamma(u, v) = \nabla_u \Omega(u, v).$$

We write

$$h_2(u, v) = \langle F(v), v - u \rangle - \Omega(u, v), \tag{27}$$

$$g_2(v) = \max_{u \in V} h_2(u, v) = \langle F(v), v - W(v) \rangle - \Omega(W(v), v), \tag{28}$$

where $W(v)$ is the unique solution of the auxiliary variational inequality AVIP(v). From (9), we have

$$\nabla g_2(v) = F(v) + (\nabla F(v))^T (v - W(v)) - \nabla_v \Omega(W(v), v). \tag{29}$$

Generic Algorithm A3.

(i) Select a feasible vector v^0, a tolerance factor ϵ, and parameters γ, β, σ in the open interval (0, 1) Set k to zero.

(ii) At step k of the algorithm, determine the search direction d^k by solving the auxiliary variational inequality problem

(AVIP (v^k))$\langle \nabla_u \Omega(W(v^k), v^k) + F(v^k), u - W(v^k) \rangle \geq 0$, $\forall u \in V$, and let $d^k = W(v^k) - v^k$. If $g_2(v^k + d^k) < \gamma g_2(v^k)$, set $v^{k+1} = v^k + d^k$. Otherwise, select the smallest integer m such that

$g_2(v^k) - g_2(v^k + \beta^m d^k) \geq -\sigma\beta^m \langle \nabla g_2(v^k), d^k \rangle$, and set $v^{k+1} = v^k + \beta^m d^k$.

This step follows from Armijo's linescarch rule.

(iii) Stop if $\| v^{k+1} - v^k \| < \epsilon$. Otherwise, increase k by one and return to Step (ii).

Assumption 7.1. The function $\Omega(u, v)$ is continuously differentiable on $V \times V$ and satisfies $\langle \nabla_u \Omega(u, v) + \nabla_v \Omega(u, v), u - v \rangle \geq 0$, $\forall u, v \in V$.

Proposition 7.1. If F is strongly monotone with modulus μ on V, Ω satisfies Assumption 7.1, and v^k is not a solution to VIP, then $d^k = W(v^k) - v^k$ satisfies

$$\langle \nabla g_2(v^k), d^k \rangle < -\eta \| d^k \|^2, \tag{30}$$

for some $\eta > 0$, i. e., d^k is a feasible decent direction for g_2 at v^k.

Proof. Let us temporarily drop the iteration index k. Since $d = W(v) - v$, it follows from (29) that

$$\begin{aligned}\langle \nabla g_2(v), d \rangle &= \langle F(v), W(v) - v \rangle - \langle \nabla F(v)^T (W(v) - v), W(v) - v \rangle \\ &\quad - \langle \nabla_v \Omega(W(v), v), W(v) - v \rangle \\ &= \langle \nabla_u \Omega(W(v), v) + F(v), W(v) - v \rangle \\ &\quad - \langle \nabla_v \Omega(W(v), v) + \nabla_u \Omega(W(v), v), W(v) - v \rangle \\ &\quad - \langle d, \nabla F(v) d \rangle. \end{aligned} \tag{31}$$

Since $W(v)$ is a solution of AVIP(v), the first term of (31) is nonpositive. From Assumption 7.1, the second term of (31) is also nonpositive. Also, the strong monotonicity of F implies

$$\langle d, \nabla F(v) d \rangle \geq \mu \| d \|^2.$$

Taking $\eta = \mu$, the result follows. □

Theorem 7.1. Global Convergence Theorem. Let F be as in Proposition 7.1. Then, for any starting point $v^0 \in V$, the sequence $\{v^k\}$ converges to the unique solution of VIP.

Proof. It is similar to the proof of Theorem 6.1. □

If

$$\Omega(u, v) = (1/2)(u - v)^T B(v)(u - v),$$

$B(v)$ is symmetric and $\nabla B(v)(u - v)$ is positive definite for all $u, v \in V$, then Assumption 7.1 is satisfied. This is obviously true if $B(v) \equiv B$, where B is a positive-definite matrix (usual projection method), and we recover the framework of Wu, Florian, and Marcotte[9].

8. Conclusions

In this paper, we presented a very general decent framework for solving VIP and analyzed its relationship with existing algorithms. It is clear that the choice of a gap function should be made in accordance with that of the underlying algorithm. As an example, it is advantageous to use the projective function jointly with the projection algorithm, and so on. Let us also mention that decomposition can be obtained from our generic algorithm. For instance, if $R^n = R^{n_1} \times R^{n_2}, \cdots, \times R^{n_N}$, $V_i \subset R^{n_i}, i = 1, \cdots, N$, and $V = V_1 \times V_2 \times \cdots, \times V_N$, a decomposition can be achieved by adequately choosing the mappings Γ and Ω. Also, coupled with the techniques of Zhu and Marcotte[11], our method can deal with the following variational inequality: Find v^* such that

$$\langle F(v^*), v - v^* \rangle + f_1(v) - f_1(v^*) \geq 0, \qquad \forall v \in V, \tag{32}$$

where f_1 is a convex and continuously differentiable function from R^n into R. We can also use the partial technique of Zhu and Marcotte[11] to solve variational inequalities where F assumes the form

$$F(u, v) = (F_1(u), F_2(v))^T,$$

where ∇F_1 is symmetric and ∇F_2 is skew-symmetric. This will be discussed in a subsequent paper.

References

[1] HARKER, P. T., and PANG, J. S., *Finite-Dimensional Variational Inequality and Nonlinear Complementarity Problems: A Survey of Theory, Algorithms, and Applications*, Mathematical Programming, Vol. 48, pp. 161-220, 1990.

[2] DAFERMOS, S., *An Iterative Scheme for Variational Inequalities*, Mathematical Programming, Vol. 26, pp. 40-47, 1983.

[3] ZANNI, L., *On the Convergence Rate of Two Projection Methods for Variational Inequalities in* R^n, Calcolo, 1992.

[4] COHEN, G., *Auxiliary Problem Principle Extended to Variational Inequalities*, Journal of Optimization Theory and Applications, Vol. 59, pp. 325-333, 1988.

[5] MARCOTTE, P., *A New Algorithm for Solving Variational Inequalities, with Application to the Traffic Assignment Problem*, Mathematical Programming, Vol. 33, pp. 339-351, 1985.

[6] MARCOTTE, P., and DUSSAULT, J. P., A *Sequential Linear Programming Algorithm for Solving Monotone Variational Inequalities*, SIAM Journal on Control and Optimization, Vol. 27, pp. 1260-1278, 1989.

[7] MARCOTTE, P., and DUSSAULT, J. P., *A Note on a Globally Convergent Newton Method for Solving Monotone Variational Inequalities*, Operations Research Letters, Vol. 6, pp. 35-42, 1987.

[8] FUKUSHIMA, M., *Equivalent Differentiable Optimization Problems and Descent Methods for*

Asymmetric Variational Inequality Problems, Mathematical Programming, Vol. 53, pp. 99-110, 1992.

[9] Wu, J. H., FLORIAN, M., and MARCOTTE, P., *A General Descent Framework for the Monotone Variational Inequality Problem*, Mathematical Programming, Vol. 61, pp. 281-300, 1993.

[10] TAJI, K., FUKUSHIMA, M., and IBARAKI, T., *A Globally Convergent Newton Method for Solving Monotone Variational Inequalities*, Mathematical Programming, Vol. 58, pp. 369-383, 1993.

[11] ZHu, D. L., and MARCOTTE, P., *Auxiliary Problem Principle and Descent Methods*, Preprint, University of Montreal, 1991.

Published in *Journal of Optimization Theory and Applications*, 1994, 80(2)

New Classes of Generalized Monotonicity *

D. ZHU** AND P. MARCOTTE***
Communicated by S. Schaible

Abstract. This paper introduces new classes of generalized monotone functions and relates them to classes previously introduced.

Key Words. Generalized monotonicity, variational inequalities.

1. Introduction

Various concepts of generalized monotone mappings have been introduced in the literature; see Karamardian and Schaible (Ref. 1) for example. The role of these concepts parallels that of generalized convexity in optimization. For instance, Schaible (Ref. 2) argued that pseudomonotone mappings could play, for variational inequality problems, a role similar to that of pseudoconvexity for minimization problems.

In this paper, we introduce new classes of monotone and pseudomonotone mappings and analyze their properties and relationships with respect to other concepts of monotonicity by means of theoretical results, examples, and counterexamples. We expect these concepts to play an important role in the convergence analysis of classical iterative algorithms. For instance, Zhu and Marcotte (Ref. 3) have shown that convergence results can be obtained under the cocoercivity assumption investigated in Section 3 of this paper.

The paper will be organized as follows: We present the basic notation in Section 2, we briefly review cocoercive mappings and their properties in Section 3, while we study in Sections 4 and 5 strictly and pseudococoercive mappings, respectively. In a short conclusion, we will raise some questions relative to these various classes.

---

*This work was supported by NSERC Grant A5789

**Invited Professor, Centre de Recherche sur les Transports, Université de Montréal, Montréal, Québec, Canada.

***Professor, Département d'Informatique et de Recherche Opérationnelle, Université de Montréal, Montréal, Québec, Canada.

2. Notation and Basic Definitions

In the paper, we will make use of the following conventions and notations: vectors in R^n are column vectors; $\langle x, y\rangle = \sum_i x_i y_i$ denotes the Euclidean inner product, $\| x \| = \sqrt{\langle x, x\rangle}$ the standard Euclidean norm, and $\| A \| = \max_{\| x \| = 1} \| Ax \|$ the induced norm of the $m \times n$ matrix A. The sets that we consider are convex. Moreover, we say that a mapping F is continuously differentiable on a convex set C if it is continuously differentiable on an open set containing C.

A mapping F is Lipschitz continuous with Lipschitz constant L if, for all x, y in C, there holds that

$$\| F(y) - F(x) \| \leq L \| y - x \| . \tag{1}$$

If f is a continuously differentiable function from C into R and if its gradient ∇f is Lipschitz continuous on C with Lipschitz constant L', then we have

$$f(x) - f(y) \leq \langle \nabla f (y), x - y\rangle + (L'/2) \| x - y \|^2. \tag{2}$$

A mapping F is monotone on the convex set $C \subset R^n$ if

$$\langle F(y) - F(x), y - x\rangle \geq 0, \tag{3}$$

for all x, y in C; it is strongly monotone on C if there exists a positive number a such that

$$\langle F(y) - F(x), y - x\rangle \geq \alpha \| y - x \|^2, \tag{4}$$

for all x, y in C; it is pseudomonotone on C if

$$\langle F(x), y - x\rangle \geq 0 \Rightarrow \langle F(y), y - x\rangle \geq 0, \tag{5}$$

for every pair of distinct points x, y in C; and it is strongly pseudomonotone on C if there exists $\beta > 0$ such that, for every pair of distinct points x, y in C,

$$\langle F(x), y - x\rangle \geq 0 \Rightarrow \langle F(y), y - x\rangle \geq \alpha \| y - x \|^2. \tag{6}$$

Clearly, any monotone map is pseudomonotone as a comparison of (3) and (5) shows. The converse of the above proposition does not hold, as can be observed via the following example:

$$F(x) = 1/(1 + x), \qquad C = \{x \in R \mid x \geq 0\}. \tag{7}$$

3. Cocoercive Mappings

This section is devoted to a discussion of cocoercive mappings as defined by Tseng (Ref. 4), and also studied by Magnanti and Perakis (Ref. 5) and by Zhu and Marcotte (Ref. 3).

Definition 3.1. The mapping F: $R^n \rightarrow R^n$ is cocoercive on $C \subset R^n$ if there exists $\alpha > 0$ such that

$$\langle F(y) - F(x), y - x\rangle \geq \alpha \| F(y) - F(x) \|^2, \tag{8}$$

for all x, y in C.

The next proposition relates cocoercive and strongly monotone mappings.

Proposition 3.1. Let F be Lipschitz continuous with constant L, and strongly monotone with modulus β. Then, F is also cocoercive with modulus β/L^2.

Proof. This is straightforward from the definitions. □

The converse of Proposition 3.1 is not true, since a constant mapping is trivially cocoercive but clearly not strongly monotone.

A cocoercive mapping is monotone, as a comparison of (3) and (8) shows, but the converse is not true, since the skew-symmetric function

$$F(x) = \begin{bmatrix} 0 & 1 \\ -1 & 0 \end{bmatrix} \begin{bmatrix} x_1 \\ x_2 \end{bmatrix}$$

is monotone but not cocoercive on R^2.

The sum of cocoercive mappings is cocoercive, and the next proposition shows that the cocoercivity property is preserved under affine transformations, including scalings and translations as particular cases.

Proposition 3.2. Let A be an $m \times n$ matrix. If the mapping F from $C \subset R^m$ into R^m is cocoercive with modulus a on C, then for any vector d in R^n, the mapping $A^T FA + d$ is cocoercive on $A^{-1}(C) \subset R^n$ with modulus $\alpha / \| A \|^2$ if A is not identically zero, and with arbitrarily large modulus if $A=0$.

Proof. Assume that A is nonzero (otherwise the result holds trivially). We have

$$\begin{aligned} & \langle [A^T F(Ay) + d] - [A^T F(Ax) + d], \acute{y} - x \rangle \\ = & \langle F(Ay) - F(Ax), Ay - Ax \rangle \\ \geq & \alpha \| F(Ay) - F(Ax) \|^2 \\ \geq & (\alpha / \| A \|^2) \| A^T F(Ay) - A^T F(Ax) \|^2 \\ \geq & (\alpha / \| A \|^2) \| [A^T F(Ay) + d] - [A^T F(Ax) + d] \|^2, \end{aligned}$$

and $A^T FA + d$ is cocoercive with modulus $\alpha / \| A \|$, as claimed. □

Theorem 3.1. Let F be a mapping from a dosed convex subset C of R^n into R^n. If the mapping $F - \alpha I$ is Lipschitz continuous with constant $\beta \leq \alpha$ on C, then F is cocoercive on C with modulus $1/2\alpha$. Conversely, if F is cocoercive with modulus $\beta \geq 1/2\alpha$ on C, then $F - \alpha I$ is Lipschitz continuous on C with Lipschitz constant a.

Proof. Let $G = F - \alpha I$. For any x, y in C, we can write

$$\begin{aligned} \| F(y) - F(x) \|^2 = & \| G(y) - G(x) + \alpha y - \alpha x \|^2 \\ = & \| G(y) - G(x) \|^2 \\ & + 2\alpha \langle G(y) - G(x), y - x \rangle + \alpha^2 \| y - x \|^2 \\ \leq & (\beta^2 + \alpha^2) \| y - x \|^2 + 2\alpha \langle G(y) - G(x), y - x \rangle \\ \leq & 2\alpha \langle [G(y) + \alpha y] - [G(x) + \alpha x], y - x \rangle, \end{aligned}$$

and this implies that

$$\langle F(y) - F(x), y - x \rangle \geq (1/2\alpha) \| F(y) - F(x) \|^2,$$

i.e., that F is cocoercive on C with modulus $1/2\alpha$.

As for the second claim, observe that

$$\begin{aligned}\|(F-\alpha I)(y)-(F-\alpha I)(x)\|^2 = & \|F(y)-F(x)\|^2 \\ & -2\alpha\langle F(y)-F(x), y-x\rangle+\alpha^2\|y-x\|^2 \\ \le & \alpha^2\|y-x\|^2,\end{aligned}$$

and $F-\alpha I$ is Lipschitz continuous on C. □

Proposition 3.3. Let the mapping $F: C\subset R^n \to R^n$ be invertible. Then, F is cocoercive on C if and only if F^{-1} is strongly monotone on the range $F(C)$ of F.

Proof. This is straightforward from the definitions. □

In the affine case, the concept of cocoercivity can be related to that of a psd-plus matrix. By definition, a matrix M is psd-plus if it is positive semidefinite, and $Mx=0$ whenever $\langle Mx, x\rangle = 0$. Recently, Luo and Tseng (Ref. 6) characterized the class of psd-plus matrices as follows: a matrix M is psd-plus if and only if it can be decomposed into the product

$$M = E^T A E,$$

where A is a positive-definite matrix. From this result, it can be shown without much difficulty that the following proposition holds.

Proposition 3.4. A matrix M is psd-plus if and only if the mapping $x\to Mx$ is cocoercive.

Proof. The result holds trivially if $M=0$. Assume that M is nonzero. If Mx is cocoercive, then we have

$$\langle Mx, x\rangle \ge \alpha \|Mx\|^2,$$

which implies that M is psd-plus.

Conversely, let M be a psd-plus matrix. Decompose M as $M=E^TAE$, where A is a positive-definite matrix. Let α be the smallest eigenvalue associated with the symmetric part of A. The number α is positive, and we can write

$$\langle Mx, x\rangle = \langle E^TAEx, x\rangle = \langle A(Ex), Ex\rangle \ge \alpha \|Ex\|^2. \tag{9}$$

Also, since M is nonzero, $\|E^TA\|$ is nonzero and we have

$$\|Mx\|^2 = \|E^TAEx\| \le \|E^TA\|^2 \|Ex\|^2. \tag{10}$$

Coupling (9) and (10), we get

$$\langle Mx, x\rangle \ge (\alpha/\|E^TA\|^2)\|Mx\|^2,$$

and so the mapping Mx is cocoercive on R^n. □

Now, we derive a differentiability characterization of cocoercivity, corresponding to the standard results for monotonicity and strong monotonicity; see Ortega and Rheinboldt (Ref. 7). In the following theorem, we say that a matrix M is psdplus with constant α if the mapping $x\to Mx$ is cocoercive with the same constant α.

Theorem 3.2. Let $F: C\subset R^n\to R^n$ be continuously differentiable on C. Then, F is cocoercive on C if and only if, for every x in C, $\nabla F(x)$ is psd- plus with uniform constant.

Proof. For every $x, y\in C$, we have, 'from the mean-value theorem [Ortega and

Rheinboldt (Ref. 7)],

$$F(x)-F(y)=\int_0^1 \nabla F(y+t(x-y))(x-y)\,dt,$$

$$\langle F(x)-F(y),\, x-y\rangle=\int_0^1 \langle \nabla F(y+t(x-y))(x-y),\, x-y\rangle dt.$$

If $\nabla F(z)$ is psd-plus for every $z\in C$, we have

$$\langle \nabla F(z)(x-y),\, x-y\rangle \geq \alpha \| \nabla F(z)(x-y)\|^2.$$

Therefore,

$$\begin{aligned}&\int_0^1 \langle \nabla F(y+t(x-y))(x-y),\, (x-y)\rangle\, dt\\ &\geq \alpha\int_0^1 \| \nabla F(y+t(x-y))(x-y)\|^2 dt\\ &\geq \alpha \left\| \int_0^1 \nabla F(y+t(x-y))(x-y)\, dt \right\|^2,\end{aligned}$$

i. e. ,

$$\langle F(x)-F(y),\, x-y\rangle \geq \alpha \| F(x)-F(y)\|^2,$$

and F is cocoercive with constant α on C.

Now, suppose that F is cocoercive on C with constant α. From the definition of ∇F, it follows that, for any x in C and any feasible direction h on C,

$$\begin{aligned}h^T\nabla F(x)h &= h^T\{\lim_{t\to 0} t^{-1}[F(x+th)-F(x)]\}\\ &\geq \lim_{t\to 0} t^{-2}\alpha \| F(x+th)-F(x)\|^2.\end{aligned}$$

Now, the mean-value theorem implies that

$$\begin{aligned}\lim_{t\to 0} t^{-2} \| F(x+th)-F(x)\|^2 &= \lim_{t\to 0}\left\| \int_0^1 \nabla F(x+sth)hds \right\|^2\\ &= \| \nabla F(x)h\|^2.\end{aligned}$$

Consequently,

$$h^T\nabla F(x)h \geq \alpha \| \nabla F(x)h\|^2,$$

and ∇F is psd-plus with constant α on C. □

Theorem 3.3. Let F be a continuously differentiable mapping from a closed set $C\subset R^n$ into R^n. If there exists an invertible matrix A and a positive number ρ such that $\| I-\rho A^T\nabla F(z)A\| \leq 1$, for all z in C, then F is cocoercive with modulus $\rho/2\| A^{-1}\|^2$ on C. Conversely, if F is cocoercive with modulus γ on C and A is any $n\times m$ matrix, then $\| I-\rho A^T\nabla F(z)A\| \leq 1$, for every $\rho\geq \| A\|^2/2\gamma$.

Proof. If

$$\| I-\rho A^T\nabla F(z)A\| \leq 1,$$

the mapping $x\to(\rho A^T\nabla F(z)A-I)x$ is Lipschitz continuous with Lipschitz constant 1. From Theorem 3.1, it follows that the affine mapping $x\to A^T\nabla F(z)Ax$ is cocoercive with modulus $\rho/2$. Since A is nonsingular, it follows that the mapping F is cocoercive with modulus $\rho/(2\| A^{-1}\|^2)$; see Proposition 3.2. Conversely, if F as a function of x

is cocoercive with modulus γ, then the affine mapping $x \to \nabla F(z)x$ is cocoercive with modulus γ for every $z \in C$, and $A^T \nabla F(z) A x$ is also cocoercive with modulus $\gamma / \| A \|^2$. From Theorem 3.1, we deduce that

$$\| I - \rho A^T \nabla F(z) A \| \leq 1, \qquad \text{for } \rho \geq \| A \|^2 / 2\gamma.$$

□

In the case where the mapping F is the gradient of a convex function f, the cocoercivity of F can be related to the convexity of f.

Proposition 3.5. A function f is convex and its gradient is Lipschitz continuous with Lipschitz constant L on C, if only if ∇f is cocoercive with constant $1/L$ on C.

Proof. Assume that ∇f is cocoercive with constant $1/L$, $L>0$; i.e., for all x, y in C,

$$\langle \nabla f(x) - \nabla f(y), x - y \rangle \geq (1/L) \| \nabla f(x) - \nabla f(y) \|^2,$$

It follows from the Schwarz inequality that

$$L \| x - y \| \geq \| \nabla f(x) - \nabla f(y) \|.$$

Thus, ∇f is Lipschitz continuous with constant L.

Now, assume that ∇f is monotone (recall that f is convex) and Lipschitz continuous with constant L. For fixed u, define the function

$$g(v) = f(v) - f(u) - \langle \nabla f(u), v - u \rangle. \tag{11}$$

Since f is convex, g is also convex and

$$\nabla g(v) = \nabla f(v) - \nabla f(u).$$

Obviously, we have

$$g(v) \geq 0, \qquad \text{for all } v \in C;$$

also,

$$g(u) = 0 \quad \text{and} \quad \nabla g(u) = 0.$$

Setting

$$f = g, \quad L' = L, \quad x = v - \nabla g(v)/L, \quad y = v$$

in (2), we obtain

$$\begin{aligned} 0 &\leq g(v - (1/L) \nabla g(v)) \\ &\leq g(v) + \langle \nabla g(v) \rangle, -(1/L) \nabla g(v) \rangle + (L/2) \| \nabla g(v)/L \|^2 \\ &= g(v) - (1/2L) \| \nabla g(v) \|^2. \end{aligned} \tag{12}$$

From (11)−(12), we get

$$\begin{aligned} 0 \leq\ & f(v) - f(u) - \langle \nabla f(u), v - u \rangle \\ & - (1/2L) \| \nabla f(u) - \nabla f(v) \|^2, \qquad \forall u, v \in C. \end{aligned} \tag{13}$$

Similarly, we obtain

$$\begin{aligned} 0 \leq\ & f(u) - f(v) - \langle \nabla f(v), u - v \rangle \\ & - (1/2L) \| \nabla f(u) - \nabla f(v) \|^2, \qquad \forall u, v \in C. \end{aligned} \tag{14}$$

Adding (13) and (14), we finally obtain

$$\langle \nabla f(v) - \nabla f(u), v - u \rangle \geq (1/L) \| \nabla f(v) - \nabla f(u) \|^2, \qquad \forall u, v \in C. \tag{15}$$

□

We close this section by mentioning a criterion of cocoercivity of a nonlinear mapping.

Proposition 3.6. See Marcotte and Wu (Ref. 8). Let F be Lipschitz continuous on C with Lipschitz constant L and twice continuously differentiable on C. If, for all x in C, $F'(x)$ and $[F'(x)]^2$ are positive semidefinite, then F is cocoercive on C with modulus $1/4L$.

4. Strictly Cocoercive Mappings

Definition 4.1. The mapping $F: C\subset R^n \to R^n$ is strictly cocoercive on C if there exists $\alpha>0$ such that, for every pair of distinct points x, y in C, we have

$$\langle F(y)-F(x),\ y-x\rangle > \alpha \| F(y)-F(x) \|^2. \tag{16}$$

Clearly, a Lipschitz continuous and strongly monotone mapping is strictly cocoercive. The converse is not true. For example, consider the mapping

$$F(x)=x^3,\qquad x\in[-1,1].$$

We have

$$\langle F(y)-F(x),\ y-x\rangle = | x^3-y^3 \| x-y |.$$

For every x, $y\in[-1,1]$, $x\neq y$, we have

$$0<| x^2+xy+y^2 |<3 \quad \text{and} \quad | x^3-y^3 \| x-y |>0;$$

thus,

$$\begin{aligned}\langle F(y)-F(x),y-x\rangle &= | x^3-y^3 |\cdot| x-y | \\ &> (1/3)\ | x^3-y^3 |\cdot| x-y |\cdot| x^2+xy+y^2 | \\ &= (1/3)\ | x^3-y^3 |^2 \\ &= (1/3)\ \| F(x)-F(y) \|^2.\end{aligned}$$

Therefore, F is strictly cocoercive. However, it is not strongly monotone, since $F''(0)=0$.

On the other hand, any strictly cocoercive mapping is strictly monotone. But the converse is not true. For example, let

$$F(x)=\sqrt{x},\qquad x\in(0,\infty).$$

F is strictly monotone, but not strictly cocoercive, since there is no $\gamma>0$ such that

$$\sqrt{x}+\sqrt{y}>\gamma,\qquad \text{for all } x,\ y \text{ in } (0,\infty).$$

Indeed F is not even cocoercive.

Obviously, strict cocoercivity implies cocoercivity, but the converse need not hold. Indeed the function

$$F(x)=\begin{cases}0, & \text{if} x\le 0,\\ x, & \text{if} x>0,\end{cases}$$

is cocoercive but not strictly cocoercive.

The above analysis has shown that strict cocoercivity defines a truly new class of monotonicity. The results of the previous section can be extended to strictly cocoercive mappings. As their proofs are similar to the corresponding proofs of Section 3, only their statements are presented.

Theorem 4.1. Let $F: C \subset R^n \to R^n$ be continuously differentiable on C. Then, F is strictly cocoercive on C if only if there exists a positive constant γ such that

$$\langle \nabla F(z)(y-x), y-x \rangle > \gamma \| \nabla F(z)(y-x) \|^2, \qquad \text{for all } x, y, z \text{ in } C, x \neq y.$$

The sum of a strictly cocoercive mapping and a cocoercive mapping is strictly cocoercive. The next proposition states that the strict cocoercivity property is preserved under affine transformations.

Proposition 4.1. Let F be a mapping from $C \subset R^m$ into R^m, and let A be an $m \times n$ matrix with full row rank. If the mapping F is strictly cocoercive on C with modulus α, then for any vector d in R^n, the mapping $A^T FA + d$ is also strictly cocoercive on $A^{-1}(C)$ with modulus $\alpha / \| A \|^2$.

Theorem 4.2. Let F be a mapping from $C \subset R^n$ into R^n. If the mapping $F - aI$ is Lipschitz continuous with constant $\beta < \alpha$ on C, then F is strictly cocoercive on C with modulus $1/2\alpha$.

Theorem 4.3. Let $F: C \subset R^n \to R^n$ be continuously differentiable on C. If, for some invertible matrix A and positive number ρ,

$$\| I - \rho A^T \nabla F(z) A \| < I, \qquad \text{for all } z \text{ in } C,$$

then F is strictly cocoercive with modulus $\rho / 2 \| A^{-1} \|^2$ on C. Conversely, if F is strictly cocoercive with modulus $\gamma > 0$ on C, then

$$\| I - \rho A^T \nabla F(z) A \| < 1, \qquad \text{for every } \rho > \| A \|^2 / 2\gamma, \text{ for any } n \times m \text{ matrix } A.$$

If F is the gradient of some convex function f, we have the following result.

Proposition 4.2. A function $f: C \subset R^n \to R$ is strictly convex and has a Lipschitz continuous gradient with Lipschitz constant L on C if and only if ∇f is strictly cocoercive with constant $1/L$ on C.

5. Pseudococoercive Mappings and Strictly Pseudocoeoercive Mappings

Definition 5.1. A mapping $F: C \subset R^n \to R^n$ is pseudococoercive on C if there exists a positive number $\beta > 0$ such that, for every pair of distinct points x, y in C, we have

$$\langle F(x), y-x \rangle \geq 0 \Rightarrow \langle F(y), y-x \rangle \geq \beta | F(y) - F(x) |^2. \qquad (17)$$

Clearly, a pseudococoercive mapping is pseudomonotone as a comparison of (5) and (17) shows. But the converse is not true. Indeed, consider the following mapping taken from Gowda (Ref. 9):

$$F(x) = \begin{bmatrix} 0 & -1 \\ 2 & 0 \end{bmatrix} \begin{bmatrix} x_1 \\ x_2 \end{bmatrix}.$$

The function F is pseudomonotone on R_+^2. Now, let

$$y_1 = 0, \qquad x_1 = 0, \qquad x_2 = 0, \qquad y_2 > 0.$$

We have

$$\left\langle \begin{pmatrix} 0 & -1 \\ 2 & 0 \end{pmatrix} \begin{pmatrix} x_1 \\ x_2 \end{pmatrix}, \begin{pmatrix} y_1 \\ y_2 \end{pmatrix} - \begin{pmatrix} x_1 \\ x_2 \end{pmatrix} \right\rangle = 2x_1 y_2 - x_2(x_1 + y_1) = 0.$$

However,

$$\langle F(y), y - x \rangle = 0$$

and

$$\| F(x) - F(y) \|^2 = (-x_2 + y^2)^2 + (2(x_1 - y_1))^2 = y_2^2 > 0,$$

and consequently F is not pseudococoercive on R_+^2.

To motivate the introduction of the class of pseudococoercive mappings, let us consider the variational inequality problem (VIP in short) that consists in finding a vector x in C that satisfies the variational inequality

$$\langle F(x), x - y \rangle \leq 0, \qquad \text{for all } x \text{ in } C. \tag{18}$$

The solution set S of VIP coincides with the set of global minimizers of the usually nonconvex gap function

$$g(x) = \max_{y \in C} \langle F(x), x - y \rangle. \tag{19}$$

If the mapping is pseudomonotone on C, S also coincides with the solution set of the convex program

$$\min_{y \in C} \bar{g}(x), \tag{20}$$

where $\bar{g}$ is the dual gap function, defined as

$$\bar{g}(x) = \max_{y \in C} \langle F(y), x - y \rangle. \tag{21}$$

The above program can be rewritten as an infinitely constrained linear program, and solved by a cutting-plane method. In Auslender (Ref. 10), it is proved that there exists a subsequence generated by the cutting-plane algo-rithm that converges to a solution of the variational inequality, provided that the set C is compact and the mapping F strongly monotone. The proof can be reproduced by substituting to the strong monotonicity assumption the weaker assumption of pseudo-cocoercivity.

The next result is stated without proof.

Proposition 5.1. Let $F: C \subset R^n \to R^n$ be Lipschitz continuous with constant L and strongly pseudomonotone with modulus β on C. Then, F is pseudococoercive on C with modulus β / L^2.

The following example shows that a pseudococoercive mapping may fail to be cocoercive or even monotone. Let

$$F(x) = 1/(1 + x) \quad \text{and} \quad C = [0, \infty].$$

For every pair of distinct points x, y in C, we have that

$$\langle F(x), y - x \rangle \geq 0 \text{ implies } y > x.$$

Thus,

$$\langle F(y), y - x \rangle = (y - x)/(1 + y)$$

$$\geq (y-x)^2/(1+y)^2(1+x)^2$$
$$= \| F(y)-F(x) \|^2, \quad \text{if} \langle F(x), y-x \rangle \geq 0.$$

This implies that F is pseudococoercive on C. But

$$\langle F(y)-F(x),\ y-x \rangle = -(y-x)^2/(1+y)(1+x) < 0 \text{ if } y \neq x,$$

which implies that F is neither cocoercive nor even monotone on C. On the other hand,

$$\langle F(y),\ y-x \rangle = (y-x)/(1+y),$$

and at $x=0$ there is no positive number β such that

$$(y-x)/(1+y) \geq \beta(y-x)^2,$$

for all positive y. This implies that F is not strongly pseudomonotone on C.

The above analysis has shown that pseudococoercivity defines a new class of generalized monotonicity.

The next result, stated without proof, shows that pseudococoercivity is preserved under affine transformations, including scalings and translations as particular cases.

Proposition 5.2. Let A be an $m \times n$ matrix. If F from R^m into R^m is pseudo-cocoercive on C with modulus α, then the mapping $A^TFA + d$ is also pseudococoercive on $A^{-1}(C)$. If A is nonzero, the modulus of $A^TFA + d$ is $\alpha / \| A \|^2$.

Definition 5.2. The mapping $F: C \subset R^n \to R^n$ is strictly pseudoco-coercive on C if there exists $\beta > 0$ such that, for every pair of distinct points x, y in C, we have

$$\langle F(x), y-x \rangle \geq 0 \Rightarrow \langle F(y), y-x \rangle > \beta \| F(y)-F(x) \|^2. \tag{22}$$

Obviously, a strictly pseudococoercive map is pseudococoercive as a comparison of (17) and (22) shows. But the converse is not true. Consider for instance the mapping of Section 4,

$$F(x) = \begin{cases} 0, & \text{if } x \leq 0, \\ x, & \text{if } x > 0. \end{cases}$$

The mapping F is cocoercive (pseudococoercive). But we observe that

$$F(x) = F(y) = 0, \text{ whenever } x \leq 0,\ y \leq 0,\ x \neq y.$$

Thus, F is not strictly pseudococoercive on R^n.

Strict pseudococoercivity is an intermediate concept between strict and strong pseudomonotonicity. Strict pseudococoercivity implies strict pseudomonotonicity, but the converse is not true. For instance, let $F(x)=x^2$ for x nonnegative.

$$\langle F(x),\ y-x \rangle \geq 0 \text{ implies that } x = 0 \text{ or } y-x \geq 0.$$

Thus, for every $y \neq x$, we have always

$$\langle F(y),\ y-x \rangle > 0,$$

and F is strictly pseudomonotone. If we take $x=0$, however, we have that

$$\langle F(y),\ y-x \rangle = y^3 \qquad F(y) = y^2,$$

and there is no positive number α such that

$$\langle F(y),\ y-x \rangle = y^3 > \alpha \| F(y)-F(x) \|^2 = ay^4,$$

for all positive y. Therefore, F is not strictly pseudococoercive.

Note that a strictly pseudococoercive mapping may fail to be strongly pseudomonotone; see the example following Proposition 5.1.

Some relationships among the various classes of generalized monotonicity can be represented by the diagram of Fig. 1.

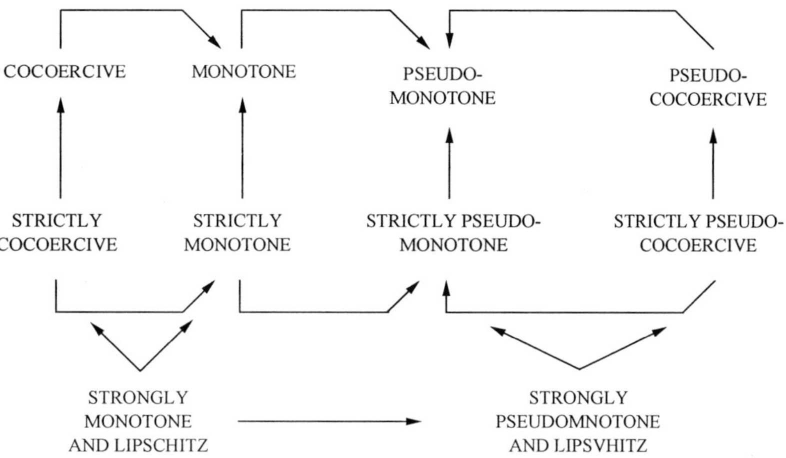

Fig. 1. Relationships between the monotonicity classes.

6. Concluding Remarks

In this paper, we introduced new classes of generalized monotonicity that we expect to play an important role in the convergence and error-bound analysis of iterative algorithms for solving variational inequalities. Recently, Karamardian, Schaible, and Crouzeix (Ref. 11) showed that, if F is linear and $C=R^n$, pseudomonotonicity implies monotonicity. We can also show that, in this situation, pseudococoercivity (respectively, cocoercivity) is equivalent to cocoercivity (respectively, strong monotonicity). But we do not know, as of now, whether the new concepts are truly distinct from previous ones in the case of affine mappings defined on general convex sets.

References

[1] KARAMARDIAN, S., and SCHAIBLE, S., *Seven Kinds of Monotone Maps*, Journal of Optimization Theory and Applications, Vol. 66, pp. 37-46, 1990.

[2] SCHAIBLE, S., *Generalized Monotonicity*, Proceedings of the 10th International Summer School on Nonsmooth Optimization, Analysis, and Applications, Erice, Italy, 1991; Edited by F. Giannessi, Gordon and Breach, Amsterdam, The Netherlands, 1992.

[3] ZHU, D., and MARCOTTE, P., *Cocoercivity and Its Role in the Convergence of Iterative Schemes for Solving Variational Inequality Problems*, Preprint, Centre de Recherche sur les Transports, Université de Montréal, 1992.

[4] TSENG, P., *Further Applications of a Splitting Algorithm to Decomposition in Variational Ine-*

qualities and Convex Programming, Mathematical Programming, Vol. 48, pp. 249-264, 1990.

[5] MAGNANTI, Z. L., and PERAKIS, G., *Convergence Conditions for Variational Inequality Algorithms*, Working Paper OR-282-93, Massachusetts Institute of Technology, 1993.

[6] Luo, Z., and TSENG, P., *A Decomposition Property for a Class of Square Matrices*, Applied Mathematical Letters, Vol. 4, pp. 67-69, 1991.

[7] ORTEGA, J. M., and RHEINBOLDT, W. C., *Iterative Solution of Nonlinear Equations in Several Variables*, Academic Press, New York, New York, 1970.

[8] MARCOTTE, P., and Wu, J. H., *On the Convergence of Projection Methods: Application to the Decomposition of Affine Variational Inequalities*, Journal of Optimization Theory and Applications, Vol. 85, pp. 347-362, 1995.

[9] GOWDA, M. S., *Pseudomonotone and Copositive Star Matrices*, Linear Algebra and Its Applications, Vol. 113, pp. 107-118, 1989.

[10] AUSLENDER, A., *Optimisation: Méthodes Numériques*, Masson, Paris, France, 1976.

[11] KARAMARDIAN, S., SCHAIBLE, S., and CROUZEIX, J. P., *Characterizations of Generalized Monotone Maps*, Journal of Optimization Theory and Applications, Vol. 76, pp. 399-413, 1993.

Published in *Journal of Optimization Theory and Applications*, 1995, 87(2)

Augmented Lagrangian Theory, Duality and Decomposition Methods for Variational Inequality Problems*

D. L. ZHU2**

Communicated by Z. Q. Luo

Abstract. In this paper, we develop the augmented Lagrangian theory and duality theory for variational inequality problems. We propose also decomposition methods based on the augmented Lagrangian for solving complex variational inequality problems with coupling constraints.

Key words. Variational inequalities, duality theory, augmented Lagrangians, decomposition methods.

1. Introduction***

It is well known that the duality theory of optimization plays an important role in both theory and applications. Powerful results of duality in linear programming and convex programming sparked a great deal of interest in duality theory for variational inequality problems (VIP). Many scientists have attempted to study this theory and related computational methods [for example Mosco[1], Fukushima and Itoh[2], Castellani and Mastroeni[3], Robinson[4] along the direction of conjugate duality. In [5], Marcotte and Zhu developed the Lagrange dual theory for variational inequalities, which is useful from a computational point of view. Based on this theoretical result, two dual decomposition methods are proposed. Convergence is proved under some stability condition. On the other hand, for optimization problems, the augmented Lagrangian methods have many advantages over the general Lagrange methods [6][7][8]. More specifically, the

---

*This work was supported by Grant NSFC 70171010.

**The author thanks Prof. Guy Cohen for his comments that helped improving the paper. Thanks are also due to two anonymous referees whose comments led to much improvement in this paper.

***Professor, Management School, Fudan University, Shanghai, China and Center for Research on Transportation, Université de Montréal, Montréal, Canada.

augmented Lagrangian dual function is differentiable and concave; it has the same saddle points as the general Lagrangian function; moreover, the former is stable; i. e., any optimal multipliers can provide the solution of the original problem. For complex optimization problems, Cohen and Zhu[8] proposed decomposition schemes using the augmented Lagrangian; many applications have shown that these algorithms are very useful.

In this paper, we develop the augmented Lagrangian duality theory and decomposition methods for VIP. In Section 2, we introduce the augmented Lagrangian duality theory for VIP. In order to facilitate the solution of the dual variational inequality problem, we examine the properties of the augmented Lagrangian dual mapping and the related augmented variational inequality system. In Section 3, we propose two augmented Lagrangian dual methods. The first one is an Uzawa-type augmented Lagrangian method. We mention that the augmented Lagrangian does not preserve separability even when this is present in the initial problem. This observation leads us to develop a second method, namely, the augmented Lagrangian decomposition for VIP in separable problems as well as nonseparable problems. In particular, if we consider a VIP involving the gradient of a convex function, we recover the augmented Lagrangian duality theory and decomposition for convex optimization problems.

Let X be a closed convex subset of R^n, let $\Theta(x)$ be a mapping from R^n to R^m, let F be a mapping from R^n to R^n, and let C be a nonempty closed convex cone in R^m with vertex at the origin, that is,

$$\alpha C+\beta C\subset C,\quad \text{for } \alpha,\ \beta\geqslant 0.$$

We consider the following variational inequality problem:

$$(\mathrm{VI}(F(x),\Gamma))\quad \text{find } x^*\in\Gamma \text{ such that}$$

$$\langle F(x^*),\ x-x^*\rangle\geqslant 0,\qquad \forall x\in\Gamma, \tag{1}$$

where

$$\Gamma=\{x\in X\mid \Theta(x)\in -C\}$$

and $\langle\cdot,\cdot\rangle$ denotes the standard Euclidean product in R^n.

When $\mathring{C}$(the interior of C) is nonempty, the constraint $\Theta(x)\in -C$ corresponds to an inequality constraint. The case $C=\{0\}$ corresponds to an equality constraint. C^* denotes the conjugate cone. Note that $C^*=R^m$ when $C=\{0\}$.

2. Definitions and Properties of the Projection Mapping

Definition 2.1. F is monotone on X if

$$\langle F(x)-F(y),x-y\rangle\geqslant 0,\quad \text{for all } x,\ y\in X. \tag{2}$$

F is cocoercive on X if there exists a positive constant γ such that

$$\langle F(x)-F(y),\ x-y\rangle\geqslant\gamma\|F(x)-F(y)\|^2,\quad \text{for all } x,\ y \text{ in } X. \tag{3}$$

F is coercive on X if X is bounded or if there exists $x^\circ\in X$ such that

$$\forall \{x^k \mid k \in N,\ x^k \in X\}, \lim \|x^k\| \to +\infty \text{ implies}$$
$$\lim \langle F(x^k),\ x^k - x^\circ \rangle / \|x^k - x^\circ\| = +\infty. \tag{4}$$

The reader interested in this and other concepts of generalized monotonicity is referred to the papers of Zhu and Marcotte [9][10], Bruck[11], and Tseng[12].

Definition 2.2. Θ is C-convex if

$$\forall x, y \in X, \forall \alpha \in [0,1], \quad \Theta(\alpha x + (1-\alpha)y) - \alpha\Theta(x) - (1-\alpha)\Theta(y) \in -C. \tag{5}$$

$\Theta(x)$ is Lipschitz with constant τ on an open subset O containing X if

$$\forall x,\ y \in \mathcal{O}, \|\Theta(x) - \Theta(y)\| \leqslant \tau \|x - y\|. \tag{6}$$

Note that (5) means that Θ is affine when $C=\{0\}$ (equality constraint case).

(CQC) Constraint Qualification Condition. When $\dot{C} \neq \varnothing$, we assume that

$$\text{(a) } \Theta(X) \cap (-\dot{C}) \neq \varnothing. \tag{7}$$

For the case $C = \{0\}$, we assume that

$$\text{(b) } 0 \in \text{interior of } \Theta(X). \tag{8}$$

Let Π denote the projection on C^*. Note that Π is equal to the identity when $C=\{0\}$. The projection $\Pi(x)$ is characterized by the following two conditions[13]:

(i) $\langle x - \Pi(x),\ \Pi(x) \rangle = 0$; (9)

(ii) $\langle x - \Pi(x), y \rangle \leqslant 0, \quad \forall y \in C^*$. (10)

Obviously, we have

$$\langle x - \Pi(x),\ y - \Pi(x) \rangle \leqslant 0, \quad \forall y \in C^*. \tag{11}$$

Furthermore, the following proposition shows that $\Pi(x)$ is cocoercive on R^n.

Proposition 2.1. The projection operator Π is cocoercive with constant 1, i.e.,

$$\langle \Pi(x) - \Pi(y),\ x - y \rangle \geqslant \|\Pi(x) - \Pi(y)\|^2. \tag{12}$$

Proof. Using (9)—(10), we obtain

$$\begin{aligned}
&\langle \Pi(x) - \Pi(y),\ x - y \rangle \\
&= \langle \Pi(x) - \Pi(y),\ (x - \Pi(x)) - (y - \Pi(y)) + \Pi(x) - \Pi(y) \rangle \\
&= \langle \Pi(x) - \Pi(y), (x - \Pi(x)) - (y - \Pi(y)) \rangle + \|\Pi(x) - \Pi(y)\|^2 \\
&= -\langle \Pi(y),\ x - \Pi(x) \rangle - \langle \Pi(x), y - \Pi(y) \rangle + \|\Pi(x) - \Pi(y)\|^2 \\
&\geqslant \|\Pi(x) - \Pi(y)\|^2.
\end{aligned}$$

Throughout this paper, is will be assumed that $\Theta(x)$ is continuous and C-convex on X. Then, it is not difficult to show that the set Γ is convex.

3. Augmented Lagrangian Dual Theory for Variational Inequality Problems

Lemma 3.1. If F is continuous, coercive, and monotone on X, then the solution set X^* of VI($F(x)$, Γ) is nonempty and any solution x^* of VI($F(x)$, Γ) also solves the optimization problem

$$\text{(OP)} \quad \min \quad \langle F(x^*), x \rangle, \tag{13a}$$
$$\text{s.t.} \quad x \in X, \tag{13b}$$

$$\Theta(x) \in -C. \tag{13c}$$

Proof. The assumptions allow us to apply Theorem 3.1 of Ekeland and Teman [14], which states that X^* is nonempty. The second claim is straightforward from the definition of the solution for VI$(F(x), \Gamma)$.

Denote

$$J(x) = \langle F(x^*), x \rangle, \quad \text{where } x^* \in X^*.$$

The Lagrangian of the optimization problem (OP) is

$$L(x, p) = J(x) + \langle p, \Theta(x) \rangle, \tag{14}$$

where p is the Lagrangian multiplier. We recall some results about the augmented Lagrangian theory for convex optimization; see Cohen and Zhu[8]. The convex optimization problem OP can be converted into the equivalent problem with (explicit) equality constraints,

$$\min_{x \in X, u \in -C} J(x), \quad \text{s.t. } \Theta(x) - u = 0.$$

The augmented Lagrangian for this problem is

$$\overline{L}_c(x, u, p) = J(x) + \langle p, \Theta(x) - u \rangle + (c/2)\|\Theta(x) - u\|^2,$$

where c is some positive number. Then, the slack variable u can be removed by defining

$$L_c(x, p) = \min_{u \in -C} \overline{L}_c(x, u, p) = J(x) + \phi(\Theta(x), p), \tag{15}$$

where $\phi: R^m \times R^m \to R$ and

$$\phi(\theta, p) = \min_{u \in C} \langle p, \theta - u \rangle + c\|\theta - u\|^2/2. \tag{16}$$

(16) is equivalent to

$$\phi(\theta, p) = \max_{q \in C^*} \langle q, \theta \rangle - \|p - q\|^2/2. \tag{17}$$

We call

$$L_c(x, p) = J(x) + \phi(\Theta(x), p)$$

the augmented Lagrangian for the convex optimization problem (OP).

Remark 3.1. For the case of an equality constraint,

$$\phi(\Theta(x), p) = \langle p, \Theta(x) \rangle + (c/2)\|\Theta(x)\|^2.$$

For the case of a finite number of scalar inequality constraints, namely,

$$\Theta(x) \leqslant 0, \quad \text{where } \Theta(x) = (g_i(x))_{i \in \{1, \cdots, m\}},$$

then

$$\phi(\Theta(x), p) = (1/2c)\sum_{i=1}^{m}[r(y_i + cg_i(x))^2 - y_i^2]$$

(see Rockafellar, Ref. 6), where

$$(1/2c)[r(y_i + cg_i(x))^2 - y_i^2] = \begin{cases} (c/2)g_i(x_i)^2 + y_i g_i(x), & \text{if } g_i(x) \geqslant -y_i/c, \\ -y_i^2/2c, & \text{if } g_i(x) \leqslant -y_i/c. \end{cases} \tag{18}$$

The functions $\phi(\theta, p)$ and $L_c(x, p)$ have some nice properties as stated in the following two theorems, the proofs of which are given in Cohen and Zhu (Ref. 8).

Theorem 3.1. Consider the function $\phi(\theta, p)$ as defined by (17). Then:

(i) ϕ is convex in θ and concave in p;

(ii) ϕ is differentiable in θ and p and we have

$$\phi'_\theta(\theta, p) = \Pi(p + c\theta), \tag{19}$$

$$\phi'_p(\theta, p) = [\Pi(p + c\theta) - p]/c. \tag{20}$$

Theorem 3.2. Consider the Lagrangian and the augmented Lagrangian functions $L(x,p)$ and $L_c(x,p)$ defined by (14) and (15), respectively. Assuming that F is continuous, coercive, and monotone on X and assuming that (CQC) holds, then:

(i) L and L_c have the same sets of saddle points $\hat{X}\times P^*$ on $X\times C^*$ and $X\times R^m$, respectively;

(ii) L_c is stable in x, i.e.,

$$\{\arg\min_x L_c(x, p^*)\} \in \hat{X}, \quad \forall p^* \in P^*. \tag{21}$$

Following Lemma 3.1, if F is continuous, coercive, and monotone on X and if (CQC) is met, then for any $x^* \in X^*$, there exists p^* such that (x^*, p^*) is the saddle point of $L(x, p)$ and $L_c(x,p)$ on $X\times C^*$, i.e.,

$$L(x^*, p) \leqslant L(x^*, p^*) \leqslant L(x, p^*), \quad \forall x \in X, \quad \forall p \in C^*, \tag{22}$$

$$L_c(x^*, p) \leqslant L_c(x^*, p^*) \leqslant L_c(x,p^*), \quad \forall x \in X, \forall p \in C^*. \tag{23}$$

In order to get the variational form of the saddle point, we study further the properties of the functions $\langle p, \Theta(x)\rangle$ and $\phi(\Theta(x), p)$.

Lemma 3.2. Consider the function $\phi(\theta, p)$ defined by (17). Then:

(i) For any $p\in C^*$, the function $\langle p,\Theta(x)\rangle$ is continuous and convex in x on X.

(ii) For any $p\in C^*$, the function $\phi(\Theta(x), p)$ is continuous and convex in x on X.

Proof.

(i) Since Θ is C-convex, then

$$\Theta(\alpha x + (1-\alpha)y) - \alpha\Theta(x) + (1-\alpha)\Theta(y) \in -C,$$
$$\forall x, y \in X, \ \forall \alpha \in [0, 1]. \tag{24}$$

Thus, for any $p\in C^*$, we get

$$\langle p, \Theta(\alpha x + (1-\alpha)y)\rangle \leqslant \langle p, \alpha\Theta(x) = (1-\alpha)\Theta(y)\rangle \tag{25}$$

Therefore, the function $\langle p,\Theta(x)\rangle$ is convex in x on X. The continuity of $\langle p,\Theta(x)\rangle$ follows from the continuity of $\Theta(x)$.

(ii) From the definition of $\phi(\theta, p)$ and (26), it follows that

$$\phi(\Theta(\alpha x + (1-\alpha)y), p) \leqslant \phi(\alpha\Theta(x) + (1-\alpha)\Theta(y), p). \tag{26}$$

However, $\phi(\theta, p)$ is convex in θ; thus,

$$\begin{aligned}\phi(\Theta(\alpha x + (1-\alpha)y), p) &\leqslant \phi(\alpha\Theta(x) + (1-\alpha)\Theta(y), p)\\ &\leqslant \alpha\phi(\Theta(x), p) + (1-\alpha)\phi(\Theta(y), p),\end{aligned}$$

which implies that $\phi(\Theta(x), p)$ is convex in x on X. The continuity of $\phi(\Theta(x),p)$ follows from the continuity of $\Theta(x)$ in x and the continuity of $\phi(\theta, p)$ in θ.

Based on Theorem 3. 1 and Lemma 3. 2, the saddle point (x^*, p^*) of (22) and (23) can be characterized by the following variational inequality systems, respectively:

(VIS) $\langle F(x^*), x-x^*\rangle + \langle p^*, \Theta(x)-\Theta(x^*)\rangle \geqslant 0, \quad \forall x \in X,$ (27)

$\langle \Theta(x^*), p-p^*\rangle \leqslant 0, \quad \forall p \in C^*;$ (28)

(AVIS1) $\langle F(x^*), x-x^*\rangle + \phi(\Theta(x), p^*) - \phi(\Theta(x^*), p^*) \geqslant 0, \quad \forall x \in X,$ (29)

$\langle \Pi(p^*+c\Theta(x^*)) - p^*, p-p^*\rangle \leqslant 0, \quad \forall p \in C^*.$ (30)

The next lemma allows us to obtain another useful formulation of AVIS1.

Lemma 3. 3. AVIS1 is equivalent to the variational inequality system

(AVIS) $\langle F(x^*), x-x^*\rangle + \langle \Pi(p^*+c\Theta(x^*)), \Theta(x)-\Theta(x^*)\rangle \geqslant 0,$

$\forall x \in X,$ (31)

$\langle \Pi(p^*+c\Theta(x^*)) - p^*, p-p^*\rangle \leqslant 0, \quad \forall p \in C^*.$ (32)

Proof. Let X^* be the solution of (29). For any $y \in X$, take

$$x_t = ty + (1-t)x^*, \quad t \in [0,1].$$

Replacing x by x_t in (29), we get

$$t\langle F(x^*), y-x^*\rangle + \phi(\Theta(ty+(1-t)x^*), p^*) - \phi(\Theta(x^*), p^*) \geqslant 0.$$

However, as in the proof for Lemma 3. 2, we note that

$$\phi(\Theta(ty+(1-t)x^*), p^*) \leqslant \phi(t\Theta(y)+(1-t)\Theta(x^*), p^*).$$

Therefore,

$$\langle F(x^*), y-x^*\rangle + \{\phi(t\Theta(y)+(1-t)\Theta(x^*), p^*) - \phi(\Theta(x^*), p^*)\}/t \geqslant 0.$$

Passing to the limit as $t \to 0$, we obtain

$$\langle F(x^*), y-x^*\rangle + \langle \phi'_\theta(\Theta(x^*), p^*), \Theta(y)-\Theta(x^*)\rangle \geqslant 0,$$

i. e. , x^* solves (31). Conversely, suppose that x^* is the solution of (31). Since $\phi(\theta, p)$ is convex and differentiable in θ, then

$$\langle \phi'_\theta(\Theta(x^*), p^*), \Theta(x)-\Theta(x^*)\rangle \leqslant \phi(\Theta(x), p^*) - \phi(\Theta(x^*), p^*),$$

$$\langle \Pi(p^*+c\Theta(x^*)), \Theta(x)-\Theta(x^*)\rangle \leqslant \phi(\Theta(x), p^*) - \phi(\Theta(x^*), p^*),$$

which imply that x^* solves (29). The proof is now complete.

Until now, we just showed that, for any solution x^* of VI$(F(x), \Gamma)$, there exists $p^* \in C^*$ such that (x^*, p^*) solves the two variational inequality systems VIS and AVIS. One natural question is whether any solution of VIS. AVIS is a solution of VI $(F(x), \Gamma)$. The next theorem provides a positive answer.

Theorem 3. 3. Assume that F is continuous, coercive, and monotone on X and that the condition (CQC) holds true. Then, the two variational inequality systems VIS and AVIS have the same nonempty solution set $X^* \times P^*$ and X^* is the solution set of VI$(F(x), \Gamma)$.

Proof. We need only to prove that, for any solution (x^*, p^*) of VIS or AVIS, x^* solves VI$(F(x), \Gamma)$. First, we suppose that (x^*, p^*) is a solution of VIS. Since

$$\langle \Theta(x^*), p-p^*\rangle \leqslant 0, \quad \forall p \in C^*,$$

then

$$\langle \Theta(x^*),\ p^* \rangle = 0 \quad \text{and} \quad \Theta(x^*) \in -C_\partial.$$

Hence, $x^* \in \Gamma$. Also, from (27), for any $x \in \Gamma$, we have that

$$\langle F(x^*), x - x^* \rangle \geqslant \langle F(x^*), x - x^* \rangle + \langle p^*, \Theta(x) - \Theta(x^*) \rangle \geqslant 0,$$

which shows that x^* solves VI($F(x)$, Γ).

Now, suppose that (x^*, p^*) solves AVIS. Taking

$$p = \Pi(p^* + c\Theta(x^*))$$

in (32), we obtain that

$$p^* = \Pi(p^* + c\Theta(x^*)).$$

Using the properties of the projection (9)—(10) with

$$x = p^* + c\Theta(x^*),$$

we get that

$$\langle \Theta(x^*), p^* \rangle = 0 \quad \text{and} \quad \langle \Theta(x^*),\ y \rangle \leqslant 0, \forall y \in C^*.$$

Thus,

$$\Theta(x^*) \in -C \quad \text{and} \quad x^* \in \Gamma.$$

Finally, from (31), for any $x \in \Gamma$, we have

$$\begin{aligned} \langle F(x^*),\ x - x^* \rangle &\geqslant \langle F(x^*), x - x^* \rangle + \langle p^*, \Theta(x) - \Theta(x^*) \rangle \\ &= \langle F(x^*),\ x - x^* \rangle + \langle \Pi(p^* + c\Theta(x^*)), \Theta(x) - \Theta(x^*) \rangle \\ &\geqslant 0, \end{aligned}$$

and thus x^* solves VI($F(x)$, Γ).

Before defining the augmented Lagrangian dual mapping, we have to study the corresponding parametric variational inequality problem:

(VI$_c(p)$)　find $x_c(p) \in X$ such that

$$\begin{aligned} &\langle F(x_c(p)), x - x_c(p) \rangle \\ &\quad + \langle \Pi(p + c\Theta(x_c(p))), \Theta(x) - \Theta(x_c(p)) \rangle \geqslant 0, \quad \forall x \in X. \end{aligned} \tag{33}$$

The next proposition shows that, for any $p \in C^*$, VI$_c(p)$ has a nonempty solution set.

Proposition 3.1. Assume that F is continuous, coercive, and monotone on X, and assume that Θ is Lipschitz continuous. Then, the parametric variational inequality problem VI$_c(p)$ has the nonempty solution set,

$$\begin{aligned} S_c(p) = \{x_c(p) \in X \mid &\langle F(x_c(p)), x - x_c(p) \rangle \\ &+ \langle \Pi(p + c\Theta(x_c(p))), \Theta(x) - \Theta(x_c(p)) \rangle \geqslant 0, \forall x \in X\}. \end{aligned}$$

Proof. With the same argument as in the proof for Lemma 3.3, VI$_c(p)$ is equivalent to VI$_c(p)$－1:

$$\begin{aligned} &\langle F(x_c(p)), x - x_c(p) \rangle \\ &\quad + \phi(\Theta(x), p) - \phi(\Theta(x_c(p)), p) \geqslant 0, \quad \forall x \in X. \end{aligned} \tag{34}$$

Now, we turn to study the existence of a solution for the parametric variational inequality problem VI$_c(p)$－1. From the assumption, F is coercive on X; i.e., if X is not bounded, there exists $x^\circ \in X$ such that

$$\forall \{x^k \mid k \in N\} \subset X, \lim \|x^k\| \to +\infty \text{ implies}$$
$$\lim \langle F(x^k), x^k - x^\circ \rangle / \|x^k - x^\circ\| = +\infty.$$

In order to use the existence result of Ekeland and Teman (Ref. 14), we have to estimate

$$\Delta = [\langle F(x^k), x^k - x^\circ \rangle + \phi(\Theta(x^k), p) - \phi(\Theta(x^\circ), p)] / \|x^k - x^\circ\|.$$

Since the function ϕ is convex and differentiable in θ with derivative $\Pi(p+c\theta)$, then

$$\Delta \geqslant \langle F(x^k), x^k - x^0 \rangle / \|x^k - x^\circ\| + \langle \Pi(p + c\Theta(x^\circ)), \Theta(x^k) - \Theta(x^\circ) \rangle / \|x^k - x^\circ\|.$$

However, the Lipschitz continuity of Θ guarantees the boundedness of the second term. Therefore, $\Delta \to +\infty$, when $\|x^k\| \to +\infty$. Finally, using the existence result of Ekeland and Teman (Ref. 14), we get the desired result.

Definition 3.1. The mapping $\Omega_c(p) = \{\Pi(p+c\Theta(x_c(p))) - p \mid x_c(p) \in S_c(p)\}$ is called the augmented Lagrangian dual mapping.

Proposition 3.1 shows that the augmented Lagrangian dual mapping $\Omega_c(p)$ is well defined on C^*. The monotonicity of F will play the key role for the study of the augmented dual theory for $\mathrm{VI}(F(x), \Gamma)$. We begin this study with the following fundamental lemma.

Lemma 3.4. If F is monotone, then $\Pi(p+c\Theta(x_c(p)))$ is constant over $S_c(p)$.

Proof. Let $x_c(p)$ and $\bar{x}_c(p)$ be two solutions of $\mathrm{VI}_c(p)$. For any $x \in X$, we have the following two inequalities:

$$\langle F(x_c(p)),\ x - x_c(p) \rangle + \langle \Pi(p + c\Theta(x_c(p))), \Theta(x) - \Theta(x_c(p)) \rangle \geqslant 0,$$
$$\langle F(\bar{x}_c(p)),\ x - \bar{x}_c(p) \rangle + \langle \Pi(p + c\Theta(\bar{x}_c(p))), \Theta(x) - \Theta(\bar{x}_c(p)) \rangle \geqslant 0.$$

From these inequalities and the cocoercivity of the projection mapping, we get

$$\begin{aligned}
&\langle F(x_c(p)) - F(\bar{x}_c(p)),\ \bar{x}_c(p) - x_c(p) \rangle \\
&\geqslant \langle \Pi(p + c\Theta(x_c(p))) - \Pi(p + c\Theta(\bar{x}_c(p))),\ \Theta(x_c(p)) - \Theta(\bar{x}_c(p)) \rangle \\
&\geqslant \|\Pi(p + c\Theta(x_c(p))) - \Pi(p + c\Theta(\bar{x}_c(p)))\|^2
\end{aligned}$$

Since F is monotone, we see that

$$\Pi(p + c\Theta(x_c(p))) = \Pi(p + c\Theta(\bar{x}_c(p))).$$

The following theorem is concerned with the augmented Lagrangian dual mapping $\Omega_c(p)$.

Theorem 3.4. Assume that F is continuous, coercive, and monotone on X, that Θ is Lipschitz continuous, and that the condition (CQC) holds. Then:

(i) the mapping $\Omega_c(p)$ is single-valued on C^*;

(ii) $\Omega_c(p)$ is continuous on C^*;

(iii) $-\Omega_c(p)$ is cocoercive on C^*.

Proof.

(i) It is straightforward from Lemma 3.4.

(ii) Let $\{p^k\}$ be a sequence such that $p^k \in C^*$ and $p^k \to p^0 \in C^*$. Take $r^k \in S_c(p^k)$

such that $r^k \to r^0$. Then, we have

$$\langle F(r^k),\ x - r^k \rangle + \langle q^k, \Theta(x) - \Theta(r^k) \rangle \geqslant 0, \quad \forall x \in X, \tag{35}$$

where

$$q^k = \Pi(p^k + c\Theta(r^k)).$$

Taking the limit in (35), from the continuity of F, Θ, Π, we get

$$\langle F(r^0),\ x - r^0 \rangle + \langle q^0, \Theta(x) - \Theta(r^0) \rangle \geqslant 0, \quad \forall x \in X, \tag{36}$$

where

$$q^0 = \Pi(p^0 + c\Theta(r^0)).$$

Since X is closed, then $r^0 \in X$, which shows that $r^0 \in S_c(p^0)$; therefore, $S_c(p)$ is u. s. c. Since

$$\Omega_c(p) = \Pi(p + c\Theta(x_c(p)) - p,$$

$\Omega_c(p)$ is also u. s. c. However, (i) shows that $\Omega_c(p)$ is singly valued on C^*; thus, $\Omega_c(p)$ must be continuous on C^*.

(iii) In this last part of the proof, for every p_1, $p_2 \in C^*$ and for $i=1, 2$, we denote

$$r_i = p_i + c\Theta(x_c(p_i)),$$
$$\Pi_i = \Pi(r_i),$$
$$\Omega_i = \Pi_i - p_i.$$

Then,

$$c\Theta(x_c(p_i)) = \Omega_i - (\Pi_i - r_i) \quad \text{and} \quad \Pi_i = \Omega_i + p_i.$$

Since $x_c(p_i)$ is a solution of the parametric variational inequality problem $\mathrm{VI}_c(p_i)$, we have

$$\langle F(x_c(p_1)), x_c(p_2) - x_c(p_1) \rangle + \langle \Pi(p_1 + c\Theta(x_c(p_1))),\ \Theta(x_c(p_2)) - \Theta(x_c(p_1)) \rangle \geqslant 0,$$

$$\langle F(x_c(p_2)), x_c(p_1) - x_c(p_2) \rangle + \langle \Pi(p_2 + c\Theta(x_c(p_2))),\ \Theta(x_c(p_1)) - \Theta(x_c(p_2)) \rangle \geqslant 0.$$

Combining these two inequalities, we obtain

$$\begin{aligned} &\langle (\Omega_1 + p_1) - (\Omega_2 + p_2), [\Omega_1 - (\Pi_1 - r_1)] - [\Omega_2 - (\Pi_2 - r_2)] \\ &\leqslant -(1/c)\langle F(x_c(p_1)) - F(x_c(p_2)), x_c(p_1) - x_c(p_2) \rangle \\ &\leqslant 0, \end{aligned}$$

or

$$\begin{aligned} &\langle (\Omega_1 - \Omega_2, p_1 - p_2 \rangle + \| \Omega_1 - \Omega_2 \|^2 \\ &\leqslant -\langle \Pi(r_1), \Pi(r_2) - r_2 \rangle + \langle \Pi(r_1), \Pi(r_1) - r_1 \rangle \\ &\quad + \langle \Pi(r_2), \Pi(r_2) - r_2 \rangle - \langle \Pi(r_2), \Pi(r_1) - r_1 \rangle \end{aligned}$$

Using the characterizations (10)$-$(11) of the projection, we obtain that

$$\langle (\Omega_1 - \Omega_2, p_1 - p_2 \rangle + \| \Omega_1 - \Omega_2 \|^2 \leqslant 0,$$

which implies that $-\Omega_c(p)$ is cocoercive.

Now, we consider the augmented Lagrangian dual variational inequality problem

DVI$(\Omega_c(p^*), C^*)$ for VI$(F(x),\Gamma)$ defined as follows: find $p^* \in C^*$ such that

$$\langle \Omega_c(p^*), p - p^* \rangle \leqslant 0, \quad \forall p \in C^*. \tag{37}$$

Clearly, the solution set is nonempty and it coincides exactly with P^*. One important question is how to recover the primal solution of VI$(F(x), \Gamma)$ whenever the optimal dual solution $p^* \in C^*$ is available. The following theorem shows that AVIS is stable, i. e., $X^* = S_c(p^*)$, where p^* solves DVI$(\Omega_c(p^*), C^*)$.

Theorem 3.5. Assume that F is continuous, coercive, and monotone on X, that Θ is Lipschitz continuous, and that the condition (CQC) holds. Then:

$$X^* = S_c(p^*), \quad \forall p^* \in P^*.$$

Proof. For any solution p^* of DVI$(\Omega_c(p^*), C^*)$, there exists $\hat{x}(p^*) \in S_c(p^*)$ such that

$$\Omega_c(p^*) = \Pi(p^* + c\Theta(\hat{x}(p^*)) - p^*;$$

i. e., $(\hat{x}(p^*), p^*)$ is a solution of AVIS. Also, from Lemma 3.2, for any $x_c(p^*) \in S_c(p^*)$, one gets

$$\Pi(p^* + c\Theta(x_c(p^*))) = \Pi(p^* + c\Theta(\hat{x}(p^*))),$$

which shows that $(x_c(p^*), p^*)$ is also a solution of AVIS; hence,

$$x_c(p^*) \in X^* \quad \text{and} \quad S_c(p^*) \subset X^*.$$

On the other hand, since $(\hat{x}(p^*), p^*)$ solves VIS and AVIS,

$$\hat{x}(p^*) \in X^*, \quad \langle p^*, \Theta(\hat{x}(p^*)) \rangle = 0, \tag{38a}$$

$$\langle F(\hat{x}(p^*)), x - \hat{x}(p^*) \rangle + \langle p^*, \Theta(x) \rangle \geqslant 0, \quad \forall x \in X. \tag{38b}$$

Let x^* be any solution of VI$(F(x), \Gamma)$. For the two solutions x^* and $\hat{x}(p^*)$, we have

$$\langle F(\hat{x}(p^*)), x^* - \hat{x}(p^*) \rangle \geqslant 0 \quad \text{and} \quad \langle F(x^*), \hat{x}(p^*) - x^* \rangle \geqslant 0.$$

Since F is cocoercive, then we obtain

$$F(x^*) = F(\hat{x}(p^*)) \quad \text{and} \quad \langle F(x^*), \hat{x}(p^*) - x^* \rangle = 0.$$

Taking $x = x^*$ in (38b), we have $\langle p^*, \Theta(x^*) \rangle \geqslant 0$, but $p^* \in C^*$ and $\Theta(x^*) \in -C$, hence $\langle p^*, \Theta(x^*) \rangle = 0$. It follows that

$$\langle F(x^*), x - x^* \rangle + \langle p^*, \Theta(x) - \Theta(x^*) \rangle \geqslant 0, \quad \forall x \in X, \tag{39}$$

which shows that (x^*, p^*) solves VIS and AVIS. Therefore,

$$x^* \in S_c(p^*) \quad \text{and} \quad X^* \subset S_c(p^*).$$

The proof is complete.

Remark 3.2. If we take F as the gradient mapping of a convex function, then F is monotone, and VIS or AVIS is equivalent to the primal and dual problem of the corresponding convex optimization problem; moreover, $\Omega_c(p)$ is just the gradient of dual function. Then, we recover the augmented Lagrangian theory for convex optimization; see Rockafellar [6], Bertsekas [7], Cohen and Zhu [8].

The above nice properties of the augmented variational inequality system AVIS and the augmented Lagrangian dual mapping $\Omega_c(p)$ encourage us to develop the useful augmented Lagrangian dual decomposition methods for VI$(F(x),\Gamma)$ as we did for optimization problems[8].

4. Decomposition Methods Based on Augmented Lagrangian

In this section, we consider the decomposition algorithms using the augmented Lagrangian for the following problem:

$$(\mathrm{VI}(F(x),\Gamma)) \quad \text{find } x^* \in K \text{ such that } \langle F(x^*), x - x^* \rangle \geqslant 0, \ \forall x \in \Gamma, \tag{40}$$

where

$$\Gamma = \{x \in X \mid \Theta(x) \in -C\}.$$

We assume that the following decomposition of X is given:

$$X = X_1 \times \cdots \times X_I, \tag{41}$$

which means that the implicit constraints defined by X are decoupled.

4.1. Uzawa-Type Augmented Lagrangian Method. As an introduction to more complex decomposition algorithms, which will be discussed later on, let us consider first a pure Uzawa algorithm for solving AVIS.

Uzawa-Type Algorithm

$$\langle F(x^k), x - x^k \rangle + \langle \Pi(p^k + c\Theta(x^k)), \Theta(x) - \Theta(x^k) \rangle \geqslant 0, \quad \forall x \in X, \tag{42}$$

$$p^{k+1} = p^k(1 - \rho/c) + (\rho/c)\Pi(p^k + c\Theta(x^k)). \tag{43}$$

Theorem 4.1. Assume that:

(i) F is continuous, coercive, and monotone on X,

(ii) Θ is Lipschitz continuous on an open subset $\mathcal{O}$ containing X,

(iii) (CQC) is met,

(iv) $0 < \rho < 2c$.

Then, any sequence $\{(x^k, p^k)\}$ generated by the algorithm is bounded and any cluster point of this sequence is a solution of AVIS over $X \times R^m$.

Proof. From the assumptions and Proposition 3.1, the solution x^k of (42) exists (it may be nonunique). Combining (42) with $x = x^*$ for any $x^* \in X^*$ and (27) with $x = x^k$ yields

$$\begin{aligned} \langle q^k - p^*, \Theta(x^*) - \Theta(x^k) \rangle &\geqslant \langle F(x^k) - F(x^*), x^k - x^* \rangle \\ &\geqslant 0, \end{aligned} \tag{44}$$

where

$$q^k = \Pi(p^k + c\Theta(x^k)).$$

It follows from property (11) of the projections that

$$\langle p - q^k, \ p^k + c\Theta(x^k) - q^k \rangle \leqslant 0, \quad \forall p \in C^*. \tag{45}$$

Combining inequality (45) with $p = p^*$ and inequality (28) with $p = q^k$ yields

$$c\langle q^k - p^*, \Theta(x^*) - \Theta(x^k) \rangle \leqslant \langle q^k - p^*, p^k - q^k \rangle. \tag{46}$$

From (44) and (46), one observes that

$$\langle q^k - p^*, p^k - q^k \rangle \geqslant 0. \tag{47}$$

On the other hand, from (43), one has that

$$\|p^{k+1}-p^*\|^2=\|p^k-p^*\|^2+(\rho^2/c^2)\|q^k-p^k\|^2$$
$$+(2\rho/c)\langle p^k-p^*,q^k-p^k\rangle. \tag{48}$$

The last term can be written as

$$(2\rho/c)\langle p^k-p^*,q^k-p^k\rangle$$
$$=-(2\rho/c)\|q^k-p^k\|^2+(2\rho/c)\langle q^k-p^*,q^k-p^k\rangle. \tag{49}$$

But the latter term is nonpositive [see (47)]. Therefore,

$$\|p^{k+1}-p^*\|^2\leqslant\|p^k-p^*\|^2+(\rho/c)(\rho/c-2)\|q^k-p^k\|^2. \tag{50}$$

Hence, with condition (iv), one concludes that the sequence of positive numbers $\{\|p^k-p^*\|\}$ is strictly decreasing unless $q^k=p^k$ for some k. In this case, from (42) and (45), it is clear that $(x^k, p^k)\in X^*\times P^*$. Thus, $\{\|p^k-p^*\|^2\}$ has a limit. In particular, $\{p^k\}$ is bounded. Moreover, $\|q^k-p^k\|\to0$; therefore, $\{q^k\}$ is also bounded. Now, we will show that $\{x^k\}$ is bounded. In fact, from (42), one gets

$$\langle F(x^k), x^k-x\rangle\leqslant\langle\Pi(p^k+c\Theta(x^k)),\Theta(x)-\Theta(x^k)\rangle$$
$$\leqslant\tau\|q^k\|\|x-x^k\|.$$

If $\{x^k\}$ is not bounded, a contradiction follows from the coercivity of F. Therefore, the sequence $\{(x^k, p^k)\}$ is bounded and has cluster points which belong to $X\times C^*$. Let $(\bar{x}, \bar{p})$ be any of the cluster points and consider a subsequence converging to it. Pass to the limit for this subsequence in (42) and (45) to get

$$\langle F(\bar{x}), x-\bar{x}\rangle+\langle\bar{p},\Theta(x)-\Theta(\bar{x})\rangle\geqslant0,\quad\forall x\in X, \tag{51}$$
$$\langle\Theta(\bar{x}),p-\bar{p}\rangle\leqslant0,\quad\forall p\in C^*. \tag{52}$$

Thus, $(\bar{x},\bar{p})\in X^*\times P^*$.

4.2. Dual Decomposition Using the Augmented Lagrangian. We note that the Uzawa-type algorithm (42)—(43) is not a decomposition algorithm even if we assume that X is decoupled; we also note that F and Θ are additive with respect to the space decomposition (41). We will consider now a decomposition algorithm using the augmented Lagrangian.

Decomposition Algorithm with Augmented Lagrangian. Here,

$$\langle\epsilon F(x^k)+K'(x^{k+1})-K'(x^k),x-x^{k+1}\rangle$$
$$+\epsilon\langle\Pi\langle p^k+c\,\Theta(x^k)),\Theta(x)-\Theta(x^{k+1})\rangle\geqslant0,\quad\forall x\in X, \tag{53}$$
$$p^{k+1}=p^k(1-\rho/c)+(\rho/c)\Pi(p^k+c\Theta(x^{k+1})), \tag{54}$$

where ϵ is a positive number and K is an auxiliary strongly convex differentiable function with derivative K'. From the point of view of decomposition, the interest of this algorithm is the following. Assume that the decomposition (41) is given. Note that this means that the implicit constraints defined by X are decoupled. However, the complex constraints $\Theta(x)\in-C$ are relaxed in this scheme. Suppose that $\Theta(x)$ is additive, i.e.,

$$\Theta(x)=\sum_{i=1}^{I}\Theta_i(x_i),$$

and that we choose an additive auxiliary function, that is,

$$K(x) = \sum_{i=1}^{I} K_i(x_i).$$

Then obviously, subproblem (53) splits into I independent subproblems with respect to the decomposition (41),

$$\langle \epsilon F_i(x^k) + K_i'(x_i^{k+1}) - K_i'(x_i^k), x_i - x_i^{k+1} \rangle$$
$$+ \epsilon \langle \Pi(p^k + c\Theta(x^k)), \Theta_i(x_i) - \Theta_i(x_i^{k+1}) \rangle \geqslant 0, \quad \forall x_i \in X_i.$$

Theorem 4.2. We assume that

(i) F is coercive and cocoercive on X,

(ii) Θ is Lipschitz continuous on an open subset $\mathcal{O}$ containing X,

(iii) (CQC) is met,

(iv) K is strongly convex with constant b and differentiable with a Lipschitz derivative over all bounded subsets of X.

Then, the solution of (53) exists and is unique. Moreover, if

(v) $0 < \epsilon < b/[(1/2)\gamma + c\tau^2]$,

(vi) $0 < \rho < 2c$ when $C = \{0\}$ (equality constraint),

or

(vii) $0 < \rho \leqslant c$ when $C \neq \{0\}$ (inequality constraint),

then the sequence (x^k, p^k) generated by algorithm (53)—(54) is bounded. Any cluster point of this sequence is an optimal solution of AVIS.

Proof. Since K is strongly convex, there exists a unique solution of (53). Let

$$q^{(k+1)/2} = \Pi(p^k + c\Theta(x^{k+1})).$$

It follows from property (11) of the projection that

$$\langle p - q^k, p^k + c\Theta(x^k) - q^k \rangle \leqslant 0, \quad \forall p \in C^*, \tag{55}$$
$$\langle p - q^{(k+1)/2}, p^k + c\Theta(x^{k+1}) - q^{(k+1)/2} \rangle \leqslant 0, \quad \forall p \in C^*. \tag{56}$$

Together with (54), for every $p^* \in P^*$, we have

$$\begin{aligned}
&\| p^{k+1} - p^* \|^2 \\
&= \| p^k - p^* \|^2 + (\rho^2/c^2) \| q^{(k+1)/2} - p^k \|^2 + (2\rho/c) \langle p^k - p^*, q^{(k+1)/2} - p^k \rangle \\
&= \| p^k - p^* \|^2 + (\rho/c)(\rho/c - 2) \| q^{(k+1)/2} - p^k \|^2 \\
&\quad + (2\rho/c) \langle q^{(k+1)/2} - p^*, q^{(k+1)/2} - p^k \rangle.
\end{aligned}$$

Using (56) with $p = p^*$, it follows that

$$\begin{aligned}
&(\epsilon/2\rho) \| p^{k+1} - p^* \|^2 \\
&\leqslant (\epsilon/2\rho) \| p^k - p^* \|^2 + (\epsilon/2c)(\rho/c - 2) \| q^{(k+1)/2} - p^k \|^2 \\
&\quad + \epsilon \langle q^{(k+1)/2} - p^*, \Theta(x^{k+1}) \rangle.
\end{aligned}$$

Combining (28) with $p = q^k$ and (53) with any $x = x^* \in X^*$, we get

$$\begin{aligned}
&\langle K'(x^k) - K'(x^{k+1}), x^* - x^{k+1} \rangle + (\epsilon/2\rho)(\| p^{k+1} - p^* \|^2 - \| p^k - p^* \|^2) \\
&\leqslant \epsilon [(1/2c)(\rho/c - 2) \| q^{(k+1)/2} - p^k \|^2 + \langle q^{(k+1)/2} - q^k, \Theta(x^{k+1}) \rangle \\
&\quad + \langle p^*, \Theta(x^*) - \Theta(x^{k+1}) \rangle + \langle F(x^k), x^* - x^{k+1} \rangle].
\end{aligned}$$

From the assumptions on K, one can show that

$$
\begin{aligned}
&\langle K'(x^k)-K'(x^{k+1}),x^*-x^{k+1}\rangle\\
&=-\langle K'(x^{k+1}),x^*-x^{k+1}\rangle+\langle K'(x^k),x^*-x^k\rangle+\langle K'(x^k),x^k-x^{k+1}\rangle\\
&\geqslant[K(x^*)-K(x^{k+1})-\langle K'(x^{k+1}),x^*-x^{k+1}\rangle]\\
&\quad-[K(x^*)-K(x^k)-\langle K'(x^k),x^*-x^k\rangle]+(b/2)\|x^k-x^{k+1}\|^2.
\end{aligned}
$$

Let

$$
G(x,\ p)=K(x^*)-K(x)-\langle K'(x),x^*-x\rangle+(\epsilon/2\rho)\|p-p^*\|^2. \tag{57}
$$

We have

$$
\begin{aligned}
&G(x^{k+1},p^{k+1})-G(x^k,p^k)\\
&=[K(x^*)-K(x^{k+1})-\langle K'(x^{k+1}),x^*-x^{k+1}\rangle]\\
&\quad-[K(x^*)-K(x^k)-\langle K'(x^k),x^*-x^k\rangle]+(\epsilon/2\rho)[\|p^{k+1}-p^*\|^2-\|p^k-p^*\|^2],\\
&\leqslant\langle K'(x^k)-K'(x^{k+1}),x^*-x^{k+1}\rangle+(\epsilon/2\rho)\|p^{k+1}-p^*\|^2\\
&\quad-\|p^k-p^*\|^2-(b/2)\|x^k-x^{k+1}\|^2,\\
&\leqslant\epsilon[(1/2c)(\rho/c-2)\|q^{(k+1)/2}-p^k\|^2+\langle q^{(k+1)/2}-q^k,\Theta(x^{k+1})\rangle\\
&\quad+\langle p^*,\Theta(x^*)-\Theta(x^{k+1})\rangle+\langle F(x^k),x^*-x^{k+1}\rangle]-(b/2)\|x^k-x^{k+1}\|^2.
\end{aligned} \tag{58}
$$

Since $(x^*,p^*)\in X^*\times P^*$ and F is cocoercive with constant γ, then

$$
\begin{aligned}
&\langle F(x^k),x^*-x^{k+1}\rangle\\
&\leqslant\langle F(x^k)-F(x^*),x^*-x^{k+1}\rangle+\langle p^*,\Theta(x^{k+1})\rangle\\
&=\langle F(x^k)-F(x^*),x^*-x^k\rangle+\langle F(x^k)-F(x^*),x^k-x^{k+1}\rangle+\langle p^*,\Theta(x^{k+1})\rangle\\
&\leqslant-\gamma\|F(x^k)-F(x^*)\|^2+\langle F(x^k)-F(x^*),x^k-x^{k+1}\rangle+\langle p^*,\Theta(x^{k+1})\rangle\\
&\leqslant(1/4\gamma)\|x^k-x^{k+1}\|^2+\langle p^*,\Theta(x^{k+1})\rangle,
\end{aligned}
$$

which is used in (58) to get

$$
\begin{aligned}
&G(x^{k+1},p^{k+1})-G(x^k,p^k)\\
&\leqslant(1/2)(\epsilon/2\gamma-b)\|x^k-x^{k+1}\|^2+\epsilon T_k,
\end{aligned} \tag{59}
$$

where

$$
T_k=(1/2c)(\rho/c-2)\|q^{(k+1)/2}-p^k\|^2+\langle q^{(k+1)/2}-q^k,\Theta(x^{k+1})\rangle.
$$

(i) Case with Equality Constraints. If $C=\{0\}$, then $C^*=R^m$ and the projection is the identity. Then,

$$
\begin{aligned}
q^k-p^k&=c\Theta(x^k),\\
q^{(k+1)/2}-p^k&=c\Theta(x^{k+1}).
\end{aligned}
$$

In this case,

$$
\begin{aligned}
T_k&=(c/2)[(\rho/c-2)\|\Theta(x^{k+1})\|^2+\|\Theta(x^{k+1})\|^2-\|\Theta(x^k)\|^2+\|\Theta(x^{k+1})-\Theta(x^k)\|^2]\\
&\leqslant(c/2)(\rho/c-2)\|\Theta(x^{k+1})\|^2+\|\Theta(x^{k+1})\|^2-\|\Theta(x^k)\|^2]+(c\tau^2/2)\|x^{k+1}-x^k\|^2.
\end{aligned}
$$

Let

$$
H(x,p)=G(x,p)-(\epsilon c/2)\|\Theta(x)\|^2. \tag{60}
$$

Then,

$$
\begin{aligned}
&H(x^{k+1},p^{k+1})-H(x^k,p^k)\\
&\leqslant(1/2)[\epsilon(1/2\gamma+c\tau^2)-b]\|x^{k+1}-x^k\|^2+(\epsilon c/2)(\rho/c-2)\|\Theta(x^{k+1})\|^2.
\end{aligned} \tag{61}
$$

From the foregoing assumptions, the sequence $\{H(x^k, p^k)\}$ is nonincreasing. Furthermore, from (57) and

$$\|\Theta(x)\| = \|\Theta(x) - \Theta(x^*)\| \leqslant \tau\|x - x^*\|,$$

we observe that

$$H(x,p) \geqslant (1/2)(b - \epsilon c\tau^2)\|x - x^*\|^2 + (\epsilon/2\rho)\|p - p^*\|^2.$$

Because $b - \epsilon c\tau^2 > 0$, the sequences $\{x^k\}$ and $\{p^k\}$ are bounded and $\{H(x^k, p^k)\}$ is convergent. Moreover, from (61), one gets that

$$\|x^{k+1} - x^k\| \to 0,$$
$$\|\Theta(x^{k+1})\| \to 0.$$

Thus,

$$\|q^{(k+1)/2} - p^k\| \to 0,$$
$$\|q^k - p^k\| \to 0.$$

(ii) Case with Inequality Constraints. We observe first that

$$\begin{aligned}&\|q^{(k+1)/2} - p^k\|^2 \\ &= \|q^{(k+1)/2} - q^k\|^2 + \|q^k - p^k\|^2 + 2\langle q^{(k+1)/2} - q^k, q^k - p^k\rangle.\end{aligned}$$

Using (55) with $p = q^{(k+1)/2}$, it follows that

$$\begin{aligned}&\|q^{(k+1)/2} - p^k\|^2 \\ &\geqslant \|q^{(k+1)/2} - q^k\|^2 + \|q^k - p^k\|^2 + 2c\langle q^{(k+1)/2} - q^k, \Theta(x^k)\rangle.\end{aligned}$$

On the other hand,

$$\begin{aligned}0 &\leqslant \|q^{(k+1)/2} - q^k + c(\Theta(x^k) - \Theta(x^{k+1}))\|^2 \\ &\leqslant \|q^{(k+1)/2} - q^k\|^2 + c^2\tau^2\|x^k - x^{k+1}\|^2 \\ &\quad + 2c\langle q^{(k+1)/2} - q^k, \Theta(x^k) - \Theta(x^{k+1})\rangle.\end{aligned}$$

With the previous two inequalities, we find that

$$\begin{aligned}&\|q^k - p^k\|^2 + 2c\langle q^{(k+1)/2} - q^k, \Theta(x^{k+1})\rangle \\ &\leqslant \|q^{(k+1)/2} - p^k\|^2 + c^2\tau^2\|x^k - x^{k+1}\|^2.\end{aligned}$$

Using this inequality to estimate T_k, we find that

$$T_k \leqslant (1/2c)[(\rho/c - 1)\|q^{(k+1)/2} - p^k\|^2 + c^2\tau^2\|x^k - x^{k+1}\|^2 - \|q^k - p^k\|^2].$$

Thus,

$$\begin{aligned}&G(x^{k+1}, p^{k+1}) - G(x^k, p^k) \\ &\leqslant (1/2)[\epsilon(1/2\gamma + c\tau^2) - b]\|x^{k+1} - x^k\|^2 \\ &\quad + (\epsilon/2c)(\rho/c - 1)\|q^{(k+1)/2} - p^k\|^2 - (\epsilon/2c)\|q^k - p^k\|^2\end{aligned}$$

As in the case of equality, we obtain that:

(a) $\{G(x^k, p^k)\}$ is nonincreasing and has a limit;

(b) $\{x^k\}$ and $\{p^k\}$ are bounded;

(c) $\|x^{k+1} - x^k\| \to 0$,

$\|q^{k+1/2} - p^k\| \to 0$,

$\|q^k - p^k\| \to 0$.

Finally, we will complete the proof for the two cases altogether. Let $(\bar{x}, \bar{p})$ be a cluster point of $\{(x^k, p^k)\}$. Consider a subsequence $\{k_i\}$ such that

$$x^{k_i} \to \bar{x}, \quad p^{k_i} \to \bar{p}.$$

Passing to the limit in (53) and (56), one concludes that

$$\langle_\epsilon (F(\bar{x}), x-\bar{x}\rangle + {}_\epsilon\langle \bar{p}, \Theta(x)-\Theta(\bar{x})\rangle \geqslant 0, \quad \forall x \in X,$$

$$\langle \Theta(\bar{x}), p-\bar{p}\rangle \leqslant 0, \quad \forall p \in C^*.$$

Thus, $(\bar{x}, \bar{p}) \in X^* \times P^*$.

Comment 4.1. When Θ is not additive, the variational inequality problem (53) should be replaced by

$$\langle_\epsilon F(x^k) + K'(x^{k+1}) - K'(x^k), x - x^{k+1}\rangle$$
$$+ {}_\epsilon\langle \Pi(p^k + c\Theta(x^k)), \Theta'(x^k)(x-x^k)\rangle \geqslant 0, \quad \forall x \in X,$$

assuming that Θ is differentiable. We shall not give a formal convergence theorem for this case, but the adaptation of the decomposition algorithm (53)—(54) and Theorem 4.2 is easy. Using this algorithm, we can get an Arrow-Hurwicz type decomposition method based on the augmented Lagrangian for the nonseparable case.

Comment 4.2. In Ref. [15], Gabay proposed the method of multipliers to variational inequalities based on the dual theory with the inverse mapping. His method is used to solve the separable problem and the convergence for the dual variable is obtained. In this paper, we propose the augmented Lagrangian dual theory and decomposition method for nonseparable variational inequalities. The convergence is obtained for both primal and dual variable.

Comment 4.3. If Γ is represented by both inequality and equality constraints, the theory established in the following are also valid, however we have to modify (CQC) as $0 \in$ interior of $(\Theta(X)+C)$.

References

[1] MOSCO, U., *Dual Variational Inequalities*, Journal of Mathematical Analysis and Applications, Vol. 40, pp. 202-206, 1972.

[2] FUKUSHIMA, M., and ITOH, T., *A Dual Approach to Asymmetric Traffic Equilibrium Problems*, Mathematica Japonica, Vol. 32, pp. 701-702, 1987.

[3] CASTELLANI, M., and MASTROENI, G., *On the Duality Theory for Finite-Dimensional Variational Inequalities*, Variational Inequalities and Network Equilibrium Problems, Edited by F. Giannessi and A. Maugeri, Plenum Publishing Corporation, New York, NY, pp. 21-23, 1995.

[4] ROBINSON, S. M., *Composition Duality and Maximal Monotonicity*, Mathematical Programming, Vol. 85, pp. 1-13, 1999.

[5] MARCOTTE, P., and ZHU, D. L., *The Dual Theory and Decomposition Methods for Monotone Variational Inequality Problems*, Preprint, 1999.

[6] ROCKAFELLAR, R. T., *A Dual Approach to Solving Nonlinear Programming Problems by Unconstrained Optimization*, Mathematical Programming, Vol. 5, pp. 354-373, 1973.

[7] BERTSEKAS, D. P., *Constrained Optimization and Lagrange Multiplier Methods*, Academic

Press, New York, NY, 1982.

[8] COHEN, G. , and ZHU,D. L. , *Decomposition-Coordination Methods in LargeScale Optimization Problems: The Nondifferentiable Case and the Use of Augmented Lagrangians*, *Advances* in Large-Scale Systems: Theory and Applications, Edited by J. B. Cruz, JAI Press, Greenwich, Connecticut, Vol. 1, pp. 203-266, 1984.

[9] ZHU, D. L. , and MARCOTTE, P. , *Cocoerciviity and Its Role in the Convergence of Iterative Schemes for Solving Variational Inequalities*, SIAM Journal on Optimization, Vol. 6, pp. 714-726, 1996.

[10] ZHU, D. L. , and MARCOTTE, P. , *New Classes of Generalized Monotonicity*, Journal of Optimization Theory and Applications, Vol. 87, pp. 457-471, 1995.

[11] BRUCK, R. E. , Jr. , *An Iterative Solution of a Variational Inequality for Certain Monotone Operators in Hilbert Space*, Bulletin of the American Mathematical Society, Vol. 81, pp. 890-892, 1975.

[12] TSENG, P. , *Further Applications of a Matrix-Splitting Algorithm to Decomposition in Variational Inequalities and Convex Programming*, Mathematical Programming, Vol. 48, pp. 249 - 264, 1990.

[13] AUSLENDER,A. , *Optimization: Méthodes Numériques*, Masson, Paris, France, 1973.

[14] EKELAND, I. , and TEMAN,R. , *Convex Analysis and Variational Problems*, North Holland, Amsterdam, Netherlands, 1976.

[15] GABAY,D. , *Applications of Method of Multipliers to Variational Inequalities*, Augmented Lagrangian Methods: Application to the Numerical Solution of Boundary-Value Problems, Edited by M. Fortin and R. Glowinski, North Holland, Amsterdam, Netherlands, 1983.

Published in *Journal of Optimization Theory and Applications*,2003,171(1)

Conditions ensuring the applicability of cutting-plane methods for solving variational inequalities*

Jean-Pierre Crouzeix · Patrice Marcotte · Daoli Zhu

Abstract. Let VIP(F,C) denote the variational inequality problem associated with the mapping F and the closed convex set C. In this paper we introduce weak conditions on the mapping F that allow the development of a convergent cutting-plane framework for solving VIP (F,C). In the process we introduce, in a natural way, new and useful notions of generalized monotonicity for which first order characterizations are presented.

Key words. variational inequalities-cutting planes-generalized monotonicity

1. Introduction**

Let D be an open convex subset of R^n and C a closed convex subset of D. Let F: $D \to R^n$ be a continuous mapping and VIP(F,C) denote the variational inequality problem associated with the mapping F and the set C. By definition, a vector $\bar{x}$ of C is a solution of VIP(F,C) if and only if there holds:

$$\langle F(\bar{x}), x-\bar{x}\rangle \geqslant 0 \quad \forall x \in C. \tag{1}$$

We denote by sol(F,C) the solution set of of VIP(F,C).

In this paper we introduce novel concepts of monotonicity and generalized monotonicity that were motivated by the need:

- to obtain weak sufficient conditions ensuring the convergence of cutting-plane methods, either classical or based on analytic centers, that make use of cutting-planes inducing inequality constraints of the generic form:

---

*J.-P. Crouzeix: LIMOS, Université Blaise Pascal, 63177 Aubière Cedex, France, e-mail: crouzeix@ucfma.univ-bpclermont.fr

P. Marcotte: DIRO, Université de Montréal, C. P. 6128, succursale Centre-Ville, Montréal, Québec, Canada H3C 3J7, e-mail: marcotte@iro.umontreal.ca

D. Zhu: CRT, Université de Montréal, C. P. 6128, succursale Centre-Ville, Montréal, Québec, Canada H3C 3J7, e-mail: daoli@crt.umontreal.ca

Mathematics Subject Classification (1991): 49J40, 90C26

**This work was partially supported by NSERC grant A 5789 and FCAR.

$$H = \{x : \langle F(x^i), x - x^i \rangle \leqslant 0\}, \tag{2}$$

where x^i denotes the current iterate;

- to analyze the differential properties of convex and pseudoconvex functions;
- to study the stability of monotonicity classes with respect to addition and af. ne transformations.

Recently, Goffin, Marcotte and Zhu [6] proved the convergence of an analytic center cutting plane method for solving variational inequalities under strengthened monotonicity conditions. While the conditions introduced by these authors are automatically satisfied by gradient or subgradient mappings of convex functions, this need not be the case for general mappings F. Hence the need for strengthened forms of monotonicity or pseudomonotonicity, whose corresponding classes will be characterized, and that will retain the key features of convex or pseudoconvex functions. As a byproduct of this analysis, we will obtain global convergence results for a general iterative scheme.

The paper is organized as follows: for ease of reference, the next section regroups all definitions of (generalized) monotonicity classes required in our study, together with their relationships to notions of convexity, and some basic properties of these mappings. Examples are provided to show that these classes are indeed distinct. Section 3 addresses the differential characterizations of the monotonicity classes previously introduced. In Sect. 4 we briefly consider the case of multivalued mappings and discuss the algorithmic implications of the various properties of the mapping F on the convergence of cutting plane and iterative methods. The concluding section concludes.

2. Classes of monotonicity

This section is divided into three subsections, the first two being devoted to the definitions and introductory results pertaining to classes of generalized monotone and generalized pseudomonotone mappings, respectively, while the third presents three basic properties satisfied by some of these classes.

2.1.　*Generalized monotone mappings*

We recall that a mapping F is **monotone** on D if, for all x, y in D:

$$\langle F(x) - F(y), x - y \rangle \geqslant 0. \tag{3}$$

We introduce the monotonicity classes that will be studied in the paper, from strongest to weakest:

monotone$^+$: The mapping F is monotone$^+$ on D if it is monotone on D and, for all x, y in D:

$$\langle F(x) - F(y), x - y \rangle = 0 \Rightarrow F(x) = F(y). \tag{4}$$

monotone$^+_*$: The mapping F is monotone$^+_*$ on D if it is monotone on D and, for all x, y in D:

$$\left.\begin{array}{r}\langle F(x),x-y\rangle=0\\ \langle F(y),x-y\rangle=0\end{array}\right\}\Rightarrow F(x)=F(y). \tag{5}$$

monotone$_*$: The mapping F is monotone$_*$ on D if it is monotone on D and:

$$\left.\begin{array}{r}x,y\in D\\ \langle F(x),x-y\rangle=0\\ \langle F(y),x-y\rangle=0\end{array}\right\}\Rightarrow\left\{\begin{array}{l}\text{there exists } k>0 \text{ such that}\\ \quad F(x)=kF(y).\end{array}\right. \tag{6}$$

According to the above definitions, we have the relationships:

$$F \text{ monotone}^+ \Rightarrow F \text{ monotone}_*^+ \Rightarrow F \text{ monotone}_* \Rightarrow F \text{ monotone}.$$

Next we show, by means of examples, that the above classes are distinct, even in the-case of linear mappings.

Example 1. Let $F(x)=(x_2,-x_1)^T$ and $D=R^2$. Obviously, F is monotone on D. Now let $x=(1,1)^T$ and $y=(0,0)^T$. We have that

$$\langle F(x),y-x\rangle=\langle F(y),y-x\rangle=0,$$

but there is no $k>0$ such that $F(x)=kF(y)$. This implies that F is not monotone$_*$.

Example 2. Let $F(x)=(x_2,-x_1)^T$ and $D\subset R^2_{++}=\{x\in R^2: x_1>0, x_2>0\}$. By definition, F is monotone$_*$ on D. Taking $x=(1,1)^T$ and $y=(2,2)^T$, we obtain:

$$\langle F(x),x-y\rangle=0$$

$$\langle F(y),x-y\rangle=0.$$

However, $F(x)\neq F(y)$. This implies that F is not monotone$_*^+$.

Example 3. Let $F(x)=(x_1-x_2,x_1)^T$ and $D\subset R^2_{++}$. We have:

$$\langle F(x)-F(y),x-y\rangle=(x_1-y_1)^2=0$$

if and only if $x_1=y_1$. If, furthermore, we have the condition

$$\langle F(x),x-y\rangle=(x_1-x_2)(x_1-y_1)+x_1(x_2-y_2)=0$$

we may infer that $x_2=y_2$ as well, i. e., F is monotone$_*^+$.

Now, setting $x=(1,2)^T$ and $y=(1,1)^T$, we obtain:

$$\langle F(x)-F(y),x-y\rangle=0.$$

However, $F(x)\neq F(y)$, which implies that F is not monotone$^+$ on D.

Proposition 1. *Let f be convex and differentiable on the convex and open set D. Then ∇f is monotone$^+$ on D.*

Proof. Let $a,b\in D$ and assume that $\langle\nabla f(a),b-a\rangle=\langle\nabla f(b),b-a\rangle$. From the convexity of the function f, we obtain:

$$\langle\nabla f(b),b-a\rangle\geqslant f(b)-f(a)\geqslant\langle\nabla f(a),b-a\rangle.$$

This implies that

$$f(b)-f(a)=\langle\nabla f(a),b-a\rangle=\langle\nabla f(b),b-a\rangle.$$

Let us introduce the convex function g defined as

$$g(x)=f(x)-\langle\nabla f(a),x-a\rangle. \tag{7}$$

The function g is always greater than or equal to $f(a)$. Since $g(a)=f(a)$ (trivially):

$$g(b)=f(b)-\langle\nabla f(a),b-a\rangle=f(a)=g(a)=\inf_{x\in D}g(x).$$

Since D is open, it follows that $\nabla g(b)=\nabla f(a)-\nabla f(b)=0$, from which we conclude that $\nabla f(a)=\nabla f(b)$, i.e., f is monotone$^+$ on D.

2.2. *Generalized pseudomonotone mappings*

We recall that a mapping F is **pseudomonotone** on D if, for all x, y in D:

$$\langle F(x), y-x\rangle \geqslant 0 \Rightarrow \langle F(y), y-x\rangle \geqslant 0. \tag{8}$$

The next definitions propose stronger forms of pseudomonotonicity that correspond to the classes of monotone mappings introduced in Sect. 2.1.

pseudomonotone$^+$: Themapping F is pseudomonotone$^+$ on D if it is pseudomonotone on D and, for all x, y in D:

$$\langle F(x)-F(y), x-y\rangle = 0 \Rightarrow F(x) = F(y). \tag{9}$$

pseudomonotone$^+_*$: The mapping F is pseudomonotone$^+_*$ on D if it is pseudomonotone on D and, for all x, y in D:

$$\left.\begin{array}{r}\langle F(x), x-y\rangle = 0\\ \langle F(y), x-y\rangle = 0\end{array}\right\} \Rightarrow F(x) = F(y). \tag{10}$$

pseudomonotone$_*$: The mapping F is pseudomonotone$_*$ on D if it is pseudomonotone on D and:

$$\left.\begin{array}{r}x, y \in D\\ \langle F(x), x-y\rangle = 0\\ \langle F(y), x-y\rangle = 0\end{array}\right\} \Rightarrow \left\{\begin{array}{l}\text{there exists } k>0 \text{ such that}\\ \qquad F(x) = kF(y).\end{array}\right. \tag{11}$$

According to the above definitions, we have the relationships:

$$\begin{aligned} F \text{ pseudomonotone}^+ &\Rightarrow F \text{ pseudomonotone}^+_*\\ &\Rightarrow F \text{ pseudomonotone}_*\\ &\Rightarrow F \text{ pseudomonotone.}\end{aligned}$$

We now show, again by means of examples, that three of the above classes are distinct. As for the fourth class of pseudomonotone$^+$ mappings, it is the least interesting one. Indeed, gradients of differentiable pseudoconvex functions fail to be pseudomonotone$^+$ without additional assumptions.

Example 4. Consider the following mapping, taken from Gowda [7]:

$$F(x) = (-x_2, 2x_1)^T.$$

The mapping F is pseudomonotone on R^2_+. Now let $y_1=0, x_1=0, x_2=0$ and $y_2>0$. We have:

$$\langle F(x), y-x\rangle = 2x_1y_2 - x_2(x_1+y_1) = 0$$

and $\langle F(y), y-x\rangle=0$. However, there is no $k>0$ such that $F(x)=kF(y)$. This implies that F is not pseudomonotone$_*$.

Example 5. Consider the function $f(x_1, x_2)=x_2/x_1$, which is pseudoconvex on $D=(0, \infty)\times R$. From the definition, we can see that $\nabla f(x)$ is pseudomonotone$_*$ on D. However, by setting $x=(1,1)^T, y=(2,2)^T$, we obtain that $\langle \nabla f(x), y-x\rangle=\langle \nabla f(y), y-x\rangle=0$ but $\nabla f(x)\neq\nabla f(y)$. This implies that ∇f is not pseudomonotone$^+_*$.

It is possible to obtain a first-order characterization of one-dimensional pseudoconvex mappings, as follows. The proof is straightforward.

Proposition 2. *Let $f:[a,b]\to\mathcal{R}$ be differentiable on the interval $[a,b]$. Then f is pseudoconvex on $[a,b]$ if and only if its derivative f' is pseudomonotone$^+$ on $[a,b]$.*

In general, gradients of pseudoconvex functions need not be pseudomonotone $^+_*$. However, this result holds for the important class of G-convex functions. We recall that a function f is G-convex if there exists a continuous real-valued increasing function G defined on the image $I_f(D)$ of D such that $G(f(x))$ is convex over D.

Proposition 3. *Let f be a differentiable G-convex function defined over the convex set $D\subset\mathcal{R}^n$ and let G be differentiable on $I_f(D)$ with $G'(t)>0$ for all $t\in I_f(D)$. Then f is pseudoconvex over D and $\nabla f(x)$ is pseudomonotone$^+_*$.*

Proof. From Proposition 8.7 in [1] we obtain that f is pseudoconvex. Thus, ∇f is pseudomonotone over D. Let a and b be two points in D and assume that

$$\langle \nabla f(a), b-a\rangle = \langle \nabla f(b), b-a\rangle = 0.$$

Since f is G-convex, we have that

$$G(f(b)) \geqslant G(f(a)) + G'(f(a))\langle \nabla f(a), b-a\rangle = G(f(a))$$
$$G(f(a)) \geqslant G(f(b)) + G'(f(b))\langle \nabla f(b), a-b\rangle = G(f(b)).$$

It follows from the above two inequalities that $G(f(a))=G(f(b))$ and, since G is strictly increasing, $f(a)=f(b)$. However, $G(f(x))$ is convex and, from Proposition 1, the mapping $F(x)=G'(f(x))\nabla f(x)$ ismonotone$^+$ over D. Furthermore, since $\langle F(a), b-a\rangle=\langle F(b), b-a\rangle=0$, we obtain that $F(a)=F(b)$ and $\nabla f(a)=\nabla f(b)$. Therefore $\nabla f(x)$ is pseudomonotone$^+_*$ over D.

Proposition 4. *Let f be pseudoconvex and differentiable on D. Then ∇f is pseudomonotone$_*$ on D.*

Proof. Let a and b be any two distinct points in D such that $\nabla f(a)\neq 0$, $\nabla f(b)\neq 0$ and

$$\langle \nabla f(a), b-a\rangle = \langle \nabla f(b), b-a\rangle = 0.$$

Since f is pseudoconvex, we have that $f(a)=f(b)$. Take any vector $v\in R^n$ such that $\langle \nabla f(a), v\rangle<0$. Since D is open, we can select a positive number t such that $a+tv$ is in D and $f(a+tv)<f(a)=f(b)$. Hence, since f is pseudoconvex, $\langle \nabla f(b), a+tv-b\rangle<0$. But $\langle \nabla f(b), a-b\rangle=0$ implies that $\langle \nabla f(b), v\rangle<0$. We permutate a and b, repeat the argument to obtain that $\langle \nabla f(a), v\rangle<0$ if and only if $\langle \nabla f(b), v\rangle<0$, and conclude that there must exist a nonnegative number k such that $\nabla f(b)=k\nabla f(a)$.

2.3. *Three basic properties*

If a mapping is pseudomonotone over D, then the (possibly empty) solution set sol(F, C) of VIP (F,C) is convex and, for every y in C, we have the important property:

$$\text{sol}(F,C) \subseteq \{x\in C: \langle F(y), y-x\rangle \geqslant 0\}. \tag{12}$$

While the above separation property is required to prove the convergence of a cutting plane method based on the sole knowledge of the vector $F(y)$, where y is usually taken as the current iterate, this condition alone is not sufficient, unless one relies on averaging schemes. In an algorithm designed to solve concave-convex games, Zuhovickii, Polyak and Primak [20] assumed strong monotonicity of F while Goffin, Marcotte and Zhu [6] introduced to this purpose the notions of monotone^{+} and pseudomonotone^{+} mappings. These notions were merely sufficient conditions to ensure that the mappings possess the crucial CUT PROPERTY:

$$\left.\begin{array}{r} x^{*} \in \mathrm{sol}(F,C) \\ \bar{x} \in C \\ \bar{x} \neq x^{*} \\ \langle F(\bar{x}),\bar{x}-x^{*}\rangle = 0 \end{array}\right\} \Rightarrow \bar{x} \in \mathrm{sol}(F,C). \tag{13}$$

Actually, the larger class of pseudomonotone$_{*}$ mappings, which corresponds to gradients of pseudoconvex functions, also satisfies the cut property. Pseudomonotonicity$_{*}$ is in some way a minimal condition ensuring that the cut property holds independently of the subset C of the open set D. Indeed, let a, $b\in \mathrm{int}(D)$ be such that $a\in \mathrm{sol}(F,C)$ and

$$\langle F(a),b-a\rangle = \langle F(b),b-a\rangle = 0$$

without any number k satisfying $F(b)=kF(a)$. Set

$$H = \{x \in D:\langle F(a),x-a\rangle = 0\}. \tag{14}$$

By construction, $a,b\in H$, $a\in \mathrm{sol}(F,C)$ but $b\notin \mathrm{sol}(F,C)$ since one can construct a vector h such that $b+h\in \mathrm{int}(D)$, $\langle F(a),h\rangle=0$ and $\langle F(b),h\rangle<0$. Hence the cut property does not hold.

Proposition 5. *If F is pseudomonotone$_{*}$ on C, then F possesses the cut property.*

Proof. Let $x^{*} \in \mathrm{sol}(F,C)$ and let $\bar{x}$ be such that $\langle F(\bar{x}),x^{*}-\bar{x}\rangle=0$. Since x^{*} is a solution of $\mathrm{VI}(F,C)$ and F is pseudomonotone$_{*}$, it follows that $F(\bar{x})=kF(x^{*})$ with k positive, and we can write, for any x in C:

$$\langle F(\bar{x}),x-\bar{x}\rangle = k\langle F(x^{*}),x-x^{*}\rangle + \langle F(\bar{x}),x^{*}-\bar{x}\rangle \geqslant 0,$$

i. e. , $\bar{x}$ is a solution of $\mathrm{VI}(F,C)$.

Next we show that the classes introduced in the previous section are invariant under affine transformations.

Proposition 6. *Let A be an $n\times m$ matrix, a a vector in R^{m} and $\bar{D}$ a convex set such that $D=A(\bar{D})+a$. Then the mapping $\bar{F}(y)=A^{T}F(Ay+a)$ is monotone (respectively monotone^{+}, monotone$^{+}_{*}$, monotone$_{*}$, pseudomonotone, pseudomonotone$^{+}_{*}$, pseudomonotone$_{*}$) whenever F is.*

Proof. The relationships:

$$\langle \bar{F}(y^{1}),y^{1}-y^{2}\rangle = \langle F(Ay^{1}+a),(Ay^{1}+a)-(Ay^{2}+a)\rangle$$
$$\langle \bar{F}(y^{2}),y^{1}-y^{2}\rangle = \langle F(Ay^{2}+a),(Ay^{1}+a)-(Ay^{2}+a)\rangle$$

imply the result.

Note that stability under addition only holds for monotone^{+} mappings. The proof is obvious.

Proposition 7. *The sum of monotone$^+$ mappings is monotone$^+$.*

3. First-order results

The main focus of this section is on first-order results and characterizations of the monotonicity classes introduced earlier. This will require the introduction of the class of psd$^+$ matrices. We recall (see Luo and Tseng [10]) that a square matrix A is **psd$^+$** if A is positive semidefinite and, for any h, there holds:

$$\langle Ah, h\rangle = 0 \Rightarrow Ah = 0.$$

It is well known that symmetric positive semidefinite matrices are psd$^+$.

We begin with the class of (pseudo) monotone$_*$ mappings.

3.1. *(Pseudo)monotone$_*$ mappings*

The following lemma will be put to heavy use throughout this subsection.

Lemma 1. Let $a, b \in D$, *F be differentiable and pseudomonotone over D and* $\langle F(a), b-a\rangle = \langle F(b), b-a\rangle = 0$. *Then, for any point x_t on the segment $[a,b]$, we have* $\langle F(x_t), b-a\rangle = 0$ *and* $\langle \nabla F(x_t)(b-a), b-a\rangle = 0$.

Proof. From the assumptions and the pseudomonotonicity of F, we have

$$\begin{aligned}\langle F(a), b-a\rangle = 0 &\Rightarrow \langle F(a), x_t - a\rangle = 0\\ &\Rightarrow \langle F(x_t), x_t - a\rangle \geqslant 0\\ &\Rightarrow \langle F(x_t), b-a\rangle \geqslant 0.\end{aligned}$$

Symmetrically, by exchanging the roles of a and b, we obtain $\langle F(x_t), a-b\rangle \geqslant 0$, $\forall t \in [0,1]$. Hence the function $\theta(t) = \langle F(x_t\rangle, b-a$ is null over the interval $[0,1]$. Thus $\theta'(t) = \langle \nabla F(x_t)(b-a), b-a = 0$ over $[0,1]$.

Proposition 8. *Let F be differentiable and (pseudo)monotone on D. Assume that there holds:*

$$\left.\begin{aligned} x, y &\in D\\ F(x) &= 0\\ F(y) &\neq 0\end{aligned}\right\} \Rightarrow \langle F(y), y-x\rangle > 0 \tag{15}$$

$$\left.\begin{aligned} &x \in D, F(x) \neq 0\\ &\langle F(x), h\rangle = \langle F'(x)h, h\rangle = 0\end{aligned}\right\} \Rightarrow \begin{cases}\text{there exists } \lambda \text{ such that}\\ F'(x)h = \lambda F(x).\end{cases} \tag{16}$$

Then F is (pseudo) monotone$_*$ on D. Whenever F is affine, the above conditions are necessary as well.

Proof. Assume that $\langle F(a), b-a\rangle = \langle F(b), b-a\rangle = 0$ for some distinct vectors $a, b \in D$. Set $h = b-a$ and $x_t = a + th$ for $t \in [0,1]$. It follows from Lemma 1 that $F(x_t), h = 0$ for all $t \in [0,1]$.

If $F(x_t) = 0$ for some $t \in [0,1]$ then, by (15), we infer that $F(x_t) = 0$ for all $t \in [0,1]$. In particular: $F(b) = kF(a) = 0$ for any real number k, i.e., F is pseudomonotone$_*$.

On the other hand, assume that $F(x_t) \neq 0$ for all $t \in [0,1]$. It follows again from

Lemma 1, by taking a differential quotient, that:

$$\langle F(x_t), h\rangle = \langle F'(x_t)h, h\rangle = 0.$$

Hence, by (16), there exists a number λ_t such that $F'(x_t)h = \lambda_t F(x_t)$.

Let us define, at all points x where F does not vanish, the mapping:

$$G(x) = F(x)/\|F(x)\|,$$

whose Jacobian matrix at x is given by the expression:

$$G'(x) = \frac{1}{\|F(x)\|}\left(I - \frac{1}{\|F(x)\|^2}F(x)F^T(x)\right)F'(x).$$

We obtain, for every $t \in [0,1]$:

$$G'(x_t)h = \frac{\lambda_t}{\|F(x_t)\|}\left(I - \frac{1}{\|F(x_t)\|^2}F(x_t)F^T(x_t)\right)F(x_t) = 0$$

from which it follows that $G(x_t) = G(a) = G(b)$, and the result is proved.

Now, let $F(x) = Ax + b$ be affine and pseudomonotone$_*$. Let h be a vector such that:

$$\langle F(x), h\rangle = \langle F'(x)h, h\rangle = 0,$$

i. e. ,

$$\langle Ax + b, h\rangle = \langle Ah, h\rangle = 0$$

or, equivalently:

$$\langle Ax + b, h\rangle = \langle A(x+h) + b, h\rangle = 0.$$

Since F is pseudomonotone$_*$, there exists a positive number k such that $A(x+h) + b = k(Ax + b)$, from which we obtain: $Ah = (k-1)(Ax+b)$, as desired.

The remainder of this subsection is concerned with properties of differentiable monotone$_*$ and pseudomonotone$_*$ mappings, thus extending previous results of Crouzeix and Ferland[5]. We recall that these authors(see also Corollary 3 in [4])proved that a differentiable mapping F is pseudomonotone on an open covex set D if and only if:

$$x, y \in D \text{ and } F(x) = 0 \Rightarrow \langle F(y), y - x\rangle \geqslant 0$$

$$x \in D,\quad F(x) \neq 0 \text{ and } \langle F(x), h\rangle = 0 \Rightarrow \langle F'(x)h, h\rangle \geqslant 0.$$

Assume that $F(x) \neq 0$. If one sets $a = F(x)$ and $A = F'(x)$, the condition:

$$\langle Ah, h\rangle \geqslant 0 \text{ whenever } \langle a, h\rangle = 0 \tag{17}$$

holds if and only if one of the following conditions holds:

- the symmetrized matrix $A + A^T$ is positive semidefinite;
- the matrix $A + A^T$ has a single negative eigenvalue (with multiplicity one) and there exists a vector v such that $(A + A^t)v = a$ and $\langle a, v\rangle \leqslant 0$.

Similar results will be proved for pseudomonotone$_*$ and monotone$_*$ mappings. But first we will need the following linear algebra result.

Lemma 2. *Let the square $n \times n$ matrix A and the vector $a \in \mathscr{R}^n$ satisfy Condition* (17). *Then the sets*

$$K = \begin{Bmatrix} \{h : \langle a, h\rangle = 0, (A + A^T)h = 0\} & \text{if } A \text{ is positive semidefinite} \\ \{h : \langle a, h\rangle = 0, (A + A^T)h = \mu a\} & \text{otherwise.} \end{Bmatrix}$$

and $K'=\{h:\langle a,h\rangle=\langle Ah,h\rangle=0\}$ *coincide.*

Proof. If $a=0$, the result is immediate. Therefore, from now on, we assume that a is nonzero.

First note that the inclusion $K\subseteq K'$ is direct.

If A is positive semidefinite, then $\langle Ah,h\rangle=0$ directly implies that $(A+A^T)h=0$. Otherwise, let O an orthogonal matrix such that $Oa=\|a\|e_1$, where e_1 denote the first vector of the canonical basis in R^n. There exist quantities α (number), β (vector in R^{n-1}), γ (vector in R^{n-1}) and B ($(n-1)\times(n-1)$ matrix) such that:

$$OAO^T=\begin{pmatrix}\alpha & \beta^T\\ \gamma & \beta\end{pmatrix},\quad O(A+A^T)O^T=\begin{pmatrix}2\alpha & \beta^T+\gamma^T\\ \beta+\gamma & B+B^T\end{pmatrix}.$$

Let $h'\in R^{n-1}$ and $h=O^T\begin{pmatrix}0\\ h\end{pmatrix}$. We have:

$$\langle a,h\rangle=\left\langle a,O^T\begin{pmatrix}0\\ h'\end{pmatrix}\right\rangle=\langle Oa,\begin{pmatrix}0\\ h\end{pmatrix}\rangle=\left\langle \|a\|e_1,\begin{pmatrix}0\\ h\end{pmatrix}\right\rangle=0$$

and Condition (17) implies that

$$\langle Ah,h\rangle=\langle (B+B^T))h',h'\rangle\geqslant 0,$$

i. e., $B+B^T$ is positive semidefinite. Since it is also symmetric, the matrix $B+B^T$ is psd$^+$.

Now let $h\in K'$ and set $\bar{h}=Oh$. Since

$$\langle a,h\rangle=\langle a,O^T\bar{h}\rangle=\langle Oa,\bar{h}\rangle=\|a\|\langle e_1,\bar{h}\rangle=0,$$

the first component of $\bar{h}$ must be zero, i. e., we can express $\bar{h}=(0,\bar{h}')$ for some $\bar{h}'\in R^{n-1}$. Next we have, since $h\in K'$:

$$\begin{aligned}0&=\langle (A+A^T)h,h\rangle\\&=\langle (A+A^T)O^Th,O^T\bar{h}\rangle\\&=\langle O(A+A^T)O^T\bar{h},\bar{h}\rangle\\&=\langle (B+B^T)\bar{h}',\bar{h}'\rangle\end{aligned}$$

and there follows, since $B+B^T$ is psd$^+$, that $(B+B^T)\bar{h}'=0$. On the other hand:

$$\begin{aligned}(A+A^T)h&=O^TO(A+A^T)O^T\bar{h}\\&=O^T\begin{pmatrix}\langle\beta+\gamma,\bar{h}'\rangle\\ 0\end{pmatrix}\\&=O^T\frac{\langle\beta+\gamma,\bar{h}'\rangle}{\|a\|}(\|a\|e_1)\\&=\frac{\langle\beta+\gamma,\bar{h}'\rangle}{\|a\|}a,\end{aligned}$$

i. e., $h\in K$.

The combination of the previous results leads to linear algebraic sufficient condition ensuring that a mapping F be monotone$_*$ or pseudomonotone$_{**}$.

Theorem 1. *Let F be pseudo (monotone) and differentiable on D. Let* $H_x=\{h:\langle F(x),h\rangle=0\}$. *Assume that, for every* $x\in D$, *the following condition holds:*

(i) *if* $F(x)=0$:

$$y\in D \text{ and } F(y)\neq 0\Rightarrow\langle F(y),y-x\rangle>0; \tag{18}$$

(iia) *if* $F(x)\neq 0$ *and* $F'(x)$ *is positive semidefinite:*

$$F'^T(x)(H_x)\subseteq(F'(x)+F'^T(x))(R^n)+F(x)R; \tag{19}$$

(iib) *if* $F(x)\neq 0$ *and* $F'(x)$ *is not positive semidefinite:*

$$F'^T(x)(H_x)\subseteq(F'(x)+F'^T(x))(H_x)+F(x)R. \tag{20}$$

Then F is (pseudo) monotone$_*$ *on D. Whenever F is affine, the condition is necessary as well.*

Proof. Note that the case where $F(x)=0$ and the necessity in the affine case are both treated in Proposition 8.

We define the set:

$$K_x=\begin{cases}\{h\in H_x:(F'(x)+F'^T(x))h=0\} & if\ F'(x) \text{is psd}\\ \{h\in H_x:(F'(x)+F'^T(x))h=\mu F(x)\}. & \text{otherwise}\end{cases} \tag{21}$$

For ease of notation, we set $a=F(x)$, $A=F'(x)K=K_x, H=H_x$ and $T=\{h:Ah=\lambda a$ for some $\lambda\}$. Notice that both K and T are linear subspaces. Condition (16) reduces to $K\subseteq T$ or, in terms of the orthogonal subspaces, equivalently to $T^\perp\subseteq K^\perp$. It is easy to see that

$$T^\perp=\{k:\langle h,k\rangle=0 \text{ for all } h\in T\}=A^T(H).$$

Furthermore, if $K=\{h\in H:(A+A^T)h=0\}$

$$K^\perp=(A+A^T)(R^n)+aR$$

and if $K=\{h\in H:(A+A^T)h=\lambda a\}$

$$K^\perp=(A+A^T)(H)+aR.$$

Then the result follows from Proposition 8.

3.2. *Psd*$^+$ *matrices and monotone*$^+$ *mappings*

In this subsection we relate differentiable monotone$^+$ mappings to the important class of psd$^+$ matrices.

Proposition 9. *Let F be monotone and differentiable on D. If, for every x in D, the Jacobian matrix* $F'(x)$ *is psd*$^+$ *then F is monotone*$^+$ *on D. If F is affine, the psd*$^+$ *condition is necessary as well.*

Proof. Let $\langle F(a),b-a\rangle=\langle F(b),b-a\rangle$. Set $h=b-a$ and, for $t\in[0,1]:x_t=a+th$. The monotonicity of F implies that, for all $t\in[0,1]$: $\langle F(x_t),h\rangle=\langle F(a),h\rangle$ and $\langle F'(x_t)h,h\rangle=0$. Hence $F'(x_t)h=0$ and we have that $F(x_t)$ must be constant for $t\in[0,1]$. We conclude that $F(b)=F(a)$, i.e., F is monotone$^+$ on D.

This results motivates an analysis of the class of psd$^+$ matrices.

Proposition 10. *Let A be a* $n\times n$ *matrix. If A and* A^2 *are both positive semidefinite on C, then A is psd*$^+$.

Proof. Let $w \in R^n$ such that $\langle Aw, w\rangle = 0$. Since A is positive semidefinite, $A + A^T$ is psd$^+$. It follows that $(A+A^T)w = 0$. Moreover,

$$0 = \|(A+A^T)w\|^2 = \|A^T w\|^2 + \|Aw\|^2 + 2\langle A^2 w, w\rangle \geqslant 2\langle A^2 w, w\rangle \geqslant 0,$$

where the last inequality follows from the positive semidefiniteness of A^2. Finally: $Aw = 0$ and A is psd$^+$.

The converse of the above proposition does not hold, as can be seen from the matrix

$$A = \begin{pmatrix} 2 & -4 \\ 4 & 1 \end{pmatrix}$$

which is psd$^+$ while its square A^2 is not positive semidefinite.

Symmetric positive semidefinite matrices are clearly psd$^+$. Assume now that A is nonzero and antisymmetric (i. e. , $A = -A^T$). Set $F(x) = Ax + a$. Then F is monotone on the whole space R^n but not monotone$^+$ on any open nonempty convex subset D of R^n. Furthermore, it is easily shown that F is monotone$_*$ on D if and only if A has rank 2 and F does not vanish on D.

Proposition 11. *Let A be an $n \times n$ positive semidefinite matrix. Then the three following conditions are equivalent:*

(*a*) *A is psd$^+$;*

(*b*) $(A+A^T)h = 0 \Rightarrow Ah = 0$;

(*c*) $A^T(R^n) \subseteq (A+A^T)(R^n)$.

Proof. • (b)⇒(a): Assume that $\langle Ah, h\rangle = 0$. Then $\langle (A+A^T)h, h\rangle = 0$. Since $(A + A^T)$ is psd$^+$, we obtain $(A+A^T)h = 0$ and, from (b), $Ah = 0$.

- (a)⇒(b): If $(A+A^T)h = 0$, then $\langle (A+A^T)h, h\rangle = 0$. Therefore $\langle Ah, h\rangle = 0$ and, from (a), we obtain that $Ah = 0$.
- (b)⇒(c): take $K = \{h : (A+A^T)h = 0\}$ and $T = \{h : Ah = 0\}$. Then $K \subseteq T$ is equivalent to $T^\perp \subseteq K^\perp$.

Theorem 2. *Assume that D is an open convex set and F is monotone and differentiable on D. Assume also that, for all $x \in D$:*

$$[F'(x) + (F'(x))^T]h = 0 \Rightarrow F'(x)h = 0. \tag{22}$$

Then F is monotone$^+$ on D. When F is affine, the condition is also necessary. A dual formulation of (22) is

$$(F'(x))^T(R^n) \subseteq [F'(x) + (F'(x))^T](R^n). \tag{23}$$

Proof. Set $A = F'(x)$. Then A is positive semidefinite. Combine Proposition 9 with Proposition 11.

3.3. *Pseudomonotone$^+_*$ and monotone$^+_*$ mappings*

Proposition 12. *Assume that F is differentiable and pseudomonotone (respectively monotone) on D. Assume in addition that for all $x \in D$ there holds:*

$$\langle F(x), h\rangle = \langle F'(x)h, h\rangle = 0 \Rightarrow F'(x)h = 0. \tag{24}$$

Then F is pseudomonotone$^+$ (respectivelymonotone$^+_*$) on D. If F is affine, the condi-

tion is necessary as well.

Proof. Assume that $\langle F(a), b-a\rangle = \langle F(b), b-a\rangle = 0$ for some $a, b \in D$, $a \neq b$. Set $h = b - a$ and $x_t = a + th$. Let $t \in [0,1]$. From Lemma 1 it follows that

$$\langle F(x_t), h\rangle = \langle F'(x_t)h, h\rangle = 0.$$

Hence $F'(x_t)h = 0$ for any $t \in [0,1]$ and $F(a) = F(b)$.

Theorem 3. *Assume that D is an open convex set and F is pseudomonotone (monotone) and differentiable on D. For $x \in D$ define $H_x = \{h : \langle F(x), h\rangle = 0\}$. Assume that for all $x \in D$ there holds:*

(i) *if $F'(x)$ is positive semidefinite then*

$$(F'(x))^T(R^n) \subseteq [F'(x) + (F'(x))^T](R^n) + RF(x), \tag{25}$$

(ii) *if $F'(x)$ is not positive semidefinite then*

$$(F'(x))^T(R^n) \subseteq [F'(x) + (F'(x))^T](H_x) + RF(x). \tag{26}$$

Then F is pseudomonotone$^+_*$. (monotone$^+_*$) on D.

Proof. As before, we set $a = F(x)$, $A = F'(x)$ and $H = Hx$.

(i) Assume that A is a positive semidefinite matrix. It is then enough to see the equivalence of the two following conditions:

(a) $\langle a, h\rangle = 0$ and $(A + A^T)h = 0 \Rightarrow Ah = 0$;

(b) $A^T(R^n) \subseteq (A + A^T)(R^n) + Ra$.

Set $K = \{h : \langle a, h\rangle = 0$ and $(A + A^T)h = 0\}$ and $T = \{h : Ah = 0\}$. Then (a) means that $K \subseteq T$ while (b) means that $T^\perp \subseteq K^\perp$.

(ii) In the case where A is not positive semidefinite, it is sufficient to prove the following equivalences:

(c) $\langle a, h\rangle = 0$ and $\langle Ah, h\rangle = 0 \Rightarrow Ah = 0$;

(d) $\langle a, h\rangle = 0$ and $(A + A^T)h + \mu a = 0 \Rightarrow Ah = 0$;

(e) $A^T(R^n) \subseteq (A + A^T)(H) + Ra$.

Conditions (c) and (d) are equivalent by Lemma 2. To prove the equivalence of (d) and (e), consider $K = \{h : \langle a, h\rangle = 0$ and $(A + A^T)h + \mu a = 0\}$ and $T = \{h : Ah = 0\}$. Proceed as above.

4. Multivalued mappings

4.1. *Multivalued generalized monotone mappings*

Recall that a multivalued mapping F is **monotone** on D if, for all x, y in D, $r_x \in F(x)$, $r_y \in F(y)$:

$$\langle r_x - r_y, x - y\rangle \geqslant 0. \tag{27}$$

monotone$^+$: The multivalued mapping F is monotone$^+$ on D if it is monotone on D and, for all x, y in D, $r_x \in F(x)$, $r_y \in F(y)$:

$$\langle r_x - r_y, x - y\rangle = 0 \Rightarrow r_y \in F(x). \tag{28}$$

monotone$^+_*$: F is monotone$^+_*$ on D if it is monotone on D and, for all x, y in D, $r_x \in$

$F(x), r_y \in F(y)$:

$$\left.\begin{array}{r}\langle r_x, x-y\rangle = 0 \\ \langle r_y, x-y\rangle = 0\end{array}\right\} \Rightarrow r_y \in F(x). \tag{29}$$

monotone$_*$: F is monotone$_*$ on D if it is monotone on D and there exists a positive constant k such that, x, y in $D, r_x \in F(x)$, $r_y \in F(y)$:

$$\left.\begin{array}{r}\langle r_x, x-y\rangle = 0 \\ \langle r_y, x-y\rangle = 0\end{array}\right\} \Rightarrow kr_y \in F(x). \tag{30}$$

As for single-valued mappings, we have the relationships:

$$F \text{ monotone}^+ \Rightarrow F \text{ monotone}_*^+ \Rightarrow F \text{ monotone}_* \Rightarrow F \text{ monotone}.$$

Multivalued monotone$^+$ mappings arise in many situations, such as subdifferentials of lower-semicontinuous convex functions or maximal monotone trimonotone multivalued mappings (see Brézis and Browder [2]).

It is known (see Minty[12]) that the subdifferential of a convex function is monotone. The next proposition strenghtens this results by providing a characterization of the subdifferential of a covex function.

Proposition 13. *A locally Lipschitz function f is proper and convex on D if and only if its generalized gradient (in Clarke's sense) is a monotone$^+$ multivalued mapping on D.*

Proof. The 'if' part of the proposition is given in Clarke [3].

Assume that f is proper, locally Lipschitz and convex on D. Then the generalized gradient $\partial f(x)$ coincides with the subdifferential of f at x. Let $x, y, z \in D$ and $r_x \in \partial f(x), r_y \in \partial f(y)$ and $\langle r_y - r_x, y-x\rangle = 0$. From the definition of a subgradient we can write:

$$\begin{aligned}\langle r_y, z-x\rangle &= \langle r_y, y-x\rangle + \langle r_y, z-y\rangle \\ &\leqslant \langle r_x, y-x\rangle + f(z) - f(y) \\ &\leqslant f(y) - f(x) + f(z) - f(y) \\ &= f(z) - f(x).\end{aligned}$$

This implies that r_y is in $\partial f(x)$, and the result follows.

We close this section by giving the definition of new class of multivalued pseudomonotone mappings.

4.2. *Multivalued generalized pseudomonotone mappings*

pseudomonotone: A multivalued mapping F is pseudomonotone on D if, for all x, y in $D, r_x \in F(x), r_y \in F(y)$, we have:

$$\langle r_x, y-x\rangle \geqslant 0 \Rightarrow \langle r_y, y-x\rangle \geqslant 0. \tag{31}$$

pseudomonotone$^+$: The mapping F is pseudomonotone$^+$ on D if it is pseudomonotone on D and, x, y in $D, r_x \in F(x), r_y \in F(y)$, we have:

$$\langle r_x - r_y, x-y\rangle = 0 \Rightarrow r_y \in F(x). \tag{32}$$

pseudomonotone$_*^+$: The mapping F is pseudomonotone$_*^+$ on D if it is pseudomonotone on

D and, x, y in D, $r_x \in F(x)$, $r_y \in F(y)$, we have:

$$\left.\begin{array}{r}\langle r_x, x-y\rangle = 0 \\ \langle r_y, x-y\rangle = 0\end{array}\right\} \Rightarrow r_y \in F(x). \tag{33}$$

pseudomonotone$_*$: The mapping F is pseudomonotone$_*$ on D if it is pseudomonotone on D and there exists a positive constant k such that, x, y in D, $r_x \in F(x)$, $r_y \in F(y)$, we have:

$$\left.\begin{array}{r}\langle r_x, x-y\rangle = 0 \\ \langle r_y, x-y\rangle = 0\end{array}\right\} \Rightarrow kr_y \in F(x). \tag{34}$$

5. Application to variational inequalities

In this section we demonstrate the usefulness of the new concepts of generalized monotonicity for the study of variational inequalities, both from the theoretical and computational points of view.

Let us first consider the case of a variational inequality VI(F,C) characterized by a single-valued continuous mapping F and a convex set C, i. e., we look for a point x^* in C that satisfies the variational inequality:

$$\langle F(x^*), x^* - x\rangle \leqslant 0 \quad \forall x \in C$$

where C is a convex, compact subset of R^n. Then, there exists at least one solution to VI(F,C).

Lemma 3. *Let F be pseudomonotone on C and $x^* \in \mathrm{sol}(F,C)$. Then every solution $\bar{x}$ of VI(F,C) lies on the hyperplane $H^* = \{y: \langle F(x^*), y-x^*\rangle = 0\}$.*

Proof. Let $y \in \mathrm{sol}(F,C)$. By definition of sol(F,C) we have:

$$\langle F(x^*), y-x^*\rangle \geqslant 0$$
$$\langle F(y), x^* - y\rangle \geqslant 0.$$

From the pseudomonotonicity of F there follows:

$$\langle F(\bar{x}), \bar{x} - x^*\rangle \geqslant 0$$
$$\langle F(x^*), x^* - \bar{x}\rangle \geqslant 0$$

and: $\langle F(x^*), \bar{x} - x^*\rangle = 0$.

Proposition 14. *Let F be a pseudomonotone$_*^+$ mapping from C into R^n. Then the mapping F is constant over the solution set X^* of VI(F,C). If F is pseudomonotone$_*$ and x and y are in X^*, then there is a $k>0$ such that $F(y)=kF(x)$.*

Proof. Let x and y be solutions of VI(F,C). By Lemma 3 we have that $\langle F(y), y-x\rangle = 0$ and $\langle F(x), y-x\rangle = 0$. If F is pseudomonotone$_*^+$ we conclude that $F(y)=F(x)$. If F is pseudomonotone$_*$ we conclude that $F(y)=kF(x)$.

If F is continuous and pseudomonotone on C, then solving VI(F,C) is equivalent to finding a point x^* in C that satisfies the system:

$$\langle F(x), x^* - x\rangle \leqslant 0 \quad \forall x \in C \tag{35}$$

or, equivalently, x^* is a global minimizer of the gap function:

$$\bar{g}(x) = \sup_{y \in C} \langle F(y), x - y \rangle. \tag{36}$$

It turns out that $\bar{g}$ is convex as a supremum of affine functions. Let us denote by $Y(x)$ the set of optimal solutions in (36). Then $Y(x)$ is compact and nonempty since C is compact and F is continuous. Furthermore, the directional derivative of $\bar{g}$ at x with respect to d is given by

$$\bar{g}'(x,d) = \max_{y \in Y(x)} \langle F(y), d \rangle.$$

Hence, if F is pseudomonotone$_*^+$, one obtains from Proposition 14 that $\bar{g}$ is differentiable at any solution x^* of VI(F,C).

Moreover, error bounds on the distance from x to the set X^* of equilibrium points can be derived. The reader is referred to [11] for further details.

The next two results plays a key role in analyzing the convergence of cutting plane or interior point algorithms for solving VI(F,C) (see Goffin et al. [6]).

Corollary 1. *Let F be pseudomonotone$_*$ on C. If $\bar{x} \in C$ is not a solution of VI(F,C), then its solution set X^* lies entirely within the open half-space $\{x : \langle F(\bar{x}), x - \bar{x} \rangle < 0\}$.*

To close this paper, we consider variational inequalities MVI(F,C)involvingmulti-valued mappings. Any solution x^* of MVI(F,C)satisfies:

$$\exists r^* \in F(x^*) : \langle r^*, x^* - x \rangle \leqslant 0 \quad \forall x \in C. \tag{37}$$

The results obtained so far for VI(F,C)can be extended to MVI(F,C). We now give a convergence result for a class of iterative algorithms for solving pseudomonotone$_*$ MVI (F,C)'s. More precisely, let {xk}be a sequence of C such that $r_k \in F(x_k)$and:

$$\lim_{k \to \infty} \langle r_k, x_k - x^* \rangle = 0,$$

then any limit point of the sequence $\{x_k\}$ is a solution of MVI(F,C), provided that F be pseudomonotone$_*$ and closed over the convex set C. Recall that a multivalued mapping $F : C \subset R^n \to R^n$ is **closed** at a point x_0 if, for any sequence $\{r_k\}$there holds:

$$\left.\begin{array}{r} x_k \to x_0 \\ r_k \in F(x_k) \\ \lim_{k \to \infty} r_k = r_0 \end{array}\right\} \Rightarrow r_0 \in F(x_0).$$

Proposition 15. *Let C be compact and F be bounded, pseudomonotone * and closed on C. Let $\{x_k\}$ be a sequence of C and $\{r_k\}$ a sequence in R^n such that $r_k \in F(x_k)$ and $\lim_{k \to \infty} \langle r_k, x_k - x^* \rangle = 0$ for some solution x^* of MVI(F,C). Then any limit point $\bar{x}$ of $\{x_k\}$ is a solution of MVI(F,C).*

Proof. Let $\{x'_k\}$ be a convergent subsequence of $\{x_k\}$ and $\bar{x}$ its limit point. Let $r'_k \in F(x_{k'})$. Since F is bounded, there exists a subsequence $\{x_{k''}\} \subset \{x_k\}$ such that $r_{k''} \in F(x_k)$ and $r_{k''} \to \bar{r}$. But F is closed hence $\bar{r} \in F(\bar{x})$ and $\langle \bar{r}, \bar{x} - x^* \rangle = 0$. From the pseudomonotonicity of F we get $\langle -r^*, \bar{x} - x^* \rangle \geqslant 0$. But x^* is a solution of MVI(F,C), thus $\langle r^*, \bar{x} - x^* \rangle = 0$. Since F is pseudomonotone$_*$, kr^* must belong to $F(\bar{x})$, for some positive number k. Finally, for any $x \in C$, we have

$$k\langle r^*, x-\bar{x}\rangle = k\langle r^*, x-x^*\rangle + k\langle r^*, x^*-\bar{x}\rangle \geqslant 0,$$

with $kr^* \in F(\bar{x})$. This implies that $\bar{x}$ is a solution of MVI(F,C).

6. Conclusion

This paper has considered new forms of generalized monotonicity. These new forms are not artificial, in that they allow to prove the convergence of an interior point cutting-plane method for solving pseudomonotone variational inequalities. Note, however, that, in the monotone case, the monotone. condition could be weakened to simple monotonicity by adopting the averaging scheme described and implemented by Nesterov and Vial [13].

References

[1] Avriel, M., Diewert, W. E., Schaible, S., Zang, I. (1988): Generalized Concavity. Plenum Press, New York

[2] Brézis, H., Browder, F. E. (1974): Some new results about Hammerstein equations. Bull. Am. Math. Soc. **80**, 567—572

[3] Clarke, F. H. (1983): Optimization and nonsmooth analysis. Wiley

[4] Crouzeix, J.-P. (1998): Characterizations of generalized convexity and generalized monotonicity. In: Crouzeix, J.-P., Martinez-Legaz, J. E., Volle, M., eds., Generalized Convexity, Generalized Monotonicity. Kluwer Academic Publishers, pp. 237—256

[5] Crouzeix, J.-P., Ferland, J. A. (1996): Criteria for differentiabel generalized monotone maps. Math. Program. **75**, 399—406

[6] Goffin, J.-L., Marcotte, P., Zhu, D. L. (1997): An analytic center cutting plane method for pseudomonotone variational inequalities. Oper. Res. Lett. **20**, 1—6

[7] Gowda, M. (1989): Pseudomonotone and copositive star matrices. Linear Algebra Appl. **113**, 107—118

[8] Karamardian, S., Schaible, S. (1990): Seven kinds of monotone maps. J. Optim. Theory Appl. **66**, 37—46

[9] Karamardian, S., Schaible, S., Crouzeix, J.-P. (1993): Characterizations of generalized monotone maps. J. Optim. Theory Appl. **76**, 399—413

[10] Luo, Z. Q., Tseng, P. (1991): A decomposition property for a class of square matrices. Appl. Math. Lett. **4**, 67—69

[11] Marcotte, P., Zhu, D. L. (1999): Weak sharp solutions and the finite convergence of algorithms for solving variational inequalities. SIAM J. Optim. **9**, 179—189

[12] Minty, G. (1963): On a monotonicity method for the solution of nonlinear equations in Banach spaces. Proc. Nat. Acad. Sci. USA **50**, 1038—1041

[13] Nesterov, Y., Vial, J.-P. (1999): Homogeneous analytic center cutting plane methods for convex problems and variational inequalities. SIAM J. Optim. **9**, 707—728

[14] Ortega, J. M., Rheinboldt, W. C. (1970): Iterative solution of nonlinear equations in several variables. Academic Press, New York

[15] Renaud, A., Cohen, G. (1997): Conditioning and regularization of nonsymmetric operators. J. Optim. Theory Appl. **92**, 127—148

[16] Schaible, S. (1977): Second-order characterizations of pseudoconvex quadratic functions. J. Optim. Theory Appl. **21**, 15—26

[17] Tseng, P. (1990): Further applications of a splitting algorithms to decomposition in variational inequalities and convex programming. Math. Program. **48**, 249—264

[18] Zhu, D. L., Marcotte, P. (1996): Co-coercivity and its role in the convergence of iterative schemes for solving variational inequality problems. SIAM J. Optim. **6**, 714—726

[19] Zhu, D. L., Marcotte, P. (1993): New classes of generalized monotonicity. J. Optim. Theory Appl. **87**, 457—471

[20] Zuhovickii, S. I., Polyak, R. A., Primak, M. E. (1969): Two methods of search of equilibrium of n-person concave games. Soviet Math. Doklady **10**, 279—282

Published in *Mathematical Programming*, 2000, Ser. A

Theory and Methodology Coupling the auxiliary problem principle with descent method S of pseudoconvex programming*

Daoli Zhu[a], Patrice Marcotte[b],**

[a] *CRT, Université de Montréal, Montréal, Canada H3C 3J7*

[b] *DIRO, Université de Montréal, Montréal, Canada H3C M7*

Abstract. The descent auxiliary problem method allows one to find the solution of minimization problems by solving a sequence of auxiliary problems which incorporate a linesearch strategy. We derive the basic algorithm and study its convergence properties within the framework of infinite dimensional pseudoconvex minimization. We also introduce a partial descent type auxiliary problem method which partially linearizes the objective functional and includes the auxiliary term only for of subset of variables. Numerous examples of this very general scheme are provided.

Keywords, Mathematical programming; Pseudoconvex programming; Descent methods

1. Introduction

For classical optimization problems, Cohen [3,4] and Cohen and Zhu [5] introduced the auxiliary problem principle as a general framework to describe and analyze computational algorithms ranging from gradient (or subgradient) algorithms to decomposition/coordination algorithms. In this paper we combine the auxiliary problem method with a descent scheme for solving smooth pseudoconvex problems. The main advantage of the new method is to weaken the convergence requirements of traditional algorithmic schemes.

Motivated by descent methods for optimization problems, we attempt to provide a unified view of this field. More specifically, we study descent methods for pseudoconvex optimization problems in which an elementary step amounts to solving an auxiliary problem, which consists in a minimization problem built around a convex cost function defined by the user.

---

*Research supported by NSERC grant A5789.

**Corresponding author.

Several examples will illustrate how various descent algorithms can be considered as specializations of the basic algorithm. Moreover our systematic approach provides guidelines for designing new algorithms and/or improving existing ones. In particular we will analyze optimization problems where the decision space is the product of two subspaces. In this method, the objective function is linearized for only a subset of variables and an auxiliary term corresponding to this subset of variables is incorporated, yielding simpler subproblems while providing a better approximation of the original problem.

By adequately choosing the auxiliary cost functional, one may introduce decomposition into the auxiliary minimization problem, provided that the decision space be specified as the product of independent subsets. An example drawn from the field of transportation will be used to illustrate how the partial auxiliary problem principle can be made to exploit efficiently the structure of a given problem.

The paper will be organized as follows. Basic results and definitions are given in Section 2. The basic descent framework is introduced in Section 3 and various realizations are presented in Section 4. Sections 5 and 6 are concerned with the partial auxiliary problem and its applications. A brief discussion (Section 7) closes the paper.

2. Preliminaries

In the paper, we will make use of the following notation: U will denote a reflexive Banach space* U^* the topological dual space of continuous linear functionals on U, V a closed convex subset of U, J a functional on U and $J'(u)$ the Gâteaux derivative (G-derivative) of J at u. If J is defined on a product space $U_1 \times U_2$, denote by $J'_u(u,v)$ (respectively $J'_v(u,v)$) the partial derivative of J with respect to the first variable (respectively the second variable). Finally let $\langle p,u\rangle$ be the scalar product with results from the action of $p \in U^*$ on $u \in U$.

Definition 1. The functional F is *convex* on V if for all u_1, u_2 in V and for all $\alpha \in [0,1]$ we have

$$F(\alpha u_1 + (1-\alpha)u_2) \leqslant \alpha F(u_1) + (1-\alpha)F(u_2). \tag{1}$$

The functional F is *strongly convex* with modulus b on V if there exists a positive constant b such that

$$F(\alpha u_1 + (1-\alpha)u_2) \leqslant \alpha F(u_1) + (1-\alpha)F(u_2) - \frac{1}{2}b \| u_1 - u_2 \|^2 \alpha(1-\alpha), \tag{2}$$

for all u_1, u_2 in V, for all $\alpha \in [0,1]$.

A Gâteaux-differentiable functional F is *pseudoconvex* on V if

*Although our theory is presented in a general, abstract setting, our research has been motivated by applications in finite dimensional spaces. Without(much) loss of generality, the reader can assume that the space of interest is the Euclidian space R^n.

$$\langle F'(u_1), u_2 - u_1 \rangle \geqslant 0 \Rightarrow F(u_2) \geqslant F(u_1), \tag{3}$$

for all u_1, u_2 in V.

It has been shown (see Güler [8]) that if F is G-differentiable on V, then the following statements are equivalent:

— F is strongly convex on V with modulus b, (4)

— $F(u_2)-F(u_1)\geqslant\langle F'(u_1), u_2-u_1\rangle+\frac{1}{2}b\,\|u_2-u_1\|^2$, (5)

— $\langle F'(u_2)-F'(u_1), u_2-u_1\rangle\geqslant b\,\|u_2-u_1\|^2$. (6)

Definition 2. The functional F is *Lipschitz continuous* with constant L on V if there exists a positive constant L such tliat

$$|F(u_2) - F(u_1)| \leqslant L \| u_2 - u_1 \| \tag{7}$$

for all u_1, u_2 in V.

Definition 3. We say that J is *coercive* on V if for all sequences $\{u^k \mid u^k \in V\}$ such that $\| u^k \| \to +\infty$(if any), we have that $J(u^k) \to +\infty$.

Theorem 1. Let F_1, F_2 *be proper convex G-differentiable functionals on* V *and* $F_1 + F_2$ *be coercive on* V. *Then, for* $u^* \in V$, *the following five conditions are equivalent*:

(i) $(F_1+F_2)(u^{*\prime})=\min\limits_{u\in V}(F_1+F_2)$ (8)

(ii) $F_1(u)-F_1(u^*)+\langle(F'_2(u^*), u-u^*\rangle\geqslant 0\quad \forall u\in V$, (9)

(iii) $F_1(u)-f_1(u^*)+\langle F_2'(u), u-u^*\rangle\geqslant 0\quad \forall u\in V$, (10)

(iv) $\langle(F_1+F_2)'(u^*), u-u^*\rangle\geqslant 0\quad \forall u\in V$, (11)

(v) $\langle(F_1+F_2)'(u), u-u^*\rangle\geqslant 0\quad \forall u\in V$, (12)

(vi) $\langle F_1'(u)+F_2'(u^*), u-u^*\rangle\geqslant 0\quad \forall u\in V$. (13)

Proof. The equivalence of (i)—(v) is shown in Ekeland and Temam [7].

(ii)⇒(vi): Since F_1 is convex and $u^* \in V$, we have

$$\langle F'_1(u, u - u^* \rangle \geqslant F_1(u) - F_1(u^*)$$

for all u in V. Together with (9) this yields

$$\langle F'_1(u) + F'_2(u^*), u - u^* \rangle \geqslant 0 \quad \forall u = V.$$

(vi)⇒(iii): Since F_2 is convex, we have

$$\langle F'_2(u^*), u - u^* \rangle \leqslant F_2(u) - F_2(u^*) \quad \forall u \in V.$$

Thus, from (13),

$$F_2(u) - F_2(u^*) + \langle F'_1(u), u - u^* \rangle \geqslant 0 \quad \forall u \in V,$$

which is the symmetric form of (iii), and we obtain the desired implication.

Remark. In Theorem 1 ablove the convexity of F_1 is necessary. For instance, consider the following example of Zhu [20]: $U=R, V=\left[-\frac{1}{2}, \frac{1}{2}\right]$, $F_1(u)=u^3$ (pesudoconvex) and $F_2=u^2$. We have $u^*=0$. However,

$$F_1(u) - F_1(u^*) + \langle F'_2(u^*), u - u^* \rangle = u^3$$

is negative in the interval $\left[-\frac{1}{2}, 0\right)$.

3. Coupling descent methods and the auxiliary problem principle

In this section we consider the mathematical programming problem
(MP)

$$\min_{u\in V}(J+J_1)(u) \tag{14}$$

where $J+J_1$ is G-differentiable and pseudoconvex on V and J_1 is convx on V. If $J+J_1$ is coercive, then a solution u^* to Problem MP exists. Given a feasible point $u^k\in V$, we will study the auxiliary problem
(AP^k)

$$\min_{u\in V}K^k(u)+\langle\varepsilon^k J'(u^k)-(K^k)'(u^k),u\rangle+\varepsilon^k J_1(u) \tag{15}$$

where $K^k(u)=K(u,u^k)$, $K(u,v)$ is differentiable and strongly convex with modulus b^k with respect to u, and continuous with respect to (u,v) *on* $V\times V$, *and* ε^k *is a positive parameter. The solution* $\hat{u}^k$ *of this strongly convex subproblem defines a feasible direction* $d^k=\hat{u}^k-u^k$ *for* $J+J_1$ *at* u^k.

Theorem 2. *Let u^k be in V and $\hat{u}^k$ be the solution to* AP^k. *If $\hat{u}^k=u^k$, then u^k is a solution to* MP. *Otherwise, the direction $d^k=\hat{u}^k-u^k$ is a feasible descent direction for $(J+J_1)(U)$ at u^k.*

Proof. Applying (vi) in Theorem 1 to the optimization problem AP^k we obtain

$$\langle(K^k)'(\hat{u}^k)-(K^k)(u^k)+\varepsilon^k[J'(u^k)+J_1'(u)],u-\hat{u}^k\rangle\geqslant 0\quad\forall u\in V. \tag{16}$$

Letting $u=u^k$ in (16) we get

$$\langle(J+J_1)'(u^k),\hat{u}^k-u^k\rangle\leqslant-\frac{1}{\varepsilon^k}\langle(K^k)'(\hat{u}^k)-(K^k)',(u^k)-u^k\rangle. \tag{17}$$

If $\hat{u}^k\neq u^k$ we obtain, from the strong convexity of $K^k(u)$ with respect to u,

$$\langle(J+J_1)'(u^k),\hat{u}^k-u^k\rangle<0,$$

i. e. that the direction $d^k=\hat{u}^k-u^k$ is a descent direction for $J+J_1$ at u^k, and its feasibility follows from the convexity of the set V.

On the other hand, if $d^k=0$, the application of (iv) in Theorem 1 to AP^k yields

$$\langle(K^k)'(\hat{u}^k)-(K^k)'(u^k)+\varepsilon^k[J'(u^k)+J_1'(\hat{u}^k)],u-\hat{u}^k\rangle\geqslant 0\quad\forall u\in V. \tag{18}$$

Letting $\hat{u}^k=u^k$ in (18) there comes

$$\langle(J+J_1)'(u^k),u-u^k\rangle\geqslant 0\quad\forall u\in V$$

and, from the pseudocovexity of $J+J_1$ on V, u^k is optimal for MP.

Theorem 2 suggests the following feasible descent algorithm. Let sequences of functional $\{K^k(u)=K(u,u^k)\}_{k\in N}$ and of positive number $\{\varepsilon^k\}_{k\in N}$ be given.

Basic Algorithm

Step 1. Choose $u^0\in V$, Set k to 0.

Step 2. Let $\hat{u}^k$ be the unique solution of the problem AP^k and set $d^k=\hat{u}^k-u^k$.
if $d^k=0$ **then** stop with $u^*=u^k$

else go to Step 3.

Step 3. Linesearch

Let $t_k \in \arg\min_{t\in[0,1]}(J+J_1)(u^k+td^k)$.

Set $u^{k+1}=u^k+t_kd^k$.

Let $k \leftarrow k+1$ and goto Step 2.

Theorem 3 (Convergence theorem). *Assume that*:

(i) $J+J_1$ *is coercive on* V;

(ii) $J+J_1$ *is pseudoconvex with continuous G-derivative on* V;

(iii) J_1 *is convex on* V;

(iv) *the functionals* $K^k(u)=K(u,u^k)$ *are G-differentiable and strongly convex on* V *with modulus* $b^k>b$, *where* b *is some positive number*;

(v) $\gamma_1<\varepsilon^k<\gamma_2$ *for some* $\gamma_1>0$ *and* $\gamma_2>\gamma_1$.

Then any accumulation point of the sequence generated by the basic algorithm is a solution to MP.

Proof. Assume that $\hat{u}^k \neq u^k$, for all k, otherwise Theorem 2 implies that an exact solution has been obtained. It follows from the sane theorem that d^k is a feasible descent direction. Thus

$$(J+J_1)(u^{k+1}) = (J+J_1)(u^k+t_kd^k) < (J+J_1)(u^k) \tag{19}$$

and $\{(J+J_1)(u^k)\}$ is a monotonically decreasing sequence which is bounded from below. We have from the coercivity assumption that the sequence $\{\hat{u}^k\}$ is bounded. We must therefore have at least one cluster point in the weak topology. Let u^* denote such a point, and let $\{u^k\}_{k\in I}$ denote a subsequence weakly converging to u^*. Notice that $u^* \in V$, since V is covex and thus weakly closed. Let $\{\hat{u}^k\}_{k\in I}$ be the sequence of the associated points generated at Step 2 of the basic algorithm. From (17) we easily obtain

$$\begin{aligned}\langle (J+J_1)'(u^k), u^k-\hat{u}^k\rangle &\geqslant \frac{b^k}{2\varepsilon^k}\|u^k-\hat{u}^k\|^2 \\ &\geqslant \frac{b}{2\gamma_2}\|u^k-\hat{u}^k\|^2,\end{aligned} \tag{20}$$

which implies that

$$\frac{b}{2\gamma_2}\|u^k-\hat{u}^k\| \leqslant \|(J+J_1)'(u^k)\|. \tag{21}$$

It follows from the continuity of $(J+J_1)'$ and the boundedness of the sequence $\{u^k\}$ that the sequence $\{a^k\}$ is also bounded. Let $\hat{u}\in V$ be the limit of a convergent subsequence $\{\hat{u}^k\}_{k\in I'}$, $I'\subset I$. Assume that $\hat{u}\neq u^*$. Taking the limit over $k\in I'$ in (20) we obtain

$$\langle (J+J_1)'(u^*), (u^*-\hat{u})\rangle \geqslant \frac{b}{\gamma_2}\|\hat{u}-u^*\|^2. \tag{22}$$

Also, since $J+J_1$ is continuous in the weak topology, we have

$$\lim_{k\to\infty, k\in I}(J+J_1)(u^k) = (J+J_1)(u^*)$$

and, consequently

$$\lim_{k\to\infty,k\in I}[(J+J_1)(u^{k+1})-(J+J_1)(u^k)]=0. \qquad (23)$$

From (23) and the linesearch rule there comes

$$\lim_{k\to\infty,k\in I}[(J+J_1)(u^k+\beta_k)(\hat{u}^k-u^k)-(J+J_1)(u^k)]\geqslant 0,$$

for every $\{\beta_k\}_{k\in I}$ such that $\beta_k\in(0,t_k)$, and $\lim_{k\in I}\beta_k=0$. Hence

$$\lim_{k\to\infty,k\in I}\frac{(J+J_1)(u^k+\beta_k(\hat{u}^k-u^k))-(J+J_1)(u^k)}{\beta_k}\geqslant 0. \qquad (24)$$

The previous inequality and and continutity of $(J+J_1)'(u)$ imply that

$$\langle (J+J_1)'(u^*),\hat{u}-u^*\rangle\geqslant 0 \qquad (25)$$

which, together with (22), implies that $u^*=\hat{u}$. Now, for every $u\in V$, Eqn. (16)yields

$$\begin{aligned}\langle J'(u^k)+J_1'(\hat{u}^k),\hat{u}^k-u\rangle &\leqslant \frac{1}{\varepsilon^k}\langle (K^k)'(\hat{u}^k)-(K^k)'(u^k),u-\hat{u}^k\rangle\\ &\leqslant \langle J'(u^k)+J_1'(\hat{u}^k),\hat{u}^k-u\rangle\\ &\leqslant \frac{1}{\gamma_1}\|(K^k)'(\hat{u}^k)-(K^k)'(u^k)\|\ \|u-\hat{u}^k\|. \qquad (26)\end{aligned}$$

Finally, taking the limit over $k\subset I'$ in (26) we obtain

$$\langle (J+J_1)'(u^*),u-u^*\rangle\geqslant 0 \quad \forall u\in V.$$

which is the desired result.

Remark. If V is bounded we can do without the assumptions $b^k>b>0$ and $\varepsilon^k<\gamma_2$.

An advantage of the auxiliary problem method is that decomposition can be achieved easily. Assume for instance that

$$U=U_1\times U_2\times\cdots\times U_N \text{ and } V=V_1\times V_2\times\cdots\times V_N. \qquad (27)$$

If $J_1=\sum_{j=1}^N J_{1j}(u_j)$, where the functionals J_{1j}'s are convex for all j, and K^k is chosen to be separable, then AP^k splits into N independent problems. As we will see in Section 5, problem AP^k can be endowed with special features, depending on the choice of K^k.

From a practical point of view, the subproblems cannot be solved exactly, and there is a trade-off to achieve between the amount of work spent on solving AP^k and the quality of the descent direction. In this section, we will present an inexact scheme, where each subproblem is solved approximately. Denote by $\psi^k(u,u^k)$ the value of the objective function of the subproblen, i. e.

$$\psi^k(u,\ u^k)=K^k(u)+\langle \varepsilon^k J'(u^k)-(K^k)'(u^k),u\rangle+\varepsilon^k J_1(u),$$

and consider the following modified algorithm.

Modified basic algorithm

Step 1. Let $u^0\in V$, set $k=0$.

Step 2. Let $\bar{u}^k$ be a ρ^k-solution of the auxiliary problem AP^k, i. e. a point satisfying

$$\psi(\bar{u}^k,u^k)\leqslant \psi^k(u,u^k)+\rho^k \quad \forall u\in V,$$
$$\psi(\bar{u}^k,u^k)\leqslant \psi^k(u^k,u^k).$$

Set $d^k=\bar{u}-u^k$.

if $d^k \approx 0$ **then** stop

else goto Step 3.

Step 3. Line search

Find $t_k = \arg\min_{t\in[0,1]}(J+J_1)(u^k+td^k)$.

Set $u^{k+1} = u^k + t_k d^k, k = k+1$ and goto Step 2.

The following results establish the global convergence of the ablove inexact scheme.

Lemma 1. *Let* $\bar{u}^k \neq u^k$ *and* $\rho^k < \frac{1}{2}b^k \| \bar{u}^k - u^k \|^2$. *Then* $d^k = \bar{u}^k - u^k$ *is a feasible descent direction for* $(J+J_1)(u)$ *at* u^k.

Proof. Since $\psi^{k\prime}_u(u^k, u^k) = \epsilon^k (J+J_1)'(u^k)$ and $\psi^k(u, u^k)$ is strongly convex in u with modulus b^k, we can use the variational inequality (iv) of Theorem 1 to obtain

$$\begin{aligned}&\varepsilon^k \langle (J+J_1)'(u^k), \bar{u}^k - u^k \rangle \\ &= \langle \psi^{k\prime}_u(u^k, u^k), \bar{u}^k - u^k \rangle \leqslant \psi^k(\bar{u}^k, u^k) - \psi^k(u^k, u^k) - \frac{1}{2}b^k \| \bar{u}^k - u^k \|^2 \\ &\leqslant -\frac{1}{2}b^k \| \bar{u}^k - u^k \|^2 + \rho^k < 0 \quad \text{if } \rho^k < \frac{1}{2}b^k \| \bar{u}^k - u^k \|^2.\end{aligned}$$

Theorem 4. *Let the assumptions of Theorem* 3 *be satisfied and let the sequence* $\{p^k\}$ *be chosen such that* $\lim_{k\to\infty}\rho^k = 0$. *Then the modified basic algorithm either terminates in a finite number of iterations or it generates an infinite sequence* $\{u^k\}$ *such that any accumulation point of the sequence* $\{u^k\}$ *is an optimal solution to MP.*

Proof. If $d^k = 0$, the algorithm stops with a ρ^k-solution. If $\rho^k \geqslant \frac{1}{2}b \| \bar{u}^k - u^k \|^2$ for infinitely many k, then $\| \bar{U}^k - u^k \| \to 0$. Otherwise, Lemma 1 applies. In both cases, the arguments in the proof of Theorem 3 imply the result.

Remark. In some instances the objective function is costly to evaluate, and even an approximate linesearch could be hard to realize. In this case it is still possible to use a predetermined sequence of stepsizes $\{\alpha_k\}$. For instance, Powell and Sheffi [18] set

$$u^{k+1} = u^k + \alpha_k(\hat{u}^k - u^k)$$

with $\alpha_k \to 0$ and $\sum \alpha_k = \infty$. This method does not require the derivative of the mapping $J+J_1$ to be Lipschitz continuous. However, $J+J_1$ needs to be strongly monotone on V, and other conditions are required as well. Furthermore, a drawback of this method is its slow (typically sublinear) rate of convergence.

As a numerical example consider the pseudoconvex mathematical programming problem, taken from Marktos [14]:

$$\begin{aligned}\min \quad & J(u_1, u_2) = u_1^3 + u_1^2 u_2 + 4u_2^3 - 8u_1^2 - 19u_1u_2 - 6u_2^2 - 9u_1 - 18u_2 \\ \text{s. t.} \quad & u_1 + u_2 \leqslant 6, \\ & -2u_1 + 3u_2 \leqslant 3,\end{aligned}$$

$$u_1, u_2 \geqslant 0.$$

We have

$$J'(u) = \begin{bmatrix} 3u_1^2 + 2u_1u_2 - 16u_1^2 - 19u_2 - 9 \\ u_1^2 + 12u_2^2 - 19u_1 - 12u_2 - 18 \end{bmatrix}.$$

Letting $K^k(u) = \frac{1}{2} \| u \|^2$ and $\varepsilon = \frac{1}{20}$, the auxiliary problem takes the form

$$\begin{aligned} \min \quad & \frac{1}{20}\langle J'(u^k), u\rangle + \frac{1}{2} \| u - u^k \|^2 \\ \text{s. t.} \quad & u_1 + u_2 \leqslant 6, \\ & -2u_1 + 3u_3 \leqslant 3 \\ & u1, u_2 \geqslant 0. \end{aligned}$$

The application of the descent auxiliary problem principe yields the sequence of iterates, function values and descent directions shown here (see also Fig 1):

$$u^0 \begin{pmatrix} 3.80 \\ 2.00 \end{pmatrix}, \quad J(u^0) = -238.37, \quad \hat{u}^0 = \begin{pmatrix} 3.84 \\ 2.16 \end{pmatrix}, \quad d^0 = \begin{pmatrix} 0.04 \\ 0.16 \end{pmatrix},$$

$$u^1 = \begin{pmatrix} 3.84 \\ 2.16 \end{pmatrix}, \quad J(u^1) = -248.20, \quad \hat{u}^1 = \begin{pmatrix} 3.95 \\ 2.05 \end{pmatrix}, \quad d^1 = \begin{pmatrix} 0.11 \\ -0.11 \end{pmatrix},$$

$$u^* = u^2 = \begin{pmatrix} 3.90 \\ 2.10 \end{pmatrix}, \quad J(u^2) = -248.35.$$

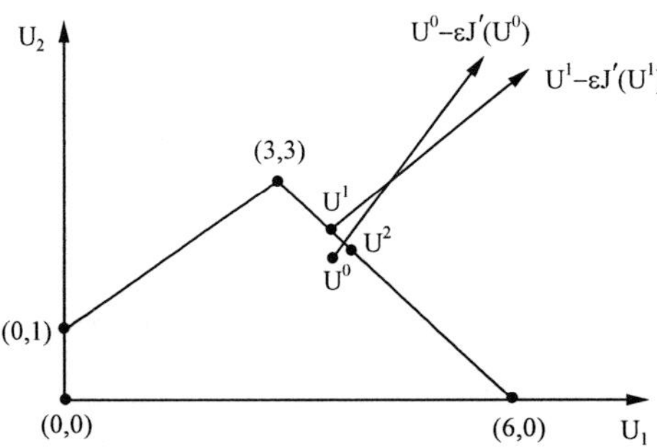

Fig. 1. A first numerical example.

If one sets ε to $+\infty$ in the previous numerical example, one recovers the Frank-Wolfe algorithm, whose directions alternate between the extreme points$(3,3)'$and $(6,0)'$, and generates a sequence that converges very slowly the optimal solution. Indeed, after 500 iterations of the Frank-Wolfe algorithm, the distance $\| u - u^* \|$ is still equal to 0.02.

4. Realizations of the descent auxiliary problem principle

In this section we consider instances of algorithms that fit our general frarmework.

The proximal point algorithm (*Martinet* [13]; *Rockafellar* [19])

Set $J=0$, and $K^k(\mathrm{u}) = \frac{1}{2} \| \mathrm{u} - \mathrm{u}^k \|^2$ in AP^k. The auxiliary problem becomes

$$\min_{u\in V} J_1(u) + \frac{1}{2\varepsilon^k} \| u - u^k \|^2, \tag{28}$$

which corresponds to the proximal iteration.

A partial linearization technique

Assume the decomposition (27) and consider the problem

$$\min_{u_j \in V_j, j=1,\cdots,n} \sum_{j=1}^{n} F_j(u_j) + G(u). \tag{29}$$

If F_j is strongly convex for all j, take $K^k = \sum_{j=1}^{n} F_j(u_j), J_1 = 0$ and $J = \sum_{j=1}^{n} F_j(u_j) + G(u)$. The auxiliary problem becomes

$$\min_{u_j \in V_j, j\in\langle 1,n\rangle} F_j(u_j) + \langle G'_{u_j}(u^k), u_j\rangle \tag{30}$$

and we recover the partial linearization technique of Larsson and Migdalas [10] as a special case. However, through the incorporation of a regularizing term, our method can deal with F'_jS that are only convex (nox *strongly* convex). Indeed, take $J_1 = \sum_{j=1}^{n} F_j(u_j)$ and $K^k = \frac{1}{2}\sum_{j=1}^{n} \| u_j - u_j^k \|^2$, yielding the strongly convex subproblems

$$\min_{u_j\in V_j} F_j(u_j) = \langle G'_{u_j}(u^k), u_j\rangle + \frac{1}{2} \| u_j - u_j^k \|^2, j = 1,\cdots,n. \tag{31}$$

A Jacobi method

Consider the problem

$$\min_{u\in V} J(u_1, u_2, \cdots, u_n). \tag{32}$$

Taking $K^k = \sum_{j-1}^{n} J(u_1^k, \cdots, u_{i-1}^k, u_i, u_{i+1}^k, \cdots, u_n^k)$, we get the n subproblems

$$\min_{u_j\in V_j} J(u_1^k, \cdots, u_{i-1}^k, u_i, u_{i+1}^k, \cdots, u_n^k). \tag{33}$$

Karmarkar's projective algorithm

The modified scheme can be used within the framework of interior point methods. Let us solve the subproblem on the (nonempty) interior V_0 of V, and consider the modified auxiliary problem

(AP_0^k)

$$\min_{u\in V_0} K^k(u) + \langle \varepsilon^k J'(u^k) - (u^k)'(u^k), u\rangle + \varepsilon^k J_1(u).$$

The cluster points of the sequence $\{u^k\} \subset V_0$ lie in V and the convergence results of Section 3 still hold. Now consider the linear program

$$\begin{aligned} \min \quad & \bar{c}^T x - \varepsilon^k \sum_{i=1}^{n} \ln x_i \\ \text{s. t.} \quad & Ax = b, \\ & x > 0, \end{aligned} \tag{35}$$

where $\bar{c}^{\mathrm{T}} = (c_1 - \varepsilon^k / x_1^k, c_2 - \varepsilon^k / x_2^k, \cdots, c_n - \varepsilon^k / x_n^k)$. One iteration of Newton's method yields the feasible descent direction

$$d^k = -\frac{1}{\varepsilon^k} XPX\bar{c} + XPe$$

where $P = (I - XA^T(AX^2A^T)^- 1AX)$, $X = \text{diag}[x_i^k]$and $e = (1, \cdots, 1)^T$.

Fractional programming

One advantage of our method is that we only require the objective $J + J_1$ to be pseudoconvex. Therefore it can be applied in the realm of generalized fractional programming considered by Avriel, Diwert, Schaible and Zang [1]:

$$\min_{x \in X^f} f_1(x) + g(x)/h(x), \tag{36}$$

where $f_1(x)$ is convex and $f_1(x) + g(x)/h(x)$ is pseudoconvex. Taking $J_1 = f_1(x)$, $J = f(x) = g(x)/h(x)$ and $K^k = \frac{1}{2} \| x - x^k \|^2$, we obtain the subproblem

$$\min_{x \in X^f} f_1(x) + \langle f'(x^k), x \rangle + \frac{1}{2} \| x - x^k \|^2, \tag{37}$$

which is easier to solve than the original problem.

Linearization methods

Consider the problem

$$\min_{x \in x^f} f(x) \tag{38}$$

and let $K^k = \frac{1}{2}(x - x^k)^T A(x^k)(x - x^k)$, where $A(x^k)$ is an $n \times n$ matrix. Depending on the choice of $A(x^k)$, we recover several well-know algorithms:

Newton's method: $A(x^k) = \nabla^2 f(x^k)$.

Quasi-Newton methods: $A(x^k) \approx \nabla^2 f(x^k)$.

Linearized Jacobi method: $A(x^k) = D(x^k)$, where $D(x^k)$ is the diagonal part of $\nabla^2 f(x^k)$.

SOR method: $A(x^k) = L(x^k) + D(x^k)/\omega$, where $L(x^k)$ is the lower triangular part of $\nabla^2 f(x^k)$ and $\omega \in (0, 2)$.

Projection method: $A(x^k) = G$, where G is a fixed, symmetric, positive definite matrix.

If the Hessian matrix $\nabla^2 f(x^k)$ is positive semidefinite on V, the convergence of Newton's method is assured. If furthermore $\nabla^2 f(x^k)$ is positive definite and Lipschitz continuous on V, then the convergence is quadratic (see Pschenichny and Danilin [17]). An application of Newton-like methodseqn be found in Bertsekas[2], Dembo and Tulowitzki[6], Pang and Yu[16], etc.

5. A partial auxiliary problem principle

In this section we address the decomposable mathematical program (DMP)

$$\min_{u \in V} (J + J_1)(u_1, u_2) \tag{39}$$

where $u=(u_1,u_2)^T$ and $V\subset U=U_1\times U_2$. We consider linearizing the sole operator J and adding an auxiliary term only for the subset of variables u_2. Denote by $(\hat{u}_1^k,\hat{u}_2^k)$ an optimal solution to the partial auxiliary problem

(PAP^k)

$$\min_{u\in V}\varepsilon^k[J(u_1,u_2^k)+J_1(u_1,u_2)]+K^k(u_2)+\langle\varepsilon^k J'_{u_2}(u_1^k,u_2^k)-(K^k)'(u_2^k),u_2\rangle. \quad (40)$$

This problem is not in general as attractive as AP^k. In particular, its objective may fail to be strongly convex in (u_1,u_2). However, the convergence of this partial scheme can be established under the following set of assumptions.

Assumption B.

(i) $J+J_1$ is jointly pseudoconvex in u_1,u_2 and its G-derivative is continuous; J_1 is jointly convex in u_1,u_2 on V.

(ii) $J(u_1,u_2)$ is strongly convex in u_1 with modulus a for all $u_2\in V$.

(iii) $J(u_1,u_2)$ is convex in u_1 and V is bounded in u_1 for every $u_2\in V$, uniformly in u_2.

(iv) $J(u_1,u_2)$ is convex in u_1, $J_1(u_1,u_2)$ is strongly convex in u_1 with modulus a_1 for every $u_2\in V$ uniformly, and Lipschitz continuous in u_2 for every $u_1\in V$, uniformly in u_1.

Let $K^k(u_2)=K(u_2,u_2^k)$, where the function $K(u_2,v_2)$ is differentiable, strongly convex with modulus b with respect to u_2, continuous with respect to v_2. Let $d^k=\hat{u}^k-u^k$ be the direction induced by the corresponding partial auxiliary problem PAP^k.

Theorem 5. *Let $\hat{u}^k$ be the solution given by* PAP^k. *If $\hat{u}^k=u^k$, then u^k is a solution to* DMP. *Otherwise, the direction $d^k=\hat{u}^k-u^k$ is a strict feasible descent direction of $(J+J_1)(u)$ at u^k.*

Proof. According to Theorem 1(iii), we have

$$\begin{aligned}&\langle(K^k)'(\hat{u}_2^k)-(K^k)'(u_2^k)+\varepsilon^k J'_{u_2}(u_1^k,u_2^k),u_2-\hat{u}_2^k\rangle\\&\quad+\varepsilon^k\{\langle J'_{u1}(\hat{u}_1,u_2^k),u_1-\hat{u}_1^k\rangle+\langle J'_1(\hat{u}^k),u-\hat{u}^k\rangle\}\geqslant 0.\end{aligned} \quad (41)$$

If $\hat{u}^k=u^k$ it follows that

$$\langle(J+J_1)'u_1(u_1^k,u_2^k),u_1-u_1^k\rangle+\langle(J+J_1)'u_2(u_1^k,u_2^k),u_2-u_2^k\rangle\geqslant 0$$

and (u_1^k,u_2^k) is a solution of DMP. By Theorem 1(v) we also have

$$\begin{aligned}&\langle(K^k)'(\hat{u}_2^k)-(K^k)'(u_2^k)+\varepsilon^k J'_{u_2}(u_1^k,u_2^k),u_2-\hat{u}_2^k\rangle\\&\quad+\varepsilon^k\{\langle J'u_1(u_1,u_2^k),u_1-\hat{u}_1^k\rangle+\langle J'_1(u),u-\hat{u}^k\rangle\}\geqslant 0\quad\forall u\in V.\end{aligned} \quad (42)$$

Setting $u=u^k$ in the above formula yields

$$\langle(J+J_1)'(u^k),u^k-\hat{u}^k\rangle\geqslant\frac{1}{\varepsilon^k}\langle(K^k)'(\hat{u}_2^k)-(K^k)'(u_2^k),\hat{u}_2^k-u_2^k\rangle. \quad (43)$$

Now (43) and the strong convexity of $K^k(u_2)$ in u_2 allow us to write

$$\langle(J+J_1)'(u_1^k,u_2^k),\hat{u}^k-u^k\rangle<0 \quad (44)$$

i. e. that the direction $d^k=\hat{u}^k-u^k$ is a descent direction for $J+J_1$ at u^k.

Next we consider the algorithm corresponding to the parital auxiliary principle.

Algorithm P

Step 1. Select $u^0 \in V$ and set $k=0$.

Step 2. Let $\hat{u}^k$ be an optimal solution of DAP^k

Set $d^k = \hat{u}^k - u^k$.

Step 3. **if** $d^k = 0$ stop.

Step 4. Linesearch

Let $t_k \in \arg\min_{t\in[0,1]}(J+J_1)(u^k+td^k)$.

Set $u^{k+1} = u^k + t_k d^k$.

$k \leftarrow k+1$ and goto Step 2.

The convergence of the preceding algorithm is proved next.

Theorem 6. *Assume that* J *and* J_1 *satis fy Assumption* B(i) *and either Assumptions* B(ii), B(iii) *or* B(iv). *Let the functionals* $K^k(u_2)=K(u_2, u_2^k)$ *be convex and their G-derivative be strongly monotone with modulus* $b^k > b > 0$ *on* V. *Let* $0<\gamma_1 \leqslant \varepsilon^k < \gamma_2 < \infty$ *for all* k. *Then algorithm* P *either terminates in a finite number of iterations or it generates an infinite sequence* $\{u^k\}$ *such that any accumulation point is an optimal solution to* DMP.

Proof. (i): If $J(U_1, u_2^k)$ is strongly convex w. r. t, to u_1 on V, we take $\overline{K}^k(u_1, u_2) = J(u_1, u_2^k) + K(u_2, u_2^k)$ and use Theorem 3 to derive the result.

(ii) From Assumption B(i), the sequence $\{u^k\}$ is bounded. If condition B(iii) is met, the definition of PAP^k yields

$$c_1 + c_2 \| u_2^k - \hat{u}_2^k \| \geqslant \frac{b}{r^2} \| u_2^k - \hat{u}_2^k \|^2 \tag{45}$$

for some constants c_1 and c_2 and, as a consequence, the sequence $\{\hat{u}_2^k\}$ is bounded. Since V is bounded, the sequence $\{\hat{u}^k\}$ is bounded as well. The rest of the proof is similar to that of Theorem 3.

(iii): Let condition B(iv) be satisfied and consider the variational inequality of Theorem 1(iv) with $u=u^k$:

$$\varepsilon^k[\langle J'(u^k), u^k - \hat{u}^k\rangle + J_1(u_1^k, u_2^k) - J_1(\hat{u}_1^k, u_2^k) + J_1(\hat{u}_1^k, u_2^k) - J_1(\hat{u}_1^k, \hat{u}_2^k)] \tag{46}$$

$$\geqslant \langle (K^k)'(\hat{u}_2^k) - (K^k)'(u_2^k), u_2^k - \hat{u}_2^k \rangle. \tag{47}$$

Together with the strong convexity of J_1 (in u_1) and K^k (in u_2) we obtain

$$\varepsilon^k[\langle J'(u^k), u^k - \hat{u}^k\rangle + \langle J'_{1u_1}(u_1^k, u_2^k), u_1^k - \hat{u}_1^k\rangle + J_1(\hat{u}_1^k, u_1^k) - J_1(\hat{u}_1^k, \hat{u}_2^k)] \tag{48}$$

$$\geqslant \varepsilon^k a_1 \| u_1^k - \hat{u}_1^k \|^2 + \frac{1}{2} b \| u_2^k - \hat{u}_2^k \|^2. \tag{49}$$

Now the boundedness of $\{u^k\}$, the continuity of $(J+J_1)'(u)$ and the Lipschitz continuity of $J_1(u_1, u_2)$ in u_2 yield

$$c_3 \| u_1^k - \hat{u}_1^k \| + c_4 \| u_2^k - \hat{u}_2^k \| \geqslant a_1 \| u_1^k - \hat{u}_1^k \|^2 + \frac{b}{\gamma_2} \| u_2^k - \hat{u}_2^k \|^2 \tag{50}$$

for some constants c_3 and c_4, and it follows that the sequence $\{\hat{u}^k\}$ is bounded. The rest of the proof is similar to that of Theorem 3.

As an example of the partial auxiliary problem principle, consider the mathematical program

$$\begin{aligned} \min \quad & J(u)+J_1(u)=u_1(u_1+2u_2)/u_2+u_2(u_2-1) \\ \text{s. t.} \quad & -1\leqslant u_1\leqslant 1, \\ & \frac{1}{2}\leqslant u_2\leqslant 2. \end{aligned}$$

The gradient of the objective function is

$$J'(u)+J_1'(u)=\begin{pmatrix} 2(u_1+u_2)/u_2 \\ (-u_1^2/u_2^2)+2u_2-1 \end{pmatrix}.$$

Setting $K^k(u_2)=\frac{1}{2}u_2^2$ and $\varepsilon=\frac{1}{2}$ we obtain, at iteration k, the partial auxiliary problem

$$\begin{aligned} \min \quad & \frac{1}{2}u_1(u_1+2u_2^k)/u_2^k+\frac{1}{2}u_2(u_2-1)+\frac{1}{2}(u_2-u_2^k)^2-\frac{1}{2}(u_1^k/u_2^k)^2u_2 \\ s.t. \quad & -1\leqslant u_1\leqslant 1, \\ & \frac{1}{2}\leqslant u_2\leqslant 2, \end{aligned}$$

which decomposes into the two simple quadratic programs

$$\min_{-1\leqslant u_1\leqslant 0}(u_1^2+2u_2^k u_1)/u_2^k$$

and

$$\min_{1/2\leqslant u_2\leqslant 2}u_2(u_2-1)+(u_2-u_2^k)^2-(u_1^k/u_2^k)^2_{u_2}.$$

The sequence of iterates produced by the algorithm, together with the function values and the descent directions, is given below (see also Fig. 2):

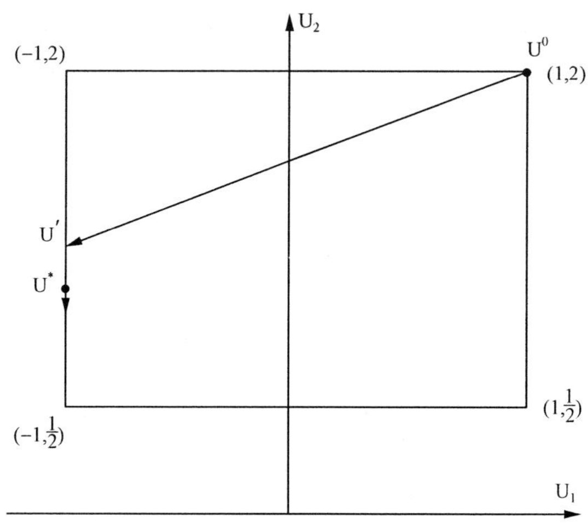

Fig. 2.　A second numerical example.

$$u^0=\begin{pmatrix}1.00\\2.00\end{pmatrix},\quad J+J_1=5.50,\hat{u}^0=\begin{pmatrix}-1.00\\1.28\end{pmatrix},\quad d^0\begin{pmatrix}-2.00\\-0.72\end{pmatrix},$$

$$u^1=\begin{pmatrix}-1.00\\1.28\end{pmatrix},\quad J+J_1=0.14,\quad \hat{u}^1=\begin{pmatrix}-1.00\\0.97\end{pmatrix},\quad d^1=\begin{pmatrix}0.00\\-0.31\end{pmatrix},$$

$$u^*=u^2=\begin{pmatrix}-1.00\\1.00\end{pmatrix},\quad J+J_1=0.00.$$

On the same example the Frank-Wolfe algorithm converges slowly (sublinearly) to the optimal solution, 'zigzagging' between the extreme points $(-1,2)^T$ and $(-1,1/2)^T$.

Remarks. If V is bounded, the conditions $b^k>b>0$ and $\varepsilon^k<\gamma_2$ are not required any more.

In the above exposition, it is assumed that the partial auxiliary problem PAP^k is solved exactly. It is clear however that an inexact scheme could be derived, exactly as was done for AP^k in Section 3 (see Theorem 4).

6. Realizations of the partial auxiliary problem principle and applications

In this section we present some specializations of the partial auxiliary problem method for which convergence is assured by Theorem 3.

The partial proximal point algorithm

We consider problem MP with $J=0$ and $K^k(u_2)=\frac{1}{2}\|u_2-u_1^k\|^2$. The auxiliary problem becomes

$$\min_{u\in V} J_1(u)+\frac{1}{2\varepsilon^k}\|u_2-u_2^k\|^2, \tag{51}$$

which constitutes a generalization of the proximal point algorithm of Ha [9].

Fractional programming

Consider the fractional programming problem

$$\min_{(x,y)} F(x,y)=\frac{\sum_{j=1}^n f_{1j}(x_j)+g(y)}{h(y)}, \tag{52}$$

where the functions f_{1j}'s are strongly convex positive for all j, g is convex nonnegative and h is a positive, concave function. Set $K^k(y)=\frac{1}{2}\|y-y^k\|^2$. The auxiliary problem is the convex program

$$\min_{(x,y)}\frac{\sum_{j=1}^n f_{1j}(x_j)}{h(y^k)}+\langle F_y'(x^k,y^k),y\rangle+\frac{1}{2\varepsilon^k}\|y-y^k\|^2. \tag{53}$$

If the auxiliary problem principle is applied to all variables, the subproblem becomes

$$\min_{(x,y)}\langle F_x'(x^k,y^k),x\rangle+\langle F_y'(x^k,y^k),y\rangle+\frac{1}{2\varepsilon^k}\{\|x-x^k\|^2+\|y-y^k\|^2\}. \tag{54}$$

Note that problem (53) is easier to solve than (54) and a better approximation of the original problem (52).

A continuous network design problem (*Marcotte* [12])

Consider the problem of determining optimal improvements to an urban road network. Let z_a denote the improvement on arc a of the network, v_a the vehicle flow on arc a, S_a the delay (congestion) function and ϕ_a the investment in upgrading arc a. This results in the system optimal network design problem

$$\min_{v\in X, z\in Y} \sum_a v_a S_a(v_a, z_a) + \phi_a(z_a) \tag{55}$$

when X denotes the set of feasible multicommodity flows are Y the set of admissible improvements. Let $K^k = \frac{1}{2}\|z\|^2$. The partial auxiliary problem PAP^k then becomes

$$\min_{v,z} \sum_a \left\{ \varepsilon_k [v_a S_a(v_a, z_a^k) + \phi_a(z_a)] + \frac{1}{2}(z_a - z_a^k)^2 - \varepsilon_k v_a^k \frac{\partial S_a}{\partial z_a}(v_a^k, z_a^k) z_a \right\} \tag{56}$$

which decomposes into a problem involving solely the z_a variables and traffic assignment problem in the v_a variables. The latter can be solved efficiently even if the network is large.

Nonlinear programming with coupling variabls (*Lasdon*[10])

The partial auxiliary problem principle yields a practical method for solving nonlinear programming with coupling variables and separable constraint sets. Consider the mathematical program

$$\min_{x,y} \quad c_0(y) + \sum_i c_i(y) x_i \tag{57}$$

$$\text{s. t.} \quad x_i \in P_i \quad \text{(convex polyhedron).} \tag{58}$$

With $K^k = \frac{1}{2}\|z\|^2$, in this case, PAP^k takes the form

$$\min_{x,y} \varepsilon^k c_0(y) + \sum_{i=1}^{n} \varepsilon_k [c_i(y^k) x_i + \langle c_i'(y^k) x^k, y\rangle] + \frac{1}{2}\|y - y^k\|^2 \tag{59}$$

which is linear and block separable in x, and nonlinear, unconstrained in y.

7. Discussions and conclusions

In this paper, we developed a unified framework for solving pseudoconvex minimization problems. By adequately selecting the auxiliary function, one may achieve the decomposition of a nonseparable problem into a sequence of separable subproblems. The main advantage of the descent approach over the standard auxiliary problem principle approach presented in [3] is that convergence is guaranteed under weaker conditions. The price to pay is the additional burden of a linesearch. Recently however, the authors [21, 22] have shown how to somewhat overcome this difficulty.

References

[1] Avriel, M., Diwert, W. E., Shaible, s., and Zang, I., *Generalized Convexity and Applications*, North-Holland, Amsterdam, 1988.

[2] Bertsekas, D. P. ,"On the Goldstein-Levitin-Polyak gradient projection method",*IEEE Transactions on Automatic Control* 21(1976) 174-184.

[3] Cohen, G. , "Optimization by decomposition and coordination: A unified approach", *IEEE Transactions on Automatic Control* 23(1978)222-232.

[4] Cohen, G. ,"Auxiliary problem principle and decomposition of optimization problems", *Joural of Optimization Theory and Applications* 32(1980)277-305.

[5] Cohen, G. , and Zhu, D. L. "Decomposition coordination methods in large scale problems: The non-differentiable case and the use of augmented Lagrangians", in: J. B. Cruz(ed.), *Advances in Large-scale Systems* 1, Chapter 8, JAI Press. Greenwich, USA. 1984.

[6] Dembo,R. S. , and Tulowitzki, U. ,"Computing equilibria on large multicommodity networks: An applicatio of truncated quadratic programming algorithms", *Networks* 18(1988)273-284.

[7] Ekeland, I. , and Temam, R. ,*Convex Analysis and Variational Problems*, North-Holland, Amsterdam, 1970.

[8] Güler, "On the convergence of the proximal point algorithm for convex minimization", *SLAM Journal on Control and Optimization* 29(1991) 403-419.

[9] Ha, C. D. ,"A generalization of the proximal point algorithm for convex minimization", *SLAM Journal on Control and Optimization* 28(1990) 503-512.

[10] Lasdon, L. S. , *Optimization Theory for Large Systems*, Macmillan, New York, 1970.

[11] Larsson, T. , and Migdalas, A. , "An algorithm for nonlinear programs over Cartesian product sets", *Optimization* 21 (1990) 535-542.

[12] Marcotte, P. ,"Network design problem with congestion effects: Acase of bilevel programming", *Mathematical Programming* 34(1986)142-162.

[13] Martinet, B. ,"Régularisation d'inéquations variationnelles par approximations successives",*Revue Francaise d' In formatique et ae Recherche Opérationnelle* 4(1970) 154-159.

[14] Martos, B. , *Nonlinear Programming*, North-Holland, Amsterdam, 1975.

[15] Ortega, J. M. , and Rheinboldt, *Iterative solution of Nonlinear Equations in Several Variables*, Academic Press, New York, 1970.

[16] Pang, J. -S. , "Linearized simplicial decomposition methods for computing traffic equilibria on network",14(1982)427-438.

[17] Pschenichny, B. N. , and Danilin, Y. , *Numerical Methods in Extremal Problems*, MIR, Moscow, 1978.

[18] Powell, W. B. , and Sheffi, Y. , "The convergence of equilibrium algorithms with predetermined step sizes", *Transportation Research* 15B(1982) 45-55.

[19] Rockafellar, R. T. ,"Augmented Lagrangians and applications of the proximal point algorithm in convex programming", *Mathmatics of Operations Research* 1(1976)97-16.

[20] Zhu, D. L. ,"Optimisation sous-différentiable et méthodes de décomposition", Ph. D. Thesis, Centre d'Automatique et Informatique, Ecole des Mines de Paris, Fontainebleau, France, 1982.

[21] Zhu, D. L. , and Marcotte, P. ,"An extended descent framework for monotone variational inequalities",*JOTA* 80(1994) 349-366.

[22] Marcotte, P. , and Zhu, D. L. "Global convergence of descent processes for solving non-strictly monotone variational inequalities", Preprint, 1992.

Published in *European Journal of Operational Research*, 1995,83

A Cutting Plane Method for Solving Quasimonotone Variational Inequalities

P. MARCOTTE

DIRO and CRT, Université al Montréal, CP 6128, succursale Centre-Ville, Montré al, Canada H3C 3J7

D. L. ZHU

CRT, Université de Montréal, CP 6128, succursale Centre-Ville, Montréal, Canada H3C 3J7 and School of Management, Fudan Univ., 220 Handan Road, Shanghai, China 200433

Abstract. We present an iterative algorithm for solving variational inequalities under the weakest monotonicity condition proposed so far. The method relies on a new cutting plane and on analytic centers.

Keywords, variational inequalities, cutting planes, analytic centers, quasimonotonicity

1. Introduction. Notation and definitions

Recently, Goffin et al. [3] developed a convergent framework for determining a solution x^* of the (primal) variational inequality $VI_P(F, X)$ associated with the continuous mapping F and the polyhedron $X=\{x:Ax\leqslant b\}$, * under an assumption slightly stronger than pseudomonotonicity. In this paper we show that their algorithm can be extended to quasi-monotone variational inequalities that satisfy a weak additional assumption if one replaces, at iteration k, the 'natural' cutting plane

$$\langle F(x^k), x - x^k \rangle = 0 \tag{1}$$

by a modified hyperplane that does not go through the current iterate x^k. This result is in some way the strongest possible in that no valid cutting plane can be derived under the sole assumption that F be quasimonotone on X.

We recall that a point x^* of X is solution of the *primal variational inequality* $VI_P(F, X)$ if there holds

$$\langle F(x^*), x - x^* \rangle \geqslant 0 \quad \forall x \in X. \tag{2}$$

* Research supported by NSERC (Canada) and FCAR (Québec).

It is a solution of the *dual variational inequality* $VI_D(F, X)$ if

$$\langle F(x), x - x^* \geqslant 0 \quad \forall x \in X. \tag{3}$$

We denote by X_P^* the set of solutions of $VI_P(F, X)$ and by X_D^* the set of solutions of $VI_D(F, X)$. While the latter set could be empty, nonemptiness of X_P^* follows from the continuity of F and the compactness of X. Whenever F is continuous, we have that $X_D^* \subseteq X_P^*$ (see Auslender [1]).

At a point x in X, we say that the mapping F *monotone* if

$$\langle F(y) - F(x), y - x\rangle \geqslant 0 \quad \forall y \in X, \tag{4}$$

pseudomonotone if

$$\langle F(x), y - x\rangle \geqslant 0 \Rightarrow \langle F(y), y - x\rangle \geqslant 0 \quad \forall_y \in X. \tag{5}$$

and *quasimonotone* if

$$\langle F(x), y - x\rangle > 0 \Rightarrow \langle F(y), y - x\rangle \geqslant 0 \quad \forall_y \in X. \tag{6}$$

If the mapping F satisfies (4) (respectively (5), (6)) for every x in X, then we say that it is monotone (respectively pseudomonotone, quasimonotone) on X. If F is pseudomonotone on X, then it is well known (see Auslender [1] again) that the solution sets X_P^* and X_D^* coincide.

2. A cutting plane-analytic center algorithm

Throughout this section we assume that F is continuous and that the solution set X_P^* is non-empty. The following proposition gives some conditions ensuring the nonemptiness of X_D^*.

Proposition 1. *If either*

(i) *F is the gradient of a differentiable quasiconvex function;*

(ii) *F is quasimonotone, $F \neq 0$ on X and X is bounded;*

(iii) *F is quasimonotone, $F \neq 0$ on X and there exists a positive number r such that, for every $x \in X$ with $\| x \| \geqslant r$, there exists $y \in X$ such that $\| y \| \leqslant r$ and $\langle F(x), y - x\rangle \leqslant 0$;*

(iv) *F is pseudomonotone at $x^* \in X_P^*$;*

(v) *there exists a point x^* in X_P^* such that F is quasimonotone at x^* and $F(x^*)$ is not normal to X at x^*,*

then X_D^* is nonempty.

Proof:

(i) Let $F = \nabla f$ andlet x^* beaglobal minimizer of f over X. Bydefinition, $f(x^*) \leqslant f(x)$ for all x in X, which implies, by quasiconvexity of f, that

$$\langle \nabla f(x), x - x^*\rangle \geqslant 0 \quad \forall x \in X,$$

i. e., since, $F = \nabla f, x^* \in x_D^*$.

(ii) and (iii) Under these assumptions, it has been shown by Hadjisavvas and Schaible [4] that the solution set of the dual variational inequality (3) is nonempty.

(iv) This is a direct consequence of the pseudomonotonicity of F at $x^* \in X_P^*$.

(v) Since $F(x^*)$ isnotnormalto X, thereexistsapoint x_0 in X such that $\langle F(x^*), x_0 - x^* \rangle > 0$. Let x be any point of X and set $x_1 = tx_0 + (1-t)x$ for $t \in (0,1]$. We have:

$$\langle f(x^*), x - x^* \rangle \geqslant 0$$

and

$$\langle F(x^*), x_t - x^* \rangle > 0.$$

Since F is quasimonotone at x^*, we obtain:

$$\langle F(x_t), x_t - x^* \rangle \geqslant 0.$$

Letting $t \to 0$ it follows from the continuity of F that $\langle F(x), x - x^* \rangle \geqslant 0$, i. e., $x^* \in X_D^*$.

Example 1 (taken from [4]). Let $X = [0, 1] \times [0, 1]$ and $t = (x_1 + \sqrt{x_1^2 + 4x_2^2})/2$. We define

$$F(x_1, x_2) = \begin{cases} (-t/(t+1), -1/(t+1)) & \text{if}(x_1, x_2) \neq (0, 0) \\ (0, -1) & \text{if}(x_1, x_2) = (0, 0). \end{cases}$$

Then F is quasimonotone on X, as condition (ii) of Proposition 1 is satisfied. Moreover, for $x^* = (1, 1) \in X_P^*$, conditions (iv) and (v) are also satisfied. In fact, $X_D^* = \{(1, 1)\}$.

Example 2 (also taken from [4]). Let $X = [0, +\infty) \times \{0\}$ and $F = (|\sin x_1|, 1)$. The function F is quasimonotone and continuous on X and $X_P^* = \{(n\pi, 0) : n \in N\}$. Condition (iv) holds for $x^* = (0, 0)$ and we have: $X_D^* = \{(0, 0)\}$.

We now introduce the elements required in the construction of algorithms for solving quasimonotone variational inequalities. Let $\Gamma(y, x): R^n \times R^n \to R^n$ denote an auxiliary mapping, continuous in x and y and strongly monotone in y, i. e.,

$$\langle \Gamma(y, x) - \Gamma(z, x), y - z \rangle \geqslant \beta \| y - z \|^2 \quad \forall y, z \in X \tag{7}$$

for some positive number β. We associate with Γ the auxiliary variational inequality $AVI_P(\Gamma, X, x)$ (see Zhu and Marcotte [8]) whose unique solution $w(x)$ satisfies:

$$\langle \Gamma(w(x), x) - \Gamma(x, x) + F(x), y - w(x) \rangle \geqslant 0 \quad \forall y \in X. \tag{8}$$

It is known that the mapping w is continuous (see Harker and Pang [5]) and that x is solution of VI_P if only if it is a . xed point of w.

Let ρ and α be positive numbers less than 1 and β, respectively. Let l, which depends on x, be the smallest nonnegative integer such that

$$\langle F(x + \rho^l (w(x) - x)), x - w(x) \rangle \geqslant \alpha \| w(x) - x \|^2. \tag{9}$$

(The existence of a finite l satisfying the above condition will be proved in Proposition 2 below.)

We introduce the composite mapping G defined, for every x in X, as:

$$G(x) = F(x + \rho^l (w(x) - x)). \tag{10}$$

If x^* is in X_P^* we have that $w(x^*)=x^*$, $l=0$ and $G(x^*)=F(x^*)$.

Proposition 2. *The operator G is well defined for every $x\in X$. Moreover, if F is Lipschitz continuous on X with Lipschitz constant L, there holds:*

$$l\leqslant\left\lceil\frac{\ln(\beta-\alpha)/L}{\ln p}\right\rceil.$$

Proof: To prove that G is well defined, we must show that $l<\infty$. From the definition of $w(x)$ we get:

$$\begin{aligned}F(x),x-w(x)&\geqslant\langle\Gamma(w(x),x)-\Gamma(x,x),w(x)-x\rangle\\&\geqslant\beta\|x-w(x)\|^2.\end{aligned}\tag{11}$$

Assume that (9) is not satisfied for any integer l, i. e.,

$$\langle F(x+\rho^l(w(x)-x)),x-w(x)\rangle<\alpha\|w(x)-x\|^2\quad\forall l.\tag{12}$$

Taking the limit (recall that F is continuous, and that $x+\rho^l(w(x)-x)\to x$, as$l\to\infty$), we obtain:

$$\langle F(x),x-w(x)\rangle\leqslant\alpha\|w(x)-x\|^2,\tag{13}$$

in contradiction with (11). (Recall that, by definition, $\alpha<\beta$.)

Now assume that F is Lipschitz continuous on X, with Lipschitz constant L. We have:

$$\begin{aligned}\langle F(x+\rho^l(w(x)-x)),x-w(x)\rangle&=\langle F(x),x-w(x)\rangle\\&\quad+\langle F(x+\rho^l(w(x)-x))-F(x),x-w(x)\rangle\\&\geqslant\beta\|w(x)-x\|^2-L\rho^l\|w(x)-x\|^2\\&=(\beta-L\rho^l)\|w(x)-x\|^2\\&\geqslant\alpha\|w(x)-x\|^2\quad\text{if}\alpha\leqslant\beta-L\rho^l,\end{aligned}$$

from which the second conclusion of the proposition follows.

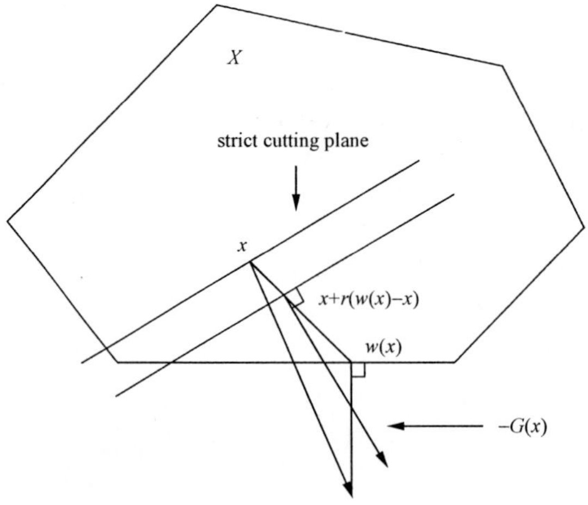

Figure 1. A strict cutting plane.

The next proposition shows that the composite mapping G possesses a property that can be used to derive a strict cutting plane at any point of X that is not solution of $VI_P(F, X)$. A geometrical illustration of the cutting plane is given in figure 1, where $\Gamma(y, x)$ has been set to $y-x$, in which case $w(x)$ is simply the projection of $x-F(x)$ onto the feasible set X.

Proposition 3. *If $x \notin X_P^*$ then, for every $y^* \in X_D^*$, we have*

$$\langle G(x), x-y^* \rangle > 0. \tag{14}$$

Proof: Let $y(x) = x+\rho^l(w(x)-x)$. We have that $G(x) = F(y(x))$ and:

$$\langle F(y(x)),\ w(x)-x \rangle \leqslant -\alpha \| w(x)-x \|^2 < 0,$$

since $x \notin X_P^*$ implies that $x \neq w(x)$. Therefore:

$$\langle F(y(x)), y(x)-x \rangle = \rho^l \langle F(y(x)), w(x)-x \rangle < 0. \tag{15}$$

However, for every $y^* \in X_D^*$ there holds

$$\langle F(y(x)), y(x)-y^* \rangle \geqslant 0. \tag{16}$$

By combining (15) and (16) we obtain

$$\langle F(y(x)), x-y^* \rangle > 0,$$

as claimed.

Recently, Magnanti and Perakis [7] proposed a unifying geometric framework for solving variational inequality problems involving mappings with strongly monotone (possibly multivalued) inverses. They used volume reduction arguments to derive convergence and complexity results. Under a strengthened pseudomonotonicity assumption, Goffin et al. [3] obtained comparable results for an analytic center cutting plane method, using potential reduction arguments. The following algorithm is a modification of the algorithm of [3] that replaces the 'natural' hyperplane $\langle F(x^k), x-x^k \rangle = 0$ bythe 'strict' hyperplane

$$\langle F(x^k+\rho^l(w(x^k)-x^k)),\ x-x^k \rangle = 0. \tag{17}$$

This yields the analytic center cutting plane algorithm described below.

EXTENDED ANALYTIC CENTER CUTTING PLANE ALGORITHM

Step 0 (initialization)

Let β be the strong monotonicity constant of $\Gamma(x, y)$ with respect to y and let $\alpha \in (0, \beta)$.

$k=0$, $A^k=A$, $bk=b$

Step 1 $X^k=\{x: A^k x \leqslant b^k\}$

Find an approximate center x^k of X^k.

Step 2 (stopping criterion)

if $gP(x^k) \leqslant \epsilon$ **then** STOP

else GOTO Step 3.

Step 3 (auxiliary variational inequality problem)

Let $w(x^k)$ satisfy the variational inequality

$$\langle F(x^k)+\Gamma(w(x^k),x^k)-\Gamma(x^k,x^k),y-w(x^k)\rangle \geqslant 0 \quad \forall y \in X.$$

Step 4 Let $y^k = x^k + \rho^{lk}(w(x^k) - x^k)$ and $G(x^k) = F(y^k)$,

where l_k is the smallest integer that satisfies

$$\langle F(x^k + \rho^{lk}(w(x^k) - x^k)), x^k - w(x^k)\rangle \geqslant \alpha \| w(x^k) - x^k \|^2.$$

Step 5 (cutting plane)

$H^k = \{x : \langle G(x^k), (x - x^k) = 0\}$

$$A^{k+1} = \begin{pmatrix} A^k \\ G(x^k)^T \end{pmatrix} \quad b^{k+1} = \begin{pmatrix} b^k \\ \langle G(x^k), x^k\rangle \end{pmatrix}$$

Increase k by one and return to Step 1.

The proof of convergence of the above algorithm is very short and relies on the following property of cutting plane methods based on approximate analytic centers[2], which we call the 'finite cut property':

Finite cut property (Goffin et al. [2]): Given a ball of radius ρ lying in the polyhedron X, there exists an iteration index $k(\rho)$ such that X^k does not contain the given ball.

Theorem 1. *Let the polyhedron X have nonempty interior. Let F be Lipschitz continuous with Lipschitz constant L on X and let the set X_D^* be nonempty. Then either the extended analytic center cutting plane algorithm stops with a solution of VI_P after a finite number of interations, or there exists a subsequence of the infinite sequence $\{x^k\}$ that converges to a point in X_P^*.*

Proof: Assume that $x^k \notin X_P^*$ for every iteration index k, and let $y^* \in X_D^*$. From Proposition 3, we know that y^*, which lies in X^k since $X_D^* \subseteq X^k$, never lies on H^k for any k. Let $\{\bar{y}_i\}_{i\in N}$ be an arbitrary sequence of points in the interior of X converging to y^*, and ϵ_i a sequence of positive numbers such that $\lim_{i\to\infty} \in i=0$ and that the sequence of closed balls $\{B(\bar{y}_i, i)\}_{i\in N}$ lies in the interior of X. Note that $\lim_{i\to\infty}\{B(\bar{y}_i, \epsilon_i)\} = \{y^*\}$.

From the finite cut property, we know that there must exist a smallest index $k(i)$ and a point $\tilde{y}_i \in B(\bar{y}_i, \epsilon_i)$ such that $\tilde{y}_i$ lies on the 'wrong' side of the hyperplane $H^{k(i)}$, i.e.,

$$\langle G(x^{k(i)}), x^{k(i)} - \tilde{y}_i < 0.$$

As $\langle G(x^{k(i)}), x^{k(i)} - y^* > 0$, there exists a point $\hat{y}_i$ on the segment $[\tilde{y}_i, y^*]$ such that $\langle G(x^{k(i)}), \hat{y}^i - x^{k(i)} = 0$. (See figure 2.)

Since X iscompact, we can extract from the sequence $\{x^{k(i)}\}_{i\in N}$ a convergent subsequence $\{x^{k(i)}\}_{i\in s}$. Denote by $\check{x}$ its limit point. We have:

$$\langle G(x^{k(i)}), \hat{y}^i - x^{k(i)}\rangle = 0 \quad \forall i \in S. \tag{18}$$

From Proposition 2, we know that the integer sequence $l_{k(i)}$ is bounded. Consequently we can extract from the sequence $\{l_{k(i)}\}_{i\in S}$ a constant subsequence $l_{k*(i)} = k^*$. Now, from the continuity of the function $w(x)$ for fixed k and the relations (9) and (18), it

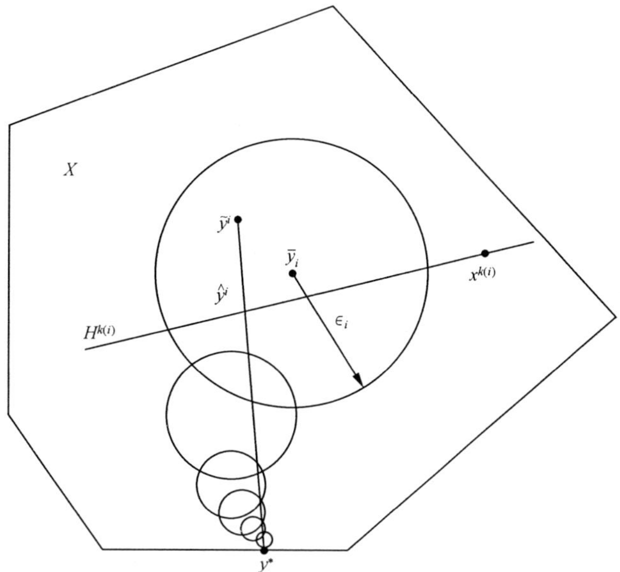

Figure 2.　Geometrical construction behind the proof.

follows by taking the limit in (18) that

$$\langle G(\check{x}), y^* - \hat{x} \rangle = 0$$

By Proposition 3, we conclude that $\check{x} \in X_P^*$.

Notes

1. The reader unfamiliar with variational inequalities is referred to [1], [5] and [6].

2. The definition of approximate analytic centers can be found in [3].

References

[1] A. Auslender, "Optimisation. Mériqdes numérques," Masson: Paris, 1976.

[2] J.-L. Goffin, Z. Q. Luo, and Y. Ye, "Complexity analysis of an interior cutting plane method for convex feasibility problems," SIAM Journal on Optimization, vol. 6, pp. 638-652, 1996.

[3] J.-L. Goffin, P. Marcotte, and D. L. Zhu, "An analytic center cutting plane method for pseudomonotone variational inequalities," Operations Research Letters, vol. 20, pp. 1-6, 1997.

[4] H. Hadjisavvas and S. Schaible, "Quasimonotone variational inequalities in Banach spaces," Journal of Optimization Theory and Applications, vol. 90, pp. 95-111, 1996.

[5] P. T. Harker and J.-S. Pang, "Finite-dimensional variational inequality and non-linear complementarity problems: A survey of theory, algorithms and applications," Mathematical Programming B, vol. 48, pp. 161-220,1990.

[6] D. Kinderlehrer and G. Stampacchia An Introduction to Variational Inequalities and their Applications, Academic Press: New York, 1980.

[7] T. L. Magnanti and G. Perakis, "A unifying geometric framework for solving variational inequalities," Mathematical Programming, vol. 71, pp. 327-351, 1995.

[8] D. L. Zhu and P. Marcotte, "An extended descent framework for monotone variational inequalities," Journal of Optimization Theory and Applications, vol. 80, pp. 349-366, 1994.

Published in *Computational Optimization and Applications*, 2001, 20

第二章　动态交通流配载和网络均衡

网络均衡模型（NEM）得到的均衡描述的是一段时间内的平均流，为了确切反映现实交通问题，必须研究动态交通网络均衡问题，即网络流和需求分布都是随时间变化的。自 20 世纪 90 年代中期开始，交通界运输的学术界和工业界把很大的注意力转向动态交通的科学研究和工程实现上。本章主要介绍了作者和蒙特利尔大学 CRT 同事们在动态交通科学方面做的研究成果。他们在 2000～2001 年提出了动态交通流分配（DTA）的基本动力学模型，解决了解的存在性问题，并提出网络流配载方法，这是动态交通系统分析领域最有深度的研究工作之一。

On the Existence of Solutions to the Dynamic User Equilibrium Problem

DAOLI ZHU

CRT, Université de Montréal, C. P. 6128, succursale Centre-Ville, Montréal H3C 3J7, Canada

PATRICE MARCOTTE

DIRO, Université de Montréal, C. P. 6128, succursale Centre-Ville, Montréal H3C 3J7, Canada

This paper is concerned with the existence of solutions to a dynamic network equilibrium problem modeled as an infinite dimensional variational inequality. Our results are based on properties of operators that map path flow departure rates to consistent time-dependent path flows and other link performance functions. The existence result requires the introduction of a novel concept that strengthens the familiar concept of First-In-First-Out (FIFO).

Following BEN-AKIVA(1985), one can identify four main elements in any dynamic network equilibrium model(DNEP): arc performance functions, path choice criterion, a demand model, and flow conservation relationships at the nodes of the network. According to this author, the extension of a static to a dynamic setting requires the determination of time-dependent arc performance functions, temporal origin-destination(OD) demand, and the assessment of queueing effects on time-varying arrival rates. In general, these relationships are not available in closed form, and, consequently, analytical properties of the model are difficult, if not impossible, to derive.

Several models of dynamic equilibrium have been proposed that involve only route choice(FRIESZ et al., 1989; MERCHANT and HEMHAUSER, 1978; SMITH, 1993; SMITH and WISTEN, 1994) or route choice and departure time choice(BEN-AKIVA, CYNA, and DE PALMA, 1984; FRIESZ et al., 1993; MAHMASSANI and HERMAN, 1984; RAN, HALL, and BOYCE, 1996; WIE et al., 1995). In all the above-mentioned models, the issue of existence of a dynamic equilibrium has not been fully addressed. In this paper, we give an ex-istence result for the dynamic User Equilibrium—Route Choice model introduced by Friesz et al. (1993), thus giving a theoretical foundation for the numerical algorithms that have been proposed for this model.

The analysis is performed under the assumption that flow throughout the network obeys the First-In-First-Out(FIFO) rule. In the absence of such a queue discipline, flow propagation can be unrealistic(see ASTARITA, 1996). We believe that analytic models should ensure that FIFO is satisfied.

A byproduct of our analysis will be a theoretical analysis of the loading procedure (see also XHU et al. , 1998) that relates the link performance functions(flow volumes, entry rates, exit rates, departure times) to the path departure rate functions. These link performance functions constitute the control variables of the dynamic network equilibrium problem, and their evaluation lies at the heart of the DNEP.

The paper is organized as follows: the mathematical formulation of the DNEP is stated in Section 1; in Section 2, we prove that, under a strengthened FIFO condition, the dynamic network constraints are consistent and that the network flow operators are well defined over their respective domains; Section 3 is devoted to the continuity properties of the link flow, path flow, and traversal time operators; from these results we derive(Section 4) the existence of a dynamic equilibrium for the route choice model with fixed departure times; in Section 5, we derive sufficient conditions that ensure the strengthened FIFO condition and hence the existence result.

1. FORMULATION OF THE DYNAMIC NETWORK SYSTEM

LET US CONSIDER a network with multiple origins and destinations, based on an underlying directed graph $G=(N,A)$ with node set N and arc set A. We denote by R the set of OD couples, by P_r the set of paths associated with the OD couple r in R, and let $P=\bigcup_{r\in R}P_r$ denote the set of all OD paths. An element σ_{ap} of the link-path incidence matrix is defined by

$$\sigma_{ap}=\begin{cases}1 & \text{if link } a \text{ belong to path } p\\ 0 & \text{otherwise.}\end{cases} \tag{1}$$

Denoting by $x_a^p(t)$ the number of vehicles traveling on arc a of path p at instant t, and by $x_a(t)$ the total number of vehicles traveling on arc a at instant t, we obtain the relationships

$$x_a(t)=\sum_{p\in P}\sigma_{ap}x_a^p(t).$$

Now let $u_a^p(t)$ (respectively, $v_a^p(t)$) denote the inflow rate into(respectively, exit rate from) link a of path p at time t. Based on these variables, the system equation for link a can be written as

$$(x_a^p)(t)=u_a^p(t)-v_a^p(t)\quad \forall p\in P_a, \tag{2}$$

where P_a is the set of paths through link a. Now, assuming that the number of vehicles on link a at the start of the period under study is equal to zero, the number of vehicles on link a at any instant t in $[0,\overline{T}]$ can be expressed as

$$x_a^p(t) = \int_0^t [u_a^p(s) - v_a^p(s)]\mathrm{d}s \quad \forall p \in P_a. \tag{3}$$

For any pair of consecutive arcs a and b of path p, flow conservation is expressed by the equation

$$v_b^p(t) = u_a^p(t). \tag{4}$$

The demand side of the model is characterized by Lipschitz continuous functions Q_r that represent the number of travelers leaving the origin node of the OD pair r at time t. The functions Q_r can be decomposed into path departure rate functions h_p according to the formula,

$$\sum_{p \in P_r} h_p(t) = Q_r(t). \tag{5}$$

The function h_p represents the control variables of the users and triggers the dynamic allocation process through the initial equation,

$$u_{o(p)}^p(t) = h_p(t), \tag{6}$$

where $o(p)$ denotes the origin node of path p.

Flow circulation within the network is governed by strictly positive, flow-dependent delay functions D_a that relate the link exit time. $\tau_a(t)$ to the time of entry t,

$$\tau_a(t) = t + D_a(x_a(t)). \tag{7}$$

The equalities and inequalities 2—7, together with obvious non-negative constraints on all flows involved, define a dynamical network system (DNS). Any solution of this system relates, in a coherent fashion, the state variables u_a^p, v_a^p, x_a^p, and τ_a to the control variables h_p. Throughout the paper, we make the assumption that the delay functions D_a are positive, strictly increasing, and continuously differentiable, and that the demand functions Q_r are bounded over the period $[0, T]$. The control vector $h = (h_p)_{p \in P}$ "lives" in the feasible set. of nonnegative, square-integrable vector functions that satisfy almost everywhere (a. e.), the initial condition 5. In Section 2, we will show that, if all links satisfy a strengthened FIFO condition, the state vectors x_a^p, u_a^p, v_a^p, and τ_a are well defined as functions of h, i. e., the DNS is well defined over the period $[0, \overline{T}]$.

2. THE DNS UNDER THE STRONG FIFO CONDITION

2.1 Some Key Concepts and Results

Before considering the existence of a dynamic network equilibrium, one must check whether the DNS is well defined. To this effect, it is natural to introduce a queue discipline that forbids vehicles overtaking each other. Unfortunately, it seems that a simple FIFO rule is not sufficient, hence the introduction of a strengthened rule, which we call "strong FIFO."

DEFINITION 2.1. *A strong FIFO condition holds at link a over the time period* $[0, t]$ *if the function* τ_a *is strongly monotone with positive modulus* γ_a, *i. e.*,

$$t_1 \geqslant t_2 \Rightarrow \tau_a(t_1) - \tau_a(t_2) \geqslant \gamma_a(t_1 - t_2) \quad (8)$$

for all t_1, t_2 *in* $[0, t]$.

Sufficient conditions that ensure the strong FIFO condition will be given in Section 4. Strong FIFO implies that the functions τ^{-1} are Lipschitz continuous (see Lemma 2.1). Note that Lipschitz continuity implies absolute continuity (see Remark 4.6 in MUKHERJEA and POTHOVEN (1978) and Definition 2.2 below), a key feature in the study of the flow functions x_a^p, u_a^p, and v_a^p. The rest of this section is devoted to definitions and theoretical results of real analysis. The results whose proof is omitted are either standard or elementary. (See KOLMOGOROV and FOMIN, 1970; Mukherjea and Pothoven, 1978; or ROYDEN, 1968.)

DEFINITION 2.2. *A real function* f *defined over the interval* $[a,b]$ *is absolutely continuous if, for any positive number* ϵ, *there exists a positive number* δ *such that, for every finite collection* $\{(x_i, x_i')\}$ *of nonoverlapping intervals with*

$$\sum_{i=1}^{n} | x_i' - x_i | < \delta$$

we have that

$$\sum_{i=1}^{n} | f(x_i') - f(x_i) | < \epsilon$$

DEFINITION 2.3. *A sequence* u_n *in a normed linear space* X *converges weakly to* $u \in X$ ($u_n \rightharpoonup u$) *if, for every bounded linear functional* F *on* X, *we have* $F(u_n) \to F(u)$ *as* $n \to \infty$.

Note that a Lipschitz continuous function is absolutely continuous.

DEFINITION 2.4. *Let* X *and* Y *be two normed linear spaces. An operator from* X *to* Y *is weakly continuous if, for every weakly converging sequence* $u_n \rightharpoonup u$, *we have that*

$$\| J(u_n) - J(u) \| \to 0 \text{ as } n \to \infty$$

THEOREM 2.1.

(i) *Any bounded and measurable function over* $[a,b]$ *is integrable over* $[a,b]$.

(ii) *Every nondecreasing function* f *is bounded and measurable on* $[a,b]$.

(iii) *Sums, differences and products of measurable functions are measurable.*

LEMMA 2.1. *Let* f *be strongly monotone with modulus* c *over the interval* $[a,b]$. *Then* f *is invertible over* $[a,b]$, *its inverse* f^{-1} *is Lipschitz continuous (with Lipschitz constant* $1/c$) *and differentiable (a. e.) over the range* $[f(a), f(b)]$ *of* f *and we have* $(f^{-1})'(x) = 1/f'(f^{-1}(x))$.

LEMMA 2.2. *Let* f *be absolutely continuous on* $[a,b]$ *with* $f'(x) \geqslant c > 0$ *for almost every* $x \in [a,b]$. *Then* f *is strongly monotone with constant* c *over* $[a,b]$.

LEMMA 2.3

(i) *Let* g *be differentiable (a. e.) on* $[a,b]$ *and* f *be integrable on* $[c,d]$, *with* $g([a,b]) \subset [c,d]$. *Let* $F(x) = \int_c^x f(t)\,\mathrm{d}t$. *We have that*

$$\int_{g(a)}^{g(x)} f(s)\mathrm{d}s = \int_{a}^{x} f(g(s))g'(s)\mathrm{d}s \tag{9}$$

for all α and x in [a,b] if and only if the function F∘g is absolutely continuous.

(ii) If g is absolutely continuous on [a,b] and f is bounded by B and integrable on [c,d], then F∘g is absolutely continuous, and (9) holds for all α and β in [a,b].

We introduce the subset $\Omega(B,T')$ of functions in $L^2[0,T']$ bounded by B:

$$\Omega(B,T') = \{u : u \in L^2[0,T'], 0 \leqslant u(t) \leqslant B\ \forall t \in [0,T']\}.$$

PROPOSITION 2.1. *Let J be the integral operator defined as*

$$Ju(t) = \int_0^t u(s)\mathrm{d}s \tag{10}$$

Then J is weakly continuous on $\Omega(B,T')$

Proof. First we prove that $Ju(t) \in L^2[0,T']$. By construction, $Ju(t)$ is of bounded variation on $[0,T']$, i. e., it can be expressed as the difference of two bounded monotone real-valued functions on $[0,T']$. From Theorem 2.1, both $Ju(t)$ and $(Ju(t))^2$ are bounded and measurable on $[0,T']$. Thus we get that $Ju(t) \in L^2[0,T']$. Let $\{u_k\}$ be a sequence converging weakly to u on $\Omega(B,T')$. Assume, by contradiction, that $\| Ju - Ju_k \|$ does not converge to zero, i. e., there exist. $\epsilon_0 > 0$ and an infinite sequence $\{n_k\}$ such that, for every k,

$$\| Ju - Ju_{n_k} \| \geqslant \epsilon_0^2$$

$$| Ju(t_{n_k}) - Ju_{n_k}(t_{n_k}) | \geqslant \frac{\epsilon_0}{\sqrt{T'}}.$$

Because $[0,T']$ is compact, there exists an infinite subsequence $\{n'_k\}$ of $\{n_k\}$ such that $t_{n'_k} \to t_0 \in [0,T']$ and

$$| Ju(t_{n'_k}) - Ju_{n'_k}(t_{n'_k}) | \geqslant \frac{\epsilon_0}{\sqrt{T'}}. \tag{11}$$

But

$$| Ju(t_{n'_k}) - Ju_{n'_k}(t_{n'_k}) \leqslant \left| \int_0^{t0} (u_{n'_k}(s) - u(s))\mathrm{d}s \right| + \left| \int_{t_0}^{t_{n'_k}} (u_{n'_k}(s)) \right|. \tag{12}$$

The first term on the right-hand side of the inequality converges to 0, because $u_{n'_k} \rightharpoonup u$. The second term also converges to 0, because $t_{n'_k} \to t_0$ and u and $u_{n'_k}$ are uniformly bounded on $[0,T']$. This is in contradiction to Eq. 11, and the operator J must therefore be weakly continuous on $\Omega(B,T')$.

2.2 Link Dynamics and the Link Flow Operator

If the entry rate functions u_a^p are known over the period $[0,T_F]$, then the theorem below assures that the functions x_a, τ_a, and v_a are well defined over their respective domain.

THEOREM 2.2. *Assume that, for some finite instant T', the entry flow rate functions $(u_a^p)_{p\in P_a}$ are well defined (a. e.), nonnegative and Lebesgue integrable over the in-*

terval $[0,T']$. *If strong FIFO holds over* $[0,T']$ *we have that*:

(*i*) τ_a *is strictly increasing and differentiable*(*a. e.*)*over* $[0,T']$;

(*ii*) τ_a^{-1} *is strictly increasing*, *Lipschitz continuous and differentiable*(*a. e.*)*over the interval* $[\tau_a(0),\tau_a(T')]$;

(*iii*) x_a *is differentiable*(*a. e.*)*on* $[0,\tau_a(T')]$.

(*iv*) $(v_a^p)_{p\in P_a}$ *are well defined*(*a. e.*), *nonnegative and Lebesgue integrable over the interval* $[0,\tau_a(T')]$.

Proof. (i), (ii), and (iii): From the definition of strong FIFO, τ_a is strongly monotone increasing, and its inverse τ_a^{-1} exists. Let $t_{a0}=\tau_a(0)$ be the instant when the first user exits link a. The flow $x_a^p(t)$ over the period $[0,t_{a0}]$ is uniquely determined by

$$x_a^p(t)=\int_0^t u_a^p(s)\mathrm{d}s, t\in[0,t_{a0}], \forall p\in P_a. \tag{13}$$

From the strong FIFO condition on $[0,T']$, the inverse function τ_a^{-1} is well defined over the interval $[t_{a0},\tau_a(T')]$ and we can write,

$$x_a^p(t)=\int_{\tau_a^{-1}(t)}^t u_a^p(s)\mathrm{d}s \quad \forall t\in[t_{a0},\tau_a(T')) \ \forall p\in P_a. \tag{14}$$

Clearly, for given$(u_a^p(t))_{p\in P_a}$ on $[0,t_{a0}]$, $(x_a^p)_{p\in P_a}$ is well defined and differentiable(a. e.)in the first period $[0,t_{a0}]$. Thus both x_a and τ_a are well defined and differentiable(a. e.)in this period. Furthermore, from the assumption and Lemma 2. 1, τ_a^{-1} is well defined, absolutely(indeed Lipschitz)continuous and differentiable(a. e.)in $[t_{a0},t_{a1}]$. From Eqs. 13—14 and Lemma 2. 3, we know that x_a and τ_a are well defined and differentiable(a. e.) in$[t_{a0},t_{a1}]$, where $t_{a1}=\tau_a(t_{a0})$. Denote $t_{ai}=\tau_a(t_{ai-1})$, $i=1,\cdots,N_u$, where $t_{aN_u}=\tau_a(T')$. An induction argument on the index i completes the proof.

(iv): Recall that$(x_a^p)'(t)=u_a^p(t)-v_a^p(t)$. Together with Eqs. 13 and 14, we obtain, from the absolute continuity of τ_a^{-1} and Lemma 2. 3, an expression for the exit flow rate function v_a:

$$v_a^p(t)=\begin{cases}0 & \text{if} \quad t\in[0,t_{a0}]\\ u_a^p(\tau_a^{-1}(t))(\tau_a^{-1})'(t) & \text{if} \quad t\in[t_{a0},\tau_a(T')].\end{cases} \tag{15}$$

It follows from(i)that$(\tau_a^{-1})(t)>0$(a. e.). Therefore, v_a^p is well defined and nonnegative (a. e.). Moreover, we have that

$$\begin{aligned}\int_0^t v_a^p(s)\mathrm{d}s &= \int_{t_{a0}}^t u_a^p(\tau_a^{-1}(s))(\tau_a^{-1})'(s)\mathrm{d}s, t\in[t_{a0},\tau_a(T')]\\ &= \int_0^{\tau_a^{-1}(t)} u_a^p(s)\mathrm{d}s,\end{aligned}$$

which shows that v_a^p is integrable over the period $[0,\tau_a(T')]$.

Now, consider, for any given arc a, the set of bounded entry flow rate functions over a period $[0,T']$:

$$\Omega(B_a,T')=\{u: u\in L^2[0,T'], 0\leqslant u(t)\leqslant B_a, t\in[0,T']\}.$$

Using Theorem 2. 2 we can prove that, under the strong FIFO condition, the link dynamics correctly defines a link flow operator x_a over the domain$(\Omega(B_a,T'))^{|P_a|}$:

$$x_a : u_a \rightarrow x_a(u_a), \forall u_a \in (\Omega(B_a,T'))^{|P_a|}, \tag{16}$$

where $|P_a|$ is the number of paths through link a. Indeed, for a given $u_a=(u_a^p)_{p\in P_a}$, we can define $x_a(u_a)$ recursively as follows:

$$x_a(t)=\left\{\begin{array}{lll} x_{a0}(t)=\sum_{p\in P_a}\int_0^t u_a^p(s)\mathrm{d}s & \text{if} & t\in[0,t_{a0}] \\ x_{a1}(t)=\sum_{p\in P_a}\int_{\tau_{a0}^{-1}(t)}^t u_a^p(s)\mathrm{d}s & \text{if} & t\in[t_{a0},t_{a1}] \\ \vdots & & \\ x_{aN_u}(t)=\sum_{p\in P_a}\int_{\tau_{aN_u-1}^{-1}(t)}^t u_a^p(s)\mathrm{d}s & \text{if} & t\in[t_{aN_a}-1,t_{aN_u}], \end{array}\right\} \tag{17}$$

where $t_{a0}=D_a(0)$, $\tau_{a0}(t)=t+D_a(x_{a0}(t))$ for t in $[0,t_{a0}]$, $t_{ai}=\tau_{ai-1}(t_{ai-1})$, $\tau_{ai}(t)=t+D_a(x_{ai}(t))$ for $t\in[t_{ai-1},t_{ai}]$, $i=1,\cdots,aN_u$ and $t_{aN_u}=\tau_{aN_u-1}(T')$.

Clearly, for given $u_a(t)$ in $[0,t_{a0}]$, $(x_{a0}(t),\tau_{a0}(t))$ is well defined in the first period. Given the link entry flow rate u_a for the periods $[t_{ai-1},t_{ai}]$, $i=1,\cdots,aN_u$, $(x_{ai}(t),\tau_{ai}(t))$ is well defined by $\tau_{ai-1}^{-1}(t)$. The latter information only depends on the information$(x_{ai-1}(t),\tau_{ai-1}(t))$ at the preceding time period. Therefore, the operator x_a is well defined. Note that this operator is exactly the dynamic link performance function proposed by Ben-Akiva(1984). If all links satisfy the strong FIFO condition on the appropriate time period, then the DNS is well defined, and so are the link flow operators x_a.

THEOREM 2.3. *Assume that $h\in\Lambda$ and that the strong FIFO condition is satisfied at all links of the transportation network. Then the flow operator $x(h)=(x_a(h))_{a\in A}$ is well defined.*

Proof. Let $\xi=\min\{t_{a0}=\tau_a(0):a\in A\}>0$ and $h\in\Lambda$. For every link $a\in A$, $u_a=(u_a^p(h(t)))_{p\in P_a}$ is well defined over the interval $[0,\xi]$. From Theorem 2.2, we have a unique solution $x_a(h)=\sum_{p\in P_a}x_a^p(t)$ where $x_a^p(t)=\int_0^t u_a^p(s)\mathrm{d}s$. The functions τ_a^{-1} and v_a^p are well defined over $[\tau_a(0),\tau_a(\xi)]$ for every link $a\in A$ with $\tau_a(\xi)\geqslant 2\xi$ and $v_a^p(t)=u_a^p(\tau_a^{-1}(t))(\tau_a^{-1})'(t)$. Note that, by obtaining the nonnegative and Lebesgue integrable exit functions $v_a^p(t)$ for all $t\in[\tau_a(0),\tau_a(\xi)]$, $p\in P_a$ and $a\in A$, we have determined $u_a^p(t)$, $p\in P_a$ on $[0,2\xi]$ for all links. Applying Theorem 2.2 again, we obtain unique solutions $x_a(t)$ on $[0,2\xi]$ and $v_a^p(t)$ on $[\tau_a(0),\tau_a(2\xi)]$ with $\tau_a(2\xi)\geqslant 3\xi$ for all $a\in A$ and $p\in P_a$. We know that v_a^p is nonnegative and Lebesgue integrable. Repeat the above process and let $\overline{T}'$ be the(finite)instant when every vehicle having entered the network during the period $[0,T]$ has reached its destination.

In at most $n=\lceil T'/\xi\rceil$ steps, we have determined nonnegative and Lebesgue integrable functions u_a for all $t\in[0,n\xi]$ and all links. By Theorem 2.2, the flow $x_a(t)$ is well defined over $[0,\tau_a(n\xi)]$. This shows that, for given $h\in\Lambda$, x_a is uniquely determined, i.

e. , the operator x_a is well defined over the set Λ, as a function of h.

3. CONTINUITY OF THE NETWORK FLOW OPERATOR

OUR OBJECTIVE IN this section is to show that the network flow operator x is weakly continuous over Λ, as a function of h. This strong result will be instrumental in analyzing the existence of solutions to both the DNS and the DNEP, and also performing sensitivity analysis for the DNS.

3.1 Strong FIFO and the DNS

Under the strong FIFO condition, the link dynamics possesses several nice properties that are stated in the next theorem.

THEOREM 3.1. *Assume that, almost everywhere over a period* $[0, T']$, *(a) for every* $p \in P_a$, *the flow entry rate function* $u_a^p(t)$ *is well defined, nonnegative, Lebesgue integrable and bounded from above by some number* B_a; *(b) the strong FIFO condition with constant* γ_a *holds over* $[0, T']$; *(c) the link traversal function* D_a *is nonnegative, nondecreasing, continuously differentiable and Lipschitz continuous with constant* L_{D_a}. *Then*:

(i) τ_a^{-1} *is Lipschitz continuous with constant* $1/\gamma_a$ *over* $[\tau_a(0), \tau_a(T')]$ *and* $(\tau_a^{-1})'(t) \leqslant 1/\gamma_a$ *(a. e.)*;

(ii) for every $p \in P_a$, $x_a^p(t) \leqslant B_a T'$, $(x_a^p)'(t) \leqslant B_a$, *and* x_a^p *is Lipschitz continuous with constant* $(1+1/\gamma_a)B_a$ *over its domain*;

(iii)

$$\gamma_a \leqslant \tau_a'(t) \leqslant 1 + L_{D_a} \mid P_a \mid B_a; \tag{18}$$

(iv) for every $p \in P_a$, $v_a^p(t) \leqslant B_a/\gamma_a$ *over its domain.*

Proof. (i) See the proof of Lemma 2.1.

(ii) For any two instants t and t' in $[0, t_{a0}]$, with $t_{a0} = \tau_a(0)$, we have

$$\mid x_a^p(t) - x_a^p(t) \mid = \left| \int_t^{t'} u_a^p(s) \mathrm{d}s \right| \leqslant B_a \mid t - t' \mid \leqslant (1 + 1/\gamma_a) B_a \mid t - t' \mid.$$

Because τ_a^{-1} is Lipschitz continuous with constant $1/\gamma_a$ on $[t_{a0}, \tau_a(T')]$, we obtain, for $t \in [t_{a0}, \tau_a(T')]$,

$$x_a^p(t) - x_a^p(t') = \left| \int_{\tau_a^{-1}(t)}^{t} t u_a^p(s) \mathrm{d}s - \int_{\tau_a^{-1}(t')} t' u_a^p(s) \mathrm{d}s \right| \leqslant \left| \int_{\tau_a^{-1}(t)}^{\tau_a^{-1}(t')} u_a^p(s) \mathrm{d}s \right| + \left| \int_t^{t'} u_a^p(s) \mathrm{d}s \right|$$
$$\leqslant (1 + 1/\gamma_a) B_a \mid t - t' \mid.$$

Therefore, x_a^p is Lipschitz continuous on $[0, \tau_a(T')]$, with constant $(1+1/\gamma_a)B_a$. Because u_a^p is bounded by B_a, Eqs. 13 and 14 directly yield

$$0 \leqslant x_a^p(t) \leqslant T' B_a.$$

Moreover, because v_a^p is nonnegative, Eq. 2 yields

$$(x_a^p)'(t) = u_a^p(t) - v_a^p(t) \leqslant u_a^p(t) \leqslant B_a.$$

(iii) First, we note that $(x_a(t))' = \sum_{p \in P_a} (x_a^p)'(t) \leqslant \mid P_a \mid B_a$. The right part of the inequality of 18 follows from the definition of τ_a and the Lipschitz continuity of D_a. By the definition of strong FIFO, the derivative of τ_a satisfies(a. e.) $\tau_a(t) \geqslant \gamma_a$.

(iv) Follows directly from Eq. 15 and(i).

The continuity of the link flow operator relies on analytical properties of integral operators that are stated below. For ease of presentation, we drop the indices a and p and present two new definitions and two preliminary results.

DEFINITION 3.1. *Let u and $\{u_k\} \in \Omega(B, T')$. We say that the sequence u_k converges to u in the integral sense on $\Omega(B, T')$ if $\int_0^t u_k(s)\mathrm{d}s \to \int_0^t u(s)\mathrm{d}s$ for every $t \in [0, T']$ and we write $u_k \to^I u$ on $\Omega(B, T')$.*

Clearly, if u_k converges weakly to $u(u_k \rightharpoonup u)$, then $u_k \to^I u$ on $\Omega(B, T')$.

DEFINITION 3.2. *Let F be an operator defined on $\Omega(B, T')$. We say that F is pseudo-weakly continuous on $\Omega(B, T')$ if $F(u_k) \to F(u)$ whenever $u_k \to^I u$ on $\Omega(B, T')$.*

Using the above definition and Proposition 2.1, we obtain that the integral operator J defined by Eq. 10 is pseudo-weakly continuous on $\Omega(B, T')$.

PROPOSITION 3.1. *Let r be a continuous real function from $[0, T']$ into $[0, T']$ and consider the functional*

$$\psi(t, u) = \int_0^{r(t)} u(s)\mathrm{d}s. \tag{19}$$

If $u_k \to^I u$ on $\Omega(B, T')$ then $\{\psi(t, u_k)\}$ converges uniformly to $\psi(t, u)$ on $[0, T']$.

Proof. For any $\epsilon > 0$ and fixed t, let $K(t)$ be an index such that

$$|\psi(t, u_k) - \psi(t, u)| \leqslant \epsilon$$

for all $k \geqslant K(t)$. Because r is continuous on $[0, T']$ and $\Omega(B, T')$ is bounded, for every instant t, there is an open neighborhood $N(t) \subset [0, T']$ such that for any t' in $N(t)$ we have $|\psi(t, u_k) - \psi(t', u_k)| \leqslant \epsilon$ and $|\psi(t, u) - \psi(t', u)| \leqslant \epsilon$. Therefore, we have $|\psi(t', u) - \psi(t', u_k)| \leqslant 3\epsilon$ for all t' in $N(t)$ and for all $k \geqslant K(t)$. By the Heine-Borel covering theorem (see page 42 of Royden, 1968), there exists a finite subcover of the compact set $[0, T']$ by elements $N(t)$. Therefore, for any $\epsilon > 0$, there exists a number K_ϵ such that, for $k \geqslant K_\epsilon$ and t in $[0, T']$,

$$|\psi(t, u) - \psi(t, u_k)| \leqslant 3\epsilon,$$

i. e., $\psi(t, u_k)$ converges uniformly to $\psi(t, u)$ on $[0, T']$.

3.2 Pseudo-Weak Continuity of the Link Flow Operator

We are now in position to study the properties of the link flow operator x. To simplify the notation, we will temporarily omit the subscript a. Consider a sequence $\{u_k\} = \{(u_k^p)_{p \in P}\}$ pseudo-weakly converging to u on $\Omega(B, T'))^{|P|}$. We will show that, for sufficient large k, there is a bijection between the "breakpoints" in the link flow nested formulations 17 of u_k and those of u. As a consequence, $N_{u_k} = N_u$. For given u_k, the function $x(u_k(t))$ can be expressed as

$$x(u_k(t))=\left\{\begin{array}{lll} x_{0k}(t)=\sum_{p\in P}\int_0^t u_k^p(s)\mathrm{d}s & \text{if} & t\in[0,t_0] \\ x_{1k}(t)=\sum_{p\in P}\int_{T0k}^{-1}(t)t\,u_k^p(s)\mathrm{d}s & \text{if} & t\in[t_0,t_{1k}] \\ \vdots & & \\ x_{N_{uk}}(t)=\sum_{p\in P}\int \tau_{N_{uk}-1(t)}^{-1}(t)t\,u_k^p(s)\mathrm{d}s & \text{if} & t\in[t_{N_{uk}-1}-1,t_{N_{uk}}] \end{array}\right\}$$

where $\tau_{0k}(t)=t+D(x_{0k}(t)),t\in[0,t_0],t_{ik}=\tau_{(i-1)k}(t_{(i-1)k}),\tau_{ik}(t)=t+D(x_{ik}(t)),t\in[t_{(i-1)k},t_{ik}],i=1,\cdots,N_{u_k}$ and $t_{N_uk}=\tau_{N_uk-1}(T')$.

PROPOSITION 3. 2. *Let $f_k\in L^2[0,T']$ be a sequence of differentiable functions with uniformly bounded derivatives that converges toward a continuous function $f\in L^2[0,T']$. Then $|f_k(t)-f(t)|$ converges uniformly to 0 on $[0,T']$.*

Proof. (i) Convergence. Suppose that $|f_k(t_1)-f(t_1)|$ does not converge to 0 for $t_1\in[0,T']$, i. e., there exists a positive number ϵ_1 and a sequence $\{k'\}$ such that, for all k',

$$|f_{k'}(t_1)-f(t_1)>\epsilon_1. \tag{20}$$

From the continuity of f, there exists a neighborhood $N(t_1)$ of t_1 such that

$$|f(t_1)-f(t)\leqslant\frac{\epsilon_1}{3}\quad\forall t\in N(t_1). \tag{21}$$

Because f_k is differentiable with uniformly bounded derivative, there exists a neighborhood $N_1(t_1)$ of t_1 such that

$$|f_{k'}(t)-f_{k'}(t_1)|\leqslant\frac{\epsilon_1}{3}\ \forall t\in N_1(t_1).$$

However, for every $t\in N(t_1)\cap N_1(t_1)$,

$$|f_{k'}(t)-f(t)|\geqslant|f_{k'}(t_1)-f(t_1)|-|f(t_1)-f(t)|-|f_{k'}(t)-f_{k'}(t_1),$$

in contradiction with the convergence of $f_k\to f$ on $L^2[0,T']$.

(ii) Uniform convergence. Assume, by contradiction, that there exists a positive number ϵ_2 and an infinite sequence $\{t(k')\}$ such that

$$|f_{k'}(t(k'))-f(t(k'))|>\epsilon_2 \tag{22}$$

Because $\{t(k')\}$ is bounded, there exists a subsequence $\{t(k'')\}$ converging to $t_2\in[0,T']$. For sufficiently large values of the index k'', we have the inequalities

$$|f_{k''}(t(k''))-f_{k''}(t_2)|\leqslant\frac{\epsilon_2}{3},$$

$$|f(t_2)-f(t(k''))|\leqslant\frac{\epsilon_2}{3},$$

$$|f_{k''}(t_2)-f(t_2)|\leqslant\frac{\epsilon_2}{3}.$$

The addition of the above inequalities contradicts Eq. 22.

THEOREM 3. 2. *Assume that*

(i) there exists a finite instant T' such that $u=(u^p)_{p\in P}$ and $u_k=(u_k^p)_{p\in P}$ are well

defined, nonnegative, Lebesgue integrable and bounded from above by B on $[0, T']$;

(*ii*) *the strong FIFO condition holds, with constant* γ;

(*iii*) *the arc traversal time function D is nonnegative, nondecreasing, differentiable and Lipschitz continuous with constant* L_D;

(*iv*) $u_k^p \to^I u^p$, $\forall p$ *on* $\Omega(B, T')$.

Then the operator sequence $\{x(u_k)\}$ *converges to* $x(u)$, *i. e.*, x *is pseudo weakly continuous on* $(\Omega(B, T'))^{|P|}$ *and* $v_k^p \to^I v^p$ *on* $\Omega(B/\gamma, \tau(T'))$, *where* v^p *is the exit flow rate corresponding to the entry flow rate* u^p.

Proof. From the assumptions and Theorem 2. 1, all functions involved are measurable and bounded, hence square integrable. Let us consider the interval $M_0 = [0, t_0]$. Because $u_k^p \to^I u^p$ on $\Omega(B, T')$, by

Proposition 2. 1, we have $x_{0k}^p \to x_0^p$ on M_0, i. e.,

$$\Delta_{0k}^p = \int_{M_0} |x_0^p(s) - x_{0k}^p(s)|^2 \mathrm{d}s \to 0.$$

By Proposition 3. 1, we have that $x_{0k}(t_0) \to x_0(t_0)$. But,

$$|\tau_0(t_0) \to \tau_{0k}(t_0)| \leqslant L_D |x_0(t_0) - x_{0k}(t_0)|.$$

Thus, $\tau_{0k}(t_0) \to \tau_0(t_0)$, i. e., $t_{1k} \to t_1$. Hence, for any $\delta > 0$, there exists an index K_0 such that for all $k \geqslant K_0$, we have

$$t_{1k} \in N_1 = (t_1 - \delta, t_1 + \delta). \tag{23}$$

Now consider the interval $M_1 = [t_0, t_1 - \delta]$ and set $t' = \tau_0(t)$. We have

$$\begin{aligned} & |x_{1k}^p(t') - x_1^p(t')|^2 \\ & \leqslant 2\left|\int_{\tau^{-1}{}_{0k}(t')}^{\tau_0^{-1}(t')} u_k^p(s)\mathrm{d}s\right|^2 + 2\left|\int_{t'}^{\tau_0^{-1}(t')} (u^p(s) - u_k^p(s))\mathrm{d}s\right|^2 \\ & \leqslant 2B^2 |\tau_0^{-1}(t') - \tau_{0k}^{-1}(t')|^2 + 2|\psi_0^p(t') - \psi_{0k}^p(t')|^2, \end{aligned}$$

where

$$\psi_0^p(t') = \int_{t'}^{\tau_0^{-1}(t')} u^p(s)\mathrm{d}s$$

and

$$\psi_{0k}^p(t') = \int_{t'}^{\tau_0^{-1}(t')} u_k^p(s)\mathrm{d}s.$$

Thus,

$$\begin{aligned} \Delta_{1k}^p &= \int_{M_1} |x_{1k}^p(t') - x_1^p(t')|^2 \mathrm{d}t' \\ &\leqslant 2B^2\int_{M_1} |\tau_0^{-1}(t') - \tau_{0k}^{-1}(t')|^2 \mathrm{d}t' + 2\int_{M_1} |\psi_0^p(t') - \psi_{0k}^p(t')|^2 \mathrm{d}t' \\ &= 2\Delta_{1k}^{p1} + 2\Delta_{1k}^{p2}. \end{aligned} \tag{24}$$

For $k \geqslant K_0$, the first term of Eq. 24 satisfies

$$\Delta_{1k}^{p1} = B^2\int_{\tau_0^{-1}(M_1)} |\tau_0^{-1}(\tau_0(t)) - \tau_0(\tau_{0k}^{-1}(t))|^2 \tau_0'(t)\mathrm{d}t$$

$$\leqslant B^2(1+L_D \mid P \mid B)\int_{\tau_0^{-1}(M1)} \mid \tau_{0k}^{-1}(\tau_{0k}(t)) - \tau_{0k}^{-1}(\tau_0(t)) \mid^2 \mathrm{d}t$$

(since $0 < \tau_0'(t) \leqslant 1 + L_D \mid P \mid B$)

$$\leqslant \frac{B^2(1+L_D \mid P \mid B)}{\gamma^2}\int_{\tau_0^{-1}(M_1)} \mid \tau_{0k}(t) - \tau_0(t) \mid^2 \mathrm{d}t$$

(from the Lipschitz continuity of τ_{0k}^{-1})

$$\leqslant \frac{L_D^2 B^2(1+L_D \mid P \mid B)}{\gamma^2}\int_{\tau_0^{-1}(M_1)} \mid x_{0k}(t) - x_0(t) \mid^2 \mathrm{d}t$$

(from the Lipschitz continuity of D)

$$\leqslant \frac{L_D^2 B^2(1+L_D \mid P \mid B)}{\gamma^2}\int_{M_0} \mid x_{0k}(t) - x_0(t) \mid^2 \mathrm{d}t$$

(since $\tau_0^{-1}(M_1) \subset M_0$)

$$= \alpha\Delta_{0k},$$

where $\alpha = L_D^2 B^2(1+L_D|P|B)/\gamma^2$.

Let us estimate the second term of Eq. 24: $\Delta_{1k}^{p2} = \int_{M_1} \mid \psi_0^p(t') - \psi_k^p(t') \mid^2 \mathrm{d}t'$. From Proposition 3. 1, ψ_k^p converges uniformly to ψ_0^p on M_1 and $\Delta_{1k}^{p2} \to 0$. We conclude that, for sufficiently large k, we have $\Delta_{1k}^p \leqslant \alpha\Delta_{0k} + \Delta_{1k}^{p2}$. Hence $\Delta_{1k}^p \to 0$ when $k \to +\infty$, i. e. , $x_{1k}^p \to x_1^p$ on M_1 for every p. Moreover, we have that $x_{1k} \to x_1$ on M_1, i. e. , $\Delta_{1k} = \int_{M_1} \mid x_1(s) - x_{1k}(s) \mid^2 \mathrm{d}s \to 0$. In contrast, the Lipschitz continuity of x and Proposition 3. 2 imply, for sufficiently large k, the relationships

$$\begin{aligned} \mid \tau_{1k}(t_1-\delta) - t_2 \mid &\leqslant \mid (t_1-\delta) - t_1 \mid + L_D \mid x_{1k}(t_1-\delta) - x_1(t_1) \mid \\ &\leqslant \delta + L_D(\mid x_1(t_1-\delta) - x_1(t_1) \mid + \mid x_{1k}(t_1-\delta) - x_1(t_1-\delta) \mid) \\ &\leqslant \delta + L_D \mid P \mid B(1+1/\gamma)\delta + L_D\delta \\ &= [1 + L_D + L_D \mid P \mid B(1+1/\gamma)]\delta \\ &= \beta\delta \\ &= \delta_2. \end{aligned}$$

As stated in the first part of this proof, we have, for $k \geqslant K_0$ and $t_{1k} \in N_1$,

$$t_{1k} = \tau_{1k}(t_0) \leqslant t_1 + \delta.$$

Thus, for sufficiently large k we have

$$[t_1+\delta, t_2-\delta_2] \subset [\tau_{1k}(t_0), \tau_{1k}(t_1-\delta)].$$

Letting $M_2 = [t_1+\delta, t_2-\delta_2]$, we get $\tau_1^{-1}(M_2) \subset M_1$. Furthermore,

$$\begin{aligned} \mid x_{1k}(t_{1k}) - x_1(t_1) \mid &= \left| \sum_{p\in P}\left(\int_{\tau_{1k}^{-1}(t_{1k})}^{t_{1k}} u_k^p(s)\mathrm{d}s - \int_{\tau_1^{-1}(t_1)}^{t_1} u^p(s)\mathrm{d}s\right)\right| \\ &= \left| \sum_{p\in P}\left(\int_{t_0}^{t_{1k}} u_k^p(s)\mathrm{d}s - \int_{t_0}^{t_1} u^p(s)\mathrm{d}s\right)\right| \\ &\leqslant \left| \sum_{p\in P}\left(\int_{t_0}^{t_1} (u_k^p(s) - u^p(s))\mathrm{d}s\right)\right| + B \mid P \mid \cdot \mid t_{1k} - t_1 \mid. \end{aligned}$$

Because, for every $p \in P$, $u_k^p \to^l u^p$ on $\Omega(B, T')$ and $t_{1k} \to t_1$, there follows $x_{1k}(t_{1k}) \to x_1(t_1)$. Also,

$$|t_{2k}-t_2|=|\tau_{1k}(t_{1k})-\tau_1(t_1)|$$
$$\leqslant |t_{1k}-t_1|+L_D|x_{1k}(t_{1k})-x_1(t_1)|$$

implies that $t_{2k}\to t_2$. We conclude that there exists $K_1\geqslant K_0$ such that for every $k\geqslant K_1$,

$$\tau_1^{-1}(M_2)\subset M_1 \text{ and } t_{2k}\in N_2=[t_1-\delta_1,t_2+\delta_2] \tag{25}$$

Consider the interval $M_2=[t_1+\delta_1,t_2-\delta_2]$. Let $t''=\tau_1(t')$. Using the same arguments as before, we obtain

$$\begin{aligned}\Delta_{2k}^p &= \int_{M_2}|x_{2k}^p(t'')-x_2^p(t'')|^2\mathrm{d}t''\\ &\leqslant 2B^2\int_{M_2}|\tau_1^{-1}(t'')-\tau_{1k}^{-1}(t'')|^2\mathrm{d}t''+2\int_{M_2}|\psi_1^p(t'')-\psi_{1k}^p(t'')|^2\mathrm{d}t''\\ &= 2\Delta_{2k}^{p1}+2\Delta_{2k}^{p1},\end{aligned}$$

where

$$\psi_1^p(t'')=\int_{t''}^{\tau_1^{-1}(t'')}u^p(s)\mathrm{d}s$$

and

$$\psi_{1k}^p(t'')=\int_{t''}^{\tau_1^{-1}(t'')}u_k^p(s)\mathrm{d}s.$$

We can also demonstrate that $\Delta_{2k}^p\to 0$ for every p and $\Delta_{2k}\to 0$. For sufficient large k, we have

$$|\tau_{2k}(t_1+\delta)-t_2|\leqslant\beta\delta=\delta_2$$
$$|\tau_{2k}(t_2-\delta_2)-t_3|\leqslant\beta\delta_2=\delta_3.$$

Letting $M_3=[t_0+\delta_2,t_3-\delta_3]$, we get $\tau_2^{-1}(M_3)\subset M_2$. We can also show that $t_{3k}\to t_3$. Thus, we conclude that there exists $K_2\geqslant K_1$ such that for any $k\geqslant K_2$, $\tau_2^{-1}(M_3)\subset M_2$ and $t_{3k}\in N_3=[t_3-\delta_3,t_3+\delta_3]$.

We pursue the above process until $k=N_u$. The analysis of this recursive scheme shows that, for sufficiently large k, the number of partitions for u_k is equal to that for u, i. e., $N_{u_k}=N_u$. If δ satisfies $\max_{1\leqslant i\leqslant N_u}\beta^{i-1}\delta<D(0)/2$, we have $\bigcap_{i=0}^{N_u}M_i=\varnothing$. For any such positive constant δ, there exists K such that for any $k\geqslant K$, we have

$$\begin{aligned}\Delta_k^p &= \int_0^{\tau(T'')}|x^p(t)-x_k^p(t)|^2\mathrm{d}t\\ &\leqslant\sum_{i=0}^{N_u}\Delta_{ik}^p+2\sum_{i=1}^{N_u}\delta_i\\ &\leqslant\sum_{i=0}^{N_u}\Delta_{ik}^p+2\delta\sum_{i=1}^{N_u}\beta^{i-1}\\ &\leqslant\sum_{i=0}^{N_u}\Delta_{ik}^p+m\delta,\end{aligned}$$

where m is some positive constant and $\Delta_{ik}^p\to 0$ when $k\to\infty$. Finally, because δ is an arbitrarily small positive number, we conclude that $\Delta_k^p\to 0$ when $k\to+\infty$, i. e., $\|x_k^p-x^p\|\to 0$. We also note that $\|x_k-x\|\to 0$and

$$\int_0^t (v_k^p(s) - v^p(s))\mathrm{d}s = \int_0^t (u_k^p(s) - u^p(s))\mathrm{d}s - (x_k^p(t) - x^p(t)) \tag{26}$$

for any t in $[0,\tau(T')]$. Because, for every $p\in P, x_k^p \to x^p$ and $u_k^p \to^I u^p$ on $\Omega(B,T')$, thus $v_k^p \to^I v^p$ on $\Omega(B/\gamma,\tau(T'))$. This completes the proof.

THEOREM 3.3(weak continuity). *Assume that*

(*i*) *there exists a finite instant* T *such that the path flow departure rate functions* $h_p, p\in P$, *are well defined on* Λ;

(*ii*) *all links satisfy the strong FIFO condition with uniform constant* γ *on* $[0,T]$;

(*iii*) *the link traversal time functions* D_a *are nonnegative, nondecreasing, continuously differentiable and Lipschitz continuous(a. e.).*

Then the flow operator $x(h)=(x_a(h))_{a\in A}$ *is well defined and weakly continuous on* Λ.

Proof. The assumptions imply the existence of a number $\overline{B}>0$ such that $h_p(t)\leqslant\overline{B}$ for all t in $[0,T]$ and all h_p in Λ. Let $h_k \rightharpoonup h$ on Λ and $\xi=\min\{t_{a0}: a\in A\}>0$. It is clear that, for all link $a\in A$ and $p\in P_a$, $u_a^p(h(t))$ and $u_a^p(h_k(t))$ are well defined on the interval $[0,\xi]$, and $u_a^p(h_k)\rightharpoonup^I u_a^p(h)$ on $\Omega(\overline{B},\xi)$. By Theorem 3.2, the functions $x_a(h_k)$ and $x_a(h)$ are well defined on $[0,\xi]$ whereas the functions $v_a^p(h_k)$ and $v_a^p(h)$, $p\in P_a$, are well defined on $[0,\tau_a(\xi)]$ for all links $a\in A$ with $\tau_a(\xi)\geqslant 2\xi$. We have that $x_a(h_k)\to x_a(h)$ and $v_a^p(h_k)\to^I v_a^p(h)$ on $\Omega(\overline{B}/\gamma,\tau_a(\xi))$. Let $B_1=\overline{B}/\gamma$. In obtaining the flow exit functions $v_a^p(h(t)), t\in[t_{a0},\tau_a(\xi)], p\in P_a, a\in A$, we simultaneously determined $u_a^p(h(t))$ and $u_a^p(h_k(t))$ on $[0,2\xi]$. Applying again Theorem 3.2, we determine uniquely $x_a(h(t)), x_a(h_k(t)), \tau_a(h(t)), \tau_a(h_k(t))$ on $[0,2\xi]$ and $v_a^p(h_k(t)), v_a^p(h(t))$ on $[0,\tau(2\xi)]$ with $\tau_a(2\xi)\geqslant 3\xi$. Moreover, we have that $v_a^p(h_k)\to^I v_a^p(h)$ on $\Omega(B_1/\gamma,\tau_a(2\xi))$. Let T' be the instant when the last vehicle exits the network. Because T' is finite, in at most $n=\lceil T'/\xi\rceil$ steps, we have determined $u_a^p(h(t))$ and $u_a^p(h_k(t))$ for all t in $[0,n\xi]$ and $u_a^p(h_k)\to^I u_a^p(h)$ on $\Omega(B_n,\tau_a(n\xi))$ with $\tau(n\xi)\geqslant(n+1)\xi$. Finally, we obtain the unique solution $x_a(h(t)), x_a(h_k(t))$ for t in $[0,T']$, and $x_a(h_k)\to x_a(h)$ when $h_k\rightharpoonup h$ on Λ. This completes the proof.

4. THE DYNAMIC USER EQUILIBRIUM PROBLEM

IN THIS SECTION, we address the existence of a solution to the dynamic user equilibrium problem.

4.1 The Path Traversal Time

Let $S_p(t,h)$ denote the traversal time for path p given that departure from the origin occurs at time t and that the path flow departure rate is $h(t)$ for t in $[0,T]$. Given a flow departure rate function $h\in\Lambda$, the traversal time $S_p(t,h)$ for users traveling on path $p=(a_{p1}, a_{p2},\ldots,a_{pn_p})$ and leaving the origin node at time t is

$$S_p(t,h) = D_{p1}(x_{p1}(t)) + \sum_{i=2}^{n_p} D_{pi}(x_{pi}(\tau_{pi-1}(t))), \tag{27}$$

where $\tau_{pi}(t)=\tau_{pi-1}(t)+D_{pi}(x_{pi}(\tau_{pi-1}(t)))$ and $\tau_{p1}(t)=t+D_{p1}(x_{p1}(t))$. If all links satisfy the strong FIFO condition, then a similar condition holds for all paths of the network, i.e., $S_p(t,h)>S_p(t',h)$ whenever $t>t'$. Hence, from Theorem 2.1, $S_p(t,h)$ is measurable and square integrable. The corresponding path travel time operator is

$$S_p(h) = S_p(t,h), \tag{28}$$

and the network traversal time operator is defined as

$$S(h) = (S_p(h))_{p\in P}. \tag{29}$$

THEOREM 4.1. *Assume that there exists a finite instant T' such that*

(i) *all path flow departure rates $h_p(t)$ are well defined over Λ;*

(ii) *all links satisfy the strong FIFO condition with a uniform constant γ over $[0, T']$;*

(iii) *the link traversal time functions D_a are nonnegative, nondecreasing, differentiable and Lipschitz continuous (a.e.) over $[0,T']$.*

Then the network traversal time operator S is weakly continuous over Λ.

Proof. We only need to prove the weak continuity of every operator $S_p(h)$ on Λ. From the assumptions, Theorem 3.3 holds, and $x(h)=(x_a(h))_{a\in A}$ is well defined and weakly continuous over Λ. Because $\tau_{p1}(h(t))=t+D_{p1}(x_{p1}(t))$, $\tau_{p1}(h)$ is weakly continuous over Λ. Moreover, $\tau_{p2}(h(t))=\tau_{p1}(t)+D_{p2}(x_{p2}(\tau_{p1}(t)))$. Thus $\tau_{p2}(h)$ is also weakly continuous over Λ. A similar argument shows that $\tau_{p3}(h),\cdots,\tau_{pn_p}(h)$ are weakly continuous over Λ. The weak continuity of S_p follows from the continuity of D_a and the weak continuity of x_a.

4.2 Definition of the Dynamic User Equilibrium Model

In Smith (1993) and Smith and Wisten (1994), a dynamic user equilibrium for the route choice problem with predetermined departure times (RC equilibrium) has been characterized as follows.

DEFINITION 4.1 (RC equilibrium). *Let $h\in\Lambda$. Then h and the user cost function $S(t,h)$ form an RC equilibrium if, for almost every instant t and for every two paths associated with a given origin-destination pair, one has*

$$S_p(t,h) > S_q(t,h) \Rightarrow h_p(t) = 0. \tag{30}$$

Smith and Wisten (1994) have characterized an RC equilibrium $h^*\in\Lambda$ as a solution of the variational inequality,

$$\sum_{r,s}\sum_{p\in P_{rs}}\int_0^T S_p(t,h^*)(h_p(s)-h_p^*(s))\mathrm{d}s \geqslant 0 \qquad \forall h(t)\in\Lambda \tag{31}$$

or, in compact form,

$$\langle S(h^*), h^*-h\rangle \leqslant 0 \qquad \forall h\in\Lambda \tag{32}$$

4.3 Existence of Solutions to the Dynamic User Equilibrium Problem

In this section, we adapt the technique developed in MARCOTTE and ZHU (1995) to prove the existence of at least one solution to variational inequality 32. The following definition will be required in the proof of the existence theorem.

DEFINITION 4.2(LIONS,1969). *Let* Λ *be a subset of a reflexive Banach space* V, V^* *its dual space, and* J *a mapping from* Λ *into* V^*. *We say that* J *is pseudomonotone (in the Lions sense) if* J *is bounded on* Λ *and, for all sequences* $\{h_k\}$ *of* Λ *converging weakly to* h, *and such that*

$$\lim\sup_k \langle J(h_k), h_k - h\rangle \leqslant 0,$$

we have

$$\lim\inf_k \langle J(h_k), h_k - y\rangle \geqslant \langle J(h), h - y\rangle \qquad \forall y \in \Lambda.$$

Note that the former definition does not correspond to the standard definition of pseudomonotonicity for point-to-set mappings(see KARAMARDIAN and SCHAIBLE, 1990). In Lions(1969), it is shown that, if J is pseudomonotone(in the Lions sense) on a nonempty, closed, convex and bounded subset Λ of a reflexive Banach space, then there exists at least one point h^* satisfying the variational inequality,

$$\langle S(h^*), h^* - h\rangle \leqslant 0 \qquad \forall h \in \Lambda.$$

THEOREM 4.2(existence of an RC equilibrium). *Let* T' *be a finite instant such that, for all* t *in* $[0, T']$, *all path flow departure rate functions* h_p *are well defined on* Λ, *all links satisfy the strong FIFO condition with constant* γ *and the link traversal functions* D_a *are nonnegative, nondecreasing, differentiable, and Lipschitz continuous (a. e.). Then the solution set of the infinite dimensional variational inequality* 32 *is nonempty.*

Proof. We proceed to check the assumptions of Lions' existence theorem.

(*i*) By construction, the set Λ is closed, convex, and bounded.

(*ii*) From Theorem 4.1, S is weakly continuous over Λ.

(*iii*) If S is not bounded, then there exists a sequence $\{h_k\}$ in Λ such that $\| S(h_k) \| \to +\infty$. But, because Λ is weakly compact, there is a subsequence $\{h_{n_k}\}$ converging weakly to h in Λ. From the weak continuity of S, we have $\| S(h_k) - S(h) \| \to 0$, a contradiction. We conclude that $S(h)$ must be bounded(a. e.).

(*iv*) Pseudomonotonicity of S: Let $\{h_k\}$ be a sequence in Λ converging weakly to h in Λ, and y an arbitrary element of Λ. We have

$$\left[\int_0^T \langle S(h_k(t)) - S(h(t)), h_k(t) - y(t)\rangle_2 \mathrm{d}t\right]^2$$

$$\leqslant \| S(h_k) - S(h) \|^2 \int_0^\tau \| h_k(t) - y(t) \|_2^2 \mathrm{d}t$$

$$\leqslant \| S(h_k) - S(h) \| 2\hat{D}^2,$$

where $\hat{D}$ is the diameter of the bounded set Λ. From(ii), we get

$$\lim_{k\to\infty}\langle S(h_k) - S(h), h_k - y\rangle = \lim_{k\to\infty}\int_0^T \langle S(h_k(t)) - S(h(t)), h_k(t) - y(t)\rangle_2 \mathrm{d}t = 0$$

and

$$\lim_{k\to\infty}\langle S(h_k),h_k-y\rangle = \lim_{k\to\infty}[\langle S(h),h_k-y\rangle + \langle S(h_k)-S(h),h_k-y\rangle]$$
$$= \langle S(h),h-y\rangle.$$

This implies, clearly, that S is pseudomonotone (in the Lions sense) over Λ.

5. A SUFFICIENT CONDITION FOR STRONG FIFO

THE FIFO AND STRONG FIFO conditions are specified with respect to a time interval. A link satisfying the FIFO condition during period $[0,T_1]$ might not satisfy it over a longer period $[0,T_2]$. From the definition of link dynamics, we have, during the initial period $[0,t_{a0}]$,

$$x_a^p(t) = \int_0^t u_a^p(s)\mathrm{d}s,$$

and the strong FIFO condition will always prevail in the time interval $[0,t_{a0}]$, provided that the link traversal time functions D_a are positive. In practice, we are interested in the strong FIFO condition over the domain $[0,T']$ of link entry flow rates. Friesz et al. (1993) have proved that the FIFO condition is met when the functions D_a are affine. We strengthen this result by showing that strong FIFO is satisfied as well.

THEOREM 5.1. *Let T' be a finite instant such that, for all t in $[0,T']$, the function $u_a^p(p\in P_a)$ is well defined, nonnegative, bounded from above by B_a, and Lebesgue integrable. Assume further that $D_a(x_a)=\alpha_a x_a+\beta_a$, where α_a is nonnegative and β_a is positive. Then*

$$v_a^p(t)\leqslant 1/\alpha_a \qquad \forall t\in[0,T'], \tag{33}$$

and strong FIFO holds with constant γ_a, i.e.,

$$\tau_a'(t)\geqslant \alpha_a\sum_{p\in P_a}u_a^p(t)+\gamma_a, \text{ with } \quad \gamma_a>0. \tag{34}$$

Proof. We will adapt the recursive technique devised by Friesz et al. (1993). In the initial period $[0,t_{a0}]$, x_a is absolutely continuous and differentiable (a.e.) and so is τ_a, with

$$\begin{aligned}\tau_a'(t) &= 1+D_a'(x_a(t))\sum_{p\in P_a}u_a^p(t)\\ &= 1+\alpha_a\sum_{p\in P_a}u_a^p(t)\\ &> \alpha_a\sum_{p\in P_a}u_a^p(t)+\frac{1}{1+\alpha_a\mid P_a\mid B_a}.\end{aligned}$$

Moreover, we have that $v_a^p(t)=0\leqslant 1/\alpha_a$ over that time period. Now assume that, at the i th period $[t_{i-1},t_i]$, x_a and τ_a are well defined (a.e.), absolutely continuous, differentiable, and that Eqs. 33 and 34 hold with $\gamma_a=1/(1+\alpha_a|P_a|B_a)^i$. We want to prove that x_a, τ_a are also absolutely continuous and Eqs. 33−34 hold for the $(i+1)$st time period $[t_i,t_{i+1}]$, with $\gamma_a=1/(1+\alpha_a|P_a|B_a)^{i-1}$, $t_i=\tau_a(t_{i-1})$, and $t_{i+1}=\tau_a(t_i)$. Because Eq. 34 holds and τ_a is absolutely continuous in the ith period, then τ_a^{-1} is well defined (by Lemma 2.1) and (Lipschitz continuous) absolutely continuous in the $(i+1)$st period (by Lemma 2.2).

Using Eqs. 2 and 14, we observe that

$$\begin{aligned} v_a^p(t) &= \frac{u_a^p(\tau_a^{-1}(t))}{\tau_a'(\tau_a^{-1}(t))} \\ &\leqslant \frac{u_a^p(\tau_a^{-1}(t))}{\alpha_a \sum_{p\in P_a} u_a^p(\tau_a^{-1}(t))} \\ &\leqslant 1/\alpha_a, \end{aligned} \tag{35}$$

i. e., Eq. 33 holds. From the knowledge of τ_a^{-1} in the $(i+1)$st period, x_a and τ_a are well defined and absolutely continuous in the $(i+1)$st period. Furthermore, based on Eqs. 2 and 14, we obtain

$$\begin{aligned} \tau_a'(t) &= 1 + D_a'(x_a(t))x_a'(t) \\ &= 1 + \alpha_a \sum_{p\in P_a} u_a^p(t) - \frac{\alpha_a \sum_{p\in P_a} u_a^p(\tau_a^{-1}(t))}{\tau_a'(\tau_a^{-1}(t))} \\ &\geqslant \alpha_a \sum_{p\in P_a} u_a^p(t) + \frac{\dfrac{1}{(1+\alpha_a \mid P_a \mid B_a)^i}}{\alpha_a \sum_{p\in P_a} u_a^p(\tau_a^{-1}(t)) + \dfrac{1}{(1+\alpha_a \mid P_a \mid B_a)^i}} \\ &\geqslant \alpha_a \sum_{p\in P_a} u_a^p(t) + \frac{1}{(1+\alpha_a \mid P_a \mid B_a)^{i+1}}, \end{aligned}$$

i. e., Eq. 34 holds with $\gamma_a = 1/(1+\alpha_a | P_a | B_a)^{i+1}$. Because $t_i - t_{i-1} \geqslant t_{a0} = D_a(0) > 0$ for all i and T' is finite, the recursion must be finite.

COROLLARY 5.1. *Let T' be a finite instant such that $h_p(t)$ is bounded by $\overline{B}$ for all p in P and all t in $[0, T']$ and assume that, for all a in A, $D_a(x_a) = \alpha_a x_a + \beta_a$, where α_a is nonnegative and β_a is positive. Then every link entry rate u_a^p is bounded by $B_a = \max\{\overline{B}, 1/\alpha\}$, where $\alpha = \min_{a\in A}\{\alpha_a\}$ and satisfies the strong FIFO condition with constant $(1+\max_{a\in A}\{\alpha_a | P_a | B_a\})^{-1}$ on the appropriate time period.*

Proof. From Eq. 35, the link exit flow rate $v_a^p(t)$ is uniformly bounded by $1/\alpha_a$. Thus the link entry flow rate u_a^p is bounded by

$$B_a = \max\{\overline{B}, 1/\alpha\}.$$

To demonstrate the strong FIFO condition, we only need to increase the system time index and repeatedly apply the argument used in the proofs of Theorem 2.3 and Theorem 5.1.

Our final result deals with the case of nonlinear traversal time functions and states that strong FIFO will be satisfied if the derivative of the link traversal time function D_a is not too large.

THEOREM 5.2. *Let T' be a finite instant such that, for all t in T' the functions $u_a^p, p \in P_a$ are well defined, nonnegative, and Lebesgue integrable, and $\sum_{p\in P_a} u_a^p(t)$ is bounded from above by $B_a (B_a \geqslant 1)$. Let the functions D_a be nonnegative, nondecreasing, and differentiable with respect to x_a. If $D_a'(x_a) < 1/(B_a + \eta)$ for some positive number*

η, then the strong FIFO condition on arc a with constant $\eta/(B_a+\eta)$.

Proof. We will prove, by induction, that

$$\sum_{p\in P_a} v_a^p(t) \leqslant B_a \tag{36}$$

and

$$\tau_a'(t) \geqslant \frac{\eta}{B_a+\eta}. \tag{37}$$

The second inequality implies that strong FIFO holds for link a.

In the initial period $[0, t_{a0}]$, x_a is absolutely continuous and differentiable(a. e.)and so is. τ_a. We have

$$\tau_a'(t) = 1 + D_a'(x_a(t))\sum_{p\in P_a} u_a^p(t) \geqslant 1 \geqslant \eta/(B_a+\eta),$$

and $\sum_{p\in P_a} v_a^p(t) = 0 \leqslant B_a$, trivially. Now suppose that, in the i th period $[t_{i-1}, t_i]$, x_a and τ_a are well defined, absolutely continuous and differentiable(a. e.), and that Eqs. 37 and 36 hold. We want to prove that Eqs. 37—36 are also satisfied in the$(i+1)$st period $[t_i, t_{i+1}]$, where $t_i=\tau_a(t_{i-1})$and $t_{i+1}=\tau_a(t_i)$. Because, in the i th period, Eq. 37 holds and τ_a is absolutely continuous in the ith period, from Lemmas 2. 1 and 2. 2, τ_a^{-1} is well defined and absolutely(indeed Lipschitz) continuous in the$(i+1)$st period. Using Lemma 2. 3, and Eqs. 2 and 14, we get

$$\begin{aligned}\sum_{p\in P_a} v_a^p(t) &= \frac{\sum_{p\in P_a} u_a^p(\tau_a^{-1}(t))}{\tau_a'(\tau_a^{-1}(t))} \\ &\leqslant \frac{[\sum_{p\in P_a} u_a^p(\tau_a^{-1}(t))](B_a+\eta)}{[\sum_{p\in P_a} u_a^p(\tau_a^{-1}(t))]+\eta} \\ &\leqslant B_a,\end{aligned}$$

i. e. , Eq. 36 holds. From the knowledge of τ_a^{-1} in the$(i+1)$st period, x_a and τ_a are well defined, absolutely continuous and differentiable(a. e.)in the$(i+1)$st period, and

$$\begin{aligned}\tau_a'(t) &= 1 + D_a'(x_a(t))x_a'(t) \\ &\geqslant 1 + \min\left\{0, \frac{\sum_{p\in P_a}(u_a^p(t)) - (v_a^p(t))}{B_a+\eta}\right\} \\ &\geqslant \frac{[\sum_{p\in P_a}(u_a^p(t))]+\eta}{B_a+\eta} \\ &\geqslant \frac{\eta}{B_a+\eta},\end{aligned}$$

i. e. , Eq. 37 holds. Finally, since $t_i - t_{i-1} \geqslant t_{a0} = D_a(0) > 0$ for every i and T' is finite, the recursion is finite.

COROLLARY 5. 2. *Let.* $\sum_{p\in P} h_p$ *be bounded from above by* $\overline{B}$ *on* $[0, T]$ *and let*

$$D_a'(x_a) \leqslant \frac{1}{|P_a|^n\overline{B}+\eta}, \tag{38}$$

where $\eta > 0$, $n = T'/\min_{a\in A} D_a(0)$ *and* T' *is the exit time of the last vehicle having entered the network before or at instant* T. *Then every total link entry flow is bounded by* $|P_a|^n \overline{B}$ *and satisfies the strong FIFO condition with constant* $\eta/(|P_a|^n \overline{B} + \eta)$.

Proof. The proof is similar to that of Corollary 5. 1, i. e. , we increase the time index and repeatedly make use of Theorem 5. 2 and the argument used in the proof of Theorem 2. 3. In contrast with the affine case, the bound on the total exit flow $\sum_{p\in P_a} v_a^p(t)$ now depends on the bound on the total entry flow rate $\sum_{p\in P_a} u_a^p(t)$. From the assumptions, we have $D_a'(x_a) \leqslant 1/(|P_a|^n \overline{B} + \eta)$, and, thus, the total entry flow rate $\sum_{p\in P_a} v_a^p(t)$ is bounded by $B_a = |P_a|^n \overline{B}$ over $[0, T']$. Thus $\tau_a(t) \geqslant \eta/(|P_a|^n \overline{B} + \eta)$ for t in $[0, T']$ and the result follows.

ACKNOWLEDGMENTS

THIS RESEARCH WAS supported by grant A5789 from National Science and Engineering Research Council of Canada and by Formation des Chercheurs et l'Aide àla Recherche(Québec).

REFERENCES

V. ASTARITA, "A Continuous Time Link Model for Dynamic Network Loading Based on Travel Time Function," in *Proceedings of the 13th International Symposium on Transportation and Traffic Theory*, J. -B. Lesort(ed.), 1996.

M. BEN-AKIVA, M. CYNA, AND A. DE PALMA, "Dynamic Models of Peak Period Congestion," *Transp. Res. B* 18B, 339—355(1984).

M. BEN-AKIVA, "Dynamic Network Equilibrium Research," *Transp. Res. A* 19A, 429—431(1985).

C. DAGANZO, "Properties of Link Travel Time Functions under Dynamic Loads," *Transp. Res. B* 29B, 95—98(1995).

O. DRISSI-KAÏTOUNI AND M. GENDREAU, "A New Dynamic Traffic Assignment Model," Publication 854, Centre de recherche sur les transports, Université de Montréal, Montréal, 1992.

T. L. FRIESZ, D. BERNSTEIN, T. E. SMITH, R. L. TOBIN, AND B. W. WEI, "A Variational Inequality Formulation of the Dynamic Network User Equilibrium Problem," *Opns. Res.* 41, 179—191(1993).

T. L. FRIESZ, F. J. LUQUE, R. L. TOBIN, AND B. W. WEI, "Dynamic Network Traffic Assignment Considered as a Continuous Time Optimal Control Problem," *Opns. Res.* 6, 893—901(1989).

S. KARAMARDIAN AND S. SCHAIBLE, "Seven Kinds of Monotone Maps," *J. Optim. Theory Appl.* 66, 37—46(1990).

A. N. KOLMOGOROV AND S. V. FOMIN, *Introductory Real Analysis*, Prentice-Hall, (1970).

J. -L. LIONS, *Quelques Méthodes de Résolution des Problémes aux Limites non Linéaires*, Dunod, Paris (1969).

H. S. MAHMASSANI AND R. HERMAN, "Dynamic User Equilibrium Departure Time and Route Choice on Idealized Traffic Arterias," *Transp. Sci.* 18, 362—384(1984).

P. MARCOTTE AND D. L. ZHU, "Equilibria with Infinitely Many Differentiated Classes of Customers," in *Complementarity and Variational Problems*, *Proceedings of the* 13*th International Conference on Complementarity Problems*: *Engineering and Economics and Applications and Computational Methods*, J.-S. Pang and M. Ferris(eds.), 234—258. SIAM, Philadelphia(1997).

D. K. MERCHANT AND G. L. NEMHAUSER, "A Model and Algorithm for the Dynamic Traffic Assignment Problem," *Transp. Sci.* 12, 182—199(1978).

A. MUKHERJEA AND K. POTHOVEN, *Real and Functional Analysis*, Plenum Press, New York (1978).

B. RAN, R. W. HALL, AND D. E. BOYCE, "A Link-Based Variational Inequality Model for Dynamic Departure Time/Route Choice," *Transp. Res. B* 30B, 31—46(1996).

H. L. ROYDEN, *Real Analysis*, MacMillan, 1968.

M. J. SMITH, "A New Dynamic Traffic Model and the Existence and Calculation of Dynamic User Equilibria on Congested Capacity-Constrained Road Network," *Transp. Res. B* 27B, 49—63(1993).

M. J. SMITH AND M. B. WISTEN, "Liapunov Methods for Dynamic Equilibrium Traffic Assignment," in *Proceedings of the second Meeting of the EURO working group on Urban Traffic and Transportations*, 223—245, INRETS, Paris, 1994.

B. W. WIE, R. L. TOBIN, T. L. FRIESZ, AND D. BERNSTEIN, "A Discrete Time, Nested Cost Operator Approach to the Dynamic Network User Equilibrium Problem," *Transp. Res. B* 29B, 79—92(1995).

Y. W. XU, J. H. WU, M. FLORIAN, P. MARCOTTE, AND D. L. ZHU, "Advances in the Continuous Dynamic Network Loading Problem," *Transp. Sci.* 33, 341—353(1999).

(Received: October 1997; revisions received: April 1999, August 1999; accepted: August 1999)

Published in *Transportation Science*, 2000, 34(4)

Advances in the Continuous Dynamic Network Loading Problem

Y. W. XU, J. H. WU, M. FLORIAN, P. MARCOTTE, and D. L. ZHU

Center for Research on Transportation, Université de Montréal, C. P. 6128, Succursale Centre-Ville, Montréal, Quebec H3C 3J7, Canada

The continuous dynamic network loading problem (CDNLP) consists in determining, on a congested network, time-dependent arc volumes, together with arc and path travel times, given the time-varying path flow departue rates over a finite time horizon. This problem constitutes an intrinsic part of the dynamic traffic assignment problem. In this paper, we present a formulation of the CDNLP where travel delays may be nonlinear functions of arc traffic volumes. We prove, under a boundedness condition, that there exists a unique solution to the problem and propose for its solution a finite-step algorithm. Some computational results are reported for a discretized version of the algorithm.

INTRODUCTION

The continuous dynamic network loading problem (CDNLP) aims at finding, on a congested network and over a fixed time period, time-dependent arc volumes, arc travel times and path travel times corresponding to given path-flow departure rate functions. This problem has recently received considerable attention, due to its importance in dynamic transportation models that assume either full information at departure nodes and the equilibrium principle (FRIESZ et al., 1989, 1993; RAN, BOYCE, and LEBLANC, 1993; WU 1994; WU, CHEN, AND FLORIAN, 1995), or take explicitly into account en-route real time information (ASTARITA, 1996; CASCETTA and CANTARELLA, 1991; FRIESZ et al. 1994; JAYAKRISHNAN, MAHMASSANI, and HU, 1994). Indeed, the CDNLP is a within-day model, in the sense of Cascetta and Cantarella (1991). Whenever disequilibrium situations are encountered (Friesz et al. 1994; NAGURNEY and ZHANG, 1995), one is confronted with both day-to-day and within-day effects.

The current solution procedures to this problem are mainly based on simulation [DYNASMART (Jayakrishnan, Mahmassani, and Hu, 1994), CONTRAM (TAYLOR, 1990)]. One advantage of the simulation approach is its detailed description of traffic phenomena. However, it is computationally intensive, especially if it is used within an interactive environment. Moreover, simulation provides little insight in the nature of the model under study. In particular, it sheds no light on the relationship between user choices(paths, departure instants)and the given path flow rates and arc volumes. Another approach to this problem is that of DAGANZO(1994, 1995), which is based on a subdivision of links into cells and describes the cell dynamics by using a finite difference approximation of the kinematic wave models.

Friesz et al. (1993) were the first to formulate the CDNLP as an essential component of the dynamic equilibrium problem, but did not propose a solution procedure. An important result of their study is that the first-in—first-out(FIFO) condition is satisfied whenever the arc traversal time functions are affine. Wu, Chen and Florian(1995) characterized the CDNLP through a system of functional equations. An approximate solution to the problem was obtained by solving a polynomial, finite-dimensional approximation of the functional system. ASTARITA(1995, 1996) considers as well a similar model of the CDNLP.

In this paper, we present a measure theoretic formulation for the CDNLP that only requires the path departure rate functions to be Lebesgue integrable. This formulation is inspired by the work of Friesz et al(1993) and is presented in a computable manner. Also, we consider the volumes in arcs and not in finer subdivisions of links, and use arc traversal functions to represent the travel time from the beginning to the end of an arc. These arc traversal functions are allowed to be nonlinear. Yet the FIFO condition will be satisfied, provided that a certain boundedness condition is satisfied. An abstract solution procedure that possesses the finite termination property will be given and numerical results will be reported on a discretized version of the infinite-dimensional procedure.

1. DEFINITIONS AND ASSUMPTIONS

LET $G=(N,A)$ DENOTE a transportation network, composed of a set of nodes N and a set of arcs A. Let $I\subseteq N\times N$ denote the set of all origin-destination(O-D) pairs, K_i the set of elementary paths connecting the origin of the O-D pair i to its destination and set: $K=\bigcup_{i\in I} K_i$. The allowable departure time period of the users is a finite interval $[0, T]$, although the time period under study(system period) $[0,\overline{T}]$ will be a longer time interval.

The CDNLP consists in determining, given path departure rate functions $h_k(t)$, the arc and path traversal time functions. Simultaneously, we will obtain a complete picture of the dynamic network, given by the arc volumes $v_a(t)$, at every instant t of the system period.

The CDNLP is a time-varying system composed of arc transfer boxes. At instant zero, there is no user in the system(the system is dormant). As time goes by, users enter the system according to exogenous path departure rate functions. The traversal time of users accessing the tail node of arc a at instant t is equal to $s_a(v(t))$, where s_a is a function of the vector $v(t)$ of arc volumes at instant t. At instant t, the system is completely determined by the vector $v(t)$. The notations used in this paper are listed below.

N	=set of nodes of the network G
A	=set of arcs of G
I	=set of all O-D pairs
K_i	=set of all paths connecting O-D pair $i \in I$
K	=set of all O-D paths: $K = \bigcup_{i \in I} K_i$
K^a	=set of all paths containing arc a
a_k^-	=arc preceding arc a on path k
$[0, T]$	=flow departure period
$[0, \overline{T}]$	=system period
$h_k(t)$	=flow departure rate for path $k (t \in [0, T])$
$b_{ka}(t)$	=entry flow rate of path k into arc a at instant $t (t \in [0, \overline{T}])$
$e_{ka}(t)$	=exit flow rate of path k out of arc a at instant $t (t \in [0, \overline{T}])$
$b_a(t)$	=entry flow rate into arc a at instant $t (t \in [0, \overline{T}])$: $b_a(t) = \sum_{k \in K^a} b_{ka}(t)$
$e_a(t)$	=exit flow rate from arc a at instant $t (t \in [0, \overline{T}])$: $e_a(t) = \sum_{k \in K^a} e_{ka}(t)$
$v_a(t)$	=traffic volume on arc a at instant $t (t \in [0, \overline{T}])$
$v(t)$	=vector of arc volumes;
$s_a(v(t))$	=traversal time of arc a at instant $t (t \in [0, \overline{T}])$
$\tau_a(t)$	=exit time of flow entering arc a at instant $t (t \in [0, \overline{T}])$
$\tau_a^{-1}(t)$	=inverse function of $\tau_a(t)$
$S_k(t)$	=path traversal time for users departing at time $t (t \in [0, T])$

Before giving a mathematical description of the CDNLP, we state our main assumptions.

ASSUMPTION 1. *At instant zero, there is no traffic volume in the network.*

ASSUMPTION 2. *Flow is conservative, i. e., it is only generated at origin nodes and absorbed at destination nodes.*

ASSUMPTION 3. *The arc traversal time of a user arriving at arc a at instant t is solely determined by the (total) traffic volume still on arc a at instant t. This implies that the arc traversal time functions s_a are separable.*

ASSUMPTION 4. *The arc traversal time functions are positive, nondecreasing, and continuously differentiable functions of total arc volumes.*

ASSUMPTION 5. *The path departure rate functions $h_k(t)$ are nonnegative, finite and Lebesgue integrable on their domain $[0, T]$.*

The preceding assumptions are not sufficient to ensure that the model is well defined. In particular, the model could yield uninterpretable results if some user could reach its destination earlier by leaving its origin node later. For this reason, we impose, throughout the paper, the FIFO condition that a user arriving later at the tail of a arc also leaves that arc later. Mathematically, this condition takes the form,

arc FIFO

$$t' > t'' \Rightarrow t' + s_a(v_a(t')) > t'' + s_a(v_a(t'')). \qquad (1)$$

2. THE MATHEMATICAL MODEL

OUR MODEL FOR THE CDNLP consists of two sets of equations and inequalities, one describing the arc dynamics and the other the path dynamics.

2.1 Arc Dynamics

Let T_a denote the latest arrival instant at the tail node of arc a, i. e. ,

$$T_a = \sup\{t \in [0, \overline{T}]: b_a(t) = 0 \text{ for all } t \in [0, \overline{T}]\}. \qquad (2)$$

From Assumption 3, $\tau_a(t)$, the exit time at the head of arc a of a user who enters the tail of the arc at time t, is equal to

$$\tau_a(t) = t + s_a(v_a(t)) \quad \text{for all} \quad t \in [0, T_a]. \qquad (3)$$

Since the functions s_a ($\forall a \in A$) are continuously differentiable, the FIFO condition is equivalent to the constraint

$$\tau_a'(t) = 1 + s_a'(v_a(t))v_a'(t) > 0 \quad \text{for all } t \in [0, \tau_a(T_a)]. \qquad (4)$$

For each arc a we define t_a^0 as the instant when the first user reaches the tail of arc a:

$$t_a^0 = \inf\{t : b_a(t) > 0 \text{ for all } t \in [0, T_a]\}.$$

We also define $\bar{t}_k^0$ as the first departure instant on path k,

$$\bar{t}_k^0 = \sup\{t : h_k(t) = 0 \text{ for all } t \in [0, T]\}.$$

and, recursively,

$$t_{ka}^0 = \begin{cases} \bar{t}_k^0 & \text{if } a \text{ is the first arc of path } k \\ \bar{t}_{ka}^0 & \text{otherwise.} \end{cases}$$

We have the relationship,

$$t_a^0 = \min\{t_{ka}^0 : k \in K^a\}.$$

The arc dynamics on arc a obey the equation

(I) $$v_a(t) = \int_0^t (b_a(y) - e_a(y))\mathrm{d}y \text{ for all } t \in [0, \tau_a(T_a)]. \qquad (5)$$

The above equation can be rewritten in three different forms, depending on the instant t. In an initial phase, flow enters and starts moving along arc a, but no flow exits from arc a, and Eq. 5 reduces to

$$v_a(t) = \int_0^t b_a(y)\mathrm{d}y \text{ for all } t \in [0, t_a^0 + s_a(0)].$$

In the final phase(t in $[T_a, \tau_a(T_a)]$), arc flow keeps exiting, but there is no entry flow. In the intermediate phase, there may exist both entering and exiting flow.

According to Eq. 4, τ_a is strictly increasing, and its inverse, τ_a^{-1}, is well defined over the interval $[s_a(0), \tau_a(T_a)]$, and we can write

(II) $$v_a(t) = \int_0^t b_a(y)\mathrm{d}y - \int_0^{\tau_a^{-1}(t)} b_a(y)\mathrm{d}y \text{ for all } t \in [s_a(0), \tau_a(T_a)].$$

Equation(II)is equivalent to the FIFO conditions. Similar results were obtained simultaneously by Astarita(1996)and HEYDECKER and ADDISON(1996).

Differentiating v_a with respect to t (see next section and the Appendix for the validity of this operation)in(I)or(II), we obtain an expression for the exit flow rate of arc a:

$$e_a(t) = \begin{cases} 0, & t \in [0, s_a(0)] \\ b_a(\tau_a^{-1}(t))(\tau_a^{-1})'(t), & t \in [s_a(0), \tau_a(T_a)]. \end{cases} \tag{6}$$

2.2 Path Dynamics

From the flow conservation assumption(Assumption 2), we have

$$b_{ka}(t) = \begin{cases} h_k(t), & \text{if } a \text{ is the first arc of path } k \\ e_{a_k^-}(t), & \text{otherwise} \end{cases} \tag{7}$$

$$b_a(t) = \sum_{k \in K^a} b_{ka}(t) \tag{8}$$

$$e_{ka}(t) = b_{ka}(\tau_a^{-1}(t))(\tau_a^{-1})'(t) \quad \text{for all } t \in [0, \tau_a(T_a)] \tag{9}$$

The travel time $S_k(t)$ of a user leaving its origin at instant t and traveling on path $k=(a_1, a_2, \cdots, a_{nk})$ is equal to $t_{nk} - t_0$, where the instants t_j are computed recursively,

$$t_0 = t \tag{10}$$

$$\begin{aligned} t_j &= \tau_{aj}(t_{j-1}) \\ &= t_{j-1} + s_{aj}(v_a(t_{j-1})) \quad j = 1, 2, \cdots, n_k \end{aligned} \tag{11}$$

for all departure instants t in $[0, T]$, and for all paths k in K. We may alternatively write $S_k(t)$ as

$$S_k(t) = \sum_{j=1}^{n_k} s_{aj}(v_a(t_{j-1})).$$

CDNLP is mathematically formulated as Eqs. 3—11, together with the nonnegativity constraints on $v_a(t)$, $b_{ka}(t)$, and $e_{ka}(t)$. Later on, we see that, under a boundness condition, the CDNLP can be simplified, whereas the arc FIFO condition Eq. 4 and the nonnegativity constraints are satisfied automatically.

3. EXISTENCE AND UNIQUENESS OF THE SOLUTION

FOR THE MODEL to be valid (i. e., satisfies the arc FIFO condition)the exit time functions τ_a must be invertible over their respective domains. This is the object of Theorem 3.1. Its proof requires the following two results. The proof of the first lemma is given in the Appendix, and the proof of the second lemma follows from Exercise 5.22 in ROYDEN(1988).

LEMMA 3.1. Let f *be absolutely continuous on* $[a, b]$ *with* $f'(x) > 0$ *for almost all* $x \in [a, b]$. *Then* f *is strictly increasing and invertible on* $[a, b]$. *Moreover, its inverse* f^{-1} *is absolutely continuous and differentiable (almost everywhere) on the interval*

$[f(a), f(b)]$, *with* $(f^{-1})'(x) = 1/f'(f^{-1}(x))$.

LEMMA 3. 2. Let g *be absolutely continuous, monotone increasing on* $[a, b]$ *and* f *be an integrable function on* $[g(a), g(b)]$. *Then, for any* $x \in [a, b]$, *there holds*

$$\frac{\mathrm{d}x}{\mathrm{d}}\int_{g(a)}^{g(x)} f(y)\mathrm{d}y = f(g(x))g'(x).$$

THEOREM 3. 1 (Nonlinear arc dynamics). *Assume that there exists a finite instant* T' *such that, for all* t *less than* T', *the entry flow rate function* b_a *is well defined, nonnegative, bounded from above by* B_a, *Lebesgue integrable, and that* $s_a'(v_a) < 1/B_a$ *for all* v_a *in the interval* $[0, V_a]$, *where* $V_a = \int_0^{T'} b_a(t)\, \mathrm{d}t$. *Then:*

(*i*) v_a *is nonnegative and differentiable almost everywhere on* $[0, \tau_a(T')]$;

(*ii*) τ_a *is strictly increasing and invertible on its domain*;

(*iii*) τ_a *and* τ_a^{-1} *are differentiable almost everywhere on their respective domains, and there exists a positive constant* ζ_a *such that* $\tau_a^{-}(t) \geqslant \zeta_a$ *for all* t *in* $[0, \tau_a(T')]$;

(*iv*) e_a *is well defined, nonnegative, Lebesgue integrable, and bounded from above by* B_a;

(*v*) *the functions* v_a, τ_a, τ_a^{-1}, *and* e_a *are well defined.*

Proof. We first notice that $s'_a(v_a(t)) < 1/B_a$ for all v_a in $[0, V_a]$ implies that $s'_a(v_a(t)) \leqslant (1/B_a) - \gamma_a$ whenever $0 < \gamma_a < 1/B_a$. Set $\zeta_a = B_a\gamma_a (< 1)$. We will subdivide the time interval $[0, T'] \subseteq T_a$ into appropriate subintervals and prove recursively the validity of the assertion for all subintervals.

Set $t_0 = t_a^0$ the instant when the first user arrives at the tail of arc a. If T' is less than t_0, there is nothing to prove. Otherwise set $t_1 = t_0 + s_a(v_a(t_0)) = t_0 + s_a(0)$ the time when the first user exits arc a. For all t in $[t_0, t_1]$, we have

$$v_a(t) = \int_0^t b_a(y)\mathrm{d}y. \tag{12}$$

It follows from a standard theorem (see Royden, 1988) that v_a is differentiable almost everywhere on $[t_0, t_1]$ and $0 \leqslant v_a(t) \leqslant V_a$ on $[t_0, t_1]$. This proves (i).

For each t in $[t_0, t_1]$, the corresponding first piece of the exit time function τ_a, denoted by τ_a^1, is defined as

$$\tau_a^1(t) = t + s_a(v_a(t)) \text{ for all } t \in [t_0, t_1], t_1 \geqslant T', \tag{13}$$

and τ_a^1 is continuously differentiable almost everywhere over $[t_0, t_1]$, with derivative

$$(\tau_a^1)'(t) = 1 + s_a'(v_a(t))b_a(t). \tag{14}$$

Since $s_a'(v_a(t))$ and $b_a(t)$ are both nonnegative, there follows

$$(\tau_a^1)'(t) \geqslant 1 \geqslant \max\{\xi_a, b_a(t)/B_a\}. \tag{15}$$

Thus, τ_a^1 is differentiable almost everywhere and strictly increasing on $[t_0, t_1]$. Now set $t_2 = \tau_a^1(t_1)$. By Lemma 3. 1, $(\tau_a^1)^{-1}$ is well defined on the interval $[t_1, t_2] = [\tau_a^1(t_0), \tau_a^1(t_1)]$, and $(\tau_a^1)^{-1}$ is differentiable almost everywhere on its domain. This yields (ii) and (iii). From Eq. 6 and Lemma 3. 2, we have

$$e_a(t) = b_a[(\tau_a^1)^{-1}(t)][(\tau_a^1)^{-1}]'(t) \geqslant 0 \text{ for all } t \in [\tau_a^1(t_0), \tau_a^1(t_1)]. \tag{16}$$

Now, by Lemma 3.1 and Eq. 15, we have

$$e_a(t) = \frac{b_a[(\tau_a^1)^{-1}(t)]}{(\tau_a^1)'[(\tau_a^1)^{-1}(t)]} \leqslant B_a, \text{ for all } t \in [t_1, t_2]. \tag{17}$$

Therefore, e_a is well defined, nonnegative, Lebesgue integrable (See Royden, 1988), and bounded from above by B_a on the interval $[t_1, t_2]$ and thus (iv) holds and (v) follows from the uniqueness of the function $(\tau_a^1)^{-1}$.

If $t_1 \geqslant T$ there is nothing left to prove. If $t_1 < T'$, we can express the arc volumes on $[t_1, t_2]$ as

$$v_a(t) = \int_0^t b_a(y)\mathrm{d}y - \int_0^t e_a(y)\mathrm{d}y,$$

with $0 \leqslant v_a(t) \leqslant V_a$, which is again differentiable almost everywhere with $v_a'(t) = b_a(t) - e_a(t)$. [note that $\tau_a^1(t_1) = \tau_a^2(t)$]. On the interval $[t_1, t_2]$, the exit time function τ_a^2 takes the form $\tau_a^2(t) = t + s_a(v_a(t))$. The function τ_a^2 is also differentiable, with derivative

$$(\tau_a^2)'(t) = 1 + s_a'(v_a(t))v_a'(t).$$

If $v'_a(t)$ is nonnegative, we readily obtain

$$(\tau_a^2)'(t) \geqslant 1 \geqslant \max\{\xi_a, b_a(t)/B_a\}.$$

Otherwise, we have

$$\begin{aligned}
(\tau_a^2)'(t) &= 1 + s_a'(v_a(t))v_a'(t) \\
&\geqslant 1 + \left(\frac{1}{B_a} - \gamma_a\right)(b_a(t) - e_a(t)) \\
&\geqslant 1 + \left(\frac{1}{B_a} - \gamma_a\right)(b_a(t) - B_a) \\
&= \left(\frac{1}{B_a} - \gamma_a\right)b_a(t) + \gamma_a B_a \\
&= \frac{b_a(t)}{B_a} - \gamma_a b_a(t) + \zeta_a \\
&\geqslant \max\left(\zeta_a, \frac{b_a(t)}{B_a}\right)
\end{aligned}$$

Therefore, τ_a^2 is also strictly increasing on $[t_1, t_2]$ by Lemma 3.1. We may conclude that the inverse function of τ_a^2 is well defined and differentiable almost everywhere ((ii)—(iii)) and its inverse, $(\tau_a^2)^{-1}$, is a well-defined function from $[t_2, t_3]$ into $[t_1, t_2]$, with $t_3 = \tau_a^2(t_2)$. Using a previous argument, we obtain that e_a is well defined, nonnegative, Lebesgue integrable, and bounded from above by B_a on $[t_2, t_3]$. This proves (iv), and (v) follows from the uniqueness of $(\tau_a^2)^{-1}$.

If $T' \leqslant t_2$, the proof is complete. Otherwise, we need to repeat the above process, which will terminate after a finite number of steps. Note that, at each step i, we have the invariant $t_i - t_{i-1} \geqslant s_a(0) > 0$ and, since T' is a finite real number, there exists a positive integer n satisfying $T' \leqslant t_{n-1}, \tau_a^{n-1}(T') \leqslant t_n$, and such that for all $i = 1, 2, \cdots, n$, (i) v_a is nonnegative and differentiable(almost everywhere)on $[t_{i-1}, t_i]$; (ii) τ_a^i is strictly increasing, thus invertible; (iii) τ_a and τ_a^{-1} are differentiable(almost everywhere)on their respective domains, with $\tau_a'(t) \geqslant \zeta_a$ and $t_{i+1} = \tau_a^i(t_i)$; (iv) $e_a(t)$ is well defined, nonnegative, Lesbesgue integrable, and bounded from above by B_a on the interval $[t_{i-1}, t_i]$, $i=1, 2, \cdots, n$; (v)all functions involved are well defined. This completes the proof.

This result provides a theoretical bound that is only sufficient for the theorem with nonlinear arc travel time functions. It may well be that steeper(larger $s_a'(v_a)$) arc travel time functions may satisfy the results. The next theorem achieves the same conclusions as Theorem 3.1, under a linearity rather than a boundedness condition on the functions s_a. A similar result has been proved in Friesz et al. (1993). Our proof of the following theorem is based on the same lines as the proof of Theorem 3.2.

THEOREM 3.2(Linear arc dynamics). *Let T' be an instant such that, for all t in $[0, T']$, the entry flow rate function b_a is fully determined, nonnegative, bounded from above by B_a, and Lebesgue integrable. Assume further that the arc traversal time function s_a is affine. Then*

(i) v_a is nonnegative and differentiable almost everywhere on $[0, \tau_a(T')]$;

(ii) τ_a is strictly increasing, hence invertible, on $[t_a^0, T_a + \tau_a(T_a)]$;

(iii) τ_a and τ_a^{-1} are differentiable almost everywhere on their respective domains and there exists a positive constant ζ_a such that $\tau_a'(t) \geqslant \zeta_a$;

(iv) e_a is well defined, nonnegative, Lebesgue integrable, and bounded from above by B_a;

(v) the functions v_a, τ_a, τ_a^{-1}, and e_a are well defined.

Proof. Let $\beta_a = s_a'(v_a)$. Without repeating the similar line of the proof as for the nonlinear dynamics, we want to show only by induction that

$$\tau_a'(t) \geqslant \beta_a b_a(t) + \frac{1}{\sum_{n=0}^{i} (\beta_a B_a)^n}$$

and

$$e_a(t) \leqslant B_a \frac{\sum_{n=0}^{i-1} (\beta_a B_a)^n}{\sum_{n=0}^{i} (\beta_a B_a)^n},$$

whenever t is in $[t_{i-1}, t_i]$. We see that

$$\tau_a'(t) = 1 + \beta_a b_a(t) \geqslant 1, \forall t \in [t_0, t_1]$$

$$\begin{aligned} e_a(t) &= \frac{b_a(\tau_a^{-1}(t))}{\tau_a'(\tau_a^{-1}(t))} \\ &= \frac{b_a(\tau_a^{-1}(t))}{1 + \beta_a b_a(\tau a_a^{-1}(t))} \\ &\leqslant \frac{B_a}{1 + \beta_a B_a}, \forall t \in [t_1, t_2]. \end{aligned} \tag{18}$$

We have

$$\begin{aligned}\tau_a'(t) &= 1+\beta_a(b_a(t)-e_a(t))\\ &\geqslant 1+\beta_a b_a(t)-\beta_a\frac{B_a}{1+\beta_a B_a}\\ &= \beta_a b_a(t)+\frac{B_a}{1+\beta_a B_a},\end{aligned}$$

where the first inequality follows from Eq. 18. We have proved for $i=1,2$. Suppose that in i th interval$(i\geqslant 2)$, we have

$$e_a(t)\leqslant\frac{B_a\sum_{n=0}^{i-2}(\beta_a B_a)^n}{\sum_{n=0}^{i-1}(\beta_a B_a)^n},$$

$$\tau_a'(t)\geqslant\beta_a b_a(t)+\frac{1}{\sum_{n=0}^{i-1}(\beta_a B_a)^n}.$$

Considering the$(i+1)$st interval, we have

$$\begin{aligned}e_a(t) &= \frac{b_a(\tau_a^{-1}(t))}{\tau_a'(\tau_a^{-1}(t))}\\ &\leqslant\frac{b_a(\tau_a^{-1}(t))}{\beta_a b_a(\tau_a^{-1}(t))+1/\sum_{n=0}^{i-1}(\beta_a B_a)^n}\\ &\leqslant\frac{B_a\sum_{n=0}^{i-1}(\beta_a B_a)^n}{\sum_{n=0}^{i}(\beta_a B_a)^n}\end{aligned}$$

and

$$\begin{aligned}\tau_a'(t) &= 1+\beta_a(b_a(t)-e_a(t))\\ &= \beta_a b_a(t)+1-\beta_a\frac{B_a\sum_{n=0}^{i-1}(\beta_a B_a)^n}{\sum_{n=0}^{i}(\beta_a B_a)^n}\\ &= \beta_a b_a(t)+\frac{1}{\sum_{n=0}^{i}(\beta_a B_a)^n}.\end{aligned}$$

We obtain the desired result.

It is difficult to generalize Theorem 3. 2 to nonlinear arc traversal time functions without making additional assumptions on b_a and/or s_a. This is because the exit flow rate will exceed the upper bound B_a whenever the condition of Theorem 3. 1 is violated and s_a is nonlinear.

We now give an example involving a single-arc network where the FIFO condition does not hold. Let $b_a(t)=1$ for $t\in[0,1)$and $b_a(1)=0$. Let $s_a(v_a(t))=1+\beta_a v_a^2(t)$. We obtain $s_a(0)=1$ and, for $t\in[0,1)$: $s_a'(v_a(t))=2\beta_a v_a(t)$, $s_a'(v_a(0))=0$. Since

$$\begin{aligned}\tau_a'(T) &= 1+s_a'(v_a(t))v_a'(t)\\ &= 1+s_a'(v_a(t))[b_a(t)-e_a(t)],\end{aligned}$$

it follows that $\tau_a'(0)=1$. Now:

$$e_a(1)=b_a(t)/\tau_a'(0)=b_a(0)=1$$

$$v_a(1) = \int_0^1 b_a(y)\mathrm{d}y = 1$$

and we have

$$\begin{aligned}\tau_a'(1) &= 1 + s_a'(v_a(1)v_a'(1)) \\ &= 1 + 2\beta_a v_a(1)(b_a(1) - e_a(1)) \\ &= 1 - 2\beta_a v_a(1) \\ &< 0\end{aligned}$$

whenever $\beta_a > 1/2$, i. e. , the FIFO condition is violated at instant $t=1$ on arc a.

In Theorems 3. 1 and 3. 2, we implicitly assumed that s_a is only dependent on the arc volume $v_a(t)$ at instant t, and not by arc volumes at other instants, or by the instant t itself. To take into account the latter effect, we can consider the more general functional form $s_a(t, v_a(t))$ for the arc traversal time function. The arc FIFO condition will still hold in this case under conditions that jointly restraint (more severely) the functions b_a and s_a.

COROLLARY 3. 1 (Satisfaction of arc FIFO). *Under the assumptions of either Theorem* 3. 1 *or Theorem* 3. 2, *the arc FIFO condition holds.*

Proof. By Theorem 3. 1, $\tau_a'(t)$ is positive. This implies that $\tau_a(t')$ is larger than $\tau_a(t'')$ whenever $t' > t''$. The result follows from Eq. 3 and the definition of the arc FIFO condition.

Although the arc FIFO condition has been stated with respect to the arcs of the network, it is clear that it also holds with respect to the paths of the network. The path FIFO is defined as

path FIFO

$$t' > t'' \Rightarrow t' + S_k(t') > t'' + S_k(t'') \; \forall t', t'' \in [0, T], \forall k \in K. \tag{19}$$

COROLLARY 3. 2 (Satisfaction of path FIFO). *Under the assumptions of either Theorem* 3. 1 *or Theorem* 3. 2, *the path FIFO condition holds.*

We note that Theorems 3. 1 and 3. 2 both imply that the CDNLP formulated as Eqs. 3—11 with the nonnegativity constraints is solvable if the network G is acyclic or if the paths of K are arc-disjoined with $T' = T_a$ for all $a \in A$. The next theorem shows that this result holds for general networks as well.

THEOREM 3. 3 (Existence). *Let the conditions of either Theorem* 3. 1 *or* 3. 2 *hold and assume that the departure rate functions* h_k *are bounded from above by some positive number* B^k. *Then there exists a finite upper bound* B_a *such that if* $s_a'(v_a(t)) < 1/B_a$ *(nonlinear case) or* $s_a'(v_a(t)) = \beta_a > 0$ *(linear case), the CDNLP has the unique solution.*

Proof. We prove the theorem by increasing system time in a stepwise manner. First, set $B_a = \sum_{k \in K_a} B^k$ and $\alpha = \min\{s_a(0) : a \in A\}$ (this latter quantity is positive). For every arc a in A, b_a is well defined on the interval $[0, \alpha]$. By Theorem 3. 1 or 3. 2, the functions τ_a, v_a are well defined over the interval $[0, \alpha]$ and the functions e_{ka}, $k \in K^a$ are well defined over the interval $[\tau_a(0), \tau_a(\alpha)]$ for all arcs a in A such that $\tau_a(\alpha) \geqslant 2\alpha$. By (iv), of Theorem 3.1, we have $e_a(t) \leqslant B_a$. In the course of obtaining the bounded exit flow functions e_a for t in $[\tau_a(0), \tau(\alpha)]$, we obtain, as well, the function b_a over the interval $[0, 2\alpha]$ and updated bounds $B_a = \sum_{k \in K^a} B_{a_{\bar{k}}}$. Using these bounds and applying Theorem 3.1(or Theorem 3.2), we have that the CDNLP admits a unique solution τ_a, v_a on $[0, 2\alpha]$ and e_{ka} on $[\tau_a(0), \tau_a(2\alpha)]$, with $\tau_a(2\alpha) \geqslant 3\alpha$. Furthermore, e_a is bounded from above by B_a.

At the beginning of the nth step($n > 1$), we have fully determined b_a on $[0, n\alpha]$ for all a in A. Applying Theorem 3.1 or Theorem 3.2 with the updated bound B_a ensures that the CDNLP admits a unique solution τ_a, v_a on $[0, n\alpha]$ and e_{ka} on $[\tau_a(0), \tau_a(n\alpha)]$ with $\tau_a(n\alpha) \geqslant (n+1)\alpha$. Also, B_a is an upper bound for e_a. But, since the functions τ_a and s_a are continuous, the path travel times are also continuous and therefore bounded on any closed time interval. This implies that $T + S_k(T)$ is finite. Let $\overline{T} = \max\{T + S_k(T) : k \in K\}$. At any instant t larger that $\overline{T}$, all flow must have reached its destination,

Since $\overline{T}$ is finite, we have determined in at most $n = \lceil \overline{T}/\alpha \rceil$ steps the upper bounds B_a and the functions b_a over the entire system period.

Since $\tau_a(t)$ is strictly increasing for all $a \in A$, it is easy to see the following corollary.

COROLLARY 3.3. *Under the conditions of the Existence Theorem, the arc FIFO condition Eq. 4 and the nonnegativity constraints in the CDNLP are satisfied automatically.*

This implies that the CDNLP can be simplified.

4. A CONCEPTUAL SOLUTION METHOD

BEING CONSTRUCTIVE, the proof of Theorem 3.3 suggests a solution method for the CDNLP. In this section, we develop an efficient algorithm, which is valid under the sole assumption that the arc exit time functions be invertible. The key observation is that the functional forms of the entry and exit flow rate and exit time functions are only modified at a finite set of instants and that, given the inverse function τ_a^{-1}, all these functions are computable. The algorithm is indeed an event-driven simulation, where events occur at the critical instants, and is outlined below.

ALGORITHM DYNALOAD

1. INITIALIZATION

$i := (0)$

$T_0 := 0$

$\overline{A} := A$

for a in A **do**

  $l_a^+ := s_a(0)$

  $l_a^- := 0$

续表

```
endfor
2. MAIN LOOP
while T_i<T or Ā≠∅ do
  i := i+1
  T_i := min{l_a^+ : a∈A}
  A_i := arg min{l_a^+ : a∈A}
  for a in Ai do
    for k in K do
      construct b_ka over [l_a^-, l_a^+] using(7)
    endfor
    construct b_a over [l_a^-, l_a^+] using(8)
    construct v_a over [l_a^-, l_a^+] using(5)
    construct τ_a over [l_a^-, l_a^+] using(3)
    construct(τ_a)^-1 over [τ_a(l_a^-), τ_a(l_a^+)]
    for k in K do
      construct e_ka over [τ_a(l̄^a), τ_a(l̄a)] using(9)
    endfor
      update l_a^- = T_i and l_a^+ = τ_a(T_i)
    endfor
    Ā := A
    for a in A do
      if b_a≡0 over [T_{i-1}, T_i] then Ā := Ā-{a}
      endif
      endfor
    endwhile
```

THEOREM 4.1 *If the FIFO condition is satisfied, then algorithm DYNALOAD finds the unique solution of the CDNLP in a finite number of iterations.*

Proof. We know that, if, at any critical instant T_i, the arc entry flow rate functions b_a and the exit time functions τ_a are well defined for all $a\in A$, for all values of t in the time interval $[0, T_i]$, then $\tau_a^{-1}(t)$ and $e_{ka}(t)$ are well defined for all t in $[T_i, T_{i+1}]$, for all a in A_{i+1} by Theorems 3.1 or 3.2 where we set $T'=T_i$. Thus, from Eq. 7, it follows that b_a is well defined all $t\in[T_i, T_{i+1}]$ in A_{i+1}.

Now we show that the solution method will stop in a finite number of iterations. Let $m=|A|$ be the number of arcs of the network, $\alpha=\min\{s_a(0) : a\in A\}$, $H_k=\int_0^T h_k(t)\mathrm{d}t$ and $H_a=\sum_{p\in K^a} H_k$. We have $S_k(T)\leqslant \overline{S}_k(T)=\sum_{a\in k} s_a(H_a)$. Let the maximum system time be $T_{\max}=\max_{k\in K}\{T+\overline{S}_k(T)\}$. Then the CDNLP will be fully solved in at most $n=O((m/\alpha)T_{\max})$ iterations.

We notice that one step mentioned in the proof of Theorem 3.3 requires at most m iterations. In practice, it is difficult to estimate the value of B_a for each arc a. This value depends on the network structure, the path flow departure rates and the arc traversal time functions. However we can adjust these parameters by trial and error.

A nice feature of the algorithm is that, during the computation, one can monitor the properties of the solutions obtained so far. If the arc FIFO condition on any arc is violated during the computation, the algorithm can be stopped, having recognized that no feasible solution to the CDNLP can be found.

5. A NUMERICAL EXAMPLE

THE ALGORITHM PRESENTED in Section 5 can theoretically solve the CDNLP in a finite number of iterations, provided that the inverse functions τ_a^{-1} is available in closed form. Otherwise, it can be used to design discretized versions of the conceptual algorithm. Here, we outline one such version and save a full discussion of the various implementations for another paper. The main purpose of this section is to provide a numerical illustration that validates our approach to the CDNLP.

Let us subdivide each interval $[T_{i-1}, T_i]$ into p subintervals of equal lengths $\Delta_i = (T_i - T_{i-1})/p$, and set $t_{ij} = T_{i-1} + j\Delta_i, j = 1, \cdots, p$. We approximate τ_a^{-1} by the Lagrange polynomial of order p going through these $p+1$ points:

$$\tau_a^{-1}(t) = \sum_{m=0}^{p} t_{im} L_m(t) \quad t \in [\tau_a(T_i), \tau_a(T_{i+1})]$$

$$L_m(t) = \frac{\prod_{m \neq j} (t - \tau_a^{-1}(t_{ij}))}{\prod_{m \neq j} (\tau_a^{-1}(t_{im}) - \tau_a^{-1}(t_{ij}))} \quad m, j = 0, \cdots, p.$$

The functions b_{ak} are interpolated in a similar fashion.

TABLE I ***Network Data***

O-D Pair	Path
(a,i)	1:(1,2,6,10)
	2:(1,5,7,10)
	3:(1,5,9,12)
	4:(3,4,7,10)
	5:(3,4,9,12)
	6:(3,8,11,12)
(a,e)	7:(1,5)
	8:(3,4)
(e,i)	9:(7,10)
	10:(9,12)
(a,c)	11:(3,8)
(c,i)	12:(11,12)
(a,g)	13:(1,2)
(g,i)	14:(6,10)

The use of Lagrange polynomial preserves the continuous differentiability of τ_a^{-1} and one can easily write down its derivative $(\tau_a^{-1})'$. Although they could theoretically yield nonincreasing functions, this was not observed in our numerical experiments.

The network for the example is given in Fig. 1. It is composed of 9 nodes, 12 arcs, 7 O-D pairs, and 14 paths (see Table I). The departure time period is set to the interval [0, 5]. The path flow rate functions are defined to be the concave functions,

$$h_k(t) = \theta_k(5t - t^2) \quad k = 1, \cdots, 14$$

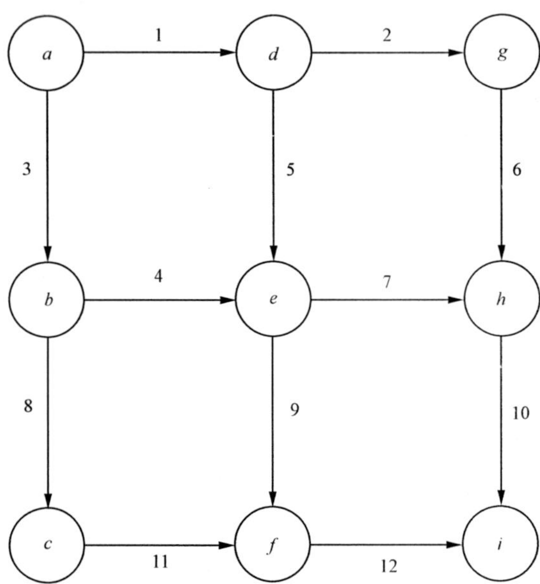

Fig. 1. The example network.

and the arc traversal time functions are defined by

$$s_a(v(t)) = \alpha_{a1} + \alpha_{a2} v_a(t) + \alpha_{a3} v_a^2(t).$$

The parameters θ_k, α_{a1}, α_{a2}, and α_{a3} are given in Table II. The degree p of the Lagrange polynomial is set to 3.

TABLE II ***Parameters for the Path Departure Rate and Arc Traversal Time Functions***

Path Departure Rate		Arc Traversal Time Functions			
k	θ_k	a	α_{a1}	α_{a2}	α_{a3}
1	0.10	1	2.0	0.2	0.013889
2	0.15	2	2.0	0.2	0.038889
3	0.18	3	1.5	0.2	0.011111
4	0.20	4	1.8	0.2	0.038889
5	0.10	5	1.5	0.2	0.033333
6	0.12	6	2.1	0.2	0.033333
7	0.20	7	1.7	0.2	0.038889

续表

Path Departure Rate		Arc Traversal Time Functions			
k	θ_k	a	α_{a1}	α_{a2}	α_{a3}
8	0.10	8	1.8	0.2	0.033333
9	0.15	9	2.0	0.2	0.038889
10	0.15	10	2.3	0.2	0.033333
11	0.12	11	2.2	0.2	0.038889
12	0.10	12	2.5	0.2	0.033333
13	0.10				
14	0.35				

The algorithm halted after 101 iterations. The computed path traversal times $S_k(t)$ are shown in Fig. 2, and the arc exit times $\tau_a(t)$ in Fig. 3. It can be checked that the FIFO condition is respected for every arc of the network. This means that even a coarse discretization could preserve the FIFO property of the model. Arc volumes and travel times are given in Figs. 4 and 5, respectively. We observe that all flow has reached its destination at instant 21 and that the departure period [0,5] differs significantly from the system period [0,21].

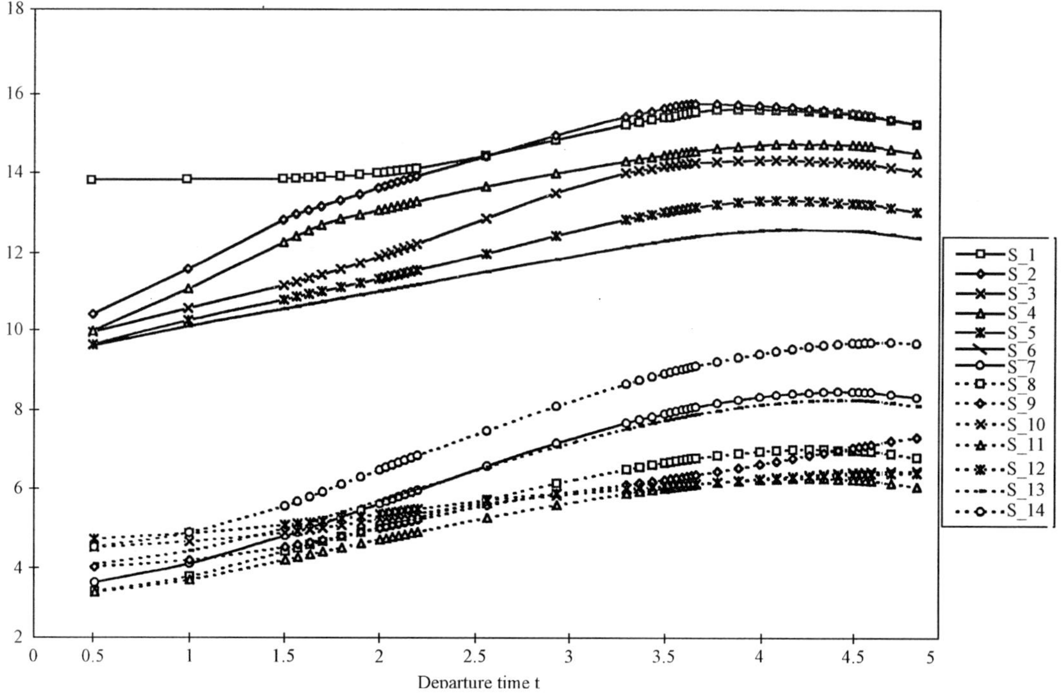

Fig. 2. Path traversal times.

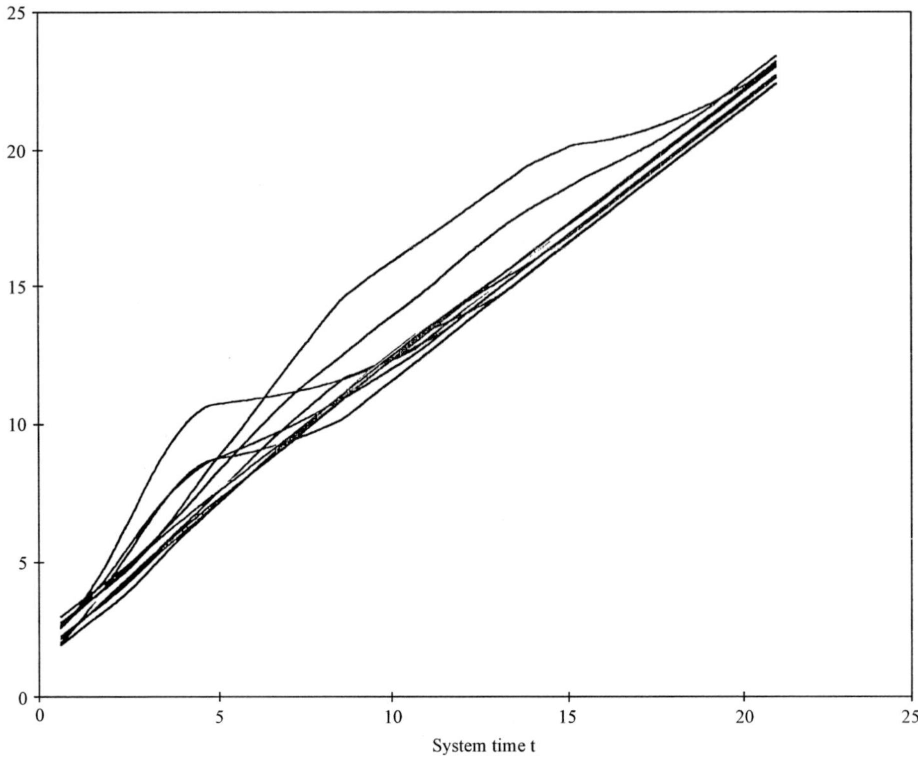

Fig. 3. Arc exit times.

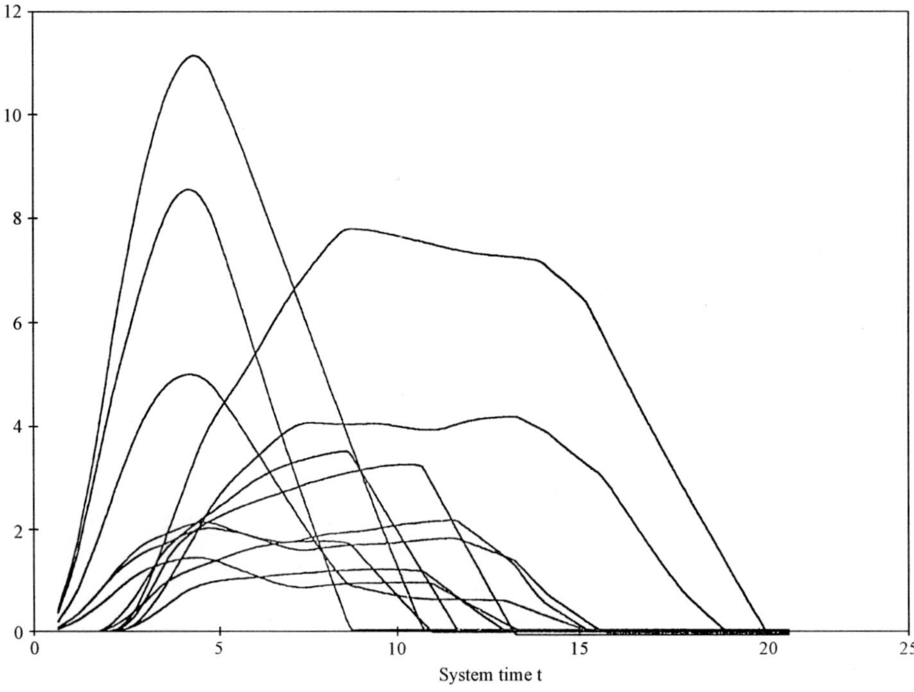

Fig. 4. Arc volumes.

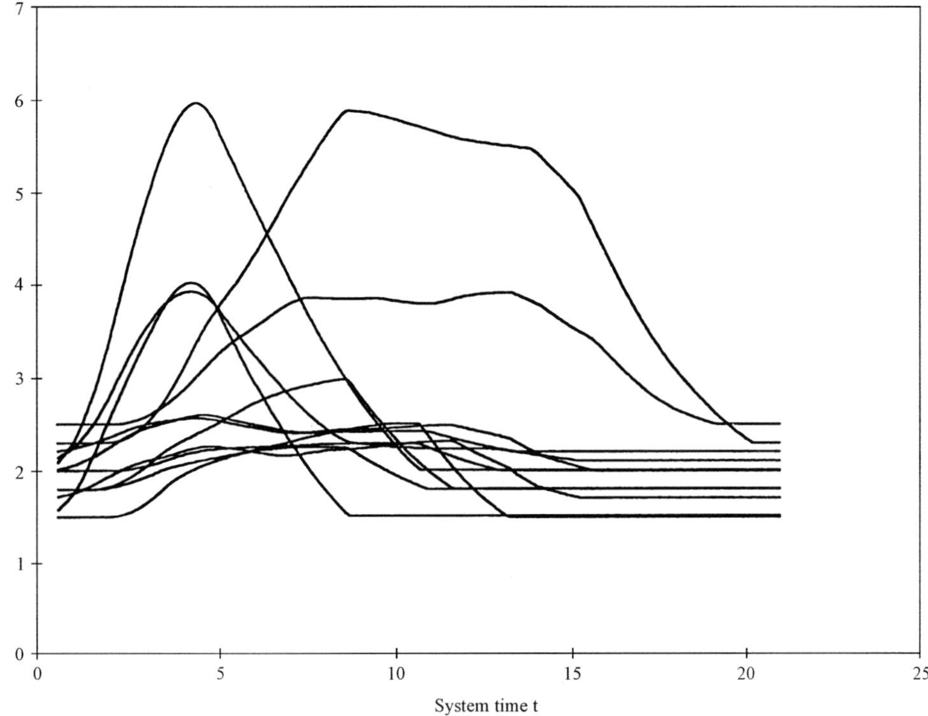

Fig. 5. Arc traversal times.

To see how flow propagates along a path, we extracted the information relevant to path 1 from Figs. 4 and 5. Figures 6 and 7 give a good indication of the flow dynamics along path 1.

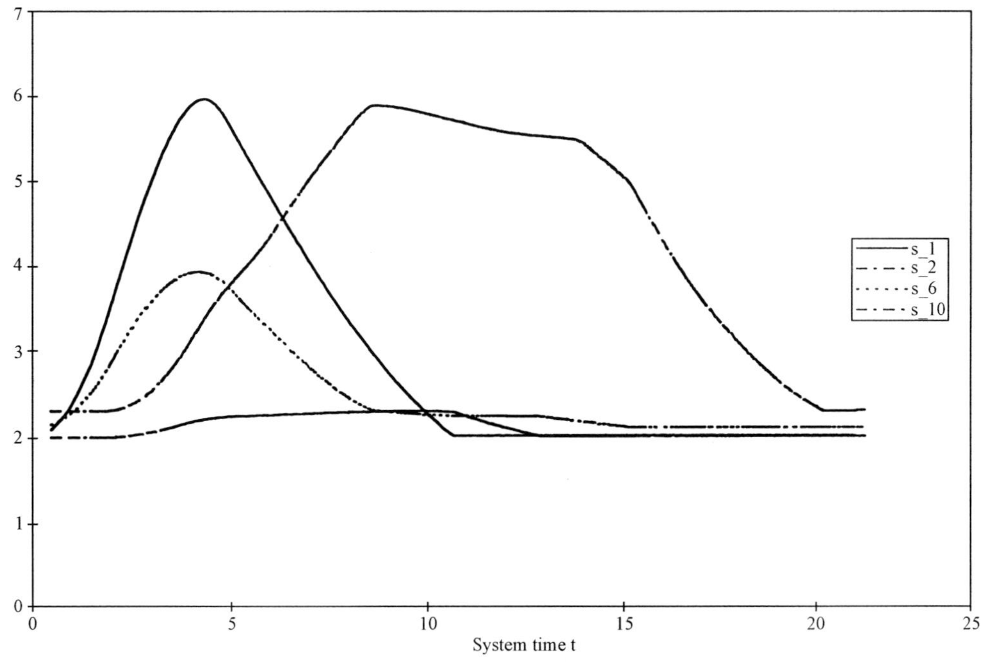

Fig. 6. Arc traversla times on path 1.

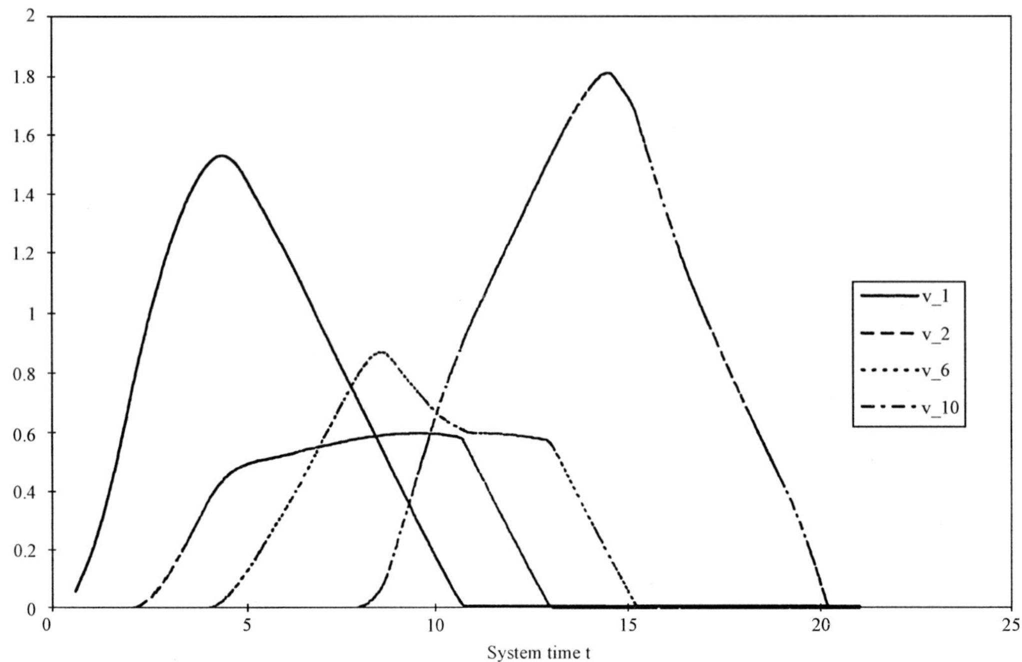

Fig. 7. Arc volumes contributed by path 1.

6. CONCLUSION

IN THIS PAPER, we have presented a formulation for the CDNLP and given sufficient conditions on the arc traversal time functions under which the FIFO condition is satisfied and the CDNLP admits a unique solution. An abstract solution method was proposed. Preliminary computational results show that a discretized version of this method performed very well on a small example. We believe that it could equally well solve the network loading problem on networks of realistic sizes(XU, WU and FLORIAN, 1998), and be embedded within a dynamic equilibrium algorithm(WU, FLORIAN and RUBIOARDANAZ, 1998).

There are many other topics for research in this area. From a theoretical point of view, it would be interesting to find weaker conditions on the traversal time functions that ensure the FIFO condition. Analytical properties of the dynamic loading operator, which maps a set of path flow departure rates to a set of path travel times, should be explored. From the numerical point of view, other discretization strategies need to be investigated, and the discretization error has to be evaluated.

APPENDIX

Proof of Lemma 3.1. The results follow from the fact that, if a function f is absolutely continuous on $[a, b]$, then it is differentiable almost everywhere on $[a, b]$. Therefore, if $a \leqslant x' < x'' \leqslant b$,

$$f(x'') - f(x') = \int_{x'}^{x''} f'(x)\mathrm{d}x > 0$$

since f' is positive(almost everywhere)on $[a, b]$. Let f^{-1} be the inverse function of f, which must exist and be strictly increasing on $[f(a), f(b)]$ since f is strictly increasing on $[a, b]$. The function f^{-1} is differentiable almost everywhere(see Royden(1988), Theorem 5.3), positive and increasing on $[f(a), f(b)]$.

Consider now the composite function$((f^{-1})' \circ f) \circ f'$. We can write, for any x in $[a, b]$,

$$\int_a^x (f^{-1})'(f(z))f'(z)\mathrm{d}z = \int_{f(a)}^{f(x)} (f^{-1})'(y)\mathrm{d}y = x - a.$$

Thus, $(f^{-1})'(f(x))f'(x) = 1$ holds almost everywhere on $[a, b]$, i. e.,

$$(f^{-1})'(x) = 1/f'(f^{-1}(x))$$

almost everywhere on $[a, b]$, as required.

ACKNOWLEDGMENTS

This research was supported in part by the National Science and Engineering Research Council of Canada (NSERC) individual operating grants OGP0157735, OGP0007406, A5789, Formation des Chercheurs et l'aide à la Recherche-Equipe and the NSERC strategic grant "Parallel software for IVHS." J. M. Rubio-Ardanaz implemented the discretized version of the algorithm. His support was greatly appreciated.

REFERENCES

V. ASTARITA, Flow Propagation Description in Dynamic Network Loading Models," in *Proceedings of 4th International Conference on Application of Advanced Technologies in Transportation Engineering*, 27—30, 1995.

V. ASTARITA, "A Continuous Time Link Model for Dynamic Network Loading Based on Travel Time Function," in *13th International Symposium on Transportation and Traffic Theory*, Lyon, France, 79—102, 1996.

E. CASCETTA AND G. E. CANTARELLA, "A Day-to-Day and Within-Day Dynamic Stochastic Assignment Model," *Transp. Res. A.* 25A, 277—291(1991).

C. F. DAGANZO, "The Cell Transmission Model I: A Dynamic Representation of Highway Traffic Consistent with the Hydrodynamic Theory," *Transp. Res. B.* 26B, 269—288(1994).

C. F. DAGANZO, "A Finite Difference Approximation of the Kinematic Wave Model of Traffic Flow," *Transp. Res. B.* 29B, 269—288(1995).

T. L. FRIESZ, J. LUQUE, R. L. TOBIN, AND B. W. WIE, "Dynamic Network Traffic Assignment Considered as a Continuous Time Optimal Control Problem," *Opns. Res.* 37, 893—901(1989).

T. L. FRIESZ, D. BERNSTEIN, T. E. SMITH, R. L. TOBIN, AND B. W. WEI, "A Variational Inequality Formulation of the Dynamic Network User Equilibrium Problem," *Opns. Res.* 41, 179—191(1993).

T. L. FRIESZ, D. BERNSTEIN, N. J. MEHTA, R. L. TOBIN, AND S. GANJALIZADEH, "Day to Day Dynamic Network Disequilibrium and Idealized Traveler Information Systems," *Opns. Res.* 42, 1120—

1136(1994).

B. G. HEYDECKER AND D. ADDISON,"An Exact Expression of Dynamic Equilibrium," 13*th International Symposium on Transportation and Traffic Theory*, 359—384, 1996.

R. JAYAKRISHNAN, H. S. MAHMASSANI, AND T. Y. HU, "An Evaluation Tool for Advanced Traffic Information and Management Systems in Urban Networks," *Transp. Res. C.* 3C, 129—147(1994).

M. J. LIGHTHILL AND J. B. WHITHAM, "On Kinematic Waves: II. A Theory of Traffic Flow in Long Crowded Roads," *Proceedings of the Royal Society* 229A, 317—345(1955).

A. NAGURNEY AND D. ZHANG, "Projected dynamical System in the Formulation, Stability Analysis, and Computation of Fixed Demand Traffic Network Equilibria." *Transp. Sci.*, 31, 147—158(1997).

B. RAN, D. E. BOYCE, AND L. J. LEBLANC, "A New Class of Instantaneous dynamic User-Optimal Traffic Assignment Models," *Opns. Res.* 41, 192—202(1993).

R. RAN AND BOYCE, D. E., dynamic Urban Transportation Network Models: Theory and Implications for Intelligent Vehicle-Highway System, *Lecture Notes in Economics and Mathematical Systems*, *Springer-Verlag*, New York, 1994.

H. L. ROYDEN, *Real Analysis* (3rd ed., Collier-Macmillan Limited, London, 1988.

N. B. TAYLOR, CONTRAM5: An Enhanced Traffic Assignment Model, Transportation Research Laboratory, Crowthorne, 1990.

M. J. SMITH, "The Existence, Uniqueness and Stability of Traffic Equilibria," *Transp. Res. B.* 13B, 295—304(1979).

M. J. SMITH, "A New dynamic Traffic Model and the Existence and Calculation of dynamic User Equilibria on Congested Capacity Constrained Road Network," *Transp. Res. B.* 27B, 49—63(1993).

M. J. SMITH AND M. B. WISTEN, "Lyapunov Methods for dynamic Equilibrium Traffic Assignment," *Proceedings of the 2nd Meeting of the EURO Working Group on Urban Traffic and Transportation*. INRETS, Paris, 233—245, 1994.

J. H. WU, "Dynamic Network Equilibrium Problem Formulated as an Infinite Variational Inequality Problem," *Proceedings of the 2nd Meeting of the EURO Working Group on Urban Traffic and Transportation*. INRETS, Paris, 247—268, 1994.

J. H. WU, Y. CHAN, AND M. FLORIAN, "The Continuous dynamic Network Loading Problem: A Mathematical Formulation and Solution Method," *Transp. Res.* 32B, 173—187(1998). ence LTD, Oxford, U. K. 51—66, 1998.

J. H. WU, M. FLORIAN, and R. M. RUBIO-ARDANAZ, "A Projection Algorithm for the Dynamic Network Equilibrium Problem," in *Proceedings of* 1998 *International Conference on Traffic and Transportation Studies*, Beijing, China. American Society of Civil Engineers, Reston, Va. 379—390, 1998.

Y. W. XU, J. H. WU, and M. FLORIAN, "An Efficient Algorithm for the Continuous Network Loading Problem: A DYNALOAD Implementation," in *Transportation Networks: Recent Methodological Advances*, Elsevier Sci

(Received, July 1996; revisions received; November 1997; accept-ed; October 1998)

Published in *Transportation Science*, 1999, 33(4)

Reliability Evaluation for Stochastic and Time-dependent Networks with Multiple Parking Facilities

Zhi-Chun Li William H. K. Lam S. C. Wong Hai-Jun Huang Dao-Li Zhu

Abstract This paper presents a fixed-point model for evaluating the reliability of stochastic and time-dependent networks with multiple parking facilities. The proposed model combines a supply model that simulates the time-dependent attributes of road and parking supplies and their variations with a demand model that simultaneously considers heterogeneous travelers' choices on departure time, route and parking location. In the proposed model, travelers are differentiated by their values of time, and parking locations are characterized by facility type. Schedule reliability and parking reliability are introduced as new performance indices for the evaluation of the level of service of a road network during time of day. A heuristic solution algorithm that uses a combination of the Monte Carlo simulation approach with the method of successive averages is proposed to estimate these two reliability measures. Numerical results show that the reliability performances of road networks are significantly influenced by the network congestion level and the capacities of road and parking facilities. The proposed model provides some new insights for assessing the impacts of various transport policies and infrastructure improvements at a strategic level.

Key words Stochastic and time-dependent network • Heterogeneous travelers • Reliability • Fixed-point model • Multiple parking facilities • Monte Carlo simulation

Nomenclature

(r,s)	an origin-destination(OD)pair
M	set of all user classes, $m\in M$
I_{rs}	set of all feasible parking locations $i, i\in I_{rs}$, between OD pair (r,s)
P_{ri}	set of all routes $p, p\in P_{ri}$, between origin r and parking location
$T^m_{ri,p}(t)$	actual route travel time of user class m departing from origin r at interval t to parking location i along route p
$c^m_a(t)$	actual travel time of user class m on link a during interval t
$\delta^{rim}_{apt}(k)$	indicator variable; it equals 1 if the flow on route p that departs from origin r at interval t to location i arrives at link a at interval k, and 0 otherwise
$y^m_i(t)$	actual parking cost of user class m entering parking location i at inter-

	val t
$\zeta_i^m(t)$	parking search time of user class m at location i at interval t
$z_i^m(t)$	parking charge of user class m entering location i at interval t, depending on the type of parking facility, parking duration and the arrival time at parking facility
$\tau_a^m(t)$	mean of the travel time of user class m on link a during interval t
$\sigma_a^m(t)$	standard deviation of the travel time of user class m on link a during interval t
$d_i^m(t)$	mean of the parking search time of user class m entering location i at interval t
$\sigma_i^m(t)$	standard deviation of the parking search time of user class m entering location i at interval t
ρ_a	parameter for measuring the degree of travel time variability on link a
λ_i	parameter for measuring the degree of parking search time variability at location i
v_a^m	parameter for measuring the perception variations of user class m on the expected travel time on link a
η_i^m	parameter for measuring the perception variations of user class m on the expected parking search time at location i
$\varphi_{rs,ip}^m(t)$	actual travel disutility of user class m departing from origin r at interval t and traveling to parking location i along route p and then walking to destination s
w_{is}^m	walking time of user class m from parking location i to destination s
$\Gamma(i,s)$	walking distance from location i to destination s
ω^m	average walking speed of user class m
$\Theta_s^m(t)$	schedule delay costs of early or late arrival at the destination s for user class m departing from origin r at interval t
$D_L^m(t)$	a dummy variable; it equals to 1 if user class m arrives at destination s late and 0 otherwise
α^m	value of time(VOT) of user class m
β^m	unit cost of arriving early at destination s for user class m
γ^m	unit cost of arriving late at destination s for user class m
θ^m	an additional discrete lateness penalty for user class m
$\mu_{rs,ip}^m(t)$	total cruise time of user class m departing at interval t for traversing OD pair(r,s) via parking location i and route p
$\Omega_{rs,ip}^m(t)$	expected travel disutility of user class m departing from origin r at interval t and traveling to location i along route p and then walking to destination s

$N(\cdot)$	density function of the normal distribution
$\Phi(\cdot)$	distribution function of the standard normal distribution
$u_a^m(k)$	inflow of user class m entering link a during interval k
$u_{apt}^{rim}(k)$	inflow to link a during interval k that departs from origin r alongroute p toward parking location i during interval t
$f_{rs,ip}^m(t)$	departure inflow of user class m on route p between OD pair(r,s) via parking location i during interval t
d_i^{0m}	free-flow parking access time of user class m at location i
C_i	capacity of parking location i
l^m	average parking duration of user class m
$h_i(t)$	hourly parking fee paid by travelers entering location i at interval t
FC_i	hourly frequency of searching for illegal parking at location i
F_i	imposed fine for illegal parking at location i
$U_{rs,ip}^m(t)$	cumulative arrivals of user class m at parking location i along route p between OD pair$(r,s)$by interval t
$U_{rs,i}^m(t)$	cumulative arrivals of user class m at parking location i between OD pair$(r,s)$by interval t
$U_i^m(t)$	total cumulative arrivals of user class m at parking location i by interval t
$V_{rs,ip}^m(t)$	cumulative departures of user class m from parking location i along route p between OD pair$(r,s)$by interval t
$V_{rs,i}^m(t)$	cumulative departures of user class m from parking location i between OD pair$(r,s)$by interval t
$V_i^m(t)$	total cumulative departures of user class m from parking location i by interval t
$D_i^m(t)$	parking accumulation at location i by user class m at interval t
$D_i(t)$	total parking accumulation at location i at interval t
$\hat{\Omega}_{rs,ip}^m(t)$	perceived expected travel disutility of user class m departing from origin r at interval t and traveling to location i along route p and then walking to destination s
$\xi_{rs,ip}^m(t)$	perception error of the expected travel disutility by user class m departing from origin r to destination s via parking location i and route p at interval t
$\xi_{ri,p}^m(t)$	perception error of the expected route travel time by user class m departing from origin r to parking location i along route p at interval t
$\xi_i^m(t)$	perception error of the expected parking search time by user class m at location i atinterval t
$\xi_a^m(t)$	perception error of the expected travel time on link a by user class m at interval t

$P_{rs,ip}^{m}(t)$ probability that the travelers in user class m between OD pair(r,s) choose interval t for departure, route p for travel and location i for parking

q_{rs}^{m} total demand of user class m between OD pair(r,s)within the study period $[0,T]$

$P_{rs,ip}^{m}(k_1,k_2|t)$ route based schedule reliability; probability of early or late arriving within a specified time threshold $[k_1,k_2]$for user class m departing from origin r at interval t to destination s via parking location i and route p

$\overline{\mu}_{rs,i}^{m}(t)$ weighted average of the travel times for all travelers in user class m departing at interval t from origin r to destination s via location i

$P_{rs,i}^{m}(k_1,k_2|t)$ OD schedule reliability; probability of early or late arriving withina a specified time threshold$[k_1,k_2]$for user class m departing at interval t from origin r to destination s via location i

$P_{i}^{m}(k_3|t)$ parking reliability; probability that the searching time for an available parking space for user class m at location i at interval t is less than the time threshold k_3

1 Introduction

Over the past several decades, significant progresses have been made in travel behavior modeling, which covers route choice models, departure time choice models, and simultaneous departure time and route choice models. Modeling parking behavior, which is an important component of travel behavior modeling, has recently received considerable attention(Thompson and Richardson 1998; Arnott and Rowse 1999; Lam et al. 1999; Wong et al. 2000; Hensher and King 2001; Dell'Orco et al. 2003; Hess and Polak 2004). More recently, Lam et al. (2006)proposed a time-dependent model for studying the joint choices of drivers on departure time, route, parking location and parking duration in a road network with multiple user classes and multiple parking facilities. Huang et al. (2005)further incorporated the activity choice of drivers into this model to study activity and travel scheduling behavior.

However, the existing studies on travel behavior modeling often ignore the variability or stochasticity of transport network itself, which introduces uncertainty to travelers such that they do not exactly know when they will arrive at their destinations. As a matter of fact, transport systems are complicated dynamic and stochastic systems. The dynamicity and stochasticity of transport systems result from various events, which range from irregular and random incidents, such as traffic accidents, vehicle breakdowns, road works, signal failures, adverse weather and earthquakes, to regular fluctuations in travel demand and capacity by time of day, day of week, and season(Taylor 1999; Bates et al. 2001; Chen et al. 2002a). Therefore, route travel time and parking search time for a given set of flows are stochastic(Tatineni et al. 1997). Furthermore, travelers may not have perfect information about a network, and thus they cannot perceive the travel time and parking search time accurately, which leads them to make the travel choice decisions stochastically. Therefore, Travelers' decisions are dependent on the attributes of road and parking facilities during a given time of day and their perceptions on the attributes of the facilities.

Mirchandani and Soroush(1987) first studied the time-stationary(static) transportation network equilibrium problem in a probabilistic and uncertain environment. Based on the studies of Ran and Boyce(1996) and Boyce et al. (1998), Liu et al. (2002) extended the work of Mirchandani and Soroush(1987) to a time-dependent problem. However, these studies mainly focused on route and/or departure time choices, and parking choice was ignored.

In fact, parking is closely tied to road usage, and every car has to park at the end of a trip. It is widely recognized that parking policy plays an important role in the planning and management of transportation systems in densely developed urban areas (Verhoef et al. 1995; Young et al. 1991; Wong et al. 2000; Lau et al. 2005). It has been observed that drivers spend a significant percentage of their total trip time searching for a parking space (Axhausen and Polak 1991), which significantly affects the level of traffic congestion and environmental quality within an urban area. Therefore, it is necessary to study the combination of travel and parking choices in a unified framework.

Reliability, as an important network performance measure, has recently become an increasingly hot issue because it is a requirement for sustained economic growth and the improvement of the quality of life (Iida and Bell 2003). As the value of time increases, people desire a reliable transport network with a high level of service, and are interested not only in saving travel time and parking search time, but also in reducing the variability of these factors (Chen et al. 2002b). Therefore, it is necessary to study the reliability performance of types of infrastructure under uncertainty.

The existing reliability studies can be classified into such categories as connectivity reliability (Bell and Iida 1997), travel time reliability (Du and Nicholson 1997; Bell et al. 1999; Clark and Watling 2005) and capacity reliability (Chen et al. 1999, 2000, 2002a, b; Yang et al. 2000; Sumalee and Kurauchi 2006). To evaluate the whole transport system more adequately, Lam and Tam (2003) first introduced parking reliability as the probability of reaching an available parking space at a given destination from an origin within a given searching time for parking. This performance index is particularly important when there is a shortage of parking spaces in urban areas. However, all of these definitions of reliability are limited to the static paradigm, and thus cannot evaluate the time-varying level of service of a road network at different times of day.

The motivation of this paper is to extend the previous studies on reliability of transport network in a static environment to a dynamic or time-dependent problem. A fixed-point model is proposed that combines a supply model that simulates the time-dependent attributes of road and parking supplies and their variations with a demand model that simultaneously considers the choices of heterogeneous travelers on departure time, route and parking location. Built on the uncertainty of a road network, schedule reliability and parking reliability in a time-dependent context are introduced as new network performance indices to evaluate the level of service of stochastic and time-dependent networks. We develop a heuristic solution algorithm that combines a Monte Carlo simulation approach with the method of successive averages to estimate these two reliability measures.

The remainder of this paper is organized as follows. In the next section, a supply model is described. Section 3 formulates a demand model. In Section 4, a supplydemand interaction model is presented as a fixed-point problem, and the existence and uniqueness of the model solution are discussed. A solution algorithm for the proposed model is developed in Section 5. In Section 6, two new reliability indices arepresented. Section7 provides a numerical experiment to illustrate the application of the proposed model. Finally, conclusions are drawn in Section 8 together with recommendations for future research.

2 Supply model

2.1 Actual travel disutility

Consider a transportation network $G=(N,A)$, where N is the set of all nodes and A is the set of all directed links. Let R denote the set of origin nodes, r represent a single origin node, $r\in R\subset N$, S denote the set of destination nodes, and s represent a single destination node, $s\in S\subset N$. Let M denote the set of all user classes and m denote a user class with a specific value of time(VOT). Let I_{rs} denote the set of all feasible parking locations i, $i\in I_{rs}$, between an origin-destination(OD)pair(r,s). Let P_{ri} be the set of all routes p, $p\in P_{ri}$, between origin r and parking location i. The whole study period $[0,T]$ is discretized into equal time intervals that are sequentially numbered $t\in T=\{0,1,\cdots,\overline{T}\}$, and δ is the interval length such that $\overline{T}\delta=T$. The value of T is sufficiently large to ensure that all travelers can complete their journeys within the study period $[0,T]$.

Let $T^m_{ri,p}(t)$ be the actual route travel time of user class m departing from origin r at interval t to parking location i along route p and $c^m_a(t)$ be the actual travel time of user class m on link a during interval t. The route travel time $T^m_{ri,p}(t)$ can be represented by the sum of all of the link travel times along this route(Chen and Hsueh 1998), i. e. ,

$$T^m_{ri,p}(t)=\sum_a\sum_{k\geqslant t}c^m_a(k)\delta^{rim}_{apt}(k),\ \forall r,i,p,m,t \tag{1}$$

where the indicator variable $\delta^{rim}_{apt}(k)$ equals 1 if the flow on route p that departs from origin r at interval t to parking location i arrives at link a at interval k, and 0 otherwise.

Let $y^m_i(t)$ be the actual parking cost of user class m entering parking location i at interval t, which consists of the searching time delay for finding an available parking space $\zeta^m_i(t)$ and the parking charge $z^m_i(t)$, i. e. ,

$$y_i^m(t) = \zeta_i^m(t) + z_i^m(t), \forall i, m, t \tag{2}$$

where the parking charge $z_i^m(t)$, defined in the next subsection, is measured in time unit by VOT of user class m.

We represent an variable and uncertain network environment by assuming that the actual link travel time of user class m, $c_a^m(t)$, on each link $a \in A$ and the actual parking search time at location i, $\zeta_i^m(t)$, during the time interval $t=0,1,\cdots,\overline{T}$ are stochastic, same as that assumed by Boyce et al. (1998). Similar to Yin and Lam(2002), we further assume that these variables follow independently the normal distribution, i. e., $c_a^m(t) \sim N(\tau_a^m(t), (\sigma_a^m(t))^2)$ and $\zeta_i^m(t) \sim N(d_i^m(t), (\sigma_i^m(t))^2)$, where $\tau_a^m(t)$ and $\sigma_a^m(t)$ are the mean and standard deviation of the travel time of user class m on link a during interval t, and $d_i^m(t)$ and $\sigma_i^m(t)$ are the mean and standard deviation of the parking search time of user class m entering parking location i at interval t. Previous studies have shown that the standard deviations of the link travel time and/or parking search time are the functions of their associated means(Richardson and Taylor 1978; Taylor 1982). In this paper, we assume that $\sigma_a^m(t)=\rho_a\tau_a^m(t)$ and $\sigma_i^m(t)=\lambda_i d_i^m(t)$, where the parameter pair(ρ_a, λ_i) is constant related to link and parking location, which reflects the degree of network variability or uncertainty. The larger the value of the pair(ρ_a, λ_i), the more unreliable the network, vice versa.

Define $\varphi_{rs,ip}^m(t)$ as the actual travel disutility of user class m departing from origin r at interval t and traveling to parking location i along route p and then walking to destination s. According to Small(1982) and Noland and Small(1995), we attribute the travel disutility to the in-vehicle travel time from origin to parking location, the parking cost at the parking location, the walking time from the parking location to the destination, an early or late schedule delay, and an additional lateness penalty term, which is formulated as

$$\varphi_{rs,ip}^m(t) = \alpha^m(T_{ri,p}^m(t) + y_i^m(t + T_{ri,p}^m(t)) + w_{is}^m) + \Theta_s^m(t) + \theta^m D_L^m(t), \forall r, s, i, p, m, t \tag{3}$$

where w_{is}^m is the walking time of user class m from location i to destination s, $\Theta_s^m(t)$ are the schedule delay costs of early or late arrival at the destination s for user class m departing from origin r at interval t, $D_L^m(t)$ is a dummy variable that is equal to 1 if user class m arrives at destination s late and 0 otherwise, α^m is the VOT of user class m, and θ^m is an additional discrete lateness penalty for user class m.

For ease of presentation, we define $\mu_{rs,ip}^m(t)$ as the *total cruise time* of user class m for traversing OD pair(r,s), which is the sum of the following components: the route travel time from origin r to location i via route p, the parking search time and the walking time, i. e.,

$$\mu_{rs,ip}^m(t) = T_{ri,p}^m(t) + \zeta_i^m(t + T_{ri,p}^m(t)) + w_{is}^m, \forall r, s, i, p, m, t \tag{4}$$

Therefore, the schedule delay costs of early or late arrival at destination s can be formulated as(Huang and Lam 2002)

$$\Theta_s^m(t) = \begin{cases} \beta^m(t_s^{m^*} - \Delta_s^m - t - \mu_{rs,ip}^m(t)), \text{if } t + \mu_{rs,ip}^m(t) < t_s^{m^*} - \Delta_s^m \\ \gamma^m(t + \mu_{rs,ip}^m(t) - t_s^{m^*} - \Delta_s^m), \text{if } t + \mu_{rs,ip}^m(t) > t_s^{m^*} + \Delta_s^m \\ 0, \text{otherwise} \end{cases} \tag{5}$$

where $[t_s^{m^*}-\Delta_s^m, t_s^{m^*}+\Delta_s^m]$ is the desired arrival time window of user class m at destination s without any schedule delay penalty, $t_s^{m^*}$ is the middle point of the time window, and $\beta^m(\gamma^m)$ is the unit cost of arriving early(late) at destination s for user class m. In accordance with empirical results(Small 1982), we assume that $0<\beta^m<\alpha^m<\gamma^m$.

2.2 Expected travel disutility

Let $\Omega_{rs,ip}^m(t)$ denote the expected value of the actual travel disutility $\varphi_{rs,ip}^m(t)$. According to Eq. (3), the expected travel disutility can be formulated as

$$\Omega_{rs,ip}^m(t)=\alpha^m(E[T_{ri,p}^m(t)]+E[y_i^m(t+T_{ri,p}^m(t))]+w_{is}^m)+E[\Theta_s^m(t)]+\theta^m E[D_L^m(t)] \tag{6}$$

In the following, we derive the components on the right hand side of Eq. (6). Note that the link travel time $c_a^m(t)$ is assumed to be a normally distributed random variable, the route travel time $T_{ri,p}^m(t)$ is then normally distributed with the mean below

$$E[T_{ri,p}^m(t)]=\sum_a\sum_{k\geqslant t}\tau_a^m(k)\delta_{apt}^{rim}(k),\ \forall r,i,p,m,t \tag{7}$$

Ignoring the uncertainties of parking charges, we formulate the expected parking cost as

$$E[y_i^m(t+T_{ri,p}^m(t))]=d_i^m(t+T_{ri,p}^m(t))+z_i^m(t),\ \forall i,m \tag{8}$$

Note that the total cruise time, $\mu_{rs,p}^m(t)$, between OD pair(r,s) in Eq. (4) is normally distributed, i. e., $\mu_{rs,ip}^m(t)\sim N(E[\mu_{rs,ip}^m(t)]),(\sigma(\mu_{rs,ip}^m(t))^2)$, where

$$E[\mu_{rs,ip}^m(t)]=\sum_a\sum_{k\geqslant t}\tau_a^m(k)\delta_{apt}^{rim}(k)+d_i^m(t+T_{rs,ip}^m(t))+w_{is}^m \tag{9}$$

$$\sigma(\mu_{rs,ip}^m(t))=\sqrt{\sum_a\sum_{k\geqslant t}(\sigma_a^m(k))^2\delta_{apt}^{ri}(k)+(\sigma_i^m(t))^2} \tag{10}$$

Therefore, the probability that travelers in user class m departing from the origin at interval t arrive late at destination s can be formulated as

$$\begin{aligned}E[D_L^m(t)]&=P\{t+\mu_{rs,ip}^m(t)>t_s^{m^*}+\Delta_s^m\}=\int_{t_s^{m^*}+\Delta_s^m-t}^{\infty}N(\xi)d\xi\\&=1-\Phi\left(\frac{t_s^{m^*}+\Delta_s^m-t-E[\mu_{rs,ip}^m(t)]}{\sigma(\mu_{rs,ip}^m(t))}\right)\end{aligned} \tag{11}$$

where $N(\cdot)$ denotes the density function of the normal distribution variable $\mu_{rs,ip}^m(t)$, and $\Phi(\cdot)$ denotes the distribution function of the standard normal distribution.

The remainder is to compute the expected value of the schedule delay cost $\Theta_s^m(t)$ given by Eq. (5). According to the probability theory, when $t+\mu_{rs,ip}^m(t)<t_s^{m^*}-\Delta_s^m$, the expected schedule delay cost of early arrival is given by

$$\begin{aligned}&\int_0^{t_s^{m^*}-\Delta_s^m-t_s}\beta_m(t_s^{m^*}-\Delta_s^m-t-\xi)N(\xi)d\xi\\&=\beta^m\frac{\sigma(\mu_{rs,ip}^m(t))}{\sqrt{2\pi}}\left(\exp\left(-\frac{1}{2}\left(\frac{t_s^{m^*}-\Delta_s^m-t-E[\mu_{rs,ip}^m(t)]}{\sigma(\mu_{rs,ip}^m(t))}\right)^2\right)-\exp\left(-\frac{1}{2}\left(-\frac{E[\mu_{rs,ip}^m(t)]}{\sigma(\mu_{rs,ip}^m(t))}\right)^2\right)\right)\\&\quad+\beta^m(t_s^{m^*}-\Delta_s^m-t-E[\mu_{rs,ip}^m(t)])\left(\Phi\left(\frac{t_s^{m^*}-\Delta_s^m-t-E[\mu_{rs,ip}^m(t)]}{\sigma(\mu_{rs,ip}^m(t))}\right)-\Phi\left(-\frac{E[\mu_{rs,ip}^m(t)]}{\sigma(\mu_{rs,ip}^m(t))}\right)\right)\end{aligned} \tag{12}$$

Similarly, when $t+\mu_{rs,ip}^{m}(t)>t_s^{m^*}+\Delta_s^m$, the expected schedule delay cost of late arrival is

$$\int_{t^{m^*}+\Delta_s^m-t_s}^{\infty}\gamma^m(t+\xi-t_s^{m^*}-\Delta_s^m)N(\xi)d\xi$$

$$=\gamma^m\frac{\sigma(\mu_{rs,ip}^m(t))}{\sqrt{2\pi}}\exp\left(-\frac{1}{2}\left(\frac{t_s^{m^*}+\Delta_s^m-t-E[\mu_{rs,ip}^m(t)]}{\sigma(\mu_{rs,ip}^m(t))}\right)^2\right)$$

$$+\gamma^m(t-t_s^{m^*}-\Delta_s^m+E[\mu_{rs,ip}^m(t)])\left(1-\Phi\left(\frac{t_s^{m^*}+\Delta_s^m-t-E[\mu_{rs,ip}^m(t)]}{\sigma(\mu_{rs,ip}^m(t))}\right)^2\right) \quad (13)$$

We now define the expected values of link and parking variables that are used in Eqs. (7)—(13). Thus far, there is no universally acceptable form of time-dependent or dynamic link travel time function. However, it is generally agreed that the link travel time function can be expressed in terms of the inflow, exit flow, and number of vehicles on the link. Chen and Hsueh(1998) further showed that the exit flow and the number of vehicles on a link can be represented by the inflow. Hence, the expected travel time of user class m on link a during interval k, $\tau_a^m(k)$, can be expressed as a function $\varphi(\cdot)$ of the inflows of all of the user classes that enter that link by interval k, i. e.,

$$\tau_a^m(k)=\varphi(u_a^m(1),u_a^m(2),\cdots,u_a^m(k)),\ \forall a,m,k \quad (14)$$

However, it should be pointed out that such travel time function may possibly violate the first-in-first-out(FIFO) discipline(Daganzo 1995). In order to satisfy the FIFO condition, it is required that the rate of change in link travel time for each link in the network is greater than-1(Ran and Boyce1996).

The inflow of the user class m that enters link a during interval k, $u_a^m(k)$, in Eq. (14) can be given by

$$u_a^m(k)=\sum_{ri}\sum_{p}\sum_{t}u_{apt}^{rim}(k),\ \forall a,m,k \quad (15)$$

where $u_{apt}^{rim}(k)$ is the inflow to link a during interval k that departs from origin r along route p toward parking location i during interval t. This link inflow can be represented by the route inflow through the use of the indicator variable $\delta_{apt}^{rim}(k)$, i. e.,

$$u_{apt}^{rim}(k)=\delta_{apt}^{rim}(k)\sum_{s}f_{rs,ip}^{m}(t),\ \forall a,p,i,r,m,t,k \quad (16)$$

where $f_{rs,ip}^m(t)$ is the departure inflow of user class m on route p between OD pair(r,s) via parking location i during interval t.

The expected searching time delay for an available parking space can be computed by the following Bureau of Public Roads(BPR) function(Lam et al. 1999, 2006)

$$d_t^m(t)=d_i^{0m}+0.31(D_i(t+T_{ri,p}^m(t))/C_i)^{4.03},\ \forall i,m,t \quad (17)$$

where d_i^{0m} is the free-flow parking access time, $D_i(t+T_{ri,pe}^m(t))$ is the parking accumulation or occupancy at location i when travelers in user class m departing at interval t from origin r arrive at location i at interval $t+T_{ri,p}^m(t)$, and C_i is the capacity of parking location i.

The parking charge is closely related to the types of parking facility. Specifically, the parking charges at off-street and charged on-street parking facilities are generally dependent on the average parking duration l^m of user class m and the arrival time interval $(t+T^m_{ri,p}(t))$ at the parking location i. The illegal parking may suffer a risk of being imposed a fine, which is dependent on the probability of being fined under the parking control policy and on the value of a fine. Considering these, we formulate the parking charge as(Bifulco 1993; Dell'Orco et al. 2003)

$$z_i^m(t)=\begin{cases}0 & \text{for free parking}\\ l^m\times h_i(t+T^m_{ri,p}(t))/\alpha^m,\ \forall i,m,t, & \text{for charged parking}\\ F_i\times\min(1,FC_i\times l^m)/\alpha^m & \text{for illegal parking}\end{cases}\tag{18}$$

where $h_i(t+T^m_{ri,p}(t))$ is the hourly parking fee at time interval $(t+T^m_{ri,p}(t))$, FC_i is the hourly frequency of searching for illegal parking at location i, F_i is the imposed fine for illegal parking, and the VOT parameter α^m converts the parking fee of user class m into an equivalent time.

The walking time depends on the distance between the parking space and the final destination and the walking speed of travelers(Bifulco 1993; Lam et al. 2006), and can be computed by

$$w_{is}^m=\frac{\Gamma(i,s)}{\omega^m},\ \forall i,s,m\tag{19}$$

where $\Gamma(i,s)$ is the walking distance from location i to destination s, and ω^m is the average walking speed of user class m(km/h).

We now derive the parking accumulation for location i that is used in Eq. (17). For a given route p between a given OD pair(r,s), the cumulative arrivals of user class m, $U^m_{rs,ip}(t)$, at parking location i along route p by the beginning of interval t is given by

$$U^m_{rs,ip}(t)=\sum_{\varsigma=1}^{t-1}\ \sum_{k:k+T^m_{ri,p}(k)=\varsigma} f^m_{rs,ip}(k),\ \forall r,s,i,p,m,t\tag{20}$$

Therefore, for a given OD pair(r,s), the cumulative arrivals, $U^m_{rs,ip}(t)$, of user class m at parking location i by interval t can be computed by

$$U^m_{rs,i}(t)=\sum_p U^m_{rs,ip}(t),\ \forall r,s,i,m,t\tag{21}$$

Hence, the total cumulative arrivals of user class m from all of the OD pairs, $U_i^m(t)$ at parking location i by interval t can be given by

$$U_i^m(t)=\sum_{rs} U^m_{rs,i}(t),\ \forall i,m,t\tag{22}$$

On the other hand, for a given OD pair(r,s) and user class m with parking duration l^m, travelers who arrive at parking location i along route p before interval$(t-l^m)$ will already have left parking location i by interval t, and thus the cumulative departures, $V^m_{rs,ip}(t)$, of user class m from parking location i along route p by the beginning of interval t is

$$V^m_{rs,ip}(t)=\sum_{\varsigma=1}^{t-1-l^m}\ \sum_{k:k+T^m_{ri,p}(k)=\varsigma} f^m_{rs,ip}(k),\ \forall r,s,i,p,m,t\tag{23}$$

Hence, for a given OD pair (r,s), the cumulative departures, $V_{rs,i}^{m}(t)$, of user class m from parking location i by interval t can be computed by

$$V_{rs,i}^{m}(t) = \sum_{p} V_{rs,ip}^{m}(t), \forall r,s,i,m,t \tag{24}$$

and thus, the total cumulative departures, $V_i^m(t)$, of user class m for all of the OD pairs from parking location i by interval t can then be computed by

$$V_i^m(t) = \sum_{rs} V_{rs,i}^{m}(t), \forall i,m,t \tag{25}$$

Therefore, the parking accumulation at location i by user class m at interval t, $D_i^m(t)$, which equals the cumulative arrivals, $U_i^m(t)$, by time t minus the cumulative departures, $V_i^m(t)$, by that time, can be represented as

$$D_i^m(t) = U_i^m(t) - V_i^m(t), \forall i,m,t \tag{26}$$

Hence, the total parking accumulation, $D_i(t)$, at location i by all user classes at interval t is

$$D_i(t) = \sum_{m} D_i^m(t), \forall i,t \tag{27}$$

3　Demand model

Due to the variability of network and inaccuracy of available information to travelers, the expected travel disutility that is perceived by travelers is a random variable. Denote $\hat{\Omega}_{rs,ip}^{m}(t)$ as the perceived expected travel disutility by user class m departing from origin r at interval t and traveling to parking location i along route p and then walking to destination s, which is formulated as the sum of systematic and random components, i. e.,

$$\hat{\Omega}_{rs,ip}^{m}(t) = \Omega_{rs,ip}^{m}(t) + \xi_{rs,ip}^{m}(t), \forall r,s,i,p,m,t \tag{28}$$

where the systematic component $\Omega_{rs,ip}^{m}(t)$ is given by Eq. (6) and $\xi_{rs,ip}^{m}(t)$ is the random error of perceiving the expected travel disutility by user class m departing from origin r to destination s at interval t, which includes the random perception error of the expected route travel time $\xi_{ri,p}^{m}(t)$ and that of the expected parking search time $\xi_i^m(t)$, i. e.,

$$\xi_{rs,ip}^{m}(t) = \alpha^m(\xi_{rs,p}^{m}(t) + \xi_i^m(t)), \forall r,s,i,p,m,t \tag{29}$$

where the VOT parameter α^m can convert the perception errors of user class m on the route travel time and the parking search time into travel disutility unit.

Up to now, we have introduced two types of random errors, one caused by the network's physical condition and another by the travelers' biased perception. Similar to Eq. (1), the perception error of the expected route travel time can be represented by the sum of all of the perception errors of the expected link travel times along this route, i. e.,

$$\xi_{rs,ip}^{m}(t) = \sum_{a} \sum_{k \geq t} \xi_a^m(k) \sigma_{apt}^{rim}(k), \forall r,s,i,p,m,t \tag{30}$$

where $\xi_a^m(k)$ is the perception error of user class m on the expected link travel time.

Suppose that travelers make choice decisions on departure time, route, and parking location in terms of the minimal perceived expected travel disutility, the probability that the travelers in user class m between OD pair(r,s)choose interval t for departure, route p for travel and location i for parking is then given by

$$P^{m}_{rs,ip}(t)=p\{\hat{\Omega}^{m}_{rs,ip}(t)<\hat{\Omega}^{m}_{rs,jp}(k)\mid\forall k\in T,j\in I_{rs},q\in P_{rs},\\ k\neq t,j\neq i,q\neq p\},\forall r,s,i,p,m,t \tag{31}$$

Clearly, $P^{m}_{rs,ip}(t)$ is dependent on the probability distributions of the random variables $\xi^{m}_{a}(t)$ and $\xi^{m}_{i}(t)$. Different hypotheses on the distributions of these two random variables lead to different choice models. As in Yin and Lam(2002), this paper assumes that $\xi^{m}_{a}(t)$and $\xi^{m}_{a}(t)$follow the normal distributions with zero means, i. e. , $\xi^{m}_{a}(t)\sim N(0;(v^{m}_{a}\tau^{m}_{a}(t))^{2})$and $\xi^{m}_{i}(t)\sim N(0,(\eta^{m}_{i}d^{m}_{i}(t))^{2})$, where the parameter pair $(v^{m}_{a},\eta^{m}_{i})$is constant related to user class, link and parking location, which measures the perception variations of the drivers in user class m on the expected link travel time and the expected parking search time, respectively. The two parameters also reflect the familiarity degree to traffic conditions by the drivers in user class m.

Therefore, the random component, $\xi^{m}_{rs,ip}(t)$, on the right hand side of Eq. (28)is also normally distributed. Thus, the model proposed in this paper is framed as a probit-based formulation. Hence, the distribution of the departure flows can be obtained with

$$f^{m}_{rs,ip}(t)=q^{m}_{rs}P^{m}_{rs,ip}(t),\forall r,s,i,p,m,t \tag{32}$$

where q^{m}_{rs} is the total demand of user class m between OD pair(r,s)during the whole study period$[0,T]$.

4 Fixed-point model for supply-demand equilibrium

Based on the discussions in previous sections, we now formally define the simultaneous departure time, route and parking location choice equilibrium conditions for a stochastic and time-dependent network as follows:

Definition 1 At equilibrium, for each OD pair and each user class, no traveler can improve his or her perceived expected travel disutility by unilaterally changing departure time, route or parking location.

Definition 1 is a generalization of stochastic dynamic user optimal route/departure time choice conditions in the literature, such as Chen and Feng(2000), Han(2003), Lo and Szeto(2004), and Lim and Heydecker(2005). Definition 1 means that at equilibrium the perceived expected travel disutilities of all of the used combinations of departure time, route and parking location are equal and minimal, and the perceived expected travel disutility of any unused combination of departure time, route and parking location is greater than or equal to the minimal perceived expected travel disutility.

It can be inferred from the demand model Eqs. (28)—(32)that the route in flow **f** is the function of the systematic component Ω, which is the function of the link travel time

$\boldsymbol{\tau}$ and the parking search time $\mathbf{d}$, which are in turn the function of route inflow $\mathbf{f}$ in terms of Eqs. (14)—(27). As a result, the supply-demand circular dependence induces the following fixed-point network equilibrium model:

$$\mathbf{f}^* = \mathbf{qP}(\boldsymbol{\Omega}(\mathbf{T}(\boldsymbol{\tau}(\mathbf{f}^*))), \mathbf{d}(\mathbf{f}^*)) \tag{33}$$

where the bolded symbols represent the vectors of corresponding variables.

Proposition 1 *A simultaneous departure time, route, and parking location choice equilibrium in a stochastic and time-dependent network is reached if and only if the fixed-point formulation Eq. (33) is satisfied.*

Equation(33) is a multi-class fixed-point problem with regard to route inflows, and therefore explicit route enumeration in both the model formulation and algorithm design are required. Some effectiv emethods have been developed to generate a set of feasible or efficient routes, in which only the routes that are most utilized are contained (Lim and Heydecker 2005). A comprehensive review of how to automatically generate the set of efficient routes on a medium-scale or even largescale network can be found in Li et al. (2007).

Note that all functions defined above are continuous with regard to route inflows. According to Brouwer's fixed-point theory, there is at least one feasible solution to the fixed-point problem Eq. (33). However, the route travel times are non-linear and non-convex due to the non-linearity and non-convexity of flow conservation constraint Eq. (16), and thus the fixed-point model Eq. (33) is non-convex. This implies that multiple local solutions may exist in the proposed model.

5 Solution algorithm

As indicated in the previous section, the fixed-point problem Eq. (33) is the result of the interaction between the supply and demand models. Its stationary solution can therefore be obtained by iteratively solving the supply model Eqs. (1)—(27) and demand model Eqs. (28)—(32), i. e.,

$$\mathbf{f}^{(1)} \rightarrow (\boldsymbol{\tau}^{(1)}, \mathbf{d}^{(1)}) \rightarrow \mathbf{f}^{(2)} \rightarrow (\boldsymbol{\tau}^{(2)}, \mathbf{d}^{(2)}) \rightarrow \cdots \rightarrow \mathbf{f}^* \tag{34}$$

Zhang et al. (2005) recently applied the iterative approach to solve a fixed-point problem for determining the stationary schedule choice of daily work activities and morning-evening commutes with bottleneck congestion. In this paper, the method of successive averages (MSA) algorithm is combined with the Monte Carlo simulation method to solve the fixed-point problem Eq. (33). The flowchart of the algorithm is given in Fig. 1, and the step-by-step procedure of the proposed solution algorithm is given as follows.

Step 1　Initialization: Choose an initial route inflow vector $\mathbf{f}^{(1)}$, and set $n=1$.

Step 2　Outer loop operation: Set sample number $\kappa=1$.

Step 3　Inner loop operation (stochastic network loading loop):

Step 3.1. Calculate the associated link inflow vector $\mathbf{u}^{(\kappa)}$, the expected link travel time $\boldsymbol{\tau}^{(\kappa)}$, and the expected parking search time $\mathbf{d}^{(\kappa)}$.

Step 3.2 Perform a Monte Carlo simulation by sampling the random link travel time, the parking search time, and the individual perception errors on them, then calculate the perceived expected travel disutility $\{\hat{\Omega}_{rs,ip}^{m(\kappa)}(t)\}$.

Step 3.3 Assign OD demand to the departure time, route and parking location combination with the minimal perceived expected travel disutility by performing all-or-nothing loading, and then yield the auxiliary route inflowe $\tilde{\mathbf{g}}^{(\kappa)}$.

Step 3.4 Update the route inflow pattern $\mathbf{g}^{(\kappa)}=[(\kappa-1)\mathbf{g}^{(\kappa-1)}+\tilde{\mathbf{g}}^{(\kappa)}]/\kappa$.

Step 3.5 If the sample number κ is less than a pre-specified sample size, then set $\kappa=\kappa+1$ and go to Step 3.1. Otherwise, set $\mathbf{g}^{(n)}=\mathbf{g}^{(\kappa)}$ and go to Step 4.

Step 4 Update: Update the route inflow pattern $\mathbf{f}^{(n+1)}=\mathbf{f}^{(n)}+(\mathbf{g}^{(n)}-\mathbf{f}_n^{(n)}/)$.

Step 5 Convergence check: If the relative gap $G=\|\mathbf{f}^{(n+1)}-\mathbf{f}^{(n)}\|/\|\mathbf{f}^{n}\|$ is smaller than a pre-specified tolerance, then stop. Otherwise, set $n=n+1$ and go to Step2.

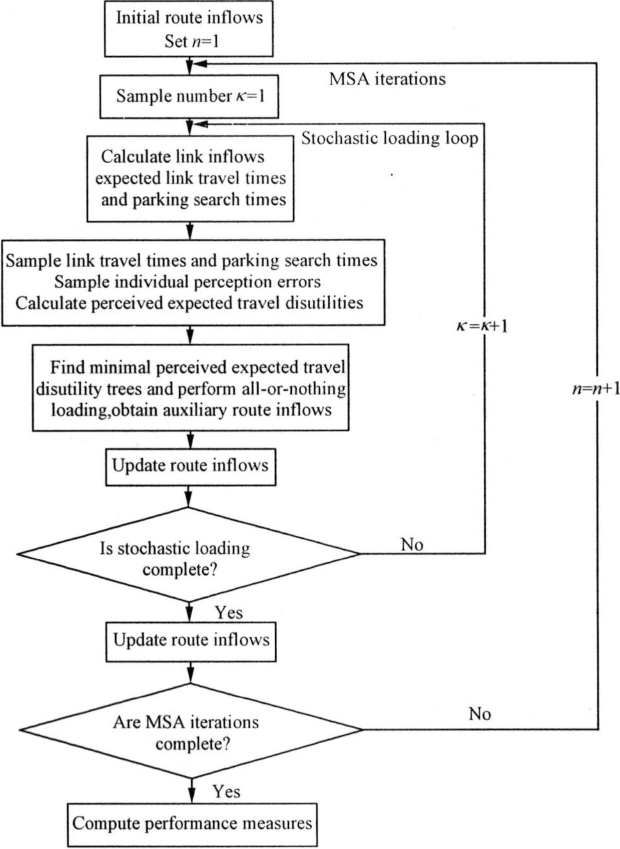

Fig. 1 Flowchart of the proposed algorithm

In Step 1, the initial route inflows can be set to zero, which signifies an empty network. In Step 3, each stochastic network loading in the inner loop generates a new minimum-disutility tree. Therefore, the total number of minimum-disutility trees that are generated in the implementation of the solution algorithm is potentially equal to the number of stochastic network loadings in the inner loop multiplied by the number of iterations that are performed for the MSA in the outer loop. The CPU time that is required for the proposed algorithm is mainly dominated by Step 3, because Monte Carlo simulation is performed in this step.

6 Measures of reliability

As stated in the introduction section, the existing studies regarding transport network reliability have been confined to the static environment, and thus cannot evaluate the time-varying level of service of transport facilities at different times of day. In the following, schedule reliability and parking reliability in a time-dependent context are introduced to assess the level of service of transport facilities during the time of day.

Definition 2 Schedule reliability is defined as the probability that a traveler between a given OD pair departing at a certain time interval arrives at destination on time or within a time threshold early or late.

We introduce two indices for measuring the schedule reliability, namely the route based index and OD based index. The former is defined as the probability that the travel time of a given route between an OD pair at a certain departure time interval is within a time threshold, whereas the latter is defined as the probability that the weighted travel time for a given OD pair at a certain departure time interval is within an acceptable level of service. The OD based schedule reliability uses all of the relevant routes that are used by travelers to determine an aggregate measure for the level of service between a given OD pair. The two schedule reliabilities are basically a dynamic or time-dependent generalization of the route and OD travel time reliabilities in a static environment (Chen et al. 2002b).

Let $P_{rs,ip}^{m}(k_1, k_2 \mid t)$ denote the schedule reliability of early arriving within a specified time threshold $[k_1, k_2]$ for travelers in user class m departing from origin r at interval t to destination s via parking location i and route p. It can mathematically be represented as

$$P_{rs,ip}^{m}(k_1, k_2 \mid t) = P\{k_1 < t_s^{m^*} - \Delta_s^m - t - \mu_{rs,ip}^m(t) < k_2\}$$

$$= \Phi\left(\frac{t_s^{m^*} - \Delta_s^m - k_1 - t - E[\mu_{rs,ip}^m(t)]}{\sigma(\mu_{rs,ip}^m(t))}\right) - \Phi\left(\frac{t_s^{m^*} - \Delta_s^m - k_2 - t - E[\mu_{rs,ip}^m(t)]}{\sigma(\mu_{rs,ip}^m(t))}\right) \quad (35)$$

Similarly, the schedule reliability of late arriving within a specified time threshold $[k_1, k_2]$ for travelers in user class m departing from r at interval t to s via parking location i and route p can be expressed by

$$P_{rs,ip}^{m}(k_1, k_2 \mid t) = P\{k_1 < t + \mu_{rs,ip}^m(t) - t_s^{m^*} - \Delta_s^m < k_2\}$$

$$= \Phi\left(\frac{t_s^{m^*} + \Delta_s^m + k_2 - t - E[\mu_{rs,ip}^m(t)]}{\sigma(\mu_{rs,ip}^m(t))}\right) - \Phi\left(\frac{t_s^{m^*} + \Delta_s^m + k_1 - t - E[\mu_{rs,ip}^m(t)]}{\sigma(\mu_{rs,ip}^m(t))}\right) \quad (36)$$

In addition, the probability of punctually arriving within the time window $[t_s^{m^*} - \Delta_s^m, t_s^{m^*} + \Delta_s^m]$ can be computed by

$$P_{rs,ip}^m(t_s^{m^*} - \Delta_s^m, t_s^{m^*} + \Delta_s^m / t\}$$

$$= \Phi\left(\frac{t_s^{m^*} + \Delta_s^m - t - E[\mu_{rs,ip}^m(t)]}{\sigma(\mu_{rs,ip}^m(t))}\right) - \Phi\left(\frac{t_s^{m^*} + \Delta_s^m - t - E[\mu_{rs,ip}^m(t)]}{\sigma(\mu_{rs,ip}^m(t))}\right) \quad (37)$$

We now define the OD based schedule reliability. Let $\overline{\mu}_{rs,i}^m(t)$ be the weighted average of the travel times for user class m departing from origin r at interval t to destination s via parking location i, i. e.,

$$\overline{\mu}_{rs,i}^m(t) = \sum_{p \in P_{ri}} f_{rs,ip}^m(t)\mu_{rs,ip}^m(t) \Big/ \sum_{p \in P_{ri}} f_{rs,ip}^m(t), \ \forall r,s,i,m,t \quad (38)$$

The numerator and denominator on the right hand side of Eq. (38) are, respectively, the total travel time and total demand of all travelers in user class m departing from origin r at interval t to destination s via parking location i. Eq. (38) can further rewritten as

$$\overline{\mu}_{rs,i}^m(t) = \sum_{p \in P_{ri}} \left(f_{rs,ip}^m(t) \Big/ \sum_{p \in P_{ri}} f_{rs,ip}^m(t)\right)\mu_{rs,ip}^m(t), \ \forall r,s,i,m,t \quad (39)$$

The route inflow, $f_{rs,ip}^m(t)$, in Eqs. (38) and (39) can be determined by Eq. (32). As $\mu_{rs,ip}^m(t)$ is normally distributed, $\overline{\mu}_{rs,i}^m(t)$ is also normally distributed with the following mean and standard deviation,

$$E[\overline{\mu}_{rs,i}^m(t)] = \sum_{p \in P_{ri}} \left(f_{rs,ip}^m(t) \Big/ \sum_{p \in P_{ri}} f_{rs,ip}^m(t)\right) E[\mu_{rs,ip}^m(t)], \ \forall r,s,i,m,t \quad (40)$$

$$\sigma[\overline{\mu}_{rs,i}^m(t)] = \sqrt{\sum_{p \in P_{ri}} \left(f_{rs,ip}^m(t) \Big/ \sum_{p \in P_{ri}} f_{rs,ip}^m(t)\right)(\sigma(\mu_{rs,ip}^m(t)))^2}, \ \forall r,s,i,m,t \quad (41)$$

Consequently, we can easily compute the OD schedule reliability, $P_{rs,i}^m(k_1, k_2 \mid t)$, of early arrival, late arrival, or punctually arriving within a specified time threshold $[k_1, k_2]$. This can be achieved by substituting $\overline{\mu}_{rs,i}^m(t)$, $E(\overline{\mu}_{rs,i}^m(t))$ and $\sigma(\overline{\mu}_{rs,i}^m(t))$ for $\overline{\mu}_{rs,ip}^m(t)$, E $(\mu_{rs,ip}^m(t))$ and $\sigma(\overline{\mu}_{rs,ip}^m(t))$ that appear in Eqs. (35), (36) and (37).

It should be pointed out that travelers are more concerned about the route based schedule reliability, whereas traffic managers and planners prefer to use the OD based schedule reliability as a proxy to evaluate the performance of road networks (Chen et al. 2002a, b).

Definition 3 Parking reliability is defined as the probability that a traveler can find an available parking space at a given destination at a certain time interval within an acceptable tim ethreshold.

This performance index is particularly important when there is a shortage of parking spaces in urban areas, and can be used to evaluate the level of service of a parking facility at different times of day. It can be mathematically formulated as.

$$P_i^m(k_3 \mid t) = P(\zeta_i^m(t) \leqslant k_3) = \Phi\left(\frac{k_3 - d_i^m(t)}{\sigma_i^m(t)}\right) \tag{42}$$

Fig. 2 Difference in specificati on of time threshold: (a) Schedule reliability; (b) Parking reliability

where $P(\zeta_i^m(t) \leqslant k_3)$ represents the probability that the searching time delay, $\zeta_i^m(t)$, for an available parking space at location i during interval t is less than the time threshold k_3.

According to the definitions of schedule reliability and parking reliability, there exists a significant difference in the specifications of their time thresholds. Figure 2(a) and (b) are used to illustrate this difference. In Fig. 2(a), $[-k_1, -k_2]$ denotes the time threshold of schedule reliability for early arrival from k_2 to k_1 time units, $[k_1, k_2]$ denotes the time threshold of schedule reliability for late arrival from k_1 to k_2 time units, and 0 denotes the time window for non-penalty (or on-time) arrival. However, the time threshold k_3 in the definition of parking reliability means that the searching time for an available parking space is within the range $[0, k_3]$, as shown in Fig. 2(b).

With different time thresholds, the schedule reliability and parking reliability introduced above can reflect the differences of the network's service levels during different time intervals of a day. This cannot be achieved in the static paradigm that only studies the issues of one interval.

7 Numerical experiments

In this section, a numerical example is employed to illustrate the model and algorithm that are proposed in this paper, and to investigate the sensitivity of reliability measures to network congestion level and infrastructure improvements, such as the capacity expansion of road links and parking facilities.

7.1 Experiment settings

The test network is shown in Fig. 3 with 2 OD pairs (1—12 and 6—12), 12 road nodes, 17 road links, and three types of parking facilities, namely A and B for off-street parking, C for on-street metered parking and D for illegal on-street parking. For brevity, it is assumed that locations A and B have the same parking characteristics. The free-flow parking access times are 0.1h and the parking capacities are 1,300 vehicles for locations A and B, and the free-flow parking access time is 0.05h and the parking capacity is 400 vehicles for location C. The average free-flow access time for illegal on-street parking is assumed to be 0.02h. The average walking distances from locations A, B, C to the destination are 1.0, 1.0, 0.5km, respectively, and 0.2km for the illegal parking. The uniform hourly parking charges for locations A, B and C are \$2.5, \$2.5 and \$0.5, respectively.

The fine due to illegal parking and hourly frequency of searching illegal parking are \$15 and 0.2, respectively. The study period runs from 06:00 to 17:00 and is divided into 66 time intervals with 10 min each. For each time interval, the following BPR-type link travel time function is a dopted:

$$\tau_a(t) = \tau_a^0(1.0 + 0.15 \times (u_a(t)/C_a)^4), \forall a, t \tag{43}$$

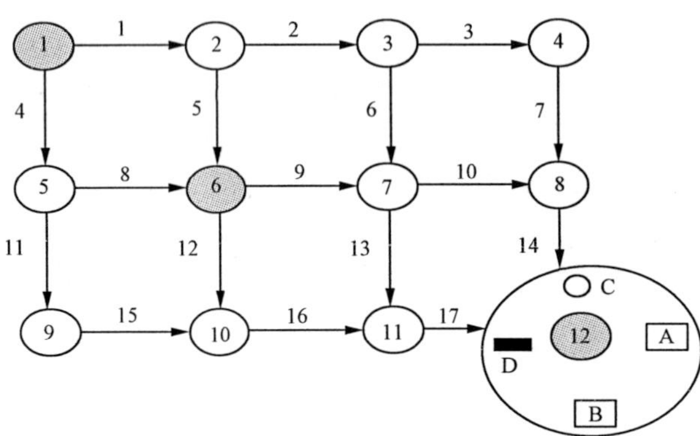

Fig. 3 The test network

where τ_a^0 and C_a are the free-flowt ravel time and the capacity of link a, respectively, and $u_a(t) = \sum_m u_a^m(t)$. The parameters of all of the link travel time functions are given in Table 1.

All of the travelers are grouped into two user classes: One class contains non-commuters who go in for non-work activities with lower VOT, and another class covers commuters who traverse for working purposes with higher VOT. The average parking durations of non-commuters and commuters are assumed to be 1 and 4 h, respectively. Hereinafter, for convenience we employ the superscript "c" to denote commuters and "nc" to denote non-commuters.

The parameters in Eqs. (3) and (5) are: $\alpha^c = 6.4$ (\$/h), $\beta^c = 3.9$ (\$/h), $\gamma^c = 15.21$ (\$/h), $\theta^c = 0.58$ (\$), $t^{c^*} = 9.0$ (h) and $\Delta^{c^*} = 0.17$ (h) for commuters; $\alpha^{nc} = 3.0$ (\$/h), $\beta^{nc} = 2.0$ (\$/h), $\gamma^{nc} = 8.0$ (\$/h), $\theta^{nc} = 0.2$ (\$), $t^{nc^*} = 14.0$ (h) and $\Delta^{nc^*} = 0.33$ (h) for non-commuters. The total demand of commuters are $q_{1,12}^c = 1600$ (veh) and $q_{6,12}^c = 800$ (veh) for OD pairs (1, 12) and (6, 12), respectively. The total demand of non-commuters are $q_{1,12}^{nc} = 800$ (veh) and $q_{6,12}^{nc} = 400$ (veh) for OD pairs (1, 12) and (6, 12), respectively. The average walking speed in Eq. (19) is $\omega^c = \omega^{nc} = 5.0$ (km/h). The parameter pair measuring network uncertainty is $(\rho_a, \lambda_i) = (0.5, 0.3)$ for all links and for all parking locations. The parameter pairs measuring perception errors of commuters and non-commuters are: $(v_a^c, \eta_i^c) = (0.2, 0.1)$ and $(v_a^{nc}, \eta_i^{nc}) = (0.3, 0.2)$ for all links and for all parking locations, respectively. The sample number in Monte Carlo simulation is $\kappa = 2{,}000$.

Table 1 Parameters of the link travel time functions

Link no.	τ_a^0(h)	C_a(veh/h)	Link no.	τ_a^0(h)	C_a(veh/h)
1	0.20	1,500	10	0.10	1,500
2	0.15	1,000	11	0.15	800
3	0.10	800	12	0.10	1,500
4	0.15	1,500	13	0.15	1,500
5	0.15	800	14	0.20	2,000
6	0.15	800	15	0.10	1,000
7	0.10	1,000	16	0.20	1,500
8	0.20	1,000	17	0.20	2,000
9	0.20	1,500			

7.2 Experiment results and analyses

The proposed solution algorithm was coded in programming language C and run on a DELL INSPIRON/510 m computer. Figure 4 shows the relative gap G against the number of outer-loop iterations in the MSA algorithm. The relative gap reaches 0.0001 after 2,000 iterations. Hence, a satisfactory equilibrium solution is achieved. However, it requires about 4,370 s of CPU time because of the need of computing the Monte Carlo simulation in each of the MSA iterations.

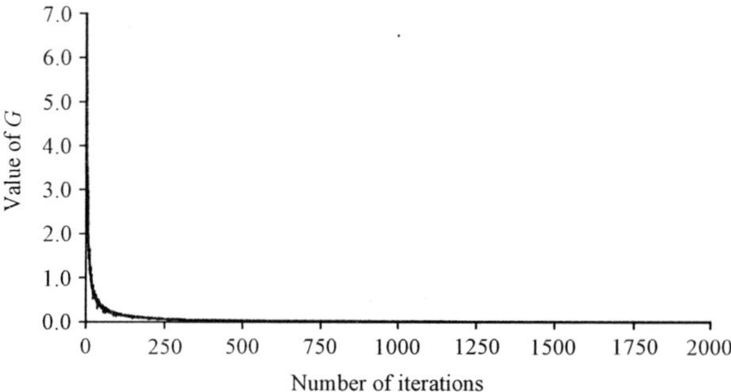

Fig. 4 Convergence of the proposed solution algorithm

Figure 5(a)and(b)show the effect of the network congestion level on schedule reliability via parking location A at different departure intervals for OD pairs(1,12)and(6,12),respectively. Only off-street location A is chosen for illustration because locations A and B have identical parking characteristics, and thus the same reliability performances. As the OD travel demands are doubled, the schedule reliability curves for departure interval 07:50—08:00 for OD pairs(1,12)and that for 08:10—08:20 for OD pair(6,12) basically remain unchanged. However, the schedule reliability curves for other intervals for these two OD pairs move backwards, which implies that the probabilities of early, on-time and late arrivals are shifted to those of on-time, late and very late arrivals, respectively. Specifically, for OD pair(1,12) and for departure interval 07:40—07:50, the probability of early arrival decreases by about 55% from 65 to 10%, and is basically translated into the probability of on-time arrival; for departure interval 08:00—08:10, the probability of on-time arrival decreases by about 60%, which leads to an increase of about 55% in the probability of arriving 10—20 min late. Similar phenomena are also observed for OD pair(6,12) that is shown in Fig. 5(b), but with a different magnitude of change.

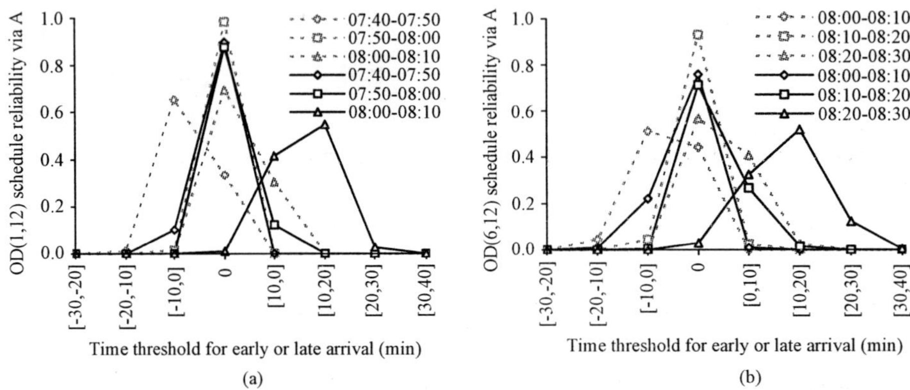

Fig. 5 Schedule reliability via location A at different departure intervals and different congestion levels(*solid lines* denote the base demand level and *dotted lines* denote half of the base demand level): (a) OD pair(1,12); (b) OD pair(6,12)

These interesting phenomena can be explained as follows. When the OD travel demands are doubled, the congestion level in the road network increases dramatically. As a result, the route travel time and parking search time for a journey increase, and thus the degree of network uncertainty increases. Accordingly, as the network congestion level increases, the departure interval with a large probability of arriving early becomes that with a large probability of on-time arrival; the departure interval with a large probability of on-time arrival becomes that with a large probability of arriving late. Furthermore, the increase in network congestion also forces the travelers to depart earlier to reduce the late-arrival penalty. As shown in Fig. 6(a), the peak of departure for commuters changes from 07:50—08:00 to 07:40—07:50 for OD pair(1,12) and from 08:10—08:20 to 08:00—08:10 for OD pair(6,12). For non-commuters, this peak moves from12:50—13:00 to 12:40—12:50 for OD pair(1,12) and from 13:10—13:20 to 13:00—13:10 for OD pair(6,12), as depicted in Fig. 6(b). It is also observed that the peak of departure for commuters or non-commuters between OD pair(1,12) occurs about 20 min earlier than that between OD pair(6,12). This is because the travel distance of travelers for OD pair (1,12) is longer than that for OD pair(6,12).

Figure 7(a) and (b) plot the curves of parking accumulation at off-street location A and on-street location C by time of day under the different demand levels. It can be ob-

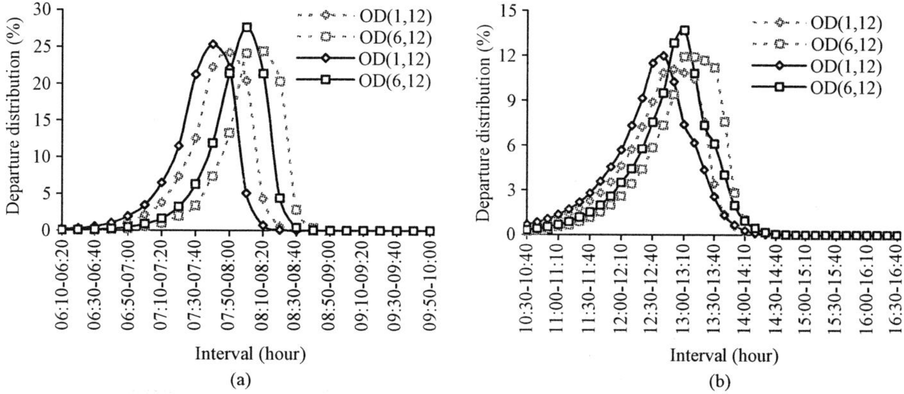

Fig. 6 Departure distribution under different congestion levels(*solid lines* denote the base demand level and *dotted lines* denote half of the base demand level):(a) Commuters;(b) Non-commuters

served that the peak of parking accumulation at location A occurs at 09:10 regardless of network congestion level. This is because this time(09:10)is the latest work start time, beyond which commuters will incur a large penalty. Therefore, to avoid the penalty, commuters have to arrive at their workplace before 09:10. Moreover, when the travel demand of non-commuters is doubled, oversaturation occurs during interval 13:40—14:10 at location C, because non-commuters prefer to park their cars at the on-street parking location regardless of congestion level. Figure 7(a)also shows that a few non-commuters choose to park at off-street parking location A as a result of the tradeoff between the high parking congestion at location C and low parking charges at location A($2.5/h). Moreover, the higher the network congestion level, the greater the demand of non-commuters who choose to park at location A. Figure 7(b)indicates that some risk-prone non-commuters will park their cars illegally on the kerbside at the risk of being fined. In particular, the peak number of illegal parking vehicles is increased by a factor of 2.5 when the demand level is doubled.

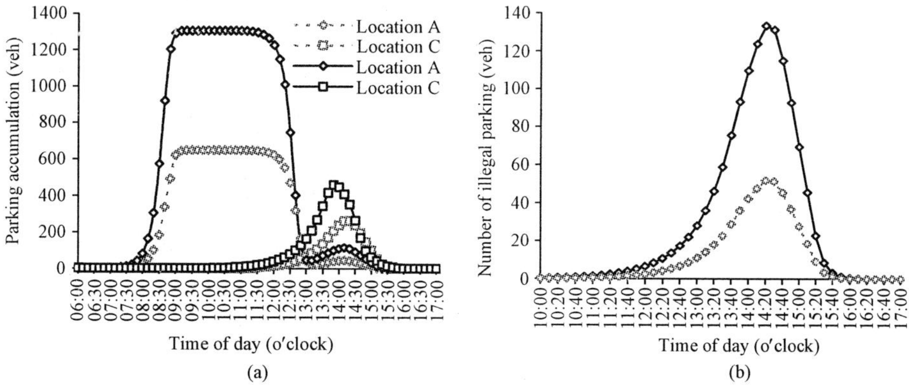

Fig. 7 (a) Parking accumulation at locations A and C;(b) Number of illegal parking(*solid lines* denote the base demand level and *dotted lines* denote half of the base demand level)

Figure 8(a)and(b)exhibit the parking reliabilities of off-street parking location A and on-street parking location C at different intervals under different congestion levels. It can be observed that the increase in OD demand leads to the decline of the parking reliabilities at locations A and C. Specifically, before the demand level is increased, travelers take at most 11 min for parking at A and 5 min for parking at C regardless of their departure interval. This is because at the low demand level, there are vacant parking spaces at both locations so that travelers can find for parking spaces easily. However, when the demand is doubled, the parking reliability from 08:30 to 09:00 at location A and that from 13:00 to 13:30 at location C are reduced. For instance, for parking location A, the searching time for a parking space needs about 12 min in 08:30—08:40 and 18 min in 08:40—08:50, and exceeds 24 min in 08:50—09:00. This is consistent with the increasing congestion for parking at location A from 08:30 to 09:00(see Fig. 7(a)). Similar observations also occur at parking location C. This shows the parking reliability that is proposed in this paper is a good proxy for measuring the level of service of parking facilities at different times of day.

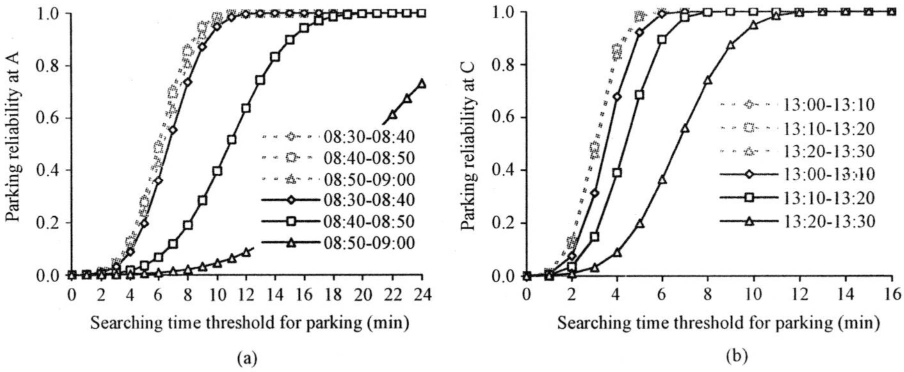

Fig. 8 Parking reliability at different intervals and different congestion levels(*solid lines* denote the base demand level and *dotted lines* denote half of the base demand level): (a) Off-street parking location A; (b) On-street parking location C

Suppose that the total demands are fixed at the base level. We examine the changes in schedule reliabilities of two routes(4-8-9-13-17 and 9-13-17) when the capacities of road links 9 and 17 that are on the two routes are increased by 1,000 vehicles/h. The results are shown in Fig. 9(a)for Route 4-8-9-13-17 for OD pair(1,12)and in Fig. 9(b)for Route 9-13-17 for OD pair(6,12). Links 9 and 11 are selected because they both reach oversaturation at the base demand level, as shown in Fig. 10. However, after the capacities of the two links are expanded, oversaturation no longer exists. Figure 9(a)and(b) show that the change in scheduled reliability of the two routes for OD pairs(1,12)and (6,12)at different times of day as a result of the link capacity expansion is very different. This means that road capacity expansion would cause the spatial equity issue(Meng and Yang 2002)as well as temporal equity issue. Therefore, it is necessary to take into account the equity issue for the design of a reliable road network.

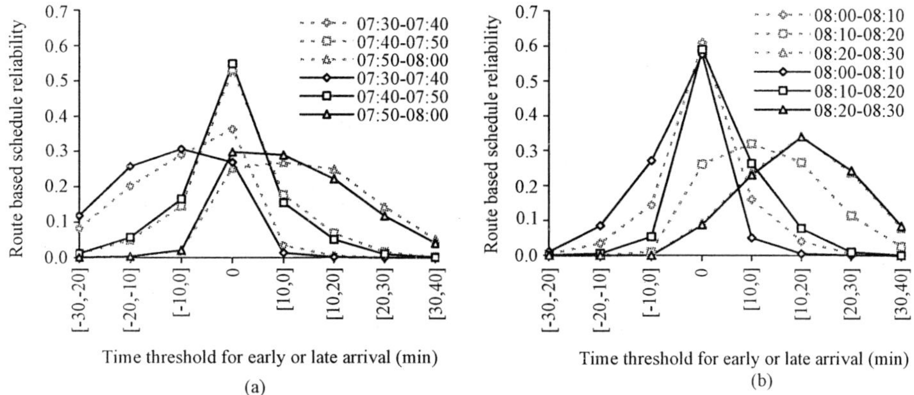

Fig. 9　Route based schedule reliability at different departure intervals before(*dotted lines*)and after(*solid lines*)link capacity expansion: (a) Route 4-8-9-13-17 between OD pair(1,12);(b) Route 9-13-17 between OD pair(6,12)

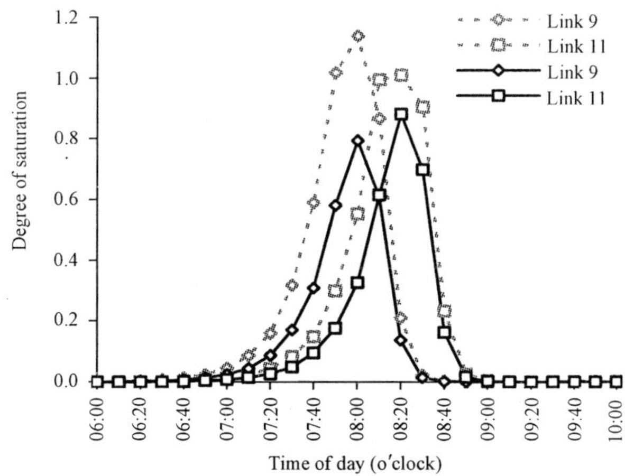

Fig. 10　Degree of saturation on links 9 and 11 before(*dotted lines*) and after(*solid lines*)link capacity expansion

Figures 11 and 12 display the changes in the vehicle number of illegal parking and the parking reliabilities of locations A and C, when the capacity of each of off-street and on-street parking locations is increased by 100 spaces. It can be seen from Fig. 11 that after parking conditions are improved, the vehicle number of illegal parking is reducedand the peak of illegal parking occurs earlier. In addition, the parking reliabilities of locations A and C are both enhanced, particularly for the parking peak periods, such as 08:50—09:00 for location A and 13:20—13:30 for location C, as shown in Fig. 12(a)and(b), respectively. Hence, the parking capacity expansion highly influences the parking behavior of travelers and the reliability performances of parking facilities.

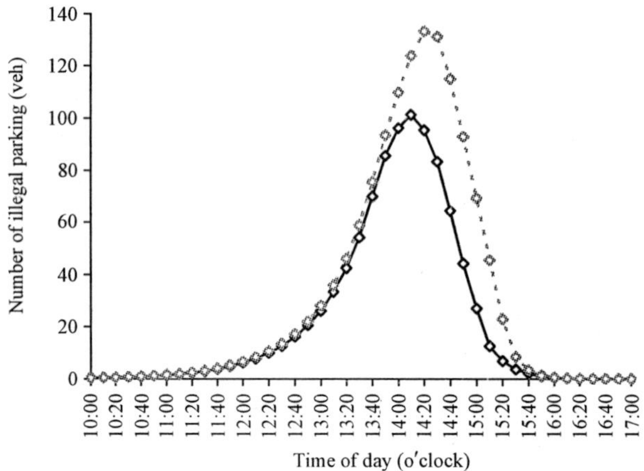

Fig. 11 Number of illegal parking before(*dotted lines*) and after(*solid lines*) parking capacity expansion

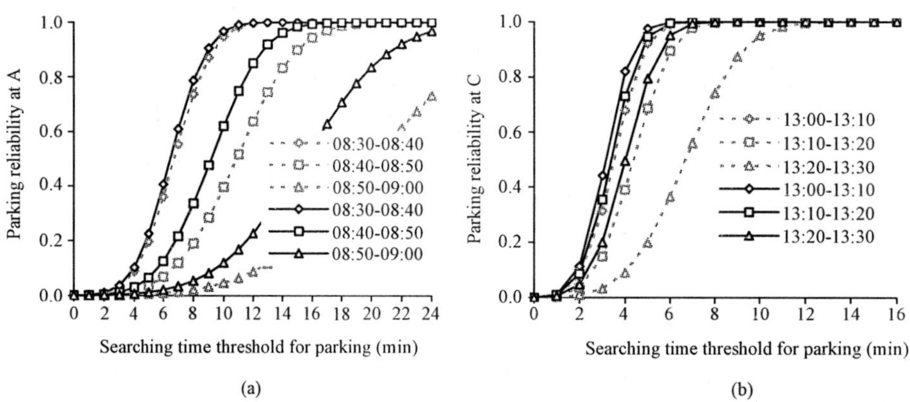

Fig. 12 Parking reliability at different intervals before(*dotted lines*) and after(*solid lines*) parking capacity expansion: (a) Off-street parking location A; (b) On-street parking location C

8 Conclusions

In this paper, two reliability measures in a time-dependent paradigm-schedule reliability and parking reliability—are introduced as new network performance indices for the assessment of the level of service of a stochastic and time-dependent road network with multiple parking facilities. The two reliability measures can be estimated by a fixed-point model, which models the travel and parking choice behavior of heterogeneous travelers. The proposed model consists of a supply model, a demand model, and a supply-demand interaction model. A heuristic solution algorithm that uses a combination of the Monte Carlo simulation approach with the method of successive average is developed to solve the proposed model. Based on the numerical results, some new insights and important findings are obtained: (1) The reliability performance of road networks during time of day depends very much on the network congestion level and infrastructure improvements; (2) Road capacity expansion may cause the temporal and spatial equity issue in terms of the schedule reliability; (3) Road congestion level and infrastructure improvements also significantly influence the departure pattern of travelers, parking behavior and the number of illegal parking.

The proposed model provides a useful tool for studying the complex temporal and spatial interaction between supply and demand under network uncertainty. The reliability indices proposed in this paper provide an effective avenue to measure the performances of road networks, and can be used to evaluat evarious transport policies for strategic planning purposes and to design a reliable transport system that includes a parking subsystem.

Several directions for future research are suggested as below: (1) to extend the model proposed in this paper to investigate the impact of route and/or parking information(Lo and Szeto 2004; Huang and Li 2007); (2) to consider the risk-taking behavior of travelers towards uncertainty(Boyce et al. 1998; Chen et al. 2002b); (3) to explicitly consider spillback queuing on roads and parking bottlenecks (Daganzo1998; Szeto and Lo 2004, 2006); (4) to study the day-to-day evolution of travel behavior of travelers across a stochastic network(Dargay and Goodwin 1995; Watling and Hazelton 2003); (5) to further validate the proposed model and solution algorithm on large-scale networks.

Acknowledgements The work that is described in this paper was supported by grants from the Research Grants Council of the Hong Kong Special Administrative Region (Project no. PolyU 5084/05E, PolyU 5143/03E and HKU 7134/03E), grants from the National Natural Science Foundation of China(Project no. 50578006, 70521001), and the China Postdoctoral Science Foundation(20060400573). The authors would like to thank two anonymous referees for their helpful comments and suggestions on an earlier draft of the paper.

References

Arnott R, Rowse J(1999) Modeling parking. J Urban Econ 45:97—124

Axhausen KW, Polak J(1991) Choice of parking: stated preference approach. Transportation 18:59—81

Bates J, Polak J, Jones P, Cook A(2001) The valuation of reliability for personal travel. Transp Res 37E: 191—229

Bell MGH, Iida Y(1997) Transportation network analysis. Wiley, Chichester

Bell MGH, Cassir C, Iida Y, Lam WHK(1999) A sensitivity-based approach to network reliability assessment. In: Ceder A(ed) Transportation and traffic theory. Elsevier, Oxford, pp283—300

Bifulco GN(1993) A stochastic user equilibrium assignment model for the evaluation of parking policies. Eur J Oper Res 71:269—287

Boyce DE, Ran B, Li Y(1998) Considering travelers' risk-taking behavior in dynamic traffic assignment. In: Bell MGH (ed) Transportation networks: recent methodological advances. Elsevier, Oxford, England, pp67—81

Chen HK, Feng G(2000) Heuristics for the stochastic/dynamic user-optimal route choice problem. Eur J Oper Res126:13—30

Chen HK, Hsueh CF(1998) A model and an algorithm for the dynamic user-optimal route choice problem. Transp Res 32B:219—234

Chen A, Yang H, Lo HK, Tang WH(1999) A capacity related reliability for transportation networks. J Adv Transp 33:183—200

Chen A, Tatineni M, Lee DH, Yang H(2000) Effect of route choice models on estimating network capacity reliability. Transp Res Rec 1733:63—70

Chen A, Yang H, Lo HK, Tang WH(2002a) Capacity reliability of a road network: an assessment methodology and numerical results. Transp Res 36B:225—252

Chen A, Ji ZW, Recker W(2002b) Travel time reliability with risk-sensitive travelers. Transp Res Rec 1783:27—33

Clark S, Watling D(2005) Modeling network travel time reliability under stochastic demand. Transp Res 39B:119—140

Daganzo CF(1995) Properties of link travel time functions under dynamic loads. Transp Res 29B:93—98

Daganzo CF(1998) Queue spillovers in transportation networks with a route choice. Transp Sci 32:3—11

Dargay JM, Goodwin PB(1995) Evaluation of consumer surplus with dynamic demand. J Transp Econ Policy 29:179—193

Dell'Orco M, Ottomanelli M, Sassanelli D(2003) Modeling uncertainty in parking choic ebehavior. Presented at the 82nd Annual Meeting of the Transportation Research Board, Washington D. C.

Du ZP, Nicholson A(1997) Degradable transportation systems: sensitivity and reliability analysis. Transp Res 31B:225—237

Han S(2003) Dynamic traffic modelling and dynamic stochastic user equilibrium assignment for general road networks. Transp Res 37B:225—249

Hensher DA, King J(2001) Parking demand and responsiveness to supply, pricing and location in the Sydney central business district. Transp Res 35A:177—196

Hess S, Polak J(2004) Mixed logit estimation of parking type choice. Presented at the 83rd annual meeting of the Transportation Research Board, Washington D. C.

Huang HJ, Lam WHK(2002) Modeling and solving the dynamic user equilibrium route and departure time choice problem in network with queues. Transp Res 36B:253—273

Huang HJ, Li ZC(2007) A multiclass, multicriteria logit-based traffic equilibrium assignment model under ATIS. Eur J Oper Res 176:1464—1477

Huang HJ, Li ZC, Lam WHK, Wong SC(2005) A time-dependent activity and travel choice model with multiple parking options. In: Mahmassani H(ed) Transportation and traffic theory. Elsevier, Oxford, pp717—739

Iida Y, Bell MGH(2003) The network reliability of transport. Elsevier, Oxford

Lam WHK, Tam ML(2003) Reliability assessment on searching time for parking in urban areas. In: Iida Y, Bell MGH(eds) The network reliability of transport. Elsevier, Oxford, pp61—78

Lam WHK, Tam ML, Yang H, Wong SC(1999) Balance of demand and supply of parking spaces. In: Ceder A(ed) Transportation and traffic theory. Elsevier, Oxford, pp707—731

Lam WHK, Li ZC, Huang HJ, Wong SC(2006) Modeling time-dependent travel choice problems in road networks with multiple user classes and multiple parking facilities. Transp Res 40B:368—395

Lau WWT, Poon PST, Tong CO, Wong SC(2005) The Hong Kong second parking demand study. Proc Inst Civ Eng Transp 158:53—59

Li ZC, Huang HJ, Lam WHK, Wong SC(2007) Time-differential pricing of road tolls and parking charges in a transport network with elastic demand. In: Bell MGH et al. (eds) Transportation and traffic theory. Elsevier, Oxford

Lim Y, Heydecker BG(2005) Dynamic departure time and stochastic user equilibrium assignment. Transp Res 39B:97—118

Liu HX, Ban XG, Ran B, Mirchandani P(2002) Analytical dynamic traffic assignment model with probabilistic travel times and perceptions. Transp Res Rec 1783:125—133

Lo HK, Szeto WY(2004) Modeling advanced traveller information services: Static versus dynamic paradigms. Transp Res 38B:495—515

Meng Q, Yang H(2002) Benefit distribution and equity in road network design. Transp Res 36B:19—35

Mirchandani P, Soroush H(1987) Generalized traffic equilibrium with probabilistic travel times and perceptions. Transp Sci 21:133—152

Noland RB, Small KA(1995) Travel-time uncertainty, departure time choice, and the cost of morning commutes. Transp Res Rec 1493:150—158

Ran B, Boyce DE(1996) Modeling dynamic transportation networks: an intelligent transportation system oriented approach. Second Revised Edition. Springer, Berlin Heidelberg New York

Richardson AJ, Taylor MAP(1978) Travel time variability on commuter journeys. High Speed Ground Transp J 12:77—99

Small KA(1982) The scheduling of commuter activities: work trips. Am Econ Rev 72:172—181

Sumalee A, Kurauchi F(2006) Network capacity reliability analysis considering traffic regulation after a major disaster. Netw Spat Econ 6:205—219

Szeto WY, Lo HK(2004) A cell-based simultaneous route and departure time choice model with elastic demand. Transp Res 38B:593—612

Szeto WY, Lo HK (2006) Dynamic traffic assignment: properties and extensions. Transportmetrica 2:31—52

Tatineni M, Boyce DE, Mirchandani P(1997) Comparisons of deterministic and stochastic network traffic loading models. Transp Res Rec 1607:16—23

Taylor MAP(1982) Travel time variability—the case of two public modes. Transp Sci 16:517—521

Taylor MAP(1999) Dense network traffic models, travel time reliability and traffic management, II: application to reliability. J Adv Transp 33:235—244

Thompson RG, Richardson AJ(1998) Aparking search model. Transp Res 32A:159—170

Verhoef E, Nijkamp P, Rietveld P(1995) The economics of regulatory parking policies: the(im) possibilities of parking policies in traffic regulation. Transp Res 29A:141—156

Watling D, Hazelton ML(2003) The dynamics and equilibria of day-to-day assignment models. Netw Spat Econ 3:349—370

Wong SC, Tong CO, Lam WCH, Fung RYC(2000) The development of parking demand models in Hong Kong. ASCE J Urban Plann Dev 126:55—74

Yang H, Lo HK, Tang WH (2000) Travel time versus capacity reliability of a road network. In: Bell MGH, Cassir C(eds) Reliability of transport networks. Research Studies, MA

Yin Y, Lam WHK(2002) Modeling risk-taking behavior in queuing networks with advanced traveler information systems. In: Taylor MAP(ed) Transportation and traffic theory. Elsevier, Oxford, pp309—328

Young W, Thompson RG, Taylor MAP(1991) A review of urban parking models. Transp Rev 11: 63—84

Zhang X, Yang H, Huang HJ, Zhang M(2005) Integrated scheduling of daily work activities and morning-evening commutes with bottleneck congestion. Transp Res 39A: 41—60

第三章　具有多类出行者多目标的交通均衡和有效收费问题

由于交通出行者的出行行为和社会经济特征(如收入、年龄、偏好、习惯)是不同的,他们乘坐的车辆(如汽车、卡车、火车、飞机等)也是不同的。所以,把单用户的交通均衡扩展到多用户的交通均衡是非常自然和必要的。由于不同用户有不同的经济特征,他们的时间、费用、舒适偏好决定了他们对交通方式与路径选择有着不同的行为。各类用户具有的特征一般是满足某些分布的。人们已认识到交通均衡是一种特殊的纳什均衡。各类用户按照自己的行为来选择出行路线与工具,选择标准也经常是多目标的,如费用、时间和舒适等。研究多类出行者多目标的交通均衡问题是20世纪90年代中期,特别是新世纪以来交通界最重要的研究方向之一。交通系统设计者非常关心如何使用交通收费、补贴以及信息引导来控制出行者的行为,使得交通系统达到某种预期目标。根据多类用户的选择偏好分布是离散还是连续的,多用户多目标交通均衡模型可分为有限维和无限维两种,无限维模型更能深刻反映现实本质,但工程实现中大部分是应用有限维模型来计算的。本章中Marcotte和Zhu(1997)研究了具有多类出行者多目标的交通均衡模型、计算方法以及控制策略设计。其研究成果在航空收益管理、交通收费、补贴等方面都有重要应用。

在最优收费问题中,人们试图找到一个合理的收费策略以使多目标多用户交通系统的均衡状态达到预期的状态,如系统最优状态,或者让系统达到某个系统目标,如污染排放小于某个值等。由于无穷维最优收费问题的约束不具有合适的约束凸性,这就导致了合理收费策略的存在性问题成为一个困难的科学研究问题。Marcotte和Zhu(2009)引进平均流概念把无限维收费问题转换为有限维问题来处理,证明了系统最优合理收费策略的存在性。而Hu,Zhu和Chen(2009)研究了合理污染收费策略问题。

EQUILIBRIA WITH INFINITELY MANY DIFFERENTIATED CLASSES OF CUSTOMERS

P. MARCOTTE* AND D. L. ZHU**

Abstract. In this work we consider a bicriterion extension of equilibrium problems formulated as variational inequalities, and propose for its solution a generalization of the Frank-Wolfe method. Under suitable monotonicity assumptions on the cost function and a reasonable regularity assumption, we prove that the Frank-Wolfe iterates converge linearly to the unique solution of our equilibrium problem.

Key words. Equilibrium, variational inequalities, Frank-Wolfe algorithm, multiobjective.

AMS subject classifications. 47H05, 49J40, 49M27, 90C25

1. Introduction and problem formulation

Consider the vroblem of determining an equilibrium state resulting from the interaction of infinitely many agents in a system, and assume that the equilibria correspond to the solutions of a finite dimensional variational inequality. More precisely, we say that a vector x in R^n is a solution of the variational inequality problem VIP(H, Ω) associated with the set Ω and the function $H: R^n \to R^n$ if it satisfies the variational inequality:

$$\langle H(x), x-y \rangle_2 \leqslant 0 \quad \forall y \in \Omega, \tag{1}$$

where $\langle . , . \rangle_2$ denotes the standard inner product in R^n. It is frequently the case that the vector x is naturally decomposed into classes

$$x = (x^1, x^2, \cdots, x^p),$$

each class being endowed with its own constraint set Ω^c and function H^c. If we assume that the function H^c takes the particular form

$$H^c(x) = F(X) + \alpha_c G(X),$$

where X is the total activity vector $X = \sum_{c=1}^{p} x^c$, the sole interaction between the clas-

* DIRO, Université de Montréal, C. P. 6128, succursale Centre-Ville, Montréal, Quebec, Canada H3C 3J7 (marcotte @iro. umontreal. ca).

** CRT, Université de Montrdal, C. P. 6128, succursale Centre-Ville, Montréal, Québec, Canada H3C 3J7 (daoli @crt. umontreal. ca).

ses is induced bv the two functions F and G. The class c is distinguished by its parameter α_c, which expresses the relative importance of the two criteria represented by the "disutility" functions F and G. For instance, if $F(X)$ represents delays, expressed in time units, and $G(X)$ represents monetary costs, then a_c represents the time equivalent of one monetary unit to an economic agent belonging to the class c. Using this notation, the equilibrium problem takes the form of the variational inequality problem: Find x^c in Ω^c such that

$$\langle F(x)+\alpha_c G(X), x^c-y^c\rangle_2 \leqslant 0 \quad \forall y^c \in \Omega^c \quad \forall_c=1,\cdots,p. \tag{2}$$

We will further reduce the multiclass equilibrium and impose that the sets Ω^c be closed, convex polyhedra of the form

$$\Omega^c = \{x^c : Ax^c = bh^c, x^c \geqslant 0\},$$

with $h^c \geqslant 0$ and $\sum_{c=1}^{p} h^c = 1$, i. e., the resource vector b is split among the classes according to the probabilities $h_1,\cdots,h_p$.

One can extend this model to cover the situation where there is a continuum of classes and where the discrete vector h^c is replaced by a measurable, almost everywhere positive and square-integrable density function $h(\alpha)$ having compact support $[0, \alpha_{\max}]$:

$$h(\alpha) > 0 \text{ a. e}$$

$$\int_0^{\alpha_{\max}} h(\alpha)\mathrm{d}\alpha = 1$$

This situation leads, for every value of the parameter α in $[0, \alpha_{\max}]$, to the equilibrium condition:

$$x(\alpha) \in \Omega(\alpha) = \{x(\alpha): Ax(\alpha) = bh(\alpha), x(\alpha) \geqslant 0\}$$

$$\langle F(X)+\alpha G(X),\ x(\alpha)-\ y(\alpha))\rangle_2 \leqslant 0 \quad \forall y(\alpha) \in \Omega(\alpha), \tag{3}$$

where the total activity vector X is now given by the formula

$$X = \int_0^{\alpha_{\max}} x(\alpha)d\alpha.$$

If the above inequality is only required to hold almost everywhere on $[0,\alpha_{\max}]$, the equilibrium conditions can be replaced by the infinite dimensional variational inequality:

$$x \in \Omega$$

$$\langle F(X)+\alpha G(X),\ x-\ y))\rangle \leqslant 0 \quad \forall y \in \Omega, \tag{4}$$

where Ω is the subset of $\{\mathcal{L}^2(0,\alpha_{\max})\}^n$ defined by the equality and nonnegativity constraints

$$\Omega = \{x \in \{\mathcal{L}^2(0,\alpha_{\max})\}^n : Ax(\alpha) = bh(\alpha), x(\alpha) \geqslant 0 \quad \forall \alpha \in [0,\alpha_{\max}]\}$$

and $\langle .,.\rangle$denotes the scalar product in $\{\mathcal{L}^2(0,\alpha_{\max})\}^n$, i. e:

$$\langle \Phi,\Psi\rangle = \int_0^{\alpha_{\max}} \langle \Phi(\alpha),\Psi(\alpha)\rangle_2 d\alpha.$$

We will denote:

$$\hat{\Omega} = \{X \in R^n : AX = b, X \geqslant 0\}.$$

This finite dimensional subset of R^n plays a key role in the analysis of the infinite dimensional variational inequality (4).

The aim of the paper is to analyze, both theoretically and algorithmically, the infinite dimensional variational inequality (4). In Section 2 we address the existence and uniqueness of solutions to (4); in Section 3 we propose a linearization algorithm for the numerical solution of (4); in section 4 we present a numerical example drawn from the context of traffic equilibrium. The concluding Section 5 will raise questions pertaining to the extension of the basic model and mention areas for future research.

2. Theoretical properties of the model

In this section we address the existence and uniqueness of a solution to the variational inequality (4) and give a necessary and sufficient condition for the function H to be monotone. Throughout the paper, we assume that a is nonnegative, that the density function h is measurable, with $\int_0^{\alpha_{\max}} h(\alpha)\,d\alpha = 1$, and has finite norm in the Hilbert space $\mathcal{L}^2(0, \alpha_{\max})$, i. e., $\| h \| = \left(\int_0^{\alpha_{\max}} h^2(\alpha)\,d\alpha\right)^{1/2} < \infty$.

The following definition will be required in the proof of the existence theorem.

DEFINITION 2.1. *Let Ω be a subset of a reflexive Banach space V, V^* its dual space and J a mapping from Ω into V^*. We say that J is pseudomonotone (in the Lions sense, see Lions [9]) if J is bounded on Ω and, for all sequences $\{x^k\}$ of Ω converging weakly to x in Ω and such that:*

$$\lim\sup_k \langle J(x^k), x^k - x\rangle \leqslant 0$$

we haue:

$$\lim\inf_k \langle j(x^k), x^k - y\rangle \geqslant \langle J(x), x - y\rangle \quad \forall y \in \Omega.$$

Note that the former definition does not correspond to the standard definition of pseudomonotonicity for point-to-set mappings (see Karamardian and Schaible [7]).

In Lions [9] it is shown that if J is pseudomonotone (in the Lions sense) on a nonempty, closed, convex and bounded subset Ω of a reflexive Banach space, then there exists at least one point x^* satisfying the variational inequality:

$$\langle J(x^*),\ x^* - x\rangle \leqslant 0 \quad \text{for all } x \text{ in } \Omega.$$

In order to demonstrate that the solution set of the variational inequality (4) is nonempty, we will check that the set Ω and the function H satisfy the assumptions of Lions' theorem.

THEOREM 2.2. *Let the real functions F and G be continuous, and the finite dimensional set $\hat{\Omega}$ be compact. Then the solution set of the infinite dimensional variational inequality (4) is nonempty.*

Proof. We check the assumptions of Lions' existence theorem, which will require us to first show that H is weakly continuous and bounded on Ω.

(i) Ω is closed, convex and bounded: By construction, the set Ω is closed and convex. Since $h(\alpha)$ has been assumed positive almost everywhere, we have:

$$\| x(\alpha) \|_2^2 \leqslant \sup_{X\in\hat{\Omega}} \| X \|_2^2 h^2(\alpha)$$

almost everywhere and, for x in Ω:

$$\| x \|^2 = \int_0^{\alpha_{\max}} \| x(\alpha) \|_2^2 d\alpha \leqslant \sup_{X\in\hat{\Omega}} \| X \|_2^2 \int_0^{\alpha_{\max}})h^2(\alpha)d\alpha.$$

This shows that Ω is bounded.

(ii) H is weakly continuous on Ω: Let $\{x^k\}$ be a sequence in Ω converging weakly to x in Ω. We have:

$$\begin{aligned} \| H(x^k) - H(x) \| &= \| (F(X^k) + \alpha G(X^k)) - (F(X) + \alpha G(X)) \| \\ &\leqslant \| F(X^k) - F(X) \| + \| \alpha(G(X^k) - G(X)) \| \\ &\leqslant \sqrt{\alpha_{\max}} \| F(X^k) - F(X) \|_2 + \alpha_{\max}^{1.5} \| G(X^k) - G(X)) \|_2. \end{aligned}$$

Since x^k converges weakly to x implies that X^k converges (strongly) to X, we conclude that

$$\lim_{k\to\infty} \| H(x^k) - H(x) \| = 0$$

and that the function H is weakly continuous on Ω.

(iii) H is bounded on Ω: Let $x^{(0)}$ be an arbitrary point in Ω. We have:

$$\begin{aligned} \| H(x) \| &= \| H(x) - H(x^{(0)}) + H(x^{(0)}) \| \\ &\leqslant \| H(x) - H(x^{(0)}) \| + \| H(x^{(0)}) \| \\ &\leqslant \sqrt{\alpha_{\max}} \| F(X) - F(X^{(0)}) \|_2 + \alpha_{\max}^{1.5} \| G(X) \\ &\quad - G(X^{(0)}) \|_2 + \| H(x^{(0)}) \| \end{aligned}$$

which is bounded, since F, G are continuous functions and $\hat{\Omega}$ is sompact.

(iv) H is pseudomonotone on Ω: Let $\{x^k\}$ be a sequence in Ω converging weakly to x in Ω, and y an arbitrary element of Ω. First we have:

$$\begin{aligned} \langle H(x^k) - H(x), x^k - y\rangle^2 &= \left[\int_0^{\alpha_{\max}} \langle H(x^k(\alpha)) - H(x(\alpha)), x^k(\alpha) - y(\alpha)\rangle_2 d\alpha\right]^2 \\ &\leqslant \| H(x^{(k)}) - H(x) \|^2 \int_0^{\alpha_{\max}} \| x^k(\alpha) - y(\alpha) \|_2^2 d\alpha \\ &\leqslant \| H(x^{(k)}) - H(x) \|^2 \hat{D}^2 \int_0^{\alpha_{\max}} h^2(\alpha)d\alpha \end{aligned}$$

where $\hat{D}$ is the diameter of the compact set $\hat{\Omega}$. This implies that

$$\lim_{k\to\infty} \langle H(x^{(k)}) - H(x), x^{(k)} - y\rangle = 0.$$

Next, coupling this result with (ii) and using the weak continuity of H, we obtain:

$$\lim_{k\to\infty} \langle H(x^k) - H(x), x^{(k)} - y\rangle = \lim_{k\to\infty} \int_0^{\alpha_{\max}} \langle H(x^k(\alpha)) - H(x(\alpha)), x^k(\alpha) - y(\alpha)\rangle_2 d\alpha = 0$$

and:

$$\begin{aligned} \lim_{k\to\infty} \langle H(x^k), x^{(k)} - y\rangle &= \lim_{k\to\infty} [\langle H(x), x^k - y\rangle + \langle H(x^k) - H(x), x^k - y\rangle] \\ &= \langle H(x), x - y\rangle. \end{aligned}$$

This implies, clearly, that H is pseudomonotone (in the Lions sense) on Ω. □

Most iterative procedures for solving variational inequalities require the defining function H to be monotone. Our next result characterizes the class of real functions F ahd G for which the function $F+\alpha G$ is monotone on$\{\mathcal{L}^2(0,\alpha_{\max})\}^n$, i. e. ,

$$\langle H(x)-H(y), x-y\rangle \geqslant 0$$

for all x, y in$\{\mathcal{L}^2(0,\alpha_{\max})\}^n$.

Note that if F is monotone and G is a multiple of F, the equilibrium problem can readily be reduced to a monotone variational inequality problem. Yet the mapping $F(X)+\alpha G$ is not monotone.

THEOREM 2. 3. *Let F and G be Lipschitz continuous and continuously differentiable on R^n. Then the function $F+\alpha G$ is monotone on $\{\mathcal{L}^2(0,\alpha_{\max})\}^n$ if only if F is monotone on R^n and G is constant on R^n.*

Proof. If F is monotone and G is constant we can write:

$$\begin{aligned}\langle H(x)-H(y), x-y\rangle &= \langle F(X)-F(Y), x-y\rangle \\ &= \int_0^{\alpha_{\max}} \langle F(X)-F(Y), x(\alpha)-y(\alpha)\rangle_2 d\alpha \\ &= \langle F(X)-F(Y), X-Y\rangle_2 \\ &\geqslant 0.\end{aligned}$$

Therefore, H is monotone on $\{\mathcal{L}^2(0,\alpha_{\max})\}^n$.

Now assume that H is monotone. Let $x\in\{\mathcal{L}^2(0,\alpha_{\max})\}^n$, $d\in R^n(d\neq 0)$ and ϵ a psoitive number. Define $y\in\{\mathcal{L}^2(0,\alpha_{\max})\}^n$ by

$$\begin{aligned} y(\alpha) &= x(\alpha)+1(1+\epsilon)d && \text{for } \alpha\in I_1 \\ y(\alpha) &= x(\alpha)-d && \text{for } \alpha\in I_2 \\ y(\alpha) &= x(\alpha) && \text{otherwise,}\end{aligned}$$

where I_1 and I_2 are disjoint intervals of the interval $[0, \alpha_{\max}]$, with common nonzero width l. Since $h(\alpha)$ is positive(almost everywhere), this implies that $\int_{I_1} h(\alpha)d\alpha$ and $\int_{I_2} h(\alpha)d\alpha$ are both nonzero. We have:

$$\begin{aligned} X-Y &= \int_{I_1}(x(\alpha)-y(\alpha))d\alpha+\int_{I_2}(x(\alpha)-y(\alpha))d\alpha \\ &= [-(1+\epsilon)d+d]l \\ &= -(\epsilon l)d.\end{aligned}$$

Let L denote a common Lipschitz constant for the functions F and G over R^n, and set

$$Q=\langle H(x)-H(y), x-y\rangle.$$

We have:

$$\begin{aligned} Q/l &= \langle H(x)-H(y), x-y\rangle/l \\ &= \frac{1}{l}\int_0^{\alpha_{\max}}\langle F(X)-F(Y), x(\alpha)-y(\alpha)\rangle_2 d\alpha \\ &\quad +\frac{1}{l}\int_0^{\alpha_{\max}}\alpha\langle G(X)-G(Y), x(\alpha)-y(\alpha)\rangle_2 d\alpha\end{aligned}$$

$$= -\epsilon\langle F(X) - F(Y), d\rangle_2 = \frac{1}{l}\left\langle G(X) - G(Y), d\left[-(1+\epsilon)\int_{I_1}\alpha d\alpha + \int_{I_2}\alpha d\alpha\right]\right\rangle_2$$

$$\leqslant \epsilon^2 L \| d \|_2^2\left(l + \int_{I_1}\alpha d\alpha\right) + \frac{1}{l}\langle G(X) - G(Y), d\rangle_2\left(\int_{I_2}\alpha d\alpha - \int_{I_1}\alpha d\alpha\right)$$

$$= \epsilon^2 L \| d \|_2^2\left(l + \int_{I_1}\alpha d\alpha\right) - \epsilon\langle \nabla G(X + \rho d)d, d\rangle_2\left(\int_{I_2}\alpha d\alpha - \int_{I_1}\alpha d\alpha\right)$$

for some positive number ρ in the interval $[0, \epsilon]$, by the mean value theorem. Thus:

$$Q/l\epsilon \leqslant \epsilon L \| d \|_2^2\left(1 + \int_{I_1}\alpha d\alpha\right) - \langle \nabla G(X + \rho d)d, d\rangle_2\left[\int_{I_2}\alpha d\alpha - \int_{I_1}\alpha d\alpha\right]$$

and:

$$\lim_{\epsilon\to 0+}\frac{Q}{l\epsilon} \leqslant -\langle \nabla G(X)d, d\rangle_2\left(\int_{I_2}\alpha d\alpha - \int_{I_1}\alpha d\alpha\right)$$

since ρ goes to zero as ϵ goes to zero.

In order that H be monotone, we must have that

$$\left(\int_{I_2}\alpha d\alpha - \int_{I_1}\alpha d\alpha\right)\langle \nabla G(X)d, d\rangle_2$$

is nonpositive for all possible selections of the intervals I_1 and I_2. This implies that $\langle \nabla G(X)d, d\rangle_2 = 0$ for all d in R^n. If we set $B = \nabla G(X)$, we can write:

$$\begin{aligned}\langle Bd, d\rangle_2 &= (1/2)\langle (B + B^t)d, d\rangle_2\\ &= (1/2)d^t O^t \Lambda O d\\ &= (1/2)(Od)^t\Lambda(Od)\\ &= 0 \quad \text{for all } d \in R^n,\end{aligned}$$

where $O^t\Lambda O$ is the orthogonal decomposition of the symmetric matrix $B + B^t$. Therefore the diagonal matrix Λ must be zero, and the eigenvalues of $B + B^t$ are all zero. This implies that the matrix $B + B^t$ is the square zero matrix of order n, i. e. , $B = -B^t$ is a skew-symmetric matrix.

To show that $B = \nabla G(X)$ must necessarily be zero, we proceed by contradiction. Let us introduce, as before, two disjoint intervals I_1 and I_2 of common width l. We have:

$$\int_{I_1}\alpha d\alpha \neq \int_{I_2}\alpha d\alpha.$$

Let v be a vector of R^n such that Bv is not equal to zero, τ a positive scalar and set:

$$u = -(\tau Bv)\Big/\left(\int_{I_1}\alpha d\alpha - \int_{I_2}\alpha d\alpha\right)$$

$$\begin{aligned}\delta(\alpha) &= (v/l) - u &&\text{for all } \alpha \in I_1\\ \delta(\alpha) &= u &&\text{for all } \alpha \in I_2\\ \delta(\alpha) &= 0 &&\text{otherwise.}\end{aligned}$$

We have, from the above definitions: $\int_0^{\alpha_{\max}}\delta(\alpha)d\alpha = ((v/l) - u)l + ul = v.$

Let $k(t) = \langle H(x + t\delta) - H(x), \delta\rangle$. To achieve the required contradiction, it is sufficient to show that $k(t)$ is negative for some value ofits argument t or, equivalently, that its derivative $k'(t)=\langle \nabla H(x)\delta,\delta\rangle$ is negative. Let us develop, using the definition of the vector u and the fact that B is a skew-symmetric matrix:

$$\begin{aligned}\langle \nabla H(x)\delta,\delta\rangle &= \lim_{t\to 0}\left\langle \frac{H(x+t\delta)-H(x)}{t},\delta\right\rangle \\ &= \lim_{t\to 0}\left\langle \frac{F(X+tv)-F(X)}{t},\delta\right\rangle + \lim_{t\to 0}\left\langle \alpha\frac{G(X+tv)-G(X)}{t},\delta\right\rangle \\ &= \int_0^{\alpha_{\max}}\langle \nabla F(X)v,\delta(\alpha)\rangle_2 d\alpha + \int_0^{\alpha_{\max}}\alpha\langle Bv,\delta(\alpha)\rangle_2 d\alpha \\ &= \langle \nabla F(X)v,v\rangle_2 + \int_{I_1}\alpha\langle Bv,(v/l)-u\rangle_2 + \int_{I_2}\alpha\langle Bv,u\rangle_2 \\ &= \langle \nabla F(X)v,v\rangle_2 + \left(\int_{I_2}\alpha d\alpha - \int_{I_1}\alpha d\alpha\right)\langle Bv,u\rangle_2 \\ &= \langle \nabla F(X)v,v\rangle_2 - \tau\langle Bv,Bv\rangle_2 \\ &= \langle \nabla F(X)v,v\rangle_2 - \tau\,\| Bv \|^2\end{aligned}$$

If we take τ larger than $\langle \nabla F(X)v,v\rangle_2/\| Bv\|_2^2$, we obtain that $k'(t)$ is negative, in contradiction with the monotonicity of H. Therefore, the Jacobian matrix $\nabla G(X)=B$ must be zero for all X in R^n and we conclude that the function G must be constant over R^n.

In order to show that F must be monotone, we write:

$$\begin{aligned}\langle F(X)-F(Y),X-Y\rangle &= \int_0^{\alpha_{\max}}\langle F(X)-F(Y),x(\alpha)-y(\alpha)\rangle_2 d\alpha \\ &= \langle F(X)-F(Y),x-y\rangle \\ &= \langle H(x)-H(y),x-y\rangle \\ &\geqslant 0,\end{aligned}$$

by monotonicity of H. This concludes the proof. □

The condition that the function G be constant for H to be monotone constitutes a severe theoretical restriction. However, we will see that it is quite natural in the application considered in section 4. From this point on we assume that G is constant on $\hat{\Omega}$, and that the function F is monotone on $\hat{\Omega}$.

We now state and prove two uniqueness results. The first involves a strict monotonicity assumption and is standard, while the second is based on a nondegeneracy condition specific to our problem.

THEOREM 2.4. *If the function F is strictly monotone on the compact polyhedron $\hat{\Omega}$, the vector X corresponding to an equilibrium solution x is unique.*

Proof. Let x and y be any two distinct solutions of the variational inequality, and let $X=\int_0^{\alpha_{\max}}x(\alpha)d\alpha$, $Y=\int_0^{\alpha_{\max}}y(\alpha)d\alpha$. We have: $\langle H(x),x-y\rangle\leqslant 0$ and $\langle H(y),y-x\rangle\leqslant 0$. This yields:

$$0\geqslant\langle H(x)-H(y),x-y\rangle$$

$$= \langle F(X) - F(Y), X - Y \rangle_2.$$

If X is not equal to Y, the last term is positive, a contradiction. □

To study the uniqueness of an equilibrium solution x, we introduce the infinite dimensional linear program LP obtained by setting X to its current value:

$$\text{LP:} \quad \min_{y \in \Omega} \langle F(X) + \alpha G, y \rangle.$$

This problem is a parametric continuous linear program of the bottleneck type (see Anderson and Nash[1]). Let $Y^i, i=1,\cdots,N$ be the extreme points of the compact polyhedron $\hat{\Omega}$, and set:

$$F^i(X) = \langle F(X), Y^i \rangle_2$$
$$G^i = \langle G, Y^i \rangle_2, \quad i = 1, \cdots, N.$$

DEFINITION 2.5. *An extreme point Y^i of $\hat{\Omega}$ is* dominated *at X if*

$$F^i(X) + \alpha G^i > \min_{j=1,\cdots,N} \{F^j(X) + \alpha G^j\}$$

for all α in $[0, \alpha_{\max}]$. If Y^i is not dominated at X, it is undominated *at X.*

If a point Y^i is dominated at X, then it is dominated in a neighborhood of X, due to the continuitv of the function F. In our studv of the local behaviour of the linear program LP, we will therefore only consider points that are undominated at X. Without loss of generality, we assume that the first $N(X)$ extreme points of $\hat{\Omega}$ are undominated at $X$and are sorted in decreasing order of their G^i values:

$$G^1 \geqslant G^2 \geqslant \cdots \geqslant G^{N(X)}.$$

We now introduce a nondegeneracy assumption involving the extreme points Y^i and the vector G that will be sufficient to ensure the uniqueness of the equilibrium solution x in Ω. This condition can always be enforced by a suitable perturbation of the cost vector G.

Condition A: $G^i \neq G^j$ for any two distinct extremal points Y^i and Y^j of the compact polyhedron $\hat{\Omega}$.

Under Condition A, we have:

$$G^1 > G^2 > \cdots > G^{N(X)}$$

and, since the extreme points considered are undominated, there holds the ordering:

$$F^1(X) < F^2(X) < \cdots < F^{N(X)}(X). \tag{5}$$

Under Condition A, we will show that the solution of the variational inequality(4) is unique. The proof of this result relies on the following preliminary lemma.

LEMMA 2.6. *Let $\alpha_0(X) = 0$, $\alpha_{N(X)}(X) = \alpha_{\max}$ and*

$$\alpha_j(X) = -(F^{j+1}(X) - F^j(X))/(G^{j+1} - G^j), \quad j = 1, \cdots, N(X) - 1.$$

If Condition A is met, then:

$$0 = \alpha_0(X) \leqslant \alpha_1(X) \leqslant \cdots \leqslant \alpha_{N(X)}(X) = \alpha_{\max}.$$

Proof. We will only prove the statement: $\alpha_1(X) \leqslant \alpha_2(X)$. The other statements are proved in a similar fashion. Assume, by contradiction, that $\alpha_1(X) > \alpha_2(X)$, i. e. :

$$-\alpha_2(X) = \frac{F^3(X) - F^2(X)}{G^3 - G^2} > \frac{F^2(X) - F^1(X)}{G^2 - G^1} = -\alpha_1(X).$$

Let:

$$\hat{\alpha}(X) = -\frac{F^3(X) - F^1(X)}{G^3 - G^1}.$$

Clearly, $\hat{\alpha}(X)$ is positive and $\alpha_2(X) < \hat{\alpha}(X) < \alpha_1(X)$. It follows that:

$$F^2(X) + \alpha G^2 > F^1(X) + \alpha G^1$$

for all $\alpha \leqslant \hat{\alpha}(X)$ and:

$$F^2(X) + \alpha G^2 > F^3(X) + \alpha G^3$$

for all $\alpha > \hat{\alpha}(X)$. This implies that the extreme point Y^2 is dominated and provides the required contradiction. □

By sorting in increasing order of magnitude the $M \leqslant N(X)$ distinct breakpoints (see Figure 1)

$$0 = \alpha_{i_0}(X) < \alpha_{i_1}(X) < \cdots < \alpha_{i_M}(X) < \alpha_{i_{M+1}}(X) = \alpha_{\max},$$

we obtain a partition of the set of breakpoints:

$$\alpha_i(X) = \begin{cases} \alpha_{i_0}(X) = 0 & if \quad i \in J_0 = \{0\} \\ \alpha_{i_0}(X) & if \quad i \in J_1 = \{1, \cdots, i_1\} \\ \cdots & \cdots \quad \cdots \\ \alpha_{i_k}(X) & if \quad i \in J_k = \{i_{k-1} + 1, \cdots, i_k\} \\ \cdots & \cdots \quad \cdots \\ \alpha_{i_{M+1}}(X) = \alpha_{\max} & if \quad i \in J_M = \{i_{M-1} + 1, \cdots, N(X)\} \end{cases}$$

For a fixed value of the parameter α, the parametric linear program LP reduces to the standard linear program:

$$\text{LP}(\alpha): \qquad \min_{y(\alpha) \in \Omega(\alpha)} \langle F(X) + \alpha G, y(\alpha) \rangle_2, \tag{6}$$

where $\Omega(\alpha) = \{y(\alpha) : Ay(\alpha) = bh(\alpha),\ y(\alpha) \geqslant 0\}$. An optimal extremal solution $y(\alpha)$ of LP is found by solving, for every value of α for which $h(\alpha)$ is positive, the finite dimensional linear program LP(α). One of its solutions is $y(\alpha) = Y^{i(\alpha)} h(\alpha)$, where:

$$\begin{aligned} \langle F(X) + \alpha G, Y^{i(\alpha)} \rangle_2 &= \min_{i=1,\cdots,N(X)} \langle F(X) + \alpha G, Y^i \rangle_2 \\ &= \min_{i=1,\cdots,N(X)} F^i(X) + \alpha G^i \\ &= F^{i(\alpha)}(X) + \alpha G^{i(\alpha)}. \end{aligned}$$

THEOREM 2.7. *Let Condition A hold. Then, for. fixed X, the in finite dimensional linear program LP admits the (almost everywhere) unique solution:*

$$y(X, \alpha) = Y^{i_k} h(\alpha) \quad \textit{for } \alpha \in [\alpha_{i_{k-1}}, \alpha_{i_k}].$$

Proof. The value function $\phi(\alpha) = F^{i(\alpha)}(X) + \alpha G^{i(\alpha)}$ is a piecewise affine, concave function of its scalar argument a. It passes through the points

$$(0, \phi(0)), (\alpha_{i_1}, \phi(\alpha_{i_1})), \cdots, (\alpha_{i_M}, \phi(\alpha_{i_M})), (\alpha_{\max}, \phi(\alpha_{\max})).$$

On each subinterval $(\alpha_{i_{k-1}}, \alpha_{i_k})$ its slope is equal to G^{i_k}. In the interior of each subinterval, the optimum of LP(α) is achieved at the extreme point Y^{i_k} of $\hat{\Omega}$. At a breakpoint α_{i_k} (see Figure 1), the optimum of LP(α) is achieved at the extreme points Y^j, $j \in J_k$, and $y(X, \alpha_{i_k})$ can be arbitrarily set to $h(\alpha_{i_k})$ times a convex combination of the Y^j's, for j in J_k. Since the number of breakpoints is finite, the solution $y(X)$ is unique, almost everywhere. □

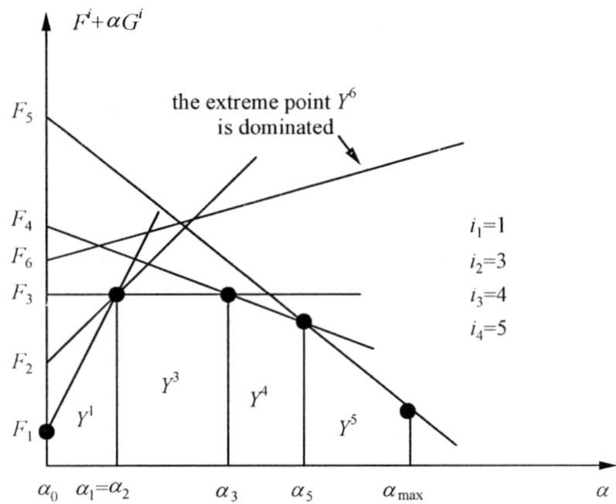

FIG. 1. *The value function*

COROLLARY 2.8. *If the equilibrium vector X^* is unique and Condition A holds, then the solution of the variational inequality* (4) *is unique, almost everywhere.*

Proof. Let x^* be an equilibrium solution and set $X^* = \int_0^{\alpha_{max}} x^*(\alpha)d\alpha$. Since the point x^* is a solution of the linear program:

$$\min_{y \in \Omega} \langle F(X^*) + \alpha G, y \rangle$$

and this solution is unique almost everywhere, x^* must be unique (almost everywhere). □

A sufficient condition for the above result to hold is clearly that F be strictly monotone on Ω. However we now prove a stronger result, namely that the (simple) monotonicity of F is a sufficient condition for the equilibrium to be unique.

THEOREM 2.9. *Let F be monotone on Ω and Condition A hold. Then, the equilibrium solution is unique.*

Proof. Let x^* and x^{**} be two solutions of the variational inequality(4). Since the function $F+\alpha G$ is monotone, we have the inequality:

$$\langle F(X)^* + \alpha G, x^{**} - x^* \rangle \leqslant 0,$$

i. e., both x^* and x^{**} are solutions of the linear program:

$$\min_{y \in \Omega} \langle F(X^*) + \alpha G, y \rangle.$$

However, Theorem (2.7) asserts that this linear program admits a unique solution, and it follows that we must have $x^* = x^{**}$. □

The remainder of this section is devoted to the study of the continuity of the mapping $x \to y(x)$, which we will denote $y(x)$, instead of simply y, to emphasize the dependence on the variable x.

THEOREM 2.10. *Let F be Lipschitz continuous on $\hat{\Omega}$, and assume that the function h is bounded on the interval $[0, \alpha_{\max}]$. Let Condition A hold. Then the function $y(x)$ is also Lipschitz continuous on Ω.*

Proof. For X' close to X we have the relationships:

$$G^1 > G^2 > \cdots > G^{N(X)}$$

$$F^1(X') < F^2(X') < \cdots < F^{N(X)}(X')$$

$$0 = \alpha_{i_0}(X') < \alpha_{i_1}(X') < \cdots < \alpha_{i_M}(X') < \alpha_{i_{M+1}}(X') = \alpha_{\max}.$$

The set of break points $\{\alpha_j(X')\}, j \in [1, \cdots, N(X)]$ defines a revised partition of the interval $[0, \alpha_{\max}]$. This set includes the breakpoints $\alpha_{i_k}(X'), k=1, \cdots M$ and, possibly, some new breakpoints $\alpha_j(X')$ for $j \in \bigcup_{k=1}^{M} J_k$.

Let $Y^{i(\alpha)}(X)$ denote the optimal solution of LP(α) and $y(X)$ the optimal solution of LP. We have, for X' close to X:

$$\begin{aligned}
\| y(X')(\alpha) - y(X)(\alpha) \|^2 &= \int_0^{\alpha_{\max}} \| y(X')(\alpha) - y(X)(\alpha) \|_2^2 d\alpha \\
&= \int_0^{\alpha_{\max}} \| Y^{i(\alpha)}(X') - Y^{i(\alpha)}(X) \|_2^2 h^2(\alpha) d\alpha \\
&\leqslant \hat{D}^2 h_{\max}^2 \max_{i \in \bigcup_{k=1}^{M} J_k} | \alpha_i(X') - \alpha_i(X) |,
\end{aligned}$$

where

$$h_{\max} = \max\{h(\alpha) : \alpha \in [0, \alpha_{\max}]\}.$$

From the definition of α_j:

$$\alpha_j(X) = -(F^{j+1}(X) - F^j(X))/(G^{j+1} - G^j), \quad j = 1, \cdots, N(X) - 1$$

and the fact that F is Lipschitz continuous, we obtain that $y(X)$ is locally Lipschitz continuous on the compact set $\hat{\Omega}$, with Lipschitz constant L_X, say. This implies that $y(X)$ is Lipschitz continuous on $\hat{\Omega}$, with Lipschitz constant L_X. Now:

$$\begin{aligned}
\| y(x') - y(x) \|^2 &= \| y(X') - y(X) \|^2 \\
&\leqslant L_X^2 \| X' - X \|_2^2 \\
&= L_X^2 \left\| \int_0^{\alpha_{\max}} (x(\alpha) - x'(\alpha)) d\alpha \right\|^2 \\
&\leqslant 2L_X^2 \int_0^{\alpha_{\max}} (x(\alpha) - x'(\alpha))^2 d\alpha \\
&= 2L_X^2 \| x - x' \|^2
\end{aligned}$$

and we conclude that $y(x)$ is Lipschitz continuous, with Lipschitz constant $\sqrt{2} L_X$, as a function of the variable (vector function) $x \in \{\mathcal{L}^2(0, \alpha_{\max})\}^n$. □

3. A solution algorithm and its convergence analysis

In this section we propose a linearization algorithm aimed at minimizing the gap function:

$$g(x) = \max_{y\in\Omega} \quad \langle H(x), x - y\rangle \qquad \text{subject to} \quad A_y = bh, \quad y \geqslant 0, \tag{7}$$

where $H(x) = F(X) + \alpha G$.

The function g is continuous and nonnegative on Ω and it is clear that x is a solution of the variational inequality (4) if and only if $g(x)=0$, i. e., x is a global optimum of the mathematical program:

$$\min_{x\in\Omega} g(x). \tag{8}$$

Note that the function g need not be convex (see Marcotte [10]). Throughout this section, we assume that the fumction F is monotone on $\hat{\Omega}$, that the function G is constant on $\hat{\Omega}$ and that Condition A holds. Under these assumptions (see Theorem 2. 3), the variational inequality (4) is monotone and, by generalizing techniques developed for the finite-dimensional case (see Marcotte [10]), it can be shown that any stationary point of (8) solves the variational inequality (4). Furthermore, under Condition A, the solution $y(x)$ of the linear program:

$$\min_{y\in\Omega}\langle H(x), x - y\rangle$$

is unique, and x solves the variational inequality (4) if and only if $y(x)=x$. It follows that g is differentiable and can be minimized using differentiable optimization technique, if F is continuously differentiable. We propose for its solution a linearization technique which constitutes, in some way, an extension to the infinite-dimensional case of the classical Frank and Wolfe algorithm, and is stated below.

LINEARIZATION ALGORITHM

ϵ: tolerance factor

$\{t_k\}$: stepsize sequence

initialization: Let $x^{(0)} \in \Omega$.

Set k to 0.

while $g(x^{(k)}) > \epsilon$ **do** $X^{(k)} = \int_0^{\alpha_{\max}} x^{(k)}(\alpha)d\alpha$

$y^{(k)} \in \arg\max_{y\in\Omega}\langle F(X^{(k)}) + \alpha G, x^{(k)} - y\rangle$

$d^{(k)} = y^{(k)} - x^{(k)}$

$x^{(k+1)} = x^{(k)} + t_k d^{(k)}$

Set k to $k+1$.

The stepsize t_k can be chosen according to several rules. We will consider four of these rules. The first assigns to all t_k's a constant, positive value; the second corresponds to the popular Armijo rule, while the third makes the sequence $\{t_k\}$ coincide with a sequence converging to zero, and whose corresponding series diverges. The fourth corresponds to a stepsize rule analyzed by Dunn [4], where it is referred to as an "open loop" stepsize rule.

Stepsize Rule A: $t_k = \bar{t}$, for some positive scalar $\bar{t}$.

Stepsize Rule B: Let γ and δ be positive numbers less than 1. We set $t_k = \delta^{i_k^*}$ where i_k^* is the smallest nonnegative integer i satisfying:

$$g(x^{(k)} + \delta^i d^{(k)}) - g(x^{(k)}) \geqslant \delta^i \gamma \langle \nabla g(x^{(k)}), d^{(k)} \rangle. \tag{9}$$

Stepsize Rule C: $\{t_k\}$ is any sequence satisfying:

$$0 < t_k \leqslant 1 \tag{10}$$

$$\lim_{k \to \infty} t_k = 0 \tag{11}$$

$$\sum_{k=0}^{\infty} t_k = +\infty. \tag{12}$$

Stepsize Rule D: $t_0 = 1$ and $t_{k+1} = t_k - (1/2)t_k^2$.

The proof of convergence of the linearization algorithm will require preliminary results that are the object of the next series of three lemmas.

LEMMA 3.1. (Polyak [12]) *Let p be a positive number, $\{u_k\}$ a sequence of positive numbers and $\{a_k\}$ a sequence of nonnegative numbers such that:*

$$u_{k+1} \leqslant u_k - a_k u_k^{1+p}.$$

Then, for all indices k, we have:

$$u_k \leqslant u_0 \left(1 + p u_0^p \sum_{i=0}^{k-1} a_i\right)^{-1/p}.$$

In particular, if $p=1$ and $a_k = a$ for all k, we obtain:

$$u_k \leqslant u_0/(1 + a u_0 k).$$

LEMMA 3.2. *Let $\{t_k\}$ and $\{u_k\}$ be two sequences of nonnegative real numbers such that $\{t_k\}$ satisfies (11) and (12) and: $\sum_{k=0}^{\infty} t_k u_k < \infty$. Then there exists a subsequence $\{u_k\}_{k \in K}$ converging to zero. If, furthermore, there exists a positive number b such that:*

$$u_{k+1} \leqslant u_k - t_k u_k + b t_k^2, \tag{13}$$

then the entire sequence $\{u_k\}$ converges to zero.

Proof. If the first conclusion of the lemma does not hold, there must exist a positive number η and an index K such that $u_k \geqslant \eta$ for all $k \geqslant K$. Therefore:

$$\sum_{k=0}^{\infty} t_k u_k \geqslant \eta \sum_{k=0}^{\infty} t_k = +\infty,$$

in contradiction with the convergence of the above series.

Now let condition (13) hold. If the sequence $\{u_k\}$ does not converge to zero, there must exist a positive number η' and an infinite subsequence $\{u_k\}_{k \in I'}$, such that $u_k \geqslant \eta'$ for all $k\in I'$ and $u_k<\eta'$ for all k in $I''=\{1,2,\ldots\}-I'$. From the first part of the lemma, we know that there exists a subsequence converging to zero, hence I'' is nonempty. Let $\tilde{K}$ be an index such that $t_k<\eta'/b$ for all $k\geqslant\tilde{K}$. (Such and index $\tilde{K}$ must exist since t_k converges to zero.) Select an index $k''\geqslant\tilde{K}$ in I'' such that $k'=k''+1$ is in I'. We have, from the choice of $\tilde{K}$:

$$u_{k+1}<u_k \quad \forall k\geqslant\tilde{K}.$$

Consequently:

$$\eta'\leqslant u_{k'}<u_{k''}<\eta',$$

which is the desired contradiction. □

LEMMA 3.3. *Let ∇F be Lipschitz continuous on $\hat{\Omega}$ and Condition A hold. Then, ∇g is Lipschitz continuous on Ω and we have:*

$$\nabla g(x)=\langle\nabla F(X),x-y(x)\rangle+H(x) \tag{14}$$

$$g'(x;y(x)-x)=\langle\nabla g(x),y(x)-x\rangle\leqslant-g(x)-\beta\|y(x)-x\|^2 \tag{15}$$

$$g(x)\geqslant\beta\|X-X^*\|_2^2, \tag{16}$$

where β denotes the strong monotonicity coefficient of F. (If F is monotone but not strongly monotone, we set β to zero.)

Proof. Under Condition A, $y(x)$ is unique and the right-hand-side of equation (14) is well-defined. The validity of (14) comes from the rule of differentiation of max-functions. Now:

$$\begin{aligned}\langle\nabla g(x),y(x)-x\rangle&=\langle\nabla F(X)(x-y(x))+H(x),y(x)-x\rangle\\&=\int_0^{\alpha_{\max}}\langle\nabla F(X)(x-y(x)),y(x)-x\rangle_2 d\alpha+\langle H(x),y(x)-x\rangle\\&\leqslant-\beta\int_0^{\alpha_{\max}}\|y(x)-x\|_2^2 d\alpha+\langle H(x),y(x)-x\rangle\\&=-g(x)-\beta\|y(x)-x\|^2.\end{aligned}$$

Finally:

$$\begin{aligned}g(x)&=\langle H(x),x-y(x)\rangle\\&\geqslant\langle H(x),x-x^*\rangle\\&\geqslant\langle F(X)-F(X^*),x-x^*\rangle\\&\geqslant\beta\|X-X^*\|_2^2,\end{aligned}$$

and the proof is complete. □

We are now in position to prove four convergence theorems, each one corresponding to a specific stepsize rule.

THEOREM 3.4. *Let $\{x^{(k)}\}$ be a sequence generated by the linearization algorithm under Stepsize Rule A. Let Condition A hold. Let ∇F be Lipschitz continuous on $\hat{\Omega}$, and F be strongly monotone on $\hat{\Omega}$ with strong monotonicity coefficient $\beta(\beta>0)$. Let* $0<$

$\bar{t}<\min\{1,\ 2\beta/L_{\nabla g}\}$ *and* $\rho=1-\bar{t}$. *Then we have*:

$$g(x^{(k+1)})\leqslant \rho g(x^{(k)}) \tag{17}$$

$$\| X^{(k)}-X^{*}\|_{2}=\mathcal{O}(\rho^{k/2}) \tag{18}$$

$$\| y(x^{(k)})-x^{*}\| =\mathcal{O}(\rho^{k/2}). \tag{19}$$

Proof. From the expression (14) of Lemma 3. 3 and the Lipschitz continuity of $y(x)$ (Theorem 2. 10) and ∇F, we deduce that ∇g is Lipschitz continuous, with Lipschitz constant $L_{\nabla g}$, say. Setting $\mathrm{d}=y(x)-x$ and using the second result of Lemma 3. 3, we can write:

$$\begin{aligned}g(x+td)-g(x)&\leqslant t\langle\nabla g(x),d\rangle+\frac{1}{2}L_{\nabla g}t^{2}\|d\|^{2}\\&\leqslant t(-g(x)-\beta\|d\|^{2})+\frac{1}{2}L_{\nabla g}t^{2}\|d\|^{2}\\&\leqslant tg(x)-t\|d\|^{2}(\beta-tL_{\nabla g}/2).\end{aligned}$$

To ensure that $x+\bar{t}d$ be feasible, we impose the constraint $\bar{t}\leqslant 1$. Furthermore, if $0<\bar{t}<\min\{1,2\beta/L_{\nabla g}\}$ and $\rho=1-\bar{t}$, we readily obtain the desired result.

Now, from Lemma 3. 3, we have:

$$\| X^{(k)}-X^{*}\|_{2}\leqslant\frac{1}{\sqrt{\beta}}\sqrt{g(x^{(k)})}\leqslant\frac{1}{\sqrt{\beta}}\rho^{k/2}g(x^{(0)}),$$

i,e., $\| X^{(k)}-X^{*}\|_{2}=\mathcal{O}(\rho^{k/2})$. Finally, since $y(x)$ is Lipschitz continuous (with Lipschitz constant $\sqrt{2}L_{X}$) as a function of X, and $y(x^{*})=x^{*}$, we have:

$$\begin{aligned}\| y(x^{(k)})-x^{*}\| &\doteq \| y(x^{(k)})-y(x^{*})\|\\&=\| y(X^{(k)})-y(X^{*})\|\\&\leqslant\sqrt{2}L_{X}\| X^{(k)}-X^{*}\|\\&\leqslant(\sqrt{2}L_{X}/\sqrt{\beta})\rho^{k/2}g(x^{(0)})\end{aligned}$$

and this implies that $y(x^{(k)})=\mathcal{O}(\rho^{k/2})$. □

In practical, large-scale applications, it will be numerically difficult to estimate the Lipschitz constant $L_{\nabla g}$. The stepsize rule B allows to achieve an implement able rule, even when F is not strongly monotone, and to achieve a linear order of convergence for the sequence $\{g(x^{(k)})\}$, without requiring the a priori knowledge of $L_{\nabla g}$.

THEOREM 3. 5. *Let* $\{x^{(k)}\}$ *be a sequence generated by the linearization algorithmunder Stepsize Rule B. Let Condition A hold. Let* ∇F *be Lipschitz continuous on* $\hat{\Omega}$. *If* $x^{(k)}$ *is not a solution of the variational inequality* (4), *then there exists an integer* i_k^{*} *satisfying* (9). *Moreover, the corresponding stepsize* $\tilde{t}_k=\delta^{i_k^{*}}$ *satisfies*:

$$\tilde{t}_{k}>2\delta(1-\gamma)\frac{-\langle\nabla g(x^{(k)}),d^{(k)}\rangle}{L_{\nabla g}\| d^{(k)}\|^{2}}.$$

Proof. Recall that the Lipschitz continuity of ∇g yields:

$$g(x^{(k)}+t_{k}d^{(k)})-g(x^{(k)})\leqslant t_{k}\langle\nabla g(x^{(k)}),d^{(k)}\rangle+\frac{1}{2}L_{\nabla G}t^{2}\| d^{(k)}\|^{2}. \tag{20}$$

If one sets $t_k \leqslant 2(\gamma-1)\langle \nabla g(x^{(k)}), d^{(k)}\rangle/(L_{\nabla g}\|d^{(k)}\|^2)$ in the above expression, there comes:

$$g(x^{(k)}+t_k d^{(k)})-g(x^{(k)}) \leqslant \gamma t_k \langle \nabla g(x^{(k)}), d^{(k)}\rangle. \tag{21}$$

There exists an integer i_k such that

$$\delta^{i_k} \leqslant 2(\gamma-1)\langle \nabla g(x^{(k)}), d^{(k)}\rangle/(L_{\nabla g}\|d^{(k)}\|^2).$$

Therefore, Stepsize Rule B will be satisfied, after a finite number of trials. If i_k^* denotes the smallest index such that (9) is met, then (9) is not met for $i=i_k^*-1$. Denoting $\tilde{t}_k=\delta^{i_k^*}$, we have:

$$\frac{1}{\delta}\tilde{t}_K > \frac{g(x^{(k)}+(1/\delta)\tilde{t}_k d^{(k)})-g(x^{(k)})}{\gamma\langle \nabla g(x^{(k)}), d^{(k)}\rangle}$$

or:

$$\gamma\tilde{t}_k\left\langle \nabla g(x^{(k)}), \frac{d^{(k)}}{\delta}\right\rangle < g\left(x^{(k)}+\tilde{t}_k\frac{d^{(k)}}{\delta}\right)-g(x^{(k)}).$$

On the other hand, from the Lipschitz continuity of ∇g, we also have:

$$g\left(x^{(k)}+\tilde{t}_k\frac{d^{(k)}}{\delta}\right)-g(x^{(k)}) \leqslant \tilde{t}_k\left\langle \nabla g(x^{(k)}), \frac{d^{(k)}}{\delta}\right\rangle+\frac{1}{2\delta^2}L_{\nabla g}\tilde{t}_k^2\|d^{(k)}\|^2. \tag{22}$$

Thus

$$\gamma\tilde{t}_k\left\langle \nabla g(x^{(k)}), \frac{d^{(k)}}{\delta}\right\rangle < \tilde{t}_k\left\langle \nabla g(x^{(k)}), \frac{d^{(k)}}{\delta}\right\rangle+\frac{1}{2\delta^2}L_{\nabla g}\tilde{t}_k^2\|d^{(k)}\|^2$$

and

$$\tilde{t}_k > 2\delta(1-\gamma)\frac{-\langle \nabla g(x^{(k)}), d^{(k)}\rangle}{L_{\nabla g}\|d^{(k)}\|^2},$$

as required. □

THEOREM 3.6. *Under the assumptions of Theorem 3.5, every weak cluster point of the sequence* $\{x^{(k)}\}$ *is a solution of the variational inequality* (4) *and we have*: $g(x^{(k)})=\mathcal{O}(1/k)$. *Furthermore, if F is strongly monotone on* $\hat{\Omega}$, *we have*: $g(x^{(k+1)})\leqslant \rho g(x^{(k)})$, $\|X^{(k)}-X^*\|_2=\mathcal{O}(\rho^{k/2})$ *and* $\|y(x^{(k)})-x^*\|=\mathcal{O}(\rho^{k/2})$, *with* $\rho=1-(2\beta\delta\gamma(1-\gamma)/L_{\nabla g})$.

Proof. From Theorem 3.5, we can write:

$$\tilde{t}_k > 2\delta(\gamma-1)\frac{\langle \nabla g(x^{(k)}), d^{(k)}\rangle}{L_{\nabla g}\|d^{(k)}\|^2} \geqslant 2\delta(\gamma-1)\frac{\langle \nabla g(x^{(k)}), d^{(k)}\rangle}{L_{\nabla g}D^2},$$

where D is the diameter of the bounded set Ω. Hence:

$$\begin{aligned} g(x^{k+1})-g(x^{(k)}) &\leqslant \gamma\tilde{t}_k\langle \nabla g(x^{(k)}), d^{(k)}\rangle \\ &< \frac{2\delta\gamma(\gamma-1)}{L_{\nabla g}D^2}\langle \nabla g(x^{(k)}), d^{(k)}\rangle^2 \\ &\leqslant \frac{2\delta\gamma(\gamma-1)}{L_{\nabla g}D^2}(g(x^{(k)}))^2 \end{aligned}$$

and, using Lemma 3.2 with $\rho=1$ *we obtain*: $g(x^{(k)})=\mathcal{O}(1/K)$.

Since Ω is closed and convex, it is also weakly compact (see Ekeland and Temam [5]) and must have a cluster point $\bar{x}$ in the weak topology. Since Ω is weakly closed and g is weakly continuous(easy to show), it follows that $\bar{x} \in \Omega$ and $g(\bar{x})=0$. If F is strongly monotone on $\hat{\Omega}$ with positive strong monotonicity coefficient β, we have:

$$\gamma \tilde{t}_k \geqslant 2\delta\gamma(\gamma-1)\frac{\langle \nabla g(x^{(k)}), d^{(k)} \rangle}{L_{\nabla g} \| d^{(k)} \|^2} \geqslant \frac{2\beta\delta\gamma(1-\gamma)}{L_{\nabla g}}.$$

Combining the above inequality with (9) (where $\tilde{t}_k = \delta^i = \delta^{i_K^*}$) we obtain:

$$g(x^{(k+1)}) = g(x^{(k)} + \tilde{t}_k d^{(k)}) \leqslant \left(1 - \frac{2\beta\delta\gamma(1-\gamma)}{L_{\nabla g}}\right) g(x^{(k)}).$$

The proof of the last statement is similar to that of the proof of geometric convergence of the sequence of iterates in Theorem 3.4. □

THEOREM 3.7. *Let* $\{x^{(k)}\}$ *be a sequence generated by the linearization algorithm under Stepsize Rule C. Let Condition A hold. Let* ∇F *be Lipschitz continuous on* $\hat{\Omega}$. *Then the sequence* $\{g(x^{(k)})\}$ *converges to zero and every weak cluster point of the sequence* $\{x^{(k)}\}$ *is a solution of the variational ineqrality*(4).

Proof. Let D, as before, denote the diameter of the bounded set Ω. We have:

$$g(x^{(k+1)}) \leqslant g(x^{(k)}) + t_k \langle \nabla g(x^{(k)}), d^{(k)} \rangle + \frac{L}{2} t_k^2 \| d^{(k)} \|^2$$

$$\leqslant g(x^{(k)}) - t_k g(x^{(k)}) + \frac{L}{2} D^2 t_k^2$$

and:

$$t_k g(x^{(k)}) \leqslant g(x^{(k)}) - g(x^{(k+1)}) + \frac{L}{2} D^2 t_k^2.$$

Summing the preceding inequality from 0 to ∞ there comes:

$$\sum_{k=0}^{\infty} t_k g(x^{(k)}) < \infty$$

and, by Lemma 3.2, the sequence $\{g(x^{(k)})\}$ converges to zero.

The proof of the last statement is obtained as in Theorem 3.5. □

THEOREM 3.8. *Under the assumptions of the previous theorem and Stepsize Rule D*, $g(x^{(k)}) = \mathcal{O}(1/k)$ *and every weak cluster point of the sequence* $\{x^{(k)}\}$ *is a solution of the variational inequality* (4).

Proof. The sequence $\{t_k\}$ satisfies the assumptions of Lemma 3.1 with $a_k = 1/2$ and $p=1$. It follows that t_k converges monotonically to zero and $t_k = \mathcal{O}(1/k)$. Now, define:

$$\sigma = \max\{g(x^{(0)}), L_{\nabla g} D^2\}.$$

We will show, by induction, that $g(x^{(k)}) \leqslant \sigma t_k$ for all indices k. The statement is clearly true for $k=0$ and, if $g(x^{(k)}) \leqslant \sigma t_k$:

$$g(x^{(k+1)}) \leqslant (1-t_k) g(x^{(k)}) + \frac{L_{\nabla g} D^2}{2} t_k^2$$

$$\leqslant (1-t_k)\sigma t_k + \frac{\sigma}{2}t_k^2$$

$$= \sigma t_k\left(1-\frac{t_k}{2}\right)$$

$$\leqslant \sigma t_{k+1}.$$

Therefore: $g(x^{(k)}) \leqslant \sigma t_k$ for all k and $g(x^{(k)}) = \mathcal{O}(t_k) = \mathcal{O}(1/k)$. □

The stepsize rules analyzed above are valid for arbitrary, continuously differentiable, monotone functions F, whether they are gradient mappings or not. If F happens to be the gradient of some real convex function f, then any solution of the variational inequality corresponds to a stationary point of the convex optimization problem:

$$\min_{x\in\Omega} \psi(x) = f(X) + \left\langle G, \int_0^{\alpha_{\max}} \alpha x(\alpha)d\alpha \right\rangle_2, \tag{23}$$

where $f(X) = \int_0^X F(t)dt$. Other stepsize rules, based on the minimization of ψ along the direction $d^{(k)}$, can be implemented. For instance, the Armijo rule would then take the standard form:

Stepsize Rule E: Let γ and δ be positive numbers less than 1. We set $t_k = \delta^{i_k^*}$ where i_k^* is the smallest nonnegative integer i satisfying:

$$\psi(x^{(k)} + \delta^i d^{(k)}) - \psi(x^{(k)}) \geqslant \delta^i \gamma \langle \nabla\psi(x^{(k)}), d^{(k)} \rangle. \tag{24}$$

and its validity can be proved in a straightforward manner. The abovementioned stepsize rule can also be implemented if F is a nonmonotone gradient mapping.

We close this section with the following remark: In the course of the linearization algorithm, it is not necessary to keep track of the iterates $x^{(k)}$, which would be cumbersome. Indeed, only the quantities

$$\left\langle G, \int_0^{\alpha_{\max}} \alpha x^{(k)}(\alpha)d\alpha \right\rangle_2$$

need be recorded and updated through the formula:

$$\left\langle G, \int_0^{\alpha_{\max}} \alpha x^{(k+1)}(\alpha)d\alpha \right\rangle_2 = \left\langle G, \int_0^{\alpha_{\max}} \alpha x^{(k)}(\alpha)d\alpha \right\rangle_2 + t_k\left\langle G, \int_0^{\alpha_{\max}} \alpha d^{(k)}(\alpha)d\alpha \right\rangle_2.$$

If the algorithm is stopped at iteration K, then $X^{(K)}$ is an approximation of the equilibrium vector X^*. Under condition A, the functional vector $y(x^{(K)}) = y(X^{(K)})$ is also a valid approximation of the equilibrium solution x^*, in a neighborhood of x^*.

4. A transportation application

In this section we consider an application of the multiclass problem to the realm of traffic assignment. This model constitutes an extension of the modesl proposed by Dial [3] and Dafermos [2] in the uncongested and separable cases, respectively. An extension to the variable demand case has been analyzed by Leurent [8], who proposed for its solution a sublinearly convergent stochastic optimization algorithm. In this context, the users of the transportation network seek to minimize their individual cost expressed as the sum of a monetary component and a time component. The latter is transformed into a monetary value, after it is multiplied by a "value-of-time" parameter $\beta = 1/\alpha$. For a user travelling between two nodes of the network, the cost of a path is defined as the sum of the costs of the arcs composing that path. More precisely, let us introduce the following notations:

$G=(N,A)$: A network with node set N and arc set A

$FS(i)$: The forward star associated with node $i \in N$

$BS(i)$: The backward star associated with node $i \in N$

α: The value of time (state variable)

$\alpha_{\max}$: An upper bound on the value of α.

l: A commodity index (origin-destination pair index)

L: The set of origin-destination couples

d^l: The demand for commodity (origin-destination) k

$h(\alpha)$: A probability density function over the values of time

$x_a^l(\alpha)$: The flow density along arc a with respect to the value of time α

$X_a(\alpha)$: The total flow density of class α along arc a: $X_a(\alpha)=\sum_{l\in L} x_a^l(\alpha)$

$x(\alpha)$: The vector of functions $x_a^1(\alpha)$, $a \in A$, $l \in L$

X_a: The total flow along arc a. One has:

$$X_a = \sum_{l \in L} \int_0^{\alpha_{\max}} x_a^1(\alpha) d\alpha = \int_0^{\infty} X_a(\alpha) d\alpha$$

σG_a: The fixed monetary cost of travel along arc a

$F_a(X)$: The delay (congestion) function associated with arc a.

The above positive constant σ is used to vary the relative importance of the time and cost components of the mapping F. As σ approaches the value zero, it is expected that the algorithm's behaviour will be similar to that of the Frank-Wolfe algorithm applied to a single-class problem.

Let Ω denote the set of all demand-feasible assignments of the multiclass flow x onto the transportation network. Then an equilibrium assignment corresponds to an origin-destination flow density vector $x_a^k(\alpha)$ that satisfies the infinite-dimensional variational inequality:

$$\left\langle F(X) + \frac{1}{\alpha}\sigma G, x - y \right\rangle \leqslant 0 \quad \forall y \in \Omega. \tag{25}$$

Note that, in the above, the state variable α divides G, instead of multiplying it. The reader is referred to Marcotte and Zhu [11] for further details.

In the standard traffic assignment model (see Florian [6]), under a strict monotonicity assumption, only the uniqueness of the total arc flow vector is guaranteed, since the decomposition of arc flows into commodity flows is not unique, in general. A key feature of the multiclass formulation of the traffic assignement model is that, under Condition A, the uniqueness of the commodity flows is achieved, even under the weaker condition of monotonicity of the delay function F.

In the remainder of this section, we present two numerical examples that illustrate the applicability of the proposed methodology. The first involves the (in)famous Braess paradox example, whose input data is given in Table 5 below. The demand from the origin node 1 to the destination node 4 is set to 6 units of flow, while the cost functions are affine and separable, namely:

$$F_a(X) = F_a(X_a) = \beta_a + \gamma_a X_a.$$

The density function of the class parameter α is triangular and its mathematical expression is:

$$h(\alpha) = \begin{cases} \alpha & \alpha \in [0,1] \\ 2-\alpha & \alpha \in [1,2] \\ 0 & \text{elsewhere.} \end{cases}$$

Since Condition A is satisfied and the mapping F is separable, the unique equilibrium solution can be found by solving the convex (indeed quadratic) optimization problem (23). In this situation, the optimal stepsize can be obtained in closed form.

The results, corresponding to three distinct values of the parameter σ, are presented in Tables 2, 3, 4 and 5. The influence of the parameter σ is readily observed: as σ increases, the monetary part of the cost mapping becomes predominant, and the convergence is faster. For very small values of σ however, the congestion part takes over, and the convergence pattern becomes similar to that of the Frank-Wolfe method applied to a single-class problem; furthermore, an inordinate number of iterations is then required in order that the total flow vectors $X^{(k)}$ and $Y^{(k)}$ agree to a few decimal places. Actually, the convergence of $X^{(k)}$ to the equilibrium solution X^*, as indicated by the value of the gap function $g(x^{(k)})$, is much faster than that of $Y^{(k)}$ towards $X^{(k)}$ (or X^*). The convergence rate is clearly seen to be influenced by the relative importance of the congestion and monetary parts of the mapping, represented by the parameter σ. This is consistent with the observation that, as σ decreases, the value of the optimal stepsize t_k becomes very small.

The second example is based on the network of the city of Sioux Falls (see Suwansirikul and Friesz [13]). It comprises 24 nodes, 76 arcs and the origin-destination matrix is full (24×23 nonzero entries). The arc congestion function is separable and of the form:

$$F_a(X_a) = \beta_a + \gamma_a (X_a/\delta)^4.$$

The distribution of the α-values is similar to that of the Braess examples. The values of the parameters β_a, γ_a and δ were taken from reference [13]. The values of the parameters G_a were randomly set to one of the three values 0, 1 or 2. The results are presented in Table 5, where the left-hand side columns correspond to a multiclass assignment and the right-hand side columns to a single-class assignment, obtained by setting all G_a's to zero.

We observe that, in the multiclass model, the convergence to equilibrium is much faster. At the 24th iteration, the value of the objective function ψ has stabilized and the gap value is less than one thousandth of the corresponding value for the singleclass model. This is all the more impressive if one were to compare the values of the gap function relative to the total cost, the latter value being more than 15 times higher for the single-class model.

5. Extensions and conclusion

The multiclass equilibrium problem considered in this paper constitutes a natural extension of classical equilibrium models in finite dimension. The multiclass model yields additional information not readily available from the single-class model, at a reasonable increase in computational cost. Areas of future research will focus on (i) relaxing Condition A to allow for nonconstant mappings $G(X)$, while keeping the same constraint structure; this corresponds to an infinite-dimensional extension of the multimodal equilibrium model first mentioned by Dafermos [2] (ii) considering more than two criteria, i. e., analyzing mappings of the form

$$H(x) = \sum_{i=1}^{q} \alpha_i F_i(X) \tag{26}$$

with $\sum_{i=1}^{q} \alpha_i = 1, \alpha_i \geqslant 0$ for all $i=1,\cdots,q$ and $(\alpha_1,\cdots,\alpha_q)$is a q-dimensional vector with density $h(\alpha_1,\cdots,\alpha_q)$. In both cases, the resulting variational inequalities involve a non-monotone mapping if more than one of the functions is not constant. However we do not know, as of now, whether their solution sets are still convex, and whether globally convergent iterative algorithms exist for their solution.

References

[1] Anderson E. J., and Nash, P., *Linear Programming in Infinite Dimensional Spaces*, John Wiley and Sons. New York. 1987.

[2] Dafermos, S. C., *A multicriteria route-mode choice traffic equilibrium model*, unpublished manuscript, befschetz Center for Dynamical Systems, June 1981.

[3] Dial, R. B., *A model and algorithm for multicriteria route-mode choice*, Transportation Research B 13B (1979)311-316

[4] Dunn, J. C., *Gradient-related constrained minimization algorithms in function spaces: convergence properties and computational implications*, Large Scale Optimization: State of the Art, W. W. Hager et al. (eds.), Kluwer Academic Publishers (1994) 95-114.

[5] Ekeland, I. and Temam, R., Analyse convexe et problèmes variationnels, Dunod, Paris (1972).

[6] Florian, M., *Nonlinear cost network models in transportation analysis*, Mathematical Programming Study 26 (1986) 167-196

[7] Karamardian, S. and Schaible, S., *Seven kinds of monotone maps*, Journal of Optimization Theory and Applications 66 (1990) 37-46

[8] Leurent, *Cost versus time equilibrium over a network*, European Journal of Operational Research 71 (1993) 205-221.

[9] Lions, J.-L., Quelques méthodes de résolution des problèmes aux limites non linéaires, Dunod, Paris, 1969.

[10] Marcotte, P., *A new algorithm for solving variational inequalities, with application to the traffic assignment problem*, Mathematical Programming 33 (1985) 339-351

[11] Marcotte, P. et Zhu, D., An *efficient algorithm for a bicriterion traffic assignment problem*, Proceeding of TRISTAN II (Triennal Symposium on Transportation Analysis), Capri, June 23-28, 1994, 891-897.

[12] Polyak, B. T., Introduction to Optimization, Optimization Software, New-York, 1987.

[13] Suwansirikul, C. and Friesz, T. L., *Equilibrium decomposed optimization: a heuristic for the continuous equilibrium network design problem*, Transportation Science 21 (1987) 254-263.

TABLE 1

Data for the Braess network example.

arc	β_a	γ_a	G_a
1-2	0	10	100
1-3	50	1	90
2-3	10	1	10
2-4	50	1	100
3-4	0	10	100

TABLE 2

Numerical results on Braess network: $\sigma=0$ (single-class).

k	$X^{(k)}$	$Y^{(k)}$	$g(x^{(k)})$	t_k	$\psi(x^{(k)})$
0	6.0000	6.0000	156.00	.0361	43.80
	0.0000	0.0000			
	6.0000	0.0000			
	0.0000	6.0000			
	6.0000	0.0000			
1	6.0000	0.0000	143.00	.0309	40.98
	0.0000	6.0000			
	3.8333	0.0000			
	2.1667	0.0000			
	3.8333	6.0000			

k	$X^{(k)}$	$Y^{(k)}$	$g(x^{(k)})$	t_k	$\psi(x^{(k)})$
9	4.0429	0.0000	1.642	.0072	38.601
	1.9571	6.0000			
	2.0610	0.0000			
	1.9819	0.0000			
	4.0180	6.0000			
49	4.0000	0.0000	00004	.0000002	38.600
	1.9999	6.0000			
	2.0000	0.0000			
	1.9992	0.0000			
	4.0000	6.0000			

TABLE 3

Numerical results on Braess network :σ=1.

k	$X^{(k)}$	$Y^{(k)}$	$g(x^{(k)})$	t_k	$\psi(x^{(k)})$
0	6.0000	0.0000	322.35	0.7462	2184.73
	0.0000	6.0000			
	6.0000	0.0000			
	0.0000	0.0000			
	6.0000	6.0000			
1	1.5228	5.8763	218.41	0.3698	2064.46
	4.4772	0.1237			
	1.5228	0.0000			
	0.0000	5.8763			
	6.0000	0.1237			
9	2.8785	2.2971	1.407	0.3482	2000.74
	3.1215	3.7029			
	0.5651	0.0000			
	2.3134	2.2971			
	3.6866	3.7029			
49	2.7348	2.7354	0.000003	0.073	1999.92
	3.2652	3.2646			
	0.3395	0.3383			
	2.3953	2.3971			
	3.6047	3.6029			

TABLE 4

Numerical results on Braess network **: σ=.001.**

k	$X^{(k)}$	$Y^{(k)}$	$g(x^{(k)})$	t_k	$\psi(x^{(k)})$
0	6.0000	0.0000	156.17	0.3615	439.75
	0.0000	6.0000			
	6.0000	0.0000			
	0.0000	0.0000			
	6.0000	6.0000			
1	3.8310	6.0000	143.07	0.3094	411.52
	2.1690	0.0000			
	3.8310	0.0000			
	0.0000	6.0000			
	6.0000	0.0000			
49	3.9980	5.6946	0.086	0.0005	387.66
	2.0021	0.3054			
	1.9987	0.0000			
	1.9924	5.6946			
	4.0001	0.3054			
9999	3.9983	4.0535	0.000023	0.00008	387.63
	2.0017	1.9465			
	1.9978	1.9076			
	2.0006	2.1459			
	3.9994	3.8541			

TABLE 5

Numerical results on Braess network **: σ=10.**

k	$X^{(k)}$	$Y^{(k)}$	$g(x^{(k)})$	t_k	$\psi(x^{(k)})$
0	6.0000	0.0000	1819.55	0.9999	17905.31
	0.0000	6.0000			
	6.0000	0.0000			
	0.0000	0.0000			
	6.0000	6.0000			
1	0.0000	0.7052	4.29	0.3927	16301.76
	5.9999	5.2948			
	0.0000	0.0000			
	0.0000	0.7052			
	6.0000	5.2948			

k	$X^{(k)}$	$Y^{(k)}$	$g(x^{(k)})$	t_k	$\psi(x^{(k)})$
3	0.3282	0.2678	0.0344	0.4283	16299.76
	5.6718	5.7322			
	0.0000	0.0000			
	0.3282	0.2678			
	5.6718	5.7322			
7	0.3005	0.3000	0.000002	0.4224	16299.74
	5.6995	5.7000			
	0.0000	0.0000			
	0.3005	0.3000			
	5.6995	5.7000			

TABLE 6

Siowx Falls results.

	multiclass			single-class		
k	$g(x^{(k)})$	t_k	$\psi(x^{(k)})$	$g(x^{(k)})$	t_k	$\psi(x^{(k)})$
0	1662.49	0.4394	1220.34	69.86	0.3141	185.65
1	95.42	0.2281	941.70	12.24	0.2054	82.99
2	59.96	0.6124	930.94	45.79	0.1650	70.70
3	81.12	0.2103	912.39	26.18	0.2858	66.86
5	49.05	0.1385	896.85	15.57	0.2594	61.35
9	2.33	1.0000	891.95	8.57	0.1331	56.67
14	1.08	0.0537	889.78	4.27	0.1401	54.26
24	0.0088	0.0011	889.75	1.55	0.0768	52.51
49	0.0027	0.0455	889.75	6.61	0.0235	51.88
99	0.0002	0.0002	889.75	0.304	0.0070	51.72
199	0.00008	0.0132	889.75	0.0097	0.0041	51.66

Published in *Complementarity and Variational Problems*, Pang, J.-S and Ferris, M. eds, SIAM, 1997

The demand functions that satisfy the weak axiom of revealed preference and generalized monotonicity

D. L. Zhu

Management School, Fudan University, China and CRT, Universite dé Montréal, Montréal, Canada

Abstract. We prove that the individual demand function satisfying the Weak Axiom of Revealed Preference and the excess demand function satisfying the Wald's Axiom are pseudomonotone$^{+}_{*}$, a new class of generalized monotonicity. With this new concept, we refine the characterization of Zhou for the individual demand function. In particular, a full characterization for the excess demand functions satisfying the Wald's Axiom is derived.

Keywords: Individual demand function; Weak axiom of revealed preference; Excess demand function; Wald's Axiom; Generalized monotonicity

JEL classification: D11

1. Introduction

The weak axiom of revealed preference (WARP) has become one of the most fundamental pieces in demand theory, since it was introduced by Samulson in 1938. Many economists have attempted to provide characterizations of demand functions that satisfy WARP. One good result in this direction was obtained by Zhou (1995). In his paper, the technique of Hildenbrand and Jerison (1989) and Slutsky matrix were used to derive a full characterization of individual demand function. However, this trick does not work for excess demand functions that do not have the Slutsky decomposition. Until now, it is not clear whether a result can be derived for excess demand functions satisfying the Wald axiom, which is the counterpart of the Weak axiom of revealed preference for demand functions. In this paper it is proved that both excess demand function and individual demand function are pseudomonotone$^{+}_{*}$, a new class of generalized monotonicity introduced recently by Crouzeix et al. (1999). In this paper, a full characterization of pseudomonotone$^{+}_{*}$ mapping is used to refind the characterization of Zhou for the individual demand functions. Furthermore a new characterization for excess demand functions satisfying the Wald axiom is also derived by our new concept of generalized monotonicity.

2. New results of generalized monotonicity

In this section we study one new class of generalized monotonicity and its characterization. First, we recall that a mapping F is **pseudomonotone** on C if, for all x, y in C

$$\langle F(x), y-x\rangle \geqslant 0 \Rightarrow \langle F(y), y-x\rangle \geqslant 0. \tag{1}$$

Recently, Crouzeix et al. (1999) introduced the pseudomonotone$^+_*$ mapping as the following.

Definition 2.1. The mapping F is pseudomonotone$^+_*$ on C if it is pseudomonotone on C and, for all x, y in C:

$$\left.\begin{array}{l}\langle F(x), x-y\rangle = 0\\ \langle F(y), x-y\rangle = 0\end{array}\right\} \Rightarrow F(x) = F(y). \tag{2}$$

Crouzeix et al. (1999) provided the following two characterizations of pseudomonotone$^+_*$ mappings.

Theorem 1. *Assume that F is differentiable and pseudomonotone on C. Assume in addition that for all $x \in C$ there holds:*

$$\langle F(x), h\rangle = \langle F'(x)h, h\rangle = 0 \Rightarrow F'(x)h = 0. \tag{3}$$

Then F is pseudomonotone$^+_*$ on D. If F is affine, the condition is necessary as well.

Theorem 2. *Assume that C is an open convex set and F is pseudomonotone and differentiable on C. For $x \in C$ define $H_x = \{h: \langle F(x), h\rangle = 0\}$. Assume that for all $x \in C$ there holds:*

(i) *if $F'(x)$ is positive semidefinite then*

$$(F'(x))^T(\mathscr{R}^n) \subseteq [F'(x) + (F'(x))^T](\mathscr{R}^n) + \mathscr{R}F(x), \tag{4}$$

(ii) *if $F'(x)$ is not positive semidefinite then*

$$(F'(x))^T(\mathscr{R}^n) \subseteq [F'(x) + (F'(x))^T](H_x) + \mathscr{R}F(x). \tag{5}$$

Then F is pseudomonotone$^+_*$ on C.

In this paper, we get one more full characterization of the pseudomonotone$^+_*$ mapping, given by the following theorem. This result will be used to explore a full characterization of demand functions that satisfy WARP.

Theorem 3. *Assume that C is an open convex set and F is differentiable on C. Then F is pseudomonotone$^+_*$ is equivalent to the following two conditions:*

(i) *for any $x \in C$ and $\langle F(x), h\rangle = 0$ implies $\langle F'(x)h, h\rangle \geqslant 0$.*

(ii) *if $F(x+h) \neq F(x)$, then there exists some $a \in [0,1)$ such that $\langle F'(x+\alpha h)h, h\rangle > 0$.*

Proof.

1. Suppose that condition (i) and (ii) hold for any $x \in C$ and $h \in R^n$. From (i), F is pseudomonotone on C, see Crouzeix and Ferland (1996). Moreover, we assume that $\langle F(x), h\rangle = 0$ and $\langle F(x+h), h\rangle = 0$. From Lemma 1 of Crouzeix et al. (1999), we observe that $\langle F'(x+\alpha h)h, h\rangle = 0$, $\forall \alpha \in [0,1]$. Comparing with condition (ii), it fol-

lows that $F(x)=F(x+h)$, i. e., F is pseudomonotone$^+_*$ on C.

2. Now suppose that F is pseudomonotone$^+_*$ on C. The pseudomonotonicity directly implies condition (i), see Crouzeix and Ferland (1996). Assume that $F(x)\neq F(x+h)$ and $\langle F(x),h\rangle=0$. Since F is pseudomonotone$^+_*$, we must have $\langle F(x+h),h\rangle>0$. Denote $g(\alpha)=\langle F(x+\alpha h),h\rangle$. Thus $g(1)>0$, $g(0)=0$. Therefore, exists $\alpha\in[0,1)$ such that $g'(\alpha)>0$, i. e., $\langle F'(x+\alpha h)h,h\rangle>0$. □

3. Individual demand function satisfying the "Weak Axiom of Revealed Preference" (WARP)

Any function f from $R^n_{++}\times R_{++}$ to R is called an individual demand function if it is homogeneous and satisfies the budget balance condition. As Samuelson argued, a reasonable demand function should satisfy some minimal consistency conditions, for example, the weak axiom of revealed preference (WARP).

$$\langle f(p',b'),p\rangle\leqslant b,\langle f(p,b),p'\rangle\leqslant b' \text{ implies } f(p,b)=f(p',b') \tag{6}$$

Definition 3.1. *Quasi-negative definiteness. For any (p,b) and h, if $\langle f(p,b),h\rangle=0$, then $\langle\partial_p f(p,b)h,h\rangle\leqslant 0$; furthermore, if $f(p+h,b)\neq f(p,b)$, then there exists some $\alpha\in[0,1)$ such that $\langle\partial_p f(p+\alpha h,b)h,h\rangle<0$.*

Zhou (1995) used the technique of Hildenbrand and Jerison (1989) and the Slutsky matrix to deduce that for any differentiable demand function f, the following ones are equivalent: (a) f satisfies WARP. (b) f satisfies Quasi-negative. Our objective of this section is to state that the concept of pseudomonotone$^+_*$ can be used directly to get Zhou's result without using the technique of Hildenbrand and Jerison and the Slutsky matrix. Before obtaining this main result, we first transform an individual demand function into a mapping with n dimension. Denote $F(\bar{p})=f(p/b,1)$, where $\bar{p}=p/b$. Using the homogeneity of the demand function, the budget-identity and WARP conditions can be written as

(i) Budget-identity

$$\langle F(\bar{p}),\bar{p}\rangle=1,\forall\bar{p} \tag{7}$$

(ii) WARP

$$\langle F(\bar{p}'),\bar{p}\rangle\leqslant 1,\langle F(\bar{p}),\bar{p}'\rangle\leqslant 1 \text{ implies } F(\bar{p})=F(\bar{p}') \tag{8}$$

Theorem 4. *For any differentiable individual demand function, the following are equivalent: (a) f satisfies WARP, (b) $-F$ is pseudomonotone$^+_*$, (c) f satisfies Quasi-negative.*

Proof. (a)⇔(b). Suppose that the demand function $F(\bar{p})$ satisfies WARP condition, we will prove that $-F$ is pseudomonotone. Assume that $\langle F(\bar{p}),\bar{p}'-\bar{p}\rangle\leqslant 0$ and

$$\langle F(\bar{p}'),\bar{p}'-\bar{p}\rangle>0. \tag{9}$$

Since $F(\bar{p})$ satisfies the budget identity and WARP conditions, then $F(\bar{p})=F(\bar{p}')$ which follows the contradiction with (9). Thus, $\langle F(\bar{p}),\bar{p}'-\bar{p}\rangle\leqslant 0$ implies $\langle F(\bar{p}'),\bar{p}'-\bar{p}\rangle\leqslant 0$. Then, $-F(\bar{p})$ *is* pseudomonotone. Furthermore, with the budget identity and WARP conditions, if $\langle F(\overline{p}), \overline{p}'-\overline{p}\rangle=0$ and $\langle F(\overline{p}'), \overline{p}'-\overline{p}\rangle=0$, we obtain $F(\overline{p})=F(\overline{p}')$. Therefore $-F(\overline{p})$ is pseudomonotone$^{+}_{*}$.

Reversely, suppose that negative demand function $-F(\overline{p})$ is pseudomonotone$^{+}_{*}$. Since $F(\overline{p})$ is demand function, then it satisfies the budget-identity condition, i. e.,

$$\langle F(\overline{p}), \overline{p}\rangle = 1 \text{ and} \langle F(\overline{p}'), \overline{p}'\rangle = 1. \tag{10}$$

Moreover, suppose that

$$\langle F(\overline{p}), \overline{p}'\rangle \leqslant 1 \text{ and} \langle F(\overline{p}'), \overline{p}\rangle \leqslant 1 \tag{11}$$

we will prove that $F(\overline{p}) = F(\overline{p}')$, i. e., $F(\overline{p})$ satisfies WARP.

In fact, from (10, 11), we obtain

$$\langle F(\overline{p}'), \overline{p}-\overline{p}'\rangle \leqslant 0 \text{ and} \langle F(\overline{p}), \overline{p}'-\overline{p}\rangle \leqslant 0. \tag{12}$$

However, from the pseudomonotonicity of $-F(\overline{p})$, we get $\langle F(\overline{p}'), \overline{p}'-\overline{p}\rangle\leqslant 0$. Furthermore, we obtain

$$\langle F(\overline{p}'), \overline{p}-\overline{p}'\rangle \leqslant 0 \text{ and} \langle F(\overline{p}), \overline{p}'-\overline{p}\rangle = 0. \tag{13}$$

Finally, since $-F(\overline{p})$ is pseudomonotone$^{+}_{*}$ then $F(\overline{p})=F(\overline{p}')$. Thus, $F(\overline{p})$ satisfies WARP.

(b) ⇔ (c). From Theorem 1, we just need to prove that the following equivalences hold.

1. $\langle F(\overline{p}), \overline{h}\rangle=0 \Leftrightarrow \langle f(p,b), h\rangle=0$,
2. $\langle F'(\overline{p})\overline{h}, \overline{h}\rangle\leqslant 0 \Leftrightarrow \langle \partial_p f(p,b)h, h\rangle\leqslant 0$,
3. $F(\overline{p}+\overline{h})\neq F(\overline{p}) \Leftrightarrow f(p+h,b)\neq f(p,b)$,
4. $\langle F'(\overline{p}+\alpha\overline{h})\overline{h}, \overline{h}\rangle<0 \Leftrightarrow \langle \partial_p f(p+\alpha h,b)h, h\rangle<0$

where $\overline{h}=h/b$.

In fact, we observe that

(i) $F(\overline{p})=f(\overline{p},1)=f(p,b)$ and $\langle F(\overline{p}), \overline{h}\rangle=\frac{1}{b}\langle f(p,b), h\rangle$,

(ii) $F'(\overline{p})=b\partial_p f(p,b)$ and $\langle F'(\overline{p})\overline{h}, \overline{h}\rangle=\frac{1}{b}\langle \partial_p f(p,b)h, h\rangle$,

(iii) $F(\overline{p}+\overline{h})=f(p+h,b)$ and $F(\overline{p})=f(p,b)$,

(iv) $F'(\overline{p}+\alpha\overline{h})=b\partial_p f(p+\alpha h,b)$.

Therefore, conclusions(1)—(4) hold. □

4. Excess demand function satisfying the "Wald axiom"

Instead of an individual demand function, in this section we consider an excess demand function $D(p)$ that is homogeneous and satisfies the Walras' identity condition:

$$\langle D(p), p\rangle = 0 \quad \forall p. \tag{14}$$

Particularly, we are interested in the excess demand function satisfying the Wald Axiom:

$$\langle D(p), p'\rangle \leqslant 0, \langle D(p'), p\rangle \leqslant 0 \quad \text{implies} D(p) = D(p') \tag{15}$$

It is obvious the Wald's axiom and Walras' identity for an excess demand function D is formally analogous to the Weak axiom of revealed preference and budget identity for an individual function f. It's very interesting if the result parallel to individual demand function satisfying WARP can be derived for an excess demand function which satisfies Wald's axiom. However, it's well known that the excess demand function doesn't have Slutsky decomposition. Therefore, as stated by Zhou (1995), his trick does not work for excess demand functions satisfying Wald's axiom. In the previous section, we observe that the concept of pseudomonotone$^{+}_{*}$ plays a key role to get the full characterizations of individual demand satisfying WARP. It is natural that, with the tool of pseudomonotone$^{+}_{*}$ we can apply the results of Section 3 to the case of the excess demand function satisfying the Wald's axiom.

Proposition 1. *The excess demand function* $D(p)$ *satisfies Wald's axiom if only if* $-D(p)$ *is pseudomonotone*$^{+}_{*}$.

Proof. See the proof: (a)$\Leftrightarrow$(b) of Theorem 4. □

As a direct application of Theorem 5, full characterization of excess demand function D(p) satisfying Wald's axiom is derived in the following theorem.

Theorem 5. *For any differentiable demand function D, the following are equivalent:* (*a*) *D satisfies Wald's axiom;* (*b*) *D satisfies two following conditions:*

(i) *for any* $p \in R^n_{++}$, $h \in R^n$ *and* $\langle D(p), h\rangle = 0$ *implies* $\langle D'(p)h, h\rangle \leqslant 0$.

(ii) *if* $D(p+h) \neq D(p)$, *then there exists some* $a \in [0,1)$ *such that* $\langle D'(p+\alpha h)h, h\rangle < 0$.

Acknowledgements

Financial support by Shanghai-Hong Kong Education and Research Center (Fudan University and The University of Hong Kong), China, is gratefully acknowledged. I would like to thank Prof. Reinhard John, Bonn University for his careful reading of the paper and helpful comments.

References

Crouzeix, J.-P., Marcotte, P., Zhu., D. L., 1999. Conditions ensuring the applicability of cutting-plane methods for solving variational inequalities. Accepted by Mathematical Programming.

Crouzeix, J.-P., Ferland, J. A., 1996. Criteria of differentiable generalized monotone maps. Mathematical Programming 75, 399-406.

Hildenbrand, W., Jerison, M., 1989. The demand theory of the weak axioms of revealed preference. Economics Letters 29, 209-213.

Zhou, L., 1995. A characterization of demand functions that satisfy the weak axiom of revealed preference. Economics Letters 49, 403-406.

Published in *Ecomonics letter*, 2001, 70.

Existence and computation of optimal tolls in multiclass network equilibrium problems

P. Marcotte[a,*], D. L. Zhu[b]

a *DIRO, Université de Montréal, C. P.* 6128, *succursale Centre-Ville, Montréal, Québec, H3C 3J7 Canada*

b *School of Management, Fudan University, Shanghai, China*

Abstract. In this work we provide a simple proof of the existence of optimal tolls for multiclass network equilibrium problems where the value-of-time parameter varies continuously throughout the population. The main argument, based on a finite-dimensional reformulation of the problem, also allows us to determine in a simple fashion revenue minimizing link toll vectors.

Keywords. Network equilibrium Multiclass Optimal tolls Pricing

1. Introduction

For a transportation network subject to congestion it is a well known fact(seeBeckman net al. [1]) that, if tolls are setto the marginal costs corresponding to link usage, then the resulting equilibrium will minimize total travel delay. Although this approach is no longer valid when the valuation of travel delay varies across the population, it is still true that the set of tolls that induces a system-optimal use of the network is nonempty. For the case of finitely many classes of customers, each characterized by its own value-of-time (VOT) parameter, Yan gand Huang[2]have shown that such tolls could be set to the optimal dual vector of a network-structured linear program (see also Marcotte and Patriksson[3]). Slightly later, although the publishingyear pre-dates that of[2], Cole et al. [4] extended the result to the infinite-dimensional case (a single origin-destination pair however), using a two-step approach. First, they provided an alternative and existential proof of Yang and Huang's result, followed by a limiting argument, where they let the number of userclasses go to infinity. Independently, Fleischer et al. [5]and Karakostas and Kolliopoulos[6]obtained similar results and made the connection with the

* Corresponding author.

E-mail addresses: marcotte@iro. umontreal. ca (P. Marcotte), dlzhu@fudan. edu. cn (D. L. Zhu).

more general class of problems known as congestion games.

The aim of this work is to provide a simple and unifying proof of these results in the slightly more general framework of variational inequalities. Initially, we believed that this could be achieved by transposing in a trivial fashion the technique of Yang and Huang to the infinite-dimensional case. Unfortunately, in the absence of constraint qualifications, the duality argument could not be invoked any longer. However, it turns out that an implicit reformulation of the problem in finite dimension is amenable to a proof almost as direct as that of Yang and Huang, and considerably shorter and simpler than that of Cole et al. As a corollary, duality results for a class of semi-infinite linear programs are derived.

The work is structured as follows. In Section 2, we introduce the finite-dimensional multiclass problem, together with its infinitedimensional counterpart. We describe Yang and Huang's linear programming approach and discuss the difficulty of extending it to the infinite case. In Section 3, we propose a new formulation of the problem, which lends itself to treatment with Yang and Huang's technique. In Section 4, we address the computation of minimal toll schedules, an issue that had previously been considered in the finite-dimensional case.

2. The multiclass network equilibrium problem

Let us consider a multicommodity network characterized by its node set N, arc set A and set K of origin-destination pairs, each pair $k \in K$ being endowed with a fixed demand b_k. Let v_p denote the flow along path p. Let P_k denote the set of paths linking an OD pair $k \in K$. Let Ω_v be the set of demand-feasible path flow vectors v, defined as

$$\Omega_v = \left\{v \geqslant 0: \sum_{p \in P_k} v_p = b_k, \forall k \in K\right\}$$

or, in vector-matrix form:

$$\Omega_v = \{v \geqslant 0: Av = b\}.$$

In parallel, we introduce arc flows x_a, together with the compatibility relationship

$$x_a = \sum_{k \in K} \sum_{p \in P_k} \delta_{ap} v_p,$$

where δ_{ap}, an entry of the arc-path in cidence matrix Δ, takes value 1 if arc a belongs to path p, and value 0 otherwise. The set of feasible arc flows is defined, implicitly, as

$$\Omega_x = \{x : \exists\, v \in \Omega_v: x = \Delta v\}.$$

With each vector x we associate a generalized cost function $\alpha F(x) + T$, where the delay function F assumes positive values, but is not required to be separable, T is a toll vector, and the scalar α represents the valuation of one unit of delay by the users. On the basis of this notation, a feasible arc flow vector x satisfies Wardrop's equilibrium conditions with respect to T if and only if it solves the variational inequality

$$\langle \alpha F(x) + T, x - y \rangle \leqslant 0 \quad \forall y \in \Omega_x. \tag{1}$$

Equivalently, a feasible path flow vector v is Wardropian if and only if it solves the variational inequality

$$\langle \Delta^t (F(\Delta v) + T), v - w \rangle \leqslant 0 \quad \forall w \in \Omega_v. \tag{2}$$

Alternatively, a vector x^* is said to be system optimal if it minimizes total travel delay, i. e.,

$$x^* \in \arg \min_{x \in \Omega_x} \langle F(x,)x \rangle.$$

and a corresponding system-optimal path flow vector is denoted by v^*. The reader is referred to Marcotte and Patriksson [3] for further details concerning these standard formulations.

In this framework, our problem consists in finding a toll vector T such that the equilibrium associated with the modified cost $\alpha F(x) + T$ coincides with the efficient assignment x^*. If the VOT parameter α is uniform throughout the population, this can be achieved by setting T to the vector of scaled marginal arc costs $\alpha \langle F'(x^*) x^* \rangle$.

Next, consider an extension of the basic framework where α varies across users. To be precise, the population is partitioned into segments, where segment $i \in I$ is endowed with its own VOT parameter α_i. We associate with class i a probability $h(\alpha_i)$, a demand vector $h(\alpha_i)b$ and the feasible sets $\Omega_x(\alpha_i) = h(\alpha_i)\Omega_x$ and $\Omega_v(\alpha_i) = h(\alpha_i)\Omega_v$. Arc and path flow vectors associated with a class indexed by $i \in I$ are denoted by $x(\alpha_i)$ and $v(\alpha_i)$, respectively. The vector of total arc flows is defined as $X = \sum_{i \in I} x(\alpha_i)$ and the vector of total path flows as $V = \sum_{i \in I} v(\alpha_i)$. In this framework, we let $x = (x(\alpha_i))i$ denote the concatenation of class link flow vectors, which must belong to the feasible set $\Omega_x = \prod_{i \in I} \Omega_x(\alpha_i)$. The path flow vector and its feasible set are defined in a similar manner. We say that a multiclass equilibrium is reached when each class is in equilibrium, i. e.,

$$\langle \alpha_i F(X) + T, x(\alpha_i) - y(\alpha_i) \rangle \leqslant 0 \quad \forall y(\alpha_i) \in \Omega_x(\alpha_i), \forall i \in I. \tag{3}$$

The latter variational inequality can be aggregated to yield the equivalent

$$\sum_{i \in I} \langle \alpha_i F(X) + T, x - y \rangle \leqslant 0 \quad \forall y \in \Omega_x. \tag{4}$$

In this context, and for the sake of notational consistency, we denote by X^* the vector of system-optimal total link flows. Yang and Huang [2] have shown that the dual vector associated with the capacity constraints of the linear program

$$\min_{x \in \Omega_x} \quad \sum_{i \in I} \alpha_i \langle F(X^*), x(\alpha_i) \rangle \tag{5}$$

$$\text{subject to} \sum_{i \in I} x(\alpha_i) \leqslant X^* \tag{6}$$

induces X^*. Actually, this technique can be used to induce any flow pattern that satisfies some mild conditions, not only systemoptimal ones.

In this work, we are concerned with the situation where the mass vector $(h(\alpha_i))_i$ is replaced by a measurable, almost everywhere positive and square-integrable function having compact support $[0, \alpha_{\max}]$, that we still denote as h. The variables of the problem are then flow densities $x(\alpha) \in \Omega_x(\alpha)$ and $v(\alpha) \in \Omega_v(\alpha)$, with

$$\Omega_v(\alpha) = \left\{ v(\alpha) \geqslant 0 : \sum_{p \in \mathcal{K}} v_p(\alpha) = h(\alpha) b, a.\,e.\ \alpha \in [0, \alpha_{\max}] \right\} \tag{7}$$

$$\Omega_x(\alpha) = \Delta \Omega_v(\alpha) = \{ x(\alpha) : \exists\, v(\alpha) \in \Omega(\alpha) : x(\alpha) = \Delta v(\alpha) \} \tag{8}$$

The parallel with the finite-dimensional case is straightforward, with class flow vectors being replaced by square-integrable flow densities, and the feasible sets being members of the class of square-integrable vector functions having compact support $[0, \alpha_{\max}]$. Total flow vectors are then obtained by integrating flow densities over $[0, \alpha_{\max}]$ and an equilibrium x is reached when, almost everywhere on $[0, \alpha_{\max}]$, there holds

$$\langle \alpha F(X) + T, x(\alpha) - y(\alpha) \rangle \leqslant 0 \quad \forall\, y(\alpha) \in \Omega_x(\alpha),\ a.\,e.\ \alpha \in [0, \alpha_{\max}] \tag{9}$$

which, through aggregation (integration), is equivalent to the (multiclass) variational inequality

$$\text{MCVI} : \langle \alpha F(X) + T, x - y \rangle_2 \leqslant 0 \quad \forall\, y \in \Omega_x, \tag{10}$$

where $\langle . , . \rangle_2$ denotes the inner product of vector functions:

$$\langle f, g \rangle_2 = \int_0^{\alpha_{\max}} \langle f(\alpha), g(\alpha) \rangle d\alpha.$$

The corresponding path flow formulation of equilibrium is then

$$\langle \Delta^t (\alpha F(\Delta V) + T), v - w \rangle \leqslant 0 \quad \forall\, w \in \Omega_v \tag{11}$$

The above problem has been investigated from a theoretical and computational point of view, and actually lends itself to a variety of finite-dimensional formulations, for which the reader is referred to Leurent [7], Marcotte [8], and Marcotte and Zhu [9].

To derive link tolls that induce the system-optimal flow pattern X^*, it is tempting to mimic the technique of Yang and Huang by considering the conic linear program

$$\text{LPCON}: \min_{x \in \Omega_x} \langle \alpha F(X^*), x \rangle_2 \tag{12}$$

$$\text{subject to} \quad \int_0^{\alpha_{\max}} x(\alpha) \mathrm{d}\alpha \leqslant X^*. \tag{13}$$

Unfortunately, no known constraint qualification applies to the above problem, that would allow us to derive optimal tolls from the dual vector associated with the capacity constraint (see Bonnans and Shapiro [10] or Shapiro [11]).

Alternatively, one could consider one of the finite-dimensional formulations proposed by Marcotte [8], such as the one based on the threshold values ("breakpoints") of the VOT parameter α that define intervals where path flows are invariant. More precisely, consider the set of vertices x^e, indexed by E of the polyhedron Ω_x and a vector $\hat{\alpha} = (\alpha_e)_{e \in E}$ of VOT values. Under mild conditions, it can be shown that the equilibrium is related to a vector $\hat{\alpha}$ in the following manner: $x(\alpha) = h(\alpha) x^e$ if and only if $\alpha \in [\alpha_{e-1}, \alpha_e]$, with $\alpha_0 = 0$ and $\alpha_{|E|} = \alpha_{\max}$. Otherwise stated, the segment $[0, \alpha_{\max}]$ can be partitioned into intervals such that, within each interval, origin-destination flows are assigned to a unique path.

This relationship between breakpoint vectors and flow densities allows for a finite-dimensional reformulation of the equilibrium problem. On the basis of this, we can write down an equivalent of LPCON, where the capacity constraints are expressed as

$$\Gamma\left(\int_{a_{i-1}}^{a_i} h(\alpha)\,\mathrm{d}\alpha\right)_{i=1,\cdots,|E|} \leqslant X^*,$$

and Γ denotes the arc-vertex incidence matrix of the multicommodity network. Unfortunately, and quite surprisingly, unless the density function h is uniform (constant over the interval $[0,\alpha_{\max}]$), no constraint qualification could be derived for these nonconvex constraints which would have ensured the existence of dual variables and hence system-optimal tolls.

3. An implicit formulation of the toll problem

In this section, we introduce a finite-dimensional and implicit formulation of the toll problem upon which a simple proof of the existence of system-optimal tolls can be based, and which paves the way to efficient algorithms for their computation. It relies on the simple factthat, in order to verify whether a flow density vector x satisfies the variational inequality MCVI, only finite quantities are required. Indeed, the left-hand side of (10) can be written as

$$\begin{aligned}\langle \alpha F(X)+T, x-y\rangle_2 &= \left\langle F(X), \int_0^{\alpha_{\max}} \alpha(x(\alpha)-y(\alpha))\,\mathrm{d}\alpha\right\rangle \\ &\quad + \left\langle T, \int_0^{\alpha_{\max}} (x(\alpha)-y(\alpha))\,\mathrm{d}\alpha\right\rangle \\ &= \langle T, X-Y\rangle + \langle F(X), \overline{X}-\overline{Y}\rangle\end{aligned}$$

where $\overline{X}$and $\overline{Y}$represent, respectively, the average flow vectors associated with the flow density vectors x and y. It follows that the sole attributes of a density vector x required to check that it satisfies the conditions of a multiclass equilibrium are its total and average flows(moments of order 0 and 1). This prompts us to define the set of joint total and average flows

$$\overline{\Omega} = \left\{(X,\overline{X}) : \exists x \in \Omega_x : X = \int_0^{\alpha_{\max}} x(\alpha)\,\mathrm{d}\alpha, \overline{X} = \int_0^{\alpha_{\max}} \alpha x(\alpha)\,\mathrm{d}\alpha\right\}$$

for which there exist feasible flow densities. The situation parallels that of arc formulation of the standardt raffic assignment problems, where the set of feasible arc flows must be compatible with flows disaggregated by origins and destinations. In contrast with the latter case, one must be careful that this set is actually a polyhedron. This is taken care of in the following lemma.

Lemma 3.1. *Assume that the function h is measurable over the interval $[0,\alpha_{max}]$.*

Then the set $\overline{\Omega}$ is a polyhedron.

Proof. The set $\overline{\Omega}$ is trivially convex and bounded, so it remains to show that the number of its extreme points and extreme rays is finite. The argument is based on the relationship between extreme pointsof $\overline{\Omega}$ and the set of vertices of Ω_x. Note that a vertex of Ω_x is characterized by an assignment of flows to unique paths, one for each origin-destination pair. Now, let $(X, \overline{X}) \in \overline{\Omega}$ and assume that, for every OD pair, the total flow X corresponding to avertex of Ω is not assigned to a single path for each OD pair. It follows that there must exist a subset S of $[0, \alpha_{\max}]$ with positive measure over which the density function h also has positive measure, and for which the flow density is not concentrated on X. Consequently, there exist total flows X^1 and X^2 such that

$$x(\alpha) = h(\alpha)\frac{X^1 + X^2}{2}$$

for $\alpha \in S$. Next we introduce, for $i = 1, 2$, the functions

$$x^i(\alpha) = \begin{cases} h(\alpha)X^i & \text{if } \alpha \in S \\ x(\alpha) & \text{else,} \end{cases}$$

the corresponding total flow vectors $X^i = \int_0^{\alpha_{\max}} x^i(\alpha)\mathrm{d}\alpha$, and finally the average flow vectors $\overline{X}^i = \int_0^{\alpha_{\max}} \alpha x^i(\alpha)\mathrm{d}\alpha$, for $i = 1, 2$. From this construction, we have that $X = 1/2(X^1 + X^2)$ and $\overline{X} = 1/2(\overline{X}^1 + \overline{X}^2)$, with $X^1 \neq X^2$. Since $(X^1, \overline{X}^1)$ and $(X^2, \overline{X}^2)$ belong to $\overline{\Omega}$ by construction, $(X, \overline{X}) = 1/2((X^1, \overline{X}^1) + (X^2, \overline{X}^2))$, and $(X, \overline{X})$ is not extremal, as claimed. This is the desired contradiction that concludes the proof. The proof concerning extreme rays involves cycles in the original graph and is similar. Actually, cyclic flows are of little interest, as one may restrict one's attention to the convex envelope of extremal flows. □

We are now in position to provide a simple proof of the existence of "optimal" tolls.

Theorem 3.1. *Assume that the function h is measurable over the interval $[0, \alpha_{\max}]$. Then there exists a system-optimal toll vector for the multiclass equilibrium problem.*

Proof. Consider the mathematical program

$$\overline{\mathrm{LP}}: \min_{(X,\overline{X})\in\overline{\Omega}} \langle F(X^*, \overline{X})\rangle$$
$$\text{subject to } X \leqslant X^*.$$

Since $\overline{\Omega}$ is a polyhedron by Lemma 3.1, the above program is linear. Since X^* is the solution that achieves the minimum system cost, the fact that the cost function F is positive implies that the total flow vector *cannot* be less, componentwise, than X^*. It follows that X^* is the only feasible, and therefore optimal, partial solution of $\overline{\mathrm{LP}}$. From strong duality, there exists an optimal multiplier λ^* such that X^* is solution of the Lagrangean dual:

$$\min_{(X,\overline{X})\in\overline{\Omega}} \langle F(X^*), \overline{X}\rangle + \langle \lambda^*, X - X^*\rangle$$

or, equivalently, of the variational inequality

$$\langle F(X^*),\overline{X}^*-\overline{Y}\rangle+\langle\lambda^*,X^*-Y\rangle\leqslant 0\quad\forall(Y,\overline{Y})\in\overline{\Omega}.$$

This last inequality precisely states that the multiclass equilibrium x^* implicit in the definition of $(X^*,\overline{X}^*)$ is compatible with the system-optimal total flow vector X^*, provided that the toll vector is set to λ^*, the optimal dual vector of $\overline{\text{LP}}$. □

Note: As occurs in the discrete case, the linear program $\overline{\text{LP}}$ possesses a structure that can be exploited for its numerical resolution. This will actually be subsumed by the analysis of the next section.

4. Optimization over the set of optimal tolls

The main result of the previous section is a constructive proof that the set of optimal tolls is nonempty. This set is actually a polyhedron upon which one may optimize a secondary objective. Motivated by the analysis of Hearn et al. [12], we address the problem that consists in finding a positive optimal toll vector whose sum is minimal, and propose an efficient algorithm for its determination. Throughout this section, we assume that the implicitly defined polyhedron $\overline{\Omega}$ assumes the form

$$\overline{\Omega}=\{(X,\overline{X})\geqslant 0: AX+\overline{A}\,\overline{X}=\overline{b}\}.$$

Then, a toll vector T is system optimal if and only if $(X^*,\overline{X}^*)$ is an optimal solution of the linear program

$$\begin{aligned}\min_{X,\overline{X}}\quad & \langle T,X\rangle+\langle F(X^*),\overline{X}\rangle\\ \text{subject to}\quad & AX+\overline{A}\,\overline{X}=\overline{b}\\ & X,\overline{X}\geqslant 0,\end{aligned}$$

whose optimality conditions (dual feasibility and complementary slackness) are expressed as

$$\begin{aligned}&\mu A\leqslant T && \langle T-\mu A,X\rangle=0\\ &\mu\overline{A}\leqslant F(X^*) && \langle F(X^*)-\mu\overline{A},\overline{X}\rangle=0.\end{aligned}$$

Replacing X and $\overline{X}$ by X^* and $\overline{X}^*$ in the above, we have that T is optimal if and only if there exists a dual vector μ such that

$$\begin{aligned}&\mu A\leqslant T && \langle T-\mu A,X^*\rangle=0\\ &\mu\overline{A}\leqslant F(X^*) && \langle F(X^*)-\mu\overline{A},\overline{X}^*\rangle=0.\end{aligned}$$

A minimum-optimal toll can then be obtained by solving the linear program

$$\begin{aligned}\text{MINTOLL:}\ \min_{T,\mu}\quad & \langle T,X^*\rangle\\ \text{subject to}\quad & \mu A\leqslant T\\ & \mu\overline{A}\leqslant F(X^*)\\ & \langle T-\mu A,X^*\rangle+\langle F(X^*)-\mu\overline{A},\overline{X}^*\rangle=0.\end{aligned}$$

Using an exact penalty scheme for the complementarity constraint (this is always valid for finite-dimensional linear programs) and dividing the objective by the penalty constant M yields

$$\min_{T,\mu}\quad \frac{1}{M}\langle T,X^*\rangle+\langle T-\mu A,X^*\rangle+\langle F(X^*)-\mu\overline{A},\overline{X}^*\rangle$$

$$\text{subject to } \mu A - T \leqslant 0$$
$$\mu \overline{A} \leqslant F(X^*),$$

whose linear programming dual is

$$\min_{(X,\overline{X})\geqslant 0} \quad \langle F(X^*), \overline{X}\rangle$$
$$\text{subject to} \quad AX + \overline{A}\,\overline{X} = AX^* + \overline{A}\,\overline{X}^*$$
$$X \leqslant (1 + 1/M)X^*$$

or, since $AX^* + \overline{A}\,\overline{X}^* = \overline{b}$,

$$\min_{(X,\overline{X})\in\overline{\Omega}} \quad \langle F(X^*), \overline{X}\rangle$$
$$\text{subject to} \quad X \leqslant (1 + 1/M)X^*.$$

Using a convex and differentiable penalty function for the bound constraint, the latter mathematical program reduces to a convex multiclass problem that can be easily and efficiently solved by the techniques described in Marcotte and Zhu [9].

5. Conclusion

While we did not address some important modeling issues, such as equity (users of efficient paths might be penalized by the optimal toll scheme; see Lawphongpanich [13]) or cost non-separability (in some practical situations, tolls are set on paths rather than arcs of the network; see Agdeppa et al. [14], Maruyamaa and Sumalee [15]), we believe that our approach could be useful in addressing these situations as well.

From the theoretical point of view, a by-product of our analysis is a duality result for a class of conic linear programs. Note also that the Lebesgue measure that we adopted could be replaced by the Lebesgue-Stieltjes measure, thus providing a framework that unifies both the discrete and continuous cases.

Acknowledgments

This research was partially supported by NSFC (China), SLADPB120 (Shanghai), NSERC (Canada), FQRNT (Québec) and MITACS.

References

[1] M. Beckmann, C. B. McGuire, C. B. Winsten, Studies in the economics of transportation, Yale University Press, New Haven, Connecticut, 1956.

[2] H. Yang, H.-J. Huang, The multi-class, multi-criteria traffic network equilibrium and systems optimum problem, Transportation Research B 38B (2004) 1-15.

[3] P. Marcotte, M. Patriksson, Traffic equilibrium, in: C. Barnhardt, G. Laporte (Eds.), Transportation. Handbooks in Operations Research and Management Science, North-Holland, 2007, pp. 623-714.

[4] R. Cole, Y. Dodis, T. Roughgarden, Pricing network edges for heterogeneous selfish users, in: Proceedings of the 35th Annual ACM Symposium on Theory of Computing, San Diego, CA, USA, June 9-11, 2003.

[5] L. Fleischer, K. Jain, M. Mahdian, Tolls for heterogeneous selfish users in multicommodity net-

works and generalized congestion games, in: Proceedings of the 45th Annual IEEE Symposium on Foundations of Computer Science, Rome, Italy, October 2004.

[6] G. Karakostas, S. G. Kolliopoulos, Edge pricing of multicommodity networks for heterogeneous selfish users, in: Proceedings of the 45th Annual IEEE Symposium on Foundations of Computer Science, Rome, Italy, October 2004.

[7] F. Leurent, Cost versus time equilibrium over a network, European Journal of Operational Research 71 (1993) 205-221.

[8] P. Marcotte, Reformulations of a bicriterion equilibrium problem, in: M. Fukushima, L. Qi (Eds.), Reformulation-Nonsmooth, Piecewise Smooth, Semismooth and Smoothing Methods, Kluwer, Dordrecht, 1999, pp. 269-292.

[9] P. Marcotte, D. L. Zhu, Equilibria with infinitely many differentiated classes of customers, in: J.-S. Pang, M. Ferris (Eds.), Complementarity and Variational Problems, State of Art, SIAM, 1997, pp. 234-258.

[10] J. F. Bonnans, A. Shapiro, Perturbation Analysis of Optimization Problems, Springer-Verlag, New York, 2000.

[11] A. Shapiro, On duality theory of conic linear programming, in: Miguel A. Goberra, Marco A. Lopez (Eds.), Semi-Infinite programming: Recent Advances, Kluwer, Dordrecht, 2001, pp. 135-165.

[12] L. Bai, D. W. Hearn, S. Lawphongpanich, Decomposition techniques for the minimum toll revenue problem, Networks 44 (2004) 142-150.

[13] S. Lawphongpanich, Y. Yin, Pareto-improving congestion tolls for road networks, Working paper, Department of Industrial and Systems Engineering, University of Florida, Gainesville, available at: http://www.ise.ufl.edu/toi/Lawphong-Yin.pdf.

[14] R. P. Agdeppa, N. Yamashita, M. Fukushima, An implicit programming approach for the road pricing problem with nonadditive route costs, Journal of Industrial and Management Optimization 4 (2008) 183-197.

[15] T. Maruyamaa, A. Sumalee, Efficiency and equity comparison of cordonand area-based road pricing schemes using a trip-chain equilibrium model, Transportation Research A 41A (2007) 655-671.

Published Operations Research Letters, 2009

Emission charging in multi-class transportation networks equilibrium problems with infinitely user classes

Yihong Hu, Kedong Chen, Daoli Zhu*

School of Management, Fudan University, Shanghai, China, 200433

Abstract. In this paper we propose an emission charging scheme in a multi-class, multi-criteria transportation network equilibrium problem with infinitely user classes. We first identify a minimum emission flow and prove that without any subsidy there exist a non-negative optimal charging scheme which could induce the minimum flow pattern or minimum total emission. A numerical example is given to show the change of the VOT distribution cause different optimal charges. We demonstrate that when designing an emission charging scheme to reduce the emission, not only network topology, demand and cost function, but also VOT distribution should be taken into consideration.

Key words: Traffic equilibrium problem; Emissions; Value of time

1. Introduction

Urban road transport is well known as a significant and increasing resource of air pollution, responsible for 13% all the anthropogenic greenhouse gases and 23% CO in the world from the fossil fuel combustion(OECD, 2005). To reduce the environmental impact of transport, various measures including new technologies, governmental legislation and market force power-road pricing are introduced. Road pricing has been widely recognized as an efficient method to internalize the externalities of transportation such as congestion, pollution, noise (Button 1993; Johansson 1997; Nagurney 2000a). Recently emission pricing has been used in practice of Low Emission Zone(LEZ) in many European cities. For example, the city of London in Feb 2008 introduced a pricing scheme(500 or 200 daily fee) for vehicles into low emission zone, expected to reduce emissions by 16 percent by 2012. The LEZ charge is addition to any congestion charge.

Nagurney(2000b) studied emission paradoxes in the transportation network equilibrium. She identified that improvement in the network like travel demand decrease or road addition could cause the total emission increasing. To circumvent such paradoxes, Nagurney and Dong (2001) proposed an optimal pricing scheme to control the emission under a total emission volume constraint which guarantees that the users seek not only to minimize the cost of the route choice but also the emissions generated. Yin and Lawphongpanich(2006) studied the optimization problem of minimizing total traffic emission and indicated that there always exists an emission charge that induces a traffic flow with minimum emission, called as first-best emission charging. They also estimated the price of anarchy of emission charging. The above works all deal with the emission charging problem with homogeneous users, i. e. users have the same response to the tolls. Empirical studies(Small et al. 2005) have demonstrated that there is significant heterogeneity among travelers which varies according to household income, gender, age and time period of trip. The travelers heterogeneity has long been incorporated in congestion pricing modeling but not in emission pricing yet.

Value of time(VOT) is a very important concept in transportation network equilibrium modeling as it describes how heterogeneous users make tradeoffs between money and time in response to toll charges. Each user in the network is given a VOT, representing his evaluation of the time. With this VOT some users choose slower route to avoid tolls while others choose toll roads to save time. VOT could be a discrete set for several distinct user classes(Nagurney 2000a; Yang and Huang 2004) or a continuous distribution across the whole population for infinitely user classes(Leurent 1996; Marcotte and Zhu 1997; Dial 1999a; Dial 1999b; Mayet and Hansen 2000). VOT's distribution may be different from city to city due to demographical reason or from time to time due to social-economic status. For example, the VOT distribution in a metropolitan city is surely different to that in a famous travel site where is full of leisure tourists. And the social development or economic crisis could in average increase or decrease traveler's evaluation of time.

This paper is aimed to incorporate user heterogeneity into emission pricing problem and therefore provide an efficient charging scheme to reduce traffic emission to a minimum. We first formulate an infinite-dimensional multiclass network equilibrium model. Then we identify the minimum emission flow and prove that without any subsidy there exist non-negative optimal tolls which could induce the minimum flow pattern or minimum total emission. Through theoretical analysis and a numerical example, we show that when making the emission policy, not only the network structure, demand, cost functions and emission functions, but also the distribution of VOT should be taken into consideration.

The rest of the paper is structured as follows. Section 2 introduces the infinite-dimensional multiclass transportation network equilibrium problem. In Section 3, we discuss the problem of minimizing the total vehicle emissions and prove that there exist optimal tolls to induce the minimum emission flow pattern. In Section 4, a numerical example with two different VOT distributions is given to show that the VOT distribution have great impact on toll changes. Section 5 gives another model formulation which allows the total emission function to be linear and prove the existence of optimal tolls under total emission constraint. Section 6 is the conclusion.

2. The multi-class network equilibrium problem

Let us consider a transportation network defined by its node set N, arc set $\mathscr{A}$ and set K of origin-destination pairs, each pair $k \in K$ being endowed with a fixed demand b_k. Let v_p denote the flow along path p. Let P_k denote the set of paths linking an OD pair $k \in K$, and by Ω_v the set of demand-feasible path flow vectors v, i. e.,

$$\Omega_v = \{v \geqslant 0 : \sum_{p \in P_k} v_p = b_k, k \in K\}$$

or, in vector-matrix form:

$$\Omega_v = \{v \geqslant 0 : Av = b\}.$$

In parallel, we introduce arc flows x_a, together with the relationship

$$x_a = \sum_{k\in K}\sum_{p\in P_k}\delta_{ap}v_p,$$

where δ_{ap}, an entry of the arc-path incidence matrix Δ, takes value 1 if arc a belongs to path p, and value 0 otherwise. The set of feasible arc flows is defined, implicitly, as

$$\Omega_x = \{x : \exists v \in \Omega_v : x = \Delta v\}.$$

With each vector x we associate a generalized cost function $\alpha F(x)+T$, where the delay function F assumes positive values, but is not required to be separable, T is a emission charging vector, and the scalar α represents the valuation of one unit of delay by the users. Based on this notation, a feasible arc flow vector x satisfies Wardrop's equilibrium conditions with respect to T if and only if it solves the variational inequality

$$\langle \alpha F(x) + T, x - y\rangle \leqslant 0 \quad \forall y \in \Omega_x. \tag{1}$$

Equivalently, a feasible pathflow vector v is Wardropian if and only if it solves the variational inequality

$$\langle \Delta^t(\alpha F(\Delta v) + T), v - w\rangle \leqslant 0 \quad \forall w \in \Omega_v. \tag{2}$$

Next, consider an extension of the basic framework where α varies across users. Precisely, the population is partitioned into segments, where segment $i\in I$ is endowed with a VOT parameter α_i[1] We associate with class i a probability $h(\alpha_i)$, a demand vector $h(\alpha_i)b$ and the feasible sets $\Omega_x(\alpha_i)=h(\alpha_i)\Omega_x$ and $\Omega_v(\alpha_i)=h(\alpha_i)\Omega_v$.

Arc and path flow vectors associated with a class indexed by $i\in I$ are denoted by $x(\alpha_i)$ and $v(\alpha_i)$, respectively. The vector of total arc flows is defined as $X = \sum_{i\in I}x(\alpha_i)$ and the vector of total path flows as $V = \sum_{i\in I}V(\alpha_i)$ In this framework, we let $x=((x(\alpha_i))_i$ denote the concatenation of class link flow vectors, which must belong to the feasible set $\Omega_x = \prod_{i\in I}\Omega_x(\alpha_i)$. The path flow vector and its feasible set are defined in a similar manner. We say that a multiclass equilibrium is reached when *each* class is in equilibrium, i. e.,

$$\langle \alpha_i F(X) + T, x(\alpha_i) - y(\alpha_i)\rangle \leqslant 0 \quad \forall y(\alpha_i) \in \Omega_x(\alpha_i), \quad \forall i \in I. \tag{3}$$

The latter variational inequality can be aggregated to yield the equivalent

$$\sum_{i\in I}\langle \alpha_i F(X) + T, x - y\rangle \leqslant 0 \quad \forall y \in \Omega_x. \tag{4}$$

Yang and Huang (2004) have shown that the dual vector associated with the capacity constraints of the linear program

$$\min_{x\in\Omega_x} \quad \sum_{i\in I}\alpha_i\langle F(X^*), x(\alpha_i)\rangle \tag{5}$$

[1] Throughout the paper we assume, strictly for ease of exposition reasons, that the probability mass function is identical for all origin-destination pairs.

$$\text{s. t.} \qquad \sum_{i \in I} x(\alpha_i) \leqslant X^* \tag{6}$$

induces system optimal flow X^*. Actually, this technique can be used to induce minimal emission flow pattern that satisfies some mild conditions, not only system-optimal ones.

In this paper, we are concerned with the situation where the mass vector$(h(\alpha_i))_i$ is replaced by a measurable, almost everywhere positive and square-integrable function that we still denote h, and having compact support $[0, \alpha_{\max}]$. The variables of the problem are thenflow densities $x(\alpha) \in \Omega_x(\alpha)$ and $v(\alpha) \in \Omega_v(\alpha)$, with

$$\Omega v(\alpha) = \{v(\alpha) \geqslant 0 : \sum_{p \in \mathcal{K}} v_p(\alpha) = h(\alpha)b, \quad \text{a. e.} \quad \alpha \in [0, \alpha_{\max}]\} \tag{7}$$

$$\begin{aligned} \Omega_x(\alpha) &= \Delta\Omega_v(\alpha) \\ &= \{x(\alpha) : \exists\, v(\alpha) \in \Omega_v(\alpha) : x(\alpha) = \Delta v(\alpha)\}. \end{aligned} \tag{8}$$

and total flow $X \in \hat{\Omega}$ with

$$\hat{\Omega} = \{X \in R^n : X = \int_0^{\alpha_{\max}} x(\alpha) d\alpha, x(\alpha) \in \Omega_x(\alpha)\} \tag{9}$$

The parallel with the finite-dimensional case is straightforward, with class flow vectors being replaced by square-integrable flow densities, and the feasible sets being members of the class of square-integrable vector functions having compact support $[0, \alpha_{\max}]$. Total flow vectors are then obtained by integrating flow densities over $[0, \alpha_{\max}]$ and an equilibrium x is reached when, almost everywhere on $[0, \alpha_{\max}]$, there holds

$$\langle \alpha F(X) + T, x(\alpha) - y(\alpha) \rangle \leqslant 0 \quad \forall\, y(\alpha) \in \Omega_x(\alpha), \quad \text{a. e.} \quad \alpha \in [0, \alpha_{\max}] \tag{10}$$

which, through aggregation(integration), is equivalent to the(multiclass) variational inequality

$$\text{MCVI}: \langle \alpha F(X) + T, x - y \rangle \leqslant 0 \quad \forall\, y \in \Omega_x, \tag{11}$$

where $\langle \cdot, \cdot \rangle$ denotes the inner product of vector functions:

$$\langle f, g \rangle = \int_0^{\alpha_{\max}} \langle f(\alpha), g(\alpha) \rangle d\alpha.$$

The corresponding path flow formulation of equilibrium is then

$$\langle \Delta^t(\alpha F(\Delta V) + T), v - w \rangle \leqslant 0 \quad \forall\, w \in \Omega_v. \tag{12}$$

Marcotte, P. and Zhu, D. L. (2009) introduce the concept of *average* flow vectors associated with the flow density vectors $x(\alpha)$:

$$\overline{X} = \int_0^{\alpha_{\max}} \alpha x(\alpha) d\alpha,$$

and define the set

$$\overline{\Omega} = \{(X, \overline{X}) : \exists\, x \in \Omega_x : X = \int_0^{\alpha_{\max}} x(\alpha) d\alpha, \overline{X} = \int_0^{\alpha_{\max}} \alpha x(\alpha) d\alpha\}.$$

Then, variational inequality MCVI can be rewrited as

$$\langle T, X - Y \rangle + \langle F(X), \overline{X} - \overline{Y} \rangle \leqslant 0, \quad \forall\, (Y, \overline{Y}) \in \overline{\Omega}.$$

The following lemma allow us to obtain a finite-dimensional and implicit formulation of the emission charging problem upon which a simple proof of the existence of optimal emission charging can be provided, and paves the way to efficient algorithms for their computation.

Lemma 1. *Assume that the function $h(\alpha)$ is measureable over the interval $[0, \alpha_{\max}]$. Then the set $\overline{\Omega}$ is a polyhedron.*

Proof. See Marcotte, P. and Zhu, D. L. (2009).

3. Emission charging scheme with minimal emission pattern

Consider emission function $E(X)$ to estimate vehicular emission (e. g. CO). The following optimization problem is called as the minimum emission problem that determines a flow pattern with the minimal emission:

$$\text{ME:} \quad \min \quad \langle E(X), x\rangle$$
$$\text{s.t.} \quad x \in \Omega_x(\alpha)$$

Let x_E denote an optimal solution of ME, i. e. x_E is a minimum total emission flow.

The problem ME can be formulated in total flow.

$$\overline{\text{ME}}: \quad \min \quad \langle E(X), X\rangle$$
$$\text{s.t.} \quad X \in \hat{\Omega}$$

with the optimal solution X_E. Denote $g(X)=\langle E(X), X\rangle$ be the total emission. In the following we introduce the relation of two vectors: $X>Y$, i. e., every component of X is larger than that of Y, there exists at least one component of X strictly larger than that of Y.

Assumption H: If $X>Y$, then $g(X)>g(Y)$.

Remark 1. *If $X>Y$ implies that $E(X)>E(Y)$, then Assumption H satisfied.*

This assumption is quite general. Many emission factor functions are decreasing with travel speed v as long as v is not too large (Yin 2006; Xia and Shao 2005; Corvalán and Vargas 2003). Note that the average speed $v_a = l_a/F_a(X)$ with l_a being arc length vector and $F_a(X)$ is non-decreasing, we can easily draw the conclusion that emission factor functions are increasing with traffic flow X. Therefore Remark 1 is satisfied.

Remark 2. *If $g(X)$ is convex and differentiable with $\nabla g(X)$ is positive on $\hat{\Omega}$., then we have*

$$\langle \nabla g(Y), X-Y\rangle \leqslant g(X)-g(Y)$$

and Assumption H is satisfied.

An instance of Remark 2 is that $E(X)$ is an afine function defined as $E(X)=MX+b$ with M is a positive semi-definite matrix. A more especial case is a constant $E(X)$ function (Nagurney 2000b; Nagurney 2001).

In this paper, the interesting problem consists in finnding an emission charging vector T such that the equilibrium associated with the modified cost $\alpha F(x)+T$ coincides with the efficient assignment x_E. If the VOT parameter α is uniform throughout the population, this can be achieved by setting T to the vector of scaled marginal arc costs $(E'(x_E)x_E+E(x_E)-F(X_E))\alpha$.

We say that T is a "valid" vector of emission charge if when added to the mapping $F(X)$, it makes a minimum total emission flow solve the following multi-criteria, multi-class user equilibrium problem,

$$\langle \alpha F(X) + T, x - y \rangle \leqslant 0, \quad \forall y \in \Omega_x(\alpha) \tag{13}$$

A valid emission charging scheme induces multi-class users to use route that lead to a minimum emission total flow.

Theorem 1. (*Existence of the valid emission charges*): *If Assumption H is satisfied on $\hat{\Omega}$, then there exists a nonnegative valid emission charging vector with minimal emission pattern.*

Proof. Consider the optimization problem

$$\begin{aligned} \text{LP:} \quad & \min \quad \langle \alpha F(X_E), x \rangle \\ & \text{s. t.} \quad \int_0^{\alpha_{\max}} x(\alpha) d\alpha \leqslant X_E \\ & \qquad\quad x \in \Omega_x \end{aligned}$$

or

$$\begin{aligned} \overline{\text{LP}}_1: \quad & \min_{(X,\overline{X}) \in \hat{\Omega}} \quad \langle F(X_E), \overline{X} \rangle \\ & \text{s. t.} \quad X \leqslant X_E \end{aligned}$$

Since $\hat{\Omega}$ is a polyhedron by Lemma 1, the above program is linear. Since X_E is the solution that achieves the minimum emission, the assumption H implies the total flow vector cannot be less component than X_E. It follows that X_E is the only feasible, and therefore optimal, partial solution of $\overline{\text{LP}}_1$. From strong duality, there exists a non-negative optimal multiplier λ^* such that X_E is the solution of the Lagrangean dual:

$$\min_{(X,\overline{X}) \in \hat{\Omega}} \langle F(X_E), \overline{X} - \overline{X}_E \rangle, + \langle \lambda^*, X - X_E \rangle$$

or, equivalently, of the variational inequality

$$\langle \alpha F(X_E) + \lambda^*, x - x_E \rangle \geqslant 0, \quad \forall x \in \Omega_x$$

i. e. λ^* is a non-negative valid emission charging vector.

4. Emission pricing depends on VOT-a numerical example

From the above proof, we can see that emission charging vector is closely related to value-of-time α. We provide a simple example in this section to show that emission pricing policy is dependent on VOT distributions, in addition to network topology, cost function and demand. In our example, the latency function is nonseparable, asymmetric affine function.

The network topology is depicted in the Fig. 1 in which there are three arcs: a, b, c connecting the O-D pair $w=(1,2)$. The latency functions on these arcs are: $F_a(X)=X_a+X_b+7$, $F_b(X)=X_b+X_c+8$, $F_c(X)=X_a+X_c+6$. The fixed demand between the OD pair is: $b=6$. The emission functions on the links are: $E_a(X)=(1/2)X_a+1$, $E_b(X)=$

$(1/3)X_b+2, E_c(X)=(1/6)X_c+3$. Clearly the total emission function $g(X)$ is the case in Remark 2 and therefore satisfies the assumption H. So we could use Theorem 1 to find the valid tolls. Through calculation we find that the minimal emission flow distribution is $X_a=2.4545, X_b=2.1818, X_c=1.3636$, and the total minimal emission is 15.8182.

The government or the regulator of network would like to design emission charges to make the minimal emissionfiow X_E as user equilibriumfiow distribution. Assume there are two different VOT distributions due to difierent social-economic conditions, we display in the below that the government should change emission tolls when $h(\alpha)$ has changed.

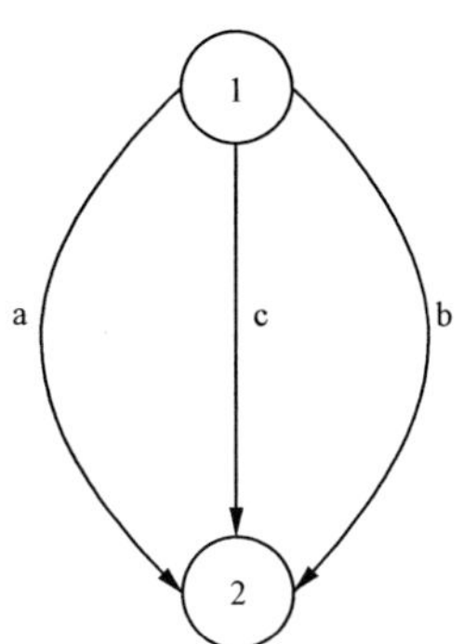

Figure 1: Network topology.

(1). First the VOT distribution $h(\alpha)$ takes the function displayed in the left in the Fig. 2: $h(\alpha)=-1/2\alpha+1$, $\alpha\in[0,2]$, which indicates that in the population there are a large part of travelers don't value time high. Through calculation we obtain the set of valid optimal tolls with the relationship: $T_a=T_b-0.0421, T_c=T_b+1.8078$ with $T_b>0.0421$ to insure the non-negativity. For example, we can let $T_b=1$, then $T_a=0.9579, T_c=2.8078$. This is one valid optimal toll in this situation.

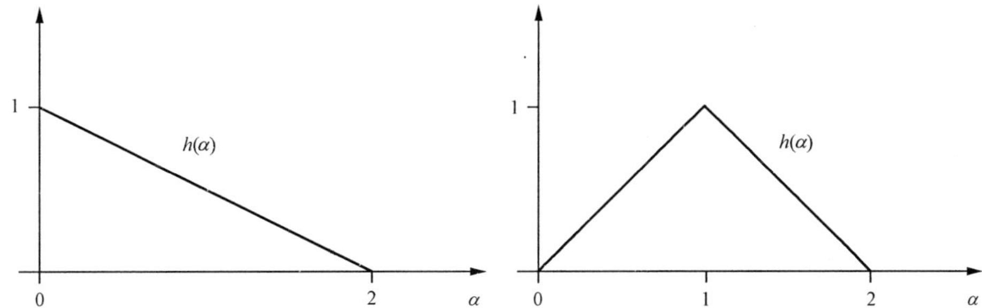

Figure 2: Left: A VOT distribution function $h(\alpha)=-1/2\alpha+1, \alpha\in[0,2]$.
Right: Another VOT distribution function $h(\alpha)=\alpha, \alpha\in[0,1], h(\alpha)=-\alpha+2, \alpha\in[1,2]$.

(2). Then due to some social economic reason such as the accelerations of life pace or demographic shift, more people value time important and the distribution becomes: $h(\alpha)=\alpha, \alpha\in[0,1], h(\alpha)=-\alpha+2, \alpha\in[1,2]$, as depicted in the right of Fig. 2. If we still use the previous tolls, it will cause the following unexpected emission cost. We can compute the network equilibrium using the algorithm presented in Marcotte and Zhu (1997) and get the network equilibrium arc flow are: $X_a=0.6420, X_b=2.6311, X_c=2.7269$. The total emission now generated is 17.8379, larger than the minimal total emission 15.8182.

Aware of the VOT distribution shift, we calculate the problem again and find the set of valid optimal tolls with the relationship: $T_a=T_b-0.0822, T_c=T_b+2.2901$. If

$T_b=1$, we must take the charging as $T_a=0.9178$, $T_c=3.2901$ to achieve the minimal total emission.

From the above example we see that for different VOT distribution, different emission charging should be placed to achieve the same emission objective.

5. Emission charging scheme with minimal total emission

In this section, we consider the emission charging scheme with minimum total emission constraint. Here we assume that total emission function $g(X)$ is linear, indicating that $E(X)$ is constant which is often assumed in emission pricing studies (Nagurney 2000; Nagurney 2001).

Theorem 2. *If $g(X)$ is linear and $\nabla g(X)$ is positive on $\hat{\Omega}$, then there exists a non-negative valid emission charing vector with minimal total emission.*

Proof. Consider the variational inequality problem: find $x\in\Omega_x$ such that

$$\langle \alpha F(X^*), x-x^*\rangle \geqslant 0, \quad \forall x\in\{x\in\Omega_x \mid g(X)\leqslant Q_E\}$$

where $Q_E=g(X_E)$.

This variational inequality can be formulated in finite dimension.

$$\langle F(X^*), \overline{X}-\overline{X}^*\rangle \geqslant 0, \quad \forall X\in\{(X,\overline{X})\in\overline{\Omega} \mid g(X)\leqslant Q_E\}$$

Since the constraint set is convex and compact, $F(X)$ is continuous, then the solution $(X^*, \overline{X}^*)$ exists. Fixed $\overline{X}^*$, consider the optimization problem

$$\begin{aligned} &\min \quad \langle \alpha F(X^*), x\rangle \\ &\text{s. t.} \quad g(X)\leqslant Q_E \end{aligned}$$

or

$$\overline{LP}_2 \quad \begin{aligned} &\min_{(X,\overline{X})\in\overline{\Omega}} \quad \langle F(X^*), \overline{X}\rangle \\ &s.t. \quad g(X)\leqslant Q_E \end{aligned}$$

Since $Q_E=g(X_E)$, X_E is the minimum total emission. we must have $g(X^*)=Q_E=g(X_E)$. Another hand for strongly duality of linear programming, there exists dual $\lambda^*\geqslant 0$ such that X^* is the solution of the Lagrangean dual:

$$\min_{(X,\overline{X})\in\overline{\Omega}} \langle F(X^*), \overline{X}-\overline{X}^*\rangle + \langle \lambda^*, g(X)-Q_E\rangle$$

or equivalent of the variational inequality: Find $x^*\in\Omega_x$

$$\langle \alpha F(X^*)+\lambda^*\nabla g(X^*), x-x^*\rangle \geqslant 0, \quad \forall x\in\Omega_x$$

Since $g(X^*)=Q_E$ and ∇g is non-negative vector on $\hat{\Omega}$, then $\lambda^*\nabla g(X^*)$ is a non-negative valid emission charging vector with minimal total emission.

6. Conclusion

In this paper, we study the problem of emission pricing in multi-class transportation network equilibrium with infinite user classes. We prove the existence of non-negative optimal tolls to realize a minimum emission flow pattern or minimum total emission. Using a simple example we show that the emission pricing policy is dependent on VOT distribution. When designing an emission pricing policy to reduce the emission, not only network topology, demand, cost functions and emission functions, but also VOT distribution should be taken into consideration. There are some questions worth further investigating, such as the proof of existence of valid emission charging when the total emission function $g(X)$ is nonlinear in Section 5.

References

Button, K. J. , 1993. Transport economics. Edward Elgar, Northampto.

Corvalán, R. M. , Vargas, D. , 2003. Experimental analysis of emission deterioration factors for light duty catalytic vehicles case study: Santiago, Chile. Transportation Research 8D, 315-322.

Dial, R. B. , 1999a. Network-optimized road pricing: Part I: A parable and a model. Operations Research 47, 1, 54-64.

Dial, R. B. , 1999b. Network-optimized road pricing: Part II: Algorithms and examples. Operations Research 47, 2, 327-336.

Johansson, O. , 1997. Optimal road-pricing: simultaneous treatment of time losses, increased fuelconsumption, and emissions. Transportation Research 2D, 77-87.

Mayet, J. , Hansen, M. , 2000. Congestion pricing with continuously distributed values of time. Journal of Transport Economics and Policy 34, 359C370.

Marcotte, P. , Zhu, D. L. , 1997. Equilibria with infinitely many differentiated classes of customers, in: Complementarity and Variational Problems, State of Art. Pang, J. -S. and Ferris, M. eds. , SIAM 234-258.

Marcotte, P. , Zhu, D. L. , 2009. Existence and computation of optimal tolls in multiclass network equilibrium problem. Operations Research Letter, in press.

Nagurney, A. , 2000a. Sustainable transportation networks. Edward Elgar Publishers, Cheltenham.

Nagurney, A. , 2000b. Congested urban transportation networks and emission paradoxes. Transportation Research 5D, 145C151.

Nagurney, A. , Dong, J. , 2001. Paradoxes in networks with zero emission links: implications for telecommunications versus transportation. Transportation Research 6D , 283-296.

Nagurney , A. , Dong, J. , 2002. A multiclass, multicriteria traffic network equilibrium model with elastic demand. Sage Urban Studies Abstracts 304, 415-517.

OECD report, 2004.

Small, K. A. , Winston, C. , Yan, J. , 2005. Uncovering the distribution of motorists' preferences for travel time and reliability. Econometrica 73, 4, 1367-1382.

Xia, L. P. , Shao, Y. P. , 2005. Modelling of trafficfiow and air pollution emission with application to Hong Kong Island. Environmental Modelling and Software 20, 1175-1188.

Yang, H. , Huang, H. J. , 2004. The multi-class, multi-criteria traffic network equilibrium and systems optimum problem. Transportation Research 38B, 1-15.

Yin, Y. , Lawphongpanich, S. , 2006. Internalizing emission exterenality on road networks. Transportation Research 11D , 292-301.

第四章 用于交通网络系统设计的二层优化与控制研究

交通系统是一个复杂的服务系统，它由服务对象和服务者、交通设施组成。交通系统设计者必须考虑出行者行为和交通网络设施等。交通系统设计和控制可归纳为一个二层优化和控制问题，在20世纪90年代，二层优化和控制及变分不等式理论和计算是交通科学领域的重要研究方向。交通科学的需求和发展促进了变分不等式和二层优化控制的发展，而后者又为交通科学与工程提供了理论工具和方法。由于二层优化控制问题是一个困难的科学问题，这个领域的研究也推动了非线性分析数学分支的发展。

本章介绍了作者和合作者在二层优化和控制的最优化条件理论以及有效计算方法方面的研究，其成果可应用于交通网络设计及收益管理。例如，Marcotte, Savard and Zhu (2009) 利用二层优化方法研究航空服务收益管理问题，其下层问题是多类出行者多目标交通均衡问题。

Mathematical structure of a bilevel strategic pricing model

Patrice Marcotte* ,Gilles Savard,Daoli Zhu

DIRO and CRT ,Université de Montréal ,C. P. 6128 ,Succursale Centre-Ville ,Montréal (Québec) ,Canada H3C 3J7 MAGI and GERAD ,École Polytechnique-Montréal ,C. P. 6079 ,Succursale Centre-ville ,Montréal (Québec) ,Canada H3C 3A7 Department of Management Science ,Fudan University ,220 Handan Road ,Shanghai 20433 ,China

Abstract. This paper is concerned with the characterization of optimal strategies for a service firm acting in an oligopolistic environment. The decision problem is formulated as a leader-follower game played on a transportation network, where the leader firm selects a revenue maximizing price schedule that takes explicitly into account the rational behavior of the customers. In the context of our analysis, the follower's problem is associated with a competitive network market involving non atomic customer groups. The resulting bilevel model can therefore be viewed as a model of product differentiation subject to structural network constraints.

Keywords: Pricing; Productivity and competitiveness; Revenue management; Economics; Game theory

1. Introduction

In the context of deregulation, much attention is being paid to the design of managerial tools for optimizing revenues. In the airline industry, a 'Yield Management' strategy (see McGill and Van Ryzin, 1999; Belobaba, 1987) consists in addressing, concurrently or sequentially, four interrelated issues: demand forecasting, pricing, seat allocation and overbooking. While an optimization model that deals simultaneously with these issues cannot be realistically considered, several attempts have been made at addressing them individually, one market at a time. However, the strong interconnections between markets, as well as the bilateral impacts of pricing and seat allocation policies, which are often designed by separate departments within an airline, point to the weaknesses of such disaggregate approaches.

---

*Corresponding author. Tel. : +1 514 343 5941; fax: +1 514 343 7121.

E-mail addresses: marcotte@iro. umontreal. ca (P. Marcotte), gilles. savard@polymtl. ca (G. Savard), dlzhu@fudan. edu. cn (D. L. Zhu).

In this paper, we consider a bilevel model of revenue management for an industry operating within an oligopolistic environment characterized by a network structure and the partition of demand into user groups, each group being endowed with its valuation of the products' attributes. Although the model could be applied to various sectors of an economy (hotels, manufacturing industry, etc.), we use as our base paradigm that of an airline whose aim is to design a revenue maximizing strategy based on jointly optimal pricing and seat allocation policies. Such a strategy takes explicitly into account the fnite capacity of the leader's fleet, as well as the behaviour of each user group. This results in a strategy that discriminates between customers, according to their willingness to pay for flights with high quality of service or short duration. While we assume that the overall demand for transportation is inelastic over the planning horizon, the demand specific to the leader airline is dependent on its fare and seat allocation policies; in that sense, the model addresses, partially, the issue of demand forecasting previously mentioned as one of the four key components of the 'Yield Management' decision process.

Two of the model's features have been widely studied in the economic literature (see Martin, 1993), namely product differentiation (Hotelling, 1929; Gabszewicz and Thisse, 1986) and customer segmentation (Gabszewicz and Thisse, 1979; Phlips and Thisse, 1982), both these features paving the way to price discrimination (Phlips, 1983). The main goal of this paper is to characterize the market structure resulting from the underlying network topology, a result previously achieved only on a simple two-node network by Leurent (1993). Our approach can also be viewed as a differential markets extension of the taxation model of Labbé et al. (1998).

Finally, the reader is referred to Loridan and Morgan (1996) for an analysis of the relationship between bilevel programs and Stackelberg (leader-follower) games.

The paper is structured as follows: in Section 2 we motivate and formulate a strategic model of revenue management, whose mathematical properties are analyzed in Section 3, and for which an algorithmic framework is developed Section 4.

2. A product differentiation model

To illustrate the concepts introduced and analyzed in this paper, let us consider a system composed of airlines (or alliances) competing for market share on overlapping networks. Such a system, corresponding to the competitive market 'Montreal-Shanghai', is shown in Fig. 1.

In this network, the cities of Vancouver, Tokyo and New York correspond to connection hubs, while the arcs represent the various fight legs. In this example, we select AC as the leader company, which operates both a single leg fight to Vancouver and a connecting fight to Shanghai, and set the travellers to be the followers. This company selects fares T_{MV} on the Montreal-Vancouver part of the trip and T_{VS} on the transpacific leg, given fixed fare schedules from its competitors. For ease of presentation, we assume that fares are associated with legs although, in real life, they are associated with fights between origin and destination nodes (see C oté et al., 2002 for the description of a fight-based model). The fight structure offered by three competing companies over the Montreal-Shanghai market is specified in Table 1.

The revenue of AC is clearly dependent on the fare structure within the system and on the demand for the entire flight composed of two legs. The demand for a given flight may be interpreted as the reaction to the market's fare structure and the attractiveness of the flight with respect to competing proposals. In the above simplistic example, flights are only differentiated by their respective duration and number of legs (i. e., number of connections plus one). In real life, passengers select a product endowed with several attributes. While price and time are the prime components of a given product, others have to be considered as well, such a the choice of a cabin (economy, business or first class) and of various features associated with a ticket (refundable or not, advance purchase, minimum stay, etc.). This results in as many as 25 products ('Fare Basis Codes') for a given flight, for which a number of aircraft seats has to be assigned. For notational simplicity, we shall not consider this seat allocation problem, and assume that all seats of the aircraft share the same attributes.

On the demand side, we assume that each traveller is characterized by a trade-off value between time and money, which we denote by the letter α. If T_a and C_a are, respectively, the fare and the travel time associated with leg a of some. flight, then the perceived disutility (cost) GC_a of a traveller of the 'group' having VOT (Value of Time) α is

$$GC_a = T_a + \alpha C_a,$$

where α is a continuous random variable with density $\psi_w(\alpha)$ that could depend on the origin-destination w. Natural and important extensions of this concept, which are not investigated in this paper, are nonlinear valuations of time and market segmentation of the VOT.

Faced with a supply for transportation from its origin node to its destination node, a customer selects the flight that minimizes its own disutility. Due to the continuity assumption on the distribution of α, the choice of the optimal flight is nonambiguous, with the exception of a finite number of values of the parameter α, whenever travel times for a given O-D pair are distinct (see Marcotte and Zhu, 1997). The demand for a given flight is obtained by integrating the density function ψ_w over the set of α values (intervals, actually) for which that flight is optimal. This yields a continuous and piecewise differential demand mapping.

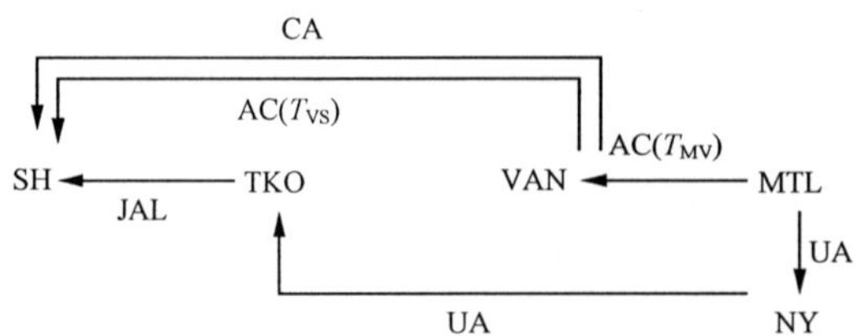

Fig. 1 Structure of the flight market.

Table 1 Flight structure for the Montreal-Shanghai market (prices in $ CAN)

Flight	Airline	Path	Rate	Travel time (hours)
1	UA+JAL	Montreal-NewYork-Tokyo-Shanghai	$ 1320	36
2	AC+CA	Montreal-Vancouver-Shanghai	T_{MV} + $ 720	26
3	AC+AC	Montreal-Vancouver-Shanghai	$T_{MV}+T_{VS}$	18

Even on a problem of very small size, as that considered a bove, the choice of revenue-maximizing fares T_{MV} and T_{VS} is far from obvious, as it depends on

- the shape of the density function ψ_w,
- the network structure (a high value of T_{MV} might make sense on the Montreal-Vancouver market but deter customers headed for China),
- the attributes (fare and duration) of the competing flights.

The algorithmic issues related to the above three points will be addressed in Section 4.

The above example, where airline flights correspond to 'products', is a case of horizontal product differentiation (see Krouse, 1990) that takes place on a transportation network, hence a nontrivial structure, and where a service is realized by a sequence of 'legs' that make up a path of the network, i. e., a 'flight'. Before giving a formal statement of the mathematical model, we set the notation, in the context of an airline network.

$G=(N,A)$ service network

N set of nodes (origins, destinations, connecting nodes) of G

$A\subset N\times N$ set of arcs (legs) of G

$A_1\subset A$ set of arcs (legs) controlled by the leader

$A_2=A\backslash A_1$ set of arcs controlled by the competition

$W\subset N\times N$ set of origin-destination pairs (flights)

K_w set of flights (network paths) connecting the origin-destination pair $w\in W$

d_w demand associated with an origin-destination $w\in W$

C_a flight duration on leg a

$T_a, a\in A_2$ fare on leg a (competition)

$\psi_w(\alpha)$ density of VOT parameter α for origin-destination pair $w\in W$

α_{max} maximum value for the VOT parameter

The decision variables for both the leader and the followers are:

$x_a(\alpha)$　flow density (group α) on leg a

x_a　total flow on leg a: $x_a = \int_0^{\alpha_{\max}} x_a(\alpha)\mathrm{d}\alpha$

$h_k(\alpha)$　flow density (group α) on path k

h_k　total flow on path k: $h_k = \int_0^{\alpha_{\max}} h_k(\alpha)\mathrm{d}\alpha$

$T_a, a\in A_1$　fare on leg a (leader)

In this system, the demand side consists of nonatomic consumers differentiated by their respective VOT parameter α. The supply side consists of products/services that are relatively close substitutes to each other, and are represented by paths in the transportation network. Consumers are assumed to make indivisible and mutually exclusive purchases of the products or services.

The origin to destination (O-D) demands give rise to arc flows $x_a(\alpha), \alpha\in A$ and the total generalized trip cost is

$$\int_0^{\infty}\sum_{a\in A}(T_a+\alpha C_a)x_a(\alpha)\mathrm{d}\alpha$$

For each origin-destination pair $w\in W$, flow feasibility is characterized by the conservation and nonnegativity constraints

$$\sum_{p\in K_w} h_p(\alpha) = d_w\psi_w(\alpha) \quad \forall w\in W\,\forall\alpha,$$

$$h_p(\alpha)\geqslant 0 \quad \forall p\in K_w\,\forall\alpha.$$

The corresponding arc flows are obtained from the balance equations:

$$x_a(\alpha) = \sum_{w\in W}\sum_{p\in K_w}\delta_{ap}h_p(\alpha) \quad \forall a\in A\,\forall\alpha, \tag{1}$$

where

$$\delta_{ap} = \begin{cases}1 & \text{if arc } a \text{ belong to path} p\\ 0 & \text{otherwise}\end{cases}$$

are the coefficients of the arc-path incidence matrix Δ, i. e., in matrix form: $x(\alpha)=\Delta h(\alpha)$. Based on this notation the sets of path (respectively arc) flow density vectors take the form

$$H(\alpha) = \left\{h(\alpha)\geqslant 0: \sum_{p\in K_w} h_p(\alpha) = d_w\psi_w(\alpha), w\in W\right\} \tag{3}$$

$$X(\alpha) = \Delta H(\alpha) = \{x(\alpha): \exists h(\alpha)\in H(\alpha): x(\alpha) = \Delta h(\alpha)\}. \tag{4}$$

For each value of the parameter α, the flow density $x(\alpha)$ solves the mathematical program (see Marcotte, 1999)

$$\min_{x(\alpha)\in X(\alpha)}\int_0^{\infty}\sum_{a\in A}(T_a+\alpha C_a)x_a(\alpha)\mathrm{d}\alpha \tag{5}$$

By regrouping the fares and delays into respective vectors T and C, we obtain the infinite-dimensional optimization problem

$$\min_{x \in X} \langle T + \alpha C, x \rangle, \tag{6}$$

where X is the set of square-integrable vector functions defined as

$$X = \{x \in \{L^2[0, \alpha_{\max})\}^{|A|} : x(\alpha) \in X(\alpha)\ \forall \alpha\}, \tag{7}$$

and$\langle \cdot , \cdot \rangle$ denotes the scalar product in $\{L^2[0, \alpha_{\max})\}^{|A|}$:

$$\langle u, v \rangle = \int_0^{\alpha_{\max}} \langle u(\alpha), v(\alpha) \rangle \mathrm{d}\alpha.$$

This demand assignment problem with product differentiation corresponds to a parametric infinite dimensional linear program of the bottleneck type (see Anderson and Nash, 1987). It will be analyzed in Section 3. At the upper level, the leader determines its profit-maximizing strategic policy by solving the mathematical program

$$\max_{T_1} \langle T_1, x_1(T_1) \rangle, \tag{8}$$

where $T_1 = (T_a)_{a \in A_1}$ and $x_1(T_1)$ is the demand for the products or services offered by the leader firm. For a given feasible policy T_1, $x_1(T_1)$ is the partial solution, with respect to the arcs controlled by the leader, of the demand assignment problem (5). We can now formulate the strategic policy design problem as the bilevel program

$$\max_{T_1 \geqslant 0} \langle T_1, x_1 \rangle$$

$$\min_{x, h} \int_0^{\alpha_{\max}} \sum_{a \in A} (T_a + \alpha C_a) x_a(\alpha) \mathrm{d}\alpha$$

$$x_a(\alpha) = \sum_{w \in W} \sum_{p \in K_w} \delta_{ak} h_p(\alpha) \quad \forall a \in A\, \forall \alpha \tag{9}$$

$$\sum_{p \in K_w} h_p(\alpha) = d_w \psi_w(\alpha) \quad \forall w \in W\, \forall \alpha$$

$$h_p(\alpha) \geqslant 0 \quad \forall p \in K_w \quad \forall w \in W\, \forall \alpha. \tag{10}$$

In this vertical format, it is understood that x_1 is the partial solution of the lower level minimization problem, parameterized by the price vector T_1.

3. The demand (lower level) assignment problem

In this section, we analyze the structure of the demand assignment problem. To this end, we express the incidence matrix Δ as

$$\Delta = \begin{pmatrix} B_1^1 & B_1^2 & \cdots & B_1^w & \cdots B_1^{|W|} \\ B_2^1 & B_2^2 & \cdots & B_2^w & \cdots B_2^{|W|} \end{pmatrix}, \tag{11}$$

where submatrices B_i^w are of dimension $|A_i| \times |K_w|$. Based on this notation, the generalized path cost vector is given by the affine function

$$\Delta^t (T + \alpha C) = D(T_1) + \alpha G \tag{12}$$

with $D(T_1) = \Delta^t T$ and $G = \Delta^t C$. Using this notation, the demand assignment problem that determines the market shares of the services (paths) reduces to

$$\min_{h \in H} \langle D(T_1) + \alpha G, h \rangle. \tag{13}$$

Restricting our attention to a single path $p \in K_w$ we express $D(T_1)$ as the affine function

$$D_p(T_1) = \langle b_1^{wp}, T_1 \rangle + \langle b_2^{wp}, T_2 \rangle,$$

where b_i^{pw} is the pth row of the transposed matrix $(B_i^w)^t$. From now on we will, for notational simplicity, only consider a single origin and, without loss of generality, assume that the demand is equal to one.

We now introduce an order relation among the paths that will be essential in characterizing market shares.

Definition 3.1. A path p is dominated at T_1 if, for all nonnegative values of α:

$$D_p(T_1) + \alpha G_p > \min_{q \in K}\{D_q(T_1) + \alpha G_q\}.$$

Conversely, if there exists a value α for which

$$D_p(T_1) + \alpha G_p \leqslant \min_{q \in K}\{D_q(T_1) + \alpha G_q\},$$

we say that the path p is undominated.

If a path is dominated at T_1, clearly it is dominated in a neighborhood around T_1.

Definition 3.2. A path p is called weakly undominated at T_1 if there exists a unique value of α such that

$$D_p(T_1) + \alpha G_p \leqslant \min_{q \in K}\{D_q(T_1) + \alpha G_q\}.$$

A path p which is undominated but not weakly undominated is strongly undominated.

We will see that, if a path is strongly undominated at T_1, then there exist *breakpoints* $(\alpha_p(T_1)$ and $\alpha_{p+1}(T_1))$ such that the dominance relationship holds strongly over the open interval $(\alpha_p(T_1), \alpha_{p+1}(T_1))$, and weakly at the endpoints of the interval.

Throughout the paper, we will make the following mild assumption, which rules out degeneracy situations (infinite profit, overlapping path cost functions, etc).

Assumption $\mathbf{H}_0$

(i) $G_p \neq G_q$ whenever $p \neq q$.

(ii) For any $T_1 \geqslant 0$, there exists at least one strongly undominated path.

(iii) There exists a value $\alpha_{\max}$ such that $\psi(\alpha) = 0$ whenever $\alpha \geqslant \alpha_{\max}$.

The dominance relationship allows us to characterize the market structure at a price vector T_1, independently of the actual market shares, in the following way:

Definition 3.3. Associated with a price vector T_1, we associate the market structure $(\mathcal{SU}, \mathcal{WU}, \mathcal{D})$ as the triplet composed of the sets of strongly undominated, weakly undominated and dominated paths, respectively.

Let M denote the number of strongly undominated paths. We set $\mathcal{SU} = \{p_{i_k}\}_{k \in \{1,\cdots,M\}} \subseteq K$, $\mathcal{WU} = \{p_{j_k}\}$ and $\mathcal{D} = \{p_{l_k}\}$ and, without loss of generality, assume that the scalars G_p are sorted in decreasing order, i. e.,

$$G_{i_1} > G_{i_2} > \cdots > G_{i_M}.$$

Note that, in all rigour, one should have written G_{pi_k} in the above. Next, we introduce

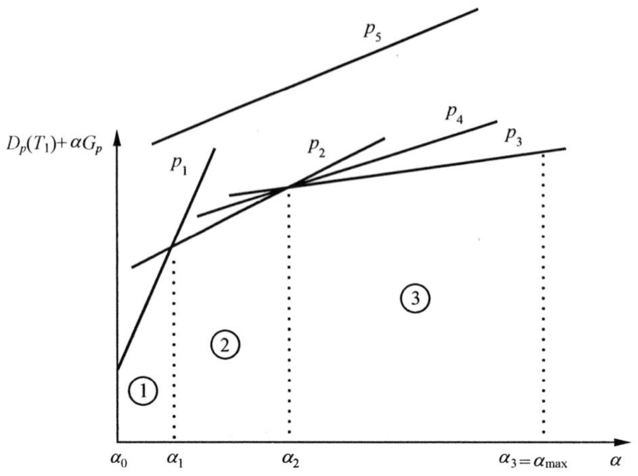

Fig. 2 Market structure.

$$\alpha_{i_k} = -\frac{D_{i_{k+1}}(T_1) - D_{i_k}(T_1)}{G_{i_{k+1}} - G_{i_k}}, \quad k = 1, \cdots, M-1,$$
$$\alpha_{i_0} = 0, \tag{14}$$
$$\alpha_{i_M} = \alpha_{\max}.$$

One possible configuration is illustrated in Fig. 2 where, for a given value of the fare vector T_1, paths 1-3 are strongly undominated, path 5 is dominated and path 4 is weakly undominated. The market shares of each path are obtained by integrating the density function ψ over the interval where this path achieves the lowest generalized cost.

The next theorem provides an analytic characterization of the market structure, for a given price vector T.

Theorem 3.1. *Under Assumption H_0, the system has the market structuree ($\mathscr{SU}$; $\mathscr{WU}$; $\mathscr{D}$) at T_1 if and only if the following conditions hold:*

(i) $0=\alpha_{i_0}<\alpha_{i_1}<\alpha_{i_2}<\cdots<\alpha_{i_{M-1}}<\alpha_{i_M}=\alpha_{\max}$.

(ii) *If $p_j \in \mathscr{D}$, then either*

— *inequality $G_{i_k} > G_j > G_{i_{k+1}}$ holds for some index $k \in [1, \cdots, M-1]$, with* $\beta_{j_k} > \alpha_{i_k} > \beta_{j_{k+1}}$, (15)

$$\text{where } \beta_{j_k} = \frac{D_j(T_1) - D_{i_k}(T_1)}{G_j - G_{i_k}} \text{ and } \beta_{j_{k+1}} = -\frac{D_j(T_1) - D_{i_{k+1}}(T_1)}{G_j - G_{i_{k+1}}};$$

— *inequality $G_{i_M} > G_j$ holds, and*

$$\beta_j = -\frac{D_j(T_1) - D_{i_M}(T_1)}{G_j - G_{i_M}} > \alpha_{i_M}; \tag{16}$$

— *inequality $G_j > G_{i_1}$ holds, and*

$$\beta_j = -\frac{D_j(T_1) - D_{i_1}(T_1)}{G_j - G_{i_1}} < 0.$$

(iii) *If* $p_j \in \mathscr{W}\mathscr{U}$, *then equality holds for either* (15) *or* (16).

Proof

- Necessity

(i) From the labelling of the strongly undominated paths, one has

$$D_{i_1}(T_1) < D_{i_2}(T_1) < \cdots < D_{i_M}(T_1).$$

If $\alpha_{i_{k-1}} > \alpha_{i_k}$ for some $k \in [1, \cdots, M-1]$ then

$$-\frac{D_{i_{k+1}}(T_1) - D_{i_k}(T_1)}{G_{i_{k+1}} - G_{i_k}} < -\frac{D_{i_k}(T_1) - D_{i_k-1}(T_1)}{G_{i_k} - G_{i_{k-1}}}$$

Let

$$\hat{\alpha} = -\frac{D_{i_{k+1}}(T_1) - D_{i_{k-1}}(T_1)}{G_{i_{k+1}} - G_{i_{k-1}}}.$$

By construction, $\hat{\alpha} \in [\alpha_{i_k}, \alpha_{i_{k-1}}]$. It follows that

$$D_{i_k}(T_1) + \alpha G_{i_k} > D_{i_{k-1}}(T_1) + \alpha G_{i_{k-1}} \quad \text{for} \quad \alpha \leqslant \hat{\alpha},$$

$$D_{i_k}(T_1) + \alpha G_{i_k} > D_{i_{k+1}}(T_1) + \alpha G_{i_{k+1}} \quad \text{for} \quad \alpha \leqslant \hat{\alpha},$$

which implies that path p_{i_k} is dominated, a contradiction. If $\alpha_{i_{k-1}} = \alpha_{i_k}$ holds, then

$$D_{i_k}(T_1) + \alpha G_{i_k} > D_{i_{k-1}}(T_1) + \alpha G_{i_{k-1}}$$

$$\text{for } \alpha < \alpha_{i_{k-1}} = \alpha_{i_k}.$$

$$D_{i_k}(T_1) + \alpha G_{i_k} > D_{i_{k+1}}(T_1) + \alpha G_{i_{k+1}}$$

for $\alpha > \alpha_{i_k}$, which implies that path p_{i_k} is weakly undominated, a contradiction.

(ii) *Case* 1. If $\beta_{j_k} \leqslant \alpha_{i_k}$, i. e.,

$$\frac{D_{i_k}(T_1) - D_j(T_1)}{G_j - G_{i_k}} \leqslant \alpha_{i_k},$$

then we have

$$D_{i_k}(T_1) - D_j(T_1) \geqslant (G_j - G_{i_k})\alpha_{i_k}$$

or, equivalently,

$$D_{i_k}(T_1) - \alpha_{i_k} G_{i_k} \geqslant D_j(T_1) + \alpha_{i_k} G_j,$$

which implies that p_j is undominated, a contradiction. The reverse inequality (15) follows from a similar argument.

Case 2. In this case, we have that $G_{i_M} > G_j$. If

$$\beta_j = -\frac{D_j(T_1) - D_{i_M}(T_1)}{G_j - G_{i_M}} \leqslant \alpha_{i_M}, \tag{17}$$

then $D_{i_M}(T_1) - D_j(T_1) \geqslant \alpha_{i_M}(G_j - G_{i_M})$, i. e., $D_{i_M}(T_1) + \alpha_{i_M} G_{i_M} \geqslant D_j(T_1) + \alpha_{i_M} G_j$, a contradiction.

Case 3. The proof is similar to that of (ii) (Case2). Item (iii) Using there sults of (i) and (ii), the proof of (iii) is readily obtained.

- Sufficiency

(i) From the assumption, we observe that

$$D_{i_M}(T_1)+\alpha_{i_{k-1}}G_{i_M}>\cdots>D_{i_{k+1}}(T_1)+\alpha_{i_{k-1}}G_{i_{k+1}}>D_{i_k}(T_1)+\alpha_{i_{k-1}}G_{i_k}$$

and

$$D_{i_M}(T_1)+\alpha_{i_k}G_{i_M}>\cdots>D_{i_{k+1}}(T_1)+\alpha_{i_k}G_{i_{k+1}}=D_{i_k}(T_1)+\alpha_{i_{k-1}}G_{i_k}.$$

It follows that

$$D_{i_j}(T_1)+\alpha G_{i_j}>D_{i_k}(T_1)+\alpha G_{i_k},\ j\in[k+1,\cdots,M]\text{ for }\forall\alpha\in(\alpha_{i_k},\alpha_{i_k}).$$

On the other hand, we have

$$D_{i_1}(T_1)+\alpha G_{i_1}>D_{i_2}(T_1)+\alpha G_{i_2}\quad\text{for }\alpha>\alpha_{i_1},$$
$$D_{i_2}(T_1)+\alpha G_{i_2}>D_{i_3}(T_1)+\alpha G_{i_3}\quad\text{for }\alpha>\alpha_{i_2},$$
$$\vdots$$
$$D_{i_{k-1}}(T_1)+\alpha G_{i_{k-1}}>D_{i_k}(T_1)+\alpha G_{i_k}\quad\text{for }\alpha>\alpha_{i_{k-1}}.$$

The above inequalities imply that p_{i_k} is strongly undominated.

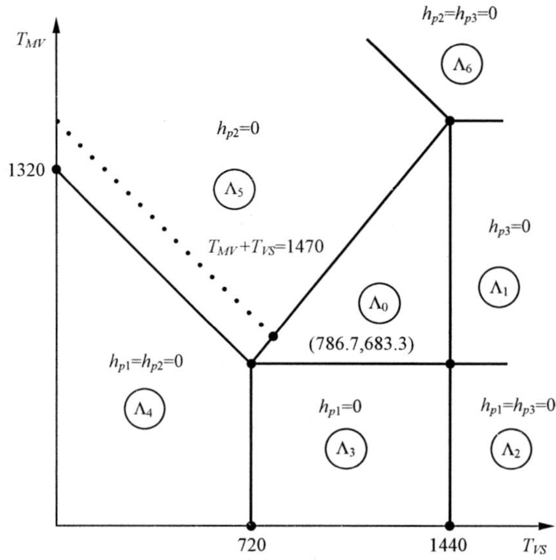

Fig. 3 Market structure for the Montreal-Shanghai example.

(ii) *Case* 1. If $\beta_{j_k}>\alpha_{i_k}>\beta_{j_{k+1}}$, then

$$D_j(T_1)+\alpha G_j>D_{i_k}(T_1)+\alpha G_{i_k}\quad\text{for }\alpha<\alpha_{i_k}<\beta_{j_k},$$
$$D_j(T_1)+\alpha G_j>D_{i_{k+1}}(T_1)+\alpha G_{i_{k+1}}\quad\text{for }\alpha>\alpha_{i_k}>\beta_{j_{k+1}}.$$

This implies that p_j is dominated.

Case 2. If $\beta_j>\alpha_{i_M}$, i. e., $(D_j(T_1)-D_{i_M}(T_1))/(G_{i_M}-G_j)>\alpha_{i_M}$, we have

$$D_j(T_1)+\alpha G_j>D_{i_M}(T_1)+\alpha G_{i_M}\text{ for all }\alpha\leqslant\alpha_{i_M}$$

and path p_j is dominated.

Case 3. The proof is similar to that of Case 2.

(iii) Obvious. This completes the proof.

The analysis of the market structure allows to perform sensitivity analysis of the lower level problem with respect to the price vector T_1. First, we investigate the regions where the market structure is invariant:

$$\Lambda_{\mathscr{SWD}} = \{T_1 \geqslant 0 : p_{i_k} \in \mathscr{SU}, k \in [1,\cdots,M];$$
$$p_{j_k} \in \mathscr{WU}, k \in [1,\cdots,N]; p_{l_k} \in \mathscr{D}, k \in [1,\cdots,S]\}. \tag{18}$$

It follows from Theorem 3.1 that the set $\Lambda_{\mathscr{SWD}}$ is a polyhedron where all demand is assigned to a fixed set of dominated paths that share the total market. Customers are associated with segments $[\alpha_{i-1},\alpha_i]$ and the market share of astrongly undominated path p_i is obtained by integrating the density function ψ over the corresponding interval. Within an interval, the generalized cost of customers are all minimized by the same strongly undominated path p_i.

Geometrically, the whole strategic policy space $R^{|A_1|}$ can be partitioned into regions, each region having its own structure, i.e.,

$$\mathrm{R}^{|A_1|} = \bigcup \Lambda_{\mathscr{SWD}} \tag{19}$$

Fig. 3 illustrates the partition corresponding to the Montreal-Shanghai market presented in the introduction. Each region Λ_i is characterized by its set of undominated paths or, equivalently, by the set of paths with null flows. In the interior of the regions, all undominated paths are strongly undominated. For instance, all paths are undominated in region Λ_0 while, in the interior of Λ_6, only path p_1 is strongly undominated. In this example, the density function ψ is uniform over the interval $[0,\alpha_{\max}]$ and any point on the dotted line is an optimal solution of the pricing problem.

4. Sensitivity analysis of demand side

In this section, we study the sensitivity of the lower level solution to the price vector T_1. To this end, we need to solve, for each value of α, the parameterized problem

$$\mathrm{LP}(T_1,\alpha): \min_{h(\alpha)\in H(\alpha)} \langle D(T_1) + \alpha G, h(\alpha)\rangle.$$

Let M (T_1) denote the number of strongly undominated paths at T_1. If the density function ψ is *strictly positive* over the interval $[0,\alpha_{\max})$, the (almost everywhere) unique solution of LP (T_1,α) is $h(\alpha)=Y^{i(\alpha)}\psi(\alpha)$, where $Y^{i(\alpha)}$ is the extremal point of the simplex: $\{y: \sum_{i\in[1,\cdots,M(T_1)]} y_i = 1, y_i \geqslant 0\}$ associated with $i(\alpha)$ that satisfies

$$D_{i(\alpha)}(T_1) + \alpha G_{i(\alpha)} = \min_{j\in[1,\cdots,M(T_1)]} D_j(T_1) + \alpha G_j. \tag{20}$$

Note that this point is unique except at the critical points α_i who are in finite number.

Theorem 4.1. *For fixed $T_1 \in \Lambda_{\mathscr{SWD}}$, the solution of the infinite-dimensional lower level program is unique (almost everywhere) and given by*

$$h(\alpha) = Y^{i_k}\psi(\alpha) \quad \textit{for } \alpha \in [\alpha_{i_{k-1}},\alpha_{i_k}), k \in [1,\cdots,M]$$

and the total path flow vector $h(T_1)$ is unambiguously defined.

Proof. The value function $\phi(\alpha) = D_{i(\alpha)}(T_1) + \alpha G_{i(\alpha)}$ is the piecewise affine concave function of its scalar argument α which interpolates the points

$$(0,\phi(0)),\quad (\alpha_{i_1},\phi(\alpha_{i_1})),\cdots,(\alpha_{i_{M-1}},\phi(\alpha_{i_{M-1}})).$$

On each subinterval $(\alpha_{i_{k-1}}, \alpha_{i_k})$ its slope is equal to G_{i_k}. In the interior of each subinterval, the optimum of LP (T_1, α) is achieved at an extreme point Y^{i_k} of the simplex. At a breakpoint α_{i_k}, the optimum of LP (T_1, α) is achieved at either one of the extreme points Y^j, say $j \in J_k$, where J_k denotes the index set of extreme points; in that case $h(\alpha_{i_k})$ can be arbitrarily set to $\psi(\alpha_{i_k})$ times a convex combination of the Y^{j}'s, for j in J_k. Since the number of breakpoints is finite, the total path flow $h(T_1)$ is unique.

Under Assumption H_0 and the market structure$(\mathscr{SU}, \mathscr{WU}, \mathscr{D})$ at T_1 exactly one of the following three inequalities must hold for a given undominated path p_j:

1. $G_{i_u} > G_j > G_{i_l}$, where $l = \arg\min\{k \mid G_{i_k} < G_j, p_{i_k} \in \mathscr{SU}\}$ and $u = \arg\max\{k \mid G_{i_k} > G_j, p_{i_k} \in \mathscr{SU}\}$;
2. $G_{i_M} > G_j$ for $p_{i_M} \in \mathscr{SU}$;
3. $G_j > G_{i_1}$ for $p_{i_1} \in \mathscr{SU}$.

We will refer to paths p_{i_u} and p_{i_l} (or p_{i_M}, p_{i_1}) as the $\mathscr{SU}$ (respectively left and right) neighbors of p_j.

The characterization of $\mathscr{WU}$ neighbors is a little more involved. Let

$$L_u = \{k \in \mathscr{WU} \mid G_{i_u} > G_k > G_j\}.$$

If L_u is nonempty, we define the left $\mathscr{WU}$ neighbor of path p_j as the path p_{ju} such that

$$G_{j_u} = \min\{G_k \mid k \in L_u\}.$$

Symmetrically, a right $\mathscr{WU}$ neighbor of path p_j satisfies

$$G_{j_l} = \mathrm{man}\{G_k \mid k \in L_l\},$$

whenever the set $L_l = \{k \in \mathscr{WU} \mid G_j > G_k > G_{i_l}\}$ is nonempty.

The notion of neighbor is key in deriving results about the local behaviour of the revenue function. For simplicity, we analyze its behaviour in the case where the set of $\mathscr{WU}$ neighbors is empty, and then proceed with some remarks about the degenerate cases. In the course of the proof, one may obviously discard dominated paths, with the exception of the path p_j under consideration.

Theorem 4.2. *Assume that the market structure $(\mathscr{SU}; \mathscr{WU}; \mathscr{D})$ holds at T_1 and let all paths be strongly undominated, with the possible exception of path p_j. Then, under Assumption H_0, we have:*

(i) *If path p_j is strongly undominated and $a \in A_1$, then $h_{p_j}(T_1)$ is partially differentiable with respect to T_a.*

(i.1) *If $a \in p_j$, then h_{p_j} has a nonpositive partial derivative with respect to T_a; moreover, if arc a belongs to all $\mathscr{SU}$ neighbors of p_j, then $\dfrac{\partial h_{p_j}(T_1)}{\partial T_a} = 0$; otherwise $\dfrac{\partial h_{p_j}(T_1)}{\partial T_a} < 0$.*

(i.2) *If $a \notin p_j$, then h_{p_j} has a nonnegative partial derivative with respect to T_a;*

moreover if arc a does not belong to all $\mathscr{SU}$ *neighbors of* p_j, *then* $\dfrac{\partial h_{p_j}(T_1)}{\partial T_a}=0$; *otherwise* $\dfrac{\partial h_{p_j}(T_1)}{\partial T_a}>0$.

(ii) *If path* p_j *is weakly undominated and* $a\in A_1$, *then* $h_{p_j}(T_1)$ *is partially side differentiable with respect to* T_a.

(ii.1) *If* $a\in p_j$, *then* h_{p_j} *has nonnegative partial side derivatives; moreover if arc a belongs to all* $\mathscr{SU}$ *neighbors of* p_j, *then* $\dfrac{\partial h_{p_j}(T_1)}{\partial T_a}=0$; *otherwise* $\dfrac{\partial^- h_{p_j}(T_1)}{\partial T_a}>0$ *and* $\dfrac{\partial^+ h_{p_j}(T_1)}{\partial T_a}=0$.

(ii.2) *If* $a\notin p_j$, *then* p_j *has nonpositive partial side derivatives; moreover, if arc a does not belong to the* $\mathscr{SU}$ *neighbors of* p_j, *then the partial derivatives of* $h_{p_j}(T_1)$ *are equal to zero; otherwise* $\dfrac{\partial^+ h_{p_j}(T_1)}{\partial T_a}<0$ *and* $\dfrac{\partial^- h_{p_j}(T_1)}{\partial T_a}=0$.

(iii) *If path* $p_j\in\mathscr{D}$ *and* $a\in A_1$, *then* $h_{p_j}(T_1)$ *is partially differentiable with respect to* T_a; *and* $\dfrac{\partial h_{p_j}(T_1)}{\partial T_a}=0$.

Proof

(i) Let $p_j\in\mathscr{SU}$ at T_1 and assume that $j=i_k$. The demand for path p_j is given by

$$h_{p_j}(T_1)=h_{p_{i_k}}(T_1)=\int_{\alpha_{i_{k-1}}(T_1)}^{\alpha_{i_k}(T_1)}\psi(\alpha)\mathrm{d}\alpha,k\in[1,\cdots,M] \tag{21}$$

with

$$\alpha_{i_k}(T_1)=-\frac{D_{i_u}(T_1)-D_{i_k}(T_1)}{G_{i_u}-G_{i_k}},k\in[1,\cdots,M-1], \tag{22}$$

$$\alpha_{i_M}=\alpha_{\max}; \tag{23}$$

$$\alpha_{i_{k-1}}(T_1)=-\frac{D_{i_l}(T_1)-D_{i_k}(T_1)}{G_{i_l}-G_{i_k}},k\in[1,\cdots,M-1], \tag{24}$$

$$\alpha_{i_0}=0. \tag{25}$$

Since $\alpha_{i_k}(T_1)$ is a linear function of T_1 then, for sufficiently small perturbation

$$\delta T_1=(0,\cdots,0(\delta T_1)_a,0,\cdots,0)^t,$$

the market structure (18) holds at $T_1+\delta T_1$, i.e.,

$$0=\alpha_{i_0}<\alpha_{i_1}(T_1+\delta T_1)<\alpha_{i_2}(T_1+\delta T_1)<\cdots<\alpha_{i_{M-1}}(T_1+\delta T_1)<\alpha_{i_M}=\alpha_{\max} \tag{26}$$

and the flow on pasth p_j is given by

$$h_{p_j}(T_1+\delta T_1)=\int_{\alpha_{i_{k-1}}(T_1+\delta T_1)}^{\alpha_{i_k}(T_1+\delta T_1)}\psi(\alpha)\mathrm{d}\alpha,k\in[1,\cdots,M]. \tag{27}$$

Therefore

$$\frac{\partial h_{p_j}(T_1)}{\partial T_a}=\frac{\partial \alpha_{i_k}(T_1)}{\partial T_a}\psi(\alpha_{i_k}(T_1))-\frac{\partial \alpha_{i_{k-1}}(T_1)}{\partial T_a}\psi(\alpha_{i_{k-1}}(T_1)), \tag{28}$$

which settles cases (i. 1) and (i. 2).

(ii) Let p_j be weakly undominated. This implies that $h_{p_j}(T_1)=0$. We will only give a proof for the case where the inequality $G_{i_u}>G_j>G_{i_l}$ holds for some $k\in[1,\cdots,M-1]$, since a similar argument is valid for the cases where $G_{i_M}>G_j$ or $G_j>G_{i_1}$.

- *Case* (ii. 1)

Let $a\in p_j$. If arc a belongs to all $\mathcal{SU}$ neighbours of p_j, then $h_{p_j}(T_1+\delta T_1)=0$. Otherwise

$$h_{p_j}(T_1+\delta T_1)=\int_{\beta_{j_k}(T_1+\delta T_1)}^{\beta_{j_{k+1}}(T_1+\delta T_1)}\psi(\alpha)\mathrm{d}\alpha, \tag{29}$$

where

$$\beta_{j_k}(T_1+\delta T_1)=-\frac{D_j(T_1+\delta T_1)-D_{i_l}(T_1+\delta T_1)}{G_j-G_{i_l}} \tag{30}$$

and

$$\beta_{j_{k+1}}(T_1+\delta T_1)=-\frac{D_j(T_1+\delta T_1)-D_{i_u}(T_1+\delta T_1)}{G_j-G_{i_u}} \tag{31}$$

From (29)—(31), the desired results follows.

- *Case* (ii. 2)

Let $a\notin p_j$. If $(\delta T_1)_a\leqslant 0$ or $(\delta T_1)>0$ and a is neither in $p_{i_{k+1}}$ nor in p_{i_k}, then $h_{p_j}(T_1+\delta T_1)=0$. Otherwise (29)—(31) is still valid and the results holds.

(iii) If p_j is dominated, then $h_{p_j}(T_1)=h_{p_j}(T_1+\delta T_1)=0$ for any sufficiently small $(\delta T_1)_a$, i. e., $\frac{\partial h_{p_j}(T_1)}{\partial T_a}=0$ for all $a\in A_1$.

Corollary 4. 1. *Under the assumptions of Theorem* 4. 2, *the path flow functions* h_{p_j} *are locally Lipschitz continuous with respect to* T_1.

Proof. In the proof of Theorem 4. 2, we showed that every breakpoint $\alpha_{i_k}(T_1)$ and $\beta_{j_k}(T)$ is linear in T_1 and that the partial side derivatives are bounded. It follows that the path flow $h_j(T_1)$, $j\in K$ is Lipschitz continuous on some neighborhood of T_1.

In the last part of this section, we consider the case where $p_j\in\mathcal{SU}$ and the inequality $G_{i_l}>G_{j_l}>G_j>G_{j_u}>G_{i_u}$ holds. For simplicity, only one pair of $\mathcal{WU}$ is considered. Note that the demand of p_j at T_1 is given by (29). Following a small perturbation δT_1, the market structure (18) at $T_1+\delta T_1$ is modified, and the flow on path p_j becomes

$$h_{p_j}(T_1+\delta T_1)=\int_{\alpha_l(T_1+\delta T_a)}^{\alpha_u(T_1+\delta T_a)}\psi(\alpha)\mathrm{d}\alpha, \tag{32}$$

where the values of the new breakpoints $\alpha_u(T_1+\delta T_a)$ and $\alpha_l(T_1+\delta T_a)$ are given in Table 2 for several cases. In the first three columns, a '1' indicates that arc a belongs to the relevant path. From Fig. 4, it is clear that the market structure is modified if only $a\in p_j$. Once sensitivity of the breakpoints is obtained, the partial (side) derivative of the path *flow* h_{p_j} with respect to T_a readily follows:

Table 2 Price sensitivity of demand function

Case	$a\in p_j$	$a\in p_{i_l}$ [$a\in p_{i_u}$]	$a\in p_{j_l}$ [$a\in p_{i_u}$]	δT_a	$\alpha_l(T_1+\delta T_a)$	$\frac{\partial\alpha_l}{\partial T_a}$	$[\alpha_u(T_1+\delta T_a)]$	$\left[\frac{\partial\alpha_u}{\partial T_a}\right]$
1	1	1	1	+/−	$\alpha_{i_{k-1}}(T_1)$	0	$\alpha_{i_k}(T_1)$	0
2	1	1	0	+	$\alpha_{i_{k-1}}(T_1)-\frac{\delta T_a}{G_j-G_{j_l}}$	$-\frac{1}{G_j-G_{j_l}}$	$\alpha_{i_k}(T_1)-\frac{\delta T_a}{G_j-G_{j_u}}$	$-\frac{1}{G_j-G_{j_u}}$
3	1	1	0	−	$\alpha_{i_{k-1}}(T_1)$	0	$\alpha_{i_k}(T_1)$	0
4	1	0	1	+	$\alpha_{i_{k-1}}(T_1)-\frac{\delta T_a}{G_j-G_{i_l}}$	$-\frac{1}{G_j-G_{i_l}}$	$\alpha_{i_k}(T_1)-\frac{\delta T_a}{G_{i_u}-G_j}$	$-\frac{1}{G_{i_u}-G_j}$
5	1	0	1	−	$\alpha_{i_{k-1}}(T_1)-\frac{\delta T_a}{G_j-G_{j_l}}$	$-\frac{1}{G_j-G_{j_l}}$	$\alpha_{i_k}(T_1)-\frac{\delta T_a}{G_j-G_{j_u}}$	$-\frac{1}{G_j-G_{j_u}}$
6	1	0	0	+	$\alpha_{i_{k-1}}(T_1)-\frac{\delta T_a}{G_j-G_{j_l}}$	$-\frac{1}{G_j-G_{j_l}}$	$\alpha_{i_k}(T_1)-\frac{\delta T_a}{G_j-G_{j_u}}$	$-\frac{1}{G_j-G_{j_u}}$
7	1	0	0	−	$\alpha_{i_{k-1}}(T_1)-\frac{\delta T_a}{G_j-G_{i_l}}$	$-\frac{1}{G_j-G_{i_l}}$	$\alpha_{i_{k-1}}(T_1)-\frac{\delta T_a}{G_{j_u}-G_j}$	$-\frac{1}{G_{j_u}-G_j}$
8	0	0	0	+/−	$\alpha_{i_{k-1}}(T_1)$	0	$\alpha_{i_k}(T_1)$	0
9	0	0	0	+	$\alpha_{i_{k-1}}(T_1)$	0	$\alpha_{i_k}(T_1)$	0
10	0	0	1	−	$\alpha_{i_{k-1}}(T_1)-\frac{\delta T_a}{G_{j_l}-G_{i_l}}$	$-\frac{1}{G_{j_l}-G_{i_l}}$	$\alpha_{i_k}(T_1)-\frac{\delta T_a}{G_j-G_{j_u}}$	$-\frac{1}{G_j-G_{j_u}}$
11	0	1	1	+	$\alpha_{i_{k-1}}(T_1)-\frac{\delta T_a}{G_j-G_{i_l}}$	$-\frac{1}{G_j-G_{i_l}}$	$\alpha_{i_k}(T_1)-\frac{\delta T_a}{G_j-G_{j_u}}$	$-\frac{1}{G_{j_u}}$
12	0	1	1	−	$\alpha_{i_{k-1}}(T_1)-\frac{\delta T_a}{G_j-G_{j_l}}$	$-\frac{1}{G_j-G_{j_l}}$	$\alpha_{i_k}(T_1)-\frac{\delta T_a}{G_j-G_{i_u}}$	$-\frac{1}{G_j-G_{i_u}}$
13	0	1	0	+	$\alpha_{i_{k-1}}(T_1)$	0	$\alpha_{i_k}(T_1)$	0
14	0	1	0	−	$\alpha_{i_{k-1}}(T_1)-\frac{\delta T_a}{G_j-G_{i_l}}$	$-\frac{1}{G_j-G_{i_l}}$	$\alpha_{i_k}(T_1)-\frac{\delta T_a}{G_{i_u}-G_j}$	$-\frac{1}{G_{i_u}-G_j}$

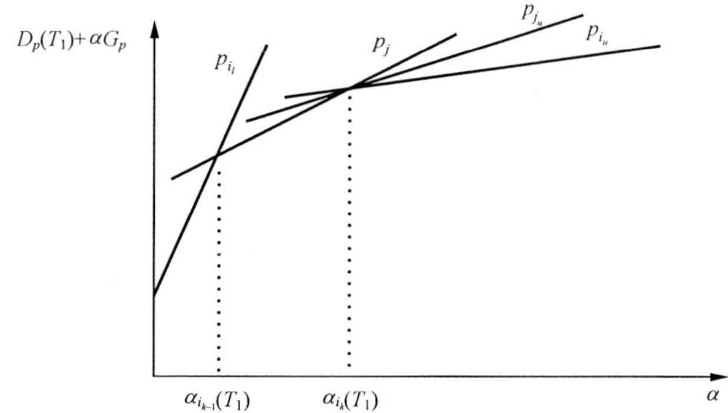

Fig. 4 Sensitivity of the markets tructure.

$$\frac{\partial h_{p_j}(T_1)}{\partial T_a}=\frac{\partial\alpha_u(T_1)}{\partial T_a}\psi(\alpha_u(T_1))-\frac{\partial\alpha_l(T_1)}{\partial T_a}\psi(\alpha_l(T_1)). \tag{33}$$

5. A piecewise optimization strategy

Based on the sensitivity results of Section 4, it is possible to solve the pricing problem by standard descent methods, for a given market structure. If one denotes by $x(T_1)$ and $h(T_1)$ the arc and path flow vectors that correspond to a price schedule T_1, the leader firm maximizes its revenue by solving the unconstrained mathematical program

$$\max_{T_1} f(T_1) = \langle T_1, x_1(T_1)\rangle = \langle B_1 T_1, h(T_1)\rangle.$$

Restricted to a given area Λ_i of the market structure $(\mathcal{SU}, \mathcal{WU}, \mathcal{D})$, the objective function takes the form

$$\begin{aligned} f_{\Lambda_i}(T_1) &= \langle B_1 T_1, h(T_1)\rangle = \sum_{k=1}^{M} \langle b_1^{i_k}, T_1\rangle h_{i_k}(T_1) \\ &= \langle b_1^{i_1}, T_1\rangle \int_0^{\alpha_{i_1}(T_1)} \psi(\alpha)\,\mathrm{d}\alpha + \langle b_1^{i_2}, T_1\rangle \int_{\alpha_{i_1}(T_1)}^{\alpha_{i_2}(T_1)} \psi(\alpha)\,\mathrm{d}\alpha + \cdots + \langle b_1^{i_M}, T_1\rangle \int_{\alpha_{i_{M-1}}(T_1)}^{\alpha_{i_M}(T_1)} \psi(\alpha)\,\mathrm{d}\alpha \\ &= \langle b_1^{i_1} - b_1^{i_2}, T_1\rangle \int_0^{\alpha_{i_1}(T_1)} \psi(\alpha)\,\mathrm{d}\alpha + \langle b_1^{i_2} - b_1^{i_3}, T_1\rangle \int_0^{\alpha_{i_2}(T_1)} \psi(\alpha)\,\mathrm{d}\alpha + \cdots \\ &\quad + \langle b_1^{i_{M-1}} - b_1^{i_M}, T_1\rangle \int_0^{\alpha_{i_{M-1}}(T_1)} \psi(\alpha)\,\mathrm{d}\alpha + \langle b_1^{i_M}, T_1\rangle. \end{aligned}$$

If one sets

$$g_j(T_1) = \langle b_1^{i_{j-1}} - b_1^{i_j}, T_1\rangle \int_0^{\alpha_{i_{j-1}}(T_1)} \psi(\alpha)\,\mathrm{d}\alpha, \quad j \in [2, \cdots, M],$$

the gradient vector and Hessian matrix of the objective take the respective forms

$$\nabla g_j(T_1) = (b_1^{i_j} - b_1^{i_{j-1}}) \int_0^{\alpha_{i_{j-1}}(T_1)} \psi(\alpha)\,\mathrm{d}\alpha + \nabla \alpha_{i_{j-1}}(T_1) \langle b_1^{i_j} - b_1^{i_{j-1}}, T_1\rangle \psi(\alpha_{i_{j-1}}(T_1)),$$

$$\begin{aligned} \nabla^2 g_j(T_1) &= 2\frac{(b_1^{i_j} - b_1^{i_{j-1}})^t (b_1^{i_j} - b_1^{i_{j-1}})}{G_{i_j} - G_{i_{j-1}}} \psi(\alpha_{i\,j-1}(T_1)) \\ &\quad + \nabla \alpha_{i_{j-1}}(T_1)(\nabla \alpha_{i_{j-1}}(T_1))^t \langle b_1^{i_{j-1}} - b_1^{i_j}, T_1\rangle \psi'(\alpha_{i_{j-1}}(T_1)) \\ &= \frac{(b_1^{i_j} - b_1^{i_{j-1}})^t (b_1^{i_j} - b_1^{i_{j-1}})}{G_{i_j} - G_{i_{j-1}}} \left[2\psi(\alpha_{i_{j-1}}(T_1)) + \frac{\langle b_1^{i_{j-1}} - b_1^{i_j}, T_1\rangle \psi'(\alpha_{i_{j-1}}(T_1))}{G_{i_j} - G_{i_{j-1}}} \right] \end{aligned}$$

A sufficient condition for the concavity of the profit function is that, for every index j, the matrix $\nabla^2 g_j(T_1)$ be negative semidefinite. This condition will be satisfied if either

1. The density function ψ is uniform over the interval $[0, \alpha_{\max}]$, i.e.,

$$\psi = \begin{cases} \dfrac{1}{\alpha_{\max}} & \text{if } \alpha \in [0, \alpha_{\max}] \\ 0 & \text{otherwise.} \end{cases}$$

2. $\psi(\alpha)$ is nondecreasing and $\langle b_1^{i_{j-1}} - b_1^{i_j}, T_1\rangle < 0$ for $j \in [2, \cdots, M]$ and $T_1 \in \Lambda$.

Since a_{i_j} is an affine function of T_1, the profit function $f(T_1)$ is piecewise concave whenever one of the above conditions holds. If the market structure is known, i.e., $R^{|A_1|} = \bigcup_i \Lambda_i$, the optimal price schedule can be obtained by solving a finite set of mathematical programs:

$$\max_i \max_{T_1 \in \Lambda_i} f_{\Lambda_i}(T_1) \tag{34}$$

where in the uniform case, the objective functions take the form

$$f_{\Lambda_i}(T_1) = \frac{1}{\alpha_{\max}}\{\langle b_1^{i_1} - b_1^{i_2}, T_1\rangle \alpha_{i_1} + \langle b_1^{i_2} - b_1^{i_3}, T_1\rangle \alpha_{i_2} + \cdots + \langle b_1^{i_{M-1}} - b_1^{i_M}, T_1\rangle \alpha_{i_{M-1}}\} + \langle b_1^{i_M}, T_1\rangle.$$

However, by adding the equalities

$$\langle b_1^{i_1} - b_1^{i_2}, T_1\rangle = (G_{i_2} - G_{i_1})\alpha_{i_1} - \langle b_2^{i_1} - b_2^{i_2}, T_2\rangle,$$

$$\langle b_1^{i_2} - b_1^{i_3}, T_1\rangle = (G_{i_3} - G_{i_2})\alpha_{i_2} - \langle b_2^{i_2} - b_2^{i_3}, T_2\rangle,$$

$$\vdots$$

$$\langle b_1^{i_{M-1}} - b_1^{i_M}, T_1\rangle = (G_{i_M} - G_{i_{M-1}})\alpha_{i_{M-1}} - \langle b_2^{i_{M-1}} - b_2^{i_M}, T_2\rangle,$$

one obtains $\langle b_1^{i_M}, T_1\rangle = \langle b_1^{i_1}, T_1\rangle + \langle b_2^{i_1} - b_2^{i_M}, T_2\rangle - [(G_{i_2} - G_{i_1})\alpha_{i_1} + \cdots + (G_{i_M} - G_{i_{M-1}})\alpha_{i_{M-1}}]$ and, finally, the quadratic expression

$$f_{\Lambda_i}(T_1) = \frac{1}{\alpha_{\max}}\left\{(G_{i_2} - G_{i_1})\left[\alpha_{i_1} - \frac{\alpha_{\max} + \frac{\langle b_2^{i_1} - b_2^{i_2}, T_2\rangle}{G_{i_2} - G_{i_1}}}{2}\right]^2 + \cdots\right.$$

$$+ (G_{i_M} - G_{i_{M-1}})\left[\alpha_{i_{M-1}} - \frac{\alpha_{\max} + \frac{\langle b_2^{i_{M-1}} - b_2^{i_M}, T_2\rangle}{G_{i_M} - G_{i_{M-1}}}}{2}\right]^2$$

$$\left. - \frac{1}{4}\sum_{j=1}^{M-1}(G_{i_{j+1}} - G_{i_j})\left(\alpha_{\max} + \frac{\langle b_2^{i_j} - b_2^{i_{j+1}}, T_2\rangle}{G_{i_{j+1}} - G_{i_j}}\right)^2\right\} + \langle b_1^{i_1}, T_1\rangle + \langle b_2^{i_1} - b_2^{i_M}, T_2\rangle.$$

Hence the functions $f_{\Lambda_i}(T_1)$ are differentiable concave quadratic functions that can be maximized by the steepest ascent algorithm or, on networks of moderate sizes, is amenable to conjugate gradient or quasi-Newton methods.

6. Back to the Air Canada example

In the introductory example of Section 2, there are three flights (paths) with respective generalized costs:

$$p_1 = 1320 + 36\alpha,$$

$$p_2 = T_{MV} + 720 + 26\alpha,$$

$$p_3 = T_{MV} + T_{VS} + 18\alpha.$$

Seven market structures correspond to seven regions $\{\Lambda_i\}_{i=0}^{6}$ in the Euclidian plane (see Fig. 3). We now proceed to analyze each region, assuming that total demand is equal to 1000 passengers and that the density function is uniform with maximal VOT equal to $\alpha_{\max} = 90$. Calculations, albeit straightforward, are tedious.

• Region 0 (Main region) This corresponds to the market structure where all services (products, flights) are competitive, i. e., in the interior of its region, all flights carry positive flow. It is described as

$$\Lambda_0 = \{T_{MV} \geqslant 0, T_{VS} \geqslant 0 : 600 \leqslant T_{MV}, 4T_{MV} - 5T_{VS} + 1200 \leqslant 0, T_{VS} \leqslant 1440\}.$$

The profit function in this area is

$$f_{\Lambda_0}(T_1) = 1000\frac{1}{3600}(-4T_{MV}^2 + 6000T_{MV} - 5T_{VS}^2 + 7200T_{VS}),$$

whose maximum $f^* \approx \$1334000$ is achieved when $T_{MV}^* = \$683$ and $T_{VS}^* = \$787$.

- Region 1: $\Lambda_1 = \{T_{MV} \geqslant 0, T_{VS} \geqslant 0: 600 \leqslant T_{MV} \leqslant 1500, T_{VS} \geqslant 1440\}, h_{p3} = 0$

—profit function: $f_{\Lambda_1}(T_1) = \frac{10}{9}(-T_{MV}^2 + 1500T_{MV})$;

—optimal profit: $f^* = \$625,000$;

—optimal solution: $T_{MV}^* = \$750 \quad T_{VS}^* \geqslant \$1440$.

- Region 2: $\Lambda_2 = \{T_{MV} \geqslant 0, T_{VS} \geqslant 0: T_{MV} \leqslant 600, T_{VS} \geqslant 1440\}, h_{p1} = h_{p3} = 0$

—profit function: $f_{\Lambda 2}(T_1) = 1000T_{MV}$;

—optimal profit: $f^* = \$600,000$;

—optimal solution: $T_{MV}^* = \$600 \quad T_{VS}^* \geqslant \$1440$.

- Region 3: $\Lambda_3 = \{T_{MV} \geqslant 0, T_{VS} \geqslant 0: T_{MV} \leqslant 600, 720 \leqslant T_{VS} \geqslant 1440\}, h_{p1} = 0$

—profit function: $f_{\Lambda 3}(T_1) = 1000 \times \frac{1}{720}(-T_{MV}^2 + 1440T_{VS}) + T_{MV}$;

—optimal profit: $f^* = \$1,320,000$;

—optimal solution: $T_{MV}^* = \$600 \quad T_{VS}^* = \$720$.

- Region4: $\Lambda_4 = \{T_{MV} \geqslant 0, T_{VS} \geqslant 0: T_{MV} + T_{VS} \leqslant 1320, T_{VS} \leqslant 720\}, h_{p_1} = h_{p_2} = 0$

—profit function: $f_{\Lambda_4}(T_1) = 1000(T_{MV} + T_{VS})$;

—optimal profit: $f^* = \$1,320,000$;

—optimal solution: Any combination in Λ_4 such that $T_{MV}^* + T_{VS}^* = \$1320$.

- Region5: $\Lambda_5 = \{T_{MV} \geqslant 0, T_{VS} \geqslant 0: 1320 \leqslant T_{MV} + T_{VS} \leqslant 2940, 4T_{MV} - 5T_{VS} + 1200 \leqslant 0\}, h_{p_2} = 0$

—profit function: $f_{\Lambda_5}(T_1) = 1000\frac{1}{1620}(-(T_{MV} + T_{VS})^2 + 2940(T_{MV} + T_{VS}))$;

—optimal profit: $f^* \approx \$1,334,000$

—optimal solution: Any combination in Λ_5 such that $T_{MV}^* + T_{VS}^* = \$1470$.

- Region 6: $\Lambda_6 = \{T_{MV} \geqslant 0, T_{VS} \geqslant 0: T_{MV} + T_{VS} \geqslant 2940, T_{MV} \geqslant 1500\}, h_{p_2} = h_{p_3} = 0$

—profit function: $f_{\Lambda_6}(T_1) = 0$;

—optimal profit: $f^* = \$0$;

—optimal solution: Any combination of fares that belongs to Λ_6.

It is interesting to take a closer look at some regions. For instance, in regions 2-4, the leader company's combination of fare and time dominates all competing proposals, and this results in Air Canada attracting all consumers to its two-leg flight. At the other end of the spectrum, Air Canada's fares in region 6 are so high that they fail to attract even passengers whose value of time is at its maximum α_{max}. In areas 0, 1 and 5, the fares set by the leader company achieve a trade-off between the number of passengers attracted and their willingness to pay.

The optimum is achieved in region 5. Since path 2 is dominated, the corresponding flow is zero, and only the sum of the fares $T_{MV}+T_{VS}$ on Air Canada's two-leg flight matters. The trade-off VOT at which passengers are indifferent between path p_1 and p_3 is the solution of the linear equation

$$1320+36\alpha=1470+18\alpha,$$

i. e., $\alpha^*=25/3$. The market share for Air Canada's two-leg flight is equal to the probability that a passenger's VOT be larger than α^*, i. e.,

$$\int_{\alpha^*}^{90}\psi(\alpha)\mathrm{d}\alpha=1-\frac{25}{3\times 90}\approx .907.$$

Therefore, at the optimum, 907 passengers fly Air Canada between Montreal and Shanghai.

7. Conclusion

In this paper, we have developed a bilevel pricing model for a service firm. Two key features of the model is that it explicitly takes into account customer behavior (thus allowing room for price discrimination) as well as the underlying network topology of the problem.

While, for ease of presentation, we restricted ourselves to a simple form of the model, its formulation can easily be extended to deal with more refined descriptions of user behavior, involving for instance more than two criteria, and to incorporate features such as: finite capacities, upper bounds on decision variables, more general functional forms of the cost functions, etc. A more ambitious goal is to integrate the current model within a dynamic framework, thus closing the gap between the bilevel pricing model and more traditional 'yield management' approaches adopted in the airline industry.

Finally, a word about algorithmic complexity. From the computational point of view, our model looks complex, as it requires the solution of alarge (exponential) number of subproblems. However our numerical experiences tend to show that, when started in a region which corresponds to flows that are (almost) all positive, convergence towards an optimal or near-optimal solution is frequently achieved. We also investigated successfully a discretization approach where the densities ψ_w are replaced by probability mass functions. The resulting approximation is then reformulated as a large mixed integer program (see Côté et al., 2002) that can be tackled either by commercial codes or heuristic procedures.

Acknowledgements

This research has been supported by NSERC (Canada), MITACS and FQRNT (Québec).

References

[1] Anderson, E. J., Nash, P., 1987. Linear Programming in Infinite-Dimensional Spaces. John Wiley and

Sons, New York, NY.

[2] Belobaba, P. P. , 1987. Airline yield management: An overview of seat inventory control. Transportation Science 21, 63-73.

[3] Côté, J. -P. , Marcotte, P. , Savard, G. 2002. A Bilevel Modeling Approach to Pricing and Fare Optimization in the Airline Industry. GERAD Research Report G-2002-71, Montreal, Canada.

[4] Gabszewicz, J. , Thisse, J. -F. , 1986. On the nature of competition with differentiated products. The Economic Journal 96, 160-172.

[5] Gabszewicz, J. , Thisse, J. -F. , 1979. Price competition, quality and income disparities. Journal of Economic Theory 20, 340-359.

[6] Hotelling, H. , 1929. Stability in competition. Economic Journal 39, 41-57.

[7] Krouse, C. K. , 1990. Theory of Industrial Economics. Basil Blackwell, Oxford, UK.

[8] Labbé, M. , Marcotte, P. , Savard, G. , 1998. A bilevel model of taxation and its application to optimal highway pricing. Management Science 44, 1595-1607.

[9] Leurent, F. , 1993. Cost versus time equilibrium over a network. European Journal of Operational Research 71, 205-221.

[10] Loridan, P. , Morgan, J. , 1996. Weak via strong Stackelberg problem: New results. Journal of Global Optimization 8, 263-287.

[11] Marcotte, P. , 1999. Reformulations of a bicriterion equilibrium problem. In: Fukushima, Masao, Qi, Liqun (Eds.), Reformulation-Nonsmooth, Piecewise Smooth, Semismooth and Smoothing Methods. Kluwer, Dordrecht, pp. 269-292.

[12] Marcotte, P. , Zhu, D. L. , 1997. Equilibria with infinitely many differentiated classes of customers. In: Pang, J. -S. , Ferris, M. (Eds.), Complementarity and Variational Problems, State of Art. SIAM, Philadelphia, USA, pp. 234-258.

[13] Martin, S. , 1993. Advanced Industrial Economics. Basil Blackwell, Oxford, UK.

[14] McGill, J. L. , Van Ryzin, G. J. , 1999. Revenue management: Research overview and prospects. Transportation Science 33, 233-256.

[15] Phlips, L. , 1983. The Economics of Price Discrimination. Cambridge University Press, Cambridge, UK.

[16] Phlips, L. , Thisse, J. -F. , 1982. Spatial competition and the theory of differential markets. Journal of Industrial Economics 31, 1-9.

Pablished in *European Journal of Operational Research*, 2009, 193

Exact and inexact penalty methods for the generalized bilevel programming problem

P. Marcotte[a,*], D. L. Zhu[b]

[a] *Département d'Informatique et de Recherche Opérationnelle, Université de Montréal, C. P. 6128, Succursale Centre-Ville. Montréal, Québec, Canada H3C 3J7*

[b] *Centre de Recherche sur les Transports, Université de Montréal, Montréal, Québec, Canada H3C 3J7*

Abstract. We consider a hierarchical system where a leader incorporates into its strategy the reaction of the follower to its decision. The follower's reaction is quite generally represented as the solution set to a monotone variational inequality. For the solution of this nonconvex mathematical program a penalty approach is proposed, based on the formulation of the lower level variational inequality as a mathematical program. Under natural regularity conditions, we prove the exactness of a certain penalty function, and give strong necessary optimality conditions for a class of generalized bilevel programs.

Key words, Optimization; Variational inequalities; Bilevel programming; Exact penalty; Descent methods

1. Introduction

We consider a two-level hierarchical system in Euclidian space where the upper level decision maker (hereafter the leader) controls a vector of variables x, and the lower level (hereafter the follower) controls a vector of variables y. The leader makes its decision first, taking into account the reaction of the follower to its course of action. The reaction $y(x)$ of the follower to the leader's decision x is a solution to an equilibrium problem represented by a variational inequality. We then obtain the generalized bilevel program, or GBLP:

$$\begin{aligned} \text{GBLP:} \quad & \min_{x\in X, y\in Y(x)} f(x, y) \\ & \text{subject to } \langle F(x, y), y - z\rangle \leqslant 0, \text{ for all } z \in Y(x), \end{aligned} \tag{1}$$

where the leader is implicitly restricted to x-vectors such that the lower level constraint

*Corresponding author.

set $Y(x)$ be nonempty. This mathematical program was first introduced by Marcotte [18] for formulating an equilibrium-constrained network design problem.

The term "follower" may denote either one, several or infinitely many "players". If it denotes a single player whose objective $g(x,y)$ is convex, then the corresponding standard bilevel program (or Stackelberg game) can be put in the form GBLP, with $F \equiv \nabla_y f$. If it denotes more than one player, then F represnts the cost mapping associated with the corresponding equilibrium solution concept: Nash equilibrium, perfect equilibrium, etc.

This difficult, nonconvex problem has drawn the attention of the mathematical community, both from the theoretical and computational points of view. (See the special issues of the journals *Computers and Operations Research* [5] and *Annals of Operations Research*[1] devoted to this topic.) The present paper studies the properties of a class of penalty functions, both exact and inexact, for the GBLP. The idea is not new. Ishizuka and Ayioshi [22] developed a double penalty scheme for the nonlinear bilevel programming problem, where the lower level problem (an optimization problem in their case) is transformed, via a quadratic penalty, into an unconstrained optimization problem or, equivalently, into a system of nonlinear equations. In a second stage, this nonlinear system is appended, again via a penalty term, to the upper level objective, to yield an unconstrained global optimization problem. Similarly, Haslinger and Neittaanmäki proposed (see [13, Chapter 10]) to penalize the state constraints associated with the lower level of their optimal shape design problem. Other schemes have also been proposed in the realm of linear bilevel programming (see [3]).

In this paper, we formulate the lower level variational inequality as a parameterized equation related to the duality gap of the lower level problem. We then use this "gap" function as a penalty term for the upper level problem. Since the gap function characterizing the lower level is nonnegative over the feasible domain, the penalty term assumes a very simple form. In the separable case, our formulation coincides with that found in a frequently overlooked paper of Fisk [8], who also penalizes the "standard" gap function. However, the exactness of this penalty scheme has not be proved by the author.

The remainder of the paper is organized as follows: We first formulate the problem; then we prove convergence results for an inexact penalty scheme as well as the exactness of penalty schemes based on some linear gap function, both under separable and nonseparable constraints; finally we show how our results can be used to derive necessary optimality conditions for the GBLP.

2. Formulation of the problem

Let C denote a continuously differentiable function from $\mathbb{R}^{n_1+n_2}$ into $\mathbb{R}^m$ and denote:

$$S = \{(x,y) \in \mathbb{R}^{n_1+n_2} \mid C(x,y) \leqslant 0\},$$

$$Y(x) = \{y \in \mathbb{R}^{n_2} \mid C(x,y) \leqslant 0\} = \{y \in \mathbb{R}^{n_2} \mid (x,y) \in S\},$$
$$X = \{x \in \mathbb{R}^{n_1} \mid Y(x) \neq \varnothing\}.$$

Let f be a continuously differentiable function from S into $\mathbb{R}$ and F a continuously differentiable, Lipschitz continuous(with Lipschitz constant L) function from S into $\mathbb{R}^{n_2}$, monotone on $Y(x)$ with respect to y for every x in X. In this paper we will consider the generalized bilevel program:

$$\begin{aligned} &\min_{x \in X, y \in Y(x)} f(x,y) \\ &\text{subject to } \langle F(x,y), y-z \rangle \leqslant 0, \forall z \in Y(x). \end{aligned} \tag{2}$$

We will assume throughout the paper that the set S is convex and compact and that, for fixed x in X, the parameterized set $Y(x)$ is convex. Under those assumptions, the GBLP is well defined, possesses at least one solution, and the solution set to the lower level variational inequality is, for fixed x in X, a compact, convex set. We will also make use of the following definitions.

Definition 1. (Dussault and Marcotte [7]) Let F be a continuous, monotone function from a convex polyhedron $X \subset \mathbb{R}^n$ into $\mathbb{R}^n$ and denote by VIP(X,F) the variational inequality problem associated with X and F, i. e. , find x^* in X such that

$$\text{VIP}(F,X): \quad \langle F(x^*), x^* - x \rangle \leqslant 0, \text{ for all } x \text{ in } X.$$

We say that VIP(F,X) is *geometrically stable* if, for any solution x^* of the variational inequality, $\langle F(x^*), x^* - x \rangle = 0$ implies that x lies on the optimal face, i. e. the minimal face of X containing the (convex) solution set to VIP(F,X).

Definition 2. Let Ω be a point-to-set mapping from X_1 into 2^{X_2}: Let $\{x_k\}$ be a sequence of points in X_1. The mapping Ω is *closed* at $x \in X_1$ if

$$\left.\begin{array}{l} x_k \in X_1 \\ x_k \to x \\ y_k \in \Omega(x_k) \\ y_k \to y \end{array}\right\} \Rightarrow y \in \Omega(x).$$

The mapping Ω is *open* at $x \in X_1$ if

$$\left.\begin{array}{l} x_k \in X_1 \\ x_k \to x \\ y \in \Omega(x) \end{array}\right\} \Rightarrow \exists \{y_k\} \text{ such that} \left\{\begin{array}{l} y_k \in X_2 \\ y_k \in \Omega(x_k) \\ y_k \to y. \end{array}\right.$$

If the mapping Ω is both closed and open at $x \in X$, we say that it is *continuous* at x.

Definition 3. The point-to-set mapping Ω is *uniformly compact* at $\bar{x}$ if there exists a nonempty neighborhood N of $\bar{x}$ such that the closure of $\bigcup_{x \in N} \Omega(x)$ is compact.

We associate with the lower level variational inequality VIP$(F(x, \cdot), Y(x))$ the *gap function*

$$G_\alpha(x,y) = \max_{z \in Y(x)} \phi(x,y,z), \tag{3}$$

where $\phi(x,y,z) = \langle F(x,y), y-z \rangle - \frac{1}{2}\alpha \| y-z \|^2$ and α is a positive number. The gap function has been used to construct descent methods for solving variational inequalities. We refer in particular to[18,19] for the linear gap function ($\alpha=0$), and to [10] for the quadratic, differentiable gap function ($\alpha>0$).

The function ϕ is concave in z (strongly concave if α is positive). Also, since G_α is nonnegative over $Y(x)$, and $G_\alpha(x,y)=0$ if an only if y is a solution to the lower level variational inequality parameterized by x, VIP($F(x,\cdot)$, $Y(x)$) can be rewritten as the nonlinear equation

$$G_\alpha(x,y) = \max_{z\in Y(x)}\phi(x,y,z) = \phi(x,y,p_\alpha(x,y)) = 0, \tag{4}$$

where $p_\alpha(x,y)$ is any solution of (3). Finally this leads to a reformulation of the GBLP as the standard mathematical program

$$\begin{aligned} \text{P1:} \quad & \min_{x\in X, y\in Y(x)} \quad f(x,y) \\ & \text{subject to} \quad G_\alpha(x,y) = 0. \end{aligned} \tag{5}$$

3. An inexact penalty approach

In this section we will approximate P1 by the penalized problem

$$P2: \min_{(x,y)\in S} q_\alpha(x,y,\mu) = f(x,y) + \mu G_\alpha(x,y), \tag{6}$$

where μ is a positive number. Problem P2 is nonlinear with convex constraints, and its objective function is continuously differentiable when a is positive. For each value of the weight μ we denote by $(x(\mu),\ y(\mu))$ a global optimum of P2. A penalty function algorithm is obtained by specifying a sequence of increasing (unbounded) weights $\{\mu_k\}$ and the associated sequence of iterates $\{(x(\mu_k),\ y(\mu_k))\}$. The main convergence result of this section relies on the following lemma.

Lemma 1. *Let* $\{(x_k=x(\mu_k), y_k=y(\mu_k))\}$ *be a sequence generated by a penalty algorithm based on the penalty function* P2. *Let* (x^*, y^*) *denote an optimal solution to the GBLP. Set* $f^*=f(x^*, y^*)$. *Then we have the relationships*

$$q_\alpha(x_k,y_k,\mu_k) \leqslant q_\alpha(x_{k+1},y_{k+1},\mu_{k+1}), \tag{7}$$

$$G_\alpha(x_k,y_k) \geqslant G_\alpha(x_{k+1},y_{k+1}), \tag{8}$$

$$f(x_k,y_k) \leqslant f(x_{k+1},y_{k+1}), \tag{9}$$

$$q_\alpha(x_k,y_k,\mu_k) \leqslant f^*. \tag{10}$$

Proof. Since x_k, $x_{k+1}\in X, y_k\in Y(x_k)$ and $Y_{k+1}\in Y(x_{k+1})$, we have

$$f(x_{k+1},y_{k+1}) + \mu_{k+1}G_\alpha(x_{k+1},y_{k+1}) \leqslant f(x_k,y_k) + \mu_{k+1}G_\alpha(x_k,y_k)$$

and

$$\begin{aligned} q_\alpha(x_{k+1},y_{k+1},\mu_{k+1}) &= f(x_{k+1},y_{k+1}) + \mu_{k+1}G_\alpha(x_{k+1},y_{k+1}) \\ &\geqslant f(x_{k+1},y_{k+1}) + \mu_k G_\alpha(x_{k+1},y_{k+1}) \\ &\geqslant f(x_k,y_k) + \mu_k G_\alpha(x_k,y_k), \text{ since } (x_k,y_k) \textit{ is } \text{optimal} \\ &= q_\alpha(x_k,y_k,\mu_k), \end{aligned}$$

and this proves (7). Also, since x_k and x_{k+1} are optimal for their respective penalized programs, we can write

$$f(x_k, y_k) + \mu_k G_\alpha(x_k, y_k) \leqslant f(x_{k+1}, y_{k+1}) + \mu_k G_\alpha(x_{k+1}, y_{k+1}).$$

Combining the above inequalities yields

$$(\mu_{k+1} - \mu_k) G_\alpha(x_{k+1}, y_{k+1}) \leqslant (\mu_{k+1} - \mu_k) G_\alpha(x_k, y_k),$$

which leads to (8), after dividing by the positive number $\mu_{k+1} - \mu_k$. Next the inequality

$$f(x_{k+1}, y_{k+1}) + \mu_k G\alpha(x_{k+1}, y_{k+1}) \geqslant f(x_k, y_k) + \mu_k G\alpha(x_k, y_k),$$

combined with (8), yields (9). Finally, observe that

$$\begin{aligned} f^* &= f(x^*, y^*) + \mu_k G_\alpha(x^*, y^*) \\ &\geqslant f(x_k, y_k) + \mu_k G_\alpha(x_k, y_k) \\ &\geqslant f(x_k, y_k). \end{aligned}$$

Proposition 1. *Let $\{x_k, y_k\}$ be a sequence generated by a penalty algorithm based on the penalty function* P2. *Any limit point of the sequence $\{x_k, y_k\}$ is a solution of the bilevel program* P1.

Proof. The set S being compact, there exists a convergent subsequence $\{(x_k, y_k)\}_{k\in K^*}$ Let$(\overline{x}, \overline{y})$ be its limit point. It follows from the continuity of f that

$$\lim_{k\in K} f(x_k, y_k) = f(\overline{x}, \overline{y}). \tag{11}$$

Let f^* be the optimal value of the GBLP. Lemma 1 implies that

$$q_\alpha^* = \lim_{k\in K} q_\alpha(x_k, y_k, \mu_k) \leqslant f^* \tag{12}$$

Subtracting (11) from (12) there comes

$$\lim_{k\in K} \mu_k G_\alpha(x_k, y_k) = q_\alpha^* - f(\overline{x}, \overline{y}) \leqslant f^* - f(\overline{x}, \overline{y}) \leqslant 0. \tag{13}$$

Since G_α is nonnegative, Eq. (13) implies that

$$\lim_{k\in K} G_\alpha(x_k, y_k) = 0. \tag{14}$$

and, using the continuity of G_α, $G_\alpha(\overline{x}, \overline{y}) = 0$, i. e., that$(\overline{x}, \overline{y})$ is feasible for problem P1. Furthermore, the inequality (10) in Lemma 1 allows to write

$$f(\overline{x}, \overline{y}) = \lim_{k\in K} f(x_k, y_k) \leqslant f^* \tag{15}$$

and this shows that $(\overline{x}, \overline{y})$ is an optimal solution of P1 or, equivalently, of the GBLP.

Example 1. Consider the bilevel problem

$$\begin{aligned} &\min_{x\in[-1,1],\, y\in[-1,1]} \quad x^2 - y \\ &\text{subject to} \quad \langle 2y, y - z\rangle \leqslant 0, \text{ for all } z \in [-1, 1]. \end{aligned} \tag{16}$$

Clearly the point (0,0) is the unique solution of the above GBLP. For $\alpha = 1$, the gap function associated with the lower-level variational inequality takes the form

$$\begin{aligned} G_1(x, y) &= \max_{-1\leqslant z\leqslant 1} \quad \langle 2y, y - z\rangle - \frac{1}{2}\| y - z \|^2 \\ &= 2y^2 \quad \text{if} -1 \leqslant y \leqslant 1. \end{aligned}$$

The corresponding penalized problem P2 is

$$\min_{-1\leqslant x\leqslant 1, -1\leqslant y\leqslant 1} \quad x^2 - y + 2\mu y^2 \tag{17}$$

and its optimal solution is $(0, 1/(4\mu))$, which converges to (0, 0) as μ goes to infinity.

4. An exact penalty function for the GBLP: the separablle cse

In the example of the previous section, there is no finite value of the penalty parameter μ for which the solution to the penalized problem agrees with the optimal solution of the GBLP. We will show that the exactness property can be achieved with the"classical" gap function G_0, introduced by Hearn[14] in an optimization setting, and corresponding to the choice $\alpha=0$ in P1. In this section we focus on the case where the set S is separable and refer to the corresponding problem as P3:

$$\text{P3:} \min_{x\in X, y\in Y} \quad f(x,y) \qquad \text{subject to} \quad \langle F(x,y), y-z\rangle \leqslant 0, \quad \forall z \in Y. \tag{18}$$

The gap formulation of the GBLP is now

$$\text{P4:} \min_{x\in X, y\in Y} \quad f(x,y) \qquad \text{subject to} \quad G_0(x,y) = 0 \tag{19}$$

and its penalized equivalent is

$$P5: \min_{x\in X, y\in Y} \quad f(x,y) + \mu G_0(x,y). \tag{20}$$

Note that the global convergence result (Proposition 1) of the previous section holds for $\alpha=0$, i. e. P5.

Example 2. Consider the bilevel problem of Example 1. The gap function G_0 of the lower level problem is

$$G_0(x,y) = \max_{-1\leqslant z\leqslant 1} \quad \langle 2y, y-z\rangle = 2y^2 + 2\mid y\mid \tag{21}$$

and the corresponding formulation P5 is

$$\min_{-1\leqslant x\leqslant 1, -1\leqslant y\leqslant 1} \quad x^2 - y + 2\mu(y^2 + \mid y\mid). \tag{22}$$

For all values of μ larger than 1/2, the optimal solution of the above penalized problem is the optimal solution of the GBLP, namely: $(x^*, y^*)=(0,0)$.

Throughout this section, it will be assumed that the set Y is the polyhedron $Y=\{y\mid By\leqslant b\}$ (where B is an $m\times n_2$ matrix and b a vector in $\mathbb{R}^m$), that the mapping F is strongly monotone with respect to the variable y and that its Jacobian $\nabla_y F$ is uniformly Lipschitz continuous with respect to the variable y, i. e. , respectively,

$$\langle \nabla_y F(x,y_2) - \nabla_y F(x,y_1), y_2 - y_1\rangle \geqslant v\parallel y_2 - y_1\parallel^2, \quad \forall x\in X, \forall y_1, y_2 \in Y, \tag{23}$$

and

$$\parallel \nabla_y F(x,y_2) - \nabla_y F(x,y_1)\parallel \leqslant L\parallel y_2 - y_1\parallel, \quad \forall x\in X, \forall y_1, y_2\in Y. \tag{24}$$

The main convergence result of this section will require preliminary results about the local behavior of the lower level variational inequality.

Lemma 2. *Let $x_0\in X$ and assume that there exists a neighborhood of the point x_0 such that* VIP$(F(x,\cdot),Y)$ *is geometrically stable inside that neighborhood. Then there exists some neighborhood N_0 of x_0 such that the minimal face containing the solutions to*

VIP $(F(x,\cdot),Y)$ *and* VIP$(F(x_0,\cdot),Y)$ *are identical.*

Proof. First note that our assumptions imply that the reaction $y(x)$ to a given upper level decision x defines a continuous function (see [21]). Let us denote by $T(x)$ and $T(x_0)$ the minimal faces containing the solutions to VIP$(F(x,\cdot)Y)$ and VIP $(F(x_0,\cdot)Y)$ respectively. We divide the proof into two parts.

(i) $T(x)\subset T(x_0)$ for all x in some neighborhood of x_0.

We argue by contradiction. Assume there exists a sequence $\{x_i\}$ converging to x_0 and a sequence of extreme points $u_l\in Y$ such that $u_l\in T(x_l)$ but $u_l\notin T(x_0)$. It follows from the geometric regularity assumption (see also [7]) that

$$\langle F(x_l,y(x_l)),u_l-y(x_l)\rangle=0. \tag{25}$$

Now we select a subsequence $\{u_l\}_{l\in L}$ such that $\lim_{l\in L}u_l=u_x$, * with $u_x\in Y-T(x_0)$. Taking the limit as $l\to\infty(l\in L)$ in (25) there comes

$$\langle F(x_0,y(x_0)),u_x-y(x_0)\rangle=0. \tag{26}$$

and this in turn implies that $u_x\in T(x_0)$, a contradiction.

(ii) $T(x_0)\subset T(x)$ for all x in some neighborhood of x_0.

We proceed by contradiction again. Assume the result does not hold. Then there must exist a sequence $\{x_l\}_{l\in L'}$ such that $T(x_l)$ is a strict subface of $T(x_0)$. Without loss of generality, we assume that the faces $T(x_l)$ are identical for all l in L'. For each $l\in L'$, consider the sequence $\{y(x_l)\}_{l\in L'}$ of solutions to the lower level variational inequality. The the minimal face containing its limit point $y(x_0)$ is a strict subface of $T(x_0)$, a contradiction.

Lemma 3. *Under the assumption of Lemma 2, there exists a neighborhood of x_0 and a positive number η such that*

$$G_0(x,y)\geqslant\eta\,\|y(x)-y\|, \tag{27}$$

for all x in that neighborhood and all y in Y.

Proof. Following a result of Marcotte and Dussault [19], for each x in N_0, there exists a positive number $\eta(x)$ such that the bound

$$G_0(x,y)\geqslant\eta(x)\,\|y(x)-y\| \tag{28}$$

holds, for all y in Y. Furthermore it is a direct consequence of the analysis leading to this result that $\eta(x)$ is a continuous function of the variable x, whenever the optimal face of the lower level variational inequality remains unchanged. Since this condition is satisfied in some neighborhood of x_0 (see Lemma 2), and $\eta(x_0)$ is positive, the set $\{\eta(x)\}$ is bounded from below by some number η, for x in the required neighborhood, and the result is proved.

Lemma 4. *Let $\tilde{y}(x,y)$ be the solution of the linearized variational inequality, i.e.,*

$$\langle F(x,y)+\nabla_yF(x,y)(\tilde{y}(x,y)-y),\tilde{y}(x,y)-z\rangle\leqslant 0,\ \forall z\in Y. \tag{29}$$

---

*Actually $\{u_l\}$ can be taken as the constant sequence $\{u_x\}$.

Then we have

$$G_0'((x,y);(0,\tilde{y}(x,y)-y))\leqslant -G_0(x,y). \tag{30}$$

Proof. This lemma is simply a restatement in our context of a result of Marcotte and Dussault [20] about the descent property of Newton's direction.

Lemma 5. *Under the assumption of Lemma 2, there exists a neighborhood of* $(x_0, y(x_0))$ *and a positive constant* γ *such that*

$$G_0'((x,y);(0,y(x)-y))\leqslant -\gamma\|y(x)-y\|, \tag{31}$$

for all x, y *in that neighborhood.*

Proof. We have that $\|\tilde{y}(x,y)-y(x)\|=\mathcal{O}(\|y(x)-y\|^2)$ (see[17]). This allows us to write

$$\begin{aligned}&G_0'((x,y);(0,y(x)-y))\\&=G_0'((x,y);(0,\tilde{y}(x,y)-y))+G_0'((x,y);(0,y(x)-\tilde{y}(x,y)))\\&\leqslant G_0'((x,y);(0,\tilde{y}(x,y)-y))+\mathcal{O}(\|y(x)-y\|^2),\end{aligned}$$

by the linearity of G_0' with respect to its second argument and the continuity and compactness assumptions,

$$\leqslant -G_0(x,y)+\mathcal{O}(\|y(x)-y\|^2), \text{by Lemma 4},$$

$$\leqslant -\eta\|y(x)-y\|+\mathcal{O}(\|y(x)-y\|^2), \text{by Lemma 3}.$$

Since $y(x)$ is a continuous function of x, there must exist a neighborhood of $(x_0, y(x_0))$ such that

$$G_0'((x,y);(0,y(x)-y))\leqslant -\gamma\|y(x)-y\|,$$

for all (x,y) in that neighborhood, for any positive number γ less than η.

We are now in position to state and prove the main result of this section.

Theorem 1. *Let* $(x^*,y^*)\in S$. *Assume that there exists a neighborhood of the point* x^* *such that* VIP$(Y, F(x,\cdot))$ *is geometrically stable inside that neighborhood. Then there exists a finite value of the penalty parameter* μ, *say* μ^*, *such that for all* μ *larger than* μ^*, (x^*,y^*) *is a global solution of* P5 *if and only if it is also a global solution of* P3.

Proof. From Proposition 1, there exists a subsequence $\{\mu_k\}_{k\in K}$ such that the solution $(x(\mu_k),y(\mu_k))$ of P5 converges to a solution $(x^*,y^*)\in S$ of GBLP. Lemma 5 ensures the existence of a neighborhood N^* of (x^*,y^*) and some positive number γ such that

$$G_0'((x,y);(0,y(x)-y))\leqslant -\gamma\|y(x)-y\|,\quad \forall (x,y)\in N^*.$$

Therefore there must exist a finite value $\tilde{\mu}$ such that $(x(\mu_k),y(\mu_k))$ lies in N^* for all values of μ_k larger than $\tilde{\mu}$ and all indices $k\in K$.

On the other hand, since f is continuously differentiable on the compact set $S=X\times Y$, we have

$$\|\nabla_y f(x,y)\|\leqslant\beta,\quad \forall x\in X, y\in Y, \tag{32}$$

for some finite number β. Let $\mu^*=\min\{\mu_k, k\in K\mid \mu_k\geqslant\tilde{\mu}, \mu_k>\beta/\gamma\}$. Assume that $G_0(x(\mu^*)$,

$y(\mu^*)$)is positive, i. e. ,that $y(x(\mu^*))\neq y(\mu^*)$. (Otherwise the solution to the penalized problem is feasible for P3, and consequently optimal for the GBLP.) We have

$$f'[(x(\mu^*),y(\mu^*));(0,y(x(\mu^*))-y(\mu^*))] \tag{33}$$

$$+\mu^* G_0'[(x(\mu^*),y(\mu^*));(0,y(x(\mu^*))-y(\mu^*))]$$

$$\leqslant (\beta-\mu^*\gamma)\parallel y(x(\mu^*))-y(\mu^*)\parallel \text{ by (32) and Lemma 5}$$

$$<0 \tag{34}$$

and$(0,y(x(\mu^*))-y(\mu^*))$is a feasible descent direction for P5, in contradiction with the (global) optimality of $(x(\mu^*),y(\mu^*))$. We conclude that $G_0(x(\mu^*),y(\mu^*))=0$. From Lemma 1, we have $G_0(x(\mu),y(\mu))=0$ for $\mu\geqslant\mu^*$. Thus $(x(\mu),y(\mu))$ is an optimal solution to the GBLP.

Conversely, let (x^*,y^*) be an optimal solution of the GBLP and consider$(x(\mu),y(\mu))$ for μ larger than μ^*. By the above analysis we have that $G_0(x(\mu),y(\mu))=0$. Therefore,

$$f(x^*,y^*)=f(x^*,y^*)+\mu G_0(x^*,y^*)$$

$$\leqslant f(x(\mu),y(\mu))+\mu G_0(x(\mu),y(\mu))$$

and this shows that (x^*,y^*) is optimal for P5, as claimed.

Corollary 1. *Let* $\mu\geqslant\mu^*$. *Then* $(\overline{x},\overline{y}))$ *is a local minimum of* P5 *if and only if it is a local minimum of* P3.

Proof. In the proof of Theorem 1, the inequality (34) holds for local as well as for glocal minima and it follows that any local minimum of P5 satisfies $G_0(\overline{x},\overline{y})=0$ and is feasible for P3, whenever $\mu\geqslant\mu^*$, i. e. , that P5 is entirely equivalent to P3. Consequently, the set of local minima of P5 coincides with that of P3.

The formulation P5 involves a nondifferentiable term. However it is possible to rewrite G_0 as

$$\begin{aligned} G_0(x,y) &= \max_{z\in Y} \langle F(x,y),y-z\rangle \\ &= \max_{e\in E} \langle F(x,y),y-u_e\rangle \\ &= \min_{\xi} \xi \\ &\quad \text{subject to } \xi\geqslant\langle F(x,y),y-u_e\rangle,\forall e\in E, \end{aligned} \tag{35}$$

where $\{u_e\}_{e\in E}$ denotes the set of extreme points of the polyhedron $Y=\{y|By\leqslant b\}$. This results in the formulation

$$\begin{aligned} &\min_{x\in X,y\in Y,\xi} f(x,y)+\mu\xi \\ &\text{subject to } \xi\geqslant\langle F(x,y),y-u_e\rangle, \quad \forall e\in E, \end{aligned} \tag{36}$$

which yields a differentiable formulation.

Alternatively, the gap function can be expressed in dual form (see [19]) as

$$\begin{aligned} G_0(x,y) &= \min_{\lambda\geqslant 0} \langle F(x,y),y\rangle+b^t\lambda \\ &\quad \text{subject to } F(x,y)+B^t\lambda=0. \end{aligned} \tag{37}$$

Replacing $G_0(x, y)$ by its dual formulation yields

$$\begin{aligned} P6: \min_{x\in X, y\in Y, \lambda\geqslant 0} \quad & f(x,y) + \mu(\langle F(x,y), y\rangle + b^t\lambda) \\ \text{subject to} \quad & F(x,y) + B^t\lambda = 0. \end{aligned} \tag{38}$$

Corollary 2. *Under the assumption of Theorem* 1, *there exists a finite value of the penalty parameter* μ. *say* μ^*, *such that for all* μ *larger than* μ^*, (x^*, y^*) *is a global solution of* P6 *if and only if it is also a global solution of* P3.

Proof. The result is a direct consequence of the equivalence between P5 and P6.

We close this section with an equivalent of Corollary 1.

Corollary 3. *Let* $\mu\geqslant\mu^*$. *Then* $(\bar{x},\bar{y})$ *is a local minimum of* P6 *if and only if it is a local minimum of* P5, *if and only if it is a local minimum of* P3.

5. An exact penalty function for the GBLP: the non-separable case

In this section we extend the analysis to the case where the set S is *not* separable with respect to the vectors of variables x and y. More specifically, we set

$$S = \{(x,y) \mid C(x,y) = Ax + By - d \leqslant 0, x \in X'\},$$

where A and B are $p\times n_1$ and $p\times n_2$ matrices respectively, and X' is a compact, convex subset of $\mathbb{R}^{n_1}$. We will still assume that the mapping F is strongly monotone with respect to the variable y and that its Jacobian with respect to y, $\nabla_y F$, is uniformly Lipschitz continuous on the set S.

At a point x_0 of X, a solution y_0 to the lower level variational inequality is characterized by the complementarity system

$$\begin{aligned} & F(x_0, y_0) + B^t\lambda_0 = 0, \\ & (Ax_0 + By_0 - d)^t\lambda_0 = 0, \\ & \lambda_0 \geqslant 0. \end{aligned} \tag{39}$$

The strong monotonicity of F implies that the lower level solution $y(x)$ is unique, for all x. Furhermore, if the gradients of the binding constraints are linearly independent and the *strict complementarity condition*

$$\lambda_{0i} > 0 \Leftrightarrow C_i(x_0, y_0) = 0, \quad \forall i, \tag{40}$$

is satisfied then, in a neighborhood of x_0, the functions $y(x)$ and $\lambda(x)$ are unique and Lipschitz continuous. (See [9] for example.)

For given x, denote by $T(x)$ the minimal face of $Y(x)$ containing the solution $y(x)$ to the lower level variational inequality. We have the following results.

Proposition 2. *Let* $x_0\in X$. *If the linear independence and strict complementarity conditions hold at* $y_0 = y(x_0)$, *there exists a neighborhood* N_0 *of* x_0 *such that* $T(x)$ *and* $T(x_0)$ *have the same topological structure for all* $x\in N_0$, *i. e.*,

$$C_i(x_0, y_0) = 0 \Leftrightarrow C_i(x, y(x)) = 0.$$

Proof. Let J denote the index set of binding constraints at (x_0, y_0) and

$$T(x_0)=\{y\mid C_i(x_0,y)=0,i\in J,C_i(x_0,y)\leqslant 0,i\notin J\}.$$

The strict complementarity condition yields

$$\lambda_i(x_0)>0\Leftrightarrow C_i(x_0,y_0)=0.$$

Since the mapping λ is continuous in the variable x, there must exist a neighborhood N_1 of x_0 such that $\lambda_i(x)>0$ whenever $C_i(x,y(x))=0$, for all $i\in J$ and $x\in N_1$.

On the other hand, the continuity of the (affine) functions C_i implies the existence of a neighborhood N_2 such that $C_i(x,y(x))<0$ for all $i\notin J$ and $x\in N_2$. Taking $N_0=N_1\cap N_2$ brings the conclusion.

Proposition 3. *Under the assumptions of Proposition 2, there exists a neighborhood N_0 of x_0 such that T is a continuous point-to-set mapping on N_0.*

Proof. Let N_0 be the neighborhood of Proposition 2, J the index set of binding constraints at x_0, and $\bar{x}\in N_0$.

(i) T is closed at $\bar{x}$. Let

$$\begin{aligned}T(\bar{x})&=\{y\mid C_i(\bar{x},y)=0,i\in J,C_i(\bar{x},y)\leqslant 0,i\notin J\}\\&=\{y\mid \bar{A}\bar{x}+\bar{B}y-\bar{d}=0,\bar{\bar{A}}\bar{x}+\bar{\bar{B}}y-\bar{\bar{d}}\leqslant 0\},\end{aligned}$$

for suitable submatrices $\bar{A},\bar{\bar{A}}$ of A and $\bar{B},\bar{\bar{B}}$ of B. Let $x_k\to\bar{x}$, $y_k\to\bar{y}$, $x_k\in N_0$ and $y_k\in T(x_k)$, for all k. We have

$$\lim_{k\to\infty}C_i(x_k,y_k)=C_i(\bar{x},\bar{y})$$

and

$$C_i(\bar{x},\bar{y})\begin{cases}=0, & \forall i\in J,\\ \leqslant 0, & \forall i\notin J,\end{cases}$$

which implies that $\bar{y}\in T(\bar{x})$, and T is closed at $\bar{x}$.

(ii) T is open at $\bar{x}$. Let x_k denote a sequence converging to the point $\bar{x}$, and $\bar{y}$ be an arbitrary point in the face $T(\bar{x})$. Let us introduce the face $T(x_k)=\{y\mid\bar{A}x_k+\bar{B}y-\bar{d}=0, \bar{\bar{A}}x_k+\bar{\bar{B}}y-\bar{\bar{d}}\leqslant 0\}$, and let $y_k=\arg\min_{y\in T(x_k)}\|\bar{y}-y\|$, i. e., y_k is the projection of $\bar{y}$ onto $T(x^k)$ and the distance from $\bar{y}$ to $T(x^k)$ is given by $\|\bar{y}-y_k\|$.

The application of Hoffman's Lemma [15] to the linear systems $\bar{A}x_k+\bar{B}y-\bar{d}=0$ and $\bar{\bar{A}}x_k+\bar{\bar{B}}y-\bar{\bar{d}}\leqslant 0$ yields:

$$\begin{aligned}\|\bar{y}-y_k\|&\leqslant\tau(\|\bar{A}x_k+\bar{B}\bar{y}-\bar{d}\|+\|(\bar{\bar{A}}x_k+\bar{\bar{B}}\bar{y}-\bar{\bar{d}})_+\|)\\&\leqslant\tau(\|\bar{A}(x_k-\bar{x})+(\bar{A}\bar{x}+\bar{B}\bar{y}-\bar{d})\|\\&\quad+\|(\bar{\bar{A}}(x_k-\bar{x}))_+\|+\|(\bar{\bar{A}}\bar{x}+\bar{\bar{B}}\bar{y}-\bar{\bar{d}})_+\|)\\&=\tau(\|\bar{A}(x_k-\bar{x})\|+\|(\bar{\bar{A}}(x_k-\bar{x}))_+\|),\end{aligned}$$

for some positive constant τ, where $(x)_+$ denotes the projection of the vector x onto the nonnegative orthant. We conclude that $\lim_{k\to\infty}\|\bar{y}-y_k\|=0$ and therefore $y_k\to\bar{y}$, as required.

Corollary 4. *Consider the function δ defined as*

$$\delta(x) = \max_{z \in T(x)} \| y(x) - z \| . \quad (41)$$

If the assumptions of Proposition 2 hold at x_0, *then there exists a neighborhood of* x_0 *such that* δ *is continuous on that neighborhood.*

Proof. The sets $Y(x)$ and $T(x)$ are uniformly compact and the point-to-set mapping T is ontinuous in a neighborhood of x_0. Also the function $y(x)$ is continuous on X. The conclusion then follows from Theorem 7 in [16].

Now, as in the previous sections, we associate with the GBLP its reformulation

$$\begin{aligned} \text{P7: } & \min_{(x,y)\in S} f(x,y) \\ & \text{subject to } G_0(x,y) = 0. \end{aligned} \quad (42)$$

and the corresponding penalty problem:

$$\text{P8: } \min_{(x,y)\in S} q_a(x,y,\mu) = f(x,y) + \mu G_0(x,y). \quad (43)$$

Lemma 6. *Under the assumptions of Proposition 2, there exist a positive constant* η *and a neighborhood* $N'(x_0,y_0)$ *of* (x_0,y_0) *such that*

$$G_0(x,y) \geqslant \eta \| y(x) - y \| , \quad \forall (x,y) \in S \cap N'(x_0,y_0). \quad (44)$$

Proof. For fixed $x \in X$, one has (see Proposition 3 of [19])

$$G_0(x,y) \geqslant \eta(x) \| y(x) - y \| , \quad \forall y \in Y(x), \quad (45)$$

where $\eta(x)$ depends continuously on the distance $\delta(x)$ of $y(x)$ to the boundary of $T(x)$. Now, Corollary 4 ensures that $\eta/(x)$ is continuous in a neighborhood of x_0. Since $\eta(x_0)$ is positive, the conclusion follows.

The next lemma parallels Lemma 5 of the preceding section and its proof is similar.

Lemma 7. *Under the assumptions of Proposition 2, there exists a neighborhood of* (x_0, y_0) *and a positive constant* γ *such that*

$$G_0'((x,y);(0,y(x)-y)) \leqslant -\gamma \| y(x) - y \| . \quad (46)$$

for all x, y *in that neighborhood.*

Lemma 7 is the key result that is required to prove the exactness of G_0 as a penalty function. The proofs are similar to the proofs of the corresponding results in Section 4, using Lemma 6 in place of Lemma 3.

Theorem 2. *Let* $(x^*, y^*) \in S$ *and let the assumptions of Proposition 2 hold at* (x^*, y^*). *Then there exists a finite value* μ^* *such that, for all* $\mu \geqslant \mu^*$, (x^*, y^*) *is a global optimum of* P8 *if and only if it is also a global optimum of* P7.

Corollary 5. *Let* $\mu \geqslant \mu^*$. *Then* $(\bar{x}, \bar{y})$ *is a local minimum of* P8 *if and only if it is a local minimum of* P7.

We note that similar results hold for the dual formulation

$$\begin{aligned} \text{P9: } & \min_{(x,y)\in S, \lambda \geqslant 0} f(x,y) + \mu[\langle F(x,y), y\rangle + (d - Ax)^t\lambda] \\ & \text{subject to } F(x,y) + B^t\lambda = 0 \end{aligned} \quad (47)$$

Example. We illustrate our main result using a two-dimensional example taken from the paper by Gauvin and Savard [12], where the lower level problem corresponds to an optimization problem. We have

$$f(x,y) = x^2 + (y-10)^2,$$
$$S = \{(x,y) \mid x+y \leqslant 20, x \leqslant 15, x,y \geqslant 0\},$$
$$F(x,y) = 4(x+2y-30).$$

Its optimal value is 20 and is reached at the unique optimal solution $(x^*, y^*)=(2, 14)$. The gap function of this problem takes the form

$$\begin{aligned} G_0(x,y) &= \max_z \{\langle 4(x+2y-30), y-z\rangle \mid 0 \leqslant z \leqslant 20-x\} \\ &= 4(x+2y-30)y - \min\{0, 4(x+2y-30)(20-x)\} \\ &= \begin{cases} 4(x+2y-30)y, & \text{if } x+2y-30 \geqslant 0, \\ 4(x+2y-30)(x+y-20), & \text{if } x+2y-30 \leqslant 0. \end{cases} \end{aligned} \tag{48}$$

Now consider the penalized problem

$$\begin{aligned} \min_{x,y} \quad & x^2 + (y-10)^2 + \mu G_0(x,y) \\ \text{subject to} \quad & x+y \leqslant 20 \\ & x \leqslant x \leqslant 15 \\ & y \geqslant 0. \end{aligned} \tag{49}$$

The above problem separates into two cases.

(i) First case: $x+2y \geqslant 30$:

$$P(\mu) = \min_{x,y\geqslant 0} \{x^2 + (y-10)^2 + 4\mu(x+2y-30)y \mid x+2y \geqslant 30, \\ x+y \leqslant 20, x \leqslant 15\} \tag{50}$$

The optimum is reached at $(x,y)=(2,14)$ and its value is 20.

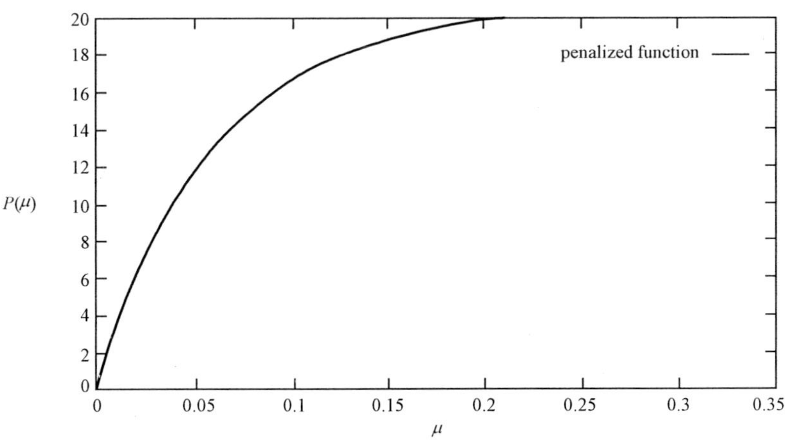

Fig. 1　Convergence of the penalized problem.

(ii) Second case: $x+2y \leqslant 30$:

$$P(\mu) = \min_{x,y\geqslant 0} \{x^2 + (y-10)^2 + 4\mu(x+2y-30)(x+y-20) \mid x+2y \leqslant 30, \\ x+y \leqslant 20, x \leqslant 15\} \tag{51}$$

If $\mu \geqslant \frac{1}{4}$, the solution is(2,14) as well. If $\mu \leqslant \frac{1}{4}$, the optimal solutiob is

$$x(\mu) = \frac{40(\mu - \mu^2)}{1 + 12\mu - 4\mu^2}, \qquad y(\mu) = \frac{10(1 + 18\mu - 4\mu^2)}{1 + 12\mu - 4\mu^2}.$$

The sequence of optimal values of the penalized function $P(\mu)$ is plotted in Fig. 1.

6. Extensions and remarks

In this paper, we presented an exact penalty scheme for an optimization problem with variational inequality constraints. Our analysis made use of the nondifferentiable gap function of the lower level variational inequality as a penalty function. In this context, our regularity assumptions could not be weakened while still retaining the key result

$$G_0'((x,y);(y(x) - y)) \leqslant -\gamma \| y(x) - y \| . \tag{52}$$

In the case where F is constant and f is affine however, the linear independence and strict complementarity conditions are not required any more: (52) is *always* valid for linear programs. Indeed, a direct proof of exactness of the gap function, in the linear case, can be found in [2]. This result can actually be extended to the situation where f is nonlinear and F assumes the form $F(x,y) = H(x) + h$.

It is also possible to extend the analysis to take into account additional upper level constraints $(x,y) \in S'$, resulting in the more general formulation:

$$\min_{(x,y) \in S' \cap S} \quad f(x,y)$$

$$\text{subject to} \quad \langle F(x,y), y - z \rangle \leqslant 0, \text{ for all } z \in Y(x).$$

A byproduct of our exactness result is the derivation of necessary optimality conditions for the GBLP. If we assume that the convex set X' can be represented as

$$X' = \{x \in \mathbb{R}^{n_1} \mid l_i(x) \leqslant 0, i = 1, \cdots, s\},$$

where the functions l_i are convex, and that its interior is nonempty(Slater's constraint qualification), then(x^*, y^*) is a (local) minimum of the GBLP only if there exist vectors v^* and w^* such that

$$\begin{aligned}
0 &\in \nabla_x f(x^*, y^*) + \mu \partial_x G_0(x^*, y^*) + \sum_{i=1}^{s} v_i^* \nabla l_i(x^*) + w^{*t} A, \\
0 &\in \nabla_y f(x^*, y^*) + \mu \partial_y G_0(x^*, y^*) + w^{*t} B, \\
& v_i^* l_i(x^*) = 0, \qquad i = 1, \cdots, s, \\
& w_j^* (Ax^* + B_j y^* - d_j) = 0, \qquad j = 1, \cdots, p, \\
& v_i^* \geqslant 0, \qquad i = 1, \cdots, s, \\
& w_j^* \geqslant 0, \qquad j = 1, \cdots, p,
\end{aligned}$$

provided that the penalty parameter μ is sufficiently large ($\mu \geqslant \mu^*$). In the separable case ($A = 0$), the expression of the Clarke generalized gradient of G_0 takes the simple form

$$\partial_x G_0(x,y) = \mathrm{CO}_{z\in\Gamma(x,y)}(\nabla_x F(x,y))^t(y-z),$$
$$\partial_y G_0(x,y) = \mathrm{CO}_{z\in\Gamma(x,y)}[F(x,y)+(\nabla_x F(x,y))^t(y-z)],$$

where $\Gamma(x,y)=\arg\min_{z\in Y(x)}(F(x,y))^t(y-z)$. The derivation of Karush-Kuhn-Tucker conditions for the GBLP can also be based on the dual formulation (47). One must be careful however that the dual feasibility constraints

$$F(x,y)+B^t\lambda=0 \tag{53}$$

satisfy some regularity (constraint qualification) condition. This will be the case if F is affine in (x,y) or under various separability conditions. As of now, we do not know whether the regularity of the system (53) is satisfied for more general classes of nonlinear functions F.

Several authors have previously proposed optimality conditions based on the reformulation of a bilevel program as an optimization program constrained by the optimality conditions, in one form or another, of the lower level program. (See [3,4].) The drawback of these approaches is that, in general, no constraint qualification holds for the KKT constraints, leading to optimality conditions that are very seldom realized in practice. Let us mention that stronger optimality results, based on local sensitivity analysis results, have been proposed by Gauvin and Savard [12].

From a practical point of view, the nonconvex and nondifferentiable problems P5 and P8 are difficult to solve. A global optimum can only be achieved by resorting to global optimization techniques such as implicit enumeration, cutting plane methods, etc. Recently, in the context of linear bilevel programming, Gendreau et al. [11] proposed an efficient heuristic for generating a high-quality initial solution, later to be used as a starting point for local search methods. This procedure was based on a primal-dual, exact penalty formulation of the linear bilevel program. Work is currently under way to adapt this technique within a nonlinear framework.

References

[1] Hierarchical Optimization, *Annals of Operations Research* 34 (1992).

[2] G. Anandalingam and D. J. White, "A solution method for the linear static Stackelberg problem using penalty functions," *IEEE Transactions on Automatic Control* AC-35 (1990) 1170-1173.

[3] J. F. Bard, "An efficient point algorithm for a linear two-stage optimization problem," *Operations Research* 31(1983)670-684.

[4] Z. Bi, P. Calamai and A. Conn, "An exact penalty method approach for the nonlinear bilevel programming problem," Report # 180-0-170591, Department of Systems Design, University of Waterloo (1991).

[5] *Computers and Operations Research* 9(1982).

[6] J. M. Danskin, "The theory of max-min, with applications," *SIAM Journal of Applied Mathematics* 14(1966)641-664.

[7] J. P. Dussault and P. Marcotte, "Conditions de régularité géométrique pour les inéquations variation-

nelles," *RAIRO* Recherche *Opérationnelle* 23(1988)1-16.

[8] C. S. Fisk, "A conceptual framework for optimal transportation systems planning with integrated supply and demand models," *Transportation Science* 20(1986)37-47.

[9] T. L. Friesz, R. T. Tobin, H-J Cho and N. J. Mehta, "Sensitivity analysis based heuristic algorithms for mathematical programs with variational inequality constraints," *Mathematical Programming* 48(1990) 265-284.

[10] M. Fukushima, "Equivalent differentiable optimization problems and descent methods for asymmetric variational inequality problems," *Mathematical Programming* 53 (1992) 99-110.

[11] M. Gendreau, P. Marcotte and G. Savard, "A hybrid tabu-ascent algorithm for the liner bilevel programming problem," forthcoming in *Journal of Global Optimization*.

[12] J. Gauvin and G. Savard, "The steepest descent method for the nonlinear bilevel programming problem," Working paper G-9037, GERAD, École Polytechnique de Montréal (1992)(first version).

[13] J. Haslinger and P. Neittaanmäiki, *Finite Element Approximation for Optimal Shape Design, Theory and Application* (Wiley, New York, 1988).

[14] D. W. Hearn, "The gap function of a convex program," *Operations Research Letters* 1 (1981) 67-71.

[15] A. J. Hoffman, "On approximate solutions of systems of linear inequalities," *Journal of Research of the National Bureau of Standards* 49(1952)263-265.

[16] W. Hogan, "Directional derivative for extremal value functions with applications to the completely convex case," *Operations Research* 21 (1973) 188-209.

[17] N. H. Josephy, "Newton's method for generalized equations," Technical Report 1966, Mathematical Research Center, University of Wisconsin, Madison, WI (1979).

[18] P. Marcotte, "A new algorithm for solving variational inequalities with application to the traffic assignment problem," *Mathematical Programming* 33 (1985) 339-351.

[19] P. Marcotte and J.-P. Dussault, "A sequential linear programming algorithm for solving monotone variational inequalities," *SIAM Journal of Control and Optimization* 27 (1989) 1260-1278.

[20] P. Marcotte and J.-P. Dussault, "A note on a globally convergent method for solving monotone variational inequalities," *Operations Research Letters* 6 (1987) 35-42.

[21] Y. Qiu and T. Magnanti, "Sensitivity analysis for variational inequalities," *Mathematics of Operations Research* 17 (1992) 61-76.

[22] Y. Ishizuka and E. Aiyoshi, "Double penalty method for bilevel optimization problems," *Annals of Operations Research* 34 (1992) 73-88.

Published in *Mathematical Programming*, 1996, 74

EXACT PENALIZATION AND NECESSARY OPTIMALITY CONDITIONS FOR GENERALIZED BILEVEL PROGRAMMING PROBLEMS*

J. J. YE**, D. L. ZHU***, AND Q. J. ZHU****

Abstract. The generalized bilevel programming problem (GBLP) is a bilevel mathematical program where the lower level is a variational inequality. In this paper we prove that if the objective function of a GBLP is uniformly Lipschitz continuous in the lower level decision variable with respect to the upper level decision variable, then using certain uniform parametric error bounds as penalty functions gives single level problems equivalent to the GBLP. Several local and global uniform para-metric error bounds are presented, and assumptions guaranteeing that they apply are discussed. We then derive Kuhn-Tucker-type necessary optimality conditions by using exact penalty formulations and nonsmooth analysis.

Key words: generalized bilevel programming problems, variational inequalities, exact penalty formulations, uniform parametric error bounds, necessary optimality conditions, nonsmooth analysis

AMS subject classifications. 49K99, 90C, 90D65

PII. S1052623493257344

1. Introduction.

We consider the following *mathematical programming problem with variational inequality constraints* (which is called the *generalized bilevel programming problem* (GBLP)):

$$\text{GBLP minimize } f(x,y) \text{ subject to } x\in X \text{ and } y\in S(x) \tag{1}$$

---

*http://www.siam.org/journals/siopt/7-2/25734.html

**Department of Mathematics and Statistics, University of Victoria, Victoria, BC, Canada V8W 3P4 (janeye@uvic.ca). The research of this author was supported by National Science and Engineering Research Council of Canada grant WFA 0123160.

***Center for Research on Transportation, University of Montréeal, C. P. 6128, Succursale Centre-Ville, Montréal, Québec, Canada H3T 1V6 (daoli@crt.umontreal.ca).

****Department of Mathematics and Statistics, Western Michigan University, Kalamazoo, MI 49008-5152 (zhu@math-stat.wmich.edu).

where $f: R^{n+m} \to R$, X is a nonempty and closed subset of R^n, and for each $x \in X$, $S(x)$ is the *solution set of a variational inequality with parameter* x,

$$S(x) = \{y \in U(x) : \langle F(x,y), y - z \rangle \leqslant 0 \quad \forall z \in U(x)\}.$$

Here $U: X \to R^m$ isaset-valued map and $F: R^{n+m} \to R^m$ is a function. Throughout this paper, we make the blanket assumption that $\mathrm{Gr}S := \{(x,y) : x \in X, y \in S(x)\}$, the graph of S, is not empty.

One can interpret the above problem as a *hierarchical decision process* where there are two decision makers and the upper level decision maker always has the first choice as follows: given a decision vector x for the upper level decision maker (the *leader*), $S(x)$ is viewed as the lower level decision maker's (the *follower's*) decision set, i. e., the set of decision vectors that the follower may use. Assuming that the game is *cooperative* (i. e., the follower's decision set $S(x)$ is not a singleton), the follower allows the leader to choose the lower level decision from $S(x)$. Having complete knowledge of the follower's possible reactions, the leader selects decision vectors $x \in X$ and $y \in S(x)$, minimizing his objective function $f(x,y)$.

If $F(x,y)$ is the partial gradient of a real-valued differentiable function (i. e., $F(x,y) = -\nabla_y g(x,y)$, where $g: R^{n+m} \to R$ is differentiable in y and $U(x)$ is convex), then the variational inequality with parameter x,

$$\langle F(x,y), y - z \rangle \leqslant 0 \quad \forall z \in U(x), \tag{2}$$

is the first-order necessary optimality condition for the following optimization problem with parameter x:

$$P_x \quad \text{minimize}_y\ g(x,y) \text{ subject to } y \in U(x) \tag{3}$$

(see, e. g., [13]). Furthermore, if $g(x,y)$ is pseudoconvex in y (i. e., $\langle \nabla_y g(x,y), y - z \rangle \leqslant 0$ implies $g(x,y) \leqslant g(x,z)$ for all $y, z \in U(x)$), then a vector $y \in U(x)$ is a solution to (2) if and only if it is a global optimal solution to (3). In this case, the mathematical programming problem with variational inequality constraints (1) is the *classical bilevel programming problem* (CBLP), or Stackelberg game (see, e. g., [1, 6, 17, 26, 29, 30, 31, 32]),

$$\text{CBLP} \quad \text{minimize } f(x,y) \quad \text{subject to } x \in X \text{ and } y \in \sum(x),$$

where $\sum(x)$ is the set of solutions for the problem P_x. The correspondence between lower level problems breaks down if F is not the partial gradient of a function with respect to y. Since problem (1) includes problems that are not classical bilevel programming problems, we call problem (1) a *generalized bilevel programming problem* (GBLP). The problem has been studied under the name "mathematical programs with equilibrium constraints" by other authors (see [12] and [19]).

In this paper we assume that

$$U(x) = \{y \in R^m : c(x,y) \leqslant 0\},$$

where c: $R^{n+m} \to R^d$ is a function. Throughout this paper we assume that f, c, and F are continuous. Under these assumptions, it is known [12, Lem. 1] that the solution set $S(x)$ of the variational inequality with parameter x is closed. Refer to [12] for the results on the existence of solutions for GBLP and CBLP.

Reducing a (generalized or classical) bilevel programming problem to a single level optimization problem is a useful strategy from both theoretical and computational points of view. There are several equivalent single level formulations for the GBLP. The Karush-Kuhn-Tucker (KKT) approach is to interpret the variational inequality constraint $y \in S(x)$ with y being a solution of the following optimization problem:

$$\text{minimize}\langle F(x,y), z\rangle \quad \text{subject to } z \in U(x),$$

and to replace this minimization problem by its KKT necessary optimality conditions. These conditions are also suffcient if the feasible region $U(x)$ is convex. Assuming that $U(x)$ is convex, $c(x,y)$ is differentiable in y and one of the usual constraint qualifications, such as the Mangasarian-Fromowitz, condition is satisfied by the system of constraints $c(x,y) \leqslant 0$ in terms of variable y at a feasible point (x^*, y^*). Then (x^*, y^*) is a solution to the GBLP if and only if there exists $u^* \in R^d$ such that (x^*, y^*, u^*) is a solution to the following problem:

$$\begin{aligned} \text{KS} \quad & \min f(x,y) \\ & \text{s.t. } F(x,y) + \nabla_y c(x,y)^{\mathrm{T}} u = 0, \\ & \qquad \langle u, c(x,y)\rangle = 0, \\ & \qquad u \geqslant 0, c(x,y) \leqslant 0, \\ & \qquad x \in X, y \in R^m. \end{aligned} \tag{4}$$

To handle general GBLPs and CBLPs where $U(x)$ *may or may not be convex*, the value function and the gap function can be used to derive equivalent single level problems. Consider the CBLP. Define the *value function* $V(x)$: $X \to [-\infty, \infty]$ by

$$V(x) := \inf\{g(x,y) : y \in U(x)\}. \tag{5}$$

Then, for any $x \in X$, we have

$$g(x,y) - V(x) \geqslant 0 \quad \forall\, y \in U(x), \text{ and } g(x,y) - V(x) = 0 \text{ if and only if } y \in \sum(x). \tag{6}$$

Thus, CBLP is equivalent to the following single level optimization problem:

$$\begin{aligned} \text{VS} \quad & \min f(x,y) \\ & \text{s.t. } g(x,y) - V(x) = 0, \\ & \qquad c(x,y) \leqslant 0, \\ & \qquad x \in X, y \in R^m. \end{aligned} \tag{7}$$

Following [14] and [25], define the *gap function* $G_0(x,y)$: $X \times R^m \to [-\infty, \infty]$ by

$$G_0(x,y) := \sup\{\langle F(x,y), y - z\rangle : z \in U(x)\}. \tag{8}$$

It is easy to see that, for any $x \in X$,

$$G_0(x,y)\geqslant 0 \quad \forall\, y\in U(x) \text{ and } G_0(x,y)=0 \text{ if and only if } y\in S(x). \tag{9}$$

Hence GBLP is equivalent to the following single level optimization problem:

$$\begin{aligned}\text{GS} \quad & \min f(x,y) \\ \text{s. t. } & G_0(x,y)=0, \\ & c(x,y)\leqslant 0, \\ & x\in X, y\in R^m,\end{aligned} \tag{10}$$

Using the single level equivalent formulations KS, VS, and GS (see (4), (7), and (10)), one can derive Fritz John-type necessary optimality conditions for the original GBLP or CBLP. (See, e. g., [30] for the derivation of Fritz John-type necessary optimality conditions for CBLP.) In deriving Kuhn-Tucker-type necessary optimality conditions, however, we need to find constraint qualifications. Unfortunately, the usual constraint qualifications such as the Mangasarian-Fromowitz condition, never hold for problems VS and GS. To see this, for convenience, we assume that $U(x)=R^m$, $X=R^n$ and that $g(x,y)$, $V(x)$, and $G_0(x,y)$ are Lipschitz continuous. Now suppose that (x^*,y^*) is a solution of GBLP. Then (6) and (9) imply the inclusions $0\in\partial(g(x^*,y^*)-V(x^*))$ and $0\in\partial G_0(x^*,y^*)$, respectively. These imply that there always exist abnormal multipliers for problems VS and GS. This is equivalent to saying that the Mangasarian-Fromowitz condition will never hold (see, e. g., [30, Prop. 3. 1] for the equivalence). This phenomenon is intrinsic in bilevel problems. Even when using the KKT approach, the usual constraint qualifications will never hold for KS as long as the lower level problem is constrained. The following is a precise statement of this fact.

Proposition 1. 1. *Let (x^*,y^*,u^*) be a solution of KS. Suppose that $I:=\{0\leqslant i\leqslant d:\ c_i(x^*,y^*)=0\}\neq\varnothing$. Then the Mangasarian-Fromowitz condition does not hold at (x^*,y^*,u^*).*

Proof. The complementary slackness condition (4) implies that $u_i^*=0\ \forall\, i\in I^c:=\{0\leqslant i\leqslant d:\ c_i(x^*,y^*)\neq 0.\}$. So

$$c_i(x^*,y^*)=0,\quad i\in I$$

and

$$-u_i^*=0,\quad i\in I^c$$

are active constraints for KS at (x^*,y^*,u^*). Set

$$\tilde{c}_i(x,y,u):=c_i(x,y),$$

$$\hat{c}_i(x,y,u):=-u_i,$$

and

$$h(x,y,u):=\langle u,c(x,y)\rangle.$$

Suppose that there exists a vector $v\in R^{n+m+d}$ such that

$$\langle v,\nabla\tilde{c}_i(x^*,y^*,u^*)\rangle=\sum_{j=1}^{n+m}v_j\nabla_j c_i(x^*,y^*)<0 \quad \forall\, i\in I$$

and

$$\langle v, \nabla \hat{c}_i(x^*, y^*, u^*) \rangle = -v_{n+m+i} < 0 \quad \forall i \in I^c,$$

where $\nabla_j c_i(x, y)$ denotes the gradient of c_i with respect to the jth component of the vector (x, y). Then

$$\langle v, \nabla h(x^*, y^*, u^*) \rangle$$

$$= \sum_{i \in I} u_i \sum_{j=1}^{n+m} v_j \nabla_j c_i(x^*, y^*) + \sum_{i \in I^c} v_{n+m+i} c_i(x^*, y^*) < 0.$$

Thus, the Mangasarian-Fromowitz condition cannot hold at (x^*, y^*, u^*).

The diffculty here is obviously due to the equality constraints (4), (7), and (10), which reflect the bilevel nature of the problem.

The partial calmness condition is identified in [30] as an appropriate constraint qualification for problem VS. It is also proved that the existence of a uniformly weak sharp minimum is a sufficient condition for partial calmness, and a parametric linear lower level problem is always partially calm.

Recently, using the theory of exact penalization for mathematical programming problems with subanalytic constraints and the theory of error bounds for quadratic inequality systems, Luo et al. [19] successfully derived various penalty functions for the single level equivalent mathematical programming problem KS. By using the theory of parametric normal equations, Luo et al. [19] also obtained some necessary and sufficient stationary point conditions for GBLP.

In this paper we use the *uniform parametric error bound* as a tool to establish (local or global) exact penalty formulations of several single level mathematical programming problems (including KS, VS, and GS) that are equivalent to GBLP. Since the exact penalty formulations move the troublesome equality constraints (4), (7), and (10) to the objective function, we can get Kuhn-Tucker-type necessary optimality conditions under the usual constraint qualifications. The concept of a uniform parametric error bound generalizes the uniformly weak sharp minimum defined in [30]. Thus, the uniform parametric error bounds derived in this paper provide many more exact penalty formulations than those in [30] for VS. Using the uniform para-metric error bound as a tool, the conditions we derived in this paper are very general and distinct (cf. Theorem 6.5) from the ones derived in [19].

The paper is arranged as follows. In the next section we introduce uniform parametric error bounds and show that they provide local and global exact penalty formulations of GBLP. In section 3, we discuss several useful uniform parametric error bounds. Kuhn-Tucker-type necessary optimality conditions for problem GBLP associated with various uniform parametric error bounds are derived in section 4. In section 5, the relationships between various uniform parametric error bounds are discussed and some examples are given showing that the various equivalent single level optimization formulations with uniform parametric error bounds and their corresponding necessary optimality conditions complement each other. In section 6, we show that uniform parametric error bounds can be used to derive exact penalty formulations for KS.

2. Partial calmness and exact penalization.

In this section we introduce uniform parametric error bounds and show that they are useful in deriving exact penalty formulations for GBLP.

Consider the following mathematical programming problem:

MP minimize $f(x)$

subject to $h(x)=0$,

$g(x)\leqslant 0$,

$x\in C$,

where $f:R^n\to R, h:R^n\to R, g:R^n\to R^m$ are lower semicontinuous and C is a closed subset in R^n. The corresponding *perturbed problem* is

MP(ε) minimize $f(x)$

subject to $h(x)=\varepsilon$,

$g(x)\leqslant 0$,

$x\in C$,

where $\varepsilon\in R$. The following definition was introduced in [30].

Definition 2.1 (partial calmness). *Let* x^* *solve* MP. *The problem* MP *is said to be* partially calm *at* x^* *provided that there exist constants* $\mu>0, \delta>0$ *such that, for all* $\varepsilon\in\delta B$ *and all* $x\in x^*+\delta B$ *that are feasible for* MP(ε), *one has*

$$f(x)-f(x^*)+\mu\,|\,h(x)\,|\geqslant 0.$$

Here B *denotes the open unit ball in* R^n. *The constants* μ *and* δ *are called the modulus and radius, respectively.*

The partial calmness condition is similar to, but different from, the calmness condition introduced by Clarke and Rockafellar (see, e. g., [5]; see also Deffnition 4.1) in that only the equality constraint $h(x)=0$ is perturbed.

The concept of calmness was shown to be closely related to "exact penalization" in [5, Prop. 6.4.3]. More precisely, if x^* is a local solution of MP and the problem MP is calm at x^*, then x^* is a local solution for a penalized problem. In the following proposition we show that the concept of partial calmness is equivalent to local exact penalization.

Proposition 2.2. *Assume that* f *is continuous. Suppose* x^* *is a local minimum of* MP *and* MP *is partially calm at* x^*. *Then there exists* $\mu^*>0$ *such that* x^* *is a local minimum of the following penalized problems for all* $\mu\geqslant\mu^*$:

MP_μ *minimize* $f(x)+\mu|h(x)|$

subject to $g(x)\leqslant 0$,

$x\in C$.

Any local minima of MP_μ *with* $\mu > \mu^*$ *with respect to the neighborhood of* x^* *in which* x^* *is a local minimum are also local minima of* MP.

Proof. Suppose that x^* is a local minimum of MP but not MP_μ for any $\mu > 0$. Then, for each positive integer k, there exists a point $x_k \in x^* + (1/k)B \subset C$ and $g(x_k) \leqslant 0$ such that

$$f(x_k) + k|h(x_k)| < f(x^*). \tag{11}$$

Since x^* is a local minimum of MP, the above inequality implies that $|h(x_k)| > 0$. Therefore,

$$0 < |h(x_k)| < \frac{f(x^*) - f(x_k)}{k}. \tag{12}$$

Taking the limit as k goes to infinity in (12), one has

$$|h(x_k)| \to 0 \text{ as } k \to \infty.$$

But then the inequality (11) contradicts the hypothesis that MP is partially calm at x^*. Thus for some $\mu^* > 0$, x^* must be a local minimum of MP_{μ^*}.

It is obvious that a local minimum of MP_{μ^*} must be a local minimum for MP_μ whenever $\mu \geqslant \mu^*$.

Conversely, let $\mu > \mu^*$ and x_μ be a local minimum of MP_μ in the neighborhood of x^* in which x^* is a local minimum. Then

$$\begin{aligned} f(x_\mu) + \mu \mid h(x_\mu) \mid &= f(x^*) \quad \text{since } x^* \text{ is a local minimum of } \mathrm{MP}_\mu, \\ &\leqslant f(x_\mu) + \frac{1}{2}(\mu + \mu^*) \mid h(x_\mu) \mid \quad \text{since } \frac{1}{2}(\mu + \mu^*) > \mu^*, \end{aligned}$$

which implies that

$$(\mu - \mu^*) \mid h(x_\mu) \mid \leqslant 0.$$

Therefore, $h(x_\mu) = 0$, which implies that x_μ is also a local minimum of MP.

Remark 2.3. Notice that in the above result, no continuity assumption is required for the function $h(x)$. When the function h is continuous, it is easy to see that if MP is partially calm at a solution x^* of MP with modulus μ and radius ε, then there exists a $\hat{\delta} \leqslant \delta$ such that x^* is a $\hat{\delta}$-local solution to the penalized problem MP_μ; i.e.,

$$f(x) + \mu \mid h(x) \mid \geqslant f(x^*) \quad \forall x \in C \text{ s.t. } g(x) \leqslant 0, x \in x^* + \delta B.$$

Therefore, in our definition of partial calmness, the restriction on the size of perturbation $\varepsilon \in \delta B$ can be removed when h is continuous, and it then corresponds to the definition of calmness given by Burke [2]. Furthermore, the infimum of μ^* in Proposition 2.2 can be taken as the modulus of partial calmness.

For any $x \in X, y \in R^m$, define the parametric distance function

$$d_{S(x)}(y) := \inf\{ \| y - z \| : z \in S(x)\}$$

to be the distance from the point y to the set $S(x)$. The GBLP is equivalent to a *mathematical programming problem involving a parametric distance function constraint*:

$$\text{DP} \qquad \text{minimize} \qquad f(x, y)$$

$$\text{subject to} \quad d_{S(x)}(y) = 0,$$
$$c(x,y) \leqslant 0,$$
$$x \in X, y \in R^m.$$

It is known (see [5, Prop. 2.4.3]) that if the objective function of a constrained optimization problem is Lipschitz continuous then the distance function is an exact penalty term. In what follows, we extend this result to the mathematical programming problem with variational inequality constraints, GBLP. The constraint implied in the parametric distance function is, in fact, in the lower level decision variable. It is natural that we only need to assume that the objective function is locally Lipschitz in the lower level decision variable uniformly in the upper level decision variable to prove the exact penalty property of the parametric distance function. We need the following definition.

From now on we shall use $N(z)$ to denote a neighborhood of z.

Definition 2.4. *Let $(x^*, y^*) \in R^{n+m}$. The function $f(x,y)$ is said to be locally Lipschitz near y^* uniformly in $x \in N(x^*)$ if there exists $L>0$ and a neighborhood $N(y^*)$ of y^* such that*

$$| f(x,y') - f(x,y) | \leqslant L | y' - y | \quad \forall y', y \in N(y^*), x \in N(x^*).$$

The following result generalizes Proposition 2.4.3 of Clarke [5] to GBLP. We omit the proof of the global result, since it is essentially the same as the local one and the converse part of the proof in Proposition 2.2.

THERORМ 2.5. *Let (x^*, y^*) be a local solution of problem DP. Assume that f is locally Lipschitz near y^* uniformly in x on a neighborhood of x^* with constant L. Then problem DP is partially calm at (x^*, y^*) with modulus L.*

Furthermore, let (x^*, y^*) be a global solution of GBLP and assume that $f(x, \cdot)$ is Lipschitz continuous in y with constant $L>0$ uniformly for all $x \in X$. Then (x^*, y^*) is a global solution of the penalized problem

$$\mathrm{DP}_\mu \quad \text{minimize} \quad f(x,y) + \mu d_{S(x)}(y)$$
$$\text{subject to} \quad c(x,y) \leqslant 0,$$
$$x \in X, y \in R^m$$

for any $\mu \geqslant L$, and any other global solution of DP_μ for any $\mu > L$ is also a global solution of GBLP.

Proof. Let $\delta>0$ be such that (x^*, y^*) is a local solution of DP in $(x^*, y^*)+2\delta B \subset X \times Y$. For any $0 \leqslant \varepsilon < \delta$, let $(x,y) \in (x^*, y^*)+\delta B$ be feasible for DP_ε; i. e., $d_{S(x)}(y)=\varepsilon$ and $c(x,y) \leqslant 0, (x,y) \in (x^*, y^*)+\delta B$. Since $S(x)$ is closed, one can choose a $y' \in S(x)$ such that $\| y' - y \| = \varepsilon$. Since (x, y') is feasible for DP and

$$\| (x,y') - (x^*, y^*) \| \leqslant \| (x,y') - (x,y) \| + \| (x,y) - (x^*, y^*) \|$$
$$\leqslant \varepsilon + \delta < 2\delta,$$

we have

$$f(x,y') \geqslant f(x^*, y^*). \tag{13}$$

Since $f(x, \cdot)$ is locally Lipschitz near y^*,

(14) $$f(x,y)-f(x,y')\geqslant -L\varepsilon.$$

Combining (13) and (14) yields

$$f(x,y)-f(x^*,y^*)+L\varepsilon\geqslant 0;$$

i. e., DP is partially calm at (x^*,y^*) with modulus L.

Theorem 2.5 shows that the distance function provides an exact penalty equivalent formulation for GBLP under very mild conditions. However, the parametric distance function is usually an implicit nonsmooth function of the data in the original problem. It is difficult to compute or estimate its Clarke generalized gradient.

To overcome this difficulty, we shall use the parametric distance function $d_{S(x)}(y)$ establishing some equivalent exact penalty formulations of GBLP. These equivalent formulations have penalty functions with computable Clarke generalized gradients.

We call a function $r(x,y): R^{n+m}\rightarrow R$ a *merit function* provided

(15) $$r(x,y)\geqslant 0 \quad \forall (x,y)\in \mathrm{Gr}U \text{ and } r(x,y)=0 \text{ if and only if } (x,y)\in \mathrm{Gr}S.$$

A merit function is called a *uniform parametric error bound* for the inclusion $y\in S(x)$ with modulus $\delta>0$ in the set $Q\subset \mathrm{Gr}U$ if it satisfies

(16) $$d_{S(x)}(y)\leqslant \delta r(x,y) \quad \forall (x,y)\in Q.$$

A merit function provides the following equivalent formulation of GBLP:

$$\begin{array}{lll} \mathrm{RP} & \text{minimize} & f(x,y) \\ & \text{subject to} & r(x,y)=0, \\ & & c(x,y)\leqslant 0, \\ & & x\in X, y\in R^m. \end{array}$$

Its corresponding penalized problem is

$$\begin{array}{lll} \mathrm{RP}_\mu & \text{minimize} & f(x,y)+\mu r(x,y) \\ & \text{subject to} & c(x,y)\leqslant 0, \\ & & x\in X, y\in R^m. \end{array}$$

Next we show that if $r(x,y)$ is a uniform parametric error bound and f is Lipschitz near y^* uniformly in x, then there exists $\mu>0$ such that the problem RP_μ is an exact penalty equivalence of RP. As in Theorem 2.5 we omit the proof for the global result.

THEOREM 2.6. *Let* (x^*,y^*) *be a local solution of problem* GBLP *and* r *be a uniform parametric error bound with modulus* $\delta>0$ *in a neighborhood of* (x^*,y^*). *Suppose that* f *is locally Lipschitz near* y^* *uniformly for all* x *in a neighborhood of* x^*. *Then there exists* $\mu^*>0$ *such that* (x^*,y^*) *is a local solution of the penalized problem* RP_μ *for all* $\mu\geqslant\delta\mu^*$ *and any local solution to* RP_μ *with* $\mu>\delta\mu^*$ *with respect to the neighborhood of* (x^*,y^*) *is also a local solution to* RP.

Furthermore, let (x^*,y^*) *be a global solution of* GBLP *and* r *be a uniform parametric error bound in* GrU. *Assume that* $f(x,\cdot)$ *is Lipschitz continuous with constant* $L>0$ *uniformly for all* $x\in X$. *Then* (x^*,y^*) *is a global solution of* RP_μ *for all* $\mu\geqslant$

δL, *and any other global solution of* RP_μ *for all* $\mu > \delta L$ *is also a global solution of* GBLP.

Proof. Being a local solution of GBLP, (x^*, y^*) is also a local solution of DP. DP is partially calm by Theorem 2.5. Thus, by Proposition 2.2, there exists a $\mu^* > 0$ such that (x^*, y^*) is also a solution to DP_{μ^*}. Hence, for all (x, y) in a neighborhood of (x^*, y^*) which are feasible for $RP_{\delta\mu^*}$, one has

$$\begin{aligned} f(x^*, y^*) + \delta\mu^* \cdot r(x^*, y^*) &= f(x^*, y^*) + \mu^* d_{S(x^*)}(y^*) && \text{since } y^* \in S(x^*), \\ &\leqslant f(x, y) + \mu^* d_{S(x)}(y) && \text{since } (x^*, y^*) \text{ solves } DP_{\mu^*}, \\ &\leqslant f(x, y) + \delta\mu^* r(x, y) && \text{by inequality (16).} \end{aligned}$$

Therefore, (x^*, y^*) is also a local solution of $RP_{\delta\mu^*}$. The proof for the converse is similar to that of the converse part of Proposition 2.2.

Remark 2.7. As in Remark 2.3 when the uniform parametric error bound r is continuous, the constant μ^* in Theorem 2.6 can be taken as the modulus of partial calmness, which is the Lipschitz constant of $f(x, \cdot)$ by virtue of Theorem 2.5.

Sometimes a uniform parametric error bound is not nicely behaved but its square is; e.g., $\sqrt{|x|}$ is not Lispchitz continuous near 0 but $|x|$ is. Therefore, we are interested in the following formulations which are equivalent to GBLP when $r(x, y)$ is a merit function.

$$\text{RSP} \qquad \begin{aligned} &\text{minimize} && f(x, y) \\ &\text{subject to} && r^2(x, y) = 0, \\ &&& c(x, y) \leqslant 0, \\ &&& x \in X, y \in R^m. \end{aligned}$$

Its penalized problem is

$$\text{RSP}_\mu \qquad \begin{aligned} &\text{minimize} && f(x, y) + \mu r^2(x, y) \\ &\text{subject to} && c(x, y) \leqslant 0, \\ &&& x \in X, y \in R^m. \end{aligned}$$

Although the penalty term $r^2(x, y)$ might be better behaved, it is smaller than $r(x, y)$ for all (x, y) that are close to (x^*, y^*). Hence, to formulate an equivalent exact penalty formulation for the problem RSP, one needs to impose a stronger condition on f. The following definition gives such a condition.

Definition 2.8. *Let* $x_0 \in X$. *The mapping* $f(x, y): R^n \times R^m \to R$ *is* upper Hölder continuous with exponent 2 near every $y \in S(x)$ uniformly for x in a neighborhood of x_0 *provided there exists* $L > 0$ *such that*

$$f(x, y') - f(x, y) \geqslant -L \| y' - y \|^2 \quad \forall y' \in N(y), y \in S(x), x \in N(x_0).$$

The constant L *is called the modulus*.

We prove that $r^2(x, y)$ provides an exact penalty formulation for GBLP if $r(x, y)$ is a uniform parametric error bound and f is upper Hölder continuous with exponent 2 near every $y \in S(x)$ uniformly in x in a neighborhood of x^*.

THEOREM 2.9. *Let* (x^*, y^*) *be a local solution of the problem* RSP. *Assume that* r *is a uniform parametric error bound with modulus* δ *in a neighborhood of* (x^*, y^*) *and that* f *is upper Hölder continuous with exponent* 2 *and modulus* $L>0$ *near every* $y\in S(x)$ *uniformly in* x *in a neighborhood of* x^*. *Then* (x^*, y^*) *is a local solution of the penalized problem* RSP_μ *for all* $\mu\geqslant\delta^2 L$, *and any local solution to* RSP_μ *with* $\mu>\delta^2\mu^*$ *in the neighborhood of* (x^*, y^*) *is also a local solution to* RSP.

Proof. Let $\alpha>0$ be such that (x^*, y^*) is a local solution of RSP in $(x^*, y^*)+\alpha(\delta+1)B\subset X\times Y$. For any $\varepsilon, 0\leqslant\varepsilon^{\frac{1}{2}}<\alpha$, Let $(x,y)\in(x^*, y^*)+\alpha B$ be such that $r^2(x,y)=\varepsilon, c(x,y)\leqslant 0$. Since $S(x)$ is closed, one can choose $y'(x)\in S(x)$ such that $\| y-y'(x)\| =d_{S(x)}(y)\leqslant \delta r(x,y)=\delta\varepsilon^{\frac{1}{2}}$. Since $(x,y'(x))$ is feasible for RSP and

$$\begin{aligned}\|(x,y'(x))-(x^*, y^*)\| &\leqslant \|(x,y'(x))-(x,y)\|+\|(x,y)-(x^*, y^*)\|\\ &\leqslant \delta\varepsilon^{\frac{1}{2}}+\alpha<\alpha(\delta+1),\end{aligned}$$

we have

$$f(x,y'(x))\geqslant f(x^*, y^*).$$

Therefore

$$\begin{aligned}&f(x,y)-f(x^*, y^*)\\ &\geqslant f(x,y)-f(x,y'(x)) \qquad \text{by optimality of } (x^*, y^*),\\ &\geqslant -L\| y-y'(x)\|^2 \qquad \text{by upper Hölder continuity of } f,\\ &=-L(d_{S(x)}(y))^2,\\ &\geqslant -L\delta^2 r^2(x,y) \qquad \text{since } r(x,y) \text{ is a uniform parametric error bound},\\ &=-L\delta^2\varepsilon;\end{aligned}$$

i. e., RSP is partially calm at (x^*, y^*) with modulus $\delta^2 L$. The rest of the proof is similar to the converse part of Proposition 2.2.

3. Some uniform parametric error bounds.

In this section we discuss some useful uniform parametric error bounds. We start with two definitions.

Definition 3.1. *Let* $\Omega\subset R^n$. *A mapping* $F(x,y): R^n\times R^m\to R^m$ *is called* strongly monotone with respect to y uniformly *in* $x\in\Omega$ *with modulus* $\mu>0$ *provided*

$$\langle F(x,y)-F(x,z), y-z\rangle\geqslant\mu\| y-z\|^2 \quad \forall y,z\in U(x), x\in\Omega.$$

Definition 3.2. *Let* $\Omega\subset R^n$. *The mapping* $F(x,y): R^n\times R^m\to R^m$ *is called* pseudostrongly monotone with respect to y uniformly in $x\in\Omega$ *with modulus* $\mu>0$ *provided*

$$\langle F(x,y), z-y\rangle\geqslant 0 \quad \textit{implies} \ \langle F(x,z), z-y\rangle\geqslant\mu\| z-y\|^2 \quad \forall y,z\in U(x), x\in\Omega.$$

3.1 Uniformly weak sharp minima for the lower level optimization problem.

Definition 3.3 (see [30]). *A family of parametric mathematical programming problems* $\{(P_x): x\in X\}$ *as defined in* (3) *is said to have uniformly weak sharp minima in* $\Omega \subset GrU$ *if there exists an* $\delta > 0$ *such that*

(17) $$d_{\sum(x)}(y) \leqslant \delta(g(x,y) - V(x)) \quad \forall (x,y) \in \Omega,$$

where $\sum(x)$ *is the solution set of the lower level optimization problem* P_x. *The constant* δ *is called the modulus of the uniformly weak sharp minima.*

By virtue of (9), $g(x,y)-V(x)$ is a merit function. When $\sum(x) = S(x)$ (e.g., when $U(x)$ is convex, $g(x,y)$ is pseudoconvex and differentiable in y), $g(x,y)-V(x)$ is obviously a uniform parametric error bound.

The next result follows easily from a result about regular points due to Ioffe (Theorem 1 and Corollary 1.1 of [8]).

Proposition 3.4. *Let* (x^*, y^*) *be an optimal solution of the CBLP. Suppose that* $g(x,y)$ *is Lipschitz continuous in* y *uniformly in* $x \in X$ *with constant* $L_g > 0$. *Assume that there exist* $\sigma > 0$ *such that for any* $(x,y) \in GrU$ *satisfying* $y \notin S(x)$ *and any* $\xi \in \partial_y g(x,y)$, $\eta \in (L_g+1)\partial d_{S(x)}(y)$ *(or* $\eta \in N_{S(x)}(y)$*)*,

$$\| \xi + \eta \| \geqslant \sigma.$$

Then

$$d_{S(x)}(y) \leqslant (1/\sigma)(g(x,y) - V(x)) \quad \forall (x,y) \in GrU.$$

Consider the bilevel programming problem where the lower level problem is the following parametric quadratic programming problem:

$$QP_x \min g(x,y) := \langle y, Px \rangle + \frac{1}{2}\langle y, Qy \rangle + p^t x + q^t y$$

$$\text{s.t. } y \in \Omega_x := \{y \in Y: Ax + By - b \leqslant 0\}.$$

Here $Q \in R^{m \times m}$ is a symmetric and positive semidefinite matrix, $p \in R^n$, $q \in R^m$, $P \in R^{m \times n}$; A and B are $d \times n$ and $d \times m$ matrices, respectively, and $b \in R^d$.

The next proposition gives a suffcient condition for the family of parametric quadratic programming problems $\{QP_x : x \in R^n\}$ to have uniformly weak sharp minima.

Proposition 3.5. *Assume that there exists a constant* $M > 0$ *such that for all* $(x,y) \in GrS$, *every element* z *of* $(N(y,\Omega x) + \text{span}(\nabla_y g(x,\bar{y}))) \cap B$ *can be expressed as*

$$z = \eta \nabla_y g(x,\bar{y}) + \xi,$$

where $|\eta| \leqslant M$ *and* $\xi \in N(y,\Omega_x)$. *Assume*

(18) $$\ker(\nabla_y^2 g(x,\bar{y}))^\perp \subset \text{span}(\nabla y g(x,\bar{y})) + N(y,\Omega_x) \quad \forall (x,y) \in GrS$$

or, equivalently,

$$(\nabla_y g(x,\bar{y}))^\perp \cap T(y,\Omega_x) \subset \ker(\nabla_y^2 g(x,\bar{y})) \quad \forall (x,y) \in GrS,$$

where $\bar{y}$ *is any element in* $S(x)$, $A^\perp := \{y \in R^m : \langle y,x \rangle = 0 \ \forall x \in A\}$ *denotes the subspace perpendicular to* A, span(d) *represents the subspace generated by the vector* d, $T(y,C)$ *is the tangent cone to the set* C *at* y, *and* $\ker(A)$ *is the nullspace of the matrix* A. *Then* $\{QP_x : x \in X\}$ *has uniformly weak sharp minima.*

Before proving the above result we first state the following description of the solution set of a convex program given in Mangasarian [21].

LEMMA 3.6. *Let S be the set of solutions to the problem* $\min\{g(y): y\in\Omega\}$ *where* $g: R^n\to R$ *is a twice continuously differentiable convex function and* Ω *is a convex subset of* R^n. *Let* $\bar{y}\in S$. *Then*

$$S=\{y\in\Omega:\nabla g(y)=\nabla g(\bar{y}),\langle\nabla g(\bar{y}),y-\bar{y}\rangle=0\}.$$

It follows that for QP_x, the solution set $S(x)$ is

$$S(x)=\Omega_x\cap\{y:\langle\nabla_y g(x,\bar{y}),y-\bar{y}\rangle=0\}\cap\{y:\nabla_y^2 g(x,\bar{y})(y-\bar{y})=0\}.$$

Since Ω_x is a polyhedral one has

(19) $$T(y,S(x))=T(y,\Omega_x)\cap(\nabla_y g(x,\bar{y}))^{\perp}\cap\ker(\nabla_y^2 g(x,\bar{y}))$$

by virtue of Corollaries 16.4.2 and 23.8.1 of Rockafellar [28].

Proof of Proposition 3.5. By virtue of Theorem 2.6 of Burke and Ferris [4], it suffices to show that for all $x\in X, y\in S(x)$, there exists an $\alpha>0$ such that

$$g'_2.(x,y;d)\geqslant\alpha\|d\|\quad\forall d\in T(y,\Omega_x)\cap N(y,S(x)),$$

where $g'_2(x,y;d)$ is the directional derivative of g with respect to y in the direction d. Note that (19) and (18) imply that

$$\begin{aligned}N(y,S(x))&=N(y,\Omega_x)+\operatorname{span}(\nabla_y g(x,\bar{y}))+\ker(\nabla_y^2 g(x,\bar{y}))^{\perp}\\&=N(y,\Omega_x)+\operatorname{span}(\nabla_y g(x,\bar{y})).\end{aligned}$$

Since $d\in T(y,\Omega_x)\cap N(y,S(x))$, one has

$$\begin{aligned}\|d\|&=\sup\{\langle z(x),d\rangle:z(x)\in B\cap N(y,S(x))\}\\&\leqslant\sup\{\langle\eta\nabla_y g(x,\bar{y})+\xi,d\rangle:|\eta|<M,\xi\in N(y,\Omega_x)\}\\&\leqslant M\langle\nabla_y g(x,\bar{y}),d\rangle=M\langle\nabla_y g(x,y),d\rangle=Mg'_2(x,y,d)\end{aligned}$$

The first inequality follows from the assumption, and the second equality follows from Lemma 3.6. Setting $\alpha=1/M$ completes the proof.

The following bilinear programming problem with parameter x is a special case of QP_x.

$$\begin{aligned}BLP_x\qquad&\min\langle y,Px\rangle+p^tx+q^ty\\\text{s.t. }&Ax+By-b\leqslant0,\\&y\in R^m.\end{aligned}$$

Proposition 3.5 has the following simple consequence.

Corollary 3.7. *The bilinear programming problem* BLP_x *has a uniformly weak sharp minima if there exists a constant* $M>0$ *such that for all* $(x,y)\in\mathrm{GrS}$, *every element* z *of* $(N(y,\Omega_x)+\operatorname{span}(Px+q))\cap B$ *can be expressed as*

$$z=\eta(Px+q)+\xi$$

where $|\eta|\leqslant M$ *and* $\xi\in N(y,\Omega_x)$.

The following example shows that the assumption in Corollary 3.7 cannot be omitted.

Example 3.8. Consider the problem

$$\min x+y$$
$$\text{s. t. } 0\leqslant x\leqslant 1, y\in \arg\min\{-xy: x+y-1\leqslant 0, y\geqslant 0\}.$$

The solution set of the lower level problem is

$$S(x)=\begin{cases}[0,1] & \text{if } x=0,\\ 1-x & \text{if } 0<x\leqslant 1.\end{cases}$$

The value function of the lower problem is

$$V(x)=\begin{cases}0 & \text{if } x=0,\\ -x(1-x) & \text{if } 0<x\leqslant 1.\end{cases}$$

It is easy to check that the assumption in Corollary 3.7 is not satisfied and there is no uniformly weak sharp minimum. In fact, if we replace the constraint $0\leqslant x\leqslant 1$ by $0<\varepsilon\leqslant x\leqslant 1$, then the assumption in Corollary 3.7 is satisfied, and uniformly weak sharp minima exist.

3.2. A standard gap bound.

Consider a parametric variational inequality with *nonseparable and linear constraints*, i. e.,

(20) $$U(x)=\{y\in R^m \mid c(x,y)=Ax+By-b\leqslant 0\},$$

where A and B are $d\times n$ and $d\times m$ matrices, respectively, and $b\in R^d$. In this case, $\forall x_0\in X, y_0\in U(x_0)$ solve the variational inequality with parameter x_0 (see (2)) if and only if there exists $\lambda_0\in R^d$ such that (x_0, y_0, λ_0) satisfies the following *complementarity system*:

$$F(x_0,y_0)+B^T\lambda_0=0,$$
$$(Ax_0+By_0-b)^T\lambda_0=0,$$
$$Ax_0+By_0-b\leqslant 0, \lambda_0\geqslant 0.$$

If the *gradients of the binding constraints* in the variational inequality (2) at (x_0, y_0), i. e., those $\nabla_y c_j(x_0,y_0)$ such that $c_j(x_0,y_0)=0, j\in\{1,2,\cdots,d\}$, are *linearly independent*, and the *strict complementarity condition*

(21) $$\lambda_{0i}>0 \Leftrightarrow c_i(x_0,y_0)=0,\quad \forall i\in\{1,2,\cdots,d\}$$

holds, then the variational inequality (2) with parameter x has a unique solution $y(x)$ for all x in a neighborhood of x_0, and the above complementarity system has a unique solution $(y(x),\lambda(x))$ for all x in a neighborhood of x_0. Furthermore, the functions $y(x)$ and $\lambda(x)$ are Lipschitz continuous, and the strict complementarity condition (21) is satisfied in a neighborhood of x_0 (see, e. g., Friesz et al. [10]).

The following result due to Marcotte and Zhu [25] shows that the gap function defined by (8) can serve as a uniform parametric error bound under certain conditions.

Proposition 3.9. *Assume that X is a compact, convex subset of R^n and $U(x)$ defined as in (20) is compact. Let the mapping F be strongly monotone with respect to y uniformly in $x\in X$, and let $\nabla_y F$ be Lipschitz continuous in y uniformly in x. Suppose*

$x_0 \in X$. *If the linear independence and strict complementarity conditions hold at* $y_0 = y(x_0)$, *then there exists a constant* $\delta > 0$ *and a neighborhood of* (x_0, y_0) *such that*

$$d_{S(x)}(y) \leqslant \delta G_0(x,y) \quad \forall (x,y) \in \mathrm{Gr}U \cap N(x_0, y_0).$$

Now we consider a parametric variational inequality with separable and linear constraints; i. e. , $U(x) = \{y \in R^m \mid By \leqslant b\}$ is a convex polyhedron. In this case we can weaken the assumptions of Proposition 3. 9.

We need the following definition due to Dussault and Marcotte [7].

Definition 3. 10. *Let F be a continuous, monotone mapping from a convex polyhedron* $X \subset R^n$ *into* R^n *and denote by* VIP(X,F) *the variational inequality problem associated with X and F; i. e. , find* x^* *in X such that*

$$\mathrm{VIP}(F,X) \qquad \langle F(x^*), x^* - x \rangle \leqslant 0 \quad \textit{for all } x \textit{ in } X.$$

We say that VIP(F,X) *is geometrically stable if, for any solution* x^* *of the variational inequality,* $\langle F(x^*), x^* - x \rangle = 0$ *implies that* x *lies on the optimal face, i. e. , the minimal face of X containing the (convex) solution set to* VIP(F,X).

The following result due to Marcotte and Zhu [25] gives a useful error bound.

Proposition 3. 11. *Assume that X is a convex polyhedron,* $U(x) = \{y: By - b \leqslant 0\}$ *is compact, and the mapping F is strongly monotone with respect to y uniformly in* $x \in X$. *Let* $x_0 \in X$ *and assume that there exists a neighborhood of* x_0 *such that* VIP$(F(x, \cdot), Y)$ *is geometrically stable inside that neighborhood. Then there exist some neighborhood* $N(x_0)$ *of* x_0 *and a positive number* $\delta > 0$ *such that*

$$d_{S(x)}(y) \leqslant \delta G_0(x,y) \quad \forall y \in U(x), x \in N(x_0).$$

3. 3. A square root standard gap bound.

The following result gives a uniform parametric error bound in terms of the square root of the gap function G_0.

Proposition 3. 12. *Assume that the mapping F is pseudostrongly monotone with respect to yuniformly in* $x \in N(x_0)$ *with modulus* μ. *Then one has*

$$d_{S(x)}(y) \leqslant \frac{\sqrt{\mu}}{\mu} \sqrt{G_0(x,y)} \quad \forall y \in U(x), x \in N(x_0).$$

Proof. Let $y(x) \in S(x)$. Then, by the definition of $S(x)$, one has

$$\langle F(x, y(x)), y - y(x) \rangle \geqslant 0 \quad \forall y \in U(x).$$

Since $y(x) \in U(x)$, it follows from the pseudostrong monotonity of F and the definition of G_0 that, for all $x \in N(x_0)$ and $y \in U(x)$, one has

$$\mu \| y(x) - y \|^2 \leqslant \langle F(x,y), y - y(x) \rangle \leqslant G_0(x,y),$$

from which the result follows readily.

3. 4. A square root differentiable gap bound.

Recently, Fukushima [11] gave an optimization formulation of a variational inequality based on the *differentiable gap function* defined as

(22) $$G_\alpha(x,y)=\max_{z\in U(x)}\{\langle F(x,y),y-z\rangle-\frac{1}{2\alpha}\|y-z\|_M^2\},$$

where $\alpha>0$ is a given constant, $\|\cdot\|_M$ denotes the elliptic norm in R^m defined by $\|z\|_M=\langle z,Mz\rangle^{\frac{1}{2}}2$, and M is a symmetric positive definite matrix. It is easy to see that the differentiable gap function G_α satisfies condition (15). The following result gives a uniform parametric error bound based on $\sqrt{G_\alpha}$.

Proposition 3. 13. *Suppose $U(x)$ is convex and $x_0\in X$. Let the mapping F be pseudostrongly monotone with respect to y uniformly in $x\in N(x_0)$. Then there exists $\delta>0$ such that*

$$d_{S(x)}(y)\leqslant\delta\sqrt{G_\alpha(x,y)}\quad\forall y\in U(x),x\in N(x_0).$$

Proof. Let $y(x)\in S(x)$. Then, by the definition of $S(x)$, one has

$$\langle F(x,y(x)),y-y(x)\rangle\geqslant 0\quad\forall y\in U(x).$$

Since $y(x)\in U(x)$, it follows from the pseudostrong monotonity of F that, for every $x\in N(x_0)$ and $y\in U(x)$,

$$\langle F(x,y),y-y(x)\rangle\geqslant\mu\|y-y(x)\|^2.$$

Let $y_t=y+t(y(x)-y)$ for $t\in[0,1]$. By the convexity of $U(x)$, $y_t\in U(x)$ for any $y\in U(x)$. It follows from the definition of $G_\alpha(x,y)$ (see (22)) that

$$\begin{aligned}G_\alpha(x,y)&\geqslant\langle F(x,y),y-y_t\rangle-\frac{1}{2\alpha}\|y-y_t\|_M^2\\&=\cdot t\langle F(x,y),y-y(x)\rangle-\frac{t^2}{2\alpha}\|y-y(x)\|_M^2\\&\geqslant\left(t\mu-\frac{t^2\|M\|}{2\alpha}\right)\|y-y(x)\|^2.\end{aligned}$$

Letting $t=\min\left\{1,\frac{\alpha\mu}{\|M\|}\right\}$ gives

$$G_\alpha(x,y)\geqslant\sigma\|y-y(x)\|^2,$$

where

$$\sigma=\begin{cases}\left(\mu-\dfrac{\|M\|}{2\alpha}\right) & \text{if } \mu\geqslant\dfrac{\|M\|}{\alpha},\\ \dfrac{\alpha\mu^2}{2\|M\|} & \text{if } \mu\leqslant\dfrac{\|M\|}{\alpha}.\end{cases}$$

This proves the result.

3.5. A projection bound.

The following projection characterization of $y\in S(x)$ is well known (see, e. g., [15]).

Lemma 3. 14. *An arbitrary vector $y\in Y$ is a solution of the variational inequality with parameter x if and only if it satisfies*

$$h(x,y)=y-\mathrm{proj}_{U(x)}(y-F(x,y))=0$$

where $\text{proj}_{U(x)}(z)$ *is the orthogonal projection of a vector* z *onto the set* $U(x)$.

It follows from the above lemma that any vector norm of $h(x,y)$ satisfies condition (15). The following result is a parametric version of [27, Thm. 3.1]. The proof is omitted since it is essentially the same as that of [27, Thm. 3.1].

Proposition 3.15. *Let* $x_0 \in X$. *Assume that the mapping* F *is strongly monotone with respect to* y *uniformly in* $N(x_0)$ *with modulus* μ, *and* F *is Lipschitz continuous in* y *with constant* $L_F>0$ *uniformly in* $x\in N(x_0)$. *Then we have*

(23) $$d_{S(x)}(y)\leqslant((L_F+1)/\mu)\parallel h(x,y)\parallel \quad \forall\, y\in U(x), x\in N(x_0).$$

Remark 3.16. An important special case of GBLP is one where $F(x,y)=Qx+My+q$ and $U(x)=R_+^m$, the nonnegative orthant in R^m. In this case, finding a solution $y\in R^m$ to the parametric variational inequality (1) reduces to the parametric linear complementarity problem of finding a $y\in R^m$ satisfying

$$y\geqslant 0, Qx+My+q\geqslant 0, \langle y, Qx+My+q\rangle = 0.$$

The uniform projection error bound holds when M is a P-matrix (see Mathias and Pang [24]) and when M is an R_0-matrix. (See Mangasarian and Ren [23] and Luo and Tseng [18].)

4. Kuhn-Tucker-type necessary optimality conditions.

In this section we derive Kuhn-Tucker-type necessary optimality conditions for GBLP.

Without loss of generality, we assume in this section that all solutions of the mathematical programming problems lie in the interior of their abstract constraint sets.

First we give a concise review of the material on nonsmooth analysis. Our reference is Clarke [5].

Consider the following mathematical programming problem:

$$\text{P} \qquad \begin{aligned} &\text{minimize} && \phi(x,y) \\ &\text{subject to} && c(x,y)\leqslant 0, \\ & && x\in X, y\in R^m. \end{aligned}$$

The corresponding perturbed problem is

$$\text{P}(\alpha) \qquad \begin{aligned} &\text{minimize} && \phi(x,y) \\ &\text{subject to} && c(x,y)+\alpha\leqslant 0, \\ & && x\in X, y\in R^m, \end{aligned}$$

where $\phi(x,y): R^{n+m}\to R$ and $c(x,y): R^{n+m}\to R^d$ are locally Lipschitz near the points of interest.

Definition 4.1 (calmness). *Let* (x^*, y^*) *solve* P. *Problem* P *is calm at* (x^*, y^*) *provided that there exist* $\delta>0$ *and* $\mu>0$ *such that for all* $\alpha\in\delta B$, *for all* $(x,y)\in(x^*, y^*)+\delta B$ *which are feasible for* $P(\alpha)$, *one has*

$$\phi(x,y)-\phi(x^*, y^*)+\mu\parallel\alpha\parallel\geqslant 0.$$

Definition 4.2 (abnormal and normal multipliers). *Let* (x,y) *be feasible for* P. *Define* $M^0(x,y)$, *the set of* abnormal multipliers *corresponding to* (x,y), *as the set*

$$M^0(x,y):=\{s\in R^d:0\in\partial c(x,y)^{\top}s,s\geqslant 0,\langle s,c(x,y)\rangle=0\}.$$

Define $M^1(x,y)$, *the set of* normal multipliers *corresponding to* (x,y), *as the set*

$$M^1(x,y):=\{s\in R^d:0\in\partial\phi(x,y)+\partial c(x,y)^{\top}s,s\geqslant 0,\langle s,c(x,y)\rangle=0\}.$$

Remark 4.3. A sufficient condition for P to be calm at (x^*,y^*) is $M^0(x^*,y^*)=\{0\}$. $M^0(x^*,y^*)=\{0\}$ if and only if the Mangasarian-Fromowitz conditions are satisfied [30].

Proposition 4.4 (Kuhn-Tucker Lagrange multiplier rule). *Let* (x^*,y^*) *solve P. Suppose* ϕ,c *are locally Lipschitz near* (x^*,y^*) *and problem P is calm at* (x^*,y^*). *Then there exists* $s\geqslant 0$ *such that*

$$0\in\partial\phi(x^*,y^*)+\partial c(x^*,y^*)^{\top}s$$

and

$$0=\langle s,c(x^*,y^*)\rangle.$$

The following theorem gives a necessary condition for optimality when an error bound $r(x,y)$ is explicitly known.

Theorem 4.5. *Let* (x^*,y^*) *be a solution of problem* GBLP. *Let* $r(x,y)$ *be a uniform parametric error bound in a neighborhood of* (x^*,y^*) *and* RP_μ *be the associated penalized problem of* RP, *where* $\mu>0$. *Assume that* f *and* r *are locally Lipschitz near* (x^*,y^*) *and the associated penalized problem* RP_μ *is calm at* (x^*,y^*). *Then there exists a nonzero vector* $s\geqslant 0$ *such that*

$$0\in\partial f(x^*,y^*)+\mu\partial r(x^*,y^*)+\partial c(x^*,y^*)^{\top}s$$

and

$$0=\langle s,c(x^*,y^*)\rangle.$$

Proof. By Theorem 2.6, (x^*,y^*) is also a solution of the associated penalized problem RP_μ. The result follows from Proposition 4.4.

However, in many cases, uniform parametric error bounds are implicit functions of the original problem data. The useful uniform parametric error bounds derived in section 4 involve the class of marginal functions or value functions. In order to derive necessary conditions in these cases, one must first study the generalized differentiability of marginal functions.

Consider the following parametric mathematical programming problem:

$$\begin{array}{lll} \mathrm{P}_\alpha & \text{minimize} & \phi(\alpha,y) \\ & \text{subject to} & c(\alpha,y)\leqslant 0, \\ & & y\in R^m. \end{array}$$

We assume that for problem P_α the functions ϕ and c are locally Lipschitz near the point of interest $y_0\in R^m$. Let y be feasible for P_α. Define

$$M_\alpha^0(y):=\{\pi\in R^d:0\in\partial_y c(\alpha,y)^{\top}\pi,\langle\pi,c(\alpha,y)\rangle=0,\pi\geqslant 0\},$$

$$M_{\alpha}^{1}(y):=\{\pi\in R^{d}:0\in\partial_{y}\phi(\alpha,y)+\partial_{y}c(\alpha,y)^{\top}\pi,\langle\pi,c(\alpha,y)\rangle=0,\pi\geqslant 0\}.$$

Let $W(\alpha)=\inf\{\phi(\alpha,y):c(\alpha,y)\leqslant 0,y\in Y\}$. The following result is an easy consequence of Corollary 1 of Theorem 6.5.2 of Clarke [5].

Proposition 4.6 (generalized differentiability of marginal functions). *Let* $\sum_{\alpha_0}$ *be the solution set to problem* P_{α_0} *and suppose it is nonempty. Suppose* $M_{\alpha_0}^{0}(\sum_{\alpha_0})=\{0\}$.

Then $W(\alpha)$ *is Lipschitz near* α_0, *and one has*

$$\partial W(\alpha_0)\subset \mathrm{clco}\{\partial_{\alpha}\phi(\alpha_0,y)+\partial_{\alpha}c(\alpha_0,y)^{\top}\pi:\ y\in\sum\nolimits_{\alpha_0},\pi\in M_{\alpha_0}^{1}(y)\},$$

where clcoA denotes the closed convex hull of the set A.

Set $G_0(x,y)=-\min\{\langle F(x,y),z-y\rangle:c(x,z)\leqslant 0,z\in R^{m}\}$. The parameter here is $\alpha=(x,y)$. Let $\sum_{(x,y)}$ denote the set of vectors at which $G_0(x,y)$ attains the maximum. By Proposition 4.6, one has the following result.

Proposition 4.7. Suppose $M_{(x^*,y^*)}^{0}(\sum_{(x^*,y^*)})=\{0\}$. *Assume that* f,F, *and* c *are locally Lipschitz near* (x^*,y^*) *and that* $\partial F(x^*,y^*)\subset\partial_x F(x^*,y^*)\times\partial_y F(x^*,y^*)$. *Then* $G_0(x,y)$ *is Lipschitz near* (x^*,y^*) *and one has*

$$\begin{aligned}&\partial G_0(x^*,y^*)\\&\subset \mathrm{co}\{(\partial x F(x^*,y^*)^{\top}(y^*-y)-\partial_x c(x^*,y)^{\top}\pi,\partial_y F(x^*,y^*)^{\top}(y^*-y)+F(x^*,y^*)):\\&\qquad\qquad y\in\sum\nolimits_{(x^*,y^*)},\pi\in M_{(x^*,y^*)}^{1}(y)\},\end{aligned}$$

where

$$M_{(x^*,y^*)}^{0}(y)=\{\pi\in R^{d}:0\in\partial_y c(x^*,y)^{\top}\pi,\pi\geqslant 0,\langle\pi,c(x^*,y)\rangle=0\},$$
$$M_{(x^*,y^*)}^{1}(y)=\{\pi\in R^{d}:0\in F(x^*,y^*)+\partial_y c(x^*,y)^{\top}\pi,\pi\geqslant 0,\langle\pi,c(x^*,y)\rangle=0\}.$$

Combining Proposition 4.7, Remark 4.3, and Theorems 2.6, 2.9, and 4.5, one has the following result.

Theorem 4.8. *Suppose* f,F, *and* c *are* C^1. *Let* (x^*,y^*) *be a solution of* GBLP. *Assume either of the following assumptions is satisfied*:

- $G_0(x,y)$ *is a uniform parametric error bound in a neighborhood of* (x^*,y^*).
- $\sqrt{G_0(x,y)}$ *is a uniform parametric error bound in a neighborhood of* (x^*,y^*) *and* f *is upper Hölder continuous with exponent 2 near every* $y\in S(x)$ *uniformly in* x *in a neighborhood of* x^*.

Suppose $M_{(x^*,y^*)}^{0}(\sum_{(x^*,y^*)})=\{0\}$. *Then there exist* $\mu>0$, $s\in R^{d}$, *positive integers* I,J, $\lambda_{ij}\geqslant 0$, $\sum_{i=1}^{I}\sum_{j=1}^{J}\lambda_{ij}=1$, $y_i\in\sum_{(x^*,y^*)}$, *and* $\pi_{ij}\in R^{d}$ *such that*

$$0=\nabla_x f(x^*,y^*)+\nabla_x c(x^*,y^*)^{\top}s+\mu\sum_{ij}\lambda_{ij}\{\nabla_x F(x^*,y^*)^{\top}(y^*-y_i)-\nabla_x c(x^*,y_i)^{\top}\pi_{ij}\},$$

$$0=\nabla_y f(x^*,y^*)+\nabla_y c(x^*,y^*)^{\top}s+\mu\sum_{ij}\lambda_{ij}\{\nabla_y F(x^*,y^*)^{\top}(y^*-y_i)+F(x^*,y^*)\}$$

$$0=\langle s,c(x^*,y^*)\rangle,s\geqslant 0,$$

$0 = F(x^*, y^*) + \nabla_y c(x^*, y_i)^\top \pi_{ij}$,
$0 = \langle \pi_{ij}, c(x^*, y_i) \rangle, \pi_{ij} \geqslant 0$.

For $G_\alpha(x,y)$, the differentiable gap function defined in (22), since y is the unique solution in the right-hand side of (22), we have $\sum_{(x,y)} = \{y\}$. By Proposition 4.6, one has the following result.

Proposition 4.9. *Suppose f, F, and c are locally Lipschitz near (x^*, y^*). Assume that $M^0_{(x^*,y^*)}(y^*) = \{0\}$. Then $G_\alpha(x,y)$ is Lipschitz near (x^*, y^*) and one has*

$$\partial G_\alpha(x^*, y^*) \subset \{(-\partial_x c(x^*, y^*)^\top \pi, F(x^*, y^*)) : \pi \in M^1_{(x^*,y^*)}(y^*)\},$$

where

$$M^1_{(x^*,y^*)}(y^*) = \{\pi \in R^d : 0 \in F(x^*, y^*) + \partial_y c(x^*, y^*)^\top \pi, \pi \geqslant 0, \langle \pi, c(x^*, y^*) \rangle = 0\}.$$

Furthermore, if c is a C^1 function and $M^1_{(x,y)}(y) = \{\pi\}$ is a singleton, then $G_\alpha(x,y)$ is C^1 and one has

$$\nabla G_\alpha(x,y) = (-\nabla_x c(x,y)^\top \pi, F(x,y)).$$

Combining Proposition 4.9, Remark 4.3, and Theorems 2.6, 2.9, and 4.5, one has the following result.

Theorem 4.10. *Let (x^*, y^*) be a solution of* GBLP. *Suppose F is locally Lipschitz near (x^*, y^*) and f and c are C^1 functions. Assume that either of the following assumptions is satisfied:*

- *$G_\alpha(x,y)$ is a uniform parametric error bound in a neighborhood of (x^*, y^*).*
- *$\sqrt{G_\alpha(x,y)}$ is a uniform parametric error bound in a neighborhood of (x^*, y^*) and f is upper Hölder continuous with exponent 2 near every $y \in S(x)$ uniformly in x in a neighborhood of x^*.*

Suppose $M^0_{(x^*,y^*)}(y^*) = \{0\}$. Then there exist $\mu > 0$, $s \in R^d$, and $\pi \in R^d$ such that

$$0 = \nabla_x f(x^*, y^*) + \nabla_x c(x^*, y^*)^\top s - \mu \nabla_x c(x^*, y^*)^\top \pi,$$
$$0 = \nabla_y f(x^*, y^*) + \nabla_y c(x^*, y^*)^\top s + \mu F(x^*, y^*),$$
$$0 = \langle s, c(x^*, y^*) \rangle = 0, s \geqslant 0,$$
$$0 = F(x^*, y^*) + \nabla_y c(x^*, y^*)^\top \pi,$$
$$0 = \langle \pi, c(x^*, y^*) \rangle, \pi \geqslant 0.$$

Remark 4.11. To shorten the exposition, we have assumed in Theorems 4.8 and 4.10 that f, F, g, and c are C^1 functions. However, these theorems can also be stated without difficulty when f, F, g, and c are merely Lipschitz continuous.

5. Relationships between various uniform parametric error bounds.

In this section, we study the relationships between various uniform parametric error bounds. Through illustrative examples we show that various equivalent single level optimization formulations with uniform parametric error bounds and their corresponding necessary optimality conditions complement each other.

The following result is easy to prove.

Proposition 5.1. *Suppose that r_S and r_B are two merit functions that satisfy the following inequality*:

$$r_S(x,y) \leqslant \delta r_B(x,y) \quad \forall (x,y) \in \mathrm{Gr}U,$$

for a constant $\delta>0$. If $r_S(x,y)$ is a uniform parametric error bound, then so is $r_B(x,y)$.

Motivated by the above result we now establish certain inequalities and equalities among various uniform parametric error bounds.

Proposition 5.2.

(1) *If the objective function $g(x,y)$ of the lower level optimization problem* (3) *is convex and C^1(continuously differentiable) in y, then*

$$g(x,y)-V(x)\leqslant G_0(x,y). \tag{24}$$

Furthermore, if the lower level problem is linear, then

$$g(x,y)-V(x)=G_0(x,y).$$

(2) *For* GBLP, *we have*

$$\sqrt{G_\alpha(x,y)}\leqslant\sqrt{G_0(x,y)}. \tag{25}$$

(3) *For (x,y) in a neighborhood of the solution (x^*,y^*) of* GBLP,

$$G_0(x,y)\leqslant\sqrt{G_0(x,y)}. \tag{26}$$

(4) *For* GBLP, *we have*

$$\| h(x,y) \| \leqslant\sqrt{2G_0(x,y)}. \tag{27}$$

Proof. (1) Let $y(x)\in \mathrm{argmin}_{y\in U(x)} g(x,y)$. By the convexity of $g(x,\cdot)$ and the definition of G_0, we have

$$\begin{aligned} G_0(x,y) &\geqslant \langle \nabla_y g(x,y), y-y(x)\rangle \\ &\geqslant g(x,y)-g(x,y(x)) \\ &= g(x,y)-V(x). \end{aligned}$$

The second assertion follows from the definitions of $V(x)$ and $G_0(x,y)$.

(2) This follows directly from the definitions of G_α and G_0.

(3) Since G_0 is continuous in (x,y) and $G_0(x^*,y^*)=0$, $G_0(x,y)<1$ in a neighborhood of the solution (x^*,y^*) of GBLP. This implies the result.

(4) Taking $\alpha=1$ and $M=I$ the identity matrix in the definition of G_α, we have

$$G_1(x,y)=\langle F(x,y), y-p(x,y)\rangle-\frac{1}{2}\| y-p(x,y)\|^2\geqslant 0,$$

where $p(x,y)=\mathrm{Proj}_{U(x)}(y-F(x,y))$. Thus

$$\begin{aligned} G_0(x,y) &\geqslant \langle F(x,y), y-p(x,y)\rangle \\ &\geqslant \frac{1}{2}\| y-p(x,y)\|^2=\frac{1}{2}\| h(x,y)\|^2. \end{aligned}$$

The proof is completed.

As shown in section 4, one of the major applications of the exact penalty formulation with uniform parametric error bounds is to derive Kuhn-Tucker-type necessary optimality conditions. For this purpose parametric error bounds must be Lipschitz continuous (see Theorem 4. 5). Among the aforementioned error bounds, G_0, h, and g-V are Lipschitz continuous under appropriate constraint qualifications on $U(x)$. The rest are generally not Lipschitz. By virtue of Proposition 5. 1, if we have an exact penalty formulation with a given uniform parametric error bound then a similar exact penalty formulation is also valid, with that error bound replaced by a larger one. Smaller error bounds generally require stronger conditions. Hence, on one hand, error bounds G_0, h, and ϕ-V can be Lipschitz continuous but require stronger conditions. On the other hand, larger bounds such as $\sqrt{G_0}$ may not be Lipschitz continuous but require weaker conditions. In the case when uniform parametric error bounds are not Lipschitz continuous, Theorems 4. 8 and 4. 10 show that stronger assumptions, such as upper Hölder continuity on the upper level objective functions, may be required. Therefore, various error bounds and their equivalent exact penalty representations complement each other. The following are some illustrative examples.

Example 5. 3. Consider the following classical bilevel programming problem:

$$\text{(P1)}\quad \min\ x^2-2y$$
$$\text{s. t. } x\in[0,2] \text{ and } y\in\operatorname{argmin}\{y^2-2xy : y\in[0,2x]\}.$$

It is easy to verify that (1,1) is the unique solution of (P1) and assumption (18) does not hold. Therefore, Proposition 3. 5 does not apply and one may suspect that (P1) does not have a uniformly weak sharp minimum. Indeed, direct calculation shows that the value function for the lower level problem is $V(x)=x^2$. Using the value function approach, problem (P1) is equivalent to the following problem:

$$\begin{aligned} &\min x^2-2y \\ &\text{s. t. } (y-x)^2=0, \\ &\qquad y\in[0,2x], x\in[0,2]. \end{aligned}$$

Here $(y-x)^2$ is not an exact penalty term for the above problem, since for any $\mu>0$ $(1, y)$ where $y\in\left(1,\frac{2+\mu}{\mu}\right)$ assigns a lower value to the objective function than (1,1) in the penalized problem

$$\begin{aligned} &\min\ x^2-2y+\mu(y-x)^2 \\ &\text{s. t. } y\in[0,2x], x\in[0,2]. \end{aligned}$$

It is clear that the function $F(x,y)=\nabla_y g(x,y)=y-x$ is strongly monotone in y uniformly for $x\in R$. The standard gap function takes the form

$$\begin{aligned} G_0(x,y) &= \max_{z\in[0,2x]}\langle y-x, y-z\rangle \\ &= y^2-xy+\max_{z\in[0,2x]}\langle y-x,-z\rangle \\ &= y^2-xy-x[(y-x)-|y-x|] \\ &= (y-x)^2+x|y-x|. \end{aligned}$$

The linear independence and the strict complementarity conditions can easily be verified at(1,1). Hence, by Proposition 3. 9, the gap function $G_0(x,y)$ is a uniform parametric error bound in a neighborhood of (1,1). Indeed, it is easy to see that (1,1) is also the unique solution of the penalized problem

$$\text{s. t. } y \in [0,2x], x \in [0,2]$$

for any $\mu > 0$.

We now slightly modify the above example to show that the strict complementarity conditions cannot be omitted from Proposition 3. 9.

Example 5. 4. Consider the same problem in Example 5. 3 with constraints $y, z \in [0,2x]$ replaced by $y, z \in [0,x]$ and with $x \in [0, 2]$ replaced by $x \in [0, \infty)$.

Again, one can check that (1,1) is the only solution to the problem. However, the gap function is different. In fact, in this example,

$$\begin{aligned} G_0(x,y) &= \max_{z\in[0,x]} \langle y-x, y-z \rangle \\ &= y^2 - xy + \max_{z\in[0,x]} \langle y-x, -z \rangle \\ &= y^2 - xy + x^2 - xy \\ &= (y-x)^2. \end{aligned}$$

Thus the equivalent single level problem involving the standard gap function is

$$\begin{aligned} \text{minimize} \quad & x^2 - 2y \\ \text{subject to} \quad & (y-x)^2 = 0, \\ & y \in [0,x], x \in [0, \infty). \end{aligned}$$

Again, $(y-x)^2$ is not an exact penalty term. This is due to the fact that the strict complementarity condition does not hold at (1,1).

$F(x,y) = y - x$ is strongly monotone; therefore, it is pseudostrongly monotone with respect to y uniformly for all $x \in R^n$. Using Propositions 3. 12, 3. 13, and 3. 15, the problem has the square root standard gap bound, the square root differentiable gap bound, and the projection bound. The differentiable gap function associated with $\alpha = 1$ and $M = I$ takes the form

$$\begin{aligned} G_1(x,y) &= \max_{z\in[0,x]} \left\{ \langle y-x, y-z \rangle - \frac{1}{2}(y-z)^2 \right\} \\ &= \frac{1}{2}(y-x)^2 \end{aligned}$$

The projection bound takes the form $|h(x,y)| = |y-x|$. Indeed, the original problem is equivalent to the following penalized problem:

$$\text{s. t. } y \in [0,x], x \in [0, \infty),$$

for all $\mu > 0$.

Note that the uniform parametric error bounds for Example 5. 4 are all Lipschitz continuous. We now give an example which has a square root standard gap bound that is not Lipschitz continuous.

Example 5.5. Consider the following classical bilevel programming problem:

$$\min (x-1)^2 + x^2(y+1)^2$$

$$\text{s.t. } x \in [-1,1] \text{ and } y \in \arg\min\left\{\left(\sin\frac{\pi}{2}x\right)y : y \in [-1,1]\right\}.$$

Here $(1,-1)$ is the optimal solution of the problem, and the solution set of the lower level problem is

$$S(x) = \begin{cases} \{1\} & \text{if } -1 \leqslant x < 0, \\ [-1,1] & \text{if } x = 0, \\ \{-1\} & \text{if } 0 < x \leqslant 1 \end{cases}$$

The standard gap function for the problem is

$$G_0(x,y) = \max\left\{\sin\frac{\pi}{2}x \cdot (y-z) : z \in [-1,1]\right\}$$

$$= \begin{cases} \sin\frac{\pi}{2}x \cdot (y-1) & -1 \leqslant x < 0, \\ 0 & x = 0, \\ \sin\frac{\pi}{2}x \cdot (y+1) & 0 < x \leqslant 1. \end{cases}$$

Since $F(x,y) = \sin\frac{\pi}{2}$ x is independent of y, F is pseudostrongly monotone with respect to y uniformly for all x in a neighborhood of 1. By Proposition 3.12, $\sqrt{G_0(x,y)}$ is an error bound in the neighborhood of $(1,-1)$. However, $\sqrt{G_0(x,y)}$ is not Lipschitz continuous near $(x^*, y^*) = (1,-1)$. Theorem 4.5 cannot be used.

We now verify that the assumptions of Theorem 4.8 are satisfied. The objective function $f(x,y) = (x-1)^2 + x^2(y+1)^2$ is upper Hölder continuous near every $y \in S(x)$ uniformly for x in a neighborhood of 1. Since the constraint set $-1 \leqslant x \leqslant 1, -1 \leqslant y \leqslant 1$ has an interior point, the Slater condition is satisfied. Theorem 4.8 implies that at $(x^*, y^*) = (1,-1)$, there must exist $\mu > 0$, $(s_1, s_2, s_3) \geqslant (0,0,0)$, an integer J, $\lambda_j \geqslant 0$, $\sum_{j=1}^{J} \lambda_j = 1$, and $\pi_j = (\pi_j^1, \pi_j^2, \pi_j^3) \in R^3$ such that

$$0 = 2(x^* - 1) + 2x^*(y^* + 1)^2 + s_3 - \mu\sum_j \lambda_j \pi_j^3,$$

$$0 = 2x^{*2}(y^* + 1) + \mu\sin\left(\frac{\pi}{2}x^*\right) + s_1 - s_2,$$

$$0 = s_1(y^* - 1),$$

$$0 = s_2(-1 - y^*),$$

$$0 = s_3(x^* - 1),$$

$$0 = \sin\left(\frac{\pi}{2}x^*\right) + \pi_j^1 - \pi_j^2,$$

$$0 = \pi_j^1(y^* - 1),$$

$$0 = \pi_j^2(-1 - y^*),$$

$$0 = \pi_j^3(x^* - 1).$$

Indeed, the above condition holds for $J=1$, $\lambda_1=1, \mu=s_2=\pi_1^2=1$, and $s_1=s_3=\pi_1^1=\pi_1^3=0$.

6. Exact penalty functions for the KKT formulation.

In this section, we assume that $c(x,y)$ is convex and differentiable in y and that one of the usual constraint qualifications holds for the inequality system $c(x,y)\leqslant 0$ in terms of variable y. Under these assumptions, besides formulating GBLP as the single level equivalent problem GS or VS, one can also formulate GBLP as the equivalent single level problem KS. We will show that some of the uniform parametric error bounds such as $G_0(x,y)$, $\sqrt{G_0(x,y)}$, and $g(x,y)-V(x)$ can not only serve as exact penalty terms themselves, but can also play an important role in deriving equivalent exact penalty formulations for KS.

The following results establish the relationships among the KKT, the standard gap, and the value function formulations of GBLP.

Proposition 6.1. *Suppose $c(x,y)$ is convex and differentiable in the y variable. Then*

$$G_0(x,y) \leqslant -\langle u, c(x,y)\rangle \text{ for all } (x,y,u)\in X\times R^m\times R^d \text{ such that}$$
$$u\geqslant 0, c(x,y)\leqslant 0, F(x,y)+\nabla_y c(x,y)^t u = 0.$$

Proof. From mathematical programming weak duality (see, e.g., [20]), one has

$$\begin{aligned}
G_0(x,y) :&= \sup\{\langle F(x,y), y-z\rangle : \forall z\in R^m \text{ s.t. } c(x,z)\leqslant 0\}\\
&= -\inf\{\langle F(x,y), z-y\rangle : \forall z\in R^m \text{ s.t. } c(x,z)\leqslant 0\}\\
&\leqslant -\sup\{\langle F(x,y), z-y\rangle + \langle u, c(x,y)\rangle : \forall (z,u)\in R^m\times R^d \text{ s.t.}\\
&\qquad u\geqslant 0, c(x,z)\leqslant 0,\\
&\qquad F(x,z)+\nabla_y c(x,z)^t u = 0\}\\
&\leqslant -\sup\{\langle u, c(x,y)\rangle : \forall (x,y,u)\in X\times R^m\times R^d \text{ s.t.}\\
&\qquad u\geqslant 0, c(x,y)\leqslant 0,\\
&\qquad F(x,y)+\nabla_y c(x,y)^t u = 0\}.
\end{aligned}$$

Combining Proposition 6.1 and (1) from Proposition 5.2, we get the following result.

Corollary 6.2. *Assume that the objective function $g(x,y)$ for the lower level optimization problem (3) and $c(x,y)$ are convex and C^1 in y. Then*

$$g(x,y)-V(x)\leqslant -\langle u, c(x,y)\rangle\ \forall (x,y,u)\in X\times R^m\times R^d \text{ such that}$$
$$u\geqslant 0, c(x,y)\leqslant 0, \nabla_y g(x,y)+\nabla c(x,y)^t u = 0.$$

Remark 6.3. Propositions 5.1 and 6.1 and Corollary 6.2 show that any condition ensuring that the standard gap function or $g(x,y)-V(x)$ provides exact penalty terms for the equivalent single level problems GS and VS, respectively, ensure that $-\langle u, c(x,y)\rangle$ is an exact penalty function for the equivalent single level problem KS. The converse is not necessarily true.

Under assumptions involving continuous subanalytic functions, Luo et al. proved in [19] that there exists a constant $N>0$ such that $(-\langle u, c(x,y)\rangle)^{1/N}$ is an exact penalty term for KS. Moreover, for the case where the mapping $F(x,y)$ is affine and the feasible region is compact, N can be taken as 1 or 2 depending on whether or not the strict complementarity condition is satisfied. To compare our results with those in [19], we summarize the related results in [19].

Theorem 6.4 (see Theorems 4 and 6 of [19]). *Consider GBLP where the lower level problem is* QP_x. *Assume that* $f(x,y)$ *is Lipschitz continuous in both variables and that the set*

$$\{(x,y)\in X\times R^m: Ax+By-b\leqslant 0\}$$

is a compact polyhedron. Suppose GBLP has a solution. Then there exist positive scalars μ^* *and* β *such that for all scalars* $\mu\geqslant\mu^*$, *any vector* (x^*, y^*) *solves GBLP if and only if for some* $u^*\in R^d$, *the triple* (x^*, y^*, u^*) *solves the following penalized problem in the variables* (x,y,u):

$$\begin{aligned}\min\ & f(x,y)+\mu\sqrt{-\langle u, Ax+By-b\rangle}\\ \text{s.t.}\ & Px+Qy+q+B^Tu=0,\\ & u\geqslant 0,\ \|u\|\leqslant\beta,\\ & Ax+By-b\leqslant 0,\\ & x\in X, y\in R^m.\end{aligned}$$

Furthermore, if the strict complementarity condition is satisfied for all (x,y,u) *in the feasible region of KS, then we can remove the square root.*

In the following result we relax most of the assumptions of Theorem 6.4 but we require stronger conditions on $F(x,y)$.

Theorem 6.5. *Consider GBLP where* $f(x,y)$ *is Lipschitz continuous in* y *uniformly in* $x\in R^n$ *with constant* L, *and* $c(x,y)$ *is convex and differentiable in* y. *Suppose that there exists a solution to GBLP.*

If $F(x,y)$ *is pseudostrongly monotone with respect to* y *uniformly in* $x\in X$ *with modulus* δ, *then any vector* (x^*, y^*) *is a global solution to GBLP if and only if for some* $u^*\in R^d$, *the triple* (x^*, y^*, u^*) *is a global solution to the following penalized problem in the variables* (x,y,u):

$$\begin{aligned}\min\ & f(x,y)+\mu\sqrt{-\langle u, c(x,y)\rangle}\\ \text{s.t.}\ & F(x,y)+\nabla_y c(x,y)^T u=0,\\ & u\geqslant 0, c(x,y)\leqslant 0,\\ & x\in X, y\in R^m,\end{aligned}$$

for all $\mu\geqslant\frac{\sqrt{\delta}}{\delta}L$.

Under the assumptions of Propositions 3.4 and 3.5, any vector (x^*, y^*) *is a global solution to GBLP if and only if for some* $u^*\in R^d$, *the triple* (x^*, y^*, u^*) *is a* *global solution to the following penalized problem in the variables* (x, y, u):

$$\begin{aligned}&\min f(x,y) - \delta\mu\langle u, c(x,y)\rangle\\ \text{s.t. } & F(x,y) + \nabla_y c(x,y)^T u = 0,\\ & u \geqslant 0, c(x,y) \leqslant 0,\\ & x \in X, y \in R^m,\end{aligned}$$

for all $\mu \geqslant L$, *where* δ *is the modulus of the uniformly weak sharp minimum.*

Proof. We only prove the first assertion, since the proof of the second is similar. Assume (x^*, y^*, u^*) is a global solution of CS. Then (x^*, y^*) is a global solution of GBLP. By Proposition 3.12, $\sqrt{G_0(x,y)}$ is a uniform parametric error bound with modulus $\frac{\sqrt{\delta}}{\delta}$. Therefore, by Theorem 2.6, (x^*, y^*) is a global solution of $RP_{\frac{\sqrt{\delta}}{\delta}\mu}$ with $r(x, y) = \sqrt{G_0(x,y)}$ for all $\mu \geqslant L$. Therefore,

$$\begin{aligned}f(x^*, y^*) &\leqslant f(x,y) + \frac{\sqrt{\delta}}{\delta}\mu\sqrt{G_0(x,y)} \quad \forall x, y \text{ s.t. } c(x,y) \leqslant 0,\\ &\leqslant f(x,y) + \frac{\sqrt{\delta}}{\delta}\mu\sqrt{-\langle u, c(x,y)\rangle} \quad \forall (x,y,u) \text{ s.t.}\\ & u \geqslant 0, c(x,y) \leqslant 0, F(x,y) + \nabla_y c(x,y)^t u = 0,\end{aligned}$$

where the last inequality follows from Proposition 6.1.

The proof of the converse is similar to the converse part in the proof of Proposition 2.2.

Even when $c(x,y)$ is convex and C^1 in y, the ranges of applications of Theorems 6.4 and 6.5 are difierent. Indeed, the following example, taken from [19], is a situation where Theorem 6.5 is applicable but Theorem 6.4 is not.

Example 6.6. Consider the problem:

$$\begin{aligned}\text{(P2)} \quad & \min x - y\\ & \text{s.t. } x \geqslant 0, \text{ and } y \in \operatorname{argmin}\left\{\frac{1}{2}y^2 : x + y \geqslant 0, y \geqslant 0\right\}.\end{aligned}$$

In [19], by direct arguments, (P2) is shown to be equivalent to the penalized problem

$$\begin{aligned}\text{(P3)} \quad & \min x - y + \mu\sqrt{u(x+y)}\\ & \text{s.t. } y - u = 0, x + y \geqslant 0,\\ & (x, y, u) \geqslant 0,\end{aligned}$$

for any $\mu > 0$. Indeed, it is easy to see that $(0,0)$ is the unique solution to the problem (P2)and$(0,0,0)$ is the unique solution of the penalized problem (P3) for any $\mu > 0$. It is also observed in [19] that Theorem 6.4 is not applicable because the feasible region is not compact. On the other hand, since $F(x,y) = y$ is strongly monotone with respect to y for all $x \in R^n$, this example does satisfy all the conditions of Theorem 6.5. By Theorem 6.5 both $\sqrt{G_0(x,y)}$ and the square root of the complementarity term are exact penalty terms. The standard gap function in this case is $G_0(x,y) = y^2$ for all $x \geqslant 0$. Therefore, (P2) is equivalent to both (P3) and the following problem:

$$\text{(P4)} \quad \min x - y + \mu \mid y \mid \quad \text{s.t.}\ x + y \geqslant 0, x \geqslant 0, y \geqslant 0.$$

Indeed, it is easy to see that $(0,0)$ is the unique solution of (P4).

Now we discuss an example to which both the KKT and the non-KKT approaches apply, but yield different equivalent single level problems.

Example 6.7. Consider the problem

$$\begin{aligned}\text{(P5)} \quad & \min x + y_1 + y_2 \\ & \text{s.t.}\ a \leqslant x \leqslant b, \\ & (y_1, y_2) \in \arg\min_{y_1, y_2}\left\{\frac{1}{2}y_1^2 + xy_1 + y_2, : \frac{1}{2}y_1 + x \geqslant 0, y_1 \geqslant 0, y_2 \geqslant 0\right\},\end{aligned}$$

where a and b are positive constants. It is obvious that $S(x)=\{(0,0)\}$ and $V(x)=0$ for all $x \geqslant 0$. $F(x,y)=(y_1+x,1)$ is not pseudostrongly monotone. Therefore, the assumptions of Propositions 3.9, 3.11, and 3.13 are not satisfied. However, one can verify that the assumptions of Proposition 3.5 are satisfied. Therefore, for any $\mu>0$, (x^*, y^*) is a solution of the original problem (P5) if and only if it is the solution of the following problem (by the value function approach):

$$\begin{aligned}\text{(P6)} \quad & \min x + y_1 + y_2 + \mu\left(\frac{1}{2}y_1^2 + xy_1 + y_2\right) \\ & \text{s.t.}\ \frac{1}{2}y_1 + x \geqslant 0, a \leqslant x \leqslant b, y_1 \geqslant 0, y_2 \geqslant 0.\end{aligned}$$

By Theorem 6.5, there exists $u^* \in R^3$ such that (x^*, y^*, u^*) is a solution of the following problem:

$$\begin{aligned}\text{(P7)} \quad & \min x + y_1 + y_2 + \mu\left(u_1\left(\frac{1}{2}y_1 + x\right) + u_2 y_1 + u_3 y_2\right) \\ & \text{s.t.}\ 0 = y_1 + x - \frac{1}{2}u_1 - u_2, \\ & 0 = 1 - u_3, \\ & a \leqslant x \leqslant b, \frac{1}{2}y_1 + x \geqslant 0, y_1 \geqslant 0, y_2 \geqslant 0, u_1 \geqslant 0, u_2 \geqslant 0\end{aligned}$$

for any $\mu>0$. Clearly, (P5) and (P6) have a unique solution $(a,0,0)$, and (P7) has a unique solution $(a,0,0,0,0,1)$. Note that the compactness of the feasible region and the strict complementarity assumptions of Theorem 6.4 fail for this example.

Examples 6.6 and 6.7 illustrate that both the KKT and the non-KKT approaches have their advantages and disadvantages. On one hand, by the KKT approach, the exact penalty term is an explicit function of the problem data, but the number of variables in the single level problem increases. On the other hand, by the non-KKT approach, although the number of variables stays the same in the equivalent single level problem, the exact penalty function needs to be computed.

Acknowledgements

We thank J. S. Treiman for his comments on an early version of this paper, which helped to improve the exposition.

References

[1] G. Anandalingam and T. L. Friesz, eds., *Hierarchical optimization*, Ann. Oper. Res., 34 (1992).

[2] J. V. Burke, *Calmness and exact penalization*, SIAM J. Control Optim., 29 (1991), pp. 493-497.

[3] J. V. Burke, *An exact penalization viewpoint of constraint optimization*, SIAM J. Control Optim., 29 (1991), pp. 968-998.

[4] J. V. Burke and M. C. Ferris, *Weak sharp minima in mathematical programming*, SIAM J. Control Optim., 31 (1993), pp. 1340-1359.

[5] F. H. Clarke, *Optimization and Nonsmooth Analysis*, Wiley-Interscience, New York, 1983.

[6] S. Dempe, *A necessary and suffcient optimality condition for bilevel programming problems*, Optimization, 25 (1992), pp. 341-354.

[7] J.-P. Dussault and P. Marcotte, *Conditions derégularité géométrique pour les inéquations variationnelles*, RAIRO Rech. Opér., 23 (1988), pp. 1-16.

[8] A. D. Ioffe, *Regular points of Lipschitz functions*, Trans. Amer. Math. Soc., 251 (1979), pp. 61-69.

[9] M. C. Ferris and O. L. Mangasarian, *Minimum principle sufficiency*, Math. Programming, 57 (1992), pp. 1-14.

[10] T. L. Friesz, R. T. Tobin, H.-J. Cho, and N. J. Mehta, *Sensitivity analysis based heuristic algorithms for mathematical programs with variational inequality constraints*, Math. Pro-gramming, 48 (1990), pp. 265-284.

[11] M. Fukushima, *Equivalent differentiable optimization problems and descent methods for asymmetric variational inequality problems*, Math. Programming, 53 (1992), pp. 99-110.

[12] P. T. Harker and J. S. Pang, *On the existence of optimal solutions to mathematical programs with equilibrium constraints*, Oper. Res. Lett., 7 (1988), pp. 61-64.

[13] P. T. HarkerandJ. S. Pang, *Finite-dimensional variational inequality and nonlinear complementarity problems: A survey of theory, algorithms and applications*, Math. Programming, 48 (1990), pp. 161-220.

[14] D. W. Hearn, *The gap function of a convex program*, Oper. Res. Lett., 1 (1982), pp. 67-71.

[15] D. Kinderlehrer and G. Stampacchia, *An Introduction to Variational Inequalities and Their Applications*, Academic Press, New York, 1980.

[16] M. Labbé, P. Marcotte, and G. Savard, *A bilevel model of taxation and its application to optimal highway pricing*, preprint.

[17] P. Loridan and J. Morgan, *A theoretical approximation scheme for Stackelberg problems*, J. Optim. Theory Appl., 11 (1989), pp. 95-110.

[18] X. D. Luo and P. Tseng, *Conditions for a projection-type error bound for the linear complemen-*

tarity problem to be global, preprint.

[19] Z. Q. Luo, J. S. Pang, D. Ralph, and S.-Q. Wu, *Exact penalization and stationarity conditions of mathematical programs with equilibrium constraints*, preprint.

[20] O. L. Mangasarian, *Nonlinear Programming*, McGraw-Hill, New York, 1969.

[21] O. L. Mangasarian, *A simple characterization of solution sets of convex programs*, Oper. Res. Lett., 7 (1988), pp. 21-26.

[22] O. L. Mangasarian and R. R. Meyer, *Nonlinear perturbation of linear programs*, SIAM J. Control Optim., 17 (1979), pp. 745-752.

[23] O. L. Mangasarian and J. Ren, *New improved error bounds for the linear complementarity problem*, Math. Programming, 66 (1994), pp. 241-255.

[24] R. Mathias and J. S. Pang, *Error bounds for the linear complementarity problem with a P-matrix*, Linear Algebra Appl., 132 (1990), pp. 123-136.

[25] P. Marcotte and D. L. Zhu, *Exact and Inexact Penalty Methods for the Generalized Bilevel Programming Problem*, Publication of Centre de recherche sur les transports, Université de Montréal, Canada, CRT-920, 1992.

[26] J. V. Outrata, *Necessary optimality conditions for Stackelberg problems*, J. Optim. Theory Appl., 76 (1993), pp. 305-320.

[27] J. S. Pang, *A posteriori error bounds for the linearly-constrained variational inequality problem*, Math. Oper. Res., 12 (1987), pp. 474-484.

[28] R. T. Rockafellar, *Convex Analysis*, Princeton University Press, Princeton, NJ, 1970.

[29] H. Von Stackelberg, *The Theory of the Market Economy*, Oxford University Press, Oxford, England, 1952.

[30] J. J. Y eand D. L. Zhu, *Optimality conditions for bilevel programming problems*, Optimization, 33 (1995), pp. 9-27.

[31] R. Zhang, *Problems of hierarchical optimization: Nonsmoothness and analysis of solutions*, Ph. D. thesis, University of Washington, Seattle, 1990.

[32] R. Zhang, *Problems of hierachical optimization infinitedimensions*, SIAM J. Optim., 4 (1994), pp. 521-536.

Published in *SIAM J. Optimization*, 1997, 7(2)

A homotopy method for solving bilevel programming problem*

Dao Li Zhu[a,**], Qing Xu[a,b], Zhenghua Lin[a,c]

[a] *School of Management, Fudan University, 220 Handan Road, Shanghai* 200433, *China*
[b] *Naval Submarine Academy, Qingdao, Shandong* 266071, *China*
[c] *Department of Mathematics, Jilin University, Changchun* 130023, *China*

Abstract. A homotopy method for solving bilevel programming problem (BLPP) is proposed. The algorithm is based on constructing the homotopy equation for BLPP. One satisable sucient condition is given to ensure that the point of homotopy path globally converges to a K-K-T point of BLPP. Numerical results are presented to show the eectiveness of this method.

MSC: 58C30; 65H20; 90C30

Keywords: Bilevel programs; Nonconvex programs; Homotopy method; Normal cone condition

1. Introduction

The bilevel programming problem, BLPP, is an optimization problem that is constrained by another optimization problem. We consider the following bilevel programming problem:

$$\text{(BLPP)} \quad \begin{aligned} &\min_{x,y} \quad f(x,y) \\ &\text{s.t.} \quad g(x,y) \leqslant 0, \\ &\min_{y} \quad F(x,y) \\ &\text{s.t.} \quad G(x,y) \leqslant 0, \end{aligned} \tag{1.1}$$

where $(x,y) \in R^{n+m}$ and f, $F: R^{n+m} \to R$, $g = (g_1, \cdots, g_{m_1})^{\mathrm{T}}: R^{n+m} \to R^{m_1}$, $G = (G_1, \cdots,$

*In memory of Professor Zhenghua Lin. This research was supported by the National Natural Science Foundation of China 70171010 and China Postdoctoral Science Foundation.

**Corresponding author. Tel.: +86-2165644781; fax: +86-215-55521353.

E-mail address: daolizhu@yahoo.com (D. L. Zhu).

$G_{m_2})^T: R^{n+m} \to R^{m_2}$. BLPP, even in the linear case, is a nonconvex optimization problem. Generally, problem (1.1) is a nonconvex and nonsmooth program.

The origin of BLPP could be traced to economic notion of a stackelberg game[22]. Today bilevel programs have a wide range of applications in engineering and economics. For example, economic planning[8], agricultural credit distribution[19], electric utility pricing and planning, [12,15], network design problem, origin-destination demand adjustment problem, discrete transit planning problem, a facility location and production problem[16,11], etc. Several algorithms have been proposed for nonlinear bilevel programming. First categories of the algorithms for BLPP is the branch-and-bound approach, Edmunds and Bard[9], Al-Khayal, Horst and Pardalos [3]; the second one is descent methods, Kolstad and Lasdon[14], Savard and Gauvin[20]. Finally, the penalty methods constitute a third category of algorithms, Aiyoshi and Shimizu[1,2,21], Ishizuka and Aiyoshi[13], Marcotte and Zhu[17], Calamai and Conn[6], Case et al. [7].

In this paper, we propose a homotopy method for solving bilevel programs. First we construct the homotopy equation for BLPP, then we prove that, under one satisable sucient condition, the point of homotopy path globally converges to a K-K-T point of BLPP. The predictor-corrector algorithm is proposed to trace numerically the homotopy equations. Finally, some numerical results are presented to show the eectiveness of this method.

2. The homotopy equation for follower's optimization problem

In what follows we consider BLPP (1.1) where f, F, g and G are sucient smooth and convex. First, we consider the follower's optimization problem,

$$\begin{aligned} \min_{y} \quad & F(x,y) \\ \text{s.t.} \quad & G(x,y) \leqslant 0. \end{aligned} \tag{2.1}$$

Assume that for given point $x \in R^n$, the set $\{y \in R^m : G(x,y) < 0\}$ is nonempty. Then optimization problem (2.1) is equivalent to the following K-K-T system.

$$\nabla_y F(x,y) + \nabla_y G(x,y) u = 0,$$
$$UG(x,y) = 0, \quad u \geqslant 0, \quad G(x,y) \leqslant 0,$$

where $u \in R_+^{m_2}$ and $U = \mathrm{diag}(u)$. Therefore, bilevel problem BLPP (1.1) can be expressed as

$$\begin{aligned} \min_{x,y} \quad & f(x,y) \\ \text{s.t.} \quad & g(x,y) \leqslant 0, \\ & \nabla_y F(x,y) + \nabla_y G(x,y) u = 0, \\ & UG(x,y) = 0, u \geqslant 0, G(x,y) \leqslant 0. \end{aligned} \tag{2.2}$$

The homotopy equation for the follower's optimization can be represented as

$$h(w,t) \triangleq \begin{pmatrix} \nabla_y F(x,y) + \nabla_y G(x,y) u \\ UG(x,y) + te \end{pmatrix} = 0, \tag{2.3}$$

where $w=(x,y,u)^{\mathrm{T}}$, $e=(1,\cdots,1)^{\mathrm{T}}\in R^{m_2}$, and $t\in(0,1]$.

Set $\tilde{f}(w)=f(x,y)$, $\tilde{g}(w)=g(x,y)$. Some feasible sets and index set are denoted as follows:

$$\Omega_1(t)\triangleq\{w\in R^{n+m}\times R_{++}^{m_2}:\tilde{g}(w)<0,h(w,t)=0\},$$
$$\Omega(t)\triangleq\Omega_1(t)\times R_{++}^{m_1}\times R^{m+m_2},$$
$$\partial\Omega_1(t)\triangleq\left\{w\in\overline{\Omega}_1(t):\prod_{i=1}^{m_1}\tilde{g}_i(w)=0\right\},$$
$$I(w)\triangleq\{i\in\{1,\cdots,m_1\}:\tilde{g}_i(w)=0\},$$
$$I_G(x,y)=\{i\in\{1,\cdots,m_2\}:G_i(x,y)=0\}。$$

Condition A.

(A. 1) $\forall t\in[0,1]$, $\Omega_1(t)$ is nonempty and bounded;

(A. 2) $\{\nabla_y G_i(x,y),i\in I_G(x,y)\}$ is a matrix of full column rank;

(A. 3) for $t\in(0,1]$, $w\in\overline{\Omega}_1(t)$, $\{\nabla\tilde{g}_i(w),i\in I(w),\nabla_w h(w,t)\}$ is full column rank;

(A. 4) $\forall w\in\overline{\Omega}_1(1)$, $\left\{w+\sum_{i\in I(w)}v_i\nabla\tilde{g}_i(w)+\nabla_w h(w,1)\lambda\right\}\cap\overline{\Omega}_1(1)=\{w\}$;

(A. 5) for any $(x,y)\in\{(x,y):g(x,y)\leqslant 0,G(x,y)\leqslant 0\}$, $\nabla_{yy}^2F(x,y)+\sum_{i=1}^{m_2}(\nabla_{yy}^2G_i(x,y)+\nabla_yG_i(x,y)\nabla_yG_i(x,y)^{\mathrm{T}})$ is positive denite.

Remark 2.1. Condition (A. 5) can guarantee the uniqueness of solution for the follower problem of BLPP. Geometrical interpretation of condition (A. 4) is that $\overline{\Omega}_1(1)$ satisfies the normal cone condition.

Lemma 2.1 (McCormick[18]). *Suppose that Condition (A. 1), (A. 2) and (A. 5) hold, and the set* $\Omega=\{(x,y)\in R^{n+m}:g(x,y)<0,G(x,y)<0\}$ *is nonempty. Then for any given point* $x\in\overline{\Omega}$ *the solution curve* $\{y(t),u(t),t\in(0,1]\}$ *for follower's homotopy equation* (2.3) *is continuous, bounded and unique, and as* $t\to 0$, $y(t)$ *tend to the solution of the follower problem.*

3. The homotopy equation for BLPP and convergence of the homotopy pathway

Consider the following parameterized programming problem:

$$\begin{aligned}\min_{x,y}\quad & f(x,y)\\ \text{s.t.}\quad & g(x,y)\leqslant 0,\\ & h(w,t)=0.\end{aligned}\tag{3.1}$$

When t is descending to 0, by Lemma 2.1, parameterized programming problem (3.1) becomes (2.2). Problem (3.1) can be state as

$$\begin{aligned}\min_{w}\quad & \tilde{f}(w)\\ \text{s.t.}\quad & \tilde{g}(w)\leqslant 0,\\ & h(w,t)=0.\end{aligned}\tag{3.2}$$

Its K-K-T system is

$$\begin{aligned}&\nabla \tilde{f}(w)+\nabla \tilde{g}(w)v+\nabla_w h(w,t)\lambda=0,\\&h(w,t)=0,\\&V\tilde{g}(w)=0,v\geqslant 0,\tilde{g}(w)\leqslant 0,\end{aligned}\qquad(3.3)$$

where $\lambda\in R^{m+m_2}$, $v\in R_+^{m_1}$ are multipliers, and $V=\mathrm{diag}(v)$. When t is descending to 0, by Lemma (2.1), (3.3) is transformed as

$$\tilde{H}(w,v,\lambda)\triangleq\begin{pmatrix}\nabla \tilde{f}(w)+\nabla \tilde{g}(w)v+\nabla_w h(w,0)\lambda\\ h(w,0)\\ V\tilde{g}(w)\end{pmatrix}=0,\quad v\geqslant 0,\tilde{g}(w)\leqslant 0.\qquad(3.4)$$

The mapping $\tilde{H}:R^{n+2m+m_1+2m_2}\to R^{n+2m+m_1+2m_2}$ is sufficient smooth with respect to (w,v,λ). (3.4) is the K-K-T system for problem (2.2).

Now, we turn to construct a homotopy equation for solving the bilevel programming problem. We define homotopy equation for BLPP:

$$H(\theta,\theta_0^0,t)\triangleq\begin{pmatrix}(1-t)(\nabla \tilde{f}(w)+\nabla \tilde{g}(w)v+\nabla_w h(w,t)\lambda+t(w-w^0)\\ h(w,t)\\ V\tilde{g}(w)-tV^0\tilde{g}(w^0)\end{pmatrix}=0,\qquad(3.4)$$

where $\theta=(w,v,\lambda)^{\mathrm{T}}$, $\theta_0^0=(w^0,v^0)^{\mathrm{T}}$, $t\in(0,1]$, $w=(x,y,u)\in R^{n+m}\times R_+^{m_2}$, $v\in R_+^{m_1}$, $\lambda\in R^{m+m_2}$, and $U=\mathrm{diag}(u)$, $V=\mathrm{diag}(v)$.

Lemma 3.1. *For any given $\theta_0^0=(w^0,v^0)\in\Omega_1(1)\times R_{++}^{m_1}$, then the equation $H(\theta,\theta_0^0,1)=0$ has a unique solution $\theta=(\theta_0^0,0)^{\mathrm{T}}$.*

Proof. When $t=1$, (3.5) becomes

$$\begin{aligned}&\nabla_w h(w,1)\lambda+w-w^0=0,\\&h(w,1)=0,\\&V\tilde{g}(w)=V^0\tilde{g}(w^0).\end{aligned}$$

By $\tilde{g}(w)<0$ and $h(w,1)=0$, we have $I(w)=\varnothing$ and $w\in\Omega_1(1)$, then by Condition (A.4) and $\nabla_w h(w,1)\lambda+w-w^0=0$, we have $\lambda=0$, $w=w^0$, hence $v=v^0$ and $\theta=(\theta_0^0,0)^{\mathrm{T}}\in\Omega(1)$.

In some cases, we rewrite (3.5) as follows form:

$$H_{\theta_0^0}(\theta,t)=H(\theta,\theta_0^0,t),$$

and the solution set of H as follows:

$$H_{\theta_0^0}^{-1}(0)=\{(\theta,t)\in\Omega(t)\times(0,1]:H_{\theta_0^0}(\theta,t)=0\}.$$

The following parameterized Sard theorem on the smooth manifold will be used in our paper.

Lemma 3.2 (Parameterized Sard theorem [4]). *Let Q, N and P be smooth manifolds of dimensions q, m and p, respectively. And let $\Phi:Q\times N\to P$ be a C^r map, where $r>$*

$max\{0, m-p\}$. If $0\in P$ is a regular value of Φ, then for almost all $a\in Q$, 0 is a regular value of $\Phi_a \equiv \Phi(a, \cdot)$.

Lemma 3.3. *If $H(\theta, \theta_0^0, t)$ is defined as (3.5) and Condition (A.1)−(A.5) is true, then for almost all $\theta^0=(\theta_0^0, 0)^T\in\Omega(1)$, 0 is the regular value of map H, and $H_{\theta_0^0}^{-1}(0)$ consists of some smooth curves, which starts from $(\theta^0, 1)$, denoted by $\Gamma_{\theta_0^0}$.*

Proof. $\forall (\theta, t)\in\Omega(t)\times(0,1]$,

$$\frac{\partial H(\theta,\theta_0^0,t)}{\partial(w,w^0,v^0)}=\begin{pmatrix} Q & -tI & 0\\ \nabla_w h(w,t)^T & 0 & 0\\ V\nabla\tilde{g}(w)^T & -tV^0\nabla_{w^0}\tilde{g}(w^0) & -t\mathrm{diag}(\tilde{g}(w^0))\end{pmatrix}$$

where

$$Q=(1-t)\left(\nabla^2\tilde{f}(w)+\sum_{i=1}^{m_1}v_i\nabla^2\tilde{g}_i(w)\right)+\sum_{i=1}^{m+m_2}\lambda_i\nabla_w^2 h_i(w,t)+tI.$$

By $w^0\in\Omega_1(1)$, $\tilde{g}(w^0)<0$, and since $\nabla_w h(w,t)$ is full column rank, then we have $\partial H(\theta, \theta_0^0, t)/\partial(w,w^0,v^0)$ is full row rank. Hence, $\partial H(\theta,\theta_0^0,t)/\partial(\theta,\theta_0^0,t)$ is also full row rank, and 0 is a regular value.

By parameterized Sard theorem on smooth manifold, for almost all $(\theta^0, 0)^T\in\Omega(t)$, 0 is a regular value of $H(\theta,\theta_0^0,t)$. By the inverse image theorem, $H_{\theta_0^0}^{-1}(0)$ consists of some smooth curves. And, because $H_{\theta_0^0}((\theta_0^0,0)T,1)=0$, there must be a smooth $\Gamma_{\theta_0^0}$ starting from$((\theta_0^0,0)^T,1)$.

Lemma 3.4. *Suppose that Condition A hold. Given $\theta^0\in\Omega(t)$, if 0 is a regular value of H, then $\Gamma_{\theta_0^0}$ is a bounded curve in $\Omega(t)\times(0,1]$.*

Proof. Suppose $\Gamma_{\theta_0^0}\subset\Omega(t)\times(0,1]$ is unbounded, then there exists $\{(\theta^k,t_k)\}\subset\Gamma_{\theta_0^0}$, and $\|(\theta^k,t_k)\|\to\infty$. Noting that (x,y) and $t\in(0,1]$ is bounded, hence, by Lemma 2.1, (x^k,y^k,u^k) is bounded, then there exists a subsequence of $\{(v_i^k,\lambda_i^k)\}$ (denoted also by $\{(v_i^k,\lambda_i^k)\}$), which goes to infinity, we set (v_i^k,λ_i^k) is unbounded. Let

$$I_1=\{i\in\{1,\cdots,m_1\}:v_i^k\to\infty\},\quad I_2=\{i\in\{1,\cdots,m+m_2\}:\lambda_i^k\to\infty\}.$$

By $H(\theta^k,\theta_0^0,t_k)=0$, i. e., (θ^k,t_k) satises

$$H(\theta,\theta_0^0,t)=\begin{pmatrix}(1-t)(\nabla\tilde{f}(w)+\nabla\tilde{g}(w)v+\nabla_w h(w,t)\lambda+t(w-w^0)\\ h(w,t)\\ V\tilde{g}(w)-tV^0\tilde{g}(w^0)\end{pmatrix}=0,$$

we have

(i) when $t^*\in[0,1)$, by $\{w^k\}$ is bounded, and $\tilde{f},\tilde{g},h$ is sucient smooth, and if $k\to\infty$, then $I_1\subset I(w)$, and

$$\left(\sum_{i\in I_1}v_i^k\nabla\tilde{g}_i(w^k)+\sum_{i\in I_2}\lambda_i^k\nabla_w h_i(w^k,t_k)\right)\Big/\min_{i\in I_1,j\in I_2}\{|v_i^k|,|\lambda_j^k|\}\to 0,$$

this contradicts to Condition (A.3);

(ii) when $t^*=1$, by the third equation of (3.5), we get $I_1=I(w)$, hence, we have

$$\sum_{i\in I} v_i^k \nabla \tilde{g}_i(w^k) + \nabla_w h(w^k, t_k)\lambda^k + w - w^0 = 0,$$

and this contradicts to Condition (A. 4). Hence, $\{(v^k, \lambda^k)\}$ is bounded, and the result is true.

By Lemmas 3. 3 and 3. 4, we get our main result.

Theorem 3. 5. *Suppose that Condition A hold. Then (3. 4) has solution as t is descending to 0, for almost all $\theta^0 \in \Omega(t)$, $H_{\theta_0^0}^{-1}(0)$ contains a smooth curve, which stars from $(\theta^0, 1)$. As $t \to 0$, the limit set $\Theta \times \{0\} \subset \Omega(1) \times \{0\}$ of $\Gamma_{\theta_0^0}$ is nonempty, and every point of Θ is a solution of (3. 4), i. e., the* K-K-T *solution. Especially, if $\Gamma_{\theta_0^0}$ is finite, and $(\theta^*, 0)$ is the end point of $\Gamma_{\theta_0^0}$, then θ^* is a the* K-K-T *solution.*

Proof. By Lemma 3. 3, for almost all $\theta^0 \in \Omega(t)$, 0 is a regular value of $H_{\theta_0^0}$, and $\Gamma_{\theta_0^0}$ consists of somes mooth curves, among them, a smooth curve is starting from $(\theta^0, 1)$.

By the classication theorem of one-dimensional smooth manifold, $\Gamma_{\theta_0^0}$ is diffeomorphic to a unit circle or the unit interval $(0, 1]$. Because

$$\frac{\partial H_{\theta_0^0}(\theta, 1)}{\partial \theta}\Big|_{\theta=(w^0, v^0, 0)}$$

$$= \begin{pmatrix} \sum_{i=1}^{m+m_2} \lambda_i \nabla_w^2 h(w^0, 1) + I & 0 & \nabla_w h(w^0, 1) \\ \nabla_w h(w^0, 1)^T & 0 & 0 \\ V^0 \nabla \tilde{g}(w^0)^T & \mathrm{diag}(\tilde{g}(w^0)) & 0 \end{pmatrix} \tag{3. 6}$$

By $\tilde{g}(w^0) < 0$, we have $\partial H_{\theta_0^0}((\theta_0^0, 0)^T, 1)/\partial\theta$ is nonsingular, hence $\Gamma_{\theta_0^0}$ is diffeomorphic to unit interval. Let (w^*, t^*) be a limit point of $\Gamma_{\theta_0^0}$, then three cases are possible.

(i) $(\theta, t^*) \in \Omega(t^*) \times \{1\}$;

(ii) $(\theta, t^*) \in \partial\Omega(t^*) \times (0, 1]$;

(iii) $(\theta, t^*) \in \partial\Omega(t^*) \times \{0\}$.

By Lemma 3. 1 and the equation $H(\theta, \theta_0^0, 1) = 0$ has only one solution$((\theta_0^0, 0)^T, 1)$ in $\Omega(1) \times \{1\}$, the case (i) is impossible. In case (ii), there must exist a sequence of $(\theta^k, t_k) \in \Gamma_{\theta_0^0}$ such that $1 \leqslant j \leqslant m_1$, $g_j(x^k, y^k) \to 0$. From the third equation (3. 5), it follows that $\| v_j^k \| \to \infty$, which contradicts Lemma 3. 4. Thus, case (ii) is impossible. As a conclusion, (iii) is the only possible case.

4. The predictor-corrector algorithm for homotopy equation

In this section, we discuss how to trace numerically the homotopy equation (3. 5). By Theorem 3. 5, for almost all $\theta^0 \in \Omega(t)$, the homotopy (3. 5) generates a smooth curve $\Gamma_{\theta_0^0}$. We call $\Gamma_{\theta_0^0}$ the homotopy path. Tracing numerically from $(\theta^0, 1)$ until $\mu \to 0$, one can find a solution of (3. 4). The tangent-vector at a point on $\Gamma_{\theta_0^0}$ has two opposite directions, one (the positive direction) makes s increase, and another (the negative direction) makes s decrease. The negative direction will lead us back to the initial point, so we must go along the positive direction. The criterion in step 1 (b) of Algorithm 1 that determines the positive direction is based on a basic theory of homotopy method(see[10, 5,4]), that is, the positive direction η at any point (w,t) on $\Gamma_{\theta_0^0}$ keeps the sign of the determinant

$$\begin{vmatrix} H'_{\theta_0^0}(\theta^0,1) \\ \eta^T \end{vmatrix}$$

invariant. Then we can determine the direction by following result.

Proposition 4.1 ([Garcia and Zangwill[10], Allgower and Georg[5]]). *If Γ is smooth, then the positive direction $\eta^{(0)}$ at the initial point $(\theta_0^0,0)^{\mathrm{T}}$ satisfies*

$$\operatorname{sign}\begin{vmatrix} H'_{\theta_0^0}(\theta^0,1) \\ \eta^T \end{vmatrix} = (-1)^{m+m_1+m_2+1}.$$

We give algorithm as follows.

Algorithm 1 (Euler-Newton method). (0) Give $t_0=1$, an initial point $\theta^0\in\Omega(1)$, step length $h_0>0$ and two small positive numbers $\varepsilon_1, t_\varepsilon>0, k:=0$.

(1) Compute a predictor point$(\theta^{(k+1,0)}, t_{k+1,0})$:

(a) Compute a unit tangent vector $\xi^{(k)}\in R^{n+2m+m_1+m_2+1}$;

(b) Determine the direction $\eta^{(k)}$ of predictor step:

If the sign of the determinant

$$\begin{vmatrix} H'_{\theta_0^0}(\theta^{(k)},t_k) \\ \xi^{(k)^{\mathrm{T}}} \end{vmatrix} = (-1)^{m+m_1+m_2+1},$$

then $\eta^{(k)}=\xi^{(k)}$, else if the sign of the determinant

$$\begin{vmatrix} H'_{\theta_0^0}(\theta^{(k)},t_k) \\ \xi^{(k)^{\mathrm{T}}} \end{vmatrix} = (-1)^{m+m_1+m_2},$$

then $\eta^{(k)}=-\xi^{(k)}$;

(c) $(\theta^{(k,0)},t_{k,0})=(\theta^{(k)},t_k)+h_k\eta^{(k)}$.

(2) Compute a corrector point $(\theta^{(k+1)},t_{k+1})$:

$$(\theta^{(k+1,j)},t_{k+1,j}) = (\theta^{(k,j-1)},t_{k,j-1}) - M^{+}_{k,j-1}H_{\theta_0^0}(\theta^{(k,j)},t_{k,j}),\quad j=1,2\cdots$$

until $\| H_{\theta_0^{(0)}}(\theta^{(k+1,j)},t_{k+1,j})\| \leqslant \varepsilon_1$. Set$(\theta^{(k+1)},t_{k+1}) = (\theta^{(k+1,j)} t_{k+1,j})$.

(3) If $t_{k+1}\leqslant t_\varepsilon$, then stop, else choose a new step-length $h_{k+1}>0$. $k:=k+1$, and go to(1).

In Algorithm 1,

$$M_{k,j-1} = H'_{\theta_0^0}(\theta^{k,j-1},t_{k,j-1}),\ \text{and}\ M^{+}=M^{\mathrm{T}}(MM^{\mathrm{T}})^{-1} \tag{4.1}$$

is the Moore-Penrose inverse of M.

5. The numerical examples

Employing the interior homotopy method, several examples problem are solved below. Simple path-following experiments show that this algorithm is effective and convenient. We set $(\overline{u}^{(0)},\overline{v}^{(0)})^T=(1,\cdots,1)^T\in R^{m_2+m_1}$, and set a small parameter $t_\varepsilon=1.e-2$ and $\varepsilon_1=1.e-6$.

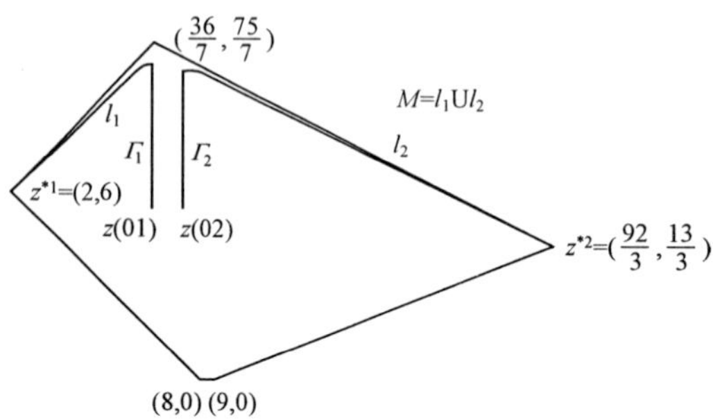

Fig. 1. The pathways Γ_i for different initial points $z^{(0i)}$, $i=1,2$.

Example 5.1. (Nonsmooth and nonconvex feasible set). Consider the bilevel optimization problem

$$
\begin{aligned}
\min_{x,y}\quad & x+5y\\
\text{s. t.}\quad & x\geqslant 0,\\
& \min_{y}\quad -y\\
& \text{s. t.}\quad y\geqslant 0,\\
& \qquad\ \ x+y\geqslant 8,\\
& \qquad\ \ -3x+2y\leqslant 6,\\
& \qquad\ \ x+4y\leqslant 48,\\
& \qquad\ \ x-5y\leqslant 9.
\end{aligned}
$$

Given x, denote the solution of the following problem by $S(x)$. Then the problem become a nonconvex optimization

$$
\begin{aligned}
\min_{x,y}\quad & x+5y\\
\text{s. t.}\quad & (x,y)\in M.
\end{aligned}
$$

The feasible set $\mathscr{M}=\{(x,y)\mid x\geqslant 0, y\in S(x)\}=l_1\cup l_2$, here $l_1=\{(2,6)+s\left(\frac{22}{7},\frac{33}{7}\right):s\in[0,1]\}$ and $l_2=\left\{\left(\frac{36}{7},\frac{75}{7}\right)+s\left(\frac{536}{21},-\frac{134}{21}\right):s\in[0,1]\right\}$. For convenience, denote $z=(x,y)^T$. The local optimal solutions are $z^{*1}=(2,6)$ and $z^{*2}=\left(30\frac{2}{3},4\frac{1}{3}\right)$.

It is easy for condition (A.1)-(A.3) and (A.5) to validate. By geometrical interpretation of condition (A.4), we can get that condition (A.4) is satised from Fig. 1. Thus, we choose the interior point of all constraints $\overline{z}^{(01)}=(5,5.5)$, then we get the corrector point$(z^{(0)},u^{(0)},v^{(0)})=(5,10.1342,1,0.0094,0.0061,0.2370,0.1478,0.010,1.0000)$, and $f(z^{(0)})=55.6710$, $\|H_0(w^{(0)},t_0)\|=8.7646$. Using Algorithm 1, when satisfying $t_k < t_\varepsilon$ and $\| H_0(w^{(k)}, t_k) \| = 8.37197e-07 < \varepsilon_1$. After 34 steps iterations, we get following result

x	g	f
2.0002	−2.0002	31.9998

y	G_1	G_2	G_3	G_4	G_5
5.9999	−5.9999	−0.0001	−0.0008	−22.0001	−36.9994

and the pathway Γ_1 is as Fig. 1;

We choose the interior point of all constraints $\bar{z}^{(01)} = (7, 5.5)$, then we get the corrector point$(z^{(0)}, u^{(0)}, v^{(0)}) = (7.0000, 9.9174, 1.0000, 0.0096, 0.0088, 0.0387, 0.2476, 0.0099, 1.0000)$, and $f(z^{(0)}) = 56.5868$, $\| H_0(w^{(0)}, t_0) \| = 8.1843$. Using Algorithm 1, when satisfying $t_k < t_\varepsilon$ and $\| H_0(w^{(k)}, t_k) \| = 2.38174e-07 < \varepsilon_1$. After 34 steps iterations, we get following result:

x	g	f
30.6481	−30.6481	52.3288

y	G_1	G_2	G_3	G_4	G_5
4.3361	−4.3361	−26.9842	−89.2720	−0.0074	−0.0326

and the pathway Γ_2 is as Fig. 1;

Example 5.2.

$$\begin{aligned} \min_{x,y} \quad & (x-3.5)^2 + (y+4)^2 \\ \text{s.t.} \quad & \min_{y} \quad (y-3)^2, \\ & \text{s.t.} \quad y^2 - x \leqslant 0. \end{aligned}$$

Given x, denote the solution of the following problem by $S(x)$. Then the problem become a nonconvex optimization

$$\begin{aligned} \min_{x,y} \quad & (x-3.5)^2 + (y+4)^2 \\ \text{s.t.} \quad & (x,y) \in M. \end{aligned}$$

Therefore, the feasible set $\mathcal{M} = \{(x,y) \mid y \in S(x)\} = l_1 \cup l_2$, here $l_1 = \{(x,y): y = \sqrt{x}, x \in [0,9]\}$ and $l_2 = \{(x,y): y = 3, x \geqslant 9\}$, the local optimal solution is $z^* = (1,1)$.

We choose the interior point of all constraints $\bar{z}^{(0)} = (4.5, -2)$, then we get the corrector point$(z^{(0)}, u^{(0)}, v^{(0)}) = (4.5000, 2.1164, 0.4175, 1.0000)$, and $f(z^{(0)}) = 38.4106$, $\| H_0(w^{(0)}, t_0) \| = 4.8673$. Using Algorithm 1, when satisfying $t_k < t_\varepsilon$ and $\| H_0(w^{(k)}, t_k) \| = 5{:}30775e-08 < \varepsilon_1$. After 18 steps iterations, we get following result:

x	f
1.0071	31.2498

y	G
1.0035	−0.0001

and the pathway Γ is as following (Fig. 2).

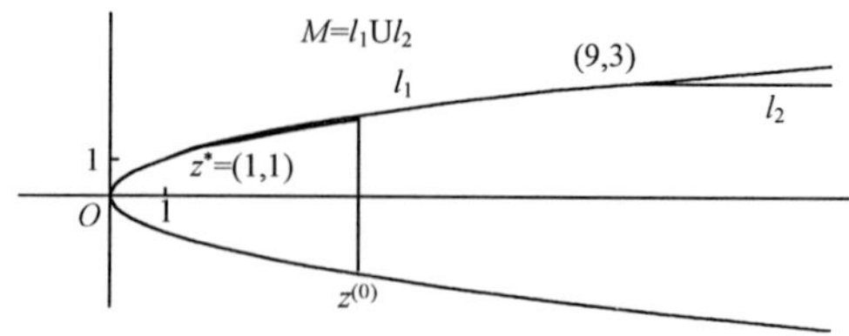

Fig. 2. The pathway Γ for the initial points $z^{(0)}$.

References

[1] E. Aiyoshi, K. Shimizu, Hierarchical decentralized systems and its new solution by a barrier method, IEEE Trans. Syst. Man Cybern. 11 (1981) 444-449.

[2] E. Aiyoshi, K. Shimizu, A solution method for the static constrained Stackelberg problem via penalty method, IEEE Trans. Automat. Contr. 34 (1992) 1111-1114.

[3] F. A. Al-Khayal, R. Horst, P. M. Pardalos, Global optimization of convex functions subject to quadratic constrains: an application in nonlinear bilevel programming, Ann. Oper. Res. 34 (1992) 125-147.

[4] E. L. Allgower, K. Georg, Numerical Continuation Methods: An Introduction, Springer, Berlin, New York, 1990.

[5] E. L. Allgower, K. Georg, Simplicial and continuation methods for approximating xed points and solutions to systems of equations, SIAM Rev. 22 (1980) 28-85.

[6] Z. Bi, P. H. Calamai, A. R. Conn, An exact penalty function approach for the nonlinear bilevel programming problem, Technical Report 180-O-170591, Department of Systems Design Engineering, University of Waterloo, 1991.

[7] L. M. Case, An l_1 penalty function approach to the nonlinear bilevel programming problem, Ph. D. Thesis, University of Waterloo, Ontario, Canada, 1999.

[8] R. G. Cassidy, M. J. L. Kriby, W. M. Raike, Ecient distribution ofresources through three level of government, Manage. Sci. 17 (8) (1971) 462.

[9] T. Edmunds, J. F. Bard, Algorithms for nonlinear bilevel mathematical programming, IEEE Trans. Syst. Man Cybern. 21 (1) (1991) 83-89.

[10] J. Fortuny-amat, B. McCarl, A representation and economic interpretation of a two-level programming problem, J. Oper. Res. Soc. 32 (1981) 783-792.

[11] C. B. Garcia, W. I. Zangwill, Pathways to Solutions, Fixed Points and Equilibria, Prentice-Hall, Englewood Clis, NJ, 1981.

[12] B. F. Hobbs, S. K. Nelson, A nonlinear bilevel model for analysis of electric utility demand-side planning issues, Ann. Oper. Res. 34 (1992) 255.

[13] Y. Ishizuka, E. Aiyoshi, Double penalty methodfor bilevel optimization problem, Ann. Oper. Res. 34 (1992) 73-88.

[14] C. D. Kolstad, L. S. Lasdon, Derivative estimation and computational experience with large bilevel mathematical programs, J. Optimiz. Theory Appl. 65 (1990) 484-499.

[15] P. B. Luh, Y. Ho, R. Muralidaran, Load adaptive pricing: an emerging tool for electric utilities, IEEE Trans. Auto. Contr. 27 (2) (1982) 320.

[16] Z. Q. Luo, J. S. Pang, D. Ralph, Mathematical Programs with Equilibrium Constraints, Cambridge University Press, Cambridge, 1996.

[17] P. Marcotte, D. L. Zhu, Exact and inexact penalty methods for the generalized bilevel programming problem, Math. Program. 74 (1996) 141-157.

[18] P. G. McCormick, The projective SUMT method for convex programming, Math. Oper. Res. 14 (1989) 203-223.

[19] H. Onal, D. H. Darmawan, S. H. Johnson III, A mulitilevel analysis of agricultural credit distribution in East Java, Indonesia, Comp. Oper. Res. 22 (2) (1995) 227.

[20] G. Savard, J. Gauvin, The steepest descent direction for the nonlinear bilevel programming problem, Oper. Res. Lett. 15 (1994) 265-272.

[21] K. Shimizu, E. Aiyoshi, A new computational method for Stackelberg and min-max problems by use of a penalty method, IEEE Trans. Automat. Contr. 26 (1981) 460-466.

[22] H. Von Stackelberg, The Theory of the Market Economy, Oxford University Press, Oxford, England, 1952.

Published in *Nonlinear Analysis*, 2004, 57

New necessary optimality conditions for bilevel programs by combined MPEC and the value function approach*

Jane J. Ye* and Daoli Zhu**

Abstract. The bilevel programming problem is a sequence of two optimization problems where the constraint region of the upper level problem is determined implicitly by the solution set to the lower level problem. The classical approach to solve such a problem is to replace the lower level problem by its Karush-Kuhn-Tucker(KKT) condition and solve the resulting mathematical programming problem with equilibrium constraints(MPEC). In general the classical approach is not valid for nonconvex bilevel programming problems. The value function approach uses the value function of the lower level problem to define an equivalent single level problem. But the resulting problem requires a strong assumption such as the partial calmness codition for the KKT condition to hold. In this paper we combine the classical and the value function approaches to derive new necessary optimality conditions under rather weak conditions. The required conditions are even weaker in the case where the classical approach or the value function approach alone are valid.

Key words necessary optimality conditions, partial calmness, constraint qualifications, nonsmooth analysis, value function, bilevel programming problems.
AMS subject classification: 90C46, 90C26

1. Introduction

In this paper we consider the following bilevel programming problem(BLPP):

$$\text{BLPP} \quad \min_{x,y} \; F(x,y) \quad \text{s. t.} \; y \in S(x), \; G(x,y) \leqslant 0$$

where $S(x)$ denotes the set of solutions of the lower level problem:

---

*Department of Mathematics and Statistics, University of Victoria, Victoria, B. C. , Canada V8P 5C2, e-mail: janeye @math. uvic. ca. Theres earch of this author was partially supported by NSERC.

**School of Management, Fudan University, Shanghai 200433, People's Republic of China. This research was supported by the National Natural Science Foundation of China, NSFC.

$$P_x: \quad \min_y \quad f(x,y)$$
$$\text{s. t.} \quad g(x,y) \leqslant 0$$

and $F, f: R^n \times R^m \to R, G: R^n \times R^m \to R^q, g: R^n \times R^m \to R^p$. We allow p or q to be zero to signify the case in which there are no explicit inequality constraints. In these cases it is clear below that certain references to such constraints are simply to be deleted.

To simplify the exposition and to concentrate on the main ideas, we assume that all defining mappings F, G, f, g are twice continuously difierentiable and we do not include equality constraints. The results can be easily generalized to the case of the presence of equality constraints in a straightforward manner.

Although the bilevel programming problem was only introduced to the optimization community in the seventies of the 20th century by Bracken and McGill[3], the first formulation of a simpler case was introduced and used on market economy by Stackelberg [17]in 1934 and hence is also known as a Stackelberg game in economic game theory. Bilevel programming problems can be used tomodel a two-level hierarchical system where the higher level(the leader) and the lower level(the follower)must find vectors $x \in R^n$ and $y \in R^m$, respectively to minimize their individual objective functions $F(x,y)$ and $f(x,y)$ subject to certain constraints. The leader is assumed to select his decision vector first and the follower after that. Under these assumptions on the order of the play, the game will proceed as follows: For any possible decision vector $x \in R^n$ chosen by the leader, the follower will react optimally by choosing his decision vector $y \in R^m$ to minimize the objective function $f(x,y)$ subject to constraints $g(x,y) \leqslant 0$. Assume also that if the solution set $S(x)$ of the lower level problem is not a singleton, the follower allows the leader to choose which of them is actually used. Hence now the leader chooses his optimal decision vector $x \in R^n$ and $y \in S(x)$ to minimize his objective function $F(x,y)$ subject to the constraints $G(x,y) \leqslant 0$. The BLLPP has been a hot research area over the last twenty years and many researchers have made contributions to the area. The reader is referred to monographs[1,8,16] for applications of bilevel programming and recent developments on the subject, and to [9,18] for a bibliography review.

The classical Karush-Kuhn-Tucker (KKT) approach (also called the first order approach) to derive necessary optimality conditions for BLPP(see e. g. [2]) was to replace the lower level problem by its KKT conditions and the problem of constraint qualification is usually neglected. This approach, however, is only applicable to *convex* bilevel programming problems, i. e. , those bilevel programming problems where the lower level problem is convex, i. e. $f(x, \cdot), g_i(x, \cdot)$ are convex functions, and a certain contraint qualification is satisfied for the lower leve. Moreover the resultiong single level proglem belongs to the class of mathmatical programs with equlibrium constraints or MPECs([11,15]) and it is known that the usual constraint qualifications such as Mangasarian Fromovitz constraint qualification(MFCQ) will never hold(see [26, Proposition

1.1]). Recently some useful optimality conditions for MPECs such as the M-stationary condition(associated with the generalized calculus developed by Mordukhovich[13])and the C-stationary condition(associated with the Clarke generalized gradient) which are weaker than the classical KKT condition and the corresponding constraint qualifications are developed (see [20,22] for detailed discussions).

Dempe [7] and Outrata [14] derived necessary conditions for the case where the solution set $S(x)=\{y(x)\}$ is a singleton by minimizing the objective function $F(x,y(x))$ over all x satisfying constraints $G(x,y(x))\leqslant 0$. This approach, however, requires that the solution set $S(x)$ is a singleton and the map $y(x)$ has certain differentiability properties.

InYe and Zhu [24,25], the following value function approach is taken to reformulate the BLPP. Define *the value function of the lower level problem* as an extended value function $V:R^n\rightarrow\overline{R}$ by

$$V(x):=\inf_y\{f(x,y):g(x,y)\leqslant 0\}$$

where $\overline{R}:=R\cup\{-\infty\}\cup\{+\infty\}$ is the extended real line and $\inf\{\varnothing\}=+\infty$ by convention. Then it is obvious that the BLLP can bereformulated as the following single level optimization problem involving the value function:

$$\begin{aligned}(\text{SP})\quad \min\quad & F(x,y)\\ s.t.\quad & f(x,y)-V(x)\leqslant 0,\\ & g(x,y)\leqslant 0,\\ & G(x,y)\leqslant 0.\end{aligned}\tag{1}$$

The above single level problem is completely equivalent to the BLPP without any convexity assumption on the lower level problem. However there are two issues needed to be addressed when using this approach. First, it is well known that $V(x)$ may not be differentiable in general even in the case where all defining functions f, g are continuously differentiable and hence the problem (SP) is in general a nonsmooth problem. To use the generalized Lagrange multiplier rule of Clarke[4], $V(x)$ is required to be Lipschitz continuous. This issue can be addressed if the lower level problem is assumed to satisfy the MFCQ at the optimal solution and the constraint mapping is assumed to be uniformly bounded. Secondly, since the constraint(1)is actually an equality constraint, the nonsmooth MFCQ for the sing lelevel problem (SP) will never be satisfied([24, Proposition3.2]). To copy with this difficulty, the partial calmness condition was suggested by [24,25]as a condition under which a local optimal solution of BLPP satisfies the generalized Lagrange multiplier rule of Clarke. This condition assumes that the local optimal solution of BLPP is a local optimal solution of the partial penalized problem where the constraint (1) is omitted but the violation of the constraint is penalized. The value function approach was further developed in Ye[21,23]using other constraint qualifications such as Abadie constraint qualification.

Unfortunately optimal solutions of many *nonconvex* bilevel programming problems where the lower level problem is not convex do not satisfy the KKT conditions derived by using either the MPEC approach or the value function approach. In this paper we derive a new KKT condition by using a new approach which is a combination of the classical KKT and the value function approach. The resulting necessary optimality condition is much more likely to hold since it contains the ones derived by using the MPEC and the value function approach as special cases. In the case where the lower level problem is convex or the lower level problem has a unique solution and a unique multiplier at the optimal solution of the bilevel problem, the resulting KKT condition reduces to either the S-stationary condition or the M-stationary condition by using the MPEC approach and in the case where the multipliers corresponding to the KKT conditions of the lower level problem are zero, it reduces to the KKT condition derived by using the value function approach. And even in these cases our sufficient conditions for the KKT conditions to hold at a local optimal solution are new and weaker than some of the existing conditions.

In this paper we adopt the following standard notation. For any two vectors a, b in R^n, we denote by $\langle a, b\rangle$ its inner product. Given a function $F: R^n \to R^m$, we denote its Jacobian by $\nabla F(z) \in R^{m\times n}$. If $m=1$, the gradient $\nabla F(z) \in R^n$ is considered as a column vector. Given a function $f: R^n \times R^m \to R$, we denote by $\nabla^2_{xy} f(x,y) := \nabla_x(\nabla_y f(x,y))$, $\nabla^2_{yy} f(x,y) := \nabla_y(\nabla_y f(x,y))$. For a subset $A \subseteq R^n$, we denote by int A, co$A$ the interior and the convex hull of A respectively. For a matrix $A \in R^{n\times m}$, A^T is its transpose.

Let $\varphi: R^n \to R$ be Lipschitz continuous near $\bar{x}$, the directional derivative and the Clarke generalized directional derivative of φ at $\bar{x}$ in direction $d \in R^n$ are defined by

$$\varphi'(\bar{x}; d) := \lim_{t\downarrow 0} \frac{\varphi(\bar{x}+td)-\varphi(\bar{x})}{t}$$

$$\varphi^\circ(\bar{x}; d) := \limsup_{x\to\bar{x}, t\downarrow 0} \frac{\varphi(x+td)-\varphi(x)}{t}$$

respectively. The Clarke generalized gradient at $\bar{x}$ is a convex and compact subset of R^n defined by

$$\partial\varphi(\bar{x}) := \{\xi \in R^n : \xi^T d \leqslant \varphi^\circ(\bar{x}; d) \quad \forall d \in R^n\}.$$

When φ is convex, the Clarke generalized gradient coincides with the subgradient in the sense of convex analysis, i. e. ,

$$\partial\varphi(\bar{x}) := \{\xi \in R^n : \xi^T(x-\bar{x}) \leqslant \varphi(x)-\varphi(\bar{x}) \quad \forall x \in R^n\}.$$

When φ is continuously differentiable, the Clarke generalized gradient is reduced to the usual gradient, i. e. , $\partial\varphi(\bar{x}) = \{\nabla\varphi(\bar{x})\}$. The following calculation rules for Clarke generalized gradients will be useful in the paper.

Proposition 1.1(see[4,5]) *Let $f, g: R^n \to R$ be Lipschitz continuous near $\bar{x} \in R^n$ and α, β be* *any real numbers. Then*

$$\partial(\alpha f+\beta g)(\overline{x})\subseteq \alpha\partial f(\overline{x})+\beta\partial g(\overline{x}).$$

We organize our paper as follows. In section 2, we use a simple example to illustrate our approach and in the mean time derive a KKT condition for the special case of the bilevel programming problem where the lower level has no constraints. In section 3 we provide our results for the general bilevel programming problem. We conclude our paper with some illustrate examples in section 4.

2. An example

To illustrate the problem and the approach, we consider the following example from Mirrlee [12].

Example 2.1 (Mirrlees' problem)

$$\text{BLPP} \quad \min \quad F(x,y)=(x-2)^2+(y-1)^2$$
$$s.t. \quad y \; minimizes f\ (x,y)=-xe^{-(y+1)^2}-e^{-(y-1)2}.$$

The first order condition for minimization of the lower level objective function with respect to y is

$$x(y+1)e^{-(y+1)2}+(y-1)e^{-(y-1)2}=0.$$

Hence each x and y, a stationary point of the lower level problem are related by the equation

$$x=\frac{1-y}{1+y}e^{4y}, \tag{2}$$

which is a smooth and connected curve as shown in Figurel.

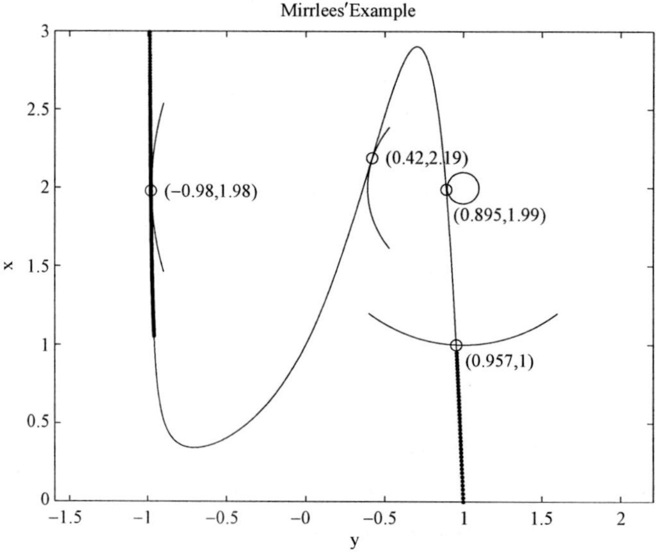

Figure 1: The first order approach fails

Since the objective of the lower level problem is not convex as afunction of y, for each fixed x, not all corresponding $y's$ lying on the curve are global optimal solutions of the lower level problem. The true global optimal solutions for the lower level problem are indentified as a disconnected curved with a jump at $\overline{x}=1$ (the darken curve in Figure1) which represents the feasible region of the bilevel program.

Although at $\overline{x}=1$, both $\overline{y}=0.957$ and $y_1=-0.957$ are the global solution of the lower level problem, the global optimal solution of the Mirrlees' problem is shown to be $\overline{x}=1, \overline{y}=0.957$. However by the classical first order approach, one would consider the optimization problem with the first order condition (2) as constraint and find three solutions $(x,y)=(0.895,1.99)$, $(x,y)=(0.42,2.19)$, $(x,y)=(-0.98,1.98)$ to the Lagrange multiplier rule. Since these three solutions do not include the optimal solution $(\overline{x},\overline{y})=(1,0.957)$, by using the first order approach, one would miss the optimal solution of the bilevel program completely.

The solution of Mirrlees' problem will not change if we add the constraint $y\in[-2, 2]$ into the lower level problem. Hence $\overline{x}=1, \overline{y}=0.957$ is still the optimal solution to the bilevel programming problem

$$\begin{aligned} \min \quad & F(x,y) = (x-2)^2+(y-1)^2 \\ s.t. \quad & y \in S(x) \end{aligned}$$

where $S(x)$ is the solution of the lower level problem

$$\min_y f(x,y) := -xe^{-(y+1)^2} - e^{-(y-1)^2} \quad s.t. \quad y \in [-2, 2].$$

The value function for the lower level problem is

$$V(x) = \min_{y\in[-2,2]} -xe^{-(y+1)^2} - e^{-(y-1)^2}$$

By the value function approach, Mirrlees' problem is equivalent to the following sing lelevel optimization problem:

$$\begin{aligned} (SP) \quad \min \quad & F(x,y) = (x-2)^2+(y-1)^2 \\ s.t. \quad & f(x,y)-V(x) \leqslant 0, \\ & y \in [-2, 2]. \end{aligned}$$

The following result can be obtained from Danskin's Theorem stated on page 99 of [5] (also see [6]).

Proposition 2.1(**Danskin'sTheorem**) *Let $S\subseteq R^m$ be a compact set and $f(x,y)$ be a function on $R^n\times R^m$ that is continuously differentiable at $\overline{x}$. Then the value function*

$$V(x) = \min\{f(x,y): y \in S\}$$

is Lipschitz and directionally differentiable at $\overline{x}$. Let $S(\overline{x})$ denote the solution of the lower level problem. Then the Clarke generalized gradientat $\overline{x}$ and the directional derivative of V at $\overline{x}$ indirection dx are

$$\partial V(\overline{x}) = co\{\nabla x f(\overline{x},y'): y' \in S(\overline{x})\}$$

and

$$V'(\overline{x};dx) = \min\{\nabla_x f(\overline{x},y')^T dx : y' \in S(\overline{x})\},$$

where coA denotes the convex hull of set A.

By Danskin's theorem, the single level problem (SP) is an optimization problem with Lipschitz continuous and continuously differentiable problem data. By the nonsmooth generalized Lagrange multiplier rule of Clarke[4, Theorem 6.1.1], there exist nonnegative scalars λ, μ not all zero such that

$$0 \in \lambda \nabla_x F(\overline{x},\overline{y}) + \mu[\nabla_x f(\overline{x},\overline{y}) - \partial V(\overline{x})], \tag{3}$$

$$0 = \lambda \nabla_y F(\overline{x},\overline{y}) + \mu \nabla_y f(\overline{x},\overline{y}). \tag{4}$$

Since $\overline{y}=0.957$ is an interior point of $[-2,2]$ and it is an optimal solution of the lower level problem, $\nabla_y f(\overline{x},\overline{y})=0$. But $\nabla_y F(\overline{x},\overline{y})\neq 0$. So the above Lagrange multiplier rule only holds if $\lambda=0$. Hence the KKT condition by using the value function approach does not hold at the optimal solution and hence will miss the optimal solution completely as well.

We now consider the following optimization problem in which we add the first order condition to the problem (SP).

$$\begin{aligned} \text{(P)} \quad \min \quad & F(x,y) = (x-2)^2 + (y-1)^2 \\ \text{s.t.} \quad & f(x,y) - V(x) \leqslant 0, \\ & \nabla_y f(x,y) = 0, \\ & y \in [-2, 2]. \end{aligned} \tag{5}$$

Since the first order condition holds at $(\overline{x},\overline{y})$, the constraint (5) is basically an extra constraint and hence $(\overline{x},\overline{y})$ is still the optimal solution of the above problem. By the no nsmooth generalized Lagrange multiplier rule of Clarke[4]. There exist $\lambda\geqslant 0$, $\mu\geqslant 0$, $\beta\in R^m$ not all zero such that

$$0 \in \lambda \nabla_x F(\overline{x},\overline{y}) + \mu[\nabla_x f(\overline{x},\overline{y}) - \partial V(\overline{x})] + \nabla^2_{xy} f(\overline{x},\overline{y})^T \beta,$$

$$0 = \lambda \nabla_y F(\overline{x},\overline{y}) + \nabla^2_{yy} f(\overline{x},\overline{y})^T \beta.$$

As verified in Mirrlees, at $\overline{x}=1$, both $\overline{y}=0.957$ and $y_1=-0.957$ are solutions of the lower level problem $P_{\overline{x}}$. Henceby Danskin's Theorem,

$$\begin{aligned} \partial V(\overline{x}) &= co\{\nabla_x f(\overline{x},\overline{y}), \nabla_x f(\overline{x},y_1)\} \\ &= \{\alpha \nabla_x f(\overline{x},\overline{y}) + (1-\alpha)\nabla_x f(\overline{x},y_1) : \alpha \in [0, 1]\}. \end{aligned}$$

Hence the nonsmooth generalized Lagrange multiplier rule of Clarke implies the existence of $\lambda\geqslant$, $\mu\geqslant 0$, $\beta\in R^m$ not all zero and $\alpha\in[0,1]$ such that

$$0 = \lambda \nabla_x F(\overline{x},\overline{y}) + \mu(1-\alpha)[\nabla_x f(\overline{x},\overline{y}) - \nabla_x f(\overline{x},y_1)] + \nabla^2_{yx} f(\overline{x},\overline{y})^T \beta,$$

$$0 = \lambda \nabla_y F(\overline{x},\overline{y}) + \nabla^2_{yy}(\overline{x},\overline{y})^T \beta.$$

It is now easy to verify that the above condition holds for $\lambda=1$, $\mu=2.05$, $\beta=-0.04918$, $\alpha=0$. Since multipliers for both the first order condition and the value function constraints are not zero, it is clear that both the first order approach and the value function approach failf or Mirrlees' problem. Actually Mirrlees pointed out in [12] that there are many similar bilevel programming problems in the class of Moral-Hazard model of Principal-Agent problems in Economics and hence it is extremely important to find an approach that will solve these types of problems.

Let us analyze why the value function approach fails even though the value function reformulation (SP) is completely equivalent to the original bilevel programming problem (BLPP). Let us consider the perturbed objective function of the bilevel programming problem:

$$F_\mu(x,y) = F(x,y) + \mu(f(x,y) - V(x))$$

for some $\mu \geqslant 0$. By Danskin's theorem, since $\nabla_x f(\bar{x},y_1) < \nabla_x f(\bar{x},\bar{y}) < 0$ one has

$$\begin{aligned} V'(\bar{x};dx) &= \min\{\nabla_x f(\bar{x},\bar{y})^T dx, \nabla_x f(\bar{x},y_1)^T dx\} \\ &= \begin{cases} \nabla_x f(\bar{x},y_1)^T dx & \text{if } dx > 0 \\ \nabla_x f(\bar{x},\bar{y})^T dx & \text{if } dx \leqslant 0. \end{cases} \end{aligned}$$

Hence the directional derivative of the perturbed objective function is

$$\begin{aligned} & F'_\mu((\bar{x},\bar{y});(dx,dy)) \\ &= \nabla F(\bar{x},\bar{y})^T(dx,dy) + \mu[\nabla f(\bar{x},\bar{y})^T(dx,dy) - V'(\bar{x};dx)] \\ &= \nabla F(\bar{x},\bar{y})^T(dx,dy) + \mu[\nabla_x f(\bar{x},\bar{y})^T dx - V'(\bar{x};dx)] \\ &= \begin{cases} \nabla F(\bar{x},\bar{y})^T(dx,dy) + \mu(f_x(\bar{x},\bar{y}) - f_x(\bar{x},y_1))^T dx & \text{if } dx > 0 \\ \nabla F(\overline{xy})^T(dx,dy) & \text{if } dx \leqslant 0 \end{cases} \\ &= \begin{cases} -2dx - 0.86dx + \mu(e^{-0.043^2} - e^{-1.957^2})dx & \text{if } dx > 0 \\ -2dx - 0.86dy & \text{if} dx \leqslant 0. \end{cases} \end{aligned}$$

It is clear that for any $\mu \geqslant 0$ and any direction (dx,dy) such that $dx=0, dy>0$,

$$F'_\mu.((\bar{x},\bar{y});(dx,dy)) < 0$$

which implies that $(\bar{x},\bar{y})$is not a local minimum of the perturbed problem min $F_\mu(x,y)$ for any $\mu \geqslant 0$ and hence the problem (SP) is not partially calm.

Let $M=\{(x,y):\nabla_y f(x,y)=0\}$ represent the set described by the first order condition (2). Then at the point $(\bar{x},\bar{y}) \in M$,the tangent plane of Matpoint $(\bar{x},\bar{y})$ is

$$T((\bar{x},\bar{y}):M) = \{(dx,dy):\nabla^2_{xy} f(\bar{x},\bar{y})dx + \nabla^2_{yy} f(\bar{x},\bar{y})dy = 0\}.$$

From Figure 1,It is easy to see that for any nonzero direction $(dx,dy) \in T((\bar{x},\bar{y}):M)$, $\frac{dx}{dy} < 0$ and $|dx| > |dy|$. When $dx \leqslant 0, dy \geqslant 0$ and $|dx| \geqslant |dy|$, we have

$$F'_\mu((\bar{x},\bar{y});(dx,dy)) = 2(\bar{x}-2)dx + 2(\bar{y}-1)dy \geqslant 0.$$

and when $dx>0, dy\leqslant 0$, since $\nabla_x f(\bar{x},\bar{y}) - \nabla_x f(\bar{x},y_1) > 0$ we can find $\mu>0$ large enough such that

$$\begin{aligned} F'_\mu((\bar{x},\bar{y});(dx,dy)) = 2(\bar{x}-2)dx &+ \mu[\nabla_x f(\bar{x},\bar{y}) - \nabla_x f(\bar{x},y_1)]^T dx \\ &+ 2(\bar{y}-1)dy \geqslant 0. \end{aligned}$$

So in every direction of the tangent plane of the curve described by the first order condition, the perturbed objective function of the bilevel programming problem is nonnegative. That is, $d=(dx,dy)=(0,0)$is an optimal solution to the following linearized perturbed problem for some $\mu > 0$:

$$\min_{d} \quad \Phi(d) := F'_{\mu}.((\bar{x},\bar{y});d)$$
$$\nabla(\nabla_y f)(\bar{x},\bar{y})d = 0.$$

Since the directional derivative is a convex function as a function of the direction, the above problem is a convex program with linear constraints. Since $d=0$ is an optimal solution, there exists $\xi \in \partial\Phi(0)$, the subgradient of Φ in the sense of convex analysis and a multiplier β such that

$$0 = \xi + \nabla(\nabla_y f)(\bar{x},\bar{y})^T\beta.$$

By the definition of subgradient in the sense of convex analysis, $\xi \in \partial\Phi(0)$ if and only if

$$F'_{\mu}((\bar{x},\bar{y});d) = \Phi(d) \geqslant \langle \xi, d \rangle \quad \forall d.$$

By the definition of the Clarke generalized gradient, the above inequality implies that $\xi \in \partial F_{\mu}(\bar{x},\bar{y})$. By the calculus rule in Proposition 1.1 it follows that

$$\xi \in \partial F_{\mu}(\bar{x},\bar{y}) \subseteq \nabla F(\bar{x},\bar{y}) + \mu(\nabla f(\bar{x},\bar{y}) - \partial V(\bar{x}) \times \{0\})$$

and consequently,

$$0 \in \nabla F(\bar{x},\bar{y}) + \mu(\nabla f(\bar{x},\bar{y}) - \partial V(\bar{x}) \times \{0\}) + \nabla(\nabla_y f)(\bar{x},\bar{y})^T\beta.$$

By Carathéodory's theorem, the convex set $coW(\bar{x}) \subseteq R^n$ can be represented by not more than $n+1$ elements at a time. Hence by Danskin's Theorem,

$$\partial V(\bar{x}) = \left\{ \sum_{i=1}^{n+1} \lambda^i \nabla_x f(\bar{x}, y^i) : \lambda^i \geqslant 0, \sum_{i=1}^{n+1} \lambda^i = 1, y^i \in S(\bar{x}) \right\}.$$

Actually we have proved the following theorem.

Theorem 2.1 *Let $(\bar{x},\bar{y})$ be a local optimal solution to the bilevel programming problem:*

$$\min \quad F(x,y)$$
$$y \in \arg\min_{y \in S} f(x,y)$$

where S is a compact subset of R^m and F, f are continuously differentiable function at $(\bar{x},\bar{y})$. Suppose that $\bar{y} \in int\, S$ and there exists $\mu \geqslant 0$ such that

$$F'_{\mu}((\bar{x},\bar{y}),d) \geqslant 0$$

for all $d=(dx,dy) \in R^{n+m}$ such that

$$\nabla^2_{yx} f(\bar{x},\bar{y})dx + \nabla^2_{yy} f(\bar{x},\bar{y})dy = 0.$$

Then there exist $\beta \in R^m$, $\lambda^i \geqslant 0, i=1,\cdots,n+1, y^i \in S(\bar{x})$ such that $\sum_{i=1}^{n+1} \lambda^i = 1$ and

$$0 = \nabla_x F(\bar{x},\bar{y}) + \mu \sum_{i=1}^{n+1} \lambda^i [\nabla_x f(\bar{x},\bar{y}) - \nabla_x f(\bar{x},y^i)] + \nabla^2_{xy} f(\bar{x},\bar{y})^T\beta,$$
$$0 = \nabla_y F(\bar{x},\bar{y}) + \nabla^2_{yy} f(\bar{x},\bar{y})^T\beta.$$

3. Combined MPEC and the value function approach

In this section we consider the general BLPP defined as in Section 1. Using the KKT condition for the lower level problem we con sider the following sing lelevel optimization problem:

$$
\begin{aligned}
(\mathrm{P}) \quad \min_{x,y,u} \quad & F(x,y) \\
s.t. \quad & f(x,y) - V(x) \leqslant 0, \\
& \nabla_y f(x,y) + u \nabla_y g(x,y) = 0, \\
& g(x,y) \leqslant 0,\ u \geqslant 0, \langle g(x,y), u \rangle = 0, \\
& G(x,y) \leqslant 0,
\end{aligned} \tag{6}
$$

where $u\nabla_y g(x,y) := \sum_{i=1}^{p} u_i \nabla_y g_i(x,y)$.

We now study the relationship of the above problem and BLPP in the following proposition.

Proposition 3.1 *Let $(\bar{x},\bar{y})$ be a local (global) optimal solution to BLPP. Suppose that at $\bar{y}$, the KKT condition holds for the lower level problem $P_{\bar{x}}$. Then there exists $\bar{u}$ such that $(\bar{x},\bar{y},\bar{u})$ is a local (global) optimal solution of (P). Conversely, suppose that $(\bar{x},\bar{y},\bar{u})$ is an optimal solutionto (P) restricting on $U(\bar{x},\bar{y})\times R^p$ where $U(\bar{x},\bar{y})$ is a neighbourhood of $(\bar{x},\bar{y})$ and the KKT condition holds at $y\in S(x)$ for lower level problem P_x for all (x,y) close to $(\bar{x},\bar{y})$, then $(\bar{x},\bar{y})$ is a local solution of BLPP.*

Proof. Let $(\bar{x},\bar{y})$ be a local optimal solution to BLPP. Then there exists $U(\bar{x},\bar{y})$, a neighbourhood of $(\bar{x},\bar{y})$ such that

$$
F(\bar{x},\bar{y}) \leqslant F(x,y) \quad \forall (x,y) \in U(\bar{x},\bar{y}) \cap \mathscr{F} \tag{7}
$$

where $\mathscr{F}$ denotes the feasible region of BLPP. Since $\bar{y}$ is the global optimal solution of the lower level problem $P_{\bar{x}}$, by the KKT condition, there exists a multiplier $\bar{u}$ such that

$$
0 = \nabla_y f(\bar{x},\bar{y}) + \sum_{i=1}^{p} \bar{u}_i \nabla_y g_i(\bar{x},\bar{y}),
$$

$$
\bar{u} \geqslant 0, \sum_{i=1}^{p} \bar{u}_i g_i(\bar{x},\bar{y}) = 0.
$$

Therefore $(\bar{x},\bar{y},\bar{u})$ is a feasible solution to problem (P). Now let (x,y,u) be a feasible solution to problem (P) such that $(x,y)\in U(\bar{x},\bar{y})$. Then it is obvious that (x,y) is a feasible solution of BLPP. By(7), $(\bar{x},\bar{y},\bar{u})$ is a local (global) optimal solution of (P).

Conversely, suppose that $(\bar{x},\bar{y},\bar{u})$ is an optimal solution to (P) on $U(\bar{x},\bar{y})\times R^p$. Then

$$
F(\bar{x},\bar{y}) \leqslant F(x,y) \quad \forall (x,y,u) \in (U(\bar{x},\bar{y}) \times R^p) \cap \mathscr{F}_1 \tag{8}
$$

where $\mathscr{F}_1$ is the feasible region of (P). Let $(x,y)\in U(\bar{x},\bar{y})$ be a feasible solution of BLPP, then by the assumption, the KKT condition holds and hence there exists u such that (x,y,u) it is a feasible solution of problem (P). The optimality of $(\bar{x},\bar{y})$ for problem BLPP follows from (8).

Suppose that the value function $V(x)$ is Lipschitz continuous near the optimal solution then the problem (P) is a mathematical programming problem with equilibrium constraints (MPEC) with continuously differentiable and Lipschitz continuous problem data. It is known that under certain constraint qualifications such as MPEC GMFCQ(a MPEC version of the MFCQ) or Linear CQ (see Ye[20,22]),a local optimal solution of (P) is a M-stationary point and under stronger constraint qualifications such as MPECLICQ, a local optimalsolution of (P) isa S-stationary point. However since the constraint (6) is actually an equality the MPEC GMFCQ and MPEC LICQ will never hold. Since the value function is usually not linear, the Linear CQ is unlikely to hold as well.

To copy with this difficulty, we consider the partially penalized problem of (P) for some $\mu \geqslant 0$

$$
\begin{aligned}
P_\mu \quad \min_{x,y,u} \quad & F_\mu(x,y):=F(x,y)+\mu(f(x,y)-V(x)) \\
s.t. \quad & \nabla_y f(x,y)+u\nabla_y g(x,y)=0, \\
& g(x,y)\leqslant 0, u\geqslant 0, \langle g(x,y),u\rangle = 0, \\
& G(x,y)\leqslant 0.
\end{aligned}
$$

As in [24,25],we say that the problem (P) is partially calm at$(\bar{x},\bar{y},\bar{u})$,a local solution to (P) if it is also a local solution to the above partially perturbed problem for some $\mu \geqslant 0$. Under the partial calmness and certain MPEC constraint qualifications, one can then obtain M-stationary and S-stationary conditions. However the partial calmness condition may be difficult to verify. In the rest of this section we introduce some conditions which are weaker and easier to verify than the partial calmness condition.

Let $\tilde{\mathscr{F}}$. denote the feasible region of the problem P_μ. Given a feasible vector $(\bar{x},\bar{y},\bar{u})\in\tilde{\mathscr{F}}$. We define the following index sets:

$$
\begin{aligned}
I_G &= I_G(\bar{x},\bar{y}):=\{i:G_i(\bar{x},\bar{y})=0\} \\
I_g &= I_g(\bar{x},\bar{y},\bar{u}):=\{i:g_i(\bar{x},\bar{y})=0,\bar{u}_i>0\} \\
I_u &= I_u(\bar{x},\bar{y},\bar{u}):=\{i:g_i(\bar{x},\bar{y})<0,\bar{u}_i=0\} \\
I_0 &= I_0(\bar{x},\bar{y},\bar{u}):=\{i:g_i(\bar{x},\bar{y})=0,\bar{u}_i=0\}.
\end{aligned}
$$

It can be shown easily that the linearization cone of the feasible region of P_μ can be described as follows:

Definition 3.1(linearization cone) *The linearization cone of* $\tilde{\mathscr{F}}$*at* $(\bar{x},\bar{y},\bar{u})$ *is the cone defined by*

$$
\mathcal{L}(\bar{x},\bar{y},\bar{u};\tilde{\mathscr{F}}):=\left\{\begin{array}{ll}
(d,v) & \nabla(\nabla_y f+\bar{u}\nabla_y g)(\bar{x},\bar{y})d+\nabla_y g(\bar{x},\bar{y})^T v=0 \\
 & \nabla G_i(\overline{xt})^T d\leqslant 0 \quad i\in I_G \\
\in R^{n+m}\times R^p: & \nabla g_i(\bar{x},\bar{y})^T d=0 \quad i\in I_g \\
 & v_i=0 \quad i\in I_u \\
 & \nabla g_i(\bar{x},\bar{y})^T d\leqslant 0, v_i\geqslant 0 \quad i\in I_0
\end{array}\right\}.
$$

Since the feasible region of a MPEC may be nonconvex, it is unreasonable to expect that the usual linearization cone of the feasible region $\tilde{\mathscr{F}}$ is equal to the tangent cone of the feasible region. However in the MPEC literature, it is known that under weak assumptions, the MPEC linearization cone defined as followsis equal to the tangent cone of the feasible region. When the tangent cone is equal to the MPEC linearization cone it is said that MPEC Abadie constraint qualification holds. The reader is referred to Ye[22]for sufficient conditions for MPEC Abadie constraint qualification to hold.

Definition 3. 2 (MPEC linearizationc one) *The MPEC linearization cone of* $\tilde{\mathscr{F}}$ at $(\bar{x}, \bar{y}, \bar{u})$ is the cone defined by

$$\mathcal{L}^{MPEC}((\bar{x},\bar{y},\bar{u});\tilde{\mathscr{F}}):\left\{\begin{array}{ll}(d,v) & \nabla(\nabla_y f+\bar{u}\nabla_y g)(\bar{x},\bar{y})h+\nabla_y g(\bar{x},\bar{y})^T v=0 \\ \in R^{n+m}\times R^p & \nabla G_i(\bar{x},\bar{y})^T d\leqslant 0 \quad i\in I_G \\ & \nabla g_i(\bar{x},\bar{y})^T d=0 \quad i\in I_g \\ & v_i=0 \quad i\in I_u \\ & \left\{\begin{array}{l}\nabla g_i(\bar{x},\bar{y})^T d\cdot v_i=0 \\ \nabla g_i(\bar{x},\bar{y})^T d\leqslant 0, v_i\geqslant 0\end{array}\right. \quad i\in I_0\end{array}\right\}$$

Theorem 3. 1 *Let* $(\bar{x},\bar{y},\bar{u})$ *be a local solution to* (P). *Suppose that the value function* $V(x)$ *is Lipschitz near* $\bar{x}$.

If

$$F_\mu^\circ((\bar{x},\bar{y});d)\geqslant 0 \quad \forall (d,v)\in \mathcal{L}^{MPEC}((\bar{x},\bar{y},\bar{u});\tilde{\mathscr{F}}) \tag{9}$$

for some $\mu\geqslant 0$, *then* $(\bar{x},\bar{y},\bar{u})$ *is a M-stationary point of* (P), *i. e. , there exist* ,$\beta\in R^m$, $\eta^g\in R^p$, $\eta^G\in R^q$ *such that*

$$0\in\nabla F(\bar{x},\bar{y})+\mu[\nabla f(\bar{x},\bar{y})-\partial V(\bar{x})]$$
$$+\nabla(\nabla_y f+\bar{u}\nabla_y g)(\bar{x},\bar{y})^T\beta+\nabla g(\bar{x},\bar{y})^T\eta^g+\nabla G(\bar{x},\bar{y})^T\eta^G, \tag{10}$$
$$\eta_i^G\geqslant 0 \quad i\in I_G, \eta_i^G=0 \quad i\notin I_G, \tag{11}$$
$$\eta_i^g=0 \quad i\in I_u, (\nabla_y g(\bar{x},\bar{y})\beta)_i=0 \quad i\in I_g, \tag{12}$$
$$\text{either } \eta_i^g>0, (\nabla_y g(\bar{x},\bar{y})\beta)_i>0 \quad \text{or} \quad \eta_i^g(\nabla_y g(\bar{x},\bar{y})\beta)_i=0 \quad i\in I_0.$$

If

$$F_\mu^\circ((\bar{x},\bar{y});d)\geqslant 0 \quad \forall (d,v)\in \mathcal{L}((\bar{x},\bar{y},\bar{u});\tilde{\mathscr{F}}) \tag{13}$$

holds for some $\mu\geqslant 0$, *then* $(\bar{x},\bar{y},\bar{u})$ *is a S-stationary point of* (P), *i. e. , there exist* $\beta\in R^m$, $\eta^g\in R^p$, $\eta^G\in R^q$ *such that* (10)-(12) *and the following condition holds*:

$$\eta_i^g\geqslant 0, (\nabla_y g(\bar{x},\bar{y})\beta)_i\geqslant 0 \quad i\in I_0.$$

Proof. By(9), $(d,v)=(0,v)$ is an optimal solution to the following linearized problem:

$$\begin{array}{lll}(P)_L & \min\limits_{(d,v)} & \Phi(d):=F_\mu^\circ((\bar{x},\bar{y});d) \\ & s.t. & (\nabla_y f+\bar{u}\nabla_y g)(\bar{x},\bar{y})d+\nabla_y g(\bar{x},\bar{y})^T v=0 \\ & & \nabla G_i(\bar{x},\bar{y})d\leqslant 0 \quad i\in I_G, \\ & & \nabla g_i(\bar{x},\bar{y})d=0 \quad i\in I_g, \\ & & v_i=0 \quad i\in I_u, \\ & & \left\{\begin{array}{l}\nabla g_i(\bar{x},\bar{y})d\cdot v_i=0, \\ \nabla g_i(\bar{x},\bar{y})d\leqslant 0, v_i\geqslant 0\end{array}\right. i\in I_0.\end{array} \tag{14}$$

The objective function of the above problem is a nonsmooth convex function and the constraint functions are all linear in variable (d, v) and (14) is a linear complementarity constraint. Although the results of [22] are stated for the case where all functions are continuously differentiable ,all results still hold for the case where the objective functions are nonsmooth but Lipschitz continuous with the classical gradient of the objective function replaced by the Clarke generalized gradient. In particular applying [22, Theorem 2. 2], we conclude that there exist multipliers $\beta \in R^m$, $\eta^g \in R^p$, $\eta^G \in R^q$, $\eta^u \in R^p$ such that

$$0 \in \partial\Phi(0) + \nabla(\nabla_y f + \overline{u}\nabla_y g)(\overline{x}, \overline{y})^T\beta + \nabla_g(\overline{x}, \overline{y})^T\eta^g + \nabla G(\overline{x}, \overline{y})^T\eta^G,$$
$$0 = \nabla_y g(\overline{x}, \overline{y})\beta - \eta^u,$$
$$\eta_i^G \geqslant 0 \quad i \in I_G, \eta_i^G = 0 \quad i \notin I_G,$$
$$\eta_i^g = 0 \quad i \in I_u, \eta_i^u = 0 \quad i \in I_g,$$
$$\text{either} \quad \eta_i^g > 0, \eta_i^u > 0 \quad \text{or} \quad \eta_i^g\eta_i^u = 0 \quad i \in I_0.$$

By the calculus rules for Clarke generalized gradients, one has

$$\partial\Phi(0) \subseteq \nabla F(\overline{x}, \overline{y})' + \mu\{\nabla f(\overline{x}, \overline{y}) - \partial V(\overline{x}) \times \{0\}\}.$$

The desired result follows from replacing η^u by $\nabla_y g(\overline{x}, \overline{y})\beta$.

Now suppose that (13) holds. Then $(d, v) = (0, v)$ is an optimal solution to the following linearized problem:

$$
\begin{aligned}
(P)_L \quad \min_{(d,v)} \quad & \Phi(d) := F_{\mu}^{\circ}.((\overline{x}, \overline{y}); d) \\
s.t. \quad & \nabla(\nabla_y f + \overline{u}\nabla_y g)(\overline{x}, \overline{y})d + \nabla_y g(\overline{x}, \overline{y})^T v = 0 \\
& \nabla G_i(\overline{x}, \overline{y})d \leqslant 0 \quad i \in I_G, \\
& \nabla_g i(\overline{x}, \overline{y})d = 0 \quad i \in I_g, \\
& v_i = 0 \quad i \in I_u, \\
& \nabla_g i(\overline{x}, \overline{y})d \leqslant 0, v_i \geqslant 0 \quad i \in I_0.
\end{aligned}
$$

The desired result follows from applying then onsmooth KKT condition to the above optimization problem.

The necessary optimality conditions obtained in Theorem 3. 1 involve the Clarke generalized gradient of the value function. There are two issues to be considered here. The first one is when the value function is Lipschitz continuous and the second one is how to express the Clarke generalized gradient of the value function in terms of the problem data of the lower level problem. For this purpose we recall the following definition and the results. Let $x \in R^n$. For any $y \in S(x)$ we denote the set of KKT multipliers for the lower level problem $P(x)$ at y as follows:

$$M^1(x, y)\left\{u \in R^p : \begin{array}{c} 0 = \nabla_y f(x, y) + \sum_{i=1}^{P} u_i \nabla_y g_i(x, y), \\ u \geqslant 0, \sum_{i=1}^{p} u_i g_i(x, y) = 0. \end{array}\right\}.$$

Recall that a set-valued map Y is called uniformly bounded around $\overline{x}$ if there exists a neighburhood U of $\bar{x}$ such that the set $\bigcup_{x \in U} Y(x)$ is bounded. The following result is a special case of Clarke [4, Theorem 6.5.2].

Proposition 3.2 (Clarke) *Assume that the set-valued map* $Y(x) := \{y \in R^m : g(x,y) \leqslant 0\}$ *is uniformly bounded around* $\bar{x}$. *Suppose that MFCQ holds at* y' *for all* $y' \in S(\bar{x})$. *Then the value function* $V(x)$ *is Lipschitz continuous near* $\bar{x}$ *and*

$$\partial V(\bar{x}) \subseteq coW(\bar{x})$$

where

$$W(\bar{x}) := \{\nabla_x f(\bar{x}, y') + u' \nabla_x g(\bar{x}, y') : y' \in S(\bar{x}), u' \in M^1(\bar{x}, y')\}. \tag{15}$$

By Carathéodory's theorem, the convex set $coW(\bar{x}) \subseteq R^n$ can be represented by not more than $n+1$ elements at a time. That is,

$$coW(\bar{x}) = \left\{ \begin{array}{c} \sum_{i=1}^{n+1} \lambda^i (\nabla_x f(\bar{x}, y^i) + u^i \nabla_x g(\bar{x}, y^i)) : \quad y^i \in S(\bar{x}), u^i \in M^1(\bar{x}, y^i), \\ \lambda^i \geqslant 0, \sum_{i=1}^{n+1} \lambda^i = 1 \end{array} \right\}.$$

We now introduce two new conditions under which our new necessary optimality conditions hold. Our new conditions do not involve either the Clarke generalized directional derivative or the Clarke generalized gradient of the value function.

Definition 3.3 *Given a feasible vector* $(\bar{x}, \bar{y}, \bar{u})$ *of* (P_μ). *We say that* (P) *is Mweakly calm at* $(\bar{x}, \bar{y}, \bar{u})$ *with modulus* μ *if*

$$[\nabla F(\bar{x}, \bar{y}) + \mu \nabla f(\bar{x}, \bar{y})]^T d - \mu \min_{\xi \in W(\bar{x})} \xi dx \geqslant 0 \quad \forall (d, v) \in \mathcal{L}^{MPEC}((\bar{x}, \bar{y}, \bar{u}); \widetilde{\mathscr{F}}). \tag{16}$$

We say that (P) *is S-weakly calm at* $(\bar{x}, \bar{y}, \bar{u})$ *with modulus* μ *if*

$$[\nabla F(\bar{x}, \bar{y}) + \mu \nabla f(\bar{x}, \bar{y})]^T d - \mu \min_{\xi \in W(\bar{x})} \xi dx \geqslant 0 \quad \forall (d, v) \in \mathcal{L}((\bar{x}, \bar{y}, \bar{u}); \widetilde{\mathscr{F}}). \tag{17}$$

Since

$$F_{\mu}^{\circ}.((\bar{x}, \bar{y}); d) = [\nabla F(\bar{x}, \bar{y}) + \mu \nabla f(\bar{x}, \bar{y})^T d + \mu(-V^{\circ})(\bar{x}; dx)$$

and

$$(-V)^{\circ}(\bar{x}; dx) = \max_{\xi \in \partial(-V)(\bar{x})}) \{\xi dx\} \leqslant \max_{\xi \in -W(\bar{x})} \{\xi dx\} = \max_{\xi \in W(\bar{x})} \{-\xi dx\} = -\min_{x \in W(\bar{x})} \{-\xi dx\},$$

the M-weakly calmness condition and the S-weakly calmness condition are weaker than the condition (9) and (13) respectively.

Theorem 3.2 *Let* $(\bar{x}, \bar{y}, \bar{u})$ *be a local solution to* (P). *Suppose that the set* $W(\bar{x})$ *as defined in* (15) *is nonempty and compact.*

If (P) *is M-weakly calm at* $(\bar{x}, \bar{y}, \bar{u})$ *with modulus* $\mu \geqslant 0$ *then there exist* $\lambda^i \geqslant 0$, $\sum_{i=1}^{n+1} \lambda^i = 1$, $y^i \in S(\bar{x})$, $u^i \in M^1(\bar{x}, y^i)$, $i = 1, 2, \cdots, n+1$, *and* $\beta \in R^m$, $\eta^g \in R^p$, $\eta^G \in R^q$ *such that*

$$0 = \nabla_x F(\bar{x}, \bar{y}) + \mu \sum_{i=1}^{n+1} \lambda^i (\nabla_x f(\bar{x}, \bar{y}) - \nabla_x f(\bar{x}, y^i) - u \nabla_x g(\bar{x}, y^i)) + \nabla_x (\nabla_y f + \bar{u} \nabla_y g)(\bar{x}, \bar{y})^T \beta + \nabla_x g(\bar{x}, \bar{y})^T \eta^g + \nabla_x G(\bar{x}, \bar{y})^T \eta^G, \tag{18}$$

$$0 = \nabla_y F(\overline{x},\overline{y}) + \mu \nabla_y f(\overline{x},\overline{y})$$
$$+ \nabla_y(\nabla_y f + \overline{u}\nabla_y g)(\overline{x},\overline{y})^T\beta + \nabla_y g(\overline{x},\overline{y})^T\eta^g + \nabla_y G(\overline{x},\overline{y})^T\eta^G, \quad (19)$$
$$\eta_i^G \geqslant 0 \quad i \in I_G, \eta_i^G = 0 \quad i \notin I_G, \quad (20)$$
$$\eta_i^g = 0 \quad i \in I_u, \quad (\nabla_y g(\overline{x},\overline{y})\beta)_i = 0 \quad i \in I_g, \quad (21)$$
$$\text{either } \eta_i^g > 0, (\nabla_y g(\overline{x},\overline{y})\beta)_i > 0 \quad \text{or} \quad \eta_i^g(\nabla_g(\overline{x},\overline{y})\beta)_i = 0 \quad i \in I_0.$$

If (P) is S-weakly calm with modulus $\mu \geqslant 0$ at $(\overline{x},\overline{u})$ then there exist $\lambda^i \geqslant 0$, $\sum_{i=1}^{n+1}\lambda^i = 1, y^i \in S(\overline{x}), u^i \in M^1(\overline{x},y^i), i = 1,2,\cdots,n+1$, and $\beta \in R^m, \eta^g \in R^p, \eta^G \in R^q$ such that (18)-(21) holds and

$$\eta_i^g \geqslant 0, \ (\nabla_y g(\overline{x},\overline{y})\beta)_i \geqslant 0 \quad i \in I_0.$$

Proof. Suppose that (P) is M-weakly calm. Then (16) holds at $(\overline{x},\overline{y},\overline{u})$ for some $\mu \geqslant 0$. Therefore $(d,v)=(0,v)$ is an optimal solution to the following linearized problem:

$$(P)_L \quad \min_{(h,v)} \quad [\nabla F(\overline{x},\overline{y}) + \mu\nabla f(\overline{x},\overline{y})]^T d - \mu \min_{\xi \in W(\overline{x})} \xi^T dx$$
$$s.t. \quad \nabla(\nabla_y f + \overline{u}\nabla_y g)(\overline{x},\overline{y})d + \nabla_y g(\overline{x},\overline{y})^T v = 0$$
$$\nabla G_i(\overline{x},\overline{y})d \leqslant 0 \quad i \in I_G,$$
$$\nabla g_i(\overline{x},\overline{y})d = 0 \quad i \in I_g$$
$$v_i = 0 \quad i \in I_u$$
$$\begin{cases} \nabla g_i(\overline{x},\overline{y})d \cdot v_i = 0 \\ \nabla g_i(\overline{x},\overline{y}) \leqslant 0, v_i \geqslant 0 \end{cases} \quad i \in I_0. \quad (22)$$

Let $\phi(z) := \min_{\xi \in W(\overline{x})} \xi^T z$. Since the set $W(\overline{x})$ is assumed to be nonempty and compact, by Danskin's theorem one has $\partial\phi(0) = coW(\overline{x})$. Therefore the Clarke generalized gradient of the objective function of the above problem at $(d,v)=(0,v)$ is included in the set described by

$$\nabla F(\overline{x},\overline{y}) + \mu[\nabla f(\overline{x},\overline{y}) - coW(\overline{x}) \times \{0\}].$$

As in the proof of Theorem 3.1, the desired result follows from applying the Mstationary condition to the above MPEC with linear complementarity constraints. The result for the S-stationary condition under the S-weak calmness condition is similarly proved and we omit the proof.

We would like to point out that a sufficient but not necessary condition for the set $W(\overline{x})$ to be nonempty and compact is that the MFCQ holds at every optimal solution of the lower level problem $P_{\overline{x}}$ and the the set-valued map $Y(x) := \{y \in R^m : g(x,y) \leqslant 0\}$ is uniformly bounded around $\overline{x}$.

4. Illustrative examples

In this section we use some nonconvex bilevel programming problems to illustrate the necessary optimality conditions we obtain in Theorem 3.2. We first examinate the example given by Vogel in his Ph. D. thesis and later included by Dempe in his recent monograph.

Example 4.1 (**Vogel** [**19**], **Dempe** [**10**])

$$\begin{aligned} \min \quad & (y+1)^2 \\ \text{s.t.} \quad & y \in S(x) := \arg\min_y \{y^3 - 3y : y \geqslant x\}, \\ & -3 \leqslant x \leqslant 2. \end{aligned}$$

It is easy to see that

$$S(x) = \begin{cases} \{x\} & \text{if} -3 \leqslant x < -2 \\ \{-2, 1\} & \text{if } x = -2 \\ \{1\} & \text{if} -2 < x \leqslant 1 \\ \{x\} & \text{if} 1 < x \leqslant 2 \end{cases}$$

and the optimal solution of the bilevel problem is $\overline{x}=\overline{y}=-2$.

If the classical KKT approach is used, then the resulting single level problem is

$$\begin{aligned} \min \quad & (y+1)^2 \\ s.t. \quad & 0 = 3y^2 - 3 - u, \\ & y \geqslant x, u \geqslant 0, \ (x-y)u = 0, \\ & -3 \leqslant x \leqslant 2. \end{aligned}$$

But the optimal solution of the above problem is $\overline{x} \leqslant -1, \overline{y}=-1, \overline{u}=0$ and the optimal solution of the bilevel program and the corresponding multiplier $\overline{x}=\overline{y}=-2, \overline{u}=9$ do not satisfy the KKT condition of the above problem. Hence the classical KKT approach fails for this example. Now

$$S(\overline{x}) = \{-2, 1\}, M^1(\overline{x}, -2) = \{9\}, M^1(\overline{x}, 1) = \{0\}, W(\overline{x}) = \{0, 9\}$$

and for any $d=(dx, dy) \in R^2$,

$$\begin{aligned} & \nabla F(\overline{x},\overline{y})^T d + \mu \nabla f(\overline{x},\overline{y})^T d - \mu \min_{\xi \in W(\overline{x})} \xi dx \\ & = \begin{cases} (-2+9\mu)dy - 9\mu dx & \text{if } dx < 0 \\ (-2+9\mu)dy & \text{if } dx \geqslant 0 \end{cases} \\ & \geqslant 0 \text{ for } \mu = 2/9. \end{aligned}$$

Hence the problem is S-weakly calm with modulus $\mu=2/9$. The KKT condition from Theorem 3.2 implies the existence of $\lambda^1 \geqslant 0, \lambda^2 \geqslant 0, \lambda^1 + \lambda^2 = 1, y^1 = \overline{y} = -2, y^2 = 1, u^1 = \overline{u} = 9, u^2 = 0, \beta \in R, \eta^g \in R$ such that

$$\begin{aligned} & 0 = \mu\lambda^1(-\overline{u}) + \mu\lambda^2(-u^2) + \eta^g \\ & 0 = 2(\overline{y}+1) + \mu(3\overline{y}^2 - 3) + 6\overline{y}\beta + (-1)\eta^g \\ & \beta = 0. \end{aligned}$$

The above KKT condition holds at $(\overline{x}, \overline{y}, \overline{u}) = (-2, -2, 9)$ with $\lambda^1=0, \lambda^2=1, \beta=0, \eta^g=0, \mu=2/9$. Since μ is not equal to zero but β is equal to zero, the value function approach works but the classical KKT approach fails. This example shows that our theorem includes the KKT condition derived by using the value function approach as a special case for nonconvex bilevel programming problem.

We now modify the objective function of the upper level problem so that it becomes the following problem.

Example 4.2

$$\begin{aligned}&\min \quad (x-1)^2+y^2\\&S.t. \quad y\in S(x):=\arg\min_y\{y^3-3y:y\geqslant x\},\\&\qquad -3\leqslant x\leqslant 2.\end{aligned}$$

It is easy to see that

$$S(x)=\begin{cases}\{x\} & \text{if } -3<x<-2\\ \{-2,1\} & \text{if } x=-2\\ \{1\} & \text{if } -2<x\leqslant 1\\ \{x\} & \text{if} 1<x\leqslant 2.\end{cases}$$

and the optimal solution of the bilevel problem is $\overline{x}=\overline{y}=1$. Now we have

$$S(\overline{x})=\{1\} \quad M^1(\overline{x},1)=\{0\}$$

and since $I^g=I^u=\varnothing$ and $I^0=\varnothing$, the linearization cone of the feasible region is

$$\mathcal{L}((\overline{x},\overline{y},\overline{u});\widetilde{\mathscr{F}})=\{(dx,dy,du):6dy=dv,dy\geqslant dx,dv\geqslant 0\}.$$

Since for all $\mu\geqslant 0$,

$$\nabla F(\overline{x},\overline{y})^Td+\mu\nabla f(\overline{x},\overline{y})^Td=2dy\geqslant 0 \quad \forall (dx,dy,dv)\in\mathcal{L}((\overline{x},\overline{y},\overline{u});\widetilde{\mathscr{F}})$$

the problem is S-weakly calm at $(\overline{x},\overline{y},\overline{u})$ with modulus $\mu\geqslant 0$. The KKT condition

$$\begin{aligned}&0=2(\overline{x}-1)+\eta^g\\&0=2\overline{y}+\mu(3\overline{y}^2-3)+6\overline{y}\beta+(-1)\eta^g\\&\eta^g\geqslant 0,\beta\leqslant 0\end{aligned}$$

holds at $(\overline{x},\overline{y},\overline{u})=(1,1,0)$ with $\beta=-1/3,\eta^g=0,\mu\geqslant 0$.

Since the solution set $S(\overline{x})$ is a singleton and the corresponding multiplier is a singleton as well for this example, our KKT condition actually reduces to the KKT condition derived by using the classical KKT approach. But the problem in this example is a nonconvex bilevel programming problem. Hence this example illustrates that our result provides a sufficient condition under which the KKT condition derived by the classical KKT approach is valid even for a nonconvex bilevel programming problem.

Example 4.3

$$\begin{aligned}&\min \quad (x-0.5)^2+(y-2)^2\\&S.t. \quad y\in S(x):=\arg\min_y\{y^3-3y:y\geqslant x-3\}\\&\qquad 0\leqslant x\leqslant 4.\end{aligned}$$

The solution set of the lower level problem can be easily obtained as

$$S(x)=\begin{cases}\{x-3\} & \text{if } 0\leqslant x<1\\ \{-2,1\} & \text{if } x=1\\ \{1\} & \text{if} 1<x\leqslant 4\end{cases}$$

and it is easy to verify that the optimal solution of the bilevel problem is $\overline{x}=\overline{y}=1$. Now

$$S(\overline{x}) = \{-2, 1\}, M^1(\overline{x}, -2) = \{9\}, M^1(\overline{x}, 1) = \{0\}, W(\overline{x}) = \{0, 9\}.$$

Since $g(\overline{x},\overline{y})=1-3-1=-3<0$ and $\overline{u}=0$, $I^g=I^0=\varnothing$ and $I^u\neq\varnothing$. The linearization cone of the feasible region is

$$\mathcal{L}((\overline{x},\overline{y},\overline{u});\widetilde{\mathcal{F}}) = \{(dx,dy,du):6dy = 0\}.$$

So one has

$$\begin{aligned}&\nabla F(\overline{x},\overline{y})^T d + \mu\nabla f(\overline{x},\overline{y})^T d - \mu \min_{\xi\in W(\overline{x})} \xi dx \\ &= \begin{cases} dx - 2dy - 9\mu dx & \text{if } dx < 0 \\ dx - 2dy & \text{if } dx \geqslant 0 \end{cases} \\ &\geqslant 0 \quad \forall (dx,dy,dv) \in \mathcal{L}((\overline{x},\overline{y},\overline{u});\widetilde{\mathcal{F}}) \text{and } \mu = 1/9.\end{aligned}$$

The KKT condition

$$\begin{aligned}&0 = 2(\overline{x}-0.5) + \mu\lambda^1(-\overline{u}) + \mu\lambda^2(-u^2) + \eta^g \\ &0 = 2(\overline{y}-2) + \mu(3\overline{y}^2-3) + 6\overline{y}\beta + (-1)\eta^g \\ &\eta^g = 0\end{aligned}$$

holds at $(\overline{x},\overline{y},\overline{u})=(1,-2,9)$ with $\lambda^1=0, \lambda^2=1, u^2=0, \beta=1/3, \eta^g=0, \mu=1/9$.

Note that since both β and μ are not equal to zero, both the classical KKT approach and the value function approach fail and only the combined KKT and the value function approach will work for this example.

References

[1] J. F. Bard, *Practical Bilevel Optimization: Algorithms and Applications*, Kluwer Academic Publications, Dordrecht, The Netherlands, 1998.

[2] J. F. Bard and J. E. Falk, *An explicit solution to the multilevel programming problem*, *Compu.* Oper. Res. 9(1982), pp. 77-100.

[3] J. Bracken and J. McGill, *Mathematical programs with optimization problems in the constraints*, Oper. Res. 21(1973), pp. 37-44.

[4] F. H. Clarke, *Optimization and Nonsmooth Analysis*, Wiley-Interscience, New York, 1983.

[5] F. H. Clarke, Yu. S. Ledyaev, R. J. SternandP. R. Wolenski, *Nonsmooth Analysis and Control Theory*, Springer, NewYork, 1998.

[6] J. M. Danskin, *The Theory of Max-Min and its Applications to Weapons Allocation Problems*, Springer, New York, 1967.

[7] S. Dempe, *A necessary and sufficient optimality condition for bilevel programming problems*, Optimization 25(1992), pp. 341-354.

[8] S. Dempe, *Foundations of Bilevel Programming*, Kluwer Academic Publishers, 2002.

[9] S. Dempe, *Annotated bibliography on bilevel programming and mathematical programs with equilibrium constraints*, Optimization 52(2003), pp. 333-359.

[10] S. Dempe, *Bilevel programming*, *Essays and* Surveys in Global Optimization, GERAD 25 Anniv. Ser. 7, Springer, New York, 2005, pp. 165-193.

[11] Z. Q. Luo, J. S. Pang and D. Ralph, *Mathematical Programs with Equilibrium Constraints*, Cam-

bridge University Press, 1996.

[12] J. Mirrlees, J. *The theory of moral hazard and unobservable behaviour-part I*, Review of Economic Studies, 66(1999), pp. 3-22.

[13] B. S. Mordukhovich, *Variational Analysis and Generalized Differentiation*, *Vol. 1: Basic Theory*, *Vol. 2: Applications*, Springer, 2004.

[14] J. V. Outrata, *Necessary optimality conditions for Stackelberg problems*, J. Optim. Theory and Appl. 76(1990), pp. 305-320.

[15] J. V. Outrata, M. Kočvara and J. Zowe, *Nonsmooth Approach to Optimization Problem with Equilibrium Constraints: Theory, Application and Numerical Results*, Kluwer, Dordrecht, TheNetherlands, 1998.

[16] K. Shimizu, Y. Ishizuka and J. F. Bard, *Nondifferentiable and Two-Level Mathematical Programming*, Kluwer Academic Publishers, Boston, 1997.

[17] H. von Stackelberg, *Marktform and Gleichgewicht* Springer-Verlag, Berlin, 1934. engl. transl.: The Theory of the Market Economy, Oxford University Press, Oxford, England, 1954.

[18] L. N. Vincente and P. H. Calamai, *Bilevel and multilevel programming: A bibliography review*. J. Global Optim. 5(1994), pp. 291-306.

[19] S. Vogel, *Zwei-Ebenen-Optimierungsaufgaben mit nichtkonvexer Zielfunktion in derunterren Ebene: Pfadverfolgung und Sprüunge*, Ph. D. thesis, Technische Universitat Bergakademie Freiberg, 2002.

[20] J. J. Ye, *Constraint qualifications and necessary optimality conditions for optimization problems with variational inequality constraints*, SIAMJ. Optim. 10(2000), pp. 943-962.

[21] J. J. Ye, *Nondifferentiable multiplier rules for optimization and bilevel optimization problems*, SIAM J. Optim. 15(2004), pp. 252-274.

[22] J. J. Ye, *Necessary and sufficient optimality conditions for mathemtical programs with equilibrium constraints*, J. Math. Anal. Appl., 307(2005), pp. 305-369.

[23] J. J. Ye, *Constraint qualifications and KKT conditions for bilevel programming problems*, Math. Oper. Res., 31(2006), pp. 811-824.

[24] J. J. Ye and D. L. Zhu, *Optimality conditions for bilevel programming problems*, Optimization33 (1995), pp. 9-27.

[25] J. J. Ye and D. L. Zhu, *A note on optimality conditions for bilevel programming problems*, Optimization39(1997), pp. 361-366.

[26] J. J. Ye, D. L. Zhu and Q. J. Zhu, *Exact penalization and necessary optimality conditions for generalized bilevel programming problems*, SIAMJ. Optim. 2(1997), pp. 481-507.

A trust region algorithm for nonlinear bilevel programming

P. Marcotte[a,*], G. Savard[b], D. L. Zhu[c]

[a] *DIRO and CRT, Université de Montréal, CP 6128, succursale Centre-ville, Montréal, QC, Canada H3C 3J7*

[b] *GERAD and Département de mathématiques et génie industriel, École Polytechnique, C. P. 6079, succursale Centre-ville, Montréal, QC, Canada H3C 3A7*

[c] *CRT, Universitedé Montréal, CP 6128, succursale Centre-ville, Montréal, QC, Canada H3C 3J7 and Fudan University, Shanghai, China*

Received 5 October 2000; received in revised form 21 June 2001; accepted 5 July 2001

Abstract. We propose to solve generalized bilevel programs by a trust region approach where the "model" takes the form of a bilevel program involving a linear program at the upper level and a linear variational inequality at the lower level. By coupling the concepts of trust region and linesearch in a novel way, we obtain an implementable algorithm that converges to a strong stationary point of the original bilevel program.

Keywords: Bilevel programming; Trust region; Linesearch

1. A trust region approach to bilevel programming

In this paper we consider bilevel programs (or MPECs, i. e., mathematical programs with equilibrium constraints, see [5]) of the form

$$\min_{x\in X, y\in Y(x)} f(x,y)$$
$$\text{s. t. } \langle F(x,y), y-y'\rangle \leqslant 0 \ \forall y' \in Y(x),$$

where the mapping F is strongly monotone with respect to the lower level variable y and where the sets X and $Y(x)=\{y: Ax+By\geqslant b\}$ are polyhedral. We propose for its solu-

* Correspondingauthor.

E-mail address: *marcotte*@IRO. umontreal. ca (P. Marcotte).

tion a trust region approach where the model is itself a bilevel program of a combinatorial nature that can be solved for a global optimum.

This approach, which mixes continuous and discrete optimization, trust regions and linesearches, is in stark contrast with more traditional descent methods whose convergence properties are frequently weak and dicult to analyze (see the works of Outrata et al. [7] or, more recently, the sequential programming scheme developed by Fukushima and Tseng[3]). Although the underlyingmotivation is quite dierent, it is related to a trust region method applied to an exact penalty reformulation of the original bilevel program, such as the one proposed by Scholtes and Stöhr [10].

The core of the algorithm consists in solving, at each iteration, the affine approximation of the original bilevel model obtained by replacing f and F by their respective rst-order developments $\overline{f}$ and $\overline{F}$ around thecurrent iterate$(\overline{x},\overline{y})$, and forcing the upper level decision vector x to lie within some distance ε(the radius of the trust region)of the current iterate, i. e. ,

$$\min_{x\in X, y\in Y(x)} \overline{f}(x,y)$$
$$\text{s. t. } \langle \overline{F}(x,y), y-y' \rangle \leqslant 0 \ \forall y' \in Y(x),$$
$$\| x-\overline{x} \| \leq \varepsilon.$$

Starting from$(\overline{x},\overline{y})$the algorithm sets the next iterate to a solution$(\overline{x}_\varepsilon,\overline{y}_\varepsilon)$ of the above linearized program, provided that the trust region model is deemed a suitable approximation to the original bilevel program, i. e. , the ratio

$$\frac{f(\overline{x},y(\overline{x}))-f(\overline{x}_\varepsilon,y(\overline{x}_\varepsilon))}{\overline{f}(\overline{x},\overline{y}(\overline{x}))-\overline{f}(\overline{x}_\varepsilon,\overline{y}(\overline{x}_\varepsilon))},$$

where $y(x)$ and $\overline{y}(x)$ represent the well-dened optimal reaction functions, is bounded away from zero. If the ratio is small, the iterate is left unchanged and the radius of the trust region is decreased; otherwise the point $\overline{x}_\varepsilon$ replaces the iterate $\overline{x}$ as the new iterate. This yields the following classical trust region algorithm which is, by construction, a descent algorithm.

Algorithm BlTrust

Step 0 [Initialization]:

- Select positive parameters ε_0 and an initial iterate $x_0 \in X$.
- Set the iteration index k to 0.

Step 1:

$\overline{x}_{\varepsilon k} \leftarrow$ solution of the linearized problem within the trust region.

Step 2:

Set $r_k=\dfrac{f(x^k,y(x^k))-f(\overline{x}_{\varepsilon_k},y(\overline{x}_{\varepsilon_k}))}{\overline{f}(x^k,\overline{y}(x^k))-\overline{f}(\overline{x}_{\varepsilon_k},y(\overline{x}_{\varepsilon_k}))}$.

if $2/3 \leqslant r_k$ **then** $x^{k+1} \leftarrow \overline{x}_{\varepsilon_k}$ and $\varepsilon_{k+1} \leftarrow 2\varepsilon_k$

if $1/3 \le r_k < 2/3$ **then** $x^{k+1} \leftarrow \overline{x}_{\varepsilon_k}$ and $\varepsilon_{k+1} \leftarrow \varepsilon_k$

if $r_k < 1/3$ **then** $x^{k+1} \leftarrow x^k$ and $\varepsilon_{k+1} \leftarrow \varepsilon_k / 2$

Step 3:

- $k \leftarrow k+1$
- Return to Step 1.

At Step 1 of the algorithm, the lower level linear variational inequality can be replaced by its Karush-Kuhn- Tucker system, to yield the equivalent primal-dual single-level program

$$\begin{aligned}
\min_{x} \quad & \overline{f}(x, y) \\
\text{s. t.} \quad & x \in X, \\
& \| x - \overline{x} \| \leqslant \varepsilon, \\
& Ax + By \geq b, \\
& \pi B = \overline{F}(x, y), \\
& \pi \geqslant 0, \\
& \pi(Ax + By - b) = 0.
\end{aligned}$$

Upon introduction of a row vector of binary variables z, the sole nonlinear constraint of the above program can be written as

$$\pi \leqslant Mz, \ Ax + By - b \leqslant M(e - z^{\mathrm{T}}),$$

where the components of the vector e are all equal to one and where M is a suitably large (nite) constant which also appears in exact penalty reformulations of the bilevel program (see [6] or [10]). Whenever the norm $\| \cdot \|$ is polyhedral, this mixed-integer program can be solved exactly for a global optimum by implicit enumeration (branch-and-bound) techniques.

Algorithm BlTrust is closely related to the trust region method applied in [10] to an exact penalization of a mathematical program with equilibrium constraints (MPEC) and where the "model" is nonsmooth. The dierence between the approaches is twofold:

- Scholtes and Stöhr apply the trust region constraint to both the upper and lower level variables. Actually, in an MPEC formulation of the bilevel program, their trust region applies as well to the lower level dual vector.
- no solution algorithm for the nonsmooth model is specied whereas, in our case, the model can be solved exactly, by an algorithm similar to that of Hansen et al. [4]. If both upper and lower level functions are mildly nonlinear, we expect that the trust region model will be in close agreement with the original program, and that a nearly globally optimal solution will be uncovered in the early stages of the procedure.

Under standard assumptions on the functions f, F and the constraint sets X and $Y(x)$, it is usually only possible to prove that the limit points of the sequence $\{x^k\}$ satisfy first-order optimality conditions in the Clarke sense (see [1]). The blanket assumption required to prove the stronger result that limit points are B-stationary, i. e. , that there do not exist feasible descent directions, is that the sequence of radii ε_k stays bounded away from zero. Rather than making such a claim, we will modify the last statement at Step 2 of the basic algorithm to incorporate a linesearch strategy that will guarantee that limit points are B-stationary, thus eliminating the requirement about trust region radii.

$$\textbf{if} \quad r_k < 1/3 \quad \textbf{then} \quad v_k \in \{\arg \min_{v \in \{2^j \varepsilon_k : 1 \leqslant j \leqslant [-\lg \varepsilon_k]\}} f(\overline{x}_v, y(\overline{x}_v))\}$$

$$x^{k+1} \in \operatorname{argmin}\{f(\overline{x}_{v_k}, y(\overline{x}_{v_k})), f(x^k, y(x^k))\}$$

$$\varepsilon_{k+1} \leftarrow \varepsilon_k / 2$$

The rationale underlying the linesearch rule is that, in the vicinity of a nonstationary point, there must exist a trust region radius ε such that $\overline{x}_\varepsilon$ improves on the current iterate x^k, even though the ratio r_k indicates that the linear model is a poor approximation of the original model; by doubling the trust region radius a nite number of times, one is able to bypass such nonstationary points. While this scheme may appear computationally costly at a rst glance, it is not unreasonable, considering that (i) "tractable" bilevel programs must involve lower level problems that can be eciently and repeatedly solved and (ii) the probability of havingto perform the linesearch is low, as conrmed by our numerical experiments.

We now present the key assumptions that will be used throughout the paper.

Assumption 1. The set X is compact.

Assumption 2. The function f and its gradient ∇f are Lipschitz continuous on $Z=\{(x,y): x\in X, y\in Y(x)\}$, with respective Lipschitz constants l and l' .

Assumption 3. The mapping F and its Jacobian are Lipschitz continuous on Z, with respective Lipschitz constants L and L'.

Assumption 4. F is uniformly strongly monotone in y, with modulus β, on Z.

Note that the above Lipschitz and monotonicity properties are shared by the rst-order approximations of f and F, respectively.

The remainder of the paper will be divided into four parts: the local behavior of the reaction functions $y(x)$ and $\overline{y}(x)$, a series of approximation lemmas, the convergence analysis and a conclusion.

2. Local behavior of $y(x)$ and $\overline{y}(x)$

Theorem 1. *The functions $y(x)$ and $y(x)$ are Lipschitz continuous on their common domain of denition $D=\{x\in X: Y(x)\neq\phi\}$.*

Proof. Under local Lipschitz and strong monotonicity assumptions on the mapping F, Dafermos[2]has shown that the reaction function $y(x)$ is Lipschitz continuous, provided that the projection operator $p_z(x)=\mathrm{proj}_{Y(x)}(z)$ is also Lipschitz continuous, for xed z. By denition, we have that

$$p_z(x) = \arg\min_{y\in Y(x)} \frac{1}{2}\| y - z \|^2$$

or equivalently, $p_z(x)$ satises the generalized equation

$$0 \in p_z(x) - z + \partial\delta(Y(x));$$

where δ denotes the indicator function of the polyhedral set $Y(x)$. It follows from Robinson[9]that the polyhedral multifunction $p_z(x)$ is upper Lipschitzian. Since the set X is compact and $p_z(x)$ is uniquely dened, we conclude that $p_z(x)$ is Lipschitz continuous on its domain, and this brings the desired result. Anidentical proof applies to the reaction function $\overline{y}(x)$. □

Theorem 2. *The functions $y(x)$ and $y(x)$ are directionally dierentiable.*

Proof. Let $c=F(x, y(x))$. Consider the linear program

$$\begin{aligned} &\min_y \quad cy \\ &\text{s. t.} \quad Ax+By\geqslant b \end{aligned}$$

and its dual

$$\begin{aligned} &\max_{\pi\geqslant 0} \quad \pi(b-Ax) \\ &\text{s. t.} \quad \pi B=c; \end{aligned}$$

The vector $y(x)$ is the optimal solution of the primal program while the optimal set of dual vectors $\pi(x)$ isupper Lipschitzian as a function of the couple(c, x). Since $c=F(x, y(x))$ is Lipschitz continuous, it follows that the multifunction $\pi(x)$ is upper Lipschitzian. This guarantees, for any feasible direction d and any real sequence $\{t_i\}_{i\in I}$ converging to zero, the existence of vectors. $\tilde{\pi}(x)\in\pi(x)$, $\tilde{\pi}(x+t_id)\in\pi(x+t_id)$and of a positive number M such that

$$\| \tilde{\pi}(x+t_id) - \tilde{\pi}(x) \| \leqslant Mt_i \quad \forall i;$$

Let

$$\pi' = \lim_{i\in I'} \frac{\tilde{\pi}(x+t_id) - \tilde{\pi}(x)}{t_i}$$

for some subset of indices I'. and let us consider, as in[8], the index sets

$$\begin{aligned} K_1 &= \{k \mid \tilde{\pi}(\overline{x}) > 0; (By(\overline{x}) + A\overline{x} - b)_k = 0\}, \\ K_2 &= \{k \mid \tilde{\pi}(\overline{x}) = 0, (By(\overline{x}) + A\overline{x} - b)_k = 0\}, \\ K_3 &= \{k \mid \tilde{\pi}(\overline{x}) = 0, (By(\overline{x}) + A\overline{x} - b)_k > 0\}. \end{aligned}$$

Let y' be a limit point of the sequence $\{[y(x+t_id)-y(x)]/=t_i\}_{i\in I}$. According to results of Qiu and Magnanti we obtain that the limit vectorsy y' and π' satisfy the linear complementarity system

$$\begin{aligned} &\pi' B - \nabla_y F(x, y)y' - \nabla_x F(x, y)d = 0; \\ &(By')_k = 0 \text{ if } k\in K_1, \\ &(By')_k = 0 \text{ if } k\in K_2 \text{ and } (\pi')_k > 0, \\ &(By')_k \geqslant 0 \text{ if } k\in K_2 \text{ and } (\pi')_k = 0, \\ &(\pi')_k \geqslant 0 \quad \text{if } k\in K_2, \end{aligned}$$

$$(\pi')_k = 0 \quad \text{if } k \in K_3.$$

The partial solution y' of the above system, which coincides with the directional derivative $y'(x;d)$, is also the unique solution of the strongly monotone variational inequality

$$\langle \nabla_x F(x,y)d + \nabla_y F(x,y)y, y - z\rangle \leqslant 0 \quad \forall z \in P,$$

where $P=\{y:(By)_k=0;k\in K_1;(By)_k\geqslant 0;k\in K_2\}$. □

The above results justify the local approximation of the function $f(x,y(x))$ by the function $\overline{f}(x,\overline{y}(x))$, since not only $\overline{y}(\overline{x})=y(\overline{x})$ and $\overline{y}'(\overline{x};d)=y'(\overline{x};d)$ but also both lower level variational inequalities, original and approximated, have identical KKT multipliers and directional derivatives.

3. Approximation results

In this section we prove that, applied to an iterate suciently close to a point which is not a strongstationary point, i. e. , a point where at least one feasible descent direction exists, algorithm BlTrust will generate a new iterate with an objective value strictly less than that of the current iterate. The proof of this result is based on three approximation lemmas, which make use of the notation described in Table 1.

Table 1 Notation

ε:	radius of the trust region
$y(x)$:	solution of the lower level variational inequality
$(\overline{x},\overline{y})$:	currentfeasibleiterate: $\overline{y}=y(\overline{x})$
$\overline{y}(x)$:	solution of the linearized lower level variational inequality
$\overline{f}(x,y)$:	linear approximation of f at $(\overline{x},\overline{y})$
$\overline{F}(x,y)$:	linear approximation of F at $(\overline{x},\overline{y})$
$(\overline{x}_\varepsilon,\overline{y}_\varepsilon=\overline{y}(\overline{x}_\varepsilon))$:	a global minimizer of the linearized bilevel program (model) within the trust region.
$(x_\varepsilon,y(x_\varepsilon))$:	a global minimizer of the bilevel program within the trust region
α:	joint Lipschitz constant of $y(x)$ and $\overline{y}(x)$
β:	uniform modulus of strong monotonicity of F with respect to its second argument y
σ:	$\sigma=\frac{1}{2}L'(1+\alpha^2)/\beta$
μ:	$\mu=l\sigma+\frac{1}{2}l'(1+\alpha^2)$
τ:	$\tau=\mu+\frac{1}{2}l'(1+\alpha^2)+l\sigma$
$\widetilde{f}$:	$\widetilde{f}(x)=f(x,y(x))$

Lemma 1. *$\| y(x_\varepsilon)-\overline{y}(x_\varepsilon) \| \leqslant\sigma\varepsilon^2$ and $\| y(\overline{x}_\varepsilon)-\overline{y}_\varepsilon \| \leqslant\sigma\varepsilon^2$.*

Proof. By denition of $y(x_\varepsilon)$ and $\overline{y}(x_\varepsilon)$ one has

$$\langle F(x_\varepsilon,y(x_\varepsilon)), y(x_\varepsilon)-\overline{y}(x_\varepsilon)\rangle \leq 0$$

and

$$\langle \overline{F}(x_\varepsilon, \overline{y}(x_\varepsilon)), \overline{y}(x_\varepsilon) - y(x_\varepsilon)\rangle \leqslant 0.$$

Subtracting those inequalities, one gets

$$\langle F(x_\varepsilon, y(x_\varepsilon)) - \overline{F}(x_\varepsilon, \overline{y}(x_\varepsilon)), y(x_\varepsilon) - \overline{y}(x_\varepsilon)\rangle \leqslant 0.$$

Adding and subtracting the term $F(x_\varepsilon, \overline{y}(x_\varepsilon))$ one obtains

$$\langle F(x_\varepsilon, y(x_\varepsilon)) - F(x_\varepsilon, \overline{y}(x_\varepsilon)) + F(x_\varepsilon, \overline{y}(x_\varepsilon)) - \overline{F}(x_\varepsilon, \overline{y}(x_\varepsilon)), y(x_\varepsilon) - \overline{y}(x_\varepsilon)\rangle \leqslant 0$$

and, using the strong monotonicity and Lipschitz continuity of F'.

$$\begin{aligned}
\beta \| y(x_\varepsilon) - \overline{y}(x_\varepsilon) \| &\leqslant \| F(x_\varepsilon, \overline{y}(x_\varepsilon)) - \overline{F}(x_\varepsilon, \overline{y}(x_\varepsilon)) \| \\
&\leqslant \frac{1}{2}L'[\| x_\varepsilon - \overline{x} \|^2 + \| \overline{y}(x_\varepsilon) - \overline{y} \|^2] \text{ by Theorem 1} \\
&\leqslant \frac{1}{2}L'[\varepsilon^2 + (\alpha\varepsilon)^2] \\
&= \beta\sigma\varepsilon^2.
\end{aligned}$$

The result follows upon division of each side of the inequality by β. The proof of the second inequality is similar. □

Lemma 2. *The dierence between the global minimum within the trust region and the true minimum is of the order of* ε^2. *More precisely*,

$$\overline{f}(\overline{x}_\varepsilon, \overline{y}_\varepsilon) - f(x_\varepsilon, y(x_\varepsilon)) \leqslant \mu\varepsilon^2.$$

Proof. Since $(\overline{x}_\varepsilon, \overline{y}_\varepsilon)$ is optimal for the model, we have

$$\begin{aligned}
\overline{f}(\overline{x}_\varepsilon, \overline{y}_\varepsilon) &\leqslant \overline{f}(x_\varepsilon, \overline{y}(x_\varepsilon)) \\
&\leqslant f(x_\varepsilon, \overline{y}(x_\varepsilon)) + \frac{1}{2} l'[\| x_\varepsilon - \overline{x} \|^2 + \| \overline{y}(x_\varepsilon) - \overline{y} \|^2] \\
&\leqslant f(x_\varepsilon, \overline{y}(x_\varepsilon)) + \frac{1}{2} l'\varepsilon^2(1 + \alpha^2) \text{ by Theorem 1} \\
&\leqslant f(x_\varepsilon, y(x_\varepsilon)) + l \| \overline{y}(x_\varepsilon) - y(x_\varepsilon) \| + \frac{1}{2}l'\varepsilon^2(1 + \alpha^2) \\
&\leqslant f(x_\varepsilon, y(x_\varepsilon)) + l\sigma\varepsilon^2 + \frac{1}{2}l'\varepsilon^2(1 + \alpha^2) \text{ by Lemma 1} \\
&= f(x_\varepsilon, y(x_\varepsilon)) + \mu\varepsilon^2.
\end{aligned}$$

□

Lemma 3. *The dierence between the value predicted by the model and the actual value of the cost function is of the order of* ε^2. *More precisely*;

$$f(\overline{x}_q, y(\overline{x}_\varepsilon)) - f(\overline{x}_\varepsilon, \overline{y}_\varepsilon) \leqslant l\sigma\varepsilon^2.$$

Proof. $f(\overline{x}_\varepsilon, y(\overline{x}_\varepsilon)) \leqslant f(\overline{x}_\varepsilon, \overline{y}_\varepsilon) + l \| y(\overline{x}_\varepsilon) - \overline{y}_\varepsilon \| \leqslant f(\overline{x}_\varepsilon, \overline{y}_\varepsilon) + l\sigma\varepsilon^2$y Lemma 1. □

Lemma 4. *The dierence between the best value of the cost function within the trust region and the actual value given by the model is of the order of* ε^2. *More precisely*,

$$| \tilde{f}(\overline{x}_\varepsilon) - \tilde{f}(x_\varepsilon) | \leqslant \tau\varepsilon^2.$$

Proof.

$$
\begin{aligned}
\tilde{f}(\bar{x}_\varepsilon) &= f(\bar{x}_\varepsilon, y(\bar{x}_\varepsilon)) \\
&\leqslant f(\bar{x}_\varepsilon, \bar{y}(\bar{x}_\varepsilon)) + l\sigma\varepsilon^2 \text{ by Lemma 3} \\
&\leqslant \bar{f}(\bar{x}_\varepsilon, \bar{y}(\bar{x}_\varepsilon)) + \frac{1}{2} l'[\|\bar{x}_\varepsilon - \bar{x}\|^2 + \|\bar{y}_\varepsilon - \bar{y}\|^2] + l\sigma\varepsilon^2 \\
&\leqslant \bar{f}(\bar{x}_\varepsilon \bar{y}, (\bar{x}_\varepsilon)) + \frac{1}{2} l'[(1+\alpha^2)\|\bar{x}_\varepsilon - \bar{x}\|^2] + l\sigma\varepsilon^2 \text{ by Theorem 1} \\
&\leqslant f(x_\varepsilon, y(x_\varepsilon)) + \mu\varepsilon^2 + \frac{1}{2} l'(1+\alpha^2)\varepsilon^2 + l\sigma\varepsilon^2 \text{ by Lemma 2} \\
&= f(x_\varepsilon, y(x_\varepsilon)) + \tau\varepsilon^2.
\end{aligned}
$$

□

Theorem 3. *If the function $\tilde{f}$ admits a feasible descent direction at $\bar{x}$, then $\tilde{f}(\bar{x}_\varepsilon) < \tilde{f}(\bar{x})$ for suciently small ε.*

Proof. Let $d(\|d\|=1)$ be a feasible descent direction at $\bar{x}$ and $\bar{t}, \theta$ be positive numbers such that

$$\tilde{f}(\bar{x}+td) \leqslant \tilde{f}(\bar{x}) - \theta t \quad \text{for all } t \in [0, \bar{t}].$$

Let $\varepsilon \in (0, \min\{\bar{t}, \theta/\tau\})$. We have, by Lemma 4

$$
\begin{aligned}
\tilde{f}(\bar{x}_\varepsilon) &\leqslant \tilde{f}(x_\varepsilon) + \tau\varepsilon^2 \\
&\leqslant \tilde{f}(\bar{x}+\varepsilon d) + \tau\varepsilon^2 \\
&\leqslant \tilde{f}(\bar{x}) - \theta\varepsilon + \tau\varepsilon^2 \\
&= \tilde{f}(\bar{x}) - \varepsilon(\theta - \tau\varepsilon) \\
&< \tilde{f}(\bar{x}).
\end{aligned}
$$

□

Theorem 4. *Let $\tilde{f}$ admit a feasible descent direction at $\tilde{x}$. Then there exists a positive number ε such that $\tilde{f}(\bar{x}_{\bar{\varepsilon}}) < \tilde{f}(\tilde{x})$ wheneverx $\|\tilde{x} - \bar{x}\| \leq \varepsilon/2$ and $\bar{\varepsilon} \in [\varepsilon, 2\varepsilon]$.*

Proof. As before, there exist positive numbers $\bar{t}, \theta$ and a feasible direction d such that $\|d\|=1$ and

$$\tilde{f}(\tilde{x}+td) \leqslant \tilde{f}(\tilde{x}) - \theta t \quad \text{for all } t \in [0, \bar{t}].$$

Let $\varepsilon \in (0, \min\{\bar{t}, \theta/8\tau\})$ and $\delta = \varepsilon/2$. We have that $\tilde{x}+\delta d$ lies in the ball (trust region) of radius ε centered at $\bar{x}$ and

$$\tilde{f}(\tilde{x}+\delta d) \leqslant \tilde{f}(\tilde{x}) - \delta\theta.$$

Since $x_{\bar{\varepsilon}}$ is optimal within the trust region

$$\tilde{f}(x_{\bar{\varepsilon}}) \leqslant \tilde{f}(\tilde{x}+\delta d) \leqslant \tilde{f}(\tilde{x}) - \delta\theta.$$

Now

$$
\begin{aligned}
\tilde{f}(\bar{x}_{\bar{\varepsilon}}) &\leqslant \tilde{f}(x_{\bar{\varepsilon}}) + \tau\bar{\varepsilon}^2 \quad \text{by Lemma 4} \\
&\leqslant \tilde{f}(\tilde{x}) - \delta\theta + \tau\bar{\varepsilon}^2 \\
&= \tilde{f}(\tilde{x}) - \varepsilon(\theta/2 - 4\tau\varepsilon) \\
&< \tilde{f}(\tilde{x})
\end{aligned}
$$

□

4. Convergence analysis

We say that a feasible point x is *strongly stationary* for a function g if there do not exist a positive number α and a sequence$\{x^i\}_{i\in I}$ converging to x such that

$$g(x^i) < g(x) - \alpha \| x - x^i \| \quad \forall i \in I.$$

Note that the set of strong stationary points may be a strict subset of points that are stationary in the Clarke sense,i. e. ,points for which the zero vector belongs to the generalized subdierential. Whenever the function g is directionally dierentiable over its domain, the set of strong stationary points coincides with the set of B-stationary points,i. e. ,the set of points where no feasible descent direction exists. In view of Theorem 4 this is the case for the function $f(x,y(x))$ of our bilevel program.

If algorithm BlTrust stops nitely then, since the directional derivatives of the model agree with those of the original objective function, it must do so at a B-stationary point, i. e. , a strong stationary point. The next theorem shows that a similar result holds for any accumulation point generated by the trust region procedure.

Theorem 5. *Let $\{x^k\}_{k\in N}$ be an innite sequence generated by algorithm BlTrust. Then any accumulation point x^* of the sequence is B-stationary, i. e, strongly stationary.*

Proof. Let $\{x^{k_i}\}_{i\in I} \to x^*$. We consider two mutually exclusive cases.

*Case*1:There exists a positive number μ such that $\varepsilon_{k_i} \geqslant \mu$ for all $i \in I$. For this case, we adapt the arguments of Scholtes and Stöhr[10]. Let $y_i(x)$ denote the solution of the lower level linearized variational inequality corresponding to the upper level vector x^i obtained at iteration i and set $f_i(x) = f(x, y_i(x))$. From the statement of the algorithm,it must occur innitely often that the ratio r_k is larger than or equal to $\frac{1}{3}$, i. e. , usingthe previous notation

$$\tilde{f}(x^{k_i}) - \tilde{f}(x^{k_i+1}) \geqslant \frac{1}{3}(\bar{f}(x^{k_i}) - \bar{f}(\bar{x}_{\varepsilon_{k_i}})). \tag{1}$$

If x^* is not B-stationary for $\tilde{f}$,then it is not B-stationary either for the function $f_*(x)$ dened as $f_*(x) = f(x, y_*(x))$ where $y_*(x)$ satises the variational inequality

$$\langle F(x^*, y(x^*)) + F'_x(x^*, y(x^*))(x - x^*) + F'_y(x^*, y(x^*))(y_*(x) - y(x^*)), y_*(x) - y\rangle \leqslant 0 \quad \forall y \in Y(x).$$

Hence,for an arbitrary $\varepsilon \in (0, \mu]$, one can find a point $\hat{x} \in R^n$ with $\| \hat{x} - x^* \| \leq \varepsilon$ such that

$$f(\hat{x}, y_*(\hat{x})) < f(x^*, y(x^*)).$$

From the assumptions and previous continuity results, we obtain that $\| y_*(x) - y_{k_i}(x) \| \to 0$ and $f(\hat{x}, y_{k_i}(\hat{x})) \to f(\hat{x}, y_*(\hat{x}))$. Furthermore,

$$f_{k_i}(x^{k_i}) - f_{k_i}(\bar{x}_{\varepsilon_{k_i}}) \geqslant f_{k_i}(x^{k_i}) - f_{k_i}(\hat{x})$$
$$\geqslant \frac{1}{2}(f(x^*, y(x^*)) - f(\hat{x}, y_*(\hat{x}))) \tag{2}$$

for every suciently large $i \in N$. This implies, in view of (1) and (2), that the series $\sum(\tilde{f}(x^{k_i}) - \tilde{f}(x^{k_i+1}))$ diverges. However, since the trust region method generates a decreasing sequence, we have

$$\sum_{i=1}^{\infty}(\tilde{f}(x^{k_i})-\tilde{f}(x^{k_i+1})]) \leqslant \sum_{i=1}^{\infty}(\tilde{f}(x^{k_i})-\tilde{f}(x^{k_i+1})) = \tilde{f}(x^{k_1})-\tilde{f}(x^{)} < \infty,$$

which is the desired contradiction to our assumption that x^* was not B-stationary.

Case 2: $\lim_{i\to\infty}\varepsilon_{k_i}=0$. Assume that the limit point x^* is not B-stationary and select ε as in Theorem 4. Let i be an index such that $\| x^{k^i}-x^* \| \leqslant \varepsilon/2$, j an integer satisfying the relationship $\varepsilon \leqslant 2^j \varepsilon_{k_i}=\varepsilon' \leqslant 2\varepsilon$. From Theorem 4, we have that $\tilde{f}(\overline{x}_{\varepsilon'})<\tilde{f}(x^*)$ which contradicts the statement that x^* was not a B-stationary limit point of the sequence $\{x^{k_i}\}$. □

Theorem 5 completes our analysis of an approximation scheme for solving bilevel programs. It examplies the power of a nonconvex approximation for solving nonconvex programs. In our case, this scheme concen-trates the combinatorial diculties on the linearized bilevel program. This decoupling of the combinatorial and nonlinear nature of the problem allows us to take full advantage of both the trust region methodology for the outer problem and of efficient combinatorial techniques for the linearized subproblem. This makes for an algorithm that possesses good convergence properties and is implementable. An apparent drawback of the method is the need to perform a costly linesearch at each iteration in order to enforce convergence to a strong stationary point. However, this technique will most likely be required only in extreme cases where the algorithm gets trapped in the vicinity of a C-stationary point, an unlikely event.

5. Conclusion

Although algorithm BlTrust is only guaranteed to generate B-stationary limit points, it has the capability to move away from nonglobal stationary points. In this respect, it is unlikely to get trapped into "weak" local solutions and holds the potential of solving to global optimality generalized bilevel programs involving mildly nonlinear functions f and F. For that reason we refer to BlTrust as a "semi-global" method.

Future work on BlTrust will focus on its implementation and on relaxingsome of the assumptions required to prove convergence to a B-stationary point. In particular, the set Y could depend nonlinearly on the upper-level vector x. Standard regularity assumptions on this set would ensure that the approximations obtained in our lemmas still hold.

References

[1] F. H. Clarke, Optimization and Nonsmooth Analysis, SIAM, Philadelphia, PA, 1990.

[2] S. Dafermos, Sensitivity analysis in variational inequalities, Math. Oper. Res. 13 (1988) 421-434.

[3] M. Fukushima, P. Tseng, An implementable active-set algorithm for computing a B-stationary point of the mathematical program with linear complementarity constraints, Technical Report 99020, Department of Applied Mathematics and Physics, Kyoto University, October 1999.

[4] P. Hansen, B. Jaumard, G. Savard, New branch-and-bound rules for linear bilevel programming, SIAM J. Sci. Statist. Comput. 13 (1992) 1194-1217.

[5] Z. Q. Luo, J. S. Pang, D. Ralph, Mathematical Programs with Equilibrium Constraints, Cambridge University Press, Cambridge, 1996.

[6] P. Marcotte, D. L. Zhu, Exact and inexact methods for the generalized bilevel programming problem, Math. Programming 74 (1996) 141-157.

[7] J. V. Outrata, M. Kocvara, J. Zowe, Nonsmooth Approach to Optimization Problems with Equilibrium Constraints, Kluwer Academic Publishers, Dordrecht, 1998.

[8] Y. Qiu, T. L. Magnanti, Sensitivity analysis for variational inequalities denedon polyhedral sets, Math. Oper. Res. 14 (1989) 410-423.

[9] S. M. Robinson, Some continuity properties of polyhedral multifunctions, Math. Programming Stud. 14 (1981) 206-214.

[10] S. Scholtes, M. Stohr, Exact penalization of mathematical programs with equilibrium constraints, SIAM J. Control Optim. 37 (1999) 617-652.

Published in *Operations Research letters* 2001,29

第五章　全球运输和港口竞争分析

随着全球经济的发展，航运业在经历了船舶大型化和集装箱化革命之后已进入现代物流时代。航运企业间竞争将从简单的航运价格提升到完整价值链意义上的集成物流服务价值竞争。港口已不再是运输的终点，而是国际运输和物流链中的一环。港口货源的形成分析、港口之间的合作和竞争已成为现代港口管理的重要内容。

港口以及国际贸易运输链对托运人的个性化服务特征，如快捷运输、挂港减少，直达航线大幅增加及价格决定了港口和国际贸易运输链的竞争力，也决定了一个港口的吞吐量和贸易量。

在本章前三篇论文中，我们利用了产品差异化、超网络理论和数据包络分析方法分别研究了全球运输和港口竞争分析及港口服务绩效评价。论文提出了基于顾客选择的Hotelling模型和方法，突破了计算港口吞吐量的传统方法，如腹地定界方法和GDP回归方法。

在本章最后一篇论文中，我们研究了世界海运网络（WMN），它由集装箱海上航线和港口所组成。我们把WMN构建为带权有向网络，通过分析其拓扑性质，发现它是一个无标度小世界网络。我们还研究了WMN的层次结构、点度和介数的一致性。最后对重要性排名世界前25位的港口的地理位置分布及特征作了分析。

港口价格竞争策略研究*

朱道立，吉阿兵

（复旦大学 管理学院，上海 200433）

摘要：在对以港口为基础的多式联运以及顾客选择行为分析的基础上，构建了出口货物的多式联运超级网络以及基于顾客选择的 Hotelling 模型。对港口价格竞争的 Nash 均衡问题进行分析和求解，并分析了港口价格策略对其腹地份额和收益的影响。

关键词：超级网络；港口竞争；Hotelling 模型；顾客选择；Nash 均衡

中图分类号：F 253.4　　　　**文献标识码：**A

港口与国际贸易相辅相成的关系，中国对外贸易的快速增长，促进了中国港口业的发展。发展港口可以带动地区经济的发展，目前，中国沿海、沿江各地纷纷投资建设新港口或提高原有港口的吞吐能力，使得港口吞吐能力的增长高于贸易量的增长，港口间相互竞争的势头已经出现。对同一个港口群内的港口而言，地理位置的靠近、交通基础设施的改善、腹地的重叠，使得这种竞争更为激烈。

关于港口竞争问题，有两个主要的研究方向，即研究港口政策对港口竞争的影响和港口竞争策略研究。其中有关港口竞争策略的研究，在 20 世纪 80 年代以前，主要集中于价格策略方面，如 Bennathan[1] 定性分析了实行价格歧视策略可以增强港口的竞争力。随着运输过程的复杂化，发货人的选择行为对港口的影响越来越大。文献[2～6]通过实证方法研究影响发货人港口选择的因素，指出港口竞争已呈现多元化，但港口的价格仍然是最重要的因素之一。以上文献大多从定性的角度来研究港口的策略问题，而 UNCTAD[1] 的研究使用了定量分析方法，以时间、成本、安全为指标，建立综合衡量港口竞争实力的公式。施欣[1] 研究了港口竞争对策模型，但没有进行深入的讨论；Luo[7] 则利用仿真的方法研究了新建港口对原有港口的影响及腹地的重新划分问题。

上述研究促进了港口竞争理论的发展，但是，这些研究在分析港口竞争策略时，很少考虑竞争港口的反应策略。较少文献分析港口的竞争策略对发货人港口选择行为的影响和对港口腹地份额的影响。

港口的收费是国际物流成本的重要组成部分，在近洋运输中港口费用大约占总运输成本的 40％～60％，在远洋运输中这一比例是 5％～10％[8]。当前，中国港口的收费由交通部统一定价，交通部已通知各港口进行价格政策研究。因此，及早研究港口的价格行为

---

* **收稿日期：**2006-04-19

基金项目：国家自然科学基金重点资助项目(70432001)

作者简介：朱道立(1945～)，男，教授，博士生导师；吉阿兵(1977～)，男，博士研究生。

对我国港口的发展具有很重要的现实意义。

传统的港口吞吐量的预测方法主要是腹地定界法、时间序列法[9]等方法。现实中这两种方法存在很大的误差，如温州在进行港口规划的过程中，最初认为直接腹地温州、台州、金华、丽水、衢州的货源大都会从温州港进出，实际上这五个地区80%以上的货源从上海港与宁波港进出。预测的偏差导致规划建设的温州港七里港区一直处于闲置状态，因此，需要新的方法进行港口吞吐量的预测。

Hotelling在1929年提出了著名的Hotelling模型[10]，后来Aspremont[11,12]等指出了Hotelling模型的缺陷，并给出均衡解存在的条件以及二次情况的修改Hotelling模型。Hotelling模型能够比较好地表示2个寡头的价格竞争行为，而港口正好具有寡头垄断的特征，本文将使用Hotelling模型来研究港口的价格策略设计问题。

1 数学模型

1.1 相关假设

1）海上运输。影响海上运输的因素有船公司的船舶配置策略和船舶计划、不同船型的经济航行速度等。由于本文研究港口的不同策略对服务需求量，特别是集装箱吞吐量的影响，在模型中用平均船速、平均费用表示船舶的海上航行特征，并认为每条船的容量足够大。同时还假设从2个港口到每个目的港都有直接的航线。在这些假设下，我们可根据航线长度、每英里的平均费用、运输速度来计算海上运输费用。

2）港口。通过一个港口的集装箱量本质上是由港口所具有的比较优势决定的，包括港口位置、航道条件、泊位数、港口收费等。对顾客而言，看到的和关心的是港口收费和货物运输过程的总时间等外在因素。航道条件、泊位数等是港口的内部因素，港口可以通过改变内部因素来改变收费和服务质量等外部因素。本文研究的重点是港口的外在因素对港口的影响，因此在模型中假设港口的内部因素是无差别的。此外，为了简化起见，假设目的港只有一个。

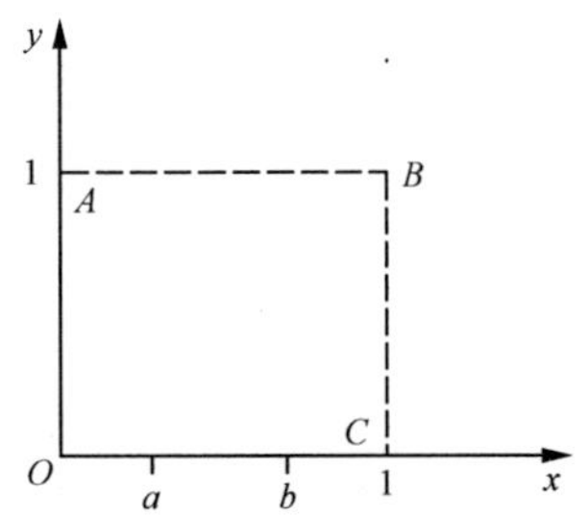

图1 港口腹地平面图

Fig. 1 Hinterland of port

3）发货人。在海运实务中，发货人本身并不选择运输路线，只是决定货源地、目的地、运输方式及到港时间，具体的路线安排由货代或船公司来决定。Tsamboulas和Kapros[13]指出货代、发货人、船公司在做运输路线决策的时候，通常遵循14个原则，其中运输费用最小是最重要的原则之一。在我们的研究中将作为发货人统一处理，并假设每个发货人的发货量为1单位。

4）港口共同腹地。与传统的腹地概念相比，这里所研究的腹地是指2个港口直接腹地的总和。如图1，假设港口1和港口2分别位于轴上的点$(a,0)$和$(b,0)$，而港口的竞争腹地为由点O,A,B,C组成的矩形Γ，假设发货人在Γ中均匀分布。

1.2 多式联运超级网络

以出口（进口的过程相反）为例来讨论发货人的选择行为和货运量的分配，为简化起见，只讨论一种货物的情况。在CIF(Cost Insurance Freight)情况下，由出口商负责货物的运输。在FOB(Free on Board)情况下，由进口商负责货物运输，其运输决策行为与CIF情况下的出口商相类似。因此，在CIF下的出口商代表发货人。

我们用一个多式联运超级网络来表示运输过程（图2）。图中最左边的方框表示2个港口所面对的共同腹地，发货人在其中均匀分布，点(x,y)表示某一个发货人。货物从发货地经过陆路运输后进入港口，再通过港口的装卸、转运活动装上轮船，经过海上运输后到达目的港并卸到码头堆场。在以往的多式联运网络中，港口只是用一个节点表示，在本图中，用两个节点和一个虚弧构成的简单网络表示港口节点，这种包含网络的网络称为超网络。

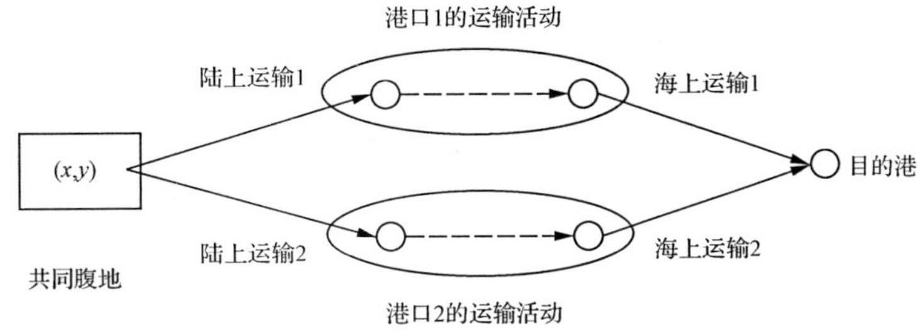

图 2　出口货物的超级运输网络

Fig. 2　Super network of export

1.3　选择模型

从图 2 中可以看出，发货人有 2 条路线可以选择，路线 1：陆上运输 1—港口 1—海上运输 1；路线 2：陆上运输 2—港口 2—海上运输 2。在做路线选择的决策过程中，发货人要考虑货物陆上的运输费用、港口的费用、海上运输费用。因此，单个发货人的选择行为就是综合比较两条路线的总费用，然后，找出总费用最小的路线。在一个发货人均匀分布的腹地中，所有发货人的选择都遵循这一原则。把单个发货人的选择行为集聚后，就形成了腹地的划分。

模型中的变量定义如下：i 表示第 i 发货人；α 表示陆上的运输费用参数；β 表示海上的运输费用参数；$f_{in}(l_{in})$表示从发货人 i 至第 n 港口的陆上费用函数；l_{in} 表示从发货人 i 至第 n 个港口的距离；p_n 表示在第 n 个港口收取单位集装箱的价格，包括港口使用费、拖轮费、引航费、装卸费等费用；l_{nd} 表示第 n 个港口到目的港 d 的海上距离。不失一般性，在本文中可以假设 $l_{2d} \geqslant l_{1_d}$；$f_{nd}(l_{nd})$表示从港口 n 到目的港 d 的海上运输费用函数。

发货人 i 利用港口 n 的总费用＝陆上运输费用＋海上运输费用＋港口费用，即

$$TC_n(i) = f_{in}(l_{in}) + f_{nd}(l_{nd}) + p_n \quad n = 1,2 \tag{1}$$

发货人 i 寻找总费用最小的路线，用公式表示为

$$\min_{n=1,2}\{TC_n(i)\}$$

文献[11]研究发现当陆上运输费用是距离平方的函数时，Hotelling 模型能够保证解的唯一性，故令 $f_{in}(l_{in}) = \alpha l_{in}^2$，$\alpha$ 为常量，$f_{nd}(l_{nd}) = \beta l_{nd}$，$\beta$ 为常数。设发货人 i 的坐标为(x,y)，则发货人至港口 1 的距离为 $l_{i1} = \sqrt{(x-a)^2+y^2}$，至港口 2 的距离为 $l_{i2} = \sqrt{(x-b)^2+y^2}$。选择最小路线的过程可表示为

$$\min_{n=1,2} TC_n(i) = \alpha l_{in}^2 + \beta l_{nd} + p_n \tag{2}$$

2　共同腹地市场份额的划分

对任意一个发货人 I，通过 2 个港口到达目的港的费用分别是 $TC_1(x,y)$和 $TC_2(x,$

y)，可用 $h(x,y)=TC_1(x,y)-TC_2(x,y)$ 表示通过 2 个港口的费用之差，我们有

$$h(x,y)=2\alpha(a-b)x+\alpha(b^2-a^2)+(p_2-p_1)+\beta(l_{2d}-l_{1d})$$

很显然，$h(x,y)$ 是与 $y\in[0,1]$ 不相关的函数。因此，记 $h(x)=h(x,y)$。特别地有

$$h(0)=p_2-p_1+c_1,\quad h(1)=p_2-p_1+c_2$$

其中，

$$c_1=(\alpha b^2+\beta l_{2d})-(\alpha a^2+\beta l_{1d})$$

$$c_2=(\alpha(1-b)^2+\beta l_{2d})-(\alpha(1-a)^2+\beta l_{1d})=c_1+2\alpha(a-b)$$

因为 $h(x)$ 是关于参数 x 的单调减函数，所以有 $h(0)\geqslant h(x)\geqslant h(1)$，$\forall x\in[0,1]$。

文献[14]通过大量的调查发现，当港口价格等港口特征无差异时，发货人一般选择较近的港口出口：即处于 $x=0$ 的发货人认为选择港口 1 的运输总成本要小于选择港口 2 的运输总成本，所以有 $c_1>0$；位于 $x=1$ 的发货人认为选择港口 2 运输的总成本小于选择港口 1 的运输总成本，有 $c_2<0$。因此，本文采取合理的假设 $c_1>0$ 和 $c_2<0$。

情况 1　$h(0)\geqslant 0$，且 $h(1)\leqslant 0$，即 $c_2\leqslant p_1-p_2\leqslant c_1$。

此时，港口 1 和港口 2 共同划分腹地。在 2 个港口之间存在一条垂直于横坐标的直线，线上的任一发货人 $(\bar{x},y)$ 到 2 个港口的费用是相等的，即 $h(\bar{x})=0$。由此可解得

$$\bar{x}=\frac{(p_2-p_1)+c_1}{2a(b-a)}=\frac{(p_2-p_1)+c_1}{c_1-c_2}\tag{3}$$

在集合 $\Gamma_1=\{(x,y)\mid x\leqslant\bar{x},y\in[0,1]\}$ 中的所有发货人都会选择港口 1，而位于集合 $\Gamma_2=\{(x,y)\mid x\geqslant\bar{x},y\in[0,1]\}$ 的发货人选择港口 2。此时，2 个港口的腹地份额分别为

$$q_1=\bar{x}=\frac{(p_2-p_1)+c_1}{c_1-c_2}\tag{4}$$

$$q_2=1-\bar{x}=\frac{(p_1-p_2)-c_2}{c_1-c_2}\tag{5}$$

情况 2　$h(1)>0$，即 $p_1-p_2<c_2$，所有发货人选择港口 1，港口 1 占全部腹地。此时的腹地份额分别是：

$$q_1=1,\quad q_2=0$$

情况 3　$h(0)<0$，即 $p_1-p_2>c_1$，所有的发货人选择港口 2，港口 2 拥有全部腹地市场。此时的市场份额分别是：

$$q_1=0,\quad q_2=1$$

3　2 个港口的竞争策略选择

每个港口都试图通过改变港口收费来改变对发货人的吸引力，从而获得较大的收益。2 个港口的收入函数分别表示为 $\pi_1(p_1,p_2)=p_1q_1$，$\pi_2(p_1,p_2)=p_2q_2$。根据上一节的分析结果，2 个港口的收入函数可表示为 p_1 和 p_2 的分段函数：

$$\pi_1(p_1,p_2)=\begin{cases}\dfrac{p_2-p_1+c_1}{c_1-c_2}p_1 & p_2+c_2\leqslant p_1\leqslant p_2+c_1\\ p_1 & p_1<p_2+c_2\\ 0 & p_1>p_2+c_1\end{cases}\tag{6}$$

$$\pi_2(p_1,p_2)=\begin{cases}\dfrac{p_1-p_2-c_2}{c_1-c_2}p_2 & p_1-c_1\leqslant p_2\leqslant p_1-c_2\\ p_2 & p_2<p_1-c_1\\ 0 & p_2>p_1-c_2\end{cases}\tag{7}$$

2 个港口之间的价格竞争是非合作竞争，可用 Nash[15] 均衡来表示。

定义 1　设 Nash 均衡解为(p_1^*,p_2^*)，则有

$$\pi_1(p_1^*,p_2^*)\geqslant\pi_1(p_1,p_2^*)\qquad\forall\, p_1\geqslant 0$$
$$\pi_2(p_1^*,p_2^*)\geqslant\pi_2(p_1^*,p_2)\qquad\forall\, p_2\geqslant 0$$

任一港口在其他港口的最优价格给定的情况下，选择自己的价格，从而达到自身的收益最大化。并且，在最优均衡状态下，任何港口都不能通过改变自身的价格来获得额外收益。为了讨论 Nash 均衡解的存在性，我们先分析函数$\pi_1(p_1,p_2)$和$\pi_2(p_1,p_2)$的性质。

命题 1　给定 p_2，函数 $\pi_1(p_1,p_2)$是 $p_1(p_1>0)$的连续的拟凹函数；给定 p_1，函数 $\pi_2(p_1,p_2)$是 $p_2(p_2>0)$的连续的拟凹函数。

证　先证明函数 $\pi_1(p_1,p_2)$的连续性。

给定 p_2，要证明分段函数 $\pi_1(p_1,p_2)$是关于 p_1 的连续函数，只需证明函数 $\pi_1(p_1,p_2)$在分割点 $\bar{p}_1=p_2+c_2$，$\bar{\bar{p}}_1=p_2+c_1$ 处是连续的。容易算得 p_1 在点 $\bar{p}_1$ 左右两边的极限存在且等于函数值 $\bar{p}_1$，所以函数 $\pi_1(p_1,p_2)$在点 $\bar{p}_1$ 处连续。同理，可知函数在 $\bar{\bar{p}}_1$ 点亦是连续的。所以函数 $\pi_1(p_1,p_2)$是关于 p_1 在$[0,\infty)$上的连续函数。

再证明函数 $\pi_1(p_1,p_2)$是关于 p_1 的拟凹函数。

对于给定的 p_2，设函数 $\pi_1(p_1,p_2)$在$[0,\infty)$的最大值在 $\hat{p}_1$ 点达到。由(6)式易得到 $\hat{p}_1$ 的表达式为

$$\hat{p}_1=\begin{cases}p_2+c_2 & p_2>c_1-2c_2\\ \dfrac{p_2+c_1}{2} & p_2\leqslant c_1-2c_2\end{cases}\tag{8}$$

根据 $\pi_1(p_1,p_2)$的表达式(6)，我们知道在$[0,\hat{p}_1]$上 $\pi_1(\cdot,p_2)$是单调上升的，而在$[\hat{p}_1,\infty]$是单调下降的，见图 3。因此，对于给定的 p_2，$\pi_1(\cdot,p_2)$是连续的单峰函数，因而也是一个连续的拟凹函数[16]。

同样的方法可以证明：对于给定的 p_1，函数 $\pi_2(p_1,\cdot)$是连续的拟凹函数，见图 4。

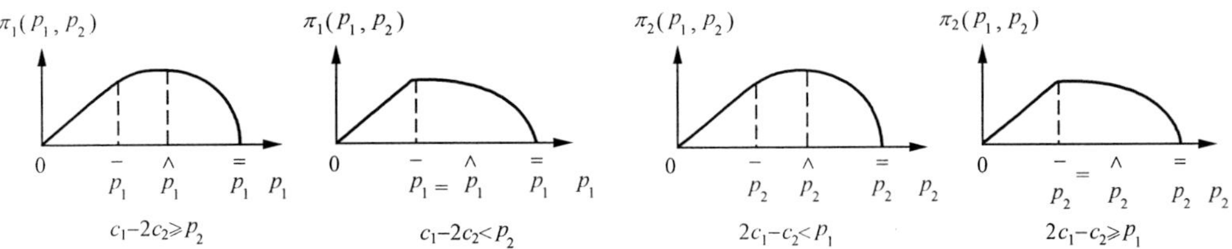

图 3　港口 1 的收入函数 $\pi_1(p_1,p_2)$

Fig. 3　Port 1 income function $\pi_1(p_1,p_2)$

图 4　港口 2 的收入函数 $\pi_2(p_1,p_2)$

Fig. 4　Port 2 income function $\pi_2(p_1,p_2)$

命题 2[15]　在本文的假设下，2 个港口之间价格竞争的 Nash 均衡解存在。

最后我们求出 Nash 均衡解。

先写出 2 个港口的价格反应函数(图 5)：

$$p_1(p_2)=\hat{p}_1=\begin{cases}p_2+c_2 & p_2>c_1-2c_2\\ \dfrac{p_2+c_2}{2} & p_2\leqslant c_1-2c_2\end{cases}\tag{9}$$

$$p_2(p_1)=\hat{p}_2=\begin{cases}p_1-c_1 & p_1>2c_1-c_2\\ \dfrac{p_1-c_1}{2} & p_1\leqslant 2c_1-c_2\end{cases}\tag{10}$$

因此，2 个港口的最佳价格决策，即 Nash 均衡解(p_1^*,p_2^*)满足方程

$$\begin{cases}p_1^*=p_1(p_2^*)\\ p_2^*=p_2(p_1^*)\end{cases}$$

根据(8)，(9)式知(p_1^*,p_2^*)满足

$$\begin{cases}p_1^*=\dfrac{p_2^*+c_1}{2}\\ p_2^*=\dfrac{p_1^*-c_2}{2}\end{cases}$$

最后得到 Nash 均衡解为

$$p_1^*=\frac{2c_1-c_2}{3},\quad p_2^*=\frac{c_1-2c_2}{3}\tag{11}$$

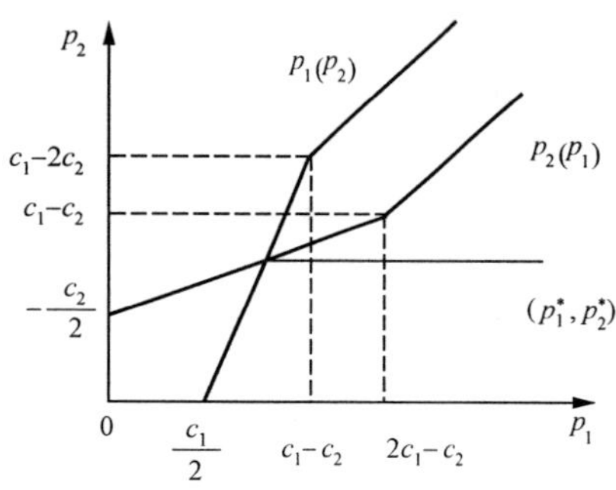

图 5 价格反应函数和 Nash 均衡解

Fig. 5 Price reaction function and Nash equilibrium solution

此时，2 个港口在均衡状态下所占有的腹地份额分别为

$$q_1^*=\frac{2c_1-c_2}{3(c_1-c_2)},\quad q_2^*=\frac{c_1-2c_2}{3(c_1-c_2)}\tag{12}$$

而港口 1,2 获得的收益分别是

$$\pi_1(p_1^*,p_2^*)=\frac{(2c_1-c_2)^2}{9(c_1-c_2)},\quad \pi_2(p_1^*,p_2^*)=\frac{(c_1-2c_2)^2}{9(c_1-c_2)}\tag{13}$$

4 分析与结论

港口在国际贸易中占有重要的地位，港口的收费和服务质量影响发货人的选择行为，而发货人的选择行为反过来又影响港口的腹地份额大小和收益的高低。本文的结论不但可以解释一些港口运营中的经济现象，而且可以为港口经营管理的决策提供参考。

把 c_1，c_2 带入(4)，(5)式可得

$$q_1=\frac{(p_2-p_1)+\beta(l_{2d}-l_{1d})+\alpha(b^2-a^2)}{2\alpha(b-a)}$$

$$q_2=\frac{(p_1-p_2)+\beta(l_{2d}-l_{1d})-\alpha(b-a)(a+b-2)}{2\alpha(b-a)}$$

可以发现港口的腹地份额与港口的价格和离目的港的距离有关系。港口的价格越高，其腹地份额越低；离目的港越近，腹地份额越高。这可解释为什么在枢纽港的周围地区仍有小港口存在的现象，比如上海港的周边地区有太仓港、嘉兴港。而在美国，东海岸港口进出的货物其目的地大都是欧洲，而西海岸港口货物的目的地大都是亚洲。

由(11)～(13)式可以看出港口的收益和最优策略与港口在腹地中的位置和对目的港

的距离有关系。在本文的假设前提下,离目的港越近的港口,其收益也越大,越远的港口其收益相应减少。

(11)式表明港口的收费与货物的海上和陆上运输费率成正比。对于单位价值较高的商品可以收取较高的费用,单位价值较低的商品收取较低的运费。这可以解释为什么不同用途的港口其收费不同,比如,大众散货的运输价格低于集装箱的运输价格,所以,集装箱码头的收费一般都高于散货码头的收费。

影响港口吞吐量的因素很多,比如腹地经济发展水平、航班密度、航道水深、港口所处地理位置,但港口价格是发货人或货主乃至船公司关心的最重要因素之一。在本文中我们综合考虑了出口货物陆上,海上、港口费用,探讨港口获得最大收益情况下的价格策略设计问题和港口在共同腹地中的市场份额问题。与以往不同的是本文所构建的多式联运的超级网络结构能表达顾客的选择行为,并且考虑其他港口的反应。港口可以通过改变自身活动来改变发货人的选择行为,而发货人的选择行为反过来又影响到港口的腹地份额大小和收益的高低。文中得出的结论对于港口企业进行科学决策具有重要的参考价值。

The Competition Strategies bet ween Regional Container Terminals

ZHU Dao-li ,JIA-bing

(*School of Management* , *Fudan University* , *Shanghai* 200433 , *China*)

Abstract: Based on the theory of customer choice ,the behavior of shippers was discussed and a super network of export was built. After that the Hotelling model was used to express the choice of port. The proof of existence of solution in Nash equilibrium condition was given. Especially a dashed line was used to describe the process conducted by ports. Conclusions revealed could be used to interpret some behaviors used by ports.

Keywords : super network ; port competition ; Hotelling model ; customer choice ; Nash equilibrium

参考文献

[1] 施欣. 港口竞争对策模型的研究[J]. 系统工程理论与实践,1998 ,**18** (9) :27-33.

[2] Bardi E J. Carrier selection from one mode[J]. *Transportation Journal* ,1973 ,**13** (1) :23-29.

[3] Brooks M. An alternative theoretical approach to the evaluation of liner shipping:Part 1,Situational factors[J]. *Maritime Policy & Management* ,1984 ,**11** (1) :35-43.

[4] Brooks M. An alternative theoretical approach to the evaluation of liner shipping:Part 2,Choicecrite-

ria[J]. *Maritime Policy & Management* ,1984 ,**12** (2) :145-155.

[5] Slack B. Containerization ,inter-port competition and port selection[J]. *Maritime Policy & Management* ,1985 , **13** (4) :293-303.

[6] Slack B. Shipping lines as agents in the port industry[J]. *Maritime Policy & Management* ,1996 , **23** (3) :289-300

[7] Luo Meifeng. Container transportation servicedemand simulation model for us coastal containerports [D]. Rhode Island:Department of environment and natural resource economics,Rhode Island University,2002.

[8] Siri P S. Port pricing structures and ship efficiency[J]. *Review of Network Economics* ,2004 , **3** (2) :135-144.

[9] 邹俊善. 现代港口经济学[M]. 北京:人民交通出版社,1997.

[10] Hotellig H. Stability in competition[J]. *Economic Journal* ,1929 ,**39** :41-57.

[11] Aspremont C D,Gabszewicz J J,Thisse J F. On hotelling's"stability in competition"[J]. *Econometrica* ,1979 , **47** (5) :1145-1150.

[12] Prescott E C. Sequential location among firms with foresight[J]. *The bell Journal of Economics* , 1977,**8** :378-393

[13] Tsamboulas D A,Kapros S. Decision-making process in intermodal transportation[M]. Washington: Transportation Research Record ,2000.

[14] Rhea E. By sea:The port nexus in the global commodity network[D]. Southen California:Political economy and public policy ,Southen California University ,2002.

[15] Nash J F. On cooperative games[J]. *Annals of Mathematics* ,1951 ,**54** :286-298.

[16] Martos B. Nonlinear programming theory and methods[M]. Amsterdam:North Holland,1975.

(本文发表于《复旦学报》(自然科学版),2006 年第 5 期)

网络外部性下的港口竞争策略设计

吉阿兵，朱道立

（复旦大学管理学院管理科学系，上海 200433）

摘要：在 Hotelling 模型的基础上发展了一个国际货物运输的路径选择模型来分析港口网络外部性与竞争、港口服务产品差异化的关系，以及港口的收费策略设计和服务质量设计问题。我们的研究发现，在均衡时港口网络外部性能够降低港口的收费，加剧了港口的竞争；港口的服务质量具有战略替代性，港口服务质量的影子价格较小的港口，倾向于采用高水平的服务质量。当陆上或海上的运输费率上升时，港口可以收取较高的费用，并获得较大的收益。

关键词：Hotelling 模型，网络外部性，港口竞争，竞争策略

中图分类号：F253.4　　　　**文献标识码：**A

1　引　言

香港作为全世界最繁忙的集装箱港口，因其更快捷、更可靠的服务仍然保留着竞争优势。但香港的政界和业界领导人担心其较高的收费会影响其竞争力，此外珠江三角洲与香港港口之间的陆上货车运输费用也使一些公司转向选择收费更低的深圳，因为从珠江三角洲运到香港，陆上运输费用可能使成本明显增加[1]。新加坡的经历表明，优质服务并不一定能确保成功。虽然仍是世界上最繁忙的转运中心和第二大集装箱港口，新加坡面临着附近收费较低的马来西亚港口的竞争。马士基-海陆 2000 年把其东南亚的运输中心转到马来西亚的丹戎帕拉帕斯港，使新加坡港丧失至少 100 万 TEU 的年吞吐量[1]。上述事例说明港口要保持竞争力，必须采取合适的竞争策略，并考虑其它与运输相关的因素的影响。*

关于港口竞争问题，有两个主要的研究方向。即研究港口政策对港口竞争的影响以及港口竞争策略的研究。其中有关港口竞争策略的研究，在 20 世纪 80 年代以前，主要集中于价格策略方面。如 Bennathan(1979)[2]定性分析了实行价格歧视策略可以增强港口的竞争力。随着运输过程的复杂化，港口费率已不再是货物运输成本的主要构成，需要关注发货人的选择行为。文献[3～6]通过实证研究的方法研究了影响发货人的港口选择因

* **收稿日期：**2005-06-27

资助项目：国家自然科学基金重点资助项目(70432001)

作者简介：吉阿兵(1977～)，男，复旦大学管理学院管理科学系，博士生；朱道立(1945～)，男，复旦大学管理学院管理科学系，教授。

素。以上的文献大多从定性的角度来研究港口的策略问题。UNCTAD(1992)[9]的研究使用了定量分析方法,以时间、成本、安全为指标,建立综合衡量港口竞争实力的公式。施欣(1998)[2]研究了港口竞争对策模型,但没有进行深入的讨论。Mei-Feng Luo(2002)[8]则利用仿真的方法研究了新建港口对原有港口的影响及腹地的重新划分问题。上述关于港口竞争的研究都没有考虑港口的竞争策略设计问题。

Hotelling 在 1929 年提出了著名的 Hotelling 模型,用于研究两个厂商的价格设计问题。Aspremont[12]等人指出了 Hotelling 的缺陷,并求出均衡解存在的条件以及二次情况的修改 Hotelling 模型。当某产品对用户的价值随着采用相同产品或兼容性产品的用户增加而增加时,就出现消费者规模经济,即所谓的网络外部性[15]。网络外部性可能是直接的,效用因用户数目增加而增加,如电话;也可能是间接的,效用因用户数目增加而导致更多的互补产品供给,如计算机。对网络外部性进行研究的文献很多,最代表性的研究者是 Katz 和 Shapiro,他们研究了网络产品(如软件)的网络外部性、产品兼容性和知识产权的关系[15~17]。其它研究者从不同的角度对此问题进行了研究[17~19]。文献[20]从产业组织理论出发,研究了线性 Hotelling 模型中网络外部性、产品差异化的关系,假设消费者的消费终端是两个厂商的经营地,厂商可以进行经营场所的选择。

本文在文献研究的基础上,使用 Hotelling 模型来研究港口的竞争策略设计问题,以及港口网络外部性与竞争、港口服务产品差异化的关系,对文献中的定理进行了拓展。与一般的 Hotelling 模型不一样的是,作为竞争主体的港口在市场中不具有位置选择性,并且,作为消费者的发货人对港口服务产品的选择不仅仅与发货人至港口的运输费用有关,还与被选择的港口至货物目的港的运输费用相关。在文中我们较为详细的描述了港口的网络外部性现象,并分析这一现象对港口价格策略和服务策略的影响。

2 港口网络外部性、运输产品的 Hotelling 模型

假设发货人在[0,1]市场中均匀分布,并且发货人肯定进行一次货物运输。港口 1 和港口 2 距 0 点的距离分别为 a、b,且 $a+b<2$。为简便起见,假设货物的目的港只有一个,为 d 点。参见图 1。

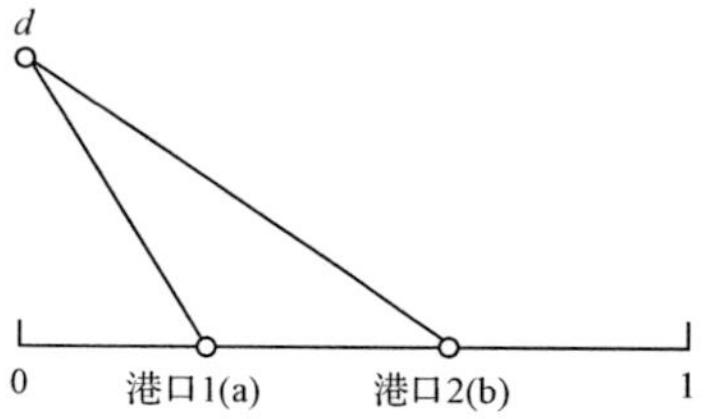

图 1 运输网络简图

与一般的 Hotelling 模型相比,本文所建的运输产品的 Hotelling 模型具有以下特点:消费者所享用产品的生产和消费同时进行,消费者的消费地不仅仅包括港口提供的服务,还包括海上运输人和陆上运输人提供的服务。作为竞争主体的港口,其在市场中的位置不可以改变,可以改变的是市场的整体规模。

为便于分析发货人的决策行为,对发货人进行国际货物进出口运输的过程简述如下:发货人向货代提出运输申请,货代接受后根据发货人的要求向船公司订舱或者发货人直接向船公司订舱,然后再由发货人或货代组织装箱及货物的陆上运输,货物进入港口道口后,由港口组织货物的堆存、装卸。船舶到港后,港口负责货物在港区内的运输和装船工作。经过海上航行后,货物在目的港卸下,再由目的港的货代组织目的地的装卸、运输、提

货等工作。货物的进口过程与之相反。由此可以看出，发货人要做出以下几个决策：货代的选择决策、港口选择决策、船公司选择决策、陆上运输方式选择决策。港口作为货代、船公司的主要活动场所以及海陆衔接的交点，显然港口的选择决策是发货人的中心决策。发货人要支付的主要费用包括陆上运输费用、海上运输费用、港口费收、货代的代理费用，理性的发货人会选择总费用最小的运输路线。

货代、船公司、港口组成的服务群体能够给发货人带来产品空间和时间上的位移，给发货人带来货物运输的一般效用外，在整个运输过程中，发货人还会受到网络外部性的影响。直接的网络外部性表现为当某一个港口相对于其它港口的服务价格更好时，很多发货人都选择这一港口，为了满足顾客增长的需要，港口会改善管理水平，采购更先进的设备，扩大港口的吞吐能力，从而降低货物在港逗留时间，给发货人带来额外效益。规模经济的效应，使得港口愿意降低船舶或货物使用港口的各种费用，降低产品的成本，增强发货人产品的国际市场竞争能力。

间接的网络外部性体现在作为港口互补服务的船公司和货代两个方面。对船公司而言，由于港口的吞吐量越来越大，船公司会把港口作为运输的枢纽港，在港口开辟直达航线，并配置更大的船型，增加航班密度来稳定原有货源或吸引更多的货源。航班密度的上升，使得发货人能够更快捷地运输货物。同时，众多船公司的相互竞争，可以降低海上的货物运输费用和享受更好的服务。那么，越来越多的发货人会选择从此港口出发，从而形成良性循环。对很多不了解国际货物运输的发货人而言，选择一个货运代理人是最佳方案。货代与港口的互补关系，港口的吞吐量越大越能吸引货代公司的进驻，发货人能够找到比较合适的代理人，港口的吞吐量随着代理人的数量增加而增加。货代市场上的相互竞争行为为发货人提供优质的服务和较低的价格，并进一步吸引发货人。因此，每个发货人的选择都间接给其他发货人带来了收益。

当然，港口的收费过低或服务质量过高，也会给发货人带来负的网络外部性。比如在某一时段内，由于进港货物太多，导致港口道路和堆场的紧张，从而引起货物或船舶滞港时间的延长，降低发货人的收益，在本文不考虑此种情况。

模型中的变量定义如下：

i：表示第 i 个发货人；

r：发货人从事国际贸易所获得的利润；

α：表示陆上的运输费用参数；

l_{in}：表示从发货人 i 至第 n 个港口的距离；

p_n：表示在第 n 个港口收取单位集装箱的价格，包括港口使费、拖轮费、引航费、装卸费等费用；

l_{nd}：表示第 n 个港口到目的港 d 的海上运输费用，若给定出发港、目的港，海上运输费用是固定的。不失一般性，在本文中可以假设 $l_{2d} \geqslant l_{1d}$；

s_n：港口 n 的服务质量；

γ：服务质量的价值系数；

x_n：发货人预期港口 n 的吞吐量；

μ：网络外部性强度。

假设陆上运输费用为二次成本函数，海上运输费用为一次成本函数，港口的市场份额，即港口的吞吐量给发货人带来正的效用，港口服务质量水平也给发货人带来正的效用。则发货人 $i(x)$ 利用港口 n 的剩余效用可表示为：

$$U_n(i) = r + \gamma s_n + \mu x_n - \alpha l_{in}^2 - l_{nd} - p_n, \quad n = 1,2 \tag{1}$$

式(1)经济解释如下：发货人通过购买运输产品获得基本剩余效用，即 $r - \alpha l_{in}^2 - l_{nd} - p_n$。与此同时，发货人还获得额外的效用。这是因为港口的服务质量越高，船舶、货物在港逗留时间越短，给船公司和发货人带来的效益越大，用 γs_n 来表达港口服务水平给发货人带来的效用，这个效用可以是节约的时间成本或者是发货人对港口服务水平的货币衡量。船代、货代作为国际货物运输的辅助行业，与港口业是互补关系，如果港口所在地区船代、货代数量比较多，船公司或者发货人就比较容易以优惠的价格购买所需的服务，从而给船公司和发货人带来正效用，用 μx_n 表示。对发货人而言，不管其路径选择如何，只要完成了货物的运输，就获得相同的运输效用 r。由于发货人必须进行运输，所以假设 r 是一个充分大的数值。则发货人的剩余效用最大化等同于支付的最小化，式(1)等价于：

$$\min_{n=1,2} TC_n(i) = p_n + \alpha l_{in}^2 + l_{nd} - \gamma s_n - \mu x_n \tag{2}$$

式(2)表示发货人在选择港口的过程中，总是选择使得货物运输总费用最小的港口。用 $h(x) = TC_2(x) - TC_1(x)$ 表示发货人 x 通过两个港口的费用之差，则有

$$\begin{aligned} h(x) &= [p_2 + \alpha(x-b)^2 + l_{2d} - \gamma s_2 - \mu x_2] - [p_1 + \alpha(x-a)^2 + l_{1d} - \gamma s_1 - \mu x_1] \\ &= 2\alpha(a-b)x + \alpha(b^2 - a^2) + (p_2 - \gamma s_2 - \mu x_2) - (p_1 - \gamma s_1 - \mu x_1) + (l_{2d} - l_{1d}) \end{aligned} \tag{3}$$

文献[8,9]的研究发现如果港口价格、港口服务质量以及其它港口特征无差异，发货人一般选择较近的港口出口。那么，当式(3)中的第三项等于第四项时，处于 $x=0$ 点的发货人会选择港口1，即 $h(0)>0$。令 $c_1 = (\alpha b^2 + l_{2d}) - (\alpha a^2 + l_{1d})$，则有 $c_1 > 0$。位于 $x=1$ 的发货人会选择港口2，即 $h(1)<0$，若令 $c_2 = c_1 + 2\alpha(a-b) = [\alpha(1-b)^2 + l_{2d}] - [\alpha(1-a)^2 + l_{1d}]$，则有 $c_2 < 0$。因此，本文采取了合理的假设 $c_1 > 0$ 和 $c_2 < 0$。通常情况下，港口的网络外部性给发货人带来的效用不会优于成本差异所带来的效用，假设 $0 < \mu < \alpha(b-a)$。

在本模型中，发货人的选择行为是通过港口最优化的行为得以体现，因为我们假设发货人是独立的和理性的。

3 港口的竞争策略设计

通常情况下，港口可以通过设计较低的收费和较高的服务质量来吸引腹地内所有的发货人，或者设计较高的收费和较高的质量，吸引注重服务质量、价格敏感度低的发货人，或者提供较低收费和较低的价格，覆盖部分发货人。我们假定腹地市场中的每一个发货人都进行选择，且港口的最高收费小于等于发货人的利润与陆上、海上运输费用的差额。

引理1 如果 $c_2 + \mu \leqslant (p_1 - \gamma s_1) - (p_2 - \gamma s_2) \leqslant c_1 - \mu$，那么两港口共同分享腹地市场。港口1的腹地份额 $q_1 = \dfrac{(p_2 - \gamma s_2) - (p_1 - \gamma s_1) + c_1 - \mu}{c_1 - c_2 - 2\mu}$，港口2的份额 $q_2 = \dfrac{(p_1 - \gamma s_1) - (p_2 - \gamma s_2) - c_2 - \mu}{c_1 - c_2 - 2\mu}$

证明 假设在两个港口之间存在一个到两个港口无差异的发货人 $\bar{x}$，由 $h(\bar{x})=0$ 可解得

$$\overline{x}=\frac{(p_2-\gamma s_2)-(p_1-\gamma s_1)+c_1-\mu}{2\alpha(b-a)-2\mu}=\frac{(p_2-\gamma s_2)-(p_1-\gamma s_1)+c_1-\mu}{c_1-c_2-2\mu} \tag{4}$$

若两个港口共同分享腹地市场，则 $0<\bar{x}<1$，即 $0<\frac{(p_2-\gamma s_2)-(p_1-\gamma s_1)+c_1-\mu}{c_1-c_2-2\mu}<1$，又因为假设 $0<\mu<\alpha(b-a)$，从而解得 $c_2+\mu\leqslant(p_1-\gamma s_1)-(p_2-\gamma s_2)\leqslant c_1-\mu$ 若 $c_2+u\leqslant(p_1-rs_1)-(p_2-rs_2)\leqslant c_1-u$ 成立，代入公式(4)，易知 $0<\bar{x}<1$ 所以共同划分腹地市场。证毕。

$$q_1=\frac{(p_2-\gamma s_2)-(p_1-\gamma s_1)+c_1-\mu}{c_1-c_2-2\mu}$$

$$q_2=1-\bar{x}=\frac{(p_1-\gamma s_1)-(p_2-\gamma s_2)-c_2-\mu}{c_1-c_2-2\mu}$$

引理 2　如果 $(p_1-\gamma s_1)-(p_2-\gamma s_2)<c_2+\mu$，则所有发货人选择港口 1，两港口的腹地份额分别是：$q_1=1,q_2=0$。

证明　如果 $(p_1-\gamma s_1)-(p_2-\gamma s_2)<c_2+\mu$ 成立，代入公式(4)可算得 $\bar{x}>1$。其含义是港口 2 直接腹地的发货人选择港口 2 从事运输的成本大于选择港口 1 的成本，那么所有的发货人都不会选择港口 2。

引理 3　如果 $(p_1-\gamma s_1)-(p_2-\gamma s_2)>c_1-\mu$，则港口 2 占领全部腹地市场，即 $q_1=0$，$q_2=1$。

证明　如果 $(p_1-\gamma s_1)-(p_2-\gamma s_2)>c_1-\mu$ 成立，代入公式(4)易知 $\bar{x}<0$。其含义是港口 1 直接腹地的发货人都会选择港口 2。

引理 1、引理 2、引理 3 的基本含义是，如果两个港口的价格和服务质量的差异，能够弥补两个港口所在运输网络上的陆上和海上运输费用差额，则发货人会选择价格和服务水平效用较大的港口。在引理 2、3 的情况下，只有一个港口存在，由于港口的投资比较大，退出的成本很高，所以，任何一个港口都不会退出市场，那么引理 2、3 所代表的情况是一种短暂的非稳定状态，在市场均衡时这种状况不可能存在。下文如果不特别说明，只讨论引理 1 所表示的状态。

定理 1　在给定港口的服务质量时，港口的均衡收费 (p_1^*,p_2^*) 和收益 (π_1^*,π_2^*) 满足以下条件：

$$\begin{aligned}p_1^*=p_1&=\max\left\{\frac{\gamma s_1-\gamma s_2+2c_1-c_2-3\mu}{3},0\right\}\\ p_2^*=p_2&=\max\left\{\frac{\gamma s_2-\gamma s_1+c_1-2c_2-3\mu}{3},0\right\}\end{aligned} \tag{5}$$

$$\begin{aligned}\pi_1^*=\pi_1&=\max\left\{\frac{(\gamma s_1-\gamma s_2+2c_1-c_2-3\mu)^2}{9(c_1-c_2-2\mu)},0\right\}\\ \pi_2^*=\pi_2&=\max\left\{\frac{(\gamma s_2-\gamma s_1+c_1-2c_2-3\mu)^2}{9(c_1-c_2-2\mu)},0\right\}\end{aligned} \tag{6}$$

证明　由引理 1、2、3 知在均衡状态下，港口 1 的市场份额是 $q_1=\frac{(p_2-\gamma s_2)-(p_1-\gamma s_1)+c_1-\mu}{c_1-c_2-2\mu}$，由 $p_1\in\arg\max p_1q_1$，可得：

$$p_1 = \frac{p_2 - \gamma s_2 + \gamma s_1 - \mu + c_1}{2}$$

同理可得 p_2 的反应函数

$$p_2 = \frac{p_1 - \gamma s_1 + \gamma s_2 - \mu - c_2}{2}$$

联立以上两式，再结合均衡价格非负约束可证明定理 1。此时，两港口的腹地份额分别是

$$q_1 = \frac{\gamma s_1 - \gamma s_2 + 2c_1 - c_2 - 3\mu}{3(c_1 - c_2 - 2\mu)} \tag{7}$$

$$q_2 = \frac{\gamma s_2 - \gamma s_1 + c_1 - 2c_2 - 3\mu}{3(c_1 - c_2 - 2\mu)} \tag{8}$$

定理 1 表明，存在网络外部性时，港口收费低于没有网络外部性时的价格，即网络外部性加剧了港口间的竞争。其原因是当某一港口的市场份额比较大时，必然吸引众多船公司进行停靠，发货人就更容易选择承担运输的船公司并获得优惠运价。同时，港口也获得规模经济效应，港口可以以更低价格提供更好的服务，这又导致港口需求的进一步增加，网络外部性效应进一步增强。

由于港口的位置具有不可移动性，当两个港口的服务质量相等时，其收费由港口在整个运输网络中的相对位置决定。从定理 1 我们还可以看出，当港口腹地扩大时，港口的收费可以定得较高，相反则价格定得较低。其原因是，腹地扩大后，陆上、海上的运输费用在总运输成本中的比重增大，港口的收费的比重相对降低，此时增加部分港口的收费对发货人的影响变小，发货人就愿意支付较高的费用。

定理 1 还表明港口的收费与港口提供的服务质量成正比，与竞争对手的服务质量成反比；港口市场份额与港口的服务质量成正比。因此，港口有通过改变服务质量水平来提高市场占有率的动机。通常情况下，港口的质量策略包括提高港口装卸效率、加强与船公司和货代的信息共享、改善海关通关条件等等。这些措施的实施需要港口进行一定的设备和管理投入，我们假定港口的服务成本是港口服务水平的二次函数，即 $\lambda_n s_n^2$。则港口的最优服务策略设计如下：

定理 2 当 $\frac{\gamma^2}{\lambda_1} \leqslant 3(c_1 - c_2 - 2\mu)$，$\frac{\gamma^2}{\lambda_2} \leqslant 3(c_1 - c_2 - 2\mu)$ 成立时，港口的最优服务策略分别是

$$s_1^* = \frac{\gamma^3 + \gamma\lambda_2(3\mu + c_2 - 2c_1)}{(\lambda_1 + \lambda_2)\gamma^2 - 3\lambda_1\lambda_2(c_1 - c_2 - 2\mu)} \tag{9}$$

$$s_2^* = \frac{\gamma^3 + \gamma\lambda_1(3\mu + 2c_2 - c_1)}{(\lambda_1 + \lambda_2)\gamma^2 - 3\lambda_1\lambda_2(c_1 - c_2 - 2\mu)} \tag{10}$$

证明 令 $R_1 = \pi_1 - \lambda_1 s_1^2$，$R_2 = \pi_2 - \lambda_2 s_2^2$，则港口利润最大化的充分条件为

$$\frac{\partial R_1}{\partial s_1} = \frac{\partial \pi_1}{\partial s_1} - 2\lambda_1 s_1 = 0$$

$$\frac{\partial R_2}{\partial s_2} = \frac{\partial \pi_2}{\partial s_2} - 2\lambda_2 s_2 = 0$$

解得

$$s_1^* = \frac{\gamma^3 + \gamma\lambda_2(3\mu + c_2 - 2c_1)}{(\lambda_1 + \lambda_2)\gamma^2 - 3\lambda_1\lambda_2(c_1 - c_2 - 2\mu)}$$

$$s_2^* = \frac{\gamma^3 + \gamma\lambda_1(3\mu + 2c_2 - c_1)}{(\lambda_1 + \lambda_2)\gamma^2 - 3\lambda_1\lambda_2(c_1 - c_2 - 2\mu)}$$

利润最大化的必要条件是

$$\frac{\partial^2 R_1}{\partial s_1^2} \leqslant 0$$

$$\frac{\partial^2 R_2}{\partial s_2^2} \leqslant 0$$

即

$$\frac{\gamma^2}{\lambda_1} \leqslant 3(c_1 - c_2 - 2\mu)$$

$$\frac{\gamma^2}{\lambda_2} \leqslant 3(c_1 - c_2 - 2\mu)$$

在定理 2 的条件成立时，服务质量的影子价格①较小的港口，其服务水平较高，并且竞争对手的服务质量影子价格越高，给港口带来的服务质量效用越高。

从定理 2 还可以看出，当港口的单位服务质量给发货人带来的单位效用确定时，港口的服务质量选择具有相互替代性，其原因在于 $\lambda_1 s_1^* + \lambda_2 s_2^* = \gamma$，所以当某个港口选择较高服务质量时，另一个港口的需求必然减小，因而收益随之降低，港口就倾向于选择较低质量水平，以便降低成本。这可以解释为什么在现代物流业兴起的背景下，各港口纷纷扩展服务范围，提高服务质量的现象。

4　分析与结论

港口作为水陆连接的枢纽，在国际贸易中占有重要的地位。但是港口的收费、服务质量(主要指港口的装卸效率)、陆上运输费用、海上运办理费用、船班密度、船代及货代的数量会影响发货人的选择行为而发货的选择行为反过来又影响到港口的腹地份额大小和收益以及其它发货人、船代、货代等的收益。

由公式(5)、(7)、(8)可以看出，网络外部性加剧了港口间的竞争，且网络外部性有提高港口市场份额的趋势。当海上费率上升后，离目的港距离较近的港口市场份额会增加，距离较近港口的最佳收费会相应较高。如果陆上的运输费率上升，港口应采取较高的收费，以便获得较大的效益。竞争对手的服务质量越高，港口应采取较低的价格策略，降低的幅度与服务质量给发货人带来的效用相关。

公式(9)、(10)表明当港口的单位服务质量给发货人带来的单位效用确定时，港口的服务质量选择具有相互替代性，所以当一个港口服务质量提高后，另一个港口要么采取较低的服务质量策略，以保持低成本，要么通过投资提高服务质量，当两者的服务质量都提高后，会给发货人或船公司带来更大的服务效用。港口的最佳服务质量与港口服务质量的影子价格成反比，如果竞争对手提高服务水平的成本相对较高，港口有提高服务质量的

① 服务质量的影子价格我们定义为提高单位服务质量所花费的成本.

动机。港口的最佳服务质量与服务质量给发货人带来的效用呈同方向变化趋势。当$\frac{\gamma}{2\lambda_1}>1$、$\frac{\gamma}{2\lambda_2}>1$成立时，港口的最佳服务质量随网络外部性的增加而增加；当$\frac{\gamma}{2\lambda_1}=1$、$\frac{\gamma}{2\lambda_2}=1$，港口的服务策略与网络外部性的关系不定；当$\frac{\gamma}{2\lambda_1}<1$、$\frac{\gamma}{2\lambda_2}<1$，港口的最佳服务质量随网络外部性的增加而减少。

在本文中，我们分析了港口价格、服务质量、海上运输费率、陆上运输费率对发货人和港口的影响，并对港口存在的网络外部性现象进行了阐述。港口的直接网络外部性体现在港口服务质量的提高和以及由此引起的产品成本的降低，港口的间接网络外部性表现为船公司和货代服务价格的下降和服务水平的上升。在均衡时港口正的网络外部性能够降低港口的收费，加剧港口间竞争；港口的服务质量具有战略替代性，港口服务质量的影子价格较小的港口，倾向于采用高水平的服务质量。我们还给出了港口的最优收费策略和服务策略。文中得出的结论对于港口企业进行科学决策具有重要的参考价值。港口负的网络外部性会降低港口的服务水平，港口采取何种措施来减少负的网络外部性的影响，尚需进一步研究。

The Port competitive Strategies with Network Externality

H A-bing, ZHU Dao-li

(School of Management, Fudan University, Shanghai 200433, China)

Abstract: Inthis paper, we constructed a selection model based on Hotelling model to express forwarders' behavior. We further analyse the relationship among port's network externality , competition , service quality and port pricing strategy and service strategy. We found the port's optimal price is lower with network externality , which fierce the competition. Ports' service quality could be substitute and the port with lower marginal service cost prefer to higher service level. When the rate of sea transport and land transport increased , the port can use positive pricing strategy to gain more profit.

Key words: Hotelling model ; network externality ; port competition ; competitive strategies

参考文献

[1] 世界经济[N]. 参考消息，2005-02-26. The World Economy[N]. Reference News ,2005-02-26.

[2] 施欣. 港口竞争对策模型的研究[J]. 系统工程理论与实践，1998，18(9)：27-33. Shi Xin. A game model of port competition[J]. Systems Engineering-Theory & Practice, 1998, 18(9): 27-33.

[3] Bardi EJ. Carrier selection from one mode[J]. Transportation Journal,1973,13(1):23-29.

[4] Brooks M. An alternative theoretical approach to the evaluation of liner shipping:Part 1,Situational factors[J]. Maritime Policy & Management , 1984 ,11(1):35-43.

[5] Brooks M. An alternative theoretical approach to the evaluation of liner shipping: Part 2 ,Choice criteria[J]. Maritime Policy & Management , 1984 ,12(2):145-155.

[6] Slack B. Containerization, inter-port competition and port selection [J]. Maritime Policy &Management, 1985. 12(4) :293-303.

[7] Slack B. Shipping lines as agents in the port industry[J]. Maritime Policy &Management , 1996 ,23 (3) :289-300.

[8] Luo Meifeng. Container transportation service demand simulation model for uscoastal container ports [D]. Diss Uni of Rhode Island , 2002.

[9] Tsamboulas , Dimitrios A , Seraphim Kapros. Decision-making process in intermodal transportation [R]. Transportation Research Record 1707 ,Paper No. 00-1304 ,2000.

[10] Eileen Rhea. By Sea:The PortNexus in the Global Commodity Network[D]. Diss Uni of Southen Califronia,2002.

[11] Hotellig H. Stability in competition[J]. Economic Journal ,1929,39 :41-57.

[12] C. D'Aspremont,Gabszewicz,etc. On hotelling's"stability in competition"[J]. Econometrica,1979, 47(5): 1145-1150.

[13] Prescott E C ,et al. Sequential location among firms with foresight[J]. The BellJournal of Economics,1977,8 :378-393.

[14] Salop S. Monopolistic Competition reconstituted or-Circular fashion in Economic thought. Federal Reserve Board ,Washington ,D. C. ,1977.

[15] Katz M,Shapiro C. Network externalities,competition and compatibility[J]. American Economic Review,1985,75:424-440.

[16] Katz M,Shapiro C. Technology adoption in the presence of networke xternalities[J]. Journal of Political Economy,1986,94:822-841.

[17] Katz M ,Shapiro C. System competition and network effects[J]. Journal of Economic Perspectives, 1994,8:93-115.

[18] Farrel J ,Saloner G. Converters ,compatibility and the control interfaces[J]. The Journal Industrial Economics ,1992 ,40:340-359.

[19] Emmanuelle Auriol , Michel Benaim. Standardization in decentralized economies[J]. The American Economic Review ,2000 ,90:550-570.

[20] Baake P,Boom A. Vertical product differentiation,network externalities, and compatibility decision [J]. International Journal of Industrial Organization ,2001,19:267-284.

[21] 汪淼军,励斌. 网络外部性、竞争和产品差异化[J]. 经济学(季刊) ,2003 ,2(2) :355-378. Wang Miaojun ,Li Bin. Network externalities ,competition ,and product's diferentiation[J]. China Economic Quarterly ,2003 ,2(2) : 355-378.

(本文发表于《系统工程理论与实践》,2006 年第 7 期)

基于极效率 DEA 模型的港口绩效评价*

吉阿兵，朱道立

（复旦大学 管理学院，上海 200433）

摘要：对集装箱港口的绩效进行评价一直是港口当局关心的问题，现有文献尚未提出比较有效的方法，尝试利用极效率（super-efficiency）DEA 模型对集装箱港口的绩效进行评价。极效率 DEA 模型能够有效地区别出有效（绩效值 1）决策单元之间的绩效差异，可以对所评价的决策单元进行有效的排序。此方法已在城市和企业的评价中得到了应用，但尚未在港口得到应用。在案例中，汉堡港最有效率，新加坡港次之，然后是香港港、泽布勒赫港和基隆港，香港港由于船舶的无效逗留时间长、新加坡港集卡数配置不合理，导致两者的绩效低于吞吐量远小于它们的港口。

关键词：极效率数据包络分析（super-efficiency DEA）；港口绩效；评价

中图分类号：U 491　　**文献标识码**：A

随着大型跨国公司进行全球布点、全球采购和全球销售，对全球运输提出了越来越高的要求。港口作为全球运输网络中的重要环节，面临着提高服务、降低成本的巨大压力。迫使港口当局采取措施，提高港口的经营绩效来满足各方面的要求。一个国家港口的效率水平和运营绩效在一定程度上反应了这个国家的国际竞争力[1]。为了在港口竞争中保持优势，既需要了解哪些因素影响港口的竞争力，也需要与其它港口的经营绩效进行比较，从而便于提出实施战略。

对港口绩效评价的研究很多，文献[2]提出了衡量港口绩效的各种指标。文献[3]用港口的实际吞吐量与最优吞吐量的比值作为衡量港口绩效的指标。文献[4]发现公路、铁路的发展使得传统意义上的港口腹地不复存在，建议以经济最优吞吐量（economic optimum throughput）为指标衡量港口绩效。以上文献都以单一指标衡量港口绩效。文献[5]用包含专家权重的模糊综合评价方法对中国集装箱港口的竞争力进行评价，但需要人为给定指标的权重，难免出现偏颇。DEA 方法能够从比较全面的角度衡量港口绩效，且不需要预先给定指标的权重。利用此方法，文献[6]利用假设数据，文献[7]利用真实数据分别对港口的绩效进行了评价。在文献中，只是区别了高低效率的港口，没有区分出高效率（效率值等于 1）港口之间的差异。本文利用极效率 DEA 模型来解决这一问题。对所

* **收稿日期**：2004-11-19

基金项目：国家自然科学基金资助项目（70171010）

作者简介：吉阿兵（1977～），男，江苏人，复旦大学管理学院博士研究生，研究方向：物流与供应链管理；朱道立，复旦大学管理学院教授，博士生导师。

选择港口进行初步的 DEA 评价，然后对高效率港口再利用极效率 DEA 模型进行评价，从而区分出高绩效港口之间效率的差异。港口类别众多，货物特性的差异导致装卸工艺的迥异，我们只对集装箱港口的绩效进行评价。

1 极效率 DEA 模型

数据包络分析(Data Envelopment Analysis，DEA)是著名运筹学家 A. Charnes，W. W. Cooper 及 E. Rhodes 在“相对效率评价”概念基础上发展起来的一种新的系统分析方法。在 1978 年出现了第一个 DEA 模型(CCR)，这是首次出现的能够处理多投入、多产出指标的非参数生产前沿分析方法。利用数学规划模型，该方法可以解决具有多输入多输出特征的同行业企业生产率评价问题。魏权龄[8,9]等学者证明了相对有效的决策单元就是在同样的情况下用多目标规划解出的 Pareto 有效解。

假设有 n 个决策单元 $DMU_j(1 \leqslant j \leqslant n)$，$DMU_j$ 的输入、输出指标向量分别为

$$x_j = (x_{1j}, x_{2j}, \cdots, x_{mj})^T > 0, y_j = (y_{1j}, \quad y_{2j}, \cdots, y_{sj})^T > 0$$

设输入、输出指标的权向量为

$$v = (v_1, v_2, \cdots, v_m)^T, \quad u = (u_1, u_2, \cdots, u_s)^T$$

建立 C^2R 模型[8]

$$\max \quad \frac{\sum_{k=1}^{s} u_k y_{kj0}}{\sum_{i=1}^{m} v_i x_{ij0}} = V_p \tag{1}$$

$$\text{s.t} \quad \frac{\sum_{r=1}^{s} u_r y_{rj}}{\sum_{i=1}^{m} v_i x_{ij}} \leqslant 1, j = 1, \cdots n$$

$$u_r \geqslant 0, \quad r = 1, \cdots, s$$

$$v_i \geqslant 0, \quad i = 1, \cdots, m$$

这是一个分式规划问题，转换后变为一个线性规划问题：

$$\begin{aligned} \max \quad & \mu^T y_0 \\ \text{s.t} \quad & \omega^T x_j \geqslant \mu^T y_i, \quad j = 1, \cdots, n \\ & \omega^T x_0 = 1 \\ & \omega \geqslant 0 \\ & \mu \geqslant 0 \end{aligned} \tag{2}$$

此线性规划问题的对偶问题为

$$\min \quad \theta_0 \tag{3}$$

$$\text{st} \quad \sum_{j=1}^{n} \lambda_j x_{ij} \leqslant \theta_o X_{io}, i = 1, \cdots, m$$

$$\sum_{j=1}^{n} \lambda_j y_{rj} \geqslant y_{r0}, \quad r = 1, \cdots, s$$

$$\lambda_j \geqslant 0, \quad j = 1, \cdots, n$$

x_{i0}、y_{r0}分别表示决策单元 DMU_0 的第 i 个输入和第 r 个输出，λ_j、θ_0 是决策变量。如果决策单元是有效的，则 $\theta_0^* = 1$。

在 DEA 模型中，如果被考察的决策单元不在参考集中，此时的 DEA 模型称为极效率(super-efficiency)DEA 模型[10]。以 CCR 模型为基础，文献[11]、[12]首次提出并利用极效率模型来识别有效 DMU 的效率差异。文献[13]、[14]、[15]给出了一系列极效率模型，并证明极效率 CCR 模型不会出现非可行解。极效率模型如下：

$$\min \quad \theta_0^{\text{sup}} \tag{4}$$

$$\text{st} \quad \sum_{\substack{j=1 \\ j \neq 0}}^{n} \lambda_j x_{ij} \leqslant \theta_0^{sup} x_{i0}, \quad i = 1, \cdots, m$$

$$\sum_{\substack{j=1 \\ j \neq 0}}^{n} \lambda_j y_{rj} \geqslant y_{r0}, \quad r = 1, \cdots, s$$

$$\lambda_j \geqslant 0, \quad j \neq 0$$

2 影响集装箱港口生产绩效的因素分析

港口的各项基础条件对客户的影响集中反映在对客户的综合服务方面。对客户而言，比较关注港口作业效率、港口的拥挤程度和船舶进港时间延滞程度等指标。港口的这些指标影响船公司的航线配置计划、船舶配置计划，进而影响发货人的港口选择行为。船公司和发货人的选择行为的结果，又影响到港口的吞吐量和竞争力。

影响港口作业效率的因素包括泊位数、设备装卸效率、堆场面积大小、集卡数、投入的人力。泊位数主要影响船舶到一能否及时进入泊位等待装卸效率，决定了船舶在泊位上有效逗留时间的长短。以上两个因素是船公司最关心的因素。当然，这里没有考虑进港航道的影响，因为，这不能反映港口的绩效。

堆场面积的大小影响码头自身的操作效率，堆场面积大，装卸过程中的翻箱率就较低，可以有更多的场吊用于船舶装卸，港口听效率就高，集卡数和投入的人力主要体现港口生产管理水平的高低，如果港口的生产管理水平高，就可以利用较少的人力、集卡完成装卸任力，反之，就需要较多的集卡和人员。尤其值得注意的是在装卸过程中，集卡数一定要配置恰当，配置少了，可能导致桥吊等待集卡，这是一种巨大的浪费；配置太多，又会使得集卡不能得到充分利用，而且会影响整个码头的操作环境。港口的硬件作业能力与港口的管理水平相互作用的结果是船舶在港的无效逗留时间。船舶在港的无效逗留时间包括：船舶在港等待泊位时间、在泊位等待装卸时间、装卸过程中由于换班或吃饭所浪费的时间。

以上影响港口的绩效的因素，我们作为 DEA 模型中的输入。港口的吞吐量、单船作业效率或单机作业效率都可以反映港口对输入的利用效果。我们采用港口的吞吐量作为 DEA 模型的输出。

由于收集数据的困难，本文中采用文献[7]所使用的数据（见附表）。计算所采用的软件是 EXCEL 中的 SPREADSHEET。

3 应用结果分析

先用模型(3)对港口的绩效进行评价，结果见下表的第二列。从表中可以看出，香港港（Hong Kong）、德国汉堡港（Ham burg）、新加坡港（Singapore）、中国台湾基隆港（Keelung）、比利时泽布勒赫港（Zeeb rugge）的相对绩效值为 1。一般情况下不给出五个港口效率的高低，但有些时候需要了解这几个港口之间效率的差异。利用模型(4)对这五个港口进行相对效率的评价，结果见表中的第三列。从中可看出，汉堡港最有效率，新加坡港次之，然后是香港港、泽布勒赫港，最后是基隆港。最终的排名见表的第四列。

从我们的结果中可以发现，香港港的吞吐量最大，在单指标的港口评价方法中，港口的绩效肯定是最高的，在我们的结果中并非如此。香港与汉堡港相比，虽然在桥吊数和泊位数上占优，但船舶在港的浪费时间上远远高于后者。船舶在港无效时间这一重要因素在我们的模型中得以充分反映。香港港可以从减少船舶在港的无效逗留时间入手来提高竞争能力。比如，把船舶无效逗留时间减为 1，香港港的绩效值增加 36%；若与汉堡港相同，其绩效值是汉堡港的 1.29 倍。

新加坡港与汉堡港相比，船舶的无效逗留时间较长，集卡配置的数量太少，影响了绩效。新加坡港与香港港相比，在桥吊数、堆场面积、船舶的无效逗留时间和工人人数上占据一定的优势，在集卡数上处于劣势，综合的结果是新加坡的绩效高于香港的绩效。由此可看出 DEA 能够综合地衡量决策单元的绩效。泽布勒赫港、基隆港与前面的三个港口相比，在各指标上的劣势比较明显，所以排名靠后。Felix stowe 港的集卡数配置严重不合理，不但使得其它设备的能力没有得到充分发挥，而且在整体上影响了港口的竞争力。O saka 的集卡数以及无效逗留时间均处于劣势，尽管其桥吊数很多。由此可以看出，极效率 DEA 模型不但可以综合衡量港口的各个方面，并对港口进行准确评价，还可以从中找出最影响港口绩效的因素。

4 结论

本文主要解决的是利用极效率 DEA 模型对港口的绩效进行综合评价。从结果中可以看出这一模型优于以往利用单一指标的方法，而且此模型还可以对有效的港口进行区别，看出各自效率的高低。

从我们的研究中可以看出汉堡港、新加坡港、香港港、泽布勒赫港、基隆港是最有效率的港口。集卡与桥吊配比程度是影响港口绩效、船舶在港的无效逗留时间是影响港口的最重要因素。因此，港口管理者对这两个因素应加以重视。

本文所采用的方法可以用于其他领域的评价或排序。

港口	CCR	SUP-CCR	排序
Melbourne	0. 2688		14
Hong Kong	1	1. 57395	3
Ham burg	1	2. 713608	1
Rotterdam	0. 5404		8
Felixstowe	0. 6311		7
Yokohama	0. 4914		10
Singapore	1	2. 01362	2
Keelung	1	1. 117875	5
Sydney	0. 3057		11
Fremantle	0. 2277		15
Brisbane	0. 2989		12
Tilbury	0. 2733		13
Zeebrugge	1	1. 565586	4
La Spezia	0. 5261		9
Tanjung Priok	0. 7418		6
Osaka	0. 2184		16

附表　1996 年港口数据表

港口	输入指标						输出指标
	桥吊数	泊位数	集卡数	堆场面积	无效逗留时间	工人数	集装箱吞吐量
M elbourne	16	12	6	1184100	8	829	904 618
Hong Kong	64	18	24	2 198 300	4	800	13 460 343
Ham burg	52	14	25	3 030 000	0. 2	1 168	3 054 320
Rotterdam	66	18	15	4 158 000	1. 7	981	4 935 616
Felix stow e	29	13	3	1 432 000	0. 6	1 824	2 042 423
Yokoham a	41	20	34	1 823 250	6	472	3 911 927
Singapore	95	17	12	2 979 211	23	978	12 943 900
Keelung	23	14	9	339 000	13	690	2 320 397
Sydney	14	11	3	1 124 500	9. 5	635	695 312
Frem antle	5	7	5	273 000	9	498	202 680
Brisbane	6	3	5	474 000	5. 5	200	249 439
Tilbury	11	4	2	519 000	4. 5	750	394772
Zeebrugge	16	9	5	2 311 100	1	210	553 175
La Spezia	8	7	8	270 000	3. 7	177	871 100
Tan jung Priok	10	6	11	310 000	50	1513	1 421 693
O saka	24	13	10	1 154 000	4	1070	987 948

注：表中集装箱吞吐量以 20 英尺标箱计算。

数据来源：澳大利亚交通与运输经济委员会；集装箱国际年鉴(1998)；L loyd 港口世界(1998)。

Efficiency Measurement of Ports Based on Super-eff iciency DEA Model

JIA-bin，ZHU Dao-li

(School of Management，Fudan University，Shanghai200433，China)

Abstract：Available studies have not provided a satisfactory answerto the problem of measuring thepórts efficiency. DEA . has been applied to a wide number of different situations whereefficiency comparisons are required The DEA technique is useful in resolving the measurement of port efficiency because the calculations are nonparam etric，can handlemultiple outputand input. In this paper，thesuperefficiency data envelopment analysis (DEA) was used to provide an efficiency measurement for selected ports and rank the selected ports. Some factors affecting ports efficiency were also been discussed in detail.

Key words：Super-efficiency DEA ；Port Efficiency；Measurement

参 考 文 献

[1] Tongzon JL. Determ inants of portperform ance and efficiency[J]. Transport ResearchA ，1995，29 (3)：245-352.

[2] Australian bureau of industry economics[R]. International Performance Indicators in the Waterfront，Research Report 47，1993.

[3] Sachish A. Productivity functions as a managerial tool in Israeliports [J]. M aritime policy and Management，1996，23 (4) ：341-369.

[4] TalleyW K. Optimum throughput and performance evaluation of marine term inals[J]. M aritime Policy and Management，1988，15 (4)：327-331.

[5] 吕永波等. 我国主要集装箱运输港口的竞争力评价研究[J]. 北方交通大学学报，2002，26 (5)：102-105.

[6] Hayuth Y. Portperformance com parison applying data envelopm ent analysis (DEA)[J]. M aritime Policy and Managem ent，1993，20 (2)：161-163.

[7] Tongzon J L. Efficiency measurem ent of selected A ustralian and other international ports using data envelopm ent analysis[J]. Transport Research A ，2001，35 (2)：113-128.

[8] 魏权龄. 评价相对有效性的 DEA 方法[M]. 北京：中国人民大学出版社，1988.

[9] 魏权龄. 数据包络分析[M]. 北京：科学出版社，2004.

[10] Chen Yao. M easuring super-efficiency in DEA in the presence of infeasibility [J]. European Journal of Operational Research，2003.

[11] Yao Chen. Ranking efficient units in DEA [J]. The International Journal of Management Science，2004，32：213-219.

[12] Banker R D ,Das S,Datar S M. Analysis of cost variances form anagem ent con trol in Hospitals[J]. Research in Governm ental and Nonprofit Accounting, 1989, 5: 268-291.

[13] Andersen P, Petersen N C. Aprocedure for ranking efficient units in data envelopment analysis[J]. Management Science, 1993, 39: 1261-1264.

[14] Zhu J. Robustness of the efficient DMU S in data envelopment analysis [J]. European Journal of Operational Research, 1996, 90: 451-460.

[15] Seiford L M,Zhu J. Stability regions formain taining efficiency in data envelopment analysis[J]. European Journal of Operational Research, 1998, 108: 127-139.

本文发表于《系统工程》,2005 年第 4 期

世界海运网络复杂拓扑性质研究

胡一竑,朱道立*

复旦大学管理学院,上海 200433

摘要: 本文实证研究世界集装箱海上运输的地理布局和组织网络。集装箱海上运输是目前海运业主要的运输方式,本文研究了由集装箱航线和世界各大港口组成的世界海运网路。我们首先分析世界海运网络是一个无标度的小世界网络。并且通过考察带权重和不带权重的度相关性,发现世界海运网络和世界航空网络一样具有明显的层级结构,而且有"富者俱乐部"现象,点度大的节点彼此之间互相连接紧密,且之间的权重很大,反映了交通运输业的轴辐射运营模式的影响。

关键词: 复杂网络;集装箱运输;地理空间网络

1 引 言

海上运输是国际贸易中的主要运输方式,承担了国际间大宗物资如原油、矿石、粮食等的运输任务,在世界经济发展中扮演了重要角色。据联合国贸易和发展会议的《2007 年世界海运回顾》[1]报导,2007 年全球海运货物总量达 74 亿吨,比前一年增长了 4.3%,一直保持总体增长态势,其中超过 70%的世界海运贸易通过集装箱班轮运输。

集装箱运输从 20 世纪 50 年代开始成为全球海运运输体系中的重要运输方式。其重要组织形式是班轮运输。班轮运输(liner shipping)通常是指固定的船舶沿着固定航线,并按预先规定和公开的船期表进行航行,沿途停靠若干固定港口,而且运价较为固定。目前集装箱运输普遍采用轴辐侍服(hub-and-spoke)的组织模式,形成由枢纽港、支线港、干线和支线航班所组成的复杂海上运输网络[9]。

海上集装箱运输网络一直是交通运输和地理科学领域关注和研究的热点。王成金和金凤君[2]采用 70 家集装箱班轮公司的数据,从经济地理的角度对中国集装箱运输的组织网络进行了研究。王成金在[3,4]中着重研究了世界集装箱港口的演变机制,并对港口地理学的研究现状作了回顾。田炜[5]从复杂网络的角度分析了世界著名船运公司马士基的海运网络。A. Fremont[35]对马士基船运公司的海运网络做了详尽的航线结构、港口情况、发展演变趋势分析。徐新平[7]研究了中国客船运输网络,提供了一个船运网络的研究实例。这些文献从不同角度对海运网络进行了探索,但仍然缺少对全球海运网络整体结构性的研究。

和其他交通运输网络相比,海运网络具有鲜明不同的特征:

(1) 公交汽车和火车一般在固定线路上双向来回运行,而大部分集装箱航线构成回路。也就是说一艘集装箱船从始发港 A 出发,次序经过一系列港口,最后直接回到港口 A,不按原路返回。这在集装箱运输里面被称为钟摆式服务(pendulum service)[9]。

(2) 由于上述第一点特征，得到的海运网络是有向和不对称的。

(3) 航线分成干线和支线航班两种类型。干线航班跨越大洋经过多个港口，有的干线航班途中会挂靠多达 30 多个港口。支线航班在临近港口之间提供短途运输，为干线航班提供服务。

本文作者把世界海运网络构建为带权有向网络，通过分析海运网络的拓扑性质，发现海运网络是一个无标度的小世界网络。度分布和公交网络类似，在 P 空间下服从截尾幂律分布，在 L 空间下服从指数分布。各种指标如点度和点度，入度和出度，点强度和点度之间都存在强烈的关联。通过考察带权重和不带权重的集聚系数和度相关性，发现世界海运网络具有明显的层级结构和"富者俱乐部"现象，和世界航空网络(WAN)极为相似。通过分析节点重要性指标:点度和介数，发现它们彼此符合一致。作者还研究了世界重要性排名前 25 名的港口地理位置分布，发现它们全部在东西航线上，而且大多数分布在亚洲和欧洲，具有地理上的不平衡特性。

2 数据来源

我们研究的数据来自国际集装箱海运数据库 CI-ONLINE[10]，包括全球 878 个海运港口和 1802 条航线，这些航线分别由 434 个船公司经营。港口分别属于不同的地区，表 1 中列出了各大洲的港口数量。

表 1 按各地区分布的港口数目

地区	港口数量
非洲	96
亚洲和中东	251
欧洲	311
北美洲	61
拉丁美洲	96
大洋洲	63
总量	878

3 L 空间和 P 空间

为了构建世界海运网络，首先我们要引入 L 空间和 P 空间的概念(图 1)。这是由 Sen 等人[12]率先提出的，后来广泛应用在城市公交、铁路网络研究中。

L 空间以公交站点(港口)为节点，在公交路线(海运航线)上相邻的两个节点之间建立连线。点度 k 代表直接相邻的节点个数，最短距离代表两点之间需要经过的站数。而在 P 空间下，如果一路车(一条航线)经过两个站(港口)，这两个站(港口)之间就建立了连接，这时候的点度 k 代表同一辆车就可以到达、不需要转车的站点数目，两个点之间的最短距离代表两个点之间的换乘次数，因此比 L 空间下的最短距离要小。P 空间考察的是站点和站点之间的连通性。

海运网络是有向的，根据文献[7]，可以将上述 L 空间和 P 空间概念进一步推广到有向

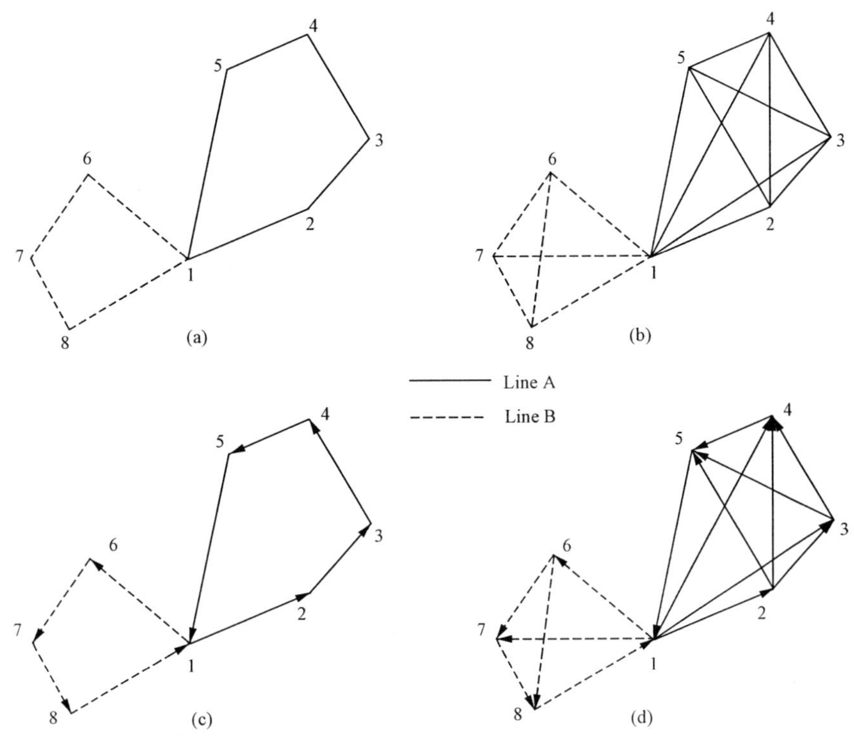

图 1　海运网络 L 空间和 P 空间的描述

注：图中实线和虚线代表两条不同的集装箱海运航线，构成闭合回路，都经过港口 1。
(a)和(b)分别代表无向 L 空间和 P 空间，(c)和(d)分别代表有向 L 空间和 P 空间。
L 空间中一条航线上依次经过的节点相连，P 空间中一条航线上所有的节点都彼此连接。

网络。图 1 中的(a)、(b)和(c)、(d)分别是对无向和有向情况下 L 空间和 P 空间的描述。A 和 B 是不同的两条航线，都经过港口 1。而且根据海运网络特点，这里的两条航线都是闭合的，航线逐次经过挂靠港口，到达目的港后，最后直接回到始发港。

表 2　世界海运网络在 L 空间和 P 空间下的基本性质

空间	节点数	连线数	平均点度	平均集聚系数	平均路径长度
L 空间	878	7 955	9.04	0.4002	3.60
P 空间	878	2 4967	28.44	0.7061	2.66

注：点度、集聚系数都是无向的。

4　世界海运网络构建和符号表述

我们基于上述概念建立了 L 空间和 P 空间下的世界海运网络，邻接矩阵分别为 A^L 和 A^P。同时我们通过计算航线数量，建立了 L 空间和 P 空间下的权重矩阵 W^L 和 W^P，其中的元素 w_{ij}^L 和 w_{ij}^P 是点 i 和点 j 之间的航班总数。世界海运网络是有向、带权、不对称的网络。

因为网络是有向的，所以我们区分点的入度和出度。记 L 空间下点 i 的入度和出度分别为 $k_{in}^L(i)$ 和 $k_{out}^L(i)$，无向情况下的点度为 $k_{un}^L(i)$。P 空间下的符号类似，分别为 $k_{in}^P(i)$，$k_{out}^P(i)$，和 $k_{un}^P(i)$。我们有如下的计算公式：

$$k_{in}^{L}(i)=\sum_{j\neq i}a_{ji}^{L} \quad (1)$$

$$k_{out}^{L}(i)=\sum_{j\neq i}a_{ij}^{L} \quad (2)$$

$$k_{un}^{L}(i)=\sum_{j\neq i}(a_{ij}^{L}+a_{ji}^{L}) \quad (3)$$

这对于空间 P 也同样适用。

同样的，我们也可以区分点强度为入强度和出强度。记 L 空间下点 i 的入强度和出强度分别为 $S_{in}^{L}(i)$ 和 $S_{out}^{L}(i)$，无向点强度（总点强度）记为 $S_{un}^{L}(i)$。计算公式如下

$$S_{in}^{L}(i)=\sum_{j\neq i}w_{ji}^{L} \quad (4)$$

$$S_{out}^{L}(i)=\sum_{j\neq i}w_{ij}^{L} \quad (5)$$

$$S_{un}^{L}(i)=\sum_{j\neq i}(w_{ij}^{L}+w_{ji}^{L}) \quad (6)$$

计算公式对 P 空间下的 $S_{in}^{P}(i)$，$S_{out}^{P}(i)$，$S_{un}^{P}(i)$ 也类似。

文中还涉及其他指标，如集聚系数和度相关性，同样根据 L 空间和 P 空间的不同，记为 $c^{L}(k)$，$c^{P}(k)$，$k_{nn}^{L}(k)$，$k_{nn}^{P}(k)$。带权的集聚系数和度相关性，我们记为 $c^{WL}(k)$，$c^{WP}(k)$，$k_{nn}^{WL}(k)$，$k_{nn}^{WP}(k)$。

5 基本拓扑性质

5.1 点度分布和度之间的相关性

我们首先研究世界海运网络的入度、出度和无向点度的分布情况。从图 2 可以看到，世界海运网络在 L 空间下的三条点度分布曲线都服从双幂律分布，且拟合后的幂指数相同。入度和出度的分布曲线在 $k=20$ 之前服从 $P(k)\sim k^{-1.08}$，点度大于 20 时，曲线向下弯折，分布变为 $P(k)\sim k^{-2.95}$。无向情况下的点度幂律指数相同，也是 1.08 和 2.95，但从 $k=30$ 开始弯折。这样的双幂律分布在很多交通网络中观察到，如世界机场网络[20]，中国机场网络[21]，美国机场网络[22]，意大利机场网络[23]。[19]认为机场连接成本的存在使得新的边不再倾向于连接点度大的点，因此导致世界航空网络中的点度分布曲线向下弯折。海运网络中也存在类似的连接成本。在繁忙的大港口，很多船只需要等待一段时间才能进入码头。船只的等待成本很高，一旦船只等待时间过长，下次航班可能就考虑改去挂靠别的港口。作者认为海运网络和航空网络中的截尾幂律分布是由交通运输网络的规模经济和拥挤效应造成的，在第五章通过模拟仿真重现了交通运输网络特性。

P 空间下的三条点度分布曲线服从指数分布，$P(k)\sim e^{-\alpha k}$，经过拟合得到入度的指数 $\alpha=0.0117$，出度的指数 $\alpha=0.0085$，无向点度的指数 $\alpha=0.0086$。世界海运网络的点度分布在 L 空间中服从幂律分布，在 P 空间中服从指数分布，这个性质和很多城市公交网络[8,13]、铁路网络[12]类似，特别的，印度铁路网络在 P 空间下的 α 指数是 0.0085，和我们的出度、无向点度的指数基本相同。

我们接着来检查入度和出度之间的关系。图 2(c)显示 L 空间和 P 空间中出度和入度都有正的相关性，且是线性相关的。因为海运航线绝大多数都是闭合的，而在构成回路的海运航线中，航线上的每个港口都有相同的入度和出度。所以入度和出度的正线性相关是可

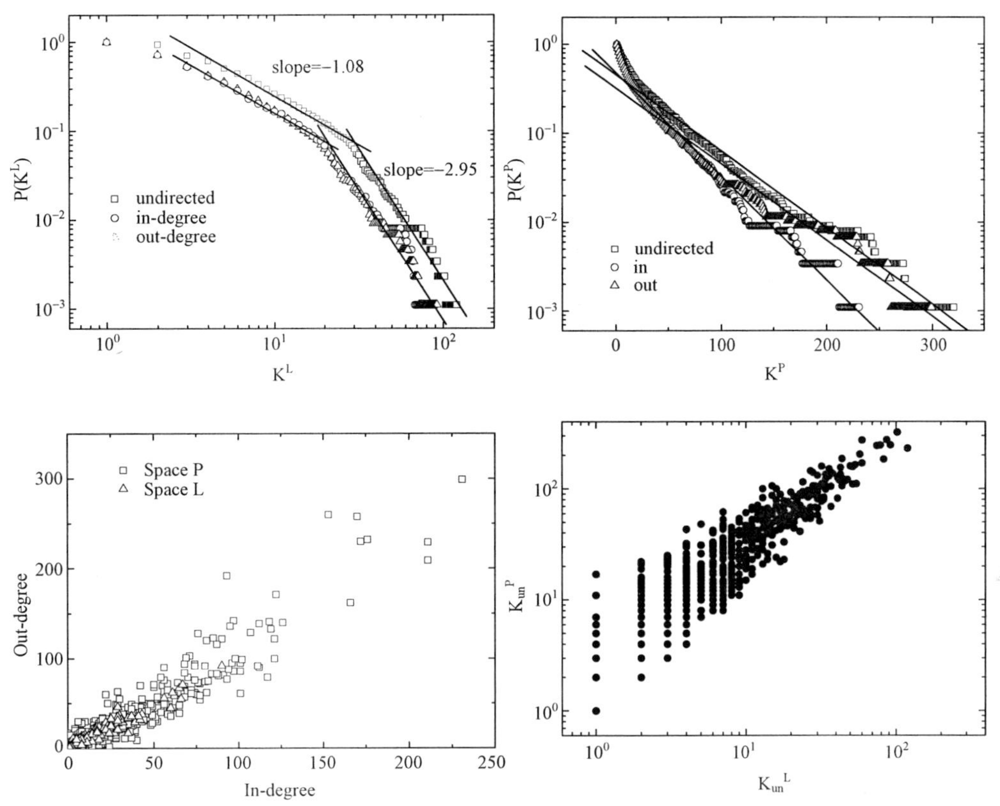

图 2　(a) L 空间下点度的累积概率分布

注：入度、出度和无向点度的累积分布曲线都服从相同指数的截尾幂律分布，分别从 $k=20$ 和 $k=30$ 左右开始弯曲。(b) P 空间下点度的累积概率分布，服从指数分布。(c) 入度和出度在 L 空间和 P 空间下都有正的线性相关性。(d) 两个空间下的无向点度，P 空间普遍比 L 空间高。

以理解的。

此外，不同空间下的点度之间有什么样的关联呢？图 2(d)中的点是无向点度，该图显示所有的点都在对角线的上方，也就是说 $k_{un}^{P} \geqslant k_{nu}^{L}$，这符合最初两个空间的定义，$P$ 空间下一条航线上的所有节点彼此之间都相互连接，节点点度必然比 L 空间大大增加。表 2 列出了两个空间中网络的基本性质。P 空间下的平均点度是 28.44，P 空间下的平均点度是 9.04，可以看到 P 空间的平均点度大大高于 L 空间。

5.2　航线长度分布

我们来看一条航线的长度即航线途经挂靠港口的次数，存在什么样的规律。如果我们记一条航线挂靠港口次数为 l，从图 3 可以看到 $P(l)$服从指数分布，在半对数图中呈一条直线，$P(l) \sim e^{-\alpha l}$，拟合指数为 $\alpha=0.13$。指数分布说明短的航线较多，长的航线随着长度增加逐渐变少。这反映了海上运输行业目前干线和支线互相配合的经营现状，挂靠港口较多的航线都是主要干线，使用大型船舶如万吨油轮，在洲与洲之间运输货物。而挂靠港口数量少的一般都是支线航线，担负区域内短途运输的任务，或者为主干线提供货物供给，构成轴辐射层次结构，这样的航线相对比较多。例如下述这条航线：Shanghai-Busan-Osaka-Nagoya-

Tokyo-Shimizu-Los Angeles-Charleston-Norfolk-New York-Antwerp-Bremerhaven-Thamesport-Rotterdam-Le Havre-NewYork-Norfolk-Charleston-Colon-LosAngeles-Oakland-Tokyo-Osaka-Shanghai 就是标准的主干线航线，从上海出发，连接了亚洲、美洲、欧洲的几个最主要的港口，最后回到上海，挂靠港口 24 次。相对的，城市公交网络和铁路网络不具有这样明显的航线长度区别。

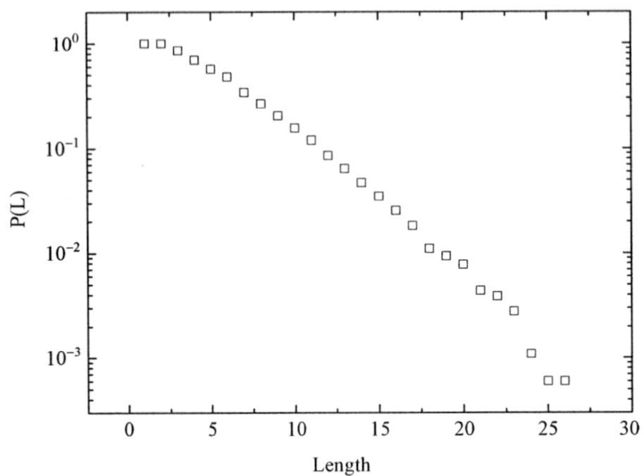

图 3 航线停靠港口数目 l 的分布曲线，服从指数分布

5.3 平均路径长度

网络中点对之间的最短路距离代表了网络内部的连通程度。图 4 是两个空间下最短距离的分布，L 空间下的最短路距离比 P 空间分布范围较宽，最大达到 10。L 空间下的平均路径长度是 3.60，P 空间下的平均路径长度是 2.66。这意味着在全世界范围内，货物平均途经 3 个港口就可以到达目的地，或者说平均经过 2 次中转可以到达目的地。相比网络的规模 $N=878$，可以说世界海运网络的平均路径长度是很小的。

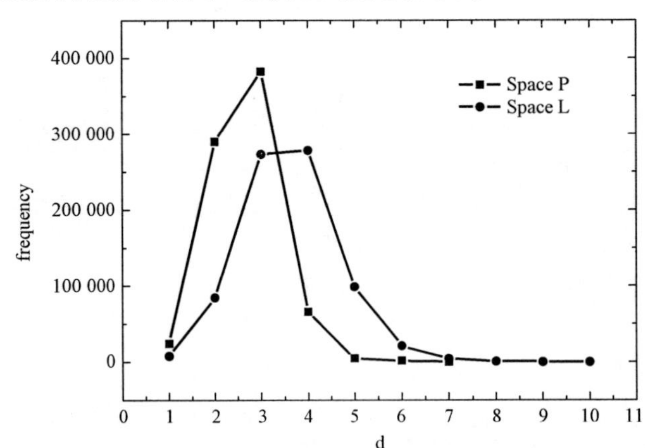

图 4 两个空间下的最短路距离频率分布图

注：L 空间下的最短路距离比 P 空间分布范围较宽

5.4 权重分布、点强度分布、点强度和点度关系

通常交通网络里的交通流量并不是平均分布的。一些边比其他边拥有更多的交通流

量，在整个网络功能中扮演更重要的角色。因此权重在交通网络中应该受到特别的关注。这里我们将研究带权海运网络的四种属性：权重分布、点强度分布、点强度和点度关系、入强度和出强度关系。结果显示在图 5 中。

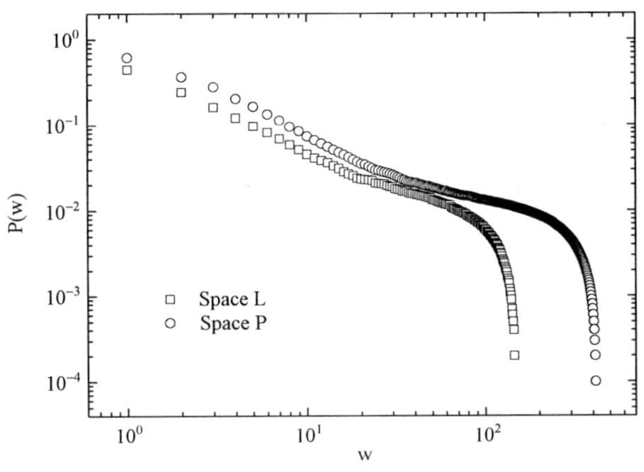

图 5 两个空间下的权重累积概率分布曲线，服从幂律分布

首先来看权重分布情况。在两个空间下权重分布基本相同，图 5 显示两条曲线在(1，100)之间是条倾斜向下的直线，服从幂律分布。

其次点强度分布也属于无标度分布。图 6 显示两个空间下的无向点强度分布曲线，尾部是一条直线，服从幂律分布，拟合后的函数是 $P(k) \sim k^{-1.3}$。

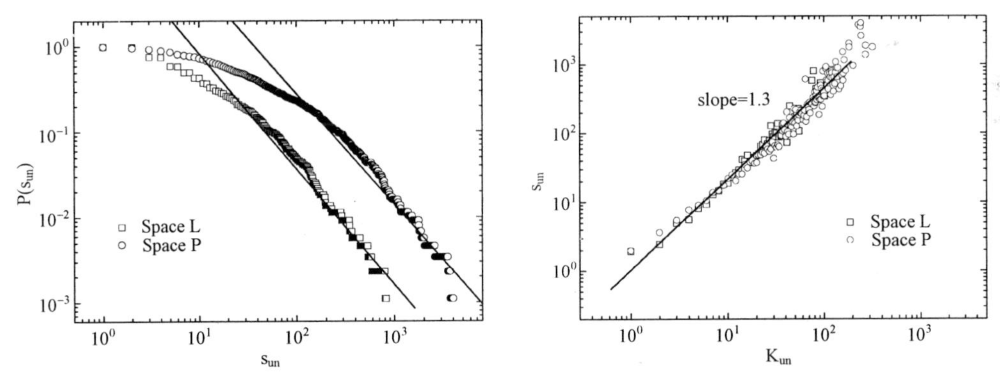

图 6 两个空间下的无向点强度分布曲线

注：左图：点强度累积概率分布曲线，服从幂律分布，幂律指数相同为－1.3

右图：点强度和点度之间的非线性关联。拟合的直线斜率都等于 1.3

最后，图 6 中两个空间下点强度和点度的关联直线拟合斜率都等于－1.3，说明世界海运网络的点强度和点度具有非线性关联，$s(k) \sim k^{-1.3}$，也就是说随着点度的增加，点强度加速增加。这符合"富者更富"的网络演化规则，也在很多实际的交通网络中得到验证，如中国航空网络、公交网络等。航班越多的港口，越容易成为实施货物合并的地方，所以会吸引更多的航班连接到港口，带来更多的流量。其中的演化规律在第五章有进一步的阐述。

6 网络结构

在这一节,我们通过分析带权和不带权的集系数和度相关指标,发现世界海运网络存在鲜明的层级结构,而且有富者俱乐部现象,枢纽港口之间航线多、流量大,构成了一个紧密联系的“俱乐部”。作者认为这种结构和海运网络中船运公司的意图最小化运营成本的最优化行为有关。

6.1 集聚系数

集聚系数是刻画网络的一个重要几何量,反映了连接在一起的点各自的近邻之中有多少是共同的近邻。集聚系数相关性是指度为 k 的节点的平均集聚系数与 k 的关系。图 7显示在两个空间下的集聚系数随着点度的增大逐渐下降,但 P 空间下的集聚系数曲线高于 L 空间。平均集聚系数在 L 空间中是 0.4,在 P 空间下是 0.7。从 P 空间下的高集聚系数,和 P 空间下网络平均最短距离 2.66 来看,我们可以得出结论,世界海运网络是一个小世界网络。

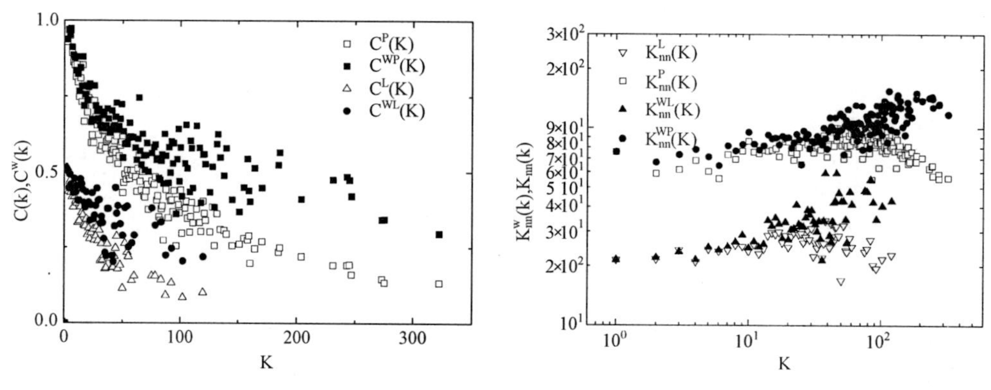

图 7 左图:集聚系数

注:P 空间下的集聚系数比 L 空间的集聚系数高,带权重的集聚系数比不带权重的集聚系数高。右图:度相关性。在两个空间中 $k_{nn,i}$都先随着点度增大而变大,随后随着点度继续增大反而开始下降。而带权的 $k^{w}_{nn,i}$一直上升。

得到的计算结果如图 7 中所示,在 L 空间和 P 空间下,带权集聚系数的曲线都位于不带权的集聚系数曲线之上,即 $C^w(k)>C(k)$,这说明了网络中的权重分布不平衡,在互相联系非常紧密的一些点之间边上权重相对较高,而互相连接不紧密的点之间权重不高。

6.2 度相关性

度相关性是指度为 k 的节点的所有近邻节点平均点度与 k 的关系,表现了节点之间互相匹配的偏好性。如果点度大的节点倾向与和点度小的节点连接,属于负相关。如果点度大的节点倾向与点度小的节点连接,则属于正相关。

图 7 显示 P 空间下的 $k_{nn,i}$高于 L 空间下的 $k_{nn,i}$。度为 k 的节点的邻连节点平均点度 $k_{nn,i}$首先随着点度增大而变大,随后随着点度继续增大反而下降。说明网络在较小的点度范围内属于正相关,在较大的点度范围则是负相关。这个结果和北美航空网络[29]、全球航空网络[28]的情况一致。当点度较小时,点度大的节点趋向连接点度小的节点,度相关性为

负。当点度变大时，点度大的节点反而趋向于连接点度同样大的节点，表现出正的度相关性。

接下来，我们来看加入权重因素以后情况会有什么变化。计算结果展示在图 7 中。可以看到，两个空间下带权重的 $k_{nn,i}^{w}$ 一直呈现上升趋势，位于 $k_{nn,i}$ 之上，即 $k_{nn,i}^{w} > k_{nn,i}$，这意味着网络中的权重大的边倾向于连接点度大的点。这个结果再一次地和北美航空网络[29]、全球航空网络[28]的情况一致。在增加了权重因素以后，我们清楚地看到世界海运网络是一个正相关匹配的网络。这个结果也和波兰公交系统的研究结果符合[12]。该研究揭示在不同规模的交通网络中度相关性不同，节点数 $N>500$ 的网络正相关，$N<500$ 的网络负相关。世界海运网络的节点数大于 500，度相关性也为正，吻合该研究结果。

6.3 富者俱乐部系数

在很多社会网络、技术网络中我们会看到这样的现象，点度大的节点互相之间连接很紧密，构成一个小团体，我们将它称为“富者俱乐部”现象。富者俱乐部系数(rich-club coefficient)被用来定量地衡量富者俱乐部现象，它首先由[26]提出，定义为如下的公式：

$$\phi(k) = \frac{2E_{>k}}{N_{>k}(N_{>k}-1)} \tag{7}$$

其中，$N_{>k}$ 定义为点度高于某个 k 值的点的数目，$E_{>k}$ 代表 $N_{>k}$ 个节点中互相连接的边的数目。这个公式代表这 $N_{>k}$ 个点中现实的边数和所有可能的边数之比。如果 $\phi(k)$ 随着 k 的增大而增大，说明点度越大的节点之间边连接的越紧密，因此可以说具有“富者俱乐部”现象。然后它在[14]中推广为 $\rho_{ran}(k)$(normalized rich-club coefficient)：

$$\rho_{ran}(k) = \phi(k)/\phi_{ran}(k) \tag{8}$$

这里 $\phi_{ran}(k)$ 是在保持点度序列不变的前提下最大程度随机化后的网络的富者俱乐部系数，具体随机化方法参见[27]中的算法。只有当 $\phi(k)$ 大于 $\phi_{ran}(k)$，我们才能说该网络明显不同于随机网络，[14]中用世界航空网络、Internet 等实际例子说明这样处理后的系数才能真正代表网络是否具有富者俱乐部的倾向性。

我们计算了世界海运网络在两个空间下的富者俱乐部系数 $\rho_{ran}(k)$。在图 8 中，我们看到两个空间下的两条曲线都高于 1，说明世界海运网络拥有富者俱乐部现象，而且曲线形状和世界航空网络很相似。

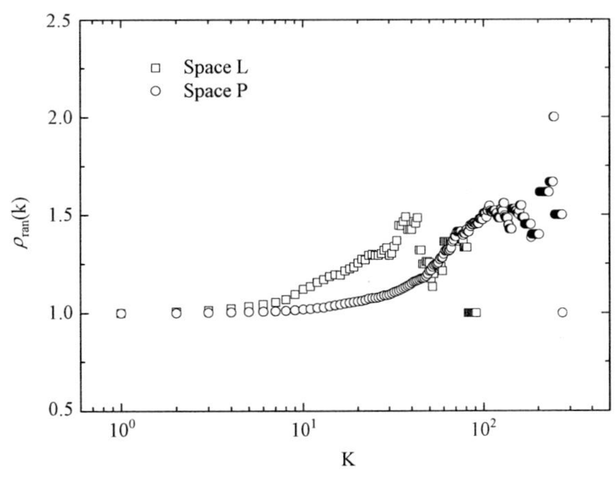

图 8 富者俱乐部系数

在 L 和 P 空间下都高于 1，说明世界海运网络拥有富者俱乐部现象综上所述，世界海运网络和世界航空网络非常相似，具有明显的层级结构，并存在“富者俱乐部”现象，点度大的节点倾向于和点度大的节点相连，点度大的节点彼此之间互相连接紧密，交通流量大大高于非枢纽节点之间的流量。相似的性质后面隐藏了相似的结构。这种结构和实际生活中航空业和海运业出于最优化目的而采用轴辐射运营模式有紧密关联，见下节的讨论。

6.4 海运网络网络结构和轴辐射运营模式的关系

世界航空网络和世界海运网络的网络结构充分反映了交通运输业的轴辐射运营模式的影响。作者认为正是因为经营者把港口或机场区分成枢纽机场或非枢纽机场，开设不同的干线航班和支线航班而造成权重分布的不均衡和网络结构的层次性，无标度性以及其他拓扑特性。

轴辐射运营模式是交通业内普遍采用的结构。这种结构能够使运输者充分利用交通里面的规模经济，采用大型运输工具在枢纽节点之间运输，达到大幅度降低运输成本的目的。交通科学的学者的一个热点研究方向是如何确定枢纽节点，如何设计枢纽节点的容量，如何合理安排其他节点到枢纽节点的航线，实现成本最优化或利润最优化的目的。常见模型包括单枢纽选址问题、多枢纽选址问题、p 枢纽选址问题（p-hub median problems）、枢纽链接选址问题（hubarc location problems）等[30,33]。

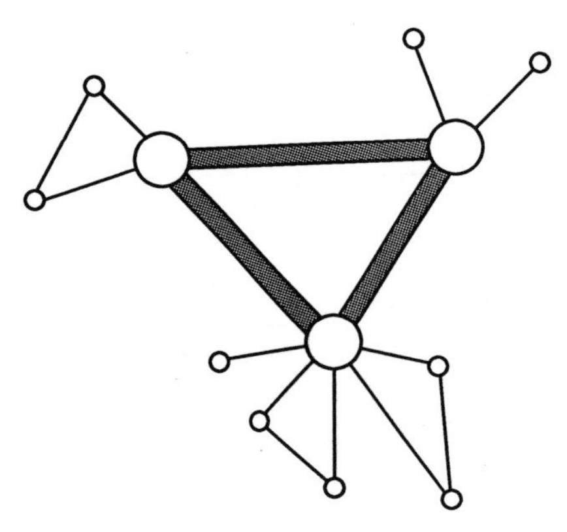

图 9 一个典型的海运网络中的轴辐射结构

注：三个枢纽节点互相之间用干线航班连接，流量很高，而其他一些节点通过支线航班和单个枢纽节点相连，支线航班顺序访问枢纽节点附近的港口，为干线航班提供货物。这个简单的结构拥有和世界海运网络同样的性质，即 $C^w(k)>C(k)$，$k_{nn}^w(k)>k_{nn}(k)$。

图 9 是一个典型的海运网络中轴辐射运营模型。图中有三个枢纽节点，互相之间完全连接，代表了干线航班，粗线代表枢纽节点之间的交通流量较大。其他节点通过连接到枢纽节点和整个网络连通，支线航班把货物运到枢纽节点，为干线航班喂给流量。这个轴辐射模型正好符合海运网络的结构特征：$c^w > c$，$k_{nn,i}^w > k_{nn,i}$。反映出航空和海运网络都是为达成最优化目的而科学设计后得到的网络。

7 节点重要性指标

在这一节，我们将研究节点重要性指标和这些指标的地理分布。首先我们回顾一下社会网络中心性分析的三个主要指标[34]：点度、介数和紧密度。点度是最自然的节点重要性指标：连接最多的最重要。点度已经在第 4.4.1 节得到详细讨论。下面我们先来讨论介数和紧密度指标。

7.1 介数(betweenness)

图 10 显示了介数的累积概率分布曲线。在两个空间中介数随着点度的增加而呈直线上升趋势，显示了清楚的幂律关系 $C^B(k)\sim k^{\alpha}$，指数在空间 L 下 $\alpha=1.66$，在空间 P 下

$\alpha=1.93$。类似的介数和点度的幂律关联也在公交汽车网络[13,?]和船运网络[7]中发现。值得注意的是，这种幂律关系加上点度本身的双幂律分布暗示着介数的概率分布也应该服从双幂律分布。这在图 10(a)中得到了证实。我们发现介数分布是双幂律分布：$P(C^B)\sim C^{-\alpha}$，在两个空间中的指数几乎是相同的，在较小的点度范围内 $\alpha=0.14\pm 0.01$，当点度较大时 $\alpha=1.0\pm 0.01$。

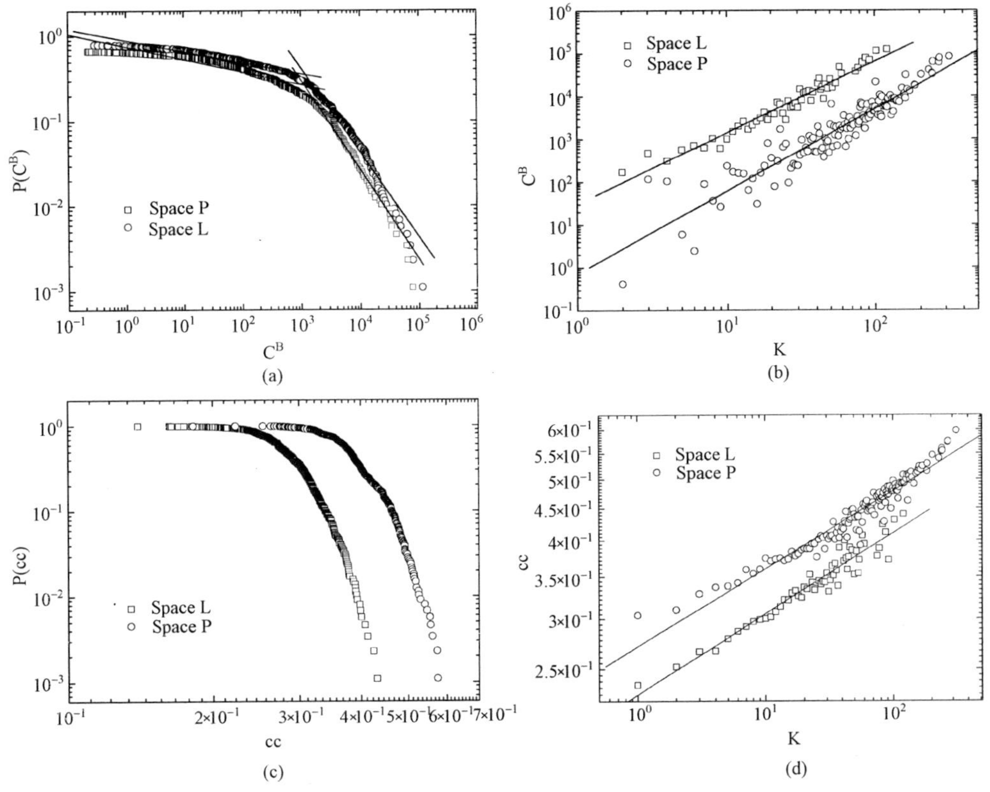

图 10　介数的累积概率分布曲线

注：左上图：介数分布，是弯折的幂律分布曲线。右上图：介数和点度相关性。在双对数图中成上升直线，拟合函数 L 空间下是 $C^B\sim k^{1.66}$，P 空间下是 $C^B\sim k^{1.93}$。左下图：紧密度分布，是弯折的幂律分布曲线。右下图：紧密度和点度相关性，都呈直线上升趋势，拟合函数 L 空间下是 $C^C\sim k^{0.128}$，P 空间下是 $C^C\sim k^{0.123}$。

7.2　紧密度(closeness centrality)

它衡量的是点 i 离网络中所有其他点的距离远近，定义为

$$C_i^C=\frac{N-1}{\sum_{j\neq i}d_{ij}}\tag{9}$$

这里的 d_{ij} 是指两点 i,j 之间的最短距离。图 10 中紧密度的分布在双对数图中尾部也服从幂律分布，拟合后的。紧密度和点度之间呈直线上升趋势，因此关联紧密。

介数和点度之间的幂律分布关系暗示两者之间具有强烈的关联，这点在世界各大港口介数和点度排名中也得到了进一步的证实。我们计算了网络中各点的点度和介数，并作了对比，列出了世界排名前 25 名的港口(表 3)。从节点重要性指标可以看到，新加坡

无论是点度还是介数，都排在全球第一名。新加坡的重要性是由其所处的地理位置决定的，它位于马六甲海峡要冲，许多国际海运航线都需要通过这里。它是全球海运中心，也是世界上最繁忙的海港之一，集装箱年吞吐量达1680万标箱。现在亚洲空运货物的16%以及亚洲航运的25%，都以新加坡为转运中心。同样的，其他名列世界前25名的港口地理位置都非常优越，处于航线必经之路，加上有些港口腹地经济贸易发展非常迅速，海上运输需求量很大，成为世界上最重要的港口之一。

表3　世界海运网络中20个最重要的港口城市

排名	港口	点度	介数	所属地区
1	新加坡	120	124 110.125 8	亚洲
2	安特卫普	102	113 368.616 1	欧洲
3	釜山	92	69 094.749 0	亚洲
4	鹿特丹	87	78 097.875 4	欧洲
5	巴生港	83	62 111.622 6	亚洲
6	香港	78	46 072.979 9	亚洲
7	上海	75	37 748.431 6	亚洲
8	汉堡港	60	40 362.462 5	欧洲
9	巴伦西亚港	60	27 346.095 6	欧洲
10	勒阿弗尔港	58	48 231.163 6	欧洲
11	焦亚陶罗港	55	20 148.466 7	欧洲
12	横滨港	54	19 716.728 7	亚洲
13	高雄港	52	15 363.578 1	亚洲
14	塞德港 *	52	16 121.847 6	非洲
15	不来梅哈芬港	50	24 998.908 8	欧洲
16	科伦坡港 *	48	15 128.362	亚洲
17	丹戎帕拉帕斯港	46	18 735.126 7	亚洲
18	吉达港 *	45	8 570.772 4	非洲
19	杰贝阿里港	44	20 137.525 5	非洲
20	宁波 *	44	12 315.951 5	亚洲
21	阿尔赫西拉斯	43	18 701.261 9	欧洲
22	巴塞罗那 *	43	15 256.390 3	欧洲
23	神户	43	8 869.731 3	亚洲
24	纽约	42	25 935.669 2	北美洲
25	金斯敦	41	23 281.322 3	北美洲

注：表中各项指标都是无向 L 空间下的。有 * 标志的港口不在介数的前20名内。

表3显示这两种指标之间的排名大致符合，如点度前25名中只有5名不在介数的前25名内。并没有出现如世界航空网络中的点度和介数大不相符的情况[20]。世界航空网络的研究曾发现点度最高的城市并不是介数最高城市的异常现象，而这种情况是由于

航空网络洲际之间明显的社团结构造成的。作者认为航空网络和海运网络之间的这种差别，是由于海运网络受到地域限制和政策限制相对比较少造成的。远洋船只可以旅行的距离比飞机远。由于国家政治和航空政策的限制，国际航班连接的机场限于可以开辟国际航班的城市。而海运网络中，集装箱海运港口大部分都是从事国际海运运输，没有航空航班有国内航班和国际航班之分，因此不会出现如航空网络那样的明显地域限制。

在图 11 中，从地理位置来看，这 25 名港口主要分布在亚洲和欧洲，包括亚洲和中东 13 个，非洲 1 个，欧洲 9 个，北美洲 1 个和拉丁美洲 1 个，地理分布不平衡。很显然，世界贸易钟摆已经偏向了远东地区，亚洲港口在当今世界集装箱港口业界占据了主导地位。此外，特别值得注意的是，这些港口都分布在东西航线上。世界上海运航线主要分为东西航线、南北航线和南南航线，东西航线主要链接亚洲、欧洲和北美洲[9,35]。世界上点度最高的港口都分布在东西航线这一事实代表了世界经济贸易在欧洲—亚洲、欧洲—美洲、亚洲—美洲之间的快速增长[1]。

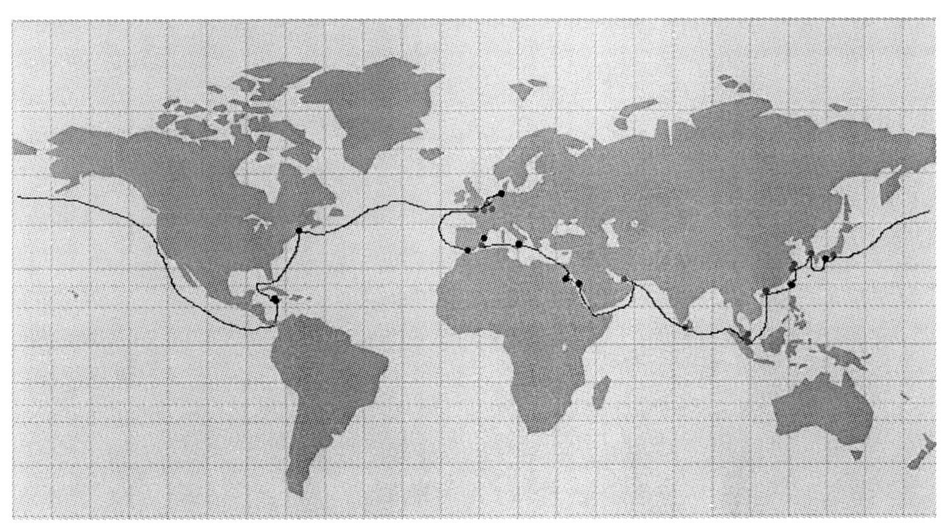

图 11　世界点度排名前 25 名的港口

注：全部都位于东西航线上。它们主要分布在亚洲和欧洲，
包括亚洲和中东 13 个，非洲 1 个，欧洲 9 个，北美洲 2 个。

8　结　论

本文在两种不同的拓扑空间中研究了由集装箱航线和世界各大港口组成的世界海运网路。我们首先分析了基本的拓扑性质，点度分布和公交网络类似，在 P 空间下服从截尾幂律分布，在 L 空间下服从指数分布。在 P 空间下，网络平均最短距离为 2.66，集聚系数为 0.7，证明了世界海运网络是一个无标度的小世界网络。并且通过考察带权重和不带权重的度相关性，发现世界海运网络和世界航空网络一样具有明显的层级结构，而且有“富者俱乐部”现象，点度大的节点彼此之间互相连接紧密，且之间的权重很大，反映了交通运输业的轴辐射运营模式的影响。

参 考 文 献

[1] United Nation. Review of maritime transport 2007[R] . http://www. ci-online. co. uk/.

[2] 王成金,金凤君. 中国海上集装箱运输的组织网络研究[J]. 地理科学,2006,26(4):392-401.

[3] 王成金. 现代港口地理学的研究进展及展望[J]. 地球科学进展,2008,23(3):244-248.

[4] 王成金. 世界集装箱港的形成演化及与国际贸易的耦合机制[J]. 地理研究,2007,26(3):558-567.

[5] 田炜,邓贵仕,武配剑,车文娇. 世界航运网络复杂性分析[J]. 大连理工大学学报,2007,47(4):605-609.

[6] Fremont Antoine. Global maritime networks: the case of Maersk[J]. Journal of transport geography, 2007,15:431-442.

[7] Xu Xinping, Hu Junhui and Liu Feng. Empirical analysis of the ship-transport network of China[J]. Chaos,2007,17:023129.

[8] Xu Xinping, Hu Junhui, Liu Feng and Liu Lianshou. Scaling and correlations ini three bus-transport networks of China[J]. Physica A,2007,374:441-448.

[9] Rodrigue Jean-Paul, et al. The geography of transport systems[M] . New York: Routledge, 2006.

[10] http://www. ci-online. co. uk/

[11] Guimerà R. , Mossa S. , Turtschi A. , and Amaral L. A. N. . The worldwide air transportation network: Anomalous centrality, community structure, and cities' global roles[J]. Proceedings of the National Academy of Sciences,2005,102(22):7791-7799.

[12] Sen P, Dasgupta S, Chatterjee A, P. A. Sreeram, G. Mukherjee, and S. S. Manna. Small world properties of the Indian railway network[J]. Physical Review E,2003,67:036106.

[13] Sienkiewicz Julian and Holyst Janusz. Statistical analysis of 22 public transport networks in Poland [J]. Physical Review E,2005,72:046127.

[14] Colizza V. , Flammini A. , Serrano M. A. , and Vespignani A. . Detecting rich-club ordering in complex networks[J]. Nature Physics,2006,2:110-115.

[15] Wasserman S. and Faust K. . Social networks analysis[M]. Cambridge University Press, Cambridege, 1994.

[16] A. -L. Barabasi, R. Albert, Nature 286 (1999) 509.

[17] M. E. J. Newman, Proc. Natl. Acad. Sci. USA 98 (2001) 404.

[18] H. Jeong B. Tombor R. Albert Z. N. Oltvai, A. -L. Barabasi, Nature 407(2000)651.

[19] L. A. N. Amaral, A. Scala, M. Barthelemy, H. E. Stanley, Proc. Natl. Acad. Sci. USA 97 (2000)11149.

[20] R. Guimera, S. Mossa, A. Turtschi and L. A. N. Amaral, Proc. Natl. Acad. Sci. USA 102(2005)7794.

[21] W. Li, X. Cai, Phys. Rev. E 69 (2004) 046106.

[22] L. P. Chi, R. Wang, H. Su, X. P. Xu, J. S. Zhao, W. Li, X. Cai, Chin. Phys. Lett. 20(8)(2003)1393.

[23] M. Guida, F. Maria, Chaos soitions and fractals 31 (2007) 527.

[24] Liping et al, Chin. Phys. Lett. 23 (12) (2006) 3384.

[25] W. Li, X. Cai, Physica A 382 (2007) 693.

[26] Zhou Shi and Mondragón R. J. . The Rich-Club phenomenon in the Internet topology[J]. IEEE Communications Letters,2004,8(3):180-182.

[27] Maslov S and Sneppen K. Science, 2002, 296: 910-913.

[28] A. Barrat, et al. , Proc. Natl. Acad. Sci. USA 101 (11) (2004) 3747.

[29] A. Barrat, M. Bartheélémy, A. Vespignani, J. of Stat. Mech. (2005) P05003.

[30] M. O'Kelly, Journal of transport geography, 6(3)(1998)171.

[31] Ross Robinson, Maritime Policy and Management 25 (1) (1998) 21.

[32] M. C. Moura, M. V. Pato, A. C. Paixa, Maritime Policy and Management 29(2)(2002)135.

[33] Bryan and M. O'Kelly, Journal of regional science, 39 (2) (1999) 275.

[34] S. Wasserman, K. Faust, Social networks analysis, Cambridge University Press, Cambridege, 1994.

[35] A. Fremont, Journal of transportation geography, 15(2007)431.

第六章　多产品需求和供应链竞争协调策略

MIT 的 Pindyck 教授和 UCL Berkely 的 Rubinfeld 教授所著的微观经济学（2001年）是世界上第一本介绍竞争环境下需求理论的经济学著作。基于顾客选择的需求理论，已成为产品竞争和供应链竞争的最重要的基本理论之一。朱道立、曹瑜（2005）介绍了我们在轿车市场预测、汽车制造和采购以及航空收益管理的应用研究，并提出了基于顾客选择的需求理论以及竞争策略设计方法。

鲁其辉、朱道立（2005）进一步深入研究了多产品的需求理论，基于顾客选择行为，建立了具有多种特征的多产品需求函数，在此基础上提出了最优供货策略，并分析了不同特征与不同竞争策略对收益的影响。徐兵、朱道立（2007）提出了具有网络外部性的产品差异化理论。

20 世纪 90 年代以来，世界经济步入全球化和信息化时代，供应链管理理论与实践使现代管理发生了重大变革，对全球经济发展产生了显著的影响。典型的供应链是供应商、制造商、批发商及零售商通过运输、库存、信息及金融设施互连而成的一个有机整体，它的目标是为最终客户提供产品和服务的有效价值，为供应链各个成员创造收益。

由于供应链的各个成员分属不同的企业，他们的利益和职责不同，所掌握的信息也有很大的局限性，这就使得他们在利益、风险方面都存在不同程度的冲突，而他们的局部利益和行为经常与供应链系统的目标不相吻合，这就导致供应链的系统性能降低和成员的收益受损。为此，我们有必要设计和使用供应链的协调机制，让供应链的各个成员共享信息，协调各个分散成员的决策行为，使他们的行为和供应链系统目标统一起来，从而提高供应链的总体性能，为顾客提供最好的服务，提高供应链的产品和服务的竞争力。

作者在 2005～2008 年主持了中国第一个关于供应链管理的自科基金重点项目，研究了供应链协调理论和方法、关键的供应链计算和分析方法、供应链协调应用技术和运营策略。

在本章第二部分的论文中，作者和合作者研究了各种供应链协调策略，特别是基于多产品需求理论的竞争环境下供应链协调策略，如质量与价格竞争供应链协调策略、基于货架空间分配决策的供应链协调；还研究了信息不对称的供应链契约设计问题，如最优激励契约、供应链线性契约、供应链产能投资问题等。

近年来，供应链间竞争和供应链网络的研究成为供应链管理的重要研究方向。通过超网络理论方法，我们用交通网络来刻画供应链结构，应用交通均衡理论来研究产品需求和系统收益及协调策略。

为了深入分析现实的供应链，实施有效的协调策略，我们必须研究一些重要分析理论工具对供应链管理的应用，如博弈论、变分不等式、二层优化与控制以及委托代理问题的有效算法。有兴趣的读者可参考我们在这方面的研究成果。

多产品竞争环境下的需求理论和竞争策略设计*

朱道立，曹 瑜
（复旦大学管理学院，上海 200433）

摘要：回顾了作者多年在汽车工业和航空公司管理中的应用研究，讨论和总结基于顾客选择的多产品竞争环境下的需求理论，以及竞争策略设计的有关理论和管理技术。这些管理思想和技术还可以应用于其他制造业和服务业，如通迅业等。

关键词：多产品竞争；顾客选择；需求理论；竞争策略设计
中国分类号：F270 **文献标识码：**A

当前，经济和管理的一个主要特点是企业面临着一个复杂多变的市场环境，具体表现为产品需求不稳定、多变，原材料、配套产品和服务的价格变化剧烈，交货期不确定等等。企业面临的问题是企业之间的竞争愈益激烈，逐渐演变为供应链之间的竞争。企业的竞争策略设计已成为企业迫切需要解决的问题。例如，企业必须考虑如何科学地制定采购和生产计划；确定其销售价格以及折扣；确定对顾客的服务水平和库存策略，以便企业自身的产品能最大限度地吸引顾客而战胜对手，从而使企业在竞争激烈的环境中立于不败之地。在复杂多变的竞争环境中，企业要科学地进行竞争策略设计和实现科学管理困难很大，关键是如何把握市场，洞悉顾客需求。

1 多产品竞争环境下的需求理论

中国经济正以相当惊人的速度往前发展，经济社会面临着翻天覆地的变化。但应注意的是，中国市场经济发展的历史很短，无论是国家和各级政府的统计数据，还是各行业的市场数据都不够完整，历史数据积累甚少。不仅如此，近 10 年来中国经济和社会变化的跳跃非常大。这些特点很难使用传统的需求理论和预测技术来指导一些行业的产品需求分析和计算。如 2003 年，中国轿车市场的需求猛增，完全出乎专家的意料，几乎所有从事市场预测的咨询公司和汽车厂商对轿车需求预测的误差都超过了 200% 。这样的预测误差对轿车的生产和销售都带来了很大的困难。近年来，中国港口快速崛起，主要港口的吞吐量猛增，但是日本港口的吞吐量却大幅下跌。我们可以把港口吞吐量看成是港口服

---

* **收稿日期：**2005-03-15 。
基金项目：国家自然科学基金重点资助项目(70432001) 。
作者简介：朱道立(1945～)，男，教授，博士研究生导师，研究方向：物流和供应链管理，最优化理论；曹瑜(1980～)，女，硕士研究生。

务产品的需求量。在复杂的竞争环境下,港口吞吐量的变化很难用传统的腹地 GDP 回归方法来解释。目前各国港口之间和我国各地港口之间的竞争甚为剧烈,因此,研究新的港口吞吐量预测方法和设计港口竞争策略成为一个非常重要的问题[5]。

M IT 的 Pindyck 教授和 UCL,Berkely 的 Rubinfeld 教授的微观经济学[7]是第一本初步介绍竞争环境下的需求理论的微观经济学教材。

基于顾客选择的需求理论是竞争环境下需求理论的最主要的内容之一,其基本内容:①在对消费者收入、购买行为和社会与经济因素分析的基础上,结合专家调查等预测方法对产品总量进行预测;②根据市场历史数据,对消费者的选择偏好分析研究;③利用市场结构、各产品的特征及顾客偏好的分析结果,结合产品差异化理论以及顾客选择理论计算产品的市场份额。如产品带有网络外部性,则需要使用定点原理等专门工具进行市场份额的计算[6]。图 1 表示基于顾客选择的需求理论的主要框架。

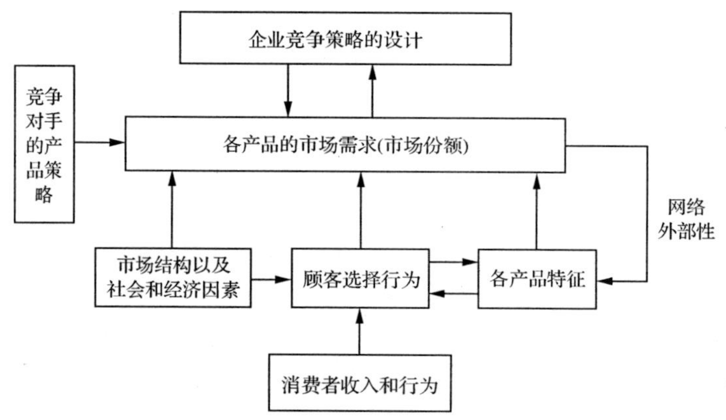

图 1　顾客选择和企业竞争策略设计

Fig. 1　Customer choice & enterprise competition policy design

基于顾客选择的产品市场预测理论的一个典型和重要的例子是汽车的需求预测。汽车需求理论和计算一直是学术界和工业界颇为关注的问题[1]。根据我们的分析,使用基于顾客选择的产品市场预测理论对于我国轿车市场比较合适。这是因为中国轿车市场的历史很短,市场不稳定,人的购买行为对中国轿车市场起了决定性的作用。

由于我国居民收入的详细统计数据不够完整,对顾客选择偏好分布的研究较为困难,因此选用离散选择的 Logit 模型进行我国轿车市场份额预测比较合理[2,4]。在 Logit 模型中,假设消费者是理性的,追求个人的效用最大化,其效用函数为

$$U_i = \theta_1 S_{i1} + \theta_2 S_{i2} + \cdots + \theta_m S_{im} + e_i = V_i + e_i$$

其中,效用值 U_i 是消费者对某种车型 i 的综合评价值,服务属性 S_{ij} 即消费者对某种车型 i 的各种评价指标 j (以下简称总指标)的评价,待定系数 θ_j 为消费者对各项总指标的偏好(即顾客偏好),从侧面反映各项总指标在消费者的购车行为中所起的作用,e_i 为随机变量。

根据我们对汽车销售公司的实地调查以及由专家调查法所获取的信息,可确定在轿车购买行为中影响消费者选择的主要产品特征,即模型中的总指标和分指标(表 1)。

通过市场调查可得到顾客对各类车型指标的评价值,其中总指标的评价是由各项分指标(以下简称分指标)的评价值加权所得,从而确定(S_{i1},S_{i2},…,S_{im})。

表 1　轿车的主要产品特性

Tab. 1 Main product characters of automobiles

总指标	分指标								
安全性	安全气囊	ABS							
使用合适性	音响系统	外后视镜	电动门窗	前排座椅调节	门锁	定速巡航系统	动力转向	变速器	可调转向盘
性能	发动机类型及排量	最高车速	0－100km/h 加速时间	制动系统					
美观性	天窗	真皮座	外观评分						
品牌	品牌满意度	品牌知名度	新颖性						

对顾客偏好 θ_j 的估计是根据轿车市场份额的历史数据，利用最小二乘法或极大似然估计法反推得到历史的顾客偏好。若采用最小二乘法，则历史的顾客偏好由求解以下公式得到：$\min\limits_{\theta_1,\theta_2,\cdots,\theta_m}\sum\limits_{i=1}^{n}(P_i-Q_i)^2$，$P_i$ 表示由 Logit 模型计算得到的历史预测销量，Q_i 表示历史实际销量。假设消费者的顾客偏好存在一个缓慢的变化过程，根据历史顾客偏好，可以采用时间序列中的指数平滑法得出需预测月份的顾客偏好。

利用以上两部分的结果，得到效用函数中确定部分 V_i 的值，再利用随机变量 e_i 的分布性质，通过推导计算，可以得出消费者选择车型 i 的概率，即各车型的市场份额

$$P_i = P\{U_i > U_j,\ j\ i\} = \frac{e^{v_i}}{\sum\limits_j e^{V_j}}$$

轿车市场份额预测的具体流程如图 2 所示。

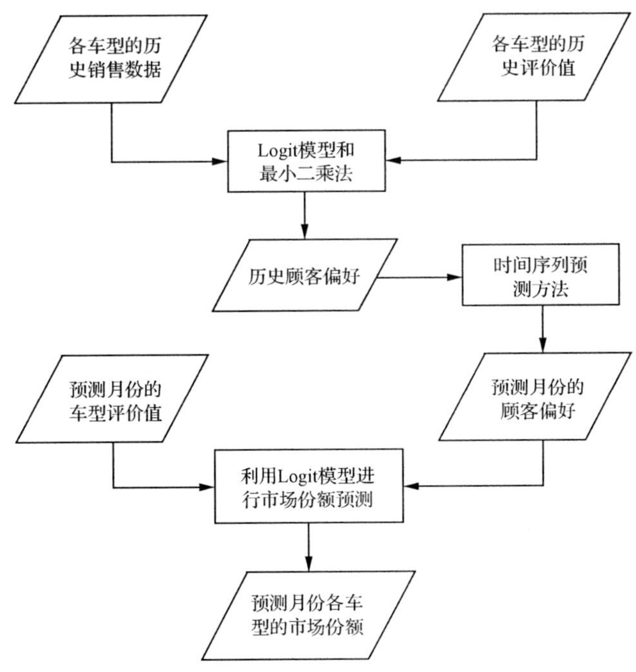

图 2　轿车市场份额预测流程

Fig. 2　market share forecasting flow of auto mobiles

我们开发的"中国轿车市场预测系统"(图 3)是一个可以根据轿车车型的历史销售数据以及各月份轿车车型的特性指标,对各轿车车型和品牌进行动态的市场份额预测,并在此基础上辅助竞争策略设计的决策支持系统[8]。

图 3　系统界面

Fig. 3　System main interface

该系统预测得到的结果非常令人满意。表 2 表示了上汽集团在某月的市场份额预测及其实际市场份额,可以看出其误差很小。

表 2　某月上汽及其他厂商实际与预测市场份额对比

Tab. 2 Actual& Forecasting Market Share of SAIC

厂商	实际销售量/辆	实际市场份额/%	预测销售量/辆	预测市场份额/%
上汽集团	43 563	46.24	45 090	47.86
其他厂商	50 656	53.73	49 129	52.14

利用该系统还可以进行产品的竞争策略设计。例如在轿车市场中,企业可以通过改变自身产品的一项或多项产品指标,而改变市场份额或改善竞争优势;利用"中国轿车市场预测系统",还可以对影响轿车需求量的各项产品指标进行敏感性分析,确定其影响程度,从而为决策者的竞争性决策提供依据和帮助。

2　竞争环境下企业的竞争策略设计

企业在竞争环境下为了争取顾客,扩大自身产品的市场份额和收益,必须要考虑顾客的需求和竞争对手的行为以及市场结构和产品特征等因素,以便设计出最优于企业本身利益的竞争策略。

如果一个企业提供的是公共服务产品,它的企业竞争策略设计还会影响到国家和地区的经济。这时企业竞争策略的设计和实现是由企业、国家和地区共同完成的。例如,日本港口的竞争实力近几年明显下降,日本神户的港口吞吐量原来是世界的第四位,现已降到 27 位,并且日本的主要港口(东京、神户和横滨)的吞吐量总和已不及我国深圳港口的吞吐量，这些情况引起了日本政府和港口的高度重视。一个港口吞吐量的大小取决于进出港口的运输量，包括货物中转量。顾客选取服务港口取决于港口费用、港口服务时间、航班设置、货物始发地—港口以及港口—货数。日本政府和港口，经过研究和论证，在今年准备扒出两大主要措施，即港口费用下降 30%，以及大幅度缩短通关时间。

企业之间的竞争有时还发生在这样的情况下，即竞争对手提供的是不同形式但又具有可替代性的产品。例如，不同模式的交通方式在客运市场展开了激烈的竞争。航空公司和铁路部门都可以为乘客提供从始发地至目的地的客运服务，而顾客选择客运方式所考虑的主要因素有价格、时间、方便性和舒适性等。几年来，我国的航空公司和铁路部门多次在价格和提速方面进行了竞争。铁路部门采取的竞争策略主要是提速和改善服务，而航空公司采取的竞争策略主要是降低价格和增设航班等。如何提速，如何降价这就是竞争策略设计问题，设计依据是估计竞争策略对市场份额的影响。

对于单个乘客而言，他有一个称为时间价值的尺度 α。乘客比较乘飞机和乘火车的总费用(将时间换算为费用)，即(飞机费用＋α^* 飞机时间)和(火车费用＋α3 火车时间)，然后决定选取何种交通客运方式。如图 3 所示，可以看到存在一个 $\hat{\alpha}$，使得时间价值较小的乘客($\alpha<\hat{\alpha}$) 愿意乘火车，时间价值较大的乘客($\alpha>\hat{\alpha}$) 愿意乘飞机。航空公司和铁路部门的竞争策略决定了 $\hat{\alpha}$ 的数值。另一方面，根据顾客收入和其他社会、经济因素分析，可以得到乘客时间价值的分布规律。因此，一旦给定航空公司和铁路部门的竞争策略，就可计算得到两种运输方式的市场份额。注意到，市场份额是竞争策略的函数，据此可以进行火车提速和飞机降价的策略设计。关于航空公司和铁路部门的竞争策略设计详见文献[9]。

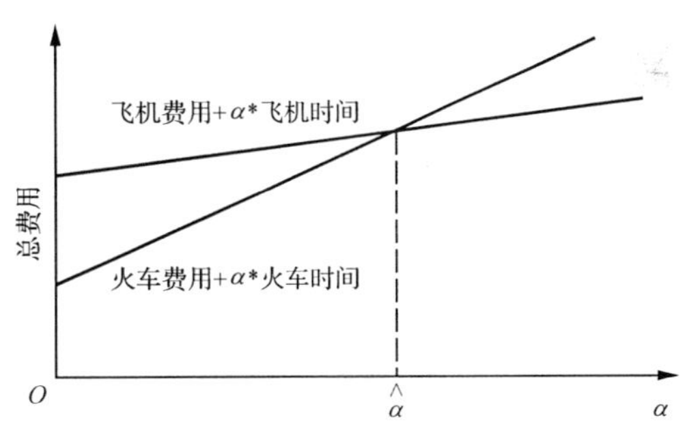

图 4　总费用和顾客选择

Fig 4　Total cost & customer choice

然而，航空公司和铁路部门对价格和速度的设计过程远比上述过程复杂得多。例如铁路部门要对不同的火车班次，不同的始发地/目的地，不同类别的乘客(如学生、老年人等)设计不同的价格和速度，而航空公司则面临着航线组织、价格设计、航空舱位分配等决策。在不同时间，对不同顾客及舱位给予不同的价格和服务，这是一个很复杂的竞争策略设计过程，现被称为航空业的收益管理。

航空公司竞争的另一个特点是竞争和合作的问题。航空公司有自己独立的航线服务，但也经常和别的航空公司合作共同负责一条航线服务，因而航空运输服务往往呈现带有网络结构的服务产品特性[3]。作者在文献[3] 中提出了航空公司收益管理(价格设计)的二层决策理论。这种理论和方法已被用于加拿大和法国的航空公司和铁路公司的管理之中。下面用一个简单的例子来说明这种理论和方法。

加拿大航空公司(下以 AC 表示)，中国国际航空公司(CA)，日本航空公司(JAL)，美国联邦航空公司(UA)在加拿大蒙特利尔市—中国上海市之间提供三条航线服务，如图 5 所示。各条航线的费用和时间见表 3。

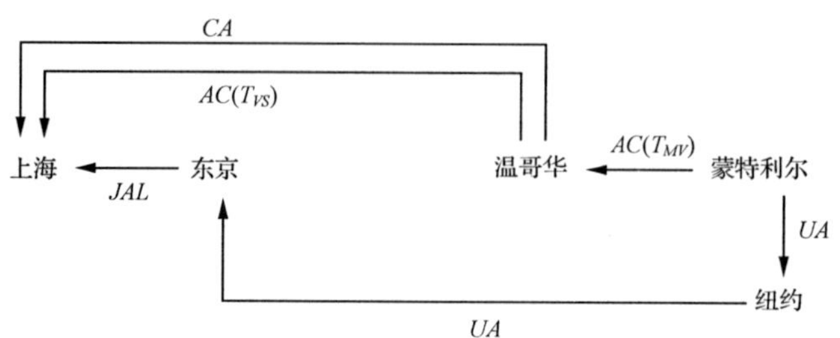

图 5 竞争和合作的航线

Fig. 5 Flight course of cooperation and competition

表 3 各航线的费用和时间

Tab 3 Cost and time of each flight course

序号	航空公司	航线	费用/$	时间/h
1	UA+JAL	蒙特利尔—纽约—日本—上海	1 320	36
2	AC+CA	蒙特利尔—温哥华—上海	T_{MV}+720	26
3	AC+AC	蒙特利尔—温哥华—上海	$T_{MV}+T_{VS}$	18

加拿大航公司的竞争策略设计问题是如何设计从蒙特利尔—温哥华的价格（T_{MV}）和温哥华—上海的价格（T_{VS}），使航空公司收益最大。在对顾客偏好和航空市场调查研究的基础上，利用顾客选择理论就可以计算得到三条航线的市场份额。注意到，这个市场份额是 T_{MV}和 T_{VS}的函数。利用二层最优化理论就可设计加拿大航空公司的最优价格[3]。进一步，我们还可以得到有关航线服务的市场结构，即各航空公司市场份额和价格之间的关系，如图 6 所示。各航空公司可以据此确定自身的竞争策略，如进入市场策略、独立市场策略等。

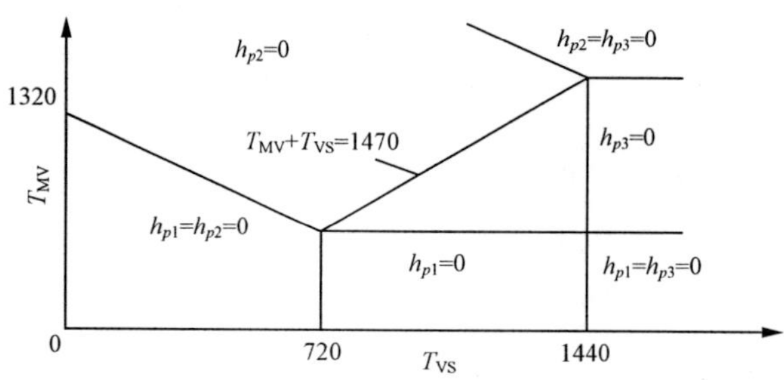

图 6 竞争策略和市场结构

Fig. 6 Market structure & competition strategy

本文从顾客选择理论出发，讨论了竞争市场预测和竞争策略设计的理论方法和技术。尽管本文较多地应用运输服务产品的例子来说明竞争策略设计，但这些思想和技术也可应用于通讯业和制造业中。

Demand Theory and Competition Policy Design in Multi-products Competition Markets

ZHU Dao-li, CAO Yu

(*School of Management Fudan university*, *Shanghai* 210093, *China*)

Abstract: Based on authors' research on managem ent in automobile and airline industries for many years, it discusses customer-choice demand theory in multi-products competition markets, and also theories and management techniques for competition policy design. These ideas and techniques can also be applied to oth-er manufacturing and service industries, such as telecomm unication industry.

Keywords: multi-products comp etition; customer choice; dem and theory; competition policy design

参考文献

[1] Chow G C. Demand for Automobiles in the United States[M]. Am sterdam: North-Holland Publishing Company, 1957.

[2] Gabszewica J, Thisse J F. On the nature of competition with differentiated products[J]. *The Econom ic Journal*, 1979a, **96**: 160-172.

[3] Marcotte P, Savard G, Zhu D L. Mathematical structure of a bileval strategic pricing model[J]. *European Journal of Operations Research*, 2005 (to be published).

[4] Kenneth E T. Discrete choice methods with simulation[M]. Cambridge: Cambridge University Press, 2002.

[5] Song D W. Port competition in concept and practice[J]. *Maritime Policy & Management*, 2003, **30** (1): 29-44.

[6] Nagurney A. Network economics: A variato inal inequality approach[M]. Dordrecht: Kluwer Academic Publishers, 1993.

[7] Pindych R S, Rubinfeld D L. Microeconomics(Fifth Edition)[M]. NJ: Prentice Hall, 2001.

[8] 朱道立，陈　霖，钱力显，等."中国轿车市场预测"项目报告[R]. 上海：上汽汽车项目评委会，2003.

[9] 祁海燕. 竞争策略设计研究和产品差异性[D]上海：复旦大学管理学院硕士论文，2002.

（本文发表于《研究与发展管理》，2005 年第 2 期）

多产品竞争环境中最优供货决策①

鲁其辉，朱道立

（复旦大学管理学院管理科学系，上海 200433）

摘要：在有多产品竞争的市场中，产品零售商首先需要了解每个产品在市场中的地位和市场份额，然后通过了解市场需求总量和销售支出情况来决定产品的供应数量，以达到利润的最大化的目标。怎样得到最优的供量问题是现代库存管理的基础性问题之一。通过引进产品特征描述和消费者一般支出的概念，给出一种市场份额的分析方法和市场份额的一些数学性质及经济特点。然后引入管理中经典库存决策模型——“报童问题”模型，分析多产品竞争环境中零售商的最优供货决策问题。最后研究了在产品的某些特征描述改变的条件下，零售商最优供货量、期望利润和市场利润总量的敏感性分析及其经济含义解释。

关键词：市场竞争；报童模型；多产品；库存问题；决策分析

中图分类号：O221　　**文献标识码**：A　　**文章编号**：1007-9807(2005)06-0043-08

0 引言

经济全球化、产品开发速度的不断加快使得市场中产品之间的竞争日趋激烈，从而使产品的零售商确定供货量变得更加困难。传统的库存决策模型中往往只考虑消费者对价格的关注。而实际上，消费者选择产品时，并不仅仅比较产品之间的价格，而且还会根据自身的偏好来同时衡量产品的其他特征。因此，通过使用只考虑与价格有关的需求来决定供货量是不很完善的。本文将引进产品特征描述的概念，通过消费者偏好形成消费者一般支出的表达式，得到产品的市场份额，然后综合考虑市场总需求量和零售商的销售支出情况给出最优决策模型。

目前，研究多产品供货决策问题的研究方向大致可以分为三类，第一类方向是研究单个零售商提供多个产品并且有多个资金和能力约束条件的情况，例如文献[1～4]。在这个方向的研究一般假定每个产品的需求函数是已知的，并且产品的市场需求量是相互独立的或者已知它们的相关系数。第二类方向是研究产品之间有替代性的问题，见文献[5,6]，它的现实背景是：如果某个产品出现了缺货时，全部或者一部分消费者将选择市场中其他同类产品。最后一类方向是考虑每个零售商具有不同的最大化效用目标的问题，见文献[7～11]，文献[12]对研究多产品供货决策问题的文献进行了详细的评述。

本文的研究方式与以上文献所不同之处主要有以下两点：①市场需求函数的不同。

---

① **收稿日期**：2003-12-15；**修订日期**：2005-09-28。

基金项目：国家自然科学基金资助项目(70432001)；复旦大学研究生创新基金资助项目。

作者简介：鲁其辉(1977～)，男，湖南益阳人，博士生。

以上文献的研究中一般假定需求函数是给定的，产品的相关性系数也是已知的，而本文是通过消费者的一般支出和偏好分布求出市场份额来得到产品的需求函数；②敏感性分析方式的不同。由于以前的研究工作中假定消费者面对产品的特征只有一个就是价格，假定产品有多个特征，因此本文研究产品的不同特征变化时，对零售商最优供货决策和收益的影响情况。

1　产品竞争描述

1.1　产品特征描述

在市场经济环境中，市场中产品是丰富多样的，消费者可以根据自身的经济状况和个人偏好进行选择。比如说，一位旅客要从上海市旅行到北京市，他面临着多种可供选择的交通方式，如，乘火车、坐飞机、坐汽车或轮船等等。但是不同的交通方式有旅行费用和旅行时间等方面的不同。一般来说，乘火车旅行花费的时间（T_1）要比坐飞机花费的时间（T_2）长，但是乘火车的旅行费用（P_1）要比坐飞机的旅行费用（P_2）低，即 $T_1>T_2$，$P_1<P_2$。因此，可以把同类商品或服务产品的共同特点提取出来作为该类产品的特征描述，例如上面旅行例子中的旅行费用 P 和旅行时间 T 作为交通方式的特征描述。下面给出同类竞争产品特征描述的。

定义 1　在一个提供同类消费结果的市场中，设有 n 种不同的产品：V_i，$i=1,\cdots,n$，把可以区别产品的 $m+1$ 个数量特征称为该类产品的特征描述。记为 $P,T_1,\cdots,T_m$。那么产品 V_i 的特征描述值为 $P_i,T_{i1},\cdots,T_{im}$。

1.2　消费者偏好及一般支出

假定　在面对具有不同特征描述的多种产品市场中，消费者按照最小的一般支出原则选择唯一一种产品消费。其中，一般支出可以分为两个部分：一个是显性支出，一般只有一个变量，它表现为货币支出，比如说上小节旅行实例中的旅行费用 P；另一个是隐形支出，它一般含有一个或多个变量，它们表现为非货币支出，比如说例中的旅行时间 T。假定消费者对于隐形支出有偏好，设对产品的特征描述 T_i 的偏好系数为 α_i，它的数量单位为（特征描述 P 的单位）/（特征描述 T_i 的单位）。例如旅行实例中旅行时间 T 的偏好系数 α 的单位是（元/h），表示消费者对支出单位时间相当的货币数量，一般称为“时间价值”（value-of-time）。下面给出消费者一般支出的定义。

定义 2　设在有 n 种不同的产品（Vi，$i=1,\cdots,n$）的市场中，产品 V_i 的特征描述为 $P_i,T_{i1},\cdots,T_{im}$。设消费者对特征描述 T_i 的偏好系数为 α_i。那么，对于产品 V_i，消费者的一般支出为

$$C_i \triangleq P_i+\sum_{j=1}^{m}\alpha_i T_{ij},i=1,\cdots,n \tag{1}$$

特别地，如果市场中只有两个同类产品且特征描述为 P 和 T，消费者面对的一般支出可简记为

产品 V_1

$$C_1=P_1+\alpha T_1 \tag{2}$$

产品 V_2

$$C_2 = P_2 + \alpha T_2$$

如果 $P_1 < P_2, T_1 > T_2, \hat{\alpha} \in (0, \alpha_{\max}]$，则两个产品的一般支出可用图 1 表示。

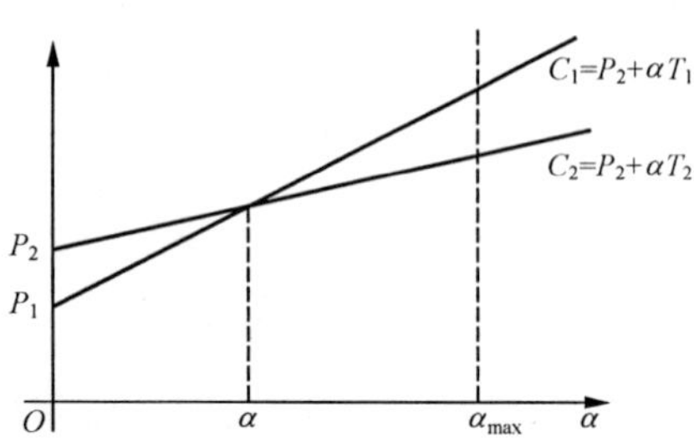

图 1 两个产品消费者一般支出示意图

Fig. 1 Customer's general cost of two kinds of products

1.3 市场份额

在市场中，不同消费者有不同的消费者偏好，可以采用市场调查的方式将消费者对产品特征 T_i 的偏好 α_i 进行统计，得到消费者偏好的概率分布。设 α_i 服从连续概率分布，分布函数为 $H_i(\alpha_i)$，概率密度函数为 $h_i(\alpha_i)$。设在销售季节时段内，到达市场的消费者总人数为 M，那么每位消费者对产品特征 T_i 的偏好 α_i 服从分布函数 $H_i(\alpha_i)$。

市场份额是指在有多个产品的市场中消费者选择某个产品的概率。下文将只考虑对于有两个竞争产品及两个特征描述的市场份额的计算。见图 1，显然，$\hat{\alpha}$ 是两个产品的一般支出的交点，即满足下式

$$P_1 + \hat{\alpha} T_1 = P_2 + \hat{\alpha} T_2$$

那么

$$\hat{\alpha} = \frac{P_2 - P_1}{T_1 - T_2} \tag{4}$$

从图 1 可以看出，对于消费者时间价值 α 属于区间$(0, \hat{\alpha}]$的消费者，不会选择产品 V_2 而只会选择产品 V_1；对于时间价值 α 属于区间$(\alpha, \alpha_{\max}]$的消费者，不会选择产品 V_1 而只会选择产品 V_2。这个特点与现实世界的情况也是相符合的。比如在例中，时间价值高的商务旅行者，一般会选择时间短的交通方式，而时间价值低的消费者将选择价格低的交通方式。

设已知消费者对产品特征 T 的偏好分布 $H(\alpha)$。则可按下式分别求出两个产品的市场份额

$$S_1 = \int_0^{\hat{\alpha}} h(\alpha) \mathrm{d}\alpha = H\left(\frac{P_2 - P_1}{T_1 - T_2}\right) \tag{5}$$

$$S_2 = \int_0^{\alpha_{\max}} h(\alpha) \mathrm{d}\alpha = 1 - H\left(\frac{P_2 - P_1}{T_1 - T_2}\right) \tag{6}$$

1.4 市场份额的特点

设在有两个产品的竞争市场中，零售商 1 在市场中提供产品 V_1，零售商 2 在市场中提供产品 V_2。下面的命题给出市场份额的特点。

命题 3 在只改变产品 V_1 的特征描述 T_1 而不改变两个产品的其他特征描述的条件下，如果零售商 1 减低 T_1，那么产品 V_1 的市场份额会增加，即$\frac{\mathrm{d}S}{\mathrm{d}T_1}<0$。同样，在不改变其他产品特征描述的条件下，如果零售商 2 减低 P_2，那么产品 V_2 的市场份额会增加，即$\frac{\mathrm{d}S_2}{\mathrm{d}p_2}<0$。

证明　由$\frac{d\hat{\alpha}}{dT_1}<0$和$\frac{dH(\hat{\alpha})}{d\hat{\alpha}}>0$可知$\frac{dS_1}{dT_1}=\frac{dH}{d\hat{\alpha}}\cdot\frac{d\hat{\alpha}}{dT_1}<0$成立。同理$\frac{dS_2}{dP_2}<0$成立。证毕。

例 1　设从上海到北京乘火车和坐飞机，消费者需要付出的旅行费用和旅行时间分别为$P_1=200, T_1=15; P_2=600, T_2=3$，消费者对旅行时间的价值$\alpha$服从均匀分布$U[0,100]$。设零售商1提供火车客运服务（产品$V_1$），零售商2提供飞行客运服务（产品$V_2$）。在上述假设条件下，根据式(5)和式(6)，容易求出产品V_1和产品V_2的市场份额分别为：33.3%和66.7%。在现实世界中，火车客运公司可以通过提高火车运行速度来减少旅行时间T_1，现在假设提速后的旅行时间为$T_1'=10$，在其他参数不变的条件下，市场份额变化为57.1%和42.9%。同样如果其他参数不变降低飞机票价为$P_2'=500$，新的市场份额为25%和75%。

2　经典报童模型

2.1　经典报童问题

经典报童问题（Newsboy 或 Newsvendor）模型在现代库存管理中有着广泛的应用，文献[13]对近几十年中报童模型的推广及应用做了详细综述。经典报童问题是指在一个销售季节短且只有一次订货机会的产品供货量决策中，零售商面对不确定的市场需求量x，从供应商批发产品或自行提供产品的单价为c。如果提供的产品过多，在销售季节过后，未售出的产品引起的库存管理和其他处理费用的平均单价为h，若出现缺货的情况，由于没有满足潜在消费者的需求而出现了机会损失，设单位产品的惩罚价为s，每售出单位产品的零售价格为P，在这些条件下，零售商在销售季节开始之前确定最优供货量Q。首先给出以下记号：

M——到达市场的消费者人数；

X——随机需求变量；

$f(x)$——X的概率密度函数；

$F(x)$——X的概率分布函数；

μ,σ^2——X的均值和方差；

$\phi(x)$——标准正态分布密度函数，即$\phi(x)=\frac{1}{\sqrt{2\pi}}e^{-x^2/2}$；

$\Phi(\cdot)$——标准正态分布函数；

$\Phi^{-1}(\cdot)$——标准正态分布函数的逆函数；

见论文[1,7～10]，在供货量的决策过程中，若零售商的供货量为Q时，他的期望收益可表达成

$$\Theta(Q)=(P+s+h)\cdot\left(\int_{\infty}^{Q}xf(x)dx-QF(Q)\right)+(P+s-c)Q-s\mu \tag{7}$$

由于模型中零售商按照最大期望收益的原则选择最优供货量，且目标函数(7)是一个严格凹函数，即$\frac{d^2\Theta(Q)}{d(Q)}<0$，那么可以通过求解$\frac{d\Theta(Q)}{dQ}=0$得到最优订货量。见文献[1]，若需求函数是正态分布$N(\mu,\sigma^2)$时，最优供货量为

$$\mathrm{EQ}_{\mathrm{Ret}} = \mu + \Phi^{-1}(\lambda)\sigma \tag{8}$$

最大期望收益为

$$\mathrm{EP}_{\mathrm{Ret}} = (P-c)\mu - ((c+h)\Phi^{-1}(\lambda) + (P+s+h)b_r(\Phi^{-1}(\lambda)))\sigma \tag{9}$$

其中：记 $b_r(\Phi^{-1}(\lambda)) = \int_{\Phi^{-1}(\lambda)}^{\infty}(y-\Phi^{-1}(\lambda))\phi(y)\mathrm{d}y$

称 λ 为系统的服务水平

$$\lambda \triangleq \frac{P+s-c}{P+s+h} \tag{10}$$

2.2 不确定性需求

下两分析两个产品竞争市场中，消费者对产品的需求情况。对于产品 V_i，由式(5)、(6)可知每个消费者对它的需求 d_i 都是满足“泊努利分布”的随机变量，均值为 S_i。设每个消费者的决策都是相互独立的。那么到达市场的 M 个消费者对产品 V_i 形成总的需求随机变量 D_i 服从“二项分布”，它的均值和方差分别为

$$\mu_i = MS_i,\quad \sigma_i^2 = MS_i(1-S_i) \tag{11}$$

见文献[14,15]，如果 MS_i 和 $M(1-S_i)$ 都大于 5，那么可以用正态分布很好的近似二项分布式(11)，因此可以假设对于产品 V_i 的需求量 x_i 的需求分布为

$$x_i \sim N(\mu_i, \sigma_i^2) \tag{12}$$

其中：μ_i，σ_i 由式(11)给出。

从上面的分析可知，若已知两个产品的特征描述和销售参数以及消费者总数和偏好分布，就可以求出最优订货量和最大期望收益。本文以下所有参数和最优值记号下加上对应产品和零售商的编号。

例 2 设两个产品的特征描述及销售参数由下表给出。

表 1 产品的特征及消费参数

Table1Products' characterizations and sale parameters

参数	P_i	T_i	c_i	s_i	h_i
产品 V_1	200	15	180	150	120
产品 V_2	500	3	450	400	100

设到达市场的人数 $M=1\ 000$，并且消费者的偏好 α 服从(0，100]上的均匀分布。那么根据式(5)、(6)、(8)和式(9)可以求出两个产品的市场份额和最优订货量、最大期望收益：$S_1=0.25$，$\mathrm{EQ}_{\mathrm{Ret\,1}}=245$，$\mathrm{EP}_{\mathrm{Ret1}}=2588$；$S_2=0.75$，$\mathrm{EQ}_{\mathrm{Ret2}}=748$，$\mathrm{EP}_{\mathrm{Ret2}}=35263$。

3 敏感性分析

本节分析产品特征描述变化对于零售商最优供货及其最大收益的影响。设市场中只有两个竞争产品 V_1，V_2，它们的产品特征描述值分别为 P_i，T_i，$i=1,2$ 且 $P_1<P_2$，$T_1>T_2$。对于现实世界来说，零售商 1 可以通过技术变革等方法进行改进产品 V_1 的特征 T_1，即降低 T_1，从而增加产品 V_1 的市场份额；零售商 2 可以通过降低产品 V_2 的价格 P_2 来增加产品 V_2 的市场份额。下面分别分析这两种情况。

3.1　T_1 变化的情况

本节分析 EQ_{Reti}，EP_{Reti}，关于 T_1 的变化情况，还将得到两个产品的收益总额 EP_{Total} 和收益增量 EPA_{Reti}，EPA_{Total} 的变化情况。当 T_1 变化为 T_1' 时，定义

$$EP_{Total}(T_1') \triangleq EP_{Ret1}(T') + EP_{Ret2}(T_1') \tag{13}$$

$$EPA_{Reti}(T_1') = \Delta EP_{Reti}(T_1') - EP_{Reti}(T_1) \quad i = 1,2 \tag{14}$$

$$EPA_{Total}(T_1') = EP_{Total}(T_1') - EP_{Total}(T_1) \tag{15}$$

例 3　首先看一个实例。设参数由例 3.1 中给出。在其他参数不变得条件下，如果产品 V_1 的特征描述 T_1 变化，两个零售商的市场份额和最优订货量、最大期望收益以及由式(13)—(15)定义的收益值的变化情况见表 2。

表 2　收益值与 T_1 的变化情况

Table 2 Profits' changing with T_1

T_1	S_1	$EQ_{Ret\,1}$	$EP_{Ret\,1}$	S_2	$EQ_{Ret\,2}$	$EP_{Ret\,2}$	EP_{Total}	$EPA_{Ret\,1}$	$EPA_{Ret\,2}$	EPA_{Total}
15	0.250	245	2 588	0.750	748	35 263	37 852	0	0	0
14	0.273	268	2 974	0.727	726	34 063	37 037	35	−111	−76
13	0.300	295	3 448	0.700	698	32 633	36 081	859	−2 630	−1 771
12	0.333	328	4 041	0.667	665	30 898	34 940	1 453	−4 365	−2 912
11	0.375	370	4 804	0.625	623	28 749	33 553	2 215	−6 414	−4 299
10	0.429	423	5 815	0.571	569	26 015	31 830	3 227	−9 248	−6 021

从表 2 可以看出，如果 T_1 减少，产品 V_1 的市场份额增加，零售商 1 的最优供应量增加、最大期望收益增加，而零售商 2 的情况恰好相反。下面通过分析表明在一般假设条件下，以上规律都成立。

下面首先给出几个假设条件：

条件 1　$\lambda_i \in (0.001, 0.999)$，$i=1,2$；

条件 2　$S_i \in (0,01, 0.99)$，$i=1,2$；

条件 3　M 充分大。

条件 1 实际上表明零售商 i 提供产品时，不会由于服务水平 λ_i 过高或过低而引起巨大的多货或缺货损失，这个条件在现实中一般总是满足的。而且容易知道，在条件 1 下，$\Phi^{-1}(\lambda_i) \in (-3.1, 3.1)$，由式(8)可知最优订货量 EQ_{Reti} 有上下界。条件 2 要求两个产品的市场份额不能太低，因为如果太低，产品基本上处于出局的状态，这不是本文研究的重点。

由数值分析可知，在条件 1 和 2 下要使下式成立：

$$\sqrt{M} > |(2S_i - 1)\Phi^{-1}(\lambda_i)| \cdot \frac{1}{2\sqrt{S_i(1-S_i)}}, \quad i = 1,2 \tag{16}$$

仅仅要求消费者到达市场的总人数满足 $M>240$。消费者到达市场的总人数 M 充分大也是本文的一个基本假设。

命题 4　设 S_i，λ_i，M，$i=1,2$ 满足条件 1,2,3。那么

$$\frac{dEQ_{Ret\,1}}{dT_1} < 0, \quad \frac{dEQ_{Ret\,2}}{dT_1} > 0 \tag{17}$$

证明 由于 $S_1+S_2=1$，零售商 1，2 的最优供货量关于 T_1 的导数分别为

$$\frac{\mathrm{dEQ}_{\mathrm{Ret}\,1}}{\mathrm{d}T_1}=\frac{\mathrm{d}(\mu_1+\Phi^{-1}(\lambda_1)\sigma_1)}{\mathrm{d}T_1}=M\frac{\mathrm{d}S_1}{\mathrm{d}T_1}+\Phi^{-1}(\lambda_1)\frac{\mathrm{d}\sigma_1}{\mathrm{d}T_1}$$

$$=\sqrt{M}\frac{\mathrm{d}S_1}{\mathrm{d}T_1}\left[\sqrt{M}+(1-2S_1)\Phi^{-1}(\lambda_1)\frac{1}{2\sqrt{S_1(1-S_1)}}\right]$$

$$\frac{\mathrm{dEQ}_{\mathrm{Ret}\,2}}{\mathrm{d}T_1}=\frac{\mathrm{d}(\mu_2+\Phi^{-1}(\lambda_2)\sigma_2)}{\mathrm{d}T_1}=\frac{\mathrm{d}(M(1-S_1)+\Phi^{-1}(\lambda_2)\sigma_1)}{\mathrm{d}T_1}=-M\frac{\mathrm{d}S_1}{\mathrm{d}T_1}+\Phi^{-1}(\lambda_2)\frac{\mathrm{d}\sigma_1}{\mathrm{d}T_1}$$

$$=-\sqrt{M}\frac{\mathrm{d}S_1}{\mathrm{d}T_1}\left[\sqrt{M}+(1-2S_2)\Phi^{-1}(\lambda_2)\cdot\frac{1}{2\sqrt{S_1(1-S_1)}}\right]$$

$$=-\sqrt{M}\frac{\mathrm{d}S_1}{\mathrm{d}T_1}\cdot\left[\sqrt{M}+(1-2S_2)\Phi^{-1}(\lambda_2)\cdot\frac{1}{2\sqrt{(1-S_2)S_2}}\right]$$

当 $(1-2S_i)\Phi^{-1}(\lambda_i)\geqslant 0, i=1,2$ 满足时，由命题 1 的结论显然式(17)成立。若 $(1-2S_1)\Phi^{-1}(\lambda_1)<0$ 时，由条件 1，2，3 有式(16)成立，则式(17)显然成立，故命题成立。　证毕。

下面分析 T_1 变化时零售商的最大期望收益的变化规律。首先，零售商 1，2 的最大期望收益关于 T_1 的导数分别为

$$\frac{\mathrm{dEp}_{\mathrm{pet}\,1}}{\mathrm{d}T_1}=(p_1-c_1)\sqrt{M}\frac{\mathrm{d}S_1}{\mathrm{d}T_1}\cdot\left[\sqrt{M}-\left(\frac{c_1+h_1}{p_1-c_1}\Phi^{-1}(\lambda_1)+\frac{P_1+s_1+h_1}{p_1-c_1}b_r(\Phi^{-1}(\lambda_1))\right)\right.$$
$$\left.(1-2S_1)\cdot\frac{1}{2\sqrt{S_1(1-S_1)}}\right]$$

$$\frac{\mathrm{dEp}_{\mathrm{Ret}\,2}}{\mathrm{d}T_1}=-(p_2-c_2)\sqrt{M}\frac{\mathrm{d}S_1}{\mathrm{d}T_1}\cdot\left[\sqrt{M}-\left(\frac{c_2+h_2}{p_2-c_2}\Phi^{-1}(\lambda_2)+\frac{P_2+s_2+h_2}{p_2-c_2}b_r(\Phi^{-2}(\lambda_2))\right)\right.$$
$$\left.(1-2S_2)\cdot\frac{1}{2\sqrt{S_2(1-S_2)}}\right]$$

令 $L(S_i)$ 定义为

$$L(S_i)\triangleq(1-2S_i)\frac{1}{2\sqrt{S_i(1-S_i)}}$$

在条件 2 下，易知 $L(S_i)\in(-5,5)$。在条件 1 下，通过数值计算可知

$$\Phi^{-1}(\lambda_i)\in(-3.1,3.1)$$
$$b_r(\Phi^{-1}(\lambda_i))\in(3.1,0)$$
$$b_r(\Phi^{-1}(\lambda_i))\geqslant\Phi^{-1}(\lambda_i)$$

因此可以求出 $B_i=\frac{c_i+h_i}{P_i-c_i}\Phi^{-1}(\lambda_i)+\frac{P_i+s_i+h_i}{P_i-c_i}\cdot b_r(\Phi^{-1}(\lambda_i))$ 的界为

$$\left(3.1\frac{P_i+s_i-c_i}{P_i-c_i},\quad 3.1\frac{P_i+c_i+s_i+2h_i}{p_i-c_i}\right)$$

那么

$$|B_i\cdot L(S_i)|\in\left(15.5\frac{P_i+s_i-c_i}{P_i-c_i},\quad 15.5\frac{P_i+c_i+s_i+2h_i}{P_i-c_i}\right)\tag{18}$$

即在条件 1，2 下上式有界，故在条件 1，2，3 下有

$$\frac{\mathrm{dEP}_{\mathrm{Ret}\,1}}{\mathrm{d}T_1}>0,\quad\frac{\mathrm{dEP}_{\mathrm{Ret}\,2}}{\mathrm{d}T_1}<0$$

通过数值计算可知，对于实例 3.1 中的算例可知 $B_i\cdot L(S_i)$ 的界为(26，120)，(28，96)。

在条件 1,2 下,要使$\frac{\mathrm{dEP}_{\mathrm{Ret\,1}}}{\mathrm{d}T_1}>0$,$\frac{\mathrm{dEP}_{\mathrm{Ret\,2}}}{\mathrm{d}T_1}<0$ 成立只需 $M\geqslant 1900$。

下面用同样的分析方式来分析 $\mathrm{EP}_{\mathrm{Total}}$与 T_1 的变化关系。首先,$\mathrm{EP}_{\mathrm{Total}}$关于 T_1 的导数为

$$\frac{\mathrm{dEP}_{\mathrm{Total}}}{\mathrm{d}T_1}=((P_1-c_1)-(P_2-c_2))\sqrt{M}\frac{\mathrm{d}S_1}{\mathrm{d}T_1}\Bigg[\sqrt{M}-\frac{1}{(P_1-c_1)-(P_2-c_2)}\left(\sum_{i=1}^{2}(c_i+h_i)\Phi^{-1}(\lambda_i)+\sum_{i=1}^{2}(P_i+s_i+h_i)b_r(\Phi^{-1}(\lambda_i))\right)(1-2S_1)\frac{1}{2\sqrt{S_1(1-S_1)}}\Bigg]$$

从上面的分析可知

$$\left|\frac{1}{(P_1-c_1)-(P_2-c_2)}\left(\sum_{i=1}^{2}(c_i+h_i)\Phi^{-1}(\lambda_i)+\sum_{i=1}^{2}(P_i+s_i+h_i)b_r(\Phi^{-1}(\lambda_i))\right)(1-2S_1)\frac{1}{2\sqrt{S_1(1-S_1)}}\right|\in\left(\frac{15.5}{|(P_1-c_1)-(P_2-c_2)|}\sum_{i=1}^{2}(P_i+s_i+c_i)\right.,$$
$$\left.\frac{15.5}{|(P_1-c_1)-(P_2-c_2)|}\sum_{i=1}^{2}(P_i+s_i+c_i+2h_i)\right)$$

从现实情况可知,销售单价(P)高的产品的单位利润($P-c$)也要高,那么可以引入下列假设条件:

条件 4

$$P_1-c_1<P_2-c_2$$

因此,在条件 1,2,3,4 下,由命题 1 可知

$$\frac{\mathrm{dEP}_{\mathrm{Total}}}{\mathrm{d}T_1}>0 \tag{19}$$

计算表明,在条件 1,2,4 下,若 $M>9000$,式(19)成立。

总结以上几条可以得到以下结论:

在条件 1,2,3,4 下,当产品 V_1 的特征描述 T_1 减少时,零售商 1 的收益将增大,零售商 2 的收益会减少,市场利润总量减少。把这些规律转化为收益增量的表达式为

$$\frac{\mathrm{dEPA}_{\mathrm{Ret\,1}}}{\mathrm{d}T_1}<0,\frac{\mathrm{dEPA}_{\mathrm{Ret\,2}}}{\mathrm{d}T_1}>0,\frac{\mathrm{dEPA}_{\mathrm{Ret\,1}}}{\mathrm{d}T_1}>0$$

例 4 中的结果可用图 2 表示。

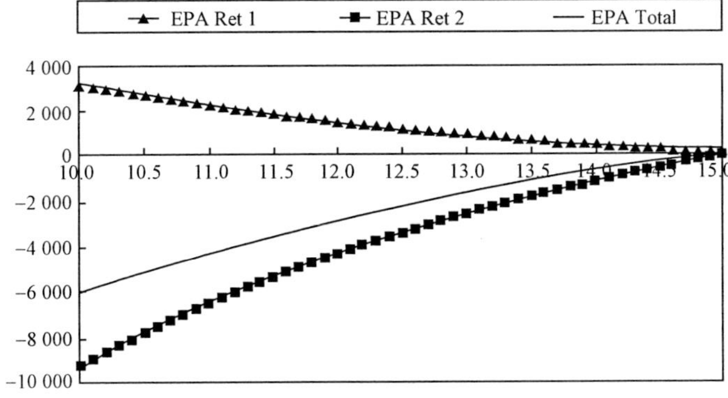

图 2　收益增量与参数 T_1 的关系图

Fig. 2Relations between profit increment and T_1

3.2 P2 变化的情况

例 4 下面再看看例 3.1 中的算例。在其他参数不变的条件下，如果产品 V_2 的特征描述 P_2 变化，两个零售商的市场份额和最优订货量、最大期望收益等量的变化情况见表 3。

表 3 收益值与 P_2 的变化情况

Table 3 Profits' changing with P_2

P_2	S_1	$EQ_{Ret\ 1}$	$EP_{Ret\ 1}$	S_2	$EQ_{Ret\ 2}$	$EP_{Ret\ 2}$	EP_{Total}	$EPA_{Ret\ 1}$	$EPA_{Ret\ 2}$	EPA_{Total}
1 000	0.667	668	27 870	0.333	341	199 334	227 204	0	0	0
900	0.583	585	24 023	0.417	423	209 337	233 322	−2 348	9 986	6 139
800	0.500	502	20 242	0.500	506	202 913	223 155	−7 629	3 579	−4 050
700	0.417	418	16 523	0.583	588	180 083	196 606	−11 348	−19 251	−30 599
600	0.333	335	12 871	0.667	669	140 811	153 682	−15 000	−58 522	−73 522
500	0.250	251	9 294	0.750	751	85 091	94 385	−18 576	−114 243	−132 819
400	0.167	168	5 817	0.833	832	12 922	18 739	−22 054	−186 412	−208 466

从表 3 可以看出，当初始价格比较高时，如果 P_2 减少，零售商 2 的最优供应量增加、最大期望收益增加；如果零售商 2 继续降低价格，他的最优供应量增加、最大期望收益反而减少。对于产品 V_1，如果零售商 2 降低价格，产品 V_1 的市场份额将减少，零售商 1 的最优供应量减少、最大期望收益减少。下面通过分析表明，在上小节的几个假设条件下，以上规律都成立。

命题 5 设 $S_i, \lambda_i, M, i=1,2$ 满足条件 1,2,3。那么

$$\frac{dEQ_{Ret\ 1}}{dP_2} > 0, \quad \frac{dEQ_{Ret2}}{dP_2} < 0 \tag{20}$$

证明 零售商 1,2 的最优供货量关于 P_2 的导数为

$$\frac{dEQ_{Ret\ 1}}{dP_2} = \sqrt{M}\frac{dS_2}{dP_2}\left[\sqrt{M} + (1-2S_1)\Phi^{-1}(\lambda_1)\frac{1}{2\sqrt{S_1(1-S_1)}}\right]$$

$$\frac{dEQ_{Ret\ 2}}{dP_2} = \sqrt{M}\frac{dS_2}{dP_2}\left[\sqrt{M} + (1-2S_2)\Phi^{-1}(\lambda_2)\frac{1}{2\sqrt{S_2(1-S_2)}}\right]$$

由命题 1 的结论和命题 2 的证明方法可知命题成立。 证毕。

零售商 1 的最大期望收益关于 P_2 的导数为

$$\frac{dEP_{Ret\ 1}}{dP_2} = (P_1 - c_1)\sqrt{M}\frac{dS_1}{dP_2}$$

$$\cdot\left[\sqrt{M} - \left(\frac{c_1+h_1}{P_1-c_1}\Phi^{-1}(\lambda_1) + \frac{P_1+s_1+h_1}{P_1-c_1}b_r(\Phi^{-1}(\lambda_1))\right)(1-2S_1)\right.$$

$$\left.\cdot\frac{1}{2\sqrt{S_1(1-S_1)}}\right]$$

按上小节同样的分析方法可知，在条件 1,2,3 下：

$$\frac{\mathrm{dEP_{Ret1}}}{\mathrm{d}P_2}>0$$

由于零售商 2 的最大期望收益及市场收益总量关于 P_2 的导数表达式非常复杂，很难通过进行严格的数学分析来得出结论，因此这里只采用数值分析的方法分析。通过大量数值算例分析得出的规律与例 4 中的规律大体相似，图 3 即表明了一个较为典型的变化关系。

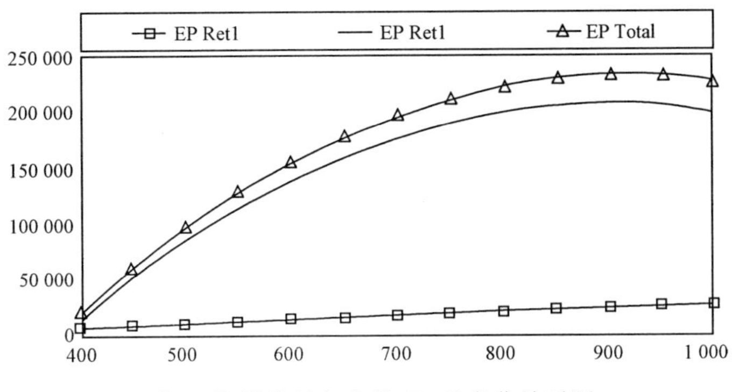

图 3 期望收益与参数 P_2 的变化关系图

Fig. 3 Relations between expected profits and parameter P_2

4 结 论

本文引进了产品特征描述和消费者一般支出的定义，以此分析市场中消费者对产品的总体需求情况，进而应用经典报童模型给出了产品的最优供货量和最大期望收益的计算公式。然后应用数值和数学分析相结合的方法分析了在产品的特征描述变化的条件下，零售商的供货量和期望收益的变化情况。

通过上面几节的分析可以得到以下主要结论：

1）产品的零售商可以通过技术变革等方法来提高产品的品质，以达到增加市场份额和收益的结果，并且竞争对手的市场份额和收益会随之减少。市场收益总量这时会减少，这是由于产品质量的提高带来了消费者福利的增加（即支出的减少）的原因。

2）如果零售商采用降低价格来提高市场份额的方法，他的收益不一定会增加，这是由于新加入的消费者带来的利润有可能不能弥补降价带来的损失，但是竞争对手会由于降价失去市场份额和部分收益，因此降价一般来说可以达到削弱竞争对手的目的，这可能是目前产品价格激烈竞争的原因之一，在降价的幅度不太大的情况下，市场收益总量这时是增加的，如果价格降低太大，市场中商家的收益都会减少，即消费者的总支出减少，从而消费者福利增加。

本文给出了一种分析多产品竞争的分析方法和一些初步研究，可以将它和其他模型相结合来分析一些更复杂的现实问题。

Optimal ordering decision in multi-products competition environment

LU Qi-hui , ZHU Dao-li

Management School, Fudan University, Shanghai 200433, China

Abstract: In a multi-product competition market, the retailers of products at first must know the state and the market shares of the products in the markets, then decide the quantities of product through analysis the market and the revenue to gain the maximum profits. It is the fundamental problem in the market inventory management that how to gain the optimal order quantity. In this paper, through introducing the concepts of product characterization description and customer general cost, we give a method of market share and some mathematical properties of market share. Then we use the classical inventory management model-"newsboy problem"model to analysis the optimal ordering decision problem in the multi-products competition environment. In the last of this paper, we give the sensitive analysis and economic explanations of retailers' optimal ordering quantity, optimal expected profits and total profit in the market.

Key words: market competition ; newsboy problem ; multi-products ; inventory problem ; decision science

参考文献

[1] Lau H S, Lau A H L. The newsstand problem: A capacitated multiple-product single-period inventory problem[J]. European Journal of Operational Research, 1996, 94 : 29-42.

[2] Moon I, Silver E A. The multi-item newsvendor problem with a budget constraint and fixed ordering costs[J]. Journal of the Operational Research Society, 2000, 51 : 602-608.

[3] 杜荣，胡奇英，陈开周. 同类产品多品牌的最优定价模型[J]. 管理科学学报，2004,7 (3):69-74. Du Rong, Hu Qiying, Chen Kaizhou. Optimal pricing model for various brands within prcdcct category[J]. Journal of Management Sciences in China, 2004, 7(3) : 69-74. (in Chinese)

[4] Mantrala M K, Raman K. Demand uncertainty and supplier's retums policies for a mlti -store stylegood retailer[J]. European Journal of Operational Research, 1999, 115 : 270-284.

[5] Khouja M, Mehrez A, Rabinowitz G. A two-item newsboy problem with substitutability[J]. Int. J. Production Economics, 1996, 44: 267-275.

[6] Agrawal N, Smith S A. Optimal retail assortments for substitutable items purchased in sets[J]. Naval Research Logistics, 2003, 50.

[7] Lin C-T, Chen C-B, Hsieh H J. Effects of centralization on expected profits in a multi-location news-

boy problem[J]. Journal of the Operational Research Society,2001,53 : 839-841.

[8] Lau A H-L ,Lau H-S. Comparative normative optimal behavior in two-echelon multiple-retailer distribution systems for a single-period product[J]. European Journal of Operational Research,2003,144 : 659-676.

[9] 符国群，佟学英. 品牌、价格和原产地如何影响消费者的购买选择[J]. 管理科学学报，2003,6(6) : 79 —84.
Fu Guoqun,Tong Xueying. How brand,price and country of origin influence consumers' purchase choices[J]. Journal of Manage-ment Sciences in China,2003,6(6) : 79-84. (in Chinese)

[10] Li J,Lau H-S,Lau A H-L. A two-product newsboy problem with satisfaction objective and independent exponential demands[J]. IIE Transaction,1991,23(1) : 29-39.

[11] Kouvelis P,Gutierrez GJ. The newsvendor problem in a global market:Optimal centralized and decentralized control policies for a two-market stochastic inventory system[J]. Management Science,1997,43(5) : 571-585.

[12] 李善民，曾昭灶. 质量差异化与产品互补型企业兼并问题[J]. 管理科学学报，2003,6(6) : 54-71.
Li Shanmin,Zeng Zhaozao. Quality differentiation and merger of complement firms[J]. Journal of Management Sciences in China,2003,6 (6) : 54-71. (in Chinese)

[13] Khouja M. The single-period(news-vendor) problem: Literature review and suggestions for future research[J]. Omega. International Journal of Management Science,1999,27 : 537-553.

[14] Lau A H-L,Lau H-S,Willet K D. Demand uncertainty and returns policies for a seasonal product: An alternative model[J]. Int. J . Production Economics,2000,66 : 1-12.

[15] Marvel H P,Peck J. Demand uncertainty and returns policies[J]. International Economic Review,1995,36(3):691-714.

具有网络外部性的扩展 Hotelling 模型*

徐　兵[1,2]，朱道立[1]

（1. 复旦大学管理学院，上海 200433；2. 南昌大学管理科学与工程系，南昌 330047）

摘要：将网络外部性引入线性运输成本下的 Hotelling 模型，研究了两家网络产品厂商首先选址，然后进行价格竞争的两阶段完全信息动态博弈问题，得到了厂商价格竞争均衡的存在性条件，推广了一般 Hotelling 模型的结论。由于网络外部性的存在，消费者效用是相互依赖的。网络产品的市场份额既是消费者选择的结果，又是消费者选择的依据。文章将交通流量分配技术和无穷维变分方法相结合，建立了刻画网络产品市场划分的模型——无穷维变分不等式，并研究了市场划分的存在性和唯一性问题。最后假定厂商定位在两端，分析了产品的网络外部性特征及单位运输成本对两个厂商竞争均衡情况的影响。

关键词：Hotelling 模型；网络外部性；Nash 均衡；无穷维变分不等式

中图分类号：F270　　**文献标识码：**A　　**文章编号：**1007-9807 (2007)01-0009 -09

0 引　言

产品差异化问题是现代产业组织理论有关市场结构与市场竞争研究的重要内容。消费者通常依据自身偏好，通过比较不同产品的价格、质量等产品属性来选择某种产品，以最大化自身效用。网络外部性（network externality）是影响消费者选择网络产品（如：电话、传真机、办公软件等）的重要因素，也是网络产品厂商进行产品差异化竞争的重要手段。网络外部性在电信、铁路、民航、软件产业、服务业等行业中广泛存在，已成为经济、营销、管理等诸多方面的研究热点。网络外部性表现为消费者使用某种产品的价值，会随着使用该产品极其兼容产品的用户总量的增加而增加，即原有的用户免费得到了由于用户数量的增加而新增加的产品价值，却无需为这一部分的价值提供相应的补偿[1~4]。例如使用 WPS 办公软件的用户越多，潜在的可相互交换信息的对象越多，WPS 办公软件越有价值；随着可刷卡消费的商店增加，使用银行卡的消费者效用越大等。

Hotelling 空间竞争模型是研究产品差异化竞争的经典模型，是分析企业选址、定价两阶段博弈的有效工具[5]。文献[6]讨论了 Hotelling 模型中最优选址问题和价格均衡的存在性条件：在线性运输成本条件下，如果两家厂商定位太近，则不存在纯战略价格均衡；在二次运输成本条件下，厂商将选址为线性城市的两端，以最大化产品差异。20 世纪

---

* 收稿日期：2004-08-23；修订日期：2006-03-29。

基金项目：国家自然科学基金重点项目(70432001)。

作者简介：徐兵(1972～)，男，江西南昌人，博士生，讲师。Email：xubing99 @sina. com.

年代之后，许多学者对 Hotelling 模型进行了多种形式的推广。文献[7，8]分别在交通费用函数为 $d(x)=bx^{a}$、$d(x)=ax+bx^{2}$ 形式下对 Hotelling 模型进行了研究。文献[9]将信息交换费用引入厂商成本函数、文献[10]假定消费者在[0，1]区间非均匀分布，分别运用 Hotelling 模型研究了厂商选址和价格竞争的两阶段博弈问题。有关 Hotelling 模型的已有研究还包括单位运输成本为内生变量的研究[11]、厂商采取歧视性定价策略的分析[12]、存在消费者购买选择的 Hotelling 模型[13]等。

把网络外部性引入 Hotelling 模型，研究两家网络产品厂商的竞争问题，在经济和管理中是非常有意义的工作。部分学者在二次运输成本假设[14，15]或厂商定位在线性城市两端情况[16]下进行了少量研究。对具有网络外部性的扩展 Hotelling 模型进行研究，首先要根据消费者选择理论求出产品的市场份额，从而获得厂商利润函数，据此再进行价格和选址决策分析。由于网络外部性的存在，消费者的选择依据又决定于产品的市场份额。因此必须用所谓的不动点定进[17]来求网络产口市场份额。现有研究网络外部性的文献，大多假定产品的网络外部性特征为特殊情况，如：产品完全不兼容且外部强度系数相同[14,15,18]等；并且通常在经济学中的理性预期假设下求网络产品市场份额：即假设消费者对销量有一个理性预期，从而得到消费者在预期销量情况下购买网络产品的效用，然后运用无差异曲线方法得到市场份额，再假设预期销量正好等于所求出的市场份额，从而确定市场划分[1～3，14～16，18]。当市场上厂商个数较多，产品网络外部性特征为一般情况时，很难用此方法来求解网络产品市场划分。

文献[19] 研究了具有多个指标以及无穷类别出行者的交通均衡问题，其中出行者对指标的偏好 α 服从某种分布。出行者由于不同的偏好而引起不同的广义出行费用，用无穷维变分不等式

$$\langle F(X)+\alpha G, x-y\rangle \leqslant 0, \forall y \in \Omega(\alpha)$$

来刻画此交通均衡问题。其中，G 为道路使用货币支付(常向量)，$F(X)$ 为道路通行时间向量(与道路流量 X 有关)，α 相当于单位货币的时间转换当量。这是个带外部性的垂直差异化问题。文献[19] 证明了这一类交通均衡问题解的存在性、唯一性，分析了解的性质及求解算法的收敛性。作者注意到，在具有网络外部性的 Hotelling 模型中，必须考虑消费者在空间中的不同分布而引起的不同交通费用，以及网络外部性的影响。本文将把空间分布的消费者对网络产品的选择问题转化为交通网络中无穷类别出行者的道路选择问题。从而网络产品市场划分可通过下面的无穷维变分不等式

$$\langle \mathrm{P}-\mathrm{U}_0-\mathrm{F}(\mathrm{X})+\mathrm{G}(\theta), x-y\rangle \leqslant 0, \quad \forall y \in \Omega(\theta)$$

来刻画。其中，P 为产品价格向量，U_0 为产品保留效用向量(常向量)，F(X)为产品网络外部效应向量(与产品市场份额 X 有关)，$\mathrm{G}(\theta)$ 为交通费用函数向量，θ 为消费者位置。与文献[19]不同，本文研究的是个带外部性的水平差异化问题。

1　网络外部性和扩展 Hotelling 模型

1.1　模型假设

如图 1，假设存在一个长度为 1 的“线性城市”，消费者总数标准化为 1，并沿城市均匀分布。用 θ 表示消费者所在位置，交通费用为线性函数，单位交通费用 $t>0$。假定 a，1－

b 处存在厂商 1 和厂商 2，提供除位置差异（即产品水平差异）及网络外部性差异之外的同质产品。两家厂商进行如下两阶段完全信息动态博弈：首先同时决定所处位置，满足 $a\geqslant 0, b\geqslant 0, a+b\leqslant 1$；然后同时决定产品价格 p_1, p_2。假设每个消费者只购买一件产品，且产品的保留效用 u_0 足够大，因而市场被完全覆盖。若不考虑网络外部性，可运用一般 Hotelling 模型来分析两个厂商的定位和价格博弈问题[6]。

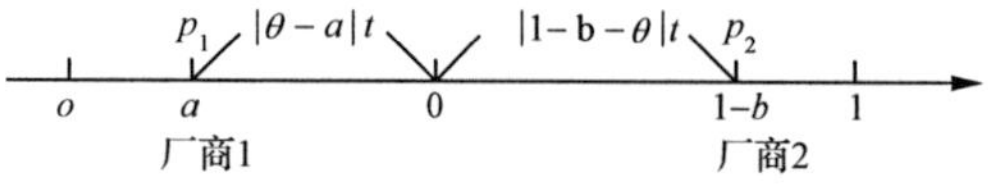

图 1　Hotelling 模型图示

Fig. 1Diagram of Hotelling model

现在建立产品具有网络外部性的扩展 Hotelling 模型。假设产品 i 的外部强度系数为 α_i，满足 $1\geqslant\alpha_i\geqslant 0$；产品 i 与产品 j 的兼容系数为 β_{ij}，满足 $1\geqslant\beta_{ij}\geqslant 0$，其中，$\beta_{ij}=1$ 表示产品 i 完全兼容产品 j，$\beta_{ij}=0$ 表示产品 i 不兼容产品 j。设 $x_i(\theta)$ 表示位置在 θ 的使用产品 i 的消费者人数，$X_i=\int_0^1 x_i(\theta)\,\mathrm{d}\theta$ 表示使用产品 i 的消费者总人数，即产品 i 的市场份额。记 $x(\theta)=(x_1(\theta), x_2(\theta))^{\mathrm{T}}, X=(X_1, X_2)^{\mathrm{T}}=\int_0^1 x(\theta)\,\mathrm{d}\theta$。产品 1,2 的网络外部效应函数分别为 $f_1(X)=\alpha_1(X_1+\beta_{12}X_2), f_2(X)=\alpha_2(X_2+\beta_{21}X_1)$。记 $\gamma_1=\dfrac{\partial f_1(X)}{\partial X_1}-\dfrac{\partial f_2(X)}{\partial X_1}=\alpha_1-\alpha_2\beta_{21}, \gamma_2=\dfrac{\partial f_2(X)}{\partial X_2}-\dfrac{\partial f_1(X)}{\partial X_2}\alpha_2-\alpha_1\beta_{12}$，即 γ_i 是由于产品 i 的需求增加而引起的产品 i 与产品 j 的网络外部性的边际增加值之差。$\gamma_i\geqslant\gamma_j$ 等价于 $\alpha_i+\alpha_i\beta_{ji}\geqslant\alpha_j+\alpha_j\beta_{ji}$ 即 γ_i, γ_j 的大小关系反映了产品 i 与产品 j 的网络外部性特征的大小关系，且 $\gamma_1+\gamma_2=\alpha_1(1-\beta_{12})+\alpha_2(1-\beta_{21})\geqslant 0$。位置在 θ 的消费者使用产品 1,2 的效用分别为

$$U_1(\theta, X)=u_0+f_1(X)-p_1-|\theta-a|\,t \tag{1}$$

$$U_2(\theta, X)=u_0+f_2(X)-p_2-|1-b-\theta|\,t \tag{2}$$

记 $P=(p_1, p_2), U_0=(u_0, u_0), F(X)=(f_1(X), f_2(X)), G(\theta)=(|\theta-a|\,t, |1-b-\theta|\,t)$。

1.2　刻画网络产品市场划分的无穷维变分方法

给定厂商位置、产品价格及网络外部性特征，消费者将根据效用最大化原则选择产品。由于存在网络外部性，消费者的效用是相互依赖的。网络产品市场份额既是消费者选择的结果又是消费者选择的依据。因此网络产品市场份额的计算是个不动点问题。将上述网络产品选择问题转化为交通网络中的出行者道路选择问题（图 2）：位置在 θ 的消费者（出行者）选择道路 1,2 从 O 到 D，所付费用分别为 $-U_1(\theta,X)$，$-U_2(\theta,X)$。每个出行者都依据费用最小原则选择道路，流量 X 对应到产品市场份额。利用文献[19]中无穷类别出行者的交通网络流量分配技术，网络产品市场份额计算等价于求：$x(\theta)\in\Omega(\theta)=\{x(\theta): x_1(\theta)+x_2(\theta)=1, x(\theta)\geqslant 0, \forall\theta\in[0,1]\}$，

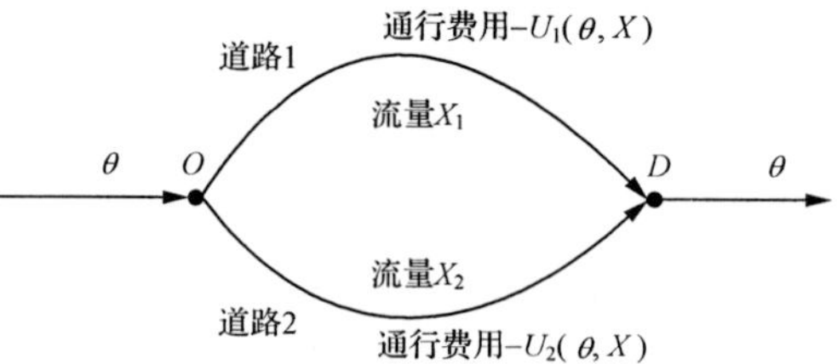

图 2　对应 Hotelling 模型的路径选择问题

Fig. 2 Path choice problem transformed from Hotelling model

$X=\int_0^1 x(\theta)\mathrm{d}\theta$，满足无穷维变分不等式

$$\langle P-U_0-F(X)+G(\theta),x-y\rangle\leqslant 0\quad\forall y\in\Omega(\theta)\tag{3}$$

设变分不等式(3)的解(即市场划分)为 X，假定此时位置在 θ 的人选择了产品 1，即 $x(\bar{\theta})=(1,0)^{\mathrm{T}}$，令 $y(\bar{\theta})=(0,1)^{\mathrm{T}}$，代入式(3)，有 $U_1(\bar{\theta},X)\geqslant U_2(\bar{\theta},X)$ 对选择产品 2 的消费者有类似结论。这表明变分不等式(3)的解，是消费者依据效用最大化原则选择产品所确定的市场划分。网络产品的市场份额对应到上述交通问题的均衡流量，有

变分不等式(3)的经济解释是：当网络产品市场中消费者的产品选择(相当于所对应的交通问题中的道路选择)达到均衡时，在其他消费者不改变产品选择的情况下，单个消费者单独改变产品选择不可能使其效用变大。

由假设，有 $x_2(\theta)=1-x_1(\theta)$，$X_2=1-X_1$。经简单推算，变分不等式(3) 可化为：求 $x_1(\theta)\in\Omega_1(\theta)=\{x_1(\theta):1\geqslant x_1(\theta)\geqslant 0,\forall\theta\in[0,1]\}$，$X_1=\int_0^1 x_1(\theta)\mathrm{d}\theta$，满足变分不等式

$$\begin{aligned}&\langle p_2-p_1-\gamma_2+(\gamma_1+\gamma_2)X_1+(|1-b-\theta|-|\theta-a|)t,\\&x_1(\theta)-y_1(\theta)\rangle\geqslant 0,\forall y_1(\theta)\in\Omega_1(\theta)\end{aligned}\tag{4}$$

定义 1　当 $a+b=1$，$\beta_{12}=\beta_{12}=\beta_{21}=1$，$p_1-p_2=\alpha_1-\alpha_2$(特别 $p_1=p$，$a_1=a_2$时，变分不等式(4)左边恒为零，此时称变分不等式(4)为退化的，否则称变分不等式(4)为非退化的。

令 $\Omega_1=\{x_1\in l(0,1):1\geqslant x_1(\theta)\geqslant 0,\forall\theta\in[0,1]\}\bar{\Omega}_1=\{X_1\in R:1\geqslant X_1\geqslant 0\}$。记

$$H(X_1)=p_2-p_1-\gamma_2+(\gamma_1+\gamma_2)X_1$$

$$M(\theta=|1-b-\theta|-|\theta-a|)t$$

$$=\begin{cases}(1-b-a)t & \text{当}\ \theta\in[0,a)\\(1-b+a-2\theta)t & \text{当}\ \theta\in[a_1-b]\\-(1-b-a)t & \text{当}\ \theta\in(1-b,1)\end{cases}$$

因此，$H(X_1)$是 $\bar{\Omega}_1$ 上的连续有界增函数，$M(\theta)$是$[0,1]$上的连续有界减函数。

变分不等式(4)只要求对任意 $\theta\in[0,1]$几乎处处成立，即不满足变分不等式(4)的 θ 的测度为零。所以变分不等式(4)等价于求 $x_1\in\bar{\Omega}_1$，满足下面的无穷维变分不等式

$$\langle H(X_1)+M(\theta),x_1-y_1\rangle_L\geqslant 0,\quad\forall y_1\in\Omega_1\tag{5}$$

其中：$\langle\rangle_L$ 为 $L(0,1)$空间内积，即：$\langle\Phi,\Psi\rangle_L=\int_0^1\langle\Phi(\theta),\Psi(\theta)\rangle\mathrm{d}\theta$。

2　厂商竞争分析

用后退归纳法，分析两家网络产品厂商间的选址、定价两阶段完全信息动态博弈的纯策略 Nash 均衡问题。首先要计算两种产品的市场份额。

2.1　网络产品通场划分的存在性与唯一性

通过研究变分不等式(4) 或(5) 解的存在性和唯一性，来分析网络产品市场划分的情况。

定义 2　设 Ω 为 Banach 空间 V 的子集，V^* 是 V 的对偶空间，J 是从 Ω 到 V^* 的映射。

如果 J 在 Ω 上有界，对 Ω 中任意弱收敛于 $x\in\Omega$ 的序列 $\{x^k\}$ 若 $\lim\sup_k\langle J(x^k),x^k-x\rangle\leqslant 0$ 有 $\lim\inf_k\langle J(x^k),x^k-y\rangle\leqslant\langle J(x),x-y\rangle$，则称 J 为Lions意义上的伪单调映射[21]。

(A) 设 Ω 为Banach空间的非空有界闭凸子集，若 J 为 Ω 上的Lions意义上的伪单调映射，则至少存在一点 $x^*\in\Omega$，满足变分不等式 $\langle J(x^*),x^*-y\rangle\leqslant 0,\forall y\in\Omega$。

定理1 由已知条件，无穷维变分不等式(5)存在均衡解，也即给定厂商位置、产品价格及网络外部性特征，则一定存在对应的市场划分。

定理1的证明方法与文献[19]的定理2.2类似，只要证明变分不等式(5)满足结论(A)所需要的条件。因为篇幅所限，本文省略证明过程。进一步，市场划分存在三种可能情况：

情况1 产品1完全占有市场，即 $x_1(\theta)=1,\forall\theta\in[0,1]$，$X_1=1$，由式(4)，充要条件为

$$p_2-p_1+\gamma_1+(|1-b-\theta|-|\theta-a|)t>0,\forall\theta\in[0,1]$$
$$\Leftrightarrow p_1<p_2+\gamma_1-(1-b-a)t \tag{6}$$

情况2 产品2完全占有市场，即 $x_1(\theta)=0,\forall\theta\in[0,1]$，$X_1=0$，由式(4)，充要条件为

$$p_2-p_1-\gamma_2+(|1-b-\theta|-|\theta-a|)t<0,\forall\theta\in[0,1]$$
$$\Leftrightarrow p_2<p_1+\gamma_2-(1-b-a)t \tag{7}$$

情况3 产品1,2同时占有市场，充要条件为

$$\gamma_1-(1-b-a)t\leqslant\quad p_1-p_2\leqslant(1-b-a)t-\gamma_2 \tag{8}$$

定义两种产品的水平差异为两家厂商的距离，即为 $1-b-a$。由上述分析可知，对非网络产品(此时 $\gamma_1=\gamma_2=0$)，产品 i 要独占市场，其价格要低于对手的价格减去两个厂商位置差异所引起的交通费用。而对网络产品，如果 $\gamma_i\geqslant(1-b-a)t$，即产品 i 的网络外部性较大，而两种产品的水平差异较小，此时即使其价格比对手高，产品 i 仍然可能独占市场；如果 $\gamma_i<0$，即产品 i 的网络外部性较低，由 $\gamma_1+\gamma_2\geqslant 0$ 可知，竞争产品的网络外部性较高，此时产品 i 要以更低的价格才能占有市场。这能部分解释Windows操作系统的高价高市场占有率，及中国联通的低价策略。

下面进一步分析厂商定位与产品网络外部性特征对市场划分的影响。

(1) 若变分不等式(4)为退化的，则 $\Omega_1(\theta)$ 中的任意元素均满足式(4)，即其有无穷多个解。此时消费者对两种产品的选择是无差异的，因此市场划分存在多种可能。

(2) 若 $2(1-b-a)t<\gamma_1+\gamma_2$，则式(8)不可能成立，即由于两种产品的水平差异小于网络外部效应的作用，市场将被一家厂商独占。进一步，如果存在价格 p_1,p_2 同时满足式(6)和式(7)，此时变分不等式(4)有两个解 $X_1=1$ 和 $X_1=0$，说明市场划分存在两种可能情况。市场最终由哪家厂商独占，取决于两种产品的网络外部性的相对大小及初始销量(又称为安装基础)。所以网络产品市场中，厂商经常在初始竞争阶段采用低价甚至亏损策略来扩大市场份额，提高其产品网络外部效应，从而将竞争对手挤出市场。例如，移动通信业中采用的入网并预存话费即送手机活动，就是一种扩大市场份额的策略。

(3) 若 $2(1-b-a)t\geqslant\gamma_1+\gamma_2$，则市场划分只能是式(6)，(7)，(8)中的一种情况。如果两种产品同时占有市场，且变分不等式(4)非退化，则二者的市场份额可唯一确定。

由上述分析，有下面的命题1和定理2成立，其中命题1的证明见文章附录。

命题1　设 $a+b<1$，且产品1，2同时占有市场，则存在 $\bar{\theta}\in[a,1-b]$，有 $x_1(\theta)=\begin{cases}1, 当\ \theta\in[0,\bar{\theta}]\\0, 当\ \theta\in(\bar{\theta},1]\end{cases}$ $X_1=\int_0^1 x_1(\theta)\mathrm{d}\theta=\bar{\theta}$ 满足变分不等式(4)。若 $t\neq\frac{1}{2}(\gamma_1+\gamma_2)$，则

$$\theta-=\frac{p_2-p_1-\gamma_2+(1-b+a)t}{2_t-\gamma_1-\gamma_2} \tag{9}$$

定理2　设变分不等式(4)非退化，若 $2(1-b-a)t\geqslant\gamma_1+\gamma_2$，则无穷维变分不等式(4)存在唯一解，即此时市场划分被唯一确定。

2.2　厂商价格竞争

假定厂商位置及产品网络外部性特征给定，研究两家厂商进行价格竞争的均衡情况。设 $2(1-b-at\geqslant\gamma_1+\gamma_2$，且 $t\neq\frac{1}{2}(\gamma_1+\gamma_2)$ 综合市场划分的三种情况，得到两种产品的市场份额及两家厂商的利润函数分别为

$$X_1(p_1,p_2)=\begin{cases}\dfrac{p_2-p_1-\gamma_2+(1-b+a)t}{2t-\gamma_1-\gamma_2} & \gamma_1-(1-b-a)t\geqslant p_1-p_2\leqslant(1-b-a)t-\gamma_2\\ 1 & p_1<p_2+\gamma_1-(1-b-a)t\\ 0 & p_1<p_2+(1-b-a)t-\gamma_2\end{cases}$$

$$X_2(p_1,p_2)=1-X_1(p_1,p_2)$$
$$\Pi_1(p_1,p_2)=p_1X_1(p_1,p_2)$$
$$\Pi_2(p_1,p_2)=p_2X_2(p_1,p_2)$$

在厂商生产成本为零的假设下，如果 $(1-b-a)t<\max\{\gamma_1,\gamma_2\}=\gamma_i$，则对任意 $p_j\geqslant 0$，存在 $0<\varepsilon_0<\gamma_i-(1-b-a)t$，若厂商 i 选取价格 $0<p_i=p_j+\gamma_i-(1-b-a)t-\varepsilon_0$，此时式(6)或式(7)成立，产品 i 将完全占有市场。这说明如果产品水平差异过小，则网络外部性强的产品将完全占有市场，即出现所谓的"赢者通吃"现象。所以有如下命题2成立。

命题2　两家厂商进行价格竞争，同时占有市场的必要条件为 $(1-b-a)t\geqslant\max\{\gamma_1,\gamma_2\}$。两家厂商之间的价格竞争是非合作博弈，均衡价格 p_1^*,p_2^* 为二者竞争的Nash均衡解，满足

$$\begin{cases}\Pi_1(p_1^*,p_2^*)\geqslant\Pi_1(p_1,p_2^*),\ \forall\ p_1\geqslant 0\\ \Pi_2(p_1^*,p_2^*)\geqslant\Pi_2(p_1^*,p_2),\ \forall\ p_2\geqslant 0\end{cases}$$

定理3　设 $(1-b-a)t\geqslant\max\{\gamma_1,\gamma_2\}$，且 $t\neq\frac{1}{2}(\gamma_1+\gamma_2)$ 有

1) 若 $a+b=1$，两家厂商进行价格竞争，存在唯一均衡点 $p_1^*=p_2^*=0$；

2) 若 $a+b<1$，两家厂商进行价格竞争，均衡价格存在的充分必要条件为

$$\frac{[(3-b+a)t-\gamma_1-2\gamma_2]^2}{2t-\gamma_1-\gamma_2}\geqslant 3[(4b+2a)t+\gamma_1-\gamma_2] \tag{10}$$

$$\left[\frac{(3+b-a)t-2\gamma_1-\gamma_2}{2t-\gamma_1-\gamma_2}\right]^2\geqslant 3[(2b+4a)t-\gamma_1+\gamma_2] \tag{11}$$

如果条件成立，对应的厂商均衡价格和利润分别为

$$\begin{cases} p_1^* = \dfrac{1}{3}[(3-b+a)t-\gamma_1-2\gamma_2] \\ p_2^* = \dfrac{1}{3}[(3+b-a)t-2\gamma_1-\gamma_2] \end{cases} \tag{12}$$

$$\begin{cases} \Pi_1^* = \dfrac{[(3-b+a)t-\gamma_1-2\gamma_2]^2}{9(2t-\gamma_1-\gamma_2)} \\ \Pi_2^* = \dfrac{[(3+b-a)t-2\gamma_1-\gamma_2]^2}{9(2t-\gamma_1-\gamma_2)} \end{cases} \tag{13}$$

定理 3 表明，如果厂商定位太近，即两种产品的水平差异过小时，则不存在纯战略价格均衡。进一步，有如下推论：

推论 1 情况 1。两种产品是非网络产品：即 $\alpha_1=\alpha_2=\beta_{12}=\beta_{21}$；

情况 2 两种产品完全兼容且网络外部强度系数相同：即 $\alpha_1=\alpha_2, \beta_{12}=\beta_{21}=1$。

针对上述两种情况均有如下结论：

若 $a+b=1$，两家厂商进行价格竞争，存在唯一均衡点：$p_1^*=p_2^*=0$；

若 $a+b<1$，两家厂商进行价格竞争，存在均衡价格的充分必要条件为

$$\left(1+\frac{a-b}{3}\right)^2 \geqslant \frac{4}{3}(a+2b)$$

$$\left(1+\frac{b-a}{3}\right)^2 \geqslant \frac{4}{3}(2a+b)$$

如果上述条件成立，对应的厂商均衡价格和利润分别为

$$p_1^*=t\left(1+\frac{a-b}{3}\right), p_2^*=t\left(1-\frac{a-b}{3}\right)$$

$$\Pi_1^*=\frac{t}{2}\left(1+\frac{a-b}{3}\right)^2$$

$$\Pi_2^*=\frac{t}{2}\left(1-\frac{a-b}{3}\right)^2$$

推论 1 中针对情况 1 的结论，正是一般 Hotelling 模型[6]的结论，所以本文具有网络外部性的扩展 Hotelling 模型是文献[6]的推广。情况 2 说明，如果两种网络产品完全兼容且网络外部强度系数相同，也即在网络外部性方面二者是无差异的，此时与非网络产品结论一样，均衡价格的存在性条件完全由产品的水平差异决定。

2.3 厂商选址决策

由推论 1 及文献[6]，对于非网络产品，如果厂商选址在中心以极小化产品水平差异，此时两种产品的均衡价格及两个厂商的利润均为零，得到 Betrand 悖论。如果产品存在很小的水平差异，两个厂商间不存在价格竞争均衡。只有当产品水平差异足够大时，才能保证均衡价格存在。假如只考虑对称定位(即 $a=b$)情况，均衡价格存在的充分必要条件为 $a=b\leqslant\dfrac{1}{4}$。

由定理 3，对于网络产品，如果厂商选扯在中心以极小化产品水平差异，此时两种产品要同时占有市场，其网络外部性特征必须完全相同，即两种产品是完全同质产品(否则网络外部性强的产品将独占市场)，此时两个厂商的利润为零，同样得到 Betrand 悖论。

只有当产品的水平差异足够大，才能保证两个厂商同时占有市场，并存在均衡价格。进一步，厂商的选址决策与网络外部性特征和单位交通费用 t 的相对大小有关。由命题 2，两个厂商要同时占有市场，单位交通费用 t 必须满足

$$t \geqslant \max\{\gamma_1, \gamma_2\}$$

假如只考虑产品对称定位决策（即 $a=b$）及 $\gamma_1=\gamma_2$ 情况，均衡价格存在的充分必要条件为

$$a = b \leqslant \frac{1}{4}\left(1-\frac{\gamma_1}{t}\right) \tag{14}$$

特别，当 $\gamma_1=\gamma_2=0$ 时，有 $a=b\leqslant\frac{1}{4}$。所以非网络产品的竞争均衡问题是网络产品竞争问题的特殊情况。另一方面，在式(10)，(11)成立的条件下，有 $\frac{\partial \Pi_1 p_1^*, p_2^*)}{\partial a} > 0$ $\frac{\partial \Pi_2 p_1^*, p_2^*)}{\partial b} > 0$，即厂商有向中心定位的倾向。在式(14)约束下，两个厂商的最佳选址为 $a=b=\frac{1}{4}\left(1-\frac{\gamma_t}{1}\right)$

3　市场结构分析

为简化起见，以 $a=b=0$，$\beta_{12}=\beta_{21}=\beta$ 这一种情况为例，研究不同市场情况下 $t, \alpha_1, \alpha_2, \beta$ 对产品市场份额、均衡价格及厂商利润的影响。假设 $t\geqslant\max\{\gamma_1,\gamma_2\}$，且 $t\neq\frac{1}{2}(\gamma_1+\gamma_2)$，可以证明此时式(10)，(11)自然满足，即保证了两家厂商能同时占有市场。厂商均衡价格及利润由式(12)，(13)给出，其中：$\gamma_1=\alpha_1-\alpha_2\beta, \gamma_2=\alpha_2-\alpha_1\beta$。

3.1　一般市场结构分析

1）网络外部强度系数大的产品，其市场份额、价格和利润均较高，因为

$$X_1^* - X_2^* = \frac{(a_1-a_2)(1+\beta)}{3[2t-(a_1+a_2)(1-\beta)]}$$

$$p_1^* - p_2^* = \frac{1}{3}(\alpha_1-\alpha_2)(1+\beta)$$

$$\Pi_1^* - \Pi_2^* = \frac{1}{3}(\alpha_1-\alpha_2)(1+\beta)$$

2）产品均衡价格随兼容系数的增加而增加，随竞争产品的外部强度系数的增加而减小；当 $1\geqslant\beta\geqslant 1/2$ 时，产品均衡价格随自身的外部强度系数的增加而增加，当 $0\leqslant\beta<1/2$ 时，产品均衡价格随自身的外部强度系数的增加而减小。因为对 $i,j=1,2,i\neq j$，有

$$\frac{\partial p_i^*}{\partial \beta} = \frac{2\alpha_i+\alpha_j}{3} \geqslant 0, \frac{\partial p_i^*}{\partial a_j} = \frac{\beta-2}{3} < 0, \quad \frac{\partial p_i^*}{\partial a_j} = \frac{2\beta-1}{3}$$

3.2　完全不兼容市场结构分析（$\beta=0$），此时有

$$\begin{cases} p_1^* = t - \dfrac{\alpha_1+2\alpha_2}{3} \\ p_2^* = t - \dfrac{2\alpha_1+\alpha_2}{3} \end{cases}$$

$$\begin{cases} \Pi_1^* = \dfrac{[3t - (\alpha_1 + 2\alpha_2)]^2}{9[2t - (\alpha_1 + \alpha_2)]} \\ \Pi_2^* = \dfrac{[3t - (2\alpha_1 + \alpha_2)]^2}{9[2t - (\alpha_1 + \alpha_2)]} \end{cases}$$

1）产品均衡价格和厂商利润随自身的外部强度系数的增加而减小，随竞争产品的外部强度系数的增加而减小。因为对 $i,j=1,2,i\neq j$，有

$$\begin{cases} \dfrac{\partial p_i^*}{\partial a_i} = -\dfrac{1}{3} < 0 \\ \dfrac{\partial p_i^*}{\partial a_j} = -\dfrac{2}{3} < 0 \end{cases}$$

$$\frac{\partial \Pi_i^*}{\partial a_i} = \frac{[3t - (\alpha_i + 2\alpha_j)](\alpha_i - t)}{9[2t - (\alpha_1 + \alpha_2)]^2} \leqslant 0$$

$$\frac{\partial \Pi_i^*}{\partial a_j} = \frac{[3t - (\alpha_i + 2a_j)](3\alpha_i + 2a_j - 5t)}{9[2t - (\alpha_1 + \alpha_2)]^2} \leqslant 0$$

2）厂商利润随 t 的增加（相当于产品水平差异变大）而增加（要求 u_0 充分大）。因为

$$\frac{\partial \Pi_1^*}{\partial t} = \frac{[(3t - (\alpha_1 + 2\alpha_2)](6t - 4\alpha_1 - 2\alpha_2)}{9[2t - (\alpha_1 + \alpha_2)]^2} \geqslant 0$$

$$\frac{\partial \Pi_2^*}{\partial t} = \frac{[(3t - (2\alpha_1 + \alpha_2)](6t - 2\alpha_1 - 4\alpha_2)}{9[2t - (\alpha_1 + \alpha_2)]^2} \geqslant 0$$

3.3 完全兼容市场结构分析($\boldsymbol{\beta=1}$)，此时有

$$\begin{cases} p_1^* = t + \dfrac{\alpha_1 - \alpha_2}{3} \\ p_2^* = t + \dfrac{\alpha_2 - \alpha_1}{3} \end{cases}$$

$$\begin{cases} \Pi_1^* = \dfrac{(3t + a_1 - a_2)^2}{18t} \\ \Pi_2^* = \dfrac{(3t + a_2 - a_1)^2}{18t} \end{cases}$$

1）产品均衡价格和厂商利润随自身的外部强度系数的增加而增加，随竞争产品的外部强度系数的增加而减小。因为对 $i,j=1,2,i\neq j$，有

$$\begin{cases} \dfrac{\partial p_i^*}{\partial a_i} = \dfrac{1}{3} < 0 \\ \dfrac{\partial p_i^*}{\partial a_j} = -\dfrac{1}{3} < 0 \end{cases}$$

$$\begin{cases} \dfrac{\partial \Pi_i^*}{\partial a_i} = \dfrac{3t + a_i - a_j}{9t} > 0 \\ \dfrac{\partial \Pi_i^*}{\partial a_j} = -\dfrac{3t + a_i - a_j}{9t} < 0 \end{cases}$$

2）厂商利润随 t 的增加（相当于产品水平差异变大）而增加（要求 u_0 充分大）。因为

$$\frac{\partial \Pi_1^*}{\partial t} = \frac{\partial \Pi_2^*}{\partial t} = \frac{(3t + \alpha_1 - \alpha_2)(3t - \alpha_1 + \alpha_2)}{18t^2} > 0$$

4　结论与进一步研究工作

本文将网络外部性引入线性运输成本下的 Hotelling 模型，针对产品网络外部性特征为一般情况，研究了两家网络产品厂商首先进行选址，然后进行价格竞争的完全信息动态博弈问题，得到了厂商价格竞争的均衡存在性条件，推广了一般 Hotelling 模型的结论。因为网络外部性作用，消费者的效用是互相依赖的。消费者选择网络产品的过程会改变产品网络外部性的大小，从而反过来影响到消费者选择。网络产品市场份额的计算是个不动点问题。本文利用无穷类别出行者的交通流量分配技术，用无穷维变分方法来刻画网络产品市场划分，并给出了网络产品市场划分的存在性与唯一性条件。最后针对厂商定位在两端，且两种产品的兼容系数相同这一情况，分析了产品网络外部强度系数、兼容系数及单位运输成本对一般市场、完全兼容市场及完全不兼容市场中两家厂商均衡价格和利润的影响。本文假定消费者对网络外部性的偏好完全相同。可进一步将本文方法推广到空间 Hotelling 模型和消费者对网络外部性的偏好不相同情况的研究。特别是，利用无穷维变分方法对存在多个厂商的市场划分及厂商竞争问题进行研究，将更能显现本文方法的有效性和意义。

Extended Hotelling model with network externality

XU Bing[1,2], *ZHU Daoli*[1]

1. Management School , Fudan University , Shanghai 200433 , China ;

2. Management Science and Engineering Department , Nanchang University , Nanchang 330047 , China

Abstract : Hotelling model with network externality and linear transportation cost functions is analyzed. Two firms , providing network products , play a twostage dynamic game with perfect information. Firstly , they simultaneously choose their location , then they compete in price. The conditions for equilibrium price are obtained. One customer's utility is dependent on the others'products choice because of network externality. Customer choice determines the market share of network products. Meanwhile the market share reversely influences customer choice. By using of transportation flow distribution and infinite dimensional variational inequality method , the market share model of network products , i. e. infinite dimensional variational inequality , is set up. Its existence and uniqueness is studied. Finally , the influence of network externality character and unit transportation cost on the firms' competition equilibrium is analyzed under the assumption that two firms choose the location at the two ends.

Key words: Hotelling model ; network externality ; Nash equilibrium ; infinite dimensional variational inequality

参考文献

[1] Katz M, Shapiro C. Network externalities, competition, and compatibility[J]. American Economic Review, 1985, 75 (3): 424-440.

[2] Katz M, Shapiro C. Technology adoption in the presence of network externalities[J] . Journal of Political Economy, 1986, 94: 824-841.

[3] Katz M, Shapiro C. Systems competition and network effects[J]. Journal of Economic Prespectives, 1994, 8: 93-115.

[4] 张铭洪. 网络外部性及其相关概念辨析[J]. 广东工业大学学报, 2002, 2 (4): 88-90. Zhang Minghong. Analyzing the network externality and correlative concepts[J]. Journal of Guangdong University of Technology(Social Sciences Edition) , 2002 , 2(4) : 88-90. (in Chinese)

[5] Hotelling H. Stability in competition[J]. Economic Journal, 1929, 39 (153): 41-57.

[6] Aspremont C D , Gabszewicz J J , Thisse J F. On Hotelling's"Stability in competition"[J]. Econometrica , 1979 , 47 (5) : 1145-1150.

[7] Economides N. Minimal and maximal product differentiation in Hotelling's duopoly[J]. Economics Letters , 1986 , 21 : 67-71.

[8] Gabszewicz J J , Thisse J F. On the nature of competition with differentiated products[J]. Economic Journal , 1986 , 96 : 160-172.

[9] Mai C C, Peng S K. Cooperation vs competition in aspatial model[J]. Regional Science and Urban Economics, 1999, 29: 463-472.

[10] 顾锋，黄培清，周东生. 消费者不均匀分布时企业的最小产品差异策略[J]. 系统工程学报, 2002, 17 (5): 32-37.
Gu Feng , Huang Peiqing , Zhou Dongsheng. Strategy of minimum product differentiation with heterogeneity[J]. Journal of Systems Engineering , 2002 , 17(5) : 32-37. (in Chinese)

[11] 曹韫建. 运输成本内生化的三阶段 Hotelling 模型[J]. 管理工程学报, 2002, 16 (1): 5-7.
Cao Yunjian. A three stage Hotelling model with endogenous transportation costs[J]. Journal of Industrial Engineering and Engineering Management , 2002 , 16(1) : 5-7. (in Chines)

[12] 曹韫建，顾新一. 歧视性定价下的两阶段水平差异模型[J]. 管理科学学报, 2002, 5 (2): 56-61.
Cao Yunjian , Gu Xinyi. Two-stage horizontal differentiation model with dscriminatory pricing[J]. Journal of gement Sciences in China , 2002 , 5(2) : 56 -61. (in Chinese)

[13] 顾 锋，薛 刚，黄培清. 32-37.
Gu Feng Xue Gang , Huang Peiqing . Hotelling'scompetition with consumer's choice [J]Systems Engieering-Theory Methodology Applycaions , 1999, 8(4): 32-37. (in Chinese)

[14] 汪淼军，历 斌. 网络外部性、竞争和产品差异化[J]. 经济学(季刊), 2003, 2(2): 355-378.
Wang Miaojun Li Bin . Network externalities, competition , and product' and differentiation[J]. China Economic Quartely, 2003, 2(2): 355-378. (in Chinese)

[15] 曹韫建，顾新一. 一类存在网络外部性的水平差异模型[J]. 管理科学学报, 2002, 5 (1): 59-64.
Cao Yunjian , Gu Xinyi. Horizontal differentiation model with network externality[J]. Journal of Management Sciences in China , 2002 , 5 (1) : 59-64. (in Chinese)

[16] 王国才，朱道立. 网络经济下企业兼容性选择与用户锁定策略研究[J]. 中国管理科学，2004，12(6)：91-95.
Wang Gaocai，Zhu Daoli. Study on the choice of compatibility and lockin tactics under network economics[J]. Chinese Journal of Management Science，2004，12(6)：91-95. (in Chinese)
[17] Aubin J P. Optima and Equilibria[M]. New York：Springer Verlag Press，1998.
[18]Lambertini L，Orsini R. Existence of equalibrium in a differented duopoly with network externalities[J]. Japanese Economic Review，2005，56：55-66.
[19] Marcotte P，Zhu D L. "Equilibrium with infinitely many differentiated classes of customers"in complementarity and variational problems[A]. InPang J S，Ferris M，ed. Proceedings of the 13th International Conference on Complementarity Problems：Engineering and Economics and Applications and Computational Methods. SIAM，Philadelphia，1997. 234-258.
[20] 黄海军. 城市交通网络平衡分析——理论与实践[M]. 北京：人民交通出版社，1994.
Huang Haijun. Urban transportation network equilibrium analysis：Theory and practice[J]. Beijing：People Traffic Publishing Company，1994. (in Chinese)
[21] Lions J L. Quelques Methods de Resolution des Problemes aux Limites non Lineaires (Solving Method for Nonlinear Limited Problem)[M]. Paris：Dunod，1969.

（本文发表于《管理科学学报》，2007 年第 1 期）

附　录

命题 1 的证明：

证明　因为 $H(X_1)$ 是单调递增函数，$M(\bar{\theta})$ 是单调递减函数，且产品 1，2 同时占有市场，所以存在市场划分点 $\bar{\theta}\in(0,1)$，在 $\bar{\theta}$ 左侧的消费者都选择产品 1，在 $\bar{\theta}$ 右侧的消费者都选择产品 2，而 $\bar{\theta}$ 为无差异点，此时 $x_1=\bar{\theta}$，令 $y(\theta)=\begin{cases}0,当\ \theta\in[0,\bar{\theta}]\\1,当\ \theta\in(\bar{\theta},1)\end{cases}$ 代入变分不等式(4)。

1）若 $\bar{\theta}\in(0,a)$，当 $\bar{\theta}<\theta<a$ 时，有 $p_2-p_1-\gamma_2+(\gamma_1+\gamma_2)\bar{\theta}+(1-b-a)t\leqslant 0$，此时式(7) 成立，即产品 2 将独占市场，矛盾。

2）若 $\theta\in(1-b,1)$，当 $1-b<\theta<\bar{\theta}$ 时，有 $p_2-p_1-\gamma_2+(\gamma_1+\gamma_2)\bar{\theta}-(1-b-a)t\geqslant 0$，此时式(6) 成立，即产品 1 将独占市场，矛盾。

所以 $\bar{\theta}\in[a_1-b]$。此时 $x(\bar{\theta})=1$ 及 $x(\bar{\theta})=0$ 均满足变分不等式(4)，有

$p_2-p_1-\gamma_2+(\gamma_1+\gamma_2)\bar{\theta}+(1-b+\alpha-2\bar{\theta})t0$ 若 $t\neq\frac{1}{2}(\gamma_1+\gamma_2)$，有式(9)成立。

证毕。

定理 3 的证明：

证明　1）若 $a+b=1$，则 $\gamma_1=\gamma_2=0$，有 $a_1=a_2$，$\beta_{12}=\beta_{21}=1$，即两种产品是完全同质产品，厂商进行 Betrand 竞争，因此 $p_1^*=p_2^*=0$。

2）若 $a+b<1$，先证必要性。因为 $(1-b-a)t\geqslant\max(\gamma_1,\gamma_2)$，两个厂商进行价格竞争，则均衡价格一定满足式(8)，而在式(8) 所确定的范围内，$\Pi_1(p_1,p_2)$ 是 p_1 的可微凹函

数，$\Pi_2(p_1, p_2)$ 是 p_2 的可微凹函数，由一阶条件

$$\begin{cases} \dfrac{\partial \Pi_1(p_1^*, p_2^*)}{\partial p_1} = \dfrac{p_2^* - 2p_1^* - \gamma_2 + (1-b+a)t}{2t - \gamma_1 - \gamma_2} = 0 \\ \dfrac{\partial \Pi_2(p_1^*, p_2^*)}{\partial p_2} = 1 - \dfrac{2p_2^* - p_1^* - \gamma_2 + (1-b+a)t}{2t - \gamma_1 - \gamma_2} = 0 \end{cases}$$

可得到式(12)，再代入厂商利润函数，得到式(13)。因为厂商利润函数不是连续函数(图3)，p_1^*，p_2^*是均衡解，必须满足

$$\begin{cases} \Pi_1(p_1^*, p_2^*) \geqslant \Pi_1(p_2^* + \gamma_1 - (1-b-a)t - \varepsilon, p_2^*) \\ \Pi_2(p_1^*, p_2^*) \geqslant \Pi_2(p_1^* + \gamma_2 - (1-b-a)t - \varepsilon) \end{cases}$$

等价于式(10)，(11)。

再证充性。假设式(10)和式(11)成立，由上述过程，只要证明式(12)的 p_1^*，p_2^*满足式(8)。用反证法。由式(10)，(11)，有

$$(p_1^*)^2 \geqslant [2t - \gamma_1 - \gamma_2][p_2^* + \gamma_1 - (1-b-a)t] \tag{15}$$

$$(p_2^*)^2 \geqslant [2t - \gamma_1 - \gamma_2][p_1^* + \gamma_2 - (1-b-a)t] \tag{16}$$

若 $p^*{}_1 < p^*{}_2 + \gamma_1 - (1-b-a)t$，由式(15)，有

$$p_2^* > 2t - \gamma_1 - \gamma_2 \Rightarrow (3-b+a)t < \gamma_1 + 2\gamma_2$$

与假设矛盾，若 $p_2^* < p_1^* + \gamma_2 - (1-b-\alpha)t$ 由式(16)，有

$$p_2^* > 2t - \gamma_1 - \gamma_2 \Rightarrow (3-b+\alpha)t < \gamma_1 + 2\gamma_2$$

与假设矛盾所以 p_1^*，p_2^*满足式(8)。　　证毕。

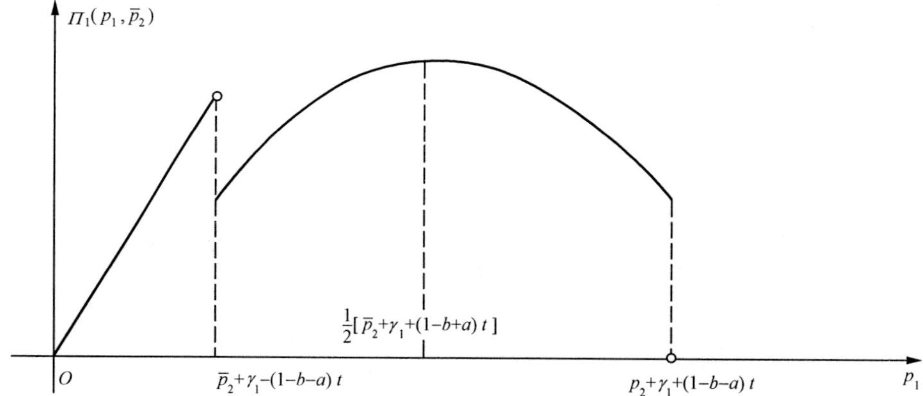

图3　厂商1的利润函数图示

Fig. 3 Diagram of the profits function of manufacturer 1

质量与价格竞争供应链的均衡与协调策略研究*

鲁其辉[1,2]，朱道立[2]

（1. 浙江大学管理学院管理科学与工程系，杭州 310058；
2. 复旦大学管理学院，上海 200433）

摘要：研究了一个两条竞争的二层供应链模型，每个制造商通过各自的分销商向顾客提供产品，供应链在产品质量和价格两个方面进行竞争。文中首先分析了三种情景中供应链竞争的均衡解：无协调情景、混合情景（仅有一条供应链采用协调策略）和协调情景。通过分析发现协调策略对于每条供应链都是一个占优策略，并且质量成本优势越大供应链在采用协调策略后的收益越大。但当两条供应链同时采用协调策略后，所有供应链的利润有可能均小于无协调情景中 的利润，即可能出现囚徒困境现象。供应链协调加剧了市场竞争，使产品平均质量提高和市场中顾客总量增加。供应链协调总是使顾客受益。

关键词：供应链管理；协调；一体化；质量竞争；价格竞争

中图分类号：O221

0　引　言

现代商业的迅速发展，使商品的种类和功能越来越多样化，消费者需求转变的频率也不断加快。企业管理者在不断改进企业内部的运作效率的同时，努力从提高产品质量角度来增强商品的吸引力，以寻求更大的竞争优势。企业只有提供比其他竞争者更高的质量水平和合适的价格水平给顾客，才能保留和吸引顾客，从而在竞争中处于不败之地。因而，质量管理理论和定价理论已经成为管理理论研究和企业界关注的焦点。

在激烈的市场竞争环境中，企业管理者已经认识到，要想取得竞争优势仅仅依靠单打独斗已经远远不能满足和适应新的市场环境。20 世纪 90 年代以来，一些运作管理专家提出了供应链管理的基本思想。供应链管理是指从最终用户到提供产品、服务和信息以及增加客户和其他利害关系者价值的原始供应商关键经营过程的集成[13]。供应链管理成为企业提高运作效率、降低成本和提高竞争力的有力武器。供应链管理中最重要的一个思想就是协调管理的思想，就是通过形成一种供应链决策机制来改善或最大化供应链绩效[5]。企业界（制造业和服务业）和学术界逐渐认识到供应链协调管理的重要性，并大

---

* 基金项目：国家自然科学基金重点项目（70432001），中国博士后科学基金资助项目（20070410166）.

作者简介：鲁其辉（1977～），男，博士，湖南益阳人，浙江大学管理学院管理科学与工程系讲师，研究方向：供应链管理、运营管理，qihuilu@zju. edu. cn.

力将供应链协调理论和方法运用于管理实践，为企业带来了巨大的效益和竞争优势。

本文将分析供应链竞争环境下质量与定价均衡，研究供应链协调对市场的影响和对供应链竞争力的影响，研究供应链竞争环境中产业平均质量和平均价格与产品的成本结构的关系。本文的研究将有助于理解供应链协调对整个产业的影响，以及提高企业竞争力的关键因素。

在两层及多层供应链中，供应链上下游之间的竞争被称为纵向竞争。如在供应链某一层中有多个企业相互竞争并且其决策相互影响，这被称为横向竞争。横向竞争可以是零售商之间的竞争[3]，也可以是多个供应商之间的竞争和制造商之间的竞争[2]等等。竞争的形式和促使竞争的因素有多种，如产品的数量、价格和可替代性等。

近年来，许多研究者开始研究关于服务水平、产品质量等竞争因素的供应链竞争均衡和协调策略。文献[14]分析了一类供应链模型，供应链系统中包含两个竞争的零售商和一个公共的制造商，模型推广了以往模型中只考虑价格竞争的传统模型，考虑了最终消费者是关于零售价格和零售商库存的服务水平敏感的。文中分析指出竞争的相对激烈程度和零售商之间协作的力度是供应链利益分配的关键因素，供应链达到协调只在一些非常特殊的条件下通过批发价格机制达到。文献[4]考虑一个供应链竞争模型，两条竞争的供应链给出同样的零售价格但在库存满足率方面进行竞争，文中考虑了三种情形：全不协调情形、协调情形和混合情形。研究发现尽管协调是供应链的占优策略，但是所有供应链均协调的情形下的收益要比均不协调的情形下的收益都低，出现了一种囚徒困境现象。文献[1]考虑了零售商之间竞争的供应链模型，每个产品的市场需求量是与市场中所有产品的价格和质量相关的，研究了在三类不同的竞争环境中的质量均衡水平，分析了质量水平与相应的竞争类型下的竞争激烈程度之间的关系。

在动态竞争环境中分析供应链管理问题也是一个日益受到关注的研究方向。文献[7]考虑了在有容量限制的服务业中服务竞争的动态模型，销售企业必须同时考虑下一阶段的容量水平和提供给顾客的产品质量水平，文中分析了一般的单阶段模型和多阶段有界模型，分析指出在产品质量水平将随着市场中竞争的激烈程度增加而提高。文献[8]考虑了在多个企业间存在市场份额竞争的情况下，顾客通过以往的购买经验选择产品，研究指出企业总是提供高质量产品的均衡不一定存在，从而指出必须在产业中发挥专业协会的监督作用以促使企业总是提供与产品价格相匹配的高质量产品。

近年，与传统的质量管理研究中基于企业内部运作的角度不同，一些学者从供应链管理的角度来研究产品的质量改进问题。文献[11]在协调和一体化概念基础上给出了战略联盟内部的质量管理的定义。文献[15]研究了供应链中不同成员在质量改进中扮演的角色，分析指出合作态度在提高产品质量中的重要作用。文献[9]采用委托代理理论的方法探讨了双边道德风险条件下的质量控制策略。

1　供应链竞争模型

本文考虑一个含有两条供应链的竞争模型(图 1)，每个供应链包含一个制造商和一个分销商，它们面对同一市场，市场中顾客选择何种产品将综合考虑所有分销商给出的价格 $p_i(i=1,2)$ 和所有产品的质量 $t_i(i=1,2)$。这里所指的产品质量为包括与消费者感知产品的相关因素，例如，产品的品牌、产品的品质以及售后服务等等，这些因素仅包含有制造商的运作效率和市场策略等对产品质量的影响因素，本文不考虑分销商的销售能力和努力程度对产品质量的影响。于是假设产品是两个性质的组合体：价格和质量，并且假定产品的质量 $t_i(i=1,2)$ 影响产品 i 的需求是正向的，即，当值 t_i 越大时，关于产品 i 的需求越大。

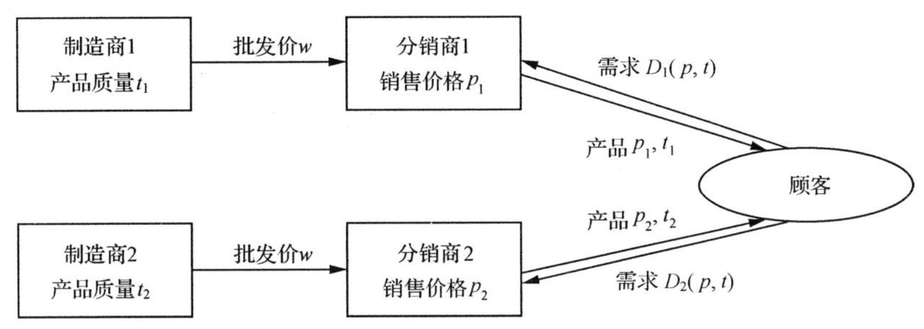

图 1　供应链竞争模型

Fig. 1 Supply Chain Compe““on model

令 $D_i(p,t)$表示产品 i 在价格向量 p 和质量向量 t 下的需求. 本文仅考虑需求 D_i 关于价格和质量是线性的情况，

$$D_i(p,t) = a_i - bp_i + cp_j + \alpha t_i - \beta t_j, i, j = 1,2, i \neq j$$

其中，$a_i(i=1,2)$，$b>0$，$c,\alpha,\beta \geqslant 0$ 为常数，且 $a_1+a_2=a$ 为常数。参数 a_i 表示产品 i 的“顾客需求基数”，反映产品对顾客的内在吸引力，a 表示整个市场的顾客内在需求，它反映了该类产品的整体市场发展水平；参数 b 表示顾客需求对产品价格的反应；参数 c 表示顾客需求对竞争产品价格的反应。这里采用文献[1] 中的设定，产品的顾客需求的反应关于自身价格的变化比竞争对手产品价格变化的反应要大，即 $b>c$。参数 α，β表示顾客需求对产品质量的反应，同样假定有 $\alpha>\beta$。文献[14]考虑了类似的需求模型，不同的是该文分析一个制造商面对两个竞争分销商的供应链模型。

制造商 i 为了使质量达到 t_i 而付出的支出为 $\gamma_i t_i^2/2$，其中二次项表示当 t_i 越大提高产品质量的支出越多，制造商之间的不同的质量成本 γ_i 反映了制造商的运作效率的差异性。假定两个不同的制造商向各自的分销商供货，且都有充足的生产能力，单位产品的生产成本为 $c_i + vt_i(i=1,2)$，它与产品质量呈正的线性关系。

设制造商向分销商供货的收入是单位产品的批发价格 w. 注意到这里假设两个制造商向各自分销商收取的批发价是相同的，这样的假设可以反映制造商的差异性主要体现在生产成本 c_i 与质量成本 γ_i 上。这里假定制造商与分销商的固定运作成本为零。

2　供应链竞争均衡解

这一节首先分析当两条供应链均不协调情景中(即成员的决策是独立的)供应链的竞争均衡解，然后分析混合情景中(其中有一条供应链采用协调策略)的竞争均衡解，最后研究两条供应链同时采用协调策略后供应链的竞争均衡解。

供应链之间的竞争按照下列顺序进行：(i) 制造商或供应链同时确定产品的质量；

(ii)供应链的所有成员都了解所有的产品的质量,以及顾客需求的参数;(iii) 分销商或供应链同时选择销售价格;(iv) 在确定的价格和质量的基础上,顾客选择产品,市场需求得以实现。

2.1 无协调情景中供应链均衡分析

在给定的产品质量 t 的条件下,两个分销商的利润函数为

$$\Pi_{Ri}(p,t)=(p_i-w)D_i(p,t)=(p_i-w)(a_i-bp_i+cp_j+\alpha t_i-\beta t_j),i,j=1,2,i\neq j$$

均衡价格的一阶条件为

$$\frac{\partial\Pi_{Ri}(p,t)}{\partial p_i}=a_i-2bp_i+cp_j+\alpha t_i-\beta t_j+bw=0,i,j=1,2,i\neq j$$

因为 $\frac{\partial^2\Pi_{Ri}(p,t)}{\partial p_i^2}=-2b<0$,分销商的利润函数关于价格是严格凹函数,同时求解以上等式可以得到均衡价格函数:

$$p_i^*(t)=\frac{1}{Z}(R_i+St_i-Vt_j),i,j=1,2,i\neq j$$

其中,$Z=4b^2-c^2,R_i=2ba_i+ca_j+(2b^2+bc)w,S=2b\alpha-c\beta,V=2b\beta-c\alpha$。

将均衡价格 $p_i^*(t)$代入分销商利润函数中得到价格均衡中分销商的利润,

$$\begin{aligned}H_{Ri}^*(t)&=(p_i^*(t)-w)(a_i-bp_i^*(t)+cp_j^*(t)+\alpha t_i-\beta t_j)\\&=b(p_i^*(t)-w)^2\\&=\frac{b}{Z^2}(R_i-wZ+St_i-Vt_j)^2,i,j=1,2,i\neq j\end{aligned}$$

价格均衡状态中,产品 i 的市场需求量为

$$D_i^*(t)=a_i-bp_i^*(t)+cp_j^*(t)+\alpha t_i-\beta t_j,$$

$$bp_i^*(t)-bw=\frac{b}{Z}(R_i-wZ+St_i-Vt_i),i,j=1,2,i\neq j$$

为了满足 $D_i^*(t)$ 在 $t_i=t_j=0$ 的情况下是正数,必须使 $R_i-wZ>0,i=1,2$,那么假设下列条件满足:

$$w<\frac{ca}{(b-c)(2b+c)}\tag{2}$$

进一步,若 $V<0$,当产品 i 的质量 t_i 保持不变,而当产品 j 的质量 t_j 增加时,产品 i 的需求随之增加,这与需求定义相矛盾,因而必须有 $V\geqslant0$,即$\frac{\alpha}{\beta}\leqslant\frac{2b}{c}$. 同样,若 $S<V$,当两个产品同时减少相同数量的质量时,分销商的市场需求增加,这也与需求定义中假设 $\alpha>\beta$ 相矛盾,因而必须有 $S\geqslant V$,即,$\frac{\alpha}{\beta}\geqslant\frac{b+c}{2b+c}$,这样设下列条件满足:

$$\frac{b+c}{2b+c}\leqslant\frac{\alpha}{\beta}\leqslant\frac{2b}{c}$$

由价格 p_1^*,p_2^*t 和市场需求 $D_i^*(t)$可以求得每个制造商的利润函数,

$$\begin{aligned}\Pi_{Mi}(t)&=(w-c_i-v_it_i)D_i^*(t)-\gamma_it_i^2/2\\&=\frac{b(w-c_iv_it_i)}{Z}(R_i-wZ+St_i-Vt_j)-\gamma_it_i^2/2\end{aligned}$$

最优质量的一阶条件为

$$\frac{\partial \Pi_{Mi}}{\partial t_i} = \frac{b}{Z}[\phi_i - \rho_i t_i + \theta_i t_j] = 0, i,j = 1,2, i \neq j$$

其中

$$\phi_i = (w - c_i)S + v_i(wZ - R_i)$$
$$\rho_i = 2v_i S + \gamma_i Z/b$$
$$\theta_i = v_i V$$

因为 $\frac{\partial^2 \Pi_{Mi}}{\partial t_i^2} = - b\rho_i/Z < 0$，那么求解上述两个方程组可得出制造商的质量均衡解：

$$t_i^* = \frac{\phi_i \rho_j + \phi_j \theta_i}{\rho_i \rho_j - \theta_i \theta_j}, i,j = 1,2, i \neq j \tag{5}$$

将质量均衡解代入以上各函数，可以得到价格均衡解 p_i^*，市场需求 D_i^*，均衡状态下供应链成员的期望利润 Π_{mi}^*，Π_{Ri}^* 和供应链的总利润 $\Pi_{SCi}^* = \Pi_{Mi}^* + \Pi_{Ri}^*$。

2.2　协调情景中供应链竞争均衡分析

供应链的各个成员在利益、风险等方面存在不同程度的冲突，这就需要对供应链上下游进行必要的协调管理，以使供应链成员的目标与供应链总体目标相一致。供应链协调(Supply Chain Coordination)是指通过形成某种联合决策机制或激励机制后提高或最大化供应链的整体利润或者降低风险的状态[10]-[5]。文献[10]总结了近年来学界和企业界提出的一些供应链协调机制。在本文分析的供应链中，制造商与分销商通过联合决策价格和质量而达到供应链整体利润的最大化。在本文中不考虑协调状态中供应链成员的利益分配问题。

当供应链达到协调时，供应链的总利润为

$$\hat{\Pi}_{SCi}(p,t)(p_i - c_i - v_i t_i)(a_i - bp_i + cp_j + at_i - \beta t_j) - \gamma_i t_i^2/2, i,j = 1,2, i \neq j$$

均衡价格的一阶条件为

$$\frac{\partial \Pi_{SCi}}{\partial p_i} = a_i - 2bp_i + cp_j + (a + bv_i)t_i - \beta t_j + bc_i = 0, i,j = 1,2, i \neq j$$

显然，供应链的利润函数关于价格也是严格凹的，同时求解以上等式可以得到均衡价格：

$$p_i^*(t)\ \frac{1}{Z}(\hat{R}_i + \hat{S}_i t_i - \hat{V}_i t_j), i,j = 1,2, i \neq j$$

其中，$\hat{R}_i = 2ba_i + ca_j + (2b^2 + bc)c_i$，$\hat{S}_i = 2b(\alpha + bv_i) - c\beta$，$\hat{V}_i = 2b\beta - c(\alpha + bv_i)$

价格均衡状态中，产品 i 的市场需求量为

$$\begin{aligned} D_i^*(t) &= a_i - bp_i^*(t) + cp_j^*(t) + at_i - \beta t_j \\ &= b(p_i^*(t) - c_i - v_i t_i) \\ &= \frac{b}{Z}\hat{R}_i - c_i Z + (\hat{S} - v_i Z)t_i - \hat{V}_i t_j), i,j = 1,2, i \neq j \end{aligned}$$

同样，为了满足 $D_i^*(t)$ 在 $t_i = t_j = 0$ 的情况下是正数，必须使 $\hat{R}_i - c_i Z > 0, i = 1,2$，那么假设下列条件满足：

$$c_i < \frac{ca + (2b - c)a_i}{(b - c)(2b + c)}, i = 1,2 \tag{6}$$

进一步，按上一小节的分析方法可知必须有 $\hat{V}_i > 0$ 和 $\hat{S}_i - v_i Z \geqslant \hat{V}_i$，这样设下列条件满足：

$$v_i < \frac{2\beta}{c} - \frac{\alpha}{b}, \quad v_i < \frac{\alpha - \beta}{b - c}$$

将均衡价格 $p_i^*(t)$ 代入供应链利润函数中得到价格均衡中供应链的利润，

$$\begin{aligned}\Pi_{SCi}^*(t) &= (p_i^*(t) - c_i - v_i t_i)(a_i - bp_i^*(t) + cp_j^*(t) + \alpha t_i - \beta t_j) - \gamma_i t_i^2/2 \\ &= b(p_i^*(t) - c_i - v_i t_i)^2 - \gamma_i t_i^2/2 \\ &= \frac{b}{Z^2}(\hat{R}_i + (\hat{S}_i - v_i Z)t_i - \hat{V}_i t_j - c_i Z)^2 - \gamma_i t_i^2/2, i,j = 1,2, i \neq j\end{aligned}$$

最优质量的一阶条件为

$$\frac{\partial \Pi_{SCi}}{\partial t_i} = \frac{2b(\hat{S}_i - v_i Z)}{Z^2}[\hat{\phi}_i - \hat{\rho}_i t_i - \hat{\theta}_i t_j] = 0, i,j = 1,2, i \neq j \tag{8}$$

其中

$$\hat{\phi}_i = \hat{R}_i - c_i Z$$

$$\hat{\rho}_i = \frac{\gamma_i Z^2}{2b(\hat{S}_i - v_i Z)} - (\hat{S}_i - v_i Z)$$

$$\hat{\theta}_i = \hat{V}_i$$

条件 1：

$$\gamma_i > 2b(v_i - \hat{S}_i/Z)^2, \quad i = 1,2 \tag{9}$$

若条件 1 满足，那么求解上述两个方程组可得出供应链的质量均衡解：

$$\hat{t}_i^* = \frac{\hat{\phi}_i\hat{\rho}_j - \hat{\phi}_j\hat{\theta}_i}{\hat{\rho}_i\hat{\rho}_j - \hat{\theta}_i\hat{\theta}_j}, i,j = 1,2, i \neq j \tag{10}$$

将质量均衡代入以上各函数，可得价格均衡解 $\hat{p}_i^*$，均衡状态下供应链的总利润 $\hat{\Pi}_{SCi}^*$

2.3 混合情景中供应链竞争均衡分析

不失一般性，假定制造商 1 与分销商 1 达成了供应链协调合同，而制造商 2 与分销商 2 仍然独立决策。那么在价格竞争中的目标函数分别为：

$$\bar{\Pi}_{SC1}(p,t) = (p_1 - c_1 - v_1 t_1)(a_1 - bp_1 + cp_2 + \alpha t_1 - \beta t_2) - \gamma_1 t_1^2/2$$

$$\bar{\Pi}_{R2}(p,t) = (p_2 - w)(a_2 - bp_2 + cp_1 + \alpha t_2 - \beta t_1)$$

最优价格的一阶条件为

$$\frac{\partial \bar{\Pi}_{SC1}(p,t)}{\partial p_1} = a_1 - 2bp_1 + cp_2 + (\alpha + bv_1)t_1 - \beta t_2 + bc_1 = 0$$

$$\frac{\partial \bar{\Pi}_{R2}(p,t)}{\partial p_2} = a_2 - 2bp_2 + cp_1 + \alpha t_2 - \beta t_1 + bw = 0$$

显然，供应链 1 与分销商 2 的利润函数关于各自价格决策变量是严格凹的，同时求解以上等式可以得到均衡价格：

$$\bar{p}_1^*(t)=\frac{1}{Z}[2ba_1+ca_2+2b^2c_1+bcw+(2b(a+bv_1)-c\beta)t_1-(2b\beta-ca)t_2]$$

$$\bar{p}_2^*(t)=\frac{1}{Z}[2ba_2+ca_1+2b^2w+bcc_1+(2ba-c\beta)t_2-(2b\beta-c(a+bv_1))t_1]$$

价格均衡状态的利润函数分别为

$$\bar{\Pi}_{SC1}(t)=b(\bar{p}_1^*(t)-c_1-v_1t_1)^2-\gamma_1t_1^2/2$$

$$\bar{\Pi}_{M2}(t)=b(w-c_2-v_2t_2)(\bar{p}_2^*(t)-w)-\gamma_2t_2^2/2$$

那么质量均衡的一阶条件为

$$\frac{\partial\bar{\Pi}_{SC1}(t)}{\partial t_1}=\frac{2b}{Z}(2b(a+bv_1)-c\beta-v_1Z(\bar{p}_1^*(t)-c_1-v_1t_1)-\gamma_1t_1=0$$

$$\frac{\partial\bar{\Pi}_{M_2}(t)}{\partial t_2}=\frac{b}{Z}[(2ba-c\beta)(w-c_2-v_2t_2)-v_2Z(\bar{p}_2^*(t)-w)]-\gamma_2t_2=0$$

由条件 1 和 $\beta_2>0$ 易推出供应链 1 和制造商 2 利润函数关于各自质量变量是严格凹的，那么同时求解上述两个方程组可得出质量均衡解 $t_i^*, i=1,2$ 将质量均衡解代入以上各函数，可得价格均衡解 p_i^*，均衡状态下的期望利润 $\bar{\Pi}_{M2}^*$，$\bar{\Pi}_{R2}^*$ 和供应链的总利润 $\bar{\Pi}_{sci}^*$

3　供应链协调分析

上一节中，已经分析了价格与质量竞争环境中供应链的均衡解，其中分别考虑了三种情景：无协调情景、协调情景和混合情景。由于均衡解的表达式非常复杂或者没有解析表达式，这一节与下一节将通过分析一些算例来分析供应链协调对供应链成员、顾客和整个产业的影响，展现供应链协调在竞争环境中的价值，研究产品的成本关系对供应链协调的价值的影响。

例 1　令市场需求参数为 $\alpha_1=\alpha_2=200, b=15, c=12, \alpha=3, \beta=2$ 在这里，首先考虑供应链关于产品的成本结构是相同的，令参数分别为 $c_1=10, c_2=10, v_1=v_2=0.06$，$\gamma=\gamma_2=0.3$。批发价等于 $w=20$。那么由上一节的结论可得到无协调情景中供应链的相应均衡解：$t_1^*=t_2^*=14.2$，$p_1^*=p_2^*=28.6$，$\Pi_{R1}^*=\Pi_{R2}^*=1101.1$，$\Pi_{M1}^*=\Pi_{M2}^*=1145.2$，$\Pi^*_{SC1}=\Pi_{SC2}^*=2246.3$。

不失一般性，假定供应链 1 形成了供应链协调，而制造商 2 与分销商 2 仍保持独立决策不变，那么相应的均衡解分别为：$\bar{t}_1^*=116.3$，$\bar{t}_2^*=22.0$，$\bar{p}_1^*=35.4$，$\bar{p}_2^*=25.3$，$\bar{\Pi}_{SC1}^*=3080.0\bar{\Pi}_{SC2}^*=2246.3$。

比较上面的均衡解可以看出，当供应链 1 采用协调策略后，供应链 1 提供的产品质量显著提高，产品价格也相应提高，而供应商 2 为了保存一定的市场竞争能力，不得不提高产品的质量，分销商 2 也只能通过降价来吸引顾客，那么也就是说，采用协调策略后的供应链 1 在市场竞争中的竞争力大大提高，而供应链 2 的竞争力被大大削弱。因此，在市场中各供应链均未采用协调策略的状态中，每条供应链都有采用协调策略的趋势，协调策略是供应链的一个占优策略。

根据一般规律，产品的生产成本对产品的市场竞争力起着关键性作用，这里将分析产品的成本结构对供应链协调的价值的影响情况。在本文的模型中主要考虑了两个关键成本参数:单位产品的可变成本参数 v_i 和固定质量成本气质量成本 r_i 之间的大小关系和 r_i 之间的大小关系也反映了供应链之间关于产品质量提高的效率优势关系。

例 2 保持例 1 中其他参数不变,但使参数 v_1 在[0.02,0.10]中变化,同样考虑无协调情景和混合情景的均衡解。图 2 中分别给出了供应链总利润和产品质量与参数 v_1 的关系。

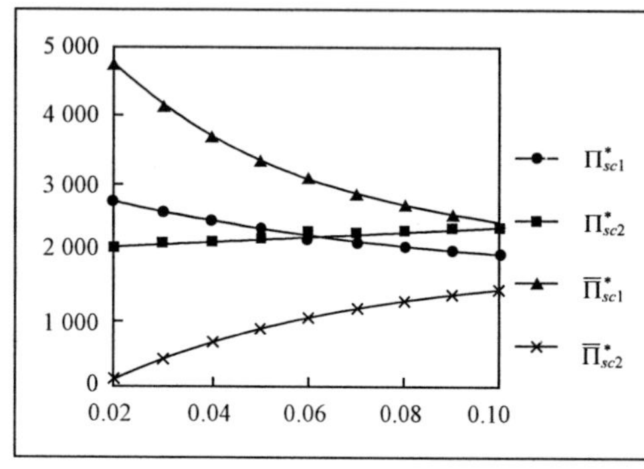

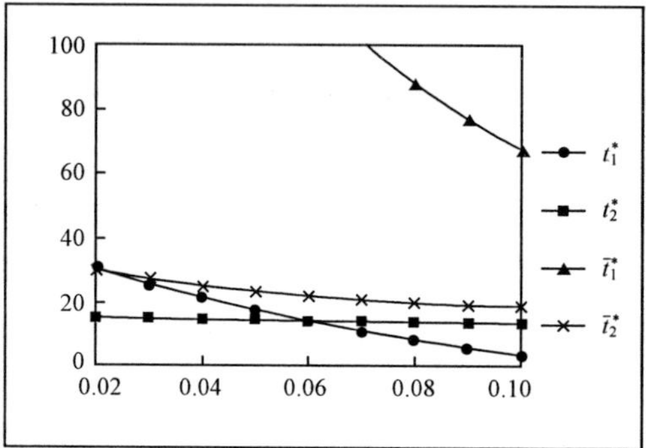

图 2 供应链总利润和产品质量均衡解与参数 v_1 的关系

Fig. 2 Relations of Supply chains' Profits and Products' Qualities in Equilibrium with parameter v_1.

进一步,同样保持例 1 中其他参数不变,但参数(v_1,γ_1)由表 1 中所示。表 1 给出了供应链的均衡解和相应的收益情况。

表 1 供应链的最优解,收益和支出与 T_1 的变化关系

Table 1. Changes of Optima ,Profits and Quality Costs with T_1

质量成本	供应链 1					供应链 2				
(v_1,γ_1)	制造商 1		分销商 1		链 1	制造商 2		分销商 2		链 2
无协调情景	t_1^*	Π^*_{M1}	p_1^*	Π^*_{R1}	Π^*_{SC1}	t_2^*	Π^*_{M2}	p_2^*	Π^*_{R2}	Π^*_{SC2}
(0.05,0.2)	23.0	1183.9	29.3	1302.0	2468.1	14.8	1107.0	28.3	1 042.6	2149.6
(0.07,0.3)	11.2	1130.0	28.3	1035.1	2165.1	14.0	1158.5	28.6	1121.9	2280.4
(0.09,0.4)	5.0	1109.6	27.8	908.2	2017.9	13.6	1185.4	28.8	1164.3	2349.74
混合情景	$\bar{t}_1^*$	—	$\bar{p}_1^*$	—	$\overline{\Pi}^*_{SC1}$	$\bar{t}_2^*$	$\overline{\Pi}^*_{M2}$	$\bar{p}_2^*$	$\overline{\Pi}^*_{R2}$	$\overline{\Pi}^*_{SC2}$
(0.05,0.2)	335.1	—	60.1	—	5414.9	31.1	81.9	21.5	32.2	114.1
(0.07,0.3)	100.9	—	34.2	—	2863.2	21.0	682.3	25.7	489.1	1171.4
(0.09,0.4)	53.1	—	28.7	—	2342.7	19.1	792.5	26.5	636.9	1429.4

由图 2 和表 1 中无协调情景中的均衡解可以看出,在无协调情景中,同于供应链的其他成本就是相同的,当产品 1 相对于产品 2 具有更大的成本优势时(即 v_1 或 γ_1 越小),供应链 1 的利润要越大于供应链 2 的利润,产品 1 的质量越高于产品 2 的质量;反之越小。因此,与传统观点相一致,提高产品质量方面拥有的效率优势越大的供应链,拥有的竞争

优势越大。

若市场中有一条供应链采用了协调策略，那么它将大幅度提高产品的质量，这也促使竞争供应链提高其产品质量。相应的，协调供应链获得比不协调情况中多的利润，而不协调供应链利润下降。又由图 2 和表 1 可以看出，若协调供应链的质量成本优势越大(这里指 v_1 或 γ_1 越小)，那么协调策略使其获益的幅度越高，并相应的使竞争供应链的损失越大。也就是说，质量成本优势越明显，供应链采用协调策略的收益越大。

进一步，由图 2 中可以看出，当协调供应链的质量成本大于无协调策略的供应链时，协调策略仍然能使供应链在提高产品质量的同时获得较高利润，也就是说，协调策略能弥补供应链在质量成本方面的劣势

由上面的分析可以看出，供应链协调是供应链的一个占优策略，这种先发优势将促使每条供应链都有采用协调策略的趋势。但是当两条供应链同时采用协调策略时，两条供应链有可能都将受损(与无协调情景中的收益相比)，也就是说，出现一种“囚徒困境”现象，譬如表 2 分析了例 1 中的供应链系统。

表 2　例 1 中供应链协调的“囚徒困境”现象

Table 2. The"Prisoner's Dilemma" for Supply Chains in Example 1.

		Supply Chain 2	
		Uncoordinated	Coordinated
Supply Chain 1	Uncoordinated	(2246.3,2246.3)	(3080.0,1035.3)
	Coordinated	(1035.3,3080.0)	(1587.1,1587.1)

从表 2 中可以看到，当某一条供应链首先采用协调策略后，其供应链比润比无协调情况中的利润要大大提高，也使竞争供应链的利润大幅降低；由于观察到利润的大幅降低，竞争供应链必将也采用协调策略，这时也使一条供应链利润增加，另一条供应链利润减少。因此，对于一些供应链系统来说，供应链协调将使系统出现“囚徒困镜”现象。

由表 2 所示，在协调情景中所有供应链的利润都要小于无协调情景中的利润，但是通过观察一些算例，这里发现对于有些供应链系统，协调情景中某条供就链的利润要大于无协调情景中利润。例如，保持例 1 中其他参数不变，但供应链 1 的质量成本参数变化为 $v_1=0.04$，$\gamma_1=0.25$，表 3 给出了不同策略下的供应链变化情况。那么这时对于供应链 1 来说，采用协调策略是它的严格占优策略，因此同时采用协调策略是这个供应链系统的均衡解。

表 3　供应链协调是供应链的竞争均衡

Table 3. Supply Chain Coordination is the Equililbrium of Supply Chain Competition.

		Supply Chain 2	
		Uncoordinated	Coordinated
Supply Chain 1	Uncoordinated	(2010.91767.3)	(4166.7,370.2)
	Coordinated	(1118.6,2677.9)	(2380.4,750.6)

下面研究竞争产品的成本关系和协调策略对整个市场中的平均质量水平和平均产品

价格的影响。类似于文献[1]中对产业平均质量的定义，这里定义无协调情景中的协调情景中的平均质量水平分别为，

$$\bar{t}^*_{uc}=\frac{t^*_1D^*_1+t^*_2D^*_2}{D^*_1+D^*_2},\bar{t}_c=\frac{\hat{t}^*_1\hat{D}^*_1+\hat{t}^*_2\hat{D}^*_2}{\hat{D}^*_1+\hat{D}^*_2}$$

并定义无协调情景中和协调情景中的平均产品价格分别为，

$$\bar{p}_{uc}=\frac{p^*_1D^*_1+p^*_2D^*_2}{D^*_1+D^*_2},\bar{p}_c=\frac{\hat{p}^*_1\hat{D}^*_1+\hat{p}^*_2\hat{D}^*_2}{\hat{D}^*_1+\hat{D}^*_2}$$

例 3 保持例 1 中其他参数不变，使参数 v_1 在 0.4 到 0.8 中取值，且参数 v_2 满足 $v_2=1.5v_1$。表 4 中给出了市场中平均质量和平均价格的变化情况，其中 $\bar{D}_{uc}=D^*_1+D^*_2$，$\bar{D}_c=\hat{D}^*_1+\hat{D}^*_2$。

由表 4 可以看出，当市场中所有制造商的生产效率提高时（表现为 v_1，v_2 变小），市场所提供的平均产品质量大幅度提高，而在协调情景中，市场中的产品质量要比无协调情景中的产品质量有很大的提高，而平均产品价格却有可能降低。在协调情景中平均价格大于无协调情景中的平均价格的情况中，平均质量的提高幅度大大高于产品价格提高的幅度。因此，协调策略加剧了产业的竞争，提高了市场中产品的质量水平，并相对的使价格大为降低，但是这都使顾客受益。同时，供应链协调使市场的需求总量大大提高，特别的，当制造商的生产效率越高，市场中顾客总量增加的幅度越大。

表 4 市场平均质量和平均价格与成本(v_1，v_2)的关系

Table 4. The relatons of average qualities and average prices with costs (v_1，v_2)

成本参数	无协调情景			协调情景		
(v_1，v_2)	$\bar{t}_{uc}$	$\bar{p}_{uc}$	D_{uc}	$\bar{t}_c$	$\bar{p}_c$	D_c
(0.040，0.060)	18.3	28.8	263.5	127.5	33.0	451.8
(0.045，0.068)	16.0	28.7	259.7	102.1	30.3	420.2
(0.050，0.075)	13.9	28.6	256.2	84.2	28.4	397.1
(0.055，0.083)	11.9	28.5	252.8	70.8	26.9	379.3
(0.060，0.090)	10.0	28.4	249.7	60.4	25.8	365.4
(0.065，0.098)	8.3	28.3	246.7	52.1	25.0	354.3
(0.070，0.105)	6.6	28.2	243.9	45.8	24.3	345.8
(0.075，0.113)	5.0	28.1	241.3	41.4	23.8	339.8
(0.080，0.120)	3.5	28.0	238.8	39.4	23.6	337.1

4 管理借鉴与结论

现代通讯技术的快速发展与应用，已经使商业竞争的模式发生了根本性的变化，单个企业之间的竞争逐渐演变成了供应链与供应链之间的竞争。本文通过分析两层供应链竞争模型中的价格与质量竞争均衡，研究了供应链竞争环境中供应链协调策略对所有供应链的影响，并刻画了质量成本结构对供应链均衡和协调策略的价值的影响，最后考虑了协调策略对市场中产品的平均质量水平、平均价格及顾客的影响。

近年来，由于市场竞争的激烈程度不断加剧，越来越多的企业开始采用供应链一体化或供应链协调策略来提高企业的竞争力。在本文的分析中，不仅指出了采用供应链协调的理由，也分析出协调策略对供应链成员可能是无效率的原因。文中说明了，对任一供应链来说，协调策略是她的一个占优策略，在这个决策中先发着能够通过提高产品质量和价格来大部分占有供应链系统的收益。然而，当其中已经有一条供应链采用了协调策略后，另一条供应链必然也要采用协调策略。那么，从长期来看，均采用协调策略是供应链系统的均衡状态。但是，协调策略并不能保证供应链取得比不协调情景中更多的利润，在有些情况中，所有供应链的收益都要比无协调情景中的利润少，这就是说，供应链协调有可能使供应链系统出现"囚徒困境"现象；在有些情况中，供应链协调使某条供应链获益，另一条供应链受损。

通过分析供应链成本结构对供应链均衡解和协调策略价值的影响，文中指出，质量提高的相对效率越高，供应链拥有的竞争优势越大；质量成本优势越明显，供应链采用协调策略的收益越大，并且协调策略能弥补供应链在质量成本方面的劣势。协调策略使市场的竞争激烈程度提高，使市场中产品的平均质量水平提高，并使平均价格降低或使平均价格提高的幅度大大小于平均质量提高的幅度。协调策略使市场中顾客总量大大增加，有利于产业的发展。从市场中产品的平均质量的提高和平均价格的变化关系来看，供应链协调策略使顾客受益。

当然，本文建立的供应链模型相对比较简单，研究者可以建立含有多个制造商和多个分销商的供应链网络模型，可以相应的得到更一般情况中的供应链竞争均衡解，并可以同样分析供应链协调对供应链系统的影响和整个市场的影响。另一个值得关注的研究问题是，与本文和以往文献所考虑的竞争因素不同，也可以考虑供应链所提供的东西不仅有产品本身还有产品所伴随的相关服务，这种产品和服务相融合的供应链竞争问题以及供应链一体化理论是很值得关注的研究问题。

Research on Equilibriums and Coordination Strategies of Supply Chains with Quality and Price Competition

LU Qihui[1,2], *ZHU Daoli*[2]

1. School of Management, Zhejiang University, Hangzhou 310058, China

2. School of Management, Fudan University, Shanghai 200433, China

Abstract: In this paper, we consider a market with two competing supply chains with common customers, each consisting of one manufacture and one retailer. We assume that supply chain competing ontwo sides: products' qualities and prices. At first we analyze the supply chain competition results in threescenarios: uncoordinated scenario, hybrid scenario (only one supply chain adopts coordination strategy) and coordinated scenario. We show that coordinating supply chain decisions is a dominant strategy for each supply chain. The coordinated supply chain has more benefits when the supply chain has more advantage of quality cost. However, supply chain profits may decrease when both channels coordinate their decisions, i. e. , there may occur the classical prisoner's dilemma in the supply chain system. The competitive intensity is higher under supply chain coordination equilibrium. The average quality levels are higher and customer amount increase in the coordination scenario. Customers benefit a lot from coordination strategy.

Keywords: Supply Chain Management;Coordination;Integration;Quality Cuality Competition; Price Competition

参考文献

[1] Banker R D,Khosla I,Sinha,K K. Quality and competition[J]. Management Science,1998,44(9): 1179-1192.

[2] Bernstein F,Federguren A. Ageneral equilibrium model for industries with price and service competition[J]. Operations Research,2004,52(6):868-886.

[3] Boyaci T. Competitive stocking and coordination in a multiple-channel distribution system[J]. IIE Transactions,2005,37:407-427.

[4] Boyaci T,Gfallego G. Supply chain coordination in a market with customer service competition[J]. Production and Operations Management ,2004,13(1):3-22

[5] Cachon G P. Supply chain coordination with contracts,Handbooks in Operations Research and Management Science :Supply Chain Management[M]. Amsterdam:North Holland ,2003.

[6] Drezner Z. Facility Location :A Survey of Applications and Methods[M]. London:Spinger,1995.

[7] Hall J,Porteus E. Customer service competition in capacitated systems[J]. Manufacturing and Service Operations Management ,2000,2(2):144-165.

[8] Kranton R E. Competition and the Incentive to Produce High Quality. Econcmica,2003,70:385-404.

[9] 李丽君,黄小原,庄小田. 双边道德风险条件下供应链的质量控制策略[J]. 管理科学学报,2004,8(1):42-47.

Ll Li-jun,HUANG Xiao-yuan. ZHUANG Xin-tian. Strategy of quality control in supply chain under double moral haxzard condition[J]. Journal of Management Sciences in china,2004,8(1):42-47. (in Chinese)

[10] Li X,Wang Q. Coordination Mechanisms of supply chain system[J]. European Journal of Operational Research,2007,179:1-16.

[11] Mellat-parast M,Digman L A. A framework for quality managment practices in stategic alliances [J]. Management Decision,2007,45(4):802-818.

[12] Pastrnack B A. Optimal pricing and returns policies for perishable commodities[J]. Marketing Science,1985,4:166-176

[13] Simchi-Levi D,Wu D,Shen,Z M. Handbook of Quantiative Supply Chain Analysis:Modeling in the E Business Era International Series in Operations Resesarch and Management science[M]. Norwell: Kluwer Acabemic Publishers,2004.

[14] Tsay A A,Agrawal N. Channel dynamics under price and service competition. Maunfacturing and Service Operations Management ,2000,2(4):372-391.

[15] Zhu K,Zhang R Q, Tsung F. Pshing quality inprovement along supply chains[J]. Management Science,2007,53(3):421-436.

供应链中基于货架空间分配的质量改进策略研究*

鲁其辉，朱道立

（复旦大学管理学院，上海，200433）

摘要： 本文考虑一个包含两个竞争的制造商和一个共同的零售商的供应链模型，制造商提供的产品是紧密可替代的，最终消费者对每个产品的需求与市场中产品的质量差异和该产品的货架空间相关。文中分析指出零售商的最优货架空间分配策略是使货架空间的比值等于产品在零售商总收益中的比值。文中研究供应链中的三种情况. 在无质量改进的情况中，文中分析产品的货架空间和市场需求与产品的潜在需求、边际收益和货架空间弹性系数的关系。在单方质量改进的情况中，分析指出产品的最优质量改进水平和货架空间随着产品的潜在需求优势增大而提高。在同时质量改进的竞争均衡中，主要结论指出，当市场需求对质量差异的反应或者货架空间弹性系数越大，质量竞争的激烈程度提高，且制造商将采用更高质量水平；零售商和有质量改进成本优势的制造商将从质量竞争受益；质量成本劣势的制造商和整个供应链在质量竞争中受损；消费者将从质量竞争中获益。

关键词： 市场竞争；顾客价值；供应链；协调；价格竞争

中图分类号： F253

0　引　言

市场需求是产品及其制造商生存和发展的关键，如何在日趋激烈的竞争环境中得到更大的市场需求，成为企业管理者最为关注的问题之一。企业为获得更大的市场需求而采用的策略是多种多样的，如，价格、质量、服务水平、广告、品牌等等，其中质量策略是最重要也是最容易打败竞争对手的策略，譬如说，在二十世纪的七十至九十年代这一时期，西方激烈的市场竞争中，欧洲和美国在很多制造产业中，如汽车、半导体、电子消费品，失去了很多市场份额给日本的制造业，其中最重要的一个原因就是日本企业能提供更优质可靠的产品（Banker et al.，1998）。当前，全球化和网络时代的来临，使市场竞争的激烈程度不断提高，在竞争环境中正确的分析产品的市场状态并设定恰当的质量策略是管理者必须考虑的关键问题。

在供应链这种多层分散式的系统结构中，每个成员都有各自的收益和风险，且拥有相应的决策手段，这些决策将影响到所有供应链成员的收益和风险。货架空间作为零售商

* 基金项目：国家自然科学基金资助项目（70432001）。

作者简介：鲁其辉（1977～），男，湖南益阳人，复旦大学管理学院博士后。

的一项稀缺资源，零售对货架空间的分配是其最重要的一个决策，这项决策不仅影响到自身的收益，而且通过影响市场需求状态来影响制造商的收益及其决策(Amrouche & Zaccour，2006)。同样，制造商的质量策略不仅影响竞争制造商的质量策略，而且通过影响市场需求状态来影响零售商的货架空间决策。因而，市场中每个产品的需求不仅与所有产品的质量相关，而且与零售商分配给产品的货架空间相关(Wang & Gerchak，2001)。在分散型的供应链结构中，零售商具有激励将更多的货架空间分配给更大收益的产品，同样制造商也具有改进产品的质量而获得更大的货架空间的激励(Desmet & Renaudin，1998)。

在竞争环境中分析质量改进策略是所关注本文的主要问题。在两层供应链模型中，本文将首先从零售商的角度，分析货架空间的最优决策问题，然后基于零售商的货架空间决策来分析制造商的质量改进策略，在无质量改进的情况下，分析货架空间和市场需求与产品的基本需求和边际收益的关系；在单方质量改进的情况下，分析质量改进决策与产品的市场状态和产品对制造商的边际收益的关系；在同时质量竞争的情况下，研究竞争均衡的性质，并分析产业中市场需求的变化情况和供应链成员的收益变化情况。

许多科研工作者在不同的供应链环境从不同的角度分析质量竞争问题，研究过程中市场需求结构和质量成本结构是研究的基本出发点。Moorthy(1988)在研究制造商的价格和质量竞争问题时，首次考虑了产品的单位生产费用与产品质量水平相关的情况，分析结果指出企业的竞争质量策略是每个企业都将提供区别于竞争对手的质量水平，分析得到的结果很好地解释了提供高质量产品的企业也得到高的边际收益的现象。Chambers et al.(2006)考虑了两阶段的价格和质量竞争问题，文中考虑了一类广义的与质量水平相关的可变单位生产成本函数，文中指出生产成本函数的形式对质量竞争均衡、企业收益和市场覆盖度有巨大的影响。Banker et al.(1998)不仅考虑了质量提高策略的固定成本，还考虑了与质量水平线性相关的单位生产成本，在三类质量竞争的环境中，分析均衡质量水平与市场竞争的激烈程度之间的关系。在本文中，将考虑产品的市场需求与所有产品的质量和产品的基本需求及货架空间相关，这种结构与市场竞争的现实状态一致，文中将考虑的质量成本中仅包含单位质量提高成本，不考虑可变单位生产成本。

货架空间分配问题是市场营销与运营管理研究工作者关注的热点问题之一，以往的研究工作大致可以分为三类。第一类研究集中于使用市场实际数据来估计货架空间的弹性系数(见文 Desmet & Renaudin，1998 和文中的文献回顾)。第二类研究工作集中于建立关于零售商的利润的货架空间分配模型并构建有效的算法进行求解(见文 Bookbinder & Zarour，2001 和文中的文献回顾)。第三类文献在两层供应链模型中，考虑制造商与零售之间关于货架空间和价格的博弈。Amrouche & Zaccour(2006)考虑零售商控制了货架空间分配和零售商自有品牌(Private Labels)的零售价格，而制造商控制了制造商品牌的批发价格，通过分析 Stackelberg 均衡模型，文中指出货架空间分配均衡解与自有品牌的需求基础密切相关。MarÍn—Herrán et al.(2006)分析了两个关于价格竞争的制造商和一个零售商(控制产品的销售价格和货架空间)的两层供应链竞争模型，文中考虑了市场需求与货架空间的弹性系数和交叉弹性系数相关的情况，指出制造商的批发价格均衡解对货架空间分配有强烈影响。这种在两层供应链结构中，考虑零售商的货架空间的决策对制造商的竞争均衡的影响的分析，为本文在基于货架空间决策的质量竞争均衡的分析提供了有益的参考。

1 供应链竞争模型

本文考虑一个两层供应链模型，包含两个竞争的制造商与一个共同的零售商，基本结构如图1所示。两个制造商(记为 $i,j\in\{1,2\},i\neq j$)以批发价格 w_i,w_j 向零售商提供相似产品，两个产品属于同一个产品类别且是可替代的。制造商 i 控制产品 i 的质量水平 q_i，假定质量水平是可测的且 $q_i\geqslant 0$。零售商仅有固定的货架空间用来分配给这两个产品，记分配给产品 i 的货架空间(这里指百分比率)为 s_i，则产品 j 的货架空间为 $s_j=1-s_j$。由于货架空间的分配费用往往是一个常数且在同类产品中几乎相同，因此这里不失一般性的假设货架空间的分配费用为零。产品 i 的零售价格为 p_i，且是一个由外部市场所决定的常数。一般的，假设 $p_i>w_i,i=1,2$。

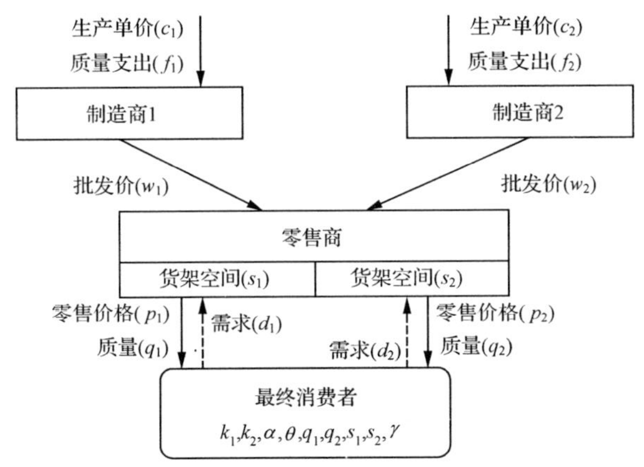

图1 供应链竞争模型

Figure 1. Supply Chain Competition Model.

扩展文献 Amrouche & Zaccour(2006)，Banker et al. (1998)和 Martín-Herrán et al. (2006)中与货架空间相关的需求模型，这里假定产品的需求与所有产品的质量和产品所获得的货架空间相关，令市场考虑需求函数为，

$$d_i(q_i,q_j,s_i)=(k_1\alpha+\theta(q_i-q_j))s_i^{\gamma},\quad i,j=1,2,i\neq j, \tag{1}$$

其中，α,k_i,θ 是正常数，且 $k_1+k_2=1$。

考虑到当 $q_j=0$ 时，当满足 $d_j>0$ 必须使 $k_j\alpha-\theta q_i>0$ 成立，即 $q_i<q_{i1}$，其中 $q_{i1}=\dfrac{k_j\alpha}{\theta}$，$(i,j=1,2,i\neq j)$。而由于生产条件或者技术的限制，制造商 i 的质量提高水平有一个极限值，设为 q_{i2}。那么，对质量水平作以下假设，

$$q_i\in[0,q_i^0],\quad q_i^0=\min\{q_{i1},q_{i2}\},\quad i=1,2 \tag{2}$$

市场需求函数关于产品的特征为线性的形式被许多研究者采纳，例如，Banker et al. (1998)，Tsay and Agrawal(2000) and Bernstein and Federguren(2004)。这种线性模型有利于分析解的性质。产品的需求函数中 $k_i\alpha+\theta(q_i-q_j)$ 表示产品的“基本需求”，参数 θ

表示市场需求对质量差异的反应。注意到两个产品的基本需求之和为常数 α，这种需求方式反映了产品的紧密可替代性。在研究中经常采用这种需求模式，例如，Tsay & Agrawal(2000)在考虑服务水平竞争时考虑了零售商的服务水平的差异对消费者需求的影响。

参数 $k_i\alpha$ 是产品 i 的潜在初始需求参数，表示在两个制造商设定的质量提高水平为 0 的情况下产品 i 的潜在需求。潜在初始需求良 $k_i\alpha$ 反映了制造商的品牌影响力、产品的基本质量水平和广告促销力度等等对产品需求的影响。不同的参数值 k_i，k_j 也从一定程度上解释了产品的相对竞争优势。本文考虑的产品质量水平是指从基本质量水平基础上的增加值，相应的支出是指为获得期望的质量水平而付出的额外费用，包括因原材料质量提高、生产工艺改进和管理水平提高等需要增加的费用。

参数 γ 是两个产品的货架空间弹性系数，相同的参数值反映了两个产品的紧密可替代性。Desmet & Renaudin(1998)通过实证分析指出，货架空间弹性系数对于不同的产品品类来说差异很大，但是绝大多数消费者产品的货架空间弹性系数是大于 0 小于 1 的，因此本文这里假设 $0<\gamma<1$。Martín-Herrán et al.(2006)在分析货架空间与产品价格竞争中采用了相同的假设。

设制造商的支出与单位生产成本及产品质量水平的提高相关，令支出函数为

$$V_i(d_i,q_i)=c_id_i+\frac{f_i}{2}q_i^2,\quad i=1,2 \tag{3}$$

其中，c_i 为单位生产成本，$f_i>0,i=1,2$。

制造商 i 的质量改进成本$\frac{f_i}{2}q_i^2$ 表明质量成本有边际收益递减的性质。Banker et al.(1998)在单层供应链模型中分析质量竞争问题时，不仅考虑了因质量提高引起的费用 $F_i(q_i)=f+\phi_iq_i^2$，而且考虑了质量水平对生产成本的影响 $c_id_i=(v+\varepsilon q_i)d_i$($\varepsilon$ 不一定为正)，这种模型有利于分析单位生产成本可变的管理问题。但由于模型变得很复杂，本文这里将不采用这种形式。Lehmann-Grube(1997)在分析基于价格竞争的质量选择模型中，不考虑质量提高的固定成本，仅考虑了质量的可变成本。

2 货架空间分配

供应链系统中的质量竞争与货架空间分配的时间发生顺序为：(i)首先两个制造商选择各自产品的质量水平，(ii)两个制造商和零售商了解到所有产品的质量水平，(iii)然后零售商分配不同的货架空间给两个产品，(iv)最后基于产品质量和货架空间，市场中消费者需求得以实现。这个模型与管理实践相一致，反映了货架空间分配晚于产品质量决策。下面将在分析质量竞争之前首先分析零售商的货架空间分配问题。

零售商的最优货架分配问题为 $\max\Pi_R(s_1,s_2)=\sum_{i=1}^{2}(p_i-w_i)d_i$。由于 $s_2=1-s_1$，那么零售商的利润函数为

$$\Pi_R(s_1)=(p_1-w_1)(k_1\alpha+\theta(q_1-q_2))s_1^{\gamma}+(p_2-w_2)(k_2a+\theta(q_2-q_1))(1-s_1)^{\gamma}$$

其一阶最优化条件为

$$\frac{d\Pi_k(s_1)}{ds_1}=(p_1-w_1)(k_1\alpha+\theta(q_1-q_2))\gamma s_1^{\gamma-1}$$

$$-(p_2-w_2)(k_2\alpha+\theta(q_2-q_1))\gamma(1-s_1)^{\gamma-1}=0$$

因为 $\gamma-1<0$，则

$$\frac{d^2\Pi_k(s_1)}{ds_1^2}=(p_1-w_1)(k_1\alpha+\theta(q_1-q_2))\gamma(\gamma-1)s_1^{\gamma-2}$$
$$+(p_2-w_2)(k_2\alpha+\theta(q_2-q_1))\gamma(\gamma-1)(1-s_1)^{\gamma-2}<0$$

那么一阶条件的解是最优解。记

$$\Psi_i=\frac{(p_j-w_j)(k_j\alpha+\theta(q_j-q_i))}{(p_i-w_i)(k_i\alpha+\theta(q_i-q_j))},\quad i,j=1,2,i\neq j,\qquad \delta=\frac{1}{\gamma-1}$$

最优货架空间解为

$$s_i^*=\frac{\Psi_i^\delta}{1+\Psi_i^\delta},i=1,2 \tag{4}$$

记 $d_i^*=d_i(q_i,q_j,s_i^*)$，$\Pi_R^*=\Pi(s_1^*,s_2^*,q_1^*,q_2^*)$。下面分析最优货架空间分配的性质。

命题 1　产品的货架空间之比等于产品对于零售商的收益之比，i. e.

$$\frac{s_1^*}{s_2^*}=\frac{(p_1-w_1)d_1^*}{(p_2-w_2)d_2^*} \tag{5}$$

证明　由方程(4)可知，$\frac{s_1^*}{s_2^*}=\Psi_1^\delta$。又因为

$$\frac{(p_1-w_i)d_1^*}{(p_2-w_2)d_2^*}=\frac{1}{\Psi_1}\left(\frac{s_1^*}{s_2^*}\right)^\gamma$$
$$=\frac{1}{\Psi_1}\Psi_1^{(\delta\cdot\gamma)}=\Psi^{(\delta\cdot\gamma-1)}=\Psi_1^\delta$$

则命题成立。口

由(5)容易得到，

$$s_i^*=\frac{(p_i-w_i)d_i^*}{\sum_{i=1}^2(p_i-w_1)d_i^*} \tag{6}$$

上式说明了产品的最优货架空间为产品的收益在零售商总收益中的比率。

由(5)和(6)可知，零售商分配给两个产品的货架空间不仅与产品的市场需求相关，而且与产品的边际收益相关，这一点说明了为什么实践中常常采用这种货架空间分配方式，譬如，在零售商分配货架空间给自有品牌(Pribate Labels)和供应商品牌(National Brand)过程中，零售商往往不是按通常的做法分配最大的货架空间给需求量最大的供应商品牌产品，而是分配相对多的货架空间给需求量小而边际收益大的自有品牌(Amrouche & Zaccour 2006)。

这里有

$$\frac{\partial\Psi_i}{\partial q_i}=-\frac{\partial\Psi_i}{\partial q_j}=-\frac{p_j-w_j}{p_j-w_j}\cdot\frac{\theta\alpha}{(k_i\alpha+\theta(q_i-q_j))^2}$$

则有，$\frac{\partial\Psi_i}{\partial q_j}<0$，$\frac{\partial\Psi_i}{\partial q_i}>0$，那么 $s_i^*(q_i,q_j)$ 的偏导数有以下性质：

$$\frac{\partial s_i^*(q_i,q_j)}{\partial q_i}=\frac{\delta\Psi_i^{\delta-1}}{(1+\Psi_i^\delta)^2}\frac{\partial\Psi_i}{\partial q_i}>0,\qquad \frac{\partial s_i^*(q_i,q_j)}{\partial q_j}=\frac{\delta\Psi_i^{\delta-1}}{(1+\Psi_i^\delta)^2}\frac{\partial\Psi_i}{\partial q_j}<0$$

而且显然有 $\frac{\partial d_i}{\partial q_i}>$，$\frac{\partial d_i}{\partial q_j}<0$。这些性质说明了，每个产品的货架空间和市场需求关于自身产品的质量水平增函数，关于竞争对手的质量水平为减函数，这个结果反映了制造商有动机提高质量水平，以得到更多的货架空间和市场需求。

3 质量改进策略研究

分析了零售商的货架空间分配决策，现在开始分析制造商质量策略问题。制造商 i 选择质量改进水平 q_i 通过最大化下列利润函数：

$$\Pi_{Mi}=(w_i-c_i)d_i^*-\frac{f_i}{2}q_i^2$$

$$=(w_i-c_i)(k_i\alpha+\theta(q_i-q_j))\left(\frac{\Psi_i^\delta}{1+\Psi_i^\delta}\right)^\gamma-\frac{f_i}{2}q_i^2,\quad i,j=1,2,i\neq j \tag{7}$$

制造商的利润函数是一个复杂的非线性函数，下面首先通过一个数值分析来得到求解单个制造商的最优策略的方法。

例 1 令两个产品的潜在基本需求的参数值为 $\alpha=2000$，$k_1=0.4$，$k_2=0.6$，其他需求参数值为 $\theta=12$，$\gamma=0.2$。支出参数值为 $c_1=10$，$c_2=12$，$\omega_1=15$，$\omega_2=17$，$f_1=2$，$f_2=5$。零售价格为 $p_1=20$，$p_2=22$。令质量水平的最大限为 $q_{12}=40$，$q_{22}=50$。为了分析货架空间和制造商利润与产品质量的关系，这里固定产品 2 的质量水平为 $q_2=0$，且使产品 1 的质量水平在 $[0,q_1^0)$ 中变化。图 2 给出了制造商的利润和产品的货架空间与产品 1 的质量水平的关系。

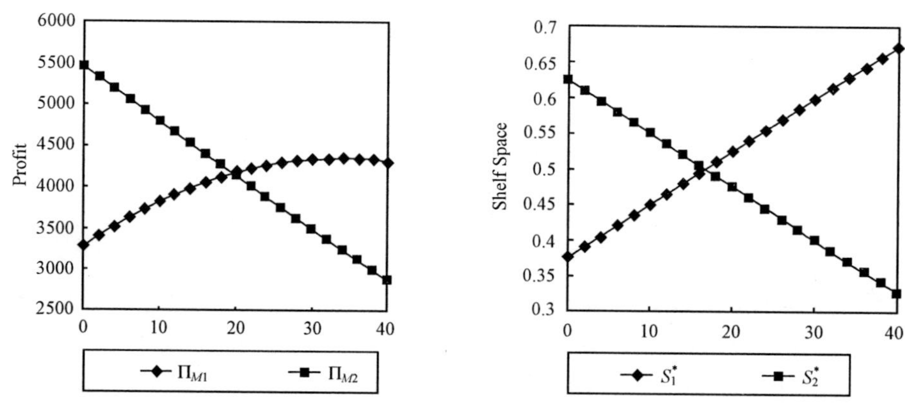

图 2 制造商利润和货架空间图

Figure 2 Graph of the two Manufactures' Profits and Shelf Space Allocation

当 $f_1=1.7$，$q_2=0$ 时，制造商 1 的利润函数在 $[0,40)$ 中满足 $\frac{\partial\Pi_{M1}(q_1,q_2)}{\partial q_1}>0$，那么这时制造商 1 的最优质量水平为 $q_1^*\approx 40$，相应的货架空间为 $s=0.672$。

当 $f_1=2$，$q_2=20$ 时，制造商 1 的利润函数在 $(0,40)$ 中存在一个最优解 $\bar{q}_1=34$ 使 $\frac{\partial\Pi}{\partial q_i}=0$，那么这时制造商 1 的最优质量水平为 $q_1^*=34$，相应的货架空间为 $s_1^*=0.614$。

从例 1 可以看到，对于给定的 q_j，为求解最优的质量水平 $q_i^*(q_j)$，必须首先在 $(0,q_i^0)$

中分析$\frac{\partial \Pi_{M1}(q_1,q_2)}{\partial q_1}=0$，的符号，若$\frac{\partial \Pi_{Mi}}{\partial q_i}$总大于零，则 $q_i^*(q_j)=q_i^0-\varepsilon$，其中 ε 表示一非常小的正数；若存在一个 $\bar{q}_i$ 使 $\frac{\partial \Pi_{Mi}}{\partial q_1}=0$ 且 Π_{Mi} 达到最大值，则 $q_i^*(q_j)=q_i^*$总之最优质量水平解为

$$q_i^*(q_j)=\begin{cases} q_i^0-\varepsilon, & \text{如果，} \frac{\partial \Pi_{Mi}(q_i,q_j)}{\partial q_i}>0, \forall q_i \in (0,q_i^0), \\ \bar{q}_i, & \text{否则。} \end{cases} \tag{8}$$

制造商的最优化问题的一阶导数为

$$\frac{\partial \Pi_{Mi}}{\partial q_i}=(w_i-c_i)\left[(k_i a+\theta(q_i-q_j))\gamma(s_i^*)^{\gamma-1}\frac{\partial s_i^*}{\partial q_i}+\theta(s_i^*)^{\gamma}\right]-f_i q_i \tag{9}$$

二阶导数为

$$\frac{\partial^2 \Pi_{Mi}}{\partial q_i^2}=(w_i-c_i)\gamma(s_i^*)^{\gamma-2}$$

$$\left[2\theta s_i^*\frac{\partial s_i^*}{\partial q_i}+(k_i\alpha+\theta(q_i-q_j))\left((\gamma-1)(s_i^*)^2+\frac{\partial^2 s_i^*}{s_i^*\partial q_i^2}\right)\right]-f_i \tag{10}$$

以上方程高度非线性，不可能得到分析解。但对于给定的质量水平 q_j，制造商 i 的目标函数 $\Pi_{Mi}(q_i)$是一个单变量的连续函数，容易用一维搜索方法求解(9)的零解而得到解 $\bar{q}_i$，从而得到最优解。

因为$\Pi_{Mi}(q_i,q_j)$是连续函数，则易知 $q_i^*(q_j)$也必定是连续的，那么可以采用迭代求解 q_1^*, q_2^*来得到均衡解$(\hat{q}_1,\hat{q}_2)$。对于示例 1，图 4 给出了反应函数 $q_1^*(q_2), q_2^*(q_1)$的关系图。容易得到制造商的均衡质量水平为$(\hat{q}_1,\hat{q}_2)=(32.89, 12.95)$。

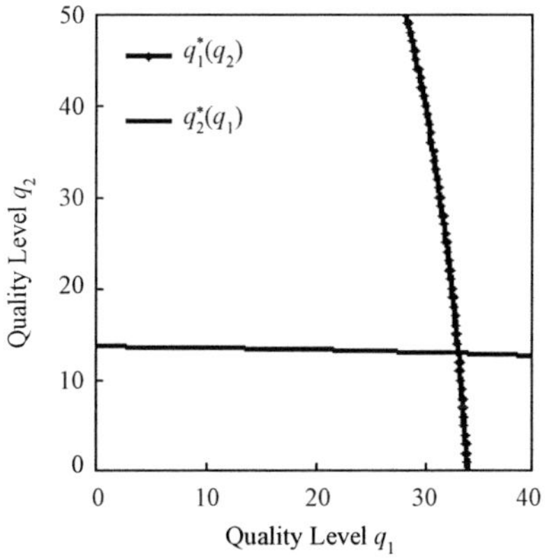

图 3 最优质量反应函数图

Figure 3 Graph of the Optimal Quality Reaction Function.

4 数值分析与管理借鉴

4.1 无质量改进情况下的货架空间分配

这里考虑两个制造商均未采用质量改进策略的基本情况，即 $q_1=q_2=0$，将主要分析产品的货架空间和市场需求与产品的基本需求参数 k_i、弹性系数 γ 和边际收益 p_i-w_i 的关系。下面考虑两种特殊情况。首先考虑边际收益相等的情况，即 $p_1=w_1=p_2=w_2$，那么有 $\Psi_i=\frac{k_j}{k_i}$，则

$$s_i^*=\frac{k_j^\delta}{k_i^\delta+k_j^\delta}, \quad d_i^*=k_i\alpha(s_i^*)^\gamma, \quad i=1,2,i\neq j$$

易知

$$\frac{\partial s_i^*}{\partial k_i}=-\delta\frac{(k_ik_j)^{\delta-1}}{(k_i^\delta+k_j^\delta)^2}>0,\quad \frac{\partial d_i^*}{\partial k_i}=\alpha(s_i^*)^\gamma+k_i\alpha\gamma(s_i^*)^{\gamma-1}\frac{\partial s_i^*}{\partial k_i}>0$$

$$\frac{\partial s_i^*}{\partial \gamma}=-\frac{1}{(\gamma-1)^2}\frac{(k_ik_j)^\delta}{(k_i^\delta+k_j^\delta)^2}\ln\frac{k_j}{k_i}$$

那么容易得到：当 $k_i<1/2$ 时，$\frac{\partial s_i^*}{\partial \gamma}<0$；$\frac{\partial s_i^*}{\partial \gamma}<0$，当 $k_i>1/2$ 时，$\frac{\partial s_i^*}{\partial \gamma}>0$，$\frac{\partial d_i^*}{\partial \gamma}>0$。当 $k_i=1/2$ 时，对任意的 γ 都有 $s_1=s_2$，$d_1=d_2$。

因此，在这种情况中，当产品 i 的潜在需求增加时(即 k_i 增大)，产品 i 的货架空间和市场需求增加. 而且当 k_i<l/2 时，货架空间的弹性系数越大，产品 i 的货架空间和市场需求越小；当机>l/2 时，货架空间的弹性系数越大，产品 i 的货架空间和市场需求越大。

下面考虑 $k_1=k_2=1/2$ 的特殊情况，这里有 $\Psi_i\frac{p_j-w_j}{p_i-w_i}$，且

$$s_i^*=\frac{(p_j-w_j)^\delta}{(p_1-w_1)^\delta+(p_2-w_2)^\delta},\quad d_i=1/2\alpha(s_i^*)^\gamma,\quad i=1,2,i\neq j$$

下面用一个示例来说明货架空间与参数的关系。

例 2 这里保持参数 p_2，w_2 不变，考虑 p_1-w_1 的变化对货架空间和市场需求的影响，Ψ_i 的值反映了产品边际收益之间的关系。考虑三种货架空间弹性系数情况，$\gamma\in\{0.2,0.4,0.6\}$。图 4 给出了货架空间与参数 Ψ_1 和 γ 的关系。

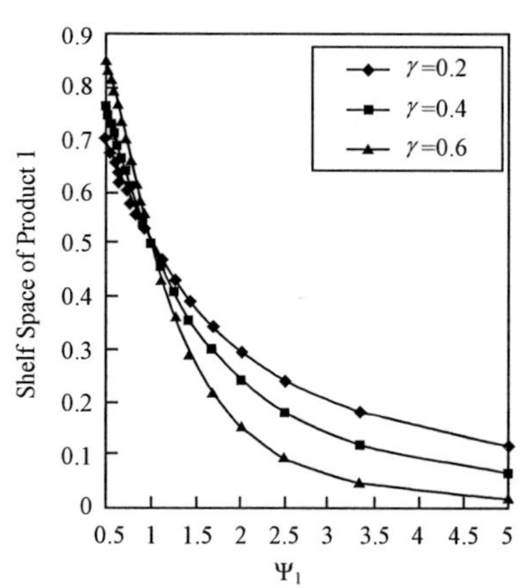

图 4 货架空间与 Ψ_1 和 γ 的关系图

Figure 4 The Relation of Shelf-space withΨ_1 and γ.

在这种特殊情况中，当 $\Psi_1=1$ 时，对任意的 γ 都有 $s_1^*=s_2^*$，$d_1^*=d_2^*$。由图 4 所示，当产品 1 的边际收益相对于产品 2 的边际收益越大时(即 Ψ_1 越小)，产品 1 的货架空间越大。而当 $p_1-w_1>p_2-w_2$ 时(即 $\Psi_1<1$ 时)，若货架空间的弹性系数越大，产品 1 的货架空间越大；当 $p_1-w_1<p_2-w_2$ 时(即 $\Psi_1>1$ 时)，若货架空间的弹性系数越大，产品 1 的货架空间越小。同样，可以说明产品 1 的市场需求与 Ψ_1 和 γ 关系与以上规律相类似。

4.2 单方质量改进策略分析

在供应链中，质量改进策略是一个提高产品的需求，进而提高产品的货架空间及制造商利润的常用方法。Amrouche & Zaccour(2006)在分析供应商如何应对零售商引入自有品牌时，指出通过创新、广告和促销等手段提升供应商品牌产品的消费者认知的质量水平，是一种有效应对自有品牌的策略。

考虑一种单方质量改进的特殊情况，制造商 1 具有潜在需求优势，即 $k_1>k_2$，而在边际收益方面处于劣势，即 $p_1-w_1<p_2-w_2$。下面通过一个示例来分析制造商通过质量改进后，产品 1 的货架空间及市场需求的变化情况。

例 3 考虑例 1 中同样的参数，并在保持参数 p_1, p_2, w_2 不变的条件下考虑 $t_1 = \frac{p_1 - w_1}{p_2 - w_2} \in \{1/4, 1/2, 3/4\}$ 三种情况下。图 5 给出了当 $q_2 = 0$ 时最优质量改进 q_1^* 及货架空间 s_1^* 与参数 k_1 和 t_1 的关系。

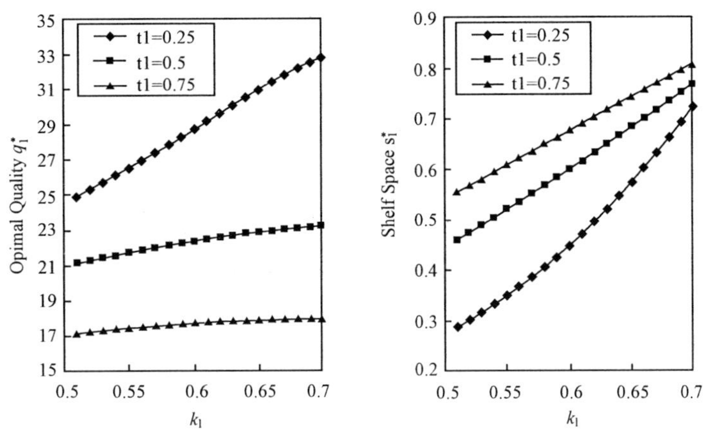

图 5 质量改进和货架空间与 k_1 和 t_1 的关系图

Figure 5 The Relation of Quality lmprovement and Shelf－space with k_1 and t_1

由图 5 可以看出，对于相同的 t_1 值，当产品 1 的内在需求优势越大时(即 k_1 增大)，产品 1 的最优质量改进水平和货架空间越大。这一点说明了，产品在市场中的地位越高，获得的货架空间越大，而能提高的质量改进的程度也随之增大，那么企业在质量改进活动中的一个最重要的管理原则就是首先要提高产品的潜在顾客需求。

对于相同的 k_1，当产品 1 的边际收益相对于产品 2 的边际收益越大(即 t_1 越大)时，产品 1 的货架空间 s_1^* 越大，但是产品 1 的最优质量改进水平 q_1^* 越小。质量水平 q_1^* 出现这种变化规律的内在原因是：在例 3 这种特殊情况中，当 t_1 越大时，制造商 1 从产品 1 所获得的边际收益 $w_1 - c_1$ 越小(因 w 越小)，那么由(9)可知，满足 $\frac{\partial \Pi_{Mi}}{\partial q_i} = 0$ 的解越小，则 q_1^* 也越小。

4.3 同时质量改进竞争均衡分析

在两个制造商同时采用质量改进策略的情况中，下面分析主要影响因素 θ 和 γ 对供应链中质量均衡解的影响。由于没有分析解，下面通过示例的分析来发现一些变化规律。

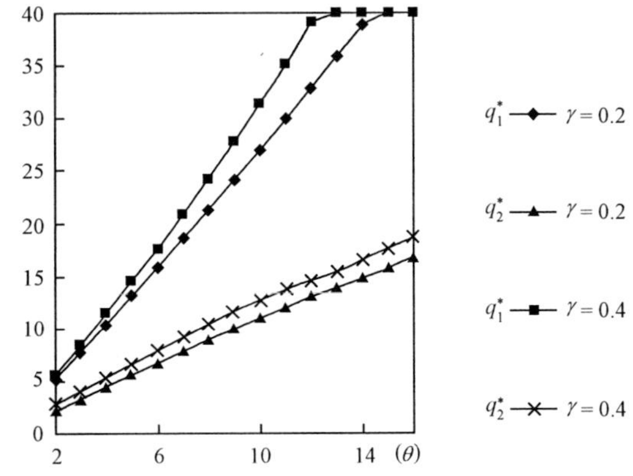

图 6 质量均衡与 θ 和 γ 的关系图

Figure 6 Relationship of Quality Equlibria with θ and γ.

例 4 考虑例 1 中的参数，但使参数 θ 在[2,16]中变化，γ 在{0.2,0.4}中取值。图 6 给出了质量均衡(q_1^*, q_2^*)与

参数 θ 和 γ 的变化关系。

由图 6 可以看出，当市场需求对质量差异的反应(即 θ)越大时，市场竞争的两个制造商都将采用更大的质量改进水平，当货架空间的弹性系数(即 γ)越大时，质量均衡水平也越大，并且由 q_1^*对 γ 的变化规律可以发现，当 γ 越大时，质量水平 q_1^*越容易达到质量改进水平的最大极限 q_1^0。

下面分析在均衡情况中货架空间、制造商利润、零售商利润和供应链的总利润与 θ 和 γ 的关系。下面表 1 给出了当 $\gamma\in\{0.2,0.4\}$时，在质量改进竞争均衡情况中，供应链中的货架空间分配和利润的比较情况。

表 1　货架空间和收益与 θ 和 γ 的变化关系

Table 1. Changes of Shelf Spaces and Profits with θ and γ

θ	$\gamma=0.2$					$\gamma=0.4$				
	s_1^*	Π_{M1}^*	Π_{M2}^*	Π_R^*	π_{scm}^*	s_1^*	Π_{M1}^*	Π_{M2}^*	Π_R^*	π_{scm}^*
2	0.380	3293	5414	8238	16 946	0.342	2591	5033	6510	14 133
4	0.391	3304	5276	8286	16 866	0.356	2598	4857	6619	14 074
6	0.409	3325	5043	8365	16 732	0.383	2614	4550	6813	13 978
8	0.437	3358	4709	8475	16 542	0.426	2649	4094	7106	13 849
10	0.475	3409	4270	8617	16 295	0.489	2722	3468	7514	13 703
12	0.525	3486	3721	8789	15 995	0.579	2874	2678	8036	13 588
14	0.587	3600	3061	8989	15 650	0.606	3017	2319	8184	13 519
16	0.607	3707	2733	9051	15 491	0.615	3091	2055	8233	13 379

在无质量改进的情况中：当 $\gamma=0.2$ 时，产品 1 的货架空间为 $s_1^0=0.376$，制造商利润为 $\Pi_{M1}^0=3289$，$\Pi_{M2}^0=5460$，零售商利润为 $\Pi_R^0=8223$，供应链的总利润 $\Pi_{scm}^0=16\ 972$；当 $\gamma=0.4$ 时，$s_1^0=0.337$，$\Pi_{M1}^0=2589$，$\Pi_{M2}^0=5089$，$\Pi_R^0=6474$，$\Pi_{scm}^0=14\ 152$。与表 1 相比较，可以看出在无质量竞争情况中供应链成员的利润要大于质量竞争情况中的利润。

由表 1 可以看出，当市场需求对质量差异的反应越大时，制造商之间关于质量的竞争越激烈，两个制造商都将采用更高的质量水平。由于在例 4 中，制造商 1 具有质量改进的优势(即 $f_1<f_2$)，可以看出，当 θ 越大，制造商 1 在质量竞争中获益更多，将不仅得到更多的货架空间，而且得到更大的利润，但制造商 2 在质量竞争中受损，将失去更多的货架空间和得到更少的利润。由于零售商将更大的货架空间转移给市场竞争力增大的产品 1，零售商将获得更大的利润。从整个供应链系统来说，当质量竞争的激烈程度提高时，系统的总利润 Π_{scm}^*下降，但从另一个方面来说，消费者从质量竞争中获益。从表 1 和图 6 可以看出，当 γ 越大时，制造商之间的质量竞争激烈程度也越大，在制造商提供更高的质量水平的同时，使供应链中所有成员的利润降低，那么同时也可以看到当质量竞争的激烈程度越高消费者获益更多。

5　结　论

在当前竞争的激烈程度不断提高的市场环境中，采用提高产品的质量来提高产品的市场需求和打败竞争对手是一种保持企业竞争力的重要手段。本文通过建立一个两层供应链模型来分析零售商的货架空间分配和制造商的质量改进竞争问题，模型中包括两个竞争的制造商和一个零售商。市场中最终消费者对每个产品的需求与市场中产品的质量差异和该产品的货架空间相关。零售商具有激励将更多的货架空间分配给更大收益的产品，文中分析指出当货架空间的比值等于产品在零售商总收益中的比值时，零售商的货架空间分配策略达到最优。

文中主要分析了供应链中质量改进的三种情况：无质量改进情况、单方质量改进情况和同时质量改进竞争情况。主要分析指出，在单方质量改进的情况中，若产品的潜在需求优势增大，那么产品的最优质量改进水平和货架空间提高。在同时质量改进的竞争均衡中，质量竞争的激烈程度和制造商采用的质量水平将随着市场需求对质量差异的反应或者货架空间弹性系数的增加而提高。对于零售商、消费者和有质量改进成本优势的制造商来说，质量竞争都将使之受益；而对于质量成本劣势的制造商和整个供应链来说，质量竞争将使之受损。

在本文中仅考虑了两个制造商的情形，在包含多个制造商的竞争中分析制造商的竞争策略和供应链竞争均衡，并分析产业中质量变化情况是一个有意义的研究方向。如果在供应链的上下游中，供应链成员通过合作和共享质量改进成本来提高产品的质量，分析合作策略的设计和竞争均衡的性质也是一个很有意义的研究课题。

Strategies of Quality Improvement in Supply Chains Based on Shelf Space Allocation

L U Qihui , ZHU Daoli

School of Management, Fudan University, Shanghai 200433, China

Abstract: This paper considers a supply chain with two competing manufacturers and a common retailer. The products provided by the two manufacturers are close substitutable. The market demand of each product is based on the deference of quality levels of products and shelf space of each product. The analysis shows that the retailer's optimal strategy of shelf space allocation is satisfying that the ratio of products' respective shelf space is equal to the ratio of products' revenues. We consider three scenarios in the supply chain. In the scenario of non-quality-improvement, we investigate relations of shelf spaces and market demands to intrinsic demands, margin profits and the elasticity of shelf space. In the scenario of one-side quality-improvement, we show that, as product's intrinsic demand increases, the optimal levels of quality improvement and shelf spaces increase. In the scenario of simultaneous qualityimprovement, the main results indicate that, as the responsiveness of market demand to the deference of quality levels or the elasticity of shelf space increases, the intensity of quality competition increase and manufacturers adopt higher quality level. The retailer and the manufacturer with cost advantageous of quality-improvement will benefit from the quality-improvement competition, while the manufacturer with cost disadvantageous of quality-improvement and the whole supply chain will lose. The consumertition.

Keywords: Shelf-Space Allocation; Nash Equilibrium; Coordination; Jointly Decision; Retail Competition

参考文献

[1] Amrouche, N. , Zaccour, G. , 2006. Shelf-space allocation of national and private brands[J]. European Journal of Operational Research ,doi:10. 1016/j. ejor. 2006. 05. 008.

[2] Banker,R. D. ,Khosla,I,k. ,Sinha,K. ,1998. Quality and competition[J]. Management Science ,44 (9),1179-1192.

[3] Bernstein,F. ,Federguren,A. ,2004. A general equilibrium mobel for industries with price and service competition[J]. Operations Research,52(6),868-886.

[4] Bookbinder, J. H. , Zarour, F. H. , 2001. Direct product profitability and retail shelf-space allocation models[J]Journal of Business Logistics,22(2),183-208.

[5] Chambers,C. ,Kouvelis,P. ,Semple,J. ,2006. Quality-based competition ,profitability,and variable cost [J]. Management Science,52(12),1884-1895.

[6] Desmet,P. ,Renaudin,V. , 1998. Estimatin of product category sales responsiveness to allocated shelf space[J]. Inter. J. of Research in Marketing,15,443-457.

[7] Lehmann-Grube,U. ,1997. Strategic choice of quality when qualify is costly: the persistence of the highquality anvantage[J]. RAND Journal of Economics,28(2),372-384.

[8] Martín-Herrán,G. ,Taboubi,S. ,Zaccour,G. ,2006. The impact of manufacturers' wholesale prices on a retailer's shelf-space and pricing decisions[J]. Decision Sciences,37(1),71-90.

[9] Moorthy,S. K. ,1998. Product and price competition in a duopoly[J]. Marketing Science ,7,141-168.

[10] Tsay,A. A. ,Agrawal,N. ,2000. Channel dynamics under price and service competition[J]. Manufacturing and Service Operations Management ,2(4),372-384.

[11] Wang Y-Z. ,Gerchak, Y. ,2001. Supply chain coordination when demand is shelf-space dependent [J]. Manufacturing & Service Operations Management,3(1),82-87.

[12] 许明辉,于刚,张汉勤,2006.具备提供服务的供应链博弈分析[J].管理科学学报,9(2),18-27.

产品随机选择下多商品流供应链网络均衡模型研究

徐兵[1,2]，朱道立[2]

（1. 南昌大学 管理科学与工程系，南昌 330047；2. 复旦大学管理学院，上海 200433）

摘要：研究产品存在产地、品牌差异情况下，具有多种商品流动的三层供应链网络均衡模型．将产地、品牌差异的影响视为随机变量，运用随机效用理论和多项式 logit 模型研究需求市场上产品随机选择问题，运用 Nash 均衡方法分析生产商之间、零售商之间的竞争行为，分别得到了供应链网络各层均衡及整体均衡的条件、经济解释和变分不等式模型，最后给出了求解算法和具体算例．

关键词：供应链网络；Nash 均衡，随机选择；变分不等式

中图分类号：F224.1；C931.1　　　　**文献标志码：**A

1　引言

随着全球化竞争的加剧，被称为“企业第三利润源”的供应链管理越采越受到企业界和学术界的重视”。供应链通常由原材料供应商、生产商、批发商、零售商和需求市场等诸多参与者组成。由于同一个参与者可能同属于若干条供应链（如同时为不同供应链服务的多商品零售商），供应链整体表现为具有一定层次结构的复杂网络。供应链网络中，参与个体的利益经常不一致（甚至冲突），但又相互依赖和影响，主要表现于同一层次成员之间的竞争关系和上下层次成员之间的协调关系。如何刻画供应链网络结构及内部成员之间的竞争与协调关系，探求供应链网络达到均衡时的条件，显得尤为紧迫和重要。*

均衡模型在经济、金融、电信、供应链、交通等领域有着广泛运用，许多学者做了大量研究[2,3]。Nagurney 运用变分不等式技术，分析了供应链网络成员间的相互关系极其决策行为，建立了单一商品流供应链网络模型[4~6]，文献[7]进一步研究了多商品流供应链网络均衡模型。文献[8]运用多项式 logit 分析方法研究了存在产地、晶牌差异情况的跨区域市场均衡模型。跨区域市场均衡是在给定各供给区域的供给函数、各需求区域的需求函数以及区域间运输成本函数情况下，不同区域的产品供给和需求、区域间的运输达到

---

* 收稿日期：2005-12-27

资助项目：国家自然科学基金（70432001）；中国博士后基金（20060400584）

作者简介：徐兵（1972～），男，江西人，复旦大学管理学院博士后，南昌大学副教授，研究方向：运筹学、物流管理；朱道立（1945～），男，上海人，复旦大学管理学院教授，博士生导师．

的平衡，其本质为弹性供给与需求下实现产销平衡的运输问题。文献[9]研究了单个需求市场、一种类型、多种规格的产品随机选择情况下的均衡模型，但文献[8,9]并不是从供应链角度采研究。由若干生产商、零售商和需求市场组成的供应链网络，其均衡状态表现为供给市场达到生产商竞争均衡、零售市场达到零售商竞争均衡以及需求市场达到供需平衡。结合上述文献，本文对供应链网络均衡问题进行了进一步研究：1）文献[4～7]通过分别建立生产商、零售商的最优化模型得到供给市场和零售市场的均衡条件，本文运用Nash均衡方法分析生产商之间、零售商之间的竞争行为，得到了与之等价的市场均衡条件；2）文献[4～7]假定不同生产商生产的同种产品完全无差异，且消费者对同种产品的选择无差异，利用确定性交通均衡原理来刻画消费者的产品选择，从而建立需求市场均衡模型。这种假设不完全符合实际，产地差异、品牌差异及消费者偏好是影响需求市场上消费者选择产品的重要因素，例如青岛啤酒和燕京啤酒，尽管市场价格不同，但由于消费者的偏好不同，在同一市场上都有一定的销量。本文假定产品存在产地、品牌差异，并将其影响视为随机变量，与文献[8]类似，运用基于随机效用理论的logit模型来刻画消费者的产品选择，并进而建立了产品随机选择下需求市场均衡的变分模型。

本文第二部分运用Nash均衡方法分析了生产商之间、零售商之间的竞争行为，分别建立了供给市场均衡和零售市场均筷的变分不等式模型；运用随机选择模型分析了消费者的产品选择行为，并建立了需求市场均衡的变分不等式模型；最后建立了产品随机选择情况下存在产地、晶牌差异的多商品流供应链网络均衡模型。第三部分给出了计算方法和算例。第四部分给出了结论及进一步研究方向。

2 产品随机选择下多商品流供应链网络均衡模型的建立

2.1 问题描述

假定供应链网络由 I 个生产商、J 个零售商和 L 个需求市场组成，分别从事生产、销售和消费某 S 种产品，用 i,j,l,s 分别表示生产商 i、零售商 j、需求市场 l 和产品 s。假设不同生产商生产的同种产品是除了产地、品牌差异外的完全同质产品，生产商（零售商）之间进行非合作竞争。每个生产商均以利润最大化为目标，决定各产品的生产量和提供给各零售商的产品供给量，供给市场均衡表现为 I 个生产商之间由于相互竞争而达到的Nash均衡。每个零售商均以利润最大化为目标，决定对各生产商的产品订购量和提供给各需求市场的产品数量，零售市场均衡表现为 J 个零售商之间由于相互竞争而达到的Nash均衡。Nash均衡理论是分析经济领域和管理实践中非合作博弈问题的有效工具[10]。考虑 N 人非合作Nash均衡问题：设凸子集 $X_i \in R^{n_i}$ 是博弈者 i 的策略集，博弈者 i 的效用函数为 $u_i: X_i \to R$，其中 $X = X_1 \times X_2 \times \cdots \times X_N$. 记 $I = \{1,2,\cdots,N\}$，$x_{-i} = (x_1, x_{i-1}, x_{i+1}, \cdots, x_N)$，$x = (x_1,\cdots,x_N) = (x_{-i}, x_{-i})$，$X_{-i} = X_1 \times \cdots \times X_{i-1} \times X_{i+1} \cdots \times X_N$，$X = X_{-i} \times X_{-i}$.

定义1 点 $x^* =,(\cdots,X_N^*)$，称为Nash均衡点，如果下式成立

$$u_i(x_i^*, x_{-i}^*) \geqslant u_i(x^i, x_{-i}^*), \forall i, \forall_{xi} \in X_i. \tag{1}$$

引理1 设对任意的 $i \in I$，函数 u_i 在 X 上连续可微。若 $x^* = (x_1^*,\cdots,x_N^*)$ 为Nash均衡点，则 x^* 也是下列变分不等式的解

$$F(x^*)^{\mathrm{T}}(x-x^*)\geqslant 0,\forall x\in X, \tag{2}$$

其中，$F(x)=-\left(\frac{\partial u_1(x)}{\partial x_1},\cdots,\frac{\partial u_N(x)}{\partial x_N}\right)^{\mathrm{T}}$。进一步，设对任意的 $i\in I$ 和任意给定的 $x_{-i}\in X_{-i}$，函数 $u_{-i}(x_i,x_{-i})$ 关于 x_{-i} 是伪凹的，则(2)也是必要条件。

需求市场上，由于同一类产品存在产地、晶牌的差异，消费者面临多种可以完全替代的选择，消费者的主观偏好对产品选择具有重要影响，可用基于效用理论的随机选择模型来刻画。由于同种商品具有相同的用户功能，其总消费量受到消费能力的限制，需求市场均衡是一种总量需求约束下的供需平衡。假定生产商与零售商之间、零售商与需求市场之间的产品交易价格为内生变量，对应到市场出清价格。供应链网络均衡表现为供给市场、零售市场和需求市场同时达到均衡时的市场出清状态此时生产商与零售商分别达到产销平衡和购销平衡。

2.2　供给市场均衡变分模型的建立

设 q_i^s 表示生产商 i 生产产品 s 的数量，$q_i=(q_i^1,\cdots,q_i^s,\cdots,q_i^s)$ 表示生产商 i 的产品生产量向量，$q=(q_1,\cdots,q_i,\cdots q_I)$ 表示所有生产商的产品生产生量向量.假设由于原材料竞争关系，生产商 i 生产产品 s 的生产成本与其他厂商的产量有关，记为 $f_i^s(q)$. 设 q_{ij}^s，$p_{ij}^s,c_{ij}^s(q_{ij}^s)$ 分别表示生产商 i 与零售商 j 交易产品 s 的数量、价格和交易成本(含运输成本)。假设 $f_i^s(q),c_{ij}^s(q_{ij}^s)$ 为连续可微凸函数.记生产商 i 与各零售商之间的交易量向量为：$Q_i=(q_{i1}^1,\cdots q_{ij}^s,\cdots,q_{ij}^s)$，$I$ 个生产商与 J 个零售商之间的交易量向量为：$Q=(Q_1,\cdots,Q_i,\cdots,Q_I)$. 生产商 i 的利润函数为：

$$R_i(q,Q)=\sum_{j=1}^{J}\sum_{s=1}^{S}p_{ij}^s q_{ij}^s-\sum_{s=1}^{S}f_i^s(q)-\sum_{j=1}^{J}\sum_{s=1}^{S}c_{ij}^s(q_{ij}^s) \tag{3}$$

供给市场均衡表观为 I 个生产商之间相互竞争的 Nash 均衡，在均衡点生产商的生产量和销售量必须满足如下产销平衡条件(4)和非负约束(5).

$$q_i^s=\sum_{j=1}^{J}q_{ij}^s,\quad \forall i,s, \tag{4}$$

$$q_{ij}^s\geqslant 0,\qquad \forall i,j,s, \tag{5}$$

记 $\Omega_i=\left\{(q_i,Q_i)\mid q_i\geqslant 0,Q_i\geqslant 0,q_i^s=\sum_{j=1}^{J}q_{ij}^s,\forall_s\right\}$，$\Omega=\Omega_1\times\Omega_2\times\cdots\times\Omega_I$。$(q^*,Q^*)\in\Omega$ 为供给市场均衡(Nash 均衡)点，充要条件为下面的不等式组成立：

$$R_i(q_i^*,Q_i^*,q_{-i}^*,Q_{-i}^*)\geqslant R_i(q_{-i},q_i,q_{-i}^*,Q_{-i}^*),\forall(q_i,Q_i)\in\Omega_I,i=1,2,\cdots,I \tag{6}$$

其中，$q_{-i}=(q_1,\cdots,q_{i-1},q_{i+1},\cdots,q_I)$，$Q_{-i}=(Q_1,\cdots,Q_{i-1},Q_{i+1},\cdots Q_I)$。(6)式表明供给市场达到均衡时，每个生产商的策略都是对于其他生产商策略的最佳反映。由假设，$R_i(q,Q)$是 Ω 上的连续可微凹函数，由引理 1，(6)式等价于下面的变分不等式：

$$\sum_{i=1}^{I}\left\{\sum_{s=1}^{S}\langle\frac{\partial f_i^s(q^*)}{\partial q_i^s},q_i^s-q_i^{s*}\rangle+\sum_{j=1}^{J}\sum_{s=1}^{S}\langle\frac{\partial c_{ij}^s q_{ij}^{s*}}{\partial q_{ij}^s}-p_{ij}^s,q_{ij}^s-q_{ij}^{s*}\rangle\right\}\geqslant 0,\quad\forall(q,Q)\in\Omega, \tag{7}$$

进一步，变分不等式(7)在 (q^*,Q^*) 点满足 Slater 约束规格。对 $\forall i,j,s$，有下面的互补问题成立[11]：

$$\begin{cases} q_i^{s*}\left(\dfrac{\partial f_i^s(q^*)}{\partial q_i^s}\right)-u_i^s=0 \\ \dfrac{\partial f_i^s(q^*)}{\partial q_i^s}-u_i^s\geqslant 0, \\ q_i^s\geqslant 0 \end{cases} \tag{8}$$

$$\begin{cases} q_{ij}^s\left(\dfrac{\partial c_{ij}^s(q_{ij}^s)}{\partial q_{ij}^s}+u_i^s-p_{ij}^s\right)=0 \\ \dfrac{\partial c_{ij}^s(q_{ij}^s)}{\partial q_{ij}^s}+u_i^s-p_{ij}^s\geqslant 0, \\ q_{ij}^s\geqslant 0 \end{cases} \tag{9}$$

其中，u_i^s 是约束条件(4)的拉格朗日乘子，相当于生产商 i 生产产品 s 所愿意承担的最小供给成本。

(8)式表明：当边际生产成本大于最小供给成本时，生产商选择不生产；仅当边际生产成本等于最小供给成本时，生产商才会进行生产.(9)式表明：当交易价格小于边际交易成本与最小供给成本之和时，生产商因无利可图选择不交易；仅当边际交易成本加上最小供给成本之和等于交易价格时，生产商才会进行交易.联合(8)式和(9)式可知，仅当边际生产成本与边际交易成本之和等于交易价格时，生产商才会组织生产并与零售商交易。

2.3 零售市场均衡变分模型的建立

设 q_{jl}^{is}，p_{jl}^{is} 分别表示零售商 j 供给需求市场 l 的由生产商 i 生产的产品 s 的数量和价格。记零售商 j 的产品购、销量向量为 $\overline{Q}_j=(q_{1j}^1,\cdots,q_{ij}^s,\cdots q_{Ij}^S,q_{jl}^{11},\cdots q_{jl}^{is},\cdots q_{jL}^{IS})$，所有零售商的产品购、销量向量为 $\overline{Q}=(\overline{Q}_1,\cdots\overline{Q}_j,\cdots,\overline{Q}_J)$。零售商销售产品 s 的主要支出成本为产品储存和展示成本，记为 $c_j^s(q_j^s)$，其中 $q_j^s=\sum_{i=1}^{I}q_{ij}^s$ 为零售商购买产品 s 的总量，假设 $c_j^s(q_j^s)$ 为连续可微凸函数。零售商 j 的利润函数为

$$R_j(\overline{Q})=\sum_{l=1}^{L}\sum_{s=1}^{S}\sum_{i=1}^{I}p_{jl}^{is}q_{ij}^s-\sum_{s=1}^{S}\sum_{i=1}^{I}p_{ij}^sq_{ij}^s-\sum_{s=1}^{S}c_j^s(q_j^s), \tag{10}$$

零售市场均表观为 J 个零售商之间相互竞的 Nash 均衡，在均衡点零售商的订购量和销售量必须满足如下购销平衡条件(11)和非负约束(12)：

$$q_{ij}^s=\sum_{l=1}^{L}q_{jl}^{is},\qquad \forall i,j,s \tag{11}$$

$$q_{ij}^s\geqslant 0,\quad q_{jl}^{is}\geqslant 0,\quad \forall i,j,l,s, \tag{12}$$

记 $\overline{\Omega}_j=\left\{\overline{\Omega}_j\mid\overline{\Omega}_j\geqslant 0,q_{ij}^s=\sum_{l=1}^{L}q_{jl}^{is},\forall i,s\right\}$，$\overline{\Omega}=\overline{\Omega}_1\times\overline{\Omega}_2\times\cdots\times\overline{\Omega}_J$.$\overline{\Omega}^*$.$\in\overline{\Omega}$ 为零售市场均衡(Nash 均衡)点，充要条件为下面的不等式组成立：

$$R_j(\overline{Q}_j^*,\overline{Q}_{-j}^*)\geqslant R_j(\overline{Q}_j,\overline{Q}_{-j}^*),\forall\overline{Q}\in\overline{Q}_j,j=1,2,\cdots,J, \tag{13}$$

其中 $\overline{\Omega}_{-j}=(\overline{\Omega}_1,\cdots\overline{\Omega}_{j-1},\overline{\Omega}_{j+1},\cdots,\overline{\Omega}_J)$。(13)式表明零售市场达到均衡时，每个零售商的策略都中对于其他零售商策略的最佳反映。由假设，$R_j(\overline{Q})$ 是 $\overline{\Omega}$ 的边续可微凹函数，由引理 1，(13)式等价与下面的变分不等式：

$$\sum_{j=1}^{J}\sum_{s=1}^{S}\sum_{i=1}^{I}\left\{\langle p_{ij}^{s}+\frac{\partial c_{i}^{s}(q_{j}^{s^{*}})}{\partial q_{ij}^{s}},q_{ij}^{s}-q_{ij}^{s^{*}}\rangle-\sum_{l=1}^{L}\langle p_{jl}^{is},q_{jl}^{is}-q_{jl}^{is*}\rangle\right\}\geqslant 0,\quad \forall \overline{Q}\in\overline{\Omega},\tag{14}$$

进一步,变分不等式(14)在 $\overline{Q}^{*}$ 点满足 SIater 约束规格. 对 $\forall i,j,l,s$, 有下面的互补问题成立[11]:

$$\begin{cases}q_{ij}^{s^{*}}\left(p_{i}^{s}j+\dfrac{\partial c_{j}^{s}(q_{j}^{s*})}{\partial q_{ij}^{s}}-u_{ij}^{s}\right)=0\\ p_{ij}^{s}+\dfrac{\partial c_{i}^{s}(q_{i}^{s^{*}})}{\partial q_{ij}^{s}}-u_{ij}^{s}\geqslant 0\\ q_{ij}^{s}\geqslant 0\end{cases}\tag{15}$$

$$\begin{cases}q_{jl}^{is}(-p_{jl}^{is}+u_{ij}^{s})=0,\\ -p_{jl}^{is}+u_{ij}^{s}\geqslant 0\\ q_{jl}^{is^{*}}\geqslant 0\end{cases}\tag{16}$$

其中, u_{ij}^{s} 是约束条件(11)的拉格朗日乘子,相当于零售商 j 销售生产商 i 生产的产品占 s 所愿意承担的最小供给成本。

(15)式表明:当边际销售成本加上产品订购价格大于最小供给成本时,零售商选择不订购;仅当边际销售成本加上产品订购价格等于最小供给成本时,零售商才会进行订购。(16)式表明:仅当最小供给成本不超过零售商供给市场时的产品要价,零售商才会进行销售,否则不销售。联合(15),(16)式可知,仅当订购价格加上边际销售成本之和等于零售商的产品要价时,零售商才会从生产商处订货并销售。

2.4 需求市场均衡变分模型的建立

设 q_{jl}^{is} 表示需求市场 l 从零售商 j 处购得生产商 i 生产的产品 s 的数量, $q_{jl}^{s}=\sum_{i=1}^{I}a_{jl}^{is}$ 为市场 l 从零售商 j 处购买产品 s 的总量, $c_{jl}^{s}=c_{jl}^{s}(q_{jl}^{s})$ 表示需求市场 l 从零售商 j 处购买产品 s 所需支付的单位交易成本,设其大于零且连续递增。需求市场 l 上的消费者选购产品时,不仅以价格作为衡量指标,还会考虑到产品在产地、品牌方面的差异。消费者的购买行为受到其对产品的主观评价的影响,可用随机效用值来度量,记为 U_{jl}^{is}. U_{jl}^{is} 是一个随机效用函数,等价于确定性的产品支付引起的负效用值项和随机主观主观观测误差项之和,可表示为

$$U_{jl}^{is}=-\theta(p_{jl}^{is}+c_{jl}^{s})+\varepsilon_{jl}^{is},\qquad \forall i,j,l,s\tag{17}$$

其中 $\theta>0$ 是成本与效用的转换系数,起到对比测度的作用。式中 $E[\varepsilon_{jl}^{is}]=0$, 并有: $E[U_{jl}^{is}]=-\theta(p_{jl}^{is}+c_{jl}^{s})$. 在需求市场 l, 零售商 j 提供的生产商 i 生产的产品 s 的销量占产品 s 的总销量的比例 w_{jl}^{is}, 等于购买产品 s 的消费者从 $I\times J$ 个生产商和零售商的组合中选择到零售商 j 处购买生产商 i 生产的产品 s 的概率。根据最大效用决策原理,该概率为:

$$w_{jl}^{is}=\mathrm{Prob}\{U_{jl}^{is}\geqslant U_{j'l}^{i's},j'=1,2,\cdots,J;i'=1,2,\cdots,I\},\tag{18}$$

且满足一般概率函数的特征:

$$0\leqslant w_{jl}^{is}\leqslant 1,\qquad \forall i,j,l,s,\tag{19}$$

$$\sum_{i=1}^{I}\sum_{j=1}^{J} w_{jl}^{is} = 1, \qquad \forall\, l,s \tag{20}$$

假设随机项 ε_{jl}^{is} 相互独立，且服从 Gumbel 分布函数：

$$F(Y) = \mathrm{Prob}\{\varepsilon_{jl}^{is} \geqslant Y\} = \exp(-e^{-Y+E}), \forall\, i,j,l,s. \tag{21}$$

其中 Y 为任意实数，$E = 0.5708\cdots$ 是欧拉常数，可得到产品随机选择的多项式 logit 模型：

$$w_{jl}^{is} = \frac{\exp[-\theta(p_{jl}^{is} + c_{jl}^{s})]}{\sum_{i=1}^{I}\sum_{j=1}^{J}\exp[-\theta(p_{j'l}^{i's} + c_{j'l}^{s})]}, \forall\, i,j,l,s. \tag{22}$$

记 $\tilde{p}_{jl}^{is} = p_{jl}^{is} + c_{jl}^{s}$ 为需求市场 l 上消费者从零售 j 处购买生产商 i 生产的产品 s 的总支付（或称销售价格），需求市场 l 上消费者购买产品 s 的平均支付（或称平均销售价格）可以表示为：

$$p_{l}^{s} = \sum_{i=1}^{I}\sum_{j=1}^{J} w_{jl}^{is\sim is} p_{jl} = \sum_{i=1}^{I}\sum_{j=1}^{I} w_{jl}^{is}(p_{jl}^{is} + c_{jl}^{s}), \forall\, l,s. \tag{23}$$

由于产品 s 具有相同的用户功能，需求市场 l 上产品 s 的总需求受到消费约束，其需求函数可表示为 $d_{l}^{s}(p_{l}^{s})$，零售商 j 提供的生产商 i 生产的产品 s 的需求函数 d_{jl}^{is} 满足：

$$d_{jl}^{is} = w_{jl}^{is} d_{l}^{s}(p_{l}^{s}), \forall\, i,j,l,s, \tag{24}$$

假设 $\tilde{p}_{jl}^{is}$ 为内生变量，由市场供求关系决定，有：

$$d_{jl}^{is}\begin{cases} = q_{jl}^{is}, \tilde{p}_{jl}^{is} \geqslant 0 \\ \leqslant q_{jl}^{is}, \tilde{p}_{jl}^{is} = 0 \end{cases}, \forall\, i,j,l,s, \tag{25}$$

上式表明需求市场上消费者愿意支付的商品价格必须大于零，供给大于需求时该商品为免费商品.

产品随机选择下需求市场均衡条件为(24)，(25)式同时成立. 根据 Iogit 模型的性质[12]，当 $\theta \to +\infty$ 时，消费者的主观误差趋于零，此时(24)，(25)式退化为

$$p_{l}^{s} = \min_{\forall\, i,j}\{p_{jl}^{is} + c_{jl}^{s}(q_{jl}^{is})\}, \qquad \forall\, l,s, \tag{26}$$

$$p_{jl}^{is} + c_{jl}^{s}\begin{cases} = p_{l}^{s}, q_{jl}^{is} \geqslant 0 \\ \geqslant p_{l}^{s}, q_{jl}^{is} = 0 \end{cases}, \forall\, i,j,l,s \tag{27}$$

$$d_{l}^{s}(p_{l}^{s})\begin{cases} = \sum_{j=1}^{J} q_{jl}^{s}, p_{l}^{s} \geqslant 0 \\ \leqslant \sum_{j=1}^{J} q_{jl}^{s}, p_{l}^{s} = 0, \end{cases} \quad \forall\, l,s \tag{28}$$

等价于确定性交通均衡原理刻画的产品完全同质的需求市场均衡条件[7]。此时同种产品要在同一市场占有市场份额，其价格必须完全相同（等于消费者愿意支付的最低价格）。

记 $\lambda_{l}^{s} = -\frac{1}{\theta}\ln\sum_{i=1}^{I}\sum_{j=1}^{I}\exp[-\theta(p_{jl}^{is} + c_{jl}^{s})]$，价格向量为 $p = (\tilde{p}_{11}^{11},\cdots,\tilde{p}_{jl}^{is},\cdots,\tilde{p}_{JL}^{IS})$，需求量向量为 $d = (d_{1}^{1},\cdots d_{l}^{s},\cdots,d_{L}^{S})$，产品销售量向量为 $\tilde{Q} = (q_{11}^{11},\cdots,q_{jl}^{is},\cdots q_{JL}^{IS})$。将消费者产品选择视为出行者的道路选择问题，由随机交通均衡配流变分模型[13]，可建立产品

随机选择下的需求市场均衡的变分模型。

定理 1　基于产品随机选择的多项式 logit 模型假设，需求市场均衡问题的解等价于：求 $(\widetilde{Q}^*,d^*,p^*)\in\widetilde{\Omega}=\{(\widetilde{Q},d,p)\geqslant 0\mid d_{jl}^{is}=q_{jl}^{is},\forall i,j,l,s\}$，使得对 $\forall(\widetilde{Q},d,p)\in\widetilde{\Omega}$，有下面的变分不等式成立：

$$\sum_{i=1}^{I}\sum_{j=1}^{J}\sum_{l=1}^{L}\sum_{s=1}^{S}\left\{\begin{array}{l}\langle(P_{jl}^{is^*}+c_{jl}^{s}(q_{jl}^{s^*}))+\frac{1}{\theta}(\mathrm{Ind}_{jl}^{is^*}-\mathrm{Ind}_{l}^{s^*})-\lambda_l^s,q_{jl}^{is}-q_{jl}^{is*}\rangle\\+\langle q_{jl}^{is^*}-d_{jl}^{is^*},\widetilde{p}_{jl}^{is}-\widetilde{p}_{jl}^{is^*}\rangle\end{array}\right\}\geqslant 0 \quad (29)$$

证明　基于产品随机选择的多项式 logit 模型假设，需求市场均衡点 $(\widetilde{Q}^*,d^*,p^*)\in\widetilde{\Omega}$ 满足(24)和(25)，等价于不动点问题(30)和变分不待式(31)成立.

$$d_{jl}^{is^*}=d_l^{s^*}\frac{\exp[-\theta(p_{il}^{is^*}+c_{il}^{s}(q_{il}^{s^*}))]}{\sum_{i=1}^{I}\sum_{j=1}^{J}\exp[-\theta(P_{j'l}^{i's}+c_{j'l}^{s})]},\qquad \forall i,j,l,s, \quad (30)$$

$$\langle q_{jl}^{is^*}+d_{jl}^{is^*},\widetilde{p}_{jl}^{is}-\widetilde{p}_{jl}^{is^*}\rangle\geqslant 0,\qquad \forall i,j,l,s, \quad (31)$$

对(30)式两边取对数，并利用 λ_1^s 进行化简，有：

$$(p_{jl}^{is*}+c_{jl}^{s}(q_{jl}^{s*}))+\frac{1}{\theta}(\ln d_{jl}^{is^*}-\ln d_l^{s^*})-\lambda_l^s=0,\quad \forall i,j,l,s \quad (32)$$

由(31)式和(32)式，$(\widetilde{Q}^*,d^*,p^*)$ 是变分不等式(29)的解。

反之，变分不等式(29)等价于互补问题：

$$\begin{cases}q_{jl}^{is^*}\left[(p_{jl}^{is^*}+c_{jl}^{s}(q_{jl}^{s^*}))+\frac{1}{\theta}(\mathrm{Ind}_{jl}^{is^*}-\mathrm{Ind}_{l}^{s^*})-\lambda_l^s\right]=0\\(p_{jl}^{is^*}+c_{jl}^{s}(q_{jl}^{s^*}))+\frac{1}{\theta}(\mathrm{Ind}_{jl}^{is^*}-\mathrm{Ind}_{l}^{s^*})-\lambda_l^s\geqslant 0\\q_{jl}^{is^*}\geqslant 0\end{cases} \quad (33)$$

$$\begin{cases}\widetilde{p}_{jl}^{is^*}(q_{jl}^{is^*}-d_{jl}^{is^*})=0\\q_{jl}^{is^*}-d_{jl}^{is^*}\geqslant 0\\\widetilde{p}_{jl}^{is^*}\geqslant 0\end{cases} \quad (34)$$

显然(34)与(25)等价. 由约束条件、对数函数的性质及互补条件(33)，可得到：

$$(p_{jl}^{is^*}+c_{jl}^{s^*}(q_{jl}^{s^*}))+\frac{1}{\theta}(\mathrm{Ind}_{jl}^{is^*}-\mathrm{Ind}_{l}^{s^*})-\lambda_I^s=0,$$

也即

$$d_{jl}^{is^*}=d_l^{s^*}\exp[-\theta(P_{jl}^{is^*}+c_{jl}^{s}(q_{jl}^{s^*})+\lambda_l^s)]=d_I^{s^*}\frac{\exp[-\theta(p_{jl}^{is^*}+c_{jl}^{s}(q_{jl}^{s^*}))]}{\sum_{i=1}^{I}\sum_{j=1}^{J}\exp[-\theta(p_{j'l}^{i's}+c_{j'l}^{s})]}$$

2.5　供应链网络均衡变分模型的建立

在市场机制的调节下，供应链网络最终将达到均衡状态肚匕时生产商提供给零售商的产品数量和价格恰好等于零售商愿意接受的产品数量和价格，并且零售商提供给需求市场的产品价格和数量恰好等于消费者愿意接受的产品价格及此价格水平下的市场需求。所以供应链网络均衡表现为生产商的生产量、生产商与零售商的交易量与交易价格、零售商与需求市场的交易量与交易价格必须同时满足变分不等式(7),(14),(29),等价于它们的和成立。本文给出如下基于产品随机选择的多项式 logit 模型假设下,多商品流供应链网络均衡的定义。

定义 2　基于产品随机选择的多项式 logit 模型假设下,多商品流供应链网络均衡状态是指供应链中产品的产量、流量以及市场价格满足变分不等式(7),(14),(29)的和。

令

$$X = \{q_i^s, q_{ij}^s, q_{jl}^{is}, \tilde{p}_{jl}^{is}\} \in \Omega = \Big\{q_i^s, q_{ij}^s, q_{jl}^{is}\tilde{q}_{jl}^{is} \geqslant 0 \mid q_i^s = \sum_{j=1}^{J} q_{ij}^s, d_{ij}^{is} = \sum_{l=1} a_{il}^{is},$$
$$d_{jl}^{is} = q_{jl}^{is}, \forall i,j,l,s\Big\},$$

根据上述定义,我们给出产品随机选择下多商品流供应链网络均衡变分模型。

定理 2　基于产品随机选择的多项式 Iogit 模型假设下,多商品流供应链网络均衡的解等价于:求 $X^* \in \Omega$,满足变分不等式:

$$\sum_{i=1}^{I}\sum_{s=1}^{S}\Big\{\langle\frac{\partial f_i^s(q^{s^*})}{\partial q_i^s}, q_i^s - q_i^{s^*}\rangle + \sum_{j=1}^{J}\langle\frac{\partial c_{ij}^s(q_{ij}^{s^*})}{\partial q_{ij}^s} + \frac{\partial c_j^s(q_j^{s^*})_j}{\partial q_{ij}^s}, q_{ij}^s - q_{ij}^{s^*}\rangle\Big\} + \sum_{i=1}^{I}\sum_{j=1}^{J}\sum_{l=1}^{L}\sum_{S=1}^{S}$$
$$\langle c_{jl}^s(q_{jl}^{s^*}) + \frac{1}{\theta}(\mathrm{Ind}_{jl}^{is^*} - \mathrm{Ind}_l^{s^*}) - \lambda_l^s, q_{jl}^{is} - q_{jl}^{is^*}\rangle + \langle q_{jl}^{is^*} - d_{jl}^{is^*}, \tilde{p}_{jl}^{is} - \tilde{p}_{jl}^{is^*}\rangle\Big\} \geqslant 0, \forall X \in \Omega \tag{35}$$

证明　将变分不等式(7),(14),(29)相加,并进行化简,可得到变分不等式(35). 反之,在变分不等式(35)中加入 $\sum_{i=1}^{I}\sum_{j=1}^{J}\sum_{s=1}^{S}\{\langle p_{ij}^s, q_{ij}^s - q_{ij}^{s^*}\rangle - \langle p_{ij}^s, q_{ij}^s - q_{ij}^{s^*}\rangle\}$ 项和 $\sum_{i=1}^{I}\sum_{j=1}^{J}\sum_{l=1}^{L}\sum_{S=1}^{S}\{\langle p_{jl}^{is^*}, q_{jl}^{is} - q_{jl}^{is^*}\rangle - \langle p_{jl}^{is^*}, q_{jl}^{is} - q_{jl}^{is^*}\rangle\}$ 项,并进行适当拆分、合并,可得到(7)(14)(29)三项和的形式。

若令 $\theta \to +\infty$,有 $\lambda_l^s \to p_l^s$ 及(26),(27),(28)式成立,变分不等式(35)退化为确定性产品选择下多商品流供应链网络均衡变分模型[7]:

$$\sum_{i=1}^{I}\sum_{s=1}^{S}\langle\frac{\partial f_i^s(q^{s^*})}{\partial q_i^s}, q_i^s - q_i^{s^*}\rangle + \sum_{i=1}^{I}\sum_{j=1}^{J}\sum_{s=1}^{S}\langle\frac{\partial c_{ij}^s(q_{ij}^{s^*})}{\partial q_{ij}^s} + \frac{\partial c_j^s(q_j^{s^*})}{\partial q_{ij}^s}, q_{ij}^s - q_i^{s^*}\rangle +$$
$$\sum_{j=1}^{J}\sum_{l=1}^{L}\sum_{s=1}^{S}\langle c_{jl}^s(q_{jl}^{s^*}) - p_l^{s^*}, q_{jl}^s - q_{jl}^{s^*}\rangle + \sum_{l=1}^{L}\sum_{s=1}^{S}\langle\sum_{j=1}^{J} q_{jl}^{s^*} - d_t^{s^*}(p_l^s), p_l^s - p_l^{s^*}\rangle \geqslant 0, \tag{36}$$

$$\text{s. t. } \forall q_i^s, q_{ij}^s, p_t^s, p_l^s \in \Theta = \Big\{q_i^s, q_{ij}^s, q_{jl}^s, p_l^s \geqslant 0 \mid q_i^s = \sum_{j=1}^{J} q_{ij}^s, \sum_{i=1}^{I} q_{ij}^s = \sum_{l=1}^{L} q_{ij}^s, d_l^s = \sum_{j=1}^{J} q_{jl}^s\Big\}$$

3　算法与算例

变分不等式(35)等价于互补问题(8),(9),(15),(16)和(24),(25)式同时成立,本文通过求解与之等价的互补问题得到变分不待式(35)的解。进一步,若 $q_{jl}^{is} > 0$, 由平衡条件有 $q_{ij}^s > 0, q_i^s > 0$,再由互补条件,有 $p_{ij}^s = \frac{\partial f_i^s(q)}{\partial q_i^s} + \frac{\partial c_{ij}^s(q_{ij}^s)}{\partial q_{ij}^s}$, $p_{ij}^{is} = p_{ij}^s + \frac{\partial c_j^s(q_j^s)}{\partial q_{ij}^s}$, 即有:

$$\tilde{p}_{jl}^{is} = \frac{\partial f_i^s(q)}{\partial q_i^s} + \frac{\partial c_{ij}^s(q_{ij}^s)}{\partial q_{ij}^s} + \frac{\partial c_j^s(q_j^s)}{\partial q_{ij}^s} + c_{jl}^s, \tag{37}$$

若将 i 视为起点，l 视为终点，q_{jl}^{is}，$\tilde{p}_{jl}^{is}$ 视为连接 i 与 l 的径径上的流量和费用，此时上述互补问题可转化为随机交能均衡流量分配问题。本文用改进的相继平均法(MSA)来求解供应链网络均衡模型[12]，算法步骤如下：

步骤 1　初始化，令 $n=1$，给定初始值 $q_{jl}^{is^n}>0$，$(\forall i,j,l,s)$ 及计算精度 ε；

步骤 2　由平衡条件得到 $q_{ij}^{s^n}$，$q_i^{s^n}$ $(\forall i,j,s)$，由(37)式计算 $\tilde{p}_{jl}^{is^n}$。

步骤 3　由(22)式计算产品选择概率 $w_{jl}^{is^n}$，由(23)式计算各市场产品的平均价格 $p_l^{s^n}$，由需求函数及(24)式分别计算此价格水平下的市场需求量 $d_l^{s^n}$ 和各产品需求量 $d_{jl}^{is^n}$；

步骤 4　更新。计算产品销量：$q_{jl}^{is^n+1}+q_{jl}^{is^n}\dfrac{1}{(n+\Delta)^{\gamma}}(d^{is^n}-q_{jl}^{is^n})$，其中 Δ,γ 为预先给定的参数，一般可选择 $\Delta\geqslant 10,1>\gamma\geqslant 0.5$(参见[8])；

步骤 5　检查收敛性。若 $\sum\limits_{i,j,l,s}|d_{jl}^{is^n}-q_{jl}^{is^{n+1}}|\leqslant\varepsilon$，则停止迭代，$q_{jl}^{is^{n+1}}$ 即为均衡解；否则令 $n=n+1$，转步骤 2。

在算法运用中，如果出现 $d_l^{s^n}<0$ 情况，则令 $d_l^{s^n}=0$；同时为减少误差，用如下(22)式的变换形式计算产品选择概率 $w_{jl}^{is^n}$：

$$w_{jl}^{is^n}=\frac{I}{\sum\limits_{i=1}^{I}\sum\limits_{j=1}^{J}\exp[-\theta(\tilde{p}_{j'l}^{i's^n}-\tilde{p}_{jl}^{is^n})]}$$

例 1　变动文献[7]中的例子：考虑一个 2 个生产商，2 个零售商和 2 个需求市场具有 2 种产品流动的简单供应链网络，其中产品 2 的成本函数和需求函数具有对称形式，且不考虑变量单位。

1)决策变量：生产商产品产量 q_i^s，生产商到零售商的产品流量 q_{ij}^s，零售商到需求市场的产品流量 q_{jl}^{is}，需求市场产品销售价格 $\tilde{p}_{jl}^{is}$。

2) 生产商 i 生产生产 s 的成本函数 $f_i^s(q)$ 为

$$f_1^1(q)=0.5(q_1^1)^2+q_1^1q_2^1+2q_1^1,\qquad f_2^1(q)=2.5(q_2^1)^2+q_1^1q_2^1+2q_2^1,$$

$$f_1^2(q)=3(q_1^2)^2+2q_1^2q_2^2+q_1^2,\qquad f_2^2(q)=3(q_2^2)^2+2q_1^2q_2^2+q_1^2$$

生产商 i 与零售商 j 交易产品 s 的交易成本(包括运输成本) $c_{ij}^s(q_{ij}^s)$ 为

$$c_{11}^1(q_{11}^1)=0.2(q_{11}^1)^2+q_{11}^1,\qquad c_{12}^1(q_{12}^1)=0.5(q_{12}^1)^2+3.5q_{12}^1,$$

$$c_{21}^1(q_{21}^1)=0.5(q_{21}^1)^2+3.5q_{21}^1,\qquad c_{22}^1(q_{22}^1)=0.5(q_{22}^1)^2+3.5q_{22}^1,$$

$$c_{11}^2(q_{11}^2)=(q_{11}^2)^2+3q_{11}^2,\qquad c_{12}^2(q_{12}^2)=(q_{12}^2)^2+3q_{12}^2,$$

$$c_{21}^2(q_{21}^2)=(q_{21}^2)^2+3q_{21}^2,\qquad c_{22}^2(q_{22}^2)=(q_{22}^2)^2+3q_{22}^2$$

零售商 j 关于产品 s 的储存与展示成本 $c_j^s=c_j^s(q_j^s)=c_j^s\left(\sum\limits_{i=1}^{2}q_{ij}^s\right)$ 为

$$c_1^1=0.1(q_{11}^1+q_{21}^1)^2,c_2^1=0.5(q_{12}^1+q_{22}^1)^2,c_1^2=(q_{11}^2+q_{21}^2)^2,c_2^2=(q_{12}^2+q_{22}^2)^2$$

需求市场 l 对产品 s 的需求函数 d_l^s 为

$$d_1^1(p^1)=-2p_1^1-1.5p_2^1+1000,\qquad d_2^1(p^1)=-2p_2^1-1.5p_1^1+1000,$$

$$d_1^2(p^2)=-1.5p_1^2-2p_2^2+1000,d_2^2(p^2)=-1.5p_2^2-2p_1^2+1000$$

需求市场 l 上的消费者到零售商 j 处购买产品 s 的单位交易成本 $\tilde{c}_{jl}^s=c_{jl}^s(q_{jl}^s)=$

$c_{jl}^{s}\left(\sum_{i=1}^{2} q_{jl}^{is}\right)$为

$$\tilde{c}_{11}^{1}=0.5(q_{11}^{1}+q_{11}^{21})+1,\quad \tilde{c}_{12}^{1}=(q_{12}^{11}+q_{12}^{21})+5,$$
$$\tilde{c}_{21}^{1}=(q_{21}^{11}+q_{21}^{21})+5,\quad \tilde{c}_{22}^{1}=(q_{22}^{11}+q_{22}^{21})+5,$$
$$\tilde{c}_{11}^{2}=2(q_{11}^{12}+q_{11}^{22})+3,\quad c_{12}^{2}=2(q_{12}^{12}+q_{12}^{22})+3,$$
$$\tilde{c}_{21}^{2}=2(q_{21}^{12}+q_{21}^{22})+3\quad c_{22}^{2}=2(q_{22}^{12}+q_{22}^{22}+3)$$

运用上述 MSA 算法求解产品随机选择下的供应链均衡问题，均衡解如表 1 至表 4 所示。

表 1　生产商产品生产量

q_i^s	产品 1 产量	产品 2 产量
生产商 1	144.17	22.68
生产商 2	9.26	22.68

表 2　生产商到零售商产品流量

q_{ij}^s	零售商 1		零售商 2	
	产品 1 流量	产品 2 流量	产品 1 流量	产品 2 流量
生产商 1	106.04	11.34	38.13	11.34
生产商 2	5.78	11.34	3.48	11.34

表 3　零售商到需求市场产品流量

q_{jl}^{is}		需求市场 1		需求市场 2	
		产品 1 流量	产品 2 流量	产品 1 流量	产品 2 流量
零售商 1	生产商 1 的产品	63.46	5.67	42.58	5.67
	生产商 2 的产品	3.46	5.67	2.32	5.76
零售商 2	生产商 1 的产品	12.50	5.67	25.63	5.67
	生产商 2 的产品	1.14	5.67	2.34	5.67

表 4　需求市场产品价格

$\tilde{q}_{jl}^{is}$		需求市场 1		需求市场 2	
		产品 1 价格	产品 2 价格	产品 1 价格	产品 2 价格
零售商 1	生产商 1 的产品	255.67	279.23	271.12	279.23
	生产商 2 的产品	258.58	279.23	274.03	279.23
零售商 2	生产商 1 的产品	257.30	279.23	271.63	279.23
	生产商 2 的产品	259.69	279.23	274.02	279.23
平均价格		256.11	279.23	271.48	279.23

对于产品 2 而言，供应链网络具有对称结构，供应链达到均衡状态时，产品 2 的产量和流量为对称均匀分布：各生产商生产产品 2 的数量相同，各生产商与同一零售商之间产品 2 的交易量相同，各零售商与不同需求市场之间产品 2 的交易量相同，不同需求市场上产品 2 的价格相同。对产品 1 而言，生产商 1 的生产效率比生产商 2 高，因此其产量也较

高:生产商1与零售商1交易比与零售商2交易的边际成本低,因此其与零售商1的交易量也较多;零售商1在需求市场1上比在需求市场2上的产品展示和储存的边际成本低,因此其在需求市场1上销量也大;需求市场1上的消费者到零售商1处比到零售商2处购买产品1的单位边际交易成本低,因此到零售商1处的购买量也大;从生产商1到零售商1,到需求市场1的产品1的生产-销售链最有效,因此其对应的产品销售价格也最低,销量也最大。可进一步对模型参数进行灵敏度分析,以获取更多信息(此处因篇幅所限而省略)。由于消费者偏好不同,在随机产品选择下同种产品即使具有不同的销售价格,也能同时拥有市场份额(如产品1),这比利用确定性交通均衡原理采刻画产品选择更符合实际。

4　结论与进一步研究工作

本文假定产品存在产地、品牌差异,并将其对消费者选择产品的影响视为随机变量,利用基于随机效用理论的Iogit模型刻画产品随机选择,建立了由生产商、零售商和需求市场组成的具有多种商品流动的三层供应链网络的变分不等式模型。相对以前的研究,随机产品选择更符合实际,能够解释同一市场上具有不同销售价格的同一产品能够同时拥有市场份额的原因,表明了产品销售价格决定于产品生产-销售链的效率。本文还给出了求解模型的算法和具体算例。本文研究未考虑时间因素,未来可结合交货时间、交货周期、库存、供应链合同、多准则偏好等因素对供应链网络均衡问题开展进一步研究。

A MultI-COmmodity Flow Supply Chain Netnork EquiIibrium Model with Stochastic Choice

XU Bing[1,2], ZHU Dao-li[2]

(1. Management Science and Engineering Department, Nanchang University, Nanchang 330047, China; 2Management School, Fudan University, Shanghai 200433, China)

Abstract: A tbee-level competitive supply chain neNork equilibrium model with multi commodity is studied in consideration of the product differentiation of region and brand. Stochastic utility theory and multinomial Iogit model are used to anaIyze stochastic choice in demand market, while the influence of region and byand is treated as stochastic variable. Competitive behavior of manufactures and retailers is analyzed by using Nash equilibrium theory. The equilibrium models of each level and whole nemork are developed by variational inequality method, along with their equilibrium conditions and economic interpretations.

Finally, an algorithm is pld forward and applied to solving a numerical example.

Key words: supply chain netnork; Nash equilibrium; stochastic choice; variational inequality

参考文献

[1] Ballou R U. 企业物流管理——供应链的规划、组织和控制[M]. 王晓东，胡瑞鹏，等译. 北京：机械工业出版社，2002. 1-19.

Ballor R H, Business Logistics Management Planning, Organization and Controlling the Supply Chain [M]. Beijng: China Machine Press, 2003. 1-19.

[2] Nagurney A. Network Economics: A Variational Inequalities Approach, Second and Revised ed[M]. Kluwer Academic Publishers, Dordrecht, 1999.

[3] 高自友，孙会君. 现代物流与交通运输系统[M]. 北京：人民交通出版社，2003. 194-203.

Cao Z Y, Sun H J. Modern Logistics and Transportation System[M]. Beijng: China Communication Press, 2003. 194-203.

[4] Nagurney A, Zhao L. Variational inequalities and networks in the formation and computation of market equilibria and disequilibria: The case of direct demand functions [J]. Transportation Science, 1993, 27(1): 4-15.

[5] Nagurney A, Dong J, Zhang D. A supply chain network equilibrium model[J]. Transportiaton Research: Part E, 2002, 38(5): 281-303.

[6] Nagurney A, Toyasaki F. Supply chain supernetworks and emvironmental Criteria[J]. Transportiaton Research: Part D, 2003, 8(3): 185-213.

[7] 张铁柱，刘志勇，滕春贤，等. 多商品流供应链网络均衡模型的研究[J]. 系统工程理论与实践，2005，25(7): 61-66.

Zhang T Z, Liu Z Y, Teng C X, et al. A multi commodity flow supply chain networkequilibrium model [J]. Systems Engineering-Theory & Practice, 2005, 25(17): 61-66.

[8] 张宁. 产品随机选择与运输的跨区域市场均衡[J]. 系统工程理论与实践，1997，17(12): 74-78.

Zhang N. Stochastic spatial price equilibrium with transportation competition and congestion[J]. Systems Engineering-Theory & Practice, 1997, 17(12): 74-78.

[9] 张宁，卢兴普. 多规格产品随机选择的均衡[J]. 系统工程理论与实践，1997，17(10): 14-17, 90.

Zhang N, Lu X P. A market equilibrium model for differentiated multi productwith stochastic choice [J]. Systems Engineering-Theory & Practice, 1997, 17(10): 14-17, 90.

[10] 徐庆，朱道立，鲁其辉. Nash 均衡、变分不等式和广义均衡问题的关系[J]. 管理科学学报，2005，8(3): 1-7.

Xu Q, Zhu D L, LU Q H. Reiations among Nash equilibrium, variational inequalities and generalized equilibrium problem[J]. Journal of Management Sciences in China, 2005, 8(3): 1-7.

[11] Harker P T, Pang J S. Finite-dimensional variational inequality and nonlinear complementarity problems: Asuvey of theory, algorithms and application[J]. Mathematical Programming, 1990, (48): 161-220.

[12] Sheffi Y. Urban Transportation Networks: Equilibrium Analysis with Mathematical Programming

Methods [M]. Prentice Hall, INC, Englewood Cliffs, New Jersey, 1985. 324-331.
[13] 周晶. 随机交通均衡配流模型及其等价的变分不等式问题[J]. 系统科学与数学, 2003, 23(1): 120-127.
Zhou J. Stochastic user equilibrium and its variational inequality probiem[J]. Journal of Systems Science & Mathematical Sciences, 2003, 23(1): 120-127.

（本文发表于《系统工程论与实践》，2007 年第 3 期）

竞争供应链的结构和链内协调策略分析

徐兵[1,2]，朱道立[2]

（1. 南昌大学管理科学与工程系，江西南昌 330031；2. 复旦大学管理学院，上海 200433）

摘要：供应链的结构及供应链竞争环境下的链内协调问题是供应链管理的核心问题。本文利用超网络方法分析供应链运作过程，建立了两条竞争供应链的超网络结构；已知产品总需求的随机分布函数，运用顾客选择理论得到每条供应链的产品需求情况；利用博弈理论和 New svendor 模型，得到了供应链竞争环境下可协调链内成员的收益共享合同。最后的算例表明：供应链协调可以提高供应链的运作效率，但协调供应链间的竞争将更激烈，可能出现囚徒困境现象。

关键词：供应链管理；协调策略；Newsvendor 模型；供应链结构

中图分类号：F274　**文章标识码：**A　**文章编号：**1007-3221(2008)05-0051-07

0 引　言

20 世纪 90 年代之后，随着经济全球化和信息技术现代化的的发展，被称为“企业第三利润源”的供应链管理越来越受到企业界和学术界的重视。文献[1] 指出未来的竞争将不再是企业与企业之间的竞争，而是供应链与供应链的竞争。供应链管理框架包括：供应链网络结构、供应链业务流程和供应链管理要素[2]。文献[3]从供应链的地理分散程度、供销渠道类型（如网络结构、层次结构、市场类型）两方面研究了供应链网络结构及不同结构下供应链运行的有效性。文献[4，5]用交通均衡模型分别研究了确定性需求和随机需求情况下三层供应链网络均衡问题，笔者用随机交通均衡模型研究了多商品流三层供应链网络均衡模型[6]。文献[7] 从供应链经济角度研究了供应链网络均衡模型及供应链竞争问题。但上述文献均未考虑库存、供应链协调等因素，未真正反应供应链内部流程。

由于企业的局部利益和行为经常与供应链整体目标不一致，必须对供应链上下游企业进行必要的协调，其中供应链合同是协调供应链的有效方法。不考虑供应链竞争情况下，协调单条供应链的研究成果已非常丰富，如回购合同在 Newsvendor 中的价格制定问题[8]、以及数量弹性合同[9]及销售折扣合同[10]的研究。文献[11] 对单条供应链协调理论

收稿日期：2008-02-07

基金项目：国家自然科学基金重点资助项目(70432001)；中国博士后基金资助项目(20060400584)；赣教技字[2007] 10 号；江西省自科基金资助项目(2007GZS2120)

作者简介：徐兵(1972～)，男，江西南昌人，博士后，副教授；研究方向：运筹学、供应链管理。

成果进行了综述。在多条供应链相互竞争环境下，供应链协调问题非常复杂，要同时考虑上下游企业间的纵向竞争与同层企业间的横向竞争，对该类问题的研究还很不充分。文献[1] 研究了供应链竞争的三种情景：供应链与供应链间完全竞争、供应网络能力竞争、渠道盟主领导下的供应网络能力竞争及三类供应链网络形态：完全分离、完全重叠、部分重叠。文献[12] 研究了两条供应链在相同的零售价格下进行顾客服务水平（即库存满足率）方面的竞争。文献[13] 研究了如何设计各类合同参数来使两条供应链组成的系统达到供应链竞争均衡和系统整体最优。但是[12, 13]中各产品需求函数或分布函数是事先给定的。

我们知道，研究供应链之间的竞争与内部协调问题，需要首先确定每条供应链的产品需求，等价于确定多种可替代产品或相关产品的需求函数。对多产品需求问题，一般文献大多假定每种产品的需求函数是已知的，并且各产品的市场需求相互独立或者已知它们之间的相互关系[12~15]。文献[16] 阐述了基于顾客选择的需求理论，即利用市场结构、各产品的特征及顾客偏好的分析结果，结合产品差异化理论以及顾客选择理论来计算产品的市场份额。文献[17] 假定消费者依据一般支出和偏好从两种产品中进行选择，将消费者的产品选择行为视为“泊努利实验”，然后用“二项分布”来表述 M 个消费者选择产品后形成的产品需求，进而用“标准正态分布”来近似该“二项分布”。与上述文章不同，本文假定两条供应链提供存在质量差异的同种产品，消费者对产品质量的偏好为连续分布，且已知两条供应链的产品总需求的随机分布函数，利用顾客选择理论得到每条供应链的产品市场份额，进而得到各产品需求的分布函数。

本文首先通过引入库存点和虚拟供应点，建立了两条竞争供应链的超网络结构，实现了供应链流程的结构化描述，并保证了流量平衡条件，在此基础上，可利用交通均衡理论将文献[4～7] 拓展至含库存和缺货情况的供应链网络均衡问题研究；然后利用顾客选择理论得到每条供应链的产品市场份额，解决了总量分解问题，即由两条供应链的总产品需求的分布函数得到每条供应链的产品需求的分布函数，并刻画了供应链竞争的本质；最后利用博弈理论和 Newsvendor 模型分析了供应链竞争环境下的链内协调问题，证明了收益共享合同是供应链协调的有效方法，利用算例表明了协调是供应链管理的主要策略，但可能出现所有供应链同时协调时收益反而下降的囚徒困境现象。

1　竞争供应链的超网络结构

如图 1 所示，假设需求市场 D 上有两条供应链：第 i 条供应链由生产商 M_i 和零售商 R_i 组成，向市场提供产品 $i(i=1, 2)$，且产品 1 和 2 是存在质量差异的同种产品。零售商 R_i 在单个销售季节之前预测销售情况，决定向生产商 M_i 的订货量 q_i 和零售价格 p_i，生产商 M_i 依据订单组织生产，并在销售季节之前完全满足零售商 R_i 的供货需求 q_i。销售产生，假设产品 i 的市场需求为 d_i，两种产品的总需求为 d。为了刻画产品的实际流动情况，在描述 R_i 的子网络内引入库存点：当订货量 q_i 大于需求量 d_i 时，有 q_i-d_i 的产品流量流向库存点（即库存量为 $\max(0,q_i-d_i)$ ）。为了刻画市场需求的实现情况，在描述需求市场 D 的子网络内引入虚拟供应点：当订货量 q_i 小于需求量 d_i 时，有 d_i-q_i 的需求由虚拟供应点供给（即缺货量为 $\max(0,d_i-q_i)$），所以零售商 R_i关于产品 i 的实际销量为

$\min(q_i, d_i)$。可见，通过引入库存点和虚拟供应点，保证了供应链超网络中零售商子网络和需求市场子网络的流量平衡条件，进而可在此基础上利用交通流量分配理论研究含库存和缺货情况的供应链网络均衡问题。

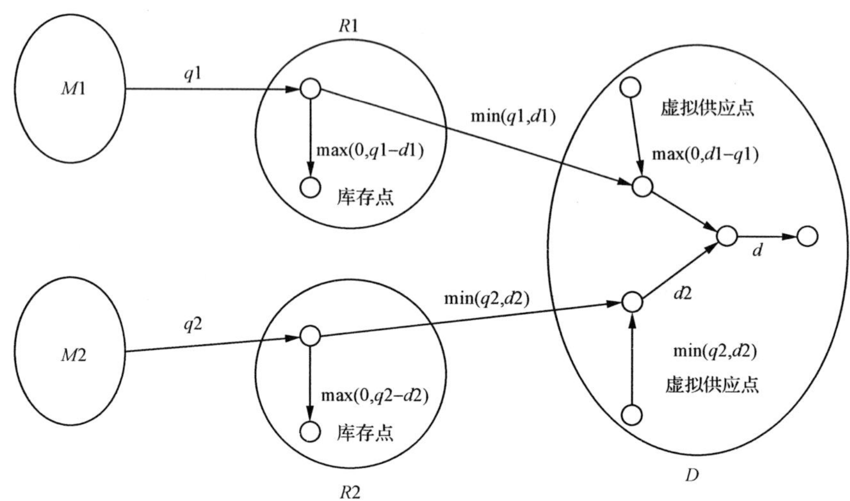

图1 两条供应链的超网络结构

2 产品需求函数的确定

假定每个零售商都面临随机需求情况下的 Newsvendor 问题。由于两条供应链提供的产品是非同质的同种产品，一般仅能通过历史数据预测销售季节市场的产品总需求。已知总需求 d 的随机分布函数 $F(x|p)$，及密度函数 $f(x|p)$，其中 $p=(p_1, p_2)$ 为两种产品的价格向量，即由于消费者收入水平的限制，总需求与价格水平有关。设 $F(x|p)$ 为严格单调增加的可微函数，$F(0|p)=0$，并存在反函数 F^{-1}，显然 F^{-1} 为严格单调增加函数。为了分析两条供应链的竞争情况，必须首先由总需求 d 的分布推导出每种产品的需求，下面结合消费者偏好和顾客选择理论对此进行分析。

假定影响消费者选择的产品特征为质量和价格（或假定两种产品仅在质量和价格两方面存在差异），产品 i 的质量 T_i 和价格 p_i 满足：$T_1 > T_2, p_1 > p_2$（即高质量产品具有高价格）。由于收入水平、年龄等方面的差异，消费者对质量的偏好（相当于质量的货币价值系数）各不相同。假设消费者对质量的偏好 α 的分布函数为 G，密度函数为 g，且 G 为严格单调增加函数，满足 $G(0)=0$。偏好为 α 的消费者购买产品 i 的效用为

$$U_i(\alpha) = U_0 + \alpha T_i - p_i \tag{1}$$

其中 U_0 为产品固有效用。令 $\Delta U(\alpha) = U_1(\alpha) - U_2(\alpha) = 0$ 得到 $\alpha_0 = (p_1 - p_2)/(T_1 - T_2)$，由顾客选择理论，消费者将选择两种产品中效用最大的产品。故选择产品 i 的消费者比例 λ_i 为

$$\lambda_1 = prob\{U_1(\alpha) \geqslant U_2(\alpha)\} = \int_{\alpha_0}^{+\infty} g(x)\,\mathrm{d}x = 1 - G(\alpha_0), \lambda_2 = 1 - \lambda_1 = G(\alpha_0) \tag{2}$$

可见 $\lambda_i = \lambda_i(p_1, p_2, T_1, T_2)$ 是价格和质量的含数，有

$$\partial\lambda_i/\partial p_i = -g(\alpha_0)/(T_1 - T_2) < 0, \quad \partial\lambda_i/\partial p_j = g(\alpha_0)/(T_1 - T_2) > 0$$

即产品 i 的市场份额随自身(对方)产品价格的上涨而下降(增加)；又 $\partial\lambda_i/\partial T_i = \alpha_0 g(\alpha_0)/(T_1 - T_2) > 0$，$\partial\lambda_i/\partial T_j = -\alpha_0 g(\alpha_0)/(T_1 - T_2) < 0$，即产品 i 的市场份额随自身(对方)产品质量的提升而增加(下降)。当 p_1, p_2, T_1, T_2 给定时，λ_i 是一个常数，此时总需求可分成固定比例的两部分：$d = d_1 + d_2$，其中 $d_i = \lambda_i d$。故 d_i 的分布函数 $F_i(x \mid p)$ 和密度函数 $f_i(x \mid p)$ 为

$$F_i(x/p) = prob(\lambda_i d \leqslant x) = F\left(\frac{x}{\lambda_i} \mid p\right), \quad f_i(x \mid p) = \frac{1}{\lambda_i} f\left(\frac{x}{\lambda_i} \mid p\right) \tag{3}$$

可见，每条供应链的产品需求与两种产品的质量、价格及消费者偏好有关。通过设计合理的价格、提升质量水平等产品相关特征来争夺市场份额是供应链竞争的主要手段。

3　供应链内部协调策略分析

3.1　模型建立

假设生产商和零售商都是风险中性，并且生产商在供应链中占主导地位，同一条供应链的生产商和零售商之间进行如下完全信息博弈：生产商 M_i 首先给零售商 R_i 提供一个合同，如果 R_i 不接受，则博弈结束，二者得到零利润；如果 R_i 接受合同，则 R_i 同时给出订货量 q_i 和零售价格 p_i；M_i 在销售季节前运送 q_i 的产品 i 给 R_i；销售产生，最后 R_i 按合同规定给 M_i 一定支付 Y_i。假设生产商 M_i 的单位成本为 c_i，满足：$c_1 > c_2$(即高质量的产品具有高成本)。零售商 R_i 的单位缺货损失为 β_i；当销售季节结束后，零售商 R_i 对未售出的商品进行降价或处理，单位商品处理价格为 v_i，满足 $v_i < c_i$(即零售商处理未售出的商品要承受一定的损失)。

记 $q = (q_1, q_2)$ 为两零售商的订购量向量，经简单推导，R_i 的期望销售量 $S_i(q,p)$，期望未销售量 $I_i(q,p)$，期望缺货量 $L_i(q,p)$ 分别为

$$S_i(q,p) = E[\min(q_i, d_i)] = q_i - \int_0^q F\left(\frac{z}{\lambda_i} \mid p\right)\mathrm{d}z$$

$$I_i(q,p) = q_i - S_i(q,p), \quad L_i(q,p) = u_i(q,p) - S_i(q,p)$$

其中 $u_i(q,p) = 0\int_0^{+\infty} x f_i(x \mid p)\mathrm{d}x = \lambda_i u(p)$ 为产品 i 的期望需求量，$u(p) = \int_0^{+\infty} x f(x \mid p)\mathrm{d}x$ 为两种产品总需求的数学期望，假设 $u(p)$ 为连续可微函数。

记 $h_i(q,p) = \int_0^q F\left(\frac{z}{\lambda_i} \mid p\right)\mathrm{d}z$，$m_i(p) = \lambda_i\beta_i u(p)$ 所以零售商 R_i 生产商 M_i 和供应链 i 的利润函数分别为

$$\begin{aligned}\pi_{Ri}(q,p) &= p_i S_i(q,p) + v_i I_i(q,p) - \beta_i L_i(q,p) - Y_i \\ &= (p_i + \beta_i)q_i - (p_i - v_i + \beta_i)h_i(q,p) - m_i(p) - Y_i\end{aligned} \tag{4}$$

$$\pi_{Mi}(q,p) = Y_i - c_i q_i \tag{5}$$

$$\pi_i(q,p) = \pi_{Ri} + \pi_{Mi} = (p_i - c_i + \beta_i)q_i - (p_i - v_i + \beta_i)h_i(q,p) - m_i(p) \tag{6}$$

定义 1　如果供应链内成员间无主从关系，各成员均以最大化自身利润为目标进行决策，

称此类供应链为分散式供应链(Decen tralized SC),此时的决策为分散化决策;如果供应链内存在盟主成员,以最大化供应链整体利润为目标支配各方决策,称此类供应链为集中式供应链(Centralized SC),此时的决策为集中化决策。

由于现实中供应链大多是分散式供应链,而分散式决策很难保证供应链的整体利润,所以如何通过设计适当的机制或合同形式来协调链内成员的决策行为,以追求供应链整体收益,达到集中式供应链的效果,是供应链管理领域近二十年来的研究热点。但供应链竞争环境下,如何协调链内成员行为的研究还有待展开。

3.2 协调策略分析

由于实施的便利性,批发价合同在供应链管理实践中非常普遍。故假定生产商 M_i 提供如下批发价合同:零售商 R_i 按单位批发价 $w_i(w_i \geqslant c_i)$ 向 M_i 定购产品,即 $Y_i = w_i q_i$。由(4)式,有

$$\pi_{Ri}(q,p) = (p_i - w_i + \beta_i)q_i - (p_i - v_i + \beta_i)h_i(q,p) - m_i(p) \tag{7}$$

命题 1 供应链竞争环境下,当零售商同时考虑价格和订货数量决策时,不管 M_j 采取何种合同形式,若 M_i 采取批发价合同,则仅当 $w_i = c_i$ 时,可协调分散式供应链 i 达到集中式供应链的效果。

证明 由(7)式,有 $\dfrac{\partial \pi_{Ri}^2(q,p)}{\partial q_i^2} = -\dfrac{p_i - v_i + \beta_i}{\lambda_i} f\left(\dfrac{q_i}{\lambda_i}/p\right) < 0$,即 $\pi_{Ri}(q,p)$ 为 q_i 的可微凹函数。由一阶条件,供应链 i 为分散式供应链情况下零售商 R_i 的最优策略(p_i^R, q^R)必须满足

$$q_i^R = \lambda_i(p_1^R, p_2^R, T_1, T_2) F^{-1}\left(\frac{p_i^R - w_i + \beta_i}{p_i^R - v_i + \beta_i}\right) \tag{8}$$

由(6)式,有

$$\frac{\partial \pi_i^2(q,p)}{\partial q_i^2} = -\frac{(p_i - v_i + \beta_i)}{\lambda_i} f\left(\frac{q_i}{\lambda_i} \mid p\right) < 0$$

即 $\pi_i(q,p)$ 为 q_i 的可微凹函数。由一阶条件,供应链 i 为集中式供应链情况下零售商 R_i 的最优策略(p_i^*, q_i^*)必须满足

$$q_i^* = \lambda_i(p_1^*, p_2^*, T_1, T_2) F^{-1} \frac{(p_i^* - c_i + \beta_i)}{p_i^* - v_i + \beta_i} \tag{9}$$

因为 F^{-1} 为严格单调增加函数,由(8)式和(9)式,仅当 $w_i = c_i$ 时,有(p_i^R, q_i^R)=(p_i^*, q_i^*)。证毕。□

分析 上述命题表明,供应链竞争环境下,如果供应商仅采用批发价合同来协调分散式供应链达到集中式供应链的效果,批发价必须等于边际成本,此时供应商的利润为 0,这缺乏现实的可行性,即批发价合同不能实现供应链协调。

下面进而研究收益共享合同的协调效果。假定生产商 M_i 提供如下收益共享合同:零售商 R_i 按单位价格 w_i 向生产商 M_i 订购产品,在销售季节结束后,R_i 将一定比例的销售收益支付给 M_i。假设 R_i 和 M_i 得到的销售收益比例分别为 $\phi_i, 1-\phi_i(0 < \phi_i \leqslant 1)$。

命题 2 供应链竞争环境下,当零售商同时考虑价格和订货数量决策时,不管 M_j 采

取何种合同形式，若 M_i 采取收益共享合同，则仅当 $w_i=\phi_i c_i$ 时，可协调供应链 i 达到集中式供应链的效果。

证明　依收益共享合同，有 $Y_i=w_i q_i+(1-\phi_i)[p_i S_i(q,p)+v_i I_i(q,p)-L_i(q,p)]$，代入(4)式，有

$$\begin{aligned}\pi_{Ri}(q,p)=&(\phi_i p_i-w_i+\phi_i\beta_i)q_i-(\phi_i p_i\\&-\phi_i v_i+\phi_i\beta_i)h_i(q,p)-\phi_i m_i(p)\end{aligned}\tag{10}$$

比较(6)式和(10)式可知，仅当 $w_i=\phi_i c_i$ 时，有 $\pi_{Ri}(q,p)=\phi_i\pi_i(q,p)$，即零售商 R_i 的利润与供应链 i 的总利润成比例关系，故此时零售商 R_i 的分散化决策等于集中化决策，命题结论成立。□

分析　命题 2 表明，收益共享合同可协调分散式供应链达到集中式供应链的效果，且生产商 M_i 可依据合同参数 ϕ_i 的不同取值来划分整条供应链的利润。因此，制定合理的合同参数，将增加供应链的整体收益，并达到链内成员的共赢。

推论 1　供应链竞争环境下，若两个生产商均采用收益共享合同，当零售商同时考虑价格和订货数量决策时，则仅当 $w_i=\phi_i c_i(i=1,2)$ 时，两条供应链可同时达到集中式供应链的效果。

可见，若两条供应链均采用批发价合同，则两条供应链均不能达到协调状态；若两条供应链均采用收益共享合同，则可同时达到协调状态(必需满足 $w_i=\phi_i c_i(i=1,2)$；若一条供应链采用批发价合同，一条采用收益共享合同，则仅一条供应链可达到协调状态。当两条供应链同时达到集中式供应链的效果时，其间的竞争体现为两条供应链均作为一个整体参与竞争，均衡状态表现为供应链间的竞争均衡。下面分析上述三种情况下零售商决策、供应链各方利润及整体利润。

4　算　例

假定产品 1 的参数为 $c_1=50,v_1=40,\beta_1=30,T_1=20$；产品 2 的参数为

$$c_2=40,v_2=30,\quad \beta_2=20,T_2=10$$

消费者对产品质量的偏好 α 为[0,2]上的均匀分布。此时 $\alpha_0=0.1(p_1-p_2)$，故仅当 $0<p_1-p_2<20$ 时，两种产品可同时拥有市场份额，并且有

$$\lambda_1=1-0.05(p_1-p_2),\quad \lambda_2=0.05(p_1-p_2)$$

为简单起见，省略变量的单位，并假定总需求量 d 为$[0,d_0(p_1,p_2)]$上的均匀分布，其中 $d_0(p_1,p_2)=1000-p_1-p_2>0$，即 $F(x|p)=x/d_0(p_1,p_2)$。下面分析如下三种情况下零售商决策、供应链各方利润和整体利润。

情况 1　两生产商均采用批发价合同：$w_1=60,w_2=50$，此时两条供应链均不协调。由(7)式，有

$$\begin{cases}\pi_{R1}(q,p)=(p_1-30)q_1-\dfrac{(p_1-10)q_1^2}{2\lambda_2 d_0(p_1,p_2)}-15\lambda_1 d_0(p_1,p_2)\\\pi_{R2}(q,p)=(p_2-30)q_2-\dfrac{(p_2-10)q_2^2}{2\lambda_2 d_0(p_1,p_2)}-10\lambda_2 d_0(p_1,p_2)\end{cases}$$

可见，$\pi_{Ri}(q,p)$是 q_i,p_i 的可微凹函数。由一阶条件 $\left(\frac{\partial\pi_{R1}}{\partial_{q1}}=\frac{\partial\pi_{R1}}{\partial_{p1}}=\frac{\partial\pi_{R2}}{\partial_{q2}}=\frac{\partial\pi_{R2}}{\partial_{p2}}=0\right)$ 得到零售商的订购量和零售价格决策，继而得到各生产商、零售商和供应链的利润（见表 1）。

情况 2 生产商 2 仍采用批发价合同：$w_2=50$，生产商 1 改用收益共享合同：$w_1=30$，$\phi_1=0.6$，此时仅供应链 1 达到协调状态，由(7)式和(10)式，有

$$\begin{cases}\pi_{R1}(q,p)=(0.6p_1-12)q_1-\dfrac{0.6(p_1-10)q_{12}}{2\lambda_1 d_0(p_1,p_2)}-9\lambda_1 d_0(p_1,p_2)\\ \pi_{R2}(q,p)=(p_2-30)q_2-\dfrac{(p_2-10)q_2^2}{2\lambda_2 d_0(p_1,p_2)}10\lambda_2 d_0(p_1,p_2)\end{cases}$$

可见，$\pi_{Ri}(q,p)$是 q_i,p_i 的可微凹函数。由一阶条件得到零售商的订购量和零售价格决策，进而得到各生产商、零售商和供应链的利润（见表 1）。

表 1　两条供应链间的三种竞争情况分析

	情况 1. 两条供应链均未协调		情况 2 供应链 1 协调，共应链 2 未协调		情况 3. 两条供应链均协调	
	$i=1$	$i=2$	$i=1$	$i=2$	$i=1$	$i=2$
p_i 的订货量 q_i	197.08	421.07	434.18	241.62	234.29	479.95
R_i 的零售价格 p_i	111.76	97.96	100.22	92.31	94.90	81.35
产品 i 的市场份额 λ_i	0.31	0.69	0.60	0.40	0.32	0.68
R_i 的利润	4028.51	12839.44	4813.10	6672.02	1949.11	8380.98
M_i 的利润	1970.83	4210.74	4341.76	2416.18	2342.86	4799.52
第 i 条供应链利润	5999.34	17050.18	9154.86	9088.20	4291.97	13180.5
两条供应链的总利润	23049.52		18243.06		17472.47	

情况 3 两生产商均采用收益共享合同：$w_1=30,\phi_1=0.6,w_2=24,\phi_2=0.6$，此时两条供应链均达到协调状态. 由(10)式，有

$$\begin{cases}\pi_{R1}(q,p)=(0.6p_1-12)q_1-\dfrac{0.6(p_1-10)q_1^2}{2\lambda_1 d_0(p_1,p_2)}-9\lambda 1 d_0(p_1,p_2)\\ \pi_{R2}(q,p)=(0.6p_2-12)q_2-\dfrac{0.6(p_2-10)q_2^2}{2\lambda_2 d_0(p_1,p_2)}-6\lambda_2 d_0(p_1,p_2)\end{cases}$$

可见，π_{Ri} 是 q_i,p_i 的可微凹函数。由一阶条件得到零售商的订购量和零售价格决策，进而得到各生产商、零售商和供应链的利润（表 1）。

分析 在情况 1、两生产商均采用批发价合同，此时两条供应链均不协调。第 1 条供应链的利润(5999.34)和产品市场份额(0.31)均远低于第 2 条供应链的利润(17050.18)和产品市场份额(0.69)，零售商 1 的利润(1970.83)和生产商 1 的利润(4028.51)较少。

在情况 2、生产商 2 仍保持情况 1 中的批发价合同不变，即供应链 2 保持不协调状态。生产商 1 转而采用收益共享合同，从而大幅提高了供应链 1 的利润(9154.86)和产品市场份额(0.60)，并同时提高了生产商 1 自身利润(4341.76)和零售商 1 的利润

(4813.76)，取得了双赢，表明了收益共享合同对供应链的协调效果。由于供应链 1 的效率和竞争力的提高，降低了供应链 2 的利润(9088.20)、产品 2 的市场份额(0.40)、生产商 2 的利润(2416.18)和零售商 2 的利润(6672.02)。

在情况 3、生产商 1 仍保持情况 2 中的收益共享合同不变，即供应链 1 保持协调状态。生产商 2 转而采用收益共享合同，从而大幅提高了供应链 2 的利润(13180.5)和产品市场份额(0.68)，并同时提高了自身利润(4799.52)和零售商 2 的利润(8380.98)，表明收益共享合同协调供应链的有效性。由于供应链 2 的效率和竞争力的提高，降低了供应链 1 的利润(4291.97)、产品 1 的市场份额(0.32)、生产商 1 的利润(2342.86)和零售商 1 的利润(1949.11)。

对比情况 1 与情况 2、以及情况 2 与情况 3 可知，只要其它供应链保持决策不变，不管其是否达到协调状态，我方供应链均可通过收益共享合同来协调自身供应链达到协调状态，从而大幅度提高供应链自身及参与企业的利润。所以协调是供应链竞争环境下供应链管理的主要策略。

对比情况 1 和情况 3，供应链 1 和供应链 2 在情况 3 中的利润较少、产品价格较低、但零售商的订货量较多，这说明以下两点：①两条供应链均实现协调后，其间的竞争越发激烈，此时全协调状态(情况 3)下各供应链的利润反而比全不协调状态(情况 1)下低。但如果我方供应链寄希望情况 1 发生而采取不协调策略，则当其它供应链由不协调转向协调时(即由情况 1 转到情况 2)，此时我方供应链利润将大幅降低，出现了一种囚徒困境现象；②供应链全部协调时系统整体运作效率将提高，从而可大幅降低产品价格、提高产品供应，即实现消费者福利的增加。

5　结束语

供应链竞争环境下，如何通过合同设计来协调供应链内部成员行为，使分散式供应链达到集中式供应链的效果，是当前迫切需要解决的问题。本文首先刻画了两条提供非同质同种产品的竞争供应链的超网络结构，为下一步运用交通均衡配流模型研究供应链网络均衡问题奠定了研究基础。然后假定消费者对产品质量的偏好为连续分布函数，运用产品差异化理论和顾客选择理论，在仅知道两条供应链的产品总需求的随机分布情况下，得到了各条供应链的产品需求分布，解决了通过总需求分解来得到各产品的需求问题。结合合同理论和博弈方法，证明了供应链竞争环境下，当零售商同时决定订购量和零售价格时，不管其它供应链采取何种合同形式，收益共享合同可以协调我方供应链达到集中式供应链效果。最后运用具体算例分析了两条供应链均不协调、仅一条协调、以及两条均协调情况下零售商决策、各方利润及供应链的利润，表明协调是供应链竞争环境下供应链管理的主要策略，且收益共享合同是协调供应链的有效方法。但是，当所有供应链均实现协调时，各条供应链的利润可能反而比所有供应链均未协调时要差，即出现了一种囚徒困境现象。未来可结合产品差异化、顾客服务水平(如缺货率)、缺货后的需求转移以及多阶段订货等因素开展进一步研究。

Analysis of the Com petitive Supply Chains'Structure and the Stra tegy for Supply Cha in Coord ination

XU Bing[1,2], ZHU Dao-li$_2$

(1. *Management Science and Engineering Department*, *Nanchang University*, *Nanchang* 330047, *China*; 2. *ManagementSchool*, *FudanUniversity*, *Shanghai* 200433, *China*)

Abstract: It is a key problem to study the structure of supply chains and supply chain coordination under the environment of SC vs. SC competition. In this paper, the super-network method is used to analyze the operation process of the supply chains and construct a super-network of the supply chains. In order to decompose to tal demand with given distribution function, customer choice theory is adopted to acquire the demand of each supply chain. By combining game theory with New svendor model, we put forw rda a revenue-share contract, which can coordinate the behaviors of the members included in a same supply chain under the environment of SC vs. SC competition. The final examp le shows that coordination strategy can improve the efficiency of supply chain operation, but the competition between coordinative supply chains is so fierce that the phenomenon of Prisoners Trap may exist.

Key words: supply chain management; coordinative strategy; newsvendor model; supply chain structure

参考文献

[1] Rice J B, Hoppe R M. SC Vs SC competition[J]. Supply Chain Management Review,2001,5(5):46-54

[2] Douglas M L,Martha C C. Issue in supply chain management [J]. Industrial Marketing Managenent,2000,29(1):65-83.

[3] Stock G N,Greis N P,Kasarda J P. Enterprise logistics and supply chain structure: the role of fit[J]. Joumal of Operations Management ,2000,18(5):531-547

[4] Nagurney A, DongJ, Zhang D. Asupply chain network equilibrium model[J]. Transportation Research Part E, 2002, 38 (5) :281-303.

[5] Dong J,ZhangD, Nagurney A. A supply chain network equilibrium model with random demands[J]. European Journal of Operational Research, 2004, 156 (1): 194-212.

[6] 徐兵,朱道立. 随机产品选择下多商品流供应链网络均衡研究[J]. 系统工程理论与

实践，2007，27 (3) ：82290，转 104.

[7] Zhang D. A network economic model for supply chain versus supply chain competition[J]. Omega，2006，34 (3):283-295.

[8] Emmons H，Gilbert S. Note. The role of returns policies in pricing and inventory decisions for catalogue goods[J]. Management Science，1998，44 (2) ：276-283.

[9] Tsay A A，Lovejoy W S. Quantity-flexibility contracts and supply chain performance[J]. Manufacturing and Service Operations Management，1999，1 (2) ：89-101.

[10] Taylor T. Supply chain coordination under channel rebates with sales effort effect [J]. Management Science，2002，48 (8)：992-1007.

[11] Cachon G P. Supply chain coordination with contracts. handbooks in operations research and management science：supply chain management[M]. edited by Steve Graves and Ton de Kok. North Holland，2003.

[12] Boyaci T,Gallego G. Supply chain coordination in a market with customer service competition[J]. Production and Operations Management，2004，13 (1) ：3-22.

[13] 甘永辉,徐兵. 供应链间的竞争与协调合同设计研究[J]. 南昌大学学报，2006，37 (2) ：43-47.

[14] Lau H S,Lau A H L. The new sstand problem：a capacitated multiple-product single-period inventoryproblem[J]. European Journal of Operational Research，1996，94 (1) ：29-42.

[15] 杜荣,胡奇英,陈开周. 同类产品多品牌的最优定价模型[J]. 管理科学学报，2004，7 (3) ：69-74.

[16] 朱道立,曹瑜. 多产品竞争环境下的需求理论和竞争策略设计[J]. 研究与发展管理，2005，17 (2) ：71-76.

[17] 鲁其辉,朱道立. 多产品竞争环境中最优供货决策[J]. 管理科学学报，2005，8 (6) ：43-50.

(本文发表于《运筹与管理》,2008 年第 5 期)

不对称信息下供应链最优激励契约的设计

徐　庆[1]，朱道立[1]，李善良[2]

（1. 复旦大学 管理学院，上海 200433；2. 苏州大学 管理学院，苏州 215021）

摘要： 对供应商和零售商之间的委托代理关系进行了分析研究，并将其归结为一个随机二层规划问题，通过给出适当的条件，证明了其解的存在性，并给出了所有的解。通过对解的分析，得到了有意义的经济学结论。

关键词： 供应链；委托代理；激励契约；二层规划

中图分类号： F830　　　**文献标志码：** A

1 引　言

供应链是供应商、制造商、批发商及零售商等通过运输、库存、信息及金融设施互连而组成的系统。由于供应链各成员企业的局部利益和行为经常与供应链系统的目标不相一致，使供应链的系统性能降低、收益受损。因此，设计和实现供应链的协调机制，提高供应链的总体性能，已引起学术界和企业界的重视. 目前，供应链协调管理，已成为一个很重要的管理问题，许多学者进行了研究[1~5]。

随着供应链时间和空间复杂性的增强，供应链企业间信息不对称现象和激励冲突变得越来越突出，学术界和企业界开始关注供应链委托代理问题的研究[6~15]。本文将研究供应商和零售商之间的委托代理关系。供应商为委托人，零售商为代理人。供应商提供产品给零售商，零售商通过自己的努力影响产品的销售量。不同的努力将直接影响销售量。一般而言，对零售商，随着努力水平的增加，销售量也将随之增加，但同时零售商付出的成本也将更多。另外，销售量还受到随机因素的影响。对供应商而言，所能观测到的只是最终的销售量，而不能观测到零售商的努力水平，而零售商知道自己的努力程度。因此作为代理人的零售商和作为委托人的供应商之间就存在信息不对称。如何有效解决供应商和零售商之间的代理问题是确保供应链有效性的一个重要因素。这个问题最终可归纳为一个不对称信息下的供应链激励契约设计问题或一个委托代理问题，本文将用二层随机规划问题表达这个问题。通过对该二层规划问题的研究。给出了该二层规划解存在的条件。并求出了该问题的全部解。从而解决了供应商面临的需要激励零售商付出哪种努

收稿日期： 2007-01-17

资助项目： 国家自然科学基金（70432001）

作者简介： 徐庆（1962～），男（汉族），博士，复旦大学管理学院，E-mail：xuqing@fudan. edu. cn.

力水平，以及当他选择这种努力水平时，应选择哪一种激励契约的问题。首先我们讨论了委托人和代理人是风险中性的情况，即效用函数是线性的。然后对严格风险喜好和严格风险厌恶的情况进行了讨论。最后对所得结果进行了分析。拉丰等人对这一问题也进行了研究[16]，但只得到了一个最优解，即一种可能实施的激励契约。与拉丰的结果相比较，本文则得到了该问题的全部解以及最优解的判别条件。因而本文的研究结果是拉丰等人工作的继续和发展。

设 e 是零售商的努力水平，本文假设仅有两种努力水平，即正努力水平，记为 $e=1$ 和零努力水平，记为 $e=0$. 令 $e=\{0,1\}$ 是零售商，即代理人的行动集。零售商付出一个努力 e，则相应的他付出一个值为 $\psi(e)$ 的成本，为讨论方便令 $\psi(1)=\psi,\psi(0)=0$。设他的效用函数在货币和努力成本之间是可分的，即 $V(t,e)=v(t)-\psi(e)$，对于供应商他所能观测到的只是最终的销售量 Q，假设市场只有两种需求 $\overline{Q},\underline{Q}$ 记 $Q=\{\overline{Q},\underline{Q}\}$ 是两个销售量。$\overline{p}(e)$（或 $\underline{p}(e)$）代表在已知行动 e 发生时，销量为 $\overline{Q}$（或 $\underline{Q}$）的概率. 显然，$\overline{p}(1)>\overline{p}(0)$，我们有 $\overline{p}(e)+\underline{p}(e)=1$。

委托人和代理人之间的契约是一个支付 $t=(\overline{t},\underline{t})$。$\overline{t}$（或 $\underline{t}$）是当销售量为 $\overline{Q}$（或 $\underline{Q}$）时代理人得到的委托人的支付。p 是产品的销售价格，c 是产品的成本，假设委托人是风险中性的，则委托人的期望效用是

$$EU(t,e)=\overline{p}(e)[(p-c)\overline{Q}-\overline{t}]+\underline{p}(e)[(p-c)\underline{Q}-\underline{t}] \tag{1}$$

$$=\overline{p}(e)[(p-c)\overline{Q}-\overline{t}]+(1-\overline{p}(e))[(p-c)\underline{Q}-\underline{t}]. \tag{2}$$

代理人的期望效用是

$$EV(t,e)=\overline{p}(e)[v(\overline{t})-\psi(e)]+\underline{p}(e)[v(\underline{t})-\psi(e)] \tag{3}$$

$$=\overline{p}(e)v(\overline{t})+(1-\overline{p}(e))v(\underline{t})-\psi(e). \tag{4}$$

代理人可以接受契约也可以拒绝契约。代理人要接受一个契约，首先必须保证他付出努力而得到的期望效用大于等于他的外在机会效用水平 V^*，此约束条件称为参与约束。同时，零售商总是选择使自己的期望效用最大的行动 e，这个约束称为激励相容约束。对委托人，他希望代理人所采取的行动 e 只能通过零售商的效用最大化来实现，委托人和代理人的关系见图 1。于是，委托代理问题（PAP）可表示为一个随机二层规划问题：

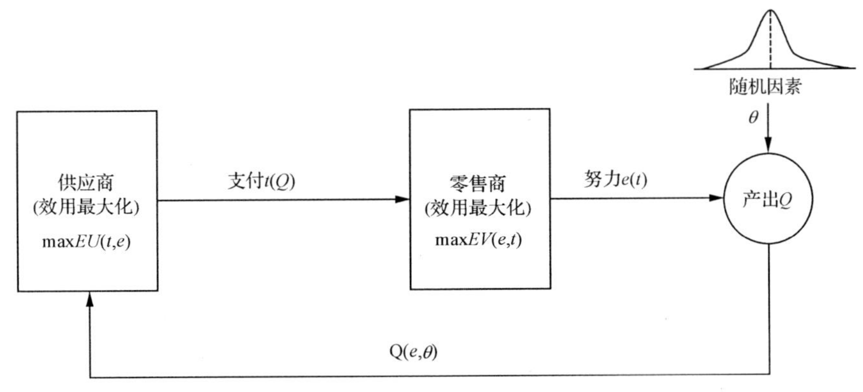

图 1　供应商和零售商关系图

$$\max_{t,e} \quad EU(t,e) \tag{5}$$

$$\text{s. t.} \quad e \in \arg\max_{e' \in \{0,1\}} EV(t,e') \tag{6}$$

$$EV(t,e) \geqslant V^* \tag{7}$$

在这个问题里，委托人是领导者，代理人是追随者，(6)式是激励相容约束，(7)式参与约束。

考虑由下式定义的期望效用最优行动函数 $e(t)$

$$EU(t,e(t)) = \max EU(t,e) \tag{8}$$

$$\text{s. t.}\, e \in \arg\max_{e' \in \{0,1\}} EV(t,e') \tag{9}$$

在研究委托代理问题解的存在性时，函数 $e(t)$ 起着重要的作用。

委托人的决策空间可分为如下三个部分：

令

$$\Gamma_1 = \{t \in R^2 \mid EV(t,1) > EV(t,0)\} = \{t \in R^2 \mid v(\bar{t}) - v(\underline{t}) < \beta\} \tag{10}$$

$$\Gamma_0 = \{t \in R^2 \mid EV(t,1) < EV(t,0)\} = \{t \in R^2 \mid v(\bar{t}) - v(\underline{t}) > \beta\} \tag{11}$$

$$\tilde{\Gamma} = \{t \in R^2 \mid EV(t,1) = EV(t,0)\} = \{t \in R^2 \mid v(\bar{t}) - v(\underline{t}) = \beta\} \tag{12}$$

其中 $\beta = \dfrac{\psi(1)}{\bar{p}(1) - \bar{p}(0)}$。因而，函数 $e(t)$ 可用另一种形式表示为

$$e(t) = \begin{cases} 1 & \text{if } t \in \Gamma_1 \\ 0 & \text{if } t \in \Gamma_0 \\ 0 \text{ 或 } 1 & \text{if } t \in \tilde{\Gamma} \end{cases}$$

(PAP)可表达成一个优化问题

$$\max_{t \in T} EU(t,e(t)) \tag{13}$$

其中决策可行集合为 $T = \{t \mid EV(t,e(t)) \geqslant V^*\}$。为了研究(PAP)的最优解的存在性，我们首先引入如下三个引理。

引理 1.1 对于 $t = (\bar{t}, \underline{t})$，函数 $EU(t,e(t))$ 是单值和上半连续的。

引理 1.2 (i) $\lim\limits_{\|t\| \to \infty} EU(t,e(t)) = -\infty$。

(ii) 存在 $\alpha > 0$ 和满足 $\|s\| \leqslant \alpha$ 的可行点 $s \in T$ 使

$$EU(t,e(t)) \leqslant EU(s,e(s))$$

对所有满足 $\|t\| \geqslant \alpha$ 的 $t \in T$。

引理 1.3 约束集合 T 是闭的。

由这三个引理，根据最优化问题解的存在性定理，我们能得到下面的结论。

定理 1.1 委托代理问题有一个最优解。

上面的引理和定理的证明见附录。

设 T^* 是(PAP)的解集。由定理 1.1，$T^* \neq \varnothing$。

为了求解(PAP)，分别固定追随者的行动 $e(t) = 1$（或 $e(t) = 0$），考虑辅助问题(FA1)

$$\max_{t} \quad EU(t,1) \tag{14}$$

$$\text{s. t.} \quad EV(t,1) \geqslant EV(t,0) \tag{15}$$

$$EV(t,1) \geqslant V^* \tag{16}$$

和(FA0)

$$\max_t \quad EU(t,0) \tag{17}$$

$$\text{s. t.} \quad EV(t,1) \geqslant EV(t,0) \tag{18}$$

$$EV(t,0) \geqslant V^* \tag{19}$$

令 F_1(或 F_0)是(FA1)(或(FA0))的可行集。

通常,供应商不能观测到零售商的努力,而只能观测到最终的销售量 Q,这样就存在了信息不对称。根据零售商的风险偏好程度,可将零售商分为风险中性和风险规避两种情况。在第 2 节和第 3 节中,我们分别讨论这两种情况下的最优契约的设计。

2 风险中性模型与最优契约设计

在这一节,考虑代理人是风险中性的,即 $v(t)=t$。在这种情况下,问题(FA1)和(FA0)是线性规划。(FA1)有下列形式

$$\max_t \quad \overline{p}(1)[(p-c)\overline{Q}-\overline{t}]+(1-\overline{p}(1))[(p-c)\underline{Q}-\underline{t}] \tag{20}$$

$$\text{s. t.} \quad (\overline{p}(1)-\overline{p}(0))\overline{t}-(\overline{p}(1)-\overline{p}(0))\underline{t}-\psi \geqslant 0 \tag{21}$$

$$\overline{p}(1)\overline{t}-(1-\overline{p}(1))\underline{t}-\psi \geqslant V^* \tag{22}$$

其 KKT 条件是

$$\overline{p}(1)-\lambda_1(\overline{p}(1)-\overline{p}(0))-\mu_1\overline{p}(1)=0 \tag{23}$$

$$(1-\overline{p}(1))+\lambda_1(\overline{p}(1)-\overline{p}(0))-\mu_1(1-\overline{p}(1))=0 \tag{24}$$

其中 λ_1,μ_1 分别是约束条件(21)和(22)的乘子。

由(23)~(24),我们得到(FA1)的最优乘子

$$\lambda_1=0,$$
$$\mu_1=1.$$

这表明参与约束(22)式是紧的。所以解集 $\hat{T}_1=\{t\in F_1 \mid \overline{p}(1)\overline{t}-(1-\overline{p}(0))\underline{t}-\psi=V^*\}$。

注意 $EU(t,1)=\alpha-\psi-EV(t,1)$,其中 $\alpha=\overline{p}(1)(p-c)\overline{Q}+(1-\overline{p}(1))(p-c)\underline{Q}$。这样在每一个解点 $\hat{t}_1\in\hat{T}_1$,委托人都有最优期望效用 $EU(\hat{t}_1,1)=\alpha-(V^*+\psi)$。然而,在每一点 $t\in F_1-\hat{T}_1$,代理人的期望效用 $EV(t,1)>V^*$。对于委托人,则有 $EU(t,1)=\alpha-\psi-EV(t,1)<\alpha-(V^*+\psi)$。

同理,固定行动 $e(t)=0$,考虑辅助问题(FA0)

$$\max_t \quad \overline{p}(0))[(p-c)\overline{Q}-\overline{t}]+(1-\overline{p}(0))[(p-c)\underline{Q}-\underline{t}] \tag{25}$$

$$\text{s. t.} \quad -(\overline{p}(1)-\overline{p}(0))\overline{t}+(\overline{p}(1)-\overline{p}(0))\underline{t}+\psi \geqslant 0 \tag{26}$$

$$\overline{p}(0)\overline{t}+(1-\overline{p}(0))\underline{t} \geqslant V^* \tag{27}$$

对(FA0)我们有最优乘子和解集

$$\lambda_0=0,$$
$$\mu_0=1.$$

这表明参与约束(27)式是紧的。所以解集 $\hat{T}_0=\{t\in F_0 \mid \overline{p}(0)\overline{t}-(1-\overline{p}(0))\underline{t}=V^*\}$。见

图 2。

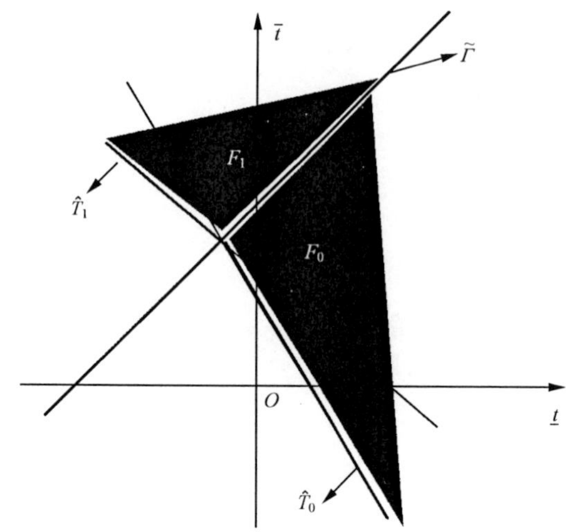

图 2 解集(零售商风险中性时)

注意 $EU(t,0)=\beta-EV(t,0)$,其中 $\beta=\bar{p}(0)(p-c)\bar{Q}+(1-\bar{p}(0)(p-c)Q$。这样在每个解点 $\hat{t}_0\in\hat{T}_0$,委托人的最优期望效用是 $EU(\hat{t}_0,0)=\beta-V^*$。然而,在每一个 $t\in F_0-\hat{T}_0$,代理人的期望效用是 $EV(t,0)>V^*$。对于委托人则有 $EU(t,0)=\beta-EV(t,0)<\beta-V^*$。

最优激励机制判别不等式 A

$$(p-c)(\bar{Q}-Q)\geqslant\frac{\psi}{\bar{p}(1)-\bar{p}(0)}. \tag{28}$$

在条件 A 下,容易得到下面的定理。

定理 2.1 当代理人是风险中性的,即 $v(t)=t$ 时,如果判别不等式(A)的严格不等式成立,则(PAP)有激励决策解集合 $\hat{T}_1$。如果判别不等式(A)的等式成立,则有解集合 $\hat{T}_1\cup\hat{T}_0$。否则,有解集合 $\hat{T}_0$。

从以上的推导和分析,我们得到如下结论。

结论 1 在信息不对称情况下,若零售商是风险中性,当条件 A 满足时,供应商选择激励零售商高努力水平,此时尽管零售商的努力水平不可观测,但道德风险不是问题,供应商无须为此付出更多的成本。零售商努力所得到的收益正好补偿了其所付出的成本。

3 风险规避模型与最优契约

在这一节,考虑风险规避的情形,即非线性情形,设 $v=v(t)$,$\bar{v}=v(\bar{t})$和 $\underline{v}=v(\underline{t})$。假设 $v(t)$是严格递增和强凹的,则 $v=v(t)$有反函数 $h=v^{-1}$,并且 h 还是严格递增和强凸的。现在,(FA1)可表达为一个凹规划(NFA1)

$$\max_{t}\quad \bar{p}(1)[(p-c)\bar{Q}-h(\bar{v})]+(1-\bar{p}(1))[(p-c)Q-h(\underline{v})] \tag{29}$$

$$\text{s.t.}\quad (\bar{p}(1)-\bar{p}(0))\bar{v}-(\bar{p}(1)-\bar{p}(0))\underline{v}-\psi\geqslant 0 \tag{30}$$

$$\bar{p}(1)\bar{v}-(1-\bar{p}(1))\underline{v}-\psi\geqslant V^* \tag{31}$$

该凹规划有唯一解 $v_1^*=(\bar{v}_1^*,\underline{v}_1^*)$,其 KKT 条件是

$$\bar{p}(1)h'(\bar{v})-\lambda_1(\bar{p}(1)-\bar{p}(0))-\mu_1\bar{p}(1)=0 \tag{32}$$

$$(1-\bar{p}(1))h'(\underline{v})+\lambda_1(\bar{p}(1)-\bar{p}(0))-\mu_1(1-\bar{p}(1))=0 \tag{33}$$

由(32)~(33),得到(NFA1)的最优乘子

$$\lambda_1=\frac{\bar{p}(1)(1-\bar{p}(1))(h'(\bar{v})-h'(\bar{v}))}{\bar{p}(1)-\bar{p}(0)}$$

$$\mu=\bar{p}(1)h'(\bar{v})+(1-\bar{p}(1))h'(\underline{v})).$$

由于 $h(\cdot)$是严格递增的,则 μ_1 是正的. 为保证 $\lambda_1>0$,我们仅需要找一个满足下列线性

系统(或保证约束(30)～(31)是紧的)的可行点：

$$(\overline{p}(1)-\overline{p}(0))\overline{v}-(\overline{p}(1)-\overline{p}(0))\underline{v}=\psi \tag{34}$$

$$\overline{p}(0)\overline{v}+(1-\overline{p}(0))\underline{v}=V^* \tag{35}$$

从这个线性系统，我们得到(FA1)的最优解 $\overline{v}_1^*=V^*+\dfrac{(1-\overline{p}(0))\psi}{\overline{p}(1)-\overline{p}(0)}$ 和 $\underline{v}_1^*=V^*-\dfrac{\overline{p}(0)\psi}{\overline{p}(1)-(0)}$。委托人有相应的最优支付 $t_1^*=(h(\overline{v}_1^*),h(\underline{v}_1^*))$ 和最优期望效用 $EU(t_1^*,1)$ $\alpha-\overline{p}(1)h(\overline{v}_1^*)-(1-\overline{p}(1))h(\overline{v}_1^*)$。

下面考虑非线性辅助问题(NFA0)

$$\max_t \quad \overline{p}(0)[(p-c)\overline{Q}-h(\overline{v})]+(1-\overline{p}(0))[(p-c)\underline{Q}-h(\underline{v})] \tag{36}$$

$$\text{s.t.}\quad -(\overline{p}(1)-\overline{p}(0)\overline{v}+(\overline{p}(1)-\overline{p}(0))\underline{v}+\psi\geqslant 0 \tag{37}$$

$$\overline{p}(0))\overline{v}+(1-\overline{p}(0))\underline{v}\geqslant V^* \tag{38}$$

其 KKT 条件是

$$\overline{p}(0)h'(\overline{v})-\lambda_1(\overline{p}(1)-\overline{p}(0))-\mu_1\overline{p}(0)=0 \tag{39}$$

$$(1-\overline{p}(0))h'(\underline{v})+\lambda_1(\overline{p}(1)-\overline{p}(0))-\mu_1(1-\overline{p}(0))=0 \tag{40}$$

由(39)～(40)，我们得到(NFA0)的最优乘子

$$\lambda_0=\frac{-\overline{p}(0)(1-\overline{p}(0))(h'(\overline{v})-h'(\underline{v}))}{\overline{p}(1)-\overline{p}(0)},$$

$$\mu_0=\overline{p}(0)h'(\overline{v})+(1-\overline{p}(0))h'(\underline{v}).$$

为保证 $\lambda_0\geqslant 0$，v_0^* 必须满足. $\overline{v}_0^*=\underline{v}_0^*$。这时可以得到(NFA0)的最优乘子：

$$\lambda_0=0 \tag{41}$$

$$\mu_0=h'(v_0^*)>0 \tag{42}$$

所以，约束 $\overline{p}(0)\overline{v}+(1-\overline{p}(0))\underline{v}\geqslant V^*$ 在$(\overline{v}_0^*,\underline{v}_0^*)$是紧的。最后我们得到 $\overline{v}_0^*=\underline{v}_0^*=V^*$，因此$(V^*,V^*)$是(NFA0)的解。见图 3，而委托人得到的最优支付为 $t_0^*=(h(V^*),h(V^*))$，最优期望效用为 $EU(t_0^*,0)=\beta-h(V^*)$。

最优激励机制判别不等式 B

$$\begin{aligned}\overline{p}(1)-\overline{p}(0)(p-c)(\overline{Q}-\underline{Q})\geqslant{}&\overline{p}(1)h\left(V^*+\frac{(1-\overline{p}(0))\psi}{\overline{p}(1)-\overline{p}(0)}\right)\\&+(1-\overline{p}(1))h\left(V^*-\frac{\overline{p}(0)\psi}{\overline{p}(1)-\overline{p}(0)}\right)-h(V^*).\end{aligned} \tag{43}$$

下面的定理容易证明。

定理 3.1　当 $v(t)$是非线性时，如果判别不等式(B)的严格不等式成立，则(PAP)有解 $t_1^*=\left(h\left(V^*+\dfrac{(1-\overline{p}(0))\psi}{\overline{p}(1)-\overline{p}(0)}\right),h\left(V^*-\dfrac{\overline{p}(0)\psi}{\overline{p}(1)-\overline{p}(0)}\right)\right)$。如果判别不等式(B)的等式成立，则有解 $t_1^*\cup t_0^*$. 否则，(PAP)有解 $t_0^*=(h(V^*),h(V^*))$。

结论 2　在信息不对称情况下，若道德风险和零售商是风险规避同时存在，当条件 B 满足时，供应商选择激励零售商付出高努力水平，激励契约为 $\overline{t}=h\left(V^*+\dfrac{(1-\overline{p}(0))\psi}{\overline{p}(1)-\overline{p}(0)}\right)$，

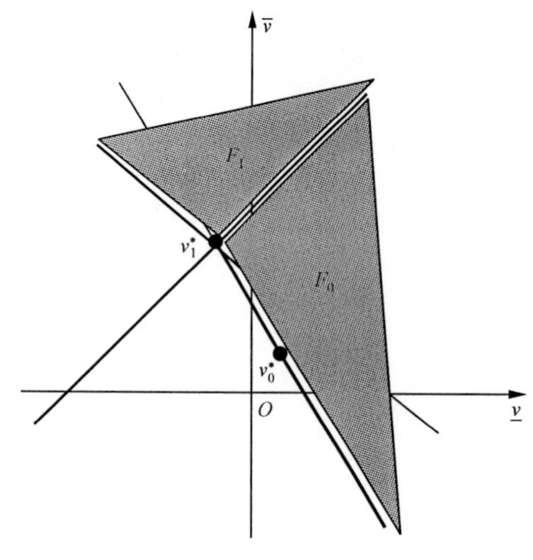

图 3　解集(零售商风险压恶时)

$t=h\left(V^*-\frac{\bar{p}(0)\psi}{\bar{p}(1)-\bar{p}(0)}\right)$，此时，供应商会付出额外的信息成本 $\bar{p}(1)h\left(V^*+\frac{(1-\bar{p}(0))\psi}{\bar{p}(1)-\bar{p}(0)}\right)+(1-\bar{p}(1))h\left(V^*-\frac{\bar{p}(0)\psi}{\bar{p}(1)-\bar{p}(0)}\right)-h(V^*)$。否则，供应商应选择激励零售商零努力水平，此时，供应商无需付出额外的信息成本。

注：如果 $v(t)=t$，即，在线性情况下，条件(B)和条件(A)是一样的。

4　附　录

引理 1.1 的证明：

证明　由定义，$EU(t,e(t))$是单值的。

令$\{t_k\}\to t_0$。由于 Γ_0 和 Γ_1 是开的，如果 $t_0\in\Gamma_0$(或 $t_0\in\Gamma_1$)，假设$\{t_k\}\subset\Gamma_0$(或$\{t_k\}\subset\Gamma_1$)。而且，$EU(t_0,0)=\lim\limits_{t_k\to t_0}EU(t_k,0)$(或 $EU(t_0 1)=$)$\lim\limits_{t_k\to t_0}EU(t_k,1)$.)

如果 $t_0\in\tilde{\Gamma}$，$\limsup\limits_{t_k\to t_0}EU(t_k,e(t_k))\leqslant EU(t_0,1)=E(t_0,e(t_0))$。所以 $EU(t,e(t))$是上半连续的。

引理 1.3 的证明：

证明　令 $t_k\in T$，$t_k\to t_0$

$$EV(t_k,e(t_k))=\bar{p}(e(t_k))v(\bar{t}^k)+(1-\bar{p}(e_{t_k}))v(\underline{t}^k)-\psi(e(t_k))\geqslant V^*$$

如果 $t_0\in\Gamma_0$ 或 $t_0\in\Gamma_1$，由于 Γ_0 和 Γ_1 是开的，则我们假设 $t_k\in\Gamma_0$ 或 $t_k\in\Gamma_1$。如果$\{t_k\}\in\Gamma_0$ 或$\{t_k\}\in\Gamma_1$。显然 $t_0\in T$。

如果 $t_0\in\tilde{\Gamma}$，$t_k=\{t_{k_1}\}\cup\{t_{k_2}\}$，其中$\{t_{k1}\}\subset\Gamma_0\cap T$，$\{t_{k_2}\}\subset(\Gamma_1\cup\tilde{\Gamma})\cap T$。则我们有

$$V^*\leqslant EV(t_{k_1},e(t_{k_1}))=EV(t_{k_1},0)\to EV(t_0,0).$$

另外，由于 $t_0\in\tilde{\Gamma}$，所以

$$EV(t_0,e(t_0))=EV(t_0,1)=EV(t_0,0)\geqslant V^*,$$

同样，我们有

$$V^*\leqslant EV(t_{k_2},e(t_{k_2}))=EV(t_{k_2},1)\to EV(t_0,1).$$

以及

$$EV(t_0,e(t_0))\geqslant V^*.$$

所以，T 是一个闭集合。

定理 1.1 的证明：

证明　考虑下列规划问题

$$\max_t EU(t,e(t)) \tag{44}$$

$$\text{s.t.}\quad t\in T \text{ and } \|t\|\leqslant\alpha \tag{45}$$

(44)的可行域是紧的。由引理 1.1,$EU(t,e(t))$上半连续的。这样(44)有一个最优解,由引理 1.2,它一定也是委托代理问题(PAP)的解。

The Supply Chain Optimal Contract Design under Asymmetrical Information

XU Qing[1] ,ZHU Dao-li[1] ,LI Shan-liang[2]

(1. Management School ,Fudan University ,Shanghai 200433 ,China ;
2. Management School,Soochow University ,Suzhou 215021 ,China)

Abstract : In this paper ,we study the principal-agent problem between the supplier and the retailer. we formulate the problem as a stochastic bi-level problem. Under suiaable conditions ,we prove the existence of solutions ,and give all the solutions. Furthermore ,we give some economic interpretations of some results obtained in this paper on the basis of analysis of the solution.

Key words: supply chain management;principal-agent problem;incentive contract;bilevel programming

参考文献

[1] Cachon G P. Supply Chain Coordination with Contracts[M]. Handbook in Operations Research and Management Science : Supply Chain Management. North-Horland ,2002.

[2] Kadiyadi V,Chintagunta P,Vilcassim N. Manufacture-retail channel interactions and implications for channel power: an empirical investigation of pricing in a local market [J]. Marketing Science, 2000,19(2):127-148.

[3] Lee H ,Whang S. Decentralized multi-echelon supply chains: Incentives and information [J]. Management Science,1999,45(5):633-640.

[4] Munson C L ,Posenblatt M J . Coordination a three-level supply chain with quantity discounts[J]. IIE Transactions ,2001 ,33 :371-384.

[5] Sudhir K. Structur al analysis of manufacturer pricing in the presence of a strategic retailer [J]. Marketing Science,2001,20(3):244-264.

[6] Basu A K,Lal R,Srinivasan V,et al. Salesforce compensation plans: An agency theoretic perspective [J]. Marketing Science,1985, 4(Fall) : 267-291.

[7] Chen Fangruo. Sales-force incentives and inventory management[J]. Manufacturing and Service Operations Management ,2000 ,2(2) : 186-202.

[8] Cachon G,Lariviere M. Capacity choice and allocation: Strategic behavior and supply chain performance [J]. Management Science, 1999 ,47(5) :629-646.

[9] Corbett C,GrooteD. A supplier'soptimal quantity discount policy under asymmetric information [J]. Management Science,2001,47 (7) :966-978.

[10] Desai P S,Srinivasan K. Demand signaling under unobservable effort in franchising: Linear and nonlinear price contracts[J]. Management Science,1995,41(10):1608-1623.

[11] Lal R,Staelin R. Salesforce compensation plans in environments with asymmetric information [J]. Marketing Science,1986,5 (summer):179-198.

[12] Lal R ,Srinivasan V. Compensation plans for single and multi-product salesforces : An application of the Holmstrom-Milgrom model [J]. Management Science,1993,39(7):777-793.

[13] Lariviere M A,Padmanabhan V. Slotting allowances and new product introductions [J]. Marketing Science,1997,16(2) :112-128.

[14] Priest G. A theory of consumer product warranty[J]. Yale Law Journal,1981,90:1297-1352.

[15] Wang Y, Gerchak Y. Capacity games in assembly systems with uncertain demand [J]. Manufacturing and Service Operations Management ,2003 ,5(3) :252-267.

[16] [法]让-雅可,拉丰(Jean-Jacques Laffont) ,大卫. 马赫蒂摩(David Maritimort) . 激励理论——委托代理模型[M]. 中国人民大学出版社,2002.
Jean-Jacques Laffont ,David Maritimort. The Theory of Incentives Ⅰ : The Pricipal-agent Model [M]. China Renmin University Press ,2002.

(本文发表于《系统工程理论与实践》,2007 年第 4 期)

合同管理中二层谈判策略*

陈祥锋，朱道立

（复旦大学管理学院，上海 200433）

摘要：从行为动机出发，就生产商和供应商之间质量争端，建立了 Nash 均衡模型，分析了合同参数对整个供应链（包括生产过程和销售过程）中产品质量的控制作用。另外，还研究了基于二层决策模型的合同管理中的谈判策略。

关键词：合同物流；合同管理；质量管理；Nash 均衡；二层决策

中图分类号：F27　**文献标识码**：A　**文章编号**：1007-9807(2002)03-0017-06

0　引　言

随着企业的发展，物流活动越来越受到重视，被认为是"企业的第三利润源"。而合同物流，则是当前物流活动的一项革新。合同物流，是指通过合同关系，使供应商提供全部或部分物资管理和配送服务的过程。其目的是基于降低成本和提高服务水平. 合同管理是合同物流的核心。

合同物流虽然意味着巨大的商机，但也潜伏着一定的风险。在实施过程中，不可轻易忽视的问题是质量的管理控制问题。采购商希望以合适的价格购买质量保证的原材料或部件；而对供应商而言，高质量的物资供应意味着成本提高，利润减少。因为高质量的物资供应需要一系列直接、间接配套服务水平的提高，如生产、运输设备的更新和创新、高质量的原材料以及更高的管理费用，等等，所以供应商在某种程度上不大愿意提供高质量的产品。

质量问题，可能形成供应链中的分裂点，严重损害了生产商和供应商、生产商和消费者之间的关系和彼此的利益. 这就是合同物流中合同管理的质量风险问题。

在传统上，主要是运用统计控制技术（如控制图表，方差样品检验等）来进行质量管理和质量控制（SQC）研究。然而，产品质量的不确定性，除了受自然和随机因素影响外，还与生产商和供应商的主观因素有关. 全面质量管理（TQC）是现代管理系统中的一个重要组成部分，其含义为要生产出满足客户要求的产品，除了用数理统计方法控制制造流程之外，还应有一系列的组织管理工作。应指出的是，在全面质量管理，人们往往忽略了生产商和供应商的人为动机，而现代合同物流管理正是从人为动机出发进行质量的管理和风

---

* 收稿日期：2000-08-16；修订日期：2002-04-04.

基金项目：国家自然科学基金资助项目（79870106）.

作者简介：陈祥锋（1973～），男，福建惠安人，博士生.

险控制。

随着研究的深入，已有一些学者，在供应链质量管理中，开始重视行为动机对质量的影响作用。Priest 研究了质量保修合同(warranty contract)中败德行为(moral hazard)的重要性[1]. Kam bhu 和 Mann & Wissink 建立模型集中分析了在生产商和消费者之间出现双向败德行为(double moralhazard)时，双方分别在生产水平(levels of quality)和关心程度(con sum er care)两方面的最优策略[2,3]。Russell & Thomas 运用模型分析了买者和卖者的行为(双向败德行为)通过质量保修合同如何影响产品的质量问题。Chew & Pisano 讨论了合同中的质量控制，并指出：同较少的供应商签定长期供应合同可提高采购品的质量[4]。Reyniers 采用博弈论工具，研究了生产技术固定下，采购商和供应商之间的质量策略[5]。Reyniers & Tapiero 就行为动机对质量的影响，以及生产技术可选择的条件下(生产高质量或生产低质量产品的技术)，建立静态博弈模型进而分析供应链中的质量问题[6]。

本文利用合同理论以及二层决策理论来研究合同物流中采购商和供应商之间的相互作用.采购商为优化自己的利益，要求供应商供应高质量的产品(价格一定的条件下)，但采购商并不了解供应商的实际选择(供应高质量产品或低质量产品)，除非对采购物资进行检验；理性的供应商追求自己的效用最大化。采购商为了让供应商的实际选择符合自己的利益，必须设计一种激励机制，来控制供应商的行为。另外，供应链的质量问题，包括两个过程，即生产过程和销售过程的质量问题假设最终产品的质量源于原材料或部件的质量，本文利用二层决策法(bi-level dicision)，构建二层决策模型，探讨了供应合同(采购过程)的合同决策变量(价格惩罚)，对最终产品(销售过程)的质量控制作用问题。

1 合同约束

合同物流中，采购商通过设计合同决策变量(本文重点研究价格惩罚项)来诱使供应商的行动符合自己的目标.为便于研究，在建模之前作如下假设：

1) 采购商对采购物资进行检验率为 y，不进行检验率为 $(1-y)$. $0\leqslant y\leqslant 1$，单位产品的检验成本为 m，销售单位最终产品的价格 θ。

2) 供应商，生产技术是可选择的，即可提供高质量的产品，也可提供低质量产品.供应低质量产品的成本为 T_1，产品不合格率为 P_1；供应高质量产品之成本为 T_2，产品不合格率为 P_2。其中 $T_1 < T_2$，$P_1 > P_2$。供应商供应低质量产品率为 x，供应高质量产品率为 $(1-x)$，$0\leqslant x\leqslant 1$。单位产品的销售价格为 π。

3) $\Delta\pi$ 为价格惩罚参数。即采购商对采购物资进行检验，如发现不合格产品存在，将采购价格降低 $\Delta\pi$。

4) 采购商对采购物资的质量要求为不合格的产品概率必须小于 p_1。

采购商拥有决定价格惩罚 $\Delta\pi$ 的权力，但 $\Delta\pi$ 的具体确定得经过采购商和供应商双方谈判后才能最终决定。事实上，$\Delta\pi$ 的选择必须受到某些约束.在进一步讨论之前，对 $\Delta\pi$ 的选择范围和合同谈判的关系先作一分析。

1) 如果 $\Delta\pi\leqslant\Delta T/\Delta P$，$\Delta T=T_2-T_1$，$\Delta P=P_1-P_2$。这时，价格惩罚 $\Delta\pi$ 小于相对产品成本差异 $\Delta T/\Delta P$ 时，供应商必定采取低质量生产，而价格惩罚 $\Delta\pi$ 失去了约束意义，这

在合同管理中不大可能出现。

2) 如果 $m<\Delta\pi P_2$，即检验成本比供应商采取高质量生产所遭受得惩罚还小，采购商定采取检验策略，此时即便是供应商全力采取高质量生产仍会受到较大的损失，因而在合同谈判中供应商必然会要求 $\Delta\pi$ 降低，使得 $\Delta\pi\leqslant m/P_2$。

3) 如果 $m>\Delta\pi P_1$，意味着 $\Delta\pi$ 太小。由于检验成本大于供应商全面采取低质量所遭受的惩罚，采购商得不偿失，只好采取不检验的策略，不能对采购物品起到质量的约束作用，这样，在合同谈判中，采购商必然要求进一步提高 $\Delta\pi$，使得 $\Delta\pi\geqslant m/P_1$，否则取消供应合同

因此，合同谈判中，对生产商(供应商)而言，$\Delta\pi$ 应满足，$\Delta\pi>\Delta T/\Delta P$ 和 $m./P_1\leqslant\Delta\pi\leqslant \mathrm{m}/\mathrm{P}_2$。

2　Nash 均衡模型

由合同理论可知，对于给定的 $\Delta\pi$，生产商和供应商的行为构成了一个 Nash 均衡模型. 即寻求均衡解 $(x^*(\Delta\pi),y^*(\Delta\pi))$ 满足 $0\leqslant x^*(\Delta\pi)\leqslant 1$ 和 $0\leqslant y^*(\Delta\pi)\leqslant 1$，以及

$$U(x^*(\Delta\pi),y^*(\Delta\pi))\geqslant U(x^*(\Delta\pi),y) \tag{1}$$

对任意 $y\in[0,1]$

$$V(x^*(\Delta\pi),y^*(\Delta\pi))\geqslant V(x,y^*(\Delta\pi))$$

对任意 $x\in[0,1]$

其中 $U(x,y)$ 为生产商的期望支付函数(the expected payoff)，即

$$\begin{aligned}U(x,y)=&[\theta-(\pi-\Delta\pi P_1)-m]xy+(\theta-\pi)x(1-y)\\&+[\theta-(\pi-\Delta\pi P_2)-m](1-x)y+(\theta-\pi)(1-x)(1-y)\end{aligned} \tag{2}$$

$V(x,y)$ 为供应商的期望支付函数，即

$$\begin{aligned}V(x,y)=&(\pi\Delta\pi P_1-T_1)xy+(\pi-T_1)x(1-y)+-(\pi-\Delta\pi P_2-T_2)(1-x)y\\&+(\pi-T_2)(1-x)(1-y)\end{aligned} \tag{3}$$

对于给定的 $\Delta\pi$ 和 y，$V(x,y)$ 为 x 的线性函数，由式(3)可计算它的斜率为

$$\frac{\mathrm{d}V}{\mathrm{d}x}=\Delta T-\Delta P\Delta\pi y$$

由此可求得反应函数 $x(y)$ 如下：

$$x(y)=\begin{cases}[0,1], & \text{如果 } y=\dfrac{\Delta T}{\Delta P\Delta\pi}\\ 1, & \text{如果 } y>\dfrac{\Delta T}{\Delta P\Delta\pi}\\ 0, & \text{如果 } y<\dfrac{\Delta T}{\Delta P\Delta\pi}\end{cases} \tag{4}$$

其中

$$\Delta T=T_2-T_1,\Delta P=P_1-P_2$$

另一方面，对给定的 $\Delta\pi$ 和 x，$U(x,y)$ 是 y 的线性函数. 由式(2)计算斜率为

$$\frac{\mathrm{d}U}{\mathrm{d}y}=\Delta\pi\Delta Px+\Delta\pi P_2-m$$

由此可求得反应函数 $y(x)$ 如下：

$$x(y)=\begin{cases}[0,1], & \text{如果 } x=\dfrac{m-\Delta\pi P_2}{\Delta P\Delta\pi}\\ 1, & \text{如果 } x>\dfrac{m-\Delta\pi P_2}{\Delta P\Delta\pi}\\ 0, & \text{如果 } x<\dfrac{m-\Delta\pi P_2}{\Delta P\Delta\pi}\end{cases} \tag{5}$$

由式(4)和(5)可得采购商和供应商的反应函数如图 1 所示：

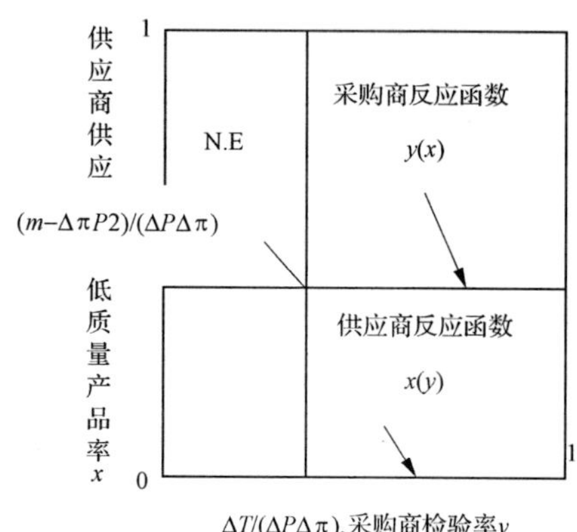

图 1　采购商和供应商反应函数图

当 $m/P_1<\Delta\pi<m/P_2$，有唯一 Nash 均衡模型(x^*,y^*)：

$$\begin{cases}x^*(\Delta\pi)=\dfrac{m-\Delta\pi P_2}{\Delta P\Delta\pi}\\ y^*(\Delta\pi)=\dfrac{\Delta T}{\Delta P\Delta\pi}\end{cases}$$

当 $\Delta\pi=m/P_1$，存在多个 Nash 均衡解，即

$$\begin{cases}x^*(\Delta\pi)=1\\ y^*(\Delta\pi)=\left[0,\dfrac{\Delta TP_1}{\Delta Pm}\right]\end{cases}$$

当 $\Delta\pi=m/P_2$，存在多个 Nash 均衡解，即

$$\begin{cases}x^*(\Delta\pi)=0\\ y^*(\Delta\pi)=\left[\dfrac{\Delta TP_2}{\Delta Pm},1\right]\end{cases}.$$

3　二层决策谈判策略

合同物流管理可以降低企业的物流成本，提高企业的快速反应速度和提高产品的质量。质量控制，是合同物流中合同管理的一个关键问题。怎样通过合同管理对供应链的质量进行控制呢？

前面已假定制成品不合格的原因是由于原材料不合格所造成的，那么引起合同物流的质量问题，主要来源于采购过程(供应合同)。一旦采购商和供应商签定了供应合同，即确定了合同的决策变量(如价格惩罚 $\Delta\pi$)，就会引起供应商和采购商行为动机的变化，从而导致了整个供应链质量问题的变化。因此合同决策变量的确定，对于整个供应链的质量控制具有重要的意义。

本文运用二层决策法(bi-level decision)来确定合同决策变量。第 1 层为销售过程(最终产品的质量问题)，第 2 层为采购过程(供应合同)，二层决策用图 2 表示：

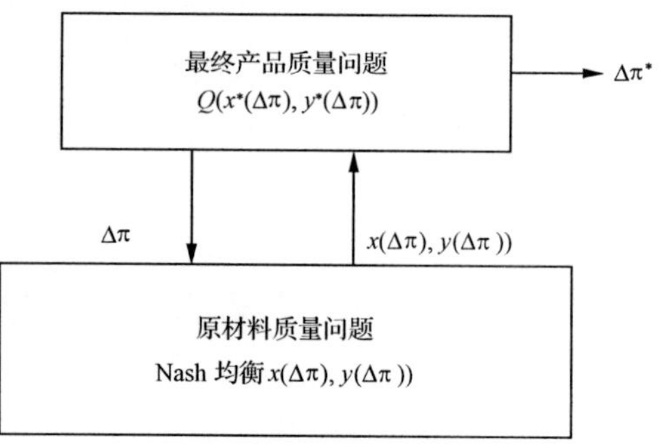

图 2　合同管理二层决策结构模型图

设 $Q(x,y)$ 为最终产品质量不合格率，经分析可构建二层决策模型如下：

$$\underset{\frac{m}{P_1}\leqslant\Delta\pi\leqslant\frac{m}{P_2}}{\text{Min}}\quad\underset{(x(\Delta\pi),y(\Delta\pi))\in NS(\Delta\pi)}{\text{Min}}\quad Q(x,y)\text{s t}\Delta\pi>\Delta T/\Delta P \tag{6}$$

其中 $NS(\Delta\pi)$ 是给定 $\Delta\pi$ 的 Nash 均衡解集合。

根据已有的假设最终产品质量不合格是由于采购商对原材料或部件不进行检验所致。所以，

$$Q(x,y)=(1-y)xP_1+(1-y)(1-x)P_2=(1-y)(x\Delta P+P_2) \tag{7}$$

情况 1　$m/P_1<\Delta\pi<m/P_2$ 此时，Nash 均衡解是唯一的，可得到

$$Q(\Delta\pi)=Q(x^*(\Delta\pi),y^*(\Delta\pi))=\frac{m}{\Delta\pi}-\frac{\Delta Tm}{\Delta P\Delta\pi^2}$$

$Q(\Delta\pi)$ 的一阶和二阶导数分别为

$$Q'(\Delta\pi)=\frac{m}{\Delta\pi^3\Delta P}(2\Delta T-\Delta\pi\Delta P)$$

$$Q''(\Delta\pi)=\frac{2m}{\Delta\pi^4\Delta P}(\Delta P\Delta\pi-3\Delta T)$$

因此，有

$$Q'(\Delta\pi)\leqslant 0,\text{如果 }\Delta\pi\geqslant\frac{2\Delta T}{\Delta P},$$

$$Q'(\Delta\pi)>0,\text{如果 }\Delta\pi<\frac{2\Delta T}{\Delta P};$$

以及

$$Q''(\Delta\pi)\leqslant 0,\text{如果 }\Delta\pi\leqslant\frac{3\Delta T}{\Delta P}$$

$$Q''(\Delta\pi)>0,\text{如果 }\Delta\pi>\frac{3\Delta T}{\Delta P}$$

当 $\Delta\pi\geqslant 2\Delta T/\Delta$ 时，$Q(\Delta\pi)P$ 的一价导数小于零，这时 $Q(\Delta\pi)$ 为减函数. 当 $\Delta\pi<2\Delta T/\Delta P$ 时，$Q(\Delta\pi)$ 的一价导数大于零，这时 $Q(\Delta\pi)$ 为增函数 $\Delta\pi\leqslant 3\Delta T/\Delta P$，$Q(\Delta\pi)$ 二价导数小于零，这时 $Q(\Delta\pi)$ 为凹函数，而当 $\Delta\pi>3\Delta T/\Delta P$，$Q(\Delta\pi)$ 为凸函数。

根据上面的分析，$Q(\Delta\pi)$ 随 $\Delta\pi$ 变化可通过图 3 表示。

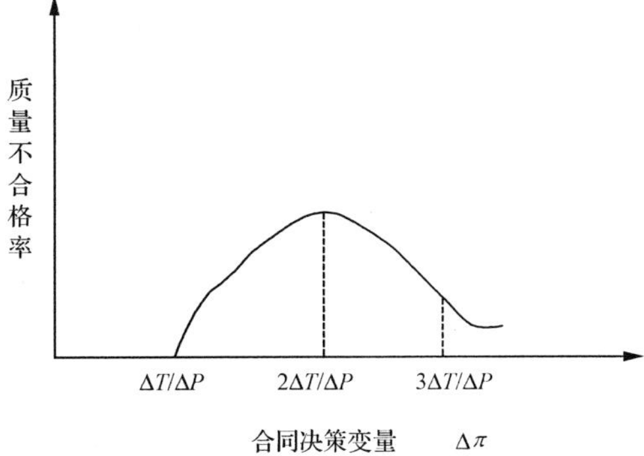

图 3　质量决策与质量不合格率关系图

情况 2　$\pi=m/P_1$

此时，Nash 均衡解是多值的，因而 $Q(\Delta\pi)$ 也是多值的，它的取值范围是 $Q(\Delta\pi)=[(1-P_1\Delta T/\Delta Pm)P_1,P_1]$。由于采购商追求最终产品的质量水平，即 $Q(\Delta\pi)$ 越小越好，那么采购商最优检验策略应为 $y\hat{}=P_1\Delta T/\Delta Pm$，其相应的最终产品不合格率为 $Q\hat{}(m/P_1)=(1-P_1\Delta T/\Delta Pm)P_1$。

情况 3　$\Delta\pi=m/P_2$

此时，Nash 均衡解为多值，因而 $Q(\Delta\pi)$ 也是多值的，它的取值范围是 $Q(\Delta\pi)=[0,(1-P_2\Delta T/\Delta Pm)P_2]$。采购商为获得最佳产品质量的最优检验策略 $y^{\hat{}}=1$，相应的最终产品不合格率 $Q^{\hat{}}(\Delta\pi)$ 为零。

由上分析，可定义最终产品质量不合格率为

$$Q^{\hat{}}(\Delta\pi)=\begin{cases}Q(\Delta\pi)\text{，如 } m/P_1<\Delta\pi<m/P_2\\(1-P_1\Delta T/m\Delta P)P_1\text{，如 } \Delta\pi=m/P_1\\0\text{，如 } \Delta\pi=m/P_2\end{cases}$$

应指出 $Q^{\hat{}}(\Delta\pi)$ 是单值函数。

在合同物流整个供应链范围内的质量问题，最应重视的是最终产品的质量情况。对生产商而言，为获得竞争优势，提高自己的声誉，获得最大的利益，要求向消费者提供高质量的产品。合同物流中，最终产品质量问题受合同的决策变量影响。由图 3 分析可知，当价格惩罚 $\Delta\pi$ 不断增加时，产品不合格率变化最先慢慢增大，然后逐渐减小。在供应合同中，采购商通过与供应商进行谈判，确定合同决策变量，这变量直接影响采购商和供应商的行为选择，间接影响了最终产品的质量。结合二层决策模型的讨论，在供应商和生产商的技术参数（$\Delta T/\Delta P,m,P_1,P_2$）给定的条件下，便可分析出生产商为获得最大利益应采用谈判策略，以作出合同决策变量的最终确定，从而有效签定供应合同。

随 $\Delta\pi$ 增加，产品不合格率先增加后减小，直观解释，这是因为生产商检验率下降，使得不合格率的原材料或部件进入生产过程增多，导致最终产品不合格率增加，而后由于 $\Delta\pi$ 继续增加，使得供应商因经营风险增加而生产出高质量的原材料或部件，引起最终产品不合格率的减小。

不同技术参数条件下，生产商的合同谈判策略是不一样的。结合二层决策模型分析可分析出不同情况下的最优谈判策略（$\Delta\pi$）和检验策略。

1）如果供应商允许 $\Delta\pi$ 取值 m/P_2，采购商的最优合同策略 $\Delta\pi^*=m/P_2$，此时最优的检验策略为 $y^*(\Delta\pi)=1$。

2）如果供应商允许 $\Delta\pi$ 取值 $m/P_2-\alpha>0$，其中 $\alpha>0$，那么

情况 1 $m/P_1\geqslant 2\Delta T/\Delta P$。此时，$Q(\Delta\pi)$ 为减函数，随着 $\Delta\pi$ 增大，最终产品质量不合格率逐渐降低。这时采购商的最优策略 $\Delta\pi^*=m/P_2-\alpha$，检验策略 $y^*(\Delta\pi^*)$ 是唯一的。从生产商的角度看，α 越小越好。

情况 2 $m/P_1<2\Delta T/\Delta P<m/P_2$. 此时，$Q(\Delta\pi)$ 在 $[m/P_1,2\Delta T/\Delta P]$ 为增函数，在 $(2\Delta T/\Delta P,m/P_2]$ 为减函数，即 $\Delta\pi$ 不断增大，最终产品不合格率先增大而后慢慢减小. 由前面分析可知，如果 $\Delta\pi$ 为 m/P_1 时，采购商最优的检验策略 $y^{\hat{}}=P_1\Delta\pi/m\Delta P$，相应的最终产品不合格率应为 $Q^{\hat{}}(m/P_1)$。因而，最优合同策略：$\Delta\pi^*=m/P_1$，如果 $Q^{\hat{}}(m/P_1)\leqslant Q^{\hat{}}(m/P_2-\alpha)$，否则 $\Delta\pi^*=m/P_2-\alpha$

情况 3 当 $m/P_1>\Delta T/\Delta P,m.P_2<2\Delta T/\Delta P$，$Q(\Delta\pi)$ 为增函数，随着 $\Delta\pi$ 增大，最终产品不合格率不断增大，最优决策变量 $\Delta\pi$ 应尽量减小。采购商应取 $\Delta\pi^*=m/P_1$，最终产品不合格率为 $Q^{\hat{}}(m/P_1)$ 和最优的检验策略 $y^{\hat{}}=P_1\Delta Tm/\Delta P$。

情况 4 $m/p_1\leqslant\Delta T/\Delta P$，$Q(\Delta\pi)$ 函数的特征与情况 3 相近。此时采购商的最优策略 $\Delta\pi^*=\Delta T/\Delta P$，最终产品不合格率为 $Q(\Delta T/\Delta P)$。

结合上述分析可得到采购商的合同策略应如表 1 表示：

表 1　采购商合同策略表

<table>
<tr><th colspan="3">供应商和技术参数约束</th><th>最优合同决策变量 $\Delta\pi^*$</th><th>最终产品不合格率 $\tilde{Q}$</th></tr>
<tr><td colspan="3">无供应商约束</td><td>m/P_2</td><td>0</td></tr>
<tr><td rowspan="6">有供应商约束</td><td>情况 1</td><td>$m/P_1 \geqslant 2\Delta T/\Delta P$</td><td>$m/P_2-\alpha$</td><td>$Q(m/P_2-\alpha)$</td></tr>
<tr><td rowspan="2">情况 2
$m/P_1 < 2\Delta T/\Delta P$</td><td>$m > (P_1+P_2)\Delta T/\Delta P$</td><td>$m/P_2-\alpha$</td><td>$Q(m/P_2-\alpha)$</td></tr>
<tr><td>$m < (P_1+P_2)\Delta T/\Delta P$</td><td>$m/P_1$</td><td>$\tilde{Q}(m/P_1)$</td></tr>
<tr><td>情况 3</td><td rowspan="2">$m/P_1 > \Delta T/\Delta P$
$m/P_2 < 2\Delta T/\Delta P$</td><td rowspan="2">$m/P_1$</td><td rowspan="2">$\tilde{Q}(m/P_1)$</td></tr>
<tr><td rowspan="2">情况 4</td></tr>
<tr><td>$m/P_1 \leqslant \Delta T/\Delta P$</td><td>$\Delta T/\Delta P$</td><td>$Q(\Delta T/\Delta P)$</td></tr>
</table>

备注：

$$\lim_{\beta\to 0} Q(m/P_1+\beta) = P_1\left(1-\frac{P_1\Delta T}{m\Delta P}\right)$$

$$\lim_{\alpha\to 0} Q(m/P_2+\alpha) = P_2\left(1-\frac{P_2\Delta T}{m\Delta P}\right)$$

下面从经济和管理角度出发对谈判策略作进一步分析。

情况 1　直观解释，当生产商的检验成本较高时，生产商的行为动机是减少检验率，为减少产品的不合格率，生产商应提高合同惩罚项（合同决策变量）威慑供应商，但必须使得合同决策变量满足供应商激励相容约束机制（incentive constraint）和参与约束机制（participation constraint），于是，生产商最优合同谈判策略 $\Delta\pi$ 应增大，即 $m/P_2-\alpha$，在谈判过程中尽可能使 α 减小。

情况 2　当检验成本适中时，最终产品的质量不合格率先增加后减小，这是因为，$\Delta\pi$ 增大，引起生产商检验率降低，使得不合格的原材料或部件进入供应链的机会增多，制成品质量不合格率增加，若 $\Delta\pi$ 增加，供应商发现风险太大——可能得不偿失，而更愿意供应较高质量的原材料或部件。当 $m>(P_1+P_2)\Delta T/\Delta P$，$\tilde{Q}(m/P_1)>Q(m/P_2-\alpha)$，即检验成本相对较高，生产商倾向于提高惩罚项减小检验率，那么生产商最优合同谈判策略 $\Delta\pi$ 取 $m/P_2-\alpha$。同理可分析，$m<(P_1+P_2)\Delta T/\Delta P$，生产商的最优合同谈判策略 $\Delta\pi$ 取 m/P_1。

情况 3 和情况 4　当生产商的检验成本较低时，$\Delta\pi$ 减小，生产商的检验率增加，从而减小最终产品的不合格率。此时，生产商应降低合同决策变量 $\Delta\pi$，发信号给供应商——将提高检验率，使得供应商选择较高质量的原材料或部件，因而生产商的最优合同谈判策略为 $\Delta\pi^*$ 为 m/P_1（情况 3）或 $\Delta\pi^*$ 为 $\Delta T/\Delta P$（情况 4）。

为更能说明问题，可通过具体的数学实例加以分析。当 $m=0.25$，$P_1=0.15$，$P_2=0.05$，$T_2=1$，$T_1=0.95$ 时，满足条件 $m/P_1\geqslant 2\Delta T/\Delta P$，根据采购商合同策略表分析结果，可以得到采购商最优合同谈判策略 $\Delta\pi$ 应增大，即 $m/P_2-\alpha$，在谈判过程中尽可能使 α 减小，从而更有效保证采购商利益。

4 结束语

全球采购、生产和配送导致了物流活动更为复杂,成本更高。同时激烈的竞争也要求公司不断地扩大产品的供给,提高快速反应速度,缩短生产周期,从而使得物流的活动更加复杂。显然,如果合同物流能得以准确的实施,那么上面的问题也就可以迎面而解。谁忽视了忽视合同物流的潜力,那将是极其危险的事。但合同物流也存在着质量等方面的风险,因此,本文建立了 Nash 均衡和二层决策模型探讨了合同管理中的质量问题。

本文所建立 Nash 均衡模型,是居于采购商和供应商在质量矛盾的问题上构建的,着重考虑人为动机对双方行为的影响,在此基础上,建立二层决策模型,分析供应合同决策变量对供应链质量影响,并探讨怎样确定最优合同决策变量来控制合同物流的质量问题。这对合同物流的质量控制和管理具有一定的理论和现实的参考价值.要使合同物流的质量问题得到合理的控制,在既定技术参数条件下,应认真考虑合同管理中决策变量的影响作用,以及变量的谈判策略,这样才能设计出有效的供应合同。

在现代的竞争中,建立伙伴关系,相当重要。合同物流中的采购商和供应商均希望建立长期的合作关系,实现纵向一体化,这就要求合同管理是一个动态的,多时段的合同谈判过程,那么模型中考虑的参数(决策变量、技术参数)是不断更新的。因而,合同物流中的 Nash 均衡模型和二层决策模型应该用动态的观点加以讨论.当然,本文模型较为简单(仅考虑价格惩罚项),未必能很好反映实际的情况。作者希望,在以后的工作中,能就这些问题上继续深入研究。

Bi-level decision in supply con tractmanagement

CHEN Xiang-f eng , ZHU Dao-li

School of Management, Fudan U niversity, Shanghai 200433, China

Abstract: From behavior motive and quality conflict between purchasing and supply, the paper sets up a N A SH model and analyzes contract parameter' s effect to quality of product in producing period. Further more, it even makes a bi-level decision model, and discusses contract parameter' seffect to quality control in supply chain, and com es up with a negoti ating strategy in contractm anagem ent as well.

Key words: contract logistics; contractm anagem ent; quality managem ent; Nash-equilibrium; bi-level decision

参考文献

[1] Priest G. A theory of consumer product warranty[J]. Yale Law Journal, 1981, 90 (3): 1297-1352.

[2] Kambhu J. Optimal production quality under asymm etric in fo rmation and moral hazard[J]. Bell-Journal of Economics, 1982, 13 (2) : 483-492 .

[3] Mann D , WissikJ. Inside vs. outside production: A contracting approach to vertical in tegration [M]. Mimeo, University of Pennsylvania, April 1983.

[4] Chew W B , Pisano G P. Vertical in tegration, long term contracts, and cost of quality [M]. Harward Business School, working paper, 1990.

[5] Reyniers D J. Supplier-customer in teraction in qualitycontrol[J]. AnnalsofOper. Res. , 1992, 34 (4): 300-307.

[6] Reyniers D J , Tapiero Charless. The delivery and controlof quality in supplier-productor contract[J]. M anagement Science , 1996, 41 (10): 1995, 1581-1589.

[7] Kambhu J. Product liability rules and moral hazard in incentive contracts[M]. Mimeo, Columbia U niversity, June 1983.

[8] Tapiero C S. Production learning and quality control[J]. IIET ransactions, 1987, 19:362-370.

[9] Cooter R D , Rubinfeld D L. Economics analysis of legal disputes and their resolution [J]. Journal of Economic Literature, 1989, 27: 1067-1097.

[10] Huberman G. Lim ited contract enforcem ent and strategic negotiation [J]. American Economic Review , 1988, 78: 471-484.

[11] Lewis T R , Sappington D E. Inflexible rules in incentiveproblems[J]. America Econom ic Review , 1989, 79:69-84.

[12] Kathryn E S. Incomplete contracts and signalizing[J]. RAND Journal of Economics , 1992, 23 (3): 71-80.

[13] 黄京华等. Agent 在电子商务环境下供应链应用研究，管理科学学报，2001，4 (5)：58-64.

（本文发表于《管理科学学报》，2002 年第 3 期）

带有快速反应策略供应链系统的补偿策略研究*

鲁其辉[1],朱道立[1],林正华[2]

(1. 复旦大学管理学院,上海 200433;2. 吉林大学数学学院,长春 130021)

摘要 过长的订购提前期往往使得零售商订货决策感到困难。快速反应策略能使零售商在获得更多更准确的市场需求信息后,调整订购量而提高收益。但是快速反应策略并不一定使供应商的利润也提高。有文章指出只有低的服务水平才能使两者利润同时提高,因而这种方法在工业应用中是不一定可行的。补偿策略是一种广泛应用的方法,能够提高产品的客户服务水平,因而研究了补偿策略在快速反应供应链系统中的作用。在某些条件下,在快速反应供应链系统中,补偿策略能使零售商与供应商一方的收益不变或者提高,另一方的收益有所提高,即 Pare to 提高。还研究了引进补偿策略后,供应链系统的最优解及期望卖出量、期望缺货量和期望残余量的变化情况。

关键词:快速反应;供应链;报童问题;定价模型;补偿策略;库存问题

中国分类号:O221　　**文献标识码**:A　　**文章编号**:1007-9807(2004)04-0014-10

0 引 言

许多工业(特别是服装工业)的季节性商品,一般有一个共同的特点,即零售商下订单和供应商交货之间的提前期非常长。例如零售商 Jaymar Ruby Slacks 的提前期是 8 个月,Oxford Shirts 的提前期是 7 个月,Liz Claiborne Apparel 的提前期是 5 个月,Benetton Apparel 的提前期是 5 个月[1]。提前期过长使得对市场需求量的预测碰到困难。零售商希望通过晚订货,缩短订货提前期,以减少预测误差,降低余货,减少缺货的可能性,而供应商希望零售商提前订货,可以更好地安排生产计划,降低生产成本。快速反应(quick response,QR)思想是缓解零售商和供应商之间订货周期矛盾的有效策略[1,2]。1992 及 1993 年连续召开的两次快速反应专题国际研讨会,充分研究了快速反应方法和它在实际领域中的广泛应用,显示了经济和社会效益。

Iyer 和 Bergen[1]实证指出,利用快速反应系统,零售商可以把 8 个月的订货时间削减至 4 个月,使 65%的预测误差减少至 35%。一般来讲,快速反应思想对于提高服务水平,提供合理的批发价格及科学的订货量,从而提高零售商和供应商的利润有相当重大的理论指导意义。但是文献[1]也指出,QR 不总是使供应商和零售商的利润同时提高,证明

* 收稿日期:2002-11-20;修订日期:2004-03-26。

基金项目:国家自然科学基金资助项目(70171010)。

作者简介:鲁其辉(1977～),男,湖南益阳人,博士生。

了在快速反应系统中,供应商的利润在某些条件下可能会减少。于是,供应商可能会为了使快速反应系统的 Pareto 提高而付诸行动。这里 Pareto 提高是指行动双方在行动完成以后,其中一方的收益不变或者提高,另一方的收益有所提高。文献[1]提出了为使快速反应系统 Pareto 提高的三种方法:提高服务水平指数,提高批发价格,使用多种同类商品。这些方法在服装工业的大量应用中证明了它们都能使快速反应系统 Pareto 提高。

Emmons 和 Gilber 在文献[3]中,Lau 和 Lau 在文献[4]中及 Lau、Lau 和 Kottas 在文献[5]中,考虑了一个简化的"带有补偿策略(RP)的供应链系统"模型(图 1),供应商首先提供两个价格:一个是在销售开始之前,提供给零售商的商品批发单价 c;另一个是在销售季节过后,零售商把未销售掉的商品退还给供应商的退货价格 v。假设供应商有无限大的生产能力,单位商品的生产费用 k 保持为一个常数。零售商根据这两个价格和对市场的需求预测决定订购量 q 和零售价格 p。

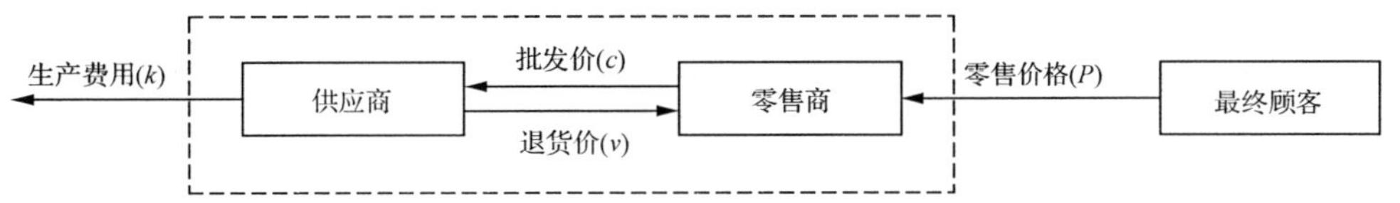

图 1　带有补偿策略供应链系统模型

Fig. 1　Supply chain model with return policies

供应商通过退货补偿能激励零售商提高对于那些需求不确定、订货提前期长、销售季节短的商品的订货量。

从系统结构的观点,在供应链系统中分别或同时引入补偿策略(RP)与快速反应策略(QR),可以得到 4 种不同的供应链系统,如图 2 所示。

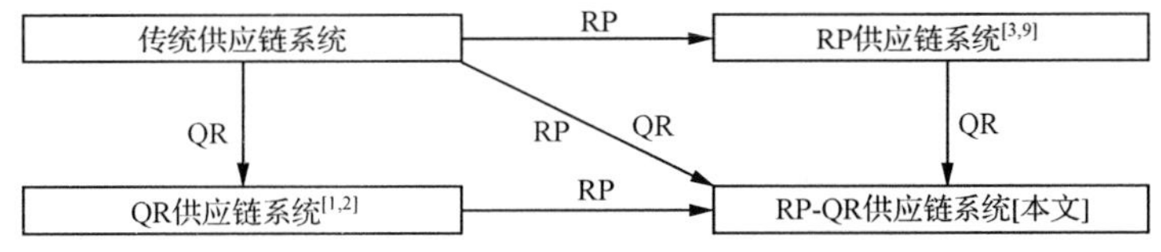

图 2　4 种不同的供应链系统

Fig. 2　Four kinds of supply chain systems

本文着重研究含补偿策略的快速反应供应链系统。分析认为,补偿策略在快速反应系统中,是既能提高系统的服务水平,又能使快速反应系统 Pareto 提高的科学决策方法。

1　模型构造

1.1　参数及记号

x——随机需求变量;

$f(x)$——x 的概率密度函数;

$F(x)$——x 的概率分布函数;

θ——需求均值随机变量;

$x|\beta$——指当 x 的均值 θ 的估计为 β 时,x 的条件需求变量,即 $x|\beta \triangleq x|(\theta|\beta)$;

$g(x|\beta)$——$x|\beta$ 的概率密度函数；

$G(x|\beta)$——$x|\beta$ 的概率分布函数；

$\phi(x)$——标准正态分布密度函数，即 $\phi(x)=\frac{1}{\sqrt{2\pi}}e^{-x^2/2}$；

$\Phi(x)$——标准正态分布函数；

p——零售商给出的单位商品的零售价；

c——供应商提供给零售商的商品批发单价；

h——销售季节过后，未售出的商品给零售商带来库存管理费用等的折合单价；

s——商品缺货时，零售商对销售机会损失给出的单位商品的惩罚价；

v——在有补偿策略系统中，供应商提供给零售商未售出商品的退货单价；

k——供应商单位商品的成本价；

q——零售商向供应商定购的商品数量，即订货量；

$a(x)$——在销售季节中，零售商实际售出的商品数量，即 $a(x)=\min\{q,x\}$。

条件 1　$p\geqslant c\geqslant \max\{v,k\}>0$ 及 $h\geqslant 0, s\geqslant 0, v>0, c>k$。

1.2　不确定性需求结构

采用文献[1]中使用的不确定性需求模型。假设需求不确定性是由两个不确定源形成的。第 1 个不确定源是关于产品固有的需求不确定性。设已知需求均值为 θ 时，在销售季节中需求是服从均值为 θ 方差为 σ 的正态分布。第 2 个不确定源是在时刻 $t=0$ 时关于 θ 估计的不确定性，设它服从均值为 μ 方差为 τ 的正态分布。文献[10]介绍了两个有用的引理。假设传统的供应链系统零售商的订购及销售分别定在 0 及 L 两个时刻（见图 3）。需要在 0 时刻预测 L 时刻的需求变量 x。

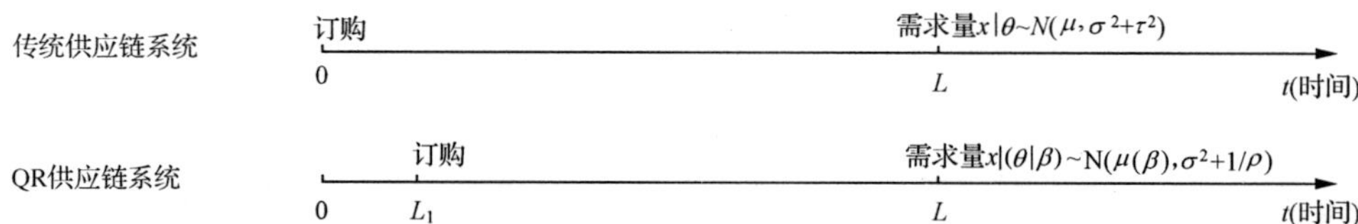

图 3　QR 供应链系统与传统供应链系统比较

Fig. 3　Compare QR supply chain with traditional supply chain

引理 1　若需求均值 $\theta\sim N(\mu,\tau^2)$，随机变量 $x|\theta\sim N(\theta,\sigma^2)$，则 $x\sim N(\mu,\sigma^2+\tau^2)$。

快速反应供应链系统（简称 QR 供应链系统）订购及销售分别定在 L_1 及 L 两个时刻，$L_1\in(0,L)$。在 L_1 时刻，零售商利用$[0,L_1]$的已知信息来预测 L 时刻的需求均值 θ，设它为 β(图 3)，再在此条件下预测需求量，即 $x|\beta$。

引理 2　若 $\theta\sim N(\mu,\tau^2)$，且 $\beta|\theta\sim N(\theta,\sigma^2)$，则 $\theta|\beta\sim N(\mu(\beta),1/\rho)$。其中，$\mu(\beta)=(\sigma^2\mu+\tau^2\beta)/(\sigma^2+\tau^2)$，$\rho=1/\sigma^2+1/\tau^2$。

设 $L_1\ll L$，且设 $\beta|\theta\sim N(\theta,\sigma^2)$，由引理 1 有 $\theta|\beta\sim N(\mu(\beta),1/\rho)$，利用新的均值估计 $\theta|\beta$，可以得到 $x|\beta\triangleq x|(\theta|\beta)$更精确的需求量估计。利用随机变量 β 的估计精度，改善随机变量 x 的估计精度。

引理 3　若随机变量 x,θ,β 定义如上，则 $x|\beta\sim N(\mu(\beta),\sigma^2+1/\rho)$。

证明　由引理 2，有 $\theta|\beta \sim N(\mu(\beta), 1/\rho)$，于是由引理 1，$x|\beta = x|(\theta|\beta) \sim N(\mu(\beta), \sigma^2 + 1/\rho)$。证明了结论。　　证毕

从上述引理看出，QR 供应链系统预测值的方差比传统供应链系统预测值的方差更小，说明应用 QR 策略能使零售商更准确地预测市场需求，QR 供应链系统比传统供应链系统具有更好的稳定性。

2　4 种供应链系统的模型及最优解

2.1　无补偿策略的传统供应链系统

在无补偿策略传统供应链系统中，零售商的收益函数及期望收益可分别表达成[1,7~9]：

$$\theta_0(q,x) = (p+s+h)a(x) - (c+h)q - sx \tag{1}$$

$$\Theta_0(q) \triangleq E\theta_0(q,x) = (p+s+h) \cdot \left(\int_{\infty}^{q} xf(x)\mathrm{d}x - qF(q)\right) + (p+s-c)q - s\mu \tag{2}$$

称 λ_0 为传统供应链系统的服务水平

$$\lambda_0 = \frac{p+s-c}{p+s+h} \tag{3}$$

记 $\Phi^{-1}(\cdot)$为标准正态分布函数的逆函数。

$$b_\tau(\Phi^{-1}(\lambda_0)) = \int_{p^{-1}(\lambda_0)}^{\infty} (y - \Phi^{-1}(\lambda 0))\phi(y)\mathrm{d}y$$

零售商的最优订货量为

$$EQ_{\text{Old}} = \mu + \Phi^{-1}(\lambda_0)\sqrt{\sigma^2 + \tau^2} \tag{4}$$

期望卖出量

$$EQ_{\text{Old-sold}} = \mu - b_\tau(\Phi^{-1}(\lambda_0)) \cdot \sqrt{\sigma^2 + \tau^2}$$

期望缺货量

$$EQ_{\text{Old-short}} = \mu - EQ_{\text{Old-sold}} = b_\tau(\Phi^{-1}(\lambda_0)) \cdot \sqrt{\sigma^2 + \tau^2}$$

期望残余量

$$EQ_{\text{Old-left}} = (\Phi^{-1}(\lambda_0) + b_\tau(\Phi^{-1}(\lambda_0))) \cdot \sqrt{\sigma^2 + \tau^2}$$

零售商与批发商的最优期望平均收益分别为

$$EP_{\text{Old-ret}} = (p-c)\mu - ((c+h)\Phi^{-1}(\lambda_0) + (p+s+h)b_\tau(\Phi^{-1}(\lambda_0))) \cdot \sqrt{\sigma^2 + \tau^2} \tag{5}$$

$$EP_{\text{Old-mfr}} = (c-k)\left(\mu + \Phi^{-1}(\lambda_0)\sqrt{\sigma^2 + \tau^2}\right) \tag{6}$$

2.2　有补偿策略的传统供应链系统(RP 供应链系统)

带有补偿策略的传统供应链系统，在该商品销售季节过后，供应商对未销售完的商品给零售商提供补偿，零售商不仅可以节省要为未销售完的商品提供费用的 h，而且可以得到补偿单价 v。因此将 2.1 中结论 h 换为 $-v$，就可以得到带补偿策略的供应链系统的结论。

零售商的最优订购量为

$$EQ_{\text{RP}} = \mu + \Phi^{-1}(\lambda_1)\sqrt{\sigma^2 + \tau^2}$$

其中：λ_1 表示有补偿策略供应链系统的服务水平

$$\lambda_1 = \frac{p+s-c}{p+s+v}$$

期望卖出量

$$EQ_{\text{RP-sold}} = \mu - b_\tau(\Phi^{-1}(\lambda_1))\sqrt{\sigma^2+\tau^2}$$

期望缺货量

$$EQ_{\text{RP-short}} = b_\tau(\Phi^{-1}(\lambda_1))\sqrt{\sigma^2+\tau^2}$$

期望残余量

$$EQ_{\text{RP-left}} = (\Phi^{-1}(\lambda_1) + b_\tau(\Phi^{-1}(\lambda_0)))\cdot\sqrt{\sigma^2+\tau^2}$$

零售商与供应商的最优平均收益分别为

$$EP_{\text{RP-ret}} = (p-c)\mu - ((c-v)\Phi^{-1}(\lambda_1) + (p+s-v)b_\tau(\Phi^{-1}(\lambda_1)))\sqrt{\sigma^2+\tau^2} \quad (8)$$

$$EP_{\text{RP-mfr}} = (c-k)\left(\mu + \Phi^{-1}(\lambda_1)\sqrt{\sigma^2+\tau^2}\right) - v(\Phi^{-1}(\lambda_1) + b_\tau(\Phi^{-1}(\lambda_1)))\sqrt{\sigma^2+\tau^2} \quad (9)$$

2.3 有补偿策略的快速反应供应链系统(QR-RP 供应链系统)

由引理 3 知，$x|\beta \sim N(\mu(\beta), \sigma^2+1/\rho)$。在快速反应供应链系统中，零售商的预测是基于对需求均值 θ 的估计量 β，得到需求变量 $x|\beta$。然后可以求出零售商与供应商收益函数。那么可以求出零售商的最优订货量 $EQ_{\text{QR-RP}}(\beta)$。估计量 β 也是服从分布 $m(\beta) \sim N(\mu, \sigma^2+\tau^2)$的。则按照 $EQ_{\text{QR-RP}} = \int_{-\infty}^{+\infty} EQ_{\text{QR-RP}}(\beta) m(\beta)\,\mathrm{d}\beta$，得到零售商的最优订货量

$$EQ_{\text{QR-RP}} = \mu + \Phi^{-1}(\lambda_1)\sqrt{\sigma^2+\frac{1}{\rho}}$$

同样可以得出下列最优值

期望卖出量

$$EQ_{\text{QR-RP-sold}} = \mu - b_\tau(\Phi^{-1}(\lambda_1))\sqrt{\sigma^2+\frac{1}{\rho}}$$

期望缺货量

$$EQ_{\text{QR-RP-short}} = b_\tau(\Phi^{-1}(\lambda_1))\sqrt{\sigma^2+\frac{1}{\rho}}$$

期望残余量

$$EQ_{\text{QR-RP-left}} = (\Phi^{-1}(\lambda_1) + b_\tau(\Phi^{-1}(\lambda_1)))\cdot\sqrt{\sigma^2+\frac{1}{\rho}}$$

零售商与供应商的最优平均收益分别为

$$EP_{\text{QR-RP-ret}} = (p-c)\mu - ((c-v)\Phi^{-1}(\lambda_1) + (p+s-v)b_\tau(\Phi^{-1}(\lambda_1)))\sqrt{\sigma^2+\frac{1}{\rho}} \quad (10)$$

$$EP_{\text{QR-RP-mfr}} = (c-k)\left(\mu + \Phi^{-1}(\lambda_1)\sqrt{\sigma^2+\frac{1}{\rho}}\right) - v(\Phi^{-1}(\lambda_1) + b_\tau(\Phi^{-1}(\lambda_1)))\sqrt{\sigma^2+\frac{1}{\rho}} \quad (11)$$

2.4 无补偿策略的快速反应供应链系统(QR 供应链系统)

文献[1]给出了无补偿策略的 QR 供应链系统的一些结论：

最优订购量

$$EQ_{\text{QR}} = \mu + \Phi^{-1}(\lambda_0)\sqrt{\sigma^2 + \frac{1}{\rho}}$$

期望卖出量

$$EQ_{\text{QR-sold}} = \mu - b_\tau(\Phi^{-1}(\lambda_0)) + \sqrt{\sigma^2 + \frac{1}{\rho}}$$

期望缺货量

$$EQ_{\text{QR-short}} = b_\tau(\Phi^{-1}(\lambda_0)) + \sqrt{\sigma^2 + \frac{1}{\rho}}$$

期望残余量

$$EQ_{\text{QR-left}} = (\Phi^{-1}(\lambda_0) + b_\tau(\Phi^{-1}(\lambda_0))) \cdot \sqrt{\sigma^2 + \frac{1}{\rho}}$$

零售商与供应商的最优平均收益分别为

$$EP_{\text{QR-ret}} = (p-c)\mu - ((c+h)\Phi^{-1}(\lambda_0) + (p+s+h)b_\tau(\Phi^{-1}(\lambda_0))) \cdot \sqrt{\sigma^2 + \frac{1}{\rho}} \quad (12)$$

$$EP_{\text{QR-mfr}} = (c-k)\left(\mu + \Phi^{-1}(\lambda_0)\sqrt{\sigma^2 + \frac{1}{\rho}}\right) \quad (13)$$

3　补偿策略在快速反应供应链系统中的影响

上节给出了 4 个不同的供应链系统零售商的订购量、期望卖出量、期望缺货量和期望残余量(图 4)等的表达式。本节着重分析不同系统中各个量之间的关系，特别是分析补偿策略在快速反应供应链系统中的影响，为供应链系统设计提供选择供应链系统结构的分析基础。下列引理的证明见附录。

	无RP	有RP
无QR	EQ_{Old} $EQ_{\text{Old-sold}}$ $EQ_{\text{Old-short}}$ $EQ_{\text{Old-left}}$ λ_0	EQ_{Rp} $EQ_{\text{Rp-sold}}$ $EQ_{\text{Rp-short}}$ $EQ_{\text{Rp-left}}$ λ_1
有QR	EQ_{QR} $EQ_{\text{QR-sold}}$ $EQ_{\text{QR-short}}$ $EQ_{\text{QR-left}}$ λ_0	$EQ_{\text{QR-RP}}$ $EQ_{\text{QR-RP-sold}}$ $EQ_{\text{QR-RP-short}}$ $EQ_{\text{QR-RP-left}}$ λ_1

图 4　4 种供应链系统的最优解

Fig. 4　Optimizations of 4 kinds of supply chain systems

首先对 QR-RP 供应链系统的平均订货量与其它系统的平均订货量做比较。

引理 4　如果条件 1 成立，那么对任何的 $\lambda_0, \lambda_1 \in (0,1)$，有 $EQ_{\text{QR-RP}} \geq EQ_{\text{QR}}$。

文献[7～9]分别考虑了补偿策略在供应链系统中的作用，其中，首要的作用是它能鼓励零售商增加订货量，这样不仅能使产品的市场占有率提高，而且能提高产品的服务水平。因此在许多供应链的交易谈判中，除了批发价格和数量是供应链双方主要关注点以外，商品的退货价格也是双方讨论的重点。下面考虑在有补偿策略的供应链系统中引入快速反应策略后，零售商订货量的变化情况。

引理 5 如果条件 1 成立，最优订货量 $EQ_{QR\text{-}RP}$ 与 EQ_{RP} 之间的关系如下：

(i) $EQ_{QR\text{-}RP}>EQ_{RP}$ 若 $\lambda_1<1/2$；

(ii) $EQ_{QR\text{-}RP}<EQ_{RP}$ 若 $\lambda_1>1/2$；

(iii) $EQ_{QR\text{-}RP}=EQ_{RP}=\mu$ 若 $\lambda_1=1/2$。

从上面的引理可以看出，如果有补偿策略供应链系统的服务水平比较低，实施快速反应策略后，零售商将提高订货量。如果服务水平已经比较高了，零售商反而会减少订货量。这主要是因为实施快速反应策略缩短了订货提前期，零售商通过对市场信息的收集，降低了预测误差，更准确地把握了市场的需求情况，这样零售商不必定购过多的商品就能够保持商品的服务水平，是 QR 策略较为明显的影响之一。

引理 6 如果条件 1 成立，最优订货量 $EQ_{QR\text{-}RP}$ 与 EQ_{Old} 之间的关系如下：

(i) 如果 $\lambda_1>\lambda_0>1/2$ 和 $0<v\leqslant(p+s)\cdot(1-t)-ht$，那么 $EQ_{QR\text{-}RP}\leqslant EQ_{Old}$；

(ii) 如果 $\lambda_0<\lambda_1\leqslant 1/2$ 或[$\lambda_1>1/2$ 且 $\lambda_0\leqslant 1/2$]或[$\lambda_1>\lambda_0>1/2$ 且 $v>(p+s)(1-t)-ht$]，那么 $EQ_{QR\text{-}RP}>EQ_{Old}$。

其中，$t=\lambda_0/\Phi\left(\dfrac{\Phi^{-1}(\lambda_0)}{y}\right)$，$y=\sqrt{\sigma^2+\dfrac{1}{\rho}}\Big/\sqrt{\sigma^2+\tau^2}$

文献[1]中也得出当 $\lambda_0\leqslant 1/2$ 时，$EQ_{QR}\geqslant EQ_{Old}$，因此在低的服务水平下，运用 QR 策略，零售商将提高订货量，故 QR 策略将使系统 Pareto 提高，即有 $EP_{QR\text{-}mft}\geqslant EP_{Old\text{-}mfr}$ 和 $EP_{QR\text{-}ret}\geqslant EP_{Old\text{-}ret}$。但是当 $\lambda_0\geqslant 1/2$ 时，$EQ_{QR}\leqslant EQ_{Old}$，即零售商的订货量将减少，从而使供应商的利润下降。QR 策略此时不能使系统 Pareto 提高。如果这时引入补偿策略来鼓励零售提高订货量，就可能增加供应商的利润，可以使供应链系统 Pareto 提高。

从引理 6 可以看出：如果传统供应链系统的服务水平已经比较高了，即 $\lambda_0>1/2$，且退货单价限制在范围 $0<v\leqslant(p+s)(1-t)-ht$ 内，零售商不会提高订货量了。反过来从引理 6 的(ii)可知，如果传统供应链系统的服务水平比较低，即 $\lambda_0<1/2$，在 QR-RP 系统中零售商将提高订货量，或者传统系统的服务水平已经比较高了，如果使退货价格提高到某一个水平以上，零售商将会提高订货量。

引理 7 如果条件 1 成立，期望缺货量、期望卖出量与期望残余量之间关系为：

$EQ_{Old\text{-}short}\geqslant EQ_{RP\text{-}short}\geqslant EQ_{QR\text{-}RP\text{-}short}$；

$EQ_{Old\text{-}short}\geqslant EQ_{QR\text{-}short}\geqslant EQ_{QR\text{-}RP\text{-}short}$；

$EQ_{Old\text{-}sold}\leqslant EQ_{RP\text{-}sold}\leqslant EQ_{QR\text{-}RP\text{-}sold}$；

$EQ_{Old\text{-}sold}\leqslant EQ_{QR\text{-}sold}\leqslant EQ_{QR\text{-}RP\text{-}sold}$；

$EQ_{QR\text{-}left}\leqslant EQ_{Old\text{-}left}\leqslant EQ_{RP\text{-}left}$；

$EQ_{QR\text{-}left}\leqslant EQ_{QR\text{-}RP\text{-}left}\leqslant EQ_{RP\text{-}left}$。

补偿策略能使商品的服务水平提高，产品的期望缺货量将减少，即 $EQ_{Old\text{-}short}\geqslant EQ_{RP\text{-}short}$，$EQ_{QR\text{-}short}\geqslant EQ_{QR\text{-}RP\text{-}short}$。快速反应策略同样也能使商品的期望缺货量减少，即 $EQ_{RP\text{-}short}\geqslant EQ_{QR\text{-}RP\text{-}short}$，$EQ_{Old\text{-}short}\geqslant EQ_{QR\text{-}short}$。反过来，补偿策略和快速反应策略能使商品的期望销售量增加，即 $EQ_{Old\text{-}sold}\leqslant EQ_{RP\text{-}sold}$，$EQ_{QR\text{-}sold}\leqslant EQ_{QR\text{-}RP\text{-}sold}$ 和 $EQ_{RP\text{-}sold}\leqslant EQ_{QR\text{-}RP\text{-}sold}$，$EQ_{Old\text{-}sold}\leqslant EQ_{QR\text{-}sold}$。对于供应链系统的期望残余量，引进快速反应策略后它将会减少，即

$EQ_{\text{QR-left}} \leqslant EQ_{\text{Old-left}}$，$EQ_{\text{QR-RP-left}} \leqslant EQ_{\text{RP-left}}$。当引进补偿策略后，零售商将增加订货量，从而使商品的期望残余量增加，即 $EQ_{\text{RP-left}} \geqslant EQ_{\text{Old-left}}$，$EQ_{\text{QR-RP-left}} \geqslant EQ_{\text{QR-left}}$。

4 系统 Pareto 提高的灵敏度分析

首先分析引入 RP 策略或 QR 策略后供应链系统中零售商的收益变化情况，然后分析供应商的收益变化情况（见图 5），最后给出系统 Pareto 提高的分析结论。下面的结论的证明参见附录。

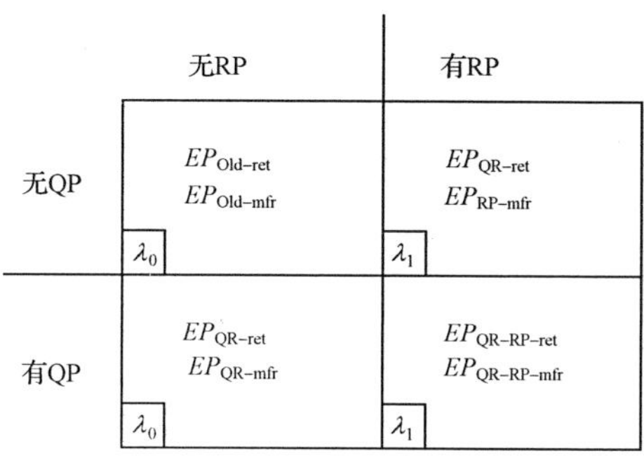

图 5　4 种供应链系统的最优期望收益

Fig. 5　Optimal expected revenue of 4 kinds of supply chain systems

引理 8　假设条件 1 成立。对于第 2 节求出的零售商平均收益，下列关系成立：

(i) 对任意的 $\lambda_0, \lambda_1 \in (0,1)$ 有 $EP_{\text{QR-RP-ret}} > EP_{\text{QR-ret}}$；

(ii) 对任意的 $\lambda_0, \lambda_1 \in (0,1)$，有 $EP_{\text{RP-ret}} \geqslant EP_{\text{Old-ret}}$；

(iii) 对任意的 $\lambda_1 \in (0,1)$，有 $EP_{\text{QR-RP-ret}} \geqslant EP_{\text{RP-ret}}$。

引理 8 给出了不同系统零售商的利润的相互关系。特别地，关系 $EP_{\text{QR-RP-ret}} > EP_{\text{QR-ret}}$，说明了把补偿策略引入 QR 供应链系统中，零售商的利润会增加。关系 $EP_{\text{RP-ret}} \geqslant EP_{\text{Old-ret}}$ 说明了对于传统供应链系统，引入补偿策略后，零售商是受益的。关系 $EP_{\text{QR-RP-ret}} > EP_{\text{RP-ret}}$ 说明，在有补偿策略的供应链系统中引入 QR 策略后，零售商的利润也将提高。因此，QR 策略和补偿策略都会促使零售商的利润提高。这也是目前许多零售企业研究和应用这两种策略的原因。对零售商来说获得退货补偿是提高期望利润的一种方法。

引理 9　假设条件 1 成立。$EP_{\text{RP-mfr}}$，$EP_{\text{QR-RP-mfr}}$ 如第 2 节中求出，那么若 $\lambda_1 \leqslant 1/2$，有 $EP_{\text{QR-RP-mfr}} \geqslant EP_{\text{RP-mfr}}$。

就是说，在服务水平比较低情况下，对于有补偿策略供应链系统，QR 策略将使供应商获益。

文献[1]的研究表明：对于无补偿策略供应链系统，当 $\lambda_0 \leqslant 1/2$ 时，$EP_{\text{RR-mft}} \geqslant EP_{\text{Old-mfr}}$，即供应商在引入 QR 策略后利润提高。因此，在服务水平比较低的情况下，引入 QR 策略将使供应商收益。

引理 10　当 $v=c$ 时，下述关系成立：

$$EP_{\text{QR-RP-mfr}} > EP_{\text{RP-mfr}}$$

证明 当 $v=c$ 时，$\lambda_1=1$，这时供应商的利润增量为

$$EP_{\text{QR-RP-mfr}} - EP_{\text{RP-mfr}} = (k\Phi^{-1}(\lambda_1) + cb_\tau(\Phi^{-1}(\lambda_1))) \cdot \left(\sqrt{\sigma^2+\tau^2} - \sqrt{\sigma^2+\frac{1}{\rho}}\right) > 0$$

证毕

QR 供应链系统引入补偿策略，这时供应商的平均收益增量的表达式为

$$EP_{\text{QR-RP-mfr}} - EP_{\text{QR-mft}} = ((c-k)(\Phi^{-1}(\lambda_1) - \Phi^{-1}(\lambda_0)) - v(\Phi^{-1}(\lambda_1) + b_\tau(\Phi^{-1}(\lambda_1)))) \cdot \sqrt{\sigma^2+\frac{1}{\rho}} \tag{14}$$

由引理 11(见附录)知道 $\Phi^{-1}(\lambda_1)+b_\tau(\Phi^{-1}(\lambda_1))$ 关于 λ_1 的函数是一个单调递增的正函数。又显然有 $\Phi^{-1}(\lambda_1)-\Phi^{-1}(\lambda_0)>0$，因此 $EP_{\text{QR-RP-mfr}}-EP_{\text{QR-mft}}$ 的正负由参数 c、v 决定。不难证明

当 $h>0$ 时，$\lim\limits_{v\to 0^+} EP_{\text{QR-RP-mfr}}-EP_{\text{QR-mft}}>0$

当 $h=0$ 时，$\lim\limits_{v\to 0^+} EP_{\text{QR-RP-mfr}}-EP_{\text{QR-mft}}=0$

显然 $EP_{\text{QR-RP-mfr}}-EP_{\text{QR-mft}}$ 关于 v 是一个连续函数。因此，当 $h>0$ 时，存在一个点 v^* 使 $EP_{\text{QR-RP-mfr}}-EP_{\text{QR-mft}}>0$，即当 $h>0$ 时，存在一个补偿策略使 QR 系统 Pareto 提高。

当 $h=0$ 时，供应商的平均收益变化情况比较复杂，下面实例说明有几个不同的情况出现。

例 1

表 1 供应链系统参数表

Tabel 1 Parameters in supply chain systems

参 数	p_i	c_i	s_i	h_i	k_i
实例 1	8.5	8	4	0	3
实例 2	12	8	2	0	4

应用数值软件可以得到下列结果(其中，$EP^i_{\text{QR-QR-mft}}$、$EP^i_{\text{QR-mfr}}$表示第 $i=1,2$ 个实例中供应商的最优利润值)：

在区间 $0<v_1<6.2$，有 $EP^1_{\text{QR-QR-mft}}>EP^1_{\text{QR1-mfr}}$；在区间 $6.2\leqslant v_1\leqslant c_1$，有$EP^1_{\text{QR-RP-mfr}}<EP^1_{\text{QR-mft}}$；

在区间 $0<v_2\leqslant c_2$，有 $EP^2_{\text{QR-RP-mfr}}<EP^2_{\text{QR-mfr}}$，当 $v^2\to 0^+$ 时，$EP^2_{\text{QR-RP-mfr}}=EP^2_{\text{QR-mft}}$。

上面的实例说明了当 $h=0$ 时，在某些条件下，存在点 v^* 使系统 Pareto 提高。在某些条件下，仅仅当 $v\to 0^+$ 时，$EP_{\text{QR-RP-mfr}}-EP_{\text{QR-mft}}=0$，当 $v\in(0,c]$时，都不能使系统 Pareto 提高。

文献[1] 指出提高批发商价格，能使供应商双方的利润同时提高，但是否存在一个 c^*、v^* 最优组合，使供应商的利润提高，有待于进一步研究。

传统供应链系统中引入补偿策略以后，供应商平均收益增量的表达式为

$$EP_{\text{QR-mft}} - EP_{\text{Old-mfr}} = ((c-k)(\Phi^{-1}(\lambda_1) - \Phi^{-1}(\lambda_0)) - v(\Phi^{-1}(\lambda_1) + b_\tau(\Phi^{-1}(\lambda_1)))) \cdot \sqrt{\sigma^2+\tau^2}$$

可以看出对供应商平均收益变化分析与在 QR 供应链系统中引入补偿策略的分析很

类似。

传统供应链系统中同时引入 QR 和 RP 策略后，供应商平均收益增量的表达式为

$$EP_{\text{QR-RP-mfr}} - EP_{\text{Old-mfr}} = \left((c-k)\left(\Phi^{-1}(\lambda_1) - \frac{\Phi^{-1}(\lambda_0)}{y} - v(\Phi^{-1}(\lambda_1) + b_\tau(\Phi^{-1}(\lambda_1)))\right)\right) \cdot \sqrt{\sigma^2 + \frac{1}{\rho}}$$

上式的分析比较复杂，仅给出它的表达式。

系统 Pareto 提高的分析结论：

1）服务水平比较低的情况下，引入 QR 策略可以使补偿策略供应链系统 Pareto 提高。由引理 8 和引理 9，关系 $EP_{\text{QR-RP-ret}} \geqslant EP_{\text{QR-ret}}$ 与 $EP_{\text{QR-RP-mfr}} \geqslant EP_{\text{RP-mfr}}$ 同时成立；

2）服务水平比较低的情况下，引入 QR 策略可以使传统供应链系统 Pareto 提高。见文献[1]；

3）当服务水平为 1 时，即 $v=c$，引入 QR 策略可以使补偿策略供应链系统 Pareto 提高。见引理 8 和引理 10；

4）在 QR 系统中引入 RP 策略，或者在传统供应链系统中引入 RP 策略，当 $h>0$ 时，存在一个 v^* 使系统 pareto 提高。当 $h=0$ 时，系统 Pareto 提高的分析比较困难，见例 1 及分析。

5　结　论

快速反应策略是一种解决季节性商品订货提前期过长带来的决策不准确问题的有效方法。但是在应用过程中也存在一些困难，只有在服务水平比较低的情况下，它才能使供应链双方的利润同时提高。本文提出了一种解决方法，即在快速反应供应链系统中，引入补偿策略。这时不仅能提高零售商的利润，而且在某种条件下，供应商的利润也将提高。并且补偿策略能激励零售商增加订货量，并且能提高商品的服务水平和减少期望缺货量。

附　录

引理 4 的证明　由于 $\lambda_0 < \lambda_1$，即有 $\Phi^{-1}(\lambda_0) < \Phi^{-1}(\lambda_1)$，因此

$$EQ_{\text{QR}} = \mu + \Phi^{-1}(\lambda_0)\sqrt{\sigma^2 + \frac{1}{\rho}} \leqslant EQ_{\text{QR-RP}} = \mu + \Phi^{-1}(\lambda_1) + \sqrt{\sigma^2 + \frac{1}{\rho}}$$

即结论成立。　　证毕

引理 5 的证明

1）由于 $\Phi^{-1}(\lambda_1) < 0$，若 $\lambda_1 < 1/2$；$\Phi^{-1}(\lambda_1) > 0$，若 $\lambda_1 > 1/2$，及

$$\sqrt{\sigma^2 + \frac{1}{\rho}} = \sqrt{\sigma^2 + \frac{\sigma^2\tau^2}{\sigma^2 + \tau^2}} < \sqrt{\sigma^2 + \tau^2}$$

有

$$\mu + \Phi^{-1}(\lambda_1)\sqrt{\sigma^2 + \tau^2} < \mu + \Phi^{-1}(\lambda_1) \cdot \sqrt{\sigma^2 + \frac{1}{\rho}},$$

若 $\lambda_1 > 1/2$。

$$\mu+\Phi^{-1}(\lambda_1)\sqrt{\sigma^2+\tau^2}>\mu+\Phi^{-1}(\lambda_1)\cdot\sqrt{\sigma^2+\frac{1}{\rho}}.$$

若 $\lambda_1>1/2$。

因此情形(i)(ii)成立。

2) 由于 $\Phi^{-1}(1/2)=0$,情形(iii)成立。 证毕

引理 6 的证明

(i) 由 $v\leqslant(p+s)(1-t)-ht$,有

$$\Phi\left(\frac{\Phi^{-1}(\lambda_0)}{y}\right)\geqslant\frac{p+s-c}{p+s-v}=\lambda_1$$

又因为正态分布函数是增函数,则

$$\frac{\Phi^{-1}(\lambda_0)}{y}\geqslant\Phi^{-1}(\lambda_1)>0$$

即 $\Phi^{-1}(\lambda_0)\sqrt{\sigma^2+\tau^2}\geqslant\Phi^{-1}(\lambda_0)\sqrt{\sigma^2+\frac{1}{\rho}}$。因此 $EQ_{\text{Old}}\geqslant EQ_{\text{QR-RP}}$。

(ii) 如果 $\lambda_1\leqslant1/2$,那么 $\Phi^{-1}(\lambda_0)<\Phi^{-1}(\lambda_1)\leqslant0$。有 $\mu+\Phi^{-1}(\lambda_0)\sqrt{\sigma^2+\tau^2}<\mu+\Phi^{-1}(\lambda_1)\sqrt{\sigma^2+\frac{1}{\rho}}$,即,$EQ_{\text{Old}}<EQ_{\text{QR-RP}}$。

如果 $\lambda_1>1/2$ 且 $\lambda_0\leqslant1/2$,那么 $\Phi^{-1}(\lambda_1)>0$,$\Phi^{-1}(\lambda_0)\leqslant0$ 显然有 $EQ_{\text{Old}}<EQ_{\text{QR-RP}}$。

如果 $\lambda_1\geqslant1/2$ 且 $v>(p+s)(1-t)-ht$,类似于(i)的证明,有 $\Phi(\Phi^{-1}(\lambda_0)/y)<\lambda_1$,于是 $\Phi^{-1}(\lambda_0)\sqrt{\sigma^2+\tau^2}<\Phi^{-1}(\lambda_1)\sqrt{\sigma^2+\frac{1}{\rho}}$,因此 $EQ_{\text{Old}}<EQ_{\text{QR-RP}}$。 证毕

引理 11 设函数

$$M(\lambda)=\Phi^{-1}(\lambda_1)+b_\tau(\Phi^{-1}(\lambda_1))$$

$$N(\lambda)=\frac{1}{\lambda}\mathrm{e}^{-\frac{(\Phi^{-1}(\lambda))^2}{2}}$$

那么 $M(\lambda)=\lambda\Phi^{-1}(\lambda)+\frac{1}{\sqrt{2\pi}}\mathrm{e}^{-\frac{(\Phi^{-1}(\lambda))^2}{2}}$ 是一个单调递增的正函数,$N(\lambda)$是一个单调递减的正函数。

证明 由于

$$\begin{aligned}\Phi^{-1}(\lambda_1)+b_\tau(\Phi^{-1}(\lambda_1))&=\Phi^{-1}(\lambda_1)+\int_{p^{-1}(\lambda_1)}^{\infty}(y-\Phi^{-1}(\lambda_1))\phi(y)\mathrm{d}y\\&=\Phi^{-1}(\lambda_1)+\int_{p^{-1}(\lambda_1)}^{\infty}y\Phi^{-1}\mathrm{d}y-\Phi^{-1}(\lambda_1)(1-\lambda_1)\\&=\lambda_1\Phi^{-1}(\lambda_1)+\frac{1}{\sqrt{2\pi}}\int_{p^{-1}(\lambda_1)}^{\infty}y\mathrm{e}^{-y/2}\mathrm{d}y\\&=\lambda_1\Phi^{-1}(\lambda_1)+\frac{1}{\sqrt{2\pi}}\mathrm{e}^{-(\Phi^{-1}(\lambda))^2/2}\end{aligned}$$

令 $\lambda=\Phi(x)$,首先根据反函数的求导规则,得

$$\frac{\mathrm{d}\Phi^{-1}(\lambda)}{\mathrm{d}\lambda}=\frac{1}{\frac{\mathrm{d}\Phi(x)}{\mathrm{d}x}}=\frac{1}{\phi(x)}=\sqrt{2\pi}\mathrm{e}^{\frac{\Phi^{-1}(\lambda)^2}{2}}$$

于是

$$\frac{\mathrm{d}M(\lambda)}{\mathrm{d}\lambda}=\Phi^{-1}(\lambda)+\lambda\frac{\mathrm{d}\Phi^{-1}(\lambda)}{\mathrm{d}\lambda}+\frac{1}{\sqrt{2\pi}}\mathrm{e}^{\frac{(\Phi^{-1}(\lambda))^2}{2}}(-\Phi^{-1}(\lambda))\frac{\mathrm{d}\Phi^{-1}(\lambda)}{\mathrm{d}\lambda}$$

$$=\lambda\frac{\mathrm{d}\Phi^{-1}(\lambda)}{\mathrm{d}\lambda}=\lambda\sqrt{2\pi}\mathrm{e}^{\frac{(\Phi^{-1}(\lambda))^2}{2}}>0$$

因此 $M(\lambda)$是一个增函数。又

$$\lim_{\lambda\to 0}M(\lambda)=\lim_{x\to-\infty}(\Phi(x)x+e^{-\frac{x^2}{2}})\Big/\sqrt{2\pi}=\lim_{x\to-\infty}x\int_{-\infty}^{x}\frac{1}{\sqrt{2\pi}}\mathrm{e}^{-\frac{t^2}{2}}\mathrm{d}t=0,$$

因此 $M(\lambda)\geqslant 0$。下面再分析 $N(\lambda)$的变化趋势

$$\frac{\mathrm{d}N(\lambda)}{\mathrm{d}\lambda}=-\frac{1}{\lambda^2}\mathrm{e}^{\frac{(\Phi^{-1}(\lambda))^2}{2}}-\frac{1}{\lambda}\mathrm{e}^{\frac{(\Phi^{-1}(\lambda))^2}{2}}\Phi^{-1}(\lambda)\frac{\mathrm{d}\Phi^{-1}(\lambda)}{\mathrm{d}\lambda}$$

$$=-\frac{1}{\lambda^2}\mathrm{e}^{\frac{(\Phi^{-1}(\lambda))^2}{2}}-\frac{\sqrt{2\pi}}{\lambda}\Phi^{-1}(\lambda)$$

$$=-\frac{\sqrt{2\pi}}{\lambda^2}\left(\frac{1}{\sqrt{2\pi}}\mathrm{e}^{\frac{(\Phi^{-1}(\lambda))^2}{2}}+\lambda\Phi^{-1}(\lambda)\right)$$

$$=-\frac{\sqrt{2\pi}}{\lambda^2}M(\lambda)\leqslant 0$$

再由 $N(\lambda)\geqslant 0$,得到 $N(\lambda)$是一个单调递减的正函数。　　证毕

引理 12　令 $b_\tau(Z)=\int_Z^\infty(y-Z)\phi(y)\,\mathrm{d}y$,则 $b_\tau(Z)$是一个单调下降正函数。

证明　如果 $Z_1\geqslant Z_2$,则

$$b_\tau(Z_1)-b_\tau(Z_2)=\int_{Z_1}^\infty(y-Z_1)\phi(y)\mathrm{d}y-\int_{Z_2}^\infty(y-Z_2)\phi(y)\mathrm{d}y$$

$$=\int_{Z_1}^\infty(y-Z_1-y+Z_2)\phi(y)\mathrm{d}y-\int_{Z_2}^{Z_1}(y-Z_2)\phi(y)\mathrm{d}y$$

$$\leqslant\int_{Z_1}^\infty(Z_2-Z_1)\phi(y)\mathrm{d}y\leqslant 0$$

显然有 $b_\tau(Z)>0$。因此结论成立。　　证毕

引理 7 的证明　由条件 1,有 $\lambda_0\leqslant\lambda_1$,及 $\Phi(\lambda_0)\leqslant\Phi(\lambda_1)$,那么由引理 12 知,$b_\tau(\Phi^{-1}(\lambda_0))\geqslant b_\tau(\Phi^{-1}(\lambda_1))\geqslant 0$,于是

$$b_\tau(\Phi^{-1}(\lambda_0))\sqrt{\sigma^2+\tau^2}\geqslant b_\tau(\Phi^{-1}(\lambda_0))\sqrt{\sigma^2+\tau^2}\geqslant b_\tau(\Phi^{-1}(\lambda_0))\sqrt{\sigma^2+\frac{1}{\rho}}$$

$$\mu-b_\tau(\Phi^{-1}(\lambda_0))\sqrt{\sigma^2+\tau^2}\leqslant\mu-b_\tau(\Phi^{-1}(\lambda_1))\sqrt{\sigma^2+\tau^2}\leqslant\mu-b_\tau(\Phi^{-1}(\lambda_1))\sqrt{\sigma^2+\frac{1}{\rho}}$$

即 $EQ_{\text{Old-short}}\geqslant EQ_{\text{RP-short}}\geqslant EQ_{\text{QR-RP-short}}$,及 $EQ_{\text{Old-sold}}\leqslant EQ_{\text{RP-sold}}\leqslant EQ_{\text{QR-RP-sold}}$。又有

$$b_\tau(\Phi^{-1}(\lambda_0))\sqrt{\sigma^2+\tau^2}\geqslant b_\tau(\Phi^{-1}(\lambda_0))\sqrt{\sigma^2+\frac{1}{\rho}}\geqslant b_\tau(\Phi^{-1}(\lambda_1))\sqrt{\sigma^2+\frac{1}{\rho}}$$

$$\mu-b_\tau(\Phi^{-1}(\lambda_0))\sqrt{\sigma^2+\tau^2}\leqslant\mu-b_\tau(\Phi^{-1}(\lambda_0))\sqrt{\sigma^2+\frac{1}{\rho}}\leqslant\mu-b_\tau(\Phi^{-1}(\lambda_1))\sqrt{\sigma^2+\frac{1}{\rho}}$$

即 $EQ_{\text{Old-short}}\geqslant EQ_{\text{QR-short}}\geqslant EQ_{\text{QR-RP-short}}$,及 $EQ_{\text{Old-sold}}\leqslant EQ_{\text{QR-sold}}\leqslant EQ_{\text{QR-RP-sold}}$。

由引理 11 有 $0\leqslant M(\lambda_0)\leqslant M(\lambda_1)$，那么

$$M(\lambda_0)\sqrt{\sigma^2+\frac{1}{\rho}}\leqslant M(\lambda_0)\sqrt{\sigma^2+\tau^2}\leqslant M(\lambda_1)\sqrt{\sigma^2+\tau^2}$$

即 $EQ_{\text{QR-left}}\leqslant EQ_{\text{Old-left}}\leqslant EQ_{\text{RP-left}}$。而且又有

$$M(\lambda_0)\sqrt{\sigma^2+\frac{1}{\rho}}\leqslant M(\lambda_1)\sqrt{\sigma^2+\frac{1}{\rho}}\leqslant M(\lambda_1)\sqrt{\sigma^2+\tau^2}$$

即 $EQ_{\text{QR-left}}\leqslant EQ_{\text{QR-RP-left}}\leqslant EQ_{\text{RP-left}}$。 证毕

引理 8 的证明

(i) 由于

$$\begin{aligned}
&(c+h)\Phi^{-1}(\lambda_0)+(p+s+h)b_\tau(\Phi^{-1}(\lambda_0))\\
&=(p+s+h)\int_{\Phi^{-1}(\lambda_0)}^{\infty}(y-\Phi^{-1}(\lambda_0))\Phi(y)\mathrm{d}y+(c+h)\Phi^{-1}(\lambda_0)\\
&=(p+s+h)\int_{\Phi^{-1}(\lambda_0)}^{\infty}y\phi(y)\mathrm{d}y-(p+s-c)\Phi^{-1}(\lambda_0)+(p+s+h)\Phi^{-1}(\lambda_0)\lambda_0\\
&=(p+s+h)\int_{\Phi^{-1}(\lambda_0)}^{\infty}y\phi(y)\mathrm{d}y\\
&=(p+s-c)\frac{1}{\lambda_0}\int_{\Phi^{-1}(\lambda_0)}^{\infty}y\phi(y)\mathrm{d}y=\frac{p+s-c}{\sqrt{2\pi}}\frac{1}{\lambda_0}\mathrm{e}^{-\frac{(\Phi^{-1}(\lambda_0))^2}{2}}
\end{aligned}$$

及

$$\begin{aligned}
&(c-v)\Phi^{-1}(\lambda_1)+(p+s-v)b_\tau(\Phi^{-1}(\lambda_1))\\
&=(p+s-v)\int_{\Phi^{-1}(\lambda_0)}^{\infty}y\phi(y)\mathrm{d}y-(p+s-c)\Phi^{-1}(\lambda_1)+(p+s-v)\Phi^{-1}(\lambda_1)\lambda_1\\
&=(p+s-v)\int_{\Phi^{-1}(\lambda_0)}^{\infty}y\phi(y)\mathrm{d}y=\frac{p+s-c}{\lambda_1\sqrt{2\pi}}\mathrm{e}^{-\frac{(\Phi^{-1}(\lambda_0))^2}{2}}
\end{aligned}$$

由引理 11，可知

$$\begin{aligned}
EP_{\text{QR-RP-ret}}-EP_{\text{QR-ret}}&=((c+h)\Phi^{-1}(\lambda_0)+(p+s+h)b_\tau(\Phi^{-1}(\lambda_0))-(c-v)\Phi^{-1}(\lambda_1)\\
&\quad-(p+s-v)b_\tau(\Phi^{-1}(\lambda_1)))\sqrt{\sigma^2+\frac{1}{\rho}}\\
&=\frac{p+s-c}{\sqrt{2\pi}}\left(\frac{1}{\lambda_0}\mathrm{e}^{-\frac{(\Phi^{-0}(\lambda_0))^2}{2}}-\frac{1}{\lambda_1}\mathrm{e}^{-\frac{(\Phi^{-1}(\lambda_1))^2}{2}}\right)\sqrt{\sigma^2+\frac{1}{\rho}}>0
\end{aligned}$$

即对任意的 $\lambda_0,\lambda_1\in(0,1)$，有 $EP_{\text{QR-RP-ret}}>EP_{\text{QR-ret}}$。

(ii) 由式(8)及(5)，得

$$\begin{aligned}
EP_{\text{RP-mfr}}-EP_{\text{Old-ret}}&=((c+h)\Phi^{-1}(\lambda_0)+(p+s+h)b_r(\Phi^{-1}(\lambda_0))-(c-v)\Phi^{-1}(\lambda_1)\\
&\quad-(p+s-v)b_r\cdot(\Phi^{-1}(\lambda_1)))\sqrt{\sigma^2+\tau^2}\\
&=\frac{p+s-c}{\sqrt{2\pi}}\cdot\left(\frac{1}{\lambda_0}\mathrm{e}^{-\frac{(\Phi^{-0}(\lambda_0))^2}{2}}-\frac{1}{\lambda_1}\mathrm{e}^{-\frac{(\Phi^{-1}(\lambda_1))^2}{2}}\right)\sqrt{\sigma^2+\tau^2}>0
\end{aligned}$$

由引理 11 及 $\lambda_0>\lambda_1$，得到 $EP_{\text{RP-mfr}}\geqslant EP_{\text{Old-ret}}$，这证明了情形(ii)。

(iii) 由式(8)及(10)

$$EP_{\text{RP-mfr}} - EP_{\text{QR-RP-ret}} = \frac{p+s-c}{(\lambda_1)\sqrt{2\pi}} e^{-\frac{(\Phi^{-1}(\lambda_0))^2}{2}} \cdot (\sqrt{\sigma^2+1/\rho} - \sqrt{\sigma^2+\tau^2}) < 0$$

因此结论成立. 证毕

引理 9 的证明 由引理 5 知,当 $\lambda_1 \leqslant 1/2$ 时,$\Phi^{-1}(\lambda_1) \leqslant 0$,$b_\tau(\Phi^{-1}(\lambda_1)) \geqslant 0$ 及 $\sqrt{\sigma^2+\tau^2} > \sqrt{\sigma^2+\frac{1}{\rho}}$,因此

$$\begin{aligned} EP_{\text{RP-mfr}} - EP_{\text{QR-RP-mfr}} &= ((c-k)\Phi^{-1}(\lambda_1) - vb_\tau(\Phi^{-1}(\lambda_1))) \cdot (\sqrt{\sigma^2+\tau^2} - \sqrt{\sigma^2+1/\rho}) \\ &= -(-(c-k)\Phi^{-1}(\lambda_1) + vb_\tau(\Phi^{-1}(\lambda_1))) \cdot (\sqrt{\sigma^2+\tau^2} - \sqrt{\sigma^2+1/\rho}) \leqslant 0 \end{aligned}$$

故 $EP_{\text{RP-mfr}} \leqslant EP_{\text{QR-RP-mfr}}$成立. 证毕

Return policies in supply chain system with quick response strategy

LU Qi-hui[1],ZHU Dao-li[1],LIN Zheng-hua[2]

1. School of Management,Fudan University,Shanghai 200433,China;

2. Mathematica Department,Jilin University,Changchun 130021,China

Abstract: With long lead-time,the wide impact of order decision is very inaccurate. Quick response strategy con-sists of dealing with this problem and enables orders to be placed closed to the start of the selling season. Retailers can adjust their order quality after gathered more and better demand information. But quick response strategy may not always make both manufacturers and retailer's benefits better. Ref 1. showed that under low service levels QR improves both retailer and manufacturer profits,but we would not observe such lower service levels in practice. The original purpose of this paper is to investigate the return polices in the supply chain system with QR strategy. Under some conditions,return policies will make QR system Pareto improving. In this paper,the author also consider changing of the expected quantity sold and the expected quantity shortage and the expected quantity left over.

Key words: quick response; supply chain; newsboy problem; pricing model; return policy; inventory problem

参 考 文 献

[1] Iyer A V,Bergen M E. Quick response in manufacture r-retailer channels[J]. Management Science, 1997,43(4): 559—570.

[2] Fisher M,Raman A. Reducing the cost of demand uncertainty through accurate response to early sales [J]. Operations Research,1996,44: 87—99.

[3] Emmons H,Gilbert S M. The role of returns policies in pricing and inventory decisions for catalogue

goods[J]. Management Science,1998,42(2): 276—283.

[4] Lau H-S,Lau A H-L. Manufacturer's pricing strategy and return policy for a single-period commodity[J]. European Journal of Operational Research,1999,116:291—304.

[5] Lau H-S,Lau A H-L,Kottas J F. Pricing/inventory decisions and profit shares in a non-integrated marketing channnel for a sin gle-period[J]. Journal of Operational Research Society, 2001, 52: 682—690.

[6] Mantrala M K,Raman K. Demand uncertainty and supplier's returns policies for a multi-store style-good retailer[J]. European Journal of Operational Research,1999,115:270—284.

[7] Lau A H-L,Lau H-S,Willet K D. Demand uncertainty and returns policies for a seasonal product:An alternative model[J]. Int J Production Economics,2000,66:1—12.

[8] Lee C H. Coordinated stocking,clearance sales,and return policies for a supply chain[J]. European Journal of Operational Research,2001,131:491—513.

[9] van Donselaar K,Kopczak L R,Wouters M. The use of advance demand information in a project-based supply chain[J]. European Journal of Operational Research,2001,130:519—538.

[10] Berger J O. Statistical Decision Theory and Bayesian Analysis[M]. Second ed. New York:Springer-Verlag,1985.

（本文发表于《管理科学学报》,2004 年第 4 期）

销售努力水平影响需求情况下的供应链回购契约

徐最[1,2]，朱道立[2]，朱文贵[2]
（1. 上海海事大学 交通运输学院，上海 200135；2. 复旦大学 管理学院，上海 200433）

摘要　考虑由一个供应商和一个零售商构成的供应链，其中需求是随机的且受到销售努力水平的影响。在销售季节到来之前，零售商需要同时确定订货数量和应采取的努力水平，本文首先分析了回购契约无法协调供应链的原因，并给出了当努力水平以两种形式影响需求时，零售商的最优努力水平和订货数量的表达式，分析了零售商的期望利润函数以及这两个决策变量关于批发价格和回购价格的变化情况。随后，提出了两种限制性回购契约，通过限制回购产品的数量来协调供应链，最后对本文涉及到的契约进行数值比较。

关键词：供应链协调；回购契约，销售努力水平
中国分类号：F830　　**文献标志码**：A

1　引　言

在有关供应链文献里，一般情况下不会刻意区分退货契约和回购契约，因为退货契约得出的结论同样适用于回购契约[1~3]，不过二者实际上是不同的。两种契约虽然都使得零售商以一定的批发价格从供应商那里采购产品，并获得关于全部剩余产品或者一部分剩余产品的补偿；但是，在退货契约下，零售商需要把货物退还给供应商，而在回购契约下，只要供应商明确零售商的剩余产品数量就可以了，不需要退货。Tsay[4]比较了二者在应用上的差别，并称回购契约为“markdown money contract”。

在产品的销售期短暂且市场需求不确定的情况下，供应商往往采用回购契约来补偿零售商，促使其多订货。宝洁公司通过采用回购契约而不是退货契约来处理剩余产品[5]，因为退货契约需要增加相应的包装、运输等成本。在服装[6]、化妆品和香水[7]、玩具[8]、专业性产品[9]以及食物[5]等行业，回购契约都得到广泛的应用。

在有关回购契约的文献里，很少考虑到零售商的销售努力行为。但是，在很多情况下，零售商的销售努力行为可以影响需求，比如把产品放在醒目的货架上、培训销售人员、雇佣更多的销售人员向顾客宣传、增加广告的投入等。销售努力带来的需求增加不仅使零售商获益也使供应商获益。对于供应商而言，当然是零售商选择越高的努力水平越好，

收稿日期：2006-11-08
资助项目：上海市教委重点学科基金（J50601）；国家自然科学基金（70432001）；复旦大学研究生创新基金
作者简介：徐最（1979～），女（满），吉林辽源人，博士。上海海事大学交通运输学院讲师。

但是如果只由零售商承担努力所付出的成本，那么他只会选择对自己最有利的努力水平，而这个选择往往不会实现供应链协调。

在不考虑销售努力水平影响需求的情况下，退货契约和回购契约都能协调供应链。但是，在产品需求受到零售商的销售努力水平影响时，Cachon[1]发现，常见的契约中只有数量折扣契约能够实现供应链协调。该契约使得供应商获得固定比例的预期销售收入，而零售商则保留所有实现的销售收入，从而使得零售商能够优化其努力水平，达到供应链协调。随后，Taylor[10]指出销售回扣(sales rebate)契约和退货契约的组合可以使得渠道协调，因为销售回扣契约和退货契约都能够激励零售商提高努力水平。然而，这个契约需要制定四个参数。何勇[11]在此基础上提出了基于回扣和惩罚策略的退货契约，即如果零售商的销售数量高于事先给定的水平，将会从供应商那里获得一定的回扣；反之，如果销售数量小于给定的水平，则会受到惩罚。该契约实际上是一个两部收费契约(two-part tariffs)即零售商获得供应链所有的销售利润，但是按事先规定的数量给供应商一定的转移支付。Krshna[12]考虑零售商要在观察到需求之后确定努力水平的情形，在满足一些特殊情况下，通过改进退货契约来协调供应链，不过这与本文考虑的情况不同。

在分析回购价格对于销售商努力水平的影响时，有的学者认为由于回购价格分担了零售商需求波动方面的风险，因此抑制了零售商提高销售努力的动机[13~16]，从而无法实现协调。Taylor[10]指出了这些结论的缺陷，认为回购价格的增加刺激零售商提高销售努力水平。但是，他没有分析回购价格对于零售商利润的影响，并且只考虑了努力水平对于需求影响的一种情况，本文对此会给出更全面的结论。

本文考虑由一个供应商和一个零售商构成的供应链，供应商向零售商提供单一产品，产品的需求是随机的，且受到零售商的销售努力水平影响。在销售季节到来之前，零售商需要同时确定订货数量和努力水平。本文首先分析了回购契约无法协调供应链的原因，并给出了当努力水平以两种形式影响需求的情况下，零售商的最优努力水平和订货数量的表达式，分析了期望利润函数以及这两个决策变量关于批发价格和回购价格的变化情况。随后，提出了两种限制性回购契约，通过限制回购产品的数量来协调供应链，最后对本文涉及到的契约进行数值比较。需要说明的是，本文接下来所提到的回购契约都是完全回购契约，即，供应商回购全部剩余产品。

2 模型描述

本文考虑由一个供应商和一个零售商构成的供应链，双方都是风险中性的。供应商通过零售商来销售产品，该产品的需求是不确定的、销售期比较短且受到零售商的销售努力水平影响。零售商在销售季节开始前需要同时决定两个变量：订货数量 q 和销售努力水平 e。销售努力水平影响销售数量，因此影响订货数量，进而影响供应商的收益。假设供应商的生产能力不受限制，边际生产成本为 c，销售价格 p 是外生给定的。变量 $D(e)$，$G(x,e)=\Pr(D(e)\leqslant x)$ 分别表示销售努力水平为 e 时产品的随机需求以及需求分布，其中需求关于努力水平是随机递增的，即 $\frac{\partial G(x,e)}{\partial e}<0$。零售商的销售努力水平为 e 时所要付出的成本为 $g(e)$，$g(e)$ 关于 e 是可微的，单调递增的和凸的，且有 $g(0)=0$。销售季节

过后，零售商从每单位剩余产品获得的残值为 v。设预期销售数量为 $S(q,e)$，其中

$$S(x,e)=E[x-(x-D(e))^{+}]=x-\int_{0}^{x}G(x,e)\mathrm{d}x.$$

那么期望剩余产品的数量为 $E(q-D(e))^{+}$，其中

$$E(x-D(e))^{+}=x-S(x,e).$$

这里假定 $S(x,e)$是关于订货数量和努力水平的二元凹函数。

本文并作如下假定：供应商和零售商都知道市场需求分布，只有一个销售季节，并且零售商只有一次订货机会。为了计算方便，这里假定零售商除了向供应商支付的费用以及努力费用外没有其它费用，未满足的需求可以损失掉，且没有惩罚成本。

3　供应链最优的努力水平和订货数量

现在考虑把供应商和零售商看作一个整体的情况。由供销双方构成的供应链面临一个产品需求是随机的销售市场，现需要决定最优的生产数量以及销售努力水平。

整个供应链的期望利润函数为

$$\begin{aligned}\Pi(q,e)&=E\{p[q-(q-D(e))^{+}]+v(q-D(e))^{+}\}-cq-g(e)\\&=pS(q,e)+v(q-S(q,e))-cq-g(e)\\&=(p-v)S(q,e)-(c-v)q-g(e)\end{aligned}\tag{1}$$

由于假定 $S(x,e)$是关于生产数量和努力水平的二元凹函数，那么整个供应链的利润也是关于这两个变量的凹函数。因此，最优的生产数量和努力水平$\{q^{0},e^{0}\}$满足如下的一阶条件：

$$\begin{cases}\dfrac{\partial\Pi(q,e)}{\partial q}=(p-v)\dfrac{\partial S(q,e)}{\partial q}-(c-v)=0,\\[2ex]\dfrac{\partial\Pi(q,e)}{\partial e}=(p-v)\dfrac{\partial S(q,e)}{\partial e}-g'(e)=0.\end{cases}\tag{2}$$

3.1　两种形式下系统最优的订货数量和努力水平

销售努力水平一般以两种形式影响需求，一种是以可加的形式，即 $D(e)=y(e)+\xi$[17]，另一种是以可积的形式，即 $D(e)=y(e)\xi$[10]。这里假定 $y(e)$是关于努力水平的单调递增的凹函数(与 Lariviere[17]的假设基本相同)，ξ表示需求中的随机变量，其分布函数和密度函数分别为 $F(\xi)$和 $f(\xi)$。两种形式比较而言，以可加的形式，销售努力行为对需求的影响是决定性的；而以可积的形式，销售努力行为对需求的影响是随机的。接下来定理1 给出在此两种形式下，整个供应链最优的努力水平以及订货数量。

定理 1

1）当努力水平以可积的形式影响需求，整个供应链的最优订货数量和努力水平$\{q^{0},e^{0}\}$分别满足

$$\begin{aligned}&\frac{g'(e^{0})}{y'(e^{0})}=(p-v)\int_{0}^{F^{-1}(r)}tf(t)\mathrm{d}t,\\&q^{0}=F^{-1}(r)y(e^{0}),\text{其中 } r=\frac{p-c}{p-v}.\end{aligned}\tag{3}$$

2）当努力水平以可加的形式影响需求，整个供应链的最优订货数量和努力水平$\{q^{0},

$e^0\}$分别满足

$$\frac{g'(e^0)}{y'(e^0)} = (p-c),$$
$$q^0 = F^{-1}(r) + y(e^0)\text{,其中 } r = \frac{p-c}{p-v}. \tag{4}$$

本定理的证明过程和定理 2 相似,这里就不证明了。

4 销售努力水平影响需求情况下的分散的供应链

在分散的供应链中,供应商和零售商相互独立,供应商通过零售商来销售产品。供应商是整个渠道的领导者,他确定契约后,零售商决定是否接受。如果接受,零售商将决定对于自己最有利的订货数量和销售努力水平。设零售商给供应商的期望转移支付为 T,并且假设由零售商来处理剩余产品,那么

供应商的期望利润函数为

$$\Pi_s(q,e) = T - cq \tag{5}$$

零售商的期望利润函数为

$$\begin{aligned}\Pi_r(q,e) &= E\{p[q-(q-D(e))^+] + v(q-D(e))^+\} - g(e) - T \\ &= pS(q,e) + v(q-S(q,e)) - g(e) - T.\end{aligned} \tag{6}$$

在由供应商和零售商构成的供应链中,供应商和零售商相互独立,双方根据各自的利润作最优的决策。如果在某种契约下,双方的决策和整个供应链的决策相一致,即,供应链的利润达到最大化,那么称该契约协调了供应链。在本文中,如果某种契约使得零售商的订货数量和努力水平的决策和整个供应链的决策相一致,那么称该契约协调了供应链。接下来分析回购契约是否能够协调此时的供应链。

4.1 回购契约

回购契约指供应商在销售季节前提供一个批发价格 w 和一个回购价格 b 给零售商,销售季节过后,对于没有卖出去的产品,供应商以每单位价格 $b(0<b<w)$补偿零售商,其中 $b<w$ 保证零售商不会从剩余产品中获利。不过,零售商仍然能够从每单位剩余产品中获得残值 v。在此契约下,零售商给供应商的转移支付为

$$T(q,e,w,b) = wq - bE(q-D(e))^+ = wq - b(q-S(q,e)).$$

供应商的期望利润函数为

$$\begin{aligned}\Pi_S(q,e) &= T(q,e,w,b) - cq = wq - b(q-S(q,e) - cq \\ &= bS(q,e) - (c+b-w)q.\end{aligned}$$

零售商的期望利润函数为

$$\begin{aligned}\Pi_r(q,e) &= E\{p[q-(q-D(e))^+\} + v(q-D(e))^+\} - T(q,e,w,b) - g(e) \\ &= pS(q,e) + (b+v)(q-S(q,e)) - g(e) - wq \\ &= (p-b-v)S(q,e) - (w-b-v)q - g(e).\end{aligned} \tag{7}$$

在不考虑销售努力水平影响需求的情况下,当批发价格和回购价格满足关系式(12)时,回购契约能够协调供应链[3]。但是,在努力水平影响需求的情况下,回购契约就无法协调供应链。

给定订货量 q，供应链最优的努力水平设为 $e^0(q)$，那么由式(1)有，

$$\frac{\partial \Pi(q,e^0(q))}{\partial e}=(p-v)\frac{\partial S(q,e^0(q))}{\partial e}-g'(e^0(q))=0. \tag{8}$$

在回购契约下，给定订货量 q，零售商的最优努力水平为 $e^b(q)$，那么由式(7)有

$$\frac{\partial \Pi_r(q,e^b(q))}{\partial e}=(p-b-v)\frac{\partial S(q,e^b(q))}{\partial e}-g'(e^b(q))=0. \tag{9}$$

比较式(8)与式(9)，由于 $b>0$，$g(e)$关于 e 是凸的，且 $S(q,e)$关于 e 是凹的，可推出，$e^b(q)<e^0(q)$，即，回购契约无法协调努力水平，也就无法协调供应链。在给定订货数量 q 下，由于零售商承担了整个供应链的全部努力成本 $g(e)$，但是只获得了部分的努力收益 $(p-b-v)S(q,e)$，因此选择的努力水平低于系统最优的努力水平。

4.2　回购价格和批发价格对于努力水平和订货数量的影响

不考虑销售努力水平对于需求的影响时，回购价格由于能够分担零售商需求波动的风险，因此回购契约能够协调供应链。但是，当考虑销售努力水平时，有的学者认为由于回购价格能够分担零售商的风险，从而抑制零售商提高销售努力水平的动机[13~16]。因此，有必要研究回购价格对于零售商两个决策变量的影响。

文[13～16]中所得的结论是在假定订货数量不变的情况下得出来的。由式(9)，就可以推出 $e^b(q)$关于 b 是单调递减的。但是，订货数量实际上也会受到回购价格的影响，也是变化的。接下来的定理 2 给出了在努力水平影响需求的两种形式下，零售商的订货数量和努力水平的表达式，以及这两个决策变量和零售商的期望利润函数关于回购价格和批发价格的变化情况。

定理 2

1）在回购契约下，当努力水平以可积的形式影响需求，零售商的最优订货数量和努力水平$\{q^b,e^b\}$分别满足

$$\begin{aligned}&\frac{g'(e^b)}{y'(e^b)}=(p-b-v)\int_0^{F^{-1}(r^b)}tf(t)\mathrm{d}t,\\&q^b=F^{-1}(r^b)y(e^b)\text{，其中 }r^b=\frac{p-w}{p-b-v}.\end{aligned} \tag{10}$$

并且$\{e^b,q^b\}$以及零售商的期望利润函数随着回购价格的增加而增加，随着批发价格的增加而递减。

2）在回购契约下，当努力水平以可加的形式影响需求，零售商的最优订货数量和努力水平$\{q^b,e^b\}$分别满足

$$\begin{aligned}&\frac{g'(e^b)}{y'(e^b)}=(p-w),\\&q^b=F^{-1}(r^b)+y(e^b)\text{，其中 }r^b=\frac{p-w}{p-b-v}.\end{aligned} \tag{11}$$

并且 e^b 与回购价格的变化无关，只是随着批发价格的增加而递减。但是，q^b 和零售商的期望利润函数随着回购价格的增加而增加，随着批发价格的增加而递减。

3）在回购契约下，如果批发价格和回购价格满足

$$\begin{aligned}&w^\lambda=\lambda_c+(1-\lambda)p,\\&b^\lambda=(1-\lambda)(p-v),0\leqslant\lambda\leqslant 1.\end{aligned} \tag{12}$$

那么，当努力水平以可积的形式影响需求时，最优订货数量和努力水平$\{q^\lambda, e^\lambda\}$为

$$\frac{g'(e^\lambda)}{y'(e^\lambda)} = \lambda(p-v)\int_0^{F^{-1}(r^b)} tf(t)\mathrm{d}t,$$
$$q^\lambda = F^{-1}(r) + y(e^\lambda),\text{其中 } r = \frac{p-c}{p-v}. \tag{13}$$

当努力水平以可加的形式影响需求时，最优订货数量和努力水平$\{q^\lambda, e^\lambda\}$为

$$\frac{g'(e^\lambda)}{y'(e^\lambda)} = \lambda(p-c),$$
$$q^\lambda = F^{-1}(r) + y(e^\lambda),\text{其中 } r = \frac{p-c}{p-v}. \tag{14}$$

无论努力水平以何种形式影响需求，零售商的努力水平、订货数量以及期望利润函数都随着回购价格(批发价格)的增加而递减。

本定理表明，回购价格对于努力水平的影响随着供应商提供的契约不同而发生变化。一般情况下，努力水平随着回购价格的增加而非降。但是，当批发价格和回购价格满足关系式(12)时，回购价格的增加促使零售商采取更低的努力水平。Taylor[10]得出了努力水平随着回购价格的增加而非降的结论，不过他假定$y(e)=e$这种特殊情况，没有给出零售商两个决策变量的具体表达形式，也没有分析期望利润函数以及订货数量关于契约中参数的变化情况，也没有考虑到定理2中的最后一部分内容。

比较式(10)、(13)和式(3)，式(11)、(14)和式(4)得出，只有当$w=c$，$b=0$，即$\lambda=1$时，供应链才能达到协调。此时，供应商以成本价格把产品销售给零售商，没有获得任何利润，而零售商获得了所有的供应链利润。显然，供应商不会提供这样的契约，即，b一定大于0，式(12)中的λ严格小于1。

正如前面所提到的，当不考虑销售努力水平影响需求的情况时，如果批发价格和回购价格满足关系式(12)，回购契约是能够协调供应链的[3]。当需求受到零售商的销售努力水平影响时，如果供应商提供的回购契约中的两个决策变量仍满足关系式(12)，那么，此时供应链不会实现协调($\lambda<1$)。但是，当λ接近1时，$\{q^\lambda, e^\lambda\}$接近于$\{q^0, e^0\}$，供应链的效率$\Pi(q^\lambda, e^\lambda)/\Pi(q^0, e^0)$接近于1。所以，当批发价格和回购价格充分小的时候，供应链几乎实现协调。

在4.1节中，我们已经推出如下的结论，即由于零售商承担了供应链所有的销售努力成本，但是没有获得全部收益，因此零售商所选择的努力水平低于整个供应链的最优的努力水平。在实际的商业活动中，供应商往往无法有效地观察到零售商的努力水平，也就不能通过契约来限制零售商的销售行为，从而引起签订契约后，零售商的降低销售努力行为，这也就是经济学上所说的“道德风险问题”。解决这个问题的一个办法就是零售商给供应商一个确定的支付，然后零售商承担所有的风险，但同时获得供应链所有的剩余利润。接下来我们通过提出两种限制性回购契约来达到这样的效果。

5 限制性回购契约

本节提出了两种限制性回购契约，批发价格固定下的限制性回购契约和带有数量溢

价的限制性回购契约。两个契约都通过限制回购产品的数量来迫使零售商采取系统最优的努力水平，不过，在回购价格相同的情况下，由于带有数量溢价的限制性回购契约的批发价格小于价格固定契约下的批发价格，因此零售商在带有数量溢价的限制性回购契约下可以获得更多的利润。

5.1　批发价格固定下的限制性回购契约

定理 3　考虑限制性回购契约$\{w^1,b^1\}$，其中$w^1=\beta c+(1-\beta)p$，$b^1=(1-\beta)(p-v)$，$0<\beta\leqslant 1$，并且规定回购产品数量为$q-S(q,e^0)$。在此回购契约下，$\{q^0,e^0\}$最大化了零售商的利润，其中$\Pi_r^1(q^0,e^0)=\beta\Pi(q^0,e^0)-(1-\beta)g(e^0)$，供应商的期望利润函数为$\Pi_s^1(q^0,e^0)=(1-\beta)\Pi(q^0,e^0)+(1-\beta)g(e^0)$，此时供应链达到协调。

证明　在限制性回购契约$\{w^1,b^1\}$下，只要订货量为q，不论产品实际剩余量是多少，零售商选择何种程度的努力水平，供应商都按照$q-S(q,e^0)$这个数量给予零售商补偿，这样，零售商给供应商的转移支付为

$$T^1(q,w^1,b^1)=w^1q-b^1(q-S(q,e^0)).$$

显然，在批发价格和回购价格给定的情况下，该转移支付只与订货数量q有关，与实际剩余产品数量无关。

在此情况下，零售商的期望利润函数为

$$\begin{aligned}\Pi_r^1(q,e)&=E\{p[q-(q-D(e))^+]+v(q-D(e))^+\}-T^1(q,w^1,b^1)-g(e)\\&=pS(q,e)+v(q-S(q,e))+b^1(q-S(q,e^0))-g(e)-w^1q\\&=(p-v)S(q,e)-(w^1-b^1-v)q-b^1S(q,e^0)-g(e)\end{aligned}\tag{15}$$

在给定订货数量q下，由于零售商承担了全部的努力成本$g(e)$，但是也获得了全部的努力收益$(p-v)S(q,e)$，因此零售商的努力水平决策和整个供应链的相同。如果零售商的订货数量为q^0，那么其选择的最优努力水平就为e^0。根据式(8)，可推出q^0最大化零售商选择努力水平为e^0的期望利润函数

$$\begin{aligned}\Pi_r^1(q,e^0)&=(p-v-b^1)S(q,e^0)-(w^1-b^1-v)q-g(e^0)\\&=\beta(p-v)S(q,e^0)-\beta(c-v)q-g(e^0).\end{aligned}$$

因此$\{q^0,e^0\}$是零售商的最优选择。此时，零售商的利润为

$$\begin{aligned}\Pi_r^1(q^0,e^0)&=\beta(p-v)S(q^0,e^0)-\beta(c-v)q^0-g(e^0)\\&=\beta\Pi(q^0,e^0)-(1-\beta)g(e^0).\end{aligned}\tag{16}$$

根据式(16)和$\Pi_s^1(q^0,e^0)=\Pi(q^0,e^0)-\Pi_r^1(q^0,e^0)$，可以得出供应商的利润。当$\beta>0$时，由于$\{q^0,e^0\}$最大化零售商的利润，因此供应链达到协调。$\beta\leqslant 1$保证供应商的利润不小于零。　　证毕

该定理表明零售商的利润随着β的增加而增加。β的取值主要由双方的谈判势力来决定。如果零售商具有更强的谈判势力，那么β就会增加，相应的批发价格和回购价格都会减少。由于销售价格和残值都是固定的，β将决定回购价格的取值，即，β越小，回购价格越高。因此可以说，对于供应商而言，采用更高的回购价格将会获得更多的利润。

5.2　带有数量溢价的限制性回购契约

定理 4　考虑限制性回购契约$\{w^2,b^2\}$，其中$w^2=\beta c+(1-\beta)p-(1-\beta)\dfrac{g(e^0)}{q}$，$b^2=$

$(1-\beta)(p-v)$，$0<\beta\leqslant 1$，并且规定回购产品数量为 $q-S(q,e^0)$。在此回购契约下，$\{q^0,e^0\}$最大化了零售商的利润，使得 $\Pi_r^2(q^0,e^0)=\beta\Pi(q^0,e^0)$，供应商的利润为 $\Pi_s^2(q^0,e^0)=(1-\beta)\Pi(q^0,e^0)$，此时供应链达到协调。

该定理的证明过程和定理 3 相似，在此不详细论证。

该回购契约的批发价格与最优努力水平有关，并且随着订货量的增加而递增，Tomlin[17]称这种契约为数量溢价(quantity premium)契约。不过，无论订货量有多大，批发价格总是严格小于 $\beta c+(1-\beta)p$。与前面的回购契约$\{w^1,b^1\}$相比，在 β 取值相同也即回购价格相同的情况下，虽然限制回购的数量都是一样的，但是由于降低了批发价格，从而使得供应商分担了一部分购买成本，因此增加了零售商的收益。

在两种限制性回购契约下，供应商根据努力水平为 e^0时的期望剩余数量来补偿零售商，从而迫使零售商选择系统最优的努力水平 e^0。由于回购的数量只和订货数量有关，与实际的剩余产品数量无关，因此，在订货数量确定的情况下，供应商的利润就是确定的，不受需求波动的影响，而零售商将承担供应链所有的风险与销售努力费用，但是也获得了所有的剩余利润，所以供应链实现了协调。在实际的商业操作过程中，供应商不需要知道零售商的实际剩余数量，只要通过订货数量就可以确定补偿数额，以及零售商给供应商的转移支付。

在回购契约下，正如 4.1 节中所分析的，供应链无法协调的原因在于零售商获得的收益和承担的成本不对等，而在限制性回购契约下，零售商了承担所有的努力成本，但是也获得了所有的由销售努力带来的剩余利润，因此供应链实现协调。这有点类似于经济学上解决“道德风险问题”的办法，即，企业所有人把产权卖给经理人，那么经理人就会全力的管理好企业，不会有“偷懒”行为。

在前言中提到的文献里 Taylor[10]和 Krishnan[12]所提出的退货契约在一定条件下可以协调供应链换，作回购契约则无法得到同样的结论。何勇[11]提出的退货契约如果换成回购契约，仍可以协调供应链。但是，供应商要想借助回扣和惩罚这两种策略协调供应链，必须以能够核实零售商的销售数量为前提，而核实往往需要一定的费用。本文提出的回购契约不需要这个前提条件，只要限制回购产品的数量就可以迫使零售商选择系统最优的努力水平，从而协调供应链。

6 数值分析

前面已经分析了回购契约无法协调的原因，并给出了回购契约下供应链的最优订货数量和努力水平的表达式。随后，提出了两种限制性回购契约来协调供应链，接下来通过数值算例对这些契约进行比较。

例 1 设 $p=9, c=8, v=4, F(x,e)=\int_0^{20} e\,\dfrac{x}{20}\mathrm{d}x, g(e)=\dfrac{1}{2}e^2$.

经过计算可以得出 $e^0=2, q^0=8, \Pi(e^0,q^0)=2$。取定 $b=2.5$，接下来的表 1 比较了在两种限制性回购契约$\{w^1,b^1\}$和$\{w^2,b^2\}$，批发价格和回购价格满足关系(1.12)时的契约$\{w^\lambda,b^\lambda\}$以及一般的回购契约$\{w,b\}$下的供应链的特征。

表 1 比较四种类型契约

契 约	$\{w^1,b^1\}$	$\{w^2,b^2\}$	$\{w^\lambda,b^\lambda\}$	$\{w,b\}$
批发价格	8.5	$8.5-1/q$	8.5	w
零售商的利润	0	1	0.5	$8(9-w)^4$
供应商的利润	2	1	1	$16(9-w)^3(3w-25)$
供应链的利润	2	2	1.5	$8(9-w)^3(5w-41)$
供应链的效率	100%	100%	75%	$4(9-w)^3(5w-41)\%$
订货数量	8	8	4	$4(9-w)^2$
努力水平	2	2	1	$32(9-w)^3$

在限制性回购契约下，由于供应链达到协调，因此零售商的最优订货数量和努力水平都等于系统的最优值。在限制性回购契约$\{w^2,b^2\}$下，供应商分担了零售商的一部分购买成本，因此其利润要低于限制性回购契约$\{w^1,b^1\}$下的利润，相应的零售商的利润就会增加。不过，由于协调了供应链，因此两种契约下供应链的利润相同。在契约$\{w^\lambda,b^\lambda\}$下，由于批发价格和回购价格满足一定的关系，因此当回购价格确定下后，批发价格也就确定了，相应的零售商努力水平和订货数量也是确定的，正如定理 2 所证明的，此时的供应链不会实现协调(因为 λ 小于 1)。在一般的回购契约$\{w,b\}$下，由于批发价格和回购价格之间没有一一对应的关系，因此，回购价格的确定只是限制了批发价格的范围(需要使得供销双方的利润不为负)。接下来的图 1 给出了在四种契约下，随着批发价格的变化，零售商的订货数量和努力水平的变化情况。

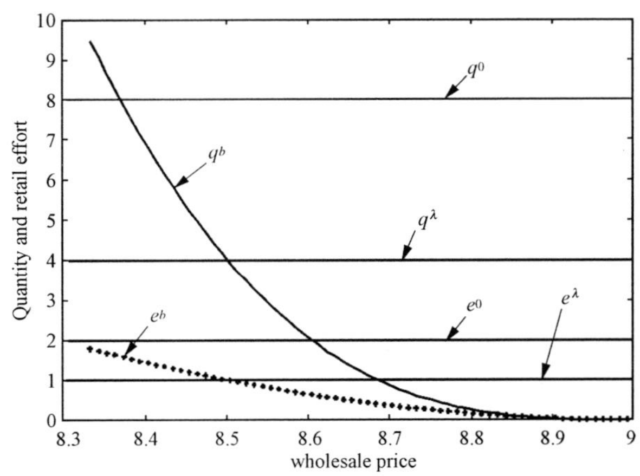

图 1 四种契约下，零售商的订货数量和努力水平关于批发价格的变化情况

从图 1 可以看出，契约$\{w^\lambda,b^\lambda\}$并没有协调供应链。契约$\{w,b\}$虽然也没有协调供应链($e^b<e^0$)，但是当批发价格足够小的时候，订货数量却可以大于协调时的订货数量($q^b>q^0$)。不过，正如定理 2 所示，订货数量和努力水平都随着批发价格的增加而递减。

取定回购价格后，如表 1 所示，在两种限制性行回购契约以及契约$\{w^\lambda,b^\lambda\}$下，供应链以及供应商、零售商的利润都是确定，只有回购契约$\{w,b\}$下的利润是受到批发价格的影响的。因此，接下来的图 2 只分析在回购契约$\{w,b\}$下，整个供应链以及供销双方的利润关于批发价格的变化情况。

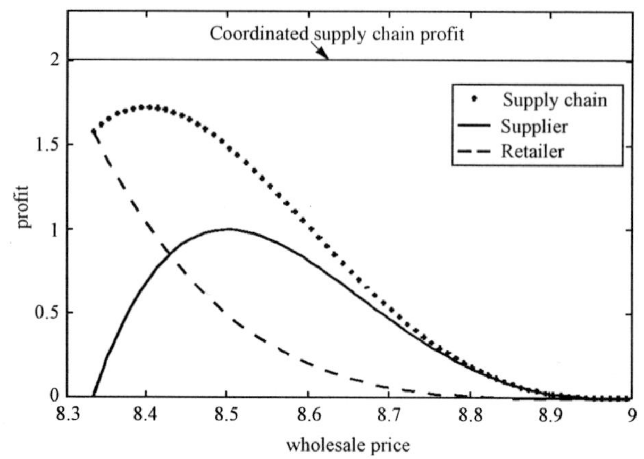

图 2 在回购契约$\{w,b\}$下，整个供应链以及供销双方的利润关于批发价格的变化情况

在回购契约$\{w,b\}$下，批发价格的增加自然导致零售商的利润降低。供应商的利润在批发价格增加的最初阶段是增加的，但是当批发价格增加所引起的利润增加小于零售商订货数量的降低所带来的利润损失时，其利润开始降低，直至当批发价格等于销售价格时，利润降为零。整个供应链的变化和供应商的类似，只不过变化的速度稍微慢一些。

从图 3 可以看出，在回购契约$\{w,b\}$下，供应链的效率关于批发价格也是先增加后减少的。契约$\{w^1,b^1\}$和契约$\{w^2,b^2\}$都使得供应链实现协调，因此，供应链的效率都达到了最大值。由于契约$\{w^\lambda,b^\lambda\}$无法协调供应链，所以，此契约下的供应链效率自然无法达到最大。

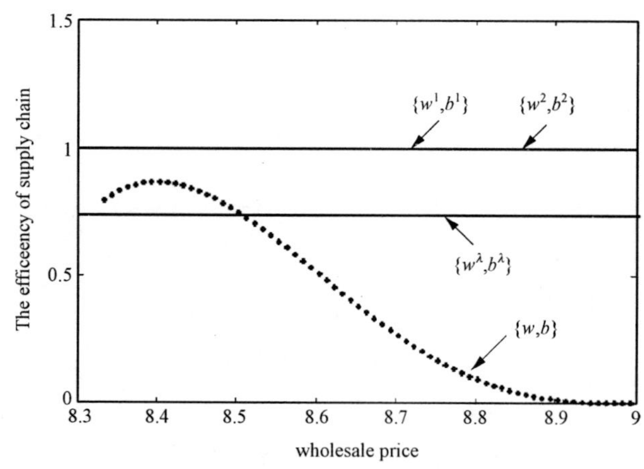

图 3 四种契约下，供应链的效率

7 结 论

本文研究了努力水平影响需求情况下的供应链。首先分析了回购契约不能协调供应链的原因，得出了当努力水平以两种形式影响需求时，零售商的努力水平和订货数量的表达式，以及零售商的期望利润函数和这两个决策变量关于批发价格和回购价格的变化情

况。证明了在不同的情况下，回购价格对于零售商的努力水平影响不同。随后提出来两种限制性回购契约，批发价格固定下的限制性回购契约$\{w^1,b^1\}$和带有数量溢价的限制性回购契约$\{w^2,b^2\}$。两种限制性契约使得供应商获得固定的收益，零售商承担供应链所有努力成本，但是获得所有的剩余利润，因此实现供应链协调。需要指出的是，本文所提出的协调供应链的限制性回购契约不需要以核实努力水平为前提，而在实际问题中，努力水平通常很难被核实或者核实费用很高，所以本文方法更具有普适性。不过由于假定供应商和零售商都知晓市场的需求分布，因此该模型更适合于一个大型企业内部引入“市场机制”的问题，因此提出更加适合供应链的协调契约是未来的研究方向。

附　录

定理 2 的证明：

证明　设需求 $D(e)=y(e)\xi$，那么

$$S(q,e)=q-[q-D(e)]^+=q-\int_0^{q/y(e)}(q-y(e)t)f(t)\mathrm{d}t$$
$$=q-y(e)\int_0^{q/y(e)}F(t)\mathrm{d}t\ .$$

根据式(7)，得出零售商的期望利润函数为

$$\Pi_r(q,e)=(p-b-v)S(q,e)-(w-b-v)q-g(e)$$
$$=(p-w)q-(p-b-v)y(e)\int_0^{q/y(e)}F(t)\mathrm{d}t-g(e).\tag{17}$$

给定努力水平 e，零售商最优的订货数量 $q^b(e)$满足

$$\frac{\partial\Pi_r(q^b(e),e)}{\partial q}=(p-w)-(p-b-v)F(q^b(e)/y(e))=0.$$

即 $q^b(e)=F^{-1}(r^b)y(e)$，其中 $r^b=\dfrac{p-w}{p-b-v}$。现在把此式代入(17)，有

$$\Pi_r(q^b(e),e)=(p-w)q^b(e)-(p-b-v)y(e)\int_0^{q^b(e)/y(e)}F(t)\mathrm{d}t-g(e)$$
$$=(p-w)y(e)F^{-1}(r^b)-(p-b-v)y(e)\int_0^{F^{-1}(r^b)}F(t)\mathrm{d}t-g(e)$$
$$=y(e)(p-b-v)\left[r^bF^{-1}(r^b)-\int_0^{F^{-1}(r^b)}F(t)\mathrm{d}t\right]-g(e)$$
$$=y(e)(p-b-v)\int_0^{F^{-1}(r^b)}tf(t)\mathrm{d}t-g(e).\tag{18}$$

由于前面假设 $y(e)$是关于 e 的凹函数，$g(e)$是关于 e 的凸函数，那么 $\Pi_r(q^b(e),e)$是关于 e 的凹函数，因此，最优的努力水平 e^b 满足

$$\left.\frac{\partial\Pi_r(q^b(e),e)}{\partial e}\right|_{e=e^b}=y'(e^b)(p-b-v)\int_0^{F^{-1}(r^b)}tf(t)\mathrm{d}t-g'(e^b)=0.$$

即

$$\frac{g'(e^b)}{y'(e^b)}=(p-b-v)\int_0^{F^{-1}(r^b)}tf(t)\mathrm{d}t.\tag{19}$$

那么，最优的订货数量 q^b 为

$$q^b = q^b(e^b) = F^{-1}(r^b)y(e^b). \tag{20}$$

如果把 $w=c, b=0$ 带入式(19)和式(20)，那么就得出定理 1 中整个供应链的最优努力水平和订货数量，此时的 $r^b=r$。

把式(19)两边关于 b 求导

$$\frac{d\dfrac{g'(e^b)}{y'(e^b)}}{de^b}\frac{\partial e^b}{\partial b} = \frac{d(p-b-v)\int^{F^{-1}(r^b)} tf(t)\mathrm{d}t}{db},$$

整理后得到

$$\frac{g''(e^b)y'(e^b)-g'(e^b)y''(e^b)}{[y'(e^b)]^2}\frac{\partial e^b}{\partial b} = \int_0^{F^{-1}(r^b)} tf(t)\mathrm{d}t.$$

由于前面假设 $y(e)$是关于 e 的单调递增的凹函数，$g(e)$是关于 e 的单调递增的凸函数，因此等式左边的第一部分不小于零的，而等式右边也不小于零的，那么有

$$\frac{\partial e^b}{\partial b} \geqslant 0.$$

再由 $F^{-1}(r^b)$关于 r^b 单调递增，r^b 关于 b 单调递增，和 $y(e^b)$关于 e 也是单调递增的，因此，由式(20)得出 q^b 关于 b 也是单调递增的。

同理，很容易证明出 e^b 关于 w 是单调递减的，又由于 r^b 关于 w 是单调递减的，进而得出 q^b 关于 w 也是单调递减的。

把 q^b 代入式(18)，得出零售商的期望利润函数为

$$\Pi_r(q^b(e^b),e^b) = y(e^b)(p-b-v)\int_0^{F^{-1}(rb)} tf(t)\mathrm{d}t - g(e^b). \tag{21}$$

把式(21)两边关于 b 求导得出

$$\frac{\partial \Pi_r(q^b(e^b),e^b)}{\partial b} = \left[y'(e^b)(p-b-v)\int_0^{F^{-1}(r^b)} tf(t)\mathrm{d}t - g'(e^b)\right]\left(\frac{\mathrm{d}e^b}{\mathrm{d}b}\right) + y(e^b)\int_0^{F^{-1}(r^b)} F(t)\mathrm{d}t. \tag{22}$$

把式(19)代入式(22)得出

$$\frac{\partial \Pi_r(q^b(e^b),e^b)}{\partial b} = y(e^b)\int_0^{F^{-1}(r^b)} F(t)\mathrm{d}t \geqslant 0.$$

因此，零售商的期望利润函数也随着回购价格的增加而递增。

同理可以得出

$$\frac{\partial \Pi_r(q^b(e^b),e^b)}{\partial b} = -y(e^b)F^{-1}(r^b) \leqslant 0.$$

即，零售商的期望利润函数也随着批发价格的增加而递减。

当需求 $D(e)=y(e)\xi$ 时，类似的会得出定理中的结论。

当 w,b 满足关系式(12)时，$r^b=r$。由式(19)和式(20)可以得出当努力水平以可积的形式影响需求时，最优努力水平和订货数量为

$$\begin{aligned} &\frac{g'(e^\lambda)}{y'(e^\lambda)} = \lambda(p-v)\int_0^{F^{-1}(r)} tf(t)\mathrm{d}t, \\ &q^\lambda = F^{-1}(r)y(e^\lambda)，其中\ r = \frac{p-c}{p-v} \end{aligned} \tag{23}$$

当努力水平以可加的形式影响需求时，由式(11)可以得出最优努水平和订货数量为

$$\frac{g'(e^{\lambda})}{y'(e^{\lambda})}=\lambda(p-c),$$

$$q^{\lambda}=F^{-1}(r)+y(e^{\lambda}),\text{其中 } r=\frac{p-c}{p-v}.$$

在证明 e^b 关于 b 单调递增的过程可知，$\frac{g'(e^{\lambda})}{y'(e^{\lambda})}$关于 λ 是单调递增的，那么由式(23)和式(24)得出，e^{λ} 和 q^{λ} 关于 λ 是单调递增的。由 w，b 和 λ 的关系可知，无论努力水平以何种形式影响需求，零售商的努力水平、订货数量都随着回购价格(批发价格)的增加而递减。

根据式(18)，得出零售商的期望利润函数为

$$\Pi_r(q^{\lambda},e^{\lambda})=y(e^{\lambda})\lambda(p-v)\int_0^{F^{-1}(r)}tf(t)\mathrm{d}t-g(e^{\lambda}). \tag{25}$$

把式(25)两边关于 λ 求导得到

$$\frac{\partial\Pi_r(q^{\lambda},e^{\lambda})}{\partial\lambda}=y(e^{\lambda})(p-v)\int_0^{F^{-1}(r)}tf(t)\mathrm{d}t\geqslant 0.$$

因此，零售商的期望利润函数也随着回购价格(批发价格)的增加而递减。

证明完毕。

Supply chain coordination under buy-back contract with sales effort effects

XU Zui[1,2], ZHU Dao-li[2], ZHU Wen-gui[2]

(1. College of Transport and Communications, Shanghai Maritime University, Shanghai 200135, China; 2. Management School, Fudan University, Shanghai 200433, China)

Abstract: Consider a supply chain consisting of a supplier and a retailer who faces a stochastic demand influenced by sales effort. Before the selling season, the retailer needs to decide his quantity as the same time as his effort level. We first analyze the reason that the buy-back contract cannot coordinate the supply chain, derive the expression of the retailer's optimal quantity and effort level under two fashions that effort influences demand, and analyze how the retailer's profit and the two decisions vary by the wholesale price and buy back price. Then, we propose two types of constrained buy-back contracts by constraining the quantity of buying back to coordinate the supply chain; finally compare the performance of the two types of contracts.

Key words: supply chain coordination; buy back contract; sales effort level

参考文献

[1] Cachon G P. Supply chain coordination with contracts[C]//Handbooks in Operation and Manage-

ments Science, Vol. 11, Supply Chain Management: Design, Coordination and Operation, 2003, 229—339.

[2] Cachon G P, Lariviere L M. Supply chain coordination with revenue sharing contracts: Strengths and limitations[J]. Management. Science, 2005, 51(1): 30—44.

[3] Lariviere M A. Supply chain contracting and coordination with stochastic demands[C]//Tayur S, Magazine M, Ganeshan R, Quantitative Models for Supply Chain Management. Masschusetts: Kluwer Academic Publishers, 1998, 233—268.

[4] Tsay A. Managing retail channel overstock: Markdown money and return policies[J]. Journal of Retailing, 2001, 77(4): 457—492.

[5] Tenser J. Procter & gamble revamps retail incentives(streamlined'97 initiative to improve efficiencies)[J]. Supermarket News, 1997, 24(March), 1.

[6] Ryan T J . Retailers expected to seek more markdown money thus yule: factors call it a bigger problem for vendors than the stock. market or Asia[J]. Daily News Record, 1998, 23(October).

[7] Parks L. All I want for christmas[J]. Drug Store News, 1996, 22(6): 26.

[8] Leccese D. Manufacturers, retailers make profitable partners: Both sides share in risks, responsibilities to enhance merchandising effort[J]. Playthings, 1993, 1(November), 30.

[9] Gallagher L. Holding the bag: Landing their first big account, entrepreneurs may think their troubles are over. They may just be beginning[J]. Forbes: 1999, 14(6), 164.

[10] Taylor T A. Supply chain coordination under channel rebates with sales effort effects[J]. Management Science, 2002, 48(8): 992—1007.

[11] 何勇，杨德礼，孟丽菊，等. 考虑努力因素的退化政策模型[J]. 系统工程理论方法应用，2005，14(6)：568—571.

He Y, Yang D L, Meng L J, et al. The return policy model with effort dependent demand[J]. Systems Engineering Theory Methodology Applications, 2005, 14(6): 568—571.

[12] Krishnan H, Kapuscinski R, Butz D A. Coordinating contracts for decentralized supply chains with retailer promotional effort[J]. Management Science, 2004, 50(1): 48—63.

[13] Chu W. Demand signaling and screening in channels of distribution[J]. Marketing Science, 1992, 11(4): 327—347.

[14] Kandel E. The right to return[J]. Journal of Law and Economics, 1996, 39: 329—356.

[15] Padmanabhan V, Png I PL. Manufacturer's returns policies and retail competition[J]. Marketing Science, 1997, 16(1): 81—94.

[16] Padmanabhan V, Png I PL. Returns policies: Making money by making good[J]. Sloan Management, 1995, 37(1): 65—72.

[17] Lariviere M A, Porteus E. Selling to the newsvendor: An analysis of priceonly contracts[J]. Manufacturing Service Operation Management, 2001, 3(4): 293—305.

[18] Tomlin B. Capacity investments in supply chains: Sharing the gain rather than sharing the pain[J]. Manufacturing & Service Operations Management, 2003, 5(4): 317—333.

（本文发表于《系统工程理论与实践》，2008 年第 4 期）

含交付时间不确定性的供应链协调策略研究*

鲁其辉，朱道立

（复旦大学管理学院管理科学系，上海 200433）

摘要：分析含有交付时间不确定性的季节性供应链管理问题。如果在供应链中共享供应商的交付时间不确定性信息，零售商可以调整订货量，减少销售损失，就有可能提高供应链的整体利润。分析指出，当交付时间不确定性程度大时，信息共享能提高改进供应链绩效的可能性，但不一定能提高供应链的整体绩效，因而，仅仅采用信息共享有应用价值，但有一定的局限性。进一步分析发现，存在能协调这种含有交付时间不确定性供应链策略，能使供应链达到整体绩效最大化，并且对供应链的利润进行分配，协调策略能有效地弥补信息共享的局限性。

关键词：供应链；信息共享；协调；交付时间；Newsvendor 模型

中国分类号：F224　　**文献标识码：**A　　**文章编号：**1007-9807(2008)02-0050-11

0　引言

经济全球化和信息经济时代的到来，使供应链管理成为现代企业管理的一个最重要的组成部分之一。供应链管理的最主要目标是减少供应链中非效率因素，提高运作与交易效率，最终提高供应链的整体绩效。本文将研究季节性产品的供应链管理问题。

在销售季节开始之前，零售商根据市场需求信息进行订货，供应商在收到订单以后开始生产与物流配送。供应商将努力做到及时交付，因为如果交付延迟而销售季节已经开始，部分市场需求将得不到满足，会引起销售损失。但是交付时间在实际运作中很难完全控制，存在许多不确定性因素和约束条件使得交付时间变得不确定，例如，能力约束、排班困难、不确定物料供应、生产工序问题等等[1]。

本文将首先分析在供应链中共享供应商的交付时间信息能否改进供应链的绩效，并分析信息共享带来的价值及其局限。供应链中的信息可以分为两种：公共信息（Common Information，指供应链成员都拥有的信息）和私有信息（Private Infor。mation，指供应链某一方拥有的独有信息）[2,3]。例如在本文研究的供应链中，“销售季节的长度和单位时间段内的需求”是公共信息，“交付时间不确定性信息”是供应商的私有信息。信息共享被

*收稿日期：2005-04-05；修订日期：2005-10-18

基金项目：国家自然科学基金资助项目（70432001），中国博士后科学基金资助项目（20070410166）

作者简介：鲁其辉（1977～），男，湖南益阳人，博士。Email：qihuilu@163. tom

认为是解决供应链“牛鞭效用(BullwhipEffect)”的主要方法之一[4,5]。从被共享的信息类型看,可以分为6种信息共享:需求信息、库存信息、销售信息、预测信息、物流配送状况信息和生产制造计划信息共享[3]。

目前,国内外研究工作者主要关注于库存信息与需求信息共享两类信息共享问题,对其他类型的信息共享问题研究较少。学术界对供应链信息共享问题的研究主要集中在信息共享的价值与信息共享的实现机制两个方面[3,6,7]。绝大部分研究工作表明信息共享具有价值,但是由于假设条件和方法不同,信息共享的价值大小不同。以往的研究没有分析信息共享的局限性。下面将指出交付时间信息共享具有局限性。

本文进一步分析发现,若供应链中引入某种协调策略,就能达到供应链整体绩效最大化的目标,这说明了协调策略能弥补信息共享的局限性。供应链协调管理的根源在于供应链的各个成员在利益、风险等方面存在不同程度的冲突,需要对供应链上下游进行必要的协调管理。当供应链中的所有决策是为了达到一个系统全局目标时,供应链才是完全协调的;而当决策者们得不到完全信息或者他们受到一些违背系统目标的利益的激励时,供应链是缺乏协调的。即便在能获取完全信息的情况下,若供应链中的各个决策者追求各自目标函数最优而不考虑系统的整体目标,这样的供应链绩效也只是次优的。供应链协调管理的研究在近20年内得到了很多的研究成果,许多协调策略被深入研究[8~10]。下面将表明采用回购策略等供应链策略能协调这种含有交付时间不确定性的供应链,并分析协调策略在这种供应链中的价值。

1 假设与记号

本文将研究最基本的供应链模型:供应-零售模型(supplier-buyer model)。在具有固定开始和结束时刻的销售季节里,零售商面对随机市场需求。零售商在销售季节开始之前向供应商订货,并要求在销售季节开始之前交付。零售商按照最大化自身期望利润为目标给出订货量。供应商在收到订单后进行生产与配送。虽然及时交付是供应商努力要去达到的目标,但各种不确定因素和约束往往造成交付时间的不确定。如果交付时间早于销售开始时间,供应商必须付出相应的库存保管等费用直至销售开始为止。反之,交付延迟的情况下,由于缺货使得零售商受到损失,这时零售商会要求供应商进行补偿。考虑常见的做法:供应商降低批发价格,使零售商的期望利润保持与没有交付延迟情况下的期望利润一致。本文采用这种假设主要出于两个主要原因:首先,因为在销售季节开始之前,零售商在及时交付的条件下订货,当交付延迟的情况出现时,供应商应该对零售商因到货延迟带来的销售损失进行补偿,这样假设零售商的期望利润始终保持不变是合理的;其次,主要考虑供应链的整体利润在信息不共享和信息共享后的关系,因此批发价的设定机制不会影响供应链的整体利润,因此令零售商的利润不变是司行的。由于供应商的交付时间直接影响零售商的销售时间长度,因而在分析季节性产品的订货和定价决策问题之前,将首先分析含有交付时间不确定性的市场需求情况。先给出一些记号。

n:销售季节的单位时间段的总数;

d_i:销售季节中单位时间段 i 内的随机需求量;

Y:产品到达零售商的时刻与销售季节开始时刻的时间差的相应销售季节的单位时

间段的个数。Y 为离散型随机变量，记它的概率分布为 $g(y)$，即，$P\{Y=Y\}=g(y)$。则 $y>0$ 表示交付时间迟于销售开始时间，$y\leqslant 0$ 表示交付时间先于或等于销售开始时间。设 Y 的取值为，$T_1, T_1+1, \cdots, 0, 1, \cdots, T_2$，$(T_1\leqslant 0, T_2\geqslant 0)$ 且 $T_2<n$。

M：当产品到达零售商以后，零售商面对的剩余销售季节内的第 1 个单位时间段的编号。注意到：若 $y>0, M=y+1$；若 $y\leqslant 0, M=1$。

X_0：货物交付时刻先于销售季节开始($y\leqslant 0$)时，零售商面对的销售季节内的市场需求量。记它的概率密度函数为 $f_0(x)$；分布函数为 $F_0(x)$；均值与方差分别记为 μ_0, σ_0^2。

X_y：货物交付时刻晚于销售季节开始($y>0$)时，零售商面对的销售季节内的市场需求量。记它的概率密度函数为 $f_y(x)$；发布函数为 $F_y(x)$；均值与方差分别为 μ_y, σ_y^2。

X：在零售商得到了供应商交付时间不确定信息的情况下，零售商分析得出的市场需求量；设 X 的概率密度函数为 $f(x)$；分布函数为 $F(x)$；X 的均值与方差分别记为 μ_X, σ_X^2。

由于零售商面对的市场需求量 X 是销售季节中时间段内需求量 d_i 累加起来的，并且它与交付时间 Y 是相关的，而且 Y, d_i 都是随机变量，则需求 X 等于下列随机个随机变量之和

$$X \triangleq d_M + \cdots + d_n. \tag{1}$$

为了深入研究销售季节内市场需求的分布情况，作下列合理的假设。

假设 1 d_i 独立同分布，并服从正态分布。均值与方差分别为 μ, σ^2。

假设 2 M 与 d_i 之间相互独立。

经典 Newsvendor 模型是分析季节性产品订货问题的基本模型，下列记号是模型中的几个记号。

P：零售商的产品销售单价。

c_0：供应商及时配送的情况下，零售商的采购批发单价；

$c_1(y)$：供应商延迟配送的时间等于 $y(y>0)$ 时，供应商提供给零售商的采购批发单价；

c_2：信息共享但不协调订货的情况下，零售商的采购批发单价；

r：在销售过程中如果出现缺货的情况，零售商设定的缺货惩罚支出费用(Shortage Cost)；

s：在销售季节过后，剩余产品能最后挽回的价值(Salvage Value)；

Q：零售商的订货量；

k：供应商生产单位产品的费用；

h：若供应商在早于销售季节开始之前交付，单位产品在单位时间段内供应商的库存保管等费用；

$\phi(x)$：标准正态分布密度函数；$\Phi(x)$：标准正态分布函数，$\Phi^{-1}(\cdot)$为其反函数。

一般地这里设模型中参数满足：$p>c_0>k>0, r\geqslant 0, s\geqslant 0, h\geqslant 0$。

2 市场需求量

下面首先分析供应商及时交付与交付延迟时间等于 y 时，零售商面对的市场需求量

的分布情况。见下面两个命题。

命题 1 若供应商及时交付，零售商面对的市场需求量 X_0 服从正态分布 $N(n\mu, n\sigma^2)$。

证明 由于供应商及时交付，有 $y\leqslant 0$，则 $M=1$。即，$X_0=d_1+\cdots+d_n$。那么由假设1,2可知市场需求量 X_0 等于 n 个独立同分布的正态分布之和，那么命题结论显然成立[11,12]。

命题 2 若供应商延迟交付，当交付时间等于 y 时，零售商面对的市场需求量 X_y 服从正态分布 $N((n-y)\mu, (n-y)\sigma^2)$。

证明 由于供应商交付延迟，有 $y>0$，则 $M=y+1$。即 $X_y=d_{y+1}+\cdots+d_n$。由假设1,2可知市场需求量 X_y 等于 $n-y$ 个独立同分布的正态分布之和，那么命题成立。

如果零售商已知供应商的不确定交付时间 Y 的分布规律，那么零售商面对的市场需求量等于随机个随机变量之和，见式(1)。由经典概率论文献[11,12]和命题1,2可知，X 的分布密度函数与分布函数分别为

$$f(x)=\sum_{y=T_1}^{T_2} f_y(x)g(y)=f_0(x)\sum_{y=T_1}^{0} g(y)+\sum_{y=1}^{T_2} f_y(x)g(y)$$

$$=\frac{1}{\sqrt{n}\sigma}\phi\left(\frac{x-n\mu}{\sqrt{n}\sigma}\right)\sum_{y=T_1}^{0} g(y)+\sum_{y=1}^{T_2}\frac{1}{\sqrt{n-y}\sigma}\phi\left(\frac{(x-(n-y)\mu)}{\sqrt{n-y}\sigma}\right)\times g(y) \tag{2}$$

$$F(x)=\sum_{y=T_1}^{T_2} F_y(x)g(y)=F_0(x)\sum_{y=T_1}^{0} g(y)+\sum_{y=1}^{T_2} F_y(x)g(y)$$

$$=\Phi\left(\frac{x-n\mu}{\sqrt{n}\sigma}\right)\sum_{y=T_1}^{0} g(y)+\sum_{y=1}^{T_2}\Phi\left(\frac{x-(n-y)\mu}{\sqrt{n-y}\sigma}\right)g(y) \tag{3}$$

那么可以由式(2)计算出 X 的均值与方差

$$\mu_X=n\mu-\mu\sum_{y=1}^{T_2} yg(y) \tag{4}$$

$$\sigma_X^2=\sigma^2\left(n\mu-\mu\sum_{y=1}^{T_2} yg(y)\right)+\left[\sum_{y=1}^{T_2} y^2 g(y)-\left(\sum_{y=1}^{T_2} yg(y)\right)^2\right]\mu^2 \tag{5}$$

可以从式(2)，(3)看出，市场需求量 X 的分布函数实际上是由正态分布组合而成，而目。是一个凸组合(由于系数 $\sum g(y)=1$)。但是，这并不能肯定地认为X近似于一下正态分布。见例1。

例 1 设交付时间 Y 的取值和相应的概率如表1。

表 1 交付时间的分布列(例 1)

Table 1 Distribution of delivery time(example 1)

y	-3	-2	-1	0	1	2	3
$g(y)$	0.1	0.2	0.2	0.2	0.1	0.1	0.1

设销售季节内单位时间段需求的均值与标准方差分别为 $\mu=100$，$\sigma=10$。销售季节

的长度 $n=20$。那么 X 的密度函数和按式(4),(5)给出的正态分布 $N(\mu_X,\sigma_X^2)$ 的密度函数 $e(x)$ 的图示

由图 1 可以看出本例中 X 的分布不近似于正态分布,因此用正态分布来作 X 为的分布不一定可行。在分析季节性产品的库存决策问题时,研究者经常分析市场需求是否能用正态分布近似的问题[13,14]文献[15]对这个方面的研究进行了评述。

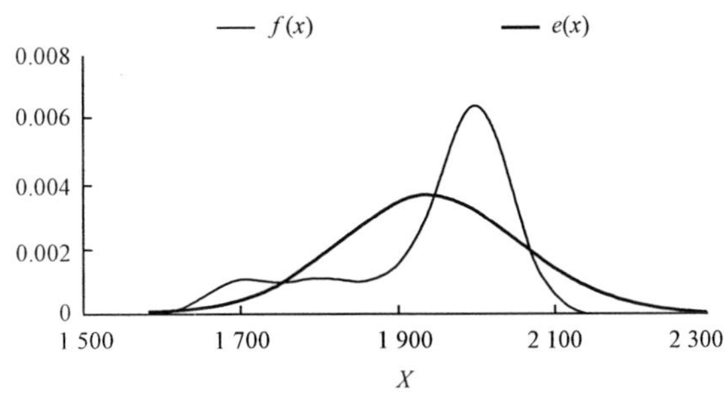

图 1 X 的分布密度函数(例 1)

Fig. 1 Density function of X (example 1)

3 信息不共享情况

下面分析在供应链信息不共享的情况下,零售商的订货决策问题,以及分析信息不共享带来的一些问题。

按命题 1,当供应商及时交付时,零售商面对的市场需求量为 X_0,满足正态分布 $N(n\mu,n\sigma^2)$。零售商按经典报童模型确定最优订货量,这时供应商给出的批发价为 c_0。见附录 A,最优订货量为,$Q_0^*=\mu_0+\phi^{-1}(\lambda_0)\sigma_0$。基中 $\lambda_0\triangleq\dfrac{p+r-c_0}{p+r-s}$。由附录 A,B,易知零售商的最大期望利润为

$$PR_{R0}=(p-s)\mu_0-(c_0-s)Q_0^*-(p+r-s)\sigma_0 b_r\left(\frac{Q_0^*-\mu_0}{\sigma_0}\right)$$

其中,$b_r(Q)\triangleq\int_Q^{+\infty}(x-Q)\phi(x)\mathrm{d}x$ 表示标准正态损失函数。

由命题 2 可知,当交付时间等于 y 时,零售商将面对 $n-y$ 个单位时间段内的需求 X_y。记 $\Theta(Q,y)$ 为交付时间等于 y 时零售商的期望收益函数。这里考虑在没有信息共享的情况下,供应商按满足零售商在及时交付时的最大期望利润不变的机制设定批发价格。当 $y>0$ 时,批发价 $c_1(Y)$ 满足万程:$\Theta(Q_0^*,y)=EP_{R0}$。由附录 A 中式(16)有

$$(p+r-s)\left(\int_{-\infty}^{Q_0^*}xf_y(x)\mathrm{d}x-Q_0^*F_y(Q_0^*)\right)+(p+r-c_1(y))Q_0^*-r\mu_y=EP_{R0}\quad(6)$$

由式(6)和附录 B 得到批发价的计算公式

$$c_1(y)=p-\frac{1}{Q_0^*}\Big[EP_{R0}+(p-s)\int_{-\infty}^{Q_0^*}(Q_0^*-x)f_y(x)\mathrm{d}x$$

$$+r\left(\mu_y-Q_0^*+\int_{-\infty}^{Q_0^*}(Q_0^*-x)f_y(x)\mathrm{d}x\right)\Big]$$

$$=p-\frac{1}{Q_0^*}\left[EP_{R0}+(p-s)\int_{-\infty}^{Q_0^*}(Q_0^*-x)f_y(x)\mathrm{d}x+r\int_{Q_0^*}^{-\infty}(x-Q_0^*)f_y(x)\mathrm{d}x\right]$$

$$=p-\frac{1}{Q_0^*}\left[EP_{R0}+(p-s)(Q_0^*-\mu_y)+(p+r-s)\int_{Q_0^*}^{-\infty}(x-Q_0^*)f_y(x)\mathrm{d}x\right]$$

$$=p-\frac{1}{Q_0^*}\left[EP_{R0}+(p-s)(Q_0^*-\mu_y)+(p+r-s)\sigma_y b_r\left(\frac{Q_0^*-\mu_y}{\sigma_y}\right)\right] \tag{7}$$

由于 $\int_{-\infty}^{Q_0^*}(Q_0^*-x)f_y(x)\mathrm{d}x>0, \int_{Q_0^*}^{-\infty}(x-Q_0^*)f_y(x)\mathrm{d}x>0$ 显然成立，因此由式(7)知对任意固定的 y 有 $c_1(y)<p$。

在供应商设定的批发价机制的基础上，可以得出供应商的最大期望利润。

$$EP_{M0}=Q_0^*\left[\sum_{y=1}^{T_2}(c_1(y)-k)g(y)+\sum_{y=T_1}^{0}(c_0-k+hy)g(y)\right]$$

$$=Q_0^*\sum_{y=1}^{T_2}c_1(y)g(y)+hQ_0^*\sum_{y=T_1}^{0}yg(y)+c_0Q_0^*\sum_{y=T_1}^{0}g(y)-kQ_0^*$$

将 $c_1(y)$ 代入上式得到

$$\begin{aligned}EP_{M0}=&(pQ_0^*-EP_{R0})\sum_{y=1}^{T_2}g(y)-\sum_{y=1}^{T_2}\Big[(p-s)(Q_0^*-\mu_y)\\&+(p+r-s)\sigma_y b_r\left(\frac{Q_0^*-\mu_y}{\sigma_y}\right)\Big]g(y)+hQ_0^*\sum_{y=T_1}^{0}yg(y)\\&+c_0Q_0^*\sum_{y=T_1}^{0}g(y)-kQ_0^*\end{aligned} \tag{8}$$

记信息不共享的情况下，供应链的利润总量为 $EP_{SC0}=EP_{R0}+EP_{M0}$。

由附录 B 知，标准正态损失函数容易计算，这样使得以上所有最优解的计算也很简单。下面给出一个数值示例。

例 2 设某产品供应商交付时间的分布及销售季节的需求按例 1 中给出。产品的销售参数为：$p=15, c_0=10, r=1, s=1$，设 $k=5, h=0.05$。

容易求出及时交付时供应链的服务水平 $\lambda_0=0.4$。当信息不共享时，零售商的最优订货量为 $Q_0^*=1988$，零售商的最大期望利润为。$EP_{R0}=9\ 741$。

如果供应商的交付时间 $y>0$，为了保证零售商的期望利润 EP_{R0} 不变，那么供应商给出的批发价格为 $c_1(1)=9.48, c_1(2)=8.77, c_1(3)=8.07$。这样可以求出供应商的期望利润 $EP_{M0}=9\ 122$。供应链的期望总利润为 $EP_{SC0}=18\ 863$。

下面分析在信息不共享的情况下，供应链出现的一些问题：

首先，供应商承担所有由交付时间不确定引起的损失。由于供应商交付时间不确定性信息没有共享，零售商的订货量按没有出现延迟交付情况的最大期望利润给出，这时供应商将承担所有由交付时间不确定引起的损失。该损失包括两部分：一是在交付延迟的情况下，由于没有满足顾客需求而引起的损失，另一个是在早于销售季节开始交付的情况下，库存保管等费用的支出。

其次，零售商的订货量不一定是最优订货量。在信息不共享的情况下，零售商按照需

求量 X_0 给出订货量。但是由于在有交付时间不确定的情况下，真实的市场需求为 X，它与交付时间 Y 相关。那么，零售商的订货量 Q_0^* 就不一定是最优订货量。

另外，供应商的利润有可能为负。由于供应商必须保证零售商的利润不会由于交付时间的不确定而改变，供应商必须在交付延迟的情况下，以降低批发单价的形式补偿零售商由于没有满足市场需求带来的销售损失。在有些情况下，供应商的期望利润可能为负数。例如，在例 2 中如果供应商的生产费用为 $k=8$，在其他参数不变的条件下，供应商的期望利润 $EP_{M0}=-232$。那么供应商就不会接受零售商的订货而退出这次交易。

从上面的分析可以看出，在信息不共享的情况下，供应链是低效率的。下面从信息共享而无协调订货和信息共享协调订货两个方面来分析这种供应链管理问题。

4　信息共享无协调策略情况

当供应商将交付时间的不确定性信息传送给零售商以后，零售商根据交付时间 Y 的分布情况，分析得出市场需求 X 的分布情况，（由式(2)，(3)给出）。当没有协调策略时，零售商的订货量按最大化自身期望利润给出。这里同样考虑供应商的批发价订价机制为保证零售商在及时交付情况下的最大期望利润不变。设供应商给出的批发价为 c_2，零售商的期望收益为

$$EP_{R2}(Q)=(p+r-s)\left(\int_{-\infty}^{Q}xf(x)\mathrm{d}x-QF(Q)\right)+(p+r-c_2)Q-r\mu_X$$

那么最优订货量 Q_2^* 满足下式

$$F(Q_2^*)=\lambda_2=\frac{p+r-c_2}{p+r-s}\tag{9}$$

相应地零售商的最大期望利润为

$$\begin{aligned}EP_{R2}&=(p+r-s)\left(\int_{-\infty}^{Q_2^*}xf(x)\mathrm{d}x-Q_2^*F(Q_2^*)\right)+(p+r-c_2)Q_2^*-r\mu_X\\&=(p+r-s)\sum_{y=T_1}^{0}g(y)\int_{-\infty}^{Q_2^*}xf_0(x)\mathrm{d}x+(p+r-s)\sum_{y=1}^{T_2}\left(\int_{-\infty}^{Q_2^*}xf_y(x)\mathrm{d}x\right)g(y)-r\mu_X\\&=(p-s)\mu_X-(c_2-s)Q_2^*-(p+r-s)\sigma_0\sum_{y=T_1}^{0}g(y)b_r\left(\frac{Q_2^*-\mu_0}{\sigma_0}\right)\\&\quad-(p+r-s)\sum_{y=1}^{T_2}\sigma_yb_r\left(\frac{Q_2^*-\mu_y}{\sigma_y}\right)g(y)\end{aligned}\tag{10}$$

下面分析供应商的批发价 c_2 的求解方法。从上面描述的供应商的定价机制，批发价 c_2 满足 $EP_{R2}(c_2)=EP_{R0}$。由式(10)可知

$$\begin{aligned}\frac{\mathrm{d}EP_{R2}(c_2)}{\mathrm{d}c_2}=&(p+r-s)\sum_{y=T_1}^{0}g(y)\times Q_2^*(c_2)f_0(Q_2^*(c_2))\frac{\mathrm{d}Q_2^*(c_2)}{\mathrm{d}c_2}\\&+(p+r-s)\sum_{y=1}^{T_2}(Q_2^*(c_2)\times f_y(Q_2^*(c_2))g(y))\frac{\mathrm{d}Q_2^*(c_2)}{\mathrm{d}c_2}\end{aligned}$$

又由式(9)可以求出

$$\frac{\mathrm{d}Q_2^*(c_2)}{\mathrm{d}c_2}=-\frac{1}{(p+r-s)f(Q_2^*(c_2))}<0.$$

因此有$\frac{dEP_{R2}(c_2)}{dc_2}<0$。那么$EP_{R2}(c_2)-EP_{R0}$关于$c_2$单调下降，可以用一元搜索方法求解$c_2$。在求解过程中必须注意：在每一步迭代中，给定一个新的批发价c_2，需要更新最优订货量Q_2^*的值，然后代人计算$EP_{R2}(c_2)$的函数值。本文下面的算例中使用二分法迭代求解。得到了供应商的批发价c_2以后，就可以求出供应商的期望利润

$$
\begin{aligned}
EP_{M2} &= Q_2^*\left[\sum_{y=1}^{T_2}(c_2-k)g(y)+\sum_{y=T_1}^{0}(c_2-k+hy)g(y)\right] \\
&= (c_2-k)Q_2^*+hQ_2^*\sum_{y=T_1}^{0}yg(y)
\end{aligned}
$$

这样得到信息共享无协调情况下供应链的最大期望总利润

$$EP_{SC2}=EP_{R2}+EP_{M2}.$$

例 3 设供应链的所有参数与例 2 中参数相同。若批发价格c_2也保持与c_0相同，那么最优订货量为 1 955，相应的零售商的最大期望利润为 9 051，供应商的利润为 9 688。

当供应商设定的批发价保证零售商的期望利润时，按上面给出的方法可以容易求解得到批发价$c_2=9.647\ 5$，最优订货量为$Q_0^*=1\ 961$。可以求得供应商的利润为$EP_{M2}=9\ 023$。供应链的期望总利润为$EP_{SC2}=18\ 738$。

由例 2 和例 3 可以看出，信息共享以后，若不采用协调策略，供应链的期望总利润与没有信息共享的期望利润相差无几，这一点引起了分析信息共享的价值与局限的必要性。

5 信息共享协调情况

当供应链成员仅仅考虑最大化自身的目标时，供应链成员的行动与供应链的总体目标不相一致，供应链的总体绩效往往较低，很难达到供应链的最优绩效(Optimal Supply Chain Performance)。研究指出，通过形成某种形式的转移支付(Transfer Payment)合同，使供应链成员的目标与供应链的总体目标相一致，就可以达到供应链的最优绩效，这里称之为供应链协调，其中的转移支付合同称之为协调策略(Coordinating Strategy 或 Coordinating Contracts)。文献[8]回顾了在不同的供应链背景环境中，一些可行的协调策略。

当供应链信息共享时，供应链得到含有交付时间不确定性信息的随机市场需求X，分布函数为$F(x)$，那么在订货决策过程中，若订货量为Q，由附录 A 易得供应链的期望收益函数

$$
\begin{aligned}
EP_{SC1}(Q) =& (p+r-s)\left(\int_{-\infty}^{Q}xf(x)dx-QF(Q)\right) \\
&+(p+r-k)Q-r\mu_X+hQ\sum_{y=T_3}^{0}yg(y) \qquad (11)
\end{aligned}
$$

由于

$$\frac{dEP_{SC1}(Q)}{dQ}=-(p+r-s)F(Q)+(p+r-k)+h\sum_{y=T_1}^{0}yg(y)$$

$$\frac{dEP_{SC1}(Q)}{dQ}=-(p+r-s)f(Q)<0$$

那么对于整个供应链来说，最优的订货量 Q_1^* 满足

$$F(Q_1^*)=\lambda_1=\frac{p+r-k+h\sum_{y=T_1}^{0}yg(y)}{p+r-s}$$

由于分布函数 $F(\cdot)$单调递增，容易一维搜索方法求解最优订货量 Q_1^*（本文在算例中都采用最简单的二分法）。当求出最优订货量 Q_1^* 以后，由式(11)就可以得到信息共享协调情况下，供应链的最大期望利润。

$$\begin{aligned}EP_{SC1}&=(p+r-s)\left(\int_{-\infty}^{Q_1^*}xf(x)\mathrm{d}x-Q_1^*F(Q_1^*)\right)+(p+r-k)Q_1^*-r\mu_X+hQ_1^*\sum_{y=T_1}^{0}yg(y)\\&=(p+r-s)\sum_{y=T_1}^{0}g(y)\int_{-\infty}^{Q_1^*}xf_0(x)\mathrm{d}x+(p+r-s)\int_{-\infty}^{Q_1^*}\left(\sum_{y=T_1}^{T_2}f_y(x)g(y)\right)\mathrm{d}x\\&\quad-(p+r-s)Q_1^*F_0(Q_1^*)\sum_{y=T_1}^{0}g(y)-(p+r-s)Q_1^*\sum_{y=T_1}^{T_2}F_y(Q^*1)g(y)\\&\quad+(p+r-k)Q_1^*-r\mu_X+hQ_1^*\sum_{y=T_1}^{0}yg(y)\\&=(p-s)\mu_X-(k-s)Q_1^*-(p+r-s)\sigma_0\times\sum_{y=T_1}^{0}g(y)b_r\left(\frac{Q_1^*-\mu_0}{\sigma_0}\right)\\&\quad-(p+r-s)\times\sum_{y=1}^{T_2}\sigma_yb_r\left(\frac{Q_1^*-\mu_y}{\sigma_y}\right)g(y)+hQ_1^*\sum_{y=T_1}^{0}yg(y)\end{aligned}\tag{12}$$

下面借鉴文献[8]中的分析方法，分析回购策略能否协调含有交付时间不确定性的供应链。在分析供应链策略能否协调供应链时，主要分析供应链策略的支付参数设计能否满足：1)供应链成员在分散决策时的最优决策解（本文中为最优订货量）与供应链达到协调时的最优解相等；2)供应链各个成员都接受协调后的利润分配。

在回购策略中，供应商收取零售商的批发价为 c，并且在销售季节过后对未售出的商品予以回购，设回购单价为 b。那么易知零售商的期望利润函数为[8]，

$$EP_R(Q,c,b)=(p+r-b)\left(\int_{-\infty}^{Q}xf(x)\mathrm{d}x-QF(Q)\right)+(p+r-c)Q-r\mu_X.$$

那么在含有回购策略的供应链中，当零售商单独决策时的最优订货量 Q_{BB}^* 必须满足

$$F(Q_{BB}^*)=\frac{p+r-c}{p+r-b}$$

考虑回购策略的参数集$\{c,b\}$，若使得对某个 $\beta\geqslant0$，有

$$p+r-b=\beta(p+r-s),$$

$$p+r-c=\beta\left(p+r-k+h\sum_{y=T_1}^{0}yg(y)\right)$$

那么当采用满足上式的参数集$\{c,b\}$以后，零售商的期望利润函数满足

$$EP_R(Q,c,b)=\beta EP_{SC1}(Q)-(1-\beta)r\mu_X.$$

由上式可知，零售商的最优订货量 Q_{BB}^* 等于供应链协调订货时的最优订货量 Q_1^*。相

应的供应商的利润函数为

$$EP_M(Q_1^*,c,b)=EP_{SC1}(Q_1^*)-EP_R(Q_1^*,c,b)$$
$$=(1-\beta)(EP_{SC1}(Q_1^*)+r\mu_X)$$

因此，当 $0\leqslant\beta<1$ 时，供应商将参与交易。设 β 使 $EP_R(Q_1^*,c,b)=PR_{R0}$。显然零售商的期望利润与参数 β 单调增加，则当 $\beta_0\leqslant\beta<1$ 时，供应链成员都将自愿采用回购策略。因此，回购策略能协调含有交付时间不确定性的供应链。文献[8]分析指出，有多种策略能协调标准形式的二层供应链。限于本文的篇幅，这里不再分析其他形式的策略。在这里，回购策略已经充分说明了可以采用协调策略来使供应链的绩效最大化。

6 信息共享和协调策略的价值与局限

得到了在不同信息结构中供应链的最优解后，这里首先用数值分析的方法，分析信息共享在含交付时间不确定性供应链中的价值与局限。表 2 给出数值分析中参数的各种取值。在数值计算时，分析每种取值组合的解，然后分析解的变化规律，这样表 2 中所有满足条件（$p>c_0>k$）的取值组合，共有 15 840 个。

表 2 参数值

Table2 Parameter Values

参数	取值
市场需求	$n=20,\mu=100,\sigma=10$
交付时间	$y=[-N,N],g(y)=1/(2N+1),N=1,\cdots,10$
零售单价(p)	135,145,155
批发单价(c_0)	100,110,120,130
生产支出(k)	85.95.105
缺货惩罚(r)	$0,0.3k,0.6k,0.9k$
挽回价值(s)	$0,0.3k,0.6k,0.9k$
库存费用(h)	$0.01k.0.001k.0.0001k$

为了分析的方便，交付时间的取值是关于 0 对称的，并且相应的概率相等。这种取值方式的设计反映了交付时间不确定性程度的不同。在数值分析中发现，在各种不同取值组合中，供应链成员中的一方或两方的期望利润可能为负值（信息共享与不共享中均出现）。当供应商的期望利润为负时，供应商不会接受零售商的订货与配送，当零售商的期望利润为负时，零售商不会订货，那么在这些情况中，供应链的交易不会实现。当剔除这些特殊情况以后，余下 13 753 个可行示例。

图 2 给出了当 N 取不同值时，有信息共享供应链的总利润 EP_{SC2} 大于无信息共享供应链的总利润 EP_{SC0} 的示例数占相应可行示例总数的比率。由于当 N 的取值越大时，交付时间的不确定程度越高，那么从图 2 中可以看出，虽然信息共享不一定能使供应链的绩效改进，但是当交付时间不确定性增加时，信息共享能提高供应链绩效的可能性增大。

图 3 中给出了信息共享后供应链利润增加的比率（$(EP_{SC2}/EP_{SC0}-1)\times100\%$）的规律图，这个比率值在 -25.81% 至 51.02% 中变化，均值为 -0.68%。在可行示例中 EP_{SC2}

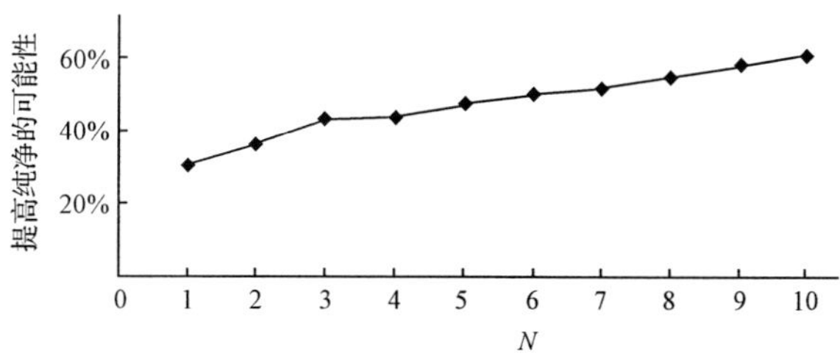

图 2　信息共事与供应链绩效提高的可能性

Fig. 2　Percentage of supply chain performance improving with information sharing

$>EP_{SC0}$的情况出现 4 155 次，$EP_{SC2}<EP_{SC0}$的情况出现 9 598 次。

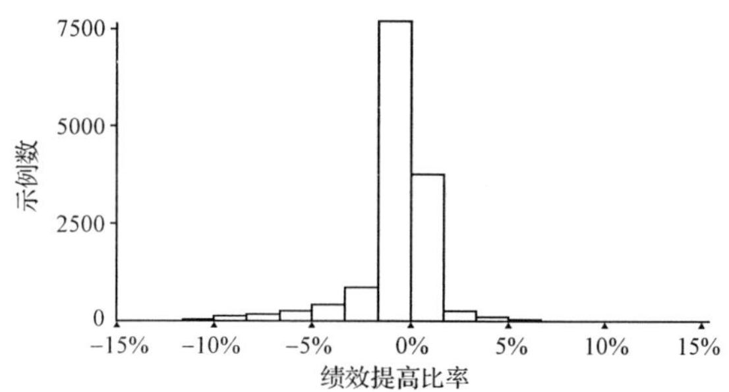

图 3　信息共享对供应链绩效提高的比率(无协调策略)

Fig. 3　Supply chain performance improving with information sharing(without coordination strategy)

供应商由于需要满足零售商的期望利润，那么它的期望利润与供应链的利润变化规律相一致。又因为供应链的总利润在信息共享后不一定提高，因而，信息共享不一定提高供应商的期望利润，在交付时间不确定性程度增加时信息共享能使供应链绩效提高的可能性增加。

上面所有的数值分析结果都说明了信息共享不一定使供应链的绩效改进。表明虽然供应链的所有成员都得到了全部信息，若在追求各自利润最大化的同时却没有考虑供应链系统的总体利益的时候，供应链的绩效将不一定得到改进。这体现了信息共享的局限性。

供应链的协调理论指出，在供应链成员之间达成某种形式的转移支付合同，就能使供应链成员的决策结果与供应链的总体目标相同，从而得到供应链的最优绩效。以下命题证明了协调后的供应链期望利润比仅有信息共享的情况要大，这一点说明了协调策略在含交付时间不确定性的供应链中的价值。

命题 3　供应链信息共享的条件下，协调订货策略能提高供应链的总利润，即

$$EP_{SC1}\geqslant EP_{SC2} \tag{13}$$

证明：由于在信息共享但不协调订货的情况下，供应链的利润总和为：

$$EP_{SC2}=EP_{R2}+EP_{M2}=(p+r-s)\sum_{y=T_1}^{0}g(y)\int_{-\infty}^{Q_2^*}xf_0(x)\mathrm{d}x$$
$$+(p+r-s)\sum_{y=1}^{T_2}\left(\int_{-\infty}^{Q_2^*}xf_y(x)\mathrm{d}x\right)g(y)$$
$$-r\mu_X+(c_2-k)Q_2^*-hQ_2^*\sum_{y=T_1}^{0}yg(y) \tag{14}$$

又由式(3),(9)可得

$$-(p+r-s)Q_2^*F_0(Q_2^*)\sum_{y=T_1}^{0}g(y)-(p+r-s)Q_2^*\sum_{y=1}^{T_2}F_y(Q_2^*)g(y)$$
$$+(p+r-k)Q_2^*=-(p+r-s)Q_2^*F(Q_2^*)+(p+r-k)Q_2^*$$
$$=-(p+r-c_2)Q_2^*+(p+r-k)Q_2^*=(c_1-k)Q_2^*$$

那么由上式,式(14)及式(12)可得

$$EP_{SC2}=EP_{SC1}(Q_2^*)\leqslant EP_{SC1}(Q_1^*)=EP_{SC1}$$

那么命题成立。

上面的分析发现,仅仅只有信息共享而没有采用某种协调策略时,供应链的绩效不一定改进。在上面的分析指出,采用协调策略能够达到供应链的最优绩效。这时就让我们想到,如果“采用协调策略供应链的总利润比没有信息共享的总利润高”成立,那么就能说明采用协调策略是提高供应链的整体绩效的有效方法,下面的命题论证这一点。

命题 4 采用信息共享和协调订货策略订货后,供应链的期望总利润大于没有信息共享供应链期望总利润,即

$$EP_{SC1}\geqslant EP_{SC0} \tag{15}$$

证明:由于无信息共享供应链的最大期望利润函数为:

$$EP_{SC0}=pQ_0^*\sum_{y=1}^{T_2}g(y)+EP_{R0}\sum_{y=T_1}^{0}g(y)-hQ_0^*\sum_{y=T_1}^{0}yg(y)$$
$$+c_0Q_0^*\sum_{y=T_1}^{0}g(y)-kQ_0^*-(p-s)\sum_{y=1}^{T_2}(Q_0^*-\mu_y)g(y)$$
$$-(p+r-s)\times\sum_{y=1}^{T_2}\int_{Q_0^*}^{+\infty}(x-Q_0^*)f_y(x)\mathrm{d}xg(y)$$
$$=pQ_0^*\sum_{y=1}^{T_2}g(y)+(p+r-s)\int_{Q_0^*}^{+\infty}(x-Q_0^*)f_0(x)\mathrm{d}x\sum_{y=T_1}^{0}g(y)$$
$$+(p+r-c_0)Q_0^*\times\sum_{y=T_1}^{0}g(y)-r\mu_0\sum_{y=T_1}^{02}g(y)-hQ_0^*\times\sum_{y=T_1}^{0}yg(y)$$
$$+c_0Q_0^*\sum_{y=T_1}^{0}g(y)-kQ_0^*-(p-s)\sum_{y=1}^{T_2}(Q_0^*-\mu_y)g(y)$$
$$-(p+r-s)\sum_{y=1}^{T_2}\int_{Q_0^*}^{-\infty}(x-Q_0^*)f_y(x)\mathrm{d}xg(y)$$

由于 $\mu_X = \mu_0 \sum_{y=T_1}^{0} g(y) + \sum_{y=1}^{T_2} \mu_y g(y)$，且

$$\mu_y - Q_0^* + \int_{Q_0^*}^{+\infty} (x - Q_0^*) f_y(x) \mathrm{d}x = \int_{+\infty}^{Q_0^*} (x - Q_0^*) f_y(x) \mathrm{d}x$$

可以得到

$$\begin{aligned} EP_{SC0} = & (p+r-s) \sum_{y=T_1}^{0} g(y) \int_{+\infty}^{Q_0^*} x f_0(x) \mathrm{d}x + (p+r-s) \int_{+\infty}^{Q_0^*} \left(\sum_{y=1}^{T_2} f_y(x) g(y) \right) \mathrm{d}x \\ & - (p+r-s) Q_0^* F_0(Q_0^*) \sum_{y=T_1}^{0} g(y) - (p+r-s) Q_0^* \sum_{y=1}^{T_2} F_y(Q_0^*) g(y) \\ & + (p+r-k) Q_0^* - r\mu_X - hQ_0^* \sum_{y=T_1}^{0} y g(y) = EP_{SC1}(Q_0^*). \end{aligned}$$

由于最大期望利润满足 $EP_{SC1} = EP_{SC1}(Q_1^*) \geqslant EP_{SC1}(Q_0^*)$。因此 $EP_{SC1} \geqslant EP_{SC0}$ 成立。

下面我们给出一个算例来说明以上结论。设供应链中市场需求参数、交付时间不确定性参数和销售参数与例 2 相同。例 3 指出，仅仅采用信息共享而不使用协调策略，供应链的总利润比没有信息共享时的总利润小。若我们使用回购策略，这时不难计算得出供应链的总利润为 $EP_{SC1}=19\ 890$，它要大于没有信息共享和仅有信息共享时的总利润。

为了进一步地理解协调策略在含有交付时间不确定性供应链中的作用和价值，下面同样使用数值分析的方法来分析模型中参数的各种取值的组合变化来得到其中的主要变化规律。在分析协调策略的价值时，这里分析采用协调策略后利润提高比率的变化规律，即分析值$((EP_{SC1}/EP_{SC2}-1)\times 100\%)$的分析规律。从示例的计算结果可知，供应链的利润增加的比例在 0%至 36.34%中变化，其均值为 1.26%。图 4 给出了汇总后的取值变化规律。

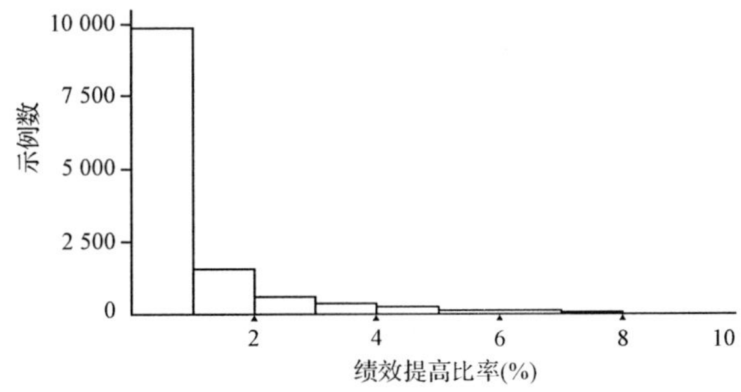

图 4　协调策略对供应链绩效提高的比率

Fig. 4　Supply chain performance increasing with coordination

由上图不难发现，协调策略对供应链的绩效提高有较大的作用。在采用协调策略以后，虽然供应链的成员仍以最大化自身收益为目标，但是这时的行动却将与供应链的总体目标相一致，能够达到最优绩效的目标，这些都说明了协调策略的巨大价值，也为供应链的一体化管理提供了理论参考依据。

7 结论

在本文的研究中，考虑了含有交付时间不确定性的季节性产品供应链。在现实商业的运作中，供应链管理者可能会经常遇到这种交付时间不确定性问题，它们的起因可能是各种各样的，比如说供应商的物料供应问题可能经常引起制造商的生产减缓或停滞，从而使交付延期；物流承运商的运输时间的不确定性也是交付时间不确定性的一个因素之一。并且供应商的交付时间经常很难完全控制。这种交付时间不确定性信息经常为供应商所独有，是一种私有信息，这种信息不对称问题是供应链管理中经常需要面对的问题。在现代信息技术的快速发展的环境中，使管理者能够越来越多的共享这种交付时间不确定信息。

本文的研究与以往关于信息共享的研究工作有一个重要的不同之处。我们的研究仔细考虑了供应链中信息的结构，区分了公共信息和私有信息，并且考虑了信息共享后的供应链的总信息。从而使我们能非常清晰的刻画在不同信息结构条件下的市场需求。这样就能用数学分析方法研究在不同信息结构下市场的需求分布，并用来分析在供应链信息不共享、信息共享无协调、信息共享协调三种情况下的供应链的期望收益函数，供应链的最优解的计算也变得很容易。

通过本文的研究发现，仅仅采用信息共享不一定能提高供应链的总利润，但是存在供应链策略能协调这种含有交付时间不确定性的供应链，采用某种协调策略能够弥补信息共享的不足，使供应链的总利润达到最大化。信息共享协调后的供应链的总利润比无信息共享和仅有信息共享的总利润都要高。本文从理论上给供应链的管理实践提供了理论依据。

附录 A：经典报童模型的最优解

设零售商面对随机市场需求量 X 满足的分布函数为 $F(x)$，那么在订货决策过程中，若零售商参考文献：的订货量为 Q 时，零售商的期望收益函数为[8]：

$$\Theta(Q)=(p+r-s)\left(\int_{-\infty}^{Q} xf(x)\mathrm{d}x-QF(Q)\right)+(p+r-c)Q-r\mu. \tag{16}$$

容易知道最优订货量 Q^* 满足 $F(Q^*)=\lambda$，其中 $\lambda\triangleq\dfrac{p+r-c}{p+r-s}$，在库存管理中称为服务水平。若需求量 X 满足正态分布 $N(\mu_X\cdot\sigma_X^2)$，最优订货量为 $Q^*=\mu_X+\Phi^{-1}(\lambda)\sigma_X$。相应的，零售商的最大期望利润为，

$$EP_R=(p-c)\mu_X-((c-s)\Phi^{-1}(\lambda)+(p+r-s)b_r(\Phi^{-1}(\lambda)))\sigma_X.$$

附录 B：一般正态分布的损失函数的计算

设 $f_y(x)=\dfrac{1}{\sqrt{2\pi}\sigma_y}\mathrm{e}^{-\frac{(x-\mu_y)^2}{2\sigma_y^2}}$，那么一般正态分布的损失函数为，

$$\begin{aligned}\int_{Q}^{+\infty}(x-Q)f_y(x)\mathrm{d}x&=\int_{Q}^{+\infty}(x-Q)\frac{1}{\sqrt{2\pi}\sigma_y}\mathrm{e}^{-\frac{(x-\mu_y)^2}{2\sigma_y^2}}\mathrm{d}x\\&=\int_{\frac{Q-\mu_y}{\sigma_y}}^{+\infty}(\mu_y+\sigma_y z-Q)\frac{1}{\sqrt{2\pi}}\mathrm{e}^{-\frac{z^2}{2}\mathrm{d}z}\end{aligned}$$

$$= \sigma_y \int_{\frac{Q-\mu_y}{\sigma_y}}^{+\infty} \left(z - \frac{Q-\mu_y}{\sigma_y}\right) \frac{1}{\sqrt{2\pi}} e^{-\frac{z^2}{2}dz}$$

$$= \sigma_y b_r \left(\frac{Q-\mu_y}{\sigma_y}\right)$$

有一些概率论书籍给出了标准正态损失函数 $b_r(y)$ 的查询表，但是它的计算也可以很容易用标准正态分布的密度和分布函数计算得出：

$$b_r(Q) = \int_Q^{+\infty} (x-Q)\phi(x)\,dx$$

$$= -\frac{1}{\sqrt{2\pi}} \int_Q^{+\infty} e^{-\frac{x^2}{2}} d\left(-\frac{x^2}{2}\right) - Q\int_Q^{+\infty} \phi(x)\,dx$$

$$= \frac{1}{\sqrt{2\pi}} e^{-\frac{Q^2}{2}} - Q(1-\Phi(Q))$$

$$= \phi(Q) - Q(1-\Phi(Q))$$

Research on coordination contacts in supply chains with uncertainty of delivery lead-time

LU Qi-hui, ZHU Dao-li

School of Management, Fudan University, Shanghai 200433, China

Abstract: In this paper, we analyze the seasonal products supply chain with uncertainty in delivery lead-time. If supplier's private information about delivery lead-time is shared in the supply chain, then retailer can adjust her order quantity to decrease the sale lost. The supply chain performance would be improved with information sharing. We point out that information sharing can increase the probability of performance of supply chain when the uncertainty of delivery time is larger. But it isn't sure that supply chain performance will be im-proved with information sharing. Then there exists value and limitation of information sharing in this type of supply chain. Under further analysis, we find that there exist supply chain contracts which can coordinate this kind of supply chain with delivery uncertainty and lead to the optimal supply chain performance. The coordination contracts can efficiently get rid of the limits of information sharing.

Key words: supply chain; information sharing; coordination; delivery lead time; newsvendor model

参 考 文 献

[1] Weng Z K, McClurg T. Coordinated ordering decisions for short life cycle products with uncertainty

in delivery time and de-mand [J]. European Journal of Operational Research, 2003, 151: 12-24.

[2] Lau A H-L, Lall H-L. Some two-echelon style-goods inventory models with asymmetric market information[J]. European Journal of Operational Research, 2001, 134: 29-42.

[3] 李刚，夏玉森，汪寿阳等．信息共享在供应链中的价值，运筹学与系统工程新进展[M]. 北京：科学出版社，2002.

Li Gang, XiaYusheng, Wang Shouyang, *et al*. The Value of Information Sharing in Supply Chains, New Advances in Oper-ation Research and System Enginneering[M]. Beijing: Science Press, 2002. (in Chinese)

[4] Lee H L, Padmanabhan P, Whang S. Information distortion in a supply chian: The bullwhip efect [J]. Management Sci-ence, 1997, 43: 546-558.

[5] 达庆利，张钦，沈厚才．供应链中牛鞭效应问题研究[J]. 管理科学学报，2003, 6(3): 86-93.

Da Qing-li, Zhang Qin, Sheng Hou-cai. Study on bullwhip effect in supply chain[J]. Joumal of Management Sciences in China, 2003, 6(3): 86-93. (inChinese)

[6] Lee H L, So K C, Tang C S. The value of information sharing in a two-level supply chain [J]. Management Science, 2000, 46(5): 626-643.

[7] 陈冬，顾培亮．供应链管理若干问题研究与进展评述[J]. 系统工程理 论与实践，2003, 23(10): 1-11.

Cheng Dang, Gu Pei-liang. Overview of the theory, methodology, application and the likely new aspects of supply chain management[J]. Systems Engineering—Theory and practice, 2003, 23(10): 1-11.

[8] Cachon G P. Supply Chain Coordination with Contracts. Handbooks in Operations Research and Management Science: Sup-ply Chain Management[M]. North Holland: Edited by Steve Graves and Ton de Kok. 2003.

[9] Padmanabhan V, Png I P L. Manufacturer's returns policies and retail competition[J]. Marketing Science, 1997: 81-94.

[10] TsayA A. Managing retail channe loveys～tock: Markdown money and retum policies[J]. Journal of Retailing, 2001, 77: 457-492.

[11] Grimmtt G R, Stirzaker D R. Probability and Ramdon Process[M]. Second Edition, New York: Oxford University Press. 1992.

[12] 费勒 w. 概率论及其应用[M]. 北京：人民邮电出版社，2006.

Feller W. An Introduction to Probability Theory and Its Applications[M]. Beijing: Posts & Telecom Pross, 2006. (in Chinese)

[13] Eppen G D, Martin R K. Determinning safety stock in the presenese of stochastic lead time and demand[J]. Management Science, 1998, 34(11): 1380-1390.

[14] Ray S, Jewkes E M. Customer lead time management when both demand and price are lead time sensitive[J]. European Journal of Operational Research, 2004, 153: 769-781.

[15] Silver E A, Pyke D F, Peterson R. Inventory Management and Production Planning and Scheduling [M]. New York: John Wiley & Sons. Inc. 1998.

（本文发表于《管理科学学报》，2008 年第 2 期）

第七章 物流金融

在物流管理的发展过程中，尽管资金流管理一直被视为现代物流管理的内在组成部分，但是，它的作用和其中所蕴藏的巨大机会长期没有得到应有的重视。随着国内外先进企业物流、信息流和资金流集成管理实践的发展，金融物流管理的概念被提出并得到广泛研究。金融物流管理是面向物流运作的全过程，应用各种集成式的服务与产品，通过信息共享、协调和组织合作等方法集成物流、资金流、信息流，从而达到降低资金流运作成本并为供应链创造价值的管理系统。

中国的中小企业在解决三角债和资金短缺的实践中，创造了诸如“物流银行”、“融通仓”等多种金融供应链管理的业务。第三方物流企业掌握货物流动信息，他们和银行、担保公司联合，能够有效控制贷款风险，因而能够提供金融供应链和金融物流的服务。以中国成通集团所属的中国储运总公司(以下简称中储)为例，中储通过与四大银行、中信实业银行、广发银行等十几家金融机构建立合作关系，2008 年开展的仓单质押授信额度突破 400 亿元，合作的范围包括中储为各个银行提供监管货物、仓单质押、动产质押、指定付款买方信贷(保兑仓)等服务。实践表明，在中国的商业环境下，金融供应链管理能够为众多企业带来收益，尤其适于解决中小企业融资难问题，从而推动中国经济向前发展。

“融通仓”作为物流金融管理领域的重要概念最早由罗齐和朱道立(2002)提出，朱道立等人系统地介绍了融通仓理论。他们认为，融通仓是一个综合性的第三方物流服务平台，不仅为银行与企业间的合作架构新桥梁，而且能够有效地融入中小企业供应链体系之中，为其提供高效的第三方物流服务。陈祥峰和朱道立(2005)接着阐述了融通仓的系统结构，并结合企业运营周期特点总结了融通仓的运作模式。朱文贵和朱道立(2007)针对融通仓中的存货质押融资业务，给出了延迟支付方式下的存货质押融资服务定价模型，可以更好地指导第三方物流企业开展该业务。马中华和朱道立(2009)进一步研究了物流企业在运作存货质押融资业务时，当银行增大融资利率以及企业投资风险大的项目时，物流企业通过调整期监管决策来保持期望收益不减的相关理论。陈祥锋和朱道立(2008)根据第三方物流企业在供应链运营中所发挥的不同角色，将具有资金约束供应链划分为三类系统结构，并分析了三种结构下相关企业的金融和运营决策问题。

关于物流金融和金融供应链的风险控制和动产质押信息监控系统的研究，有兴趣的读者参见作者有关的论文。

第三方物流服务创新:融通仓及其运作模式初探

罗齐[1] 朱道立[2] 陈伯铭[3]

(1,2. 复旦大学管理学院 上海市 200433;3.广州市侨泰房地产公司 广州市 510275)

摘要: 现代第三方物流服务创新已成为行业发展的重要特征。本文提出了一种推动质押贷款,促进中小企业发展的融通仓模式。融通仓是一个综合性的第三方物流服务平台,不仅为银行与企业间的合作架构新桥梁,帮助中小企业解决融资难题,而且能有效地融入中小企业供应链体系之中,为其提供高效的第三方物流服务。文章还分析了融通仓获得金融机构的授信额度和成立独特的信用担保体系两种运作模式。

关键词: 物流创新　供应链　质押贷款　融通仓

中图分类号: F253

文献标识码: A　　**文章编号:** 1007-8266-(2002)02-0011-04

如何与金融机构协作,进行第三方物流服务创新,满足中小企业对金融服务和第三方物流服务的迫切需求,促进中小企业发展,已经成为我国物流业界和研究人员关注的重要问题。本文将就此问题,以最具发展前景的质押贷款业务为重点,探讨第三方物流面向金融服务的创新模式。*

一、质押贷款及其外部条件瓶颈

央行不断山台扶持中小企业发展的政策,但商业银行在具体操作中往往是“想贷不敢贷”,根本原因并不在于银行信贷或资本市场的歧视,而在于中小企业过于分散和信贷风险较高。根据《贷款通则》第九条,贷款分为信用贷款、担保贷款和票据贴现三种基本类型,其中担保贷款系指保证贷款、抵押贷款、质押贷款。中小企业信用级别低,可抵押资产普遍较少,也难以得到大企业提供的担保,在经营活动中商业票据使用较少,要获得银行提供的信用贷款、保证贷款、抵押贷款、票据贴现等服务在目前状况下仍然很困难。

---

* [作者简介] 罗齐,1975 年生,男,复旦大学管理学院博士生;朱道立,1946 年生,男,复旦大学管理学院教授,复旦大学现代物流研究中心主任,博士生导师;陈伯铭,1959 年生,男,复旦大学管理学院博士,广州市侨泰房地产公司总经理。

贷款质押指借款人或者第三人(出质人)将质物交付贷款人(质权人)占有,以该质物为贷款债权担保,如果借款人不履行贷款债务,贷款人有权从质物中优先受偿的一种担保方式,按质物属性分为动产质押与权利质押。近年来我国金融机构开展的质押贷款业务主要为股票等可转让有价证券质押。为数不多的动产质押(主要质物为原材料)案例都发生在大型国有企业和三资企业,金融机构对质物的占有权带有较强的信用特征。面对中小企业的质押贷款业务尽管充满诱惑,但由于存在诸多外部条件瓶颈而陷于停滞状态,而许多中小企业迫于短期资金压力转而以高昂的成本向各地兴起的典当行获得类似于动产质押的融资。金融机构开展面向中小企业的质押贷款业务面临以下外部条件瓶颈:

1) 中小企业真正可以并愿意用于质押的财产主要为具有较强变现能力的在一定时期内处于存储状态的原材料、产成品等动产。对于依法可以转让的股份、股票及其他有价证券,中小型工贸企业在资金紧张时通常趋向于直接将其变现。对于依法可以转让的商标专用权、专利权、著作权中的财产权等权利,其价值评估存在很大不确定性,难以为金融机构接受。

2) 金融机构如何实现对动产质物的评有权。金融机构不得从事除金融服务以外的其他领域的经营活动,要实现对动产质物的占有权必须借助除借款人之外的第三方提供质物监管与仓管服务。面对为数众多的中小企业,金融机构不可能为每一笔业务代借款人寻找合适的质物监管或仓管人,同时也不愿接受质物分散存放在各借款人自己的仓库中。

3) 质物的价值计估。近年来国内的动产质押,由于贷款额度大,质物价值计估过程及费用都能够为借款人接受。而对中小企业的小额质押贷款,必须有便捷而可靠的价值计估操作。

4) 企业用于质押的物品对其产销供应链运行有很大影响,要求金融机构在实现对质物占有权的同时尽量降低对借款人正常产销活动的影响。对质物的仓管与监管必须要能够良好融入借款人产销供应链之中。

二、融通仓涵义与服务功能

融通仓作为一种开业界之先河的新型业态,其内涵和外延尚待进一步探讨和丰富。在此,将融通仓的定义分为广义与狭义两个阶段。广义的融通仓是指在工业经济和金融、商贸、物流等第三产业发达的区域创生的一种跨行业的综合性第三产业高级业态,以物流运作为起点,综合发展信用担保,电子商务平台,传统商业平台和房产开发。狭义的融通仓是指以周边中小企业为主要服务对象,以流动商品仓储为基础,涵盖中小企业信用整合与再造、物流配送、电子商务与传统商业的综合性服务平台。本文主要探讨狭义融通仓的服务功能与运作模式。狭义的融通仓首先是一个以质押物资仓管与监管、价值计估、公共仓储、物流配送、拍卖为核心的综合性第三方物流服务平台,它不仅为银企间的合作构架新桥梁,也将良好地融入企业供应链体系之中,成为中小企业重要的第三方物流服务提供者,其服务功能主要有以下两个方面:

第一,融通仓提供的一体化服务可以解决质押贷款业务的外部条件瓶颈。

在质押业务中,融通仓根据质押人与金融机构签订的质押贷款合同以及三方签订的仓储协议约定,根据质物寄存地点的不同,对客户企业提供两种类型的服务:①对寄存在

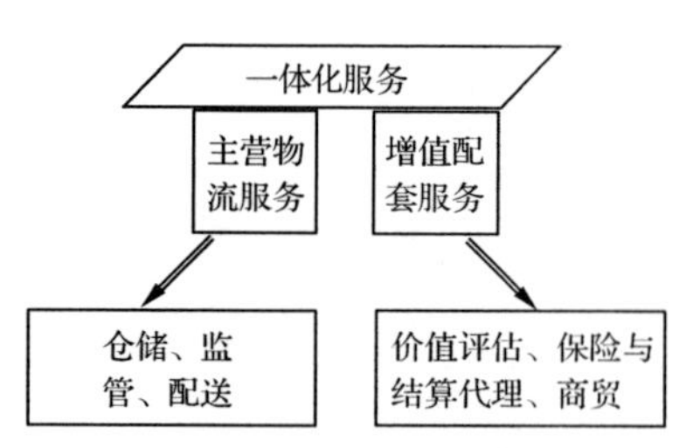

图 1　融通仓针对质押贷款业务提供一体化服务

融通仓之仓储中心的质物提供仓储管理和监管服务；②对寄存在质押人经金融机构确认的其他仓库中的质物提供监管服务，必要时才提供仓储管理服务。

借助融通仓的参与，针对中小企业的动产质押贷款业务的可操作性大大增强。在中小企业的生产经营活动中，原材料采购与产成品销售普遍存在批量性和季节性特征，这类物资的库存往往占用了大量宝贵资金。融通仓借助其良好的仓储、配送和商贸条件，吸引辐射区域内的中小企业，作为其第三方仓储中心，并帮助企业以存放于融通仓的动产获得金融机构的质押贷款融资。融通仓不仅为金融机构提供了可信赖的质物监管，述帮助质押贷款主体双方良好地解决质物价值计估、拍卖等难题，并有效融入中小企业产销供应链当中，提供良好的第三方物流服务。同时，融通仓也将商贸平台作为发展目标之一，借助“前店后仓”的运作模式，成为聚集区域内众多中小企业的采购与销售平台。

第二，信用整合与信用再造功能。

融通仓作为联结中小企业与金融机构的综合性服务平台，具有整合和再造会员企业信用的重要功能。融通仓与金融机构不断巩固和加强合作关系，依托融通仓设立中小企业信用担保体系，金融机构授予融通仓相当的信贷额度，以便于金融机构、融通仓和企业更加灵活地开展质押贷款业务。充分发挥融通仓对中小企业信用的整合和再造功能，可帮助中小企业更好地解决融资问题。

三、融通仓运作模式初探

融通仓的运作必须服务于上述两个基本功能，融入中小企业（会员企业）产销供应链，促进金融机构对中小企业的金融服务，整合和再造企业信用。

1. 融通仓选址与布局

融通仓的选址应在工业经济和金融、商贸、物流等第三产业发达的区域的中心地带，有效配送辐射半径为10～20公里，辐射区域内中小企业众多。在珠江三角洲，苏浙沪等地区都有许多良好的目标选址。融通仓储中心本着为金融机构和企业提供一体化服务的目标，需要着重考虑客户的需求，从客户的角度出发，帮助客户灵活开展质押贷款业务，降低质押贷款业务的成本，提高质押贷款业务运作的效率。这就需要对融通仓的仓储配送网络进行灵活而科学的设计。

“分布式”仓储，也可以称为“网络”仓储。融通仓在目标区域中心建设项目基地，其主要模块之一是质押与公共仓储团地，在距离基地较远的地区以贴近客户的原则设立或者租赁一定规模的子仓库，拓展融通仓的服务范围和辐射半径，实现“分布式”仓储配送的整体布局。图 2 中企业 A(B,…)和企业 a(b,…)同属于融通仓仓储团地辐射半径以内的客户源；企业 A(B,…)距离融通仓较近，其开展质押贷款时，需要将质物直接存放在融通仓仓储团地内部；企业 a(b,…)距离融通仓仓储团地较远，主要通过子仓库获得融通仓提供的仓储配送服务。

2. 融通仓融入会员企业原材料采购供应链之中

由于自身规模与实力的局限，中小企业的原材料采购通常需要以现款结算方式进行，尽管造成资金压力，多数原材料仍难采用零星购买方式。融通仓能够有效融入会员企业原材料采购供应链之中，帮助企业缓解资金压力和改善物流配送。

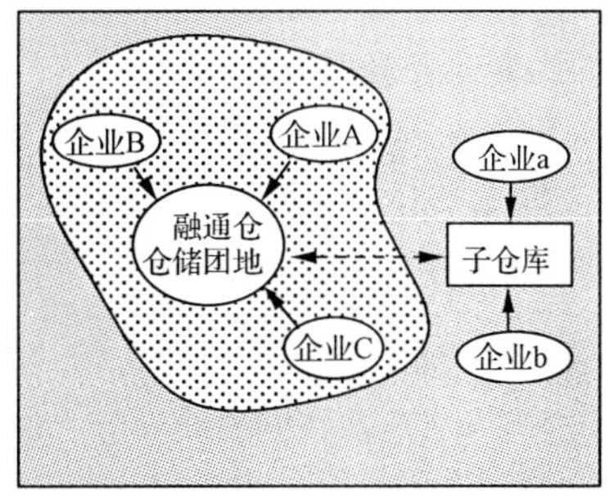

图2 整体布局："分布式"仓储配送

企业先获得贷款采购原材料，然后将采购的原材料交付给融通仓储中心仓储作质押。在贷款期间分多次偿还，并由融通仓协助完成物料配送。应对措施之一：金融机构先开出银行承兑汇票交给企业，企业凭银行承兑汇票向供应商采购原材料，将原材料准确无误地计估后交付给融通仓仓储中心入库，金融机构在银行承兑汇票到期时将汇票兑现，将款项划拨给原材料供应商账户。

应对措施之二："先抵押，后质押"。企业先以金融机构认同的动产作抵押，获得银行承兑汇票用于购买原材料，待原材料评计估并交付融通仓仓储中心入库后，金融机构在银行承兑汇票到期时将汇票兑现，并将抵押贷款转为以该批原材料为质押物的质押贷款。

3. 融通仓融入会员区域分销供应链之中

由于市场需求存在季节性特征，通用型产成品库存将占用中小企业大量资金。如果企业的主要产品销售旺季为冬季，产品库存从5月开始就逐渐增加，企业一方面需租用临时仓库用于产成品的存放，同时也被库存占据了大量的资金。金融机构开展的质押贷款业务辅助以融通仓仓储中心的配套物流服务，不仅可为该企业提供宝贵的融资机会，盘活库存资金占用，也为其提供了优质的第三方物流服务。

应对措施：企业产成品下生产线后直接运至融通仓存储，以备销售旺季之所需。以该批成品库存作质押，获得金融机构质押贷款，并以产品销售收入分批偿还贷款。为保障金融机构的利益，企业在质押权人金融机构开设专门账户，接收销售货款，此时通常要求企业实行款到发货的销售政策，如果企业与金融机构另有约定，金融机构亦可按企业接到的销售订单确认质物山库出请。融通仓此时作为企业分销供应链的一环，提供优良的仓储服务，并作为质押人企业的承运人或协助其承运人及时安排货物出库与发运，保证企业产品分销物流的顺畅。

4. 融通仓对会员企业的信用整合和再造

融通仓的重要意义还在于对中小企业信用的整合和再造。获得金融机构的授信额度和成立独特的信用担保体系是信用整合和再造的两个重要模式。

模式一：融通仓享有金融机构相当的授信额度

融通仓向金融机构按中小企业信用担保管理的有关规定和要求提供信用担保，金融机构授予融通仓一定的信贷额度。该模式有利于企业更加便捷地获得融资，减少原先质押贷款中一些繁琐的环节；有利于融通仓拓展服务范围，加强同企业的客户关系管理，提高对质押贷款全过程监控的能力；有利于金融机构更加灵活地开展质押贷款服务，优化其质押贷款的业务流程和工作环节，降低贷款的风险。

金融机构根据融通仓仓储中心的规模，经营业绩，运营现状，资产负债比例以及信用程度，授予融通仓储中心一定的信贷额度，融通仓储中心可以直接利用这些信贷额度向相关企业提供灵活的质押贷款业务，由融通仓直接监控质押贷款业务的全过程，金融机构则基本上不参与该质押贷款项目的具体运作：

1）融通仓直接同需要质押贷款的会员企业接触、沟通和谈判，代表金融机构同贷款企业签订质押借款合同和仓储管理服务协议，向企业提供质押融资的同时，为企业寄存的质物提供仓储管理服务和监管服务，从而将申请贷款和质物仓储两项任务整合操作，提高质押贷款业务运作效率。

2）贷款企业在质物仓储期间需要不断进行补库和出库，企业出具的入库单或出库单需要经过金融机构的确认，然后融通仓根据金融机构的入库或出库通知进行审核；而现在这些相应的凭证只需要经过融通仓的确认，即融通仓确认的过程就是对这些凭证进行审核的过程，中间省去了金融机构确认、通知、协调和处理等许多环节，缩短补库和山库操作的周期，在保证金融机构信贷安全的前提下，提高贷款企业产销供应链运作效率。

模式二：融通仓构建中小企业信用担保体系

·融通仓争取成立信用担保体系。在起步阶段，对于货主企业直接以寄存货物向金融机构申请质押贷款有难度的，融通仓储中心可以将其寄存货物作为反担保抵押物，通过担保实现贷款；当业务已全面启动后，融通仓将寄存货物反担保实现贷款与寄存货物质押结合起来，在银企之间搭建桥梁。

1）融通仓可以直接为中小企业申请质押贷款提供担保，间接地提高中小企业的信用。融通仓开展的担保必须取得有关部门和金融机构的支持，有必要向有关部门申请批准取得纳入信用担保体系的资格，享受扶持政策，以支撑担保业务的发展，扶持中小企业的壮大。

2）融通仓以自身担保能力组织企业联保或互助担保。具体做法可灵活多样，可以若干企业联合向融通仓担保，再由融通仓向金融机构担保，实现中小企业融资；融通仓担保能力与中小企业担保物结合起来直接向金融机构担保，实现融资；组织动员信用较高的企业为其他企业担保等。

融通仓作为一种跨行业的第三产业高级业态，将首先在珠江三角洲，苏浙沪等中小企业众多且充满活力的地区孕育和发展。在上述地区，已经有少量以商贸为核心的专业性市场同时具备了一定的金融与物流服务功能。如位于浙江嘉兴的中国茧丝绸交易市场，作为我国最重要的茧、丝、绸的交易中心，它同时也为进场会员企业提供质押贷款、担保和原料配送业务。可以预言，以第三方物流服务和促进面向中小企业的金融服务为核心的融通仓必将具有广阔的发展前景。

A Third-party Logistics Service lnnovation: Financing Warehouse and lts Operation Model

Luo,qi,zhu daoli,Chen Boming

Abstract: We discuss a 3PL service innovation towards finnance services. Through 3PL service,it is easier for the medium and small-sized enterprise to obtain hypothecation loan support from commercial banks. We also present an innovation concept of financing warehouse,and discuss its service functions and operation models.

Key words: logistics service innovation,supply chain,hypothecation loan,financing warehouse

参 考 文 献

[1] 中国人民银行.贷款通则.中国人民银行,1996.

[2] 中华人民共和国担保法.1995 年 6 月 30 日第八届全国人民代表大会常务委员会第十四次会议通过.

[3] 朱道立,龚国华,罗齐.物流和供应链管理[M].复旦大学出版社.

(本文发表于《中国流通经济》,2002 年第 2 期)

融通仓与物流金融服务创新

陈祥锋/CHEN Xiang-feng，石代伦/SHi Dai-lun，朱道立/ZHU Dao-li
复旦大学管理学院，上海 200433
School of Management，FudanUniversity，Shanghai 200433，China

摘要：融通仓是一种物流和金融的集成式服务。首先给出融通仓的定义并阐述其系统结构；其次结合企业运营周期特点总结了融通仓的运作模式；最后探讨了融通仓的一个理论框架和风险管理系统。

关键词：融通仓，物流，供应链管理，金融服务创新

中图分类号：F253.9　**文献标识码**：A　**文章编号**：1000-7857-(2005)09-0030-04

1　前言

供应链管理是当前管理科学中一个非常活跃的领域，引起了学者和实践工作者的极大关注。* 供应链管理包括对物流、资金流和信息流的计划、控制和管理(图 1)。但是，物流和资金流的管理往往是分开的：采购、生产、销售等部门负责物流；而资金流管理则是财会和出纳等部门的职能。这种物流和资金流的分离管理丧失了一些供应链整合和协调的

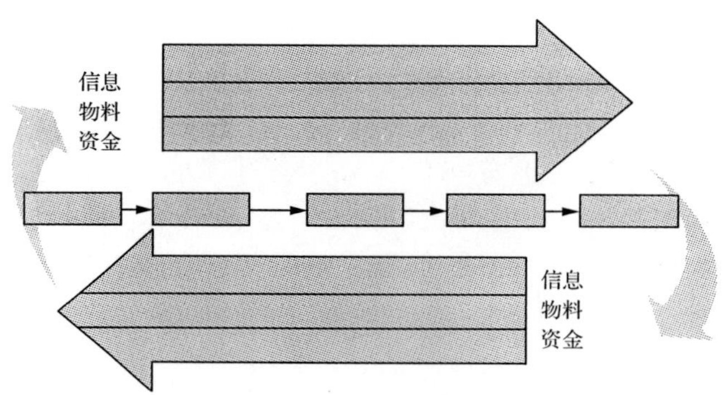

图 1　供应链物流、资金流和信息流的集成管理

* 收稿日期：2005-01-26

基金项目：国家自然科学基金重点项目(70432001)、国家自然科学基金面上项目(70271033)资助

作者简介：陈祥锋，男，上海市邯郸路 220 号复旦大学管理学院，讲师，主要研究方向为金融供应链和供应链合同管理等；E-mail：chenxf@fudan.edu.cn

宝贵机会[1]。物流和资金流的集成既能实现物流、资金流和信息流的统一管理与协调，又可成为企业的一个重要的利润源泉，从而进一步提高供应链效率并能够增强其竞争力。例如：Dell 公司 2003 年的销售额为 450 亿美元，平均每天销售额为 1.23 亿美元，而其现金周期为 5 天，HP 和 IBM 为 30～90 天。这使得 Dell 的现金周期至少比竞争对手少 35 天，共计节省运营资金 43.05 亿美元。按 5.88％利率计算，Dell 从现金管理方面比竞争对手多获取净利润 2.53 亿美元。在个人电脑行业利润率逐年减少的大环境下，从现金管理方面的额外利润是 Dell 多年成功的重要因素之一。

2 融通仓是一种物流和金融的集成式创新服务

2.1 融通仓的定义

融通仓这个词最早由罗齐和朱道立在 2000 年提出[2]。随着实践和理论的不断深入，作者对其内涵又进行了相应的拓广和发展，并于 2004 年 11 月在“2004 年中国物流创新大会”上被评选为中国物流的十大创新模式之一。顾名思义，“融”指金融，“通”指物资的流通，“仓”指物流的仓储。在此文中融通仓是指融、通、仓三者的集成，统一管理和综合协调[3]。因此融通仓是一种把物流、信息流和资金流综合管理的创新，其内容包括物流服务、金融服务、中介服务和风险管理服务，以及这些服务间的组合与互动。融通仓的核心思想是在各种流的整合和互补互动关系中寻找机会和时机；其目的是为了提升顾客服务质量、提高经营效率、减少运营资本、拓宽服务内容、减少风险、优化资源使用、协调多方行为、提升供应链整体绩效和增加整个供应链竞争力等等。

2.2 融通仓的发展历程

1999 年，一个第三方物流公司——中国储运公司，与银行合作，开始向客户提供简单的质押融资业务。2000 年，复旦大学朱道立教授主持广东顺德物流基地项目时首次提出了“融通仓”的概念，并组织人员开始相关理论的研究[4]。2001 年，TCL 应用融通仓思想开拓手机市场，通过向全国销售商提供大部分运营资金，成功地在短期内取得全国手机销量第一的业绩。同年，UPS 完成对 First International 的并购，开始提供融通仓式的服务。除传统包裹和企业物流业务外，UPS 推出了包括代开信用证、兑付出口票据、代理海关业务、提供货款融资等服务。2003 年，UPS 的金融物流集成服务成功地解决了 WALMART 和东南亚供应商之间的物流和付款拖欠太久的问题。2004 年，NOKIA 在广州使用类似 TCL 的融通仓模式抢占手机市场份额；DHL 在上海为客户提供物流和关税融资服务；中国储运集团提供仓单质押贷款业务，规模超过人民币 40 亿元。由此可见，融通仓服务的实践发展很快，而理论研究相对较慢。

2.3 融资和风险管理问题是融通仓产生的根本原因

2.3.1 融资问题

国内银行主要接受固定资产抵押贷款，因为固定资产的不可移动性使之作为抵押物，易于监管[5,6]。但是很多企业（特别是中小型企业）可用作抵押的固定资产有限，所以融资规模较小，不能满足企业发展和运营的资金需求。然而，企业的流动资产如存货、权利单证（如仓单、应付和应收款项单据凭证等）往往占企业总资产的较大比例[7]。由于流动资产的监管困难，金融机构往往不愿意开展基于动产的贷款业务。融通仓则通过对流动资产的有效监管来帮助银行和企业解决“企业想借借不到，银行想贷又怕贷”的困境：物流服务代理银行监管流动资产；金融服务则为企业提供融资及其他配套服务

2.3.2 风险管理问题

金融机构贷款存在信用风险，企业有还不起贷款的可能性[8]。融通仓对流动资产的有效监管可以降低基于动产融资贷款项目的风险。另外，由于未来的不确定性，原材料、部件、半成品和产成品的价格会波动，数量会变化，从而引发很多供应链风险[9,10]。融通仓不仅可以通过监管服务来降低银行的贷款风险，而且可以运用银行业近几十年发展起来的成熟的风险管理理论和方法（如金融衍生工具、期货和期权等）帮助企业降低供应链风险，进一步提高供应链整体效率。

2.3.3 其他原因

当前商业环境中还存在着需要融通仓服务的其他因素，包括：①中国信用体制的相对不健全；②进出口贸易增长引发大量融资和风险控制需求；③部分企业运营资金不足；④物流企业市场拓展的需求；⑤物流和资金流的统一管理可提高企业利润空间；⑥供应链竞争的需要；等等。

3 融通仓的服务内容

3.1 核心服务

融通仓是物流、金融、中介和风险管理服务的集成。其中物流和金融是核心，两者之间既相互联系又相互促进。金融靠物流对实物的监管来控制风险，而物流需要金融提供的资金来保障各个环节的最优配置。融通仓的物流服务包括运输、配送、仓储、加工、包装、装卸和信息服务等；金融服务包括融资、资产的评估、监管和处理、应付/应收帐款和现金管理、商业票据（如信用证）和银行授信转贷等。

3.2 附加服务

融通仓还包括中介和风险管理等附加服务，为客户提供增值和配套服务。中介服务内容包括海关业务代理、税金代理、进出口代理、货运代理、帐单和支付款管理、融通仓业务咨询等。风险管理业务包括客户信用风险评估和管理、资金兑现管理、系统风险分析、期权与期货交易、风险管理咨询等。融通仓提供商可以根据自身能力和市场的需要选择合适的集成式服务（可以是核心服务、附加服务或两者的任意组合），为客户提供高质量的定制服务。

3.3 融通仓职能

融通仓通过物流、融资、资金结算、风险管理等职能来加强供应链管理。

3.3.1 物流和融资职能

该职能贯穿企业物流的整个过程，包括采购、生产、加工、仓储、运输、装卸、配送和售后服务等。一旦某个环节出现资金缺口，融通仓可协助解决融资问题，而当融资风险出现时，其物流职能则通过对实物的监管来减少资金提供者的损失。

3.3.2 资金结算职能

融通仓服务发生后必然会产生大量的结算和支付需求。通过融通仓的商贸交易，除传统的买卖双方外，还涉及第三方物流公司、银行、仓储企业、中介公司等，结算和支付比

较复杂。资金结算功能提供专业的结算和支付解决方案，直接或间接地提供诸如金融结算、资金划拨等配套的附加值服务。

3.3.3　风险管理职能

在融通仓商贸交易中，各种各样的风险几乎伴随着业务范围的每个流程：采购过程、运输过程、装卸搬运过程、仓储过程、流通加工过程、包装过程、配送过程和信息服务过程。风险管理职能包括一整套涵盖融通仓各个环节的风险管理解决方案，帮助融通仓参与者发现、防范、量化、控制和规避风险。

物流，资金流和信息流是现代商贸活动中的3个重要因素。物流和信息流的集成管理在过去10～20年中带来了管理的信息化和现代化。人们过去对物流和资金流的整合关注不多，但是现在，越来越多的人发现，物流和金融的集成创新孕育着无限商机和可观的利润。融通仓服务和职能的目的，就是用资金流盘活物流，或用物流拉动资金流。因此，参与的物流、生产、中介和金融企业都可以通过融通仓模式实现多方共赢。

4　融通仓系统结构与设计

融通仓是一个较为复杂的系统，不仅涉及到多个企业之间的合作和协调，而且需要有一套关键理论和技术的支撑。因此，用系统思想来研究和设计融通仓服务模式，是保证其成功运营和健康发展的关键之一。

4.1　融通仓系统主体

融通仓系统主体包括金融机构、第三方物流企业、融资企业、供应链主导企业等等。系统主体间关系如图2所示。

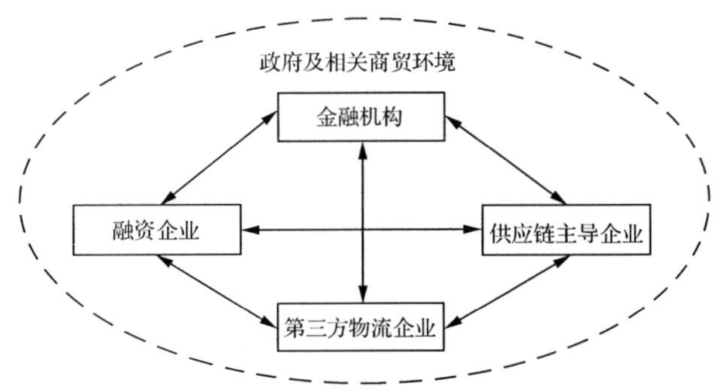

图2　融通仓系统主体及相互关系

金融机构泛指能够提供资本的机构，如银行、担保公司等；第三方物流企业是提供质押物（动产）的物流服务和资产管理服务（监管、拍卖等）的承载者；融资企业指融通仓服务的需求者；供应链主导企业往往规模较大，实力较强，所以能够通过担保、提供出质物或者承诺回购等方式帮助融资企业解决融资担保困难，从而保证与融资企业良好的合作关系和稳定的供货来源或分销渠道；政府和相关商贸环境主要指税务、海关、银行等机构和有关的政策和法规，以及相关的会计、法律、拍卖等业务环境和流程。

4.2　融通仓服务的提供者

融通仓服务的提供者可以是第三方物流企业，也可以是进出口公司、供应商和金融机构（银行、保险公司和担保公司）等（如图3）。

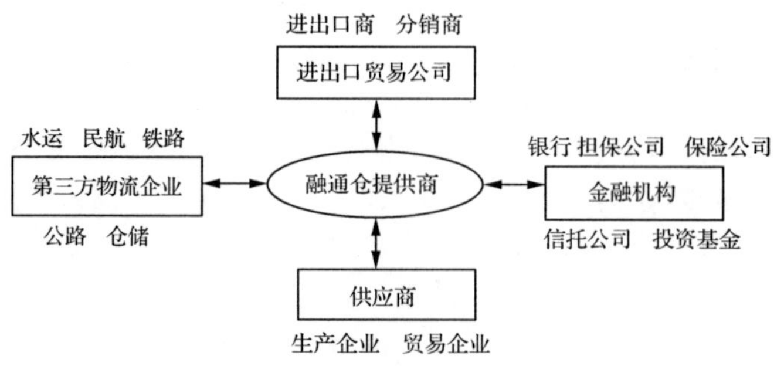

图3 融通仓服务提供商

4.3 融通仓系统结构

按系统的拓扑结构，把融通仓分为“纵向融通仓”、“横向融通仓”、“星状融通仓”和“网络融通仓”4类。以下对每种结构作简单的说明。

4.3.1 纵向融通仓

纵向融通仓的提供商利用自有资本，或者与金融机构合作，为融通仓服务的需求方提供金融和物流集成式服务，以降低供应链物流成本，提高供应链整体效益，并达到供应链中各企业多赢的局面。纵向融通仓的结构如图4所示。

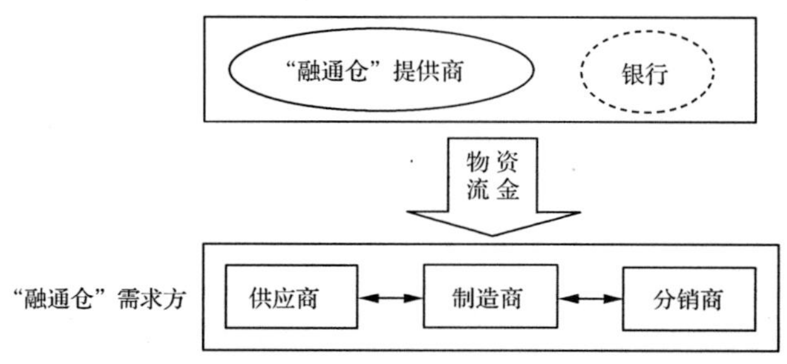

图4 纵向融通仓结构图

4.3.2 横向融通仓

横向融通仓的提供者(供应链节点企业或第三方企业，如从事期货产品或期权产品的经纪人)应用金融衍生工具和供应链风险管理方法，帮助融通仓服务需求方在风险事件发生时减少损失或增加供应链整体收益。横向融通仓的结构见图5。

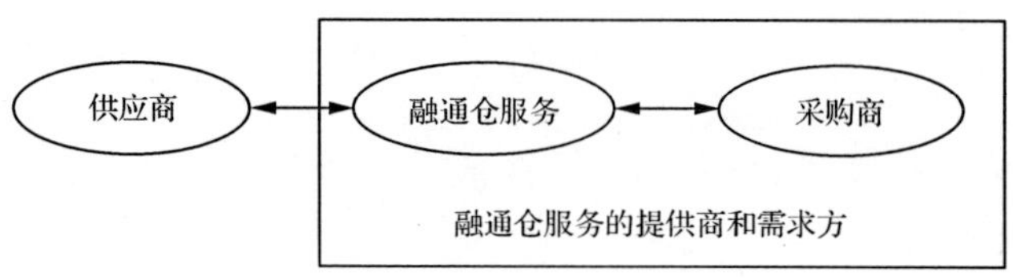

图5 横向融通仓结构图

4.3.3 星状融通仓

星状融通仓是一种金融和物流集成式服务平台，为众多的企业提供“融”、“通”和“仓”的服务。其结构见图 6。星状融通仓既可以为广大商贸交易提供融资服务，又可以提供货运代理或运输、仓储等物流服务，同时协助控制相关风险。网络融通仓提供形式多样的融通仓服务，是集横向融通仓、纵向融通仓和星状融通仓而成的融通仓服务网络。随融通仓的进一步发展和普适，结构较复杂的网络融通仓服务将会出现。利用图论知识和简单计算，我们可以证明网络融通仓可以简化商业交易的复杂度，供应链的竞争和合作可以通过融通仓来实现。

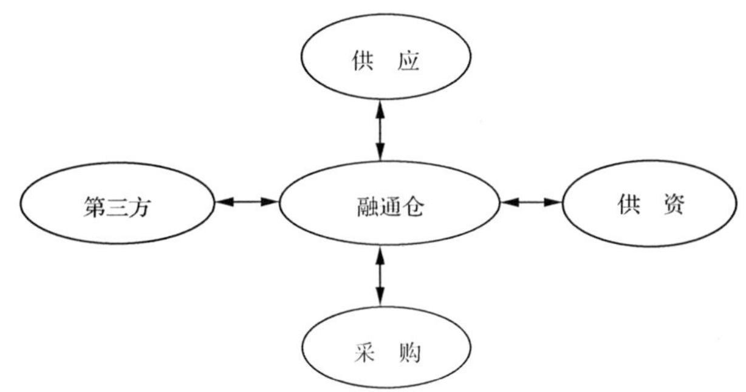

图 6 星状融通仓示意图

5 融通仓运营周期与运作模式

5.1 运营周期

企业运营过程中出现资金缺口或供应链风险发生的可能点见图 7。

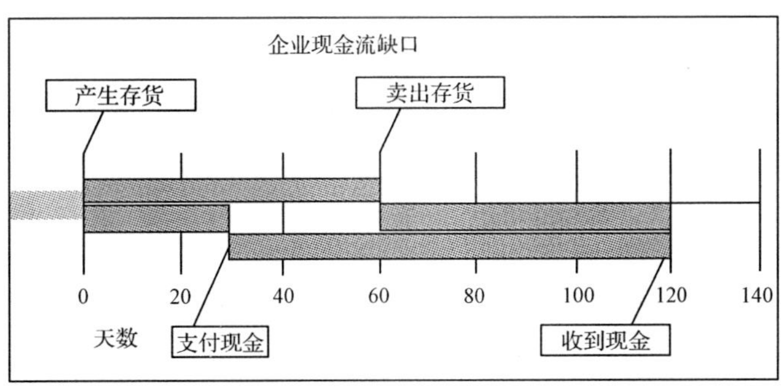

图 7 企业运营周期、资金缺口和可能风险点

如图 7 所示，企业运营周期可以分为以下 3 个阶段，不同阶段将产生不同融通仓需求和相应的运作模式。

1）第 1 阶段主要是企业采购原材料、部件、半成品或制成品的时期。此期间采购物品价格的波动或其他风险将会影响整个供应链的运营，所以融通仓的风险管理职能最为需要。另外，采购期一旦出现资金缺口，融通仓可以通过应付帐款管理来解决融资问题。

2）第 2 阶段即“支付现金”至“卖出存货”时期，为资金缺口期，此时期企业较大部分资产以动产(如库存资产等)形式存在。应用动产进行融资能大大减少企业资金压力,但是出资方必须考虑如何在流动中监管动产。融通仓作为物流和金融服务集成服务,恰好可以通过物流来监管作为融资质押物的动产。

3)第3阶段即"卖出存货"至"收到现金"时期,也可能成为资金缺口期,此时企业拥有应收帐款单据,可通过应收帐款管理来解决融资问题。

5.2 运作模式

根据企业运营过程中的风险和资金缺口需求,融通仓可以有3种模式。

5.2.1 基于动产管理的融通仓运作模式

基于动产管理的融通仓运作模式主要适用于纵向融通仓和星状融通仓,存在上述融资企业运营中"支付现金"至"卖出存货"的资金缺口期。融资模式体现为动产抵押和质押贷款(以供应链企业中的存货、仓单等动产作为质押物进行融资)。这种模式把"死"的物资或权利凭证向"活"的资产转换,加速"动产"的流通,创造更大的利润空间。具体应用的业务形式主要有"仓单质押"、"动产抵押和质押"、"保兑仓"等。

5.2.2 基于资金管理的融通仓运作模式

基于资金管理的融通仓运作模式主要用于纵向融通仓和星状融通仓的结构中。主要业务形式表现为"应付帐款管理"和"应收帐款管理",即使用应付或应收帐款的单据凭证作为担保信物向金融机构申请贷款。其中"应付帐款管理"适用企业运营周期的采购阶段,而"应收帐款管理"适用融资企业"卖出存货"至"收到现金"的资金缺口期。

5.2.3 基于风险管理的融通仓运作模式

基于风险管理的融通仓运作模式适用于企业运营周期的各个阶段,系统结构体现为横向融通仓服务。例如,在企业采购期,原材料价格波动或需求变化将会导致供应链风险。基于风险管理的融通仓运作模式则借助金融衍生工具(如期权、期货等)来管理风险,从而提高供应链绩效。

融通仓服务可以一定程度降低供应链风险,但是,融通仓服务本身又有其固有风险,如市场风险、商业环境风险、运营风险和信用风险等。有效风险管理是成功实施融通仓服务的关键。如图8所示,融通仓相关企业可以通过调整战略、战术、组织结构和风险控制机制,利用金融衍生工具和保险产品以及运营控制来有效管理融通仓相关风险。

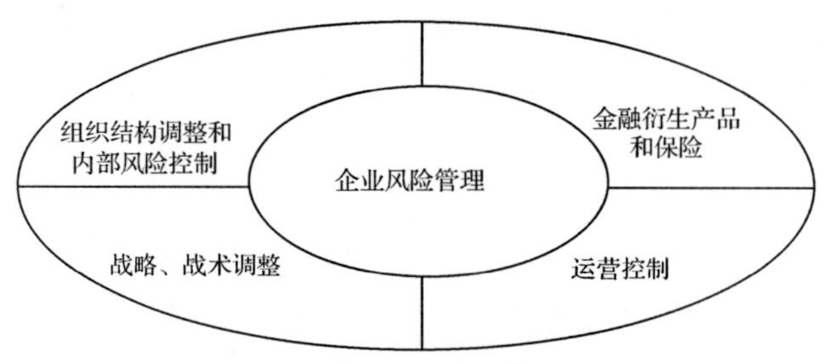

图8 融通仓风险管理框架

6　结束语

物流服务的发展、金融机构创新意识的增强、中小型企业的融资困境、进出口贸易高速增长、供应链风险管理、供应链竞争等等因素，为融通仓的发展提供了广阔前景。由于融通仓具有较复杂的系统结构，其具体的实施将伴随着一定的风险。因此，融通仓的运用对企业既是机遇，又是挑战。

当前融通仓实践缺乏系统的理论指导。本文介绍一个融通仓的系统理论框架，旨在抛砖引玉，希望更多学者能对融通仓感兴趣，发展出更多更好的融通仓理论。本文的理论框架只是一个开始，很多工作还有待发展。今后的研究可以在融通仓的系统结构设计、融通仓运营和风险的控制技术、融通仓的决策支持系统、融通仓业务流程、融通仓的宏观经济商业环境等领域进行探索。

Finance, Transportation and Warehouse: Innovative Service Integrating Logistics and Finance

Abstract: Finance, Transportation and Warehouse (FTW) is a new term for innovative service integrating logistics and finance. FTW was defined and its system structure was presented. Based on the cash-flow characteristics during different stages of a firm's operating cycle, three operational modes for FTW were summarized. Finally, a theoretical framework for the analysis of FTW was proposed.

Key Words: finance-transportation and warehouse, logistics, supply chain management, financial service innovation

CLC Num ber: F253.9　**Docum ent Code**: A　**Article ID**: 1000-7857(2005)09-0030-04

参 考 文 献(References)

[1] 罗齐，朱道立，陈伯铭. 第三方物流服务创新：融通仓及其运作模式初探[J]. 中国流通经济，2002，(2)：11-14

[2] 任文超. 物资银行及其实践[J]. 科学决策，1998，2：15-18

[3] 陈祥锋，石代伦，朱道立. 融通仓物流项目运作模式[J]. 复旦大学物流管理研究中心，2002

[4] 褚方鸿. 物流创新打开第三利润源泉的钥匙[J]. 物流技术与应用，2004，(12)：40-44

[5] Coulter J, Onumal G. The role of warehouse receipt systems in enhanced commodity marketing and rural live lihoods in Africa[J]. Food Policy, 2002, 27: 319～337

[6] Christa Hainz. Bank competition and credit markets in transition economics[J]. Journal of Comparative Economics, 2003, 31: 223-245

[7] Buraschi A, Monini D. Liquidity risk and special [J]. Journal of Financial Economics, 2002,

64:243-268

[8] Cetin Ciher. Information contest of volume:an investigation of Tokyo commodity futures markets[J]. Pacific-Basin Finance Journal,2002,10:201-215

[9] Erik Lehmann,Doris Neubergen. Do lending relationships matter? evidence from bank survey data in Germany[J]Journal of Economic Behavior & Organization,2001,45:339～359

[10] Michael E sykwta. Future trading and supply contract in the oilre fine industry[J]. Journal of Corporate Finance,1996,2:317～2334

（本文发表于《科技导报》,2005 年第 9 期）

延迟支付方式下的存货质押融资服务定价模型

朱文贵[1]，朱道立[1]，徐　最[2]

（1. 复旦大学管理学院，上海 200433；2. 上海海事大学交通运输学院，上海 200135）

摘要：研究在供应商允许零售商采用延迟支付方式的条件下，第三方物流企业向零售商提供存货质押融资服务的定价模型，在分析零售商行动策略的基础上，给出了存货质押融资服务的定价方法。

关键词：延迟支付；存货质押融资；定价

中图分类号：F276　　　　**文献标志码：**A

1　引言

企业在运营过程中，由于采购、生产和销售各环节的不确定性，会出现资金短缺的问题。我国的中小企业由于融资渠道不足等原因，难以解决这个问题。这不仅会阻碍其自身发展，还会影响供应链上的其他企业的收益[1]. 比如，中小零售商为了满足季节性商品的市场需求，需要提前采购大量的商品，而此时的资金往往不足以支付采购成本。这就容易导致零售商无法采购适量的商品，从而丧失市场机会，进而影响到整个供应链的收益。

解决这个问题需要供应链参与企业的相互合作，目前常见的方式有两种：一是供应商允许零售商延迟支付货款. 即，零售商收到货物之后并不需要立即支付货款，而是可以在允许的时间范围内进行支付，这个时间范围也称为信用期，在信用期内支付货款可以不用支付利息. 二是为零售商提供服务的第三方物流企业开展存货质押融资服务，拓宽零售商的融资渠道。即，第三方物流企业与银行合作，对零售商存储在其仓库中的货物进行质押，从而提供贷款. 典型的有中国储运公司的“授信质押服务”和中外运公司的“货押监管服务”，二者均以流动货物为质押品向货主提供贷款。*

对于第一种方式，国外研究的文献较多。Goyal[2] 研究了延迟支付方式下的采购模

* 收稿日期：2007-09-26

资助项目：国家自然科学基金（70432001）

作者简介：朱文贵（1978），男，福建人，博士生，研究方向：物流与供应链管理，E-mail：041025033@fudan.edu.cn；朱道立（1946），男，上海人，教授，博士生导师，研究方向：管理科学、运筹学，E-mail：dlzhu@fudan.edu.cn；徐最（1979），女，吉林人，讲师，研究方向：供应链管理，运筹学。

型,得出了经济订货批量公式. Aggarwal 和 Jaggi [3] 分析了延迟支付方式下易逝品的经济订货批量。Chung 和 Chu 等[4,5]进一步研究了 Gyoal 提出的模型,简化了求解经济订货批量的算法,并研究了 Aggarwal 等提出的模型的凸性。最近有一些文献(如,Ouyang[6];Chang[7])研究了在供应商使用现金折扣和允许延迟支付的情况下,零售商的经济订货批量。对于延迟支付方式下的订货,还有相当多模型,包括 Hwang 和 Shinn[8] 提出的运费有折扣且需求是价格的函数的采购模型,Sarker 和 Jamal 等[9] 考虑了延迟支付要收取利息情况下零售商的付款策略,Salameh 和 Abboud 等[10] 研究了延迟支付条件下,需求均匀而提前期随机的持续补货策略。Arcelus 和 Srinivasan[11] 结合三种数量折扣方式考虑了延迟支付的经济订货批量模型,Chang 等[12] 考虑了采购数量达到一定条件时才能延迟支付货款的模型。

对于第二种方式,目前的理论研究较少。国内的这项业务刚刚起步,尽管许多学者在实践的基础上对其运作模式和风险控制等进行了详细的分析[13,14],然而并没有进行定量研究。特别是,对于两种方式相结合的定量研究,即延迟支付方式下的存货质押融资服务,更没有相关的成果,难以指导第三方物流企业开展该项服务。

本文研究在供应商允许零售商延迟支付并给予现金折扣的条件下,第三方物流企业提供存货质押融资服务的定价方法。第三方物流企业作为领导者,决定融资服务的价格,使得自身利润最大;零售商作为跟随者,决定其支付货款的时间和采购周期,使得自身成本最小。

2 定价模型

2.1 模型假设与参数符号

假设条件:

①供应商提供给零售商两种支付货款的方式,一是在收货时立即支付货款,则获得现金折扣,二是在信用期时点支付货款,不获得现金折扣,也不需要利息支出。②商品的需求均匀稳定,不允许缺货。③零售商订货周期均匀。考虑多个周期的情形。④零售商初始资金为零,销售收入放在可获取利息的账户里,在支付供应商货款的时候以销售收入支付,不足时就需要通过存货质押融资进行支付。⑤零售商融资的资金在采购周期末还给第三方物流企业。⑥第三方物流企业资金的保留利息率与零售商销售收入可获取的利息率相同。⑦信息对称。

参数符号:

D——商品年需求量;

$I(t)$——时间 t 时的库存水平,$0 \leqslant t \leqslant T$;

M——信用期;

P_i——零售商行动策略,$i=1-3$;

Q——零售商订货量;

T——零售商的订货周期;

h—— 不计资金利息的单位商品年持有成本;

c—— 单位商品价格;

I_e——销售收入可获得的年利率；

I_p——存货质押融资服务的费率（质押融资服务占用的资金的年利率），$I_p \geq I_e$；

S——单位订货成本；

r—— 零售商立即支付货款所能获得的现金折扣率，$0<r<1$；

C——零售商的年总成本；

π_L——第三方物流企业提供存货质押融资服务的利润。

2.2 零售商的成本函数

零售商的行动策略 P_i 需要同时决定支付货款的时间和订货周期（即订货量决策）两个变量。根据支付货款时间的不同，零售商的策略可以分为立即支付策略和延迟支付策略，在延迟支付策略中，根据零售商制定的订货周期与信用期的大小关系，又有两种情况，一种是订货周期小于或等于信用期，另一种是订货周期大于信用期。所以，零售商总共有以下三种行动策略，如图 1 所示。

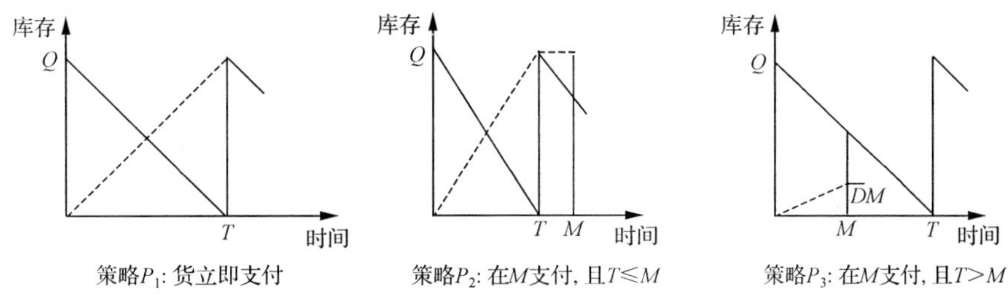

图 1 延迟支付条件下零售商的行动策略

在一个订货周期内，零售商库存 $I(t)$ 随着满足需求而减小，其变化遵循 $\frac{\mathrm{d}I(t)}{\mathrm{d}(t)}$ 又由于期末库存 $I(T)=0$，所以 $I(t)=D(T-t)$)，$Q=I(0)=DT$。

零售商的年总成本由五个部分组成：年总成本 $C=$ 订货费用＋ 持有成本＋货款＋融资费用－利息收入。其中，前两项成本与零售商采取的行动策略无关，分别为，

$$\text{年订货费用} = S/T, \text{年持有成本} = \frac{h\int_0^T I(t)\,\mathrm{d}t}{T} = \frac{hDt}{2}$$

后三项成本与零售商采取的行动策略相关，分三种情况讨论。

情况 1：零售商采取行动策略 P_1，即到货付款，获取现金折扣

由于获得现金折扣，此时零售商年支付的货款 $= \frac{cDT(1-r)}{T} = cD(1-r)$，

根据假设④和⑤，此时零售商需要从第三方物流企业融资，

$$\text{年融资费用} = \frac{cDT^2(1-r)I_p}{T} = cDT(1-r)I_p \tag{1}$$

年利息收入 $= \frac{cI_e\int_0^T DT\,\mathrm{d}t}{T} = \frac{cDTI_e}{2}$。

所以，零售商的年总成本 $C_1=\frac{S}{T}+\frac{DTh}{2}+cD(1-r)+cDT(1-r)I_p-\frac{cDTI_e}{2}$ (2)

情况 2：零售商采取行动策略 P_2，即在 M 时点付款，且 $T\leqslant M$

由于不获得现金折扣，此时零售商年支付的货款 $=\frac{cDT}{T}=cD$，

根据假设④，此时零售商需要从第三方物流企业融资，

$$\text{年利息收入}=\frac{cI_e\int_0^T Dtdt+cDT(M-T)I_e}{T}=cDI_e\left(M-\frac{T}{2}\right),$$

所以，零售商的年总成本 $C_2=\frac{S}{T}+\frac{DTh}{2}+cD-cDI_e\left(M-\frac{T}{2}\right)$ (3)

情况 3：零售商采取行动策略 P_3，即在 M 时点付款，且 $T>M$

由于不获得现金折扣，此时零售商年支付的货款 $=\frac{cDT}{T}=cD$，

根据假设④和⑤，此时零售商需要从第三方物流企业融资，年融资费用 $=\frac{cD(T-TM)^2I_p}{T}$ (4)

$$\text{年利息收入}=\frac{\left(cI_e\int_0^M Dtdt\right)+\left(cI_e\int_0^{T-M} Dtdt\right)}{T}=\frac{cDI_e[M^2+(T-M)^2]}{2T}$$

所以，零售商的年总成本，

$$C_3=\frac{S}{T}+\frac{DTh}{2}+cD+\frac{cD(T-M)^2I_p}{T}-\frac{cDI_e[M^2+(T-M)^2]}{2T} \tag{5}$$

2.3 零售商的行动策略求解

根据式(2)、(3)、(5)，可得零售商三种策略下相应成本函数的一阶和二阶导数为

$$\frac{dC_1}{dT}=-\frac{S}{T^2}+\frac{Dh}{2}+cD(1-r)I_p-\frac{1}{2}cDI_e \tag{6}$$

$$\frac{d^2C_1}{dT^2}=\frac{2S}{T^3}>0 \tag{7}$$

$$\frac{dC_2}{dT}=-\frac{S}{T^2}+\frac{Dh}{2}+\frac{cDI_e}{2} \tag{8}$$

$$\frac{d^2C_2}{dT^2}=\frac{2S}{T^3}>0 \tag{9}$$

$$\frac{dC_3}{dT}=-\frac{S+cDM^2(I_p-I_e)}{T^2}+\frac{Dh}{2}+\frac{1}{2}cD(2I_p-I_e) \tag{10}$$

$$\frac{d^2C_3}{dT^2}=\frac{2[S+cDM^2(I_p-I_e)]}{T^3}>0 \tag{11}$$

由(7)可知，零售商在立即支付策略 P_1 下的成本函数为凸函数，令 $\frac{dC_1}{dT}=0$，可得零售商此时的最优订货周期为

$$T_1^*=\sqrt{\frac{2S}{Dh+2cD(1-r)I_p-cDI_e}}\text{，当 } Dh+2cD(1-r)I_p-cDI_e>0 \tag{12}$$

$$T_1^* \to \infty \text{ 当 } Dh + 2cD(1-r)I_p - cDI_e \leqslant 0 \tag{13}$$

(13) 可以解释为由于融资的利息过低,零售商将一直保留着贷款来获取利息。

由(9)和(11)可知,零售商在延迟支付策略 P_2 和 P_3 下的成本函数均为凸函数,又由(8)和(10)可知,$\left.\frac{\mathrm{d}C_2}{\mathrm{d}T}\right|_{T=M}=\left.\frac{\mathrm{d}C_3}{\mathrm{d}T}\right|_{T=M}$,所以,零售商在延迟支付策略下的成本函数在 $T>0$时为凸函数(而不仅仅是分段凸函数)。

令 $\frac{\mathrm{d}C_2}{\mathrm{d}T,}=0$ 可得零售商在策略 P_2 下的最优订货周期为

$$T_2^* = \sqrt{\frac{2S}{Dh + cDI_e}} \tag{14}$$

$$\text{由 } T_2^* \leqslant M \text{ 可得}, 2S \leqslant DM^2(h + cI_e) \tag{15}$$

令 $\frac{\mathrm{d}C_3}{\mathrm{d}T,}=0$ 可得零售商在策略 P_3 下的最优订货周期为

$$T_3^* = \sqrt{\frac{2[S + cDM^2(I_p - I_e)]}{Dh + 2cDI_p - cDI_e}}, \text{当 } Dh + 2cDI_p - cDIe > 0 \tag{16}$$

$$T_3^* \to \infty, \text{当 } Dh + 2cDI_p - cDI_e \leqslant 0 \tag{17}$$

(17) 可以解释为由于融资的利息过低,零售商将一直保留着贷款来获取利息。

$$\text{当 } Dh + 2cDI_p - cDI_e > 0 \text{ 时,由 } T_3^* > M \text{ 可得}, 2S > DM^2(h + cI_e) \tag{18}$$

因此,零售商最优的行动策略由下列命题给出:

命题 1. 零售商要使其成本最小,需要根据不同条件采取不同的行动策略:

① 当 $2S \leqslant DM^2(h + cI_e)$ 时,

如果 $Dh + 2cD(1-r)I_p - cDI_e \leqslant 0$,则零售商选择立即支付策略 P_1,此时 $T^* \to \infty$;

如果 $Dh + 2cD(1-r)I_p - cDI_e > 0$,则 $C(T^*) = \min\{C_1(T_1^*), C_2(T_2^*)\}$,所以零售商选择行动策略 P_1 或 P_2 中成本较小的一个。

② 当 $2S > DM^2(h + cI_e)$时,

如果 $Dh + 2cDI_p - cDI_e \leqslant 0$,则零售商可选择 P_1 或 P_3,此时 $T^* \to \infty$;

如果 $Dh + 2cDI_p - cDI_e > 0$ 且 $Dh + 2cD(1-r)I_p - cDI_e \leqslant 0$,则零售商选择 P_1,此时 $T^* \to \infty$;

如果 $Dh + 2cD(1-r)I_p - cDI_e > 0$,则 $C(T^*) = \min\{C_1(T_1^*), C_3(T_3^*)\}$,所以零售商可选择行动策略 P_1 或 P_3 中成本较小的一个。

证明: 由式(12)~(18)可得上述命题。

2.4 第三方物流企业对存货质押融资服务的定价

第三方物流企业的目的是使得自身利润最大化,因此,在制定存货质押融资服务费率 I_p 的时候,需要考虑该费率引起的零售商行动策略的变化情况。根据命题 1,考虑两种情况下的定价策略。

① 当 $2S \leqslant DM^2(h + cI_e)$ 时,

为避免出现 $T^* \to \infty$(此时零售商将不偿还贷款),由 $Dh + 2cD(1-r)I_p - cDI_e > 0$ 得,$I_p > \frac{cD}{Dh + 2cD(1-r)I_e}$

为避免零售商选择策略 P_2(此时零售商不需要融资服务)，由 $C_1(T_1^*) \leqslant C_2(T_2^*)$ 可得 I_p 的取值范围，令集合 $A_1 = \{I_p \mid C_1(T_1^*) \leqslant C_2(T_2^*)\}$。

② 当 $2S > DM^2(h + cI_e)$ 时，

为避免出现 $T^* \to \infty$(此时零售商将不偿还贷款)，由 $Dh + 2cD(1-r)I_p - cDI_e > 0$ 得，$I_p > \dfrac{cD}{Dh + 2cD(1-r)I_e}$，

如果 $C_1(T_1^*) \leqslant C_3(T_3^*)$，则零售商选择策略 P_1，此时可得 I_p 的取值范围，令集合 $A_2 = \{I_p \mid C_1(T_1^*) \leqslant C_3(T_3^*)\}$；如果 $C_1(T_1^*) > C_3(T_3^*)$，则零售商选择策略 P_3，此时可得 I_p 的取值范围，令集合 $A_3 = \{I_p \mid C_1(T_1^*), C_3(T_3^*)\}$，即 $A_3 = \overline{A}_2$。

因此，第三方物流企业提供质押融资服务的定价策略由下列命题给出：

命题 2. 第三方物流企业要使其利润最大，需要根据不同条件制定不同的费率，令集合 $A_4 = \left\{I_p \mid I_p \geqslant I_e \text{ 且 } I_p > \dfrac{cD}{Dh + 2cD(1-r)} I_e\right\}$，则：

① 当 $2S \leqslant DM^2(h + cI_e)$ 时，制定费率使得 $\max\limits_{I_p} \pi^L = cD(1-r)T_1^* I_p$，$I_p \in \{A_1 \cap A_4\}$，

② 当 $2S > DM^2(h + cI_e)$ 时，制定费率使得 $\max\limits_{I_p} \pi_L = \max\{\pi_{L1}, \pi_{L2}\}$，其中，$\pi_{L1} = \max\limits_{I_p} \{cD(1-r)T_1^* I_p\}$，$I_p \in \{A_2 \cap A_4\}$，$\pi_{L2} \max\limits_{I_p} \left\{\dfrac{cD(M - T_3^*)^2 I_p}{T_3^*}\right\}$，$I_p \in \{A_3 \cap A_4\}$

3 算例

算例 1 假设 $D = 5000$ 单位/年，$h = 3$ 元/单位/年，$I_e = 0.01$/年，$S = 30$ 元，$c = 25$ 元/单位，$r = 0.02$，$M = 60/365$ 年(表 1)。

表 1 算例 1 中费率对零售商成本和第三方物流企业利润影响情况的分析表

I_p	T_1^*	C_1	T_2^*	C_2	π_L
0.694	0.018 069	125 773.6	0.060 764	125 781.94	1 536.109
0.695	0.018 057	125 775.8	0.060 764	125 781.94	1 537.298
0.696	0.018 045	125 778	0.060 764	125 781.94	1 538.486
0.697	0.018 033	125 780.2	0.060 764	125 781.94	1 539.674
0.698	0.018 021	125 782.3	0.060 764	125 781.94	0
0.699	0.018 009	125 784.5	0.060 764	1 25781.94	0
0.7	0.017 997	125 786.7	0.060 764	125 781.94	0

由于 $DM^2(h + cI_e) \approx 439$，所以 $2S \leqslant DM^2(h + cI_e)$. 利用命题 2 给出的方法，由 $I_p > \dfrac{cD}{Dh + 2cD(1-r)}) I_e$ 得 $I_p > 0.0048$，所以，$A_4 = \{I_p \mid I_p \geqslant 0.01\}$，又由 $C_1(T_1^*) \leqslant C_2(T_2^*)$ 得 $I_p \leqslant 0.697$，所以 $A_1 = \{I_p \mid I_p \leqslant 0.697\}$。根据(1)，此时第三方物流企业的利润函数为 $cDT_1^*(1-r)I_p$，在 $I_p = 0.697$ 时达到最大，所以，质押融资服务的费率定为 0.697，此时零售商选择立即支付策略(图 2)。

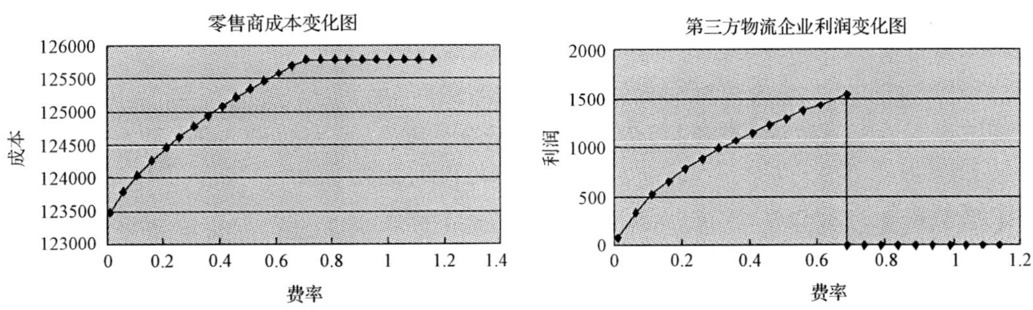

图 2　算例 1 中费率对零售商成本和第三方物流企业利润的影响情况的分析图

算例 2　假设 $D=5000$ 单位/年，$h=3$ 元/单位/年，$I_e=0.01$/年，$S=30$ 元，$c=25$ 元/单位，$r=0.02$，$M=10/365$ 年(表 2)．

表 2　算例 2 中费率对零售商成本和第三方物流企业利润影响情况的分析表

I_p	T_1^*	C_1	T_2^*	C_3	π_L
0.916	0.015 872	126 225.7	0.030 782	126 232.6	1 780.999
0.917	0.015 864	126 227.6	0.030 779	126 232.65	1782.027
0.918	0.015 856	126 229.5	0.030 775	126 232.7	1 783.054
0.919	0.015 848	126 231.5	0.030 772	126 232.74	1784.081
0.92	0.015 839	126 233.4	0.030 769	126 232.79	0.461 819
0.921	0.015 831	126 235.3	0.030 766	126 232.83	0.460 974
0.922	0.015 823	126 237.2	0.030 762	126 232.88	0.460 131
0.923	0.015 815	126 239.1	0.030 759	126 232.93	0.45929

由于 $DM^2(h+cI_e)\approx 12$，所以 $2S>DM^2(h+cI_e)$。利用命题 2 给出的方法，由 $I_p>\dfrac{cD}{Dh+2cD(1-r)}I_e$ 得 $I_p>0.0048$，所以，$A_4=\{I_p \mid I_p\geqslant 0.01\}$。由 $C_1(T_1^*)\leqslant C_3(T_3^*)$ 得 $I_p\leqslant 0.919$，所以 $A_3=\{I_p \mid I_p\leqslant 0.919\}$，当 $I_p=0.919$ 时第三方物流企业利润达到最大，此时的利润 $\pi_{L1}=1784$；又由 $C_1(T_1^*)>C_3(T_3^*)$ 得 $I_p>0.919$，所以 $A_3=\{I_p \mid I_p>0.919\}$，第三方物流企业的利润函数在 $I_p=0.919$ 时达到上限，此时的利润上限 $\pi_{L2}=0.46$。显然，质押融资服务的费率将定为 0.919，零售商同样选择立即支付策略(图 3)。

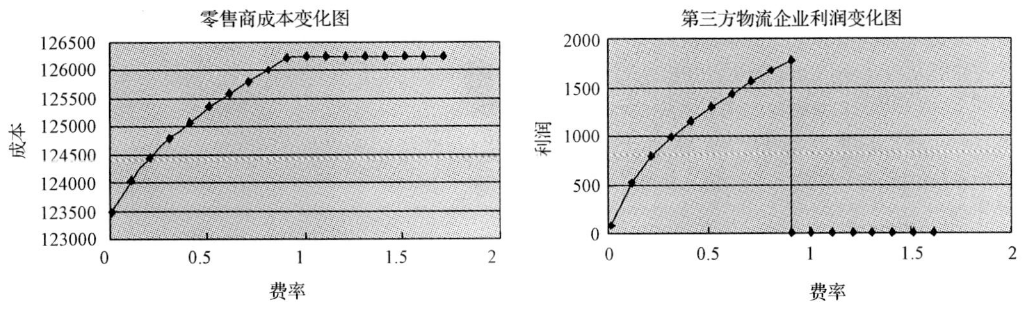

图 3　算例 2 中费率对零售商成本和第三方物流企业利润的影响情况的分析图

4 结束语

在以往的研究中，针对解决企业资金短缺问题，有一些文章研究了存货质押融资服务的运作模式等，但是缺乏对该服务的定量研究；对延迟支付方式的研究虽然较多，但是大多从优化零售商采购的角度出发，很少考虑到供应链上的其他企业。本文围绕解决企业资金短缺问题，首次将延迟支付方式与存货质押融资服务结合起来研究，不仅给出了在现金折扣情况下的零售商行动策略，而且以此为基础，进一步给出了第三方物流企业制定存货质押融资服务费率的方法，能够为相关企业推广该业务提供理论指导。

这些研究可以在以下几个方面进行拓展：①商品损耗率不均匀的情况，比如服从指数分布等，适合于对一些特殊的商品进行分析. ②对零售商库存策略假设的改变，将其变为允许缺货等更为一般的条件。③需求函数可以进一步拓展为随购买量、价格等变化而变化的函数。

Pricing Model for Inventory Impawn Financing under Conditions of Permissible Delay in Payments

ZHU Wen-gui[1], ZHU Dao-Li[1], XU Zui[2]

(1. Management School, Fudan University, Shanghai 200433, China; 2 Transport & Communications School, Shangghai Maritime University, Shanhai 200135, China)

Abstract: This paper studies the pricing model for inventory impawn financing by third part logistics provider when supplier permits the retailer delayed payments. It formulates the pricing method based on the retailer's policy analysis.

Key words: delay in payments; inventory impawn financing; pricing

参考文献

[1] 徐文丽. 中小企业融资难：中国经济发展的瓶颈之一[J]. 探索与争鸣，2004，12：30-31.

Xu WenIi. it is difficuit to finance for medium and small enterprises; A bottieneck in the deveIopm of chinese economy[J]. Expioration and Free Views, 2004, 12: 30-31.

[2] Goyal S K. Economic order quantity under conditions of permissible delay in payments[J]. The Journail of the Operational Research Society, 1985, 36(4): 335-338.

[3] Aggarwal S P, Jaggi C K. Ordering polictes of deteriorting items under permissibie delay in payments [J]. The Journal of the Operational Research Society, 1995, 46(5): 558-662.

[4] Chung K J. A theorem on the determnation of economic order quantity under conditions of permissble delay in payment[J]. Computers and Operations Research, 1998, 25(1): 49-52.

[5] Chu P, Chung KJ, Lan S P. Economic order quantity of deteriorating items under permissible delay in payments[J]. Computers and Operations Research, 1998, 25(10): 817-824.

[6] Ouyang L Y, Wu C C, Chuang K W. Economic order quantity with partial backorders under supplier credit[J]. Journal of Information & Optimization Sciences, 2003, 24: 255-267.

[7] Chang C T. Extended economic order quantity model under cash discount and payment delay[J]. International Journal of Information and Management Sciences, 2002, 13(3): 57-69.

[8] Hwang H, Shinn S W. Retailer's pricing and lot sizing policy for exponentially deteriorating products under the condition of permissible delay in payments[J]. Computers and Operations Research, 1997, 24(6): 539-547.

[9] Sarker B R, Jamal A M M, Wang SJ . Optimal payment time under permissible delay in payment for products with deterioration[J]. Production Planning & Control, 2000, 11(4): 380-390.

[10] Salameh M K, Abboud N E, El-Kassar A N, et al. Continuous review inventory model with delay in payments[J]. International Journal of Production Economics, 2003, 85(1): 91-95.

[11] Arcelus F J, Srinivasan G. Delay of payments for extraordinary purchases[J]. The Journal of the Operational Research Society, 1993, 44(8): 785-795.

[12] Chang C T, OuyangL Y, Teng, Jinn Tsair. An EOQ model for deteriorating items under supplier credits linked to ordering quantity[J]. Applied Mathematical Modelling, 2003, 27(12): 983-996.

[13] 罗齐，朱道立，陈伯铭. 第三方物流服务创新：融通仓及其运作模式初探[J]. 中国流通经济，2002，2：11-14.

Luo Qi, Zhu Daoli, Chen Boming. A third party logistics service innovation: financing warehouse and its operation model[J]. China Business and Market, 2002, 2: 11-14.

[14] 于洋，冯耕中. 物资银行业务运作模式及风险控制研究[J]. 管理评论，2003，15(9)：45-50.

Yu Yang, Feng Gengzhong. The study on material bank operation model and risk control[J]. Management Review, 2003, 15(9): 45-50.

ZHU Dao2li1, XU Zui2200433, China ; 21Transport & Communications School, Shanghai Maritime

（本文发表于《系统工程理论与实践》2007 年第 12 期）

资金约束供应链中物流提供商的系统价值研究*

陈祥锋，朱道立
（复旦大学管理学院，上海 200433）

摘要：根据第三方物流企业在供应链运营中所发挥的不同角色，把具有资金约束供应链分为三种类型的系统结构：传统结构，代理结构和控制结构。分析了三种结构下相关企业的金融和运营决策问题。分析结果表明：1)由于信息不对称，在传统结构中，融资服务不能为资金约束供应链创造价值，然而在代理结构和控制结构中，融资服务以及第三方物流企业的运作将为资金约束供应链创造新的价值；2)在第三方物流企业三种类型的角色中，控制角色是资金不足供应链中最优的角色.

关键词：供应链；第三方物流；资金约束；融资服务

中图分类号：F253.2；F253.9；F830.56　　**文献标识码：**A　　**文章编号：**100-5781(2008)06-06-08

0　引言

供应链管理强调的是物料流、信息流和资金流的协调和管理，然而绝大多数供应链管理的文献仅关注供应链中物料流和信息流的协调和管理．例如，Graves 等[1]和 Simchi-Levi 等[2]汇集大量的供应链研究文献，这些文献研究了供应链的生产计划/库存决策，产能决策，以及供应链绩效等，却忽略了资金流对供应链决策的影响．显然，在供应链管理中，忽略考虑资金流对运营决策的影响，所获得的只能是次优的决策[3]．**

本文把包含资金约束企业所组成的供应链称之为资金约束供应链．在资金约束供应链中，企业由于受到资金限制，可能无法实现其最优的运营决策，这将会影响到供应链各企业及整体的效益．然而，如资金不足企业能够获得融资服务，并实现，其最优的运营决策，那么融资服务可能为资金不足供应链创造新的价值．

当前，国内关于解决供应链资金约束问题的实践非常活跃．例如，出现了物流金融，融通仓，仓单质押等相关的业务创新．这些业务的本质是基于物流和金融的集成服务——金

* 收稿日期：2008-06-02；修订日期：2008-09-15.

基金项目：国家自然科学基金青年基金资助项目(70502008；70872012)；教育部人文社会科学一般项目青年基金资助项目(05JC630068)国家自然科学基金重点资助项目(70432001)；上海市重点学科建设资助项目(B210).

** 作者简介：陈祥锋(1973 —)，男，福建泉州人，博士，讲师，研究方向：供应链合同、金融和运营交叉，E-mail：chenxf@fudan.edu.cn；朱道立(1945 —)，男，上海人，博士，教授，博士导师，研究方向：管理科学.

融物流，其理论基础主要体现为第三方物流(3PL)企业贯穿供应链的采购、生产、和销售阶段，对供应链企业的运行信息和信用信息了解最多，因而可以协助金融机构监控供应链中借款企业的运营情况，从而降低金融机构所提供融资服务的信用风险.

国内外关于物流金融领域的理论研究比较活跃. 例如，艾东[4]就银行角度分析了中小企业物流金融服务中的风险管理问题；陈祥锋等[5]结合融通仓的实践讨论了物流金融的定义以及相关系统思想；杨宇等[6]就共生理论和价值链理论分析了物流金融的价值；胡愈等[7]综述分析了物流金融相关的运作问题；李齐[8]发展了物流金融的概念，比较分析了我国供应链融资方案相关模式和问题；李毅学[9]等研究了仓单质押贷款中质押率的决策问题. 尽管近年来国内关于物流金融研究的文献发展较快，但是更多是定性方面的研究.

在国际上，关于物流金融的研究较少，相关的文献更多是集中在抵押贷款方面，例如，Buraschi 等[10]。分析了抵押贷款中抵押物品的价值变化和流动风险；Christa[11]研究了在过渡经济学中银行竞争能力和抵押物规模之间的关系. 总之，就已有的国内外研究文献而言，很少有从理论模型上对这种物流和金融的集成服务进行系统的理论解释.

本文的目的是从理论上探索 3PL 企业在资金约束供应链的作用，分析 3PL 企业在供应链扮演不同的角色及如何影响供应链相关企业的决策和价值. 基于此，从理论上详细分析物流金融的相关的决策和价值研究，并从理论上探讨物流金融最有效率的运营模式或者 3PL 企业在资金约束供应链中最有效的角色.

1　资金约束供应链的三种系统结构

随着经济发展和竞争的加剧，3PL 企业在供应链扮演的角色会越来越丰富. 甚至，在资金约束供应链中，3PL 企业可以被认为是供应链企业中的成员之一，其运作的效率和提供服务可能会影响到供应链的竞争能力. 为深人了解 3PL 企业对资金约束供应链价值的影响，本文根据 3PL 企业在资金不足供应链中所提供不同服务，尝试性地把供应链系统分为三种模式：传统模式(con-Vention、代理模式(delegation model)和控制模式(control mode1). 与此相对应，3PL 企业在资金约束供应链所扮演的角色分别表示为传统角色，代理角色和控制角色.

1.1　传统模式

在传统模式中，参与者有供应商，零售商，3PL 企业和银行. 零售商为资金不足的企业，可能到融资市场寻求银行的贷款服务. 3PL 企业所提供的激励仅仅是物流提供商的激励，即为供应链中的企业提供专业的物流服务，使得供应链的企业可以专注于自身的核心业务. 传统模式见图 1.

1.2　代理模式

在代理模式中，参与者与传统结构相同. 资金不足的零售商企业往往会求助于银行以获得贷款服务. 然而银行由于担心企业的信用风险较大，可能不愿意提供贷款服务. 这可能会影响供应链的效益. 由于 3PL 企业往往参与供应链的整个过程，包括采购、生产和销售等过程，对供应链各相关企业的运营状况了解较深. 如果 3PL 企业与银行结成联盟，可以在一定程度上帮助银行监控借款企业的实际运营情况和质押物的动态等，这在一定的程度上可能降低借款企业的信用风险，从而使得银行可能愿意为资金不足的供应链提供商业贷款. 代理模式见图 2.

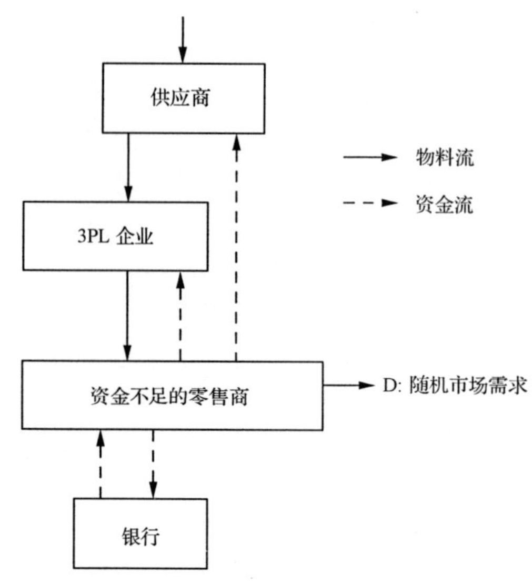

图 1　资金约束供应链系统的传统模式图

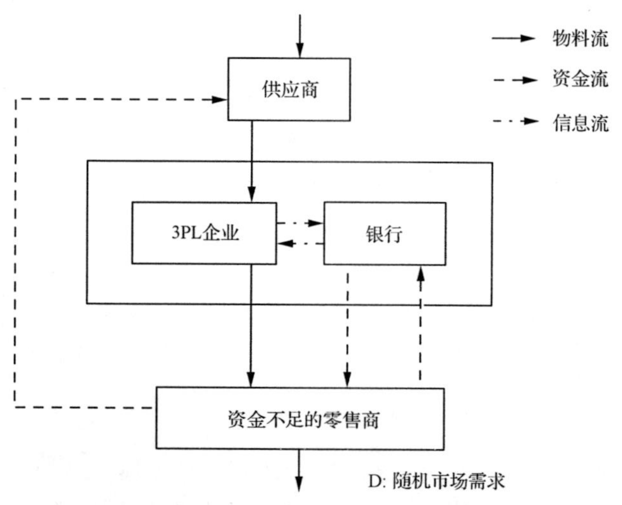

图 2　资金约束供应链系统的代理模式图

在代理模式中，3PL 在资金不足的供应链中将提供两种不同的激励：其一，是物流提供商的激励；其二是金融服务商的激励（其可以协助金融机构监控和监管借款企业，激励金融机构为供应链中资金不足企业提供融资服务）.

1.3　控制模式

在控制模式中，参与者主要是供应商、资金不足的零售商，和 3PL 企业. 由于 3PL 企业拥有自身独特优势，可以了解和掌握供应链整个环节的信息，以及各相关企业的运营实际，在一定情况下，3PL 企业甚至可以在资金不足的供应链中起到主导的作用，扮演着控制角色. 在实践中也存在着这样的情况. 例如，有些较大物流企业利用自身优势，替代资金不足的零售商进行较大规模的采购，然后再根据具体需要分销给资金不足的零售商，并且愿意为资金不足的零售商提供延迟支付信用合同.在这个机制下,具有控制角色的3PL企业将体现出三个方面的激励:其一,是传统物流提供商的激励;其二,是金融机构的激励;第三,是供应商的激励.控制模式见图3.

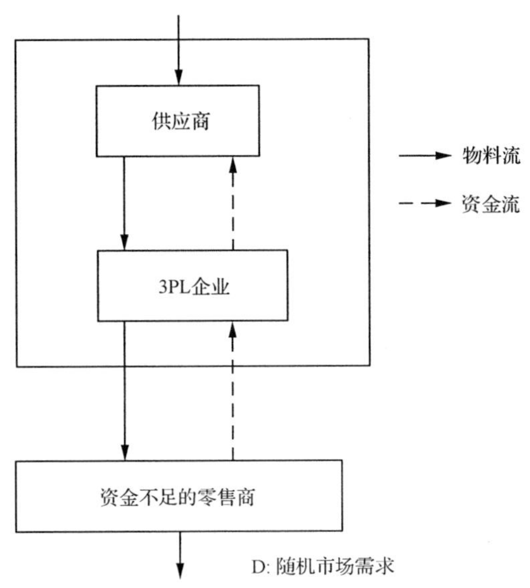

图3　资金约束供应链系统的控制模式图

2　资金约束供应链模型描述与假设

假设,资金约束供应链系统中所有的参与者都是风险中性的投资者,并且产品市场的实际需求 D 是随机的,且符合增加失败率分布(IFRD) 特性[12,13] 并且密度函数为 $f(D)$ 分布函数为 $F(D)$.另外,$\overline{F}(D) = 1 - F(D)$.

2.1　商业银行的利率决策模型与假设

假设商业银行存在于竞争的金融市场,并具有足量的资金提供贷款服务,银行提供商业贷款的利率为 r.在期初 $t=0$ 时,银行对初始资金为B的零售商提供贷款合同 $r(B)$,贷款规模为 $L(B)$;当 $t=T$ 时,零售商产生一个随机收益 $\tau = \mathrm{pmin}(D,Q)$,其中 p 为零售价格,Q 为采购量.由此可知,银行的收益为 $\min[\tau, L(B)(1+\tau(B))]$.

由于银行是风险中性的,其对风险是无差异的,因此,在竞争的金融市场中,银行提供贷款的期望收益将等于其无风险收益.于是,银行的收益以及利率决策可以通过式(1)表示.

$$\prod{}^{\mathrm{B}} = E\{\min[\tau, L(B)(1+r(b))]\} = L(B) \qquad (1)$$

2.2　零售商的最优订货决策模型与假设

假设零售商是资金不足的,并且是有限责任制的,其初始资金为 B.采购产品的批发价格为 w_{p},物流服务的价格为 w_{1},零售价格 p 为1.在销售周期开始时($t=0$),$B < wQ$,$w = w_{\mathrm{p}} + w_{1}$.零售商可以从竞争的金融市场获得商业贷款 $L(B) = (wQ - B)^{+}$,并且贷款的利率为 r.在销售周期结束时($t=T$),零售商的销售收入 τ 得到实现,由上面可知 τ 是

随机变量，且受市场需求 D 和零售商的采购量 Q 影响. 因为，零售商是有限责任制的企业，当销售收入 τ 大于贷款的本金和利息 $(1+r)(wQ-B)^{+}$，零售商将支付商业贷款的本金和利息，否则全部的销售收入归债权人所有. 于是给定销售合同 (w) 和贷款合同 (r)，零售商的最优化问题为

$$\Pi^{\mathrm{R}} = \max_{Q\geqslant 0} E[\min(D,Q) - (wQ-B).(1+r))^{+} - B] \tag{2}$$

2.3 供应商和 3PL 企业的收益模型与假设

假设供应商是被动的角色，其通过提供批发价合同销售产品，且销售收入依靠零售商的订货数量. 所以供应商的收益可以表示为

$$\Pi^{\mathrm{S}} = (w_{\mathrm{p}} - c)Q \tag{3}$$

其中，c 为供应商的生产成本.

在传统和代理模式中，假设 3PL 企业的销售收入是以提供的物流服务而获得的收益. 令 Π_{T}^{1}，Π_{D}^{1} 和 Π_{C}^{1} 分别表示传统、代理和控制供应链模式下 3PL 的收益。

假设 Q_{T}、$Q_{\mathrm{D}}Q_{c}$ 和为传统、代理和控制模式下零售商的最优采购量，c′为 3PL 企业提供物流服务的单位成本，于是 3PL 的收益可以表示为

$$\Pi_{\mathrm{T}}^{1} = (w_{1} - c')Q_{\mathrm{T}} \tag{4}$$

$$\Pi_{\mathrm{D}}^{1} = (w_{1} - c')Q_{\mathrm{D}} \tag{5}$$

在控制结构中，假设 3PL 可以向资金不足的零售商提供延迟支付的信用合同，于是，3PL 企业的收益可以表示为

$$\Pi_{\mathrm{C}}^{1} = B + E(\min(\min(D,Q_{C}),(wQ_{c} - B))) - (c' + w_{\mathrm{p}})Q_{\mathrm{C}} \tag{6}$$

3 物流提供商的系统价值分析

假设银行是根据企业的初始资产 B 来评判零售商的信用风险的，银行对企业的具体初始资产和经营睛况的信息是不对称的[14]. 另外，还假设，3PL 物流企业由于贯穿整个供应链的采购、生产和销售过程，其对零售商的运营状况的信息(例如，采购多少物品，以及具体的销售情况，等等)是对称的。

3.1 物流提供商对资金约束供应链传统模式系统的价值影响

在传统模式下的供应链，3PL 企业仅是提供物流服务，其收益是随着零售商的订货量 Q_{T} 的增加而增加的。同样的，供应商的角色也是被动的，其收益同样受 Q_{T} 影响。所以，在传统模式下的供应链，重点讨论零售商与银行之间的博弈问题。

根据假设，银行可以根据企业的资产评定企业的信用，例如零售商的初始资产 B 较大，则表示其信用水平较好，信用风险较低，银行将提供利率较低的商业贷款。然而，银行与零售商之间存在着信息不对称，因而零售商有激励向银行提供虚假的信息。下面的命题 1 将对此问题进行描述。

命题 1　在传统模式的供应链中，当银行与零售商之间存在着运营信息不对称时，给定贷款合同 $r(B)$，资金不足的零售商(初始资金为 $B \leqslant wQ^{\mathrm{N}}$，其中 $Q^{\mathrm{N}} = \overline{F}^{-1}(w)$) 有激励去夸大其初始资金为 $\widetilde{B} \geqslant B$，以获得更低利率的贷款.

证明　假设资金不足的零售商的初始资金额为 B。如果该零售商向银行夸大其初始

资金为 $\tilde{B} > B$，该零售商将获得贷款合同 $r(\tilde{B})$. 由式(2)，可以求得 $d\Pi^{R}/d\tilde{B} > 0$ 这说明零售商夸大其初始资金将会获得更大的收益，所以原命题得证。

证毕

根据命题 1，由于在传统模式的供应链中，零售商总是有激励去夸大自身的初始资金以获得更多的收益，而这个收益是在银行增加损失的基础上获得的。由于银行处于竞争的金融市场，其商业贷款的最终期望收益为零，但是这个结论是基于对称信息而获得的。但是，在信息不对称环境中，由于零售商有激励夸大其初始资金，会导致银行得到负的期望收益。因此，作为理性的银行，将会退出融资市场。由此可见，在传统模式中，由于信息不对称，资金不足的企业不能从竞争的金融市场获得融资服务。

命题 2 在传统模式的供应链中，当银行与零售商之间存在着运营信息不对称时，银行将会拒绝向资金不足零售商提供融资服务，零售商的最优订货量为 Q_{T}^{*} 并且 $Q_{T}^{*} = \min\left(\frac{B}{w}, Q^{N}\right)$.

证明 在传统模式的供应链中，零售商的最优化问题可以表述如下。

$$\Pi_{T}^{R} = \max_{Q_{T}}\left(\int_{0}^{Q} Df(D)dD + \int_{Q}^{\infty} Qf(D)dD - wQ\right) \tag{7}$$

$$S.t. \quad 0 \leqslant wQ \leqslant B \tag{8}$$

由式(7)可知，在传统模式下，零售商的最优问题相当于传统报童模型下的优化问题，求解式(7)，可得 $Q_{N} = \overline{F}^{-1}(w)$. 由于零售商是具有资金限制的，因此，由式(7)和式(8)，可得 $Q_{T}^{*} = \min\left(\frac{B}{w}, Q^{N}\right)$ 证毕。

命题 2 说明，资金约束将可能影响供应链的收益。当 $B < wQ^{N}$，零售商的最优订货量只能是 B/w，而不能实现传统报童模型的最优订货量 Q^{N}。

3.2 物流提供商对资金约束供应链代理模式系统的价值影响

在代理模式的供应链中，银行和 3PL 企业是联盟的关系。作为伙伴关系，银行和 3PL 企业将会共享零售商的运营信息。尽管银行还是提供商业贷款合同 $r(B)$，但从 3PL 企业中，银行可以获得零售商实际支付货款 wQ_{D}。的信息，因而可以判断零售商提供的信用信息是否真实。所以，在代理模式的供应链中，零售商实际没有机会说谎。如果零售商说谎，银行可以根据 3PL 提供的信息及时调整贷款规模，使得零售商收益更少。

命题 3 在代理模式的供应链中，当银行与零售商之间存在着运营信息的不对称时，零售商愿意如实向银行提供信息，银行愿意向零售商提供融资服务。

命题 3 的证明与命题 1 证明相似，所以省略。由命题 3 可知，在代理模式的供应链下，由于 3PL 企业与银行的联盟，使得原有银行与零售商之间的信息不对称问题变成信息对称的问题，因而，银行有激励为资金不足的零售商提供融资服务，以解决供应链资金不足的问题。

下面给出引理 1，用于证明关于代理结构中零售商和银行决策问题的命题 4。

引理 1 给定 $r_{f} \geqslant 0, y > 0$，对于任意随机变量 $X \geqslant 0$，当且仅当 $E(X) \geqslant y(1+r_{f})$ 时，总存在一个唯一的实数 $r > r_{f}$，使得 $y(1+r_{f}) = E(\min(X, y(1+r)))$。

证明 首先证明，当 $E(X) \geqslant y(1+r_f)$ 时，存在一个实数 $r > r_f$ 使得 $y = \mathrm{E}(\min(X, y(1+r)))$。当 $r \in (r_f, +\infty)$，定义

$$G(r) = E(\min)(X, y(1+r))) - y(1+r_f)$$

可得

$$\begin{aligned} G(r_f) &= E(\min(X, y(1+r))) - y(1+r_f) \\ &\leqslant \min(E(X)), y(1+r_f)) - y(1+r_f) \end{aligned} \tag{9}$$

$$G(+\infty) = E(\min(X, Y(1+\infty))) - y \geqslant E(X) - y(1+r_f) \tag{10}$$

由 $E(X) \geqslant y(1+r_f)$，得 $G(r_f) \leqslant 0, G(+\infty) > 0$，故 $G(r_f)G(+\infty) \leqslant 0$。

再根据 $G(r_f)$ 的连续性知，至少存在一点 $r \in (r_f +\infty)$，满足 $G(r) = 0$。

其次，证明当 $E(x) < y(1+r_f)$，不存在 $r > r_f$ 满足 $y(1+r_f) = \mathrm{E}(\min(X, y(1+r)))$。根据 Jensen 不等式，得

$$\begin{aligned} \mathrm{E}(\min(X, y(1+r))) &\leqslant \min(\mathrm{E}(x), y(1+r)) \\ &< Y(1+r_f) \end{aligned}$$

由此可得，当 $\mathrm{E}(X) \geqslant Y(1+r_f)$ 条件成立时，至少存在一个 $r > r_f$ 满足 $y(1+r_f) = \mathrm{E}(\min(X, y(1+r)))$。

令 $\Phi(r) = \mathrm{E}(\min\tau y(GY(1+r))) - y$ 可得 $\frac{\mathrm{d}\Phi(r)}{\mathrm{d}r} = \int_{y(1+r)}^{\infty} yf(\tau)\mathrm{d}\tau > 0$ 即 $\Phi(r)$ 是关于 r 的单调增函数. 所以，存在唯一解 $\mathrm{r}^* > 0$ 满足

$$\mathrm{E}(\min(\tau, (wQ - b)(1+r))) = (wQ - B)$$

证毕。

命题 4 在代理结构的供应链中，零售商最优的订货量 $Q_D^* = Q_N$，银行的最优利率为 $r^* > 0$，并且 r^* 是方程 $\mathrm{E}(\min(\tau, (wQ - B)(1+r))) = (wQ - B)$ 的唯一解。

证明 由式(1)和式(2)可得，代理结构下零售商的最优化问题

$$\Pi_D^R = \min_{Q_D \geqslant 0} \mathrm{E}((\min(D, Q) - L(B)(1+r)) - B) \tag{11}$$

$$\text{s.t} \quad E(min)(\tau, L(B)(1+r(B))) = L(B) \tag{12}$$

$$L(B) = (wQ - B)^+ \tag{13}$$

把式(10)，式(11)代人式(9)可得零售商的优化问题如下。

$$\Pi_D^R = \min\left(\int_0^Q Df(D)\mathrm{d}D + \int_Q^{\infty} Qf(D)\mathrm{d}D - wQ + B\right) \tag{14}$$

显然式(14)的最优化问题与式(7)一致，因而 $Q_D^* = Q^N$

根据引理 1，令 $r_f = 0, X = \tau, y = (wQ - B)$，可以容易得到存在着唯一的 $r^* > 0$ 满足方程 $\mathrm{E}(\min(\tau, (wQ - B)(1+r))) = (wQ - B)$。 证毕。

由命题 2 和 4 可知，在代理模式下，零售商的最优订货量总是大于传统模式下的最优订货量，即 $Q^*\mathrm{D} \geqslant Q_T^*$。根据式(3)～(6) 可知，在代理模式下，供应商和 3PL 企业的收

益。总是大于传统模式下的收益。

显然，命题 2 和 4 的结论就是当前金融物流实践的理论基础。在传统的模式下，由于信息不对称，银行不愿意为资金不足的零售商提供融资服务。然而，在代理模式下，即便是银行与零售商之间存在信息不对称，由于存在与 3PL 企业的联盟激励，银行愿意为资金不足的零售商提供融资服务，从而为资金不足的供应链创造了价值，并使得所有参与者的收益得到了增加。

3.3　物流提供商对资金约束供应链控制模式系统的价值影响

在控制模式下，3PL 企业的角色是主动的，其将替代资金不足的零售商进行采购，然后再把所采购产品提供给零售商。在控制模式下的 3PL 企业，往往是规模较大的，信誉较好的，拥有大量的资金或者可以通过融资获得金融市场的资金支持。由于 3PL 企业主营的收入来自于物流服务，而物流服务的收益又取决于零售商的采购量。当零售商处于资金不足时，有限的资金将会限制零售商的采购量，从而影响 3PL 企业的总收益。所以，3PL 可能有激励向资金不足的零售商提供延迟支付信用合同，间接为资金不足的零售商提供融资服务。此时，供应商的角色是被动的，只需考虑零售商与 3PL 企业之间的博弈问题。

在控制模式中，3PL 企业的角色是三元的，既是供应商的角色，又是 3PL 企业的角色和金融机构的角色。其不仅为资金不足的零售商提供产品服务，物流服务，还提供金融服务。于是，根据式(2)，零售商的最优化问题可以用式(15) 表述。

$$\Pi_{\mathrm{C}}^{\mathrm{R}}=\max_{Q_{\mathrm{C}}\geqslant 0}(\mathrm{E}(\min(D,Q_{\mathrm{C}})-(wQ_{\mathrm{C}}-B))^{+}-B) \tag{15}$$

尽管供应商提供的延迟支付不考虑利率，但是他可根据零售商的信用水平(如初始资金 B)来调节批发价格，以弥补自己可能出现的融资损失。下面将阐述这个问题。同时，由于 3PL 企业贯穿整个供应链过程，零售商没有机会向 3PL 企业提供虚假的运营信息。

命题 5　在控制模式的供应链中，在 3PL 企业愿意为资金不足的企业提供延迟支付信用合同时，零售商的最优收益为 Q_{C}^{*}，并且，Q_{C}^{*} 是方程 $\overline{F}(Q)=w\overline{F}(wQ-B)$ 的解。

证明　根据式(15)，可得

$$\frac{\mathrm{d}\Pi_{\mathrm{C}}^{\mathrm{R}}}{\mathrm{d}Q_{\mathrm{C}}}=\overline{F}(Q_{\mathrm{C}})-w\overline{F}(wQ_{\mathrm{C}})-B \tag{16}$$

$$\frac{\mathrm{d}^2\Pi_{\mathrm{C}}^{\mathrm{R}}}{\mathrm{d}Q_{\mathrm{C}}^2}=-w\overline{F}(wQ_{\mathrm{C}}-B)(h(Q_{\mathrm{C}}))-wh(wQ_{\mathrm{C}}-B) \tag{17}$$

当需求满足前面的假设时，容易证明 $\Pi_{\mathrm{C}}^{\mathrm{R}}$ 是关于 Q_{C} 的凹函数，并且一阶条件成立，由式(16)可以求得 Q_{C}^{*}　　证毕。

在控制模式下，3PL 企业与资金不够的零售商分享市场风险，使得零售商在控制模式下的边际成本乱，$w\overline{F}(wQ-B)$ 小于代理模式下的边际成本 w，因而零售商有激励采购更多的产品以较充分利用市场的需求情况，从而也增加了整个供应链的收益。

命题 6　如果在控制模式下零售商接受的批发价格，与代理模式下的批发价格相等，资金不足零售商最优采购量 Q_{C}^{*} 将大于代理模式下的最优采购量 Q_{D}^{*}。并且零售商的总收益 $\Pi_{\mathrm{C}}^{\mathrm{R}}$ 也大于代理模式下的总收益 $\Pi_{\mathrm{D}}^{\mathrm{R}}$。(证明略)

在控制模式中，由于 3PL 企业愿意与资金不足的零售业分担市场风险，激励零售商增加订货量,从而增加了资金约束供应链的整体收益。

4 关于物流提供商在资金约束供应链系统中的作用与分析

3PL 企业在不同的供应链模式扮演了不同的角色,而不同的角色将会对供应链产生不同的效果,特别是对那些资金不足的供应链而言。

在传统模式的供应链中,3PL 企业仅仅是传统的物流服务提供商。此时,它的作用是非常有限的,并且是被动的,并不能给资金不足的供应链创造新的价值。

在代理模式的供应链中,3PL 企业与金融机构结成联盟,进行优势互补,共享供应链的信息。这个联盟可以为资金不足的供应链提供物流和金融集成的服务,可以解决供应链资金不足的问题,从而激励零售商实现其本身的最优采购量。显然,在代理模式中,3PL 企业可以为资金约束供应链创造新的价值。同时,在代理模式中,3PL 企业的角色是二元的,既是传统的物流服务提供商,又是金融服务的提供商。

在控制模式中,3PL 企业的角色就变得更加复杂,它将包含三个方面的角色,即扮演传统物流提供商的角色,又扮演金融提供商的角色,同时还扮演了产品供应商的角色。由于 3PL 企业在控制模式的供应链中,扮演了丰富角色,不仅解决了零售商资金不足的问题,又确保了供应链产品的供应问题,这将大大增强零售商的采购热情,使得供应链之间的协作和协调问题更加紧密。因此,在控制模式中,3PL 企业也可能为供应链创造新的价值。

那么,究竟是代理角色还是控制角色才是 3PL 企业在资金不足的供应链中的最优角色?

在代理模式中,金融机构仅仅是关心自身的投资收益或者资金安全,并没有提供一种机制与资金不足的零售商共享市场的风险。在这类的融资服务中,由于零售商的市场风险并没有得到降低,因而并没有对供应链传统的问题"双边际效应(double marginalization efect)"产生任何的影响,此时的供应链仍旧是没有效率的[15]。根据命题 4,融资服务可以解决供应链中的资金不足问题,创造新的价值,但是供应链最高的收益永远不会超过传统报童模型下的最高收益。

在控制模式中,3PL 企业获得收益可能是多方面的,例如供应商收益(向供应商批量采购可能获得价格折扣优惠,然后再代售给零售商可获得一定的收益)、物流服务提供商收益(向供应链提供物流服务而获得的收益)和金融服务收益(由于 3PL 企业提供融资服务有一定的风险,它将收取一定的风险费用。在控制模式中,这种风险收益可以通过提高批发价 w 来实现)等等。由此可见,在控制模式中,信用合同可以为 3PL 企业提供一种与零售商共享市场风险的机制,从而在一定程度上降低零售商的市场风险,于是可能激励零售商实现超过传统报童模型的最优订货量。这将降低供应链"双边际效应"的影响,部分地协调了供应链。因而,3PL 企业的控制角色将是资金约束供应链的最优角色。

当前,资金不足成为了很多企业的发展瓶颈,物流金融作为一种创新的融资服务已经得到了业界很大的重视。相关的物流金融运作模式不断地创新。在这些创新中,一些企业甚至应用到了本文讨论的第三方物流最优角色——控制角色。例如,国内某著名的第三方物流提供商为资金不足的中小企业提供了化工原料的替代采购和物流服务,在整个供应链中发挥了控制的角色。同样，国内某上市的第三方物流公司为一些IT相关的生产企业提供了国际替代采购和全程物流服务，不仅解决部分企业资金不足的困境，而且大大提高了企业所在供应链的效率和竞争能力。

5 结束语

在实践中，金融物流已成为当前物流行业一个新的竞争热点。然而，无论是学者还是实践者很多人都没能对金融物流业务作出较系统的理论解释。虽然，国内已有很多学者发表了相关的研究论文，但绝大多数的论文主要是从定性的角度来表述金融物流相关概念的思想和模式。这些研究并未能从严格的理论意义上进行分析。

本文应用了博弈论和信息经济学相关的理论，从模型上解释了金融物流的理论意义。结合3PL企业在资金不足的供应链发挥的不同激励，把3PL企业在资金不足供应链扮演的角色分为值。传统角色的3PL企业仅能帮助供应链管理和协调供应链中物米流和信息流之间供应和需求不区配的问题。在代理角色中，3PL企业通过与金融机构结成联盟，为资金不足的供应链提供物流和金融机构结成联盟，为资金不足的供应链提供物流和金融服务，创造了新的价值。在控制角色中，3PL企业代替供应商销售产品(或替代零售商采购产品)，并为资金不足供应链提从物流和金融的服务，创造了新的更大的供应链的价值。模型结果显示，3PL企业的控制角色是资金约束供应链的最优角色。

本文的结果表明，在代理模式的控制模式中，3PL企业可以真正帮助供应链，管理和协调物料流，资金流和信息流之间供应和需求不匹配的问题。

System value of 3PL to the supply chain with capital constraints

CHEN Xiang-feng, ZHU Dao-li

(School of Management, Fudan University, Shanghai 200433, China)

Abstract: Based on The different roIes of 3PL (third party Iogistics) firms in a capital-constrained suppiy chain, this paper dividis the structures of suppIy chain into three different fypes: convention model, deIegation model, and control model, and investigates the operational and financial decisions of firms under the rsuppIy chain with different type. The paper shows that the financing serv-ice can not create vaIue for the capital-constrained suppIy chain under convention model with the asymmetric infofmation, whiIe financing service with the support from 3PL firm in both deIegation and control models could create value for the supply chain with capital constraints. Furthemore, the paper shows that the roie of control mode for the 3PL firm is the optimal roie in the capital-constrain-ed suppiy chain , compared with the other two roles.

Key words: supoly chain management; 3PL(third party Iogistics); capital constraints; financing service

参考文献

[1] Graves S, ed Kok T. Handbooks in Operations Research and Management Science: SuppIy Chain Management[M]. Morth-Holland: EIsevier, 2003.

[2] Simchi-Levi D, Wu S D, Shen Z. Handbook of Quantitative SuppIy Chain Anaiysis: ModeIing in the Business Era[M]. New York: KIuwer Academic PubIisher, 2004.

[3] Chen X F, Wan G. The Impact of Financial Services on a Budget-constrained SuppIy Chain under WhoIesaIe Contract[R]. Shanghai: Fudan University, 2008.

[4] 艾东. 中小企业物流融资风险管理探讨[J]. 经济研究参考, 2005, 6(68): 11-14.

[5] 陈祥锋, 石代伦, 朱道立. 融通仓与金融物流创新[J]科技导报, 2005, 23(9)44-48.

[6] 杨宇, 聂娜, 周晶. 基于共生理论的物流金融价值增值作用分析[J]. 东南大学学报, 2007, 37(11): 249-252.

[7] 胡愈, 柳恩维. 物流金融及其运作问题讨论综述[J]. 经济理论与经济管理, 2008, (2): 75-79.

[8] 李齐. 我国供应链融资方案的比较与思考[J]. 现代经济, 2008, 7(3): 1-3.

[9] 李毅学, 冯耕中, 徐渝. 价格随机波动下存货质押融资业务质押率研究[J]. 系统工程理论与实践, 2007, 27(12): 42-49.

[10] Buraschi D M. Liquidity risk and speciaIness[J]. Journal of Financial Economics, 2002, 64(2): 243-284.

[11] Christa H. Bank competition and credit markets in transition economics [J]. Jounal of Comparative Economics, 2003, 31(2): 223-245.

[12] Cachon P G. SuppIy chain coordination with contracts[A]. In: Handbooks IN Operations Research and Management Scievce: SuppIy Chain Management[M]. Edited by: Graves S, Kok de T. North-Holland: EIsevier, 2003.

[13] Lariviere M A. A note on probabiIity distributions with increasing generaIized faiIure rates [J]. Operations Research, 2006, 54(10): 602-604.

[14] 陈祥锋, 朱道立, 应雯琚. 资金约束与供应链融资和运营决策研究[J]管理科学学报, 2008, 11(3): 70-78.

[15] Spengier J. Vertical integration and antitrust poIicy[J]. Journal of PoIitical Economy, 1950, 58(4): 357-352.

(本文发表于《系统工程学报》, 2008 年第 6 期)

物流企业在存货质押融资中的决策问题研究*

马中华　朱道立
（复旦大学管理学院，上海 200433）

摘要：物流企业在存货质押融资业务中帮助银行实现了质押商品的有效监管，文中主要考察物流企业的决策问题，分别给出了在银行增大融资利率，以及企业投资风险大的项目时，物流企业通过调整其监管决策来保持期望收益不减的相关理论结果。并通过比较物流企业提供监管服务与银行采取激励机制两种情况下银行在存货质押融资业务中的收益，证明了只有当物流企业提供的监管满足一定条件时，才能够获得参与存货质押融资业务的机会。

关键词：存货质押融资，物流决策，投资激励，融资收益

中图分类号：F830.56，F253.9

0　引言

存货质押融资指企业将库存产品作为担保向银行出质，同时将质物转交给具有合法保管动产资格的物流企业监管，以获得融资的业务。物流企业利用行业特点，帮助银行实现对企业有效监管，在融资模式中具有重要的地位[1]。如果将贷款资金视为商品，通过物流企业，银行和企业间建立了一种与供应链中节点企业间相类似的商品供求关系。在供应链管理中，对多方竞争以及决策相互影响问题的研究已有大量成果[2][3][4]。随着供应链结构日益复杂，委托代理问题也已引起关注[5][6]。本文考察物流企业监管决策等问题：第二部分给出不同情形下物流企业决策模型；第三部分给出投资激励的决策模型；第四部分总结。**

1　物流企业的决策模型

假设在贷款周期初，企业将数量为 u_0，价格为 v_0 的商品质押给银行，并交由物流企业监管，企业支付的物流费用为 l；贷款数量为 B，融资利率为 r，银行支付给物流企业监管费用 m；设贷款周期长为 $T=1$，在贷款周期末，质押商品价格为 v，由市场决定，随机波动，分布函数为 $F(v)$，密度函数为 $f(v)$；企业在周期末应偿还贷款本息 $B(1+r)$，银行

* 基金项目：加家自然科学基金资助项目(70432001)；中国博士后科学基金(20080430610)

** 作者简介：马中华(1979－)，女，辽宁西丰人，博士后，研究方向：金融物流，Email：mazhonghua@fudan.edu.cn；朱道立(1946－)，男，上海人，教授，博士生导师，研究方向：管理科学、运筹学。

资金成本 $B(1+r_0)$，r_0 为存款利率；企业将贷款投资于短期项目，项目收益率为 $r+\theta,\theta\geqslant 0$；设项目失败概率和收益相关，为 $\mu(\theta,r)$，满足 $0\leqslant\mu(\theta,r)\leqslant 1,\mu'_\theta(\theta,r)>0,\mu'_r(\theta,r)>0$。在贷款周期末，如果投资项目成功，则企业收回 $B(1+r+\theta)$。如果项目失败，设借款企业收回资本为 τB，其中 $\tau\geqslant 0$ 为投资残值率，一般 $0\leqslant\tau\leqslant 1$，即投资失败时只能收回部分投资。

假设只当项目失败，并质押商品价格降到贷款本息之下时，企业违约，记违约概率 P，

$$P=\mu(\theta,r)p,\tag{1}$$

其中，p 为贷款周期末，满足 $p=p(u_0v\leqslant B(1+r))=F\left(\frac{B(1+r)}{u_0}\right)$。

企业不违约，银行收益 $B(r-_{r_0})$；企业违约，银行收益 $u_0v-b(1+r0)$，有期望收益 F

$$F=(1-P)B(r-r_0)+P\left(u_0\int vf(v)dv-B(1+r_0)\right)-m\tag{2}$$

物流企业在企业违约时损失 a_0。假设监管程度为 e，参照文[7]中努力程度成本函数，

$$\phi(e)=z\text{In}(1-e),0\leqslant e\leqslant 1,\tag{3}$$

其中，z 是一个给定的负数。这里 $\phi(0)=0$，即不付出努力时，成本为 0。$\phi(1)=+\infty$，即努力为 1 时，成本无穷大。由 $\phi'(e)=\frac{-z}{1-e}>0$，及 $\phi''(e)=\frac{-z}{(1-e)^2}>0$，可见边际成本递增。分别考虑企业违约及按照合约偿还贷款的情况，得物流企业期望收益 L

$$L=m+l-\phi(e)-Pa_0\tag{4}$$

企业将贷款 B 投资于收益为 $r+\theta$，失败概率为 $\mu(\theta,\mathrm{r})$ 的项目，在贷款周期末，如果企业违约，则其收益为 $B-u_0v-1$，如果企业不违约，则项目成功情况下的收益为 $B\theta-l$。假设企业不违约时的收益为 $B\theta-l$。因此，企业的期望收益 C 满足

$$C=P\left(B-u_0\int vf(v)dv\right)+(1-P)B\theta-l\tag{5}$$

在存货质押融资业务中，银行决定融资利率 r，物流企业决定监管程度 e，企业决定投资项目 θ，并且三方都是风险中性的，都以期望收益最大化为目标。

1.1 融资利率给定条件下物流企业的决策

物流企业通过提供质押商品价格信息，以便银行及时调整保证金数量[8]，降低贷款风险，因此假设贷款周期末质押商品价格小于贷款本息和概率

$$p_e=(1-e)p\tag{6}$$

由(3)式，物流企业监管不能完全消除价格波动带来的风险。由(1)式及(6)式，知 P，

$$P=\mu(\theta,r)p_e=(1-e)\mu(\theta,r)p\tag{7}$$

由(5)式企业期望收益 $C_r=(1-e)\mu(\theta,r)p\left(B-u_0\int vf(v)dv\right)+(1-(1-e)\mu(\theta,r)p)B\theta-l$。

在给定融资利率 r 条件下，监管程度 e 不是企业决策量，在 r,e 给定情况下，确定企业的最优投资决策。设 $\mu(\theta,r)=\alpha+\beta(\theta+r),\alpha\geqslant 0,\beta>0$，令 $C'_r(\theta)=0$，有

$$\tilde{\theta}\,\frac{(1-e)p\left(\beta B-\beta u_0\int vf(v)dv-\alpha B-\beta Br\right)+B}{2(1-e)\beta pB}\tag{8}$$

注意到 $C''_r(e) = -2(1-e)\beta pB < 0$，知 $\tilde{\theta}$ 使得企业的期望收益 C_r 取得最大值。

$r+\tilde{\theta}$ 为企业选择的最优投资项目收益。假设物流企业能够观察到这一信息，并将(8)作为融资企业的反应曲线，将 $\tilde{\theta}$ 带入到(7)式中，并且由(4)式有物流企业的收益为

$$L_r = l + m - z\text{In}(1-e) - \frac{a_0}{2B}(1-e)p\left(\beta B - \beta u_0\int vf(v)dv + B\alpha + \beta Br\right) - \frac{a_0}{2}。$$

令 $L'_r(e) = 0$，得

$$\tilde{e}\ \frac{2Bz}{a_0 p\left(\beta B - \beta u_0\int vf(v)dv + Ba + \beta Br\right)} + 1 \tag{9}$$

注意到 $L''_r(e) = \frac{z}{(1-e)^2} < 0$，知 $\tilde{e}$ 为给定融资利率 r 时，物流企业的最优监管程度。

结论 1：由(9)式，当银行增大融资利率 r 时，由 $\tilde{e}$ 是 r 的增函数，有物流企业的最优监管程度 $\tilde{e}$ 随之增大。如果融资利率 r 增大，则企业选择投资风险大的项目才有利可图，从而违约概率增大，物流企业增大监管程度才能保证期望收益不减，与本文理论结果相一致。

结论 2：将 $\tilde{e}$ 带入到(8)中，得企业的最优投资项目为

$$\tilde{\theta} = \frac{(2z-a_0)\left(\beta B - \beta u_0\int vf(v)dv\right) - (2z+a_0)(\alpha B + \beta Br)}{4\beta Bz} \tag{10}$$

1）当 $2z + a0 > 0$ 时，如果增大融资利率，企业会选择投资收益大的项目。因为 $z > -\frac{a_0}{2}$，由物流企业监管成本函数(3)，成本随监管程度 e 增大而增大的速度较快，从而相对减轻了对企业约束，所以企业通过投资收益大的项目来保证收益；

2）当 $2z + a_0 < 0$ 时，可以类似 1)得到相应的结论；

3）当 $2z + a_0 = 0$ 时，银行融资利率与企业的投资项目选择无关。

1.2 投资项目给定条件下物流企业的决策

给定 θ 与 e 条件下，银行选择最优融资利率使收益最大。由(7)和(2)式得期望收益

$$F_\theta(1-(1-e)\mu(\theta,r)p)B(r-r_0) + (1+e)\mu(\theta,r)p\left(u_0\int vf(v)dv - B(1+r_0)\right) - m$$

同样设 $\mu(\theta) = \alpha + \beta(r+\theta)$，$\alpha \geqslant 0$，$\beta > 0$，令 $F'_\theta(r)=0$，得

$$\tilde{r}\ \frac{B-(1-e)pB(\alpha+\beta\theta) + (1-e)\beta p\left(u_0\int vf(v)dv - B\right)}{2(1-e)\beta pB} \tag{11}$$

由 $F''_\theta(r) = -2(1-e)\beta pB < 0$，得 $\tilde{r}$ 为使得 F_θ 取得最大值的融资利率。

物流企业观察到银行的决策信息，并将(11)式作为银行的反应曲线，进而选择监管程度。注意到(7)式，由(4)式，并将 $\tilde{y}$ 带入，有

$$L_\theta = l + m - z\text{In}(1-e) - \frac{B + (1-e)pB(\alpha+\beta\theta) + (1-e)\beta p\left(u_0\int vf(v)dv - B\right)}{2B}a_0$$

令 $L'_\theta(e) = 0$，有

$$\tilde{e} = \frac{2Bz}{pa_0\left(B(\alpha+\beta\theta)+\beta\left(u_0\int vf(v)dv - B\right)\right)} + 1 \tag{12}$$

注意到 $L''_\theta(e) = \frac{z}{(1-e)^2} < 0$，知 $\tilde{e}$ 为使得 L_e 取得最大值的监管程度。

结论 3：由(12)式给出的物流企业最优监管程度 $\tilde{e}$ 知，$\tilde{e}$ 为 θ 的增函数，当企业投资风险高的项目时，物流企业最优监管程度也随之增大，即可以通过监管程度增强来控制风险。

结论 4：将 $\tilde{e}$ 带入到(11)式中，有银行的最优融资利率为

$$\tilde{r} = \frac{-(2z+a_0)B(\alpha+\beta\theta)+(2z-a_0)\beta\left(u_0\int vf(v)dv - B\right)}{4\beta Bz}$$

1）当 $2z+a_0>0$ 时，如果企业投资收益大的项目，银行会增大融资利率来保证收益。这是因为 $z>-\frac{a_0}{2}$，由物流企业的监管成本函数(3)，其成本随监管程度 e 增大而增大的速度较快，相对减轻了对企业的约束，所以银行只能通过增大融资利率保证收益；

2）当 $2z+a_0<0$ 时，可以类似 1)得到相应的结论；

3）当 $2z+a_0=0$ 时，银行融资利率与企业的投资无关。

2. 具有投资激励的模型

如果没有物流企业监管，银行可以减小融资利率以及承诺贷款优惠方式鼓励借款企业按照合约偿还贷款，设银行提供的激励与企业投资项目收益相关，为 $k(1-\eta(\theta))$，$0\leqslant \eta(\theta)\leqslant 1$。

1）银行提供给融资企业激励 $k(1-\eta(\theta))$ 的条件下，银行的收益及决策。给定物流企业监管 e 及融资利率 r，注意(7)式，由(5)式得企业期望收益

$$C_k = (1-e)\mu(\theta,r)p\left(B-u_0\int vf(v)dv\right)+(1-(1-e)\mu(\theta,r)p)B\theta - l + k(1-\eta(\theta))$$

同样设 $\mu(\theta,r)=\alpha+\beta(\theta+r)$，$\alpha\geqslant 0$，$\beta>0$，以及 $\eta(\theta)=\gamma\theta$，$0\leqslant\gamma\leqslant 1$，则由 $C''_k,(\theta)=-2(1-e)\frac{pB}{n}<0$，令 $C'_k(\theta)=0$，有使得 C_k 取得最大值的 $\stackrel{\approx}{\theta}$，

$$\stackrel{\approx}{\theta} \frac{(1-e)\beta p\left(B-u_0\int vf(v)dv - Br\right)-(1-e)\alpha pB + B - k\gamma}{2(1-e)\beta pB} \tag{13}$$

注意到银行的收益函数(2)式，以及(7)式得带有激励情况下银行的期望收益为

$$F_k = (1-(1-e)\mu(\stackrel{\approx}{\theta},r)p)B(r-r_0)+(1-e)\mu(\stackrel{\approx}{\theta},r)p\left(u_0\int vf(v)dv - B(1+r_0)\right) - m - k(1-\eta(\stackrel{\approx}{\theta})) \tag{14}$$

进而有使得 F_k 取得最大值的融资利率，

$$\stackrel{\approx}{r} = \frac{u_0\int vf(v)dv - B}{B} + \frac{B-(1-e)\alpha pB}{2(1-e)\beta pB}, \tag{15}$$

则由(14)式，银行的期望收益为 $F_k(\tilde{\tilde{r}},\tilde{\tilde{\theta}}$。)

2) 银行不提供给融资企业激励的条件下，银行的收益状况。当 $k=0$ 时，融资企业期望收益为

$$C_e=(1-e)\mu(\theta,r)p\left(B-u_0\int vf(v)dv\right)+(1-(1-e)\mu(\theta,r)pB\theta-l$$

进而求得使 C_e 取得最大值的 $\tilde{\theta}$，满足

$$\tilde{\theta}=\frac{(1-e)\beta p\left(B-u_0\int vf(v)dv-Br\right)-(1-e)\alpha pB+B}{2(1-e)\beta pB}$$

银行将 $\tilde{\theta}$ 作为融资企业的反应函数，得银行的期望收益

$$F_e=(1-(1-e)\mu(\tilde{\theta},r)p)B(r-r_0)+(1-e)\mu(\tilde{\theta},r)p\left(u_0\int vf(v)dv-B(1+r_0)\right)-m, \tag{16}$$

可得 F_e 取得最大值的融资利率，$\tilde{r}\ \frac{u_0\int vf(v)dv-B}{B}+\frac{B-(1-e)\alpha pB}{2(1-e)\beta pB}$。显然，只当时，即

$$F_k(\tilde{\tilde{r}},\tilde{\tilde{\theta}})>F_e(\tilde{r},\tilde{\theta})$$

$$F_k(\tilde{\tilde{r}},\tilde{\tilde{\theta}})-F_e(\tilde{r},\tilde{\theta})=-\frac{\gamma^2}{2(1-e)\beta pB}k^2+\left[\frac{\gamma}{2(1-e)\beta p}(1-(1-e)p\alpha)+\frac{B-u_0\int vf(v)dv}{B}\gamma-1\right]k\geqslant 0 \tag{18}$$

银行才会采用投资激励 $k(1-\eta(\theta))$。

结论 5：由(18)式，当 $B\gamma(1-(1-e)p\alpha)+2(1-e)\beta p\left(\left(B-u_0\int vf(v)dv\right)\gamma-B\right)>0$ 时，k 满足 $0\leqslant k\leqslant\frac{B\gamma(1-(1-e)p\alpha)+2(1-e)\beta p\left(\left(B-u_0\int vf(v)dv\right)\gamma-B\right)}{\gamma^2}$，即银行采取激励措施会比不采取激励措施获得更多的收益，并且 k 最优值为

$$k^*=\frac{1}{2\gamma^2}\left(B\gamma(1-(1-e)p\alpha)+2(1-e)\beta p\left(\left(B-u_0\int vf(v)dv\right)\gamma-B\right)\right) \tag{19}$$

当 $B\gamma(1-(1-e)p\alpha)+2(1-e)\beta p\left(\left(B-u_0\int vf(v)dv\right)\gamma-B\right)\leqslant 0$ 时，k 的取值为零，即银行拒绝采取激励。

当激励 $k^*=\frac{1}{2\gamma^2}\left(B\gamma(1-(1-e)p\alpha)+2(1-e)\beta p\left(\left(B-u_0\int vf(v)dv\right)\gamma-B\right)\right)$，由(14)及(15)式有银行收益 $F_k(\tilde{\tilde{r}}\tilde{\tilde{\theta}},k^*)$。如果银行不采取激励，在物流企业监管下，银行收益可由(16)式，即 $F_e(\tilde{\tilde{r}},\tilde{\tilde{\theta}},)$ 设物流企业监管程度 e^*，收益 $F_e(\tilde{\tilde{r}},\tilde{\tilde{\theta}},e^*)$。由

$$F_k(\tilde{\tilde{r}},\tilde{\tilde{\theta}},k^*)=F_e(\tilde{\theta},\tilde{r},e^*) \tag{20}$$

可得如果监管程度由银行采取激励的 e 调整为不采取激励的 e^*，可保证银行期望收益不变。

结论 6：如果没有物流企业帮助银行监管企业的运营投资，即 $e=0$，则银行选择投资激励 $k^{**}=\frac{1}{2\gamma^2}\left(B\gamma(1-p\alpha)+2\beta p\left(\left(B-u_0\int vf(v)dv\right)\gamma-B\right)\right)$，可获得收益与监管程度为 e^{**} 时收益相同，$F_k(\tilde{\tilde{r}},\tilde{\tilde{\theta}},k^*)_{e=0}=F_e(\tilde{\theta},\tilde{r},e^{**})$。$k^{**}$，$e^{**}$ 为(19)和(20)式中 $e=0$ 情形。

3. 总结

本文考察了物流企业在存货质押融资中的决策问题，给出了监管作用与银行激励机制具有一定等价关系的结论。如果物流企业不能够提供有力监管，银行会因为企业信用级别低以及质押商品价格波动而面临较大贷款风险，因此在实践应用中，现代化大规模的物流企业参与到存货质押融资业务中，正说明了本文结论：只有当物流企业提供监管给银行带来的收益大于银行激励机制能够获得的收益情况下，银行才会接受物流企业提供监管服务。

Research of the Logistics Enterprises Decision-making in the Inventory Financing

Ma Zhonghua, Zhu Daoli

(School of Management, Fudan University, Shanghai, 200433)

Abstract: In the inventory financing business, logistics enterprises supply supervision of the pledge. In this paper, the decision-making of the logistics enterprises is considered. With deferent situation including the bank increasing the interest rate and the enterprises investing the projects with more risk, logistics enterprises keep the profit unreduced through adjusting the supervision. And through comparing the profit of the bank in inventory financing, with situations that supervision of logistics enterprises and investment incentive mechanisms, the conclusion are given that the logistics enterprises participate the inventory financing business only when it can provide a large degree of supervision.

Keywords: inventory financing, logistics decision-making, investment incentive mechanisms, financing profits.

参考文献

[1] 陈祥峰,朱道立.现代物流金融服务创新——金融物流[J].物流技术,2005,No.3:4-6,15.

[2] Jeuland A.,Shugan S. Managing channel profits[J]. Marketing Science,1983,2(3):239-272.

[3] 葛静燕,黄培清.基于博弈论的闭环供应链定价策略分析[J].系统工程学报, 2008,23(1):111-115.

[4] 田厚平,郭亚军,王学军.一类基于进化博弈的多主多从 Stackelberg 对策算法[J].系统工程学报, 2005,20(3):303-307.

[5] Wang Y.,Gerchak Y. Capacity games in assembly systems with uncertain demand[J]. Manufacturing and Service Operations Management,2003,5(3):252-267.

[6] Corbett C.,Groote D. A supplier's optimal quantity discount policy under asymmetric information [J]. Management Science,2000,46(3):444-450.

[7] 王文辉,冯耕中,苏潇. 分散决策下存货质押融资业务的信贷合约设计[J]. 复旦学报(自然科学版),2008,47(2):266-272.

[8] Wenhui Wang,Gengzhong Feng,Xiao Su. Research on credit contract design of inventory financing business under distributed decision[J]. Journal of Fudan University, 2008,47(2):266-272.

[9] 李毅学,徐渝,冯耕中,王非.标准存货质押融资业务贷款价值比率研究[J].运筹与管理, 2006,15(6):78-82,99.

Houping Tian,Yajun Guo,Xuejun Wang. Algorithm of Stacklberg game with multiple leaders-followers based on evolutionary game theory. Journal of Systems Engineering, 2005, 20(3):303-307.

Jingyan Ge,Peiyuan Huang. Price decision analysis for closed-loop supply chain based on game theory. Journal of Systems Engineering,2008,23(1):111-115.

Xiangfeng Chen, Daoli Zhu. Innovation of logistics' finance service——finance logistics [J]. Logistics Technology,2005,No.3:4-6,15.

Yixue Li,Yu Xu,Gengzhong Feng,Fei Wang. Research on Ionan-to vaIue ratios of standard inventory financing,Operations Research and Management Science,2006,15(6):78-82,99.

补偿契约模式下的供应链产能投资研究

徐最，朱道立，朱文贵
复旦大学管理学院，上海 200433

摘要：研究由一个制造商和一个供应商构成的供应链，后者是为前者提供定制化产品的唯一厂商。产 品的需求是随机的，供应商在观察到需求前进行产能投资，制造商在观察到需求后开始下订单，随后，供应商根据订单进行生产。由于供应商独自承担产能过剩带来的损失。因此往往建造低于实现系统利润最大化的产能水平。提出了两种补偿契约，促使供应商建造更多的产能，前者使得供应商能够建造比批发价格契约下更高的产能水平，而后者使渠道协调。最后对批发价格契约、线性补偿契约和非线性补偿契约 3 种契约的利润进行了比较。

关键词：供应链；协调；产能；补偿契约

中图分类号：F253　　**文献标识码**：A　　**文章编号**：1000-7857(2007)07-0071-06

0　引言

在由上游企业和下游企业构成的供应链中，由于产品的需求具有随机性，下游企业往往会减少订货。为了促使下游企业增加订货，上游企业会采取各种契约来分担其风险，比如采用退货契约(return contract)[1]、数量柔性契约 fquantity-flexibility contract)[2]、销售回扣契约(sales rebate contract)[3]、数量折扣契约(quantity-dis-count contract)[4]以及期权契约(option contract)[5]等。不过，以上这些研究都建立在假定上游企业有足够的生产能力满足下游企业的订货要求、上游企业如果不能满足下游企业的订货要求则会受到很大的惩罚的基础之上。可是，在现实中，上游企业的产能水平往往是有限的，并且有时候很难辨别两种情况，即，上游企业不愿意满足下游企业的需求，或者因为一些外力因素导致无法满足订货需求。*

在一些高科技行业，制造商往往要求供应商生产定制化产品。在了解市场需求之前，制造商只是提供某种契约，在看到市场需求后才下最终订单(订单的数量与市场需求相同)。供应商需要在看到市场需求前投资建造产能，接到订单后开始生产，订单的完成率

---

* 收稿日期：2006-11-15

基金项目：国家自然科学基金重点项目(70432001)

作者简介：徐最，女，上海邯郸路 220 号复旦大学管理学院，博士研究生，主要从事供应链管理方面的研究；E-mail：gdxuzui@163.com

朱道立，男，上海邯郸路 220 号复旦大学管理学院，教授，主要从事供应链管理方面的研究；E-mail：dlzhu@fudan.edu.cn

受到产能水平的限制。较长的前置时间以及需求的随机性使得供应商很难准确预测市场需求，因此会出现产能过剩或不足的现象。如果产能过剩，供应商则不得不承担损失；如果产能不足，制造商则将因为供应商的产能限制而减少销售。因此，对于制造商而言，供应商建造的产能越多越好，而供应商考虑到产能过剩带来的损失，往往会减少产能。

面对这样的问题，制造商希望找到适当的契约促使供应商建造足够多的产能。Cachon[6]最先提出了供应商可能不会按照制造商的订货要求建造产能的问题。不过，他考虑了比较极端的情形，认为，由于产能投资比较复杂，受到很多因素的影响，制造商往往难以识别以及向第三方核实供应商的产能水平，或者虽能核实，但其费用很高，因此制造商将无法惩罚建造低于事先规定产能水平的供应商。在此情况下，确定承诺契约（firm commitment contract）和期权契约等同于批发价格契约 wholesale price contract）。在Cachon研究的基础上，Tomlin[7]考虑了比较实际的情况。虽然无法核实供应商的产能水平，但是，在某些情况下还是能够辨别供应。商是否按照规定的产能水平进行建造。如果最终订单（市场需求）低于事先规定的产能水平，那么制造商无法核实供应商是否按照给定的水平建造了足够多的产能；但是，如果最终订单高于事先规定的产能水平，那么制造商就可以核实并惩罚建造低于事先规定产能水平的供应商。Tomlin[7]指出，在此情况下，与批发价格契约相比.确定承诺契约以及期权契约都会提高供应商的产能水平。Erkoc和Wu[8]也考虑了不能完全识别供应商产能水平的情况，不过，是从供应商的角度提供契约，通过设计适当的契约来消除制造商的顾虑。

为了降低产能过剩的风险，供应商往往建造低于制造商需求的产能水平。由于可以在某种程度上识别供应商是否建造规定的产能水平，Tomlin[7]通过惩罚的方式，促使供应商提高产能水平。本文提出通过补偿的方式，采用补偿契约分担供应商产能过剩的风险，从而促使供应商建造更多的产能。即，如果供应商能够完全满足制造商最终下的订单，制造商对于从供应商那里购买到的每一件产品都会给予补偿，但是，如果供应商不能完全满足制造商的订单，供应商将不会获得任何补偿。

本文提出了两种补偿契约——线性补偿契约和非线性补偿契约。与批发价格契约相比，线性补偿契约可以提高供应商的产能水平，而非线性补偿契约可以协调供应链，促使供应商建造系统最优的产能水平，最后对批发价格契约和这两种补偿契约进行比较。

1 模型描述

本文讨论由一个制造商和一个供应商构成的供应链。供应商向制造商提供一个定制的关键的零配件，后者把零配件组装到自己的产品中然后销售，假定一个零配件对应于一个产品。具体的过程如图1所示。

在这过程中，制造商是看到需求后才下最终订单，因此订单数量就等于市场需求数量。

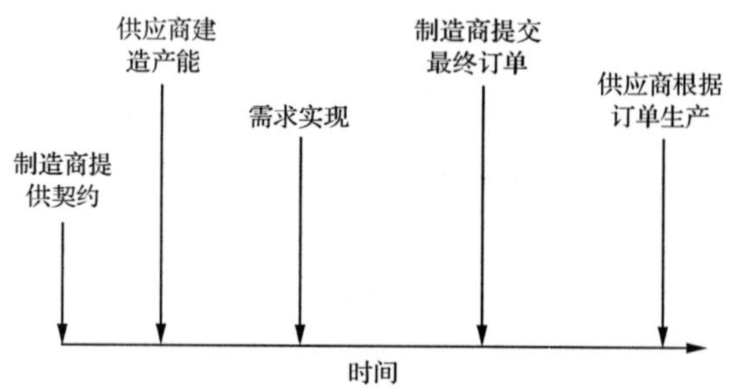

图1 整个供应链的具体过程

Fig. 1 The whoie process of the suppIy chain

产品的需求 x 是随机的，需求分布函数和密度函数分别为 $f(x)$，$f(x)$，其中 $x\in[0,\infty)$。假定 $F(x)$ 是二次连续可微的，$\overline{F}(x)=1-f(x)$，$f(x)>0$，$\forall x\in[0,\infty)$。零配件的边际产能投资成本为 $c_k>0$，边际生产成本为 $c_p>0$。零配件的固定销售价格为 r，且 $r>c_k+c_p$。

设 $S(k)$ 是产能水平为 k 时的期望销售数量

$$S(k)=E(k-(k-x)^+)=\int_0^k xf(x)\mathrm{d}x+\int_k^{+\infty}kf(x)\mathrm{d}x$$
$$=k-\int_0^k F(x)\mathrm{d}x=\int_0^k\overline{F}(x)\mathrm{d}x$$

其中 $(k-x)^+=\max\{(k-x),0\}$。为了计算方便，假定剩余产品对于双方而言没有任何价值，也没有缺货损失，并且，最后双方都能观察到市场需求。

1.1 系统最优的产能水平

如果供应商和制造商同属于一家企业，那么就会有一个中央决策者决定系统最优的产能水平。

整个供应链的期望利润函数为

$$\Pi(k)=(r-c_p)S(k)-c_kk$$

由于 $S(k)$ 是关于 k 的凹函数，因此可以求出系统最优的产能水平 k^*，其满足

$$\overline{F}(k^*)=\frac{c_k}{r-c_p}\tag{1}$$

在现实经济活动中，供应商和制造商往往属于不同的企业，他们根据各自的利润分别决策。制造商往往只考虑如何设计契约使得自已的利润达到是最大化，而不是整个系统利润最大化。这样，根据制造商提供的契约，供应商选择的产能水平往往低于系统最优的产能水平，因此供应链的利润无法达到最大化，即无法实现协调。在有关供应链的研究中，很多学者都研究如何设计适当的契约来协调供应链，如果不协调，如何改进已有的契约来提高供应链的效率。系统的最优产能水平也称为标杆解，通过与标杆解比较，可以判断出供应链是否协调，不协调时的供应链效率如何。Cachon[6] 考虑的基本模型与本文相同，指出批发价格契约无法协调供应链。本文接下来首先给出了批发价格契约下的供应商产能水平，随后分别给出了线性补偿契约和非线性补偿契约。与批发价格契约相比，线

性补偿契约可以促使供应商建造更多的产能，提高了供应链的效率，而非线性补偿契约可以促使供应商建造系统最优的产能水平，从而协调了供应链。

1.2　批发价格契约

在批发价格契约下，制造商向供应商提供一个批发价格 w。如果供应商接受该契约，那么其期望利润函数可写为

$$\Pi_s^w(k) = (w - c_p)S(k) - c_k k$$

该利润函数是关于 k 的凹函数，给定批发价格 w，那么供应商的最优产能水平 k 满足

$$\overline{F}(k) = \frac{c_k}{w - c_p} \tag{2}$$

由于 $\overline{F}(k)$ 是严格单调函数，因此 w 和 k 是一一对应的。这样可以推出，如果制造商提供的批发价格为 $w(k) = \frac{c_k}{\overline{F}(k)} + c_p$，那么供应商的最优产能水平为

制造商的期望利润函数可写为 k。

$$\Pi_M^w(k) = (r - w(k))S(k) = \left(r - \frac{c_k}{\overline{F}(k)} - c_p\right)S(k) \tag{3}$$

制造商的问题是选择最优的批发价格来最大化其利润。Cachon[6] 指出如果制造商的期望利润函数是关于 k 的凹函数，那么制造商所应提供的最优批发价格为 $w(k_w^*)$，其中 k_w^* 满足

$$\overline{F}(k_w^*) = \frac{c_k}{r - c_p}\left(1 + \frac{f(k_w^*)}{\overline{F}(k_w^*)}S(k_w^*)\right) \tag{4}$$

比较式(1)和式(4)，不难发现批发价格契约无法协调供应链（$k_w^* > k^*$）。由于供应商承担整个供应链产能投资的所有费用 $c_k k$，却得不到所有的利润 $(r - c_p)S(k)$，因此供应商选择的产能水平低于实现系统利润最大化的水平。如果制造商能够给予供应商一部分产能投资方面的补偿，供应商将会提高产能水平。接下来给出的两种契约就能达到这样的效果。

2　补偿契约

由于不愿承担产能投资过剩带来的损失，供应商会降低产能水平，如果制造商能够分担这部分损失，供应商将会提高产能水平。虽然制造商无法核实供应商的产能水平，但是能够在一定程度上判断供应商的产能是否过剩。

如果供应商无法满足制造商的订货要求（订货要求等同于市场需求），则不会出现产能过剩的情况，此时，供应商没有产能过剩方面的损失，制造商也无需分担其损失，只需要提供一个批发价格；如果供应商能够满足市场需求，就有可能出现产能过剩的情况，对于从供应商那里采购的每一件产品，除了提供批发价格外，还提供一个补偿价格，这样制造商就可以分担供应商产能过剩的损失，促使供应商提高产能水平。

本节提出了两种补偿契约——线性补偿契约和非线性补偿契约。线性契约下的补偿价格是固定的，而非线性契约下的补偿价格与制造商的采购数量有关。与批发价格契约相比. 线性补偿契约可以促使供应商建造更多的产能，提高了供应链的效率，而非线性补

偿契约可以促使供应商建造系统最优的产能水平，从而协调了供应链。

2.1 线性补偿契约

考虑如下的线性补偿契约 $\{w,c_k\}$：制造商向供应商提供一个批发价格 w，如果供应商能够满足所有的市场需求，制造商将提供一个价格为 c_k 的补偿，此时的单位产品实际购买价格为 $w+c_k$；如果只能满足一部分市场需求，那么没有任何补偿。这样，该契约的转移支付函数可写为

$$T(Q,k,w,c_k)=\begin{cases}(w+c_k)Q & 0\leqslant Q\leqslant k\\ wk & Q>k\end{cases}$$

Q 是制造商的订购数量，由于制造商在看到需求后才订货，因此 $Q=x$，x 是市场需求。

在线性补偿契约下，供应商的期望利润函数为

$$\begin{aligned}\Pi_S^{LR}(k)&=E(T(Q,k,w,c_k))-c_pS(k)-c_kk\\&=\int_0^k(w+c_k)xf(x)\mathrm{d}x+\int_k^{+\infty}wkf(x)\mathrm{d}x-c_pS(k)-c_kk\\&=(w-c_p)S(k)-c_kk+c_k\int_0^k xf(x)\mathrm{d}x\end{aligned}\tag{5}$$

给定 w，该利润函数关于 k 的一阶和二阶导函数分别为

$$\frac{\mathrm{d}(\Pi_S^{LR}(k))}{dk}=(w-c_p)\overline{F}(K)-c_k(1-f(k)k)\tag{6}$$

$$\frac{\mathrm{d}^2\,\Pi_S^{LR}(k))}{dk^2}=-f(k)(w-c_p-c_k)+c_kkf'(k)\tag{7}$$

引理 1 如果 $f(x)$ 关于 k 是严格单调递减的，制造商提供的批发价格为 $w(k)=c_k\dfrac{(1-f(k)^k)}{\overline{F}(k)}+c_p$，那么供应商的最优产能水平为 k。

证明 如果 $f(x)$关于 k 是严格单调递减的，即 $f'(x)<0$，可以推出

$$F(k)=\int_0^k f(t)\mathrm{d}t>f(k)k\tag{8}$$

根据式(8)，有

$$w(k)=c_k\left(\frac{(1-f(k)^k)}{\overline{F}(k)}\right)+c_p>c_k+c_p\tag{9}$$

由 $f'(x)<0$ 和式(9)，可以推出供应商的利润函数是关于 k 的严格凹函数。由于 $w(k)$的表达式使得式(6)为零，因此，如果批发价格为：$w(k)=c_k\dfrac{(1-f(k)^k)}{\overline{F}(k)}+c_p$，那么供应商的最优产能水平为 k。

根据引理 1，制造商的问题是找到合适的批发价格来最大化自己的利润。制造商此时的期望利润函数为

$$\begin{aligned}\Pi_M^{LR}(k)&=rS(k)E(T(Q,k,w,c_k))\\&=(r-w(k))S(k)-c_k\int_0^k xf(x)\mathrm{d}x\end{aligned}$$

$$= \left[r - c_p - c_k \left(\frac{1 - f(k)k}{\overline{F}(k)} \right) \right] S(k) - c_k \int_0^k x f(x) \mathrm{d}x \tag{10}$$

定理 1　如果 $f(x)$是关于 k 的严格单调递减函数，且制造商的期望利润函数式(10)是关于 k 的凹函数，那么制造商的最优线性补偿契约为 $\{w(k_{LR}^*), c_k\}$，其中 k_{LR}^* 满足

$$\overline{F}(k_{LR}^*) = \frac{c_k}{r - c_p} \left(1 + \frac{f(k_{LR}^*)}{\overline{F}(k_{LR}^*)^2} S(k_{LR}^*) \right) -$$

$$\frac{c_k}{r - c_p} \left[\frac{f(k_{LR}^*)}{\overline{F}(k_{LR}^*)} + k_p \frac{f'(k_{LR}^*)\overline{F}(k_{LR}) + f(k_{LR}^*)}{\overline{F}^2(k_{LR})} \right] S(k_{LR}^*) \tag{11}$$

并且，如果需求分布的失败率(failure rate)关于 k 是非单调递减的，那么，与批发价格契约相比，制造商将会获得更多的利润. 而供应商的利润将会降低，但是供应链的利润增加。

证明　由于假定制造商的期望利润函数式(10)是关于 k 的凹函数，把函数式(10)关于 k 求一阶导数，可以得出式(11)。比较式(4)和式(11)，可以看出在线性补偿契约下，供应商将会提高产能水平 $(k_w^* < k_{LR}^*)$，因此供应链的利润增加。

根据制造商在批发价格契约下的期望利润函数式(3)，有

$$\begin{aligned} \Pi_M^{LR}(k) &= \left(r - \frac{c_k}{\overline{F}(k) - c_p} \right) S(k) + c_k \left[S(k) \left(\frac{kf(k)}{\overline{F}(k)} \right) - \int_0^k x f(x) \mathrm{d}x \right] \\ &= \Pi_M^w(k) + c_k \left[S(k) \frac{kf(k)}{\overline{F}(k)} - \int_0^k x f(x) \mathrm{d}x \right] \end{aligned} \tag{12}$$

设 $G(k) = S(k) \dfrac{kf(k)}{\overline{F}(k)} - \int_0^k x f(x) \mathrm{d}x, h(k) \dfrac{f(k)}{\overline{F}(k)}$，后者是需求分布的失败率，假定是非单调递减的，即 $h'(k) \geqslant 0$。正态分布和均匀分布都满足这个性质，伽马分布和威布尔分布在一些参数限制下也具有这个性质[9]，而指数分布的失败率是常数，因此也是非减的。

由于 $G'(k) = S(k)h(k) + S(k)kh'(k) > 0, \forall k > 0$，并且 $G(0) = 0, G(k)$ 关于 k 是连续的，因此 $G(k) > 0, \forall k > 0$。由式(12)，有 $\Pi_S^{LR}(k) > 0, \forall k > \Pi_M^w(k)$，那么 $\Pi_S^{LR}(k_{LR}^*) > \Pi_M^w(k)$，即在线性补偿契约下，制造商将比在批发价格契约下获得更多的利润。

类似地，供应商的期望利润函数可以写为

$$\begin{aligned} \Pi_S^{LR}(k) &= \Pi(k) - \Pi_M^{LR}(k) \\ &= \Pi_S^w(k) + \Pi_M^w(k) - \Pi_M^{LR}(k) \\ &= \Pi_S^w(k) - G(k) \end{aligned}$$

由前面的分析得到，当 $k > 0$，有 $\Pi_S^{LR}(k) < \Pi_S^w(k_w^*)$，那么 $\Pi_S^{LR}(k_{LR}^*) < \Pi_S^w(k_w^*)$，即在线性补偿契约下，与批发价格契约相比，供应商将获得更少的利润。

2.2　非线性补偿契约

考虑非线性补偿契约 $\{w, h(Q)\}$，其中 Q 是制造商的订货数量。具体过程如下：制造商向供应商提供一个批发价格 w，如果供应商能够满足所有的市场需求，制造商将提供一个价格为 $h(Q)$的补偿，此时的单位产品实际购买价格为 $w + h(Q)$；如果只能满足一部分市场需求，那么没有任何补偿。这样，该契约的转移支付函数可写为

$$T(Q,k,w,h(Q))=\begin{cases}(w+h(Q))Q & 0\leqslant Q\leqslant k\\ wk & Q>k\end{cases}$$

Q 是制造商的订购数量，由于制造商在看到需求后才订货，因此 $Q=x$，x 是市场需求。

定理 2 在契约，$\{w,h(Q)\}$ 下，其中 $h(Q)\ \dfrac{\theta c_k}{f(Q)Q}$，$w=(1-\theta)r+\theta$，$0<\theta\leqslant 1$，给定产能水平 k，制造商和供应商的期望利润函数分别为 $\theta\Pi(k)$ 和 $(1-\theta)\Pi(k)$，因此供应链协调。

证明 给定产能水平 k，在契约 $\{w,h(Q)\}$ 下，供应商的期望利润函数为

$$\begin{aligned}\Pi_S^{NR}(k)&=E(T(Q,k,w,c_k))-c_pS(k)-c_kk\\&=\int_0^k(w+h(x))xf(x)\mathrm{d}x+\int_k^{+\infty}wkf(x)\mathrm{d}x-c_pS(k)-c_kk\\&=\int_0^k\left(w+\frac{\theta c_k}{f(x)x}\right)xf(x)\mathrm{d}x+\int_k^{+\infty}wkf(x)\mathrm{d}x-c_pS(k)-c_kk\\&=\int_0^k(wxf(x)+\theta c_k)\mathrm{d}x+\int_k^{+\infty}wkf(x)\mathrm{d}x-c_pS(k)-c_kk\\&=wS(k)-(1-\theta)c_kk-c_pS(k)\\&=(1-\theta)[(r-c_p)S(k)-c_kk]=(1-\theta)\Pi(k)\end{aligned}$$

那么制造商的期望利润函数为

$$\Pi_M^{NR}(k)=\Pi(k)-\Pi_S^{NR}(k)=\theta\Pi(k)$$

因此供应链协调。$\theta>0$ 保证制造商的利润大于零。

该定理表明制造商获得了比例为 θ 的供应链利润。这样非线性补偿契约协调了供应链并且能任意分配供应链的利润。这个利润分割的比例主要由双方的谈判势力来决定。如果制造商具有更强的谈判势力，那么 θ 就会增加。

如果 $h(Q)=\dfrac{\theta c_k}{f(Q)Q}$ 关于 Q 单调递增，那么补偿价格随着订货数量的增加而递增，这就和 Tomlint[7] 提出的数量溢价契约相类似，可以很容易地证明正态分布满足这个条件。定理 2 表明，如果补偿价格 h 随着订货数量的变化而改变并且满足一定关系，供应链可以达到协调。

3 三种契约的比较

在本文考虑的供应链中，供应商与制造商同样承担产能不足的风险，但是供应商独自承担产能过剩的风险。批发价格契约没有区别对待这两方面的风险，约供应商同样的价格。本文提出的补偿契约区别对待这两方面的风险，制造商为了补偿供应商产能过剩的风险，给予供应商一定的补偿，使得在产能过剩的情况下（包括能够满足市场需求），供应商获得比产能不足情况下更高的购买价格，这样促使供应商提高产能水平，整个供应链的利润也随之提高。线性补偿契约的每单位产品的补偿价格是固定的，因此只是提高了一部分产能水平，还无法协调；而非线性补偿契约的每单位产品的补偿价格随着订货数量的变化而改变，并且在满足一定条件下，使系统达到协调。表 1 列出了在 3 种契约下的制造商、供应商和供应链的利润。

表 1　3 种契约下的利润

Tabie 1　Profits under three kinds of contracts

	批发价格契约	线性补偿契约	非线性补偿契约
制造商的利润	$\Pi_M^w(k_w^*)$	$\Pi_M^{LR}(k_{LR}^*)$	$\theta\,\Pi(k^*)$
供应商的利润	$\Pi_S^w(k_w^*)$	$\Pi_M^{LR}(k_{LR}^*)$	$(1-\theta)\,\Pi(k^*)$
供应链的利润	$\Pi(k_w^*)$	$\Pi(k_{LR}^*)$	$\Pi(k^*)$

下面通过一个数值算例来比较 3 种契约下的利润。

图 2 显示了在 3 种契约下。制造商、供应商和供应链的利润的大小关系。在 3 种契约下，供应链的利润依次增加(比较 A,B 和 C3 点)。在线性补偿契约下，与批发价格契约相比，由于供应链的产能水平得到了提高 ($k_w^* < k_{LR}^*$)，因此制造商的利润(比较点 F 和点 D)得到了提高，不过供应商的利润降低(比较 AF 和 BD 的线段长度)。在非线性补偿契约下，供应链达到协调，最优的产能水平为 k，供应链的利润为 $\Pi(k^*)$ (点 C)。制造商的利润由系数 θ 来决定，而 θ 的取值由双方的谈判势力来确定。图中给出了在 θ 的 3 种取值情况下，制造商的利润或者大于在线性补偿契约下的利润(比较 E 点和 D 点)，或者小于在线性补偿契约下的利润(比较 G 点和 D 点)，甚至小于批发价格契约下的利润(比较 H 点和 F 点)，所以具体采用非线性补偿契约还是线性补偿契约与制造商的谈判能力有关。不过，非线性补偿契约虽然可以协调供应链，但是制造商会更愿意采用线性补偿契约，因为其执行起来比较方便。

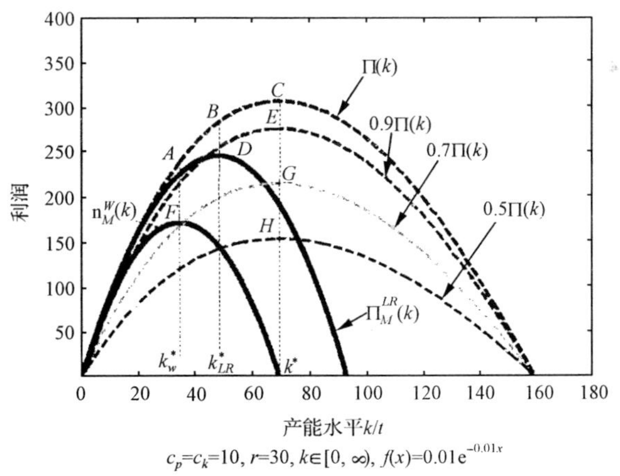

图 2　比较 3 种契约下的利润

Fig. 2　Comparison of profits under three kinds of contracts

4　结论

本文考虑了在无法完全核实供应商的产能水平的情况下. 如何提供适当的契约促使供应商建造更高的产能水平。提出了 2 种补偿契约，线性补偿契约和非线性补偿契约，通过分担供应商产能过剩的风险，促使供应商提高产能水平。与批发价格契约相比，线性补偿契约可以提高供应商的产能水平，而非线性补偿契约可以协调供应链，促使供应商建造系统最优的产能水平。通过对批发价格契约以及两种补偿契约的比较得出，对于制造商而言，线性补偿契约优于批发价格契约，非线性补偿契约不定优于线性补偿契约。但是，线性补偿契约执行起来比非线性补偿契约更方便。本文的研究丰富了关于供应商产能投资方面的问题。提出了新的解决办法来提高产能水平，但这方面的问题还有待进一步研究。

Capacity Investments in Supply Chain with Rebate Contracts

XU Zui, ZHU Daoli, ZHU Wenui

School of Management, Fudan University, Shanghai 200433, China

Abstract: In this paper, a supply chain consisting of one supplier and one manufacturer, with the latter being the only source for a customized product is considereel. Demand is stochastic, the supplier has to invest in capacity befor eseeing the demand, and the manufacturer makes his final order after seeing the demand. To allow for the loss of overcapacity, the supplier will build less capacity than what is the optimal for the supply chain. In this paper, two kinds of rebate contracts are put forward, the former caninduce the supplier to invest in more capacity than under the wholesale price contract, the latter coordinates the supply chain. Finally the three kinds of contracts are compared.

Koy Words: supply chain; coordination; capacity; rebate contract

CLC Number: F253 **Document COde**: A **Artle ID**: 1000-7857(2007)07-0071-06

参考文献

[1] PASTERNACK B A. Optimal pricing and return policies for perishable commodities [J]. Market Science, 1985, 4(2): 166-176.

[2] TSAY A. Quantity-flexibility contract and supplier-CUS-tomer incentives[J], Management Science, 1999, 45(10): 1339-1358.

[3] TAYLOR T A. Supply chain coordination under channel rebates with sales effort effects[J]. Management Science, 2002, 48(8): 992-1007.

[4] CACHON G P. Supply chain coordination with contracts [M]//Handbooks in operation and managements science. Supply chain management: design, coordination and operation. North Holland Press, 2004.

[5] BARNES-SCHUSTER D, BASSOK Y, ANUPINDI R. Coor-dination and flexibility in supply contracts with options[J]. Manufacturing & Service Operations Management, 2002, 4(3): 171-207.

[6] CACHON G P, A LARIVIERE M. Contracting to assuresupply: how to share demand forecasts in a supply chain[J]. Management Science, 2001, 47(5): 629-646.

[7] TOMLIN B. Capacity investments in supply chains: sharing the gain rather than sharing the pain [J]. Manufacturing & Service Operations Management, 2003, 5(4): 317-333.

[8] ERKOC M, WU S D. Managing high-tech capacity expansion via reservation contracts[J]. Production and Operations Management, 2005, 14(2): 232-251.

[9] BARLOW R E, PROSCHAN F. Mathemtical theory of reliability[M]. New York: John Wiley & Sons. 1965.

（本文发表于《科技导报》，2007 年第 7 期）